Corporate Financial Accounting 15e

Carl S. Warren
Professor Emeritus of Accounting
University of Georgia, Athens

Jefferson P. Jones
Associate Professor of Accounting
Auburn University

CENGAGE

Australia • Brazil • Mexico • Singapore • United Kingdom • United States

CENGAGE

Corporate Financial Accounting, **15e**
Carl S. Warren
Jefferson P. Jones

Senior Vice President, Higher Ed Product,
   Content, and Market Development: Erin Joyner

Product Director: Jason Fremder

Sr. Product Manager: Matt Filimonov

Sr. Content Developer: Diane Bowdler

Product Assistant: Aiyana Moore

Executive Marketing Manager: Robin LeFevre

Sr. Digital Project Manager: Jessica Robbe

Sr. Digital Content Specialist: Tim Ross

Sr. Content Project Manager: Tim Bailey

Production Service: Lumina Datamatics

Sr. Art Director: Michelle Kunkler

Cover and Internal Design: Ke Design/Trish
   Knapke

Cover Images: Map: hkeita/Shutterstock.com
   Pushpins: Olivier Le Moal/Shutterstock.com

Intellectual Property
   Analyst: Reba Frederics
   Project Manager: Erika Mugavin

For product information and technology assistance, contact us at
**Cengage Customer & Sales Support, 1-800-354-9706
or support.cengage.com.**

For permission to use material from this text or product, submit all
requests online at **www.cengage.com/permissions.**

Microsoft Excel® is a registered trademark of Microsoft Corporation.
© 2017 Microsoft.

Library of Congress Control Number: 2017953692

ISBN: 978-1-337-39816-9

Cengage
20 Channel Street
Boston, MA 02210
USA

Cengage is a leading provider of customized learning solutions
with employees residing in nearly 40 different countries and sales in more
than 125 countries around the world. Find your local representative at:
www.cengage.com.

Cengage products are represented in Canada by
Nelson Education, Ltd.

To learn more about Cengage platforms and services, register or access
your online learning solution, or purchase materials for your course,
visit **www.cengage.com.**

Printed at CLDPC, USA, 02-20

Roadmap for Success

Warren/Jones *Corporate Financial Accounting, 15e*, provides a sound pedagogy for giving students a solid foundation in business and accounting. Warren/Jones covers the fundamentals AND motivates students to learn by showing how accounting is important to businesses.

Warren/Jones is successful because it reaches students with a combination of new and tried-and-tested pedagogy.

This revision includes a range of new and existing features that help Warren/Jones provide students with the context to see how accounting is valuable to business. These include:

- New! Make a Decision section
- New! Pathways Challenge

Warren/Jones also includes a thorough grounding in the fundamentals that any business student will need to be successful. These key features include:

- Stepwise approach to accounting cycle
- Presentation style designed around the way students learn
- Updated schema
- At the start of each chapter, **a schema, or roadmap, shows students what they are going to learn and how it is connected to the larger picture**. In the early chapters, the schema illustrates how the steps in the accounting cycle are interrelated. In later chapters, the schema shows how each chapter's topics are connected to the financial statements.

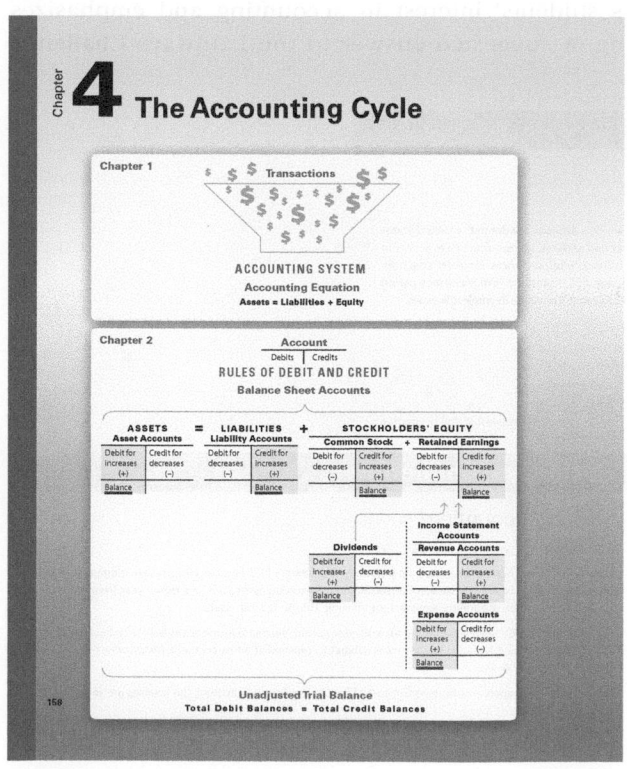

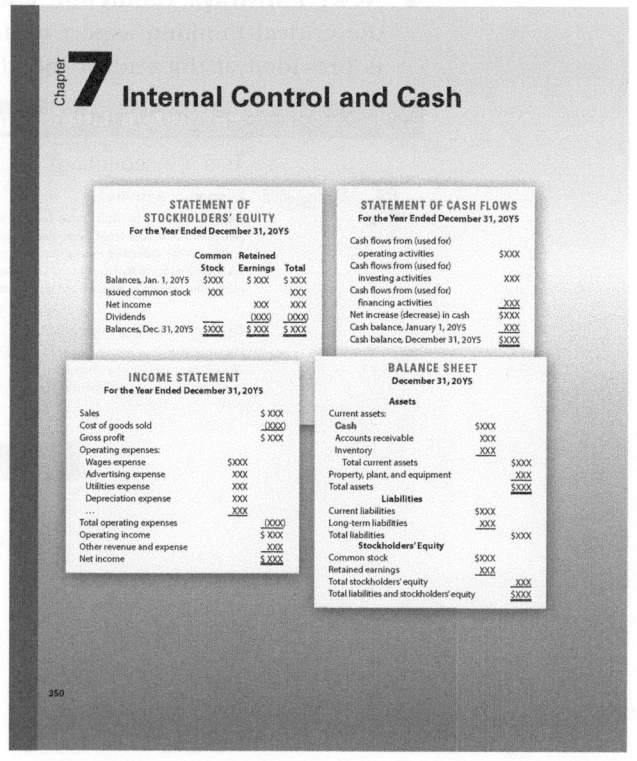

- **Link to the "opening company" of each chapter** calls out examples of how the concepts introduced in the chapter are connected to the opening company. **This shows how accounting is used in the real world by real companies**.

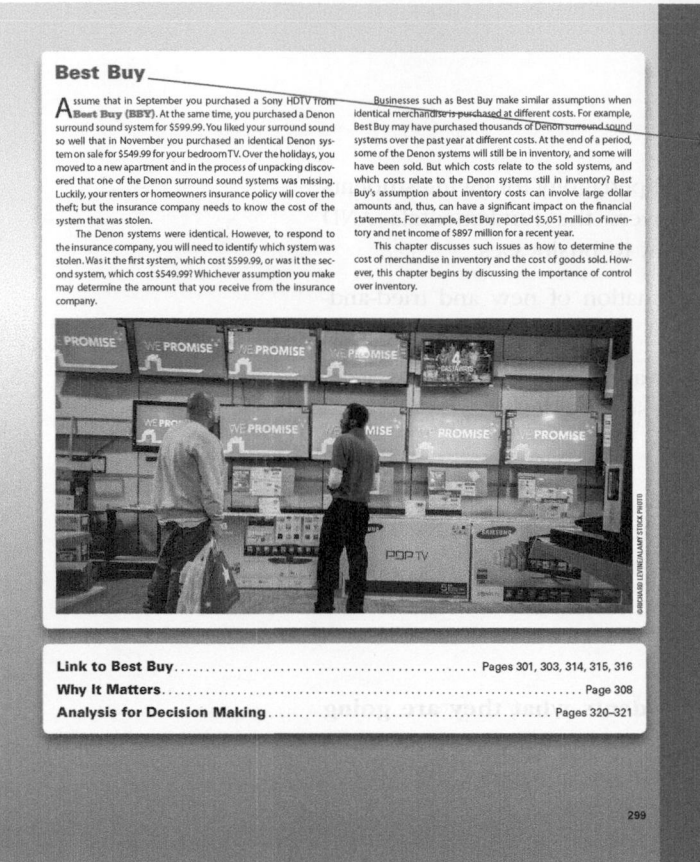

Best Buy

Assume that in September you purchased a Sony HDTV from **Best Buy (BBY)**. At the same time, you purchased a Denon surround sound system for $599.99. You liked your surround sound so well that in November you purchased an identical Denon system on sale for $549.99 for your bedroom TV. Over the holidays, you moved to a new apartment and in the process of unpacking discovered that one of the Denon surround sound systems was missing. Luckily, your renters or homeowners insurance policy will cover the theft; but the insurance company needs to know the cost of the system that was stolen.

The Denon systems were identical. However, to respond to the insurance company, you will need to identify which system was stolen. Was it the first system, which cost $599.99, or was it the second system, which cost $549.99? Whichever assumption you make may determine the amount that you receive from the insurance company.

Businesses such as Best Buy make similar assumptions when identical merchandise is purchased at different costs. For example, Best Buy may have purchased thousands of Denon surround sound systems over the past year at different costs. At the end of a period, some of the Denon systems will still be in inventory, and some will have been sold. But which costs relate to the sold systems, and which costs relate to the Denon systems still in inventory? Best Buy's assumption about inventory costs can involve large dollar amounts and, thus, can have a significant impact on the financial statements. For example, Best Buy reported $5,051 million of inventory and net income of $897 million for a recent year.

This chapter discusses such issues as how to determine the cost of merchandise in inventory and the cost of goods sold. However, this chapter begins by discussing the importance of control over inventory.

Best Buy uses scanners to screen customers as they leave the store for merchandise that has not been purchased. In addition, Best Buy stations greeters at the store's entrance to keep customers from bringing in bags that can be used to shoplift merchandise. *Link to Best Buy*

299

- **New! Pathways Challenge** encourages students' interest in accounting and emphasizes the critical thinking aspect of accounting. A suggested answer to the Pathways Challenge is provided at the end of the chapter.

Pathways Challenge

This is Accounting!

Economic Activity

Verizon Communications Inc. (VZ) is the largest wireless service provider in the United States with over 114 million retail subscribers. To deliver its products and services, Verizon must have access to spectrum—the radio frequencies that carry sound, data, and video to wireless devices. However, spectrum is a limited resource that the Federal Communications Commission (FCC) licenses to businesses for a period of 10 years, subject to renewal. In a recent year, Verizon acquired almost $10 billion in wireless licenses.

Critical Thinking/Judgment

How should Verizon account for its acquisition of wireless licenses?
What is the useful life of a wireless license?
Should Verizon expense (amortize) the cost of its wireless licenses?

Suggested answer at end of chapter.

Pathways Challenge

This is Accounting!

Information/Consequences

Because a wireless license does not exist physically, **Verizon's (VZ)** wireless licenses are intangible assets. All of the costs of acquiring a wireless license should be recorded as an asset. In a recent year, Verizon reported almost $87 billion of wireless licenses, representing 35% of its total assets.

Even though the FCC license is granted for a 10-year period, Verizon considers this license to have an indefinite useful life. This is because the license is subject to renewal at a low cost and, historically, the FCC has renewed Verizon's licenses.

Verizon does not expense (amortize) the cost of its wireless licenses. Instead, the licenses are reviewed for any impaired value.

Suggested Answer

■ Located in each chapter, **Why It Matters** shows students how accounting is important to businesses with which they are familiar. A Concept Clip icon indicates which Why It Matters features have an accompanying concept clip video in CNOWv2. ▶ CONCEPT CLIP

Why It Matters ▶ CONCEPT CLIP

Fixed Assets

Fixed assets often represent a significant portion of a company's total assets. The table that follows shows the fixed assets as a percent of total assets for some select companies across a variety of industries. As can be seen, the type of industry will impact the proportion of fixed assets to total assets. Retail has the highest percent of fixed assets to total assets, while social media and software are on the lower end of the scale. High-tech service companies often use fewer fixed assets to deliver their services than will companies that use stores, equipment, planes, cell towers, or theme parks.

Company	Industry	Percent of Fixed Assets to Total Assets
McDonald's Corporation (MCD)	Food Retail	69%
Target Corporation (TGT)	Merchandise Retail	63%
Delta Air Lines, Inc. (DAL)	Transportation	48%
Verizon Communications Inc. (VZ)	Communications	35%
The Walt Disney Company (DIS)	Entertainment	30%
Facebook, Inc. (FB)	Social Media	13%
Microsoft Corporation (MSFT)	Software	9%

Fixed assets have important properties that require management attention:

■ Fixed assets require a long-term commitment. Mistakes in acquiring fixed assets can be very costly and difficult to reverse; thus, managers must take special care in acquiring fixed assets.
■ Fixed assets wear out over time and need to be replaced. Managers must monitor fixed assets and know when to replace fixed assets due to wear and tear or obsolescence.

■ Fixed assets need to be maintained during use. Managers need to develop maintenance programs to keep the investment in fixed assets productive.
■ Fixed assets often require significant funds to purchase. Managers must acquire funding internally or by other sources to finance the purchase of fixed assets.

■ To aid comprehension and to demonstrate the impact of transactions, **journal entries include the net effect of the transaction on the accounting equation**.

20Y8				
Jan.	3	Inventory	2,510	
		Cash		2,510
		Purchased inventory from Bowen Co.		

$$A = L + E$$
$$+ -$$

Purchases of inventory on account are recorded as follows:

Jan.	4	Inventory	9,250	
		Accounts Payable—Thomas Corporation		9,250
		Purchased inventory on account.		

$$A = L + E$$
$$+ \quad +$$

- **The link between the journal entry and the accounting equation is also included in the accompanying CengageNOWv2 course** in the accounting cycle chapters, reminding students of the link—but not requiring them to actively make the link.

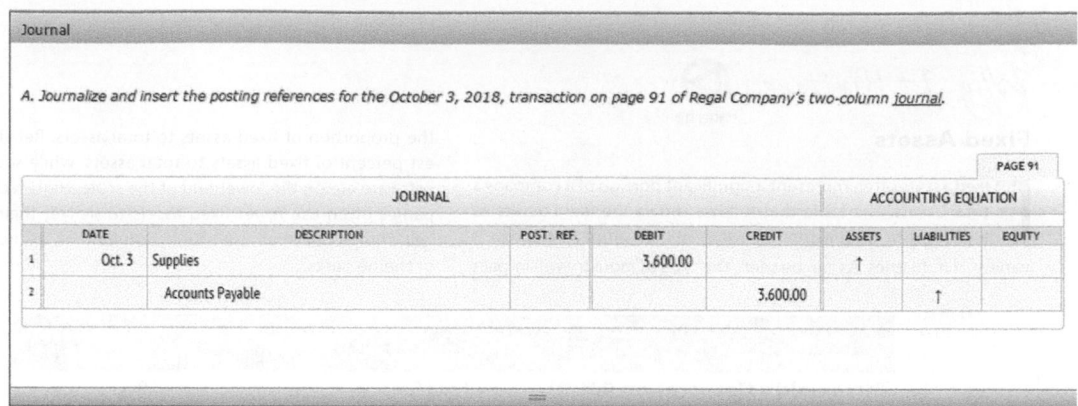

A. Journalize and insert the posting references for the October 3, 2018, transaction on page 91 of Regal Company's two-column journal.

								PAGE 91	
		JOURNAL					ACCOUNTING EQUATION		
	DATE	DESCRIPTION	POST. REF.	DEBIT	CREDIT	ASSETS	LIABILITIES	EQUITY	
1	Oct. 3	Supplies		3,600.00		↑			
2		Accounts Payable			3,600.00		↑		

- To aid learning and problem solving, throughout each chapter new, **Check Up Corners** provide students with step-by-step guidance on how to solve problems. Problem-solving tips help students avoid common errors.

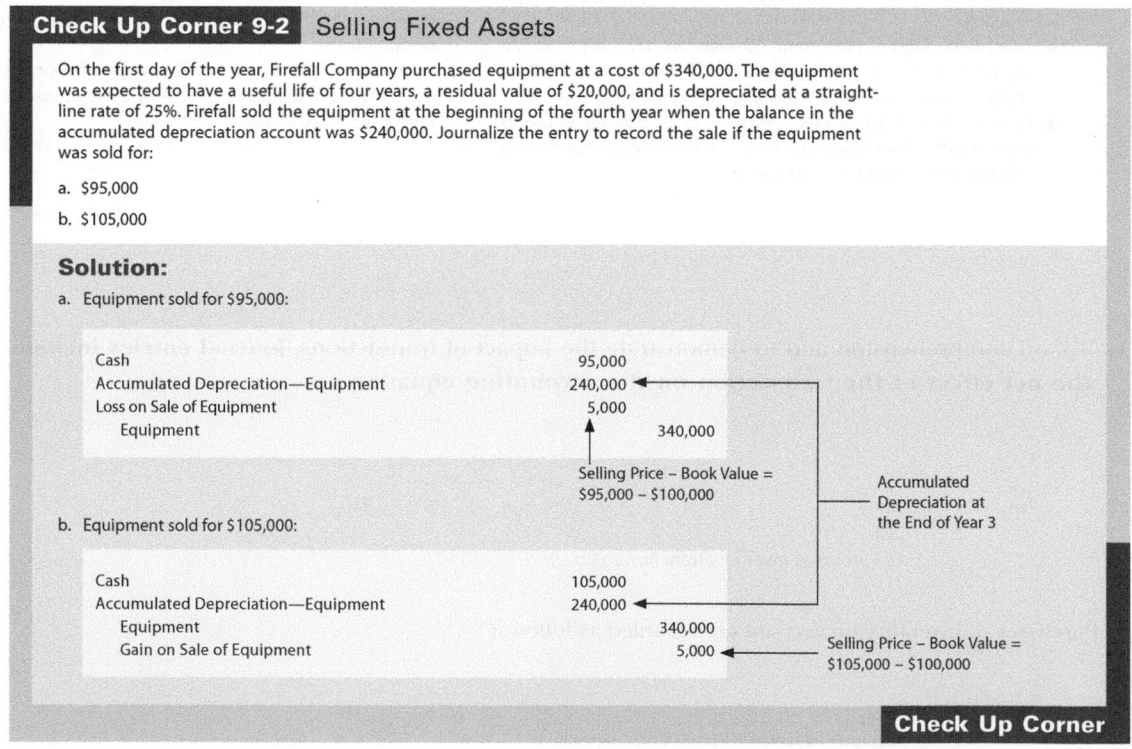

Check Up Corner 9-2   Selling Fixed Assets

On the first day of the year, Firefall Company purchased equipment at a cost of $340,000. The equipment was expected to have a useful life of four years, a residual value of $20,000, and is depreciated at a straight-line rate of 25%. Firefall sold the equipment at the beginning of the fourth year when the balance in the accumulated depreciation account was $240,000. Journalize the entry to record the sale if the equipment was sold for:

a. $95,000

b. $105,000

Solution:

a. Equipment sold for $95,000:

Cash	95,000	
Accumulated Depreciation—Equipment	240,000	
Loss on Sale of Equipment	5,000	
Equipment		340,000

Selling Price – Book Value =
$95,000 – $100,000

Accumulated Depreciation at the End of Year 3

b. Equipment sold for $105,000:

Cash	105,000	
Accumulated Depreciation—Equipment	240,000	
Equipment		340,000
Gain on Sale of Equipment		5,000

Selling Price – Book Value =
$105,000 – $100,000

Check Up Corner

- **Analysis for Decision Making** highlights how businesses use accounting information to make decisions and evaluate the health of a business. This provides students with context of why accounting is important to a business.

Analysis for Decision Making

Fixed Asset Turnover Ratio

Objective 7
Describe and illustrate the fixed asset turnover ratio to assess the efficiency of a company's use of its fixed assets.

The **fixed asset turnover ratio** measures the number of sales dollars earned per dollar of fixed assets. The higher the ratio, the more efficiently a company is using its fixed assets in generating sales. The ratio is computed as follows:

$$\text{Fixed Asset Turnover Ratio} = \frac{\text{Sales}}{\text{Average Book Value of Fixed Assets}}$$

To illustrate, the following data (in millions) were taken from a recent financial statement of **McDonald's Corporation (MCD):**

Sales	$24,621.9
Fixed assets (net):	
Beginning of year	21,257.6
End of year	23,117.6

McDonald's fixed asset turnover ratio for the year is computed as follows (rounded to one decimal place):

$$\text{Fixed Asset Turnover Ratio} = \frac{\text{Sales}}{\text{Average Book Value of Fixed Assets}}$$
$$= \frac{\$24,621.9}{(\$21,257.6 + \$23,117.6) \div 2}$$
$$= \frac{\$24,621.9}{\$22,187.6} = 1.1$$

Is 1.1 efficient? To answer this question, McDonald's fixed asset turnover ratio can be compared to other quick-service restaurant companies, as shown in Exhibit 14. **Yum! Brands (YUM)** operates KFC, Pizza Hut, and Taco Bell quick-service restaurants. The other restaurants are likely familiar by name.

- **Make a Decision** in the end-of-chapter material gives students a chance to analyze and compare real companies.

Make a Decision
Fixed Asset Turnover Ratio

REAL WORLD

MAD 9-1   Analyze and compare Amazon.com to Netflix   Obj. 7
Amazon.com, Inc. (AMZN) is the world's leading Internet retailer of merchandise and media. Amazon also designs and sells electronic products, such as e-readers. **Netflix, Inc. (NFLX)** is one of the world's leading Internet television networks. Both companies compete in the digital media and streaming space. However, Netflix is more narrowly focused in the digital streaming business than is Amazon.

Sales and average book value of fixed assets information (in millions) are provided for Amazon and Netflix for a recent year as follows:

	Amazon.com	Netflix
Sales	$135,987	$8,830
Average book value of fixed assets	25,476	212

a. Compute the fixed asset turnover ratio for each company. Round to one decimal place.
b. ⟶ Which company is more efficient in generating sales from fixed assets?
c. ⟶ Interpret your results.

REAL WORLD

MAD 9-2   Analyze and compare Alaska Air, Delta Air Lines, and Southwest Airlines Obj. 7
Alaska Air Group (ALK), **Delta Air Lines (DAL)**, and **Southwest Airlines (LUV)** reported the following financial information (in millions) in a recent year:

	Alaska Air Group	Delta Air Lines	Southwest Airlines
Sales	$5,931	$39,639	$20,425
Average book value of fixed assets	5,234	23,707	16,323

a. Determine the fixed asset turnover ratio for each airline. Round to one decimal place.
b. ⟶ Based on the fixed asset turnover ratio, which airline appears to be the most efficient in the use of its fixed assets?
c. ⟶ The most important fixed asset to an airline is the aircraft. Given this, what factors might influence the efficient use of fixed assets for an airline?

- At the end of each chapter, **Let's Review** is a new chapter summary and self-assessment feature that is designed to help busy students prepare for an exam. It includes a summary of each learning objective's key points, key terms, multiple-choice questions, exercises, and a sample problem that students may use to practice.
- Sample multiple-choice questions allow students to practice with the type of assessments they are likely to see on an exam.
- Short exercises and a longer problem allow students to apply their knowledge.
- **Answers** provided at the end of the Let's Review section let students check their knowledge immediately.
- **Take It Further** in the end-of-chapter activities allows instructors to assign other special activities related to ethics, communication, and teamwork.

CengageNOWv2

CengageNOWv2 is a powerful course management and online homework resource that provides control and customization to optimize the student learning experience. Included are many proven resources, such as algorithmic activities, a test bank, course management tools, reporting and assessment options, and much more.

Motivation: Set Expectations and Prepare Students for the Course

CengageNOWv2 helps motivate students and get them ready to learn by reshaping their misconceptions about the introductory accounting course and providing a powerful tool to engage students.

CengageNOWv2 Start-Up Center

Students are often surprised by the amount of time they need to spend outside of class working through homework assignments in order to succeed. The CengageNOWv2 Start-Up Center will help students identify what they need to do and where they need to focus in order to be successful with a variety of new resources.

- What Is Accounting? Module ensures students understand course expectations and how to be successful in the introductory accounting course. This module consists of two assignable videos: *Introduction to Accounting* and *Success Strategies*. The Student Advice Videos offer advice from real students about what it takes to do well in the course.
- Math Review Module, designed to help students get up to speed with necessary math skills, includes math review assignments and Show Me How math review videos to ensure that students have an understanding of basic math skills.
- How to Use CengageNOWv2 Module focuses on learning accounting, not on a particular software system. Quickly familiarize your students with CengageNOWv2 and direct them to all of its built-in student resources.

Motivation: Prepare Them for Class

With all the outside obligations accounting students have, finding time to read the textbook before class can be a struggle. Point students to the key concepts they need to know before they attend class.

- **Video: Tell Me More.** Short Tell Me More lecture activities explain the core concepts of the chapter through an engaging auditory and visual presentation. Available either on a stand-alone basis or as an assignment, they are ideal for all class formats—flipped model, online, hybrid, or face-to-face.

Fixed Asset Turnover Ratio

- The **fixed asset turnover ratio** measures the number of sales dollars earned per dollar of fixed assets.
- The fixed asset turnover ratio is computed as follows:

$$\text{Fixed Asset Turnover Ratio} = \frac{\text{Sales}}{\text{Average Book Value of Fixed Assets}}$$

- The higher the ratio, the more efficiently a company is using its fixed assets in generating sales.

Provide Help Right When Students Need It

The best way to learn accounting is through practice, but students often get stuck when attempting homework assignments on their own.

- **Video: Show Me How.** Created for the most frequently assigned end-of-chapter items, Show Me How problem demonstration videos provide a step-by-step model of a similar problem. Embedded tips help students avoid common mistakes and pitfalls.

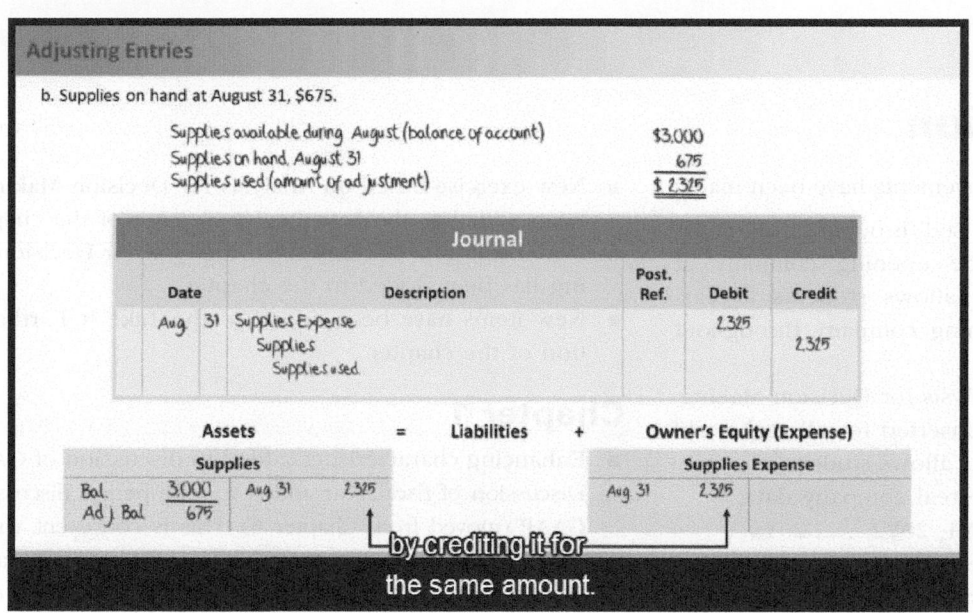

SHOW ME HOW

Help Students Go Beyond Memorization to True Understanding

Students often struggle to understand how concepts relate to one another. For most students, an introductory accounting course is their first exposure to both business transactions and the accounting system. While these concepts are already difficult to master individually, their combination and interdependency in the introductory accounting course often pose a challenge for students.

■ **Mastery Problems.** Mastery Problems enable you to assign problems and activities designed to test students' comprehension and mastery of difficult concepts.

MindTap eReader

The MindTap eReader for Warren/Jones' *Corporate Financial Accounting* is the most robust digital reading experience available. Hallmark features include:

■ Fully optimized for the iPad.
■ Note taking, highlighting, and more.
■ Embedded digital media.
■ The MindTap eReader also features ReadSpeaker®, an online text-to-speech application that vocalizes, or "speech-enables," online educational content. This feature is ideally suited for both instructors and learners who would like to listen to content instead of (or in addition to) reading it.

New to This Edition

In all chapters, the following improvements have been made:

■ Chapter schemas have been revised throughout.
■ New list of references to the opening company at the beginning of the chapter allows students to easily locate the ties to the opening company throughout the chapter.
■ New learning objective for Analysis for Decision Making.
■ Stock ticker symbol has been inserted for all real-world (publicly listed) companies. This allows students to easily use financial websites to locate real company data.
■ Years are now identified as 20Y1, 20Y2, …., 20Y9.
■ New Pathways Challenge feature added, consistent with the work of the Pathways Commission. This feature emphasizes the critical thinking aspect of accounting. A Suggested Answer to the Pathways Challenge is provided at the end of the chapter.
■ New Make a Decision section at the end of the Analysis for Decision Making allows students and instructors to easily locate the real-world company end-of-chapter materials related to Analysis for Decision Making. Also, the continuing company analysis is identified and referenced in this Make a Decision section.

■ New exercise based on Analysis for Decision Making has been added to the Let's Review section of the chapter.
■ New Basic Exercise based on Analysis for Decision Making has been added to the chapter.
■ New items have been added to the Take It Further section of the chapter.

Chapter 1

■ Enhancing characteristics added to discussion of GAAP.
■ Discussion of fiscal year added to time period discussion of GAAP (moved from Chapter 6). This is consistent with use of fiscal years throughout Chapters 1–4 and with the fact that many publicly traded companies use fiscal years not ending in December 31.
■ The statement of stockholders' equity replaces the retained earnings statement. This is consistent with the financial reporting of publicly held companies who report a statement of stockholders' equity rather than a retained earnings statement.
■ Exhibit 8 revised to show the interrelationships of the statement of stockholders' equity with the income statement and balance sheet.

Chapter 2

- Revised the discussion of correcting entries and inserted new exhibit to better enhance student understanding.

Chapter 3

- Exhibit 1 (Accruals) has been revised to make it consistent with Exhibit 2 (Deferrals).
- The chapter has been changed so that accruals are discussed and illustrated first, followed by deferrals. Accruals are the simplest adjustment (no entry has been made). Thus, the chapter discussion now goes from simple to complex, which facilitates student understanding of this complex topic.

Chapter 4

- New learning objectives for Appendices 1 and 2.
- The statement of stockholders' equity replaces the retained earnings statement. This is consistent with the financial reporting of publicly held companies that report a statement of stockholders' equity rather than a retained earnings statement.
- Exhibit 1 revised to show the interrelationships of the statement of stockholders' equity with the income statement and balance sheet.
- Simplified and updated the closing process so that *two* rather than *four* closing entries are required. Doing so eliminates the temporary (clearing) account Income Summary, which students have difficulty understanding.
- Exhibit 8 (Accounting Cycle) revised and made more readable.

Chapter 5

- Chapter has been retitled as "Accounting for Retail Businesses." Using *Retail* in the title rather than *Merchandising* is more current terminology that students can identify with.
- Schema revised to only focus on the financial statements and the key accounts that will be discussed within the chapter.
- New learning objective and separate discussion for the adjusting process of a retail business.
- New learning objective and Appendix "Gross Method of Recording Sales Discounts." This gives instructors flexibility as to whether to cover the net or gross methods of accounting for sales discounts.
- Chart of Accounts for Retail Businesses (Exhibit 2) has been moved earlier in the chapter so that students can focus on the new accounts specific to retail businesses.

- Customer refunds, allowances, and returns discussion has been simplified to progress from simple to complex, as summarized in Exhibit 7.
- Closing process for a retail business has been revised to use a two-entry closing process.
- The statement of stockholders' equity replaces the retained earnings statement. This is consistent with the financial reporting of publicly held companies that report a statement of stockholders' equity rather than a retained earnings statement.

Chapter 6

- New Check Up Corner on weighted average inventory method has been added.
- New exhibit on weighted average flow of costs has been added.
- Weighted average illustration has been added to Check Up Corner 6-3.
- Added an illustration of the lower of cost or net realizable for inventory applied by different *classes* of inventory (Exhibit 10).

Chapter 7

- Presentation of bank reconciliation has been reformatted.

Chapter 9

- New Check Up Corner on selling fixed assets was added.
- Lease discussion was modified to reflect the latest accounting standard.

Chapter 10

- Simplified Exhibit 1 by removing cash/sales discounts.

Chapter 11

- Present value formulas have been added to Appendix 1, "Present Value Concepts and Pricing Bonds Payable."

Chapter 12

- Added brief discussion of different classes of common stock (Classes A, B, and C).

Appendix D Investments

- The investments appendix has been updated to be consistent with *Financial Instruments, Subtopic 825-10, FASB Accounting Standards Update*, Financial Accounting Standards Board, Norwalk, CT, January 2016.

Acknowledgements

The many enhancements to this edition of *Corporate Financial Accounting* are the direct result of reviews, surveys, and focus groups with instructors at institutions across the country. We would like to take this opportunity to thank those who have helped us better understand the challenge of the financial accounting course and provided valuable feedback on our content and digital assets.

Rick Andrews, Sinclair Community College

Surasakdi Bhamornsiri, University of North Carolina at Charlotte

Alan Blankley, University of North Carolina at Charlotte

Salma Boumediene, Montana State University Billings

Louise Burney, University of Mississippi

James N. Cannon, Iowa State University

Jack Cathey, University of North Carolina at Charlotte

Donna Chadwick, Sinclair Community College

Ming Lu Chun, Santa Monica College

Anne Clem, Iowa State University

Stephan Davenport, University of Tennessee Chattanooga

David Deboskey, San Diego State

Desiree Elias, Florida International University

Jim Emig, Villanova University

Valerie Evans, Kansas State University

John Giles, North Carolina State University

Marcye Hampton, University of Central Florida

Christopher Harper, Grand Valley State University

Melanie Hicks, Liberty University

Jose Hortensi, Miami Dade College

Md Safayat Hossain, Florida International University

Su-Jane Hsieh, San Francisco State University

Aileen Huang, Santa Monica College

Julie Ying Huang, University of Louisville

Ann Kelley, Providence College

Charles Leflar, University of Arkansas

Eric Martin, University of Tennessee

Robert A. Martin, Kennesaw State University

Michelle McFeaters, Grove City College

Dawn McKinley, Harper College

Jill Mitchell, Northern Virginia Community College – Alexandria

DeeAnne Lynn Peterson-Meyer, University of Wisconsin – Eau Claire

Jeffery Reinking, University of Central Florida – Orlando

Jenny Resnick, Santa Monica College

Vernon Richardson, University of Arkansas

Patrick Rogan, Cosumnes River College

Jennifer Schneider, University of North Georgia

Mary Sheil, Kennesaw State University

Mona Stephens, Southern New Hampshire University

Linda Stoller, Bentley University

Nirmalee Summers, University of Wisconsin – La Crosse

Dominique Svarc, Harper College

Bill Urquhart, Florida Atlantic University

Rodney Vogt, Kansas State University

Rick Warne, University of Cincinnati

Vivian Winston, Indiana University

Jan Workman, East Carolina University

Glen Young, Texas A&M University – College Station

Mustafa Younis, Tulane University

Fang Zhao, Florida International University

Terri Ziegler, Ohio State University

Special thanks to our Financial Accounting Advisory Board Members:

Reb Beatty, Anne Arundel Community College

Amy Bourne, Oregon State University

Rachel Brassine, East Carolina University

Gregory Brookins, Santa Monica College

Marci Butterfield, University of Utah

Lawrence Chui, University of St. Thomas

Jerrilyn Eisenhauer, Tulsa Community College – Southeast

Shari Fowler, Indiana University – East

Micah Frankel, California State University – East Bay

Steven Hegemann, University of Nebraska – Lincoln

Todd Jensen, Sierra College

Sergey Komissarov, University of Wisconsin – La Crosse

Anthony Kurek, Eastern Michigan University

Joseph Larkin, Saint Joseph's University

Gary Laycock, Ivy Tech Community College – Terre Haute

Kristy McAuliffe, San Jacinto College

Melanie McCoskey, University of Akron

Allison McLeod, University of North Texas

Don Minyard, University of Alabama

Micki Nickla, Ivy Tech Community College – Gary

John Robertson, Arkansas State University

Philip Slater, Forsyth Technical Community College

Bob Urell, Irvine Valley College

Alycia Marie Winegardner, University of Tennessee – Knoxville

About the Authors

Carl S. Warren

Dr. Carl S. Warren is Professor Emeritus of Accounting at the University of Georgia, Athens. Dr. Warren has taught classes at the University of Georgia, University of Iowa, Michigan State University, and University of Chicago. He has focused his teaching efforts on principles of accounting and auditing. Dr. Warren received his PhD from Michigan State University and his BBA and MA from the University of Iowa. During his career, Dr. Warren published numerous articles in professional journals, including *The Accounting Review, Journal of Accounting Research, Journal of Accountancy, The CPA Journal*, and *Auditing: A Journal of Practice and Theory*. Dr. Warren has served on numerous committees of the American Accounting Association, the American Institute of Certified Public Accountants, and the Institute of Internal Auditors. He has consulted with numerous companies and public accounting firms. His outside interests include handball, golfing, skiing, backpacking, motorcycling, and fly-fishing. He also enjoys interacting with his five grandchildren, Bella and Mila (twins), Jeremy, and Brooke and Robbie (twins).

Jefferson P. Jones

Dr. Jefferson P. Jones is an Associate Professor of Accounting in the School of Accountancy at Auburn University where he teaches financial accounting and applied financial research courses. He received his Bachelor's in Accounting and Master of Accountancy degrees from Auburn University and his PhD from Florida State University. Dr. Jones has received numerous teaching awards, including the Auburn University Beta Alpha Psi Outstanding Teaching Award (eight times); the Auburn University Outstanding Master of Accountancy Professor Teaching Award (five times); the Auburn University Outstanding Distance Master of Accountancy Teaching Award (three times); and the Auburn University College of Business McCartney Teaching Award. In addition, he has made numerous presentations around the country on research and pedagogical issues. Dr. Jones has public accounting experience as an auditor with Deloitte and Touche, holds a CPA certificate in the state of Alabama (inactive), and is a member of the American Accounting Association, the American Institute of Certified Public Accountants (AICPA), and the Alabama Society of CPAs (ASCPA). His research interests focus on financial accounting, specifically investigating the quality of reported accounting information, and accounting education. He has published articles in numerous journals, including *Advances in Accounting, Review of Quantitative Finance and Accounting, Issues in Accounting Education, International Journal of Forecasting*, and *The CPA Journal*. When not at work, Dr. Jones enjoys playing golf and watching college football.

Brief Contents

Contents

5 Accounting for Retail Businesses 232

6 Inventories 298

7 Internal Control and Cash 350

8 Receivables 396

9 Long-Term Assets: Fixed and Intangible 442

14 Financial Statement Analysis 686

What Successful Students Are Saying

In a recent survey, students who had taken financial accounting courses listed the following actions as important steps to success in these courses:

- Complete assigned homework
- Attend class and pay attention during the lecture
- Study
- Ask for help or get a tutor
- Complete ungraded practice assignments or review exercises

❏ Did you read the chapter from the required textbook prior to attending class?
❏ Did you attend class?
❏ Did you take notes during class?
❏ Did you ask questions of the professor either during or after class when you did not understand a concept being taught?
❏ Did you complete all assigned homework?
❏ Did you complete ungraded practice assignments or review exercises to better learn and understand accounting concepts?
❏ Did you obtain an explanation from the professor for incorrect answers?
❏ Did you utilize additional resources provided such as demonstration videos & tutorials?

Successful students spent an average of four hours per week outside of class time studying, including completing assigned homework.

You just need to put in the effort. If you work through the homework problems and show up to class, you will do well.

—Brandy J. Gibson, Business Administration Major Ivy Tech Community College

Do not put off homework – it is more important than you know – and when in need – ASK FOR HELP!!

—Sally Cross, Accounting Major Ivy Tech Community College

You need to attend every class and pay attention. Take good notes and do all the homework.

—Melinda Lallier, Accounting Major Community College of Rhode Island

Come to class every day – if you miss a class, you miss a lot of notes and example problems. Homework is vital and so is studying for tests – you need to learn the different formulas and equations.

—Shannon Green, General Business Major Community College of Rhode Island

Anyone can succeed at learning & understanding accounting concepts!
<u>How?</u> Preparation, time management, & practice!

Corporate Financial
Accounting 15e

1 Introduction to Accounting and Business

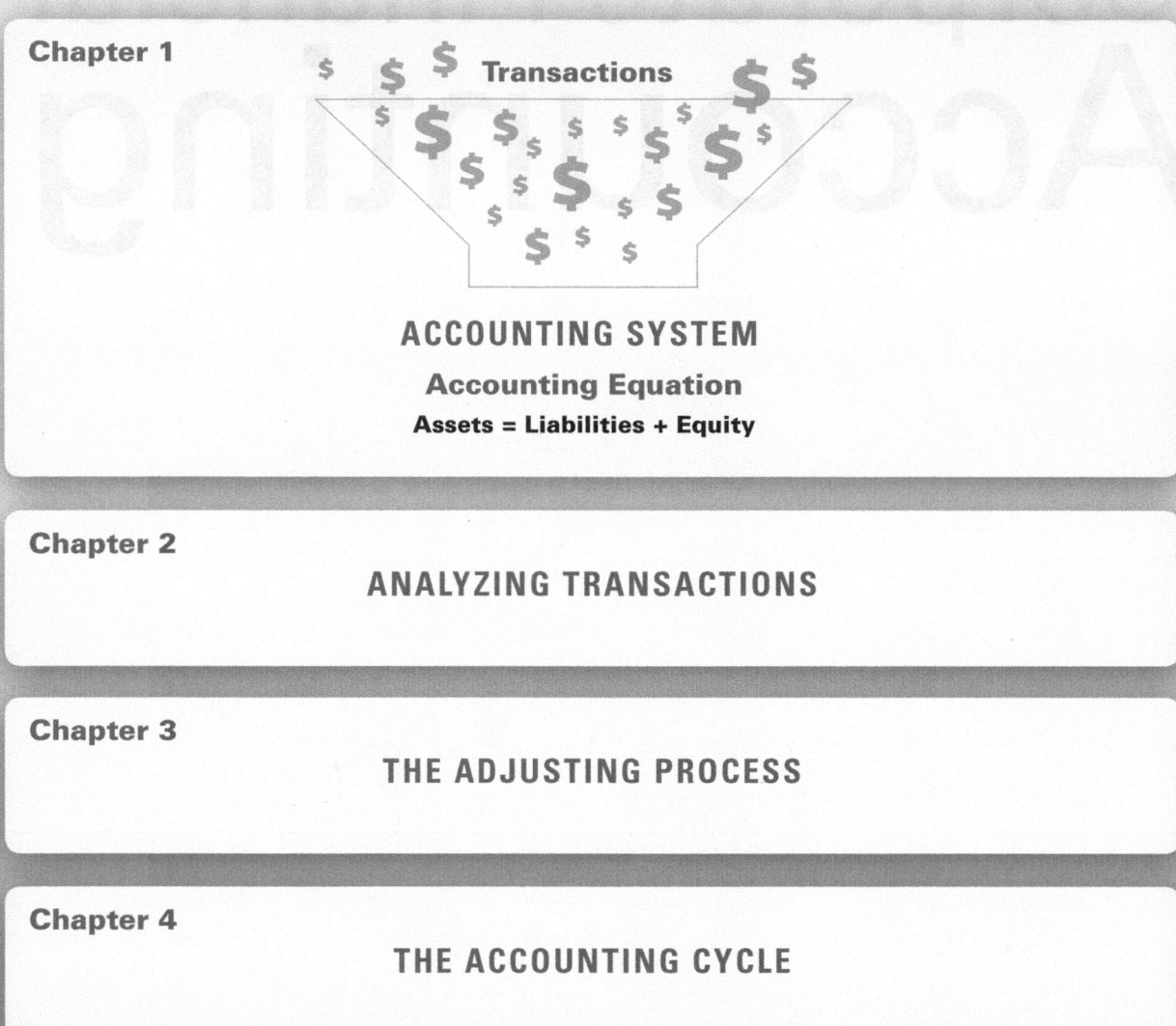

Chapter 1

Transactions

ACCOUNTING SYSTEM

Accounting Equation

Assets = Liabilities + Equity

Chapter 2

ANALYZING TRANSACTIONS

Chapter 3

THE ADJUSTING PROCESS

Chapter 4

THE ACCOUNTING CYCLE

Twitter, Inc.

When two teams pair up for a game of football, there is often a lot of noise. The band plays, the fans cheer, and fireworks light up the scoreboard. Obviously, the fans are committed and care about the outcome of the game. Just like fans at a football game, the owners of a business want their business to "win" against their competitors in the marketplace. While having your football team win can be a source of pride, winning in the marketplace goes beyond pride and has many tangible benefits. Companies that are winners are better able to serve customers, provide good jobs for employees, and make money for their owners.

Twitter, Inc. (TWTR) is one of the most visible companies on the Internet. It provides a real-time information network where members can post messages, called tweets, for free. Millions post tweets every day throughout the world.

Do you think Twitter is a successful company? Does it make money? How would you know? Accounting helps to answer these questions.

This textbook introduces you to accounting, the language of business. Chapter 1 begins by discussing what a business is, how it operates, and the role that accounting plays.

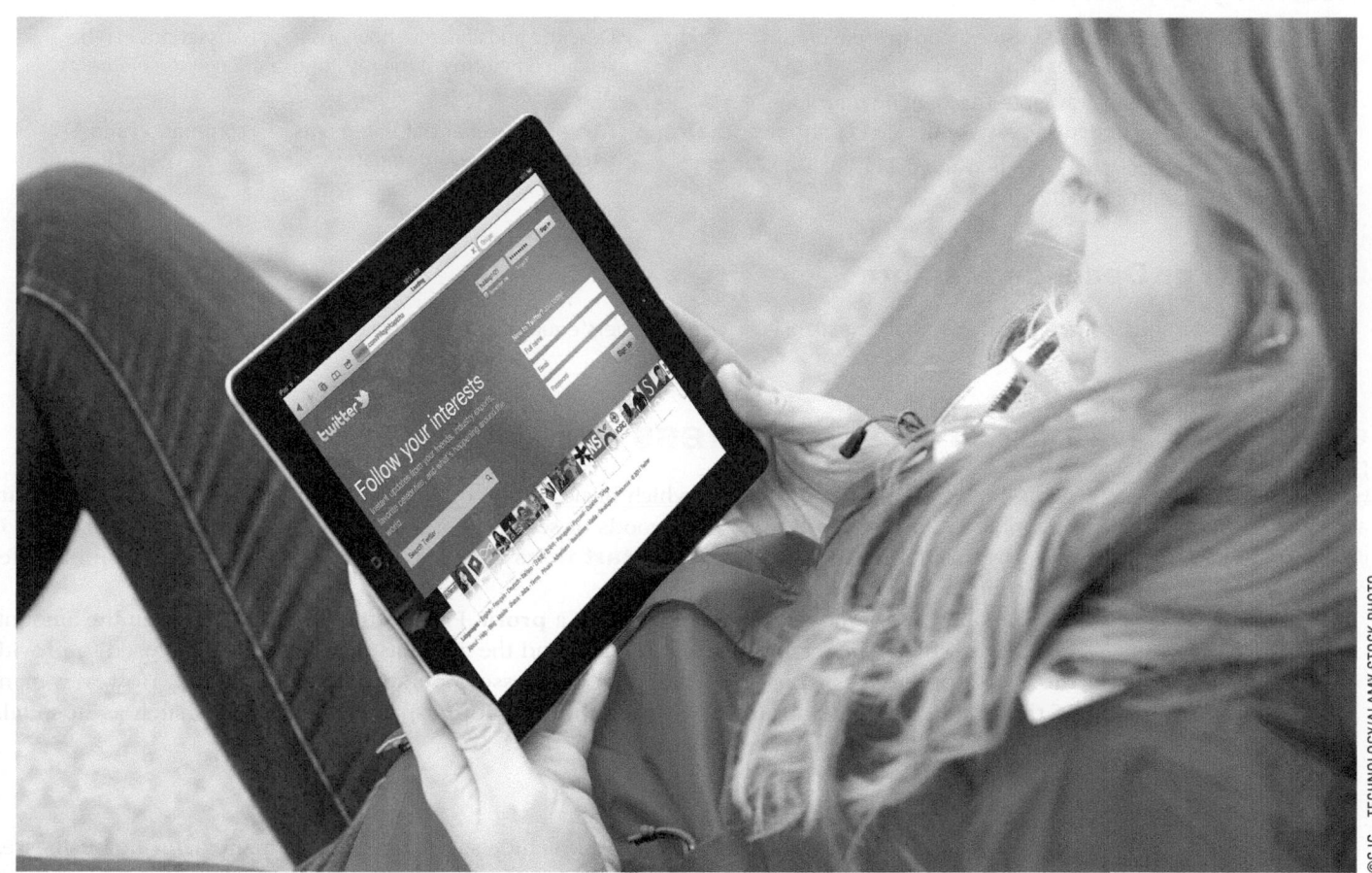

©CJG – TECHNOLOGY/ALAMY STOCK PHOTO

What's Covered

Introduction to Accounting and Business

Nature of Business
- Types of Business (Obj. 1)
- Role of Accounting (Obj. 1)
- Ethics (Obj. 1)

Nature of Accounting
- Managerial and Financial Accounting (Obj. 1)
- Career Opportunities (Obj. 1)

Analyzing Business Transactions
- Generally Accepted Accounting Principles (Obj. 2)
- Accounting Equation (Obj. 3)
- Transactions (Obj. 4)

Financial Statements
- Income Statement (Obj. 5)
- Statement of Stockholders' Equity (Obj. 5)
- Balance Sheet (Obj. 5)
- Statement of Cash Flows (Obj. 5)

Learning Objectives

Obj. 1 Describe the nature of business and the role of accounting and ethics in business.

Obj. 2 Describe generally accepted accounting principles, including the underlying assumptions and principles.

Obj. 3 State the accounting equation and define each element of the equation.

Obj. 4 Describe and illustrate how business transactions can be recorded in terms of the resulting change in the elements of the accounting equation.

Obj. 5 Describe the financial statements of a corporation and explain how they interrelate.

Analysis for Decision Making

Obj. 6 Describe and illustrate the use of the ratio of liabilities to stockholders' equity in evaluating a company's financial condition.

Objective 1
Describe the nature of business and the role of accounting and ethics in business.

Nature of Business and Accounting

A **business**[1] is an organization in which basic resources (inputs), such as materials and labor, are assembled and processed to provide goods or services (outputs) to customers. Businesses come in all sizes, from a local coffee house to **Starbucks (SBUX)**, which sells over $15 billion of coffee and related products each year.

The objective of most businesses is to earn a **profit**. Profit is the difference between the amounts received from customers for goods or services and the amounts paid for the inputs used to provide the goods or services. This text focuses on businesses operating to earn a profit. However, many of the same concepts and principles also apply to not-for-profit organizations such as hospitals, churches, and government agencies.

Types of Businesses

Three types of businesses operating for profit include service, retail, and manufacturing businesses. Some examples of each type of business follow:

- **Service businesses** provide services rather than products to customers.
    Delta Air Lines (DAL) (transportation services)
    The Walt Disney Company (DIS) (entertainment services)
- **Retail businesses** sell products they purchase from other businesses to customers.
    Wal-Mart Stores, Inc. (WMT) (general merchandise)
    Amazon.com (AMZN) (Internet books, music, videos, ...)
- **Manufacturing businesses** change basic inputs into products that are sold to customers.
    Ford Motor Company (F) (cars, trucks, vans)
    Merck & Co., Inc. (MRK) (pharmaceutical drugs)

Link to Twitter   **Twitter** is a service company that provides a platform for individuals to send text messages called tweets.

---

[1] A complete glossary of terms appears at the end of the text.

Role of Accounting in Business

The role of accounting in business is to provide information for managers to use in operating the business. In addition, accounting provides information to other users in assessing the economic performance and condition of the business.

Thus, **accounting** can be defined as an information system that provides reports to users about the economic activities and condition of a business. You could think of accounting as the "language of business." This is because accounting is the means by which businesses' financial information is communicated to users.

note:

Accounting is an information system that provides reports to users about the economic activities and condition of a business.

> **Twitter** communicates to investors in an annual report that includes accounting information.

Link to Twitter

The process by which accounting provides information to users is as follows:

1. Identify users.
2. Assess users' information needs.
3. Design the accounting information system to meet users' needs.
4. Record economic data about business activities and events.
5. Prepare accounting reports for users.

As illustrated in Exhibit 1, users of accounting information can be divided into two groups: internal users and external users.

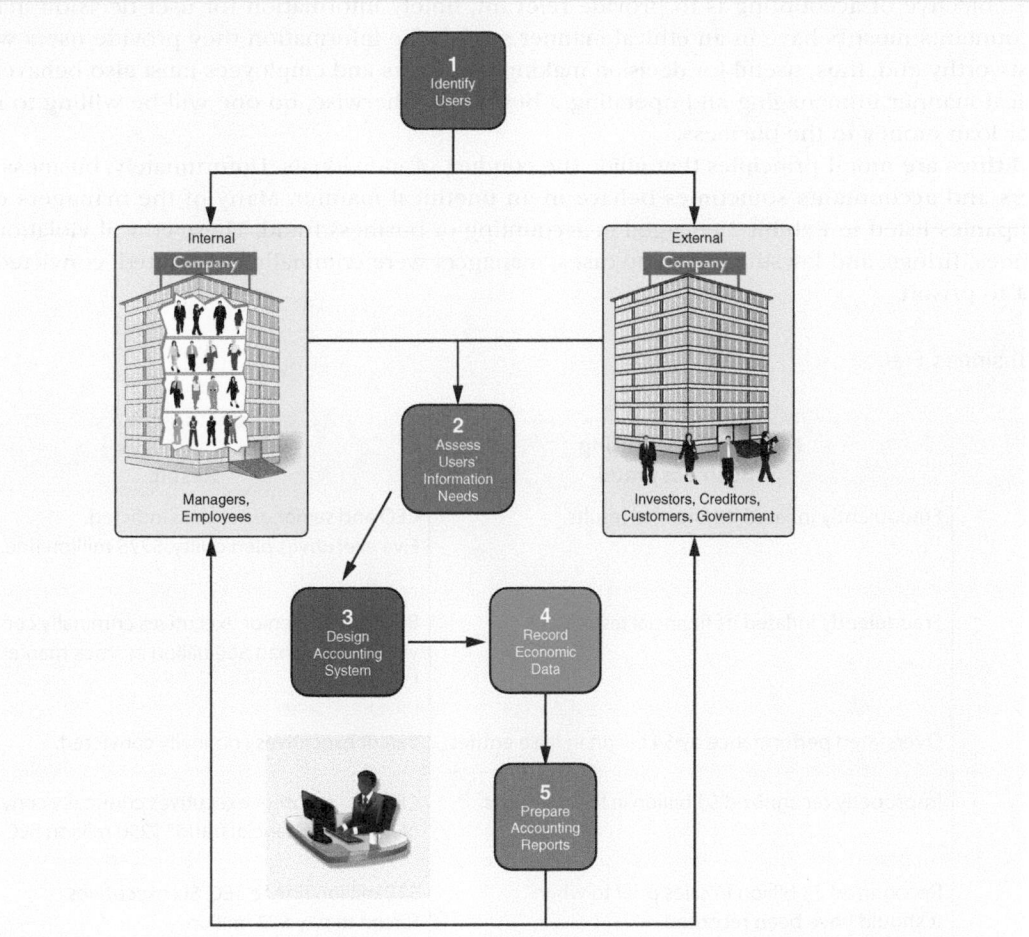

Exhibit 1

Accounting as an Information System

Managerial Accounting Internal users of accounting information include managers and employees. These users are directly involved in managing and operating the business. The area of accounting that provides internal users with information is called **managerial accounting**, or **management accounting**.

The objective of managerial accounting is to provide relevant and timely information for managers' and employees' decision-making needs. Often, such information is sensitive and is not distributed outside the business. Examples of sensitive information might include information about customers, prices, and plans to expand the business. Managerial accountants employed by a business are employed in **private accounting**.

Financial Accounting External users of accounting information include investors, creditors, customers, and the government. These users are not directly involved in managing and operating the business. The area of accounting that provides external users with information is called **financial accounting**.

The objective of financial accounting is to provide relevant and timely information for the decision-making needs of users outside of the business. For example, financial reports on the operations and condition of the business are useful for banks and other creditors in deciding whether to lend money to the business. **General-purpose financial statements** are one type of financial accounting report that is distributed to external users. The term *general-purpose* refers to the wide range of decision-making needs that these reports are designed to serve. Later in this chapter, general-purpose financial statements are described and illustrated.

Link to Twitter   **Twitter** is a service company that provides a platform for individuals to send text messages called tweets.

Role of Ethics in Accounting and Business

ETHICS

The objective of accounting is to provide relevant, timely information for user decision making. Accountants must behave in an ethical manner so that the information they provide users will be trustworthy and, thus, useful for decision making. Managers and employees must also behave in an ethical manner in managing and operating a business. Otherwise, no one will be willing to invest in or loan money to the business.

Ethics are moral principles that guide the conduct of individuals. Unfortunately, business managers and accountants sometimes behave in an unethical manner. Many of the managers of the companies listed in Exhibit 2 engaged in accounting or business fraud. These ethical violations led to fines, firings, and lawsuits. In some cases, managers were criminally prosecuted, convicted, and sent to prison.

Exhibit 2   Accounting and Business Frauds

Company	Nature of Accounting or Business Fraud	Result
Computer Associates International, Inc.	Fraudulently inflated its financial results.	CEO and senior executives indicted. Five executives pled guilty. $225 million fine.
Enron	Fraudulently inflated its financial results.	Bankrupcty. Senior executives criminally convicted. More than $60 billion in stock market losses.
HealthSouth	Overstated performance by $4 billion in false entries.	Senior executives criminally convicted.
Qwest Communications International, Inc.	Improperly recognized $3 billion in false receipts.	CEO and six other executives criminally convicted of "massive financial fraud." $250 million SEC fine.
Xerox Corporation	Recognized $3 billion in sales prior to when it should have been recorded.	$10 million fine to SEC. Six executives forced to pay $22 million.

What went wrong for the managers and companies listed in Exhibit 2? The answer normally involved one or both of the following two factors:

- **Failure of Individual Character:** Ethical managers and accountants are honest and fair. However, managers and accountants often face pressures from supervisors to meet company and investor expectations. In many of the cases in Exhibit 2, managers and accountants justified small ethical violations to avoid such pressures. However, these small violations became big violations as the company's financial problems became worse.

- **Culture of Greed and Ethical Indifference:** By their behavior and attitude, senior managers set the company culture. In most of the companies listed in Exhibit 2, the senior managers created a culture of greed and indifference to the truth.

As a result of the accounting and business frauds shown in Exhibit 2, Congress passed laws to monitor the behavior of accounting and business. For example, the **Sarbanes-Oxley Act (SOX)** was enacted. SOX established a new oversight body for the accounting profession called the **Public Company Accounting Oversight Board (PCAOB)**. In addition, SOX established standards for independence, corporate responsibility, and disclosure.

How does one behave ethically when faced with financial or other types of pressure? Guidelines for behaving ethically follow:[2]

1. Identify an ethical decision by using your personal ethical standards of honesty and fairness.
2. Identify the consequences of the decision and its effect on others.
3. Consider your obligations and responsibilities to those who will be affected by your decision.
4. Make a decision that is ethical and fair to those affected by it.

Twitter's "Code of Business Conduct and Ethics" can be found at https://investor.twitterinc.com/corporate-governance.cfm. *Link to Twitter*

Opportunities for Accountants

Numerous career opportunities are available for students majoring in accounting. Currently, the demand for accountants exceeds the number of new graduates entering the job market. This is partly due to the increased regulation of business caused by the accounting and business frauds shown in Exhibit 2. Also, more and more businesses have come to recognize the importance and value of accounting information.

As indicated earlier, accountants employed by a business are employed in private accounting. Private accountants have a variety of possible career options within a company. Some of these career options are shown in Exhibit 3 along with their starting salaries. As shown in Exhibit 3, several private accounting careers have certification options. Accountants who provide audit services, called *auditors*, verify the accuracy of financial records, accounts, and systems.

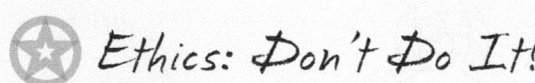

Ethics: Don't Do It!

Bernie Madoff

Bernard L. "Bernie" Madoff was sentenced to 150 years in prison for defrauding thousands of investors in one of the biggest frauds in American history. Madoff's fraud started several decades earlier when he began a "Ponzi scheme" in his investment management firm, Bernard L. Madoff Investment Securities LLC.

In a Ponzi scheme, the investment manager uses funds received from new investors to pay a return to existing investors, rather than basing returns on the investments' actual performance. As long as the investment manager is able to attract new investors, he or she will have new funds to pay existing investors and continue the fraud. While most Ponzi schemes collapse quickly when the investment manager runs out of new investors, Madoff's reputation, popularity, and personal contacts provided a steady stream of investors, which allowed the fraud to survive for decades.

Source: Bernie Madoff

---

[2] Many companies have ethical standards of conduct for managers and employees. In addition, the Institute of Management Accountants and the American Institute of Certified Public Accountants have professional codes of conduct, which can be obtained from their Web sites at www.imanet.org and www.aicpa.org, respectively.

Exhibit 3 Accounting Career Paths and Salaries

Accounting Career Track	Description	Career Options	Annual Starting Salaries*	Certification
Private Accounting	Accountants employed by companies, government, and not-for-profit entities.	Bookkeeper	$40,000	
		Payroll clerk	$40,000	Certified Payroll Professional (CPP)
		General accountant	$51,000	
		Budget analyst	$53,000	
		Cost accountant	$55,000	Certified Management Accountant (CMA)
		Internal auditor	$62,000	Certified Internal Auditor (CIA)
		Information technology auditor	$71,000	Certified Information Systems Auditor (CISA)
Public Accounting	Accountants employed individually or within a public accounting firm in audit, tax, or management advisory services.	Large firms (over $250 million in revenue)	$68,000	Certified Public Accountant (CPA)
		Mid-size firms ($25–$250 million in revenue)	$61,000	Certified Public Accountant (CPA)
		Small firms (less than $25 million in revenue)	$56,000	Certified Public Accountant (CPA)

*Average salaries rounded to the nearest thousand. Salaries may vary by size of company and region.
Source: Robert Half *2017 U.S. Salary Guide (Finance and Accounting)*, Robert Half International, Inc. (www.roberthalf.com/workplace-research/salary-guides).

Accountants and their staff who provide services on a fee basis are said to be employed in **public accounting**. In public accounting, an accountant may practice as an individual or as a member of a public accounting firm. Public accountants who have met a state's education, experience, and examination requirements may become **Certified Public Accountants (CPAs)**. CPAs typically perform general accounting, audit, or tax services. As can be seen in Exhibit 3, CPAs have slightly better starting salaries than private accountants. Career statistics indicate, however, that these salary differences tend to disappear over time. The American Institute of Certified Public Accountants (AICPA) provides information and resources for students interested in accounting at www.startheregoplaces.com.

Because all functions within a business use accounting information, experience in private or public accounting provides a solid foundation for a career. Many positions in industry and in government agencies are held by individuals with accounting backgrounds.

Why It Matters
CONCEPT CLIP

Pathways Commission

The Pathways Commission recently issued its study titled *Charting a National Strategy for the Next Generation of Accountants.* The Commission was made up of diverse members and was jointly sponsored by the American Institute of Certified Public Accountants (AICPA) and the American Accounting Association (AAA). The Commission emphasized the importance of accounting for a prosperous society and good decision making. The Commission also emphasized that accountants must be critical thinkers who are comfortable addressing the shades of gray required by accounting judgments.

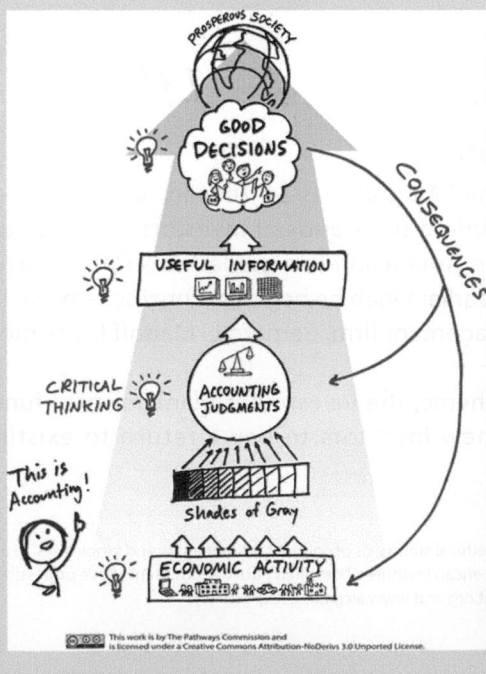

Source: *Charting a National Strategy for the Next Generation of Accountants,* The Pathways Commission, July 2012.

Generally Accepted Accounting Principles (GAAP)

Financial information in the United States is based on **generally accepted accounting principles (GAAP)**. GAAP is a collection of *accounting standards*, *principles*, and *assumptions* that define how financial information will be reported.

- **Accounting standards** are the rules that determine the accounting for individual business transactions.
- **Accounting principles** and **assumptions** provide the framework upon which accounting standards are constructed.

Within the United States, the **Financial Accounting Standards Board (FASB)** has the primary responsibility for developing accounting standards. The FASB maintains an electronic database, called the **Accounting Standards Codification**, that contains all the accounting standards that make up GAAP. Changes in the FASB Codification are made using **Accounting Standards Updates**.

The **Securities and Exchange Commission (SEC)**, an agency of the U.S. government, has authority over the accounting and financial disclosures for companies whose shares of ownership (stock) are traded and sold to the public. The SEC normally accepts the accounting standards set forth by the FASB. However, the SEC may issue *Staff Accounting Bulletins* on accounting matters that may not have been addressed by the FASB.

Outside the United States, most countries use accounting standards and principles adopted by the **International Accounting Standards Board (IASB)**. The IASB issues *International Financial Reporting Standards* (IFRS). Major differences between FASB and IASB accounting principles are identified throughout the chapters of this text and in Appendix C.

Characteristics of Financial Information

The primary goal of financial accounting is to provide information that is useful for decision making. To be useful, financial reports must possess two important characteristics: *relevance* and *faithful representation*.

- **Relevant** information has the potential to impact decision making.
- **Faithful representation** means that the information accurately reflects an entity's economic activity or condition.

The characteristics of relevant and faithful representation are enhanced by the following:

- **Comparability** allows users to identify similarities and differences among reported items.
- **Verifiability** allows users to agree on the meaning of reported items.
- **Timeliness** requires distribution of financial reports in time to influence a user's decision.
- **Understandability** requires clear and concise financial reports that facilitate user interpretation and analysis.

International Connection

IFRS International Financial Reporting Standards (IFRS)

IFRS are considered to be more "principles-based" than U.S. GAAP, which is considered to be more "rules-based." For example, U.S. GAAP consists of approximately 17,000 pages, which include numerous industry-specific accounting rules. In contrast, IFRS allow more judgment in deciding how business transactions are recorded. Many believe that the strong regulatory and litigation environment in the United States is the cause for the more rules-based GAAP approach. Regardless, IFRS and GAAP share many common principles.*

*Differences between U.S. GAAP and IFRS are further discussed and illustrated in Appendix C.

Assumptions

Financial accounting and generally accepted accounting principles are based upon the following assumptions:

- Monetary unit
- Time period
- Business entity
- Going concern

The **monetary unit assumption** requires that financial reports be expressed in a single money unit, or currency. This provides a common measurement of the effects of economic events and transactions on an entity. The monetary unit used is normally determined by the country in which the company operates. For example, in the United States, the U.S. dollar is used as the monetary unit.

The **time period assumption** allows a company to report its economic activities on a regular basis for a specific period of time. In doing so, financial condition and changes in financial condition are reported periodically on a consistent basis. In the United States, reports are normally required on a yearly basis supplemented with quarterly reports.

Link to Twitter   **Twitter** publishes quarterly as well as yearly financial reports that are available at https://investor.twitterinc.com.

The annual accounting period adopted by a company is called its **fiscal year**. The fiscal year most commonly used is the calendar year beginning January 1 and ending December 31. However, other periods are not unusual, especially for companies organized as corporations. For example, a corporation may adopt a fiscal year that ends when business activities have reached the lowest point in its annual operating cycle, which allows more time to prepare financial reports. Such a fiscal year is called the **natural business year**. For example, a company's fiscal year could begin August 1, 20Y7, and end on July 31, 20Y8, as follows:

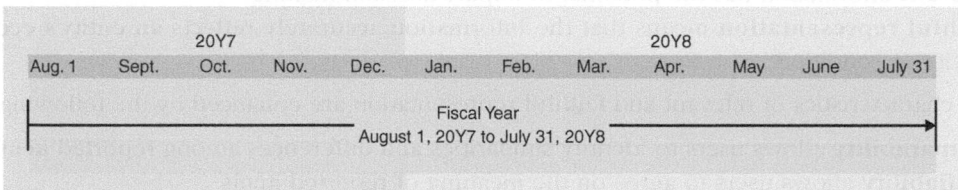

	20Y7				20Y8					
Aug. 1	Sept.	Oct.	Nov.	Dec.	Jan.	Feb.	Mar.	Apr.	May	June	July 31

Fiscal Year
August 1, 20Y7 to July 31, 20Y8

The **business entity assumption** limits the economic data in financial reports to that directly related to the activities of the business. In other words, the business is viewed as an entity separate from its owners, creditors, or other businesses. For example, the accountant for a business with one owner would record the activities of the business only and would not record the personal activities, property, or debts of the owner.

A business entity may take the form of a proprietorship, partnership, corporation, or limited liability company (LLC). Each of these forms and their major characteristics are listed in Exhibit 4.

The three types of businesses discussed earlier—service, retail, and manufacturing—may be organized as proprietorships, partnerships, corporations, or limited liability companies.

Because of the large amount of resources required to operate a manufacturing business, most manufacturers such as **Ford Motor Company (F)** are corporations. Most large retailers such as **Wal-Mart Stores (WMT)** and **The Home Depot (HD)** are also corporations. Companies

Exhibit 4 Forms of Business Entities

Form of Business Entity	Characteristics and Advantages	Examples
Proprietorship is owned by one individual.	• 70% of business entities in the United States. • Easy and inexpensive to organize. • Resources are limited to those of the owner. • Used by small businesses.	• A & B Painting
Partnership is owned by two or more individuals.	• 10% of business organizations in the United States (combined with limited liability companies). • Combines the skills and resources of more than one person.	• Jones & Smith, Architects
Corporation is organized under state or federal statutes as a separate legal taxable entity.	• Generates 90% of business revenues. • 20% of the business organizations in the United States. • Ownership is divided into shares called stock. • Can obtain large amounts of resources by issuing stock. • Used by large businesses.	• **Alphabet Inc. (GOOG)** • **Apple Inc. (AAPL)** • **Ford Motor Company (F)**
Limited liability company (LLC) combines the attributes of a partnership and a corporation.	• 10% of business organizations in the United States (combined with partnerships). • Often used as an alternative to a partnership. • Has tax and legal liability advantages for owners.	• **Boston Basketball Partners, LLC**

Although **Twitter** is organized as a corporation in Delaware, its principal offices are in San Francisco. *Link to Twitter*

organized as corporations often include Inc. as part of their name to indicate that they are incorporated. For example, Twitter's legal name is **Twitter, Inc.**

The **going concern assumption** requires that financial reports be prepared assuming that the entity will continue operating into the future. This assumption justifies reporting items such as equipment, buildings, and land at their initial or historical cost rather than liquidation or forced sale values.

Pathways Challenge

This is Accounting!

Economic Activity

Over 20 years ago, **Starbucks (SBUX)** and **Pepsi (PEP)** created a business, called **The North American Coffee Partnership**. The business combined Starbucks' expertise in coffee with Pepsi's ability to manufacture, market, and sell ready-to-drink coffee products. Its first product, Frappuccino, took off and today the business dominates the ready-to-drink market with over $1.5 billion in annual sales.

Critical Thinking/Judgment

Should the $1.5 billion in annual sales be reported as part of Starbucks' annual report?
Should the $1.5 billion in annual sales be reported as part of Pepsi's annual report?
Should the $1.5 billion in annual sales be reported as part of a separate business's annual report?

Suggested answer at end of chapter.

Principles

In addition to the preceding characteristics and assumptions, the following four principles are an integral part of financial accounting:

- Measurement
- Historical cost
- Revenue recognition
- Expense recognition

The **measurement principle** determines the amount that will be recorded and reported. The measurement principle requires that amounts be *objective* and verifiable. An amount is objective if it is based upon independent, unbiased evidence. An amount is *verifiable* if it can be confirmed by a third party. Transactions between two independent parties, called **arm's-length transactions**, provide amounts that are objective and verifiable.

To illustrate, assume that Aaron Publishers purchased the following building from Schenk Enterprises on February 20, 20Y1, for $150,000:

Price listed by Schenk Enterprises on January 1, 20Y1	$160,000
Aaron Publishers' initial offer to buy on January 31, 20Y1	140,000
Aaron Publishers' purchase price on February 20, 20Y1	150,000
Estimated selling price on December 31, 20Y3	220,000
Assessed value for property taxes, December 31, 20Y3	190,000

Aaron Publishers would record the building at the February 20, 20Y1, purchase price of $150,000. This amount is both objective and verifiable, as it was the result of a transaction between two independent parties. Recording an item at its initial transaction price is called the **historical cost principle** or **cost principle**. Under the historical cost principle, amounts do not normally change until another transaction occurs.

To illustrate, the fact that the preceding building has an estimated selling price of $220,000 on December 31, 20Y3, indicates that the building's value has increased. However, the $220,000 is not recorded in the accounting records because Aaron Publishers has not sold the building. If, however, Aaron sells the building on January 9, 20Y4, for $240,000, a profit of $90,000 ($240,000 − $150,000) would be recorded by Aaron Publishers.

Revenue is the amount earned (received) from providing services or selling goods to customers. The **revenue recognition principle** determines when revenue is recorded in the accounting records. Normally, revenue is recorded when the services have been performed or goods are delivered to the customer.

Expenses are amounts used to generate revenue. The **expense recognition principle**, sometimes called the *matching principle*, requires expenses to be recorded in the same period as the related revenue. Doing so allows the reporting of a profit or loss for the period.

Objective 3

State the accounting equation and define each element of the equation.

The Accounting Equation

The resources owned by a business are its **assets**. Examples of assets include cash, land, buildings, and equipment. The rights or claims to the assets are divided into two types: (1) the rights of creditors and (2) the rights of owners. The rights of creditors are the debts of the business and are called **liabilities**. The rights of owners are called **equity**. Since stockholders own a corporation, equity is called **stockholders' equity**. For a proprietorship, partnership, or limited liability company, equity is called **owner's equity**.

The following equation shows the relationship among assets, liabilities, and equity:

Assets = Liabilities + Equity

This equation is called the **accounting equation**. Liabilities usually are shown before equity in the accounting equation because creditors have first rights to the assets.

Throughout this text, we use the corporate form of business. However, most of the concepts and principles described and illustrated also apply to proprietorships, partnerships, and limited liability companies.

Given any two amounts, the accounting equation may be solved for the third unknown amount. To illustrate, if the assets owned by a corporation amount to $100,000 and the liabilities amount to $30,000, the stockholders' equity is equal to $70,000, computed as follows:

Assets	−	Liabilities	=	Stockholders' Equity
$100,000	−	$30,000	=	$70,000

Twitter's accounting equation for a recent year is: Assets ($6,870 million) = Liabilities ($2,265 million) + Stockholders' Equity ($4,605 million).

Link to Twitter

Business Transactions and the Accounting Equation

Objective 4
Describe and illustrate how business transactions can be recorded in terms of the resulting change in the elements of the accounting equation.

Paying a monthly bill, such as a telephone bill of $168, affects a business's financial condition because it now has less cash on hand. Such an economic event or condition that directly changes an entity's financial condition or its results of operations is a **business transaction**. For example, purchasing land for $50,000 is a business transaction. In contrast, a change in a business's credit rating does not directly affect cash or any other asset, liability, or stockholders' equity amount.

Why It Matters

The Accounting Equation

The accounting equation serves as the basic foundation for the accounting systems of all companies. The accounting equation is used by the smallest business, such as the local convenience store, to the largest business, such as **The Coca-Cola Company (KO)**. Some examples taken from recent financial reports of well-known companies follow:

Company	Assets*	=	Liabilities	+	Stockholders' Equity
Alphabet Inc. (GOOG)	$147,461	=	$27,130	+	$120,331
The Coca-Cola Company (KO)	$90,093	=	$64,539	+	$25,554
DuPont (DD)	$41,166	=	$31,173	+	$9,993
eBay (EBAY)	$17,785	=	$11,209	+	$6,576
McDonald's (MCD)	$37,939	=	$30,851	+	$7,088
Microsoft Corporation (MSFT)	$193,694	=	$121,697	+	$71,997
Southwest Airlines Co. (LUV)	$21,312	=	$13,954	+	$7,358
Wal-Mart Stores, Inc. (WMT)	$199,581	=	$119,035	+	$80,546

*Amounts are shown in millions of dollars.

note:

All business transactions can be stated in terms of changes in the elements of the accounting equation.

All business transactions can be stated in terms of changes in the elements of the accounting equation. How business transactions affect the accounting equation can be illustrated by using some typical transactions. As a basis for illustration, a business organized by Chris Clark is used.

Assume that on November 1, 20Y3, Chris Clark organizes a corporation that will be known as **NetSolutions**. The first phase of Chris's business plan is to operate NetSolutions as a service business assisting individuals and small businesses in developing Web pages and installing computer software. Chris expects this initial phase of the business to last one to two years. During this period, Chris plans on gathering information on the software and hardware needs of customers. During the second phase of the business plan, Chris plans to expand NetSolutions into a personalized retailer of software and hardware for individuals and small businesses.

Each transaction during NetSolutions' first month of operations is described in the following paragraphs. The effect of each transaction on the accounting equation is then shown.

| **Transaction a** | *Nov. 1, 20Y3   Chris Clark deposited $25,000 in a bank account in the name of NetSolutions in exchange for shares of common stock in the corporation.* |

A corporation issues **common stock** to investors as proof of their ownership rights.[3]

This transaction increases Cash under Assets (on the left side of the equation) by $25,000. To balance the equation, Common Stock under Stockholders' Equity (on the right side of the equation) increases by the same amount.

The effect of this transaction on NetSolutions' accounting equation is as follows:

$$\text{Assets} = \text{Stockholders' Equity}$$

Cash		Common Stock
a. 25,000	=	25,000

The preceding accounting equation is only for the business, NetSolutions. Under the business entity assumption, Chris's personal assets, such as a home or personal bank account, and personal liabilities are excluded from the equation.

| **Transaction b** | *Nov. 5, 20Y3   NetSolutions paid $20,000 for the purchase of land as a future building site.* |

The land is located in a business park with access to transportation facilities. Chris Clark plans to rent office space and equipment during the first phase of the business plan. During the second phase, Chris plans to build an office and a warehouse for NetSolutions on the land.

The purchase of the land changes the makeup of the assets, but it does not change the total assets. The items in the equation prior to this transaction and the effect of the transaction follow. The new amounts are called *balances*.

$$\text{Assets} = \text{Stockholders' Equity}$$

	Cash	+	Land		Common Stock
Bal.	25,000			=	25,000
b.	−20,000		+20,000		
Bal.	5,000		20,000		25,000
		25,000		=	25,000

| **Transaction c** | *Nov. 10, 20Y3   NetSolutions purchased supplies for $1,350 and agreed to pay the supplier in the near future.* |

You have probably used a credit card to buy clothing or other merchandise. In this type of transaction, you received clothing for a promise to pay your credit card bill in the future. That is, you received an asset and incurred a liability to pay a future bill. NetSolutions entered into a similar transaction by purchasing

[3] To simplify, we assume that NetSolutions issued no-par stock. Types of stock as well as par and stated values are discussed in Chapter 12.

supplies for $1,350 and agreeing to pay the supplier in the near future. This type of transaction is called a purchase *on account* and is often described as follows: *Purchased supplies on account, $1,350.*

The liability created by a purchase on account is called an **account payable**. Items such as supplies that will be used in the business in the future are called **prepaid expenses**, which are assets. Thus, the effect of this transaction is to increase assets (Supplies) and liabilities (Accounts Payable) by $1,350, as follows:

	Assets			=	**Liabilities + Stockholders' Equity**		
	Cash	+ Supplies +	Land		Accounts Payable +	Common Stock	
Bal.	5,000		20,000	=		25,000	
c.		+1,350			+1,350		
Bal.	5,000	1,350	20,000		1,350	25,000	
		26,350		=		26,350	

Nov. 18, 20Y3 *NetSolutions received cash of $7,500 for providing services to customers.*	**Transaction d**

You may have earned money by painting houses or mowing lawns. If so, you received money for rendering services to a customer. Likewise, a business earns money by selling goods or services to its customers. This amount is called revenue.

During its first month of operations, NetSolutions received cash of $7,500 for providing services to customers. The receipt of cash increases NetSolutions' assets and also increases stockholders' equity in the business. The revenues of $7,500 are recorded in a Fees Earned column to the right of Common Stock. The effect of this transaction is to increase Cash and Fees Earned by $7,500, as follows:

	Assets			=	**Liabilities +**	**Stockholders' Equity**	
	Cash	+ Supplies +	Land		Accounts Payable +	Common Stock +	Fees Earned
Bal.	5,000	1,350	20,000	=	1,350	25,000	
d.	+7,500						+7,500
Bal.	12,500	1,350	20,000		1,350	25,000	7,500
		33,850		=		33,850	

Different terms are used for the various types of revenues. As illustrated for NetSolutions, revenue from providing services is recorded as **fees earned**. Revenue from the sale of merchandise is recorded as **sales**. Other examples of revenue include rent, which is recorded as **rent revenue**, and interest, which is recorded as **interest revenue**.

Instead of receiving cash at the time services are provided or goods are sold, a business may accept payment at a later date. Such revenues are described as *fees earned on account* or *sales on account*. For example, if NetSolutions had provided services on account instead of for cash, transaction (d) would have been described as follows: *Fees earned on account, $7,500.*

In such cases, the firm has an asset, called an **account receivable**, which is a claim against the customer. The effect of the transaction increases Accounts Receivable and Fees Earned. When customers pay their accounts, Cash increases and Accounts Receivable decreases.

Why It Matters

Round-Tripping

Accounting principles require that a transaction have *commercial substance*. Commercial substance means that the transaction has an economic impact on the entity. An example of a transaction lacking commercial substance is round-tripping. Round-tripping is a situation whereby a company "sells" goods and services to another company and then, under a prearranged agreement, the customer resells the exact same goods and services back to the original company. Round-tripping has been used by companies to artificially inflate their sales. However, such agreements do not have commercial substance, since there is no economic change to either company after the round-trip. Thus, round-tripped sales are not transactions from an accounting perspective.

Transaction e	Nov. 30, 20Y3	NetSolutions paid the following expenses during the month: wages, $2,125; rent, $800; utilities, $450; and miscellaneous, $275.

During the month, NetSolutions spent cash or used up other assets in earning revenue. Assets used in this process of earning revenue are called expenses. Expenses include supplies used and payments for employee wages, utilities, and other services.

NetSolutions paid the following expenses during the month: wages, $2,125; rent, $800; utilities, $450; and miscellaneous, $275. Miscellaneous expenses include small amounts paid for such items as postage, coffee, and newspapers. The effect of expenses is the opposite of revenues in that expenses reduce assets and stockholders' equity. Like fees earned, the expenses are recorded in columns to the right of Common Stock. However, since expenses reduce stockholders' equity, the expenses are entered as negative amounts. The effect of this transaction is as follows:

	Assets			=	**Liabilities +**		**Stockholders' Equity**				
					Accounts	Common	Fees	Wages	Rent	Utilities	Misc.
	Cash	+ Supplies	+ Land		Payable +	Stock	+ Earned −	Exp. −	Exp. −	Exp. −	Exp.
Bal.	12,500	1,350	20,000 =		1,350	25,000	7,500				
e.	−3,650							−2,125	−800	−450	−275
Bal.	8,850	1,350	20,000		1,350	25,000	7,500	−2,125	−800	−450	−275

30,200 = 30,200

Businesses usually record each revenue and expense transaction as it occurs. However, to simplify, NetSolutions' revenues and expenses are summarized for the month in transactions (d) and (e).

Transaction f	Nov. 30, 20Y3	NetSolutions paid creditors on account, $950.

When you pay your monthly credit card bill, you decrease the cash and decrease the amount you owe to the credit card company. Likewise, when NetSolutions paid $950 to creditors during the month, it reduced assets and liabilities, as follows:

	Assets			=	**Liabilities +**		**Stockholders' Equity**				
					Accounts	Common	Fees	Wages	Rent	Utilities	Misc.
	Cash	+ Supplies	+ Land		Payable +	Stock	+ Earned −	Exp. −	Exp. −	Exp. −	Exp.
Bal.	8,850	1,350	20,000 =		1,350	25,000	7,500	−2,125	−800	−450	−275
f.	−950				−950						
Bal.	7,900	1,350	20,000		400	25,000	7,500	−2,125	−800	−450	−275

29,250 = 29,250

Paying an amount on account is different from paying an expense. The paying of an expense reduces stockholders' equity, as illustrated in transaction (e). Paying an amount on account reduces the amount owed on a liability.

Transaction g	Nov. 30, 20Y3	Chris Clark determined that the cost of supplies on hand at the end of the month was $550.

The cost of the supplies on hand (not yet used) at the end of the month is $550. Thus, $800 ($1,350 − $550) of supplies must have been used during the month. This decrease in supplies is recorded as an expense, as follows:

	Assets			=	**Liabilities +**		**Stockholders' Equity**					
					Accounts	Common	Fees	Wages	Rent	Supplies	Utilities	Misc.
	Cash	+ Supplies	+ Land		Payable +	Stock	+ Earned −	Exp. −	Exp. −	Exp. −	Exp. −	Exp.
Bal.	7,900	1,350	20,000 =		400	25,000	7,500	−2,125	−800		−450	−275
g.		−800								−800		
Bal.	7,900	550	20,000		400	25,000	7,500	−2,125	−800	−800	−450	−275

28,450 = 28,450

Nov. 30, 20Y3 Paid dividends, $2,000.	**Transaction h**

Dividends are distributions of earnings to stockholders. The payment of dividends decreases cash and stockholders' equity. Like expenses, dividends are recorded in a separate column to the right of Common Stock as a negative amount. The effect of the payment of dividends of $2,000 is as follows:

	Assets			=	Liabilities +				Stockholders' Equity					
					Accounts	Common			Fees	Wages	Rent	Supplies	Utilities	Misc.
	Cash +	Supp. +	Land	=	Payable +	Stock	− Dividends +		Earned −	Exp. −	Exp. −	Exp. −	Exp. −	Exp.
Bal.	7,900	550	20,000	=	400	25,000			7,500	−2,125	−800	−800	−450	−275
h.	−2,000						−2,000							
Bal.	5,900	550	20,000		400	25,000	−2,000		7,500	−2,125	−800	−800	−450	−275

26,450 = 26,450

Dividends should not be confused with expenses. Dividends do not represent assets or services used in the process of earning revenues. Instead, dividends are considered a distribution of earnings to stockholders.

Summary

The transactions of **NetSolutions** are summarized in Exhibit 5. Each transaction is identified by letter, and the balance of each accounting equation element is shown after every transaction.

Exhibit 5 Summary of Transactions for NetSolutions

	Assets			=	Liabilities +				Stockholders' Equity					
					Accounts	Common			Fees	Wages	Rent	Supplies	Utilities	Misc.
	Cash	+ Supp. +	Land	=	Payable +	Stock	− Dividends +		Earned −	Exp. −	Exp. −	Exp. −	Exp. −	Exp.
a.	+25,000					+25,000								
b.	−20,000		+20,000											
Bal.	5,000		20,000			25,000								
c.		+1,350			+1,350									
Bal.	5,000	+1,350	20,000		+1,350	25,000								
d.	+7,500								+7,500					
Bal.	12,500	1,350	20,000		1,350	25,000			7,500					
e.	−3,650									−2,125	−800		−450	−275
Bal.	8,850	1,350	20,000		1,350	25,000			7,500	−2,125	−800		−450	−275
f.	−950				−950									
Bal.	7,900	1,350	20,000		400	25,000			7,500	−2,125	−800		−450	−275
g.		−800										−800		
Bal.	7,900	550	20,000		400	25,000			7,500	−2,125	−800	−800	−450	−275
h.	−2,000						−2,000							
Bal.	5,900	550	20,000		400	25,000	−2,000		7,500	−2,125	−800	−800	−450	−275

26,450 = 26,450

You should note the following:

- The effect of every transaction *is an increase or a decrease in one or more of the accounting equation elements.*
- The two sides of the accounting equation are *always equal.*
- The stockholders' equity is *increased by amounts invested by stockholders (common stock).*
- The stockholders' equity is *increased by revenues and decreased by expenses.*
- The stockholders' equity is *decreased by dividends paid to stockholders.*

Classifications of Stockholders' Equity

Stockholders' equity is classified as:

- Common Stock
- Retained Earnings

Common stock is shares of ownership distributed to investors of a corporation. It represents the portion of stockholders' equity contributed by investors. For **NetSolutions**, shares of common stock of $25,000 were distributed to Chris Clark in exchange for investing in the business.

Retained earnings is the stockholders' equity created from business operations through revenue and expense transactions. For NetSolutions, retained earnings of $3,050 were created by its November operations (revenue and expense transactions), computed as follows:

NetSolutions Retained Earnings
November Operations
(Revenue and Expense Transactions)

	Fees Earned	−	Wages Exp.	−	Rent Exp.	−	Supplies Exp.	−	Utilities Exp.	−	Misc. Exp.
Transaction d.	+7,500										
Transaction e.			−2,125		−800				−450		−275
Transaction g.							−800				
Balance, Nov. 30	7,500		−2,125		−800		−800		−450		−275

$3,050

Stockholders' equity created by investments by stockholders (common stock) and by business operations (retained earnings) are reported separately. Since dividends are distributions of earnings to stockholders, dividends reduce retained earnings. NetSolutions paid $2,000 in dividends during November, thus reducing retained earnings to $1,050 ($3,050 − $2,000).

The effects of investments by stockholders, dividends, revenues, and expenses on stockholders' equity are illustrated in Exhibit 6.

Exhibit 6

Effects of Transactions on Stockholders' Equity

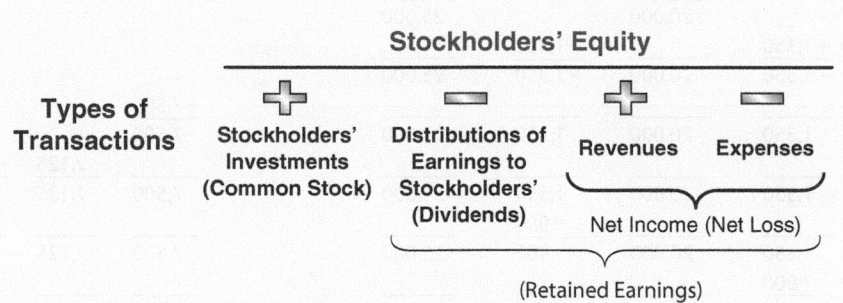

Check Up Corner 1-1   Business Transactions and the Accounting Equation

Drive Time Delivery is a local delivery service operating in Cleveland, Ohio. On February 1, Drive Time has the following balances: Cash, $32,500; Accounts Receivable, $5,000; Accounts Payable, $2,500; Common Stock, $32,500; Fees Earned, $5,000; Wages Expense, $2,500.

Drive Time Delivery completed the following transactions during February:

a. Received cash from owner as an additional investment in common stock, $20,000.

b. Paid creditors on account, $2,000.

c. Received cash from customers on account, $5,000.

d. Billed customers for delivery services on account, $18,000.

e. Paid wages expense, $10,000.

f. Paid utilities expense, $3,000.

g. Paid dividends, $4,500.

Indicate the effect that each of these transactions has on the following accounting equation elements: Cash, Accounts Receivable, Accounts Payable, Common Stock, Dividends, Fees Earned, Wages Expense, Utilities Expense.

Solution:

Each transaction affects one or more accounting equation elements.

		Assets		=	Liabilities +			Stockholders' Equity				
	Cash	+	Accounts Receivable	=	Accounts Payable	+	Common Stock	− Dividends	+ Fees Earned	− Wages Expense	− Utilities Expense	
Bal.	32,500		5,000		2,500		32,500		5,000	−2,500		
a.	20,000						20,000					
b.	−2,000				−2,000							
c.	5,000		−5,000									
d.			18,000						18,000			
e.	−10,000									−10,000		
f.	−3,000										−3,000	
g.	−4,500							−4,500				
Bal.	38,000		18,000		500	+	52,500	−4,500	23,000	−12,500	−3,000	

56,000 = 56,000

Check Up Corner

Financial Statements

Objective 5
Describe the financial statements of a corporation and explain how they interrelate.

After transactions have been recorded and summarized, reports are prepared for users. The accounting reports providing this information are called **financial statements**. The primary financial statements of a corporation are the income statement, statement of stockholders' equity, balance sheet, and statement of cash flows. The order in which the financial statements are prepared and the nature of each statement are described in Exhibit 7.

Exhibit 7
Financial Statements

Order Prepared	Financial Statement	Description of Statement
1.	Income statement	A summary of the revenue and expenses *for a specific period of time*, such as a month or a year.
2.	Statement of stockholders' equity	A summary of the changes in stockholders' equity that have occurred *during a specific period of time*, such as a month or a year.
3.	Balance sheet	A list of the assets, liabilities, and stockholders' equity *as of a specific date*, usually at the close of the last day of a month or a year.
4.	Statement of cash flows	A summary of the cash receipts and cash payments for a *specific period of time*, such as a month or a year.

The four financial statements and their interrelationships are illustrated in Exhibit 8, The data for the statements are taken from the summary of **NetSolutions**' transactions in Exhibit 5.

All financial statements are identified by the name of the business, the title of the statement, and the *date* or *period of time*. The data presented in the income statement, the statement of stockholders' equity, and the statement of cash flows are for a period of time. The data presented in the balance sheet are for a specific date.

Exhibit 8

Financial
Statements for
NetSolutions

NetSolutions
Income Statement
For the Month Ended November 30, 20Y3

Fees earned..		$ 7,500
Expenses:		
Wages expense	$2,125	
Rent expense	800	
Supplies expense...	800	
Utilities expense	450	
Miscellaneous expense	275	
Total expenses		(4,450)
Net income		$ 3,050

NetSolutions
Statement of Stockholders' Equity
For the Month Ended November 30, 20Y3

	Common Stock	Retained Earning	Total
Balances, November 1, 20Y3	$ 0	$ 0	$ 0
Issued common stock..............................	25,000		25,000
Net income		3,050	3,050
Dividends		(2,000)	(2,000)
Balances, November 30, 20Y3	$ 25,000	$ 1,050	$ 26,050

NetSolutions
Balance Sheet
November 30, 20Y3

Assets

Cash		$ 5,900
Supplies..		550
Land		20,000
Total assets		$26,450

Liabilities

Accounts payable		$ 400

Stockholders' Equity

Common stock...	$25,000	
Retained earnings..	1,050	
Total stockholders' equity....................................		26,050
Total liabilities and stockholders' equity		$26,450

NetSolutions
Statement of Cash Flows
For the Month Ended November 30, 20Y3

Cash flows from (used for) operating activities:		
Cash received from customers	$ 7,500	
Cash paid for expenses and to creditors	(4,600)	
Net cash flows from operating activities		$ 2,900
Cash flows from (used for) investing activities:		
Cash paid for acquisition of land		(20,000)
Cash flows from (used for) financing activities:		
Cash received from issuing common stock.........................	$ 25,000	
Cash dividends	(2,000)	
Net cash flows from financing activities		23,000
Net increase in cash...		$ 5,900
Cash balance, November 1, 20Y3		0
Cash balance, November 30, 20Y3................................		$ 5,900

Income Statement

The income statement reports the revenues and expenses for a period of time, based on the revenue and expense recognition principles. These principles match revenues and their related expenses so that they are reported in the same period. The excess of the revenue over the expenses is called **net income**, **net profit**, or **earnings**. If the expenses exceed the revenue, the excess is a **net loss**.

note:
When revenues exceed expenses, it is referred to as *net income, net profit,* or *earnings.* When expenses exceed revenues, it is referred to as *net loss.*

For a recent year, **Twitter** reported a net loss of $521 million.

Link to Twitter

The revenue and expenses for **NetSolutions** were shown in Exhibit 5 as separate increases and decreases. Net income for a period increases the stockholders' equity (retained earnings) for the period. A net loss decreases stockholders' equity (retained earnings) for the period.

The revenue, expenses, and net income of $3,050 for NetSolutions are reported in the income statement in Exhibit 8. The order in which the expenses are listed in the income statement varies among businesses. Most businesses list expenses in order of size, beginning with the larger items. Miscellaneous expense is usually shown as the last item, regardless of the amount.

Statement of Stockholders' Equity

The statement of stockholders' equity reports the changes in stockholders' equity for a period of time. It is prepared *after* the income statement, because the net income or net loss for the period is reported in the Retained Earnings column. It is prepared *before* the balance sheet, because the amount of common stock and retained earnings at the end of the period is reported on the balance sheet. Because of this, the statement of stockholders' equity is viewed as the connecting link between the income statement and the balance sheet.

NetSolutions had three types of transactions during November that affected its stockholders' equity:

- Common stock of $25,000 issued to Chris Clark.
- Revenues and expenses, which resulted in net income of $3,050.
- Dividends of $2,000 paid to stockholders (Chris Clark).

These transactions are summarized in the statement of stockholders' equity for **NetSolutions** shown in Exhibit 8.

Changes in each stockholders' equity element are reported in a separate column on the statement of stockholders' equity. Since NetSolutions was organized on November 1, there are no beginning balances for Common Stock or Retained Earnings. During November, common stock of $25,000 was issued and thus, is entered in the Common Stock column. Net income of $3,050 and dividends of $2,000 are entered in the Retained Earnings column, yielding an ending balance of $1,050. Each change is carried over to the Total column. After all changes are entered, the columns are totaled, representing the final balances as of November 30. These ending balances for Common Stock and Retained Earnings and the total stockholders' equity are reported on the November 30, 20Y3, balance sheet shown in Exhibit 8.

The ending common stock and retained earnings balances for November become the beginning balances for December. To illustrate, assume that during December NetSolutions issued no common stock, earned net income of $4,055, and paid dividends of $2,000. The statement of stockholders' equity for December would be as follows:

	Common Stock	Retained Earnings	Total
NetSolutions			
Statement of Stockholders' Equity			
For the Month Ended December 31, 20Y3			
Balances, December 1, 20Y3..............	$25,000	$1,050	$26,050
Net income		4,055	4,055
Dividends................................		(2,000)	(2,000)
Balances, December 31, 20Y3	$25,000	$3,105	$28,105

Instead of a statement of stockholders' equity, companies may report a **retained earnings statement**. This is often the case when a company has few (if any) common stock transactions. In such cases, only retained earnings changes from period to period.

To illustrate, a retained earnings statement for NetSolutions for December is as follows:

NetSolutions		
Retained Earnings Statement		
For the Month Ended December 31, 20Y3		
Retained earnings, December 1, 20Y3.....		$1,050
Net income	$4,055	
Dividends	(2,000)	
Increase in retained earnings.............		2,055
Retained earnings, December 31, 20Y3....		$3,105

Since most large companies report a statement of stockholders' equity, the statement of stockholders' equity will be used throughout the remainder of this text.

Balance Sheet

The balance sheet in Exhibit 8 reports the amounts of **NetSolutions**' assets, liabilities, and stockholders' equity as of November 30, 20Y3, in a vertical format. This form of balance sheet is commonly used and is called the **report form**.[4]

The asset and liability amounts are taken from the last line of the summary of transactions in Exhibit 5. The amounts for common stock, retained earnings, and total stockholders' equity are taken from the statement of stockholders' equity.

The Assets section of the balance sheet presents assets in the order that they will be converted into cash or used in operations. Cash is presented first, followed by receivables, supplies, prepaid insurance, and other assets. The assets of a more permanent nature are shown next, such as land, buildings, and equipment.

In the Liabilities section of the balance sheet in Exhibit 8, accounts payable is the only liability. When there are two or more liabilities, each should be listed and the total amount of liabilities presented as follows:

Liabilities		
Accounts payable	$12,900	
Wages payable	2,570	
Total liabilities		$15,470

---

[4] An alternative form of balance sheet reports assets, liabilities, and stockholders' equity in a horizontal format, called the account form.

Statement of Cash Flows

The statement of cash flows consists of the following three sections, as shown in Exhibit 8:

1. operating activities
2. investing activities
3. financing activities

Cash Flows from Operating Activities This section reports a summary of cash receipts and cash payments from operations. The net cash flow from operating activities normally differs from the amount of net income for the period. In Exhibit 8, **NetSolutions** reported net cash flows from operating activities of $2,900 and net income of $3,050. This difference occurs because revenues and expenses may not be recorded at the same time that cash is received from customers or paid to creditors.

Cash Flows from Investing Activities This section reports the cash transactions for the acquisition and sale of relatively permanent assets. Exhibit 8 reports that **NetSolutions** paid $20,000 for the purchase of land during November.

Cash Flows from Financing Activities This section reports the cash transactions related to cash investments by stockholders, borrowings, and dividends. Exhibit 8 shows that Chris Clark invested $25,000 in exchange for common stock of **NetSolutions**. NetSolutions also paid $2,000 of dividends during November.

For a recent year, **Twitter** reported $763 million of cash inflows from operating activities, $598 million of cash used for investing activities, $88 million of cash used for financing activities, and net increase in cash of $77 million.

Link to Twitter

Preparing NetSolutions' Statement of Cash Flows Preparing the statement of cash flows requires that each of the November cash transactions for **NetSolutions** be classified as an operating, investing, or financing activity. Using the summary of transactions shown in Exhibit 5, the November cash transactions for NetSolutions are classified as follows:

Transaction	Amount	Cash Flow Activity
a.	$25,000	Financing (Issued common stock)
b.	−20,000	Investing (Purchase of land)
d.	7,500	Operating (Fees earned)
e.	−3,650	Operating (Payment of expenses)
f.	−950	Operating (Payment of account payable)
h.	−2,000	Financing (Paid dividends)

Transactions (c) and (g) are not listed since they did not involve a cash receipt or payment. In addition, the payment of accounts payable in transaction (f) is classified as an operating activity because the account payable arose from the purchase of supplies, which are used in operations. Using the preceding classifications of November cash transactions, the statement of cash flows is prepared as shown in Exhibit 8.[5]

The ending cash balance shown on the statement of cash flows is also reported on the balance sheet as of the end of the period. To illustrate, the ending cash of $5,900 reported on the November statement of cash flows in Exhibit 8 is also reported as the amount of cash on hand in the November 30, 20Y3, balance sheet.

Since November is NetSolutions' first period of operations, the net cash flow for November and the November 30, 20Y3, cash balance are the same amount, $5,900, as shown in Exhibit 8. In later periods, NetSolutions will report in its statement of cash flows a beginning cash balance, an

---

[5] This method of preparing the statement of cash flows is called the "direct method." This method and the indirect method are discussed further in Chapter 13.

increase or a decrease in cash for the period, and an ending cash balance. For example, assume that for December NetSolutions has a decrease in cash of $3,835. The last three lines of NetSolutions' statement of cash flows for December would be as follows:

Decrease in cash	$(3,835)
Cash as of December 1, 20Y3	5,900
Cash as of December 31, 20Y3	$ 2,065

Interrelationships Among Financial Statements

Financial statements are prepared in the order of the income statement, statement of stockholders' equity, balance sheet, and statement of cash flows. This order is important because the financial statements are interrelated. These interrelationships for **NetSolutions** are shown in Exhibit 8 and are described in Exhibit 9.[6]

Exhibit 9 Financial Statement Interrelationships

Financial Statements	Interrelationship	NetSolutions Example (Exhibit 8)
Income Statement *and* Statement of Stockholders' Equity	Net income or net loss reported on the income statement is also reported on the statement of stockholders' equity as either an addition (net income) to or deduction (net loss) from the beginning retained earnings.	NetSolutions' net income of $3,050 for November is added to the beginning retained earnings on November 1, 20Y3, of $0 on the statement of stockholders' equity.
Statement of Stockholders' Equity *and* Balance Sheet	Common stock, retained earnings, and total stockholders' equity at the end of the period are reported on the statement of stockholders' equity and balance sheet.	NetSolutions' common stock of $25,000, retained earnings of $1,050, and total stockholders' equity of $26,050 as of November 30, 20Y3, are also reported on the balance sheet.
Balance Sheet *and* Statement of Cash Flows	The cash reported on the balance sheet is also reported as the end-of-period cash on the statement of cash flows.	Cash of $5,900 reported on the balance sheet as of November 30, 20Y3, is also reported on the November statement of cash flows as the end-of-period cash.

The preceding interrelationships are important in analyzing financial statements and the impact of transactions on a business. In addition, these interrelationships serve as a check on whether the financial statements are prepared correctly. For example, if the ending cash on the statement of cash flows does not agree with the balance sheet cash, then an error has occurred.

[6] Depending on the method of preparing the cash flows from operating activities section of the statement of cash flows, net income (or net loss) may also appear on the statement of cash flows. This interrelationship or method of preparing the statement of cash flows, called the "indirect method," is described and illustrated in Chapter 13.

Check Up Corner 1-2 | Financial Statements

Levart Travel Service's assets and liabilities at December 31, 20Y6, and its revenue and expenses for the year follow.

Accounts payable	$ 12,200	Land	$ 90,000
Accounts receivable	31,350	Miscellaneous expense	12,950
Cash	53,050	Office expense	63,000
Common stock	100,000	Supplies	3,350
Fees earned	263,200	Wages expense	131,700

The retained earnings were $30,000 on January 1, 20Y6, the beginning of the year. During the year, no common stock was issued and dividends of $20,000 were paid.

a. Prepare an income statement for the year ended December 31, 20Y6.

b. Prepare a statement of stockholders' equity for the year ended December 31, 20Y6.

c. Prepare a balance sheet as of December 31, 20Y6.

d. Indicate the interrelationships of these three financial statements.

Solution: The income statement reports revenues and expenses **for the period**.

The statement of stockholders' equity **connects** the income statement to the balance sheet.

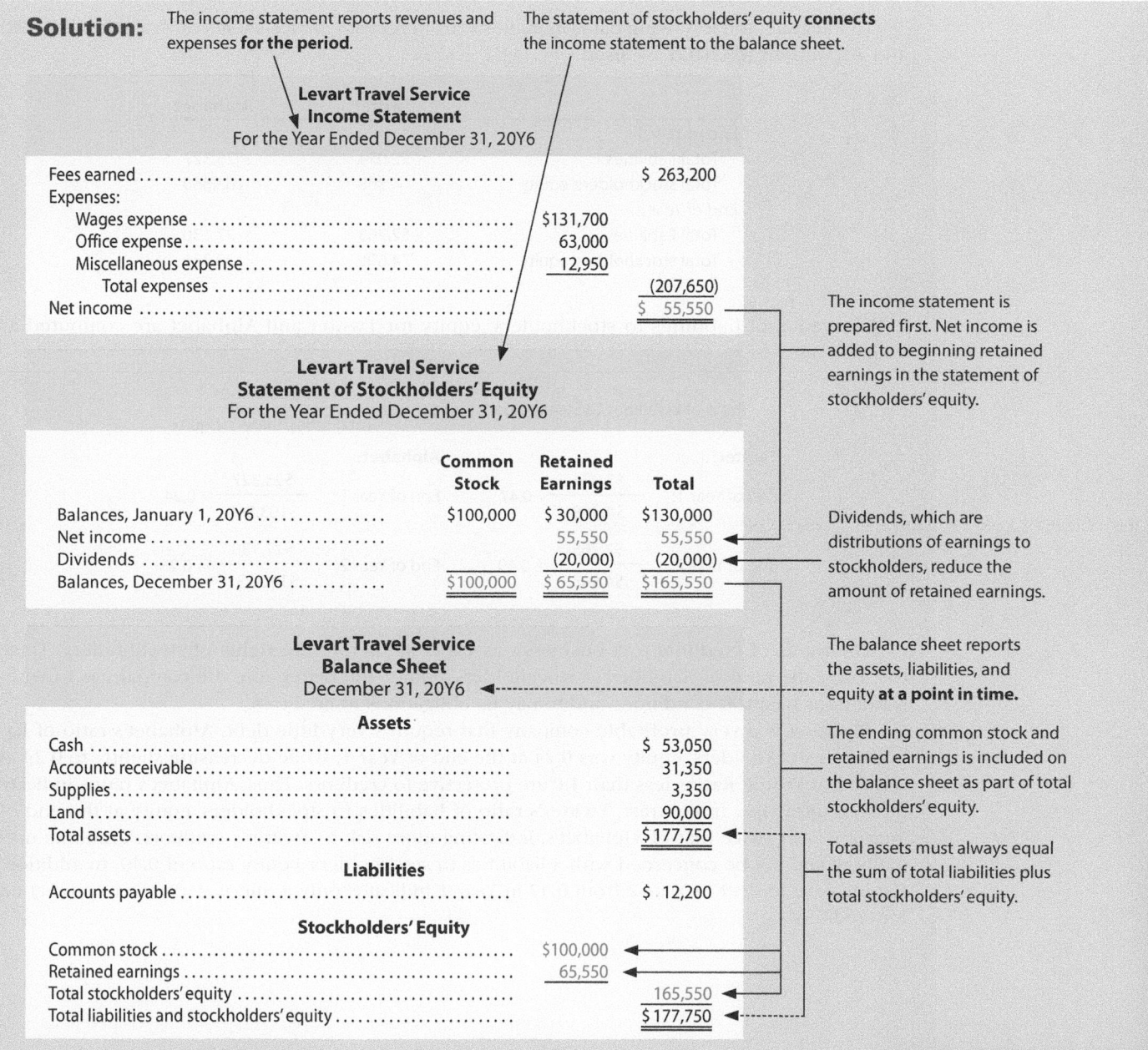

Levart Travel Service
Income Statement
For the Year Ended December 31, 20Y6

Fees earned		$ 263,200
Expenses:		
Wages expense	$131,700	
Office expense	63,000	
Miscellaneous expense	12,950	
Total expenses		(207,650)
Net income		$ 55,550

The income statement is prepared first. Net income is added to beginning retained earnings in the statement of stockholders' equity.

Levart Travel Service
Statement of Stockholders' Equity
For the Year Ended December 31, 20Y6

	Common Stock	Retained Earnings	Total
Balances, January 1, 20Y6	$100,000	$ 30,000	$130,000
Net income		55,550	55,550
Dividends		(20,000)	(20,000)
Balances, December 31, 20Y6	$100,000	$ 65,550	$165,550

Dividends, which are distributions of earnings to stockholders, reduce the amount of retained earnings.

Levart Travel Service
Balance Sheet
December 31, 20Y6

The balance sheet reports the assets, liabilities, and equity **at a point in time.**

Assets

Cash	$ 53,050
Accounts receivable	31,350
Supplies	3,350
Land	90,000
Total assets	$ 177,750

The ending common stock and retained earnings is included on the balance sheet as part of total stockholders' equity.

Liabilities

Accounts payable	$ 12,200

Stockholders' Equity

Common stock	$100,000
Retained earnings	65,550
Total stockholders' equity	165,550
Total liabilities and stockholders' equity	$ 177,750

Total assets must always equal the sum of total liabilities plus total stockholders' equity.

Analysis for Decision Making

Objective 6
Describe and illustrate the use of the ratio of liabilities to stockholders' equity in evaluating a company's financial condition.

Ratio of Liabilities to Stockholders' Equity

The basic financial statements illustrated in this chapter are useful to bankers, creditors, stockholders, and others in analyzing and interpreting the financial performance and condition of a company. Various tools and techniques that are often used to analyze and interpret a company's financial performance and condition are described and illustrated in the Analysis for Decision Making section. We begin with a method for analyzing the ability of a company to pay its creditors.

The relationship between liabilities and stockholders' equity can be expressed as a **ratio of liabilities to stockholders' equity**, as follows:

$$\text{Ratio of Liabilities to Stockholders' Equity} = \frac{\text{Total Liabilities}}{\text{Total Stockholders' Equity}}$$

To illustrate, the following data (in millions) from recent balance sheets of **Twitter (TWTR)** and **Alphabet (GOOG)** are used.

	Twitter	Alphabet
End of Year 1		
Total liabilities	$2,074	$ 25,327
Total stockholders' equity	4,368	103,860
End of Year 2		
Total liabilities	$2,265	$ 27,130
Total stockholders' equity	4,605	120,331

The ratios of liabilities to stockholders' equity for Twitter and Alphabet are computed as follows:

$$\text{Ratio of Liabilities to Stockholders' Equity} = \frac{\text{Total Liabilities}}{\text{Total Stockholders' Equity}}$$

Twitter:

End of Year 1: $\dfrac{\$2,074}{\$4,368} = 0.47$

End of Year 2: $\dfrac{\$2,265}{\$4,605} = 0.49$

Alphabet:

End of Year 1: $\dfrac{\$25,327}{\$103,860} = 0.24$

End of Year 2: $\dfrac{\$27,130}{\$120,331} = 0.23$

The rights of creditors to a business's assets come before the rights of stockholders. Thus, the lower the ratio of liabilities to stockholders' equity, the better able the company is to withstand poor business conditions and to pay its obligations to creditors.

Alphabet is a very profitable company that requires very little debt. Alphabet's ratio of liabilities to stockholders' equity was 0.24 at the end of Year 1, while decreasing slightly to 0.23 at the end of Year 2. Ratios less than 1.0 are protective to creditors. Thus, Alphabet's ratios indicate little creditor risk. In contrast, Twitter's ratio of liabilities to stockholders' equity at the end of Year 2 is over twice that of Alphabet's, indicating more risk to Twitter's creditors. Creditors normally would not be concerned with a liabilities to stockholders' equity ratio of 0.49. In addition, the increase to 0.49 in Year 2 from 0.47 in Year 1 indicates only a minor decrease in protection for creditors.

Make a Decision	Ratio of Liabilities to Stockholders' Equity

Compare Amazon.com to Best Buy (MAD 1-1)
(Continuing company analysis)

Analyze Home Depot for Three Years (MAD 1-2)

Analyze Lowe's for Three Years (MAD 1-3)

Compare Home Depot and Lowe's (MAD 1-4)

Compare Papa John's and Yum! Brands (MAD 1-5)

Make a Decision

Let's Review

Chapter Summary

1. A business provides goods or services (outputs) to customers with the objective of earning a profit. Three types of businesses include service, retail, and manufacturing businesses. Accounting is an information system that provides reports to users about the economic activities and condition of a business. Ethics are moral principles that guide the conduct of individuals. Good ethical conduct depends on individual character and company culture. Accountants are engaged in private accounting or public accounting.

2. Generally accepted accounting principles (GAAP) are used in preparing financial statements. To be useful, financial reports should provide information that is relevant and a faithful representation of the economic activity or condition, which are enhanced by comparability, verifiability, timeliness, and understandability. GAAP is based upon the assumptions of monetary unit, time period, business entity, and going concern. The principles of measurement, historical cost, revenue recognition, and expense recognition are an integral part of GAAP. The Financial Standards Board (FASB), Securities and Exchange Commission (SEC), and International Accounting Standards Board (IASB) develop standards that are incorporated into GAAP.

3. The resources owned by a business and the rights or claims to these resources may be stated in the form of an equation, as follows: Assets = Liabilities + Equity

4. All business transactions can be stated in terms of the change in one or more of the three elements of the accounting equation.

5. The primary financial statements of a corporation are the income statement, the statement of stockholders' equity, the balance sheet, and the statement of cash flows. The income statement reports a period's net income or net loss, which is also reported on the statement of stockholders' equity. The ending common stock and retained earnings reported on the statement of stockholders' equity are also reported on the balance sheet. The ending cash balance is reported on the balance sheet and the statement of cash flows.

6. The relationship between liabilities and stockholders' equity can be expressed as a ratio of liabilities to stockholders' equity, which is computed as total liabilities ÷ total stockholders' equity. Since the rights of creditors to a business's assets come before the rights of stockholders, the lower the ratio the better able the company is to withstand poor business conditions and to pay its obligations to creditors.

Key Terms

account payable (15)
account receivable (15)
accounting (5)
accounting assumptions (9)
accounting equation (12)
accounting principles (9)
accounting standards (9)
Accounting Standards Codification (9)
Accounting Standards
   Updates (9)
arm's-length transactions (12)
assets (12)
balance sheet (19)
business (4)
business entity assumption (10)
business transaction (13)
Certified Public Accountant
   (CPA) (8)
common stock (14)
comparability (9)
corporation (11)
cost principle (12)
dividends (17)
earnings (21)
equity (12)
ethics (6)
expense recognition principle (12)
expenses (12)
faithful representation (9)

fees earned (15)
financial accounting (6)
Financial Accounting Standards
   Board (FASB) (9)
financial statements (19)
fiscal year (10)
generally accepted accounting
   principles (GAAP) (9)
general-purpose financial
   statements (6)
going concern assumption (11)
historical cost principle (12)
income statement (19)
interest revenue (15)
International Accounting
   Standards Board (IASB) (9)
liabilities (12)
limited liability company
   (LLC) (11)
management (or managerial)
   accounting (5)
manufacturing business (4)
measurement principle (12)
monetary unit assumption (10)
natural business year (10)
net income (or net profit) (21)
net loss (21)
owner's equity (12)
partnership (11)
prepaid expenses (15)

private accounting (6)
profit (4)
proprietorship (11)
public accounting (8)
Public Company Accounting
   Oversight Board (PCAOB) (7)
ratio of liabilities to stockholders'
   equity (26)
relevant (9)
rent revenue (15)
report form (22)
retail business (4)
retained earnings (18)
retained earnings statement (22)
revenue (12)
revenue recognition principle (12)
sales (15)
Sarbanes-Oxley Act (SOX) (7)
Securities and Exchange
   Commission (SEC) (9)
service business (4)
statement of cash flows (19)
statement of stockholders' equity (19)
stockholders' equity (12)
timeliness (9)
time period assumption (10)
understandabilty (9)
verifiability (9)

Practice

Multiple-Choice Questions

1. A profit-making business operating as a separate legal entity and in which ownership is divided into shares of stock is known as a:
    a. proprietorship.   c. partnership.
    b. service business.   d. corporation.

2. The resources owned by a business are called:
    a. assets.   c. retained earnings.
    b. liabilities.   d. common stock.

3. A listing of a business entity's assets, liabilities, and stockholders' equity as of a specific date is a(n):
    a. balance sheet.   c. statement of stockholders' equity.
    b. income statement.   d. statement of cash flows.

4. If total assets increased $20,000 during a period and total liabilities increased $12,000 during the same period, the amount and direction (increase or decrease) of the change in stockholders' equity for that period is a(n):
    a. $32,000 increase.   c. $8,000 increase.
    b. $32,000 decrease.   d. $8,000 decrease.

5. If revenue was $45,000, expenses were $37,500, and dividends were $10,000, the amount of net income or net loss would be:
   a. $45,000 net income.
   b. $7,500 net income.
   c. $37,500 net loss.
   d. $2,500 net loss.

Answers provided after Problem. Need more practice? Find additional multiple-choice questions, exercises, and problems in CengageNOWv2.

Exercises

1. Cost principle

Obj. 2

On February 22, Kountry Repair Service extended an offer of $200,000 for land that had been priced for sale at $250,000. On April 3, Kountry Repair accepted the seller's counteroffer of $230,000 and bought the land for this amount. On September 15, the land was assessed at a value of $185,000 for property tax purposes. On January 9 of the next year, Kountry Repair was offered $300,000 for the land by a national retail chain. At what value should the land be recorded in Kountry Repair Service's records?

2. Accounting equation

Obj. 3

Dream-It LLC is a motivational consulting business. At the end of its accounting period, December 31, 20Y2, Dream-It has assets of $780,000 and liabilities of $150,000. Using the accounting equation, determine the following amounts:

a. Stockholders' equity as of December 31, 20Y2.

b. Stockholders' equity as of December 31, 20Y3, assuming that assets increased by $90,000 and liabilities increased by $25,000 during 20Y3.

3. Transactions

Obj. 4

Arrowhead Delivery Service is owned and operated by Gates Deeter. The following selected transactions were completed by Arrowhead Delivery during August:

1. Received cash in exchange for common stock, $25,000.
2. Paid creditors on account, $3,750.
3. Billed customers for delivery services on account, $22,400.
4. Received cash from customers on account, $11,300.
5. Paid dividends, $6,000.

Indicate the effect of each transaction on the following accounting equation elements: Assets, Liabilities, Common Stock, Dividends, Revenue, and Expense. To illustrate, the answer to (1) follows:

(1) Asset (Cash) increases by $25,000;
Common Stock increases by $25,000.

4. Income statement

Obj. 5

The revenues and expenses of Ousel Travel Service for the year ended November 30, 20Y8, follow:

Fees earned	$1,475,000
Office expense	320,000
Miscellaneous expense	28,000
Wages expense	885,000

Prepare an income statement for the year ended November 30, 20Y8.

5. Statement of stockholders' equity

Obj. 5

Using the income statement for Ousel Travel Service from Exercise 4, prepare a statement of stockholders' equity for the year ended November 30, 20Y8. Shane Ousel invested an additional $50,000 in the business in exchange for common stock during the year and cash dividends of $30,000 were paid. As of December 1, 20Y7, common stock had a balance of $100,000 and retained earnings had a balance of $566,000.

6. Balance sheet

Obj. 5

Using the following data for Ousel Travel Service as well as the statement of stockholders' equity from Exercise 5, prepare a balance sheet as of November 30, 20Y8:

Accounts payable	$ 62,500
Accounts receivable	186,000
Cash	308,000
Common stock	150,000
Land	480,000
Supplies	16,500

7. Statement of cash flows

Obj. 5

A summary of cash flows for Ousel Travel Service for the year ended November 30, 20Y8, follows:

Cash receipts:	
Cash received from customers	$1,465,000
Cash received from issuing common stock	50,000
Cash payments:	
Cash paid for operating expenses	1,230,000
Cash paid for land	150,000
Cash paid for dividends	30,000

The cash balance as of December 1, 20Y7, was $203,000.

Prepare a statement of cash flows for Ousel Travel Service for the year ended November 30, 20Y8.

8. Ratio of liabilities to stockholders' equity

Obj. 6

The following data were taken from Mesa Company's balance sheet:

	Dec. 31, 20Y6	Dec. 31, 20Y5
Total liabilities	$547,800	$518,000
Total stockholders' equity	415,000	370,000

a. Compute the ratio of liabilities to stockholders' equity.

b. Has the creditor's risk increased or decreased from December 31, 20Y5, to December 31, 20Y6?

Answers provided after Problem. Need more practice? Find additional multiple-choice questions, exercises, and problems in CengageNOWv2.

Problem

Cecil Jameson, Attorney-at-Law, is organized as a corporation and operated by Cecil Jameson. On July 1, 20Y4, the company has the following assets, liabilities, and common stock: cash, $1,000; accounts receivable, $3,200; supplies, $850; land, $10,000; accounts payable, $1,530; common stock, $10,000. Office space and office equipment are currently being rented, pending the construction of an office complex on land purchased last year. Business transactions during July are summarized as follows:

a. Received cash from clients for services, $3,928.

b. Paid creditors on account, $1,055.

c. Received cash from Cecil Jameson as an additional investment in exchange for common stock, $3,700.

d. Paid office rent for the month, $1,200.

e. Charged clients for legal services on account, $2,025.

f.   Purchased supplies on account, $245.

g.   Received cash from clients on account, $3,000.

h.   Received invoice for paralegal services from Legal Aid Inc. for July (to be paid on August 10), $1,635.

i.   Paid the following: wages expense, $850; utilities expense, $325; answering service expense, $250; and miscellaneous expense, $75.

j.   Determined that the cost of supplies on hand was $980; therefore, the cost of supplies used during the month was $115.

k.   Paid dividends, $1,000.

Instructions

1.   Determine the amount of retained earnings as of July 1, 20Y4.

2.   State the assets, liabilities, and stockholders' equity as of July 1 in equation form similar to that shown in this chapter. In tabular form below the equation, indicate the increases and decreases resulting from each transaction and the new balances after each transaction.

3.   Prepare an income statement for July, a statement of stockholders' equity for July, and a balance sheet as of July 31, 20Y4.

4.   (*Optional*) Prepare a statement of cash flows for July.

Need more practice? Find additional multiple-choice questions, exercises, and problems in CengageNOWv2.

Answers

Multiple-Choice Questions

1.   **d** A corporation, organized in accordance with state or federal statutes, is a separate legal entity in which ownership is divided into shares of stock (answer d). A proprietorship (answer a) is an unincorporated business owned by one individual. A service business (answer b) provides services to its customers. It can be organized as a proprietorship, partnership, corporation, or limited liability company. A partnership (answer c) is an unincorporated business owned by two or more individuals.

2.   **a** The resources owned by a business are called assets (answer a). The debts of the business are called liabilities (answer b), the stockholders' equity created from business operations through revenue and expense transactions is retained earnings (answer c), and shares of ownership in a corporation are common stock (answer d).

3.   **a** The balance sheet is a listing of the assets, liabilities, and stockholders' equity of a business at a specific date (answer a). The income statement (answer b) is a summary of the revenue and expenses of a business for a specific period of time. The statement of stockholders' equity (answer c) summarizes the changes in common stock and retained earnings during a specific period of time. The statement of cash flows (answer d) summarizes the cash receipts and cash payments for a specific period of time.

4.   **c** The accounting equation is:

Assets = Liabilities + Stockholders' Equity

Therefore, if assets increased by $20,000 and liabilities increased by $12,000, stockholders' equity must have increased by $8,000 (answer c), as indicated in the following computation:

Assets	=	Liabilities	+	Stockholders' Equity
$20,000	=	$12,000	+	Stockholders' Equity
$20,000 − $12,000	=			Stockholders' Equity
$ 8,000	=			Stockholders' Equity

5. **b** Net income is the excess of revenue over expenses, or $7,500 (answer b). If expenses exceed revenue, the difference is a net loss. Dividends are the opposite of investing in the business and do not affect the amount of net income or net loss.

Exercises

1. $230,000. Under the historical cost principle, the land should be recorded at the cost to Kountry Repair Service.

2. a.
$$A = L + SE$$
$$\$780,000 = \$150,000 + SE$$
$$SE = \$630,000$$

   b.
$$A = L + SE$$
$$\$90,000 = \$25,000 + SE$$
$$SE = \$65,000$$
   SE on December 31, 20Y3 = $630,000 + $65,000
   SE on December 31, 20Y3 = $695,000

3. (1) Asset (Cash) increases by $25,000;
   Common Stock increases by $25,000.
   (2) Asset (Cash) decreases by $3,750;
   Liability (Accounts Payable) decreases by $3,750.
   (3) Asset (Accounts Receivable) increases by $22,400;
   Revenue (Delivery Service Fees) increases by $22,400.
   (4) Asset (Cash) increases by $11,300;
   Asset (Accounts Receivable) decreases by $11,300.
   (5) Asset (Cash) decreases by $6,000;
   Dividends increases by $6,000.

4.

Ousel Travel Service Income Statement For the Year Ended November 30, 20Y8		
Fees earned...		$ 1,475,000
Expenses:		
Wages expense...	$885,000	
Office expense	320,000	
Miscellaneous expense.....................................	28,000	
Total expenses...		(1,233,000)
Net income..		$ 242,000

5.

Ousel Travel Service Statement of Stockholders' Equity For the Year Ended November 30, 20Y8	Common Stock	Retained Earnings	Total
Balances, December 1, 20Y7...............................	$100,000	$566,000	$666,000
Issued common stock	50,000		50,000
Net income...		242,000	242,000
Dividends...		(30,000)	(30,000)
Balances, November 30, 20Y8.............................	$150,000	$778,000	$928,000

6.

Ousel Travel Service Balance Sheet November 30, 20Y8		
Assets		
Cash		$308,000
Accounts receivable		186,000
Supplies		16,500
Land		480,000
Total assets		$990,500
Liabilities		
Accounts payable		$ 62,500
Stockholders' Equity		
Common stock	$150,000	
Retained earnings	778,000	
Total stockholders' equity		928,000
Total liabilities and stockholders' equity		$990,500

7.

Ousel Travel Service Statement of Cash Flows For the Year Ended November 30, 20Y8		
Cash flows from (used for) operating activities:		
Cash received from customers	$ 1,465,000	
Cash paid for operating expenses	(1,230,000)	
Net cash flows from operating activities		$ 235,000
Cash flows from (used for) investing activities:		
Cash paid for purchase of land		(150,000)
Cash flows from (used for) financing activities:		
Cash received from issuing common stock	$ 50,000	
Cash dividends	(30,000)	
Net cash flows from financing activities		20,000
Net increase in cash		$ 105,000
Cash balance, December 1, 20Y7		203,000
Cash balance, November 30, 20Y8		$ 308,000

8.

		Dec. 31, 20Y6	Dec. 31, 20Y5
a.	Total liabilities	$547,800	$518,000
	Total stockholders' equity	$415,000	$370,000
	Ratio of liabilities to stockholders' equity	1.32*	1.40**

     *$547,800 ÷ $415,000

     **$518,000 ÷ $370,000

b. Decreased

Need more help? Watch step-by-step videos of how to compute answers to these Exercises in CengageNOWv2.

Problem

1.

$$\text{Assets} - \text{Liabilities} = \text{Stockholders' Equity}$$
$$(\$1,000 + \$3,200 + \$850 + \$10,000) - \$1,530 = \text{Common Stock} + \text{Retained Earnings}$$
$$\$15,050 - \$1,530 = \$10,000 + \text{Retained Earnings}$$
$$\$3,520 = \text{Retained Earnings}$$

2.

	Assets				=	Liabilities +				Stockholders' Equity							
	Cash +	Accts. Rec. +	Supp. +	Land =		Accts. Pay. +	Common Stock +	Retained Earnings	− Dividends +	Fees Earned −	Paralegal Exp. −	Rent Exp. −	Wages Exp. −	Utilities Exp. −	Answering Service Exp. −	Supp. Exp. −	Misc. Exp.
Bal.	1,000	3,200	850	10,000		1,530	10,000	3,520									
a.	+3,928									3,928							
Bal.	4,928	3,200	850	10,000		1,530	10,000	3,520		3,928							
b.	−1,055					−1,055											
Bal.	3,873	3,200	850	10,000		475	10,000	3,520		3,928							
c.	+3,700						+3,700										
Bal.	7,573	3,200	850	10,000		475	13,700	3,520		3,928							
d.	−1,200											−1,200					
Bal.	6,373	3,200	850	10,000		475	13,700	3,520		3,928		−1,200					
e.		+ 2,025								+ 2,025							
Bal.	6,373	5,225	850	10,000		475	13,700	3,520		5,953		−1,200					
f.			+245			+245											
Bal.	6,373	5,225	1,095	10,000		720	13,700	3,520		5,953		−1,200					
g.	+3,000	−3,000															
Bal.	9,373	2,225	1,095	10,000		720	13,700	3,520		5,953		−1,200					
h.						+1,635					−1,635						
Bal.	9,373	2,225	1,095	10,000		2,355	13,700	3,520		5,953	−1,635	−1,200					
i.	−1,500												−850	−325	−250		−75
Bal.	7,873	2,225	1,095	10,000		2,355	13,700	3,520		5,953	−1,635	−1,200	−850	−325	−250		−75
j.			−115													−115	
Bal.	7,873	2,225	980	10,000		2,355	13,700	3,520		5,953	−1,635	−1,200	−850	−325	−250	−115	−75
k.	−1,000								−1,000								
Bal.	6,873	2,225	980	10,000		2,355	13,700	3,520	−1,000	5,953	−1,635	−1,200	−850	−325	−250	−115	−75

3.

Cecil Jameson, Attorney-at-Law
Income Statement
For the Month Ended July 31, 20Y4

Fees earned..		$ 5,953
Expenses:		
Paralegal expense..	$1,635	
Rent expense	1,200	
Wages expense	850	
Utilities expense	325	
Answering service expense	250	
Supplies expense	115	
Miscellaneous expense	75	
Total expenses..		(4,450)
Net income		$ 1,503

Cecil Jameson, Attorney-at-Law
Statement of Stockholders' Equity
For the Month Ended July 31, 20Y4

	Common Stock	Retained Earnings	Total
Balances, July 1, 20Y4................................	$10,000	$ 3,520	$13,520
Issued common stock	3,700		3,700
Net income		1,503	1,503
Dividends		(1,000)	(1,000)
Balances, July 31, 20Y4..............................	$13,700	$ 4,023	$17,723

Cecil Jameson, Attorney-at-Law
Balance Sheet
July 31, 20Y4

Assets

Cash	$ 6,873
Accounts receivable	2,225
Supplies	980
Land	10,000
Total assets	$20,078

Liabilities

Accounts payable	$ 2,355

Stockholders' Equity

Common stock	$13,700	
Retained earnings	4,023	
Total stockholders' equity		17,723
Total liabilities and stockholders' equity		$20,078

4. *(Optional)*

Cecil Jameson, Attorney-at-Law
Statement of Cash Flows
For the Month Ended July 31, 20Y4

Cash flows from (used for) operating activities:		
Cash received from customers	$ 6,928*	
Cash paid for operating expenses	(3,755)**	
Net cash flows from operating activities		$3,173
Cash flows from (used for) investing activities		—
Cash flows from (used for) financing activities:		
Cash received from issuing common stock	$ 3,700	
Cash paid for dividends	(1,000)	
Net cash flows from financing activities		2,700
Net increase in cash		$5,873
Cash balance, July 1, 20Y4		1,000
Cash balance, July 31, 20Y4		$6,873

*$6,928 = $3,928 + $3,000
**$3,755 = $1,055 + $1,200 + $1,500

Discussion Questions

1. Name some users of accounting information.

2. What is the role of accounting in business?

3. Why are most large companies like **Microsoft (MSFT), PepsiCo (PEP), Caterpillar (CAT)**, REAL WORLD and **AutoZone (AZO)** organized as corporations?

4. Josh Reilly is the owner of Dispatch Delivery Service. Recently, Josh paid interest of $4,500 on a personal loan of $75,000 that he used to begin the business. Should Dispatch Delivery Service record the interest payment? Explain.

5. On July 12, Reliable Repair Service extended an offer of $150,000 for land that had been priced for sale at $185,000. On September 3, Reliable Repair accepted the seller's counteroffer of $167,500. Describe how Reliable Repair Service should record the land.

6. a. Land with an assessed value of $750,000 for property tax purposes is acquired by a business for $900,000. Ten years later, the plot of land has an assessed value of $1,200,000 and the business receives an offer of $2,000,000 for it. Should the monetary amount assigned to the land in the business records now be increased?

   b. Assuming that the land acquired in (a) was sold for $2,125,000, how would the various elements of the accounting equation be affected?

7. Describe the difference between an account receivable and an account payable.

8. A business had revenues of $679,000 and operating expenses of $588,000. What was the amount of (a) net loss or (b) net income?

9. A business had revenues of $640,000 and operating expenses of $715,000. What was the amount of (a) net loss or (b) net income?

10. The financial statements are interrelated. (a) What item of financial or operating data appears on both the income statement and the statement of stockholders' equity? (b) What item appears on both the balance sheet and the statement of stockholders' equity? (c) What item appears on both the balance sheet and the statement of cash flows?

Basic Exercises

SHOW ME HOW

BE 1-1 Cost principle   Obj. 2
On June 25, Ritts Roofing extended an offer of $250,000 for land that had been priced for sale at $300,000. On July 9, Ritts accepted the seller's counteroffer of $275,000. On October 1, the land was assessed at a value of $280,000 for property tax purposes. On December 22, Ritts was offered $305,000 for the land by a national retail chain. At what value should the land be recorded in Ritts Roofing's records?

SHOW ME HOW

BE 1-2 Accounting equation   Obj. 3
Be-The-One is a motivational consulting business. At the end of its accounting period, December 31, 20Y2, Be-The-One has assets of $395,000 and liabilities of $97,000. Using the accounting equation, determine the following amounts:

a. Stockholders' equity as of December 31, 20Y2.

b. Stockholders' equity as of December 31, 20Y3, assuming that assets decreased by $65,000 and liabilities increased by $36,000 during 20Y3.

SHOW ME HOW

BE 1-3 Transactions   Obj. 4
Interstate Delivery Service is owned and operated by Katie Wyer. The following selected transactions were completed by Interstate Delivery during May:

1. Received cash in exchange for common stock, $18,000.
2. Paid advertising expense, $4,850.
3. Purchased supplies on account, $2,100.
4. Billed customers for delivery services on account, $14,700.
5. Received cash from customers on account, $8,200.

Indicate the effect of each transaction on the following accounting equation elements: Assets, Liabilities, Common Stock, Dividends, Revenue, and Expense. To illustrate, the answer to (1) follows:

(1) Asset (Cash) increases by $18,000; Common Stock increases by $18,000.

SHOW ME HOW

BE 1-4 Income statement   Obj. 5
The revenues and expenses of Paradise Travel Service for the year ended May 31, 20Y6, follow:

Fees earned	$900,000
Office expense	300,000
Miscellaneous expense	15,000
Wages expense	450,000

Prepare an income statement for the year ended May 31, 20Y6.

SHOW ME HOW

BE 1-5 Statement of stockholders' equity   Obj. 5
Using the income statement for Paradise Travel Service from Basic Exercise 1-4, prepare a statement of stockholders' equity for the year ended May 31, 20Y6. Everett McCauley invested an additional $40,000 in the business in exchange for common stock, and $10,000 of dividends were paid during the year. Common stock had a balance of $60,000 and retained earnings had a balance of $300,000 as of June 1, 20Y5.

SHOW ME HOW

BE 1-6 Balance sheet
Obj. 5

Using the following data for Paradise Travel Service as well as the statement of stockholders' equity from Basic Exercise 1-5, prepare a balance sheet as of May 31, 20Y6:

Accounts payable	$ 18,000
Accounts receivable	38,000
Cash	52,000
Common stock	100,000
Land	450,000
Supplies	3,000

SHOW ME HOW

BE 1-7 Statement of cash flows
Obj. 5

A summary of cash flows for Paradise Travel Service for the year ended May 31, 20Y6, follows:

Cash receipts:	
Cash received from customers	$880,000
Cash received from issuing common stock	40,000
Cash payments:	
Cash paid for operating expenses	758,000
Cash paid for land	150,000
Cash paid as dividends	10,000

The cash balance as of June 1, 20Y5, was $50,000.

Prepare a statement of cash flows for Paradise Travel Service for the year ended May 31, 20Y6.

SHOW ME HOW

BE 1-8 Ratio of liabilities to stockholders' equity
Obj. 6

The following data were taken from Alvarado Company's balance sheet:

	Dec. 31, 20Y4	Dec. 31, 20Y3
Total liabilities	$4,085,000	$2,880,000
Total stockholders' equity	4,300,000	3,600,000

a. Compute the ratio of liabilities to stockholders' equity for each year.
b. Has the creditor's risk increased or decreased from December 31, 20Y3, to December 31, 20Y4?

Exercises

REAL WORLD

EX 1-1 Types of businesses
Obj. 1

The following is a list of well-known companies:

1. **Alcoa Inc. (AA)**
2. **Boeing (BA)**
3. **Caterpillar (CAT)**
4. **Citigroup Inc. (C)**
5. **CVS (CVS)**
6. **Dow Chemical Company (DOW)**
7. **eBay Inc. (EBAY)**
8. **FedEx (FDX)**
9. **Ford Motor Company (F)**
10. **Gap Inc. (GAP)**
11. **H&R Block (HRB)**
12. **Hilton Hospitality, Inc. (HLT)**
13. **Procter & Gamble (PG)**
14. **SunTrust (STI)**
15. **Wal-Mart Stores, Inc. (WMT)**

a. Indicate whether each of these companies is primarily a service, retail, or manufacturing business. If you are unfamiliar with the company, use the Internet to locate the company's home page or use the finance Web site of **Yahoo** (finance.yahoo.com).
b. For which of the preceding companies is the accounting equation relevant?

ETHICS

EX 1-2   Professional ethics

Obj. 1

A fertilizer manufacturing company wants to relocate to Yellowstone County. A report from a fired researcher at the company indicates the company's product is releasing toxic by-products. The company suppressed that report. A later report commissioned by the company shows there is no problem with the fertilizer.

➤ Should the company's chief executive officer reveal the content of the unfavorable report in discussions with Yellowstone County representatives? Discuss.

EX 1-3   Business entity assumption

Obj. 2

Ozark Sports sells hunting and fishing equipment and provides guided hunting and fishing trips. Ozark is owned and operated by Eric Griffith, a well-known sports enthusiast and hunter. Eric's wife, Linda, owns and operates Lake Boutique, a women's clothing store. Eric and Linda have established a trust fund to finance their children's college education. The trust fund is maintained by Missouri State Bank in the name of the children, Mark and Steffy.

a.   For each of the following transactions, identify which of the entities listed should record the transaction in its records:

Entities	
L	Lake Boutique
M	Missouri State Bank
O	Ozark Sports
X	None of the above

1.   Linda authorized the trust fund to purchase mutual fund shares.

2.   Linda purchased two dozen spring dresses from a St. Louis designer for a special spring sale.

3.   Eric paid a breeder's fee for an English springer spaniel to be used as a hunting guide dog.

4.   Linda deposited a $2,000 personal check in the trust fund at Missouri State Bank.

5.   Eric paid a local doctor for his annual physical, which was required by the workers' compensation insurance policy carried by Ozark Sports.

6.   Eric received a cash advance from customers for a guided hunting trip.

7.   Linda paid her dues to the YWCA.

8.   Linda donated several dresses from inventory for a local charity auction for the benefit of a women's abuse shelter.

9.   Eric paid for dinner and a movie to celebrate their twelfth wedding anniversary.

10.   Eric paid for an advertisement in a hunters' magazine.

b.   ➤ What is a business transaction?

✔ Starbucks, $5,884

SHOW ME HOW   REAL WORLD

EX 1-4   Accounting equation

Obj. 3

The total assets and total liabilities (in millions) of **McDonald's Corporation (MCD)** and **Starbucks Corporation (SBUX)** follow:

	McDonald's	Starbucks
Assets	$37,939	$14,330
Liabilities	30,851	8,446

Determine the stockholders' equity of each company.

✔ Dollar Tree, $4,407

SHOW ME HOW   REAL WORLD

EX 1-5   Accounting equation

Obj. 3

The total assets and total liabilities (in millions) of **Dollar Tree Inc. (DLTR)** and **Target Corporation (TGT)** follow:

	Dollar Tree	Target
Assets	$15,901	$40,262
Liabilities	11,494	27,305

Determine the stockholders' equity of each company.

✔ a. $1,895,000

SHOW ME HOW

EX 1-6 Accounting equation
Obj. 3

Determine the missing amount for each of the following:

	Assets	=	Liabilities	+	Stockholders' Equity
a.	X	=	$550,000	+	$1,345,000
b.	$776,500	=	X	+	$588,800
c.	$14,750,000	=	$4,455,000	+	X

✔ b. $4,120,000

SHOW ME HOW

EX 1-7 Accounting equation
Obj. 3, 4

Inspirational Inc. is a motivational consulting business. At the end of its accounting period, October 31, 20Y2, Inspirational has assets of $5,250,000 and liabilities of $1,600,000. Using the accounting equation and considering each case independently, determine the following amounts:

a. Stockholders' equity as of October 31, 20Y2.

b. Stockholders' equity as of October 31, 20Y3, assuming that assets increased by $800,000 and liabilities increased by $330,000 during 20Y3.

c. Stockholders' equity as of October 31, 20Y3, assuming that assets decreased by $600,000 and liabilities increased by $140,000 during 20Y3.

d. Stockholders' equity as of October 31, 20Y3, assuming that assets increased by $440,000 and liabilities decreased by $90,000 during 20Y3.

e. Net income (or net loss) during 20Y3, assuming that as of October 31, 20Y3, assets were $6,140,000, liabilities were $1,950,000, and no additional common stock was issued or dividends paid.

EX 1-8 Asset, liability, and stockholders' equity items
Obj. 3

Indicate whether each of the following is identified with (1) an asset, (2) a liability, or (3) stockholders' equity:

a. accounts payable

b. accounts receivable

c. fees earned

d. supplies

e. supplies expense

f. utilities expense

EX 1-9 Effect of transactions on accounting equation
Obj. 4

What is the effect of each of the following transactions on the three elements (assets, liabilities, and stockholders' equity) of the accounting equation?

a. Invested cash in business in exchange for common stock.

b. Paid for business expenses.

c. Paid dividends.

d. Purchased supplies on account.

e. Received cash for services performed.

EX 1-10 Effect of transactions on accounting equation
Obj. 4

✔ a. (1) increase $183,000

SHOW ME HOW

a. A vacant lot acquired for $115,000 is sold for $298,000 in cash. What is the effect of the sale on the total amount of the seller's (1) assets, (2) liabilities, and (3) stockholders' equity?

b. Assume that the seller owes $80,000 on a loan for the land. After receiving the $298,000 cash in (a), the seller pays the $80,000 owed. What is the effect of the payment on the total amount of the seller's (1) assets, (2) liabilities, and (3) stockholders' equity?

c. ▬▬▶ Is it true that a transaction always affects at least two elements (Assets, Liabilities, or Stockholders' Equity) of the accounting equation? Explain.

EX 1-11 Effect of transactions on stockholders' equity
Obj. 4

Indicate whether each of the following types of transactions will either (a) increase stockholders' equity or (b) decrease stockholders' equity:

1. Issued common stock in exchange for cash.

2. Received cash for services performed for customers.

3. Paid business expenses.

4. Paid dividends.

EX 1-12   Transactions

Obj. 4

The following selected transactions were completed by Cota Delivery Service during July:

1. Received cash in exchange for common stock, $35,000.
2. Purchased supplies for cash, $1,100.
3. Paid rent for October, $4,500.
4. Paid advertising expense, $900.
5. Received cash for providing delivery services, $33,000.
6. Billed customers for delivery services on account, $58,000.
7. Paid creditors on account, $2,900.
8. Received cash from customers on account, $27,500.
9. Determined that the cost of supplies on hand was $300 and $8,600 of supplies had been used during the month.
10. Paid cash dividends, $2,500.

Indicate the effect of each transaction on the accounting equation by listing the numbers identifying the transactions, (1) through (10), in a column, and inserting at the right of each number the appropriate letter from the following list:

a. Increase in an asset, decrease in another asset.
b. Increase in an asset, increase in a liability.
c. Increase in an asset, increase in stockholders' equity.
d. Decrease in an asset, decrease in a liability.
e. Decrease in an asset, decrease in stockholders' equity.

EX 1-13   Nature of transactions

Obj. 4

✔ d. $22,800

SHOW ME HOW

Teri West operates her own catering service. Summary financial data for July are presented in equation form as follows. Each line designated by a number indicates the effect of a transaction on the equation. Each increase and decrease in stockholders' equity, except transaction (5), affects net income.

	Assets			= Liabilities +		Stockholders' Equity				
	Cash +	Supplies +	Land	= Accounts Payable +	Common Stock +	Retained Earnings −	Dividends +	Fees Earned −	Expenses
Bal.	40,000	3,000	82,000	7,500	50,000	67,500			
1.	+71,800							+71,800	
2.	−15,000		+15,000						
3.	−47,500								−47,500
4.		+1,100		+1,100					
5.	−5,000						−5,000		
6.	−4,000			−4,000					
7.		−1,500							−1,500
Bal.	40,300	2,600	97,000	4,600	50,000	67,500	−5,000	71,800	−49,000

a. ▬▬▬▶ Describe each transaction.
b. What is the amount of the net increase in cash during the month?
c. What is the amount of the net increase in stockholders' equity during the month?
d. What is the amount of the net income for the month?
e. How much of the net income for the month was retained in the business?

EX 1-14   Net income and dividends

Obj. 5

The income statement for the month of February indicates a net income of $17,500. During the same period, $25,500 in cash dividends were paid.

▬▬▬▶ Would it be correct to say that the business incurred a net loss of $8,000 during the month? Discuss.

✔ Blue: Net income, $410,000

SHOW ME HOW

EX 1-15   Net income and stockholders' equity for four businesses
Obj. 5

Four different corporations, Amber, Blue, Coral, and Daffodil, show the same balance sheet data at the beginning and end of a year. These data, exclusive of the amount of stockholders' equity, are summarized as follows:

	Total Assets	Total Liabilities
Beginning of the year	$1,220,000	$ 990,000
End of the year	1,730,000	1,150,000

On the basis of the preceding data and the following additional information for the year, determine the net income (or loss) of each company for the year. (*Hint*: First, determine the amount of increase or decrease in stockholders' equity during the year.)

Amber: No additional common stock was issued and no dividends were paid.

Blue: No additional common stock was issued, but dividends of $60,000 were paid.

Coral: Additional common stock of $140,000 was issued, but no dividends were paid.

Daffodil: Additional common stock of $140,000 was issued and dividends of $60,000 were paid.

EX 1-16   Balance sheet items
Obj. 5

From the following list of selected items taken from the records of Bobcat Appliance Service as of a specific date, identify those that would appear on the balance sheet:

1. Accounts Payable
2. Cash
3. Common Stock
4. Fees Earned
5. Land
6. Rent Expense
7. Retained Earnings
8. Supplies
9. Supplies Expense
10. Wages Payable

EX 1-17   Income statement items
Obj. 5

Based on the data presented in Exercise 1-16, identify those items that would appear on the income statement.

SHOW ME HOW   EXCEL TEMPLATE

EX 1-18   Statement of stockholders' equity
Obj. 5

Financial information related to Organic Products Company for the month ended June 30, 20Y9, is as follows:

Net income for June	$ 115,000
Dividends paid in June	25,000
Common stock, June 1, 20Y9	180,000
Common stock issued in June	50,000
Retained earnings, June 1, 20Y9	1,630,000

a.   Prepare a statement of stockholders' equity for the month ended June 30, 20Y9.

b.   ➤ Why is the statement of stockholders' equity prepared before the June 30, 20Y9, balance sheet?

SHOW ME HOW   EXCEL TEMPLATE

EX 1-19   Income statement
Obj. 5

Imaging Services was organized on March 1, 20Y5. A summary of the revenue and expense transactions for March follows:

Fees earned	$482,000
Wages expense	300,000
Rent expense	41,500
Supplies expense	3,600
Miscellaneous expense	1,900

Prepare an income statement for the month ended March 31.

EX 1-20 Missing amounts from balance sheet and income statement data

Obj. 5

✔ (a) $135,000

SHOW ME HOW

One item is omitted in each of the following summaries of balance sheet and income statement data for the following four different corporations:

	Freeman	Heyward	Jones	Ramirez
Beginning of the year:				
Assets	$ 900,000	$490,000	$115,000	(d)
Liabilities	360,000	260,000	81,000	$120,000
End of the year:				
Assets	1,260,000	675,000	100,000	270,000
Liabilities	330,000	220,000	80,000	136,000
During the year:				
Additional common stock issued	(a)	150,000	10,000	55,000
Dividends	75,000	32,000	(c)	39,000
Revenue	570,000	(b)	115,000	115,000
Expenses	240,000	128,000	122,500	128,000

Determine the missing amounts, identifying them by letter. (*Hint:* First determine the amount of increase or decrease in stockholders' equity during the year.)

EX 1-21 Balance sheets, net income

Obj. 5

✔ b. $135,000

SHOW ME HOW   EXCEL TEMPLATE

Financial information related to Ebony Interiors for February and March 20Y3 is as follows:

	February 28, 20Y3	March 31, 20Y3
Cash	$320,000	$380,000
Accounts receivable	800,000	960,000
Supplies	30,000	35,000
Accounts payable	310,000	400,000
Common stock	200,000	200,000
Retained earnings	?	?

a. Prepare balance sheets for Ebony Interiors as of February 28 and March 31, 20Y3.

b. Determine the amount of net income for March, assuming that no additional common stock was issued and no dividends were paid during the month.

c. Determine the amount of net income for March, assuming that no additional common stock was issued, but dividends of $50,000 were paid during the month.

EX 1-22 Financial statements

Obj. 5

REAL WORLD

Each of the following items is shown on the financial statements of **Exxon Mobil Corporation (XOM)**:

1. Accounts payable
2. Cash equivalents
3. Crude oil inventory
4. Equipment
5. Exploration expenses
6. Income taxes payable
7. Investments
8. Long-term debt
9. Marketable securities
10. Notes and loans payable
11. Notes receivable
12. Operating expenses
13. Prepaid taxes
14. Sales
15. Selling expenses

a. Identify the financial statement (balance sheet or income statement) in which each item would appear.

b. Can an item appear on more than one financial statement?

c. Is the accounting equation relevant for Exxon Mobil Corporation? Explain.

EX 1-23 Statement of cash flows

Obj. 5

Indicate whether each of the following activities would be reported on the statement of cash flows as (a) an operating activity, (b) an investing activity, or (c) a financing activity:

1. Cash received by issuing common stock.
2. Cash received for fees earned from customers.
3. Cash paid for land and building.
4. Cash paid for dividends.

SHOW ME HOW

EX 1-24 Statement of cash flows

Obj. 5

A summary of cash flows for Parker Consulting Group for the year ended January 31, 20Y4, follows:

Cash receipts:	
Cash received from customers	$1,200,000
Cash received from issuing common stock	90,000
Cash payments:	
Cash paid for operating expenses	800,000
Cash paid for land	300,000
Cash paid for dividends	36,000

The cash balance as of February 1, 20Y3, was $66,000.

Prepare a statement of cash flows for Parker Consulting Group for the year ended January 31, 20Y4.

EX 1-25 Financial statements

Obj. 5

✔ Correct amount of total assets is $51,500.

We-Sell Realty was organized as a corporation on August 1, 20Y7, by the issuance of common stock of $15,000. We-Sell Realty is owned and operated by Omar Farah, the sole stockholder. The following statements for We-Sell Realty were prepared after its first month of operations:

We-Sell Realty
Income Statement
August 31, 20Y7

Sales commissions		$140,000
Expenses:		
Office salaries expense	$87,000	
Rent expense	18,000	
Automobile expense	7,500	
Miscellaneous expense	2,200	
Supplies expense	1,150	
Total expenses		(115,850)
Net income		$ 25,000

Omar Farah
Statement of Stockholders' Equity
For the Year Ended August 31, 20Y6

	Retained Earnings	Total
Balances, August 1, 20Y7	$ 0	$ 0
Net income	25,000	25,000
Dividends	(10,000)	(10,000)
Balances, August 31, 20Y7	$ 15,000	$ 15,000

Balance Sheet
For the Month Ended August 31, 20Y7

Assets

Cash	$ 8,900
Accounts payable	22,350
Total assets	$31,250

Liabilities

Accounts receivable	$38,600
Supplies	4,000

Stockholders' Equity

Retained earnings	30,000
Total liabilities and stockholders' equity	$72,600

a.   Identify the errors contained within the presented financial statements for We-Sell Realty.

b.   Prepare a corrected set of financial statements for We-Sell Realty.

Problems: Series A

PR 1-1A   Transactions
Obj. 4

✔ Cash bal. at end of April: $63,450.

SHOW ME HOW

On April 1 of the current year, Morgan Jones established a business to manage rental property. She completed the following transactions during April:

a. Opened a business bank account with a deposit of $60,000 in exchange for common stock.

b. Purchased office supplies on account, $1,800.

c. Received cash from fees earned for managing rental property, $22,300.

d. Paid rent on office and equipment for the month, $7,000.

e. Paid creditors on account, $1,100.

f. Billed customers for fees earned for managing rental property, $3,600.

g. Paid automobile expenses for month, $750, and miscellaneous expenses, $1,000.

h. Paid office salaries, $4,000.

i. Determined that the cost of supplies on hand was $250; therefore, the cost of supplies used was $1,550.

j. Paid dividends, $5,000.

Instructions
1. Indicate the effect of each transaction and the balances after each transaction, using the following tabular headings:

Assets			= Liabilities +		Stockholders' Equity						
Cash +	Accounts Receivable +	Supplies =	Accounts Payable +	Common Stock −	Dividends +	Fees Earned −	Rent Expense −	Salaries Expense −	Supplies Expense −	Auto Expense −	Misc. Expense

2. ▬▬▬▶ Briefly explain why issuing common stock and revenues increased stockholders' equity, while dividends and expenses decreased stockholders' equity.

3. Determine the net income for April.

4. How much did April's transactions increase or decrease stockholders' equity?

PR 1-2A   Financial statements
Obj. 5

✔ 1. Net income: $402,000

SHOW ME HOW   EXCEL TEMPLATE

The assets and liabilities of Global Travel Agency on December 31, 20Y5, and its revenue and expenses for the year are as follows:

Accounts payable	$ 108,000	Miscellaneous expense	$ 19,500
Accounts receivable	539,000	Rent expense	56,000
Cash	200,000	Supplies	6,000
Common stock	575,000	Supplies expense	12,700
Fees earned	940,000	Utilities expense	34,800
Land	1,500,000	Wages expense	415,000

Common stock was $525,000 and retained earnings was $1,250,000 as of January 1, 20Y5. During the year, additional common stock of $50,000 was issued for cash, and dividends of $90,000 were paid.

Instructions
1. Prepare an income statement for the year ended December 31, 20Y5.
2. Prepare a statement of stockholders' equity for the year ended December 31, 20Y5.
3. Prepare a balance sheet as of December 31, 20Y5.
4. What items appears on both the statement of stockholders' equity and the balance sheet?

PR 1-3A   Financial statements
Obj. 5

✔ 1. Net income: $31,200

EXCEL TEMPLATE

Seth Feye established Reliance Financial Services on July 1, 20Y2. Reliance Financial Services offers financial planning advice to its clients. The effect of each transaction and the balances after each transaction for July follow:

	Cash	+ Accounts Receivable	+ Supplies =	Accounts Payable +	Common Stock	− Dividends +	Fees Earned	− Salaries Expense	− Rent Expense	− Auto Expense	− Supplies Expense	− Misc. Expense
a.	+50,000				+50,000							
b.			+7,000	+7,000								
Bal.	50,000		7,000	7,000	50,000							
c.	−3,600			−3,600								
Bal.	46,400		7,000	3,400	50,000							
d.	+110,000						+110,000					
Bal.	156,400		7,000	3,400	50,000		110,000					
e.	−33,000								−33,000			
Bal.	123,400		7,000	3,400	50,000		110,000		−33,000			
f.	−20,800									−16,000		−4,800
Bal.	102,600		7,000	3,400	50,000		110,000		−33,000	−16,000		−4,800
g.	−55,000							−55,000				
Bal.	47,600		7,000	3,400	50,000		110,000	−55,000	−33,000	−16,000		−4,800
h.			−4,500								−4,500	
Bal.	47,600		2,500	3,400	50,000		110,000	−55,000	−33,000	−16,000	−4,500	−4,800
i.		+34,500					+ 34,500					
Bal.	47,600	34,500	2,500	3,400	50,000		144,500	−55,000	−33,000	−16,000	−4,500	−4,800
j.	−15,000					−15,000						
Bal.	32,600	34,500	2,500	3,400	50,000	−15,000	144,500	−55,000	−33,000	−16,000	−4,500	−4,800

Instructions

1. Prepare an income statement for the month ended July 31, 20Y2.
2. Prepare a statement of stockholders' equity for the month ended July 31, 20Y2.
3. Prepare a balance sheet as of July 31, 20Y2.
4. (*Optional*) Prepare a statement of cash flows for the month ending July 31, 20Y2.

PR 1-4A Transactions; financial statements
Obj. 4, 5

✔ 2. Net income: $39,750

On August 1, 20Y9, Brooke Kline established Western Realty. Brooke completed the following transactions during the month of August:

a. Opened a business bank account with a deposit of $35,000 in exchange for common stock.
b. Purchased supplies on account, $2,750.
c. Paid creditor on account, $1,800.
d. Earned sales commissions, receiving cash, $52,800.
e. Paid rent on office and equipment for the month, $4,500.
f. Paid dividends, $3,000.
g. Paid automobile expenses for month, $1,100, and miscellaneous expenses, $1,200.
h. Paid office salaries, $5,250.
i. Determined that the cost of supplies on hand was $1,750; therefore, the cost of supplies used was $1,000.

Instructions

1. Indicate the effect of each transaction and the balances after each transaction, using the following tabular headings:

	Assets	= Liabilities +				Stockholders' Equity					
Cash +	Supplies =	Accounts Payable +	Common Stock	− Dividends +	Sales Commissions	− Salaries Expense	− Rent Expense	− Auto Expense	− Supplies Expense	− Misc. Expense	

2. Prepare an income statement for August, a statement of stockholders' equity for August, and a balance sheet as of August 31.

PR 1-5A Transactions; financial statements Obj. 4, 5

✔ 3. Net income: $63,775

EXCEL TEMPLATE

D'Lite Dry Cleaners is owned and operated by Joel Palk. A building and equipment are currently being rented, pending expansion to new facilities. The actual work of dry cleaning is done by another company at wholesale rates. The assets, liabilities, and common stock of the business on July 1, 20Y4, are as follows: Cash, $45,000; Accounts Receivable, $93,000; Supplies, $7,000; Land, $75,000; Accounts Payable, $40,000; Common Stock, $60,000. Business transactions during July are summarized as follows:

a. Joel Palk invested additional cash in exchange for common stock with a deposit of $35,000 in the business bank account.

b. Paid $50,000 for the purchase of land adjacent to land currently owned by D'Lite Dry Cleaners as a future building site.

c. Received cash from customers for dry cleaning revenue, $32,125.

d. Paid rent for the month, $6,000.

e. Purchased supplies on account, $2,500.

f. Paid creditors on account, $22,800.

g. Charged customers for dry cleaning revenue on account, $84,750.

h. Received monthly invoice for dry cleaning expense for July (to be paid on August 10), $29,500.

i. Paid the following: wages expense, $7,500; truck expense, $2,500; utilities expense, $1,300; miscellaneous expense, $2,700.

j. Received cash from customers on account, $88,000.

k. Determined that the cost of supplies on hand was $5,900; therefore, the cost of supplies used during the month was $3,600.

l. Paid dividends, $12,000.

Instructions

1. Determine the amount of retained earnings as of July 1, 20Y4.
2. State the assets, liabilities, and stockholders' equity as of July 1 in equation form similar to that shown in this chapter. In tabular form below the equation, indicate increases and decreases resulting from each transaction and the new balances after each transaction.
3. Prepare an income statement for July, a statement of stockholders' equity for July, and a balance sheet as of July 31.
4. (*Optional*) Prepare a statement of cash flows for July.

PR 1-6A Missing amounts from financial statements Obj. 5

✔ (k) $750,000

The financial statements at the end of Wolverine Realty's first month of operations are as follows:

Wolverine Realty
Income Statement
For the Month Ended April 30, 20Y0

Fees earned..		$ (a)
Expenses:		
Wages expense	$300,000	
Rent expense	100,000	
Supplies expense	(b)	
Utilities expense	20,000	
Miscellaneous expense	25,000	
Total expenses...		(475,000)
Net income		$ 275,000

Wolverine Realty
Statement of Stockholders' Equity
For the Month Ended April 30, 20Y0

	Common Stock	Retained Earnings	Total
Balances, April 1, 20Y0........................	$ 0	$ 0	$ 0
Issued common stock.........................	(c)		(c)
Net income		(d)	(d)
Dividends		(125,000)	(125,000)
Balances, April 30, 20Y0......................	$ (c)	$ (e)	$ (f)

Wolverine Realty
Balance Sheet
April 30, 20Y0

Assets

Cash	$462,500
Supplies	12,500
Land	150,000
Total assets	$ (g)

Liabilities

Accounts payable	$ 100,000

Stockholders' Equity

Common stock..	$375,000	
Retained earnings..	(h)	
Total stockholders' equity...................................		(i)
Total liabilities and stockholders' equity...................		$ (j)

Wolverine Realty
Statement of Cash Flows
For the Month Ended April 30, 20Y0

Cash flows from (used for) operating activities:		
Cash received from customers.................................	$ (k)	
Cash paid for expenses and to creditors.....................	(387,500)	
Net cash flows from operating activities		$ (l)
Cash flows from (used for) investing activities:		
Cash paid for land..		(m)
Cash flows from (used for) financing activities:		
Cash received from issuing common stock	$ (n)	
Cash paid for dividends.....................................	(o)	
Net cash flows from financing activities....................		(p)
Net increase (decrease) in cash.............................		$ (q)
Cash balance, April 1, 20Y0		0
Cash balance, April 30, 20Y0		$ (r)

Instructions

By analyzing the interrelationships among the four financial statements, determine the proper amounts for (a) through (r).

Problems: Series B

PR 1-1B Transactions **Obj. 4**

✔ Cash bal. at end of March: $48,650

SHOW ME HOW

Amy Austin established an insurance agency on March 1 of the current year and completed the following transactions during March:

a. Opened a business bank account with a deposit of $50,000 in exchange for common stock.
b. Purchased supplies on account, $4,000.
c. Paid creditors on account, $2,300.
d. Received cash from fees earned on insurance commissions, $13,800.
e. Paid rent on office and equipment for the month, $5,000.
f. Paid automobile expenses for month, $1,150, and miscellaneous expenses, $300.
g. Paid office salaries, $2,500.
h. Determined that the cost of supplies on hand was $2,700; therefore, the cost of supplies used was $1,300.
i. Billed insurance companies for sales commissions earned, $12,500.
j. Paid dividends, $3,900.

Instructions

1. Indicate the effect of each transaction and the balances after each transaction, using the following tabular headings:

Assets			= Liabilities +		Stockholders' Equity						
	Accounts		Accounts	Common		Fees	Rent	Salaries	Supplies	Auto	Misc.
Cash +	Receivable +	Supplies =	Payable +	Stock	− Dividends	+ Earned	− Expense	− Expense	− Expense	− Expense	− Expense

(Continued)

2. ➤ Briefly explain why issuing common stock and revenues increased stockholders' equity, while dividends and expenses decreased stockholders' equity.

3. Determine the net income for March.

4. How much did March's transactions increase or decrease stockholders' equity?

PR 1-2B Financial statements

Obj. 5

✔ 1. Net income: $200,000

SHOW ME HOW   EXCEL TEMPLATE

The assets and liabilities of Wilderness Travel Service on April 30, 20Y7, and its revenue and expenses for the year are as follows:

Accounts payable	$ 25,000	Rent expense	$ 75,000
Accounts receivable	210,000	Supplies	9,000
Cash	156,000	Supplies expense	12,000
Common stock	35,000	Taxes expense	10,000
Fees earned	875,000	Utilities expense	38,000
Miscellaneous expense	15,000	Wages expense	525,000

Common stock was $25,000 and retained earnings was $155,000 as of May 1, 20Y6. During the year, additional common stock of $10,000 was issued for cash, and dividends of $40,000 were paid.

Instructions

1. Prepare an income statement for the year ended April 30, 20Y7.
2. Prepare a statement of stockholders' equity for the year ended April 30, 20Y7.
3. Prepare a balance sheet as of April 30, 20Y7.
4. What item appears on both the income statement and statement of stockholders' equity?

PR 1-3B Financial statements

Obj. 5

✔ 1. Net income: $10,900

Jose Loder established Bronco Consulting on August 1, 20Y1. The effect of each transaction and the balances after each transaction for August follow:

	Assets			= Liabilities +				Stockholders' Equity					
	Cash	+ Accounts Receivable	+ Supplies	= Accounts Payable	+ Common Stock	− Dividends	+ Fees Earned	− Salaries Expense	− Rent Expense	− Auto Expense	− Supplies Expense	− Misc. Expense
a.	+75,000				+75,000							
b.			+9,000	+9,000								
Bal.	75,000		9,000	9,000	75,000							
c.	+92,000						+92,000					
Bal.	167,000		9,000	9,000	75,000		92,000					
d.	−27,000								−27,000			
Bal.	140,000		9,000	9,000	75,000		92,000		−27,000			
e.	−6,000			−6,000								
Bal.	134,000		9,000	3,000	75,000		92,000		−27,000			
f.		+33,000					+33,000					
Bal.	134,000	33,000	9,000	3,000	75,000		125,000		−27,000			
g.	−23,000									−15,500		−7,500
Bal.	111,000	33,000	9,000	3,000	75,000		125,000		−27,000	−15,500		−7,500
h.	−58,000							−58,000				
Bal.	53,000	33,000	9,000	3,000	75,000		125,000	−58,000	−27,000	−15,500		−7,500
i.			−6,100								−6,100	
Bal.	53,000	33,000	2,900	3,000	75,000		125,000	−58,000	−27,000	−15,500	−6,100	−7,500
j.	−5,000					−5,000						
Bal.	48,000	33,000	2,900	3,000	75,000	−5,000	125,000	−58,000	−27,000	−15,500	−6,100	−7,500

EXCEL TEMPLATE

Instructions

1. Prepare an income statement for the month ended August 31, 20Y1.
2. Prepare a statement of stockholders' equity for the month ended August 31, 20Y1.
3. Prepare a balance sheet as of August 31, 20Y1.
4. (*Optional*) Prepare a statement of cash flows for the month ending August 31, 20Y1.

PR 1-4B Transactions; financial statements

Obj. 4, 5

✔ 2. Net income: $10,850

On April 1, 20Y8, Maria Adams established Custom Realty. Maria completed the following transactions during the month of April:

a. Opened a business bank account with a deposit of $24,000 in exchange for common stock.

b. Paid rent on office and equipment for the month, $3,600.

c. Paid automobile expenses for month, $1,350, and miscellaneous expenses, $600.

d. Purchased supplies on account, $1,200.

e. Earned sales commissions, receiving cash, $19,800.

f. Paid creditor on account, $750.

g. Paid office salaries, $2,500.

h. Paid dividends, $3,500.

i. Determined that the cost of supplies on hand was $300; therefore, the cost of supplies used was $900.

Instructions

1. Indicate the effect of each transaction and the balances after each transaction, using the following tabular headings:

Assets		= Liabilities +		Stockholders' Equity							
Cash + Supplies	=	Accounts Payable	+ Common Stock	− Dividends +	Sales Commissions	Rent − Expense −	Salaries Expense −	Auto Expense −	Supplies Expense −	Misc. Expense	

2. Prepare an income statement for April, a statement of stockholders' equity for April, and a balance sheet as of April 30.

PR 1-5B Transactions; financial statements

Obj. 4, 5

✔ 3. Net income: $40,150

EXCEL TEMPLATE

Bev's Dry Cleaners is owned and operated by Beverly Zahn. A building and equipment are currently being rented, pending expansion to new facilities. The actual work of dry cleaning is done by another company at wholesale rates. The assets, liabilities, and common stock of the business on November 1, 20Y3, are as follows: Cash, $39,000; Accounts Receivable, $80,000; Supplies, $11,000; Land, $50,000; Accounts Payable, $31,500; Common Stock, $50,000. Business transactions during November are summarized as follows:

a. Beverly Zahn invested additional cash in exchange for common stock with a deposit of $21,000 in the business bank account.

b. Purchased land adjacent to land currently owned by Bev's Dry Cleaners to use in the future as a parking lot, paying cash of $35,000.

c. Paid rent for the month, $4,000.

d. Charged customers for dry cleaning revenue on account, $72,000.

e. Paid creditors on account, $20,000.

f. Purchased supplies on account, $8,000.

g. Received cash from customers for dry cleaning revenue, $38,000.

h. Received cash from customers on account, $77,000.

i. Received monthly invoice for dry cleaning expense for November (to be paid on December 10), $29,450.

j. Paid the following: wages expense, $24,000; truck expense, $2,100; utilities expense, $1,800; miscellaneous expense, $1,300.

k. Determined that the cost of supplies on hand was $11,800; therefore, the cost of supplies used during the month was $7,200.

l. Paid dividends, $5,000.

Instructions

1. Determine the amount of retained earnings as of November 1.

2. State the assets, liabilities, and stockholders' equity as of November 1 in equation form similar to that shown in this chapter. In tabular form below the equation, indicate increases and decreases resulting from each transaction and the new balances after each transaction.

3. Prepare an income statement for November, a statement of stockholders' equity for November, and a balance sheet as of November 30.

4. (*Optional*) Prepare a statement of cash flows for November.

PR 1-6B   Missing amounts from financial statements

Obj. 5

✔ I. $208,000   The financial statements at the end of Atlas Realty's first month of operations follow:

Atlas Realty
Income Statement
For the Month Ended May 31, 20Y6

Fees earned...		$ 400,000
Expenses:		
Wages expense	$ (a)	
Rent expense	48,000	
Supplies expense	17,600	
Utilities expense	14,400	
Miscellaneous expense	4,800	
Total expenses..		(288,000)
Net income		$ (b)

Atlas Realty
Statement of Stockholders' Equity
For the Month Ended May 31, 20Y6

	Common Stock	Retained Earnings	Total
Balances, May 1, 20Y6	$ 0	$ 0	$ 0
Issued common stock	(c)		(c)
Net income		(d)	(d)
Dividends		(e)	(e)
Balances, May 31, 20Y6	$ (c)	$ (f)	$ (g)

Atlas Realty
Balance Sheet
May 31, 20Y6

Assets

Cash	$123,200
Supplies...	12,800
Land	(h)
Total assets	$ (i)

Liabilities

Accounts payable	$ 48,000

Stockholders' Equity

Common stock..	$ (j)	
Retained earnings..	(k)	
Total stockholders' equity...................................		(l)
Total liabilities and stockholders' equity....................		$ (m)

Atlas Realty
Statement of Cash Flows
For the Month Ended May 31, 20Y6

Cash flows from (used for) operating activities:		
Cash received from customers....................................	$ (n)	
Cash paid for expenses and to creditors.........................	(252,800)	
Net cash flows from operating activities		$ (o)
Cash flows from (used for) investing activities:		
Cash paid for acquisition of land		(120,000)
Cash flows from (used for) financing activities:		
Cash received from issuing common stock	$160,000	
Cash paid for dividends	(64,000)	
Net cash flows from financing activities.......................		(p)
Net increase (decrease) in cash		$ (q)
Cash balance, May 1, 20Y6		0
Cash balance, May 31, 20Y6		$ (r)

Instructions

By analyzing the interrelationships among the four financial statements, determine the proper amounts for (a) through (r).

Continuing Problem

✔ 2. Net income: $1,340

Peyton Smith enjoys listening to all types of music and owns countless CDs. Over the years, Peyton has gained a local reputation for knowledge of music from classical to rap and the ability to put together sets of recordings that appeal to all ages.

During the last several months, Peyton served as a guest disc jockey on a local radio station. In addition, Peyton has entertained at several friends' parties as the host deejay.

On June 1, 20Y5, Peyton established a corporation known as PS Music. Using an extensive collection of music MP3 files, Peyton will serve as a disc jockey on a fee basis for weddings, college parties, and other events. During June, Peyton entered into the following transactions:

June 1. Deposited $4,000 in a checking account in the name of PS Music in exchange for common stock.

2. Received $3,500 from a local radio station for serving as the guest disc jockey for June.

2. Agreed to share office space with a local real estate agency, Pinnacle Realty. PS Music will pay one-fourth of the rent. In addition, PS Music agreed to pay a portion of the wages of the receptionist and to pay one-fourth of the utilities. Paid $800 for the rent of the office.

4. Purchased supplies from City Office Supply Co. for $350. Agreed to pay $100 within 10 days and the remainder by July 5, 20Y5.

6. Paid $500 to a local radio station to advertise the services of PS Music twice daily for two weeks.

8. Paid $675 to a local electronics store for renting digital recording equipment.

12. Paid $350 (music expense) to Cool Music for the use of its current music demos to make various music sets.

13. Paid City Office Supply Co. $100 on account.

16. Received $300 from a dentist for providing two music sets for the dentist to play for her patients.

22. Served as disc jockey for a wedding party. The father of the bride agreed to pay $1,000 in July.

25. Received $500 for serving as the disc jockey for a cancer charity ball hosted by the local hospital.

29. Paid $240 (music expense) to Galaxy Music for the use of its library of music demos.

30. Received $900 for serving as PS disc jockey for a local club's monthly dance.

30. Paid Pinnacle Realty $400 for PS Music's share of the receptionist's wages for June.

30. Paid Pinnacle Realty $300 for PS Music's share of the utilities for June.

30. Determined that the cost of supplies on hand is $170. Therefore, the cost of supplies used during the month was $180.

30. Paid for miscellaneous expenses, $415.

30. Paid $1,000 royalties (music expense) to National Music Clearing for use of various artists' music during the month.

30. Paid dividends, $500.

Instructions

1. Indicate the effect of each transaction and the balances after each transaction, using the following tabular headings:

Assets			=	Liabilities +				Stockholders' Equity							
											Office	Equipment					
	Accts.			Accounts	Common		Fees	Music	Rent	Rent	Advertising	Wages	Utilities	Supplies	Misc.
Cash +	Rec. +	Supplies =	Payable +	Stock	− Dividends	+ Earned −	Exp. −	Exp. −	Exp. −	Exp. −	Exp. −	Exp. −	Exp. −	Exp.

2. Prepare an income statement for PS Music for the month ended June 30, 20Y5.
3. Prepare a statement of stockholders' equity for PS Music for the month ended June 30, 20Y5.
4. Prepare a balance sheet for PS Music as of June 30, 20Y5.

Make a Decision
Ratio of Liabilities to Stockholders' Equity

REAL WORLD

MAD 1-1   Compare Amazon.com to Best Buy   Obj. 6

Amazon.com, Inc. (AMZN) is one of the largest Internet retailers in the world. We will use Amazon as a continuing company exercise to reinforce the various tools and techniques for analyzing financial statements. We will begin with the ratio of liabilities to stockholders' equity.

Ratios can be used to compare companies in the same industry. For Amazon, there are a number of competitors that sell media, electronic, and other merchandise. **Best Buy, Inc. (BBY)** is one such company. The following total liabilities and stockholders' equity information (in millions) is provided for Amazon and Best Buy for the end of a recent year:

	Amazon	Best Buy
Total assets	$64,747	$13,519
Total liabilities	51,363	9,141
Total stockholders' equity	13,384	4,378

a.   Compute the ratio of liabilities to stockholders' equity for each company. Round to two decimal places.

b.   ────▶ What conclusions regarding the margin of protection to creditors can you draw for these two companies?

SHOW ME HOW

REAL WORLD

MAD 1-2   Analyze The Home Depot for three years   Obj. 6

The Home Depot, Inc. (HD), is the world's largest home improvement retailer and one of the largest retailers in the United States based on sales volume. Home Depot operates over 2,200 stores that sell a wide assortment of building, home improvement, and lawn and garden items.

Home Depot recently reported the following end-of-year balance sheet data (in millions):

	Year 3	Year 2	Year 1
Total assets	$42,549	$39,946	$40,518
Total liabilities	36,233	30,624	27,996
Total stockholders' equity	6,316	9,322	12,522

a.   Compute the ratio of liabilities to stockholders' equity for all three years. Round to two decimal places.

b.   ────▶ What conclusions regarding the margin of protection to creditors can you draw from the trend in this ratio for the three years?

REAL WORLD

MAD 1-3   Analyze Lowe's for three years   Obj. 6

Lowe's Companies, Inc. (LOW), a major competitor to **The Home Depot, Inc. (HD)** in the home improvement retail business, operates over 1,800 stores. Lowe's recently reported the following end-of-year balance sheet data (in millions):

	Year 3	Year 2	Year 1
Total assets	$31,266	$31,721	$32,732
Total liabilities	23,612	21,753	20,879
Total stockholders' equity	7,654	9,968	11,853

a.   Compute the ratio of liabilities to stockholders' equity for all three years. Round to two decimal places.

b.   ────▶ What conclusions regarding the margin of protection to creditors can you draw from the trend in this ratio for the three years?

REAL WORLD

MAD 1-4   Compare The Home Depot and Lowe's   Obj. 6

Using your answers for **The Home Depot, Inc. (HD)** in MAD 1-2 and **Lowe's Companies, Inc. (LOW)** in MAD 1-3, compare and interpret Home Depot's ratio of liabilities to stockholders' equity to that of Lowe's.

REAL WORLD

MAD 1-5 Compare Papa John's and Yum! Brands   Obj. 6

The following total liabilities and stockholders' equity information (in millions) is provided for **Papa John's International, Inc. (PZZA)** and **Yum! Brands, Inc. (YUM)** at the end of a recent year:

	Papa John's	Yum! Brands
Total assets	$495	$8,075
Total liabilities	444	7,164
Total stockholders' equity	51	911

Yum! Brands is a much larger company than is Papa John's; however, both companies compete internationally in the fast food business. Papa John's is primarily in the carry-out and delivery pizza business, while Yum! Brands is in the quick-service restaurant business with its Pizza Hut, Taco Bell, and KFC brands.

a. Compute the ratio of liabilities to stockholders' equity for each company. Round to one decimal place.

b. What conclusions regarding the margin of protection to creditors can you draw for these two companies?

c. Which company is more risky to creditors?

Take It Further

ETHICS

TIF 1-1 Business versus personal expenses

Marco Brolo is one of three partners who own and operate Silkroad Partners, a global import–export business. Marco is the partner in charge of recording partnership transactions in the accounts. On his way to work one day, Marco's car broke down. At the repair shop, Marco learned that his car's engine had significant damage, and it will cost over $2,000 to repair the damage. He does not have enough money in his bank account to cover the cost of the repair, and his credit cards are at their limit. This car is the only form of transportation that Marco has to get to and from work every day. He does not use his car for any business travel.

After considering his options, Marco decides to take $2,000 from the partnership for the repair, and record it as an expense of the partnership. He believes that this is appropriate since he needs his car to get to work every day.

1. Is Marco behaving ethically? Why?
2. Who is affected by Marco's decision?
3. What other alternatives might Marco consider?

TEAM ACTIVITY   ETHICS

TIF 1-2 Loan from bank

Colleen Fernandez, president of Rhino Enterprises, applied for a $175,000 loan from First Federal Bank. The bank requested financial statements from Rhino Enterprises as a basis for granting the loan. Colleen has told her accountant to provide the bank with a balance sheet. Colleen has decided to omit the other financial statements because there was a net loss during the past year.

In groups of three or four, discuss the following questions:

1. Is Colleen behaving in a professional manner by omitting some of the financial statements?
2. a. What types of information about their businesses would owners be willing to provide bankers? What types of information would owners not be willing to provide?
    b. What types of information about a business would bankers want before extending a loan?
    c. What common interests are shared by bankers and business owners?

TIF 1-3   Real-world annual report

In teams, select a public company that interests you. Obtain the company's most recent annual report on Form 10-K. The Form 10-K is a company's annually required filing with the Securities and Exchange Commission (SEC). It includes the company's financial statements and accompanying notes. The Form 10-K can be obtained either (a) from the investor relations section of the company's Web site or (b) by using the company search feature of the SEC's EDGAR database service found at www.sec.gov/edgar/searchedgar/companysearch.html.

Based on the information in the company's most recent annual report, answer the following questions:

1. What is the official name of the company?
2. Where are the company's principal offices located?
3. Who is the company's chief executive officer?
4. Is the company primarily a service, retail, or manufacturing business?
5. How does the company describe its business?
6. Which financial statements are included in the annual report?

TIF 1-4   Causes of fraud

There are two common causes of business and accounting fraud:

- a failure of individual character, and
- a culture of greed or ethical indifference within an organization.

➤ Write a brief memo describing how these two factors could lead to accounting fraud.

TIF 1-5   Net income

On January 1, 20Y5, Dr. Marcie Cousins established Health-Wise Medical, a medical practice organized as a corporation. The following conversation occurred the following August between Dr. Cousins and a former medical school classmate, Dr. Avi Abu, at an American Medical Association convention in Seattle:

Dr. Abu: Marcie, good to see you again. Why didn't you call when you were in Miami? We could have had dinner together.

Dr. Cousins: Actually, I never made it to Miami this year. My husband and kids went up to our Vail condo twice, but I got stuck in Jacksonville. I opened a new consulting practice this January and haven't had any time for myself since.

Dr. Abu: I heard about it…Health…something…right?

Dr. Cousins: Yes, Health-Wise Medical. My husband chose the name.

Dr. Abu: I've thought about doing something like that. Are you making any money? I mean, is it worth your time?

Dr. Cousins: You wouldn't believe it. I started by opening a bank account with $25,000, and my July bank statement has a balance of $80,000. Not bad for six months—all pure profit.

Dr. Abu: Maybe I'll try it in Miami! Let's have breakfast together tomorrow and you can fill me in on the details.

➤ Comment on Dr. Cousins' statement that the difference between the opening bank balance ($25,000) and the July statement balance ($80,000) is pure profit.

TIF 1-6   Transactions and financial statements for a proprietorship

Lisa Duncan, a junior in college, has been seeking ways to earn extra spending money. As an active sports enthusiast, Lisa plays tennis regularly at the Phoenix Tennis Club, where her family has a membership. The president of the club recently approached Lisa with the proposal that she manage the club's tennis courts. Lisa's primary duty would be to supervise the operation of the club's four indoor and ten outdoor courts, including court reservations.

In return for her services, the club would pay Lisa $325 per week, plus Lisa could keep whatever she earned from lessons. The club and Lisa agreed to a one-month trial, after which both would consider an arrangement for the remaining two years of Lisa's college career. On this basis, Lisa organized Serve-N-Volley. During September 20Y2, Lisa managed the tennis courts and entered into the following transactions:

a.   Opened a business account by depositing $950.

b.   Paid $300 for tennis supplies (practice tennis balls, etc.).

c.   Paid $275 for the rental of video equipment to be used in offering lessons during September.

d.   Arranged for the rental of two ball machines during September for $250. Paid $100 in advance, with the remaining $150 due October 1.

e.   Received $1,750 for lessons given during September.

f.   Received $600 in fees from the use of the ball machines during September.

g.   Paid $800 for salaries of part-time employees who answered the telephone and took reservations while Lisa was giving lessons.

h.   Paid $290 for miscellaneous expenses.

i.   Received $1,300 from the club for managing the tennis courts during September.

j.   Determined that the cost of supplies on hand at the end of the month totaled $180; therefore, the cost of supplies used was $120.

k.   Withdrew $400 for personal use on September 30.

As a friend and accounting student, you have been asked by Lisa to aid her in assessing the venture.

1.   Indicate the effect of each transaction and the balances after each transaction, using the following tabular headings:

Assets	=	Liabilities +				Owner's Equity			
			Lisa	Lisa					
		Accounts	Duncan,	Duncan,	Fees	Salaries	Rent	Supplies	Misc.
Cash + Supplies =		Payable	+ Capital	− Drawing	+ Earned	− Expense	− Expense	− Expense	− Expense

2.   Prepare an income statement for September.

3.   Prepare a statement of owner's equity for September. The statement of owner's equity for a proprietorship is similar to the statement of stockholders' equity for a corporation. The balance of the owner's capital as of the beginning of the period is listed first. Any investments made by the owner during the period are then listed, the net income (net loss) is added (subtracted), and any owner's withdrawals are subtracted to determine the increase (decrease) in owner's equity for the period. This increase (decrease) is then added to (subtracted from) the beginning owner's equity to determine the owner's equity as of the end of the period.

4.   Prepare a balance sheet as of September 30.

5.   a.   Assume that Lisa Duncan could earn $10 per hour working 30 hours a week as a waitress. Evaluate which of the two alternatives, working as a waitress or operating Serve-N-Volley, would provide Lisa with the most income per month.

     b.   ▬▬▶ Discuss any other factors that you believe Lisa should consider before discussing a long-term arrangement with the Phoenix Tennis Club.

Pathways Challenge

This is Accounting!

Information/Consequences

Under the business entity assumption, **The North American Coffee Partnership** is a business entity separate from its owners—**Starbucks** and **Pepsi**. Thus, the $1.5 billion in sales are reported on its financial reports and not those of Starbucks or Pepsi. However, Starbucks and Pepsi report their share of the partnership as an investment.

Suggested Answer

2 Analyzing Transactions

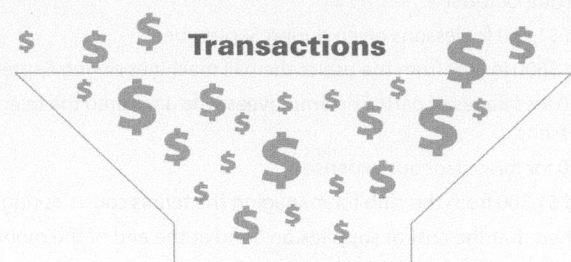

Chapter 1

$ $ $ Transactions $ $

ACCOUNTING SYSTEM

Accounting Equation

Assets = Liabilities + Equity

Chapter 2

Account

Debits	Credits

RULES OF DEBIT AND CREDIT

Balance Sheet Accounts

ASSETS = **LIABILITIES** + **STOCKHOLDERS' EQUITY**

Asset Accounts

Debit for increases (+)	Credit for decreases (–)
Balance	

Liability Accounts

Debit for decreases (–)	Credit for increases (+)
	Balance

Common Stock

Debit for decreases (–)	Credit for increases (+)
	Balance

Retained Earnings

Debit for decreases (–)	Credit for increases (+)
	Balance

Dividends

Debit for increases (+)	Credit for decreases (–)
Balance	

Income Statement Accounts

Revenue Accounts

Debit for decreases (–)	Credit for increases (+)
	Balance

Expense Accounts

Debit for increases (+)	Credit for decreases (–)
Balance	

UNADJUSTED TRIAL BALANCE

Total Debit Balances = Total Credit Balances

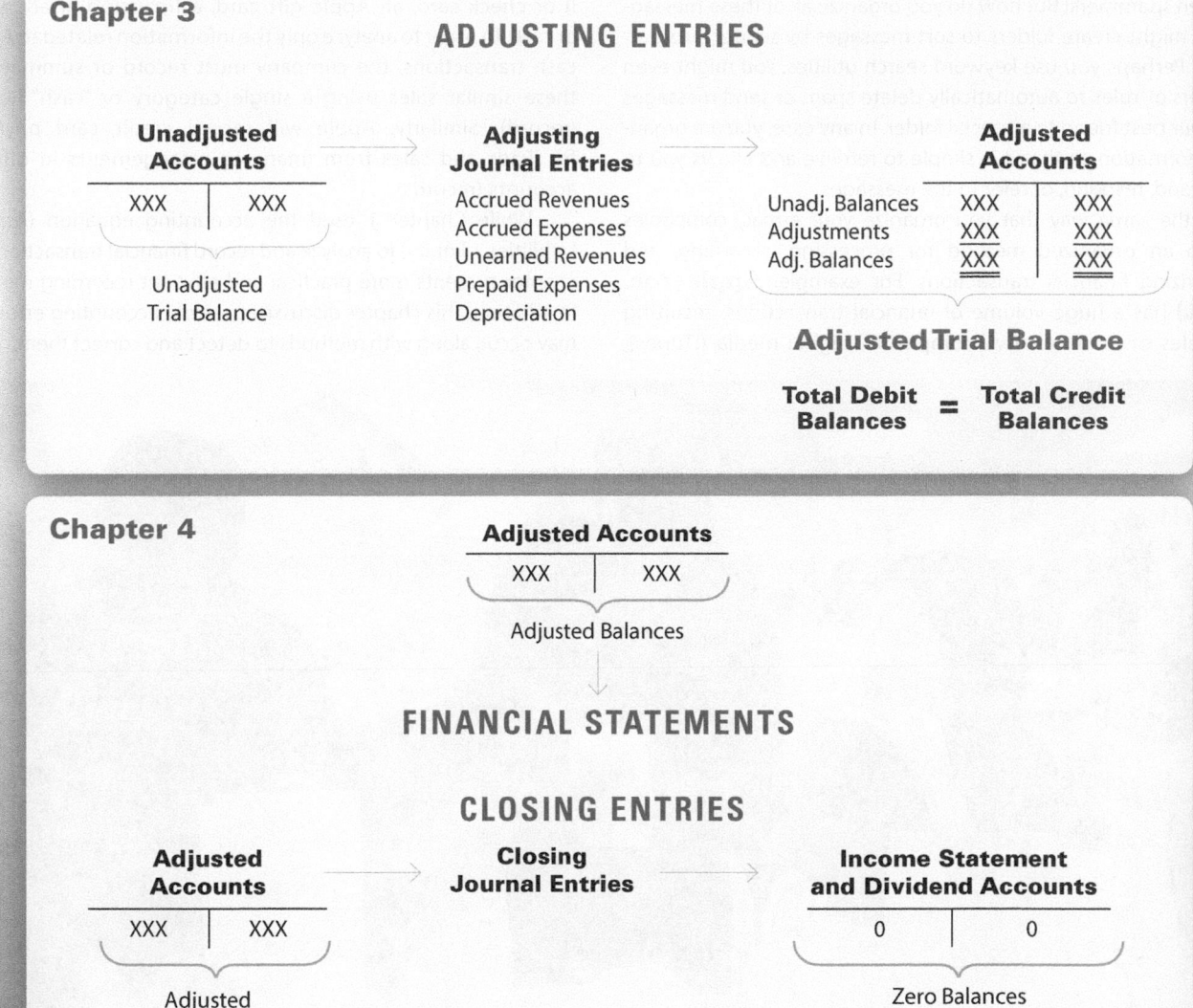

Chapter 3

ADJUSTING ENTRIES

Unadjusted Accounts

XXX	XXX

Unadjusted Trial Balance

Adjusting Journal Entries

Accrued Revenues
Accrued Expenses
Unearned Revenues
Prepaid Expenses
Depreciation

Adjusted Accounts

Unadj. Balances	XXX	XXX
Adjustments	XXX	XXX
Adj. Balances	XXX	XXX

Adjusted Trial Balance

$$\text{Total Debit Balances} = \text{Total Credit Balances}$$

Chapter 4

Adjusted Accounts

XXX	XXX

Adjusted Balances

↓

FINANCIAL STATEMENTS

CLOSING ENTRIES

Adjusted Accounts

XXX	XXX

Adjusted Balances

Closing Journal Entries

Income Statement and Dividend Accounts

0	0

Zero Balances

Balance Sheet Accounts

XXX	XXX

Post-Closing Trial Balance

Apple Inc.™

Every day it seems like we get an incredible amount of incoming e-mail messages—from friends, relatives, subscribed e-mail lists, and even spammers! But how do you organize all of these messages? You might create folders to sort messages by sender, topic, or project. Perhaps you use keyword search utilities. You might even use filters or rules to automatically delete spam or send messages from your best friend to a special folder. In any case, you are organizing information so that it is simple to retrieve and allows you to understand, respond, or refer to the messages.

In the same way that you organize your e-mail, companies develop an organized method for processing, recording, and summarizing financial transactions. For example, **Apple Inc. (AAPL)** has a huge volume of financial transactions, resulting from sales of its innovative computers, digital media (iTunes),

iPods, iPhones, and iPads. When Apple sells an iPad, a customer has the option of paying with a credit card, a debit or check card, an Apple gift card, a financing arrangement, or cash. In order to analyze only the information related to Apple's cash transactions, the company must record or summarize all these similar sales using a single category or "cash" account (record). Similarly, Apple will record credit card payments for iPads and sales from financing arrangements in different accounts (records).

While Chapter 1 used the accounting equation (Assets = Liabilities + Equity) to analyze and record financial transactions, this chapter presents more practical and efficient recording methods. In addition, this chapter discusses possible accounting errors that may occur, along with methods to detect and correct them.

©SPENCER PLATT/GETTY IMAGES

Link to Apple . . . . Pages 60, 62, 71, 73, 75

What's Covered

Analyzing Transactions

Elements of Accounting Systems
- Accounts (Obj. 1)
- Journal (Obj. 2)
- Ledger (Obj. 2)

Analyzing and Recording Transactions
- Double-Entry Accounting System (Obj. 2)
- Journalizing (Obj. 2, 3)
- Posting (Obj. 3)

Preparing a Trial Balance
- Steps in Preparation (Obj. 4)
- Interpretation (Obj. 4)
- Types of Errors (Obj. 4)

Learning Objectives

Obj. 1 Describe the characteristics of an account and a chart of accounts.

Obj. 2 Describe and illustrate journalizing transactions using the double-entry accounting system.

Obj. 3 Describe and illustrate the journalizing and posting of transactions to accounts.

Obj. 4 Prepare an unadjusted trial balance and explain how it can be used to discover errors.

Analysis for Decision Making

Obj. 5 Describe and illustrate the use of horizontal analysis in evaluating a company's performance and financial condition.

Using Accounts to Record Transactions

Objective 1
Describe the characteristics of an account and a chart of accounts.

In Chapter 1, the November transactions for **NetSolutions** were recorded using the accounting equation format shown in Exhibit 1. However, this format is not efficient or practical for companies that have to record thousands or millions of transactions daily. As a result, accounting systems are designed to show the increases and decreases in each accounting equation element as a separate record. This record is called an **account**.

To illustrate, the Cash column of Exhibit 1 records the increases and decreases in cash. Likewise, the other columns in Exhibit 1 record the increases and decreases in the other accounting equation elements. Each of these columns can be organized into a separate account.

Exhibit 1 NetSolutions' November Transactions

	Assets			= Liabilities +		Stockholders' Equity						
				Accounts	Common		Fees	Wages	Rent	Supplies	Utilities	Misc.
	Cash +	Supp. +	Land =	Payable +	Stock	– Dividends +	Earned –	Exp. –	Exp. –	Exp. –	Exp. –	Exp.
a.	+25,000				+25,000							
b.	–20,000		+20,000									
Bal.	5,000		20,000		25,000							
c.		+1,350		+1,350								
Bal.	5,000	1,350	20,000	1,350	25,000							
d.	+7,500						+7,500					
Bal.	12,500	1,350	20,000	1,350	25,000		7,500					
e.	–3,650							–2,125	–800		–450	–275
Bal.	8,850	1,350	20,000	1,350	25,000		7,500	–2,125	–800		–450	–275
f.	–950			–950								
Bal.	7,900	1,350	20,000	400	25,000		7,500	–2,125	–800		–450	–275
g.		–800								–800		
Bal.	7,900	550	20,000	400	25,000		7,500	–2,125	–800	–800	–450	–275
h.	–2,000					–2,000						
Bal.	5,900	550	20,000	400	25,000	–2,000	7,500	–2,125	–800	–800	–450	–275

An account, in its simplest form, has three parts.

- A title, which is the name of the accounting equation element recorded in the account
- A space for recording increases in the amount of the element
- A space for recording decreases in the amount of the element

The account form that follows is called a **T account** because it resembles the letter T. The left side of the account is called the *debit* side, and the right side is called the *credit* side.[1]

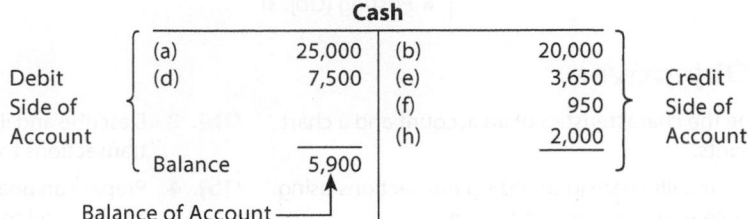

Title

Left side	Right side
debit	*credit*

note:

Amounts entered on the left side of an account are debits, and amounts entered on the right side of an account are credits.

The amounts shown in the Cash column of Exhibit 1 would be recorded in a cash account as follows:

Cash

	(a)	25,000	(b)	20,000	
Debit	(d)	7,500	(e)	3,650	Credit
Side of			(f)	950	Side of
Account			(h)	2,000	Account
	Balance	5,900			

Balance of Account ⟶

Recording transactions in accounts must follow certain rules. For example, increases in assets are recorded on the **debit** (left side) of an account. Likewise, decreases in assets are recorded on the **credit** (right side) of an account. The excess of the debits of an asset account over its credits is the **balance of the account**.

To illustrate, the receipt (increase in Cash) of $25,000 in transaction (a) is entered on the debit (left) side of the cash account. The letter or date of the transaction is also entered into the account. That way, if any questions later arise related to the entry, the entry can be traced back to the underlying transaction data. In contrast, the payment (decrease in Cash) of $20,000 to purchase land in transaction (b) is entered on the credit (right) side of the account.

The balance of the cash account of $5,900 is the excess of the debits over the credits, computed as follows:

Debits ($25,000 + $7,500)	$ 32,500
Less credits ($20,000 + $3,650 + $950 + $2,000)	(26,600)
Balance of Cash as of November 30, 20Y3	$ 5,900

The balance of the cash account is inserted in the account, in the Debit column. In this way, the balance is identified as a debit balance.[2] This balance represents NetSolutions' cash on hand as of November 30, 20Y3. This balance of $5,900 is reported on the November 30, 20Y3, balance sheet for **NetSolutions** as shown in Exhibit 8 of Chapter 1.

Link to Apple   In a recent balance sheet, **Apple Inc.** reported $20.5 billion of cash.

In an actual accounting system, a more formal account form replaces the T account. Later in this chapter, a four-column account is illustrated. The T account, however, is a simple way to illustrate the effects of transactions on accounts and financial statements. For this reason, T accounts are often used in business to explain transactions.

Each of the columns in Exhibit 1 can be converted into an account form in a similar manner as was done for the Cash column of Exhibit 1. However, as mentioned earlier, recording increases and decreases in accounts must follow certain rules. These rules are discussed after the chart of accounts is described.

Chart of Accounts

A group of accounts for a business entity is called a **ledger**. A list of the accounts in the ledger is called a **chart of accounts**. The accounts are normally listed in the order in which they appear in the financial statements. The balance sheet accounts are listed first, in the order of assets,

---

[1] The terms *debit* and *credit* are derived from the Latin *debere* and *credere*.

[2] The totals of the Debit and Credit columns may be shown separately in an account. When this is done, these amounts should be identified in some way so that they are not mistaken for entries or the ending balance of the account.

liabilities, and stockholders' equity. The income statement accounts are then listed in the order of revenues and expenses.

Assets **Assets** are resources owned by the business entity. These resources can be physical items, such as cash and supplies, or intangibles that have value. Examples of intangible assets include patent rights, copyrights, and trademarks. Assets also include accounts receivable, prepaid expenses (such as insurance), buildings, equipment, and land.

Liabilities **Liabilities** are debts owed to outsiders (creditors). Liabilities are often identified on the balance sheet by titles that include *payable*. Examples of liabilities include accounts payable, notes payable, and wages payable. Cash received before services are delivered creates a liability to perform the services. These future service commitments are called *unearned revenues*. Examples of *unearned revenues* include magazine subscriptions received by a publisher and tuition received at the beginning of a term by a college.

Stockholders' equity **Stockholders' equity** is the stockholders' right to the assets of the business. Stockholders' equity is represented by the balance of the **common stock** and **retained earnings** accounts. A **dividends** account represents distributions of earnings to stockholders.

Revenues **Revenues** are increases in assets and stockholders' equity as a result of selling services or products to customers. Examples of revenues include fees earned, fares earned, commissions revenue, and rent revenue.

Expenses **Expenses** result from using up assets or consuming services in the process of generating revenues. Examples of expenses include wages expense, rent expense, utilities expense, supplies expense, and miscellaneous expense.

Illustration of Chart of Accounts A chart of accounts should meet the needs of a company's managers and other users of its financial statements. The accounts within the chart of accounts are numbered for use as references. A numbering system is normally used, so that new accounts can be added without affecting other account numbers.

Exhibit 2 is **NetSolutions**' chart of accounts that is used in this chapter. Additional accounts will be introduced in later chapters. In Exhibit 2, each account number has two digits. The first digit indicates the major account group of the ledger in which the account is located. Accounts beginning with 1 represent assets; 2, liabilities; 3, stockholders' equity; 4, revenue; and 5, expenses. The second digit indicates the location of the account within its group.

Balance Sheet Accounts	Income Statement Accounts
1. Assets	**4. Revenue**
11 Cash	41 Fees Earned
12 Accounts Receivable	**5. Expenses**
14 Supplies	51 Wages Expense
15 Prepaid Insurance	52 Supplies Expense
17 Land	53 Rent Expense
18 Office Equipment	54 Utilities Expense
2. Liabilities	59 Miscellaneous Expense
21 Accounts Payable	
23 Unearned Rent	
3. Stockholders' Equity	
31 Common Stock	
32 Retained Earnings	
33 Dividends	

Exhibit 2
Chart of Accounts for NetSolutions

Each of the columns in Exhibit 1 has been assigned an account number in the chart of accounts shown in Exhibit 2. In addition, Accounts Receivable, Prepaid Insurance, Office Equipment, Unearned Rent, and Retained Earnings have been added. These accounts will be used in recording NetSolutions' December transactions.

Objective 2

Describe and illustrate journalizing transactions using the double-entry accounting system.

Double-Entry Accounting System

All businesses use what is called the **double-entry accounting system**. This system is based on the accounting equation and requires:

- Every business transaction to be recorded in at least two accounts.
- The total debits recorded for each transaction to be equal to the total credits recorded.

The double-entry accounting system also has specific **rules of debit and credit** for recording transactions in the accounts.

Link to Apple   **Apple** records transactions using generally accepted accounting principles and double-entry accounting.

Balance Sheet Accounts

The debit and credit rules for balance sheet accounts are as follows:

Balance Sheet Accounts					
ASSETS **Asset Accounts**		**= LIABILITIES** **Liability Accounts**		**STOCKHOLDERS' EQUITY** **+ Stockholders' Equity Accounts**	
Debit for increases (+)	Credit for decreases (–)	Debit for decreases (–)	Credit for increases (+)	Debit for decreases (–)	Credit for increases (+)

Income Statement Accounts

The debit and credit rules for income statement accounts are based on their relationship with stockholders' equity. As shown for balance sheet accounts, stockholders' equity accounts are increased by credits. Because revenues increase stockholders' equity, revenue accounts are increased by credits and decreased by debits. Because stockholders' equity accounts are decreased by debits, expense accounts are increased by debits and decreased by credits. Thus, the rules of debit and credit for revenue and expense accounts are as follows:

Income Statement Accounts			
Revenue Accounts		**Expense Accounts**	
Debit for decreases (–)	Credit for increases (+)	Debit for increases (+)	Credit for decreases (–)

Why It Matters

The Hijacking Receivable

A company's chart of accounts should reflect the basic nature of its operations. Occasionally, however, transactions take place that give rise to unusual accounts. The following is a story of one such account.

Before strict airport security was implemented across the United States, several airlines experienced hijacking incidents. One such incident occurred when a **Southern Airways** jet en route from Memphis to Miami was hijacked during a stop-over in Birmingham, Alabama. The three hijackers boarded the plane in Birmingham armed with handguns and grenades. At gunpoint, the hijackers took the plane, the plane's crew, and the passengers to nine American cities, Toronto, and eventually to Havana, Cuba.

During the long flight, the hijackers demanded a ransom of $10 million. Southern Airways, however, was only able to come up with $2 million. Eventually, the pilot talked the hijackers into settling for the $2 million when the plane landed in Chattanooga for refueling.

Upon landing in Havana, the Cuban authorities arrested the hijackers and, after a brief delay, sent the plane, passengers, and crew back to the United States. The hijackers and the $2 million stayed in Cuba.

How did Southern Airways account for and report the hijacking payment in its subsequent financial statements? As you might have analyzed, the initial entry credited Cash for $2 million. The debit was to an account entitled "Hijacking Payment." This account was reported as a type of receivable under "other assets" on Southern Airways' balance sheet. The company maintained that it would be able to collect the cash from the Cuban government and that, therefore, a receivable existed. In fact, Southern Airways was later repaid $2 million by the Cuban government, which was, at that time, attempting to improve relations with the United States.

Statement of Stockholders' Equity Accounts (Dividends)

The debit and credit rules for recording dividends are based on the effect of dividends on stockholders' equity (retained earnings). Since dividends decrease stockholders' equity (retained earnings), the dividends account is increased by debits. Likewise, the dividends account is decreased by credits. Thus, the rules of debit and credit for the dividends account are as follows:

Dividends Account	
Debit for increases (+)	Credit for decreases (–)

Normal Balances

The sum of the increases in an account is usually equal to or greater than the sum of the decreases in the account. Thus, the **normal balance of an account** is either a debit or credit depending on whether increases in the account are recorded as debits or credits. For example, because asset accounts are increased with debits, asset accounts normally have debit balances. Likewise, liability accounts normally have credit balances.

The rules of debit and credit and the normal balances of the various types of accounts are summarized in Exhibit 3. Debits and credits are sometimes abbreviated as Dr. for debit and Cr. for credit.

Exhibit 3 Rules of Debit and Credit, Normal Balances of Accounts

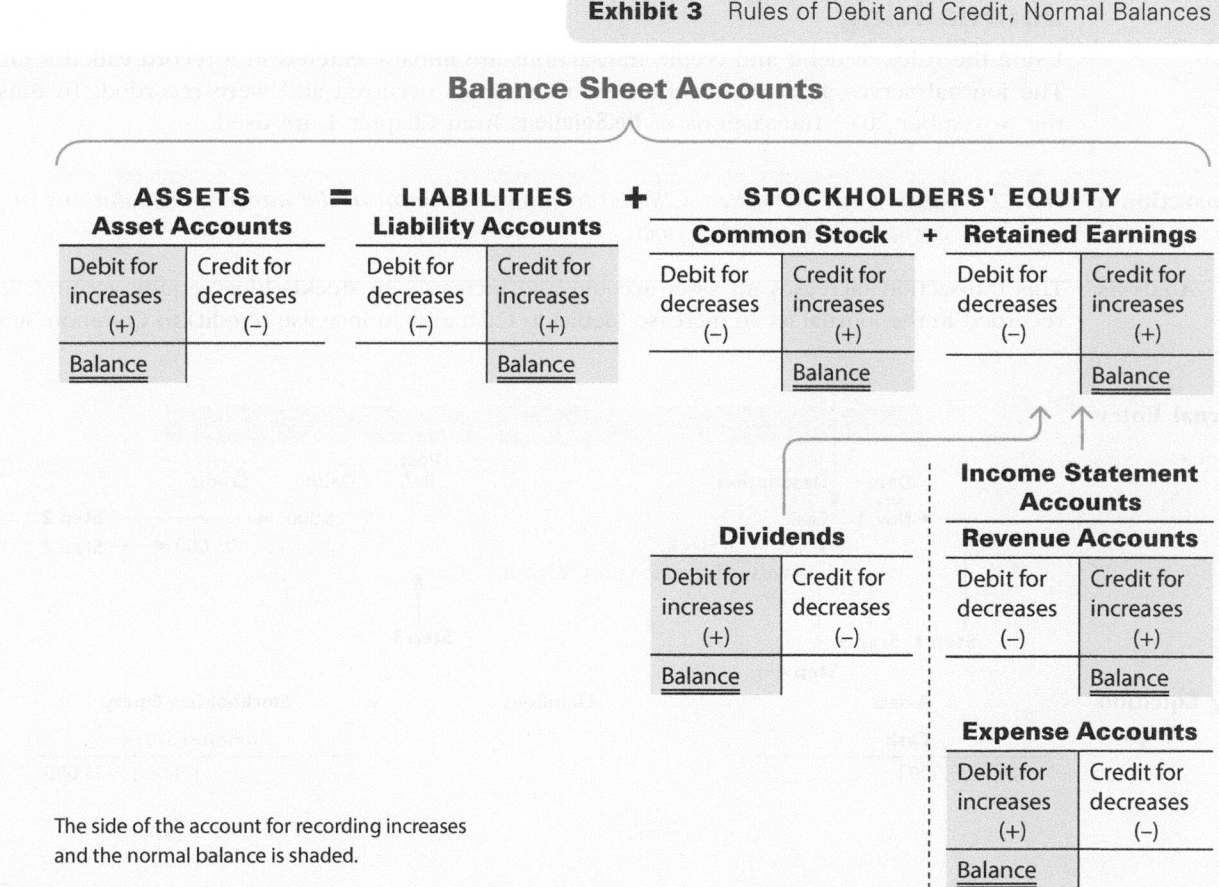

The side of the account for recording increases and the normal balance is shaded.

When an account normally having a debit balance has a credit balance, or vice versa, an error may have occurred or an unusual situation may exist. For example, a credit balance in the office equipment account could result only from an error. This is because a business cannot have more decreases than increases of office equipment. On the other hand, a debit balance in an accounts payable account could result from an overpayment.

Check Up Corner 2-1   Balance Sheet Accounts

David Simmons, M.D., organized Simmons Urgent Care Inc. by investing cash in exchange for common stock. In addition, the clinic purchased medical supplies and office equipment on account.

Identify the balance sheet accounts that Simmons Urgent Care used to record these transactions. For each account, indicate if it is an asset, liability, or stockholders' equity account and whether its normal balance is a debit or a credit.

Solution:

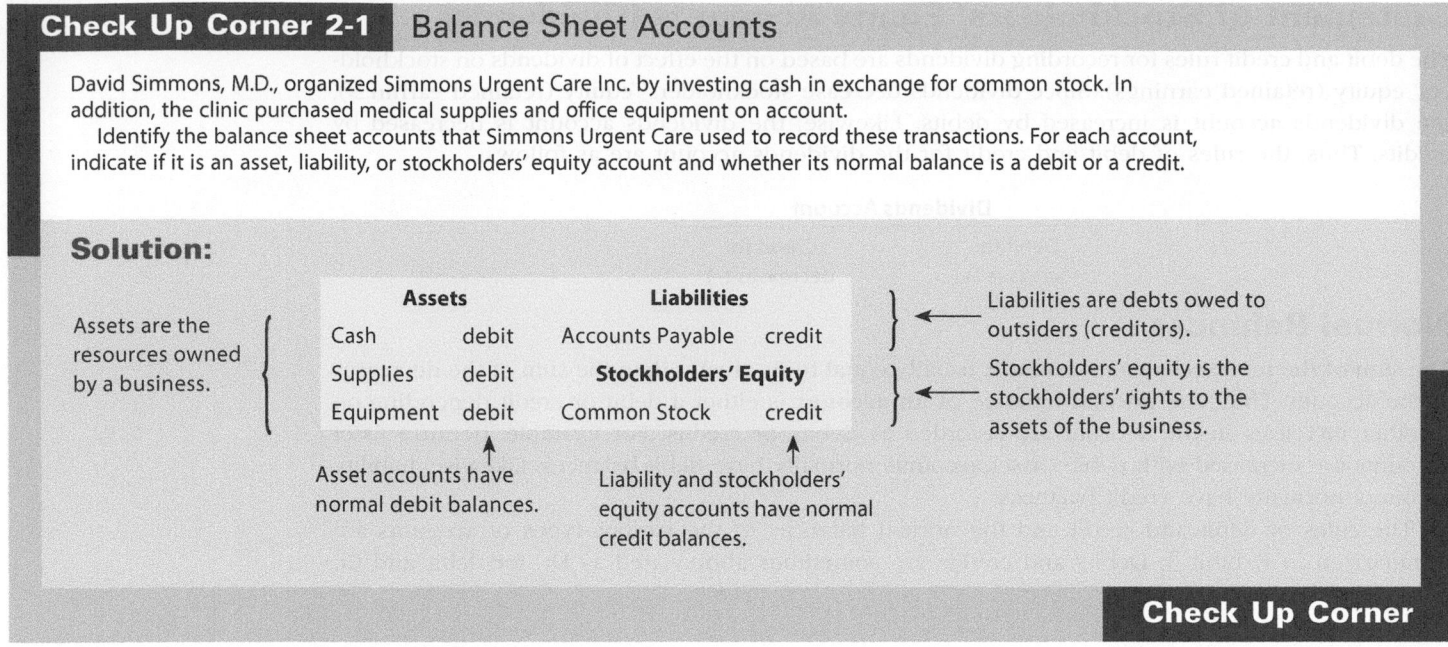

Assets are the resources owned by a business.

Assets		**Liabilities**	
Cash	debit	Accounts Payable	credit
Supplies	debit	**Stockholders' Equity**	
Equipment	debit	Common Stock	credit

Asset accounts have normal debit balances.

Liability and stockholders' equity accounts have normal credit balances.

Liabilities are debts owed to outsiders (creditors).

Stockholders' equity is the stockholders' rights to the assets of the business.

Check Up Corner

Journalizing

Using the rules of debit and credit, transactions are initially entered in a record called a **journal**. The journal serves as a record of when transactions occurred and were recorded. To illustrate, the November 20Y3 transactions of **NetSolutions** from Chapter 1 are used.

Transaction a	*Nov. 1*	*Chris Clark deposited $25,000 in a bank account in the name of NetSolutions in exchange for common stock.*

Analysis   This transaction increases an asset account and increases an stockholders' equity account. It is recorded in the journal as an increase (debit) to Cash and an increase (credit) to Common Stock.

Journal Entry

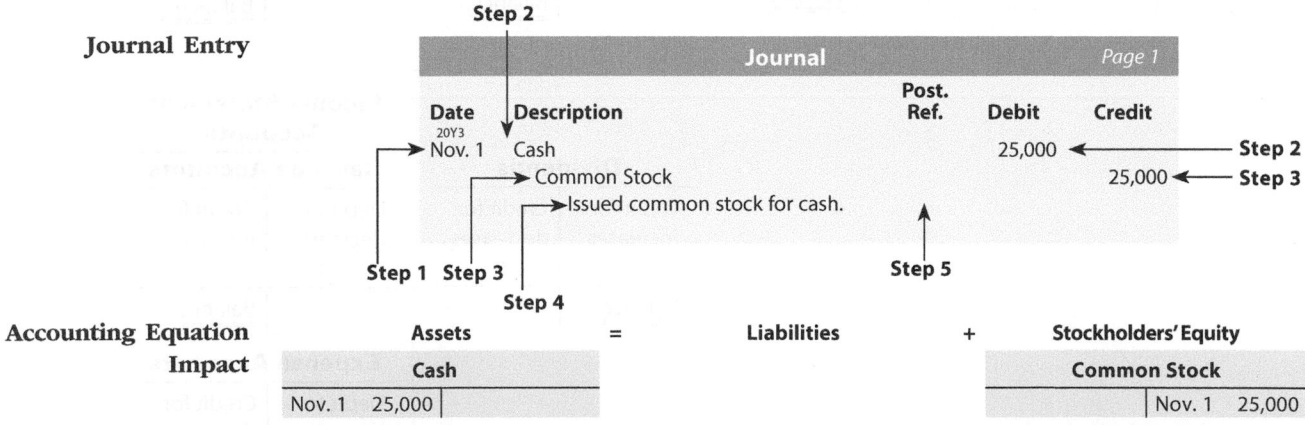

Step 2

Journal   *Page 1*

Date	Description	Post. Ref.	Debit	Credit
20Y3				
Nov. 1	Cash		25,000	◄── Step 2
	Common Stock			25,000 ◄── Step 3
	Issued common stock for cash.			

Step 1   Step 3

Step 4

Step 5

Accounting Equation Impact

	Assets	=	Liabilities	+	Stockholders' Equity	
	Cash				**Common Stock**	
Nov. 1	25,000					Nov. 1 25,000

The transaction is recorded in the journal using the following steps:

- Step 1. The date of the transaction is entered in the Date column.
- Step 2. The title of the account to be debited is recorded in the left-hand margin under the Description column, and the amount to be debited is entered in the Debit column.
- Step 3. The title of the account to be credited is listed below and to the right of the debited account title, and the amount to be credited is entered in the Credit column.
- Step 4. A brief description may be entered below the credited account.
- Step 5. The Post. Ref. (Posting Reference) column is left blank when the journal entry is initially recorded. This column is used later in this chapter when the journal entry amounts are transferred to the accounts in the ledger.

The process of recording a transaction in the journal is called **journalizing**. The entry in the journal is called a **journal entry**. The form of the journal illustrated is called the **two-column journal**. Other forms of journals are described and illustrated in online Appendix F, *Special Journals*.

A useful method for analyzing and journalizing transactions is as follows:

(a) Carefully read the description of the transaction to determine whether an asset, a liability, a stockholders' equity, a revenue, an expense, or a dividends account is affected.

(b) For each account affected by the transaction, determine whether the account increases or decreases.

(c) Determine whether each increase or decrease should be recorded as a debit or a credit, following the rules of debit and credit shown in Exhibit 3.

(d) Record the transaction using a journal entry.

Exhibit 4 summarizes terminology that is often used in describing a transaction along with the related accounts that would be debited and credited.

| | Journal Entry Account | |
Common Transaction Terminology	Debit	Credit
Received cash for services provided	Cash	Fees Earned
Services provided on account	Accounts Receivable	Fees Earned
Received cash on account	Cash	Accounts Receivable
Purchased on account	Asset account	Accounts Payable
Paid on account	Accounts Payable	Cash
Paid cash	Asset or expense account	Cash
Issued common stock	Cash and/or other assets	Common Stock
Paid dividends	Dividends	Cash

Exhibit 4
Transaction Terminology and Related Journal Entry Accounts

The remaining transactions of **NetSolutions** for November are analyzed and journalized.

Nov. 5 *NetSolutions paid $20,000 for the purchase of land as a future building site.*	**Transaction b**

This transaction increases one asset account and decreases another. It is recorded in the journal as a $20,000 increase (debit) to Land and a $20,000 decrease (credit) to Cash.

Analysis

Nov. 5	Land		20,000	
	Cash			20,000
	Purchased land for building site.			

Journal Entry

Assets	=	Liabilities	+	Stockholders' Equity

Accounting Equation Impact

Land
| Nov. 5 20,000 | |

Cash
| | Nov. 5 20,000 |

Transaction c	Nov. 10 NetSolutions purchased supplies on account for $1,350.

Analysis This transaction increases an asset account and increases a liability account. It is recorded in the journal as a $1,350 increase (debit) to Supplies and a $1,350 increase (credit) to Accounts Payable.

Journal Entry

Nov. 10	Supplies	1,350	
	Accounts Payable		1,350
	Purchased supplies on account.		

Accounting Equation Impact

Assets	=	Liabilities	+	Stockholders' Equity
Supplies		**Accounts Payable**		
Nov. 10 1,350		Nov. 10 1,350		

Transaction d	Nov. 18 NetSolutions received cash of $7,500 from customers for services provided.

Analysis This transaction increases an asset account and increases a revenue account. It is recorded in the journal as a $7,500 increase (debit) to Cash and a $7,500 increase (credit) to Fees Earned.

Journal Entry

Nov. 18	Cash	7,500	
	Fees Earned		7,500
	Received fees from customers.		

Accounting Equation Impact

Assets	=	Liabilities	+	Stockholders' Equity (Revenue)
Cash				**Fees Earned**
Nov. 18 7,500				Nov. 18 7,500

Transaction e	Nov. 30 NetSolutions incurred the following expenses: wages, $2,125; rent, $800; utilities, $450; and miscellaneous, $275.

Analysis This transaction increases various expense accounts and decreases an asset (Cash) account. You should note that regardless of the number of accounts, *the sum of the debits is always equal to the sum of the credits in a journal entry.* It is recorded in the journal with increases (debits) to the expense accounts (Wages Expense, $2,125; Rent Expense, $800; Utilities Expense, $450; and Miscellaneous Expense, $275) and a decrease (credit) to Cash, $3,650.

Journal Entry

Nov. 30	Wages Expense	2,125	
	Rent Expense	800	
	Utilities Expense	450	
	Miscellaneous Expense	275	
	Cash		3,650
	Paid expenses.		

Accounting Equation Impact

Assets	=	Liabilities	+	Stockholders' Equity (Expense)
Cash				**Wages Expense**
	Nov. 30 3,650			Nov. 30 2,125
				Rent Expense
				Nov. 30 800
				Utilities Expense
				Nov. 30 450
				Miscellaneous Expense
				Nov. 30 275

| Nov. 30 NetSolutions paid creditors on account, $950. | Transaction f |

This transaction decreases a liability account and decreases an asset account. It is recorded in the journal as a $950 decrease (debit) to Accounts Payable and a $950 decrease (credit) to Cash. | **Analysis**

Journal Entry

Nov. 30	Accounts Payable	950	
	Cash		950
	Paid creditors on account.		

| **Assets** | **=** | **Liabilities** | **+** | **Stockholders' Equity** | **Accounting Equation Impact** |

Cash		**Accounts Payable**
	Nov. 30 950	Nov. 30 950

| Nov. 30 NetSolutions determined that the cost of supplies on hand at November 30 was $550. | Transaction g |

NetSolutions purchased $1,350 of supplies on November 10. Thus, $800 ($1,350 – $550) of supplies must have been used during November. This transaction is recorded in the journal as an $800 increase (debit) to Supplies Expense and an $800 decrease (credit) to Supplies. | **Analysis**

Journal Entry

Nov. 30	Supplies Expense	800	
	Supplies		800
	Supplies used during November.		

| **Assets** | **=** | **Liabilities** | **+** | **Stockholders' Equity (Expense)** | **Accounting Equation Impact** |

Supplies		**Supplies Expense**
	Nov. 30 800	Nov. 30 800

| Nov. 30 Paid dividends, $2,000. | Transaction h |

This transaction decreases assets and stockholders' equity. This transaction is recorded in the journal as a $2,000 increase (debit) to Dividends and a $2,000 decrease (credit) to Cash. | **Analysis**

Journal Entry

Journal					Page 2
Date	**Description**		**Post. Ref.**	**Debit**	**Credit**
20Y3					
Nov. 30	Dividends			2,000	
	Cash				2,000
	Paid dividends.				

| **Assets** | **=** | **Liabilities** | **+** | **Stockholders' Equity (Dividends)** | **Accounting Equation Impact** |

Cash		**Dividends**
	Nov. 30 2,000	Nov. 30 2,000

 *Ethics: Don't Do It!*

Will Journalizing Prevent Fraud?

While journalizing transactions reduces the possibility of fraud, it by no means eliminates it. For example, embezzlement can be hidden within the double-entry bookkeeping system by creating fictitious suppliers to whom checks are issued.

Check Up Corner 2-2 Journal Entries

Selected transactions from Simmons Urgent Care Inc.'s first month of operations are as follows:

Jan. 1. David Simmons deposited $30,000 in a bank account in the name of Simmons Urgent Care Inc. in exchange for common stock.

2. Purchased medical supplies on account, $6,000.

6. Paid cash to creditors on account, $3,200.

7. Purchased office equipment on account, $62,500.

Prepare journal entries to record these transactions, and illustrate their impact on the accounting equation using T accounts.

Solution:

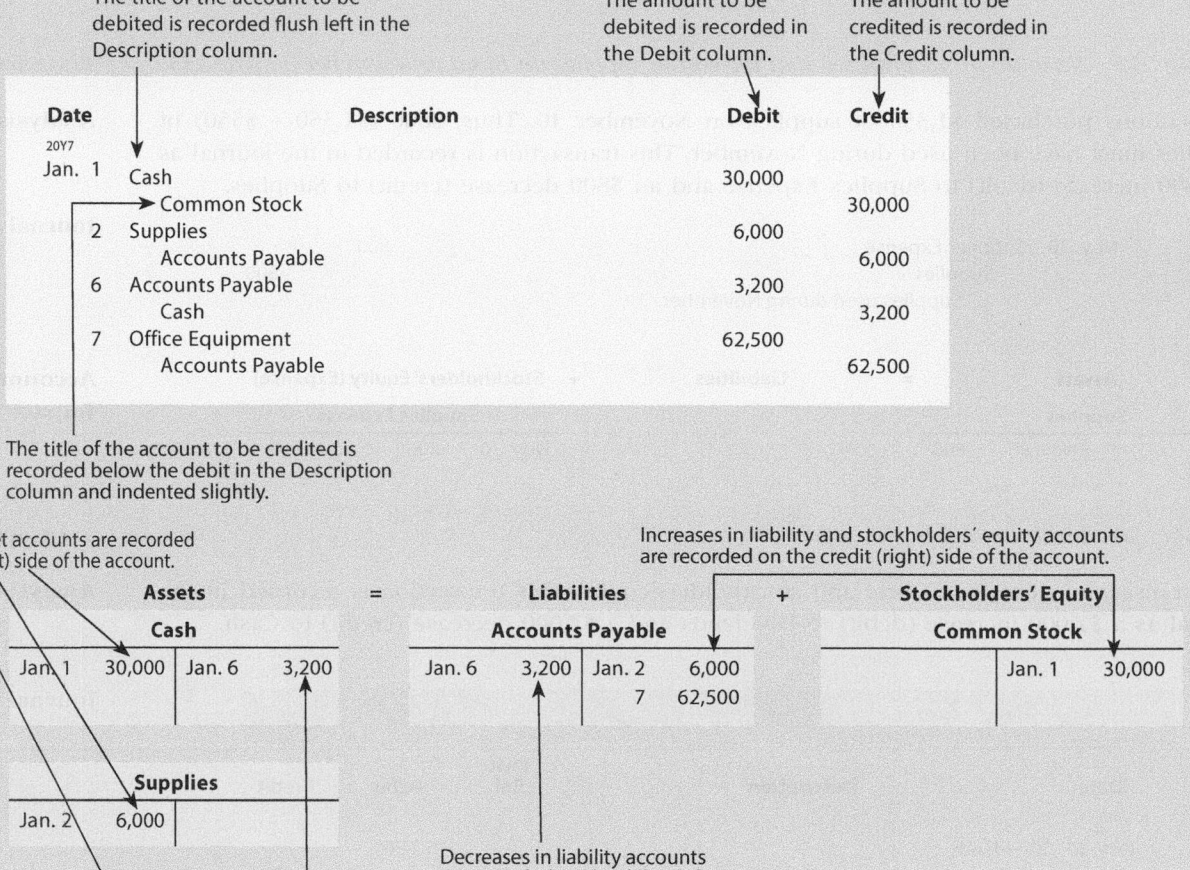

The title of the account to be debited is recorded flush left in the Description column.

The amount to be debited is recorded in the Debit column.

The amount to be credited is recorded in the Credit column.

Date	Description	Debit	Credit
20Y7			
Jan. 1	Cash	30,000	
	Common Stock		30,000
2	Supplies	6,000	
	Accounts Payable		6,000
6	Accounts Payable	3,200	
	Cash		3,200
7	Office Equipment	62,500	
	Accounts Payable		62,500

The title of the account to be credited is recorded below the debit in the Description column and indented slightly.

Increases in asset accounts are recorded on the debit (left) side of the account.

Increases in liability and stockholders' equity accounts are recorded on the credit (right) side of the account.

Assets = **Liabilities** + **Stockholders' Equity**

Cash

| Jan. 1 | 30,000 | Jan. 6 | 3,200 |

Accounts Payable

| Jan. 6 | 3,200 | Jan. 2 | 6,000 |
| | | 7 | 62,500 |

Common Stock

| | | Jan. 1 | 30,000 |

Supplies

| Jan. 2 | 6,000 | |

Decreases in liability accounts are recorded on the debit (left) side of the account.

Office Equipment

| Jan. 7 | 62,500 | |

Decreases in asset accounts are recorded on the credit (right) side of the account.

Check Up Corner

Objective 3

Describe and illustrate the journalizing and posting of transactions to accounts.

Posting Journal Entries to Accounts

As illustrated, a transaction is first recorded in a journal. Periodically, the journal entries are transferred to the accounts in the ledger. The process of transferring the debits and credits from the journal entries to the accounts is called **posting**.

The December 20Y3 transactions of **NetSolutions** are used to illustrate posting from the journal to the ledger. By using the December transactions, an additional review of analyzing and journalizing transactions is provided.

Dec. 1	NetSolutions paid a premium of $2,400 for an insurance policy for liability, theft, and fire. The policy covers a one-year period.	**Transaction**

Advance payments of expenses, such as for insurance premiums, are assets called **prepaid expenses**. For NetSolutions, the asset purchased is insurance protection for 12 months. This transaction is recorded as a $2,400 increase (debit) to Prepaid Insurance and a $2,400 decrease (credit) to Cash.

Analysis

Dec.	1	Prepaid Insurance		15	2,400	
		Cash		11		2,400
		Paid premium on one-year policy.				

Journal Entry

Assets	=	**Liabilities**	+	**Stockholders' Equity**

Accounting Equation Impact

Cash	11
	Dec. 1 2,400

Prepaid Insurance	15
Dec. 1 2,400	

Exhibit 5 shows the posting of the preceding December 1 transaction. In Exhibit 5, the T account has been replaced by a **standard four-column account**. In addition to Debit and Credit columns for recording transactions, the standard account form also has Balance (Debit and Credit) columns. These Balance columns are used to indicate the account balance after each transaction, sometimes called a *running balance*.

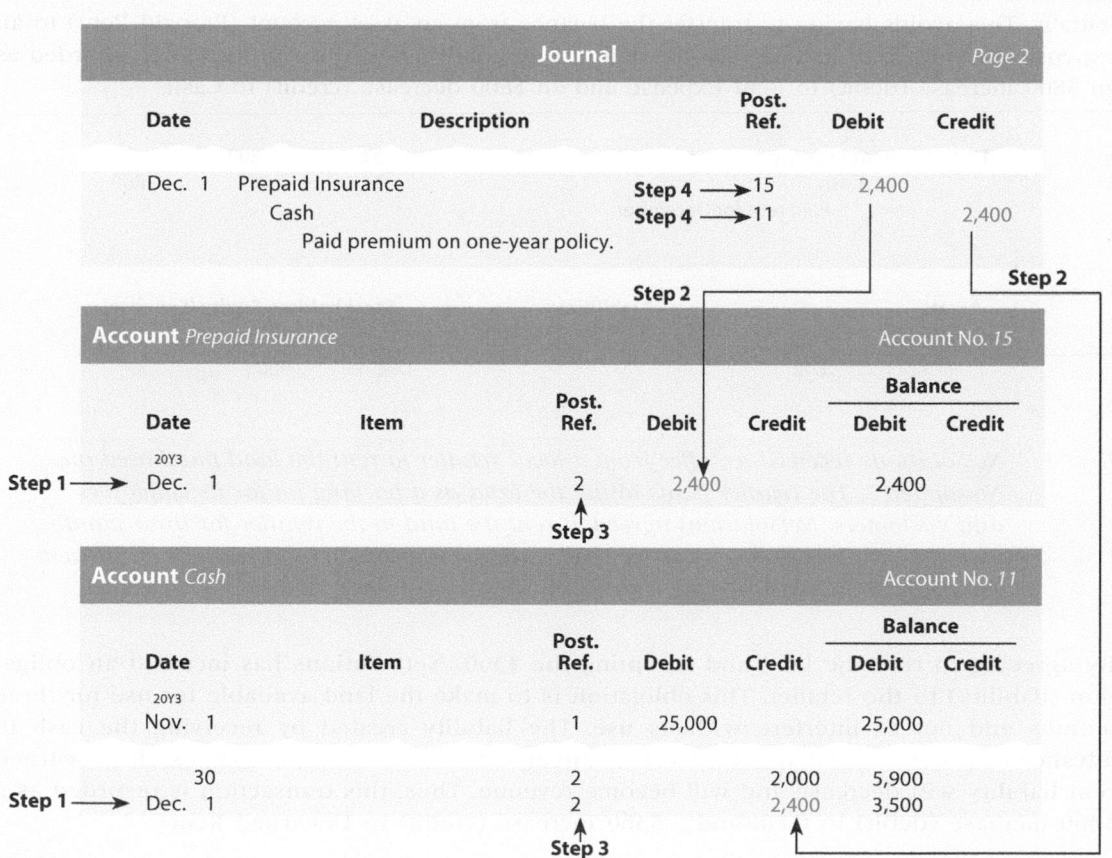

Exhibit 5
Diagram of the Recording and Posting of a Debit and a Credit

The debits and credits for each journal entry are posted to the accounts in the order in which they occur in the journal. To illustrate, the debit portion of the December 1 journal entry is posted to the prepaid account in Exhibit 5 using the following four steps:

- Step 1. The date (Dec. 1) of the journal entry is entered in the Date column of Prepaid Insurance.
- Step 2. The amount (2,400) is entered into the Debit column of Prepaid Insurance.
- Step 3. The journal page number (2) is entered in the Posting Reference (Post. Ref.) column of Prepaid Insurance.
- Step 4. The account number (15) is entered in the Posting Reference (Post. Ref.) column in the journal.

As shown in Exhibit 5, the credit portion of the December 1 journal entry is posted to the cash account in a similar manner.

The remaining December transactions for **NetSolutions** are analyzed and journalized in the following paragraphs. These transactions are posted to the ledger later in this chapter. To simplify, some of the December transactions are stated in summary form. For example, cash received for services is normally recorded on a daily basis. However, only summary totals are recorded at the middle and end of the month for NetSolutions.

Transaction	*Dec. 1*	*NetSolutions paid rent for December, $800. The company from which NetSolutions is renting its office space now requires the payment of rent on the first of each month, rather than at the end of the month.*

Analysis The advance payment of rent is an asset, much like the advance payment of the insurance premium in the preceding transaction. However, unlike the insurance premium, this prepaid rent will expire in one month. When an asset is purchased with the expectation that it will be used up in a short period of time, such as a month, it is normal to debit an expense account initially. This avoids having to transfer the balance from an asset account (Prepaid Rent) to an expense account (Rent Expense) at the end of the month. Thus, this transaction is recorded as an $800 increase (debit) to Rent Expense and an $800 decrease (credit) to Cash.

Journal Entry

Dec. 1	Rent Expense		53	800
	Cash		11		800
	Paid rent for December.			

Accounting Equation Impact

Assets		=	Liabilities	+	Stockholders' Equity (Expense)	
Cash	11				**Rent Expense**	53
Dec. 1	800				Dec. 1	800

Transaction	*Dec. 1*	*NetSolutions received an offer from a local retailer to rent the land purchased on November 5. The retailer plans to use the land as a parking lot for its employees and customers. NetSolutions agreed to rent the land to the retailer for three months, with the rent payable in advance. NetSolutions received $360 for three months' rent beginning December 1.*

Analysis By agreeing to rent the land and accepting the $360, NetSolutions has incurred an obligation (liability) to the retailer. This obligation is to make the land available for use for three months and not to interfere with its use. The liability created by receiving the cash in advance of providing the service is called **unearned revenue**. As time passes, the unearned rent liability will decrease and will become revenue. Thus, this transaction is recorded as a $360 increase (debit) to Cash and a $360 increase (credit) to Unearned Rent.

				Journal Entry
Dec. 1	Cash	11	360	
	Unearned Rent	23		360
	Received advance payment for three months' rent on land.			

Assets	=	Liabilities	+	Stockholders' Equity	**Accounting Equation**
					Impact

Cash	11		Unearned Rent	23
Dec. 1	360		Dec. 1	360

In a recent balance sheet, **Apple** reported over $11 billion in unearned revenue, sometimes called *deferred revenue*.

Link to Apple

Dec. 4	NetSolutions purchased office equipment on account from Executive Supply Co. for $1,800.	**Transaction**

The asset (Office Equipment) and liability accounts (Accounts Payable) increase. This transaction is recorded as an $1,800 increase (debit) to Office Equipment and an $1,800 increase (credit) to Accounts Payable.

Analysis

Journal Entry

Dec. 4	Office Equipment	18	1,800	
	Accounts Payable	21		1,800
	Purchased office equipment on account.			

Assets	=	Liabilities	+	Stockholders' Equity	**Accounting Equation**
					Impact

Office Equipment	18		Accounts Payable	21
Dec. 4	1,800		Dec. 4	1,800

In a recent balance sheet, **Apple** reported equipment, buildings, and land of over $27 billion.

Link to Apple

Dec. 6	NetSolutions paid $180 for a newspaper advertisement.	**Transaction**

An expense increases, and an asset (Cash) decreases. Expense items that are expected to be minor in amount are normally included as part of the miscellaneous expense. This transaction is recorded as a $180 increase (debit) to Miscellaneous Expense and a $180 decrease (credit) to Cash.

Analysis

Journal Entry

Dec. 6	Miscellaneous Expense	59	180	
	Cash	11		180
	Paid for newspaper advertisement.			

Assets	=	Liabilities	+	Stockholders' Equity (Expense)	**Accounting Equation**
					Impact

Cash	11		Miscellaneous Exp.	59
	Dec. 6	180	Dec. 6	180

Why It Matters

Computerized Accounting Systems

Computerized accounting systems like QuickBooks and PeachTree are widely used by even the smallest companies. These systems simplify the journalizing process and eliminate the need for manual posting. For example, in a computerized accounting system, when a customer payment is processed, the date, customer name, and payment amount are entered in the "Receive Payment" window. The entered data are automatically journalized and posted to the ledger accounts.

Transaction	*Dec. 11 NetSolutions paid creditors $400.*

Analysis   A liability (Accounts Payable) and an asset (Cash) decrease. This transaction is recorded as a $400 decrease (debit) to Accounts Payable and a $400 decrease (credit) to Cash.

Journal Entry

Dec. 11	Accounts Payable	21	400	
	Cash	11		400
	Paid creditors on account.			

Accounting Equation Impact

Assets	=	Liabilities	+	Stockholders' Equity

Cash	11
Dec. 11	400

Accounts Payable	21
Dec. 11	400

Transaction	*Dec. 13 NetSolutions paid a receptionist and a part-time assistant $950 for two weeks' wages.*

Analysis   This transaction is similar to the December 6 transaction, where an expense account is increased and Cash is decreased. This transaction is recorded as a $950 increase (debit) to Wages Expense and a $950 decrease (credit) to Cash.

Journal Entry

Journal					*Page 3*
Date	**Description**		**Post. Ref.**	**Debit**	**Credit**
20Y3					
Dec. 13	Wages Expense		51	950	
	Cash		11		950
	Paid two weeks' wages.				

Accounting Equation Impact

Assets	=	Liabilities	+	Stockholders' Equity (Expense)

Cash	11
Dec. 13	950

Wages Expense	51
Dec. 13	950

Transaction	*Dec. 16 NetSolutions received $3,100 from fees earned for the first half of December.*

Analysis   An asset account (Cash) and a revenue account (Fees Earned) increase. This transaction is recorded as a $3,100 increase (debit) to Cash and a $3,100 increase (credit) to Fees Earned.

Journal Entry

Dec. 16	Cash	11	3,100	
	Fees Earned	41		3,100
	Received fees from customers.			

Accounting Equation Impact

Assets	=	Liabilities	+	Stockholders' Equity (Revenue)

Cash	11
Dec. 16	3,100

Fees Earned	41
Dec. 16	3,100

Transaction	*Dec. 16 Fees earned on account totaled $1,750 for the first half of December.*

Analysis   When a business agrees that a customer may pay for services provided at a later date, an **account receivable** is created. An account receivable is a claim against the customer. An account receivable is an asset, and the revenue is earned even though no cash has been received. Thus, this transaction is recorded as a $1,750 increase (debit) to Accounts Receivable and a $1,750 increase (credit) to Fees Earned.

Journal Entry

Dec. 16	Accounts Receivable	12	1,750	
	Fees Earned	41		1,750
	Fees earned on account.			

Accounting Equation Impact

Assets	=	Liabilities	+	Stockholders' Equity (Revenue)
Accounts Receivable 12				**Fees Earned** 41
Dec. 16 1,750				Dec. 16 1,750

Dec. 20 *NetSolutions paid $900 to Executive Supply Co. on the $1,800 debt owed from the December 4 transaction.*

Transaction

This is similar to the transaction of December 11. This transaction is recorded as a $900 decrease (debit) to Accounts Payable and a $900 decrease (credit) to Cash.

Analysis

Journal Entry

Dec. 20	Accounts Payable	21	900	
	Cash	11		900
	Paid creditors on account.			

Accounting Equation Impact

Assets	=	Liabilities	+	Stockholders' Equity
Cash 11		**Accounts Payable** 21		
Dec. 20 900		Dec. 20 900		

On a recent balance sheet, **Apple** reported $37.3 billion in accounts payable.

Link to Apple

Dec. 21 *NetSolutions received $650 from customers in payment of their accounts.*

Transaction

When customers pay amounts owed for services they have previously received, one asset increases and another asset decreases. This transaction is recorded as a $650 increase (debit) to Cash and a $650 decrease (credit) to Accounts Receivable.

Analysis

Journal Entry

Dec. 21	Cash	11	650	
	Accounts Receivable	12		650
	Received cash from customers on account.			

Accounting Equation Impact

Assets	=	Liabilities	+	Stockholders' Equity
Cash 11				
Dec. 21 650				

Accounts Receivable 12
Dec. 21 650

Dec. 23 *NetSolutions paid $1,450 for supplies.*

Transaction

One asset account (Supplies) increases, and another asset account (Cash) decreases. This transaction is recorded as a $1,450 increase (debit) to Supplies and a $1,450 decrease (credit) to Cash.

Analysis

Journal Entry

Dec. 23	Supplies	14	1,450	
	Cash	11		1,450
	Purchased supplies.			

Accounting Equation Impact

Assets	=	Liabilities	+	Stockholders' Equity
Cash 11				
Dec. 23 1,450				

Supplies 14
Dec. 23 1,450

Transaction	*Dec. 27* *NetSolutions paid the receptionist and the part-time assistant $1,200 for two weeks' wages.*

Analysis This transaction is similar to the transaction of December 13. This transaction is recorded as a $1,200 increase (debit) to Wages Expense and a $1,200 decrease (credit) to Cash.

Journal Entry

Dec.	27	Wages Expense	51	1,200	
		Cash	11		1,200
		Paid two weeks' wages.			

Accounting Equation Impact

Assets		=	Liabilities	+	Stockholders' Equity (Expense)	
Cash	11				**Wages Expense**	51
Dec. 27	1,200				Dec. 27	1,200

Transaction	*Dec. 31* *NetSolutions paid its $310 telephone bill for the month.*

Analysis This is similar to the transaction of December 6. This transaction is recorded as a $310 increase (debit) to Utilities Expense and a $310 decrease (credit) to Cash.

Journal Entry

Dec.	31	Utilities Expense	54	310	
		Cash	11		310
		Paid telephone bill.			

Accounting Equation Impact

Assets		=	Liabilities	+	Stockholders' Equity (Expense)	
Cash	11				**Utilities Expense**	54
Dec. 31	310				Dec. 31	310

Transaction	*Dec. 31* *NetSolutions paid its $225 electric bill for the month.*

Analysis This is similar to the preceding transaction. This transaction is recorded as a $225 increase (debit) to Utilities Expense and a $225 decrease (credit) to Cash.

Journal Entry

Journal					Page 4
Date	**Description**		**Post. Ref.**	**Debit**	**Credit**
20Y3					
Dec. 31	Utilities Expense		54	225	
	Cash		11		225
	Paid electric bill.				

Accounting Equation Impact

Assets		=	Liabilities	+	Stockholders' Equity (Expense)	
Cash	11				**Utilities Expense**	54
Dec. 31	225				Dec. 31	225

Transaction	*Dec. 31* *NetSolutions received $2,870 from fees earned for the second half of December.*

Analysis This is similar to the transaction of December 16. This transaction is recorded as a $2,870 increase (debit) to Cash and a $2,870 increase (credit) to Fees Earned.

Journal Entry

Dec.	31	Cash	11	2,870	
		Fees Earned	41		2,870
		Received fees from customers.			

Accounting Equation Impact

Assets		=	Liabilities	+	Stockholders' Equity (Revenue)	
Cash	11				**Fees Earned**	41
Dec. 31	2,870				Dec. 31	2,870

| Dec. 31 Fees earned on account totaled $1,120 for the second half of December. | Transaction |

This is similar to the transaction of December 16. This transaction is recorded as a $1,120 increase (debit) to Accounts Receivable and a $1,120 increase (credit) to Fees Earned. — **Analysis**

Journal Entry

Dec.	31	Accounts Receivable	12	1,120	
		Fees Earned	41		1,120
		Fees earned on account.			

Accounting Equation Impact

Assets	=	Liabilities	+	Stockholders' Equity (Revenue)
Accounts Receivable 12				**Fees Earned** 41
Dec. 31 1,120				Dec. 31 1,120

On a recent balance sheet, **Apple** reported $15.8 billion in accounts receivable. — *Link to Apple*

| Dec. 31 Paid dividends, $2,000. | Transaction |

This transaction decreases stockholders' equity and assets. This transaction is recorded as a $2,000 increase (debit) to Dividends and a $2,000 decrease (credit) to Cash. — **Analysis**

Journal Entry

Dec.	31	Dividends	33	2,000	
		Cash	11		2,000
		Paid dividends.			

Accounting Equation Impact

Assets	=	Liabilities	+	Stockholders' Equity (Dividends)
Cash 11				**Dividends** 33
Dec. 31 2,000				Dec. 31 2,000

In a recent year, **Apple** paid $12 billion in dividends. — *Link to Apple*

Exhibit 6 shows the ledger for **NetSolutions** after the transactions for both November and December have been posted.

Pathways Challenge

This is Accounting!

Economic Activity

Coupons (paper or digital) encourage customers to buy products or shop at stores and online websites. A recent study revealed that over 2.2 billion coupons are redeemed per year. Almost one-third of the shoppers using coupons buy more of a product and purchase it sooner.* Assume that you purchase $100 of groceries from Kroger, give the cashier a $10 **Kroger (KR)** discount coupon, and charge your debit card for $90.

* *Source:* 2016 Inmar Promotion Industry Analysis

Critical Thinking/Judgment

Should Kroger record the sale as $100 or $90?
Instead of a Kroger coupon, assume the coupon was issued by **General Mills (GIS)**.
Should Kroger record the sale as $100 or $90?

Suggested answer at end of chapter.

Exhibit 6 General Ledger for NetSolutions

Ledger

Account *Cash*   Account No. *11*

Date	Item	Post. Ref.	Debit	Credit	Balance Debit	Balance Credit
20Y3						
Nov. 1		1	25,000		25,000	
5		1		20,000	5,000	
18		1	7,500		12,500	
30		1		3,650	8,850	
30		1		950	7,900	
30		2		2,000	5,900	
Dec. 1		2		2,400	3,500	
1		2		800	2,700	
1		2	360		3,060	
6		2		180	2,880	
11		2		400	2,480	
13		3		950	1,530	
16		3	3,100		4,630	
20		3		900	3,730	
21		3	650		4,380	
23		3		1,450	2,930	
27		3		1,200	1,730	
31		3		310	1,420	
31		4		225	1,195	
31		4	2,870		4,065	
31		4		2,000	2,065	

Account *Accounts Receivable*   Account No. *12*

Date	Item	Post. Ref.	Debit	Credit	Balance Debit	Balance Credit
20Y3						
Dec. 16		3	1,750		1,750	
21		3		650	1,100	
31		4	1,120		2,220	

Account *Supplies*   Account No. *14*

Date	Item	Post. Ref.	Debit	Credit	Balance Debit	Balance Credit
20Y3						
Nov. 10		1	1,350		1,350	
30		1		800	550	
Dec. 23		3	1,450		2,000	

Account *Prepaid Insurance*   Account No. *15*

Date	Item	Post. Ref.	Debit	Credit	Balance Debit	Balance Credit
20Y3						
Dec. 1		2	2,400		2,400	

Account *Land*   Account No. *17*

Date	Item	Post. Ref.	Debit	Credit	Balance Debit	Balance Credit
20Y3						
Nov. 5		1	20,000		20,000	

Account *Office Equipment*   Account No. *18*

Date	Item	Post. Ref.	Debit	Credit	Balance Debit	Balance Credit
20Y3						
Dec. 4		2	1,800		1,800	

Account *Accounts Payable*   Account No. *21*

Date	Item	Post. Ref.	Debit	Credit	Balance Debit	Balance Credit
20Y3						
Nov. 10		1		1,350		1,350
30		1	950			400
Dec. 4		2		1,800		2,200
11		2	400			1,800
20		3	900			900

Account *Unearned Rent*   Account No. *23*

Date	Item	Post. Ref.	Debit	Credit	Balance Debit	Balance Credit
20Y3						
Dec. 1		2		360		360

Account *Common Stock*   Account No. *31*

Date	Item	Post. Ref.	Debit	Credit	Balance Debit	Balance Credit
20Y3						
Nov. 1		1		25,000		25,000

Account *Dividends*   Account No. *33*

Date	Item	Post. Ref.	Debit	Credit	Balance Debit	Balance Credit
20Y3						
Nov. 30		2	2,000		2,000	
Dec. 31		4	2,000		4,000	

Exhibit 6 General Ledger for NetSolutions *(Concluded)*

Account *Fees Earned* — Account No. 41

Date	Item	Post. Ref.	Debit	Credit	Balance Debit	Balance Credit
20Y3						
Nov. 18		1		7,500		7,500
Dec. 16		3		3,100		10,600
16		3		1,750		12,350
31		4		2,870		15,220
31		4		1,120		16,340

Account *Wages Expense* — Account No. 51

Date	Item	Post. Ref.	Debit	Credit	Balance Debit	Balance Credit
20Y3						
Nov. 30		1	2,125		2,125	
Dec. 13		3	950		3,075	
27		3	1,200		4,275	

Account *Supplies Expense* — Account No. 52

Date	Item	Post. Ref.	Debit	Credit	Balance Debit	Balance Credit
20Y3						
Nov. 30		1	800		800	

Account *Rent Expense* — Account No. 53

Date	Item	Post. Ref.	Debit	Credit	Balance Debit	Balance Credit
20Y3						
Nov. 30		1	800		800	
Dec. 1		2	800		1,600	

Account *Utilities Expense* — Account No. 54

Date	Item	Post. Ref.	Debit	Credit	Balance Debit	Balance Credit
20Y3						
Nov. 30		1	450		450	
Dec. 31		3	310		760	
31		4	225		985	

Account *Miscellaneous Expense* — Account No. 59

Date	Item	Post. Ref.	Debit	Credit	Balance Debit	Balance Credit
20Y3						
Nov. 30		1	275		275	
Dec. 6		2	180		455	

Trial Balance

Errors may occur in posting debits and credits from the journal to the ledger. One way to detect such errors is by preparing a **trial balance**. Double-entry accounting requires that debits must always equal credits. The trial balance verifies this equality. The steps in preparing a trial balance are as follows:

- Step 1. List the name of the company, the title of the trial balance, and the date the trial balance is prepared.
- Step 2. List the accounts from the ledger, and enter their debit or credit balance in the Debit or Credit column of the trial balance.
- Step 3. Total the Debit and Credit columns of the trial balance.
- Step 4. Verify that the total of the Debit column equals the total of the Credit column.

The trial balance for **NetSolutions** as of December 31, 20Y3, is shown in Exhibit 7. The account balances in Exhibit 7 are taken from the ledger shown in Exhibit 6. Before a trial balance is prepared, each account balance in the ledger must be determined. When the standard four-column account form is used as in Exhibit 6, the balance of each account appears in the Balance column on the same line as the last posting to the account.

The trial balance shown in Exhibit 7 is titled an **unadjusted trial balance**. This is to distinguish it from other trial balances that will be prepared in later chapters. These other trial balances include an adjusted trial balance and a post-closing trial balance.[3]

Objective 4
Prepare an unadjusted trial balance and explain how it can be used to discover errors.

[3] The adjusted trial balance will be discussed in Chapter 3 and the post-closing trial balance in Chapter 4.

Exhibit 7
Trial Balance

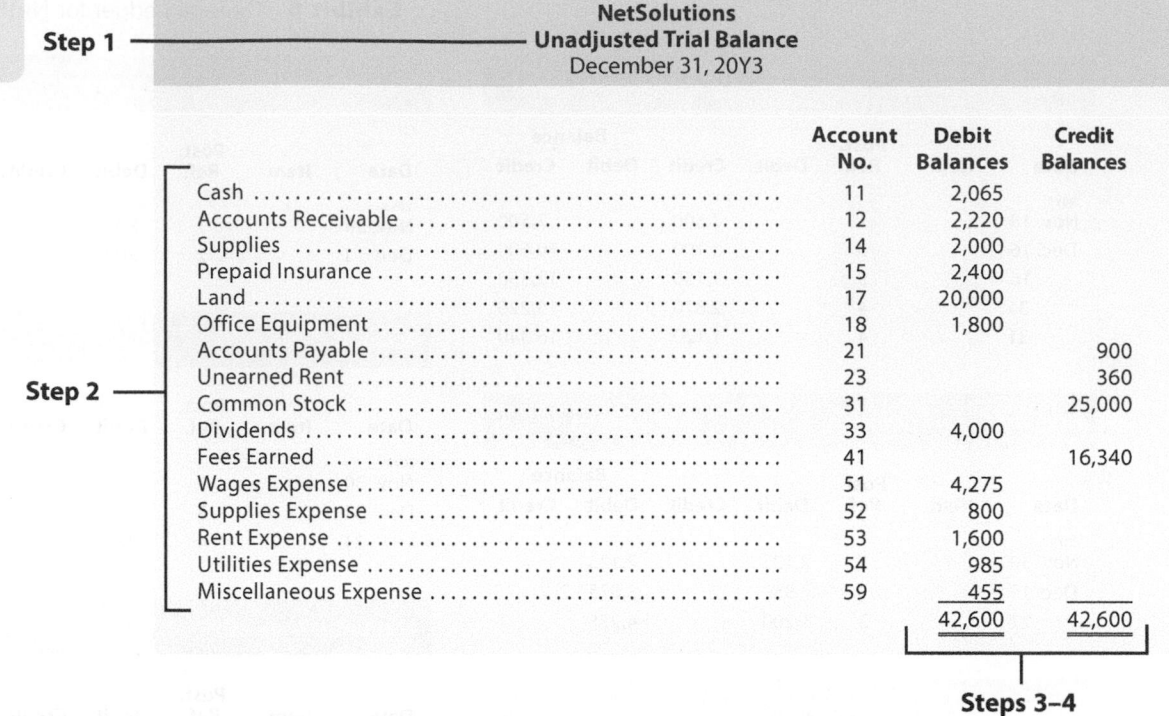

	Account No.	Debit Balances	Credit Balances
Cash	11	2,065	
Accounts Receivable	12	2,220	
Supplies	14	2,000	
Prepaid Insurance	15	2,400	
Land	17	20,000	
Office Equipment	18	1,800	
Accounts Payable	21		900
Unearned Rent	23		360
Common Stock	31		25,000
Dividends	33	4,000	
Fees Earned	41		16,340
Wages Expense	51	4,275	
Supplies Expense	52	800	
Rent Expense	53	1,600	
Utilities Expense	54	985	
Miscellaneous Expense	59	455	
		42,600	42,600

NetSolutions
Unadjusted Trial Balance
December 31, 20Y3

Step 1

Step 2

Steps 3–4

Errors Affecting the Trial Balance

If the trial balance totals are not equal, an error has occurred. In this case, the error must be found and corrected. A method useful in discovering errors is as follows:

1. If the difference between the Debit and Credit column totals is 10, 100, or 1,000, an error in addition may have occurred. In this case, re-add the trial balance column totals. If the error still exists, recompute the account balances.

2. If the difference between the Debit and Credit column totals can be evenly divisible by 2, the error may be due to the entering of a debit balance as a credit balance, or vice versa. In this case, review the trial balance for account balances of one-half the difference that may have been entered in the wrong column. For example, if the Debit column total is $20,640 and the Credit column total is $20,236, the difference of $404 ($20,640 − $20,236) may be due to a credit account balance of $202 that was entered as a debit account balance.

3. If the difference between the Debit and Credit column totals is evenly divisible by 9, trace the account balances back to the ledger to see if an account balance was incorrectly copied from the ledger. Two common types of copying errors are transpositions and slides. A **transposition** occurs when the order of the digits is copied incorrectly, such as writing $542 as $452 or $524. In a **slide**, the entire number is copied incorrectly one or more spaces to the right or the left, such as writing $542.00 as $54.20 or $5,420.00. In both cases, the resulting error will be evenly divisible by 9.

4. If the difference between the Debit and Credit column totals is not evenly divisible by 2 or 9, review the ledger to see if an account balance in the amount of the error has been omitted from the trial balance. If the error is not discovered, review the journal postings to see if a posting of a debit or credit may have been omitted.

5. If an error is not discovered by the preceding steps, the accounting process must be retraced, beginning with the last journal entry.

The trial balance does not provide complete proof of the accuracy of the ledger. It indicates only that the debits and the credits are equal. This proof is of value, however, because errors often affect the equality of debits and credits.

Errors Not Affecting the Trial Balance

An error may occur that does not cause the trial balance totals to be unequal. Such an error may be discovered when preparing the trial balance or may be indicated by an unusual account balance. For example, a credit balance in the supplies account indicates an error has occurred. This is because a business cannot have "negative" supplies. When such errors are discovered, they should be corrected. If the error has already been journalized and posted to the ledger, a **correcting journal entry** is normally prepared.

To illustrate, assume that on May 5 a $12,500 purchase of office equipment for cash was incorrectly journalized and posted as a debit to Supplies and a credit to Cash for $12,500, as follows:

May 5	Supplies	14	12,500	
	Cash	11		12,500

The error was discovered on May 31. Before making a correcting journal entry, the journal entry that was made in error is compared to the entry that should have been made. By comparing these two journal entries, the correcting journal entry can be determined, as shown in Exhibit 8.

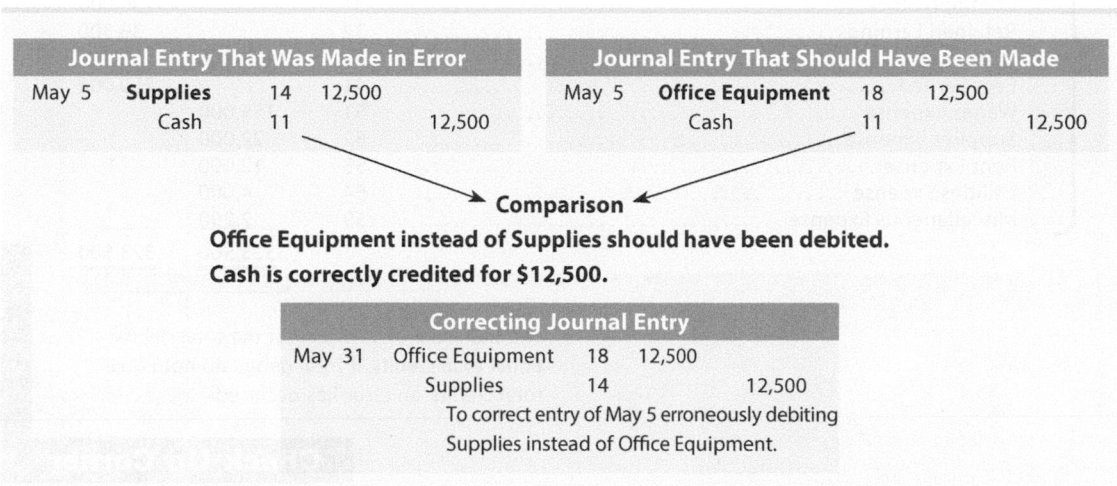

Exhibit 8
Correcting Journal Entry

Exhibit 8 indicates that the correcting journal entry debits Office Equipment and credits Supplies for $12,500. Because correcting journal entries are unusual, an explanation is often inserted below the correcting journal entry. After the correcting journal entry is posted, the office equipment and supplies accounts will have correct balances.

Check Up Corner 2-3 Trial Balance

The accounts of Simmons Urgent Care Inc. as of December 31, 20Y7, are listed in alphabetical order as follows. All accounts have normal balances.

21	Accounts Payable	$ 7,200		18	Office Equipment	$ 62,500
12	Accounts Receivable	22,000		53	Rent Expense	12,000
11	Cash	21,000		32	Retained Earnings	36,300
31	Common Stock	30,000		14	Supplies	7,800
33	Dividends	15,000		52	Supplies Expense	22,000
41	Fees Earned	250,000		54	Utilities Expense	4,000
59	Miscellaneous Expense	2,200		51	Wages Expense	155,000

Prepare an unadjusted trial balance, listing the accounts in their normal order.

(Continued)

Solution:

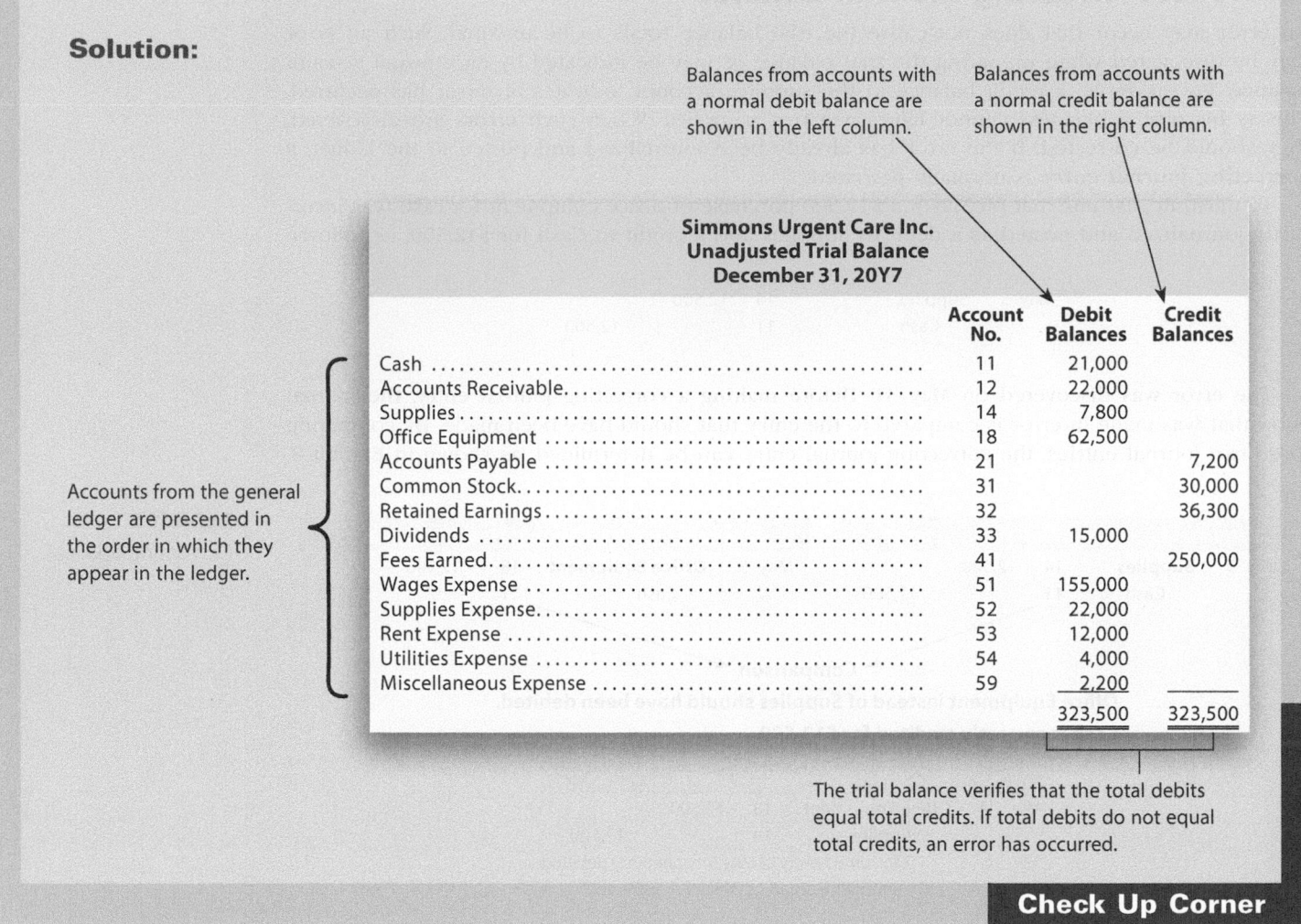

Balances from accounts with a normal debit balance are shown in the left column.

Balances from accounts with a normal credit balance are shown in the right column.

Accounts from the general ledger are presented in the order in which they appear in the ledger.

Simmons Urgent Care Inc.
Unadjusted Trial Balance
December 31, 20Y7

	Account No.	Debit Balances	Credit Balances
Cash	11	21,000	
Accounts Receivable	12	22,000	
Supplies	14	7,800	
Office Equipment	18	62,500	
Accounts Payable	21		7,200
Common Stock	31		30,000
Retained Earnings	32		36,300
Dividends	33	15,000	
Fees Earned	41		250,000
Wages Expense	51	155,000	
Supplies Expense	52	22,000	
Rent Expense	53	12,000	
Utilities Expense	54	4,000	
Miscellaneous Expense	59	2,200	
		323,500	323,500

The trial balance verifies that the total debits equal total credits. If total debits do not equal total credits, an error has occurred.

Check Up Corner

Analysis for Decision Making

Objective 5

Describe and illustrate the use of horizontal analysis in evaluating a company's performance and financial condition.

Horizontal Analysis

A single item in a financial statement, such as net income, is often useful in interpreting the financial performance of a company. However, a comparison with prior periods often makes the financial information even more useful. For example, comparing net income of the current period with the net income of the prior period will indicate whether the company's operating performance has improved.

In **horizontal analysis**, the amount of each item on a current financial statement is compared with the same item on an earlier statement. The increase or decrease in the *amount* of the item is computed together with the *percent* of increase or decrease. When two statements are being compared, the earlier statement is used as the base for computing the amount and the percent of change.

To illustrate, the horizontal analysis of two income statements for J. Holmes, Attorney-at-Law follows:

			Increase/(Decrease)	
	20Y7	**20Y6**	**Amount**	**Percent**
Fees earned	$187,500	$150,000	$37,500	25.0%*
Expenses:				
Wages expense	$ (60,000)	$ (45,000)	$15,000	33.3%
Rent expense	(15,000)	(12,000)	3,000	25.0%
Utilities expense	(12,500)	(9,000)	3,500	38.9%
Supplies expense	(2,700)	(3,000)	(300)	(10.0)%
Miscellaneous expense	(2,300)	(1,800)	500	27.8%
Total expenses	$ (92,500)	$ (70,800)	$21,700	30.6%
Net income	$ 95,000	$ 79,200	$15,800	19.9%

J. Holmes, Attorney-at-Law — Income Statements — For the Years Ended December 31

*$37,500 ÷ $150,000

The horizontal analysis for J. Holmes, Attorney-at-Law, indicates both favorable and unfavorable changes. The increase in fees earned of 25.0% is favorable as is the decrease in supplies expense. Unfavorable changes include the increase in wages expense, rent expense, utilities expense, and miscellaneous expense. These expenses increased the same as or faster than the increase in revenues, with total operating expenses increasing by 30.6%. Overall, net income increased by $15,800, or 19.9%, a favorable change.

The significance of the various increases and decreases in the revenue and expense items should be investigated to see if operations could be further improved. For example, the increase in utilities expense of 38.9% was the result of renting additional office space for use by a part-time law student in performing paralegal services. This explains the increase in rent expense of 25.0% and the increase in wages expense of 33.3%. The increase in revenues of 25.0% reflects the fees generated by the new paralegal.

The preceding example illustrates how horizontal analysis can be useful in interpreting and analyzing the income statement. Horizontal analyses can also be performed for the balance sheet, the statement of stockholders' equity, and the statement of cash flows.

Make a Decision   Horizontal Analysis

Analyze Amazon.com (MAD 2-1)
(Continuing company analysis)

Analyze Chipotle Mexican Grill (MAD 2-2)

Analyze Vera Bradley, Inc. (MAD 2-3)

Analyze Target (MAD 2-4)

Analyze Wal-Mart (MAD 2-5)

Compare Target and Wal-Mart (MAD 2-6)

Make a Decision

Let's Review

Chapter Summary

1. The simplest form of an account, a T account, has three parts: (1) a title, which is the name of the item recorded in the account; (2) a left side, called the debit side; and (3) a right side, called the credit side. Periodically, the debits in an account are added, the credits in the account are added, and the balance of the account is determined. The system of accounts that make up a ledger is called a chart of accounts.

2. Transactions are initially entered in a record called a journal. The rules of debit and credit for recording increases or decreases in accounts are shown in Exhibit 3. Each transaction is recorded so that the sum of the debits is always equal to the sum of the credits. The normal balance of an account is indicated by the side of the account (debit or credit) that receives the increases.

3. Transactions are journalized and posted to the ledger using the rules of debit and credit. The debits and credits for each journal entry are posted to the accounts in the order in which they occur in the journal.

4. A trial balance is prepared by listing the accounts from the ledger and their balances. The totals of the Debit column and Credit column of the trial balance must be equal. If the two totals are not equal, an error has occurred. Errors may occur even though the trial balance totals are equal. Such errors may require a correcting journal entry.

5. In horizontal analysis, the amount of each item on a current financial statement is compared with the same item on an earlier statement. The increase or decrease in the amount of the item is computed together with the percent of increase or decrease. When two statements are being compared, the earlier statement is used as the base for computing the amount and the percent of change. Horizontal analysis can be performed on any of the four financial statements.

Key Terms

account (59)
account receivable (72)
assets (61)
balance of the account (60)
chart of accounts (60)
common stock (61)
correcting journal entry (79)
credit (60)
debit (60)
dividends (61)
double-entry accounting system (62)

expenses (61)
horizontal analysis (80)
journal (64)
journal entry (65)
journalizing (65)
ledger (60)
liabilities (61)
normal balance of an account (63)
posting (68)
prepaid expenses (69)
retained earnings (61)

revenues (61)
rules of debit and credit (62)
slide (78)
standard four-column account (69)
stockholders' equity (61)
T account (60)
transposition (78)
trial balance (77)
two-column journal (65)
unadjusted trial balance (77)
unearned revenue (70)

Practice

Multiple-Choice Questions

1. A debit may signify a(n):
   a. increase in an asset account.
   b. decrease in an asset account.
   c. increase in a liability account.
   d. increase in the stockholders' equity (common stock) account.

2. The type of account with a normal credit balance is:
   a. an asset.
   b. stockholders' equity (dividend).
   c. a revenue.
   d. an expense.

3. A debit balance in which of the following accounts would indicate a likely error?
   a. Accounts Receivable
   b. Cash
   c. Fees Earned
   d. Miscellaneous Expense

4. The receipt of cash from customers in payment of their accounts would be recorded by:
   a. a debit to Cash and a credit to Accounts Receivable.
   b. a debit to Accounts Receivable and a credit to Cash.
   c. a debit to Cash and a credit to Accounts Payable.
   d. a debit to Accounts Payable and a credit to Cash.

5. The form listing the titles and balances of the accounts in the ledger on a given date is the:
   a. income statement.
   b. balance sheet.
   c. statement of stockholders' equity.
   d. trial balance.

Answers provided after Problem. Need more practice? Find additional multiple-choice questions, exercises, and problems in CengageNOWv2.

Exercises

---

1. Rules of debit and credit and normal balances
Obj. 2

State for each account whether it is likely to have (a) debit entries only, (b) credit entries only, or (c) both debit and credit entries. Also, indicate its normal balance.

1. Accounts Receivable
2. Commissions Earned
3. Notes Payable
4. Common Stock
5. Rent Revenue
6. Wages Expense

---

2. Journal entry for asset purchase
Obj. 2

Prepare a journal entry for the purchase of office equipment on October 27 for $32,750, paying $6,550 cash and the remainder on account.

---

3. Journal entry for fees earned
Obj. 3

Prepare a journal entry on March 16 for fees earned on account, $9,450.

---

4. Journal entry for dividends
Obj. 3

Prepare a journal entry on December 23 for dividends paid of $20,000.

---

5. Missing amount from an account
Obj. 3

On July 1, the cash account balance was $37,450. During July, cash payments totaled $115,860, and the July 31 balance was $29,600. Determine the cash receipts during July.

---

6. Trial balance errors
Obj. 4

For each of the following errors, considered individually, indicate whether the error would cause the trial balance totals to be unequal. If the error would cause the trial balance totals to be unequal, indicate whether the debit or credit total is higher and by how much.

a. The payment of an insurance premium of $5,400 for a three-year policy was debited to Prepaid Insurance for $5,400 and credited to Cash for $4,500.

b. A payment of $270 on account was debited to Accounts Payable for $720 and credited to Cash for $720.

c. A purchase of supplies on account for $1,600 was debited to Supplies for $1,600 and debited to Accounts Payable for $1,600.

---

7. Correcting entries
Obj. 4

The following errors took place in journalizing and posting transactions:

a. Rent expense of $4,650 paid for the current month was recorded as a debit to Miscellaneous Expense and a credit to Rent Expense.

b. The payment of $3,700 from a customer on account was recorded as a debit to Cash and a credit to Accounts Payable.

Journalize the entries to correct the errors. Omit explanations.

8. Horizontal analysis

Two income statements for Fuller Company follow:

Fuller Company
Income Statements
For the Years Ended December 31

	20Y4	20Y3
Fees earned	$ 680,000	$ 850,000
Expenses	(541,875)	(637,500)
Net income	$ 138,125	$ 212,500

Prepare a horizontal analysis of Fuller Company's income statements.

Answers provided after Problem. Need more practice? Find additional multiple-choice questions, exercises, and problems in CengageNOWv2.

Problem

J. F. Outz, M.D., organized Hearts Inc. three years ago to practice cardiology. During April 20Y7, Hearts Inc. completed the following transactions:

Apr. 1. Paid office rent for April, $800.

3. Purchased equipment on account, $2,100.

5. Received cash on account from patients, $3,150.

8. Purchased X-ray film and other supplies on account, $245.

9. One of the items of equipment purchased on April 3 was defective. It was returned with the permission of the supplier, who agreed to reduce the account for the amount charged for the item, $325.

12. Paid cash to creditors on account, $1,250.

17. Paid cash for renewal of a six-month property insurance policy, $370.

20. Discovered that the balances of the cash account and the accounts payable account as of April 1 were overstated by $200. A payment of that amount to a creditor in March had not been recorded. Journalize the $200 payment as of April 20.

24. Paid cash for laboratory analysis, $545.

27. Paid dividends, $1,250.

30. Recorded the cash received in payment of services (on a cash basis) to patients during April, $1,720.

30. Paid salaries of receptionist and nurses, $1,725.

30. Paid various utility expenses, $360.

30. Recorded fees charged to patients on account for services performed in April, $5,145.

30. Paid miscellaneous expenses, $132.

Hearts Inc.'s account titles, numbers, and balances as of April 1 (all normal balances) are listed as follows: Cash, 11, $4,123; Accounts Receivable, 12, $6,725; Supplies, 13, $290; Prepaid Insurance, 14, $465; Equipment, 18, $19,745; Accounts Payable, 22, $765; Common Stock, 31, $10,000; Retained Earnings, 32, $20,583; Dividends, 33, $0; Professional Fees, 41, $0; Salary Expense, 51, $0; Rent Expense, 53, $0; Laboratory Expense, 55, $0; Utilities Expense, 56, $0; Miscellaneous Expense, 59, $0.

Instructions

1. Open a ledger of standard four-column accounts for Hearts Inc. as of April 1. Enter the balances in the appropriate balance columns and place a check mark (✓) in the Posting Reference column. (*Hint:* Verify the equality of the debit and credit balances in the ledger before proceeding with the next instruction.)

2. Journalize each transaction in a two-column journal.

3. Post the journal to the ledger, extending the month-end balances to the appropriate balance columns after each posting.

4. Prepare an unadjusted trial balance as of April 30.

Need more practice? Find additional multiple-choice questions, exercises, and problems in CengageNOWv2.

Answers

Multiple-Choice Questions

1. **a** A debit may signify an increase in an asset account (answer a) or a decrease in a liability or stockholders' equity (common stock) account. A credit may signify a decrease in an asset account (answer b) or an increase in a liability or stockholders' equity (common stock) account (answers c and d).

2. **c** Liability, stockholders' equity (common stock), and revenue (answer c) accounts have normal credit balances. Asset (answer a), stockholders' equity (dividend) (answer b), and expense (answer d) accounts have normal debit balances.

3. **c** Accounts Receivable (answer a), Cash (answer b), and Miscellaneous Expense (answer d) would all normally have debit balances. Fees Earned should normally have a credit balance. Hence, a debit balance in Fees Earned (answer c) would indicate a likely error in the recording process.

4. **a** The receipt of cash from customers on account debits (increases) the asset Cash and credits (decreases) the asset Accounts Receivable, as indicated by answer a. Answer b has the debit and credit reversed, and answers c and d involve transactions with creditors (accounts payable) and not customers (accounts receivable).

5. **d** The trial balance (answer d) is a listing of the balances and the titles of the accounts in the ledger on a given date, so that the equality of the debits and credits in the ledger can be verified. The income statement (answer a) is a summary of revenue and expenses for a period of time. The balance sheet (answer b) is a presentation of the assets, liabilities, and stockholders' equity on a given date. The statement of stockholders' equity (answer c) is a summary of the changes in common stock and retained earnings for a period of time.

Exercises

1. 1. Debit and credit entries, normal debit balance
    2. Credit entries only, normal credit balance
    3. Debit and credit entries, normal credit balance
    4. Credit entries only, normal credit balance
    5. Credit entries only, normal credit balance
    6. Debit entries only, normal debit balance

2.

Oct. 27	Office Equipment	32,750	
	Cash		6,550
	Accounts Payable		26,200

3.

Mar. 16	Accounts Receivable	9,450	
	Fees Earned		9,450

4.

Dec. 23	Dividends	20,000	
	Cash		20,000

5. Using the following T account, solve for the amount of cash receipts (indicated by ? below).

Cash			
July 1 Bal.	37,450	115,860	Cash payments
Cash receipts	?		
July 31 Bal.	29,600	_____	

$29,600 = $37,450 + Cash receipts − $115,860
Cash receipts = $29,600 + $115,860 − $37,450 = $108,010

6. a. The totals are unequal. The debit total is higher by $900 ($5,400 − $4,500).
    b. The totals are equal because both the debit and credit entries were journalized and posted for $720.
    c. The totals are unequal. The debit total is higher by $3,200 ($1,600 + $1,600).

7. a.

Rent Expense	4,650	
Miscellaneous Expense		4,650

Rent Expense	4,650	
Cash		4,650

Note: The first entry in (a) reverses the incorrect entry, and the second entry records the correct entry. These two entries could also be combined into one entry as shown below; however, preparing two entries would make it easier for someone to understand later what happened and why the entries were necessary.

Rent Expense	9,300	
Miscellaneous Expense		4,650
Cash		4,650

b.

Accounts Payable	3,700	
Accounts Receivable		3,700

8.

Fuller Company
Income Statements
For the Years Ended December 31

	20Y4	20Y3	Increase/(Decrease) Amount	Increase/(Decrease) Percent
Fees earned	$ 680,000	$ 850,000	$(170,000)	(20.0)%
Expenses	(541,875)	(637,500)	(95,625)	(15.0)%
Net income	$ 138,125	$ 212,500	$ (74,375)	(35.0)%

Need more help? Watch step-by-step videos of how to compute answers to these Exercises in CengageNOWv2.

Problem

1., 2., and 3.

Journal				Page 27
Date	**Description**	**Post. Ref.**	**Debit**	**Credit**
20Y7				
Apr. 1	Rent Expense	53	800	
	Cash	11		800
	Paid office rent for April.			
3	Equipment	18	2,100	
	Accounts Payable	22		2,100
	Purchased equipment on account.			
5	Cash	11	3,150	
	Accounts Receivable	12		3,150
	Received cash on account.			
8	Supplies	13	245	
	Accounts Payable	22		245
	Purchased supplies.			
9	Accounts Payable	22	325	
	Equipment	18		325
	Returned defective equipment.			
12	Accounts Payable	22	1,250	
	Cash	11		1,250
	Paid creditors on account.			
17	Prepaid Insurance	14	370	
	Cash	11		370
	Renewed six-month property policy.			
20	Accounts Payable	22	200	
	Cash	11		200
	Recorded March payment to creditor.			

Journal				Page 28
Date	**Description**	**Post. Ref.**	**Debit**	**Credit**
20Y7				
Apr. 24	Laboratory Expense	55	545	
	Cash	11		545
	Paid for laboratory analysis.			
27	Dividends	33	1,250	
	Cash	11		1,250
	Paid dividends.			
30	Cash	11	1,720	
	Professional Fees	41		1,720
	Received fees from patients.			
30	Salary Expense	51	1,725	
	Cash	11		1,725
	Paid salaries.			
30	Utilities Expense	56	360	
	Cash	11		360
	Paid utilities.			
30	Accounts Receivable	12	5,145	
	Professional Fees	41		5,145
	Recorded fees earned on account.			
30	Miscellaneous Expense	59	132	
	Cash	11		132
	Paid expenses.			

Account *Cash*   Account No. *11*

Date	Item	Post. Ref.	Debit	Credit	Balance Debit	Balance Credit
20Y7						
Apr. 1	Balance	🕐			4,123	
1		27		800	3,323	
5		27	3,150		6,473	
12		27		1,250	5,223	
17		27		370	4,853	
20		27		200	4,653	
24		28		545	4,108	
27		28		1,250	2,858	
30		28	1,720		4,578	
30		28		1,725	2,853	
30		28		360	2,493	
30		28		132	2,361	

Account *Accounts Receivable*   Account No. *12*

Date	Item	Post. Ref.	Debit	Credit	Balance Debit	Balance Credit
20Y7						
Apr. 1	Balance	🕐			6,725	
5		27		3,150	3,575	
30		28	5,145		8,720	

Account *Supplies*   Account No. *13*

Date	Item	Post. Ref.	Debit	Credit	Balance Debit	Balance Credit
20Y7						
Apr. 1	Balance	🕐			290	
8		27	245		535	

Account *Prepaid Insurance*   Account No. *14*

Date	Item	Post. Ref.	Debit	Credit	Balance Debit	Balance Credit
20Y7						
Apr. 1	Balance	🕐			465	
17		27	370		835	

Account *Equipment*   Account No. *18*

Date	Item	Post. Ref.	Debit	Credit	Balance Debit	Balance Credit
20Y7						
Apr. 1	Balance	🕐			19,745	
3		27	2,100		21,845	
9		27		325	21,520	

Account *Accounts Payable*   Account No. *22*

Date	Item	Post. Ref.	Debit	Credit	Balance Debit	Balance Credit
20Y7						
Apr. 1	Balance	🕐				765
3		27		2,100		2,865
8		27		245		3,110
9		27	325			2,785
12		27	1,250			1,535
20		27	200			1,335

Account *Common Stock*   Account No. *31*

Date	Item	Post. Ref.	Debit	Credit	Balance Debit	Balance Credit
20Y7						
Apr. 1	Balance	🕐				10,000

Account *Retained Earnings*   Account No. *32*

Date	Item	Post. Ref.	Debit	Credit	Balance Debit	Balance Credit
20Y7						
Apr. 1	Balance	🕐				20,583

Account *Dividends*   Account No. *33*

Date	Item	Post. Ref.	Debit	Credit	Balance Debit	Balance Credit
20Y7						
Apr. 27		28	1,250		1,250	

Account *Professional Fees*   Account No. *41*

Date	Item	Post. Ref.	Debit	Credit	Balance Debit	Balance Credit
20Y7						
Apr. 30		28		1,720		1,720
30		28		5,145		6,865

Account *Salary Expense*   Account No. *51*

Date	Item	Post. Ref.	Debit	Credit	Balance Debit	Balance Credit
20Y7						
Apr. 30		28	1,725		1,725	

(Continued)

Account *Rent Expense*						Account No. *53*
Date	Item	Post. Ref.	Debit	Credit	Balance Debit	Balance Credit
20Y7 Apr. 1		27	800		800	

Account *Utilities Expense*						Account No. *56*
Date	Item	Post. Ref.	Debit	Credit	Balance Debit	Balance Credit
20Y7 Apr. 30		28	360		360	

Account *Laboratory Expense*						Account No. *55*
Date	Item	Post. Ref.	Debit	Credit	Balance Debit	Balance Credit
20Y7 Apr. 24		28	545		545	

Account *Miscellaneous Expense*						Account No. *59*
Date	Item	Post. Ref.	Debit	Credit	Balance Debit	Balance Credit
20Y7 Apr. 30		28	132		132	

4.

J. F. Outz, M.D.
Unadjusted Trial Balance
April 30, 20Y7

	Account No.	Debit Balances	Credit Balances
Cash	11	2,361	
Accounts Receivable.....................................	12	8,720	
Supplies	13	535	
Prepaid Insurance	14	835	
Equipment..	18	21,520	
Accounts Payable	22		1,335
Common Stock..	31		10,000
Retained Earnings.......................................	32		20,583
Dividends...	33	1,250	
Professional Fees..	41		6,865
Salary Expense	51	1,725	
Rent Expense	53	800	
Laboratory Expense	55	545	
Utilities Expense	56	360	
Miscellaneous Expense	59	132	
		38,783	38,783

Discussion Questions

1. What is the difference between an account and a ledger?

2. Do the terms *debit* and *credit* signify increase or decrease or can they signify either? Explain.

3. McIntyre Company adheres to a policy of depositing all cash receipts in a bank account and making all payments by check. The cash account as of December 31 has a credit balance of $1,850, and there is no undeposited cash on hand. (a) Assuming no errors occurred during journalizing or posting, what caused this unusual balance? (b) Is the $1,850 credit balance in the cash account an asset, a liability, stockholders' equity, a revenue, or an expense?

4. eCatalog Services Company performed services in October for a specific customer, for a fee of $7,890. Payment was received the following November. (a) Was the revenue earned in October or November? (b) What accounts should be debited and credited in (1) October and (2) November?

5. If the two totals of a trial balance are equal, does it mean that there are no errors in the accounting records? Explain.

6. Assume that a trial balance is prepared with an account balance of $8,900 listed as $9,800 and an account balance of $1,000 listed as $100. Identify the transposition and the slide.

7. Assume that when a purchase of supplies of $2,650 for cash was recorded, both the debit and the credit were journalized and posted as $2,560. (a) Would this error cause the trial balance to be out of balance? (b) Would the trial balance be out of balance if the $2,650 entry had been journalized correctly but the credit to Cash had been posted as $2,560?

8. Assume that Muscular Consulting erroneously recorded the payment of $7,500 of dividends as a debit to Salary Expense. (a) How would this error affect the equality

of the trial balance? (b) How would this error affect the income statement, statement of stockholders' equity, and balance sheet?

9. Assume that Sunshine Realty Co. borrowed $300,000 from Columbia First Bank and Trust. In recording the transaction, Sunshine erroneously recorded the receipt as a debit to Cash, $300,000, and a credit to Fees Earned, $300,000. (a) How would this error affect the equality of the trial balance? (b) How would this error affect the income statement, statement of stockholders' equity, and balance sheet?

10. Checking accounts are one of the most common forms of deposits for banks. Assume that Surety Storage has a checking account at Ada Savings Bank. What type of account (asset, liability, stockholders' equity, revenue, expense, dividends) does the account balance of $11,375 represent from the viewpoint of (a) Surety Storage and (b) Ada Savings Bank?

Basic Exercises

SHOW ME HOW

BE 2-1 Rules of debit and credit and normal balances   Obj. 2

State for each account whether it is likely to have (a) debit entries only, (b) credit entries only, or (c) both debit and credit entries. Also, indicate its normal balance.

1. Accounts Payable	4. Miscellaneous Expense
2. Cash	5. Insurance Expense
3. Dividends	6. Fees Earned

SHOW ME HOW

BE 2-2 Journal entry for asset purchase   Obj. 2

Prepare a journal entry for the purchase of office supplies on November 2 for $1,600, paying $500 cash and the remainder on account.

SHOW ME HOW

BE 2-3 Journal entry for fees earned   Obj. 3

Prepare a journal entry on August 13 for cash received for services rendered, $9,000.

SHOW ME HOW

BE 2-4 Journal entry for dividends   Obj. 3

Prepare a journal entry on June 30 for dividends of $11,500.

SHOW ME HOW

BE 2-5 Missing amount from an account   Obj. 3

On August 1, the supplies account balance was $1,025. During August, supplies of $3,110 were purchased, and $1,324 of supplies were on hand as of August 31. Determine supplies expense for August.

SHOW ME HOW

BE 2-6 Trial balance errors   Obj. 4

For each of the following errors, considered individually, indicate whether the error would cause the trial balance totals to be unequal. If the error would cause the trial balance totals to be unequal, indicate whether the debit or credit total is higher and by how much.

a. The payment of cash for the purchase of office equipment of $12,900 was debited to Land for $12,900 and credited to Cash for $12,900.

b. The payment of $1,840 on account was debited to Accounts Payable for $184 and credited to Cash for $1,840.

c. The receipt of cash on account of $3,800 was recorded as a debit to Cash for $8,300 and a credit to Accounts Receivable for $3,800.

SHOW ME HOW

BE 2-7 Correcting entries

Obj. 4

The following errors took place in journalizing and posting transactions:

a. The receipt of $8,400 for services rendered was recorded as a debit to Accounts Receivable and a credit to Fees Earned.

b. The purchase of supplies of $2,500 on account was recorded as a debit to Office Equipment and a credit to Supplies.

Journalize the entries to correct the errors. Omit explanations.

SHOW ME HOW

BE 2-8 Horizontal analysis

Obj. 5

Two income statements for Paragon Company follow:

Paragon Company
Income Statements
For the Years Ended December 31

	20Y7	20Y6
Fees earned	$ 1,416,000	$1,200,000
Expenses	(1,044,000)	(900,000)
Net income	$ 372,000	$ 300,000

Prepare a horizontal analysis of Paragon Company's income statements.

Exercises

REAL WORLD

EX 2-1 Chart of accounts

Obj. 1

The following accounts appeared in recent financial statements of **Delta Air Lines (DAL)**:

Accounts Payable	Flight Equipment
Advanced Payments for Equipment	Frequent Flyer (Obligations)
Air Traffic Liability	Fuel Inventory
Aircraft Fuel (Expense)	Landing Fees (Expense)
Aircraft Maintenance (Expense)	Parts and Supplies Inventories
Aircraft Rent (Expense)	Passenger Commissions (Expense)
Cargo Revenue	Passenger Revenue
Cash	Prepaid Expenses
Contract Carrier Arrangements (Expense)	Taxes Payable

Identify each account as either a balance sheet account or an income statement account. For each balance sheet account, identify it as an asset, a liability, or stockholders' equity. For each income statement account, identify it as a revenue or an expense.

EX 2-2 Chart of accounts

Obj. 1

Superior Interiors is owned and operated by Ken Lopez, an interior decorator. In the ledger of Superior Interiors, the first digit of the account number indicates its major account classification (1—assets, 2—liabilities, 3—stockholders' equity, 4—revenues, 5—expenses). The second digit of the account number indicates the specific account within each of the preceding major account classifications.

Match each account number with its most likely account in the list that follows. The account numbers are 11, 12, 13, 21, 31, 32, 33, 41, 51, 52, and 53.

Accounts Payable	Land
Accounts Receivable	Miscellaneous Expense
Cash	Retained Earnings
Common Stock	Supplies Expense
Dividends	Wages Expense
Fees Earned	

EX 2-3 Chart of accounts

Obj. 1

LeadCo School is a newly organized business that teaches people how to inspire and influence others. The list of accounts to be opened in the general ledger is as follows:

Accounts Payable	Prepaid Insurance
Accounts Receivable	Rent Expense
Cash	Retained Earnings
Common Stock	Supplies
Dividends	Supplies Expense
Equipment	Unearned Rent
Fees Earned	Wages Expense
Miscellaneous Expense	

List the accounts in the order in which they should appear in the ledger of LeadCo School and assign account numbers. Each account number is to have two digits: the first digit is to indicate the major classification (1 for assets, etc.), and the second digit is to identify the specific account within each major classification (11 for Cash, etc.).

EX 2-4 Rules of debit and credit

Obj. 1, 2

The following table summarizes the rules of debit and credit. For each of the items a through l, indicate whether the proper answer is a debit or a credit.

	Increase	Decrease	Normal Balance
Balance sheet accounts:			
Asset	(a)	Credit	(b)
Liability	Credit	(c)	(d)
Stockholders' equity:			
Common Stock	Credit	(e)	(f)
Retained Earnings	(g)	(h)	Credit
Dividends	Debit	Credit	(i)
Income statement accounts:			
Revenue	(j)	(k)	Credit
Expense	(l)	Credit	Debit

EX 2-5 Normal entries for accounts

Obj. 2

During the month, Gates Labs Co. has a substantial number of transactions affecting each of the following accounts. State for each account whether it is likely to have (a) debit entries only, (b) credit entries only, or (c) both debit and credit entries.

1. Accounts Payable
2. Accounts Receivable
3. Cash
4. Fees Earned
5. Insurance Expense
6. Dividends
7. Utilities Expense

EX 2-6 Normal balances of accounts

Obj. 1, 2

Identify each of the following accounts of Liken Services Co. as asset, liability, stockholders' equity, revenue, or expense, and state in each case whether the normal balance is a debit or a credit:

a. Accounts Payable
b. Accounts Receivable
c. Cash
d. Common Stock
e. Dividends
f. Fees Earned
g. Land
h. Rent Expense
i. Supplies
j. Utilities Expense

SHOW ME HOW

EX 2-7   Transactions

Obj. 2

Innovative Consulting Co. has the following accounts in its ledger: Cash, Accounts Receivable, Supplies, Office Equipment, Accounts Payable, Common Stock, Retained Earnings, Dividends, Fees Earned, Rent Expense, Advertising Expense, Utilities Expense, Miscellaneous Expense.

Journalize the following selected transactions for October 20Y2 in a two-column journal. Journal entry explanations may be omitted.

Oct. 1.   Paid rent for the month, $2,500.
     4.   Paid advertising expense, $1,000.
     5.   Paid cash for supplies, $1,800.
     6.   Purchased office equipment on account, $11,500.
    12.   Received cash from customers on account, $7,500.
    20.   Paid creditor on account, $2,700.
    27.   Paid cash for miscellaneous expenses, $700.
    30.   Paid telephone bill for the month, $475.
    31.   Fees earned and billed to customers for the month, $42,400.
    31.   Paid electricity bill for the month, $900.
    31.   Paid dividends, $1,500.

SHOW ME HOW

EX 2-8   Journalizing and posting

Obj. 2, 3

On February 11, 20Y9, Quick Fix Company purchased $2,250 of supplies on account. In Quick Fix's chart of accounts, the supplies account is No. 15, and the accounts payable account is No. 21.

a. Journalize the February 11, 20Y9, transaction on page 73 of Quick Fix Company's two-column journal. Include an explanation of the entry.

b. Prepare a four-column account for Supplies. Enter a debit balance of $400 as of February 1, 20Y9. Place a check mark (✓) in the Posting Reference column.

c. Prepare a four-column account for Accounts Payable. Enter a credit balance of $18,300 as of February 1, 20Y9. Place a check mark (✓) in the Posting Reference column.

d. Post the February 11, 20Y9, transaction to the accounts.

e. ━━━▶ Do the rules of debit and credit apply to all companies?

SHOW ME HOW   EXCEL TEMPLATE

EX 2-9   Transactions and T accounts

Obj. 2, 3

The following selected transactions were completed during July of the current year:

1. Billed customers for fees earned, $112,700.
2. Purchased supplies on account, $4,500.
3. Received cash from customers on account, $88,220.
4. Paid creditors on account, $3,100.

a. Journalize these transactions in a two-column journal, using the appropriate number to identify the transactions. Journal entry explanations may be omitted.

b. Post the entries prepared in (a) to the following T accounts: Cash, Supplies, Accounts Receivable, Accounts Payable, Fees Earned. To the left of each amount posted in the accounts, place the appropriate number to identify the transaction.

c. ━━━▶ Assume that the unadjusted trial balance on July 31 shows a credit balance for Accounts Receivable. Does this credit balance mean an error has occurred?

EX 2-10   Cash account balance

Obj. 1, 2, 3

During the month, Bavarian Auto Co. received $1,245,000 in cash and paid out $974,200 in cash.

a. ━━━▶ Does this information indicate that Bavarian Auto Co. had net income of $270,800 during the month? Explain.

b. If the balance of the cash account is $421,000 at the end of the month, what was the cash balance at the beginning of the month?

EX 2-11 Account balances

Obj. 1, 2, 3

a. During February, $186,500 was paid to creditors on account, and purchases on account were $201,400. Assuming the February 28 balance of Accounts Payable was $59,900, determine the account balance on February 1.

b. On October 1, the accounts receivable account balance was $115,800. During October, $449,600 was collected from customers on account. Assuming the October 31 balance was $130,770, determine the fees billed to customers on account during October.

c. On April 1, the cash account balance was $46,220. During April, cash receipts totaled $248,600 and the April 30 balance was $56,770. Determine the cash payments made during April.

EX 2-12 Retained earnings account balance

Obj. 1, 2

As of January 1, Retained Earnings had a credit balance of $314,000. During the year, dividends totaled $10,000, and the business incurred a net loss of $320,000.

a. Compute the balance of Retained Earnings as of the end of the year.

b. ➤Assuming that there have been no recording errors, will the balance sheet prepared at December 31 balance? Explain.

EX 2-13 Identifying transactions

Obj. 1, 2

Rocky Mountain Tours Co. is a travel agency. The nine transactions recorded by Rocky Mountain Tours during June 20Y2, its first month of operations, are indicated in the following T accounts:

Cash				Equipment			Dividends	
(1)	40,000	(2)	4,000	(3)	15,000		(9)	1,500
(7)	13,100	(3)	5,000					
		(4)	6,175					
		(6)	6,000					
		(9)	1,500					

Accounts Receivable				Accounts Payable			Service Revenue	
(5)	20,500	(7)	13,100	(6)	6,000	(3)	10,000	
							(5)	20,500

Supplies				Common Stock		Operating Expenses	
(2)	4,000	(8)	2,200	(1)	40,000	(4)	6,175
						(8)	2,200

Indicate for each debit and each credit: (a) whether an asset, liability, stockholders' equity, dividend, revenue, or expense account was affected and (b) whether the account was increased (+) or decreased (−). Present your answers in the following form, with transaction (1) given as an example:

	Account Debited		Account Credited	
Transaction	Type	Effect	Type	Effect
(1)	asset	+	stockholders' equity	+

EX 2-14 Journal entries

Obj. 1, 2

Based upon the T accounts in Exercise 2-13, prepare the nine journal entries from which the postings were made. Journal entry explanations may be omitted.

EX 2-15 Trial balance

Obj. 4

Based upon the data presented in Exercise 2-13, (a) prepare an unadjusted trial balance, listing the accounts in their proper order. (b) Based upon the unadjusted trial balance, determine the net income or net loss.

✔ Total of Credit column:
$6,500,000

SHOW ME HOW

EX 2-16   Trial balance

Obj. 4

The accounts in the ledger of Seaside Furniture Company as of August 20Y5 are listed in alphabetical order as follows. All accounts have normal balances. The balance of the cash account has been intentionally omitted.

Accounts Payable	$ 118,600	Notes Payable	$ 75,000
Accounts Receivable	660,500	Prepaid Insurance	21,600
Cash	?	Rent Expense	390,000
Common Stock	150,000	Retained Earnings	1,814,400
Dividends	36,000	Supplies	11,200
Fees Earned	4,330,000	Supplies Expense	23,700
Insurance Expense	18,000	Unearned Rent	12,000
Land	1,850,000	Utilities Expense	82,000
Miscellaneous Expense	30,200	Wages Expense	2,950,000

Prepare an unadjusted trial balance, listing the accounts in their normal order and inserting the missing figure for cash.

EX 2-17   Effect of errors on trial balance

Obj. 4

Indicate which of the following errors, each considered individually, would cause the trial balance totals to be unequal:

a.   A fee of $21,000 earned and due from a client was not debited to Accounts Receivable or credited to a revenue account, because the cash had not been received.

b.   A receipt of $11,300 from an account receivable was journalized and posted as a debit of $11,300 to Cash and a credit of $11,300 to Fees Earned.

c.   A payment of $4,950 to a creditor was posted as a debit of $4,950 to Accounts Payable and a debit of $4,950 to Cash.

d.   A payment of $5,000 for equipment purchased was posted as a debit of $500 to Equipment and a credit of $500 to Cash.

e.   Payment of cash dividends of $19,000 was journalized and posted as a debit of $1,900 to Salary Expense and a credit of $19,000 to Cash.

Indicate which of the preceding errors would require a correcting entry.

EX 2-18   Errors in trial balance

Obj. 4

✔ Total of Credit column:
$525,000

The following preliminary unadjusted trial balance of Ranger Co., a sports ticket agency, does not balance:

Ranger Co.
Unadjusted Trial Balance
August 31, 20Y1

	Debit Balances	Credit Balances
Cash	77,600	
Accounts Receivable	37,750	
Prepaid Insurance		12,000
Equipment	19,000	
Accounts Payable		29,100
Unearned Rent		10,800
Common Stock	40,000	
Retained Earnings	70,000	
Dividends	13,000	
Service Revenue		385,000
Wages Expense		213,000
Advertising Expense	16,350	
Miscellaneous Expense		18,400
	273,700	668,300

When the ledger and other records are reviewed, you discover the following: (1) the debits and credits in the cash account total $77,600 and $62,100, respectively; (2) a billing of $9,000 to a customer on account was not posted to the accounts receivable account; (3) a payment of $4,500 made to a creditor on account was not posted to the accounts payable account;

(4) the balance of the unearned rent account is $5,400; (5) the correct balance of the equipment account is $190,000; and (6) each account has a normal balance.

Prepare a corrected unadjusted trial balance.

EX 2-19 Effect of errors on trial balance

Obj. 4

The following errors occurred in posting from a two-column journal:

1. A credit of $6,000 to Accounts Payable was not posted.
2. An entry debiting Accounts Receivable and crediting Fees Earned for $5,300 was not posted.
3. A debit of $2,700 to Accounts Payable was posted as a credit.
4. A debit of $480 to Supplies was posted twice.
5. A debit of $3,600 to Cash was posted to Miscellaneous Expense.
6. A credit of $780 to Cash was posted as $870.
7. A debit of $12,620 to Wages Expense was posted as $12,260.

Considering each case individually (i.e., assuming that no other errors had occurred), indicate: (a) by "yes" or "no" whether the trial balance would be out of balance; (b) if answer to (a) is "yes," the amount by which the trial balance totals would differ; and (c) whether the Debit or Credit column of the trial balance would have the larger total. Answers should be presented in the following form, with error (1) given as an example:

	(a)	(b)	(c)
Error	Out of Balance	Difference	Larger Total
1.	yes	$6,000	debit

EX 2-20 Errors in trial balance

Obj. 4

✔ Total of Credit column: $1,450,000

Identify the errors in the following trial balance. All accounts have normal balances.

SHOW ME HOW

Ensemble Co.
Unadjusted Trial Balance
For the Year Ending December 31, 20Y8

	Debit Balances	Credit Balances
Cash	42,900	
Accounts Receivable		123,500
Prepaid Insurance	27,000	
Equipment	300,000	
Accounts Payable	52,000	
Salaries Payable		4,800
Common Stock		40,000
Retained Earnings		137,200
Dividends		5,000
Service Revenue		1,216,000
Salary Expense	660,000	
Advertising Expense		275,000
Miscellaneous Expense	16,600	
	1,801,500	1,801,500

EX 2-21 Entries to correct errors

Obj. 4

SHOW ME HOW

The following errors took place in journalizing and posting transactions:

a. Insurance of $18,000 paid for the current year was recorded as a debit to Insurance Expense and a credit to Prepaid Insurance.
b. Dividends of $10,000 were recorded as a debit to Wages Expense and a credit to Cash.

Journalize the entries to correct the errors. Omit explanations.

EX 2-22 Entries to correct errors

Obj. 4

SHOW ME HOW

The following errors took place in journalizing and posting transactions:

a. Cash of $8,800 received on account was recorded as a debit to Fees Earned and a credit to Cash.
b. A $1,760 purchase of supplies for cash was recorded as a debit to Supplies Expense and a credit to Accounts Payable.

Journalize the entries to correct the errors. Omit explanations.

Problems: Series A

PR 2-1A   Entries into T accounts and trial balance   Obj. 1, 2, 3, 4

✔ 3. Total of Debit column: $100,525

Marjorie Knaus, an architect, organized Knaus Architects on January 1, 20Y4. During the month, Knaus Architects completed the following transactions:

a. Issued common stock to Marjorie Knaus in exchange for $30,000.
b. Paid January rent for office and workroom, $2,500.
c. Purchased used automobile for $28,500, paying $6,000 cash and giving a note payable for the remainder.
d. Purchased office and computer equipment on account, $8,000.
e. Paid cash for supplies, $2,100.
f. Paid cash for annual insurance policies, $3,600.
g. Received cash from client for plans delivered, $9,000.
h. Paid cash for miscellaneous expenses, $2,600.
i. Paid cash to creditors on account, $4,000.
j. Paid installment due on note payable, $1,875.
k. Received invoice for blueprint service, due in February, $5,500.
l. Recorded fees earned on plans delivered, payment to be received in February, $31,400.
m. Paid salary of assistants, $6,000.
n. Paid gas, oil, and repairs on automobile for January, $1,300.

Instructions

1. Record these transactions directly in the following T accounts, without journalizing: Cash, Accounts Receivable, Supplies, Prepaid Insurance, Automobiles, Equipment, Notes Payable, Accounts Payable, Common Stock, Professional Fees, Salary Expense, Blueprint Expense, Rent Expense, Automobile Expense, Miscellaneous Expense. To the left of the amount entered in the accounts, place the appropriate letter to identify the transaction.

2. Determine account balances of the T accounts. Accounts containing a single entry only (such as Prepaid Insurance) do not need a balance.

3. Prepare an unadjusted trial balance for Knaus Architects as of January 31, 20Y4.

4. Determine the net income or net loss for January.

PR 2-2A   Journal entries and trial balance   Obj. 1, 2, 3, 4

✔ 4. c. $6,770

SHOW ME HOW   EXCEL TEMPLATE

On October 1, 20Y6, Jay Crowley established Affordable Realty, which completed the following transactions during the month:

a. Jay Crowley transferred cash from a personal bank account to an account to be used for the business in exchange for common stock, $40,000.
b. Paid rent on office and equipment for the month, $4,800.
c. Purchased supplies on account, $2,150.
d. Paid creditor on account, $1,100.
e. Earned sales commissions, receiving cash, $18,750.
f. Paid automobile expenses (including rental charge) for month, $1,580, and miscellaneous expenses, $800.
g. Paid office salaries, $3,500.
h. Determined that the cost of supplies used was $1,300.
i. Paid dividends, $1,500.

Instructions

1. Journalize entries for transactions (a) through (i), using the following account titles: Cash, Supplies, Accounts Payable, Common Stock, Dividends, Sales Commissions, Rent Expense, Office Salaries Expense, Automobile Expense, Supplies Expense, Miscellaneous Expense. Explanations may be omitted.

2. Prepare T accounts, using the account titles in (1). Post the journal entries to these accounts, placing the appropriate letter to the left of each amount to identify the transactions. Determine the account balances after all posting is complete. Accounts containing only a single entry do not need a balance.

3. Prepare an unadjusted trial balance as of October 31, 20Y6.

4. Determine the following:

   a. Amount of total revenue recorded in the ledger.

   b. Amount of total expenses recorded in the ledger.

   c. Amount of net income for October.

5. Determine the increase or decrease in retained earnings for October.

PR 2-3A **Journal entries and trial balance**   Obj. 1, 2, 3, 4

✔ 3. Total of Credit column:
$130,550

SHOW ME HOW   EXCEL TEMPLATE

On November 1, 20Y9, Lexi Martin established an interior decorating business, Heritage Designs. During the month, Lexi completed the following transactions related to the business:

Nov. 1. Lexi transferred cash from a personal bank account to an account to be used for the business in exchange for common stock, $50,000.

1. Paid rent for period of November 1 to end of month, $4,000.

6. Purchased office equipment on account, $15,000.

8. Purchased a truck for $38,500 paying $5,000 cash and giving a note payable for the remainder.

10. Purchased supplies for cash, $1,750.

12. Received cash for job completed, $11,500.

15. Paid annual premiums on property and casualty insurance, $2,400.

23. Recorded jobs completed on account and sent invoices to customers, $22,300.

24. Received an invoice for truck expenses, to be paid in November, $1,250.

Enter the following transactions on Page 2 of the two-column journal:

29. Paid utilities expense, $4,500.

29. Paid miscellaneous expenses, $1,000.

30. Received cash from customers on account, $9,000.

30. Paid wages of employees, $6,800.

30. Paid creditor a portion of the amount owed for equipment purchased on November 6, $3,000.

30. Paid dividends, $2,500.

Instructions

1. Journalize each transaction in a two-column journal beginning on Page 1, referring to the following chart of accounts in selecting the accounts to be debited and credited. (Do not insert the account numbers in the journal at this time.) Explanations may be omitted.

11	Cash	31	Common Stock
12	Accounts Receivable	33	Dividends
13	Supplies	41	Fees Earned
14	Prepaid Insurance	51	Wages Expense
16	Equipment	53	Rent Expense
18	Truck	54	Utilities Expense
21	Notes Payable	55	Truck Expense
22	Accounts Payable	59	Miscellaneous Expense

2. Post the journal to a ledger of four-column accounts, inserting appropriate posting references as each item is posted. Extend the balances to the appropriate balance columns after each transaction is posted.

3. Prepare an unadjusted trial balance for Heritage Designs as of November 30, 20Y9.

4. Determine the excess of revenues over expenses for November.

5. ▬▬▶ Can you think of any reason why the amount determined in (4) might not be the net income for November?

PR 2-4A   Journal entries and trial balance

Obj. 1, 2, 3, 4

✔ 4. Total of Debit column:
$532,525

Elite Realty acts as an agent in buying, selling, renting, and managing real estate. The unadjusted trial balance on March 31, 20Y3, follows:

Elite Realty
Unadjusted Trial Balance
March 31, 20Y3

	Account No.	Debit Balances	Credit Balances
Cash	11	26,300	
Accounts Receivable.....................................	12	61,500	
Prepaid Insurance	13	3,000	
Office Supplies..	14	1,800	
Land	16	—	
Accounts Payable	21		14,000
Unearned Rent..	22		—
Notes Payable..	23		—
Common Stock..	31		10,000
Retained Earnings.......................................	32		36,000
Dividends	33	2,000	
Fees Earned...	41		240,000
Salary and Commission Expense.........................	51	148,200	
Rent Expense	52	30,000	
Advertising Expense.....................................	53	17,800	
Automobile Expense	54	5,500	
Miscellaneous Expense	59	3,900	
		300,000	300,000

The following business transactions were completed by Elite Realty during April 20Y3:

Apr. 1. Paid rent on office for month, $6,500.

2. Purchased office supplies on account, $2,300.

5. Paid insurance premiums, $6,000.

10. Received cash from clients on account, $52,300.

15. Purchased land for a future building site for $200,000, paying $30,000 in cash and giving a note payable for the remainder.

17. Paid creditors on account, $6,450.

20. Returned a portion of the office supplies purchased on April 2, receiving full credit for their cost, $325.

23. Paid advertising expense, $4,300.

Enter the following transactions on Page 19 of the two-column journal:

27. Discovered an error in computing a commission; received cash from the salesperson for the overpayment, $2,500.

28. Paid automobile expense (including rental charges for an automobile), $1,500.

29. Paid miscellaneous expenses, $1,400.

30. Recorded revenue earned and billed to clients during the month, $57,000.

30. Paid salaries and commissions for the month, $11,900.

30. Paid dividends, $4,000.

30. Rented land purchased on April 15 to local merchants association for use as a parking lot in May and June, during a street rebuilding program; received advance payment of $10,000.

Instructions

1. Record the April 1, 20Y3, balance of each account in the appropriate balance column of a four-column account, write *Balance* in the item section, and place a check mark (✓) in the Posting Reference column.

2. Journalize the transactions for April in a two-column journal beginning on Page 18. Journal entry explanations may be omitted.

3. Post to the ledger, extending the account balance to the appropriate balance column after each posting.

4. Prepare an unadjusted trial balance of the ledger as of April 30, 20Y3.

5. Assume that the April 30 transaction for salaries and commissions should have been $19,100. (a) Why did the unadjusted trial balance in (4) balance? (b) Journalize the correcting entry. (c) Is this error a transposition or slide?

PR 2-5A Corrected trial balance

Obj. 4

✔ 1. Total of Debit column: $650,000

The Lexington Group has the following unadjusted trial balance as of May 31, 20Y6:

The Lexington Group
Unadjusted Trial Balance
May 31, 20Y6

	Debit Balances	Credit Balances
Cash	20,350	
Accounts Receivable..	37,000	
Supplies..	1,100	
Prepaid Insurance	200	
Equipment...	171,175	
Notes Payable...		36,000
Accounts Payable		26,000
Common Stock...		50,000
Retained Earnings...		94,150
Dividends	15,000	
Fees Earned...		429,850
Wages Expense	270,000	
Rent Expense	63,000	
Advertising Expense...	25,200	
Miscellaneous Expense	5,100	
	608,125	636,000

The debit and credit totals are not equal as a result of the following errors:

a. The cash entered on the trial balance was overstated by $7,000.

b. A cash receipt of $8,200 was posted as a debit to Cash of $2,800.

c. A debit of $16,500 to Accounts Receivable was not posted.

d. A return of $125 of defective supplies was erroneously posted as a $1,250 credit to Supplies.

e. An insurance policy acquired at a cost of $3,600 was posted as a credit to Prepaid Insurance.

f. The balance of Notes Payable was understated by $9,000.

g. A credit of $10,000 in Accounts Payable was overlooked when determining the balance of the account.

h. A debit of $5,000 for dividends was posted as a credit to Retained Earnings.

i. The balance of $60,300 in Rent Expense was entered as $63,000 in the trial balance.

j. Gas, Electricity, and Water Expense, with a balance of $16,350, was omitted from the trial balance.

Instructions

1. Prepare a corrected unadjusted trial balance as of May 31, 20Y6.

2. ⟶ Does the fact that the unadjusted trial balance in (1) is balanced mean that there are no errors in the accounts? Explain.

Problems: Series B

PR 2-1B Entries into T accounts and trial balance

Obj. 1, 2, 3, 4

✔ 3. Total of Debit column: $69,550

Ken Jones, an architect, organized Jones Architects on April 1, 20Y2. During the month, Jones Architects completed the following transactions:

a. Transferred cash from a personal bank account to an account to be used for the business in exchange for common stock, $18,000.

b. Purchased used automobile for $19,500, paying $2,500 cash and giving a note payable for the remainder.

c. Paid April rent for office and workroom, $3,150.

d. Paid cash for supplies, $1,450.

e. Purchased office and computer equipment on account, $6,500.

f. Paid cash for annual insurance policies on automobile and equipment, $2,400.

g. Received cash from a client for plans delivered, $12,000.

h. Paid cash to creditors on account, $1,800.

i. Paid cash for miscellaneous expenses, $375.

(Continued)

j. Received invoice for blueprint service, due in May, $2,500.

k. Recorded fees earned on plans delivered, payment to be received in May, $15,650.

l. Paid salary of assistant, $2,800.

m. Paid cash for miscellaneous expenses, $200.

n. Paid installment due on note payable, $300.

o. Paid gas, oil, and repairs on automobile for April, $550.

Instructions

1. Record these transactions directly in the following T accounts, without journalizing: Cash, Accounts Receivable, Supplies, Prepaid Insurance, Automobiles, Equipment, Notes Payable, Accounts Payable, Common Stock, Professional Fees, Rent Expense, Salary Expense, Blueprint Expense, Automobile Expense, Miscellaneous Expense. To the left of each amount entered in the accounts, place the appropriate letter to identify the transaction.

2. Determine account balances of the T accounts. Accounts containing a single entry only (such as Prepaid Insurance) do not need a balance.

3. Prepare an unadjusted trial balance for Jones Architects as of April 30, 20Y2.

4. Determine the net income or net loss for April.

PR 2-2B Journal entries and trial balance   Obj. 1, 2, 3, 4

✔ 4. c. $4,550

SHOW ME HOW   EXCEL TEMPLATE

On August 1, 20Y7, Rafael Masey established Planet Realty, which completed the following transactions during the month:

a. Rafael Masey transferred cash from a personal bank account to an account to be used for the business in exchange for common stock, $17,500.

b. Purchased supplies on account, $2,300.

c. Earned sales commissions, receiving cash, $13,300.

d. Paid rent on office and equipment for the month, $3,000.

e. Paid creditor on account, $1,150.

f. Paid dividends, $1,800.

g. Paid automobile expenses (including rental charge) for month, $1,500, and miscellaneous expenses, $400.

h. Paid office salaries, $2,800.

i. Determined that the cost of supplies used was $1,050.

Instructions

1. Journalize entries for transactions (a) through (i), using the following account titles: Cash, Supplies, Accounts Payable, Common Stock, Dividends, Sales Commissions, Rent Expense, Office Salaries Expense, Automobile Expense, Supplies Expense, Miscellaneous Expense. Journal entry explanations may be omitted.

2. Prepare T accounts, using the account titles in (1). Post the journal entries to these accounts, placing the appropriate letter to the left of each amount to identify the transactions. Determine the account balances, after all posting is complete. Accounts containing only a single entry do not need a balance.

3. Prepare an unadjusted trial balance as of August 31, 20Y7.

4. Determine the following:

    a. Amount of total revenue recorded in the ledger.

    b. Amount of total expenses recorded in the ledger.

    c. Amount of net income for August.

5. Determine the increase or decrease in retained earnings for August.

PR 2-3B Journal entries and trial balance   Obj. 1, 2, 3, 4

✔ 3. Total of Credit column: $70,300

SHOW ME HOW   EXCEL TEMPLATE

On October 1, 20Y4, Jay Pryor established an interior decorating business, Pioneer Designs. During the month, Jay completed the following transactions related to the business:

Oct. 1. Jay transferred cash from a personal bank account to an account to be used for the business in exchange for common stock, $18,000.

      4. Paid rent for period of October 4 to end of month, $3,000.

      10. Purchased a used truck for $23,750, paying $3,750 cash and giving a note payable for the remainder.

      13. Purchased equipment on account, $10,500.

      14. Purchased supplies for cash, $2,100.

Oct. 15. Paid annual premiums on property and casualty insurance, $3,600.

15. Received cash for job completed, $8,950.

Enter the following transactions on Page 2 of the two-column journal:

21. Paid creditor a portion of the amount owed for equipment purchased on October 13, $2,000.

24. Recorded jobs completed on account and sent invoices to customers, $14,150.

26. Received an invoice for truck expenses, to be paid in November, $700.

27. Paid utilities expense, $2,240.

27. Paid miscellaneous expenses, $1,100.

29. Received cash from customers on account, $7,600.

30. Paid wages of employees, $4,800.

31. Paid dividends, $3,500.

Instructions

1. Journalize each transaction in a two-column journal beginning on Page 1, referring to the following chart of accounts in selecting the accounts to be debited and credited. (Do not insert the account numbers in the journal at this time.) Journal entry explanations may be omitted.

11 Cash	31 Common Stock
12 Accounts Receivable	33 Dividends
13 Supplies	41 Fees Earned
14 Prepaid Insurance	51 Wages Expense
16 Equipment	53 Rent Expense
18 Truck	54 Utilities Expense
21 Notes Payable	55 Truck Expense
22 Accounts Payable	59 Miscellaneous Expense

2. Post the journal to a ledger of four-column accounts, inserting appropriate posting references as each item is posted. Extend the balances to the appropriate balance columns after each transaction is posted.

3. Prepare an unadjusted trial balance for Pioneer Designs as of October 31, 20Y4.

4. Determine the excess of revenues over expenses for October.

5. ⬛▬▬ Can you think of any reason why the amount determined in (4) might not be the net income for October?

PR 2-4B Journal entries and trial balance   Obj. 1, 2, 3, 4

✔ 4. Total of Debit column: $945,000

Valley Realty acts as an agent in buying, selling, renting, and managing real estate. The unadjusted trial balance on July 31, 20Y8, follows:

Valley Realty
Unadjusted Trial Balance
July 31, 20Y8

	Account No.	Debit Balances	Credit Balances
Cash	11	52,500	
Accounts Receivable	12	100,100	
Prepaid Insurance	13	12,600	
Office Supplies	14	2,800	
Land	16	—	
Accounts Payable	21		21,000
Unearned Rent	22		—
Notes Payable	23		—
Common Stock	31		17,500
Retained Earnings	32		70,000
Dividends	33	44,800	
Fees Earned	41		591,500
Salary and Commission Expense	51	385,000	
Rent Expense	52	49,000	
Advertising Expense	53	32,200	
Automobile Expense	54	15,750	
Miscellaneous Expense	59	5,250	
		700,000	700,000

(Continued)

The following business transactions were completed by Valley Realty during August 20Y8:

Aug. 1. Purchased office supplies on account, $3,150.

2. Paid rent on office for month, $7,200.

3. Received cash from clients on account, $83,900.

5. Paid insurance premiums, $12,000.

9. Returned a portion of the office supplies purchased on August 1, receiving full credit for their cost, $400.

17. Paid advertising expense, $8,000.

23. Paid creditors on account, $13,750.

Enter the following transactions on Page 19 of the two-column journal:

29. Paid miscellaneous expenses, $1,700.

30. Paid automobile expense (including rental charges for an automobile), $2,500.

31. Discovered an error in computing a commission during July; received cash from the salesperson for the overpayment, $2,000.

31. Paid salaries and commissions for the month, $53,000.

31. Recorded revenue earned and billed to clients during the month, $183,500.

31. Purchased land for a future building site for $75,000, paying $7,500 in cash and giving a note payable for the remainder.

31. Paid dividends, $1,000.

31. Rented land purchased on August 31 to a local university for use as a parking lot during football season (September, October, and November); received advance payment of $5,000.

Instructions

1. Record the August 1 balance of each account in the appropriate balance column of a four-column account, write *Balance* in the item section, and place a check mark (✓) in the Posting Reference column.

2. Journalize the transactions for August in a two-column journal beginning on Page 18. Journal entry explanations may be omitted.

3. Post to the ledger, extending the account balance to the appropriate balance column after each posting.

4. Prepare an unadjusted trial balance of the ledger as of August 31, 20Y8.

5. Assume that the August 31 transaction for dividends should have been $10,000. (a) Why did the unadjusted trial balance in (4) balance? (b) Journalize the correcting entry. (c) Is this error a transposition or slide?

✔ 1. Total of Debit column: $712,500

PR 2-5B   Corrected trial balance   **Obj. 4**

Tech Support Services has the following unadjusted trial balance as of January 31, 20Y5:

Tech Support Services
Unadjusted Trial Balance
January 31, 20Y5

	Debit Balances	Credit Balances
Cash	25,550	
Accounts Receivable...	44,050	
Supplies..	6,660	
Prepaid Insurance	3,600	
Equipment..	162,000	
Notes Payable..		75,000
Accounts Payable		13,200
Common Stock...		18,000
Retained Earnings..		83,850
Dividends	33,000	
Fees Earned..		534,000
Wages Expense	306,000	
Rent Expense	62,550	
Advertising Expense..	23,850	
Gas, Electricity, and Water Expense	17,000	
	684,260	724,050

The debit and credit totals are not equal as a result of the following errors:

a. The cash entered on the trial balance was overstated by $8,000.

b. A cash receipt of $4,100 was posted as a debit to Cash of $1,400.

c. A debit of $12,350 to Accounts Receivable was not posted.

d. A return of $235 of defective supplies was erroneously posted as a $325 credit to Supplies.

e. An insurance policy acquired at a cost of $3,000 was posted as a credit to Prepaid Insurance.

f. The balance of Notes Payable was overstated by $21,000.

g. A credit of $3,450 in Accounts Payable was overlooked when the balance of the account was determined.

h. A debit of $6,000 for dividends was posted as a debit to Retained Earnings.

i. The balance of $28,350 in Advertising Expense was entered as $23,850 in the trial balance.

j. Miscellaneous Expense, with a balance of $4,600, was omitted from the trial balance.

Instructions

1. Prepare a corrected unadjusted trial balance as of January 31, 20Y5.

2. ➡ Does the fact that the unadjusted trial balance in (1) is balanced mean that there are no errors in the accounts? Explain.

Continuing Problem

✔ 4. Total of Debit column: $40,750

The transactions completed by PS Music during June 20Y5 were described at the end of Chapter 1. The following transactions were completed during July, the second month of the business's operations:

July 1. Peyton Smith made an additional investment in PS Music in exchange for common stock by depositing $5,000 in PS Music's checking account.

1. Instead of continuing to share office space with a local real estate agency, Peyton decided to rent office space near a local music store. Paid rent for July, $1,750.

1. Paid a premium of $2,700 for a comprehensive insurance policy covering liability, theft, and fire. The policy covers a one-year period.

2. Received $1,000 on account.

3. On behalf of PS Music, Peyton signed a contract with a local radio station, KXMD, to provide guest spots for the next three months. The contract requires PS Music to provide a guest disc jockey for 80 hours per month for a monthly fee of $3,600. Any additional hours beyond 80 will be billed to KXMD at $40 per hour. In accordance with the contract, Peyton received $7,200 from KXMD as an advance payment for the first two months.

3. Paid $250 on account.

4. Paid an attorney $900 for reviewing the July 3 contract with KXMD. (Record as Miscellaneous Expense.)

5. Purchased office equipment on account from Office Mart, $7,500.

8. Paid for a newspaper advertisement, $200.

11. Received $1,000 for serving as a disc jockey for a party.

13. Paid $700 to a local audio electronics store for rental of digital recording equipment.

14. Paid wages of $1,200 to receptionist and part-time assistant.

Enter the following transactions on Page 2 of the two-column journal:

16. Received $2,000 for serving as a disc jockey for a wedding reception.

18. Purchased supplies on account, $850.

21. Paid $620 to Upload Music for use of its current music demos in making various music sets.

22. Paid $800 to a local radio station to advertise the services of PS Music twice daily for the remainder of July.

23. Served as disc jockey for a party for $2,500. Received $750, with the remainder due August 4, 20Y5.

27. Paid electric bill, $915.

28. Paid wages of $1,200 to receptionist and part-time assistant.

29. Paid miscellaneous expenses, $540.

30. Served as a disc jockey for a charity ball for $1,500. Received $500, with the remainder due on August 9, 20Y5.

31. Received $3,000 for serving as a disc jockey for a party.

31. Paid $1,400 royalties (music expense) to National Music Clearing for use of various artists' music during July.

31. Paid dividends, $1,250.

(Continued)

PS Music's chart of accounts and the balance of accounts as of July 1, 20Y5 (all normal balances), are as follows:

11	Cash	$3,920	41	Fees Earned	$6,200
12	Accounts Receivable	1,000	50	Wages Expense	400
14	Supplies	170	51	Office Rent Expense	800
15	Prepaid Insurance	—	52	Equipment Rent Expense	675
17	Office Equipment	—	53	Utilities Expense	300
21	Accounts Payable	250	54	Music Expense	1,590
23	Unearned Revenue	—	55	Advertising Expense	500
31	Common Stock	4,000	56	Supplies Expense	180
33	Dividends	500	59	Miscellaneous Expense	415

Instructions

1. Enter the July 1, 20Y5, account balances in the appropriate balance column of a four-column account. Write *Balance* in the Item column, and place a check mark (✓) in the Posting Reference column. (*Hint:* Verify the equality of the debit and credit balances in the ledger before proceeding with the next instruction.)

2. Analyze and journalize each transaction in a two-column journal beginning on Page 1, omitting journal entry explanations.

3. Post the journal to the ledger, extending the account balance to the appropriate balance column after each posting.

4. Prepare an unadjusted trial balance as of July 31, 20Y5.

Make a Decision
Horizontal Analysis

REAL WORLD

MAD 2-1　Analyze Amazon.com　　　　　　　　　　　　　　　　　　　　Obj. 5

Amazon.com, Inc. (AMZN) is the largest Internet retailer in the United States. Amazon's income statements for two recent years follow:

Amazon.com, Inc.
Income Statements
For the Years Ended December 31
(in millions)

	Year 2	Year 1
Revenues:		
Product sales	$ 94,665	$ 79,268
Service sales	41,322	27,738
Total revenues	$ 135,987	$ 107,006
Operating expenses:		
Cost of sales	$ (88,265)	$ (71,651)
Fulfillment	(17,619)	(13,410)
Marketing	(7,233)	(5,254)
Technology and content	(16,085)	(12,540)
General and administrative	(2,432)	(1,747)
Other operating expense (income), net	(167)	(171)
Total operating expenses	$(131,801)	$(104,773)
Operating income	$ 4,186	$ 2,233

a. Prepare a horizontal analysis of the income statements. Round percentages to one decimal place.

b. ▬▬▶ Interpret the results of the horizontal analysis.

MAD 2-2　Analyze Chipotle Mexican Grill　　　　　　　　　　　　　　　　Obj. 5

Chipotle Mexican Grill, Inc. (CMG) is a quick-service restaurant providing a focused menu of burritos, tacos, and salads. Chipotle's income statements for the end of two recent years are as follows:

REAL WORLD

Chipotle Mexican Grill, Inc.
Income Statements
For the Years Ended December 31
(in thousands)

	Year 2	Year 1
Revenue	$ 3,904,384	$ 4,501,223
Expenses:		
Food, beverage, packing	$(1,365,580)	$(1,503,835)
Labor	(1,105,001)	(1,045,726)
Rent (occupancy)	(293,636)	(262,412)
General and administrative	(641,953)	(514,963)
Other	(463,647)	(410,698)
Total expenses	$(3,869,817)	$(3,737,634)
Operating income	$ 34,567	$ 763,589

a. Prepare a horizontal analysis of the two income statements. Round percentages to one decimal place.

b. Interpret the horizontal analysis.

c. Can you think of a reason why Chipotle's revenues and operating income may have decreased so significantly in Year 2?

MAD 2-3 Analyze Vera Bradley, Inc. **Obj. 5**

Vera Bradley, Inc. (VRA) is a leading designer, producer, and retailer of fashion handbags, accessories, and travel items for women. Income statements for two recent years for Vera Bradley are as follows:

Vera Bradley, Inc.
Income Statements
For the Years Ended January 31
(in millions)

	Year 2	Year 1
Revenue	$ 502.6	$ 509.0
Expenses:		
Cost of merchandise sold	$(221.4)	$(240.0)
Selling, general, admin. expenses	(236.8)	(208.7)
Other expenses	(16.8)	(21.9)
Total expenses	$(475.0)	$(470.6)
Operating income	$ 27.6	$ 38.4

a. Prepare a horizontal analysis of the two income statements.

b.  Assume you are a stockholder of Vera Bradley. Would you be inclined to view Vera Bradley's change in operating income favorably or unfavorably?

MAD 2-4 Analyze Target **Obj. 5**

The following data (in millions) are taken from the financial statements of **Target Corporation (TGT)**, the owner of Target stores:

	Year 2	Year 1
Revenue	$ 73,785	$ 72,618
Operating expenses	(68,875)	(68,083)
Operating income	$ 4,910	$ 4,535

a. For Target, determine the amount of change in millions and the percent of change rounded to one decimal place from Year 1 to Year 2 for:
1. Revenue
2. Operating expenses
3. Operating income

b.  What conclusions can you draw from your analysis of the revenue and total operating expenses?

REAL WORLD

MAD 2-5   Analyze Wal-Mart   Obj. 5

The following data (in millions) are taken from the financial statements of **Wal-Mart Stores, Inc. (WMT)**:

	Year 2	Year 1
Revenue	$ 482,130	$ 485,651
Operating expenses	(458,025)	(458,504)
Operating income	$ 24,105	$ 27,147

a. For Walmart, determine the amount of change in millions and the percent of change rounded to one decimal place from Year 1 to Year 2 for:

    1. Revenue   2. Operating expenses   3. Operating income

b.   Comment on the results of your horizontal analysis in requirement (a).

MAD 2-6   Compare Target and Wal-Mart   Obj. 5

           Based upon MAD 2-4 and MAD 2-5, compare the two-year change in operating results between **Target (TGT)** and **Wal-Mart (WMT)**.

REAL WORLD

Take It Further

ETHICS

TIF 2-1   Trial balance shortcut

Buddy Dupree is the accounting manager for On-Time Geeks, a tech support company for individuals and small businesses. As part of his job, Buddy is responsible for preparing the company's trial balance. His supervisor placed a "hard deadline" of Friday at 5 PM for the completion of the trial balance. Unfortunately, Buddy was unable to get the trial balance to balance by the due date. The credit side of the trial balance exceeded the debit side by $3,000. To make the deadline, Buddy decided to add a $3,000 debit to the vehicles account balance. He selected the vehicles account because it will not be significantly affected by the additional $3,000.

1.   Is Buddy behaving ethically? Why?
2.   Who is affected by Buddy's decision?
3.   How should Buddy have handled this situation?

TEAM ACTIVITY   REAL WORLD

TIF 2-2   Real-world annual report

In teams, select a public company that interests you. Obtain the company's most recent annual report on Form 10-K. The Form 10-K is a company's annually required filing with the Securities and Exchange Commission (SEC). It includes the company's financial statements and accompanying notes. The Form 10-K can be obtained either (a) from the investor relations section of the company's website or (b) by using the company search feature of the SEC's EDGAR database service found at www.sec.gov/edgar/searchedgar/companysearch.html.

Based on the information in the company's most recent annual report, answer the following questions:

1. What amount of total assets does the company report on its balance sheet?
2. What amount of total liabilities does the company report on its balance sheet?
3. Using the accounting equation, determine the company's stockholders' equity. Compare this amount to the amount of stockholders' equity reported on the company's balance sheet.
4. How many years of information are reported on the company's income statement?
5. How many years of information are reported on the company's balance sheet?
6.   What is the difference between the information reported on the income statement and the information reported on the balance sheet?

COMMUNICATION

TIF 2-3   Job opportunities for business analysts

The complexity of the current business and regulatory environment has increased the demand for individuals in all fields of business who have the ability to analyze business transactions and interpret their effects on the financial statements. Search the Internet or your local newspaper for job opportunities in business. One possible website is www.careerbuilder.com.

           Select a job opportunity to explore further. Write a brief memo to your instructor describing how the ability to analyze business transactions and interpret their effects on the financial statements would be needed for the job opportunity you have selected.

TIF 2-4 Recording your tuition

State College requires students to pay tuition each term before classes begin. Students who have not paid their tuition are not allowed to enroll or to attend classes.

What journal entry do you think State College would use to record the receipt of the students' tuition payments? Describe the nature of each account in the entry.

TIF 2-5 Recording transactions

The following discussion took place between Tony Cork, the office manager of Hallmark Data Company, and a new accountant, Cassie Miles:

Cassie: I've been thinking about our method of recording entries. It seems that it's inefficient.

Tony: In what way?

Cassie: Well—correct me if I'm wrong—it seems like we have unnecessary steps in the process. We could easily develop a trial balance by posting our transactions directly into the ledger and bypassing the journal altogether. In this way, we could combine the recording and posting process into one step and save ourselves a lot of time. What do you think?

Tony: We need to have a talk.

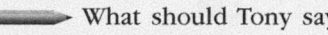 What should Tony say to Cassie?

TEAM ACTIVITY

TIF 2-6 Debits and credits

The following excerpt is from a conversation between Kate Purvis, the president and chief operating officer of Light House Company, and her neighbor, Dot Evers:

Dot: Kate, I'm taking a course in night school, "Intro to Accounting." I was wondering—could you answer a couple of questions for me?

Kate: Well, I will if I can.

Dot: Okay, our instructor says that it's critical we understand the basic concepts of accounting, or we'll never get beyond the first test. My problem is with those rules of debit and credit . . . you know, assets increase with debits, decrease with credits, etc.

Kate: Yes, pretty basic stuff. You just have to memorize the rules. It shouldn't be too difficult.

Dot: Sure, I can memorize the rules, but my problem is I want to be sure I understand the basic concepts behind the rules. For example, why can't assets be increased with credits and decreased with debits like revenue? As long as everyone did it that way, why not? It would seem easier if we had the same rules for all increases and decreases in accounts. Also, why is the left side of an account called the debit side? Why couldn't it be called something simple . . . like the "LE" for Left Entry? The right side could be called just "RE" for Right Entry. Finally, why are there just two sides to an entry? Why can't there be three or four sides to an entry?

In a group of four or five, select one person to play the role of Kate and one person to play the role of Dot.

1. After listening to the conversation between Kate and Dot, help Kate answer Dot's questions.
2. What information (other than just debit and credit journal entries) could the accounting system gather that might be useful to Kate in managing Light House Company?

Pathways Challenge

This is Accounting!

Information/Consequences

If the $10 coupon is issued by **Kroger (KR)**, the sale is recorded as $90. In addition, debit card transactions are considered cash transactions. Thus, the sale with a $10 Kroger discount coupon would be recorded by Kroger as follows:

Cash	90	
Sales		90

If the $10 coupon is issued by **General Mills (GIS)**, Kroger would submit the coupon to General Mills for a $10 reimbursement. Thus, Kroger would have an accounts receivable from General Mills, and Kroger would record the sale as $100, as follows:

Cash	90	
Accounts Receivable	10	
Sales		100

Suggested Answer

3 The Adjusting Process

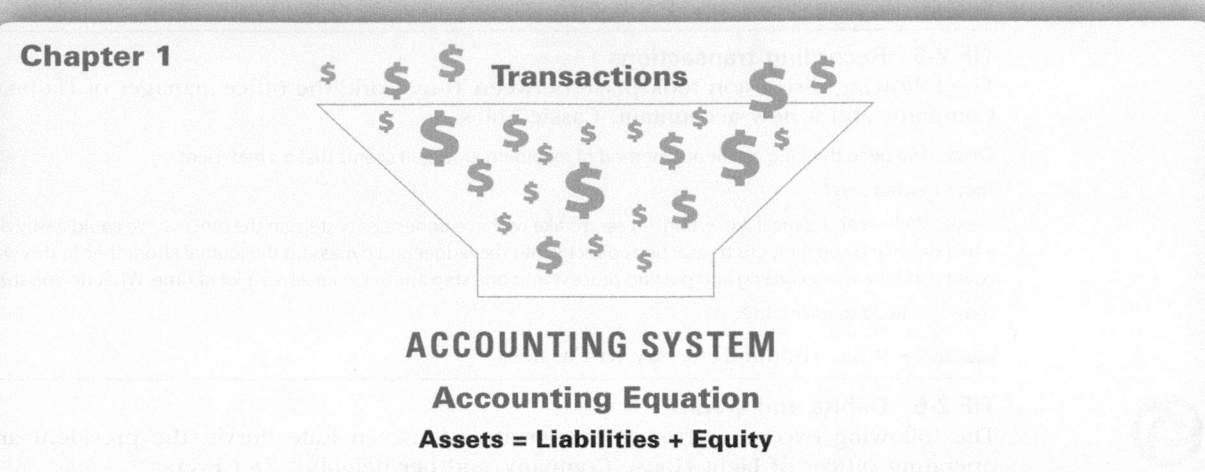

Chapter 1

$ $ $ **Transactions** $ $

ACCOUNTING SYSTEM

Accounting Equation

Assets = Liabilities + Equity

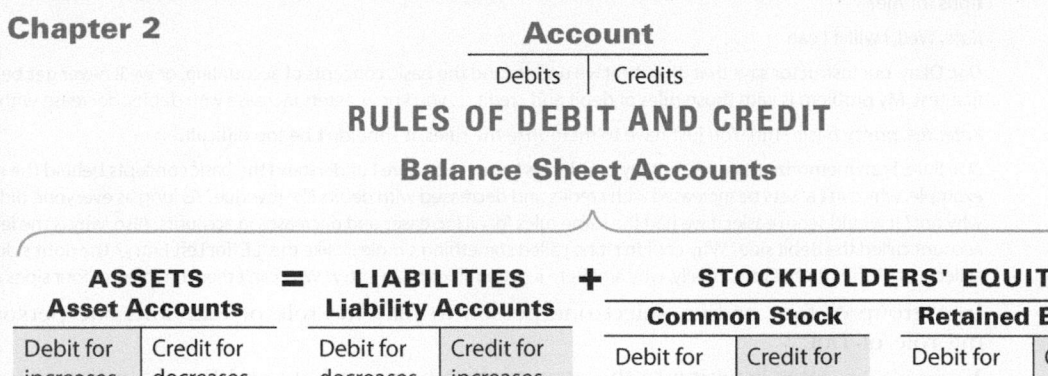

Chapter 2

Account

| Debits | Credits |

RULES OF DEBIT AND CREDIT

Balance Sheet Accounts

| **ASSETS** | **=** | **LIABILITIES** | **+** | **STOCKHOLDERS' EQUITY** |

Asset Accounts

Debit for increases (+)	Credit for decreases (−)
Balance	

Liability Accounts

Debit for decreases (−)	Credit for increases (+)
	Balance

Common Stock

Debit for decreases (−)	Credit for increases (+)
	Balance

Retained Earnings

Debit for decreases (−)	Credit for increases (+)
	Balance

Dividends

Debit for increases (+)	Credit for decreases (−)
Balance	

Income Statement Accounts

Revenue Accounts

Debit for decreases (−)	Credit for increases (+)
	Balance

Expense Accounts

Debit for increases (+)	Credit for decreases (−)
Balance	

UNADJUSTED TRIAL BALANCE

Total Debit Balances = Total Credit Balances

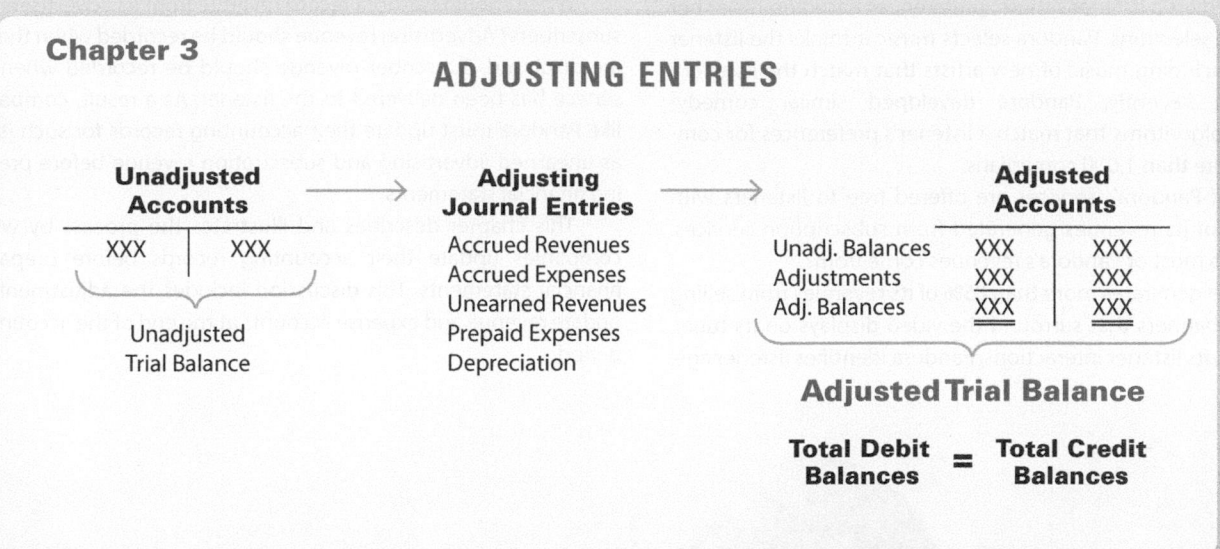

Chapter 3

ADJUSTING ENTRIES

Unadjusted Accounts		Adjusting Journal Entries	Adjusted Accounts		
XXX	XXX	Accrued Revenues	Unadj. Balances	XXX	XXX
		Accrued Expenses	Adjustments	XXX	XXX
Unadjusted Trial Balance		Unearned Revenues	Adj. Balances	XXX	XXX
		Prepaid Expenses			
		Depreciation			

Adjusted Trial Balance

Total Debit Balances = **Total Credit Balances**

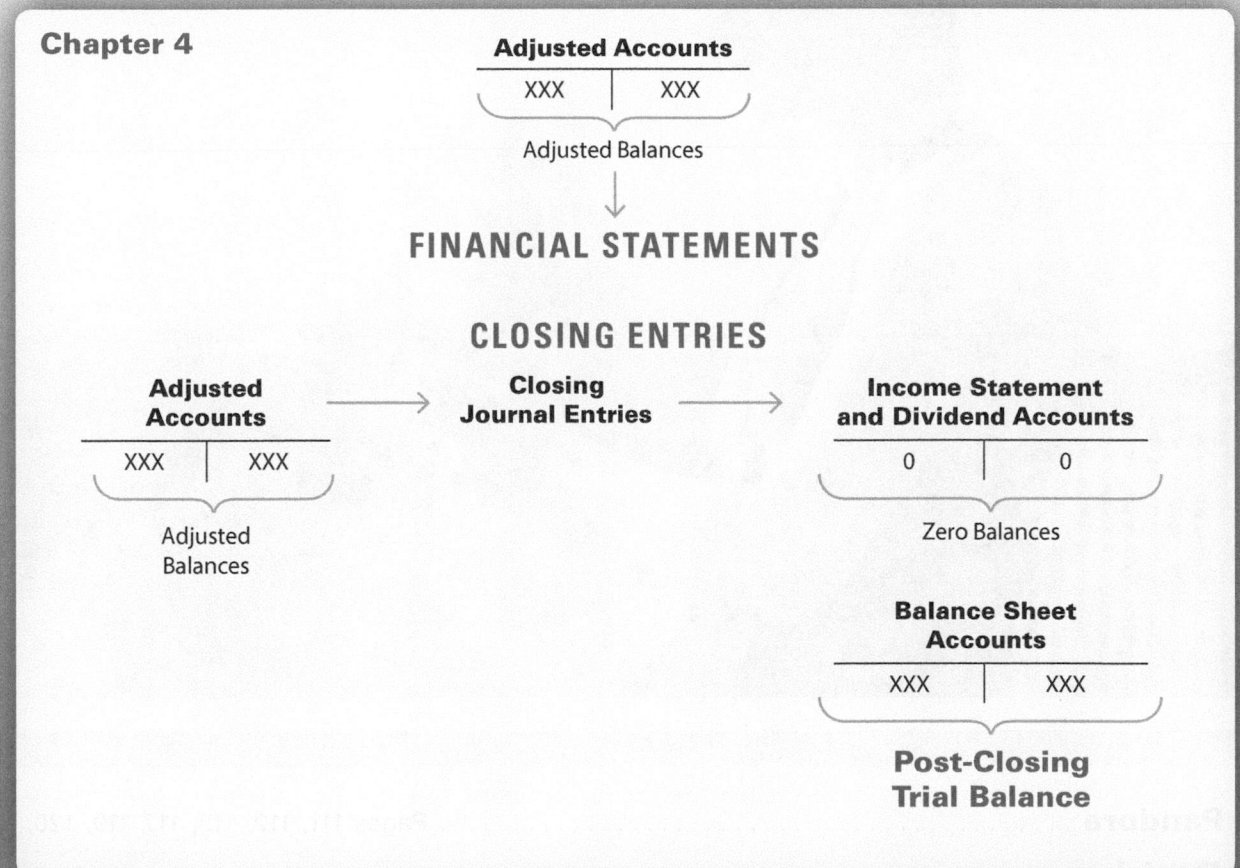

Chapter 4

Adjusted Accounts

XXX	XXX

Adjusted Balances

↓

FINANCIAL STATEMENTS

CLOSING ENTRIES

Adjusted Accounts		Closing Journal Entries	Income Statement and Dividend Accounts	
XXX	XXX		0	0

Adjusted Balances

Zero Balances

Balance Sheet Accounts

XXX	XXX

Post-Closing Trial Balance

Pandora Media, Inc.

Do you use an Internet-based music service such as **Pandora Media, Inc. (P)**? Using playlist-generating algorithms, Pandora predicts a listener's music preferences based on his or her initial music selections. Pandora selects music it thinks the listener will enjoy, including music of new artists that match the listener's preferences. Recently, Pandora developed similar comedy-generating algorithms that match a listener's preferences for comedy with more than 1,000 comedians.

Most of Pandora's services are offered free to listeners with only 12.5% of its revenues generated from subscription services. So, where do most of Pandora's revenues come from?

Pandora generates more than 85% of its revenues from selling advertising banners that surround the video displays on its tuner. By analyzing its listener interactions, Pandora identifies listener age, gender, zip code, and content preferences. These attributes can then be matched with advertiser needs and desires.

When should Pandora record revenue from its advertisers and subscribers? Advertising revenue should be recorded when the ads are displayed. Subscriber revenue should be recorded when the service has been delivered to the listener. As a result, companies like Pandora must update their accounting records for such items as unearned advertising and subscription revenue before preparing financial statements.

This chapter describes and illustrates the process by which companies update their accounting records before preparing financial statements. This discussion includes the adjustments to update revenue and expense accounts at the end of the accounting period.

©JORDAN SIEMENS/ICONICA/GETTY IMAGES

What's Covered

The Adjusting Process

Nature of Adjusting Process	Adjusting Entries for Accruals	Adjusting Entries for Deferrals	Adjusting Entries for Depreciation	Concluding the Adjusting Process
■ Accrual v. Cash Basis (Obj. 1)	■ Accrued Revenues (Obj. 2)	■ Unearned Revenues (Obj. 3)	■ Fixed Assets (Obj. 4)	■ Summary (Obj. 5)
■ Revenue and Expense Recognition (Obj. 1)	■ Accrued Expenses (Obj. 2)	■ Prepaid Expenses (Obj. 3)	■ Accumulated Depreciation (Obj. 4)	■ Adjusted Trial Balance (Obj. 6)
■ Accruals (Obj. 1)			■ Book Value (Obj. 4)	
■ Deferrals (Obj. 1)				

Learning Objectives

Obj. 1 Describe the nature of the adjusting process.

Obj. 2 Prepare adjusting entries for accruals.

Obj. 3 Prepare adjusting entries for deferrals.

Obj. 4 Prepare adjusting entries for depreciation.

Obj. 5 Summarize the adjusting process.

Obj. 6 Prepare an adjusted trial balance.

Analysis for Decision Making

Obj. 7 Describe and illustrate the use of vertical analysis in evaluating a company's performance and financial condition.

Nature of the Adjusting Process

Objective 1
Describe the nature of the adjusting process.

In Chapter 2, the November and December transactions for **NetSolutions** were recorded using the double-entry accounting system. After the transactions were recorded, an unadjusted trial balance was prepared on December 31 verifying that the total debit balances equal the total credit balances. Before financial statements can be prepared, however, some accounts in the unadjusted trial balance must be adjusted. These adjustments are necessary because the transactions for NetSolutions were recorded using the accrual basis of accounting.

Accrual and Cash Basis of Accounting

Under the **accrual basis of accounting**, revenues are reported on the income statement in the period in which a service has been performed or a product has been delivered. Cash may or may not be received from customers during this period. For example, a cleaning company will record revenue after it cleans an office building, even if it is not paid for several weeks. The accrual basis of accounting also requires expenses to be recorded when they are incurred, not necessarily when cash is paid.

Pandora uses the accrual basis of accounting in preparing its financial statements.

Link to Pandora

Although generally accepted accounting principles (GAAP) require the accrual basis of accounting, most individuals and some businesses use the cash basis of accounting. Under the **cash basis of accounting**, revenues and expenses are reported on the income statement in the period in which cash is received or paid. For example, fees are recorded when cash is received from clients; likewise, wages are recorded when cash is paid to employees. The net income (or net loss) is the difference between the cash receipts (revenues) and the cash payments (expenses).

Small service businesses may use the cash basis because they have few receivables and payables. For example, attorneys, physicians, and real estate agents may use the cash basis.

For them, the cash basis provides financial statements similar to those of the accrual basis. For most large businesses, however, the cash basis will not provide accurate financial statements for user needs. For this reason, the accrual basis is required by GAAP and is used in this text.

Revenue and Expense Recognition

To be useful for decision making, financial statements must be provided on a periodic basis. As a result, the economic life of a business is divided into time periods such as a month, quarter of a year, or full year. Under accrual accounting, the net income of a period is reported using revenue and expense recognition principles.

Under the **revenue recognition principle**, revenues are recorded when earned, which is when the services have been performed or products have been delivered to customers.[1] Revenue is normally measured as the assets received, such as cash or accounts receivable.[2]

Link to Pandora   Subscription revenues from **Pandora**'s customers are recorded equally over the subscription periods. For example, a yearly subscription would be recorded equally over 12 months.

Under the **expense recognition principle**, the expenses incurred in generating revenue must be reported in the same period as the related revenue. This is also called the **matching principle**. By matching revenues and expenses, net income or loss for the period is properly reported on the income statement. Adjusting entries are required to properly match revenues and expenses.

Link to Pandora   **Pandora** computes royalty expense paid to an artist for a song that is streamed to listeners based upon the number of times it is played/streamed.

The Adjusting Process

At the end of an accounting period, an unadjusted trial balance is prepared to verify that the total debit balances equal the total credit balances. Many of these account balances are reported in the financial statements without change. For example, the balances of the cash and land accounts are normally the amounts reported on the balance sheet.

Some accounts on the unadjusted trial balance, however, require adjustments for the following reasons:

- Some expenses are not recorded daily. For example, the daily use of supplies would require many entries with small amounts. Also, the amount of supplies on hand on a day-to-day basis is normally not needed.
- Some revenues and expenses are incurred as time passes rather than as separate transactions. For example, rent received in advance (unearned rent) expires and becomes revenue with the passage of time. Likewise, prepaid insurance expires and becomes an expense with the passage of time.
- Some revenues and expenses may be unrecorded at the end of the accounting period. For example, a company may have provided services to customers that it has not billed or recorded at the end of the accounting period. Likewise, a company may not pay its employees until the next accounting period even though the employees have earned their wages in the current period.

The analysis and updating of accounts at the end of the period before the financial statements are prepared is called the **adjusting process**. The journal entries that bring the accounts up to

---

[1] As will be illustrated later in this chapter, revenues may also be measured as a decrease in a liability such as unearned revenue.
[2] As will be illustrated later in this chapter, revenues may also be measured as a decrease in a liability such as unearned revenue.

date at the end of the accounting period are called **adjusting entries**. All adjusting entries affect at least one income statement account and one balance sheet account. Thus, an adjusting entry will always involve a revenue or an expense account *and* an asset or a liability account.

Types of Accounts Requiring Adjustment

The two general classifications of accounts requiring adjustment are as follows:

- Accruals
- Deferrals

Accruals An **accrual** occurs when revenue has been earned or an expense has been incurred but has not been recorded. If the accrual is for revenue, the adjusting entry debits an asset (Accounts Receivable) and credits a revenue account. If the accrual is for an expense, the adjusting entry debits an expense account and credits a related liability account such as Accounts Payable or Wages Payable. Exhibit 1 summarizes the accounting for accruals.

ACCRUED REVENUE			
Initial Recording		**End-of-Period Adjustment**	
Transaction	**Journal Entry**	**Adjustment Data**	**Adjusting Entry***
Revenue has been earned.	No journal entry has been made.	Revenue earned.	Accounts Receivable XXX Revenue XXX
ACCRUED EXPENSE			
Initial Recording		**End-of-Period Adjustment**	
Transaction	**Journal Entry**	**Adjustment Data**	**Adjusting Entry***
Expense has been incurred.	No journal entry has been made.	Expense incurred.	Expense XXX Accounts Payable XXX

Exhibit 1
Accruals

 * An adjusting entry will always involve a revenue or an expense account and an asset or a liability account.

Deferrals A **deferral** occurs when cash related to a future revenue or expense has been initially recorded as a liability or an asset. If the cash received is related to future revenue, it is initially recorded as a liability called **unearned revenue**. The adjusting entry in the period when the revenue is earned debits an unearned revenue account and credits a revenue account. If the cash paid is related to a future expense, it is initially recorded as an asset called **prepaid expense**. The adjusting entry in the period when the expense is incurred debits an expense account and credits a prepaid expense (asset) account. Exhibit 2 summarizes the accounting for deferrals.

UNEARNED REVENUE			
Initial Recording		**End-of-Period Adjustment**	
Transaction	**Journal Entry**	**Adjustment Data**	**Adjusting Entry***
Cash has been received for revenue that will be earned in a future period.	Cash XXX Unearned Revenue XXX	Revenue has been earned.	Unearned Revenue XXX Revenue XXX
PREPAID EXPENSE			
Initial Recording		**End-of-Period Adjustment**	
Transaction	**Journal Entry**	**Adjustment Data**	**Adjusting Entry***
Cash has been paid for a future expense.	Prepaid Expense XXX Cash XXX	Prepaid expense has been used to generate revenue.	Expense XXX Prepaid Expense XXX

Exhibit 2
Deferrals

 * An adjusting entry will always involve a revenue or an expense account and an asset or a liability account.

Objective 2
Prepare adjusting
entries for accruals.

Adjusting Entries for Accruals

To illustrate adjusting entries, the December 31, 20Y3, unadjusted trial balance of **NetSolutions**, shown in Exhibit 3, is used.

Exhibit 3
Unadjusted
Trial Balance for
NetSolutions

		NetSolutions Unadjusted Trial Balance December 31, 20Y3		
		Account No.	Debit Balances	Credit Balances
Cash		11	2,065	
Accounts Receivable		12	2,220	
Supplies		14	2,000	
Prepaid Insurance		15	2,400	
Land		17	20,000	
Office Equipment		18	1,800	
Accounts Payable		21		900
Unearned Rent		23		360
Common Stock		31		25,000
Dividends		33	4,000	
Fees Earned		41		16,340
Wages Expense		51	4,275	
Supplies Expense		52	800	
Rent Expense		53	1,600	
Utilities Expense		54	985	
Miscellaneous Expense		59	455	
			42,600	42,600

An expanded chart of accounts for NetSolutions is shown in Exhibit 4. The additional accounts used in this chapter are highlighted. The rules of debit and credit shown in Exhibit 3 of Chapter 2 are used to record the adjusting entries.

Exhibit 4
Expanded Chart
of Accounts for
NetSolutions

Balance Sheet Accounts

1. Assets
   11 Cash
   12 Accounts Receivable
   14 Supplies
   15 Prepaid Insurance
   17 Land
   18 Office Equipment
   19 Accumulated Depreciation—Office Equipment

2. Liabilities
   21 Accounts Payable
   22 Wages Payable
   23 Unearned Rent

3. Stockholders' Equity
   31 Common Stock
   32 Retained Earnings
   33 Dividends

Income Statement Accounts

4. Revenue
   41 Fees Earned
   42 Rent Revenue

5. Expenses
   51 Wages Expense
   52 Supplies Expense
   53 Rent Expense
   54 Utilities Expense
   55 Insurance Expense
   56 Depreciation Expense
   59 Miscellaneous Expense

Accrued Revenues

During an accounting period, some revenues are recorded only when cash is received. Thus, at the end of an accounting period, there may be revenue that has been earned *but has not been recorded*. In such cases, the revenue is recorded by increasing (debiting) an asset account and increasing (crediting) a revenue account.

To illustrate, assume that **NetSolutions** signed an agreement with Dankner Co. on December 15. The agreement provides that NetSolutions will answer computer questions and render assistance to Dankner Co.'s employees. The services will be billed to Dankner Co. on the fifteenth of each month at a rate of $20 per hour. As of December 31, NetSolutions had provided 25 hours of assistance to Dankner Co. The revenue of $500 (25 hours × $20) will be billed on January 15. However, NetSolutions earned the revenue in December.

The claim against the customer for payment of the $500 is an account receivable (*an asset*). Thus, the accounts receivable account is increased (debited) by $500, and the fees earned account is increased (credited) by $500. The adjusting journal entry and T accounts are as follows:

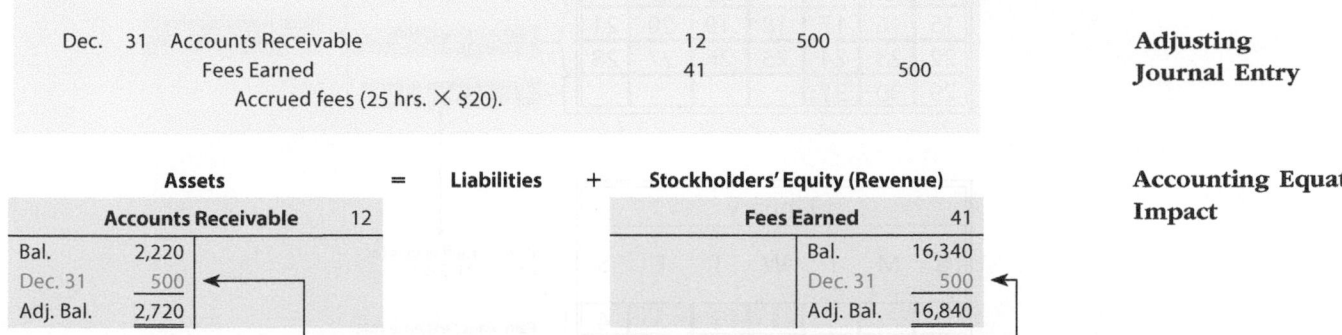

Dec.	31	Accounts Receivable	12	500	
		Fees Earned	41		500
		Accrued fees (25 hrs. × $20).			

Adjusting Journal Entry

Assets	=	**Liabilities**	+	**Stockholders' Equity (Revenue)**

Accounts Receivable 12		**Fees Earned** 41
Bal. 2,220		Bal. 16,340
Dec. 31 500 ←		Dec. 31 500 ←
Adj. Bal. 2,720		Adj. Bal. 16,840

Accounting Equation Impact

The adjusting entry is highlighted in the T accounts to separate it from other transactions. After the adjusting entry is posted, Accounts Receivable has a balance of $2,720 and Fees Earned has a balance of $16,840.

If the adjustment for the accrued revenue ($500) is not recorded, Fees Earned and the net income will be understated by $500 on the income statement. On the balance sheet, assets (Accounts Receivable) and stockholders' equity (Retained Earnings) will be understated by $500. The effects of omitting this adjusting entry are as follows:

	Amount of Misstatement
Income Statement	
Revenues understated by	$ (500)
Expenses correctly stated	XXX
Net income understated by	$ (500)
Balance Sheet	
Assets understated by	$ (500)
Liabilities correctly stated	$ XXX
Stockholders' equity understated by	(500)
Total liabilities and stockholders' equity understated by	$ (500)

Pandora's accrued revenues from advertising are recorded in its accounts receivable at the end of the year.   *Link to Pandora*

Accrued Expenses

Some types of services used in earning revenues are paid for *after* the service has been performed. For example, wages expense is used hour by hour but is paid only daily, weekly, biweekly, or monthly. At the end of the accounting period, the amount of such *accrued* but unpaid items is an expense and a liability.

For example, if the last day of the employees' pay period is not the last day of the accounting period, an accrued expense (wages expense) and the related liability (wages payable) must be recorded by an adjusting entry. This adjusting entry is necessary so that expenses are properly matched to the period in which they were incurred in earning revenue.

To illustrate, **NetSolutions** pays its employees biweekly. During December, NetSolutions paid wages of $950 on December 13 and $1,200 on December 27. These payments covered pay periods ending on those days as shown in Exhibit 5.

Exhibit 5
Accrued Wages

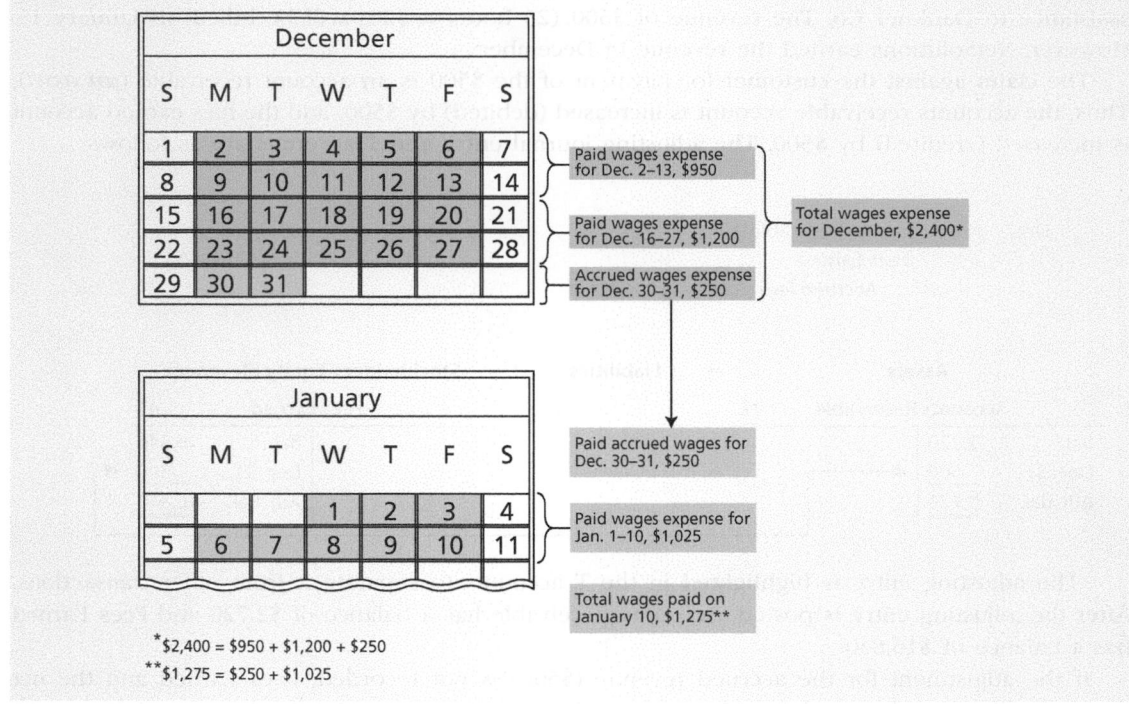

As of December 31, NetSolutions owes $250 of wages to employees for Monday and Tuesday, December 30 and 31. Thus, the wages expense account is increased (debited) by $250, and the wages payable account is increased (credited) by $250. The adjusting journal entry and T accounts are as follows:

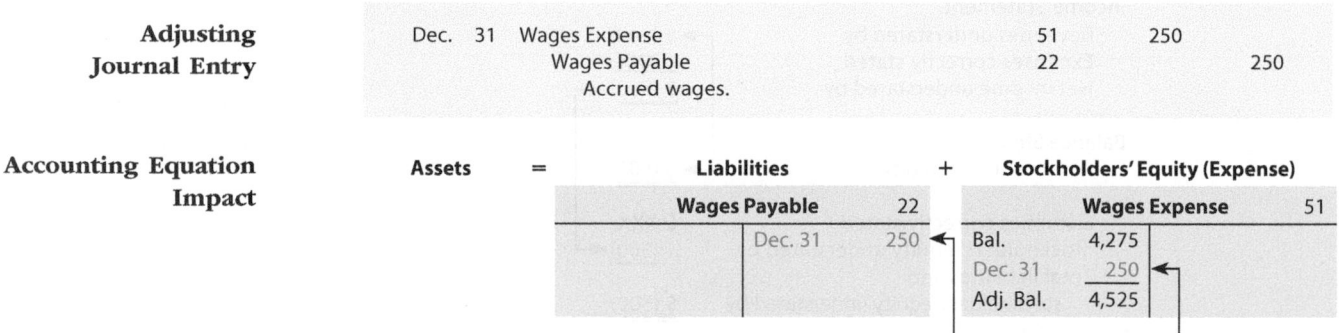

After the adjusting entry is posted, the debit balance of the wages expense account is $4,525. This balance of $4,525 is the wages expense for two months, November and December. The credit balance of $250 in Wages Payable is the liability for wages owed on December 31.

As shown in Exhibit 5, NetSolutions paid wages of $1,275 on January 10. This payment includes the $250 of accrued wages recorded on December 31. Thus, on January 10, the wages payable account is decreased (debited) by $250. Also, the wages expense account is increased (debited) by $1,025 ($1,275 – $250), which is the wages expense for January 1–10. Finally, the cash account is decreased (credited) by $1,275. The journal entry for the payment of wages on January 10 follows:[3]

Jan.	10	Wages Expense	51	1,025	
		Wages Payable	22	250	
		Cash	11		1,275

[3] To simplify the subsequent recording of the following period's transactions, some accountants use what is known as reversing entries for certain types of adjustments. Reversing entries are discussed and illustrated in an appendix to Chapter 4.

If the adjustment for wages ($250) is not recorded, Wages Expense will be understated by $250, and the net income will be overstated by $250 on the income statement. On the balance sheet, liabilities (Wages Payable) will be understated by $250, and stockholders' equity (Retained Earnings) will be overstated by $250. The effects of omitting this adjusting entry are as follows:

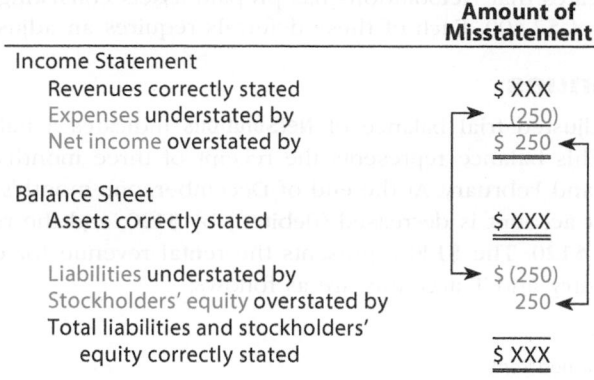

	Amount of Misstatement
Income Statement	
Revenues correctly stated	$ XXX
Expenses understated by	(250)
Net income overstated by	$ 250
Balance Sheet	
Assets correctly stated	$ XXX
Liabilities understated by	$ (250)
Stockholders' equity overstated by	250
Total liabilities and stockholders' equity correctly stated	$ XXX

In a recent balance sheet, **Pandora** reported accrued royalties payable of $94 million, which it pays to owners of the music it plays.   *Link to Pandora*

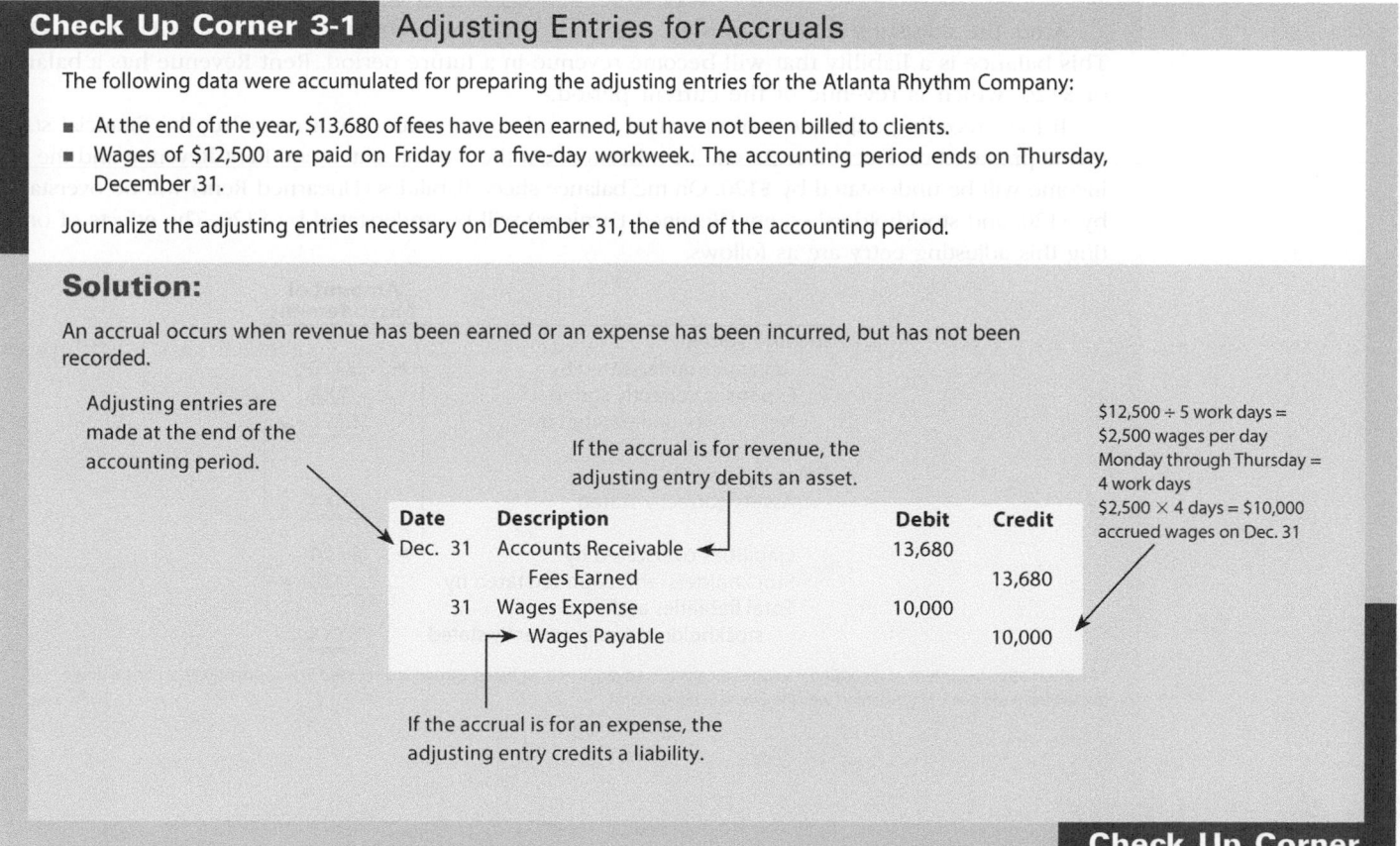

Check Up Corner 3-1 | Adjusting Entries for Accruals

The following data were accumulated for preparing the adjusting entries for the Atlanta Rhythm Company:

- At the end of the year, $13,680 of fees have been earned, but have not been billed to clients.
- Wages of $12,500 are paid on Friday for a five-day workweek. The accounting period ends on Thursday, December 31.

Journalize the adjusting entries necessary on December 31, the end of the accounting period.

Solution:

An accrual occurs when revenue has been earned or an expense has been incurred, but has not been recorded.

Adjusting entries are made at the end of the accounting period.

If the accrual is for revenue, the adjusting entry debits an asset.

$12,500 ÷ 5 work days = $2,500 wages per day
Monday through Thursday = 4 work days
$2,500 × 4 days = $10,000 accrued wages on Dec. 31

Date	Description	Debit	Credit
Dec. 31	Accounts Receivable	13,680	
	Fees Earned		13,680
31	Wages Expense	10,000	
	Wages Payable		10,000

If the accrual is for an expense, the adjusting entry credits a liability.

Check Up Corner

Adjusting Entries for Deferrals

The unadjusted trial balance for **NetSolutions** in Exhibit 3 indicates Unearned Rent of $360. In addition, Exhibit 3 indicates that NetSolutions has prepaid assets consisting of Supplies of $2,000 and Prepaid Insurance of $2,400. Each of these deferrals requires an adjusting entry.

Unearned Revenues

The December 31 unadjusted trial balance of **NetSolutions** indicates a balance in the unearned rent account of $360. This balance represents the receipt of three months' rent on December 1 for December, January, and February. At the end of December, one month's rent has been earned. Thus, the unearned rent account is decreased (debited) by $120, and the rent revenue account is increased (credited) by $120. The $120 represents the rental revenue for one month ($360 ÷ 3). The adjusting journal entry and T accounts are as follows:

Adjusting Journal Entry

Dec.	31	Unearned Rent	23	120	
		Rent Revenue	42		120
		Rent earned ($360 ÷ 3 months).			

Accounting Equation Impact

Assets = Liabilities + Stockholders' Equity (Revenue)

Unearned Rent	23
Dec. 31 120	Bal. 360
	Adj. Bal. 240

Rent Revenue	42
	Dec. 31 120

After the adjusting entry is posted, the unearned rent account has a credit balance of $240. This balance is a liability that will become revenue in a future period. Rent Revenue has a balance of $120, which is revenue of the current period.[4]

If the preceding adjustment of unearned rent and rent revenue is not recorded, the financial statements prepared on December 31 will be misstated. On the income statement, Rent Revenue and the net income will be understated by $120. On the balance sheet, liabilities (Unearned Rent) will be overstated by $120, and stockholders' equity (Retained Earnings) will be understated by $120. The effects of omitting this adjusting entry are as follows:

	Amount of Misstatement
Income Statement	
Revenues understated by	$(120)
Expenses correctly stated	XXX
Net income understated by	$(120)
Balance Sheet	
Assets correctly stated	$XXX
Liabilities overstated by	$ 120
Stockholders' equity understated by	(120)
Total liabilities and	
stockholders' equity correctly stated	$XXX

[4] An alternative treatment of recording revenues received in advance of their being earned is discussed in an appendix that can be downloaded from the book's companion website (www.cengage.com).

Why It Matters

Earning Revenues from Season Tickets

Madison Square Garden Company (MSG) owns the New York Knicks basketball team and the New York Rangers hockey team. The company sells season tickets prior to the season. The amounts received for season tickets are recognized as unearned revenue, a current liability. MSG recognizes revenue and reduces unearned revenue as the games are played through the season.

In a recent balance sheet, **Pandora** reported deferred revenue of $28 million.

Link to Pandora

Prepaid Expenses

The December 31, 20Y3, unadjusted trial balance of **NetSolutions** indicates a balance in the supplies account of $2,000. In addition, the prepaid insurance account has a balance of $2,400. Each of these accounts requires an adjusting entry.

Supplies The balance in NetSolutions' supplies account on December 31 is $2,000. Some of these supplies (paper, envelopes, etc.) were used during December, and some are still on hand (not used). If either amount is known, the other can be determined. It is normally easier to determine the cost of the supplies on hand at the end of the month than to record daily supplies used.

Assuming that on December 31 the amount of supplies on hand is $760, the amount to be transferred from the asset account to the expense account is $1,240, computed as follows:

Supplies available during December (balance of account)	$ 2,000
Supplies on hand, December 31	(760)
Supplies used (amount of adjustment)	$ 1,240

At the end of December, the supplies expense account is increased (debited) for $1,240, and the supplies account is decreased (credited) for $1,240 to record the supplies used during December. The adjusting journal entry and T accounts for Supplies and Supplies Expense are as follows:

Adjusting Journal Entry

	Journal			Page 5	
Date	Description	Post. Ref.	Debit	Credit	
20Y3					
Dec. 31	Supplies Expense	52	1,240		
	Supplies	14		1,240	
	Supplies used ($2,000 − $760).				

Accounting Equation Impact

| Assets | = | Liabilities | + | Stockholders' Equity (Expense) |

Supplies	14			Supplies Expense	52
Bal.	2,000	Dec. 31	1,240	Bal.	800
Adj. Bal.	760			Dec. 31	1,240
				Adj. Bal.	2,040

After the adjusting entry is recorded and posted, the supplies account has a debit balance of $760. This balance is an asset that will become an expense in a future period.

Why It Matters
CONCEPT CLIP

Sports Signing Bonus

The **National Football League (NFL)**, **National Basketball Association (NBA)**, and **National Hockey League (NHL)** all have team salary caps that are used to create parity in the sport league. The salary cap limits the total salaries that a team can pay each year. Teams use signing bonuses as a way to reduce the impact of salaries on the salary cap. Under cap rules, the bonus is spread over the length of the player's contract. For example, if a player receives a $6 million bonus for a six-year contract, the player will receive the complete $6 million upon signing the contract, but only $1 million will be applied to the salary cap for each year of the contract. This is similar to how GAAP also accounts for the bonus. The bonus is treated as a prepaid salary expense that is amortized over the life of the contract. If a player is released prior to the end of the contract, any remaining unamortized balance is expensed immediately.

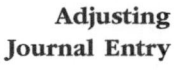

Link to Pandora   In a recent balance sheet, **Pandora** reported prepaid expenses and other current assets of $33 million.

Prepaid Insurance The debit balance of $2,400 in **NetSolutions**' prepaid insurance account represents a December 1 prepayment of insurance for 12 months. At the end of December, the insurance expense account is increased (debited), and the prepaid insurance account is decreased (credited) by $200, the insurance for one month. The adjusting journal entry and T accounts for Prepaid Insurance and Insurance Expense are as follows:

Adjusting Journal Entry

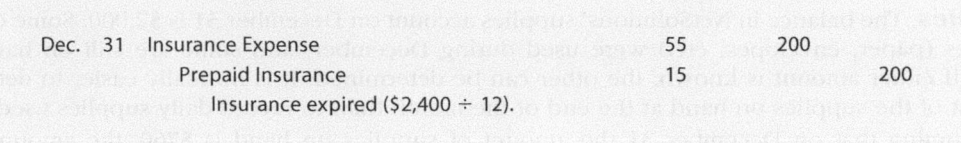

Dec.	31	Insurance Expense	55	200	
		Prepaid Insurance	15		200
		Insurance expired ($2,400 ÷ 12).			

Accounting Equation Impact

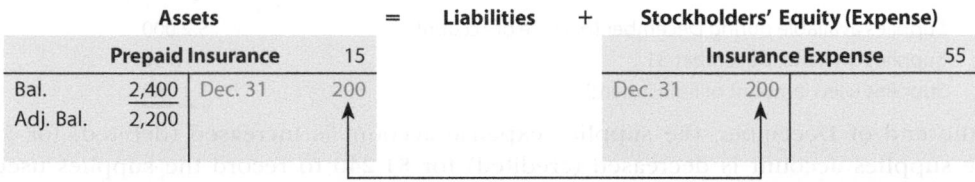

Assets	=	Liabilities	+	Stockholders' Equity (Expense)

	Prepaid Insurance	15		Insurance Expense	55
Bal.	2,400	Dec. 31 200		Dec. 31 200	
Adj. Bal.	2,200				

After the adjusting entry is recorded and posted, the prepaid insurance account has a debit balance of $2,200. This balance is an asset that will become an expense in future periods. The insurance expense account has a debit balance of $200, which is an expense of the current period.

If the preceding adjustments for supplies ($1,240) and insurance ($200) are not recorded, the financial statements prepared as of December 31 will be misstated. On the income statement, Supplies Expense and Insurance Expense will be understated by a total of $1,440 ($1,240 + $200), and net income will be overstated by $1,440. On the balance sheet, Supplies and Prepaid Insurance will be overstated by a total of $1,440. Because net income increases retained earnings, stockholders' equity will also be overstated by $1,440 on the balance sheet. The effects of omitting these adjusting entries on the income statement and balance sheet are as follows:

	Amount of Misstatement
Income Statement	
Revenues correctly stated	$ XXX
Expenses understated by	(1,440)
Net income overstated by	$1,440
Balance Sheet	
Assets overstated by	$1,440
Liabilities correctly stated	$ XXX
Stockholders' equity overstated by	1,440
Total liabilities and	
stockholders' equity overstated by	$1,440

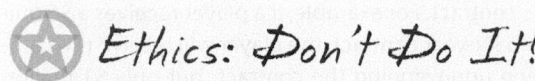

Ethics: Don't Do It!

Free Issue

Office supplies are often available to employees on a "free issue" basis. This means that employees do not have to "sign" for the release of office supplies but merely obtain the necessary supplies from a local storage area as needed. Just because supplies are easily available, however, doesn't mean they can be taken for personal use. There are many instances where employees have been terminated for taking supplies home for personal use.

Payments for prepaid expenses are sometimes made at the beginning of the period in which they will be *entirely used or consumed*. To illustrate, the following December 1 transaction of NetSolutions is used:

> Dec. 1 *NetSolutions paid rent of $800 for the month.*

On December 1, the rent payment of $800 represents Prepaid Rent. However, the Prepaid Rent expires daily, and at the end of December there will be no asset left. In such cases, the payment of $800 is recorded as Rent Expense rather than as Prepaid Rent. In this way, no adjusting entry is needed at the end of the period.[5]

Check Up Corner 3-2 | **Adjusting Entries for Deferrals**

Selected unadjusted account balances for Atlanta Rhythm Company on December 31 are as follows:

	Debit Balances	Credit Balances
Supplies	$ 2,700	
Prepaid Insurance	12,000	
Unearned Fees		$44,900

The following adjustment data were accumulated on December 31:

- Supplies on hand at December 31, $1,100.
- Insurance premiums expired during the year, $10,000.
- Unearned fees on December 31, $15,600.

Journalize the adjusting entries necessary on December 31.

Solution:

A deferral occurs when cash has been received for a future revenue, or cash has been paid for a future expense.

Adjusting entries are made at the end of the accounting period.

If the deferral is for an expense, the adjusting entry credits an asset.

Date	Description	Debit	Credit
Dec. 31	Supplies Expense	1,600	
	Supplies		1,600
31	Insurance Expense	10,000	
	Prepaid Insurance		10,000
31	Unearned Fees	29,300	
	Fees Earned		29,300

$2,700 unadjusted supplies balance − $1,100 supplies on hand at year-end.

If the deferral is for a revenue, the adjusting entry debits a liability.

$44,900 unadjusted unearned fees balance − $15,600 unearned fees at year-end.

Check Up Corner

---

[5] An alternative treatment of recording the cost of supplies, rent, and other prepayments of expenses is discussed in an appendix that can be downloaded from the book's companion website (www.cengage.com).

Objective 4
Prepare adjusting entries for depreciation.

Adjusting Entries for Depreciation

Fixed assets, or **plant assets**, are physical resources that are owned and used by a business and are permanent or have a long life. Examples of fixed assets include land, buildings, and equipment. In a sense, fixed assets are a type of *long-term* prepaid expense. However, because of their unique nature and long life, they are discussed separately from other prepaid expenses.

Fixed assets, such as office equipment, are used to generate revenue much like supplies are used to generate revenue. Unlike supplies, however, there is no visible reduction in the quantity of the equipment. Instead, as time passes, the equipment loses its ability to provide useful services. This decrease in usefulness is called **depreciation**.

All fixed assets, except land, lose their usefulness and, thus, are said to **depreciate**. As a fixed asset depreciates, a portion of its cost should be recorded as an expense. This periodic expense is called **depreciation expense**.

The adjusting entry to record depreciation expense is similar to the adjusting entry for supplies used. The depreciation expense account is increased (debited) for the amount of depreciation. However, the fixed asset account is not decreased (credited). This is because both the original cost of a fixed asset and the depreciation recorded since its purchase are reported on the balance sheet. Instead, an account entitled **Accumulated Depreciation** is increased (credited).

Accumulated depreciation accounts are called **contra accounts**, or **contra asset accounts**. This is because accumulated depreciation accounts are deducted from their related fixed asset accounts on the balance sheet. The normal balance of a contra account is opposite to the account from which it is deducted. Because the normal balance of a fixed asset account is a debit, the normal balance of an accumulated depreciation account is a credit.

The normal titles for fixed asset accounts and their related contra asset accounts are as follows:

Fixed Asset Account	Contra Asset Account
Land	None—Land is not depreciated.
Buildings	Accumulated Depreciation—Buildings
Store Equipment	Accumulated Depreciation—Store Equipment
Office Equipment	Accumulated Depreciation—Office Equipment

The December 31, 20Y3, unadjusted trial balance of **NetSolutions** (Exhibit 3) indicates that NetSolutions owns two fixed assets: land and office equipment. Land does not depreciate; however, an adjusting entry is recorded for the depreciation of the office equipment for December. Assume that the office equipment depreciates $50 during December. The depreciation expense account is increased (debited) by $50, and the accumulated depreciation—office equipment account is increased (credited) by $50.[6] The adjusting journal entry and T accounts are as follows:

Adjusting Journal Entry

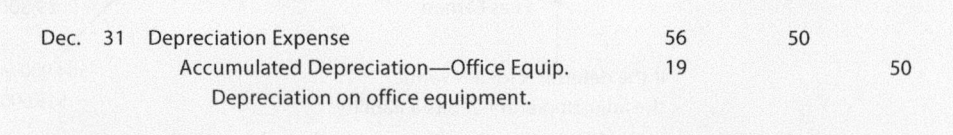

Dec.	31	Depreciation Expense		56	50
		Accumulated Depreciation—Office Equip.		19	50
		Depreciation on office equipment.			

Accounting Equation Impact

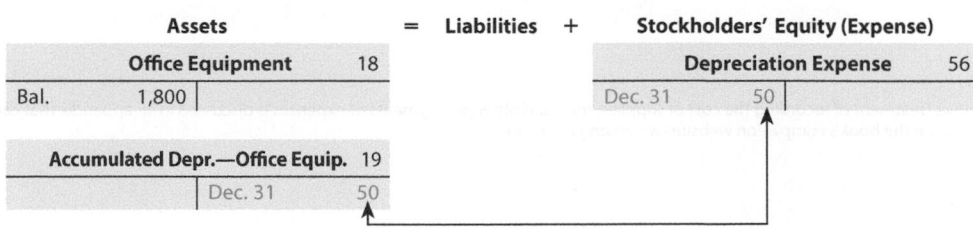

Assets	= Liabilities +	Stockholders' Equity (Expense)
Office Equipment 18		**Depreciation Expense** 56
Bal. 1,800		Dec. 31 50

Accumulated Depr.—Office Equip. 19
Dec. 31 50

---

[6] Methods of computing depreciation expense are described and illustrated in Chapter 9.

After the adjusting journal entry is recorded and posted, the office equipment account still has a debit balance of $1,800. This is the original cost of the office equipment that was purchased on December 4. The accumulated depreciation—office equipment account has a credit balance of $50. The difference between these two balances is the cost of the office equipment that has not yet been depreciated. This amount, called the **book value of the asset** (or **net book value**), is computed as follows:

Book Value of Asset   = Cost of Asset – Accumulated Depreciation of Asset

Book Value of Office Equipment = Cost of Office Equipment – Accumulated Depr. of Office Equipment
= $1,800 – $50
= $1,750

The office equipment and its related accumulated depreciation are reported on the December 31, 20Y3, balance sheet as follows:

Office equipment	$1,800	
Accumulated depreciation	(50)	$1,750

In a recent balance sheet, **Pandora** reported property, plant, and equipment of $213 million, accumulated depreciation of $89 million, and a net book value of $124 million.

Link to Pandora

The market value of a fixed asset usually differs from its book value. This is because depreciation is an *allocation* method, not a *valuation* method. That is, depreciation allocates the cost of a fixed asset to expense over its estimated life. Depreciation does not measure changes in market values, which vary from year to year. Thus, on December 31, 20Y3, the market value of NetSolutions' office equipment could be more or less than $1,750.

If the adjustment for depreciation ($50) is not recorded, Depreciation Expense on the income statement will be understated by $50, and the net income will be overstated by $50. On the balance sheet, assets (the book value of Office Equipment) and stockholders' equity (Retained Earnings) will be overstated by $50. The effects of omitting the adjustment for depreciation are as follows:

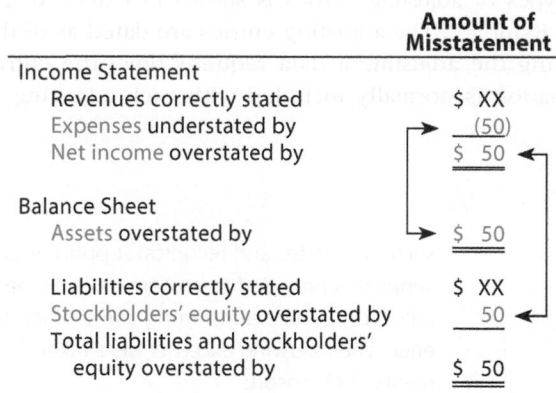

	Amount of Misstatement
Income Statement	
Revenues correctly stated	$ XX
Expenses understated by	(50)
Net income overstated by	$ 50
Balance Sheet	
Assets overstated by	$ 50
Liabilities correctly stated	$ XX
Stockholders' equity overstated by	50
Total liabilities and stockholders' equity overstated by	$ 50

Check Up Corner 3-3 Depreciation

Selected account balances for Atlanta Rhythm Company on December 31 are as follows:

	Debit Balances	Credit Balances
Equipment	$40,000	
Accumulated Depreciation—Equipment		$12,000

Depreciation on equipment during the year is $4,000.

a. Journalize the adjusting entry necessary for depreciation on December 31.
b. Compute the book value of the equipment that will be reported on the balance sheet.

Solution:

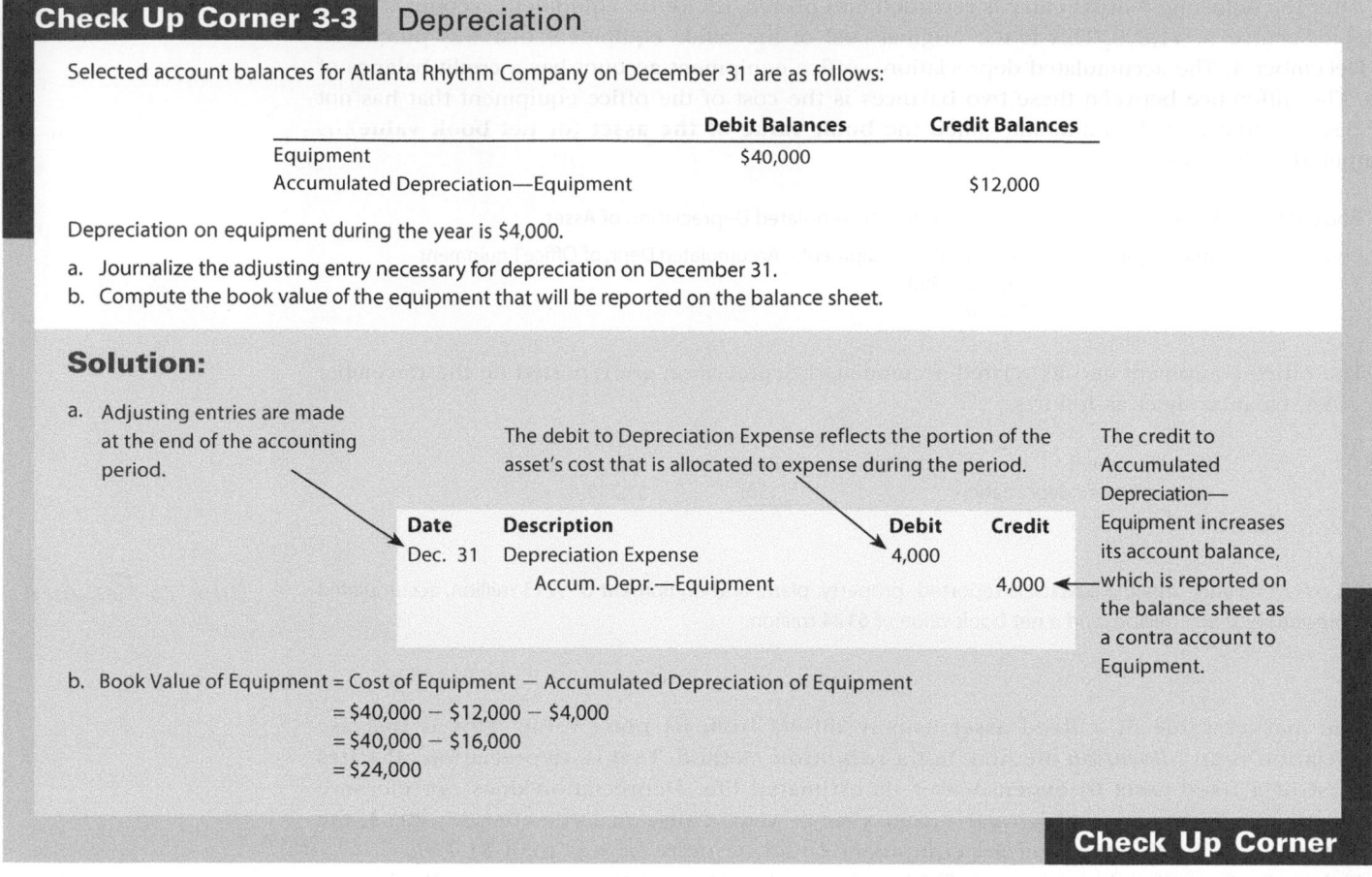

a. Adjusting entries are made at the end of the accounting period.

The debit to Depreciation Expense reflects the portion of the asset's cost that is allocated to expense during the period.

The credit to Accumulated Depreciation—Equipment increases its account balance, which is reported on the balance sheet as a contra account to Equipment.

Date	Description	Debit	Credit
Dec. 31	Depreciation Expense	4,000	
	Accum. Depr.—Equipment		4,000

b. Book Value of Equipment = Cost of Equipment − Accumulated Depreciation of Equipment
= $40,000 − $12,000 − $4,000
= $40,000 − $16,000
= $24,000

Check Up Corner

Objective 5
Summarize the adjusting process.

Summary of Adjusting Process

A summary of the basic types of adjusting entries is shown in Exhibit 6. The adjusting entries for **NetSolutions** are shown in Exhibit 7. The adjusting entries are dated as of the last day of the period. However, because collecting the adjustment data requires time, the entries are usually recorded at a later date. An explanation is normally included with each adjusting entry.

Why It Matters

Microsoft's Deferred Revenues

Microsoft Corporation (MSFT) develops, manufactures, licenses, and supports a wide range of computer software products, including Windows® operating systems, Word®, Excel®, and the Xbox® gaming system. When Microsoft sells its products, it incurs an obligation to support its software with technical support and periodic updates. As a result, not all the revenue is earned on the date of sale; some of the revenue on the date of sale is unearned. The portion of revenue related to support services, such as updates and technical support, is earned as time passes and support is provided to customers. Thus, each year Microsoft makes adjusting entries transferring some of its unearned revenue to revenue. The following excerpts were taken from recent financial statements of Microsoft:

	Year 2	Year 1
Unearned revenue (in millions)	$33,909	$25,318

The Year 2 balance is equal to 40% of Year 2 revenues, indicating the significant impact of unearned revenue to Microsoft's operating results. During Year 3, Microsoft expects to recognize $27,468 of revenue from the $33,909 of unearned revenue. At the same time, Microsoft will record additional unearned revenue from Year 3 sales.

Exhibit 6 Summary of Adjustments

			ACCRUED REVENUES			
Examples	**Reason for Adjustment**	**Adjusting Entry**		**Examples from NetSolutions**	**Financial Statement Impact if Adjusting Entry Is Omitted**	
Services performed but not billed, interest to be received	Services have been provided to the customer, but have not been billed or recorded. Interest has been earned, but has not been received or recorded.	Asset Dr. Revenue Cr.		Accounts Receivable 500 Fees Earned 500	Income Statement: Revenues Expenses Net income Balance Sheet: Assets Liabilities Stockholders' equity (Retained earnings)	Understated No effect Understated Understated No effect Understated

			ACCRUED EXPENSES			
Wages or salaries incurred but not paid, interest incurred but not paid	Expenses have been incurred, but have not been paid or recorded.	Expense Dr. Liability Cr.		Wages Expense 250 Wages Payable 250	Income Statement: Revenues Expenses Net income Balance Sheet: Assets Liabilities Stockholders' equity (Retained earnings)	No effect Understated Overstated No effect Understated Overstated

			UNEARNED REVENUES			
Unearned rent, magazine subscriptions received in advance, fees received in advance of services	Cash received before the services have been provided is recorded as a liability. Some services have been provided to the customer before the end of the accounting period.	Liability Dr. Revenue Cr.		Unearned Rent 120 Rent Revenue 120	Income Statement: Revenues Expenses Net income Balance Sheet: Assets Liabilities Stockholders' equity (Retained earnings)	Understated No effect Understated No effect Overstated Understated

			PREPAID EXPENSES			
Supplies, prepaid insurance	Prepaid expenses (assets) have been used or consumed in the business operations.	Expense Dr. Asset Cr.		Supplies Expense 1,240 Supplies 1,240 Insurance Expense 200 Prepaid Insurance 200	Income Statement: Revenues Expenses Net income Balance Sheet: Assets Liabilities Stockholders' equity (Retained earnings)	No effect Understated Overstated Overstated No effect Overstated

			DEPRECIATION			
Depreciation of equipment and buildings	Fixed assets depreciate as they are used or consumed in the business operations.	Expense Dr. Contra Asset Cr.		Depreciation Expense 50 Accum. Depreciation— Office Equipment 50	Income Statement: Revenues Expenses Net income Balance Sheet: Assets Liabilities Stockholders' equity (Retained earnings)	No effect Understated Overstated Overstated No effect Overstated

Exhibit 7
Adjusting Entries—
NetSolutions

		Journal			Page 5
Date		Description	Post. Ref.	Debit	Credit
		Adjusting Entries			
20Y3					
Dec. 31	Accounts Receivable		12	500	
	Fees Earned		41		500
		Accrued fees (25 hrs. × $20).			
31	Wages Expense		51	250	
	Wages Payable		22		250
		Accrued wages.			
31	Unearned Rent		23	120	
	Rent Revenue		42		120
		Rent earned ($360 ÷ 3 months).			
31	Supplies Expense		52	1,240	
	Supplies		14		1,240
		Supplies used ($2,000 – $760).			
31	Insurance Expense		55	200	
	Prepaid Insurance		15		200
		Insurance expired ($2,400 ÷ 12 months).			
31	Depreciation Expense		56	50	
	Accum. Depreciation—Office Equipment		19		50
		Depreciation on office equipment.			

NetSolutions' adjusting entries are posted to the ledger shown in Exhibit 8. The adjustments are highlighted in Exhibit 8 to distinguish them from other transactions.

Exhibit 8 Ledger with Adjusting Entries—NetSolutions

Account Cash — Account No. 11

Date	Item	Post. Ref.	Debit	Credit	Balance Debit	Balance Credit
20Y3						
Nov. 1		1	25,000		25,000	
5		1		20,000	5,000	
18		1	7,500		12,500	
30		1		3,650	8,850	
30		1		950	7,900	
30		2		2,000	5,900	
Dec. 1		2		2,400	3,500	
1		2		800	2,700	
1		2	360		3,060	
6		2		180	2,880	
11		2		400	2,480	
13		3		950	1,530	
16		3	3,100		4,630	
20		3		900	3,730	
21		3	650		4,380	
23		3		1,450	2,930	
27		3		1,200	1,730	
31		3		310	1,420	
31		4		225	1,195	
31		4	2,870		4,065	
31		4		2,000	2,065	

Account Accounts Receivable — Account No. 12

Date	Item	Post. Ref.	Debit	Credit	Balance Debit	Balance Credit
20Y3						
Dec. 16		3	1,750		1,750	
21		3		650	1,100	
31		4	1,120		2,220	
31	Adjusting	5	500		2,720	

Account Supplies — Account No. 14

Date	Item	Post. Ref.	Debit	Credit	Balance Debit	Balance Credit
20Y3						
Nov. 10		1	1,350		1,350	
30		1		800	550	
Dec. 23		3	1,450		2,000	
31	Adjusting	5		1,240	760	

Exhibit 8 Ledger with Adjusting Entries—NetSolutions *(Continued)*

Account *Prepaid Insurance* — Account No. *15*

Date	Item	Post. Ref.	Debit	Credit	Balance Debit	Balance Credit
20Y3						
Dec. 1		2	2,400		2,400	
31	Adjusting	5		200	2,200	

Account *Land* — Account No. *17*

Date	Item	Post. Ref.	Debit	Credit	Balance Debit	Balance Credit
20Y3						
Nov. 5		1	20,000		20,000	

Account *Office Equipment* — Account No. *18*

Date	Item	Post. Ref.	Debit	Credit	Balance Debit	Balance Credit
20Y3						
Dec. 4		2	1,800		1,800	

Account *Accum. Depr.—Office Equip.* — Account No. *19*

Date	Item	Post. Ref.	Debit	Credit	Balance Debit	Balance Credit
20Y3						
Dec. 31	Adjusting	5		50		50

Account *Accounts Payable* — Account No. *21*

Date	Item	Post. Ref.	Debit	Credit	Balance Debit	Balance Credit
20Y3						
Nov. 10		1		1,350		1,350
30		1	950			400
Dec. 4		2		1,800		2,200
11		2	400			1,800
20		3	900			900

Account *Wages Payable* — Account No. *22*

Date	Item	Post. Ref.	Debit	Credit	Balance Debit	Balance Credit
20Y3						
Dec. 31	Adjusting	5		250		250

Account *Unearned Rent* — Account No. *23*

Date	Item	Post. Ref.	Debit	Credit	Balance Debit	Balance Credit
20Y3						
Dec. 1		2		360		360
31	Adjusting	5	120			240

Account *Common Stock* — Account No. *31*

Date	Item	Post. Ref.	Debit	Credit	Balance Debit	Balance Credit
20Y3						
Nov. 1		1		25,000		25,000

Account *Dividends* — Account No. *33*

Date	Item	Post. Ref.	Debit	Credit	Balance Debit	Balance Credit
20Y3						
Nov. 30		2	2,000		2,000	
Dec. 31		4	2,000		4,000	

Account *Fees Earned* — Account No. *41*

Date	Item	Post. Ref.	Debit	Credit	Balance Debit	Balance Credit
20Y3						
Nov. 18		1		7,500		7,500
Dec. 16		3		3,100		10,600
16		3		1,750		12,350
31		4		2,870		15,220
31		4		1,120		16,340
31	Adjusting	5		500		16,840

Account *Rent Revenue* — Account No. *42*

Date	Item	Post. Ref.	Debit	Credit	Balance Debit	Balance Credit
20Y3						
Dec. 31	Adjusting	5		120		120

Account *Wages Expense* — Account No. *51*

Date	Item	Post. Ref.	Debit	Credit	Balance Debit	Balance Credit
20Y3						
Nov. 30		1	2,125		2,125	
Dec. 13		3	950		3,075	
27		3	1,200		4,275	
31	Adjusting	5	250		4,525	

(Continued)

Exhibit 8   Ledger with Adjusting Entries—NetSolutions *(Concluded)*

Account Supplies Expense					Account No. 52	
		Post.			**Balance**	
Date	**Item**	**Ref.**	**Debit**	**Credit**	**Debit**	**Credit**
20Y3						
Nov. 30		1	800		800	
Dec. 31	Adjusting	5	1,240		2,040	

Account Rent Expense					Account No. 53	
		Post.			**Balance**	
Date	**Item**	**Ref.**	**Debit**	**Credit**	**Debit**	**Credit**
20Y3						
Nov. 30		1	800		800	
Dec. 1		2	800		1,600	

Account Utilities Expense					Account No. 54	
		Post.			**Balance**	
Date	**Item**	**Ref.**	**Debit**	**Credit**	**Debit**	**Credit**
20Y3						
Nov. 30		1	450		450	
Dec. 31		3	310		760	
31		4	225		985	

Account Insurance Expense					Account No. 55	
		Post.			**Balance**	
Date	**Item**	**Ref.**	**Debit**	**Credit**	**Debit**	**Credit**
20Y3						
Dec. 31	Adjusting	5	200		200	

Account Depreciation Expense					Account No. 56	
		Post.			**Balance**	
Date	**Item**	**Ref.**	**Debit**	**Credit**	**Debit**	**Credit**
20Y3						
Dec. 31	Adjusting	5	50		50	

Account Miscellaneous Expense					Account No. 59	
		Post.			**Balance**	
Date	**Item**	**Ref.**	**Debit**	**Credit**	**Debit**	**Credit**
20Y3						
Nov. 30		1	275		275	
Dec. 6		2	180		455	

Objective 6

Prepare an adjusted trial balance.

Adjusted Trial Balance

After the adjusting entries are posted, an **adjusted trial balance** is prepared. The adjusted trial balance verifies the equality of the total debit and credit balances before the financial statements are prepared. If the adjusted trial balance does not balance, an error has occurred. However, as discussed in Chapter 2, errors may occur even though the adjusted trial balance totals agree. For example, if an adjusting entry were omitted, the adjusted trial balance totals would still agree.

Exhibit 9 shows the adjusted trial balance for **NetSolutions** as of December 31, 20Y3. Chapter 4 discusses how financial statements, including a classified balance sheet, are prepared from an adjusted trial balance.

Pathways Challenge

This is Accounting!

Economic Activity

Delta Air Lines (DAL) offers air transportation service to 323 destinations in 57 countries and serves more than 180 million passengers each year. In an effort to retain and increase passenger loyalty, Delta encourages its passengers to join its SkyMiles (frequent flyer) program. Passengers earn mileage credits for award travel as well as earn "elite" status that includes early boarding and free checked baggage. SkyMiles credits never expire.

Assume that during December 20Y6 you flew on Delta Air Lines using a ticket you purchased for $1,000 that earned 2,000 mileage credits that you plan to use in 20Y7.

Critical Thinking/Judgment

Should Delta record $1,000 as revenue for 20Y6?

How should Delta account for the 2,000 mileage credits?

Can you think of an adjusting entry related to the 2,000 mileage credits for the year ending December 31, 20Y6, that Delta might have to record?

Suggested answer at end of chapter.

NetSolutions Adjusted Trial Balance December 31, 20Y3	Account No.	Debit Balances	Credit Balances
Cash	11	2,065	
Accounts Receivable...................................	12	2,720	
Supplies..	14	760	
Prepaid Insurance	15	2,200	
Land	17	20,000	
Office Equipment	18	1,800	
Accumulated Depreciation—Office Equipment..............	19		50
Accounts Payable	21		900
Wages Payable..	22		250
Unearned Rent...	23		240
Common Stock	31		25,000
Dividends	33	4,000	
Fees Earned..	41		16,840
Rent Revenue	42		120
Wages Expense	51	4,525	
Supplies Expense..	52	2,040	
Rent Expense	53	1,600	
Utilities Expense	54	985	
Insurance Expense	55	200	
Depreciation Expense	56	50	
Miscellaneous Expense	59	455	
		43,400	43,400

Exhibit 9
Adjusted Trial Balance

Analysis for Decision Making

Vertical Analysis

Comparing each item on a financial statement with a total amount from the same statement is useful in analyzing relationships within the financial statement. **Vertical analysis** is the term used to describe such comparisons.

In vertical analysis of a balance sheet, each asset item is stated as a percent of the total assets. Each liability and stockholders' equity item is stated as a percent of total liabilities and stockholders' equity. In vertical analysis of an income statement, each item is stated as a percent of revenues or fees earned.

Vertical analysis is also useful for analyzing changes in financial statements over time. To illustrate, a vertical analysis of two years of income statements for J. Holmes, Attorney-at-Law, follows:

Objective 7
Describe and illustrate the use of vertical analysis in evaluating a company's performance and financial condition.

J. Holmes, Attorney-at-Law Income Statements For the Years Ended December 31	20Y7		20Y6	
	Amount	Percent*	Amount	Percent*
Fees earned	$ 187,500	100.0%	$ 150,000	100.0%
Expenses:				
Wages expense...........................	$ (60,000)	(32.0)%	$ (45,000)	(30.0)%
Rent expense	(15,000)	(8.0)%	(12,000)	(8.0)%
Utilities expense	(12,500)	(6.7)%	(9,000)	(6.0)%
Supplies expense	(2,700)	(1.4)%	(3,000)	(2.0)%
Miscellaneous expense	(2,300)	(1.2)%	(1,800)	(1.2)%
Total expenses........................	$ (92,500)	(49.3)%	$ (70,800)	(47.2)%
Net income.................................	$ 95,000	50.7%	$ 79,200	52.8%

*Rounded to one decimal place

The preceding vertical analysis indicates both favorable and unfavorable changes affecting the income statement of J. Holmes, Attorney-at-Law. The increase in wages expense of 2% (32.0% − 30.0%) is an unfavorable change, as is the increase in utilities expense of 0.7% (6.7% − 6.0%). A favorable change is the decrease in supplies expense of 0.6% (2.0% − 1.4%). Rent expense and miscellaneous expense as a percent of fees earned were constant. The net result of these changes is that net income decreased as a percent of fees earned from 52.8% to 50.7%.

The analysis of the various percentages shown for J. Holmes, Attorney-at-Law, can be enhanced by comparisons with industry averages. Such averages are published by trade associations and financial information services. Any major differences between industry averages should be investigated.

Make a Decision

Vertical Analysis

Analyze Amazon.com (MAD 3-1)
(Continuing company analysis)

Analyze Pandora Media (MAD 3-2)

Analyze World Wrestling Entertainment (MAD 3-3)

Analyze Chipotle Mexican Grill (MAD 3-4)

Analyze Nike (MAD 3-5)

Analyze and compare AT&T and Verizon Communications (MAD 3-6)

Make a Decision

Let's Review

Chapter Summary

1. The accrual basis of accounting requires that revenues are reported in the period in which they are earned and expenses are matched with the revenues they generate. The updating of accounts at the end of the accounting period is called the adjusting process. Each adjusting entry affects an income statement and balance sheet account. The two general classifications for accounts requiring adjustment are accruals and deferrals. Accruals include accrued revenues and accrued expenses. Deferrals include unearned revenues and prepaid expenses.

2. Adjusting entries for accruals include accrued revenues and expenses. The adjusting entry for an accrued revenue debits Accounts Receivable and credits a revenue account such as Fees Earned. The adjusting entry for an accrued expense debits an expense account such as Wages Expense and credits a liability account such as Wages Payable.

3. Adjusting entries for deferrals include unearned revenues and prepaid expenses. The adjusting entry for an unearned revenue debits an unearned revenue account such as Unearned Rent and credits a revenue account such as Rent Revenue. The adjusting entry for an accrued expense debits an expense account such as Wages Expense and credits a liability account such as Wages Payable.

4. The adjusting entry for depreciation of a fixed asset debits Depreciation Expense and credits a contra asset account, Accumulated Depreciation. The book value of a fixed asset equals its cost less its accumulated depreciation. Land is a fixed asset that does not depreciate.

5. A summary of adjustments, including the type of adjustment, reason for the adjustment, the adjusting entry, and the effect of omitting an adjustment on the financial statements, is shown in Exhibit 6.

6. After all of the adjusting entries have been posted, the equality of the total debit balances and the total credit balances is verified by an adjusted trial balance.

7. Vertical analysis compares each item on a financial statement with a total amount from the same statement. It

is useful in analyzing relationships within the financial statement. In vertical analysis of a balance sheet, each asset item is stated as a percent of the total assets. Each liability and stockholders' equity item is stated as a percent of total liabilities and stockholders' equity. In vertical analysis of an income statement, each item is stated as a percent of total revenues or fees earned.

Key Terms

accrual (113)
accrual basis of accounting (111)
Accumulated Depreciation (122)
adjusted trial balance (128)
adjusting entries (113)
adjusting process (112)
book value of the asset
　(or net book value) (123)

cash basis of accounting (111)
contra accounts (or contra
　asset accounts) (122)
deferral (113)
depreciate (122)
depreciation (122)
depreciation expense (122)
expense recognition principle (112)

fixed assets (or plant assets) (122)
matching principle (112)
prepaid expense (113)
revenue recognition principle (112)
unearned revenue (113)
vertical analysis (129)

Practice

Multiple-Choice Questions

1. Which of the following items represents a deferral?
   a. Prepaid insurance
   b. Wages payable
   c. Fees earned
   d. Accumulated depreciation

2. The balance in the unearned rent account for Jones Co. as of December 31 is $1,200. If Jones Co. failed to record the adjusting entry for $600 of rent earned during December, the effect on the balance sheet and income statement for December would be:
   a. assets understated $600; net income overstated $600.
   b. liabilities understated $600; net income understated $600.
   c. liabilities overstated $600; net income understated $600.
   d. liabilities overstated $600; net income overstated $600.

3. If the supplies account, before adjustment on May 31, indicated a balance of $2,250, and supplies on hand at May 31 totaled $950, the adjusting entry would be:
   a. debit Supplies, $950; credit Supplies Expense, $950.
   b. debit Supplies, $1,300; credit Supplies Expense, $1,300.
   c. debit Supplies Expense, $950; credit Supplies, $950.
   d. debit Supplies Expense, $1,300; credit Supplies, $1,300.

4. If the estimated amount of depreciation on equipment for a period is $2,000, the adjusting entry to record depreciation would be:
   a. debit Depreciation Expense, $2,000; credit Equipment, $2,000.
   b. debit Equipment, $2,000; credit Depreciation Expense, $2,000.
   c. debit Depreciation Expense, $2,000; credit Accumulated Depreciation, $2,000.
   d. debit Accumulated Depreciation, $2,000; credit Depreciation Expense, $2,000.

5. If the adjusting entry for accrued wages of $7,500 was omitted, the adjusted trial balance totals would be:

a. unequal, the debit total would exceed the credit total by $7,500.

b. unequal, the debit total would exceed the credit total by $15,000.

c. unequal, the credit total would exceed the credit total by $7,500.

d. equal, assuming no other errors or omissions.

Answers provided after Problem. Need more practice? Find additional multiple-choice questions, exercises, and problems in CengageNOWv2.

Exercises

---

1. Accounts requiring adjustment   Obj. 1, 2, 3
Indicate with a Yes or No whether or not each of the following accounts normally requires an adjusting entry:

a. Accumulated Depreciation   c. Land   e. Supplies

b. Dividends   d. Salaries Payable   f. Unearned Rent

---

2. Type of adjustment   Obj. 1, 2, 3
Classify the following items as (1) accrued revenue, (2) accrued expenses, (3) unearned revenue, or (4) prepaid expense:

a. Cash received for services not yet rendered   c. Rent revenue earned but not received

b. Insurance paid for the next year   d. Salaries owed but not yet paid

---

3. Adjustment for accrued revenues   Obj. 2
At the end of the current year, $23,570 of fees have been earned but have not been billed to clients. Journalize the adjusting entry to record the accrued fees.

---

4. Adjustment for accrued expense   Obj. 2
We-Sell Realty Co. pays weekly salaries of $11,800 on Friday for a five-day workweek ending on that day. Journalize the necessary adjusting entry at the end of the accounting period, assuming that the period ends on Wednesday.

---

5. Adjustment for unearned revenue   Obj. 3
The balance in the unearned fees account, before adjustment at the end of the year, is $272,500. Journalize the adjusting entry required, assuming the amount of unearned fees at the end of the year is $189,750.

---

6. Adjustment for prepaid expense   Obj. 3
The supplies account had a beginning balance of $3,375 and was debited for $6,450 for supplies purchased during the year. Journalize the adjusting entry required at the end of the year, assuming the amount of supplies on hand is $2,980.

---

7. Adjustment for depreciation   Obj. 4
The estimated amount of depreciation on equipment for the current year is $6,880. Journalize the adjusting entry to record the depreciation.

8. Effect of omitting adjustments   Obj. 5

For the year ending August 31, Mammalia Medical Co. mistakenly omitted adjusting entries for (1) depreciation of $5,800, (2) fees earned that were not billed of $44,500, and (3) accrued wages of $7,300. Indicate the combined effect of the errors on (a) revenues, (b) expenses, and (c) net income for the year ended August 31.

9. Effect of errors on adjusted trial balance   Obj. 6

For each of the following errors, considered individually, indicate whether the error would cause the adjusted trial balance totals to be unequal. If the error would cause the adjusted trial balance totals to be unequal, indicate whether the debit or credit total is higher and by how much.

a. The adjustment of $9,800 for accrued fees earned was journalized as a debit to Accounts Receivable for $9,800 and a credit to Fees Earned for $8,900.

b. The adjustment of depreciation of $3,600 was omitted from the end-of-period adjusting entries.

10. Vertical analysis   Obj. 7

Two income statements for Hemlock Company follow:

Hemlock Company
Income Statements
For the Years Ended December 31

	20Y5	20Y4
Fees earned	$ 725,000	$ 615,000
Expenses	(432,875)	(356,700)
Net income	$ 290,000	$ 258,300

a. Prepare a vertical analysis of Hemlock Company's income statements.

b. Does the vertical analysis indicate a favorable or an unfavorable change?

Answers provided after Problem. Need more practice? Find additional multiple-choice questions, exercises, and problems in CengageNOWv2.

Problem

Three years ago, T. Roderick organized Harbor Realty. At July 31, 20Y2, the end of the current year, the unadjusted trial balance of Harbor Realty follows:

Harbor Realty Unadjusted Trial Balance July 31, 20Y2	Debit Balances	Credit Balances
Cash	3,425	
Accounts Receivable	7,000	
Supplies	1,270	
Prepaid Insurance	620	
Office Equipment	51,650	
Accumulated Depreciation—Office Equipment		9,700
Accounts Payable		925
Wages Payable		0
Unearned Fees		1,250
Common Stock		5,000
Retained Earnings		24,000
Dividends	5,200	
Fees Earned		59,125
Wages Expense	22,415	
Depreciation Expense	0	
Rent Expense	4,200	
Utilities Expense	2,715	
Supplies Expense	0	
Insurance Expense	0	
Miscellaneous Expense	1,505	
	100,000	100,000

The data needed to determine year-end adjustments follow:

* Supplies on hand at July 31, 20Y2, $380.
* Insurance premiums expired during the year, $315.
* Depreciation of equipment during the year, $4,950.
* Wages accrued but not paid at July 31, 20Y2, $440.
* Accrued fees earned but not recorded at July 31, 20Y2, $1,000.
* Unearned fees on July 31, 20Y2, $750.

Instructions

1. Prepare the necessary adjusting journal entries on July 31. Include journal entry explanations.

2. Determine the balance of the accounts affected by the adjusting entries, and prepare an adjusted trial balance.

Need more practice? Find additional multiple-choice questions, exercises, and problems in CengageNOWv2.

Answers

Multiple-Choice Questions

1. **a** A deferral is the delay in recording an expense already paid, such as prepaid insurance (answer a). Wages payable (answer b) is considered an accrued expense or accrued liability. Fees earned (answer c) is a revenue item. Accumulated depreciation (answer d) is a contra item to a fixed asset.

2. **c** The failure to record the adjusting entry debiting Unearned Rent, $600, and crediting Rent Revenue, $600, would have the effect of overstating liabilities by $600 and understating net income by $600 (answer c).

3. **d** The balance in the supplies account, before adjustment, represents the amount of supplies available. From this amount ($2,250) is subtracted the amount of supplies on hand ($950) to determine the supplies used ($1,300). Since increases in expense accounts are recorded by debits and decreases in asset accounts are recorded by credits, answer d is the correct entry.

4. **c** Since increases in expense accounts (such as depreciation expense) are recorded by debits and it is customary to record the decreases in usefulness of fixed assets as credits to accumulated depreciation accounts, answer c is the correct entry.

5. **d** Assuming no other errors or omissions, the adjusted trial balance totals would be equal even though the adjusting entry for accrued wages was omitted. This illustrates that equal debit and credit totals on a trial balance don't necessarily mean that errors don't exist in the accounts.

Exercises

1. a. Yes c. No e. Yes
   b. No d. Yes f. Yes

2. a. Unearned revenue c. Accrued revenue
   b. Prepaid expense d. Accrued expense

3.

Dec. 31	Accounts Receivable	23,570	
	Fees Earned		23,570
	Accrued fees.		

4.

Dec. 31	Salaries Expense	7,080	
	Salaries Payable		7,080
	Accrued salaries [($11,800 ÷ 5 days) × 3 days].		

5.

Dec. 31	Unearned Fees	82,750	
	Fees Earned		82,750
	Fees earned ($272,500 – $189,750).		

6.

Dec. 31	Supplies Expense	6,845	
	Supplies		6,845
	Supplies used ($3,375 + $6,450 – $2,980).		

7.

Dec. 31	Depreciation Expense	6,880	
	Accumulated Depreciation—Equipment		6,880
	Depreciattion on equipment.		

8. a. Revenues were understated by $44,500.
   b. Expenses were understated by $13,100 ($5,800 + $7,300).
   c. Net income was understated by $31,400 ($44,500 – $13,100).

9. a. The totals are unequal. The debit total is higher by $900 ($9,800 – $8,900).
   b. The totals are equal because the adjusting entry was omitted.

10. a.

Hemlock Company
Income Statements
For the Years Ended December 31

| | 20Y5 | | 20Y4 | |
	Amount	Percent	Amount	Percent
Fees earned	$ 725,000	100%	$ 615,000	100%
Expenses	(435,000)	(60)%	(356,700)	(58)%
Net income	$ 290,000	40%	$ 258,300	42%

b. An unfavorable trend of increasing operating expenses and decreasing operating income is indicated.

Need more help? Watch step-by-step videos of how to compute answers to these Exercises in CengageNOWv2.

Problem

1.

	Journal			
Date	**Description**	**Post. Ref.**	**Debit**	**Credit**
20Y2 July 31	Supplies Expense		890	
	Supplies			890
	Supplies used ($1,270 – $380).			
31	Insurance Expense		315	
	Prepaid Insurance			315
	Insurance expired.			
31	Depreciation Expense		4,950	
	Accumulated Depreciation—Office Equipment			4,950
	Depreciation expense.			
31	Wages Expense		440	
	Wages Payable			440
	Accrued wages.			
31	Accounts Receivable		1,000	
	Fees Earned			1,000
	Accrued fees.			
31	Unearned Fees		500	
	Fees Earned			500
	Fees earned ($1,250 – $750).			

2.

Harbor Realty Adjusted Trial Balance July 31, 20Y2		
	Debit Balances	Credit Balances
Cash	3,425	
Accounts Receivable	8,000	
Supplies	380	
Prepaid Insurance	305	
Office Equipment	51,650	
Accumulated Depreciation—Office Equipment		14,650
Accounts Payable		925
Wages Payable		440
Unearned Fees		750
Common Stock		5,000
Retained Earnings		24,000
Dividends	5,200	
Fees Earned		60,625
Wages Expense	22,855	
Depreciation Expense	4,950	
Rent Expense	4,200	
Utilities Expense	2,715	
Supplies Expense	890	
Insurance Expense	315	
Miscellaneous Expense	1,505	
	106,390	106,390

Discussion Questions

1. How are revenues and expenses reported on the income statement under (a) the cash basis of accounting and (b) the accrual basis of accounting?

2. Is the matching concept related to (a) the cash basis of accounting or (b) the accrual basis of accounting?

3. Why are adjusting entries needed at the end of an accounting period?

4. What is the difference between *adjusting entries* and *correcting entries*?

5. Identify the four different categories of adjusting entries frequently required at the end of an accounting period.

6. If the effect of the debit portion of an adjusting entry is to increase the balance of an asset account, which of the following statements describes the effect of the credit portion of the entry?

   a. Increases the balance of a revenue account.

   b. Increases the balance of an expense account.

   c. Increases the balance of a liability account.

7. If the effect of the credit portion of an adjusting entry is to increase the balance of a liability account, which of the following statements describes the effect of the debit portion of the entry?

   a. Increases the balance of a revenue account.

   b. Increases the balance of an expense account.

   c. Increases the balance of an asset account.

8. Does every adjusting entry have an effect on determining the amount of net income for a period? Explain.

9. On November 1 of the current year, a business paid the November rent on the building that it occupies. (a) Do the rights acquired at November 1 represent an asset or an expense? (b) What is the justification for debiting Rent Expense at the time of payment?

10. (a) Explain the purpose of the two accounts: Depreciation Expense and Accumulated Depreciation. (b) What is the normal balance of each account? (c) Is it customary for the balances of the two accounts to be equal in amount? (d) In what financial statements, if any, will each account appear?

Basic Exercises

SHOW ME HOW

BE 3-1 Accounts requiring adjustment   Obj. 1, 2, 3
Indicate with a Yes or No whether or not each of the following accounts normally requires an adjusting entry:

a. Building   c. Wages Expense   e. Common Stock
b. Cash   d. Miscellaneous Expense   f. Prepaid Insurance

SHOW ME HOW

BE 3-2 Type of adjustment   Obj. 1, 2, 3
Classify the following items as (1) accrued revenue, (2) accrued expense, (3) unearned revenue, or (4) prepaid expense:

a. Cash received for use of land next month   c. Rent expense owed but not yet paid
b. Fees earned but not received   d. Supplies on hand

SHOW ME HOW

BE 3-3 Adjustment for accrued revenues   Obj. 2
At the end of the current year, $17,555 of fees have been earned but have not been billed to clients. Journalize the adjusting entry to record the accrued fees.

SHOW ME HOW

BE 3-4 Adjustment for accrued expense   Obj. 2
Prospect Realty Co. pays weekly salaries of $27,600 on Monday for a six-day workweek ending the preceding Saturday. Journalize the necessary adjusting entry at the end of the accounting period, assuming that the period ends on Friday.

SHOW ME HOW

BE 3-5 Adjustment for unearned revenue   Obj. 3
On June 1, 20Y2, Herbal Co. received $18,900 for the rent of land for 12 months. Journalize the adjusting entry required for unearned rent on December 31, 20Y2.

SHOW ME HOW

BE 3-6 Adjustment for prepaid expense   Obj. 3
The prepaid insurance account had a beginning balance of $11,500 and was debited for $18,000 of premiums paid during the year. Journalize the adjusting entry required at the end of the year, assuming the amount of unexpired insurance related to future periods is $13,000.

SHOW ME HOW

BE 3-7 Adjustment for depreciation   Obj. 4
The estimated amount of depreciation on equipment for the current year is $7,700. Journalize the adjusting entry to record the depreciation.

SHOW ME HOW

BE 3-8 Effect of omitting adjustments   Obj. 5
For the year ending April 30, Urology Medical Services Co. mistakenly omitted adjusting entries for (1) $1,400 of supplies that were used, (2) unearned revenue of $6,600 that was earned, and (3) insurance of $9,000 that expired. Indicate the combined effect of the errors on (a) revenues, (b) expenses, and (c) net income for the year ended April 30.

SHOW ME HOW

BE 3-9 Effect of errors on adjusted trial balance   Obj. 6
For each of the following errors, considered individually, indicate whether the error would cause the adjusted trial balance totals to be unequal. If the error would cause the adjusted trial balance totals to be unequal, indicate whether the debit or credit total is higher and by how much.

a. The adjustment for accrued wages of $5,200 was journalized as a debit to Wages Expense for $5,200 and a credit to Accounts Payable for $5,200.

b. The entry for $1,125 of supplies used during the period was journalized as a debit to Supplies Expense of $1,125 and a credit to Supplies of $1,152.

SHOW ME HOW

BE 3-10 Vertical analysis

Obj. 7

Two income statements for Cornea Company follow:

Cornea Company
Income Statements
For the Years Ended December 31

	20Y9	20Y8
Fees earned	$1,640,000	$1,300,000
Expenses	(869,200)	(715,000)
Net income	$ 770,800	$ 585,000

a. Prepare a vertical analysis of Cornea Company's income statements.
b. Does the vertical analysis indicate a favorable or an unfavorable trend?

Exercises

EX 3-1 Classifying types of adjustments

Obj. 1, 2, 3

Classify the following items as (a) accrued revenue, (b) accrued expense, (c) unearned revenue, or (d) prepaid expense:

1. A two-year premium paid on insurance policy.
2. Fees earned but not yet received.
3. Fees received but not yet earned.
4. Salary owed but not yet paid.
5. Subscriptions received in advance by a magazine publisher.
6. Supplies on hand.
7. Taxes owed but payable in the following period.
8. Utilities owed but not yet paid.

EX 3-2 Classifying adjusting entries

Obj. 1, 2, 3

The following accounts were taken from the unadjusted trial balance of Murray Co., a congressional lobbying firm. Indicate whether or not each account would normally require an adjusting entry. If the account normally requires an adjusting entry, use the following notation to indicate the type of adjustment:

AE—Accrued Expense
AR—Accrued Revenue
PE—Prepaid Expense
UR—Unearned Revenue

To illustrate, the answer for the first account follows:

Account	Answer
Accounts Receivable	Normally requires adjustment (AR).
Building	
Cash	
Common Stock	
Interest Receivable	
Land	
Prepaid Rent	
Salaries Payable	
Supplies	
Unearned Fees	
Wages Expense	

SHOW ME HOW

EX 3-3 Adjusting entry for accrued fees
Obj. 2

At the end of the current year, $59,500 of fees have been earned but have not been billed to clients.

a. Journalize the adjusting entry to record the accrued fees.

b. ━━━━▶ If the cash basis rather than the accrual basis had been used, would an adjusting entry have been necessary? Explain.

EX 3-4 Effect of omitting adjusting entry
Obj. 2, 5

The adjusting entry for accrued wages was omitted at July 31, the end of the current year. Indicate which items will be in error, because of the omission, on (a) the income statement for the current year and (b) the balance sheet as of July 31. Also indicate whether the items in error will be overstated or understated.

✔ a. Amount
of entry:
$5,100

SHOW ME HOW

EX 3-5 Adjusting entries for accrued salaries
Obj. 2

Paradise Realty Co. pays weekly salaries of $25,500 on Friday for a five-day workweek ending on that day. Journalize the necessary adjusting entry at the end of the accounting period, assuming that the period ends (a) on Monday and (b) on Thursday.

EX 3-6 Determining wages paid
Obj. 2

The wages payable and wages expense accounts at August 31, after adjusting entries have been posted at the end of the first month of operations, are shown in the following T accounts:

Wages Payable		Wages Expense	
	Bal. 5,250	Bal. 275,000	

Determine the amount of wages paid during the month.

EX 3-7 Effect of omitting adjusting entry
Obj. 2, 5

Accrued salaries owed to employees for October 30 and 31 are not considered in preparing the financial statements for the year ended October 31. Indicate which items will be erroneously stated, because of the error, on (a) the income statement for the year and (b) the balance sheet as of October 31. Also indicate whether the items in error will be overstated or understated.

EX 3-8 Effect of omitting adjusting entry
Obj. 2, 5

When preparing the financial statements for the month ended January 31, accrued salaries owed to employees for January 30 and 31 were overlooked. The accrued salaries were included in the first salary payment in February. Indicate which items will be erroneously stated, because of failure to correct the initial error, on (a) the income statement for the month of February and (b) the balance sheet as of February 28.

SHOW ME HOW

EX 3-9 Adjusting entries for unearned fees
Obj. 3

The balance in the unearned fees account, before adjustment at the end of the year, is $18,000. Journalize the adjusting entry required if the amount of unearned fees at the end of the year is $3,600.

EX 3-10 Effect of omitting adjusting entry
Obj. 3, 5

At the end of October, the first month of the business year, the usual adjusting entry transferring rent earned to a revenue account from the unearned rent account was omitted. Indicate which items will be incorrectly stated, because of the error, on (a) the income statement for October and (b) the balance sheet as of October 31. Also indicate whether the items in error will be overstated or understated.

SHOW ME HOW

EX 3-11 Adjusting entry for supplies
Obj. 3

The balance in the supplies account, before adjustment at the end of the year, is $9,000. Journalize the adjusting entry required if the amount of supplies on hand at the end of the year is $1,575.

SHOW ME HOW

EX 3-12   Determining supplies purchased   Obj. 3
The supplies and supplies expense accounts at December 31, after adjusting entries have been posted at the end of the first year of operations, are shown in the following T accounts:

Supplies				Supplies Expense		
Bal.	2,550			Bal.	7,120	

Determine the amount of supplies purchased during the year.

EX 3-13   Effect of omitting adjusting entry   Obj. 3, 5
At March 31, the end of the first month of operations, the usual adjusting entry transferring prepaid insurance expired to an expense account is omitted. Which items will be incorrectly stated, because of the error, on (a) the income statement for March and (b) the balance sheet as of March 31? Also indicate whether the items in error will be overstated or understated.

SHOW ME HOW

EX 3-14   Adjusting entries for prepaid insurance   Obj. 3
The balance in the prepaid insurance account, before adjustment at the end of the year, is $27,000. Journalize the adjusting entry required under each of the following *alternatives* for determining the amount of the adjustment: (a) the amount of insurance expired during the year is $20,250; (b) the amount of unexpired insurance applicable to future periods is $6,750.

SHOW ME HOW

EX 3-15   Adjusting entries for prepaid insurance   Obj. 3
The prepaid insurance account had a balance of $3,000 at the beginning of the year. The account was debited for $32,500 for premiums on policies purchased during the year. Journalize the adjusting entry required under each of the following *alternatives* for determining the amount of the adjustment: (a) the amount of unexpired insurance applicable to future periods is $4,800; (b) the amount of insurance expired during the year is $30,700.

SHOW ME HOW

EX 3-16   Adjusting entries for unearned and accrued fees   Obj. 2, 3
The balance in the unearned fees account, before adjustment at the end of the year, is $97,770. Of these fees, $39,750 have been earned. In addition, $24,650 of fees have been earned but have not been billed. Journalize the adjusting entries (a) to adjust the unearned fees account and (b) to record the accrued fees.

✔ b. $57,320

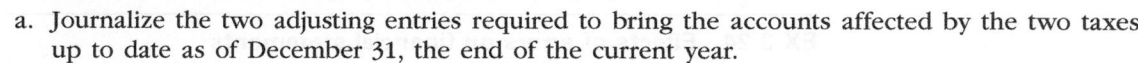

SHOW ME HOW

EX 3-17   Adjusting entries for prepaid and accrued taxes   Obj. 2, 3
A-Z Construction Company was organized on May 1 of the current year. On May 2, A-Z Construction prepaid $18,480 to the city for taxes (license fees) for the *next* 12 months and debited the prepaid taxes account. A-Z Construction is also required to pay in January an annual tax (on property) for the *previous* calendar year. The estimated amount of the property tax for the current year (May 1 to December 31) is $45,000.

a. Journalize the two adjusting entries required to bring the accounts affected by the two taxes up to date as of December 31, the end of the current year.

b. What is the amount of tax expense for the current year?

EX 3-18   Adjustment for depreciation   Obj. 4
The estimated amount of depreciation on equipment for the current year is $8,200. Journalize the adjusting entry to record the depreciation.

SHOW ME HOW

EX 3-19   Determining fixed asset's book value   Obj. 4
The balance in the equipment account is $3,150,000, and the balance in the accumulated depreciation—equipment account is $2,075,000.

a. What is the book value of the equipment?

b.   Does the balance in the accumulated depreciation account mean that the equipment's loss of value is $2,075,000? Explain.

REAL WORLD

EX 3-20 Book value of fixed assets
Obj. 4

In a recent balance sheet, **Microsoft Corporation (MSFT)** reported *Property, Plant, and Equipment* of $38,156 million and *Accumulated Depreciation* of $19,800 million.

a. What was the book value of the fixed assets?

b. ➤ Would the book value of Microsoft's fixed assets normally approximate their fair market values?

REAL WORLD

EX 3-21 Effects of errors on financial statements
Obj. 2, 5

For a recent period, the balance sheet for **Costco Wholesale Corporation (COST)** reported accrued expenses of $3,498 million. For the same period, Costco reported income before income taxes of $3,619 million. Assume that the adjusting entry for $3,498 million of accrued expenses was not recorded at the end of the current period. What would have been the income (loss) before income taxes?

REAL WORLD

EX 3-22 Effects of errors on financial statements
Obj. 2, 5

For a recent year, the balance sheet for **The Campbell Soup Company (CPB)** includes accrued expenses of $604 million. The income before taxes for Campbell for the year was $849 million.

a. Assume the adjusting entry for $604 million of accrued expenses was not recorded at the end of the year. By how much would income before taxes have been misstated?

b. What is the percentage of the misstatement in (a) to the reported income of $849 million? Round to one decimal place.

✔ 1. a. Revenue
understated, $34,900

EX 3-23 Effects of errors on financial statements
Obj. 2, 3, 5

The accountant for Healthy Life Company, a medical services consulting firm, mistakenly omitted adjusting entries for (a) unearned revenue earned during the year ($34,900) and (b) accrued wages ($12,770). Indicate the effect of each error, considered individually, on the income statement for the current year ended July 31. Also indicate the effect of each error on the July 31 balance sheet. Set up a table similar to the following, and record your answers by inserting the dollar amount in the appropriate spaces. Insert a zero if the error does not affect the item.

	Error (a)		Error (b)	
	Over-stated	Under-stated	Over-stated	Under-stated
1. Revenue for the year would be	$___	$___	$___	$___
2. Expenses for the year would be	$___	$___	$___	$___
3. Net income for the year would be	$___	$___	$___	$___
4. Assets at July 31 would be	$___	$___	$___	$___
5. Liabilities at July 31 would be	$___	$___	$___	$___
6. Stockholders' equity at July 31 would be	$___	$___	$___	$___

EX 3-24 Effects of errors on financial statements
Obj. 2, 3, 5

If the net income for the current year had been $196,400 in Exercise 3-23, what would have been the correct net income if the proper adjusting entries had been made?

SHOW ME HOW

EX 3-25 Adjusting entries for depreciation; effect of error
Obj. 4, 5

On December 31, a business estimates depreciation on equipment used during the first year of operations to be $13,900.

a. Journalize the adjusting entry required as of December 31.

b. If the adjusting entry in (a) were omitted, which items would be erroneously stated on (1) the income statement for the year and (2) the balance sheet as of December 31?

SHOW ME HOW

EX 3-26 Adjusting entries from trial balances
Obj. 6

The unadjusted and adjusted trial balances for American Leaf Company on October 31, 20Y2, follow:

American Leaf Company
Trial Balances
October 31, 20Y2

	Unadjusted		Adjusted	
	Debit Balances	Credit Balances	Debit Balances	Credit Balances
Cash	16		16	
Accounts Receivable............................	38		44	
Supplies..	12		10	
Prepaid Insurance	20		8	
Land	26		26	
Equipment......................................	40		40	
Accumulated Depreciation—Equipment.........		8		12
Accounts Payable		26		26
Wages Payable.................................		0		2
Common Stock..................................		20		20
Retained Earnings		72		72
Dividends	8		8	
Fees Earned....................................		74		80
Wages Expense	24		26	
Rent Expense	8		8	
Insurance Expense	0		12	
Utilities Expense	4		4	
Depreciation Expense	0		4	
Supplies Expense...............................	0		2	
Miscellaneous Expense	4		4	
	200	200	212	212

Journalize the five entries that adjusted the accounts at October 31, 20Y2. None of the accounts were affected by more than one adjusting entry.

EX 3-27 Adjusting entries from trial balances Obj. 6

✔ Corrected trial balance totals, $369,000

The accountant for Eva's Laundry prepared the following unadjusted and adjusted trial balances. Assume that all balances in the unadjusted trial balance and the amounts of the adjustments are correct. Identify the errors in the accountant's adjusting entries, assuming that none of the accounts were affected by more than one adjusting entry.

Eva's Laundry
Trial Balances
May 31, 20Y9

	Unadjusted		Adjusted	
	Debit Balances	Credit Balances	Debit Balances	Credit Balances
Cash	7,500		7,500	
Accounts Receivable............................	18,250		23,250	
Laundry Supplies................................	3,750		6,750	
Prepaid Insurance*	5,200		1,600	
Laundry Equipment	190,000		177,000	
Accumulated Depreciation—Laundry Equipment....		48,000		48,000
Accounts Payable		9,600		9,600
Wages Payable.................................				1,000
Common Stock		35,000		35,000
Retained Earnings..............................		75,300		75,300
Dividends	28,775		28,775	
Laundry Revenue................................		182,100		182,100
Wages Expense	49,200		49,200	
Rent Expense	25,575		25,575	
Utilities Expense	18,500		18,500	
Depreciation Expense			13,000	
Laundry Supplies Expense			3,000	
Insurance Expense			600	
Miscellaneous Expense	3,250		3,250	
	350,000	350,000	358,000	351,000

* $3,600 of insurance expired during the year.

Problems: Series A

SHOW ME HOW   EXCEL TEMPLATE

PR 3-1A   Adjusting entries

Obj. 2, 3, 4

On March 31, the following data were accumulated to assist the accountant in preparing the adjusting entries for Potomac Realty:

- The supplies account balance on March 31 is $5,620. The supplies on hand on March 31 are $1,290.
- The unearned rent account balance on March 31 is $5,000 representing the receipt of an advance payment on March 1 of four months' rent from tenants.
- Wages accrued but not paid at March 31 are $2,290.
- Fees accrued but unbilled at March 31 are $16,825.
- Depreciation of office equipment is $4,600.

Instructions

1. Journalize the adjusting entries required at March 31.
2. ⬤▬▬▶ Briefly explain the difference between adjusting entries and entries that would be made to correct errors.

SHOW ME HOW

PR 3-2A   Adjusting entries

Obj. 2, 3, 4, 5

Selected account balances before adjustment for Atlantic Coast Realty at July 31, the end of the current year, are as follows:

	Debits	Credits
Accounts Receivable	$ 75,000	
Equipment	345,700	
Accumulated Depreciation—Equipment		$112,500
Prepaid Rent	9,000	
Supplies	3,350	
Wages Payable		—
Unearned Fees		12,000
Fees Earned		660,000
Wages Expense	325,000	
Rent Expense	—	
Depreciation Expense	—	
Supplies Expense	—	

Data needed for year-end adjustments are as follows:
- Unbilled fees at July 31, $11,150.
- Supplies on hand at July 31, $900.
- Rent expired, $6,000.
- Depreciation of equipment during year, $8,950.
- Unearned fees at July 31, $2,000.
- Wages accrued but not paid at July 31, $4,840.

Instructions

1. Journalize the six adjusting entries required at July 31, based on the data presented.
2. What would be the effect on the income statement if the adjustments for unbilled fees and accrued wages were omitted at the end of the year?
3. What would be the effect on the balance sheet if the adjustments for unbilled fees and accrued wages were omitted at the end of the year?
4. What would be the effect on the "Net increase or decrease in cash" on the statement of cash flows if the adjustments for unbilled fees and accrued wages were omitted at the end of the year?

PR 3-3A Adjusting entries

Obj. 2, 3, 4, 5

Trident Repairs & Service, an electronics repair store, prepared the following unadjusted trial balance at the end of its first year of operations:

Trident Repairs & Service
Unadjusted Trial Balance
November 30, 20Y3

	Debit Balances	Credit Balances
Cash	10,350	
Accounts Receivable	67,500	
Supplies	16,200	
Equipment	116,100	
Accounts Payable		25,750
Unearned Fees		18,000
Common Stock		50,000
Retained Earnings		111,500
Dividends	13,500	
Fees Earned		294,750
Wages Expense	124,500	
Rent Expense	92,000	
Utilities Expense	51,750	
Miscellaneous Expense	8,100	
	500,000	500,000

For preparing the adjusting entries, the following data were assembled:

- Fees earned but unbilled on November 30 were $7,000.
- Supplies on hand on November 30 were $1,300.
- Depreciation of equipment was estimated to be $7,200 for the year.
- The balance in unearned fees represented the November 1 receipt in advance for services to be provided. During November, $13,500 of the services were provided.
- Unpaid wages accrued on November 30 were $4,800.

Instructions

1. Journalize the adjusting entries necessary on November 30, 20Y3.

2. Determine the revenues, expenses, and net income of Trident Repairs & Service before the adjusting entries.

3. Determine the revenues, expense, and net income of Trident Repairs & Service after the adjusting entries.

4. Determine the effect of the adjusting entries on Retained Earnings.

PR 3-4A　Adjusting entries

Obj. 2, 3, 4, 5, 6

Good Note Company specializes in the repair of music equipment and is owned and operated by Robin Stahl. On June 30, 20Y6, the end of the current year, the accountant for Good Note prepared the following trial balances:

Good Note Company
Trial Balances
June 30, 20Y6

	Unadjusted		Adjusted	
	Debit Balances	Credit Balances	Debit Balances	Credit Balances
Cash	38,250		38,250	
Accounts Receivable	89,500		89,500	
Supplies	11,250		2,400	
Prepaid Insurance	14,250		3,850	
Equipment	290,450		290,450	
Accumulated Depreciation—Equipment		94,500		106,100
Automobiles	129,500		129,500	
Accumulated Depreciation—Automobiles		54,750		62,050
Accounts Payable		24,930		26,130
Salaries Payable		—		8,100
Unearned Service Fees		18,000		9,000
Common Stock		100,000		100,000
Retained Earnings		224,020		224,020
Dividends	75,000		75,000	
Service Fees Earned		733,800		742,800
Salary Expense	516,900		525,000	
Rent Expense	54,000		54,000	
Supplies Expense	—		8,850	
Depreciation Expense—Equipment	—		11,600	
Depreciation Expense—Automobiles	—		7,300	
Utilities Expense	12,900		14,100	
Taxes Expense	8,175		8,175	
Insurance Expense	—		10,400	
Miscellaneous Expense	9,825		9,825	
	1,250,000	1,250,000	1,278,200	1,278,200

Instructions

Journalize the seven entries that adjusted the accounts at June 30. None of the accounts were affected by more than one adjusting entry.

✔ 2. Total of Debit
column: $776,900

EXCEL TEMPLATE

PR 3-5A Adjusting entries and adjusted trial balances

Obj. 2, 3, 4, 5, 6

Sears Editing Company is a small editorial services company owned and operated by Deloris Sears. On January 31, 20Y1, the end of the current year, Sears Editing Company's accounting clerk prepared the following unadjusted trial balance:

Sears Editing Company
Unadjusted Trial Balance
January 31, 20Y1

	Debit Balances	Credit Balances
Cash	7,500	
Accounts Receivable	38,400	
Prepaid Insurance	7,200	
Supplies	1,980	
Land	112,500	
Building	150,250	
Accumulated Depreciation—Building		87,550
Equipment	135,300	
Accumulated Depreciation—Equipment		97,950
Accounts Payable		12,150
Unearned Rent		6,750
Common Stock		75,000
Retained Earnings		146,000
Dividends	15,000	
Fees Earned		324,600
Salaries and Wages Expense	193,370	
Utilities Expense	42,375	
Advertising Expense	22,800	
Repairs Expense	17,250	
Miscellaneous Expense	6,075	
	750,000	750,000

The data needed to determine year-end adjustments are as follows:

- Unexpired insurance at January 31, $2,400.
- Supplies on hand at January 31, $250.
- Depreciation of building for the year, $6,600.
- Depreciation of equipment for the year, $3,500.
- Rent unearned at January 31, $2,750.
- Accrued salaries and wages at January 31, $1,800.
- Fees earned but unbilled on January 31, $15,000.

Instructions

1. Journalize the adjusting entries using the following additional accounts: Salaries and Wages Payable; Rent Revenue; Insurance Expense; Depreciation Expense—Building; Depreciation Expense—Equipment; and Supplies Expense.

2. Determine the balances of the accounts affected by the adjusting entries, and prepare an adjusted trial balance.

PR 3-6A Adjusting entries and errors

Obj. 2, 3, 4, 5

✔ 2. Corrected net
income: $137,750

EXCEL TEMPLATE

At the end of April, the first month of operations, the following selected data were taken from the financial statements of Shelby Crawford, an attorney:

Net income for April	$120,000
Total assets at April 30	750,000
Total liabilities at April 30	300,000
Total stockholders' equity at April 30	450,000

In preparing the financial statements, adjustments for the following data were overlooked:

- Supplies used during April, $2,750.
- Unbilled fees earned at April 30, $23,700.
- Depreciation of equipment for April, $1,800.
- Accrued wages at April 30, $1,400.

Instructions

1. Journalize the entries to record the omitted adjustments.

2. Determine the correct amount of net income for April and the total assets, liabilities, and stockholders' equity at April 30. In addition to indicating the corrected amounts, indicate the effect of each omitted adjustment by setting up and completing a columnar table similar to the following. The adjustment for supplies used is presented as an example.

	Net Income	Total Assets	=	Total Liabilities	+	Total Stockholders' Equity
Reported amounts	$120,000	$750,000		$300,000		$450,000
Corrections:						
Supplies used	(2,750)	(2,750)		0		(2,750)
Unbilled fees earned	_____	_____		_____		_____
Equipment depreciation	_____	_____		_____		_____
Accrued wages	_____	_____		_____		_____
Corrected amounts	══════	══════		══════		══════

Problems: Series B

PR 3-1B Adjusting entries

Obj. 2, 3, 4

SHOW ME HOW   **EXCEL TEMPLATE**

On May 31, the following data were accumulated to assist the accountant in preparing the adjusting entries for Oceanside Realty:

- Fees accrued but unbilled at May 31 are $19,750.
- The supplies account balance on May 31 is $12,300. The supplies on hand at May 31 are $4,150.
- Wages accrued but not paid at May 31 are $2,700.
- The unearned rent account balance at May 31 is $9,000, representing the receipt of an advance payment on May 1 of three months' rent from tenants.
- Depreciation of office equipment is $3,200.

Instructions

1. Journalize the adjusting entries required at May 31.

2. ⟶ Briefly explain the difference between adjusting entries and entries that would be made to correct errors.

SHOW ME HOW

PR 3-2B   Adjusting entries

Obj. 2, 3, 4, 5

Selected account balances before adjustment for Intuit Realty at November 30, the end of the current year, follow:

	Debits	Credits
Accounts Receivable	$ 75,000	
Equipment	250,000	
Accumulated Depreciation—Equipment		$ 12,000
Prepaid Rent	12,000	
Supplies	3,170	
Wages Payable		—
Unearned Fees		10,000
Fees Earned		400,000
Wages Expense	140,000	
Rent Expense	—	
Depreciation Expense	—	
Supplies Expense	—	

Data needed for year-end adjustments are as follows:

* Supplies on hand at November 30, $550.
* Depreciation of equipment during year, $1,675.
* Rent expired during year, $8,500.
* Wages accrued but not paid at November 30, $2,000.
* Unearned fees at November 30, $4,000.
* Unbilled fees at November 30, $5,380.

Instructions

1. Journalize the six adjusting entries required at November 30, based on the data presented.

2. What would be the effect on the income statement if the adjustments for equipment depreciation and unearned fees were omitted at the end of the year?

3. What would be the effect on the balance sheet if the adjustments for equipment depreciation and unearned fees were omitted at the end of the year?

4. What would be the effect on the "Net increase or decrease in cash" on the statement of cash flows if the adjustments for equipment depreciation and unearned fees were omitted at the end of the year?

PR 3-3B   Adjusting entries

Obj. 2, 3, 4, 5

Crazy Mountain Outfitters Co., an outfitter store for fishing treks, prepared the following unadjusted trial balance at the end of its first year of operations:

Crazy Mountain Outfitters Co.
Unadjusted Trial Balance
April 30, 20Y5

	Debit Balances	Credit Balances
Cash	11,400	
Accounts Receivable	72,600	
Supplies	7,200	
Equipment	112,000	
Accounts Payable		12,200
Unearned Fees		19,200
Common Stock		20,000
Retained Earnings		117,800
Dividends	10,000	
Fees Earned		305,800
Wages Expense	157,800	
Rent Expense	55,000	
Utilities Expense	42,000	
Miscellaneous Expense	7,000	
	475,000	475,000

(Continued)

For preparing the adjusting entries, the following data were assembled:

- Supplies on hand on April 30 were $1,380.
- Fees earned but unbilled on April 30 were $3,900.
- Depreciation of equipment was estimated to be $3,000 for the year.
- Unpaid wages accrued on April 30 were $2,475.
- The balance in unearned fees represented the April 1 receipt in advance for services to be provided. Only $14,140 of the services was provided between April 1 and April 30.

Instructions

1. Journalize the adjusting entries necessary on April 30, 20Y5.

2. Determine the revenues, expenses, and net income of Crazy Mountain Outfitters Co. before the adjusting entries.

3. Determine the revenues, expense, and net income of Crazy Mountain Outfitters Co. after the adjusting entries.

4. Determine the effect of the adjusting entries on Retained Earnings.

PR 3-4B Adjusting entries

Obj. 2, 3, 4, 5, 6

The Signage Company specializes in the maintenance and repair of signs, such as billboards. On March 31, 20Y6, the accountant for The Signage Company prepared the trial balances shown at the top of the following page.

Instructions

Journalize the seven entries that adjusted the accounts at March 31. None of the accounts were affected by more than one adjusting entry.

The Signage Company
Trial Balances
March 31, 20Y6

	Unadjusted		Adjusted	
	Debit Balances	Credit Balances	Debit Balances	Credit Balances
Cash	4,750		4,750	
Accounts Receivable	17,400		17,400	
Supplies	6,200		2,175	
Prepaid Insurance	9,000		1,150	
Land	100,000		100,000	
Buildings	170,000		170,000	
Accumulated Depreciation—Buildings		51,500		61,000
Trucks	75,000		75,000	
Accumulated Depreciation—Trucks		12,000		17,000
Accounts Payable		6,920		8,750
Salaries Payable		—		1,400
Unearned Service Fees		10,500		3,850
Common Stock		50,000		50,000
Retained Earnings		206,400		206,400
Dividends	7,500		7,500	
Service Fees Earned		162,680		169,330
Salary Expense	80,000		81,400	
Depreciation Expense—Trucks	—		5,000	
Rent Expense	11,900		11,900	
Supplies Expense	—		4,025	
Utilities Expense	6,200		8,030	
Depreciation Expense—Buildings	—		9,500	
Taxes Expense	2,900		2,900	
Insurance Expense	—		7,850	
Miscellaneous Expense	9,150		9,150	
	500,000	500,000	517,730	517,730

PR 3-5B Adjusting entries and adjusted trial balances

Obj. 2, 3, 4, 5, 6

Reece Financial Services Co., which specializes in appliance repair services, is owned and operated by Joni Reece. Reece Financial Services' accounting clerk prepared the following unadjusted trial balance at July 31, 20Y9:

✔ 2. Total of Debit column: $420,300

EXCEL TEMPLATE

Reece Financial Services Co.
Unadjusted Trial Balance
July 31, 20Y9

	Debit Balances	Credit Balances
Cash	10,200	
Accounts Receivable..	34,750	
Prepaid Insurance	6,000	
Supplies	1,725	
Land	50,000	
Building	155,750	
Accumulated Depreciation—Building...............................		62,850
Equipment..	45,000	
Accumulated Depreciation—Equipment...........................		17,650
Accounts Payable		3,750
Unearned Rent		3,600
Common Stock		60,000
Retained Earnings		93,550
Dividends	8,000	
Fees Earned..		158,600
Salaries and Wages Expense....................................	56,850	
Utilities Expense	14,100	
Advertising Expense	7,500	
Repairs Expense..	6,100	
Miscellaneous Expense	4,025	
	400,000	400,000

The data needed to determine year-end adjustments are as follows:

- Depreciation of building for the year, $6,400.
- Depreciation of equipment for the year, $2,800.
- Accrued salaries and wages at July 31, $900.
- Unexpired insurance at July 31, $1,500.
- Fees earned but unbilled on July 31, $10,200.
- Supplies on hand at July 31, $615.
- Rent unearned at July 31, $300.

Instructions

1. Journalize the adjusting entries using the following additional accounts: Salaries and Wages Payable; Rent Revenue; Insurance Expense; Depreciation Expense—Building; Depreciation Expense—Equipment; and Supplies Expense.

2. Determine the balances of the accounts affected by the adjusting entries, and prepare an adjusted trial balance.

PR 3-6B Adjusting entries and errors Obj. 2, 3, 4, 5

✔ 2. Corrected net income: $128,700

EXCEL TEMPLATE

At the end of August, the first month of operations, the following selected data were taken from the financial statements of Tucker Jacobs, an attorney:

Net income for August	$112,500
Total assets at August 31	650,000
Total liabilities at August 31	225,000
Total stockholders' equity at August 31	425,000

In preparing the financial statements, adjustments for the following data were overlooked:

- Unbilled fees earned at August 31, $31,900.
- Depreciation of equipment for August, $7,500.
- Accrued wages at August 31, $5,200.
- Supplies used during August, $3,000.

Instructions

1. Journalize the entries to record the omitted adjustments.

2. Determine the correct amount of net income for August and the total assets, liabilities, and stockholders' equity at August 31. In addition to indicating the corrected amounts, indicate

(Continued)

the effect of each omitted adjustment by setting up and completing a columnar table similar to the following. The first adjustment is presented as an example.

	Net Income	Total Assets	=	Total Liabilities	+	Total Stockholders' Equity
Reported amounts	$112,500	$650,000		$225,000		$425,000
Corrections:						
Unbilled fees earned	+31,900	+31,900		0		+31,900
Equipment depreciation						
Accrued wages						
Supplies used						
Corrected amounts						

Continuing Problem

✔ **3. Total of Debit column: $42,340**

The unadjusted trial balance that you prepared for PS Music at the end of Chapter 2 should appear as follows:

PS Music
Unadjusted Trial Balance
July 31, 20Y5

	Account No.	Debit Balances	Credit Balances
Cash	11	9,945	
Accounts Receivable.	12	2,750	
Supplies	14	1,020	
Prepaid Insurance	15	2,700	
Office Equipment	17	7,500	
Accounts Payable	21		8,350
Unearned Revenue	23		7,200
Common Stock	31		9,000
Dividends	33	1,750	
Fees Earned.	41		16,200
Wages Expense	50	2,800	
Office Rent Expense	51	2,550	
Equipment Rent Expense	52	1,375	
Utilities Expense	53	1,215	
Music Expense	54	3,610	
Advertising Expense.	55	1,500	
Supplies Expense.	56	180	
Miscellaneous Expense	59	1,855	
		40,750	40,750

The data needed to determine adjustments are as follows:

- During July, PS Music provided guest disc jockeys for KXMD for a total of 115 hours. For information on the amount of the accrued revenue to be billed to KXMD, see the contract described in the July 3 transaction at the end of Chapter 2.
- Supplies on hand at July 31, $275.
- The balance of the prepaid insurance account relates to the July 1 transaction at the end of Chapter 2.
- Depreciation of the office equipment is $50.
- The balance of the unearned revenue account relates to the contract between PS Music and KXMD, described in the July 3 transaction at the end of Chapter 2.
- Accrued wages as of July 31 were $140.

Instructions

1. Prepare adjusting journal entries. You will need the following additional accounts:

    18 Accumulated Depreciation—Office Equipment
    22 Wages Payable
    57 Insurance Expense
    58 Depreciation Expense

2. Post the adjusting entries, inserting balances in the accounts affected.
3. Prepare an adjusted trial balance.

Make a Decision
Vertical Analysis

REAL WORLD

MAD 3-1 Analyze Amazon.com
Obj. 7

Amazon.com, Inc. (AMZN) is the largest Internet retailer in the United States. Amazon's income statements through operating income for two recent years are as follows (in millions):

Amazon.com, Inc.
Income Statements
For the Years Ended December 31
(in millions)

	Year 2	Year 1
Revenues:		
Product sales	$ 94,665	$ 79,268
Service sales	41,322	27,738
Total revenues	$ 135,987	$ 107,006
Operating expenses:		
Cost of sales	$ (88,265)	$ (71,651)
Fulfillment	(17,619)	(13,410)
Marketing	(7,233)	(5,254)
Technology and content	(16,085)	(12,540)
General and administrative	(2,432)	(1,747)
Other operating expense (income), net	(167)	(171)
Total operating expenses	$ (131,801)	$ (104,773)
Operating income	$ 4,186	$ 2,233

a. Prepare a vertical analysis of the two income statements. Round percentages to one decimal place.

b. ➤ Use the vertical analysis to explain the increase in operating income.

MAD 3-2 Analyze Pandora Media
Obj. 7

REAL WORLD

Pandora Media, Inc. (P) provides Internet music platform services in North America. Pandora's income statements through operating income for two recent years are as follows (in thousands):

Pandora Media, Inc.
Income Statements
For the Years Ended January 31
(in thousands)

	Year 2	Year 1
Revenues:		
Advertising	$ 1,072,490	$ 933,305
Subscription	225,786	220,571
Ticketing service	86,550	10,167
Total revenues	$ 1,384,826	$ 1,164,043
Expenses:		
Cost of revenues	$ (894,922)	$ (697,341)
Sales and marketing	(491,455)	(398,169)
General and administrative	(175,572)	(153,943)
Product development	(141,636)	(84,581)
Total expenses	$ (1,703,585)	$ (1,334,034)
Operating income (loss)	$ (318,759)	$ (169,991)

a. Prepare a vertical analysis of the two income statements.

b. ➤ Interpret the vertical analysis.

REAL WORLD

MAD 3-3 Analyze World Wrestling Entertainment

Obj. 7

World Wrestling Entertainment, Inc. (WWE) is a sports media and entertainment company primarily focused on professional wrestling. WWE's income statements through operating income for two recent years are as follows (in thousands):

World Wrestling Entertainment, Inc.
Income Statements
For the Years Ended December 31
(in thousands)

	Year 2	Year 1
Revenues	$ 729,216	$ 658,768
Expenses:		
Cost of revenues	$ (430,032)	$ (379,316)
Selling, general, and administrative expenses	(219,132)	(192,773)
Depreciation and other expenses	(24,411)	(29,885)*
Total expenses	$ (673,575)	$ (619,974)
Operating income (loss)	$ 55,641	$ 38,794

*$7,125 is related to expenses of abandoning a media project in Year 1.

a. Prepare a vertical analysis of the income statements for both years.
b. ➤ Interpret the vertical analysis.

REAL WORLD

MAD 3-4 Analyze Chipotle Mexican Grill

Obj. 7

Chipotle Mexican Grill, Inc. (CMG) is a quick-service restaurant providing a focused menu of burritos, tacos, and salads. Chipotle's income statements through operating income for two recent years are as follows (in thousands):

Chipotle Mexican Grill, Inc.
Income Statements
For the Years Ended December 31

	Year 2	Year 1
Revenues	$ 3,904,384	$ 4,501,223
Expenses:		
Food, beverage, packing	$ (1,365,580)	$ (1,503,835)
Labor	(1,105,001)	(1,045,726)
Rent (occupancy)	(293,636)	(262,412)
General and administrative	(641,953)	(514,963)
Other	(463,647)	(410,698)
Total expenses	$ (3,869,817)	$ (3,737,634)
Operating income	$ 34,567	$ 763,589

a. Prepare a vertical analysis of the two income statements. Round percentages to one decimal place.
b. ➤ Interpret the vertical analysis.

MAD 3-5 Analyze Nike

Obj. 7

The following data are taken from recent financial statements of **Nike, Inc. (NKE)** (in millions):

	Year 2	Year 1
Revenues (sales)	$ 32,376	$ 30,601
Operating income	4,502	4,175

a. Determine the amount of change (in millions) and percent of change in operating income from Year 1 to Year 2. Round to one decimal place.
b. Determine the percentage relationship between operating income and sales for Year 2 and Year 1. Round to one decimal place.
c. ➤ What conclusions can you draw from your analyses?

REAL WORLD

MAD 3-6   Analyze and Compare AT&T and Verizon Communications   Obj. 7

The following income statement data for **AT&T Inc. (T)** and **Verizon Communications Inc. (VZ)** were taken from their recent annual reports (in millions):

	AT&T	Verizon
Revenues	$163,786	$125,980
Cost of services (expense)	(76,884)	(51,424)
Selling, general, and administrative expenses	(36,347)	(31,569)
Depreciation and other expenses	(26,208)	(15,928)
Operating income	$ 24,347	$ 27,059

a. Prepare a vertical analysis of the income statement for AT&T. Round to one decimal place.
b. Prepare a vertical analysis of the income statement for Verizon. Round to one decimal place.
c. ━━━▶ Based on Requirements (a) and (b), how does AT&T compare to Verizon?

Take It Further

ETHICS

TIF 3-1   Unearned rent

Chris P. Bacon is the chief accountant for CV Industries, a large manufacturing company. In addition to its normal business activities, the company has excess warehouse space that it rents out to local businesses. Because the typical renter is a small business, CV Industries requires renters to make lease payments for the entire rental period on the day the lease is signed. As a result, CV Industries typically reports a large unearned rent balance on its balance sheet.

After making adjusting entries for the current year, Chris prepares the adjusted trial balance and notices that the company's earnings will decline significantly. He presents the adjusted trial balance to the company's CFO, Antonio Beldin, who is concerned about the earnings decline. Mr. Beldin notices the large unearned rent balance and proposes making an additional end-of-period adjusting entry to recognize the entire unearned rent balance as revenue in the current period. Chris protests, reminding Mr. Beldin that the adjusting entry for unearned rent has already been made. Mr. Beldin assures Chris that his proposal is acceptable, reminding Chris that "because we have already received the cash, we have the right to recognize the revenue in the current period." He instructs Chris to make the additional adjusting journal entry. Chris is hesitant to follow these instructions, but he is sensitive to the company's emphasis on earnings growth and makes the adjusting entry as instructed.

1. ━━━▶ Is Chris behaving ethically? Why?
2. ━━━▶ Who is affected by Chris's decision?

ETHICS

TIF 3-2   Loan application

Daryl Kirby opened Squid Realty Co. on January 1, 20Y3. At the end of the first year, the business needed additional capital. On behalf of Squid Realty Co., Daryl applied to Ocean National Bank for a loan of $375,000. Based on Squid Realty Co.'s financial statements, which had been prepared on a cash basis, the Ocean National Bank loan officer rejected the loan as too risky.

After receiving the rejection notice, Daryl instructed his accountant to prepare the financial statements on an accrual basis. These statements included $65,000 in accounts receivable and $25,000 in accounts payable. Daryl then instructed his accountant to record an additional $30,000 of accounts receivable for commissions on property for which a contract had been signed on December 28, 20Y3. The title to the property is to transfer on January 5, 20Y4, when an attorney formally records the transfer of the property to the buyer.

Daryl then applied for a $375,000 loan from Free Spirit Bank, using the revised financial statements. On this application, Daryl indicated that he had not previously been rejected for credit.

━━━▶ Discuss the ethical and professional conduct of Daryl Kirby in applying for the loan from Free Spirit Bank.

TEAM ACTIVITY   REAL WORLD

TIF 3-3 Real-world annual report

In teams, select a public company that interests you. Obtain the company's most recent annual report on Form 10-K. The Form 10-K is a company's annually required filing with the Securities and Exchange Commission (SEC). It includes the company's financial statements and accompanying notes. The Form 10-K can be obtained either (a) from the investor relations section of the company's website or (b) by using the company search feature of the SEC's EDGAR database service found at www.sec.gov/edgar/searchedgar/companysearch.html.

1. Based on the information in the company's most recent annual report, answer the following questions:

    a. In what industry does the company operate?
    b. How many years of information are reported on the company's income statement?
    c. How much net income (loss) does the company report on its income statement for each year presented?
    d. How much revenue does the company report on its income statement for each year presented?
    e. Within the notes to the financial statements, find the note on significant accounting policies. Based on the information in this note, when does the company recognize revenue?

2. ━━━▶ Based solely on the company's net income, has the company's performance improved, remained constant, or deteriorated over the periods presented? Briefly explain your answer.

REAL WORLD

TIF 3-4 Passenger airline revenue

Delta Air Lines, Inc. (DAL) is a major passenger airline headquartered in the United States. Most Delta passengers purchase their tickets several weeks prior to taking the trip and use a credit card such as VISA or American Express to pay for their ticket. The credit card company pays the airline at the time the flight is booked, several weeks prior to the flight.
━━━▶ Write a brief memo to your instructor explaining when Delta should recognize revenue from ticket sales.

TIF 3-5 Adjustments and financial statements

Several years ago, your brother opened Magna Appliance Repairs. He made a small initial investment and added money from his personal bank account as needed. He withdrew money for living expenses at irregular intervals. As the business grew, he hired an assistant. He is now considering adding more employees, purchasing additional service trucks, and purchasing the building he now rents. To secure funds for the expansion, your brother submitted a loan application to the bank and included the most recent financial statemets (which follow) prepared from accounts maintained by a part-time bookkeeper.

Magna Appliance Repairs
Income Statement
For the Year Ended October 31, 20Y9

Service revenue		$ 675,000
Less: Rent paid	$ 187,200	
Wages paid	148,500	
Supplies paid	42,000	
Utilities paid	39,000	
Insurance paid	21,600	
Miscellaneous payments	54,600	(492,900)
Net income		$ 182,100

Magna Appliance Repairs
Balance Sheet
October 31, 20Y9

Assets

Cash	$ 95,400
Amounts due from customers...	112,500
Truck	332,100
Total assets	$ 540,000

Equities

Owner's capital	$ 540,000

After reviewing the financial statements, the loan officer at the bank asked your brother if he used the accrual basis of accounting for revenues and expenses. Your brother responded that he did and that is why he included an account for "Amounts Due from Customers." The loan officer then asked whether or not the accounts were adjusted prior to the preparation of the statements. Your brother answered that they had not been adjusted.

1. ▬▬▶ Why do you think the loan officer suspected that the accounts had not been adjusted prior to the preparation of the statements?
2. Indicate possible accounts that might need to be adjusted before an accurate set of financial statements could be prepared.

Pathways Challenge

This is Accounting!

Information/Consequences

Delta Air Lines (DAL) should not record the entire $1,000 as revenue for 20Y6. Instead, Delta should allocate the $1,000 revenue to (1) the flight flown in December and (2) the 2,000 mileage credits. Only the portion allocated to the flight flown in December should be recorded as revenue of 20Y6.

The portion of the $1,000 allocated to the 2,000 mileage credits should be recorded as unearned revenue (liability). Only when the mileage credits are redeemed will they be recorded as revenue.

At the end of its accounting period, Delta will need to update its estimates for mileage credits (unearned revenue), including mileage credits for tickets that have been purchased for flights that are yet to be flown.

Suggested Answer

4 The Accounting Cycle

Chapter 1

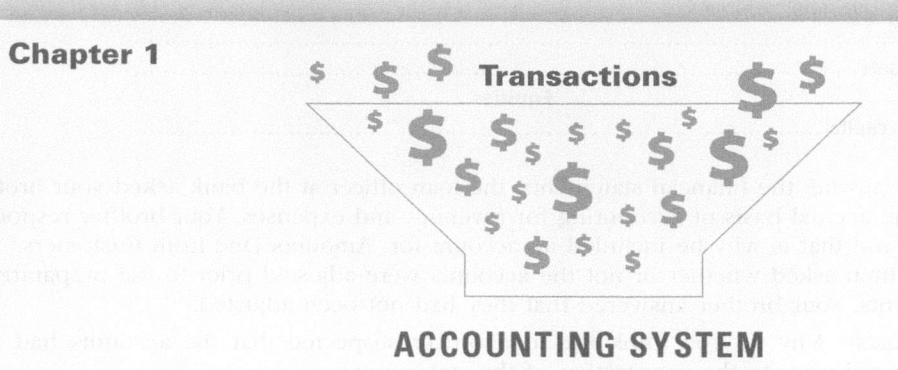

Transactions

ACCOUNTING SYSTEM

Accounting Equation

Assets = Liabilities + Equity

Chapter 2

Account

Debits	Credits

RULES OF DEBIT AND CREDIT

Balance Sheet Accounts

ASSETS = LIABILITIES + STOCKHOLDERS' EQUITY

Asset Accounts

Debit for increases (+)	Credit for decreases (−)
Balance	

Liability Accounts

Debit for decreases (−)	Credit for increases (+)
	Balance

Common Stock

Debit for decreases (−)	Credit for increases (+)
	Balance

+ Retained Earnings

Debit for decreases (−)	Credit for increases (+)
	Balance

Dividends

Debit for increases (+)	Credit for decreases (−)
Balance	

Income Statement Accounts

Revenue Accounts

Debit for decreases (−)	Credit for increases (+)
	Balance

Expense Accounts

Debit for increases (+)	Credit for decreases (−)
Balance	

Unadjusted Trial Balance

Total Debit Balances = Total Credit Balances

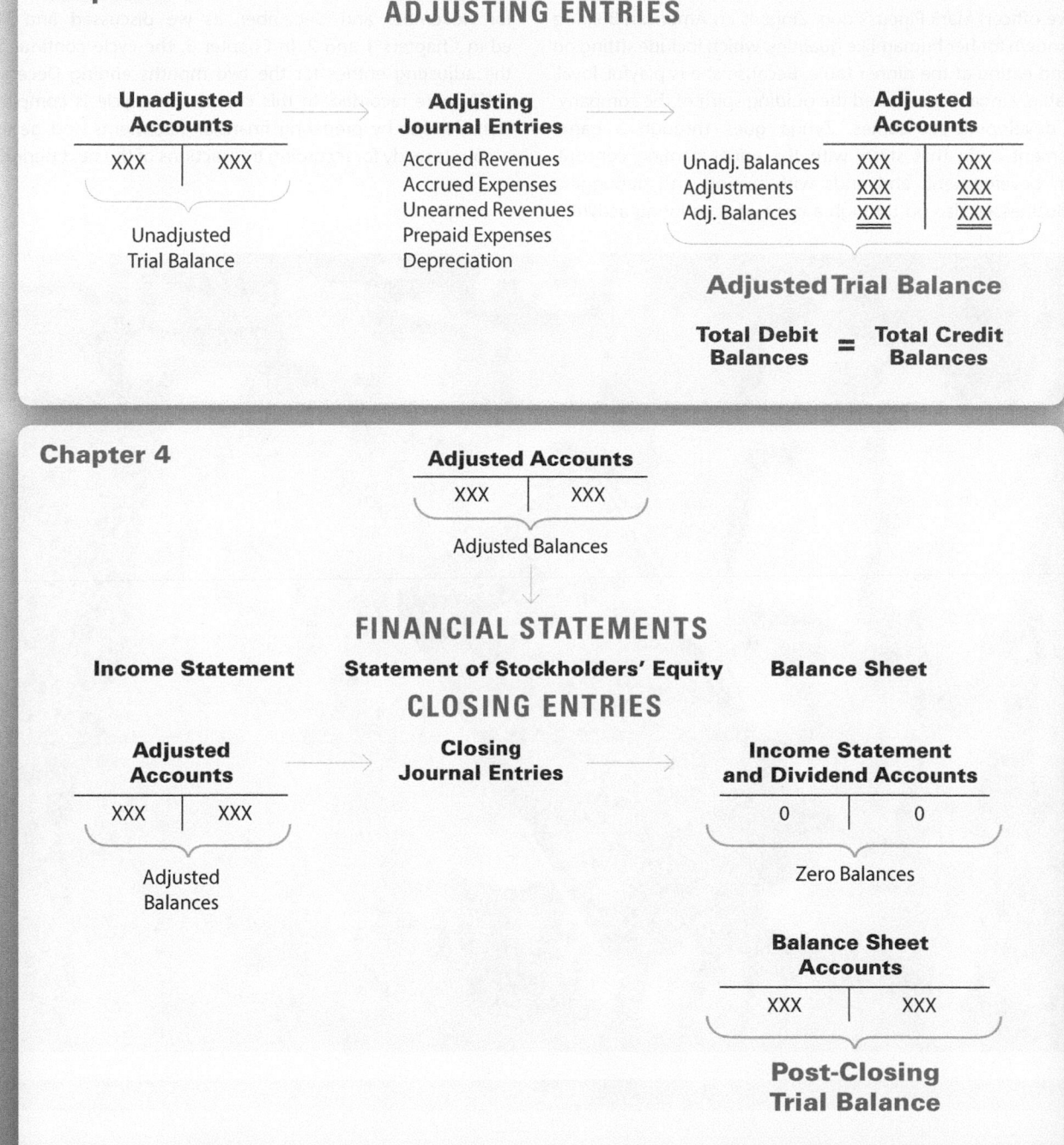

Chapter 3

ADJUSTING ENTRIES

Unadjusted Accounts

| XXX | XXX |

Unadjusted
Trial Balance

Adjusting Journal Entries

Accrued Revenues
Accrued Expenses
Unearned Revenues
Prepaid Expenses
Depreciation

Adjusted Accounts

Unadj. Balances	XXX	XXX
Adjustments	XXX	XXX
Adj. Balances	XXX	XXX

Adjusted Trial Balance

Total Debit
Balances **=** Total Credit
Balances

Chapter 4

Adjusted Accounts

| XXX | XXX |

Adjusted Balances

FINANCIAL STATEMENTS

Income Statement   **Statement of Stockholders' Equity**   **Balance Sheet**

CLOSING ENTRIES

Adjusted Accounts

| XXX | XXX |

Adjusted
Balances

Closing Journal Entries

Income Statement and Dividend Accounts

| 0 | 0 |

Zero Balances

Balance Sheet Accounts

| XXX | XXX |

Post-Closing Trial Balance

Zynga, Inc.

Zynga Inc. (ZNGA) is a leading provider of social games with more than 240 million active players per month. Zynga's games, such as CastleVille Legends, FarmVille, Mafia Wars, and Words With Friends, can be played on a variety of platforms including Facebook, Google Android, and Apple IOS.

Zynga was founded in 2007 and is named after CEO (chief executive officer) Mark Pincus's dog. Zinga is an American Bulldog who is known for her human-like qualities, which include sitting on chairs and eating at the dinner table. Because she is playful, loyal, and lovable, Zinga is considered the guiding spirit of the company.

In developing its games, Zynga goes through a game development cycle that starts with the initial gaming concept, program development, and ends with testing and debugging errors. Businesses also go through a cycle of accounting activities that begins with recording transactions and ends with preparing financial statements and getting the accounting records ready for recording the next period's transactions.

In Chapter 1, the initial accounting cycle for **NetSolutions** began with Chris Clark's investment in the business on November 1, 20Y3. The cycle continued with recording NetSolutions' transactions for November and December, as we discussed and illustrated in Chapters 1 and 2. In Chapter 3, the cycle continued when the adjusting entries for the two months ending December 31, 20Y3, were recorded. In this chapter, the cycle is completed for NetSolutions by preparing financial statements and getting the accounts ready for recording transactions of the next period.

Source: Zynga.com

©JAHI CHIKWENDIU/THE WASHINGTON POST/GETTY IMAGES

Link to Zynga . . . . Pages 163, 165, 166

Make a Decision . . . . Page 227

What's Covered

The Accounting Cycle

Preparing Classified Financial Statements
- Flow of Accounting Information (Obj. 1)
- Income Statement (Obj. 2)
- Statement of Stockholders' Equity (Obj. 2)
- Balance Sheet (Obj. 2)

Closing the Accounts
- Closing Entries (Obj. 3)
- Post-Closing Trial Balance (Obj. 3)

The Accounting Cycle
- Summary (Obj. 4)
- Illustration (Obj. 5)

Learning Objectives

Obj. 1 Describe the flow of accounting information from the unadjusted trial balance into the adjusted trial balance and financial statements.

Obj. 2 Prepare financial statements from adjusted account balances.

Obj. 3 Prepare closing entries.

Obj. 4 Describe the accounting cycle.

Obj. 5 Illustrate the accounting cycle for one period.

Analysis for Decision Making

Obj. 6 Describe and illustrate the use of working capital and the current ratio in evaluating a company's financial condition.

Appendices 1 and 2

Obj. App 1 Describe and illustrate the end-of-period spreadsheet.
Obj. App 2 Describe and illustrate the use of reversing entries.

Flow of Accounting Information

Objective 1
Describe the flow of accounting information from the unadjusted trial balance into the adjusted trial balance and financial statements.

The process of adjusting the accounts and preparing financial statements is one of the most important in accounting. Using the **NetSolutions** illustration from Chapters 1–3 and an end-of-period spreadsheet, the flow of accounting data in adjusting accounts and preparing financial statements is summarized in Exhibit 1.

The end-of-period spreadsheet in Exhibit 1 begins with the unadjusted trial balance. The unadjusted trial balance verifies that the total of the debit balances equals the total of the credit balances. If the trial balance totals are unequal, an error has occurred. Any errors must be found and corrected before the end-of-period process can continue.

The adjustments for NetSolutions from Chapter 3 are shown in the Adjustments columns of the spreadsheet. Cross-referencing (by letters) the debit and credit of each adjustment is useful in reviewing the effect of the adjustments on the unadjusted account balances. The adjustments are normally entered in the order in which the data are assembled. If the titles of the accounts to be adjusted do not appear in the unadjusted trial balance, the accounts are inserted in their proper order in the Account Title column. The total of the Adjustments columns verifies that the total debits equal the total credits for the adjusting entries. The total of the Debit column must equal the total of the Credit column.

The adjustments in the spreadsheet are added to or subtracted from the amounts in the Unadjusted Trial Balance columns to arrive at the amounts inserted in the Adjusted Trial Balance columns. In this way, the Adjusted Trial Balance columns of the spreadsheet illustrate the effect of the adjusting entries on the unadjusted accounts. The totals of the Adjusted Trial Balance columns verify that the totals of the debit and credit balances are equal after adjustment.

Exhibit 1 End-of-Period Spreadsheet and Flow of Accounting Data—NetSolutions

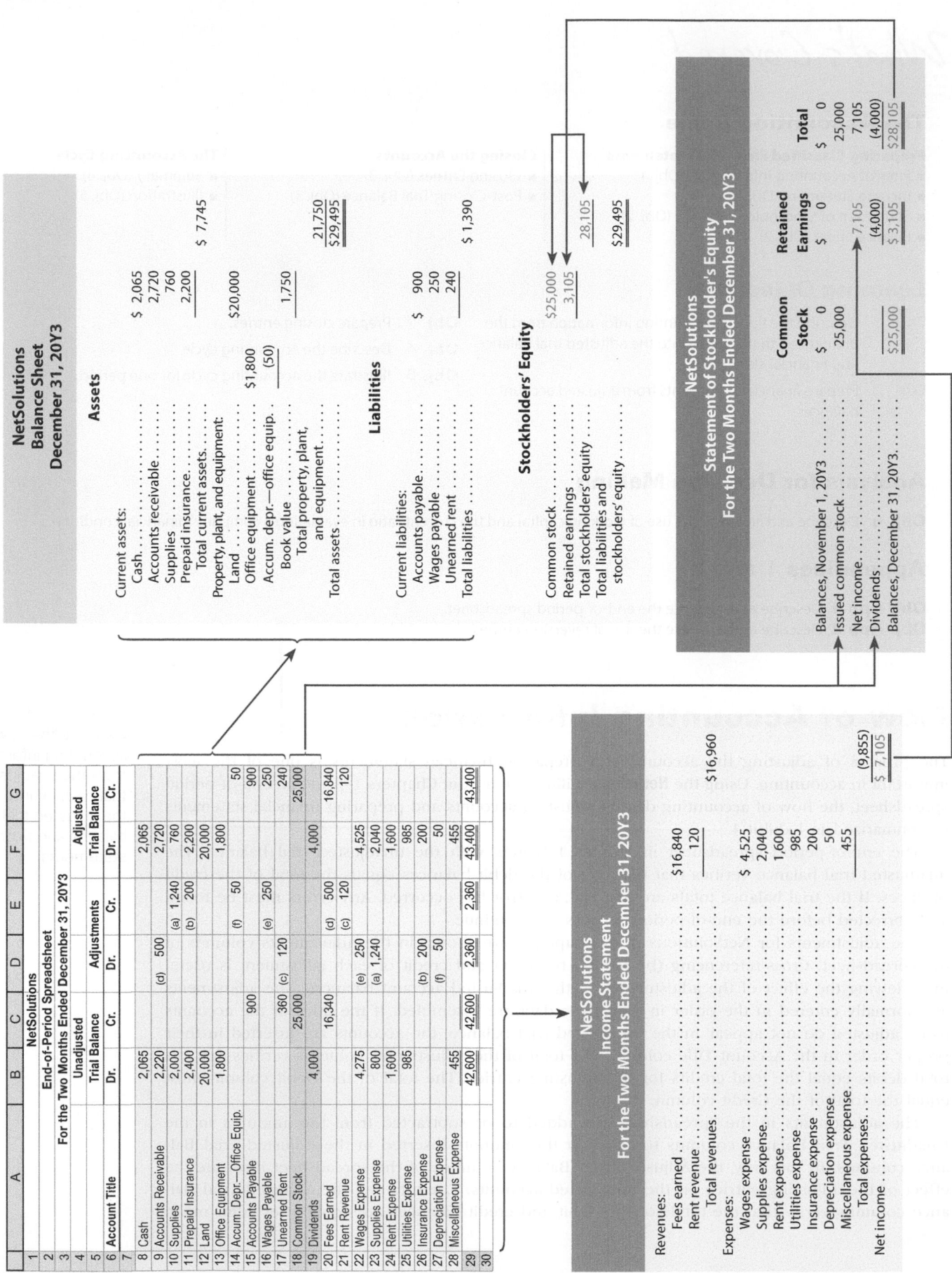

NetSolutions
Balance Sheet
December 31, 20Y3

Assets

Current assets:
Cash	$ 2,065	
Accounts receivable	2,720	
Supplies	760	
Prepaid insurance	2,200	
Total current assets		$ 7,745

Property, plant, and equipment:
Land		$20,000	
Office equipment	$1,800		
Accum. depr.—office equip.	(50)	1,750	
Total property, plant, and equipment			21,750
Total assets			$29,495

Liabilities

Current liabilities:
Accounts payable	$ 900	
Wages payable	250	
Unearned rent	240	
Total liabilities		$ 1,390

Stockholders' Equity

Common stock	$25,000	
Retained earnings	3,105	
Total stockholders' equity		28,105
Total liabilities and stockholders' equity		$29,495

NetSolutions
Statement of Stockholder's Equity
For the Two Months Ended December 31, 20Y3

	Common Stock	Retained Earnings	Total
Balances, November 1, 20Y3	$ 0	$ 0	$ 0
Issued common stock	25,000		25,000
Net income		7,105	7,105
Dividends		(4,000)	(4,000)
Balances, December 31, 20Y3	$25,000	$ 3,105	$28,105

NetSolutions
End-of-Period Spreadsheet
For the Two Months Ended December 31, 20Y3

	A	B	C	D	E	F	G
		Unadjusted Trial Balance		Adjustments		Adjusted Trial Balance	
6	Account Title	Dr.	Cr.	Dr.	Cr.	Dr.	Cr.
8	Cash	2,065				2,065	
9	Accounts Receivable	2,220		(d) 500		2,720	
10	Supplies	2,000			(a) 1,240	760	
11	Prepaid Insurance	2,400			(b) 200	2,200	
12	Land	20,000				20,000	
13	Office Equipment	1,800				1,800	
14	Accum. Depr.—Office Equip.				(f) 50		50
15	Accounts Payable		900				900
16	Wages Payable				(e) 250		250
17	Unearned Rent		360	(c) 120			240
18	Common Stock		25,000				25,000
19	Dividends	4,000				4,000	
20	Fees Earned		16,340		(d) 500		16,840
21	Rent Revenue				(c) 120		120
22	Wages Expense	4,275		(e) 250		4,525	
23	Supplies Expense	800		(a) 1,240		2,040	
24	Rent Expense	1,600				1,600	
25	Utilities Expense	985				985	
26	Insurance Expense			(b) 200		200	
27	Depreciation Expense			(f) 50		50	
28	Miscellaneous Expense	455				455	
29		42,600	42,600	2,360	2,360	43,400	43,400

NetSolutions
Income Statement
For the Two Months Ended December 31, 20Y3

Revenues:
Fees earned	$16,840	
Rent revenue	120	
Total revenues		$16,960

Expenses:
Wages expense	$ 4,525	
Supplies expense	2,040	
Rent expense	1,600	
Utilities expense	985	
Insurance expense	200	
Depreciation expense	50	
Miscellaneous expense	455	
Total expenses		(9,855)
Net income		$ 7,105

Exhibit 1 illustrates the flow of accounts from the adjusted trial balance into the financial statements as follows:

1. The revenue and expense accounts (spreadsheet lines 20–28) flow into the income statement.

2. The common stock and dividends accounts (spreadsheet lines 18 and 19) flow into the statement of stockholders' equity. The net income of $7,105 also flows into the statement of stockholders' equity from the income statement.

3. The asset and liability accounts (spreadsheet lines 8–17) flow into the balance sheet. The end-of-period common stock and retained earnings also flow into the balance sheet from the statement of stockholders' equity.

To summarize, Exhibit 1 illustrates the process by which accounts are adjusted. In addition, Exhibit 1 illustrates how the adjusted accounts flow into the financial statements. The financial statements for NetSolutions can be prepared directly from Exhibit 1.

The spreadsheet in Exhibit 1 is not required. However, many accountants prepare such a spreadsheet, sometimes called a *work sheet*, as part of the normal end-of-period process. The primary advantage in doing so is that it allows managers and accountants to see the effect of adjustments on the financial statements. This is especially useful for adjustments that depend upon estimates. Such estimates and their effect on the financial statements are discussed in later chapters.[1]

Financial Statements

Objective 2
Prepare financial statements from adjusted account balances.

Using the adjusted trial balance shown in Exhibit 1, the financial statements for **NetSolutions** can be prepared. The income statement, the statement of stockholders' equity, and the balance sheet are shown in Exhibit 2.

Income Statement

The income statement is prepared directly from the Adjusted Trial Balance columns of the Exhibit 1 spreadsheet, beginning with fees earned of $16,840. The expenses in the income statement in Exhibit 2 are listed in order of size, beginning with the larger items. Miscellaneous expense is the last item, regardless of its amount.

In a recent income statement, **Zynga** reported a net loss from operations of $108 million.

Link to Zynga

Statement of Stockholders' Equity

The statement of stockholders' equity is prepared by entering the beginning balances for common stock and retained earnings as of November 1, 20X3. Since **NetSolutions** began operations on November 1, these balances are zero in Exhibit 2.

The common stock of $25,000 that was issued during the period is entered in the Common Stock column. During the period, NetSolutions earned net income of $7,105, which increases retained earnings and is therefore entered in the Retained Earnings column. NetSolutions paid dividends of $4,000 during the period, which reduces retained earnings and is therefore entered as a deduction in the Retained Earnings column. Entries in each row are added across and the total is entered in the Total column. Finally, all of the columns are totaled to arrive at the ending balances for Common Stock and Retained Earnings and the total of stockholders' equity as of December 31, 20Y3.

For the following period, the beginning balances of Common Stock and Retained Earnings for NetSolutions are the ending balances that were reported for the previous period. For example, assume that during 20Y4, NetSolutions issued no additional common stock, earned net income

---

[1] Appendix 1 to this chapter describes and illustrates how to prepare an end-of-period spreadsheet that includes financial statement columns.

Exhibit 2

Financial Statements—
NetSolutions

NetSolutions
Income Statement
For the Two Months Ended December 31, 20Y3

Revenues:		
Fees earned	$16,840	
Rent revenue	120	
Total revenues		$16,960
Expenses:		
Wages expense	$ 4,525	
Supplies expense	2,040	
Rent expense	1,600	
Utilities expense	985	
Insurance expense	200	
Depreciation expense	50	
Miscellaneous expense	455	
Total expenses		(9,855)
Net income		$ 7,105

NetSolutions
Statement of Stockholders' Equity
For the Two Months Ended December 31, 20Y3

	Common Stock	Retained Earnings	Total
Balances, November 1, 20Y3	$ 0	$ 0	$ 0
Issued common stock	25,000		25,000
Net income		7,105	7,105
Dividends		(4,000)	(4,000)
Balances, December 31, 20Y3	$25,000	$ 3,105	$28,105

NetSolutions
Balance Sheet
December 31, 20Y3

Assets

Current assets:			
Cash		$ 2,065	
Accounts receivable		2,720	
Supplies		760	
Prepaid insurance		2,200	
Total current assets			$ 7,745
Property, plant, and equipment:			
Land		$20,000	
Office equipment	$1,800		
Accum. depr.—office equip.	(50)		
Book value		1,750	
Total property, plant, and equip.			21,750
Total assets			$29,495

Liabilities

Current liabilities:		
Accounts payable	$ 900	
Wages payable	250	
Unearned rent	240	
Total liabilities		$ 1,390

Stockholders' Equity

Common stock	$25,000	
Retained earnings	3,105	
Total stockholders' equity		28,105
Total liabilities and stockholders' equity		$29,495

of $149,695, and paid dividends of $24,000. The statement of stockholders' equity for the year ending December 31, 20Y4, for NetSolutions would be as follows:

NetSolutions Statement of Stockholders' Equity For the Year Ended December 31, 20Y4			
	Common Stock	Retained Earnings	Total
Balances, January 1, 20Y4	$25,000	$ 3,105	$ 28,105
Net income		149,695	149,695
Dividends.............................		(24,000)	(24,000)
Balances, December 31, 20Y4	$25,000	$128,800	$153,800

Zynga does not pay dividends and in recent financial statements reported a net loss of $108 million and a retained earnings deficit (debit balance) of $1.6 billion.

Link to Zynga

Balance Sheet

The balance sheet is prepared directly from the Adjusted Trial Balance columns of the Exhibit 1 spreadsheet, beginning with cash of $2,065. The asset and liability amounts are taken from the spreadsheet. The common stock and retained earnings amounts are taken from the statement of stockholders' equity, as illustrated in Exhibit 2.

The balance sheet in Exhibit 2 shows subsections for assets and liabilities. Such a balance sheet is a *classified balance sheet*. These subsections are described next.

Assets Assets are commonly divided into two sections on the balance sheet: (1) current assets and (2) property, plant, and equipment.

Current Assets Cash and other assets that are expected to be converted to cash or sold or used up usually within one year or less, through the normal operations of the business, are called **current assets**. In addition to cash, the current assets may include notes receivable, accounts receivable, supplies, and other prepaid expenses.

Notes receivable are amounts that customers owe. They are written promises to pay the amount of the note and interest. Accounts receivable are also amounts customers owe, but they are less formal

note:

Two common classes of assets are current assets and property, plant, and equipment.

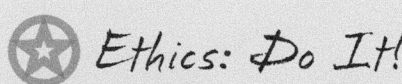

Ethics: Do It!

CEO's Health?

How much and what information to disclose in financial statements and to investors presents a common ethical dilemma for managers and accountants. For example, Steve Jobs, co-founder and CEO of **Apple Inc. (AAPL)**, had been diagnosed and treated for pancreatic cancer. Apple Inc. had insisted that the status of Steve Jobs's health

was a "private" matter and did not have to be disclosed to investors. Apple maintained this position even though Jobs was a driving force behind Apple's innovation and financial success.

Steve Jobs's health deteriorated significantly, however, and that disclosure was eventually provided. On October 5, 2011, Steve Jobs died at the age of 56.

than notes. Accounts receivable normally result from providing services or selling merchandise on account. Notes receivable and accounts receivable are current assets because they are usually converted to cash within one year or less.

Property, Plant, and Equipment The **Property, plant, and equipment** section may also be described as **fixed assets** or **plant assets**. These assets include equipment, machinery, buildings, and land. With the exception of land, as discussed in Chapter 3, fixed assets depreciate over a period of time. The original cost, accumulated depreciation, and book value of each major type of fixed asset are normally reported on the balance sheet or in the notes to the financial statements.

Link to Zynga In a recent balance sheet, **Zynga** reported current assets of $965 million; property, plant, and equipment and other assets of $941 million; and total assets of $1,906 million.

note:
Two common classes of liabilities are current liabilities and long-term liabilities.

Liabilities Liabilities are the amounts the business owes to creditors. Liabilities are commonly divided into two sections on the balance sheet: (1) current liabilities and (2) long-term liabilities.

Current Liabilities Liabilities that will be due within a short time (usually one year or less) and that are to be paid out of current assets are called **current liabilities**. The most common liabilities in this group are notes payable and accounts payable. Other current liabilities may include wages payable, interest payable, taxes payable, and unearned fees.

Long-Term Liabilities Liabilities that will not be due for a long time (usually more than one year) are called **long-term liabilities**. If NetSolutions had long-term liabilities, they would be reported below the current liabilities. As long-term liabilities come due and are to be paid within one year, they are reported as current liabilities. If they are to be renewed rather than paid, they would continue to be reported as long term. When an asset is pledged as security for a liability, the obligation may be called a *mortgage note payable* or a *mortgage payable*.

Link to Zynga In a recent balance sheet, **Zynga** reported current liabilities of $244 million, long-term and other liabilities of $81 million, and total liabilities of $325 million.

Stockholders' Equity The stockholders' right to the assets of the business is presented on the balance sheet below the Liabilities section. The stockholders' equity of NetSolutions consists of common stock and retained earnings. The stockholders' equity is added to the total liabilities, and this total must be equal to the total assets.

Link to Zynga In a recent balance sheet, **Zynga** reported common stock of $3,221 million, a retained earnings deficit of $1,640 million, and total stockholders' equity of $1,581 million.

Check Up Corner 4-1 | Financial Statements from Adjusted Trial Balance

The following account balances were taken from the adjusted trial balance for Laser Corrective Vision Company, a health care company, for the fiscal year ended December 31, 20Y2:

Common Stock	$175,000	Miscellaneous Expense	$ 8,500
Depreciation Expense	25,000	Rent Expense	20,000
Dividends	6,000	Salaries Expense	165,000
Fees Earned	312,000	Supplies Expense	15,500
Insurance Expense	6,000	Utilities Expense	12,000

On January 1, 20Y2, Retained Earnings had a balance of $100,000. During 20Y2, common stock of $50,000 was issued.

Prepare an income statement and statement of stockholders' equity for Laser Corrective Vision.

Solution:

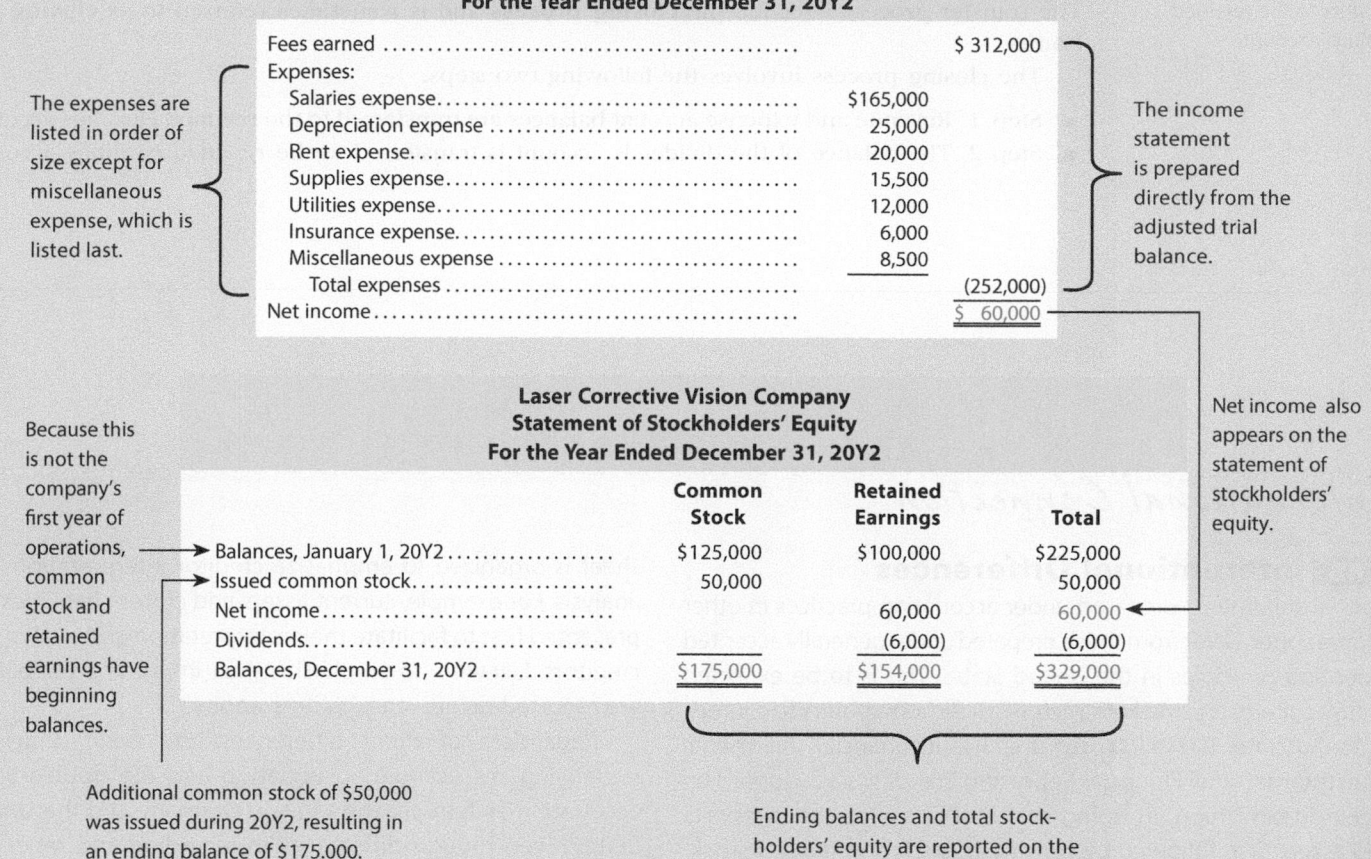

Laser Corrective Vision Company
Income Statement
For the Year Ended December 31, 20Y2

The expenses are listed in order of size except for miscellaneous expense, which is listed last.

Fees earned		$ 312,000
Expenses:		
Salaries expense	$165,000	
Depreciation expense	25,000	
Rent expense	20,000	
Supplies expense	15,500	
Utilities expense	12,000	
Insurance expense	6,000	
Miscellaneous expense	8,500	
Total expenses		(252,000)
Net income		$ 60,000

The income statement is prepared directly from the adjusted trial balance.

Laser Corrective Vision Company
Statement of Stockholders' Equity
For the Year Ended December 31, 20Y2

Because this is not the company's first year of operations, common stock and retained earnings have beginning balances.

	Common Stock	Retained Earnings	Total
Balances, January 1, 20Y2	$125,000	$100,000	$225,000
Issued common stock	50,000		50,000
Net income		60,000	60,000
Dividends		(6,000)	(6,000)
Balances, December 31, 20Y2	$175,000	$154,000	$329,000

Net income also appears on the statement of stockholders' equity.

Additional common stock of $50,000 was issued during 20Y2, resulting in an ending balance of $175.000.

Ending balances and total stockholders' equity are reported on the December 31, 20Y2, balance sheet.

Check Up Corner

Objective 3
Prepare closing entries.

Closing Entries

As discussed in Chapter 3, the adjusting entries are recorded in the journal at the end of the accounting period. For **NetSolutions**, the adjusting entries are shown in Exhibit 7 of Chapter 3. After the adjusting entries are posted to NetSolutions' ledger, shown later in this chapter, the ledger agrees with the data reported on the financial statements shown in Exhibit 2.

The balances of the accounts reported on the balance sheet are carried forward from year to year. Because they are relatively permanent, these accounts are called **permanent accounts** or **real accounts**. For example, Cash, Accounts Receivable, Equipment, Accumulated Depreciation, Accounts Payable, Common Stock, and Retained Earnings are permanent accounts.

The balances of the accounts reported on the income statement are not carried forward from year to year. Also, the balance of the dividends account, which is reported on the statement of stockholders' equity, is not carried forward. Because these accounts report amounts for only one period, they are called **temporary accounts** or **nominal accounts**. Temporary accounts are not carried forward because they relate only to one period. For example, the Fees Earned of $16,840 and Wages Expense of $4,525 for NetSolutions shown in Exhibit 2 are for the two months ending December 31, 20Y3, and should not be carried forward to 20Y4.

At the beginning of the next period, temporary accounts should have zero balances. To achieve this, temporary account balances are transferred to permanent accounts at the end of the accounting period. The journal entries that transfer these balances are called **closing entries**. The transfer process is called the **closing process** and is sometimes referred to as **closing the books**.

The closing process involves the following two steps:

- Step 1. Revenue and expense account balances are transferred to the retained earnings account.
- Step 2. The balance of the dividends account is transferred to the retained earnings account.

note:

Closing entries transfer the balances of temporary accounts to the retained earnings account.

International Connection

IFRS International Differences

Financial statements prepared under accounting practices in other countries often differ from those prepared under generally accepted accounting principles in the United States. This is to be expected because cultures and market structures differ from country to country.

To illustrate, **BMW Group** prepares its financial statements under International Financial Reporting Standards as adopted by the European Union. In doing so, BMW's balance sheet reports fixed assets first, followed by current assets. It also reports stockholders' equity before the liabilities. In contrast, balance sheets prepared under U.S. accounting principles report current assets followed by fixed assets and current liabilities followed by long-term liabilities and stockholders' equity. The U.S. form of balance sheet is organized to emphasize creditor interpretation and analysis. For example, current assets and current liabilities are presented first to facilitate their interpretation and analysis by creditors. Likewise, to emphasize their importance, liabilities are reported before stockholders' equity.*

Regardless of these differences, the basic principles underlying the accounting equation and the double-entry accounting system are the same in Germany and the United States. Even though differences in recording and reporting exist, the accounting equation holds true: The total assets still equal the total liabilities and stockholders' equity.

*Examples of U.S. and IFRS financial statement reporting differences are further discussed and illustrated in Appendix C.

The two closing journal entries required by the closing process are as follows:[2]

Closing Entry (1): Debit each revenue account for its balance, credit each expense account for its balance, and credit (net income) or debit (net loss) the retained earnings account.

Closing Entry (2): Debit the retained earnings account for the balance of the dividends account and credit the dividends account for its balance.

Exhibit 3 diagrams the closing process.

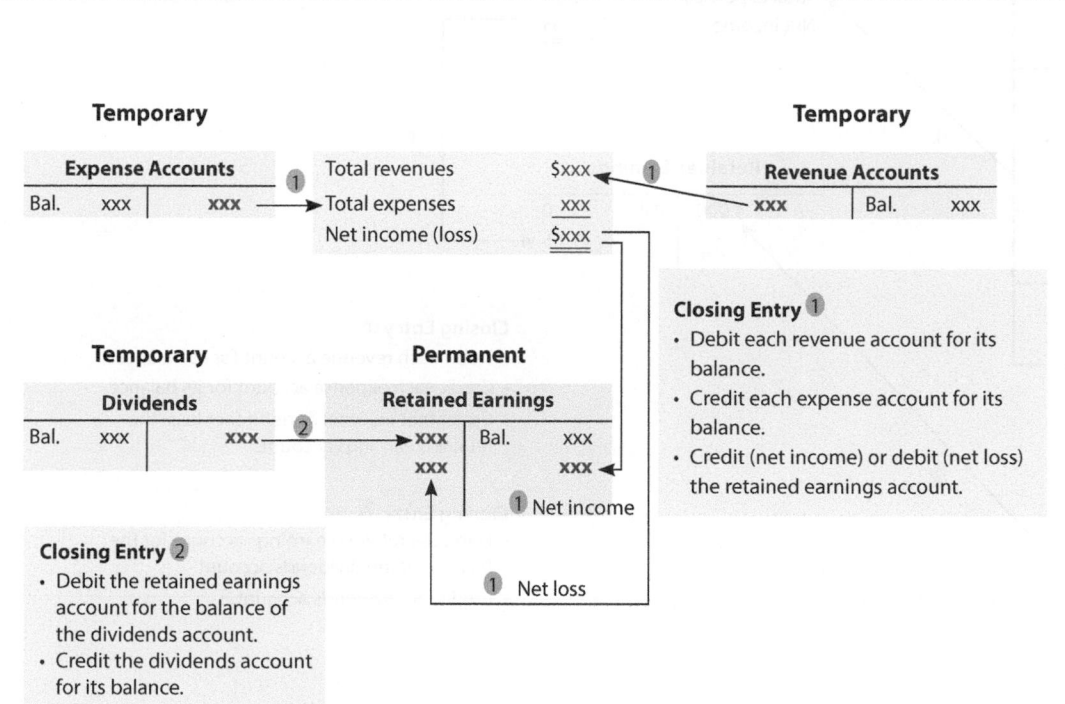

Exhibit 3
The Closing Process

Closing entries are recorded in the journal and are dated as of the last day of the accounting period. In the journal, closing entries are recorded immediately following the adjusting entries. The caption, *Closing Entries*, is often inserted above the closing entries to separate them from the adjusting entries.

Journalizing and Posting Closing Entries

A flowchart of the two closing entries for NetSolutions is shown in Exhibit 4. The balances in the accounts are those shown in the Adjusted Trial Balance columns of the end-of-period spreadsheet shown in Exhibit 1.

The closing entries for NetSolutions are shown in Exhibit 5. The account titles and balances for these entries may be obtained from the end-of-period spreadsheet, the adjusted trial balance, the income statement, the statement of stockholders' equity, or the ledger.

[2] It is possible to close the temporary revenue and expense accounts using a "clearing" account such as Income Summary, Revenue and Expense Summary, or Profit and Loss Summary. In this case, four closing entries are made. The first entry closes the revenue accounts to Income Summary. The second entry closes the expense accounts to Income Summary. The third entry closes Income Summary to Retained Earnings. The fourth entry closes Dividends to Retained Earnings.

Exhibit 4   Flowchart of Closing Entries for NetSolutions

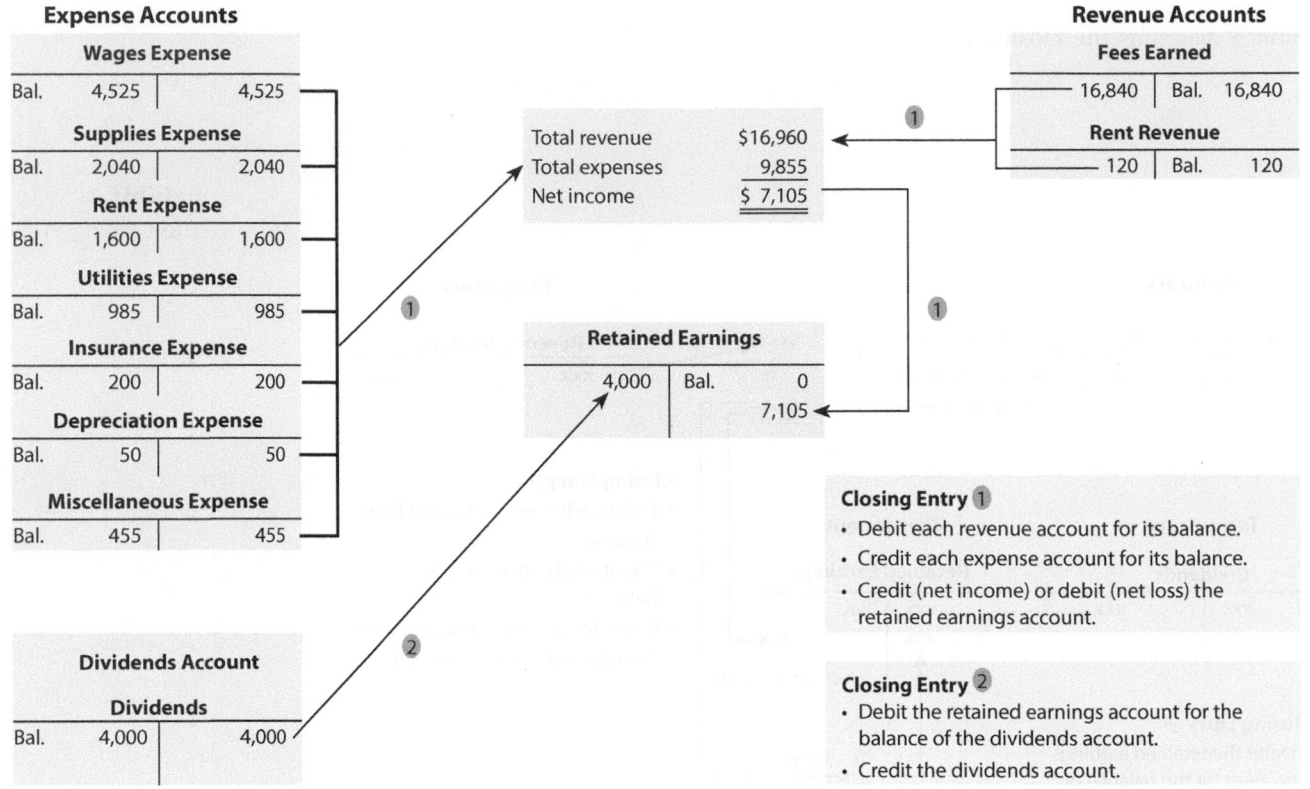

Closing Entry ①
- Debit each revenue account for its balance.
- Credit each expense account for its balance.
- Credit (net income) or debit (net loss) the retained earnings account.

Closing Entry ②
- Debit the retained earnings account for the balance of the dividends account.
- Credit the dividends account.

Exhibit 5

Closing Entries, NetSolutions

Date		Description	Post. Ref.	Debit	Credit
		Closing Entries			
20Y3 Dec.	31	Fees Earned	41	16,840	
		Rent Revenue	42	120	
		Wages Expense	51		4,525
		Supplies Expense	52		2,040
		Rent Expense	53		1,600
		Utilities Expense	54		985
		Insurance Expense	55		200
		Depreciation Expense	56		50
		Miscellaneous Expense	59		455
		Retained Earnings	32		7,105
	31	Retained Earnings	32	4,000	
		Dividends	33		4,000

Journal   Page 6

The closing entries are posted to NetSolutions' ledger as shown in Exhibit 6. After the closing entries are posted, NetSolutions' ledger has the following characteristics:

- The balance of Retained Earnings of $3,105 agrees with the amount reported on the statement of stockholders' equity and the balance sheet.
- The revenue, expense, and dividends accounts will have zero balances.

As shown in Exhibit 6, the closing entries are normally identified in the ledger as "Closing." In addition, a line is often inserted in both balance columns after a closing entry is posted. This separates next period's revenue, expense, and dividend transactions from those of the current period. Next period's transactions will be posted directly below the closing entry.

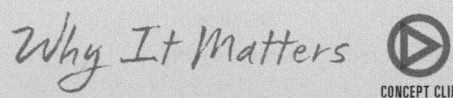

CONCEPT CLIP

Temporary Accounts on Your Pay Stub

At the end of every pay period, employees receive a paycheck (or direct deposit) and a pay stub. The pay stub might look something like this:

Sample Company Name, Sample Company Address, 95220				**EARNINGS STATEMENT**	

EMPLOYEE NAME	SOCIAL SEC. ID	EMPLOYEE ID	CHECK No.	PAY PERIOD	PAY DATE
James Robert	XXX-XX-6666	151515	259248	01/23/Y8–01/29/Y8	01/31/Y8

INCOME	RATE	HOURS	CURRENT TOTAL	DEDUCTIONS	CURRENT TOTAL	YEAR-TO-DATE
GROSS WAGES			1,000.00	FICA MED TAX	14.50	72.50
				FICA SS TAX	62.00	310.00
				FED TAX	159.50	797.50

Temporary Accounts

YTD GROSS	YTD DEDUCTIONS	YTD NET PAY	TOTAL	DEDUCTIONS	NET PAY
5,000.00	1,180.00	3,820.00	1,000.00	236.00	764.00

Each of the year-to-date accounts shown on the pay stub are temporary accounts. Each account describes the increases and decreases in the net cash received for the employee's work over the year. Increases are the gross pay, while decreases are deductions, such as Medicare taxes, social security taxes, and federal withholding taxes (FICA MED TAX, FICA SS TAX, and FED TAX in the illustration). These amounts are accumulated so that year-to-date summaries are provided as the year progresses. This is similar to income statement accounts that accumulate revenues and expenses over the period. At the end of the year, all of the year-to-date accounts are reset to zero to prepare for the next year's accumulation. This is similar to closing income statement accounts, which are also set to zero at the beginning of the new period.

Exhibit 6 Ledger with Closing Entries—NetSolutions

Account *Cash* Account No. *11*

Date	Item	Post. Ref.	Debit	Credit	Balance Debit	Balance Credit
20Y3						
Nov. 1		1	25,000		25,000	
5		1		20,000	5,000	
18		1	7,500		12,500	
30		1		3,650	8,850	
30		1		950	7,900	
30		2		2,000	5,900	
Dec. 1		2		2,400	3,500	
1		2		800	2,700	
1		2	360		3,060	
6		2		180	2,880	
11		2		400	2,480	
13		3		950	1,530	
16		3	3,100		4,630	
20		3		900	3,730	
21		3	650		4,380	
23		3		1,450	2,930	
27		3		1,200	1,730	
31		3		310	1,420	
31		4		225	1,195	
31		4	2,870		4,065	
31		4		2,000	2,065	

Account *Accounts Receivable* Account No. *12*

Date	Item	Post. Ref.	Debit	Credit	Balance Debit	Balance Credit
20Y3						
Dec. 16		3	1,750		1,750	
21		3		650	1,100	
31		4	1,120		2,220	
31	Adjusting	5	500		2,720	

Account *Supplies* Account No. *14*

Date	Item	Post. Ref.	Debit	Credit	Balance Debit	Balance Credit
20Y3						
Nov. 10		1	1,350		1,350	
30		1		800	550	
Dec. 23		3	1,450		2,000	
31	Adjusting	5		1,240	760	

Account *Prepaid Insurance* Account No. *15*

Date	Item	Post. Ref.	Debit	Credit	Balance Debit	Balance Credit
20Y3						
Dec. 1		2	2,400		2,400	
31	Adjusting	5		200	2,200	

Account *Land* Account No. *17*

Date	Item	Post. Ref.	Debit	Credit	Balance Debit	Balance Credit
20Y3						
Nov. 5		1	20,000		20,000	

Account *Office Equipment* Account No. *18*

Date	Item	Post. Ref.	Debit	Credit	Balance Debit	Balance Credit
20Y3						
Dec. 4		2	1,800		1,800	

Account *Accum. Depr.—Office Equip.* Account No. *19*

Date	Item	Post. Ref.	Debit	Credit	Balance Debit	Balance Credit
20Y3						
Dec. 31	Adjusting	5		50		50

Account *Accounts Payable* Account No. *21*

Date	Item	Post. Ref.	Debit	Credit	Balance Debit	Balance Credit
20Y3						
Nov. 10		1		1,350		1,350
30		1	950			400
Dec. 4		2		1,800		2,200
11		2	400			1,800
20		3	900			900

Account *Wages Payable* Account No. *22*

Date	Item	Post. Ref.	Debit	Credit	Balance Debit	Balance Credit
20Y3						
Dec. 31	Adjusting	5		250		250

Account *Unearned Rent* Account No. *23*

Date	Item	Post. Ref.	Debit	Credit	Balance Debit	Balance Credit
20Y3						
Dec. 1		2		360		360
31	Adjusting	5	120			240

Account *Common Stock* Account No. *31*

Date	Item	Post. Ref.	Debit	Credit	Balance Debit	Balance Credit
20Y3						
Nov. 1				25,000		25,000

Exhibit 6 Ledger, NetSolutions *(Concluded)*

Account *Retained Earnings* — Account No. *32*

Date	Item	Post. Ref.	Debit	Credit	Balance Debit	Balance Credit
20Y3						
Nov. 1						0
Dec. 31	Closing	6		7,105		7,105
31	Closing	6	4,000			3,105

Account *Dividends* — Account No. *33*

Date	Item	Post. Ref.	Debit	Credit	Balance Debit	Balance Credit
20Y3						
Nov. 30		2	2,000		2,000	
Dec. 31		4	2,000		4,000	
31	Closing	6		4,000	—	

Account *Fees Earned* — Account No. *41*

Date	Item	Post. Ref.	Debit	Credit	Balance Debit	Balance Credit
20Y3						
Nov. 18		1		7,500		7,500
Dec. 16		3		3,100		10,600
16		3		1,750		12,350
31		4		2,870		15,220
31		4		1,120		16,340
31	Adjusting	5		500		16,840
31	Closing	6	16,840		—	—

Account *Rent Revenue* — Account No. *42*

Date	Item	Post. Ref.	Debit	Credit	Balance Debit	Balance Credit
20Y3						
Dec. 31	Adjusting	5		120		120
31	Closing	6	120		—	—

Account *Wages Expense* — Account No. *51*

Date	Item	Post. Ref.	Debit	Credit	Balance Debit	Balance Credit
20Y3						
Nov. 30		1	2,125		2,125	
Dec. 13		3	950		3,075	
27		3	1,200		4,275	
31	Adjusting	5	250		4,525	
31	Closing	6		4,525	—	—

Account *Supplies Expense* — Account No. *52*

Date	Item	Post. Ref.	Debit	Credit	Balance Debit	Balance Credit
20Y3						
Nov. 30		1	800		800	
Dec. 31	Adjusting	5	1,240		2,040	
31	Closing	6		2,040	—	—

Account *Rent Expense* — Account No. *53*

Date	Item	Post. Ref.	Debit	Credit	Balance Debit	Balance Credit
20Y3						
Nov. 30		1	800		800	
Dec. 1		2	800		1,600	
31	Closing	6		1,600	—	—

Account *Utilities Expense* — Account No. *54*

Date	Item	Post. Ref.	Debit	Credit	Balance Debit	Balance Credit
20Y3						
Nov. 30		1	450		450	
Dec. 31		3	310		760	
31		4	225		985	
31	Closing	6		985	—	—

Account *Insurance Expense* — Account No. *55*

Date	Item	Post. Ref.	Debit	Credit	Balance Debit	Balance Credit
20Y3						
Dec. 31	Adjusting	5	200		200	
31	Closing	6		200	—	—

Account *Depreciation Expense* — Account No. *56*

Date	Item	Post. Ref.	Debit	Credit	Balance Debit	Balance Credit
20Y3						
Dec. 31	Adjusting	5	50		50	
31	Closing	6		50	—	—

Account *Miscellaneous Expense* — Account No. *59*

Date	Item	Post. Ref.	Debit	Credit	Balance Debit	Balance Credit
20Y3						
Nov. 30		1	275		275	
Dec. 6		2	180		455	
31	Closing	6		455	—	—

Check Up Corner 4-2 Closing Entries

After the accounts have been adjusted at December 31, the end of the year, the following balances are taken from the ledger of Wyatt Services Co.:

Retained Earnings	$615,850
Dividends	25,000
Fees Earned	380,450
Wages Expense	250,000
Rent Expense	65,000
Supplies Expense	18,250
Miscellaneous Expense	6,200

Journalize the closing entries.

Solution:

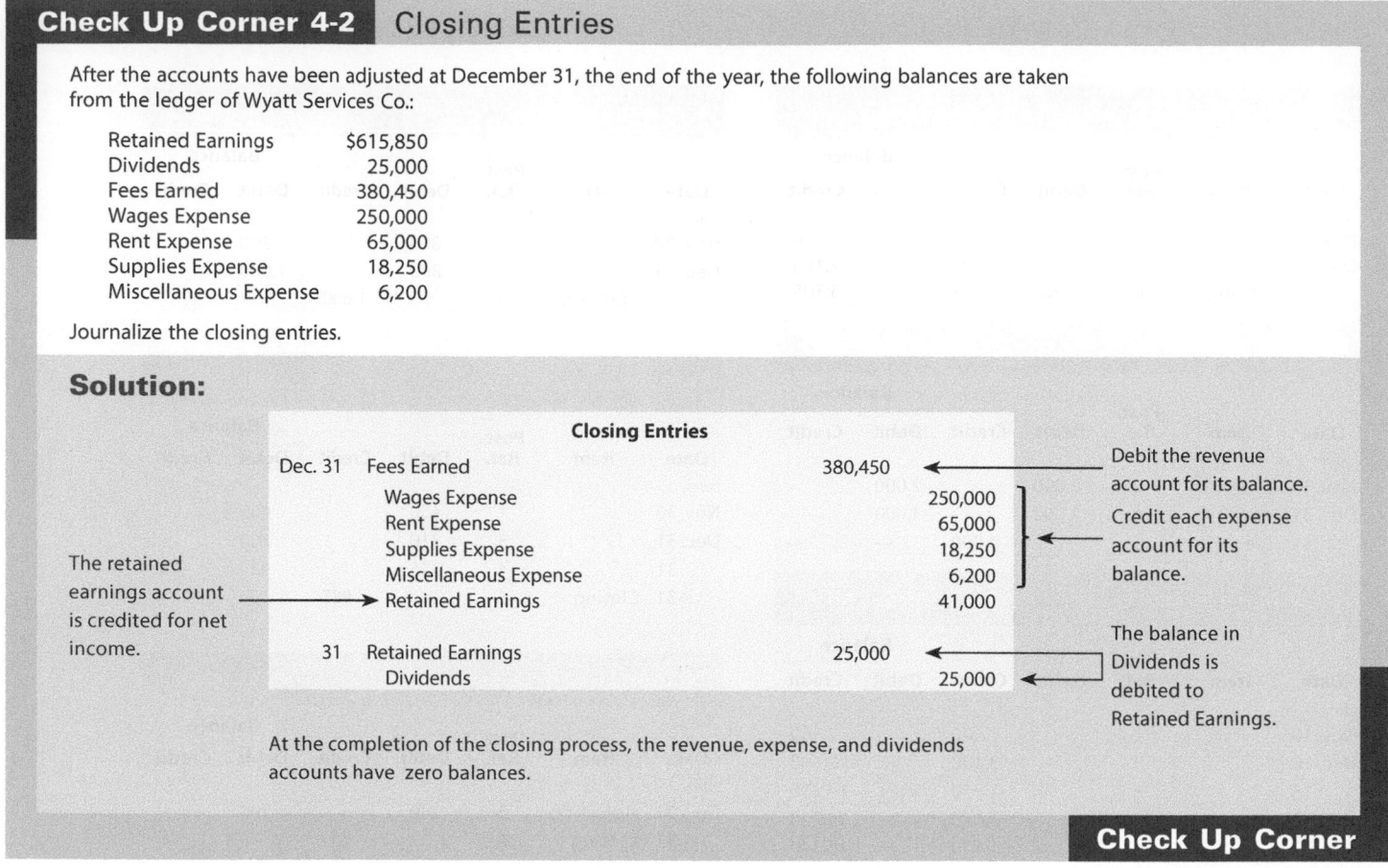

Closing Entries

Dec. 31	Fees Earned	380,450	
	Wages Expense		250,000
	Rent Expense		65,000
	Supplies Expense		18,250
	Miscellaneous Expense		6,200
	Retained Earnings		41,000
31	Retained Earnings	25,000	
	Dividends		25,000

Debit the revenue account for its balance.

Credit each expense account for its balance.

The retained earnings account is credited for net income.

The balance in Dividends is debited to Retained Earnings.

At the completion of the closing process, the revenue, expense, and dividends accounts have zero balances.

Check Up Corner

Post-Closing Trial Balance

A post-closing trial balance is prepared after the closing entries have been posted. The purpose of the post-closing (after closing) trial balance is to verify that the ledger is in balance at the beginning of the next period. The accounts and amounts should agree exactly with the accounts and amounts listed on the balance sheet at the end of the period. The post-closing trial balance for **NetSolutions** is shown in Exhibit 7.

Exhibit 7

Post-Closing Trial Balance, NetSolutions

NetSolutions
Post-Closing Trial Balance
December 31, 20Y3

	Account No.	Debit Balances	Credit Balances
Cash.	11	2,065	
Accounts Receivable.	12	2,720	
Supplies.	14	760	
Prepaid Insurance	15	2,200	
Land.	17	20,000	
Office Equipment.	18	1,800	
Accumulated Depreciation—Office Equipment.	19		50
Accounts Payable.	21		900
Wages Payable.	22		250
Unearned Rent.	23		240
Common Stock.	31		25,000
Retained Earnings.	32		3,105
		29,545	29,545

Accounting Cycle

The accounting process that begins with analyzing and journalizing transactions and ends with the post-closing trial balance is called the **accounting cycle**. The steps in the accounting cycle are as follows:

- Step 1. Transactions are analyzed and recorded in the journal.
- Step 2. Transactions are posted to the ledger.
- Step 3. An unadjusted trial balance is prepared.
- Step 4. Adjustment data are assembled and analyzed.
- Step 5. An optional end-of-period spreadsheet is prepared.
- Step 6. Adjusting entries are journalized and posted to the ledger.
- Step 7. An adjusted trial balance is prepared.
- Step 8. Financial statements are prepared.
- Step 9. Closing entries are journalized and posted to the ledger.
- Step 10. A post-closing trial balance is prepared.[3]

Exhibit 8 illustrates the accounting cycle in graphic form. It also illustrates how the accounting cycle begins with transactions that flow through the accounting system into the financial statements.

Pathways Challenge

This is Accounting!

Economic Activity

Financial statements report the results of operations for a period of time and the financial condition as of a specific date. However, a company usually does not report (issue) its financial statements for several weeks or months after the end of its fiscal year. This is because time is needed to adjust the accounts, prepare the financial statements, and have the financial statements examined (audited) by an independent certified public accounting (CPA) firm. During this time, significant business transactions or events may occur. For example, on February 16, 2017, the board of directors of **The Cheesecake Factory Incorporated (CAKE)** declared a dividend. The dividend was declared after its fiscal year ended on January 3, 2017, but before the financial statements were reported.

Critical Thinking/Judgment

What are the effects of a dividend payment on the accounts and accounting equation?

Should the financial statements of The Cheesecake Factory for the period ending January 3, 2017, be adjusted to reflect the effects of the dividend declared on February 16, 2017?

Should financial statements ever be adjusted for transactions or events that occur after the end of an accounting period but before the issuance of that period's financial statements?

Suggested answer at end of chapter.

---

[3] Some accountants include the journalizing and posting of "reversing entries" as the last step in the accounting cycle. Because reversing entries are not required, they are described and illustrated in Appendix 2 to this chapter.

Exhibit 8
Accounting Cycle

Chapter 1

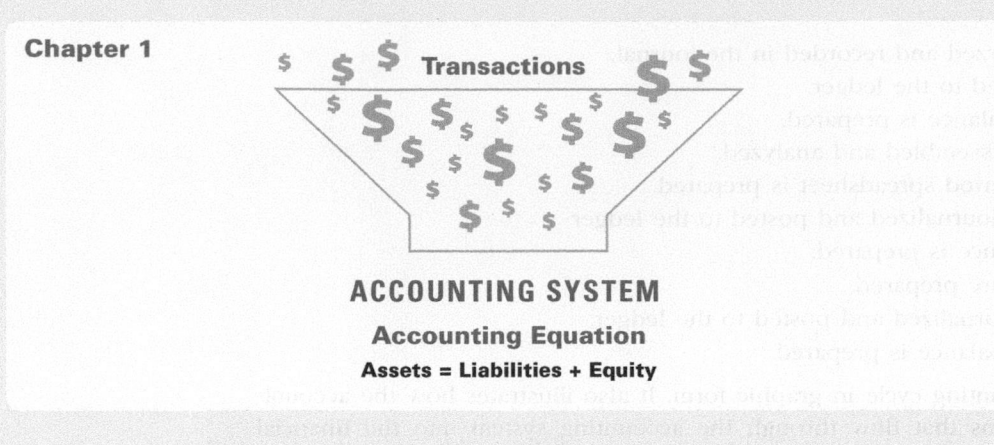

Transactions

ACCOUNTING SYSTEM

Accounting Equation

Assets = Liabilities + Equity

Accounting Cycle

Chapter 2

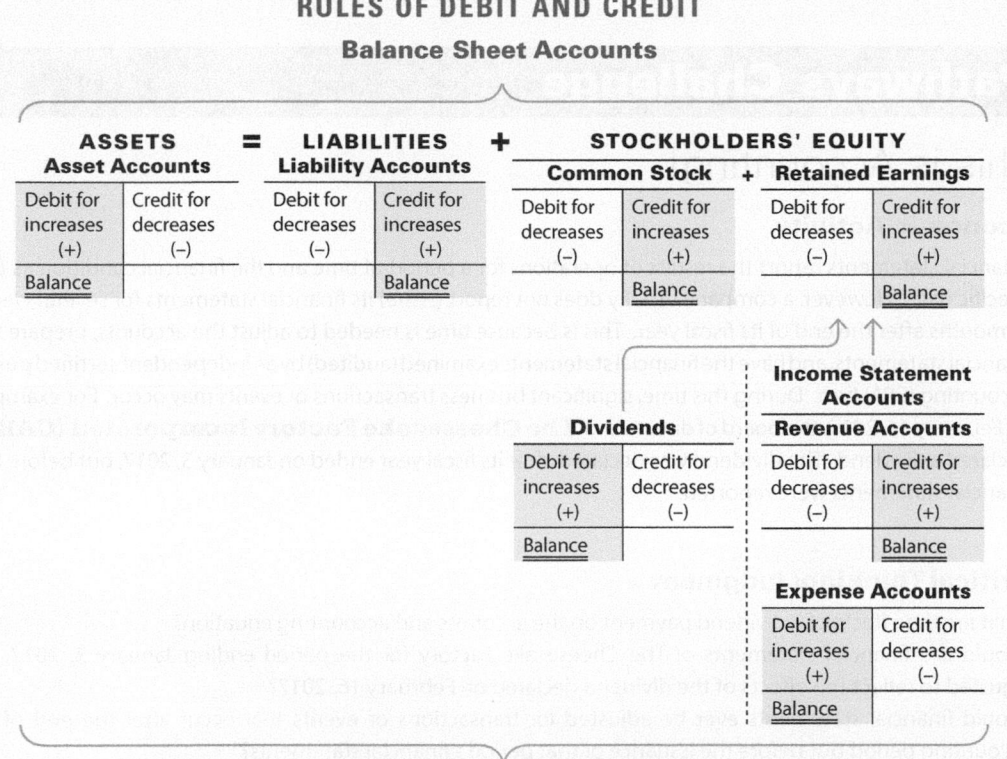

Account

| Debits | Credits |

RULES OF DEBIT AND CREDIT

Balance Sheet Accounts

ASSETS = **LIABILITIES** + **STOCKHOLDERS' EQUITY**

Asset Accounts

| Debit for increases (+) | Credit for decreases (−) |
| Balance | |

Liability Accounts

| Debit for decreases (−) | Credit for increases (+) |
| | Balance |

Common Stock

| Debit for decreases (−) | Credit for increases (+) |
| | Balance |

+ Retained Earnings

| Debit for decreases (−) | Credit for increases (+) |
| | Balance |

Dividends

| Debit for increases (+) | Credit for decreases (−) |
| Balance | |

Income Statement Accounts

Revenue Accounts

| Debit for decreases (−) | Credit for increases (+) |
| | Balance |

Expense Accounts

| Debit for increases (+) | Credit for decreases (−) |
| Balance | |

Unadjusted Trial Balance

Total Debit Balances = Total Credit Balances

Step 1.
Transactions are analyzed and recorded in the journal.

Step 2.
Transactions are posted to the ledger.

Step 3.
An unadjusted trial balance is prepared.

Exhibit 8
Accounting Cycle *(Concluded)*

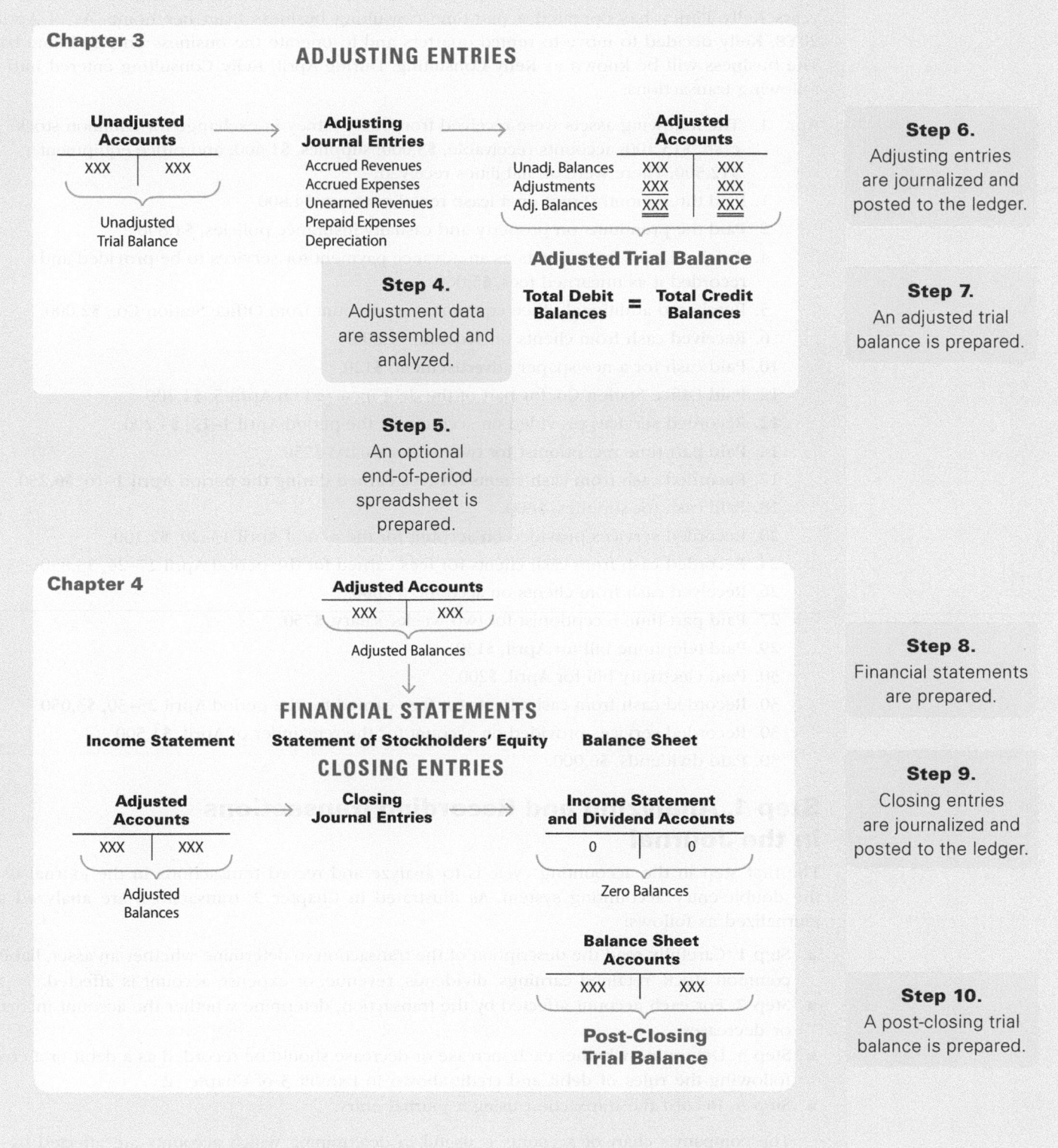

Objective 5

Illustrate the accounting cycle for one period.

Illustration of the Accounting Cycle

In this section, the complete accounting cycle for one period is illustrated. Assume that for several years Kelly Pitney has operated a part-time consulting business from her home. As of April 1, 20Y8, Kelly decided to move to rented quarters and to operate the business on a full-time basis. The business will be known as Kelly Consulting. During April, Kelly Consulting entered into the following transactions:

Apr. 1. The following assets were received from Kelly Pitney in exchange for common stock: cash, $13,100; accounts receivable, $3,000; supplies, $1,400; and office equipment, $12,500. There were no liabilities received.

1. Paid three months' rent on a lease rental contract, $4,800.

2. Paid the premiums on property and casualty insurance policies, $1,800.

4. Received cash from clients as an advance payment for services to be provided and recorded it as unearned fees, $5,000.

5. Purchased additional office equipment on account from Office Station Co., $2,000.

6. Received cash from clients on account, $1,800.

10. Paid cash for a newspaper advertisement, $120.

12. Paid Office Station Co. for part of the debt incurred on April 5, $1,200.

12. Recorded services provided on account for the period April 1–12, $4,200.

14. Paid part-time receptionist for two weeks' salary, $750.

17. Recorded cash from cash clients for fees earned during the period April 1–16, $6,250.

18. Paid cash for supplies, $800.

20. Recorded services provided on account for the period April 13–20, $2,100.

24. Recorded cash from cash clients for fees earned for the period April 17–24, $3,850.

26. Received cash from clients on account, $5,600.

27. Paid part-time receptionist for two weeks' salary, $750.

29. Paid telephone bill for April, $130.

30. Paid electricity bill for April, $200.

30. Recorded cash from cash clients for fees earned for the period April 25–30, $3,050.

30. Recorded services provided on account for the remainder of April, $1,500.

30. Paid dividends, $6,000.

Step 1. Analyzing and Recording Transactions in the Journal

The first step in the accounting cycle is to analyze and record transactions in the journal using the double-entry accounting system. As illustrated in Chapter 2, transactions are analyzed and journalized as follows:

- Step 1. Carefully read the description of the transaction to determine whether an asset, liability, common stock, retained earnings, dividends, revenue, or expense account is affected.
- Step 2. For each account affected by the transaction, determine whether the account increases or decreases.
- Step 3. Determine whether each increase or decrease should be recorded as a debit or a credit, following the rules of debit and credit shown in Exhibit 3 of Chapter 2.
- Step 4. Record the transaction using a journal entry.

The company's chart of accounts is useful in determining which accounts are affected by the transaction. The chart of accounts for Kelly Consulting is shown in Exhibit 9.

11	Cash	31	Common Stock
12	Accounts Receivable	32	Retained Earnings
14	Supplies	33	Dividends
15	Prepaid Rent	41	Fees Earned
16	Prepaid Insurance	51	Salary Expense
18	Office Equipment	52	Rent Expense
19	Accumulated Depreciation	53	Supplies Expense
21	Accounts Payable	54	Depreciation Expense
22	Salaries Payable	55	Insurance Expense
23	Unearned Fees	59	Miscellaneous Expense

Exhibit 9
Chart of Accounts for Kelly Consulting

After analyzing each of Kelly Consulting's transactions for April, the journal entries are recorded as shown in Exhibit 10.

Step 2. Posting Transactions to the Ledger

Periodically, the transactions recorded in the journal are posted to the accounts in the ledger. The debits and credits for each journal entry are posted to the accounts in the order in which they occur in the journal. As illustrated in Chapters 2 and 3, journal entries are posted to the accounts using the following four steps:

- Step 1. The date is entered in the Date column of the account.
- Step 2. The amount is entered into the Debit or Credit column of the account.
- Step 3. The journal page number is entered in the Posting Reference column.
- Step 4. The account number is entered in the Posting Reference (Post. Ref.) column in the journal.

The journal entries for Kelly Consulting have been posted to the ledger shown in Exhibit 18.

Step 3. Preparing an Unadjusted Trial Balance

An unadjusted trial balance is prepared to determine whether any errors have been made in posting the debits and credits to the ledger. The unadjusted trial balance shown in Exhibit 11 does not provide complete proof of the accuracy of the ledger. It indicates only that the debits and the credits are equal. This proof is of value, however, because errors often affect the equality of debits and credits. If the two totals of a trial balance are not equal, an error has occurred that must be discovered and corrected.

The unadjusted account balances shown in Exhibit 11 were taken from Kelly Consulting's ledger on pages 186–188, before any adjusting entries were recorded.

Step 4. Assembling and Analyzing Adjustment Data

Before the financial statements can be prepared, the accounts must be updated. The four types of accounts that normally require adjustment include prepaid expenses, unearned revenue, accrued revenue, and accrued expenses. In addition, depreciation expense must be recorded for fixed assets other than land. The following data have been assembled on April 30, 20Y8, for analysis of possible adjustments for Kelly Consulting:

a. Insurance expired during April is $300.
b. Supplies on hand on April 30 are $1,350.
c. Depreciation of office equipment for April is $330.
d. Accrued receptionist salary on April 30 is $120.
e. Rent expired during April is $1,600.
f. Unearned fees on April 30 are $2,500.

Exhibit 10

Journal Entries for April, Kelly Consulting

	Journal			Page 1
Date	**Description**	**Post. Ref.**	**Debit**	**Credit**
20Y8				
Apr. 1	Cash	11	13,100	
	Accounts Receivable	12	3,000	
	Supplies	14	1,400	
	Office Equipment	18	12,500	
	Common Stock	31		30,000
1	Prepaid Rent	15	4,800	
	Cash	11		4,800
2	Prepaid Insurance	16	1,800	
	Cash	11		1,800
4	Cash	11	5,000	
	Unearned Fees	23		5,000
5	Office Equipment	18	2,000	
	Accounts Payable	21		2,000
6	Cash	11	1,800	
	Accounts Receivable	12		1,800
10	Miscellaneous Expense	59	120	
	Cash	11		120
12	Accounts Payable	21	1,200	
	Cash	11		1,200
12	Accounts Receivable	12	4,200	
	Fees Earned	41		4,200
14	Salary Expense	51	750	
	Cash	11		750

	Journal			Page 2
Date	**Description**	**Post. Ref.**	**Debit**	**Credit**
20Y8				
Apr. 17	Cash	11	6,250	
	Fees Earned	41		6,250
18	Supplies	14	800	
	Cash	11		800
20	Accounts Receivable	12	2,100	
	Fees Earned	41		2,100
24	Cash	11	3,850	
	Fees Earned	41		3,850
26	Cash	11	5,600	
	Accounts Receivable	12		5,600
27	Salary Expense	51	750	
	Cash	11		750
29	Miscellaneous Expense	59	130	
	Cash	11		130

	Journal				_Page 2_
Date	**Description**	**Post. Ref.**	**Debit**	**Credit**	
30	Miscellaneous Expense	59	200		
	Cash	11		200	
30	Cash	11	3,050		
	Fees Earned	41		3,050	
30	Accounts Receivable	12	1,500		
	Fees Earned	41		1,500	
30	Dividends	33	6,000		
	Cash	11		6,000	

Exhibit 10

Journal Entries for April, Kelly Consulting _(Concluded)_

Kelly Consulting
Unadjusted Trial Balance
April 30, 20Y8

	Account No.	Debit Balances	Credit Balances
Cash	11	22,100	
Accounts Receivable	12	3,400	
Supplies	14	2,200	
Prepaid Rent	15	4,800	
Prepaid Insurance	16	1,800	
Office Equipment	18	14,500	
Accumulated Depreciation	19		0
Accounts Payable	21		800
Salaries Payable	22		0
Unearned Fees	23		5,000
Common Stock	31		30,000
Dividends	33	6,000	
Fees Earned	41		20,950
Salary Expense	51	1,500	
Rent Expense	52	0	
Supplies Expense	53	0	
Depreciation Expense	54	0	
Insurance Expense	55	0	
Miscellaneous Expense	59	450	
		56,750	56,750

Exhibit 11

Unadjusted Trial Balance, Kelly Consulting

Step 5. Preparing an Optional End-of-Period Spreadsheet

Although an end-of-period spreadsheet is not required, it is useful in showing the flow of accounting information from the unadjusted trial balance to the adjusted trial balance. In addition, an end-of-period spreadsheet is useful in analyzing the impact of proposed adjustments on the financial statements. The end-of-period spreadsheet for Kelly Consulting is shown in Exhibit 12.

	A	B	C	D	E	F	G
1		Kelly Consulting					
2		End-of-Period Spreadsheet					
3		For the Month Ended April 30, 20Y8					
4		Unadjusted				Adjusted	
5		Trial Balance		Adjustments		Trial Balance	
6	Account Title	Dr.	Cr.	Dr.	Cr.	Dr.	Cr.
7							
8	Cash	22,100				22,100	
9	Accounts Receivable	3,400				3,400	
10	Supplies	2,200			(b) 850	1,350	
11	Prepaid Rent	4,800			(e) 1,600	3,200	
12	Prepaid Insurance	1,800			(a) 300	1,500	
13	Office Equipment	14,500				14,500	
14	Accumulated Depr.				(c) 330		330
15	Accounts Payable		800				800
16	Salaries Payable				(d) 120		120
17	Unearned Fees		5,000	(f) 2,500			2,500
18	Common Stock		30,000				30,000
19	Dividends	6,000				6,000	
20	Fees Earned		20,950		(f) 2,500		23,450
21	Salary Expense	1,500		(d) 120		1,620	
22	Rent Expense			(e) 1,600		1,600	
23	Supplies Expense			(b) 850		850	
24	Depreciation Expense			(c) 330		330	
25	Insurance Expense			(a) 300		300	
26	Miscellaneous Expense	450				450	
27		56,750	56,750	5,700	5,700	57,200	57,200
28							

Step 6. Journalizing and Posting Adjusting Entries

Based on the adjustment data shown in Step 4, adjusting entries for Kelly Consulting are prepared as shown in Exhibit 13. Each adjusting entry affects at least one income statement account and one balance sheet account. Explanations for each adjustment including any computations are normally included with each adjusting entry.

Each of the adjusting entries shown in Exhibit 13 is posted to Kelly Consulting's ledger shown in Exhibit 18. The adjusting entries are identified in the ledger as "Adjusting."

Step 7. Preparing an Adjusted Trial Balance

After the adjustments have been journalized and posted, an adjusted trial balance is prepared to verify the equality of the total of the debit and credit balances. This is the last step before preparing the financial statements. If the adjusted trial balance does not balance, an error has occurred and must be found and corrected. The adjusted trial balance for Kelly Consulting as of April 30, 20Y8, is shown in Exhibit 14.

Step 8. Preparing the Financial Statements

The most important outcome of the accounting cycle is the financial statements. The income statement is prepared first, followed by the statement of stockholders' equity and then the balance sheet. The statements can be prepared directly from the adjusted trial balance, the end-of-period spreadsheet, or the ledger. The net income or net loss shown on the income statement is reported on the statement of stockholders' equity along with any dividends. The ending retained earnings is reported on the balance sheet with common stock as part of stockholders' equity. Stockholders' equity is then added with total liabilities to equal total assets.

Journal				Page 3
Date	**Description**	**Post. Ref.**	**Debit**	**Credit**
	Adjusting Entries			
20Y8				
Apr. 30	Insurance Expense	55	300	
	Prepaid Insurance	16		300
	Expired insurance.			
30	Supplies Expense	53	850	
	Supplies	14		850
	Supplies used ($2,200 – $1,350).			
30	Depreciation Expense	54	330	
	Accumulated Depreciation	19		330
	Depreciation of office equipment.			
30	Salary Expense	51	120	
	Salaries Payable	22		120
	Accrued salary.			
30	Rent Expense	52	1,600	
	Prepaid Rent	15		1,600
	Rent expired during April.			
30	Unearned Fees	23	2,500	
	Fees Earned	41		2,500
	Fees earned ($5,000 – $2,500).			

Exhibit 13
Adjusting Entries, Kelly Consulting

Kelly Consulting
Adjusted Trial Balance
April 30, 20Y8

	Account No.	**Debit Balances**	**Credit Balances**
Cash	11	22,100	
Accounts Receivable	12	3,400	
Supplies	14	1,350	
Prepaid Rent	15	3,200	
Prepaid Insurance	16	1,500	
Office Equipment	18	14,500	
Accumulated Depreciation	19		330
Accounts Payable	21		800
Salaries Payable	22		120
Unearned Fees	23		2,500
Common Stock	31		30,000
Dividends	33	6,000	
Fees Earned	41		23,450
Salary Expense	51	1,620	
Rent Expense	52	1,600	
Supplies Expense	53	850	
Depreciation Expense	54	330	
Insurance Expense	55	300	
Miscellaneous Expense	59	450	
		57,200	57,200

Exhibit 14
Adjusted Trial Balance, Kelly Consulting

The financial statements for Kelly Consulting are shown in Exhibit 15. Kelly Consulting earned net income of $18,300 for April. As of April 30, 20Y8, Kelly Consulting has total assets of $45,720, total liabilities of $3,420, and total stockholders' equity of $42,300.

Exhibit 15
Financial Statements,
Kelly Consulting

Kelly Consulting
Income Statement
For the Month Ended April 30, 20Y8

Fees earned..		$23,450
Expenses:		
Salary expense...	$1,620	
Rent expense..	1,600	
Supplies expense	850	
Depreciation expense	330	
Insurance expense	300	
Miscellaneous expense	450	
Total expenses.......................................		(5,150)
Net income		$18,300

Kelly Consulting
Statement of Stockholders' Equity
For the Month Ended April 30, 20Y8

	Common Stock	Retained Earnings	Total
Balances, April 1, 20Y8	$ 0	$ 0	$ 0
Issued common stock	30,000		30,000
Net income............................		18,300	18,300
Dividends		(6,000)	(6,000)
Balances, April 30, 20Y8	$30,000	$12,300	$42,300

Kelly Consulting
Balance Sheet
April 30, 20Y8

Assets

Current assets:		
Cash...	$22,100	
Accounts receivable	3,400	
Supplies	1,350	
Prepaid rent...	3,200	
Prepaid insurance	1,500	
Total current assets................................		$31,550
Property, plant, and equipment:		
Office equipment..	$14,500	
Accumulated depreciation	(330)	
Total property, plant, and equipment		14,170
Total assets..		$45,720

Liabilities

Current liabilities:		
Accounts payable.......................................	$ 800	
Salaries payable	120	
Unearned fees...	2,500	
Total liabilities...		$ 3,420

Stockholders' Equity

Common stock	$30,000	
Retained earnings	12,300	
Total stockholders' equity		42,300
Total liabilities and stockholders' equity		$45,720

Step 9. Journalizing and Posting Closing Entries

As described earlier in this chapter, two closing entries are required at the end of an accounting period. These two closing entries are as follows:

Closing Entry (1): Debit each revenue account for its balance, credit each expense account for its balance, and credit (net income) or debit (net loss) the retained earnings account.

Closing Entry (2): Debit the retained earnings account for the balance of the dividends account, and credit the dividends account for its balance.

The two closing entries for Kelly Consulting are shown in Exhibit 16. The closing entries are posted to Kelly Consulting's ledger as shown in Exhibit 18. After the closing entries are posted, Kelly Consulting's ledger has the following characteristics:

- The balance of Retained Earnings of $12,300 agrees with the amount reported on the statement of stockholders' equity and the balance sheet.
- The revenue, expense, and dividends accounts will have zero balances.

The closing entries are normally identified in the ledger as "Closing." In addition, a line is often inserted in both balance columns after a closing entry is posted. This separates next period's revenue, expense, and dividend transactions from those of the current period.

	Journal			*Page 4*
Date	**Description**	**Post. Ref.**	**Debit**	**Credit**
	Closing Entries			
20Y8				
Apr. 30	Fees Earned	41	23,450	
	Salary Expense	51		1,620
	Rent Expense	52		1,600
	Supplies Expense	53		850
	Depreciation Expense	54		330
	Insurance Expense	55		300
	Miscellaneous Expense	59		450
	Retained Earnings	32		18,300
30	Retained Earnings	32	6,000	
	Dividends	33		6,000

Exhibit 16
Closing Entries, Kelly Consulting

Step 10. Preparing a Post-Closing Trial Balance

A post-closing trial balance is prepared after the closing entries have been posted. The purpose of the post-closing trial balance is to verify that the ledger is in balance at the beginning of the next period. The accounts and amounts in the post-closing trial balance should agree exactly with the accounts and amounts listed on the balance sheet at the end of the period.

The post-closing trial balance for Kelly Consulting is shown in Exhibit 17. The balances shown in the post-closing trial balance are taken from the ending balances in the ledger shown in Exhibit 18. These balances agree with the amounts shown on Kelly Consulting's balance sheet in Exhibit 15.

Exhibit 17
Post-Closing
Trial Balance, Kelly
Consulting

Kelly Consulting
Post-Closing Trial Balance
April 30, 20Y8

	Account No.	Debit Balances	Credit Balances
Cash	11	22,100	
Accounts Receivable	12	3,400	
Supplies	14	1,350	
Prepaid Rent	15	3,200	
Prepaid Insurance	16	1,500	
Office Equipment	18	14,500	
Accumulated Depreciation	19		330
Accounts Payable	21		800
Salaries Payable	22		120
Unearned Fees	23		2,500
Common Stock	31		30,000
Retained Earnings	32		12,300
		46,050	46,050

Exhibit 18 Ledger, Kelly Consulting

Account Cash   Account No. 11

Date	Item	Post. Ref.	Debit	Credit	Balance Debit	Balance Credit
20Y8						
Apr. 1		1	13,100		13,100	
1		1		4,800	8,300	
2		1		1,800	6,500	
4		1	5,000		11,500	
6		1	1,800		13,300	
10		1		120	13,180	
12		1		1,200	11,980	
14		1		750	11,230	
17		2	6,250		17,480	
18		2		800	16,680	
24		2	3,850		20,530	
26		2	5,600		26,130	
27		2		750	25,380	
29		2		130	25,250	
30		2		200	25,050	
30		2	3,050		28,100	
30		2		6,000	22,100	

Account Accounts Receivable   Account No. 12

Date	Item	Post. Ref.	Debit	Credit	Balance Debit	Balance Credit
20Y8						
Apr. 1		1	3,000		3,000	
6		1		1,800	1,200	
12		1	4,200		5,400	
20		2	2,100		7,500	
26		2		5,600	1,900	
30		2	1,500		3,400	

Account Supplies   Account No. 14

Date	Item	Post. Ref.	Debit	Credit	Balance Debit	Balance Credit
20Y8						
Apr. 1		1	1,400		1,400	
18		2	800		2,200	
30	Adjusting	3		850	1,350	

Account Prepaid Rent   Account No. 15

Date	Item	Post. Ref.	Debit	Credit	Balance Debit	Balance Credit
20Y8						
Apr. 1		1	4,800		4,800	
30	Adjusting	3		1,600	3,200	

Account Prepaid Insurance   Account No. 16

Date	Item	Post. Ref.	Debit	Credit	Balance Debit	Balance Credit
20Y8						
Apr. 2		1	1,800		1,800	
30	Adjusting	3		300	1,500	

Exhibit 18 Ledger, Kelly Consulting *(Continued)*

Account *Office Equipment*   Account No. *18*

Date	Item	Post. Ref.	Debit	Credit	Balance Debit	Balance Credit
20Y8						
Apr. 1		1	12,500		12,500	
5		1	2,000		14,500	

Account *Accumulated Depreciation*   Account No. *19*

Date	Item	Post. Ref.	Debit	Credit	Balance Debit	Balance Credit
20Y8						
Apr. 30	Adjusting	3		330		330

Account *Accounts Payable*   Account No. *21*

Date	Item	Post. Ref.	Debit	Credit	Balance Debit	Balance Credit
20Y8						
Apr. 5		1		2,000		2,000
12		1	1,200			800

Account *Salaries Payable*   Account No. *22*

Date	Item	Post. Ref.	Debit	Credit	Balance Debit	Balance Credit
20Y8						
Apr. 30	Adjusting	3		120		120

Account *Unearned Fees*   Account No. *23*

Date	Item	Post. Ref.	Debit	Credit	Balance Debit	Balance Credit
20Y8						
Apr. 4		1		5,000		5,000
30	Adjusting	3	2,500			2,500

Account *Common Stock*   Account No. *31*

Date	Item	Post. Ref.	Debit	Credit	Balance Debit	Balance Credit
20Y8						
Apr. 1		1		30,000		30,000

Account *Retained Earnings*   Account No. *32*

Date	Item	Post. Ref.	Debit	Credit	Balance Debit	Balance Credit
20Y8						
Apr. 1						0
30	Closing	4		18,300		18,300
30	Closing	4	6,000			12,300

Account *Dividends*   Account No. *33*

Date	Item	Post. Ref.	Debit	Credit	Balance Debit	Balance Credit
20Y8						
Apr. 30		2	6,000		6,000	
30	Closing	4		6,000	—	—

Account *Fees Earned*   Account No. *41*

Date	Item	Post. Ref.	Debit	Credit	Balance Debit	Balance Credit
20Y8						
Apr. 12		1		4,200		4,200
17		2		6,250		10,450
20		2		2,100		12,550
24		2		3,850		16,400
30		2		3,050		19,450
30		2		1,500		20,950
30	Adjusting	3		2,500		23,450
30	Closing	4	23,450		—	—

Account *Salary Expense*   Account No. *51*

Date	Item	Post. Ref.	Debit	Credit	Balance Debit	Balance Credit
20Y8						
Apr. 14		1	750		750	
27		2	750		1,500	
30	Adjusting	3	120		1,620	
30	Closing	4		1,620	—	—

(Continued)

Exhibit 18 Ledger, Kelly Consulting *(Concluded)*

Account *Rent Expense*					Account No. 52	
		Post.			Balance	
Date	Item	Ref.	Debit	Credit	Debit	Credit
20Y8						
Apr. 30	Adjusting	3	1,600		1,600	
30	Closing	4		1,600	—	—

Account *Insurance Expense*					Account No. 55	
		Post.			Balance	
Date	Item	Ref.	Debit	Credit	Debit	Credit
20Y8						
Apr. 30	Adjusting	3	300		300	
30	Closing	4		300	—	—

Account *Supplies Expense*					Account No. 53	
		Post.			Balance	
Date	Item	Ref.	Debit	Credit	Debit	Credit
20Y8						
Apr. 30	Adjusting	3	850		850	
30	Closing	4		850	—	—

Account *Miscellaneous Expense*					Account No. 59	
		Post.			Balance	
Date	Item	Ref.	Debit	Credit	Debit	Credit
20Y8						
Apr. 10		1	120		120	
29		2	130		250	
30		2	200		450	
30	Closing	4		450	—	—

Account *Depreciation Expense*					Account No. 54	
		Post.			Balance	
Date	Item	Ref.	Debit	Credit	Debit	Credit
20Y8						
Apr. 30	Adjusting	3	330		330	
30	Closing	4		330	—	—

Analysis for Decision Making

Objective 6
Describe and illustrate the use of working capital and the current ratio in evaluating a company's financial condition.

Working Capital and Current Ratio

The ability to convert assets into cash is called **liquidity**, while the ability of a business to pay its debts is called **solvency**. Two financial measures for evaluating a business's short-term liquidity and solvency are *working capital* and the *current ratio*.

Working capital is the excess of the current assets of a business over its current liabilities:

Working Capital = Current Assets – Current Liabilities

Current assets are more liquid than long-term assets, because they can be more readily turned into cash to meet short-term obligations. Thus, an increase in a company's current assets increases or improves its liquidity because these assets are available for uses other than paying current liabilities.

A positive working capital implies that the business is able to pay its current liabilities and is solvent. Thus, an increase in working capital increases or improves a company's short-term solvency.

To illustrate, **NetSolutions**' working capital at the end of 20Y3 is $6,355, computed as follows from Exhibit 1:

Working Capital = Current Assets – Current Liabilities
= $7,745 – $1,390
= $6,355

This amount of working capital implies that NetSolutions is able to pay its current liabilities.

The **current ratio** is another means of expressing the relationship between current assets and current liabilities. The current ratio is computed by dividing current assets by current liabilities:

$$\text{Current Ratio} = \frac{\text{Current Assets}}{\text{Current Liabilities}}$$

To illustrate, the current ratio for NetSolutions on December 31, 20Y3 is 5.6, computed as follows:

$$\text{Current Ratio} = \frac{\text{Current Assets}}{\text{Current Liabilities}}$$
$$= \frac{\$7,745}{\$1,390}$$
$$= 5.6 \text{ (Rounded)}$$

The current ratio is more useful than working capital in making comparisons across companies or with industry averages.

Make a Decision | Working Capital and Current Ratio

Analyze and compare Amazon.com to Best Buy (MAD 4-1) (Continuing company analysis)

Analyze and compare Zynga, Electronic Arts, and Take-Two (MAD 4-2)

Analyze and compare Foot Locker and The Finish Line (MAD 4-3)

Analyze Under Armour (MAD 4-4)

Analyze Sears Holding Corporation (MAD 4-5)

Analyze and compare Alphabet (Google) and Microsoft (MAD 4-6)

Make a Decision

Appendix 1 End-of-Period Spreadsheet

Accountants often use spreadsheets for analyzing and summarizing data. Such spreadsheets are not a formal part of the accounting records. This is in contrast to the chart of accounts, the journal, and the ledger, which are essential parts of an accounting system. Spreadsheets are usually prepared by using a computer program such as Microsoft's Excel.®

As illustrated earlier in this chapter, an end-of-period spreadsheet is used to summarize adjusting entries and their effects on the accounts. As illustrated in the chapter, the financial statements for **NetSolutions** can be prepared directly from the spreadsheet's Adjusted Trial Balance columns shown in Exhibit 1.

Some accountants prefer to expand the end-of-period spreadsheet shown in Exhibit 1 to include financial statement columns. Exhibits 19 through 23 illustrate the step-by-step process of how to prepare this spreadsheet. As a basis for illustration, NetSolutions is used.

Step 1. Enter the Title

The spreadsheet is started by entering the following data:

1. Name of the business: *NetSolutions*
2. Type of spreadsheet: *End-of-Period Spreadsheet*
3. The period of time: *For the Two Months Ended December 31, 20Y3*

Exhibit 19 shows the preceding data entered for NetSolutions.

Step 2. Enter the Unadjusted Trial Balance

Enter the unadjusted trial balance on the spreadsheet. The spreadsheet in Exhibit 19 shows the unadjusted trial balance for NetSolutions at December 31, 20Y3.

Exhibit 19   Spreadsheet with Unadjusted Trial Balance Entered

	A	B	C	D	E	F	G	H	I	J	K
1					NetSolutions						
2					End-of-Period Spreadsheet						
3					For the Two Months Ended December 31, 20Y3						
4		Unadjusted				Adjusted					
5		Trial Balance		Adjustments		Trial Balance		Income Statement		Balance Sheet	
6	**Account Title**	Dr.	Cr.	Dr.	Cr.	Dr.	Cr.	Dr.	Cr.	Dr.	Cr.
7											
8	Cash	2,065									
9	Accounts Receivable	2,220									
10	Supplies	2,000									
11	Prepaid Insurance	2,400									
12	Land	20,000									
13	Office Equipment	1,800									
14	Accum. Depr.—Office Equip.										
15	Accounts Payable		900								
16	Wages Payable										
17	Unearned Rent		360								
18	Common Stock		25,000								
19	Dividends	4,000									
20	Fees Earned		16,340								
21	Rent Revenue										
22	Wages Expense	4,275									
23	Supplies Expense	800									
24	Rent Expense	1,600									
25	Utilities Expense	985									
26	Insurance Expense										
27	Depreciation Expense										
28	Miscellaneous Expense	455									
29		42,600	42,600								
30											

The spreadsheet is used for summarizing the effects of adjusting entries. It also aids in preparing financial statements.

Step 3. Enter the Adjustments

The adjustments for NetSolutions from Chapter 3 are entered in the Adjustments columns, as shown in Exhibit 20. Cross-referencing (by letters) the debit and credit of each adjustment is useful in reviewing the spreadsheet. It is also helpful for identifying the adjusting entries that need to be recorded in the journal. This cross-referencing process is sometimes referred to as *keying* the adjustments.

Exhibit 20 Spreadsheet with Unadjusted Trial Balance and Adjustments

	A	B	C	D	E	F	G	H	I	J	K
1				NetSolutions							
2				End-of-Period Spreadsheet							
3				For the Two Months Ended December 31, 20Y3							
4		Unadjusted				Adjusted					
5		Trial Balance		Adjustments		Trial Balance		Income Statement		Balance Sheet	
6	Account Title	Dr.	Cr.	Dr.	Cr.	Dr.	Cr.	Dr.	Cr.	Dr.	Cr.
7											
8	Cash	2,065									
9	Accounts Receivable	2,220		(d) 500							
10	Supplies	2,000			(a) 1,240						
11	Prepaid Insurance	2,400			(b) 200						
12	Land	20,000									
13	Office Equipment	1,800									
14	Accum. Depr.—Office Equip.				(f) 50						
15	Accounts Payable		900								
16	Wages Payable				(e) 250						
17	Unearned Rent		360	(c) 120							
18	Common Stock		25,000								
19	Dividends	4,000									
20	Fees Earned		16,340		(d) 500						
21	Rent Revenue				(c) 120						
22	Wages Expense	4,275		(e) 250							
23	Supplies Expense	800		(a) 1,240							
24	Rent Expense	1,600									
25	Utilities Expense	985									
26	Insurance Expense			(b) 200							
27	Depreciation Expense			(f) 50							
28	Miscellaneous Expense	455									
29		42,600	42,600	2,360	2,360						
30											

The adjustments on the spreadsheet are used in preparing the adjusting journal entries.

The adjustments are normally entered in the order in which the data are assembled. If the titles of the accounts to be adjusted do not appear in the unadjusted trial balance, the accounts are inserted in their proper order in the Account Title column.

The adjusting entries for NetSolutions are entered in the Adjustments columns as follows:

(a) **Supplies.** The supplies account has a debit balance of $2,000. The cost of the supplies on hand at the end of the period is $760. The supplies expense for December is the difference between the two amounts, or $1,240 ($2,000 – $760). The adjustment is entered as (1) $1,240 in the Adjustments Debit column on the same line as Supplies Expense and (2) $1,240 in the Adjustments Credit column on the same line as Supplies.

(b) **Prepaid Insurance.** The prepaid insurance account has a debit balance of $2,400. This balance represents the prepayment of insurance for 12 months beginning December 1. Thus, the insurance expense for December is $200 ($2,400 ÷ 12). The adjustment is entered as (1) $200 in the Adjustments Debit column on the same line as Insurance Expense and (2) $200 in the Adjustments Credit column on the same line as Prepaid Insurance.

(c) **Unearned Rent.** The unearned rent account has a credit balance of $360. This balance represents the receipt of three months' rent, beginning with December. Thus, the rent revenue for December is $120 ($360 ÷ 3). The adjustment is entered as (1) $120 in the Adjustments Debit column on the same line as Unearned Rent and (2) $120 in the Adjustments Credit column on the same line as Rent Revenue.

(d) **Accrued Fees.** Fees accrued at the end of December but not recorded total $500. This amount is an increase in an asset and an increase in revenue. The adjustment is entered as (1) $500 in the Adjustments Debit column on the same line as Accounts Receivable and (2) $500 in the Adjustments Credit column on the same line as Fees Earned.

(e) **Wages.** Wages accrued but not paid at the end of December total $250. This amount is an increase in expenses and an increase in liabilities. The adjustment is entered as (1) $250 in the Adjustments Debit column on the same line as Wages Expense and (2) $250 in the Adjustments Credit column on the same line as Wages Payable.

(f) **Depreciation.** Depreciation of the office equipment is $50 for December. The adjustment is entered as (1) $50 in the Adjustments Debit column on the same line as Depreciation Expense and (2) $50 in the Adjustments Credit column on the same line as Accumulated Depreciation—Office Equipment

After the adjustments have been entered, the Adjustments columns are totaled to verify the equality of the debits and credits. The total of the Debit column must equal the total of the Credit column.

Step 4. Enter the Adjusted Trial Balance

The adjusted trial balance is entered by combining the adjustments with the unadjusted balances for each account. The adjusted amounts are then extended to the Adjusted Trial Balance columns, as shown in Exhibit 21.

To illustrate, the cash amount of $2,065 is extended to the Adjusted Trial Balance Debit column since no adjustments affected Cash. Accounts Receivable has an initial balance of $2,220 and a debit

Exhibit 21 Spreadsheet with Unadjusted Trial Balance, Adjustments, and Adjusted Trial Balance Entered

	A	B	C	D	E	F	G	H	I	J	K
1				NetSolutions							
2				End-of-Period Spreadsheet							
3				For the Two Months Ended December 31, 20Y3							
4		Unadjusted				Adjusted					
5		Trial Balance		Adjustments		Trial Balance		Income Statement		Balance Sheet	
6	Account Title	Dr.	Cr.	Dr.	Cr.	Dr.	Cr.	Dr.	Cr.	Dr.	Cr.
7											
8	Cash	2,065				2,065					
9	Accounts Receivable	2,220		(d) 500		2,720					
10	Supplies	2,000			(a) 1,240	760					
11	Prepaid Insurance	2,400			(b) 200	2,200					
12	Land	20,000				20,000					
13	Office Equipment	1,800				1,800					
14	Accum. Depr.—Office Equip.				(f) 50		50				
15	Accounts Payable		900				900				
16	Wages Payable				(e) 250		250				
17	Unearned Rent		360	(c) 120			240				
18	Common Stock		25,000				25,000				
19	Dividends	4,000				4,000					
20	Fees Earned		16,340		(d) 500		16,840				
21	Rent Revenue				(c) 120		120				
22	Wages Expense	4,275		(e) 250		4,525					
23	Supplies Expense	800		(a) 1,240		2,040					
24	Rent Expense	1,600				1,600					
25	Utilities Expense	985				985					
26	Insurance Expense			(b) 200		200					
27	Depreciation Expense			(f) 50		50					
28	Miscellaneous Expense	455				455					
29		42,600	42,600	2,360	2,360	43,400	43,400				
30											

The adjusted trial balance amounts are determined by adding the adjustments to or subtracting the adjustments from the trial balance amounts. For example, the Wages Expense debit of $4,525 is the trial balance amount of $4,275 plus the $250 adjustment debit.

adjustment of $500. Thus, $2,720 ($2,220 + $500) is entered in the Adjusted Trial Balance Debit column for Accounts Receivable. The same process continues until all account balances are extended to the Adjusted Trial Balance columns.

After the accounts and adjustments have been extended, the Adjusted Trial Balance columns are totaled to verify the equality of debits and credits. The total of the Debit column must equal the total of the Credit column.

Step 5. Extend the Accounts to the Income Statement and Balance Sheet Columns

The adjusted trial balance amounts are extended to the Income Statement and Balance Sheet columns. The amounts for revenues and expenses are extended to the Income Statement columns. The amounts for assets, liabilities, and stockholders' equity (Common Stock, Retained Earnings, Dividends) are extended to the Balance Sheet columns.[4]

The first account listed in the Adjusted Trial Balance columns is Cash with a debit balance of $2,065. Cash is an asset, is listed on the balance sheet, and has a debit balance. Therefore, $2,065 is extended to the Balance Sheet Debit column. Accounts Receivable and the other balance sheet accounts are extended in the same manner. Fees Earned is the first account extended to the Income Statement columns. Its balance of $16,840 is extended to the Income Statement Credit column. The same process continues until all account balances have been extended to the proper columns, as shown in Exhibit 22.

Exhibit 22 Spreadsheet with Amounts Extended to Income Statement and Balance Sheet Columns

	A	B	C	D	E	F	G	H	I	J	K
1					NetSolutions						
2					End-of-Period Spreadsheet						
3					For the Two Months Ended December 31, 20Y3						
4		Unadjusted				Adjusted					
5		Trial Balance		Adjustments		Trial Balance		Income Statement		Balance Sheet	
6	Account Title	Dr.	Cr.	Dr.	Cr.	Dr.	Cr.	Dr.	Cr.	Dr.	Cr.
7											
8	Cash	2,065				2,065				2,065	
9	Accounts Receivable	2,220		(d) 500		2,720				2,720	
10	Supplies	2,000			(a) 1,240	760				760	
11	Prepaid Insurance	2,400			(b) 200	2,200				2,200	
12	Land	20,000				20,000				20,000	
13	Office Equipment	1,800				1,800				1,800	
14	Accum. Depr.—Office Equip.				(f) 50		50				50
15	Accounts Payable		900				900				900
16	Wages Payable				(e) 250		250				250
17	Unearned Rent		360	(c) 120			240				240
18	Common Stock		25,000				25,000				25,000
19	Dividends	4,000				4,000				4,000	
20	Fees Earned		16,340		(d) 500		16,840		16,840		
21	Rent Revenue				(c) 120		120		120		
22	Wages Expense	4,275		(e) 250		4,525		4,525			
23	Supplies Expense	800		(a) 1,240		2,040		2,040			
24	Rent Expense	1,600				1,600		1,600			
25	Utilities Expense	985				985		985			
26	Insurance Expense			(b) 200		200		200			
27	Depreciation Expense			(f) 50		50		50			
28	Miscellaneous Expense	455				455		455			
29		42,600	42,600	2,360	2,360	43,400	43,400				
30											

The revenue and expense amounts are extended to (entered in) the Income Statement columns.

The asset, liability, common stock, and dividends amounts are extended to (entered in) the Balance Sheet columns.

[4] The balance of the dividends account is extended to the Balance Sheet columns because the spreadsheet does not have separate Statement of Stockholders' Equity columns.

Step 6. Total the Income Statement and Balance Sheet Columns, Compute the Net Income or Net Loss, and Complete the Spreadsheet

After the account balances are extended to the Income Statement and Balance Sheet columns, each of the columns is totaled. The difference between the two Income Statement column totals is the amount of the net income or the net loss for the period. This difference (net income or net loss) will also be the difference between the two Balance Sheet column totals.

If the Income Statement Credit column total (total revenue) is greater than the Income Statement Debit column total (total expenses), the difference is the net income. If the Income Statement Debit column total is greater than the Income Statement Credit column total, the difference is a net loss.

As shown in Exhibit 23, the total of the Income Statement Credit column is $16,960, and the total of the Income Statement Debit column is $9,855. Thus, the net income for NetSolutions is $7,105, computed as follows:

Total of Income Statement Credit column (revenues)	$16,960
Total of Income Statement Debit column (expenses)	(9,855)
Net income (excess of revenues over expenses)	$ 7,105

Exhibit 23 Completed Spreadsheet with Net Income Shown

	A	B	C	D		E	F	G	H	I	J	K
1					NetSolutions							
2					End-of-Period Spreadsheet							
3					For the Two Months Ended December 31, 20Y3							
4		Unadjusted					Adjusted					
5		Trial Balance		Adjustments			Trial Balance		Income Statement		Balance Sheet	
6	Account Title	Dr.	Cr.	Dr.		Cr.	Dr.	Cr.	Dr.	Cr.	Dr.	Cr.
7												
8	Cash	2,065					2,065				2,065	
9	Accounts Receivable	2,220		(d)	500		2,720				2,720	
10	Supplies	2,000				(a) 1,240	760				760	
11	Prepaid Insurance	2,400				(b) 200	2,200				2,200	
12	Land	20,000					20,000				20,000	
13	Office Equipment	1,800					1,800				1,800	
14	Accum. Depr.—Office Equip.					(f) 50		50				50
15	Accounts Payable		900					900				900
16	Wages Payable					(e) 250		250				250
17	Unearned Rent		360	(c)	120			240				240
18	Common Stock		25,000					25,000				25,000
19	Dividends	4,000					4,000				4,000	
20	Fees Earned		16,340			(d) 500		16,840		16,840		
21	Rent Revenue					(c) 120		120		120		
22	Wages Expense	4,275		(e)	250		4,525		4,525			
23	Supplies Expense	800		(a)	1,240		2,040		2,040			
24	Rent Expense	1,600					1,600		1,600			
25	Utilities Expense	985					985		985			
26	Insurance Expense			(b)	200		200		200			
27	Depreciation Expense			(f)	50		50		50			
28	Miscellaneous Expense	455					455		455			
29		42,600	42,600	2,360		2,360	43,400	43,400	9,855	16,960	33,545	26,440
30	Net income								7,105			7,105
31									16,960	16,960	33,545	33,545
32												

The difference between the Income Statement column totals is the net income (or net loss) for the period. The difference between the Balance Sheet column totals is also the net income (or net loss) for the period.

The amount of the net income, $7,105, is entered in the Income Statement Debit column and the Balance Sheet Credit column. *Net income* is also entered in the Account Title column. Entering the net income of $7,105 in the Balance Sheet Credit column has the effect of transferring the net balance of the revenue and expense accounts to the retained earnings account.

If there was a net loss instead of net income, the amount of the net loss would be entered in the Income Statement Credit column and the Balance Sheet Debit column. *Net loss* would also be entered in the Account Title column.

After the net income or net loss is entered on the spreadsheet, the Income Statement and Balance Sheet columns are totaled. The totals of the two Income Statement columns must now be equal. The totals of the two Balance Sheet columns must also be equal.

Preparing the Financial Statements from the Spreadsheet

The spreadsheet can be used to prepare the income statement, the statement of stockholders' equity, and the balance sheet shown in Exhibit 2. The income statement is normally prepared directly from the spreadsheet. The expenses are listed in the income statement in Exhibit 2 in order of size, beginning with the larger items. Miscellaneous expense is the last item, regardless of its amount.

The statement of stockholders' equity is prepared by first listing the beginning-of-the-period balances of common stock and retained earnings. These beginning-of-the-period balances are taken from the ledger. Any additional common stock issued during the period and the net income for the period are then added to the beginning balances. A net loss would be subtracted from the beginning balance of retained earnings. Also, dividends are subtracted from the beginning balance of retained earnings. Finally, the columns are totaled to arrive at the end of the period balances for common stock and retained earnings.

The balance sheet can be prepared directly from the spreadsheet columns except for the ending balance of retained earnings. The ending balance of retained earnings is taken from the statement of stockholders' equity.

When a spreadsheet is used, the adjusting and closing entries are normally not journalized or posted until after the spreadsheet and financial statements have been prepared. The data for the adjusting entries are taken from the Adjustments columns of the spreadsheet. The data for the first closing entry are taken from the Income Statement columns of the spreadsheet. The amount for the second closing entry is the dividends account balance that appears in the Balance Sheet Debit column of the spreadsheet.

Appendix 2 Reversing Entries

Objective App 2
Describe and illustrate the use of reversing entries.

Some adjusting entries recorded at the end of an accounting period affect how transactions are recorded in the next period. For this reason, some companies add another step to the accounting cycle. This additional step records journal entries on the first day of the next period that are the exact *opposite* of the related adjusting entry from the last day of the prior period. These journal entries are called **reversing entries**.

To illustrate, the **NetSolutions** data for accrued wages from Chapter 3 are used. These data are summarized in Exhibit 24.

Exhibit 24
Accrued Wages

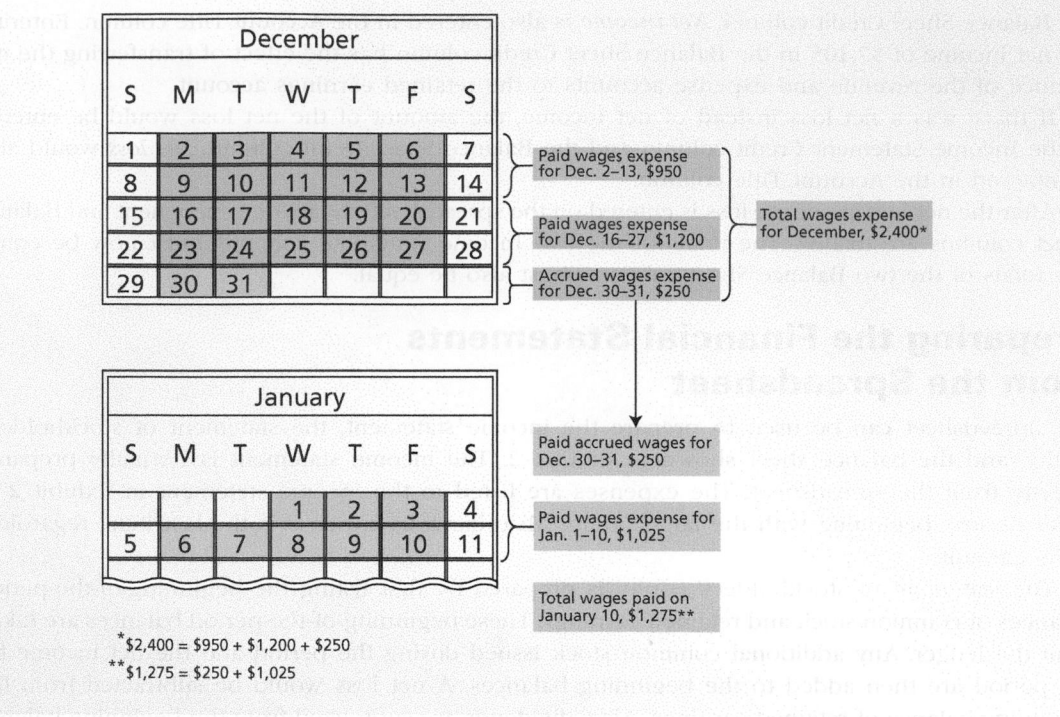

Based upon Exhibit 24, accrued wages for December 30 and 31 of $250 were recorded with the following adjusting entry:

20Y3				
Dec.	31	Wages Expense	51	250
		Wages Payable	22	250

Exhibit 25 shows Wages Payable and Wages Expense after the adjusting entry has been recorded and posted. Wages Payable has a credit balance of $250 and Wages Expense has a debit balance of $4,525.

Exhibit 25
Wages Expense and
Wages Payable

After Adjustment

Account *Wages Payable*					Account No. *22*	
					Balance	
Date	Item	Post. Ref.	Debit	Credit	Debit	Credit
20Y3						
Dec. 31	Adjusting	5		250		250

Account *Wages Expense*					Account No. *51*	
					Balance	
Date	Item	Post. Ref.	Debit	Credit	Debit	Credit
20Y3						
Nov. 30		1	2,125		2,125	
Dec. 13		3	950		3,075	
27		3	1,200		4,275	
31	Adjusting	5	250		4,525	

After the closing entries are recorded, Wages Expense has a zero balance. Since Wages Payable is a liability account, it is not closed. Thus, Wages Payable has a credit balance of $250 as of January 1, 20Y4.

On January 10, 20Y4, NetSolutions pays wages of $1,275. The *normal* entry for paying wages is as follows:

Jan.	10	Wages Expense	51	1,275	
		Cash	11		1,275

However, the preceding entry is incorrect. Specifically, Wages Payable should have been debited for $250, and the wages for January 1–10 are $1,025 ($1,275 – $250), not $1,275. The correct entry to record the January 10 payroll is as follows:

Jan.	10	Wages Payable	22	250	
		Wages Expense	51	1,025	
		Cash	11		1,275

Because the correct entry is not the same as the normal journal entry, there is a chance that Wages Payable will be overlooked and an error made. To avoid this and to simplify the recording of next period's transactions, many companies use reversing entries.

A reversing entry is the opposite of the adjusting entry to which it relates. For example, the reversing entry for the accrued payroll for NetSolutions is as follows:

Jan.	1	Wages Payable	22	250	
		Wages Expense	51		250
		Reversing entry.			

Reversing entries are recorded on the first day of the subsequent accounting period. Exhibit 26 shows the wages payable and wages expense accounts after the reversing entry has been recorded and posted.

After Reversing Entry

Account Wages Payable   Account No. 22

		Post.			Balance	
Date	Item	Ref.	Debit	Credit	Debit	Credit
20Y3						
Dec. 31	Adjusting	5		250		250
20Y4						
Jan. 1	Reversing	7	250		—	—

Account Wages Expense   Account No. 51

		Post.			Balance	
Date	Item	Ref.	Debit	Credit	Debit	Credit
20Y3						
Nov. 30		1	2,125		2,125	
Dec. 13		3	950		3,075	
27		3	1,200		4,275	
31	Adjusting	5	250		4,525	
31	Closing	6		4,525	—	—
20Y4						
Jan. 1	Reversing	7		250		250

Exhibit 26
Wages Expense and
Wages Payable

Exhibit 26 indicates that on January 1, Wages Payable has a zero balance and Wages Expense has a credit balance of $250. The Wages Expense credit balance of $250 is only temporary. Wages Expense will have a debit balance as soon as the first payroll is paid on January 10.

To illustrate, the January 10 payroll of $1,275 would be recorded in the normal manner as follows:

Jan.	10	Wages Expense	51	1,275	
		Cash	11		1,275

After the preceding entry is posted, Wages Expense will have a debit balance of $1,025 ($1,275 − $250), which is the correct wages expense for January 1–10.

The use of reversing entries is optional. However, in computerized accounting systems, routine transactions are processed in standard manner. In such cases, reversing entries are useful in avoiding errors and simplifying the recording of the subsequent period's transactions.

Let's Review

Chapter Summary

1. Exhibit 1 illustrates the end-of-period process by which accounts are adjusted and how the adjusted accounts flow into the financial statements.

2. Using the end-of-period spreadsheet shown in Exhibit 1, the income statement, statement of stockholders' equity, and balance sheet can be prepared. A classified balance sheet has sections for current assets; property, plant, and equipment; current liabilities; long-term liabilities; and stockholders' equity.

3. Two entries are required in closing the temporary accounts. The first entry closes the revenue and expense accounts to the retained earnings account. The second entry closes the dividends account to the retained earnings account. After the closing entries have been posted to the ledger, the balance in the account agrees with the amount reported on the statement of stockholders' equity and balance sheet. In addition, the revenue, expense, and dividends accounts will have zero balances.

4. The 10 basic steps of the accounting cycle are as follows:
    1. Transactions are analyzed and recorded in the journal.
    2. Transactions are posted to the ledger.
    3. An unadjusted trial balance is prepared.
    4. Adjustment data are assembled and analyzed.
    5. An optional end-of-period spreadsheet is prepared.
    6. Adjusting entries are journalized and posted to the ledger.
    7. An adjusted trial balance is prepared.
    8. Financial statements are prepared.
    9. Closing entries are journalized and posted to the ledger.
    10. A post-closing trial balance is prepared.

5. The complete accounting cycle for Kelly Consulting for the month of April is described and illustrated in this chapter.

6. The ability to convert assets into cash is called liquidity, while the ability of a business to pay its debts is called solvency. Two financial measures for evaluating a business's liquidity and solvency are working capital and the current ratio. Working capital is computed by subtracting current liabilities from current assets. An excess of current assets over current liabilities implies that the business is able to pay its current liabilities. The current ratio is computed by dividing current assets by current liabilities. The current ratio is more useful than working capital in making comparisons across companies or with industry averages.

Key Terms

accounting cycle (175)
closing entries (168)
closing process (168)
closing the books (168)
current assets (165)
current liabilities (166)

current ratio (189)
fixed (plant) assets (166)
liquidity (188)
long-term liabilities (166)
notes receivable (165)
permanent (real) accounts (168)

property, plant, and equipment (166)
reversing entries (195)
solvency (188)
temporary (nominal) accounts (168)
working capital (188)

Practice

Multiple-Choice Questions

1. Which of the following accounts in the Adjusted Trial Balance columns of the end-of-period spreadsheet (work sheet) would be reported on the statement of stockholders' equity?
   a. Utilities Expense
   b. Rent Revenue
   c. Dividends
   d. Miscellaneous Expense

2. Which of the following accounts would be classified as a current asset on the balance sheet?
   a. Office Equipment
   b. Land
   c. Accumulated Depreciation
   d. Accounts Receivable

3. Which of the following accounts would not be closed to the retained earnings account at the end of a period?
   a. Fees Earned
   b. Wages Expense
   c. Rent Expense
   d. Accumulated Depreciation

4. Which of the following accounts would not be included in a post-closing trial balance?
   a. Cash
   b. Fees Earned
   c. Accumulated Depreciation
   d. Retained Earnings

5. Which of the following steps of the accounting cycle precedes the journalizing and posting of adjusting entries?
   a. A post-closing trial balance is prepared.
   b. An unadjusted trial balance is prepared.
   c. Financial statements are prepared.
   d. An adjusted trial balance is prepared.

Answers provided after Problem. Need more practice? Find additional multiple-choice questions, exercises, and problems in CengageNOWv2.

Exercises

1. Flow of accounts into financial statements   Obj. 1
The balances for the accounts that follow appear in the Adjusted Trial Balance columns of the end-of-period spreadsheet. Indicate whether each account would flow into the income statement, statement of stockholders' equity, or balance sheet.

1. Accounts Receivable
2. Depreciation Expense—Equipment
3. Retained Earnings
4. Office Equipment
5. Rent Revenue
6. Supplies Expense
7. Unearned Revenue
8. Wages Payable

2. Statement of stockholders' equity
Obj. 2

Marcie Davies owns and operates Gemini Advertising Services. On January 1, 20Y5, Common Stock had a balance of $75,000, and Retained Earnings had a balance of $618,500. During the year, Marcie invested an additional $40,000 in exchange for common stock, and $15,000 of dividends were paid. For the year ended December 31, 20Y5, Gemini Advertising reported a net income of $92,330. Prepare a statement of stockholders' equity for the year ended December 31, 20Y5.

3. Classified balance sheet
Obj. 2

The following accounts appear in an adjusted trial balance of San Jose Consulting. Indicate whether each account would be reported in the (a) Current assets; (b) Property, plant, and equipment; (c) Current liabilities; (d) Long-term liabilities; or (e) Stockholders' equity section of the December 31, 20Y8, balance sheet of San Jose Consulting.

1. Building
2. Common Stock
3. Notes Payable (due in five years)
4. Prepaid Rent
5. Salaries Payable
6. Supplies
7. Taxes Payable
8. Unearned Service Fees

4. Closing entries
Obj. 3

After the accounts have been adjusted at October 31, the end of the fiscal year, the following balances were taken from the ledger of Smart Delivery Services Co.:

Retained Earnings	$3,550,000
Dividends	40,000
Fees Earned	1,145,000
Wages Expense	740,000
Rent Expense	65,000
Supplies Expense	14,750
Miscellaneous Expense	8,800

Journalize the two entries required to close the accounts.

5. Accounting cycle
Obj. 4

From the following list of steps in the accounting cycle, identify the two steps that are missing:

a.   Transactions are analyzed and recorded in the journal.
b.   An unadjusted trial balance is prepared.
c.   Adjustment data are assembled and analyzed.
d.   An optional end-of-period spreadsheet is prepared.
e.   Adjusting entries are journalized and posted to the ledger.
f.   An adjusted trial balance is prepared.
g.   Closing entries are journalized and posted to the ledger.
h.   A post-closing trial balance is prepared.

6. Working capital and current ratio
Obj. 6

Current assets and current liabilities for HQ Properties Company follow:

	20Y2	20Y1
Current assets	$2,175,000	$1,900,000
Current liabilities	1,500,000	1,250,000

a.   Determine the working capital and current ratio for 20Y2 and 20Y1.
b.   ━━━━► Does the change in the current ratio from 20Y1 to 20Y2 indicate a favorable or an unfavorable change?

Answers provided after Problem. Need more practice? Find additional multiple-choice questions, exercises, and problems in CengageNOWv2.

Problem

Three years ago, T. Roderick organized Harbor Realty. At July 31, 20Y6, the end of the fiscal year, the following end-of-period spreadsheet was prepared:

	A	B	C	D	E	F	G
1		Harbor Realty					
2		End-of-Period Spreadsheet					
3		For the Year Ended July 31, 20Y6					
4		Unadjusted				Adjusted	
5		Trial Balance		Adjustments		Trial Balance	
6	Account Title	Dr.	Cr.	Dr.	Cr.	Dr.	Cr.
7							
8	Cash	3,425				3,425	
9	Accounts Receivable	7,000		1,000		8,000	
10	Supplies	1,270			890	380	
11	Prepaid Insurance	620			315	305	
12	Office Equipment	51,650				51,650	
13	Accumulated Depreciation		9,700		4,950		14,650
14	Accounts Payable		925				925
15	Unearned Fees		1,250	500			750
16	Wages Payable				440		440
17	Common Stock		5,000				5,000
18	Retained Earnings		24,000				24,000
19	Dividends	5,200				5,200	
20	Fees Earned		59,125		1,000		60,625
21					500		
22	Wages Expense	22,415		440		22,855	
23	Depreciation Expense			4,950		4,950	
24	Rent Expense	4,200				4,200	
25	Utilities Expense	2,715				2,715	
26	Supplies Expense			890		890	
27	Insurance Expense			315		315	
28	Miscellaneous Expense	1,505				1,505	
29		100,000	100,000	8,095	8,095	106,390	106,390
30							

Instructions

1. Prepare an income statement, a statement of stockholders' equity, and a balance sheet. No additional common stock was issued during 20Y6.

2. On the basis of the data in the end-of-period spreadsheet, journalize the closing entries.

Need more practice? Find additional multiple-choice questions, exercises, and problems in CengageNOWv2.

Answers

Multiple-Choice Questions

1. **c** Dividends (answer c) would be reported on the statement of stockholders' equity. Utilities Expense (answer a), Rent Revenue (answer b), and Miscellaneous Expense (answer d) would all be reported on the income statement.

2. **d** Cash or other assets that are expected to be converted to cash or sold or used up within one year or less through the normal operations of the business are classified as current assets on the balance sheet. Accounts Receivable (answer d) is a current asset, since it will normally be converted to cash within one year. Office Equipment (answer a), Land (answer b), and Accumulated Depreciation (answer c) are all reported in the Property, plant, and equipment section of the balance sheet.

3. **d** Since all revenue and expense accounts are closed at the end of the period, Fees Earned (answer a), Wages Expense (answer b), and Rent Expense (answer c) would all be closed to Retained Earnings. Accumulated Depreciation (answer d) is a contra asset account that is not closed.

4. **b** Since the post-closing trial balance includes only balance sheet accounts (all of the revenue, expense, and dividend accounts are closed), Cash (answer a), Accumulated Depreciation (answer c), and Retained Earnings (answer d) would appear on the post-closing trial balance. Fees Earned (answer b) is a temporary account that is closed prior to preparing the post-closing trial balance.

5. **b** An unadjusted trial balance is prepared before the adjusting entries are journalized and posted. The post-closing trial balance (answer a) is the last step in the accounting cycle. The financial statements are prepared (answer c) after the adjusting entries are journalized and posted. The adjusted trial balance (answer d) is performed as the next step after the adjusting entries are journalized and posted.

Exercises

1. 1.   Balance sheet   5.   Income statement
    2.   Income statement   6.   Income statement
    3.   Statement of stockholders' equity   7.   Balance sheet
    4.   Balance sheet   8.   Balance sheet

2.

Gemini Advertising Services			
Statement of Stockholders' Equity			
For the Year Ended December 31, 20Y5			
	Common Stock	Retained Earnings	Total
Balances, January 1, 20Y5	$ 75,000	$618,500	$693,500
Issued common stock.	40,000		40,000
Net income.		92,330	92,330
Dividends		(15,000)	(15,000)
Balances, December 31, 20Y5	$115,000	$695,830	$810,830

3. 1.   Property, plant, and equipment   5.   Current liabilities
    2.   Stockholders' equity   6.   Current assets
    3.   Long-term liabilities   7.   Current liabilities
    4.   Current assets   8.   Current liabilities

4.

Journal		
Closing Entries		
Oct. 31 Fees Earned	1,145,000	
Wages Expense		740,000
Rent Expense		65,000
Supplies Expense		14,750
Miscellaneous Expense		8,800
Retained Earnings		316,450
31 Retained Earnings	40,000	
Dividends		40,000

5. The following two steps are missing: (1) posting the transactions to the ledger and (2) the preparation of the financial statements. Transactions should be posted to the ledger after step (a). The financial statements should be prepared after step (f).

6.

a.

	20Y2	20Y1
Current assets.	$2,175,000	$1,900,000
Current liabilities	1,500,000	1,250,000
Working capital	$ 675,000	$ 650,000
Current ratio.	1.45	1.52
	($2,175,000 ÷ $1,500,000)	($1,900,000 ÷ $1,250,000)

b. The decrease from 1.52 to 1.45 indicates an unfavorable change.

Need more help? Watch step-by-step videos of how to compute answers to these Exercises in CengageNOWv2.

Problem

1.

Harbor Realty Income Statement For the Year Ended July 31, 20Y6		
Fees earned..		$ 60,625
Expenses:		
Wages expense	$22,855	
Depreciation expense	4,950	
Rent expense	4,200	
Utilities expense	2,715	
Supplies expense	890	
Insurance expense	315	
Miscellaneous expense	1,505	
Total expenses..		(37,430)
Net income		$ 23,195

Harbor Realty Statement of Stockholders' Equity For the Year Ended July 31, 20Y6			
	Common Stock	Retained Earnings	Total
Balances, August 1, 20Y5	$5,000	$24,000	$29,000
Net income		23,195	23,195
Dividends		(5,200)	(5,200)
Balances, July 31, 20Y6	$5,000	$41,995	$46,995

Harbor Realty Balance Sheet July 31, 20Y6		
Assets		
Current assets:		
Cash...	$ 3,425	
Accounts receivable	8,000	
Supplies	380	
Prepaid insurance	305	
Total current assets....................................		$12,110
Property, plant, and equipment:		
Office equipment..	$ 51,650	
Accumulated depreciation.................................	(14,650)	
Total property, plant, and equipment		37,000
Total assets...		$49,110
Liabilities		
Current liabilities:		
Accounts payable..	$ 925	
Unearned fees	750	
Wages payable	440	
Total liabilities...		$ 2,115
Stockholders' Equity		
Common stock	$ 5,000	
Retained earnings	41,995	
Total stockholders' equity		46,995
Total liabilities and stockholders' equity		$49,110

2.

			Journal			
Date			**Description**	**Post. Ref.**	**Debit**	**Credit**
20Y6			Closing Entries			
July	31	Fees Earned			60,625	
			Wages Expense			22,855
			Depreciation Expense			4,950
			Rent Expense			4,200
			Utilities Expense			2,715
			Supplies Expense			890
			Insurance Expense			315
			Miscellaneous Expense			1,505
			Retained Earnings			23,195
	31	Retained Earnings			5,200	
			Dividends			5,200

Discussion Questions

1. Why do some accountants prepare an end-of-period spreadsheet?

2. Describe the nature of the assets that compose the following sections of a balance sheet: (a) Current assets and (b) Property, plant, and equipment.

3. What is the difference between a current liability and a long-term liability?

4. What types of accounts are referred to as temporary accounts?

5. Why are closing entries required at the end of an accounting period?

6. What is the difference between adjusting entries and closing entries?

7. What is the purpose of the post-closing trial balance?

8. (a) What is the most important output of the accounting cycle? (b) Do all companies have an accounting cycle? Explain.

9. Which step of the accounting cycle is optional?

10. (a) What is the difference between liquidity and solvency? (b) What is the difference between working capital and the current ratio?

Basic Exercises

SHOW ME HOW

BE 4-1 Flow of accounts into financial statements   Obj. 1

The balances for the accounts that follow appear in the Adjusted Trial Balance columns of the end-of-period spreadsheet. Indicate whether each account would flow into the income statement, statement of stockholders' equity, or balance sheet.

1. Accumulated Depreciation—Building
2. Cash
3. Fees Earned
4. Insurance Expense
5. Prepaid Rent
6. Supplies
7. Dividends
8. Wages Expense

SHOW ME HOW

BE 4-2 Statement of stockholders' equity
Obj. 2

Scott Lockhart owns and operates AAA Delivery Services. On January 1, 20Y7, Common Stock had a balance of $40,000, and Retained Earnings had a balance of $815,500. During the year, no additional common stock was issued, and $10,000 of dividends were paid. For the year ended December 31, 20Y7, AAA Delivery reported a net income of $67,250. Prepare a statement of stockholders' equity for the year ended December 31, 20Y7.

SHOW ME HOW

BE 4-3 Classified balance sheet
Obj. 2

The following accounts appear in an adjusted trial balance of Bridgewater Consulting. Indicate whether each account would be reported in the (a) Current assets; (b) Property, plant, and equipment; (c) Current liabilities; (d) Long-term liabilities; or (e) Stockholders' equity section of the December 31, 20Y0, balance sheet of Bridgewater Consulting.

1. Accounts Payable
2. Accounts Receivable
3. Accumulated Depreciation—Building
4. Cash

5. Common Stock
6. Note Payable (due in ten years)
7. Supplies
8. Wages Payable

SHOW ME HOW

BE 4-4 Closing entries
Obj. 3

After the accounts have been adjusted at November 30, the end of the fiscal year, the following balances were taken from the ledger of Diamond Landscaping Co.:

Retained Earnings	$2,550,000
Dividends	25,000
Fees Earned	1,150,000
Wages Expense	613,750
Rent Expense	120,000
Supplies Expense	9,150
Miscellaneous Expense	11,000

Journalize the two entries required to close the accounts.

SHOW ME HOW

BE 4-5 Accounting cycle
Obj. 4

From the following list of steps in the accounting cycle, identify the two steps that are missing:

a. Transactions are analyzed and recorded in the journal.
b. Transactions are posted to the ledger.
c. An unadjusted trial balance is prepared.
d. An optional end-of-period spreadsheet is prepared.
e. Adjusting entries are journalized and posted to the ledger.
f. An adjusted trial balance is prepared.
g. Financial statements are prepared.
h. A post-closing trial balance is prepared.

SHOW ME HOW

BE 4-6 Working capital and current ratio
Obj. 6

Current assets and current liabilities for Brimstone Company follow:

	20Y4	20Y3
Current assets	$1,586,250	$1,210,000
Current liabilities	705,000	550,000

a. Determine the working capital and current ratio for 20Y4 and 20Y3.

b.  Does the change in the current ratio from 20Y3 to 20Y4 indicate a favorable or an unfavorable change?

Exercises

EX 4-1 Flow of accounts into financial statements
Obj. 1, 2

The balances for the accounts that follow appear in the Adjusted Trial Balance columns of the end-of-period spreadsheet. Indicate whether each account would flow into the income statement, statement of stockholders' equity, or balance sheet.

1. Accounts Payable
2. Accounts Receivable
3. Cash
4. Dividends
5. Fees Earned
6. Supplies
7. Unearned Rent
8. Utilities Expense
9. Wages Expense
10. Wages Payable

EX 4-2 Classifying accounts
Obj. 1, 2

Balances for each of the following accounts appear in an adjusted trial balance. Identify each as (a) asset, (b) liability, (c) revenue, or (d) expense.

1. Accounts Receivable
2. Equipment
3. Fees Earned
4. Insurance Expense
5. Prepaid Advertising
6. Prepaid Rent
7. Rent Revenue
8. Salary Expense
9. Salary Payable
10. Supplies
11. Supplies Expense
12. Unearned Rent

EX 4-3 Financial statements from the end-of-period spreadsheet
Obj. 1, 2

SHOW ME HOW

Demo Consulting is a consulting firm owned and operated by Jesse Flatt. The following end-of-period spreadsheet was prepared for the year ended August 31, 20Y9:

	A	B	C	D	E	F	G
1	Demo Consulting						
2	End-of-Period Spreadsheet						
3	For the Year Ended August 31, 20Y9						
4		Unadjusted				Adjusted	
5		Trial Balance		Adjustments		Trial Balance	
6	Account Title	Dr.	Cr.	Dr.	Cr.	Dr.	Cr.
7							
8	Cash	182,500				182,500	
9	Accounts Receivable	234,500				234,500	
10	Supplies	27,600			22,600	5,000	
11	Land	775,000				775,000	
12	Office Equipment	400,000				400,000	
13	Accumulated Depreciation		60,200		11,800		72,000
14	Accounts Payable		41,500				41,500
15	Salaries Payable				13,500		13,500
16	Common Stock		100,000				100,000
17	Retained Earnings		810,000				810,000
18	Dividends	30,000				30,000	
19	Fees Earned		1,480,000				1,480,000
20	Salary Expense	829,600		13,500		843,100	
21	Supplies Expense			22,600		22,600	
22	Depreciation Expense			11,800		11,800	
23	Miscellaneous Expense	12,500				12,500	
24		2,491,700	2,491,700	47,900	47,900	2,517,000	2,517,000
25							

Based on the preceding spreadsheet, prepare an income statement, statement of stockholders' equity, and balance sheet for Demo Consulting. During the year ended August 31, 20Y9, $15,000 of additional common stock was issued.

SHOW ME HOW

EX 4-4 Financial statements from the end-of-period spreadsheet

Obj. 1, 2

Triton Consulting is a consulting firm owned and operated by Jayson Neese. The following end-of-period spreadsheet was prepared for the year ended April 30, 20Y3:

	A	B	C	D	E	F	G
1		Triton Consulting					
2		End-of-Period Spreadsheet					
3		For the Year Ended April 30, 20Y3					
4		Unadjusted				Adjusted	
5		Trial Balance		Adjustments		Trial Balance	
6	Account Title	Dr.	Cr.	Dr.	Cr.	Dr.	Cr.
7							
8	Cash	21,500				21,500	
9	Accounts Receivable	51,150				51,150	
10	Supplies	2,400			1,650	750	
11	Office Equipment	32,000				32,000	
12	Accumulated Depreciation		4,500		900		5,400
13	Accounts Payable		3,350				3,350
14	Salaries Payable				2,000		2,000
15	Common Stock		20,000				20,000
16	Retained Earnings		52,200				52,200
17	Dividends	10,000				10,000	
18	Fees Earned		279,000				279,000
19	Salary Expense	240,000		2,000		242,000	
20	Supplies Expense			1,650		1,650	
21	Depreciation Expense			900		900	
22	Miscellaneous Expense	2,000				2,000	
23		359,050	359,050	4,550	4,550	361,950	361,950
24							

Based on the preceding spreadsheet, prepare an income statement, statement of stockholders' equity, and balance sheet for Triton Consulting. During the year ended April 30, 20Y3, common stock of $5,000 was issued.

✔ Net income, $335,850

SHOW ME HOW

EX 4-5 Income statement

Obj. 2

The following account balances were taken from the adjusted trial balance for Urgent Messenger Service, a delivery service firm, for the fiscal year ended November 30, 20Y1:

Depreciation Expense	$ 12,200	Rent Expense	$ 80,000
Fees Earned	990,000	Salaries Expense	502,400
Insurance Expense	5,750	Supplies Expense	7,150
Miscellaneous Expense	6,650	Utilities Expense	40,000

Prepare an income statement.

✔ Net loss, $(49,250)

SHOW ME HOW

EX 4-6 Income statement; net loss

Obj. 2

The following revenue and expense account balances were taken from the ledger of Acorn Health Services Co. after the accounts had been adjusted on January 31, 20Y7, the end of the fiscal year:

Depreciation Expense	$10,000	Service Revenue	$634,900
Insurance Expense	9,000	Supplies Expense	4,100
Miscellaneous Expense	8,150	Utilities Expense	44,700
Rent Expense	60,000	Wages Expense	548,200

Prepare an income statement.

✔ a. Net income:
$1,820

EX 4-7 Income statement

Obj. 2

FedEx Corporation (FDX) had the following revenue and expense account balances (in millions) for a recent year ending May 31:

Depreciation Expense	$2,631	Purchased Transportation	$ 9,966
Fuel Expense	2,399	Rentals and Landing Fees	2,854
Maintenance and Repairs Expense	2,108	Revenues	50,365
Other Expense (Income) Net	9,086	Salaries and Employee Benefits	18,581
Provision for Income Taxes	920		

a. Prepare an income statement.

b. ━━━▶ Compare your income statement with the income statement that is available at FedEx's website (http://investors.fedex.com). Under Annual Report, select Download PDF. What similarities and differences do you see?

✔ Retained earnings,
Dec. 31, 20Y2:
$4,690,800

SHOW ME HOW

EX 4-8 Statement of stockholders' equity

Obj. 2

Climate Control Systems Co. offers its services to residents in the Spokane area. Selected accounts from the ledger of Climate Control Systems for the fiscal year ended December 31, 20Y2, are as follows:

Common Stock		
	Jan. 1	75,000
	Feb. 15	25,000

Retained Earnings				Dividends			
Dec. 31	160,000	Jan. 1 (20Y2)	4,150,800	Mar. 31	40,000	Dec. 31	160,000
		Dec. 31	700,000	June 30	40,000		
				Sept. 30	40,000		
				Dec. 31	40,000		

Prepare a statement of stockholders' equity for the year.

✔ Retained earnings,
April 30, 20Y5: $439,300

EX 4-9 Statement of stockholders' equity; net loss

Obj. 2

Selected accounts from the ledger of Restoration Arts for the fiscal year ended April 30, 20Y5, are as follows:

Common Stock		
	May 1 (20Y4)	10,000
	July 1	7,500

Retained Earnings				Dividends			
Apr. 30	31,200	May 1 (20Y4)	475,500	July 31 (20Y4)	1,250	Apr. 30	5,000
30	5,000			Oct. 31	1,250		
				Jan. 31	1,250		
				Apr. 30 (20Y4)	1,250		

Prepare a statement of stockholders' equity for the year.

EX 4-10 Classifying assets

Obj. 2

Identify each of the following as (a) a current asset or (b) property, plant, and equipment:

1. Accounts Receivable
2. Building
3. Cash

4. Equipment
5. Prepaid Insurance
6. Supplies

EX 4-11 Balance sheet classification

Obj. 2

At the balance sheet date, a business owes a mortgage note payable of $375,000, the terms of which provide for monthly payments of $1,250.

➤ Explain how the liability should be classified on the balance sheet.

EX 4-12 Balance sheet

Obj. 2

✔ Total assets: $800,000

SHOW ME HOW

Dynamic Weight Loss Co. offers personal weight reduction consulting services to individuals. After all the accounts have been closed on June 30, 20Y7, the end of the fiscal year, the balances of selected accounts from the ledger of Dynamic Weight Loss are as follows:

Accounts Payable	$ 51,200	Prepaid Insurance	$ 8,400
Accounts Receivable	187,500	Prepaid Rent	6,000
Accumulated Depreciation—Equipment	186,000	Retained Earnings	620,300
Cash	?	Salaries Payable	7,500
Common Stock	100,000	Supplies	11,200
Equipment	325,900	Unearned Fees	21,000
Land	375,000		

Prepare a classified balance sheet that includes the correct balance for Cash.

EX 4-13 Balance sheet

Obj. 2

✔ (b) Corrected balance sheet, total assets: $625,000

The following balance sheet was prepared by Labyrinth Services Co. for its year ended August 31, 20Y3.

Labyrinth Services Co.
Balance Sheet
For the Year Ended August 31, 20Y3

Assets

Current assets:		
Cash	$ 18,500	
Accounts payable	31,300	
Supplies	6,500	
Prepaid insurance	16,600	
Land	225,000	
Total current assets		$297,900
Property, plant, and equipment:		
Building	$400,000	
Equipment	97,000	
Total property, plant, and equipment		635,400
Total assets		$933,300

Liabilities

Current liabilities:		
Accounts receivable	$ 41,400	
Accumulated depreciation—building	155,000	
Accumulated depreciation—equipment	25,000	
Net income	118,200	
Total liabilities		$339,600

Stockholders' Equity

Wages payable	$ 6,500	
Common stock	75,000	
Retained earnings	512,200	
Total stockholders' equity		593,700
Total liabilities and stockholders' equity		$933,300

a. List the errors in the preceding balance sheet.

b. Prepare a corrected balance sheet.

EX 4-14 Identifying accounts to be closed

Obj. 3

From the list that follows, identify the accounts that should be closed at the end of the fiscal year:

a. Accounts Payable
b. Accumulated Depreciation—Equipment
c. Depreciation Expense—Equipment
d. Equipment
e. Common Stock
f. Dividends

g. Fees Earned
h. Land
i. Supplies
j. Supplies Expense
k. Wages Expense
l. Wages Payable

EX 4-15 Closing entries with net income

Obj. 3

Automation Services Co. offers its services to companies desiring to use technology to improve their operations. After the accounts have been adjusted at December 31, the end of the fiscal year, the following balances were taken from the ledger of Automation Services:

Fees Earned	$ 614,500
Dividends	45,000
Rent Expense	140,000
Retained Earnings	3,250,000
Supplies Expense	18,200
Wages Expense	320,000
Miscellaneous Expense	8,700

Journalize the closing entries.

SHOW ME HOW

EX 4-16 Closing entries with net loss

Obj. 3

Summit Services Co. offers its services to individuals desiring to improve their personal images. After the accounts have been adjusted at May 31, the end of the fiscal year, the following balances were taken from the ledger of Summit Services:

Fees Earned	$1,150,000	Supplies Expense	$ 19,300
Dividends	5,000	Wages Expense	915,000
Rent Expense	200,000	Miscellaneous Expense	31,900
Retained Earnings	450,000		

Journalize the closing entries required to close the accounts.

EX 4-17 Identifying permanent accounts

Obj. 3

Which of the following accounts will usually appear in the post-closing trial balance?

a. Accounts Payable
b. Accumulated Depreciation
c. Cash
d. Common Stock
e. Dividends
f. Depreciation Expense

g. Fees Earned
h. Office Equipment
i. Salaries Expense
j. Salaries Payable
k. Supplies

EX 4-18 Post-closing trial balance

Obj. 3

An accountant prepared the following post-closing trial balance:

Security Services Co.
Post-Closing Trial Balance
July 31, 20Y0

	Debit Balances	Credit Balances
Cash	41,100	
Accounts Receivable	317,400	
Supplies		5,000
Equipment		162,750
Accumulated Depreciation—Equipment	73,300	
Accounts Payable	82,500	
Salaries Payable		5,500
Unearned Rent	12,000	
Common Stock	65,000	
Retained Earnings	287,950	
	879,250	173,250

Prepare a corrected post-closing trial balance. Assume that all accounts have normal balances and that the amounts shown are correct.

EX 4-19 Steps in the accounting cycle

Obj. 4

Rearrange the following steps in the accounting cycle in proper sequence:

a. A post-closing trial balance is prepared.

b. Adjustment data are asssembled and analyzed.

c. Adjusting entries are journalized and posted to the ledger.

d. An adjusted trial balance is prepared.

e. An optional end-of-period spreadsheet is prepared.

f. An unadjusted trial balance is prepared.

g. Closing entries are journalized and posted to the ledger.

h. Financial statements are prepared.

i. Transactions are analyzed and recorded in the journal.

j. Transactions are posted to the ledger.

Appendix 1
EX 4-20 Completing an end-of-period spreadsheet

List (a) through (j) in the order they would be performed in preparing and completing an end-of-period spreadsheet.

a. Add the Debit and Credit columns of the Unadjusted Trial Balance columns of the spreadsheet to verify that the totals are equal.

b. Add the Debit and Credit columns of the Balance Sheet and Income Statement columns of the spreadsheet to verify that the totals are equal.

c. Add or deduct adjusting entry data to trial balance amounts, and extend amounts to the Adjusted Trial Balance columns.

d. Add the Debit and Credit columns of the Adjustments columns of the spreadsheet to verify that the totals are equal.

e. Add the Debit and Credit columns of the Balance Sheet and Income Statement columns of the spreadsheet to determine the amount of net income or net loss for the period.

(Continued)

f.   Add the Debit and Credit columns of the Adjusted Trial Balance columns of the spreadsheet to verify that the totals are equal.

g.   Enter the adjusting entries into the spreadsheet, based on the adjustment data.

h.   Enter the amount of net income or net loss for the period in the proper Income Statement column and Balance Sheet column.

i.   Enter the unadjusted account balances from the general ledger into the Unadjusted Trial Balance columns of the spreadsheet.

j.   Extend the adjusted trial balance amounts to the Income Statement columns and the Balance Sheet columns.

Appendix 1
EX 4-21   Adjustment data on an end-of-period spreadsheet

✔ Total of Adjustments Debit column: $31

EXCEL TEMPLATE

Alert Security Services Co. offers security services to business clients. The trial balance for Alert Security Services has been prepared on the following end-of-period spreadsheet for the year ended October 31, 20Y3:

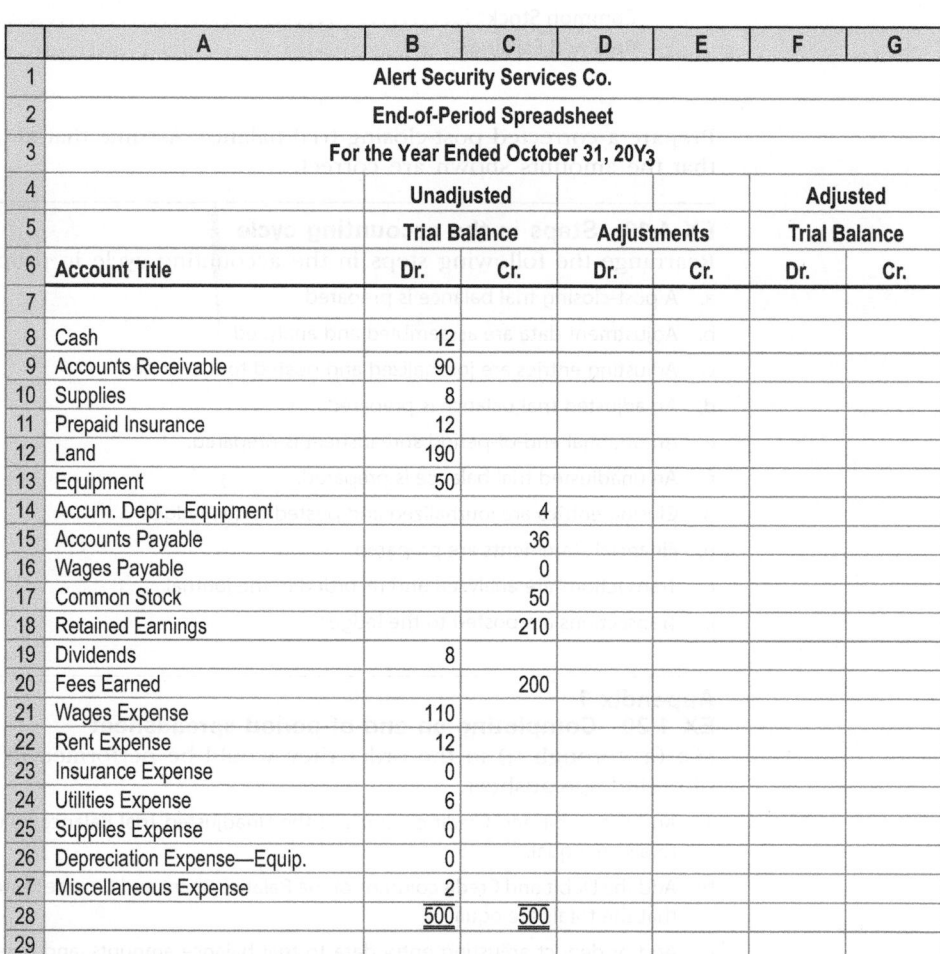

	A	B	C	D	E	F	G
1		Alert Security Services Co.					
2		End-of-Period Spreadsheet					
3		For the Year Ended October 31, 20Y3					
4		Unadjusted				Adjusted	
5		Trial Balance		Adjustments		Trial Balance	
6	Account Title	Dr.	Cr.	Dr.	Cr.	Dr.	Cr.
7							
8	Cash	12					
9	Accounts Receivable	90					
10	Supplies	8					
11	Prepaid Insurance	12					
12	Land	190					
13	Equipment	50					
14	Accum. Depr.—Equipment		4				
15	Accounts Payable		36				
16	Wages Payable		0				
17	Common Stock		50				
18	Retained Earnings		210				
19	Dividends	8					
20	Fees Earned		200				
21	Wages Expense	110					
22	Rent Expense	12					
23	Insurance Expense	0					
24	Utilities Expense	6					
25	Supplies Expense	0					
26	Depreciation Expense—Equip.	0					
27	Miscellaneous Expense	2					
28		500	500				
29							

The data for year-end adjustments are as follows:

a.   Fees earned, but not yet billed, $13.

b.   Supplies on hand, $4.

c.   Insurance premiums expired, $10.

d.   Depreciation expense, $3.

e.   Wages accrued, but not paid, $1.

Enter the adjustment data, and place the balances in the Adjusted Trial Balance columns.

Appendix 1
EX 4-22   Completing an end-of-period spreadsheet

✔ Net income: $65

EXCEL TEMPLATE

Alert Security Services Co. offers security services to business clients. Complete the following end-of-period spreadsheet for Alert Security Services Co.:

	A	B	C	D	E	F	G
1	**Alert Security Services Co.**						
2	**End-of-Period Spreadsheet**						
3	**For the Year Ended October 31, 20Y3**						
4		**Adjusted Trial Balance**		**Income Statement**		**Balance Sheet**	
5	**Account Title**	**Dr.**	**Cr.**	**Dr.**	**Cr.**	**Dr.**	**Cr.**
6	Cash	12					
7	Accounts Receivable	103					
8	Supplies	4					
9	Prepaid Insurance	2					
10	Land	190					
11	Equipment	50					
12	Accum. Depr.—Equipment		7				
13	Accounts Payable		36				
14	Wages Payable		1				
15	Common Stock		50				
16	Retained Earnings		210				
17	Dividends	8					
18	Fees Earned		213				
19	Wages Expense	111					
20	Rent Expense	12					
21	Insurance Expense	10					
22	Utilities Expense	6					
23	Supplies Expense	4					
24	Depreciation Expense—Equip.	3					
25	Miscellaneous Expense	2					
26		517	517				
27	Net income (loss)						
28							

Appendix 1
EX 4-23   Financial statements from an end-of-period spreadsheet

✔ Retained earnings, October 31, 20Y3: $267

EXCEL TEMPLATE

Based on the data in Exercise 4-22, prepare an income statement, statement of stockholders' equity, and balance sheet for Alert Security Services Co. During the year ended October 31, 20Y3, common stock of $10 was issued.

Appendix 1
EX 4-24   Adjusting entries from an end-of-period spreadsheet
Based on the data in Exercise 4-21, prepare the adjusting entries for Alert Security Services Co.

Appendix 1
EX 4-25   Closing entries from an end-of-period spreadsheet
Based on the data in Exercise 4-22, prepare the closing entries for Alert Security Services Co.

Appendix 2
EX 4-26   Reversing entry

The following adjusting entry for accrued wages was recorded on December 31:

Dec. 31	Wages Expense	5,500	
	Wages Payable		5,500

a. Journalize the reversing entry that would be made on January 1 of the next period.

b. Assume that the first paid period of the following year ends on January 6 and that wages of $61,375 were paid. Journalize the entry to record the payment of the January 6 wages.

c. Journalize the entry to record the payment of the January 6 wages assuming that a reversing entry was not made on January 1.

d. What is wages expense for the period January 1–6?

Appendix 2
EX 4-27   Adjusting and reversing entries

On the basis of the following data, (a) journalize the adjusting entries at December 31, the end of the current fiscal year, and (b) journalize the reversing entries on January 1, the first day of the following year:

1. Sales salaries are uniformly $11,750 for a five-day workweek, ending on Friday. The last payday of the year was Friday, December 26.

2. Accrued fees earned but not recorded at December 31, $51,300.

Appendix 2
EX 4-28   Adjusting and reversing entries

On the basis of the following data, (a) journalize the adjusting entries at June 30, the end of the current fiscal year, and (b) journalize the reversing entries on July 1, the first day of the following year:

1. Wages are uniformly $66,000 for a five-day workweek, ending on Friday. The last payday of the year was Thursday, June 27.

2. Accrued fees earned but not recorded at June 30, $25,000.

Appendix 2
EX 4-29   Entries posted to wages expense account

Portions of the wages expense account of a business follow:

Account *Wages Expense*					**Account No.** *53*	
		Post.			Balance	
Date	Item	Ref.	Dr.	Cr.	Dr.	Cr.
20Y8						
Dec. 26	(1)	125	15,400		800,000	
31	(2)	126	9,250		809,250	
31	(3)	127		809,250	—	—
20Y9						
Jan. 1	(4)	128		9,250		9,250
2	(5)	129	14,800		5,550	

a. Indicate the nature of the entry (payment, adjusting, closing, reversing) from which each numbered posting was made.

b. Journalize the complete entry from which each numbered posting was made.

Appendix 2
EX 4-30   Entries posted to wages expense account
Portions of the salaries expense account of a business follow:

Account Salaries Expense					Account No. 62	
		Post.			**Balance**	
Date	Item	Ref.	Dr.	Cr.	Dr.	Cr.
20Y6						
Dec. 27	(1)	29	22,000		1,200,000	
31	(2)	30	13,200		1,213,200	
31	(3)	31		1,213,200	—	—
20Y7						
Jan. 1	(4)	32		13,200		13,200
2	(5)	33	24,000		10,800	

a. Indicate the nature of the entry (payment, adjusting, closing, reversing) from which each numbered posting was made.

b. Journalize the complete entry from which each numbered posting was made.

Problems: Series A

PR 4-1A   Financial statements and closing entries   **Obj. 1, 2, 3**

✔ 1. Net income, $137,400

SHOW ME HOW

EXCEL TEMPLATE

Beacons Company maintains and repairs warning lights, such as those found on radio towers and lighthouses. Beacons Company prepared the following end-of-period spreadsheet at December 31, 20Y5, the end of the fiscal year:

	A	B	C	D	E	F	G
1		Beacons Company					
2		End-of-Period Spreadsheet					
3		For the Year Ended December 31, 20Y5					
4		Unadjusted				Adjusted	
5		Trial Balance		Adjustments		Trial Balance	
6	Account Title	Dr.	Cr.	Dr.	Cr.	Dr.	Cr.
7							
8	Cash	10,800				10,800	
9	Accounts Receivable	38,900		9,100		48,000	
10	Prepaid Insurance	4,200			3,150	1,050	
11	Supplies	2,730			2,180	550	
12	Land	98,000				98,000	
13	Building	400,000				400,000	
14	Accum. Depr.—Building		205,300		12,000		217,300
15	Equipment	101,000				101,000	
16	Accum. Depr.—Equipment		85,100		4,800		89,900
17	Accounts Payable		15,700				15,700
18	Salaries & Wages Payable				5,000		5,000
19	Unearned Rent		2,100	1,100			1,000
20	Common Stock		75,000				75,000
21	Retained Earnings		128,100				128,100
22	Dividends	10,000				10,000	
23	Fees Earned		363,700		9,100		372,800
24	Rent Revenue				1,100		1,100
25	Salaries & Wages Expense	158,100		5,000		163,100	
26	Advertising Expense	21,700				21,700	
27	Utilities Expense	16,400				16,400	
28	Depr. Exp.—Building			12,000		12,000	
29	Repairs Expense	8,850				8,850	
30	Depr. Exp.—Equipment			4,800		4,800	
31	Insurance Expense			3,150		3,150	
32	Supplies Expense			2,180		2,180	
33	Misc. Expense	4,320				4,320	
34		875,000	875,000	37,330	37,330	905,900	905,900
35							

(Continued)

Instructions

1. Prepare an income statement for the year ended December 31, 20Y5.

2. Prepare a statement of stockholders' equity for the year ended December 31, 20Y5. During the year, common stock of $25,000 was issued.

3. Prepare a balance sheet as of December 31, 20Y5.

4. Based upon the end-of-period spreadsheet, journalize the closing entries.

5. Prepare a post-closing trial balance.

PR 4-2A   Financial statements and closing entries   Obj. 2, 3

✔ 1. Retained earnings, November 30: $185,800

Foxy Investigative Services is an investigative services firm that is owned and operated by Shirley Vickers. On November 30, 20Y8, the end of the fiscal year, the accountant for Foxy Investigative Services prepared an end-of-period spreadsheet, a part of which follows:

	A	F	G
1	Foxy Investigative Services		
2	End-of-Period Spreadsheet		
3	For the Year Ended November 30, 20Y8		
4		Adjusted Trial Balance	
5			
6	Account Title	Dr.	Cr.
7			
8	Cash	27,500	
9	Accounts Receivable	71,800	
10	Supplies	3,550	
11	Prepaid Insurance	750	
12	Building	330,500	
13	Accumulated Depreciation—Building		184,100
14	Accounts Payable		16,100
15	Salaries Payable		6,600
16	Unearned Rent		1,500
17	Common Stock		40,000
18	Retained Earnings		70,300
19	Dividends	30,000	
20	Service Fees		675,500
21	Rent Revenue		9,000
22	Salaries Expense	435,000	
23	Rent Expense	55,000	
24	Supplies Expense	11,850	
25	Depreciation Expense—Building	10,000	
26	Utilities Expense	8,800	
27	Repairs Expense	4,250	
28	Insurance Expense	3,000	
29	Miscellaneous Expense	11,100	
30		1,003,100	1,003,100

Instructions

1. Prepare an income statement, a statement of stockholders' equity, and a balance sheet.

2. Journalize the entries that were required to close the accounts at November 30, 20Y8. No additional common stock was issued during the year ended November 30, 20Y8.

3. If Retained Earnings had instead decreased $46,000 after the closing entries were posted, and the dividends remained the same, what would have been the amount of net income or net loss?

PR 4-3A T accounts, adjusting entries, financial statements, and closing entries; optional end-of-period spreadsheet

Obj. 2, 3

✔ 5. Net income:
$10,700

EXCEL TEMPLATE

The unadjusted trial balance of Epicenter Laundry at June 30, 20Y6, the end of the fiscal year, follows:

Epicenter Laundry
Unadjusted Trial Balance
June 30, 20Y6

	Debit Balances	Credit Balances
Cash..	11,000	
Laundry Supplies	26,500	
Prepaid Insurance...	9,600	
Laundry Equipment..	232,600	
Accumulated Depreciation		125,400
Accounts Payable...		11,800
Common Stock		40,000
Retained Earnings		65,600
Dividends	5,000	
Laundry Revenue..		232,200
Wages Expense...	125,200	
Rent Expense...	40,000	
Utilities Expense..	19,700	
Miscellaneous Expense...	5,400	
	475,000	475,000

The data needed to determine year-end adjustments are as follows:

(a) Laundry supplies on hand at June 30 are $8,600.

(b) Insurance premiums expired during the year are $5,700.

(c) Depreciation of laundry equipment during the year is $6,500.

(d) Wages accrued but not paid at June 30 are $1,100.

Instructions

1. For each account listed in the unadjusted trial balance, enter the balance in a T account. Identify the balance as "June 30 Bal." In addition, add T accounts for Wages Payable, Depreciation Expense, Laundry Supplies Expense, and Insurance Expense.

2. *(Optional)* Enter the unadjusted trial balance on an end-of-period spreadsheet and complete the spreadsheet. Add the accounts listed in part (1) as needed.

3. Journalize and post the adjusting entries. Identify the adjustments by "Adj." and the new balances as "Adj. Bal."

4. Prepare an adjusted trial balance.

5. Prepare an income statement, a statement of stockholders' equity, and a balance sheet. During the year ended June 30, 20Y6, additional common stock of $7,500 was issued.

6. Journalize and post the closing entries. Identify the closing entries by "Clos."

7. Prepare a post-closing trial balance.

EXCEL TEMPLATE

PR 4-4A   Ledger accounts, adjusting entries, financial statements, and closing entries; optional spreadsheet   Obj. 2, 3

✔ 5. Net income: $51,150

The unadjusted trial balance of Lakota Freight Co. at March 31, 20Y4, the end of the year, follows:

Lakota Freight Co.
Unadjusted Trial Balance
March 31, 20Y4

	Account No.	Debit Balances	Credit Balances
Cash	11	12,000	
Supplies	13	30,000	
Prepaid Insurance	14	3,600	
Equipment	16	110,000	
Accumulated Depreciation—Equipment	17		25,000
Trucks	18	60,000	
Accumulated Depreciation—Trucks	19		15,000
Accounts Payable	21		4,000
Common Stock	31		26,000
Retained Earnings	32		70,000
Dividends	33	15,000	
Service Revenue	41		160,000
Wages Expense	51	45,000	
Rent Expense	53	10,600	
Truck Expense	54	9,000	
Miscellaneous Expense	59	4,800	
		300,000	300,000

The data needed to determine year-end adjustments are as follows:

(a) Supplies on hand at March 31 are $7,500.

(b) Insurance premiums expired during year are $1,800.

(c) Depreciation of equipment during year is $8,350.

(d) Depreciation of trucks during year is $6,200.

(e) Wages accrued but not paid at March 31 are $600.

Instructions

1. For each account listed in the trial balance, enter the balance in the appropriate Balance column of a four-column account and place a check mark (✓) in the Posting Reference column.

2. *(Optional)* Enter the unadjusted trial balance on an end-of-period spreadsheet and complete the spreadsheet. Add the accounts listed in part (3) as needed.

3. Journalize and post the adjusting entries, inserting balances in the accounts affected. Record the adjusting entries on Page 26 of the journal. The following additional accounts from Lakota Freight Co.'s chart of accounts should be used: Wages Payable, 22; Supplies Expense, 52; Depreciation Expense—Equipment, 55; Depreciation Expense—Trucks, 56; Insurance Expense, 57.

4. Prepare an adjusted trial balance.

5. Prepare an income statement, a statement of stockholders' equity, and a balance sheet. During the year ended March 31, 20Y4, additional common stock of $6,000 was issued.

6. Journalize and post the closing entries. Record the closing entries on Page 27 of the journal. Indicate closed accounts by inserting a line in both Balance columns opposite the closing entry.

7. Prepare a post-closing trial balance.

PR 4-5A Complete accounting cycle Obj. 4, 5

✔ 8. Net income:
$33,475

EXCEL TEMPLATE

For the past several years, Steffy Lopez has operated a part-time consulting business from his home. As of July 1, 20Y2, Steffy decided to move to rented quarters and to operate the business, which was to be known as Diamond Consulting, on a full-time basis. Diamond entered into the following transactions during July:

July 1. The following assets were received from Steffy Lopez in exchange for common stock: cash, $13,500; accounts receivable, $20,800; supplies, $3,200; and office equipment, $7,500. There were no liabilities received.

1. Paid two months' rent on a lease rental contract, $4,800.

2. Paid the premiums on property and casualty insurance policies, $4,500.

4. Received cash from clients as an advance payment for services to be provided, and recorded it as unearned fees, $5,500.

5. Purchased additional office equipment on account from Office Station Co., $6,500.

6. Received cash from clients on account, $15,300.

10. Paid cash for a newspaper advertisement, $400.

12. Paid Office Station Co. for part of the debt incurred on July 5, $5,200.

12. Recorded services provided on account for the period July 1–12, $13,300.

14. Paid receptionist for two weeks' salary, $1,750.

Record the following transactions on Page 2 of the journal:

17. Recorded cash from cash clients for fees earned during the period July 1–17, $9,450.

18. Paid cash for supplies, $600.

20. Recorded services provided on account for the period July 13–20, $6,650.

24. Recorded cash from cash clients for fees earned for the period July 17–24, $4,000.

26. Received cash from clients on account, $12,000.

27. Paid receptionist for two weeks' salary, $1,750.

29. Paid telephone bill for July, $325.

31. Paid electricity bill for July, $675.

31. Recorded cash from cash clients for fees earned for the period July 25–31, $5,200.

31. Recorded services provided on account for the remainder of July, $3,000.

31. Paid dividends, $12,500.

Instructions

1. Journalize each transaction in a two-column journal starting on Page 1, referring to the following chart of accounts in selecting the accounts to be debited and credited. (Do not insert the account numbers in the journal at this time.)

11	Cash	31	Common Stock
12	Accounts Receivable	32	Retained Earnings
14	Supplies	33	Dividends
15	Prepaid Rent	41	Fees Earned
16	Prepaid Insurance	51	Salary Expense
18	Office Equipment	52	Rent Expense
19	Accumulated Depreciation	53	Supplies Expense
21	Accounts Payable	54	Depreciation Expense
22	Salaries Payable	55	Insurance Expense
23	Unearned Fees	59	Miscellaneous Expense

2. Post the journal to a ledger of four-column accounts.

3. Prepare an unadjusted trial balance.

(Continued)

4. At the end of July, the following adjustment data were assembled. Analyze and use these data to complete parts (5) and (6).

   (a) Insurance expired during July is $375.
   (b) Supplies on hand on July 31 are $1,525.
   (c) Depreciation of office equipment for July is $750.
   (d) Accrued receptionist salary on July 31 is $175.
   (e) Rent expired during July is $2,400.
   (f) Unearned fees on July 31 are $2,750.

5. *(Optional)* Enter the unadjusted trial balance on an end-of-period spreadsheet and complete the spreadsheet.

6. Journalize and post the adjusting entries. Record the adjusting entries on Page 3 of the journal.

7. Prepare an adjusted trial balance.

8. Prepare an income statement, a statement of stockholders' equity, and a balance sheet.

9. Prepare and post the closing entries. Record the closing entries on Page 4 of the journal. Indicate closed accounts by inserting a line in both the Balance columns opposite the closing entry.

10. Prepare a post-closing trial balance.

Problems: Series B

PR 4-1B   Financial statements and closing entries   Obj. 1, 2, 3

✔ 3. Total assets:
$342,425

Last Chance Company offers legal consulting advice to prison inmates. Last Chance prepared the end-of-period spreadsheet that follows at June 30, 20Y3, the end of the fiscal year.

SHOW ME HOW   EXCEL TEMPLATE

	A	B	C	D	E	F	G
1		Last Chance Company					
2		End-of-Period Spreadsheet					
3		For the Year Ended June 30, 20Y3					
4		Unadjusted				Adjusted	
5		Trial Balance		Adjustments		Trial Balance	
6	Account Title	Dr.	Cr.	Dr.	Cr.	Dr.	Cr.
7							
8	Cash	5,100				5,100	
9	Accounts Receivable	22,750		3,750		26,500	
10	Prepaid Insurance	3,600			1,300	2,300	
11	Supplies	2,025			1,500	525	
12	Land	80,000				80,000	
13	Building	340,000				340,000	
14	Accum. Depr.—Building		190,000		3,000		193,000
15	Equipment	140,000				140,000	
16	Accum. Depr.—Equipment		54,450		4,550		59,000
17	Accounts Payable		9,750				9,750
18	Salaries & Wages Payable				1,900		1,900
19	Unearned Rent		4,500	3,000			1,500
20	Common Stock		90,000				90,000
21	Retained Earnings		271,300				271,300
22	Dividends	20,000				20,000	
23	Fees Earned		280,000		3,750		283,750
24	Rent Revenue				3,000		3,000
25	Salaries & Wages Expense	145,100		1,900		147,000	
26	Advertising Expense	86,800				86,800	
27	Utilities Expense	30,000				30,000	
28	Travel Expense	18,750				18,750	
29	Depr. Exp.—Equipment			4,550		4,550	
30	Depr. Exp.—Building			3,000		3,000	
31	Supplies Expense			1,500		1,500	
32	Insurance Expense			1,300		1,300	
33	Misc. Expense	5,875				5,875	
34		900,000	900,000	19,000	19,000	913,200	913,200
35							

Instructions

1. Prepare an income statement for the year ended June 30, 20Y3.

2. Prepare a statement of stockholders' equity for the year ended June 30, 20Y3. During the year ended June 30, 20Y3, additional common stock of $20,000 was issued.

3. Prepare a balance sheet as of June 30, 20Y3.

4. On the basis of the end-of-period spreadsheet, journalize the closing entries.

5. Prepare a post-closing trial balance.

PR 4-2B   Financial statements and closing entries   Obj. 2, 3

✔ 1. Retained earnings, October 31: $288,000

The Gorman Group is a financial planning services firm owned and operated by Nicole Gorman. As of October 31, 20Y9, the end of the fiscal year, the accountant for The Gorman Group prepared an end-of-period spreadsheet, part of which follows:

	A	F	G
1	The Gorman Group		
2	End-of-Period Spreadsheet		
3	For the Year Ended October 31, 20Y9		
4		Adjusted	
5		Trial Balance	
6	Account Title	Dr.	Cr.
7			
8	Cash	11,000	
9	Accounts Receivable	28,150	
10	Supplies	6,350	
11	Prepaid Insurance	9,500	
12	Land	75,000	
13	Buildings	250,000	
14	Accumulated Depreciation—Buildings		117,200
15	Equipment	240,000	
16	Accum. Depr.—Equipment		151,700
17	Accounts Payable		33,300
18	Salaries Payable		3,300
19	Unearned Rent		1,500
20	Common Stock		25,000
21	Retained Earnings		195,000
22	Dividends	20,000	
23	Service Fees		468,000
24	Rent Revenue		5,000
25	Salaries Expense	291,000	
26	Depreciation Expense—Equipment	17,500	
27	Rent Expense	15,500	
28	Supplies Expense	9,000	
29	Utilities Expense	8,500	
30	Depreciation Expense—Buildings	6,600	
31	Repairs Expense	3,450	
32	Insurance Expense	3,000	
33	Miscellaneous Expense	5,450	
34		1,000,000	1,000,000

Instructions

1. Prepare an income statement, a statement of stockholders' equity, and a balance sheet. During the year, no additional common stock was issued.

2. Journalize the entries that were required to close the accounts at October 31.

3. If the balance of Retained Earnings had instead increased $115,000 after the closing entries were posted, and the dividends remained the same, what would have been the amount of net income or net loss?

PR 4-3B   T accounts, adjusting entries, financial statements, and closing entries; optional end-of-period spreadsheet

Obj. 2, 3

✔ 5. Net income:
$27,350

EXCEL TEMPLATE

The unadjusted trial balance of La Mesa Laundry at August 31, 20Y5, the end of the fiscal year, follows:

La Mesa Laundry
Unadjusted Trial Balance
August 31, 20Y5

	Debit Balances	Credit Balances
Cash...	3,800	
Laundry Supplies	9,000	
Prepaid Insurance...	6,000	
Laundry Equipment.......................................	180,800	
Accumulated Depreciation		49,200
Accounts Payable...		7,800
Common Stock..		15,000
Retained Earnings		80,000
Dividends	2,400	
Laundry Revenue...		248,000
Wages Expense...	135,800	
Rent Expense..	43,200	
Utilities Expense..	16,000	
Miscellaneous Expense..................................	3,000	
	400,000	400,000

The data needed to determine year-end adjustments are as follows:

(a) Wages accrued but not paid at August 31 are $2,200.

(b) Depreciation of equipment during the year is $8,150.

(c) Laundry supplies on hand at August 31 are $2,000.

(d) Insurance premiums expired during the year are $5,300.

Instructions

1. For each account listed in the unadjusted trial balance, enter the balance in a T account. Identify the balance as "Aug. 31 Bal." In addition, add T accounts for Wages Payable, Depreciation Expense, Laundry Supplies Expense, and Insurance Expense.

2. *(Optional)* Enter the unadjusted trial balance on an end-of-period spreadsheet and complete the spreadsheet. Add the accounts listed in part (1) as needed.

3. Journalize and post the adjusting entries. Identify the adjustments by "Adj." and the new balances as "Adj. Bal."

4. Prepare an adjusted trial balance.

5. Prepare an income statement, a statement of stockholders' equity, and a balance sheet. During the year ended August 31, 20Y5, common stock of $3,000 was issued.

6. Journalize and post the closing entries. Identify the closing entries by "Clos."

7. Prepare a post-closing trial balance.

PR 4-4B Ledger accounts, adjusting entries, financial statements, and closing entries; optional end-of-period spreadsheet

Obj. 2, 3

✔ 5. Net income: $46,150

The unadjusted trial balance of Recessive Interiors at January 31, 20Y2, the end of the year, follows:

EXCEL TEMPLATE

Recessive Interiors
Unadjusted Trial Balance
January 31, 20Y2

	Account No.	Debit Balances	Credit Balances
Cash	11	13,100	
Supplies	13	8,000	
Prepaid Insurance	14	7,500	
Equipment	16	113,000	
Accumulated Depreciation—Equipment	17		12,000
Trucks	18	90,000	
Accumulated Depreciation—Trucks	19		27,100
Accounts Payable	21		4,500
Common Stock	31		30,000
Retained Earnings	32		96,400
Dividends	33	3,000	
Service Revenue	41		155,000
Wages Expense	51	72,000	
Rent Expense	52	7,600	
Truck Expense	53	5,350	
Miscellaneous Expense	59	5,450	
		325,000	325,000

The data needed to determine year-end adjustments are as follows:

(a) Supplies on hand at January 31 are $2,850.
(b) Insurance premiums expired during the year are $3,150.
(c) Depreciation of equipment during the year is $5,250.
(d) Depreciation of trucks during the year is $4,000.
(e) Wages accrued but not paid at January 31 are $900.

Instructions

1. For each account listed in the unadjusted trial balance, enter the balance in the appropriate Balance column of a four-column account and place a check mark (✓) in the Posting Reference column.

2. *(Optional)* Enter the unadjusted trial balance on an end-of-period spreadsheet and complete the spreadsheet. Add the accounts listed in part (3) as needed.

3. Journalize and post the adjusting entries, inserting balances in the accounts affected. Record the adjusting entries on Page 26 of the journal. The following additional accounts from Recessive Interiors' chart of accounts should be used: Wages Payable, 22; Depreciation Expense—Equipment, 54; Supplies Expense, 55; Depreciation Expense—Trucks, 56; Insurance Expense, 57.

4. Prepare an adjusted trial balance.

5. Prepare an income statement, a statement of stockholders' equity, and a balance sheet. During the year ended January 31, 20Y2, additional common stock of $7,500 was issued.

6. Journalize and post the closing entries. Record the closing entries on Page 27 of the journal. Indicate closed accounts by inserting a line in both Balance columns opposite the closing entry.

7. Prepare a post-closing trial balance.

✔ **8. Net income:**
$53,775

EXCEL TEMPLATE

PR 4-5B Complete accounting cycle

Obj. 4, 5

For the past several years, Jeff Horton has operated a part-time consulting business from his home. As of April 1, 20Y6, Jeff decided to move to rented quarters and to operate the business, which was to be known as Rosebud Consulting, on a full-time basis. Rosebud entered into the following transactions during April:

Apr. 1. The following assets were received from Jeff Horton in exchange for common stock: cash, $20,000; accounts receivable, $14,700; supplies, $3,300; and office equipment, $12,000. There were no liabilities received.

1. Paid three months' rent on a lease rental contract, $6,000.

2. Paid the premiums on property and casualty insurance policies, $4,200.

4. Received cash from clients as an advance payment for services to be provided and recorded it as unearned fees, $9,400.

5. Purchased additional office equipment on account from Smith Office Supply Co., $8,000.

6. Received cash from clients on account, $11,700.

10. Paid cash for a newspaper advertisement, $350.

12. Paid Smith Office Supply Co. for part of the debt incurred on April 5, $6,400.

12. Recorded services provided on account for the period April 1–12, $21,900.

14. Paid receptionist for two weeks' salary, $1,650.

Record the following transactions on Page 2 of the journal:

17. Recorded cash from cash clients for fees earned during the period April 1–16, $6,600.

18. Paid cash for supplies, $725.

20. Recorded services provided on account for the period April 13–20, $16,800.

24. Recorded cash from cash clients for fees earned for the period April 17–24, $4,450.

26. Received cash from clients on account, $26,500.

27. Paid receptionist for two weeks' salary, $1,650.

29. Paid telephone bill for April, $540.

30. Paid electricity bill for April, $760.

30. Recorded cash from cash clients for fees earned for the period April 25–30, $5,160.

30. Recorded services provided on account for the remainder of April, $2,590.

30. Paid dividends, $18,000.

Instructions

1. Journalize each transaction in a two-column journal starting on Page 1, referring to the following chart of accounts in selecting the accounts to be debited and credited. (Do not insert the account numbers in the journal at this time.)

11	Cash	31	Common Stock
12	Accounts Receivable	32	Retained Earnings
14	Supplies	33	Dividends
15	Prepaid Rent	41	Fees Earned
16	Prepaid Insurance	51	Salary Expense
18	Office Equipment	52	Supplies Expense
19	Accumulated Depreciation	53	Rent Expense
21	Accounts Payable	54	Depreciation Expense
22	Salaries Payable	55	Insurance Expense
23	Unearned Fees	59	Miscellaneous Expense

2. Post the journal to a ledger of four-column accounts.

3. Prepare an unadjusted trial balance.

4. At the end of April, the following adjustment data were assembled. Analyze and use these data to complete parts (5) and (6).

(a) Insurance expired during April is $350.

(b) Supplies on hand on April 30 are $1,225.

(c) Depreciation of office equipment for April is $400.

(d) Accrued receptionist salary on April 30 is $275.

(e) Rent expired during April is $2,000.

(f) Unearned fees on April 30 are $2,350.

5. *(Optional)* Enter the unadjusted trial balance on an end-of-period spreadsheet and complete the spreadsheet.

6. Journalize and post the adjusting entries. Record the adjusting entries on Page 3 of the journal.

7. Prepare an adjusted trial balance.

8. Prepare an income statement, a statement of stockholders' equity, and a balance sheet.

9. Prepare and post the closing entries. Record the closing entries on Page 4 of the journal. Indicate closed accounts by inserting a line in both the Balance columns opposite the closing entry.

10. Prepare a post-closing trial balance.

Continuing Problem

✔ **2. Net income: $4,955**

The unadjusted trial balance of PS Music as of July 31, 20Y5, along with the adjustment data for the two months ended July 31, 20Y5, are shown in Chapter 3. Based upon the adjustment data, the following adjusted trial balance was prepared:

PS Music
Adjusted Trial Balance
July 31, 20Y5

	Account No.	Debit Balances	Credit Balances
Cash	11	9,945	
Accounts Receivable.................................	12	4,150	
Supplies..	14	275	
Prepaid Insurance	15	2,475	
Office Equipment	17	7,500	
Accumulated Depreciation—Office Equipment..........	18		50
Accounts Payable	21		8,350
Wages Payable......................................	22		140
Unearned Revenue..................................	23		3,600
Common Stock	31		9,000
Dividends	33	1,750	
Fees Earned...	41		21,200
Music Expense	54	3,610	
Wages Expense	50	2,940	
Office Rent Expense	51	2,550	
Advertising Expense.................................	55	1,500	
Equipment Rent Expense	52	1,375	
Utilities Expense	53	1,215	
Supplies Expense....................................	56	925	
Insurance Expense	57	225	
Depreciation Expense	58	50	
Miscellaneous Expense	59	1,855	
		42,340	42,340

Instructions

1. *(Optional)* Using the data from Chapter 3, prepare an end-of-period spreadsheet.

2. Prepare an income statement, a statement of stockholders' equity, and a balance sheet.

3. Journalize and post the closing entries. The retained earnings account is #32 in the ledger of PS Music. Indicate closed accounts by inserting a line in both Balance columns opposite the closing entry.

4. Prepare a post-closing trial balance.

Comprehensive Problem 1

✔ 8. Net income,
$33,425

EXCEL TEMPLATE

Kelly Pitney began her consulting business, Kelly Consulting, on April 1, 20Y8. The accounting cycle for Kelly Consulting for April, including financial statements, was illustrated in this chapter. During May, Kelly Consulting entered into the following transactions:

May 3.   Received cash from clients as an advance payment for services to be provided and recorded it as unearned fees, $4,500.
5.   Received cash from clients on account, $2,450.
9.   Paid cash for a newspaper advertisement, $225.
13.   Paid Office Station Co. for part of the debt incurred on April 5, $640.
15.   Recorded services provided on account for the period May 1–15, $9,180.
16.   Paid part-time receptionist for two weeks' salary including the amount owed on April 30, $750.
17.   Recorded cash from cash clients for fees earned during the period May 1–16, $8,360.

Record the following transactions on Page 6 of the journal:
20.   Purchased supplies on account, $735.
21.   Recorded services provided on account for the period May 16–20, $4,820.
25.   Recorded cash from cash clients for fees earned for the period May 17–23, $7,900.
27.   Received cash from clients on account, $9,520.
28.   Paid part-time receptionist for two weeks' salary, $750.
30.   Paid telephone bill for May, $260.
31.   Paid electricity bill for May, $810.
31.   Recorded cash from cash clients for fees earned for the period May 26–31, $3,300.
31.   Recorded services provided on account for the remainder of May, $2,650.
31.   Paid dividends, $10,500.

Instructions

1. The chart of accounts for Kelly Consulting is shown in Exhibit 9, and the post-closing trial balance as of April 30, 20Y8, is shown in Exhibit 17. For each account in the post-closing trial balance, enter the balance in the appropriate Balance column of a four-column account. Date the balances May 1, 20Y8, and place a check mark (✓) in the Posting Reference column. Journalize each of the May transactions in a two-column journal starting on Page 5 of the journal and using Kelly Consulting's chart of accounts. (Do not insert the account numbers in the journal at this time.)

2. Post the journal to a ledger of four-column accounts.

3. Prepare an unadjusted trial balance.

4. At the end of May, the following adjustment data were assembled. Analyze and use these data to complete parts (5) and (6).

   (a)   Insurance expired during May is $275.
   (b)   Supplies on hand on May 31 are $715.
   (c)   Depreciation of office equipment for May is $330.
   (d)   Accrued receptionist salary on May 31 is $325.
   (e)   Rent expired during May is $1,600.
   (f)   Unearned fees on May 31 are $3,210.

5. *(Optional)* Enter the unadjusted trial balance on an end-of-period spreadsheet and complete the spreadsheet.

6. Journalize and post the adjusting entries. Record the adjusting entries on Page 7 of the journal.

7. Prepare an adjusted trial balance.

8. Prepare an income statement, a statement of stockholders' equity, and a balance sheet.

9. Prepare and post the closing entries. Record the closing entries on Page 8 of the journal. Indicate closed accounts by inserting a line in both the Balance columns opposite the closing entry.

10. Prepare a post-closing trial balance.

Make a Decision
Working Capital and Current Ratio

REAL WORLD

MAD 4-1 Analyze and compare Amazon.com to Best Buy
Obj. 6

Amazon.com, Inc. (AMZN) is the largest Internet retailer in the United States. **Best Buy, Inc. (BBY)** is a leading retailer of technology and media products in the United States. Amazon and Best Buy compete in similar markets; however, Best Buy sells through both traditional retail stores and the Internet, while Amazon sells only through the Internet. The current assets and current liabilities from recent balance sheets for both companies are provided as follows (in millions):

	Amazon	Best Buy
Current assets	$45,781	$9,886
Current liabilities	43,816	6,925

a. Compute the working capital for each company.

b. Which company has the largest working capital?

c. ➤ Is working capital a good measure of relative liquidity in comparing the two companies? Explain.

d. Compute the current ratio for both companies. Round to one decimal place.

e. Which company has the larger relative liquidity based on the current ratio?

REAL WORLD

MAD 4-2 Analyze and compare Zynga, Electronic Arts, and Take-Two
Obj. 6

Data (in millions) from recent financial statements of **Zynga Inc. (ZNGA)**, **Electronic Arts Inc. (EA)**, and **Take-Two Interactive Software, Inc. (TTWO)** are as follows:

	Zynga		Electronic Arts		Take-Two	
	Year 2	Year 1	Year 2	Year 1	Year 2	Year 1
Current assets	$966	$1,112	$4,354	$3,720	$2,045	$1,780
Current liabilities	244	236	2,418	2,747	1,220	966

a. Compute the working capital for Year 2 and Year 1 for each company.

b. Which company has the largest working capital?

c. Compute the current ratio for Year 2 and Year 1 for each company. Round to one decimal place.

d. For Year 2, rank the companies from most liquid to least liquid based upon the current ratio.

REAL WORLD

MAD 4-3 Analyze and compare Foot Locker and The Finish Line
Obj. 6

The Foot Locker, Inc. (FL) and **The Finish Line, Inc. (FINL)** are two retail athletic footwear chains. The current assets and current liabilities from recent balance sheets for both companies are as follows (in millions):

	Foot Locker		The Finish Line	
	Year 2	Year 1	Year 2	Year 1
Current assets	$2,606	$2,456	$521	$531
Current liabilities	700	696	221	191

a. Compute the working capital for Year 2 and Year 1 for each company.

b. Compute the current ratio for Year 2 and Year 1 for each company. Round to one decimal place.

c. ➤ If you were a supplier to these two companies, in which company would you feel most confident about receiving payment?

d. ➤ For each company, did liquidity improve or decline between the two years?

REAL WORLD

MAD 4-4   Analyze Under Armour   Obj. 6

The following year-end data were taken from recent balance sheets of **Under Armour, Inc. (UA)** (in millions):

	December 31	
	Year 2	Year 1
Current assets	$1,965.2	$1,498.8
Current liabilities	685.8	478.8

a. Compute the working capital and the current ratio as of December 31, Year 2 and Year 1. Round to one decimal place.

b. ━━━▶ What conclusions concerning the company's ability to meet its short-term obligations can you draw from part (a)?

REAL WORLD

MAD 4-5   Analyze Sears Holding Corporation   Obj. 6

Sears Holdings Corporation (SHLD) is one of the largest mall-based retailers in the United States. The following year-end data were taken from a recent Sears balance sheet (in millions):

	December 31	
	Year 2	Year 1
Current assets	$6,045	$5,863
Current liabilities	5,438	5,595

a. Compute the working capital and the current ratio as of December 31, Year 1 and Year 2. Round to two decimal places.

b. ━━━▶ What conclusions concerning the company's ability to meet its short-term obligations can you draw from part (a)?

REAL WORLD

MAD 4-6   Analyze and compare Alphabet (Google) and Microsoft   Obj. 6

Alphabet Inc. (GOOG) and **Microsoft Corporation (MSFT)** design and distribute consumer and enterprise software, including overlaps in search, business productivity, and mobile operating systems. Alphabet's primary source of revenue is from advertising, while Microsoft's is from software subscription and support fees. The following year-end data (in millions) were taken from recent balance sheets for both companies:

	Microsoft		Alphabet	
	Year 2	Year 1	Year 2	Year 1
Current assets	$139,660	$122,797	$105,408	$90,114
Current liabilities	59,357	49,647	16,756	19,310

a. Compute the working capital for each company for both years.

b. Which company has the larger working capital at the end of Year 2?

c. ━━━▶ Is working capital a good measure of relative liquidity in comparing the two companies? Explain.

d. Compute the current ratio for both companies. Round to one decimal place.

e. ━━━▶ Which company has the larger relative liquidity based on the current ratio?

f. ━━━▶ Based on your analysis, comment on the short-term debt-paying ability of these two companies.

Take It Further

ETHICS

TIF 4-1   Loan to company president

New Wave Images is a graphics design firm that prepares its financial statements using a calendar year. Manny Kinn, the company treasurer and vice president of finance, has prepared a classified balance sheet as of December 31. In January, this balance sheet will be submitted along with an application for a loan from First Peoples Community Bank. An excerpt from the balance sheet follows:

Cash	$ 25,000
Accounts receivable	85,000
......	
Total assets	$250,000

The accounts receivable balance includes a $56,000 loan to Tom Morrow, the company president. Tom borrowed the money from New Wave 18 months earlier for a down payment on a new home. Tom has orally assured Manny that he will pay off the loan within the next year. Because Tom is the company president, Manny treats the amount due as a trade account receivable. In addition, Manny knows that the bank will consider a large balance in trade accounts receivable more favorably than a large personal loan to a single individual. Manny reported the $56,000 in the same manner on the preceding year's balance sheet.

1. ▬▬▶ Is Manny behaving ethically by reporting the loan to Tom as a trade account receivable? Why?
2. ▬▬▶ Who will be affected by Manny's decision?

TEAM ACTIVITY   REAL WORLD

TIF 4-2   Annual reports: Zynga and Wal-Mart

In teams, access a recent annual report of **Zynga (ZNGA)** and **Wal-Mart (WMT)**. The Form 10-K is a company's annually required filing with the Securities and Exchange Commission (SEC). It includes the company's financial statements and accompanying notes. The Form 10-K can be obtained either (a) from the investor relations section of the company's website or (b) by using the company search feature of the SEC's EDGAR database service found at www.sec.gov/edgar/searchedgar/companysearch.html.

Compare the balance sheets of the two companies as follows:

1. What is each company's fiscal year?
2. Which balance sheet items do the two companies have in common?
3. ▬▬▶ What balance sheet account stands out as different between the two companies? Why does this difference exist?

COMMUNICATION

TIF 4-3   Communication

Your friend, Daniel Nat, recently began work as the lead accountant for Asheville Company. Dan prepared the following balance sheet for December 31, 20Y5:

Asheville Company Balance Sheet December 31, 20Y5	
Assets	
Land...	$100,000
Accounts payable.......................................	10,000
Accounts receivable....................................	12,500
Cash...	10,000
Common stock..	115,000
Total assets..	$247,500

(Continued)

Liabilities	
Equipment	$125,000
Retained earnings..	120,000
Wages payable...	2,500
Total liabilities	$247,500

➤ White a brief memo to Daniel explaining the errors in Asheville Company's balance sheet and provide the correct presentation for the balance sheet.

TIF 4-4 Minus for supplies?

The following is an excerpt from a telephone conversation between Ben Simpson, president of Main Street Co., and Tami Lundgren, owner of Reliable Employment Co.:

Ben: Tami, you're going to have to do a better job of finding me a new computer programmer. That last guy was great at programming, but he didn't have any common sense.

Tami: What do you mean? The guy had a master's degree with straight A's.

Ben: Yes, well, last month he developed a new financial reporting system. He said we could do away with manually preparing an end-of-period spreadsheet and financial statements. The computer would automatically generate our financial statements with "a push of a button."

Tami: So what's the big deal? Sounds to me like it would save you time and effort.

Ben: Right! The balance sheet showed a minus for supplies!

Tami: Minus supplies? How can that be?

Ben: That's what I asked.

Tami: So, what did he say?

Ben: Well, after he checked the program, he said that it must be right. The minuses were greater than the pluses. . . .

Tami: Didn't he know that Supplies can't have a credit balance—it must have a debit balance?

Ben: He asked me what a debit and credit were.

Tami: I see your point.

1. ➤ Comment on (a) the desirability of computerizing Main Street Co.'s financial reporting system, (b) the elimination of the end-of-period spreadsheet in a computerized accounting system, and (c) the computer programmer's lack of accounting knowledge.

2. ➤ Explain to the programmer why Supplies could not have a credit balance.

TIF 4-5 Financial statements and loan

Assume that you recently accepted a position with Five Star National Bank & Trust as an assistant loan officer. As one of your first duties, you have been assigned the responsibility of evaluating a loan request for $300,000 from West Gate Auto Co., a small corporation. In support of the loan application, Joan Whalen, owner, submitted a "Statement of Accounts" (trial balance) for the first year of operations ended October 31, 20Y3.

West Gate Auto Co. Statement of Accounts October 31, 20Y3		
Assets		
Cash...	5,000	
Billings Due from Others	40,000	
Supplies (chemicals, etc.)...	7,500	
Building	222,300	
Equipment	50,000	
Amounts Owed to Others		31,000
Investment in Business...		179,000
Service Revenue		215,000
Wages Expense	75,000	
Utilities Expense	10,000	
Rent Expense	8,000	
Insurance Expense	6,000	
Other Expenses	1,200	
	425,000	425,000

1.  Explain to Joan Whalen why a set of financial statements (income statement, statement of stockholders' equity, and balance sheet) would be useful to you in evaluating the loan request.

2. In discussing the "Statement of Accounts" with Joan Whalen, you discovered that the accounts had not been adjusted at October 31. Analyze the "Statement of Accounts" and indicate possible adjusting entries that might be necessary before an accurate set of financial statements could be prepared.

3.  Assuming that an accurate set of financial statements will be submitted by Joan Whalen in a few days, what other considerations or information would you require before making a decision on the loan request?

Pathways Challenge

This is Accounting!

Information/Consequences

The payment of a dividend results in a decrease in stockholders' equity (debit to Dividends) and a decrease in assets (credit to Cash).

Because the dividend occurred after the end of the fiscal year ended on January 3, 2017, it does not affect the amounts reported in that year's financial statements. However, investors may find this information useful, and the dividend should be disclosed in the notes to the financial statements. For example, **The Cheesecake Factory Incorporated (CAKE)** included the following note in its financial statements for the year ending January 3, 2017:

On February 16, 2017, our Board approved a quarterly cash dividend of $0.24 per share to be paid on March 21, 2017 to the stockholders of record on March 8, 2017.

Yes. A transaction or event may occur after the end of a fiscal year that provides evidence of a condition that existed at the balance sheet date or affects an estimate used in preparing the financial statements. For example, a lawsuit that existed at the end of the year may be settled at an amount different than previously expected. In this case, the financial statements should be adjusted for this "subsequent event."

Suggested Answer

STATEMENT OF STOCKHOLDERS' EQUITY
For the Year Ended December 31, 20Y5

	Common Stock	Retained Earnings	Total
Balances, Jan. 1, 20Y5	$XXX	$ XXX	$ XXX
Issued common stock	XXX		XXX
Net income		XXX	XXX
Dividends		(XXX)	(XXX)
Balances, Dec. 31, 20Y5	$XXX	$ XXX	$ XXX

STATEMENT OF CASH FLOWS
For the Year Ended December 31, 20Y5

Cash flows from (used for) operating activities	$XXX
Cash flows from (used for) investing activities	XXX
Cash flows from (used for) financing activities	XXX
Net increase (decrease) in cash	$XXX
Cash balance, January 1, 20Y5	XXX
Cash balance, December 31, 20Y5	$XXX

INCOME STATEMENT
For the Year Ended December 31, 20Y5

Sales		$ XXX
Cost of goods sold		(XXX)
Gross profit		$ XXX
Operating expenses:		
Wages expense	$XXX	
Advertising expense	XXX	
Utilities expense	XXX	
Depreciation expense	XXX	
...	XXX	
Total operating expenses		(XXX)
Operating income		$ XXX
Other revenue and expense		XXX
Net income		$ XXX

BALANCE SHEET
December 31, 20Y5

Assets		
Current assets:		
Cash	$XXX	
Accounts receivable	XXX	
Inventory	XXX	
Total current assets		$XXX
Property, plant, and equipment		XXX
Total assets		$XXX
Liabilities		
Current liabilities	$XXX	
Long-term liabilities	XXX	
Total liabilities		$XXX
Stockholders' Equity		
Common stock	$XXX	
Retained earnings	XXX	
Total stockholders' equity		XXX
Total liabilities and stockholders' equity		$XXX

Dollar Tree, Inc.

When you are low on cash but need to pick up party supplies, housewares, or other consumer items, where do you go? Many shoppers are turning to **Dollar Tree, Inc. (DLTR)**, a leading operator of discount variety stores with more than 13,500 stores in North America. Its stores operate under the brand names Dollar Tree and Family Dollar. All merchandise is $1 at Dollar Tree stores, while Family Dollar offers merchandise for $10 or less. The stores typically carry more than 7,000 items, consisting of basic, everyday items as well as seasonal, closeout, and promotional items.

The accounting for a retailer, like Dollar Tree, is more complex than for a service company. This is because a service company sells only services and has no inventory. With Dollar Tree's locations and merchandise, the company must design its accounting system to not only record the receipt of goods for resale, but also to keep track of what merchandise is available for sale as well as where the merchandise is located. In addition, Dollar Tree must record the sales and costs of the goods sold for each of its stores. Finally, Dollar Tree must record such data as delivery costs, merchandise discounts, and merchandise returns.

This chapter focuses on the accounting principles and concepts for a retail business. In doing so, the basic differences between retail and service company activities are highlighted. The financial statements of a retail business and accounting for merchandise transactions are also described and illustrated.

©KIT LEONG/SHUTTERSTOCK.COM

What's Covered

Accounting for Retail Businesses

Nature of Retail Businesses	**Purchase Transactions**	**Sales Transactions**	**Retail Financial Statements**
■ Operating Cycle (Obj. 1)	■ Purchase Discounts (Obj. 2)	■ Customer Discounts (Obj. 2)	■ Adjusting Process (Obj. 3)
■ Income Statement (Obj. 1)	■ Purchase Returns and	■ Customer Returns and	■ Single-Step Income Statement (Obj. 4)
■ Subsidiary Ledgers (Obj. 2)	Allowances (Obj. 2)	Allowances (Obj. 2)	■ Multiple-Step Income Statement (Obj. 4)
■ Inventory Systems (Obj. 2)	■ Freight (Obj. 2)	■ Freight (Obj. 2)	■ Statement of Stockholders' Equity (Obj. 4)
	■ Buyer/Seller Transactions	■ Buyer/Seller Transactions	■ Balance Sheet (Obj. 4)
	(Obj. 2)	(Obj. 2)	■ Closing Entries (Obj. 4)

Learning Objectives

Obj. 1 Distinguish between the activities and financial statements of service and retail businesses.

Obj. 2 Describe and illustrate the accounting for merchandise transactions.

Obj. 3 Describe and illustrate the adjusting process for a retail business.

Obj. 4 Describe and illustrate the financial statements and closing entries for a retail business.

Analysis for Decision Making

Obj. 5 Describe and illustrate the use of the asset turnover ratio in evaluating a company's operating performance.

Obj. App 1 Describe and illustrate the gross method of recording sales discounts.

Obj. App 2 Describe and illustrate the periodic system of accounting for merchandise transactions.

Objective 1
Distinguish between the activities and financial statements of service and retail businesses.

Nature of Retail Businesses

The activities of a service business differ from those of a retail business. These differences are reflected in the operating cycles of a service and retail business as well as in their financial statements.

Operating Cycle

The **operating cycle** is the process by which a company spends cash, generates revenues, and receives cash from customers. The operating cycle of a service and retail business differs in that a retail business must purchase merchandise for sale to customers. The operating cycle for a retail business is shown in Exhibit 1.

Exhibit 1

The Operating Cycle for a Retail Business

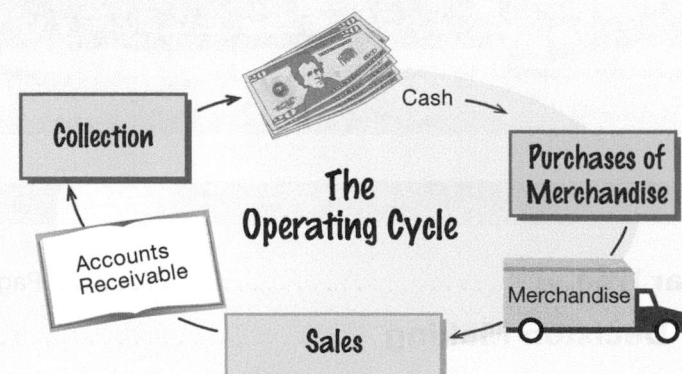

The time in days to complete an operating cycle differs significantly among retail businesses. Grocery stores normally have short operating cycles because of the nature of their merchandise. For example, many grocery items, such as milk, must be sold within their expiration dates of a week or two. In contrast, jewelry stores often carry expensive items that are displayed months before being sold to customers.

Financial Statements

The differences between service and retail businesses are also reflected in their financial statements. For example, these differences are illustrated in the following condensed income statements:

Service Business		Retail Business	
Fees earned	$ XXX	Sales	$ XXX
Operating expenses	(XXX)	Cost of goods sold	(XXX)
Operating income	$ XXX	Gross profit	$ XXX
		Operating expenses	(XXX)
		Operating income	$ XXX

The revenue activities of a service business involve providing services to customers. On the income statement for a service business, the revenues from services are reported as *fees earned*. The operating expenses incurred in providing the services are subtracted from the fees earned to arrive at *operating income*.

In contrast, the revenue activities of a retail business involve the buying and selling of merchandise. A retail business first purchases merchandise to sell to its customers. When this merchandise is sold, the revenue is reported as **sales**, and its cost is recognized as an expense. This expense is called the **cost of goods sold** or *cost of merchandise sold*. The cost of goods sold is subtracted from sales to arrive at gross profit. This amount is called **gross profit** because it is the profit *before* deducting operating expenses. The operating expenses are subtracted from gross profit to arrive at operating income.

Merchandise on hand (not sold) at the end of an accounting period is called **inventory** or *merchandise inventory*. Inventory is reported as a current asset on the balance sheet.

In a recent income statement, **Dollar Tree** reported the following (in billions):

Sales	$ 20.7
Cost of goods sold	(14.3)
Gross profit	$ 6.4
Operating expenses	(4.7)
Operating income	$ 1.7

On its balance sheet, it reported inventory of $2.9 billion.

Link to Dollar Tree

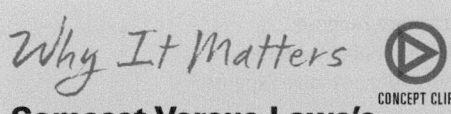

Why It Matters

CONCEPT CLIP

Comcast Versus Lowe's

Comcast Corporation (CMCSA) is a service business that offers cable communications, broadcast television (NBC television), filmed entertainment (Universal Pictures), and theme parks (Universal Parks) to its customers. **Lowe's Companies, Inc. (LOW)** is a large home improvement retailer. The differences in the operations of a service and retail business are illustrated in their recent income statements, as follows.

Comcast Corporation
Condensed Income Statement
(in millions)

Revenue	$ 80,403
Programming and production expenses	(24,463)
Selling and administrative expenses	(29,523)
Depreciation and amortization expenses	(9,558)
Operating income	$ 16,859

Source: Comcast Corporation, *Form 10-K for the Fiscal Year Ended December 31, 2016.*

Lowe's Companies, Inc.
Condensed Income Statement
(in millions)

Sales	$ 65,017
Cost of goods sold	(42,553)
Gross profit	$ 22,464
Selling, general, and administrative expenses	(15,129)
Depreciation expense	(1,489)
Operating income	$ 5,846

Source: Lowe's Companies, Inc., *Form 10-K for the Fiscal Year Ended February 3, 2017.*

As a retail company, Lowe's subtracts cost of goods sold from sales to disclose gross profit. As a service company, Comcast does not show cost of goods sold, nor a gross profit line. Rather, service expenses are subtracted from revenue straight to operating income.

Objective 2

Describe and illustrate the accounting for merchandise transactions.

Merchandise Transactions

This section illustrates merchandise transactions for **NetSolutions** after it becomes a retailer of computer hardware and software. During 20Y6, Chris Clark implemented the second phase of NetSolutions' business plan. In doing so, Chris notified clients that beginning July 1, 20Y7, NetSolutions would no longer offer consulting services. Instead, it would become a retailer.

NetSolutions' business strategy is to offer personalized service to individuals and small businesses that are upgrading or purchasing new computer systems. NetSolutions' personal service includes a no-obligation, on-site assessment of the customer's computer needs. By providing personalized service and follow-up, Chris feels that NetSolutions can compete effectively against such retailers as **Best Buy (BBY)** and **Office Depot (ODP)**.

Chart of Accounts for Retail Business

NetSolutions merchandise transactions are recorded in accounts using the rules of debit and credit that were described and illustrated in Chapter 2. However, since merchandise transactions differ from those of a service business, NetSolutions adopted a new chart of accounts shown in Exhibit 2.

Exhibit 2

Chart of Accounts for NetSolutions as a Retail Business

Balance Sheet Accounts	Income Statement Accounts
100 Assets	**400 Revenues**
110 Cash	410 Sales
112 Accounts Receivable	**500 Costs and Expenses**
115 Inventory	510 Cost of Goods Sold
116 Estimated Returns Inventory	520 Sales Salaries Expense
117 Office Supplies	521 Advertising Expense
118 Prepaid Insurance	522 Depreciation Expense—
120 Land	Store Equipment
123 Store Equipment	523 Delivery Expense
124 Accumulated Depreciation—	529 Miscellaneous Selling Expense
Store Equipment	530 Office Salaries Expense
125 Office Equipment	531 Rent Expense
126 Accumulated Depreciation—	532 Depreciation Expense—
Office Equipment	Office Equipment
200 Liabilities	533 Insurance Expense
210 Accounts Payable	534 Office Supplies Expense
211 Salaries Payable	539 Misc. Administrative Expense
212 Unearned Rent	**600 Other Revenue**
213 Customer Refunds Payable	610 Rent Revenue
215 Notes Payable	**700 Other Expense**
300 Stockholders' Equity	710 Interest Expense
310 Common Stock	
311 Retained Earnings	
312 Dividends	

The accounts related to merchandising transactions are highlighted in blue in Exhibit 2. The nature of these accounts will be described and illustrated as the related merchandising transactions are discussed.

As shown in Exhibit 2, NetSolutions' chart of accounts now consists of three-digit account numbers. The first digit indicates the major financial statement classification (1 for assets, 2 for liabilities, etc.). The second digit indicates the subclassification (e.g., 11 for current assets and 12 for noncurrent assets). The third digit identifies the specific account (e.g., 110 for Cash and 123 for Store Equipment).

Subsidiary Ledgers

The accounting system for retail businesses is often modified to more efficiently record transactions. For example, the accounting system should be designed to provide information on the amounts due from various customers (accounts receivable) and amounts owed to various creditors (accounts payable). A separate account for each customer and creditor could be added to the ledger. However, as the number of customers and creditors increases, the ledger will become large and awkward to use.

A large number of individual accounts with a common characteristic can be grouped together in a separate ledger, called a **subsidiary ledger**. The primary ledger, which contains all of the balance sheet and income statement accounts, is then called the **general ledger**. Each subsidiary ledger is represented in the general ledger by a summarizing account, called a **controlling account**. The sum of the balances of the accounts in the subsidiary ledger must equal the balance of the related controlling account. Thus, a subsidiary ledger is a secondary ledger that supports a controlling account in the general ledger.

Common subsidiary ledgers are:

- The **accounts receivable subsidiary ledger**, or *customers ledger*, lists the individual customer accounts in alphabetical order. The controlling account in the general ledger is Accounts Receivable.
- The **accounts payable subsidiary ledger**, or *creditors ledger*, lists individual creditor accounts in alphabetical order. The controlling account in the general ledger is Accounts Payable.
- The **inventory subsidiary ledger**, or *inventory ledger*, lists individual inventory by item (bar code) number. The controlling account in the general ledger is Inventory. An inventory subsidiary ledger is used in a perpetual inventory system.

Most retail companies also use computerized accounting systems that record similar transactions in separate journals, which generate purchase, sales, and inventory reports. These separate journals are called **special journals**. However, for simplicity, the journal entries in this chapter will be illustrated using a two-column general journal.[1]

Purchases Transactions

There are two systems for accounting for merchandise transactions: perpetual and periodic. In a **perpetual inventory system,** each purchase and sale of merchandise is recorded in the inventory account and related subsidiary ledger. In this way, the amount of merchandise available for sale and the amount sold are continuously (perpetually) updated in the inventory records. In a **periodic inventory system**, the inventory does not show the amount of merchandise available for sale and the amount sold. Instead, a listing of inventory on hand, called a **physical inventory**, is prepared at the end of the accounting period. This physical inventory is used to determine the cost of inventory on hand at the end of the period and the cost of goods sold during the period.

Most retail companies use computerized perpetual inventory systems. Such systems use bar codes or radio frequency identification codes embedded in a product. An optical scanner or radio frequency identification device is then used to read the product codes and track inventory on hand and sold.

Because computerized perpetual inventory systems are widely used, this chapter illustrates merchandise transactions using a perpetual inventory system. The periodic system is described and illustrated in an appendix at the end of this chapter.

Dollar Tree uses point-of-sale computerized software to plan purchases and track inventory. This system automatically reorders key items based on sales and inventory levels.

Link to Dollar Tree

---

[1] Subsidiary ledgers and special journals are further described and illustrated in an online appendix at www.cengage.com.

Under the perpetual inventory system, cash purchases of merchandise are recorded as follows:

$$\begin{array}{c} A = L + E \\ + \; - \end{array}$$

	20Y8			
	Jan. 3	Inventory	2,510	
		Cash		2,510
		Purchased inventory from Bowen Co.		

Purchases of inventory on account are recorded as follows:

$$\begin{array}{c} A = L + E \\ + \quad + \end{array}$$

	Jan. 4	Inventory	9,250	
		Accounts Payable—Thomas Corporation		9,250
		Purchased inventory on account.		

The terms of purchases on account are normally indicated on the **invoice** or bill that the seller sends the buyer. An example of an invoice sent to **NetSolutions** by Alpha Technologies is shown in Exhibit 3.

Exhibit 3
Invoice

Alpha Technologies
1000 Matrix Blvd.
San Jose, CA 95116-1000

Invoice
106-8

Made in U.S.A.

SOLD TO	CUSTOMER ORDER NO.	ORDER DATE
NetSolutions	412	Jan. 3, 20Y8
5101 Washington Ave.		
Cincinnati, OH 45227-5101		

DATE SHIPPED	HOW SHIPPED AND ROUTE	TERMS	INVOICE DATE
Jan. 5, 20Y8	US Express Trucking Co.	2/10, n/30	Jan. 5, 20Y8

FROM	F.O.B.
San Jose	Cincinnati

QUANTITY	DESCRIPTION	UNIT PRICE	AMOUNT
20	HC9 Printer/Fax/Copiers	150.00	3,000.00

The terms for when payments for merchandise are to be made are called the **credit terms**. If payment is required on delivery, the terms are cash or net cash. Otherwise, the buyer is allowed an amount of time, known as the **credit period**, in which to pay. The credit period usually begins with the date of the sale as shown on the invoice.

If payment is due within a stated number of days after the invoice date, such as 30 days, the terms are net 30 days. These terms may be written as *n/30*.[2] If payment is due by the end of the month in which the sale was made, the terms are written as *n/eom*.

[2] The word *net* as used here does not have the usual meaning of a number after deductions have been subtracted, as in *net income*.

Why It Matters

Apple's Credit Terms

Working capital efficiency is influenced by the relationship between the suppliers' and customers' credit terms. If the suppliers' credit terms are longer than the customers' credit terms, then the company is able to use suppliers to finance the operating cycle. For example, **Apple (AAPL)** is able to collect on sales within an average of approximately 30 days. However, Apple uses an average of approximately 100 days to pay its suppliers. Thus, Apple collects faster than it pays, allowing Apple to use the suppliers' money as an interest-free loan for the 70-day (100 days – 30 days) difference.

Source: Apple®

Purchases Discounts To encourage the buyer to pay before the end of the credit period, the seller may offer a discount. For example, a seller may offer a 2% discount if the buyer pays within 10 days of the invoice date. If the buyer does not take the discount, the total invoice amount is due within 30 days. These terms are expressed as 2/10, n/30 and are read as "2% discount if paid within 10 days, net amount due within 30 days." The credit terms of 2/10, n/30 are summarized in Exhibit 4, using the invoice in Exhibit 3.

Exhibit 4 Credit Terms

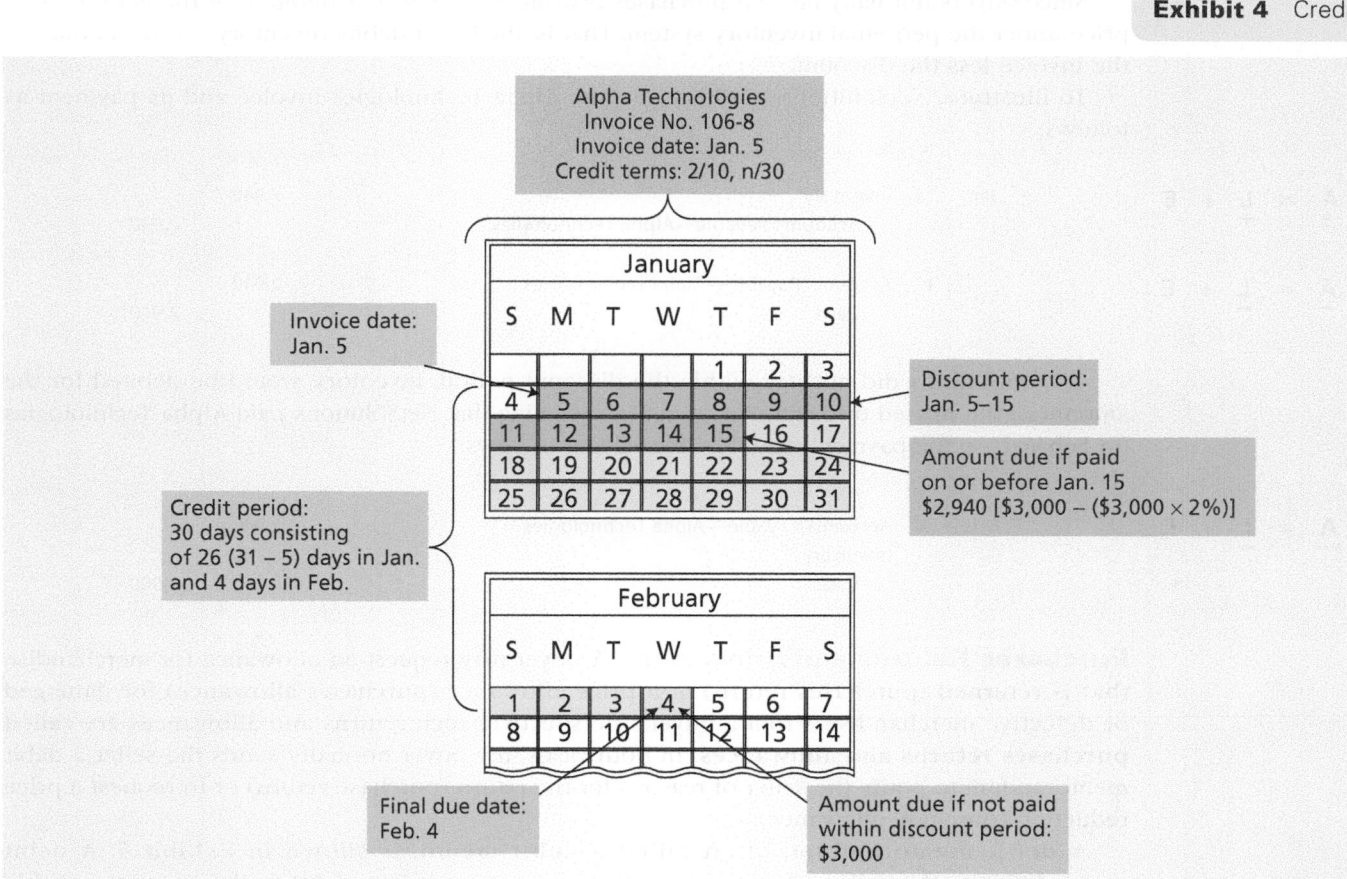

Discounts taken by the buyer for early payment of an invoice are called **purchases discounts**. Purchases discounts taken by a buyer reduce the cost of the merchandise purchased. Even if the buyer has to borrow to pay within a discount period, it is normally to the buyer's advantage to do so. For this reason, accounting systems are normally designed so that all available discounts are taken.

To illustrate, the invoice shown in Exhibit 3 is used. The last day of the discount period is January 15 (invoice date of January 5 plus 10 days). Assume that in order to pay the invoice on January 15, **NetSolutions** borrows $2,940, which is $3,000 less the discount of $60 ($3,000 × 2%). If an annual interest rate of 6% and a 360-day year is also assumed, the interest on the loan of $2,940 for the remaining 20 days of the credit period is $9.80 ($2,940 × 6% × 20 ÷ 360).[3]

The net savings to NetSolutions of taking the discount is $50.20, computed as follows:

Discount of 2% on $3,000	$60.00
Interest for 20 days at a rate of 6% on $2,940	(9.80)
Savings from taking the discount	$50.20

The savings can also be seen by comparing the interest rate on the money *saved* by taking the discount and the interest rate on the money *borrowed* to take the discount. The interest rate

---

[3] To simplify computations and rounding, we use a 360-day year rather than a 365-year.

on the money saved in the prior example is estimated by converting 2% for 20 days to a yearly rate, as follows:

$$2\% \times \frac{360 \text{ days}}{20 \text{ days}} = 2\% \times 18 = 36\%$$

NetSolutions borrowed $2,940 at 6% to take the discount. If NetSolutions does not take the discount, it *pays* an estimated interest rate of 36% for using the $2,940 for the remaining 20 days of the credit period. Thus, buyers should normally take all available purchase discounts.

Since buyers normally take all purchases discounts, Inventory is debited for the net purchase price under the perpetual inventory system. That is, the buyer debits Inventory for the amount of the invoice less the discount.

To illustrate, NetSolutions would record the Alpha Technologies invoice and its payment as follows:

A = L + E + +	Jan. 5 Inventory	2,940
	Accounts Payable—Alpha Technologies	2,940
A = L + E − −	15 Accounts Payable—Alpha Technologies	2,940
	Cash	2,940

If NetSolutions did not pay within the discount period, inventory would be debited for the amount of the missed discount. For example, assuming that NetSolutions paid Alpha Technologies on February 4, the payment would be recorded as follows:

A = L + E +− −	Feb. 4 Accounts Payable—Alpha Technologies	2,940
	Inventory	60
	Cash	3,000

Purchases Returns and Allowances A buyer may request an allowance for merchandise that is returned (purchases return) or a price allowance (purchases allowance) for damaged or defective merchandise. From a buyer's perspective, such returns and allowances are called **purchases returns and allowances**. In both cases, the buyer normally sends the seller a debit memorandum to notify the seller of reasons for the return (purchase return) or to request a price reduction (purchase allowance).

A **debit memorandum**, often called a **debit memo**, is shown in Exhibit 5. A debit memo informs the seller of the amount the buyer proposes to *debit* to the account payable due the seller. It also states the reasons for the return or the request for the price allowance.

The buyer may use the debit memo as the basis for recording the return or allowance or wait for approval from the seller (creditor). In either case, the buyer debits Accounts Payable and credits Inventory.

To illustrate, **NetSolutions** records the return of the inventory indicated in the debit memo in Exhibit 5 as follows:

A = L + E − −	Mar. 7 Accounts Payable—Maxim Systems	900
	Inventory	900
	Debit Memo No. 18.	

Before paying an invoice, a buyer may return inventory or be granted a price allowance for an invoice with a purchase discount. In this case, the amount of the return is recorded at its invoice amount less the discount.

To illustrate, assume the following data concerning a purchase of inventory by NetSolutions on May 2:

May 2. Purchased $5,000 of inventory on account from Delta Data Link, terms 2/10, n/30.
   4. Returned inventory with an invoice amount of $1,000 that was purchased on May 2.
  12. Paid for the purchase of May 2 less the return and discount.

Exhibit 5
Debit Memo

NetSolutions   **No. 18**
5101 Washington Ave.
Cincinnati, OH 45227-5101

DEBIT MEMO

TO	DATE
Maxim Systems	March 7, 20Y8
7519 East Wilson Ave.	
Seattle, WA 98101-7519	

WE DEBITED YOUR ACCOUNT AS FOLLOWS

10	Server Network Cards, your invoice No. 7291,	@90.00	900.00
	are being returned via parcel post. Our order specified No. 825X.		

NetSolutions would record these transactions as follows:

May	2	Inventory		4,900	
		Accounts Payable—Delta Data Link			4,900
		Purchased inventory			
		[$5,000 − ($5,000 × 2%)].			

$$\underset{+}{A} = \underset{+}{L} + E$$

	4	Accounts Payable—Delta Data Link		980	
		Inventory			980
		Returned portion of merchandise purchased			
		[$1,000 − ($1,000 × 2%)].			

$$\underset{-}{A} = \underset{-}{L} + E$$

	12	Accounts Payable—Delta Data Link		3,920	
		Cash			3,920
		($4,900 − $980).			

$$\underset{-}{A} = \underset{-}{L} + E$$

Check Up Corner 5-1   Purchases Transactions

On August 10, Knopfler Company purchased inventory on account from Fray Co. for $11,500, terms 2/10, n/30. Knopfler returned inventory with an invoice amount of $2,500 on August 14 and received full credit. Journalize Knopfler's entries for (a) the purchase, (b) the return, and (c) the payment of the invoice on August 18.

Solution:

The discount terms of 2/10 mean that the seller will reduce the amount due by 2% if the buyer pays within 10 days.

a.	Aug. 10	Inventory	11,270	
		Accounts Payable—Fray Co.		11,270

Inventory is debited and Accounts Payable is credited for the net purchase price: $11,500 − ($11,500 × 2% discount)

b.	Aug. 14	Accounts Payable—Fray Co.	2,450	
		Inventory		2,450

The return reduces Inventory and Accounts Payable and is recorded at the invoice amount less the applicable discount: $2,500 − ($2,500 × 2%)

c.	Aug. 18	Accounts Payable—Fray Co.	8,820	
		Cash		8,820

The remaining account payable ($11,270 − $2,450) is paid in cash within the 10-day discount period.

The account payable was paid in cash within the 10-day discount period.

Check Up Corner

Pathways Challenge

This is Accounting!

Economic Activity

To make sure that they have an adequate supply of inventory, many companies enter into contracts to purchase merchandise and other inventory at a future date. For example, in recent financial statements, **Starbucks Corporation (SBUX)** reported that it had entered into $466 million of contracts (commitments) to purchase coffee in the future at a fixed price. It had another $641 million of similar contracts (commitments) where the price was to be determined at a later date.

Source: Starbucks Corporation, 10-K for the year ended October 2, 2016.

Critical Thinking/Judgment

How should Starbucks record and/or report these contracts (commitments) to purchase coffee?
If the market price of coffee falls below the agreed-upon fixed price, should Starbucks recognize a loss?
If the market price of coffee rises above the agreed-upon fixed price, should Starbucks recognize a gain?

Suggested answer at end of chapter.

Sales Transactions

Revenue from merchandise sales is usually recorded as *Sales*. Sometimes a business may use the title *Sales of Merchandise*.

Cash Sales A retail business may sell merchandise for cash. Cash sales are normally entered on a cash register and recorded in the accounts. To illustrate, assume that on March 3, **NetSolutions** sells merchandise for $1,800. These cash sales are recorded as follows:

A = L + E
+   + Rev

20Y8				
Mar.	3	Cash	1,800	
		Sales		1,800
		To record cash sales.		

Using the perpetual inventory system, the cost of goods sold and the decrease in inventory are also recorded. In this way, the inventory account indicates the amount of inventory on hand (not sold).

To illustrate, assume that the cost of goods sold on March 3 is $1,200. The entry to record the cost of goods sold and the decrease in the inventory is as follows:

A = L + E
−   − Exp

Mar.	3	Cost of Goods Sold	1,200	
		Inventory		1,200
		To record the cost of goods sold.		

Sales may be made to customers using credit cards such as MasterCard or VISA. Such sales are recorded as cash sales. This is because these sales are normally processed by a clearinghouse that contacts the bank that issued the card. The issuing bank then electronically transfers cash directly to the retailer's bank account.[4] Thus, the retailer normally receives cash within a few days of making the credit card sale.

Link to Dollar Tree

Dollar Tree normally receives cash from credit card sales within three business days, and thus records credit card sales as cash sales.

[4] CyberSource is one of the major credit card clearinghouses. For a more detailed description of how credit card sales are processed, see the following CyberSource Web page: www.cybersource.com, click on Products, and under Payment Processing, click on Payment Cards, and then on How it Works.

If customers use MasterCards to pay for their purchases, the sales would be recorded exactly as shown in the first March 3 entry illustrated in this section. Any processing fees charged by the clearinghouse or issuing bank are periodically recorded as an expense. To illustrate, assume that NetSolutions paid credit card processing fees of $4,150 on March 31. These fees would be recorded as follows:

Mar.	31	Credit Card Expense	4,150	
		Cash		4,150
		To record service charges on credit card sales for the month.		

$\underset{-}{A} = L + \underset{- \text{Exp}}{E}$

Instead of using MasterCard or VISA, a customer may use a credit card that is not issued by a bank. For example, a customer might use an American Express card. If the seller uses a clearinghouse, the clearinghouse will collect the receivable and transfer the cash to the retailer's bank account, similar to the way it would have if the customer had used MasterCard or VISA. Large businesses, however, may not use a clearinghouse. In such cases, nonbank credit card sales must first be reported to the card company before cash is received. Thus, a receivable is created with the nonbank credit card company. However, because most retailers use clearinghouses to process both bank and nonbank credit cards, all credit card sales will be recorded as cash sales.

Dollar Tree only accepts cash, checks, credit cards, and debit cards from its customers.

Link to Dollar Tree

Sales on Account

A retail business may sell merchandise on account. The seller records such sales as a debit to Accounts Receivable and a credit to Sales. An example of an entry for a **NetSolutions** sale on account of $18,000 follows. The cost of goods sold was $10,800.

Mar.	10	Accounts Receivable—Digital Technologies	18,000	
		Sales		18,000
		Invoice No. 7172.		

$\underset{+}{A} = L + \underset{+ \text{Rev}}{E}$

	10	Cost of Goods Sold	10,800	
		Inventory		10,800
		Cost of merchandise sold on Invoice No. 7172.		

$\underset{-}{A} = L + \underset{- \text{Exp}}{E}$

Because **Dollar Tree** does not sell merchandise to customers on account, but only accepts cash, checks, credit cards, and debit cards, it did not report any accounts receivable on a recent balance sheet.

Link to Dollar Tree

Customer Discounts

A seller may grant customers a variety of discounts, called **customer discounts**, as incentives to encourage customers to act in a way benefiting the seller. For example, a seller may offer customer discounts to encourage customers to purchase in volume or order early.

A common discount, called a **sales discount**, encourages customers to pay their invoice early. For example, a seller may offer credit terms of 2/10, n/30, which provides a 2% sales discount if the invoice is paid within 10 days. If not paid within 10 days, the total invoice amount is due within 30 days.[5]

To illustrate the accounting for sales discounts, assume that **NetSolutions** sold $18,000 of merchandise to Digital Technologies on March 10 with credit terms 2/10, n/30. The March 10 sale would be recorded as follows:[6]

Mar.	10	Accounts Receivable—Digital Technologies	17,640	
		Sales [$18,000 − ($18,000 × 2%)]		17,640

$\underset{+}{A} = L + \underset{+ \text{Rev}}{E}$

[5] From the buyer's perspective, a sales discount is referred to as a purchases discount, which was discussed earlier in this chapter.
[6] The accounting for customer discounts other than sales discounts is discussed in advanced accounting courses.

The sale to Digital Technologies is recorded by NetSolutions at the most likely amount expected to be received, which is $17,640.[7] This is the invoice amount of $18,000 less the sales discount of $360 ($18,000 × 2%). This method of recording sales discounts is called the **net method**. An alternative method of recording sales discounts, called the *gross method*, is illustrated in Appendix 1 to this chapter.

The payment by Digital Technologies on March 19 is recorded as follows:

$$\begin{array}{c} A = L + E \\ +\; - \end{array}$$

Mar.	19	Cash	17,640	
		Accounts Receivable—Digital Technologies		17,640

If Digital Technologies did not pay within the discount period, NetSolutions would receive $18,000 and Sales would be credited for the amount of the discount. For example, assuming that Digital Technologies paid NetSolutions on April 9, the payment would be recorded by NetSolutions as follows:

$$\begin{array}{c} A = L + E \\ +\; - \qquad + \text{ Rev} \end{array}$$

Apr.	9	Cash	18,000	
		Accounts Receivable—Digital Technologies		17,640
		Sales		360

Customer Refunds A buyer may receive merchandise that is defective, damaged during shipment, or does not meet the buyer's expectations. If the customer has already paid for the merchandise, the seller may pay the buyer a **cash refund**.

When the seller pays a refund, the seller debits Customer Refunds Payable and credits Cash. **Customer Refunds Payable** is a liability account for estimated refunds that will be paid to customers. It is recorded at the end of the accounting period as part of the adjusting process.[8]

To illustrate, assume that on March 4 **NetSolutions** pays Blake & Sons a refund of $900 for merchandise that was damaged in shipment. Blake & Sons has agreed to keep the merchandise and make any necessary repairs. NetSolutions would record the payment of the refund as follows:

$$\begin{array}{c} A = L + E \\ -\quad - \end{array}$$

Mar.	4	Customer Refunds Payable	900	
		Cash		900

Customer Allowances A buyer who receives defective or damaged merchandise may not have paid for the merchandise. For example, the buyer may have purchased the merchandise on account and, thus, has an outstanding accounts receivable balance. In this case, the seller may grant a **customer allowance** against the customer's account receivable. When this is done, the seller sends the buyer a **credit memorandum**, or **credit memo**, indicating its intent to credit the customer's account receivable.

To illustrate, assume that **NetSolutions** grants Blake & Sons a customer allowance of $900. NetSolutions notifies Blake & Sons of the allowance by issuing the credit memo shown in Exhibit 6.

The credit memo indicates that NetSolutions intends to reduce Blake & Sons' accounts receivable for $900 due to merchandise damaged in shipment. NetSolutions would record the granting of the customer allowance as follows:

$$\begin{array}{c} A = L + E \\ -\quad - \end{array}$$

Mar.	4	Customer Refunds Payable	900	
		Accounts Receivable—Blake & Sons		900

---

[7] *Revenue from Contracts with Customers, Topic 606, FASB Accounting Standards Update,* Financial Accounting Standards Board, Norwalk, CT, May 2014, para. 606-10-32b.
[8] The adjusting process for retail businesses is illustrated later in this chapter.

NetSolutions		No. 321	**Exhibit 6** Credit Memo
5101 Washington Ave.			
Cincinnati, OH 45227-5101			

CREDIT MEMO

TO	DATE
Blake & Sons	March 4, 20Y8
7608 Melton Avenue	
Los Angeles, CA 90025-3942	

WE CREDITED YOUR ACCOUNT AS FOLLOWS

Allowance for merchandise damaged in shipment	900

Dollar Tree does not offer refunds and all sales are final.

Link to Dollar Tree

Customer Returns In the preceding examples, Blake & Sons did not return merchandise. When customers return merchandise for a cash refund or allowance, an additional entry must be made. This additional entry debits Inventory and credits Estimated Returns Inventory for the seller's original cost of the returned merchandise. **Estimated Returns Inventory** is a current asset account for the estimated amount of merchandise that will be returned by customers. It is recorded at the end of the accounting period as part of the adjusting process.[9]

To illustrate, assume that on January 15 Bormann Enterprises returned merchandise with a selling price of $3,000 for a cash refund. The merchandise originally cost **NetSolutions** $2,100. NetSolutions would record the cash refund and the return with the following two entries:

Jan.	15	Customer Refunds Payable		3,000	
		Cash			3,000
	15	Inventory		2,100	
		Estimated Returns Inventory			2,100

$$\underset{-}{A} = \underset{-}{L} + E$$

$$\underset{+\,-}{A} = L + E$$

The first entry records the cash refund payment of $3,000. The second entry records the receipt of the $2,100 of returned merchandise by debiting Inventory and crediting Estimated Returns Inventory.[10]

If Bormann Enterprises had an outstanding accounts receivable balance on January 15, NetSolutions could have issued a $3,000 credit memo to Bormann Enterprises. In this case, NetSolutions would have credited Accounts Receivable—Bormann Enterprises instead of Cash.

The journal entries to record customer refunds, allowances, and returns are summarized in Exhibit 7.

Exhibit 7 Journal Entries to Record Customer Refunds, Allowances, and Returns

	Cash Refund Paid		Credit Memorandum Issued	
Customer does not return merchandise	Customer Refunds Payable XXX		Customer Refunds Payable XXX	
	Cash	XXX	Accounts Receivable..........	XXX
Customer returns merchandise	Customer Refunds Payable XXX		Customer Refunds Payable XXX	
	Cash	XXX	Accounts Receivable..........	XXX
	Inventory...................... XXX		Inventory...................... XXX	
	Estimated Returns Inventory.....	XXX	Estimated Returns Inventory.....	XXX

[9] The adjusting process for retail businesses is illustrated later in the chapter.

[10] Because of wear, tear, and damage, companies may segregate returned items from normal inventory by using a separate returns inventory account.

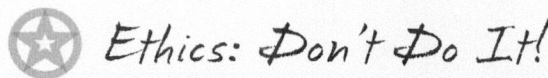

Ethics: Don't Do It!

The Case of the Fraudulent Price Tags

One of the challenges for a retailer is policing its sales return policy. There are many ways in which customers can unethically or illegally abuse such policies. In one case, a couple was accused of attaching a company's store price tags to cheaper merchandise bought or obtained elsewhere. The couple then returned the cheaper goods and received the substantially higher refund amount. Company security officials discovered the fraud and had the couple arrested after they had allegedly bilked the company for more than $1 million.

Source: Jack L. Hayes International, Inc., *28th Annual Retail Theft Survey*, 2016.

Check Up Corner 5-2 | Sales Transactions

On December 30, Burrows Inc. sold $12,000 of merchandise to Wall Company on account, with terms 2/10, n/30. The merchandise cost Burrows $8,000. On January 3, Wall determines that a portion of the merchandise received does not operate properly, and Burrows issues a credit memo for the returned items. The invoice amount of the returned merchandise is $3,000, which cost Burrows $2,000. Journalize the entries by Burrows to record (a) the December 30 sale, (b) the January 3 return, and (c) the receipt of the amount due from Wall on January 6.

Solution:

a.	Dec. 30	Accounts Receivable—Wall Company	11,760	
		Sales		11,760
	30	Cost of Goods Sold	8,000	
		Inventory		8,000

The sale is recorded at the invoice amount ($12,000) less the 2% discount ($240).

b.	Jan. 3	Customer Refunds Payable	2,940	
		Accounts Receivable—Wall Company		2,940
		Inventory	2,000	
		Estimated Returns Inventory		2,000

The customer refund is recorded at the invoice amount ($3,000) less the 2% discount ($60).

When goods are returned, Estimated Returns Inventory is credited and Inventory is debited for the original cost of the inventory.

Instead of paying a cash refund, the seller grants the customer an allowance against its account receivable.

Customer Refunds Payable is a liability account for estimated refunds and allowances.

The account receivable was paid in cash within the 10-day discount period.

c.	Jan. 6	Cash	8,820	
		Accounts Receivable—Wall Company		8,820

The remaining account receivable ($11,760 − $2,940) is paid in cash within the discount period.

Check Up Corner

Freight

Purchases and sales of merchandise often involve freight. The terms of a sale indicate when ownership (title and control) of the merchandise passes from the seller to the buyer. This point determines whether the buyer or the seller pays the freight costs.[11]

---

[11] The passage of title also determines whether the buyer or seller must pay other costs, such as the cost of insurance, while the merchandise is in transit.

The ownership of the merchandise may pass to the buyer when the seller delivers the merchandise to the freight carrier. In this case, the terms are said to be **FOB (free on board) shipping point**. This term means that the buyer pays the freight costs from the shipping point to the final destination. Such costs are part of the buyer's total cost of purchasing inventory and are added to the cost of the inventory by debiting Inventory.

note:
The buyer bears the freight costs if the shipping terms are FOB shipping point.

To illustrate, assume that on June 10, NetSolutions purchased merchandise as follows:

June 10. Purchased merchandise from Magna Data, $1,200 terms FOB shipping point.
     10. Paid freight of $50 on June 10 purchase from Magna Data.

NetSolutions would record these two transactions as follows:

June	10	Inventory	1,200	
		Accounts Payable—Magna Data		1,200
		Purchased merchandise, terms FOB		
		shipping point.		
	10	Inventory	50	
		Cash		50
		Paid shipping cost on merchandise		
		purchased.		

$$A = L + E$$
$$+ \quad +$$

$$A = L + E$$
$$+ -$$

The ownership of the merchandise may pass to the buyer when the buyer receives the merchandise. In this case, the terms are said to be **FOB (free on board) destination**. This term means that the seller pays the freight costs from the shipping point to the buyer's final destination. When the seller pays the delivery charges, the seller debits Delivery Expense or Freight Out. Delivery Expense is reported on the seller's income statement as a selling expense.

note:
The seller bears the freight costs if the shipping terms are FOB destination.

To illustrate, assume that NetSolutions sells merchandise as follows:

June 15. Sold merchandise to Kranz Company on account, $700, terms FOB destination. The cost of the goods sold is $480.
     15. NetSolutions pays freight of $40 on the sale of June 15.

NetSolutions records the sale, the cost of the sale, and the freight cost as follows:

June	15	Accounts Receivable—Kranz Company	700	
		Sales		700
		Sold merchandise, terms FOB destination.		
	15	Cost of Goods Sold	480	
		Inventory		480
		Recorded cost of goods sold to		
		Kranz Company.		
	15	Delivery Expense	40	
		Cash		40
		Paid shipping cost on merchandise sold.		

$$A = L + E$$
$$+ \qquad\quad + \text{ Rev}$$

$$A = L + E$$
$$- \qquad\quad - \text{ Exp}$$

$$A = L + E$$
$$- \qquad\quad - \text{ Exp}$$

The seller may prepay the freight, even though the terms are FOB shipping point. The seller will then add the freight to the invoice. The buyer debits Inventory for the total amount of the invoice, including the freight. Any discount terms would not apply to the prepaid freight.

To illustrate, assume that NetSolutions sells merchandise as follows:

June 20. Sold merchandise to Planter Company on account, $800, terms FOB shipping point. NetSolutions paid freight of $45, which was added to the invoice. The cost of the goods sold is $360.

NetSolutions records the sale, the cost of the sale, and the freight as follows:

A = L + E + + Rev	June	20	Accounts Receivable—Planter Company	800	
			Sales		800
			Sold merchandise, terms FOB shipping point.		
A = L + E – – Exp		20	Cost of Goods Sold	360	
			Inventory		360
			Recorded cost of goods sold to Planter Company.		
A = L + E + –		20	Accounts Receivable—Planter Company	45	
			Cash		45
			Prepaid shipping cost on merchandise sold.		

Shipping terms, the passage of title (control), and whether the buyer or seller is to pay the freight costs are summarized in Exhibit 8.

Exhibit 8 Freight Terms

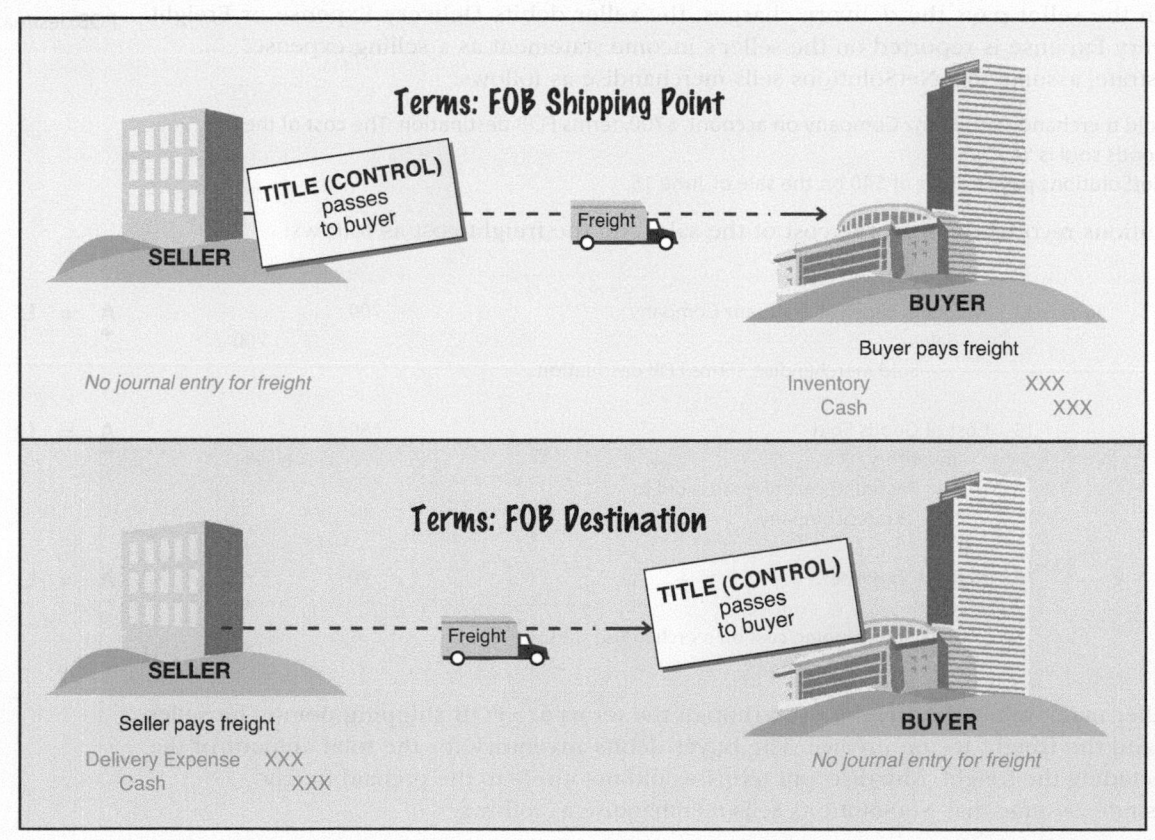

Terms: FOB Shipping Point

TITLE (CONTROL) passes to buyer

SELLER   Freight   BUYER

Buyer pays freight

No journal entry for freight

Inventory	XXX
Cash	XXX

Terms: FOB Destination

TITLE (CONTROL) passes to buyer

SELLER   Freight   BUYER

Seller pays freight

Delivery Expense	XXX
Cash	XXX

No journal entry for freight

Summary: Recording Inventory Transactions

Recording inventory transactions under the perpetual inventory system has been described and illustrated in the preceding sections. These transactions involved purchases, purchases returns and allowances, freight, cost of goods sold (from sales), and customer returns. Exhibit 9 summarizes how these transactions are recorded in T account form.

Exhibit 9 Recording Inventory Transactions

Inventory			
Purchases (net of discounts)	XXX	Purchases returns and allowances (net of discounts)	XXX
Freight for merchandise purchased FOB shipping point	XXX	Cost of goods sold	XXX
Customer returns	XXX		

Estimated Returns Inventory			
Adjusting entry for estimated customer returns	XXX	Customer returns	XXX

Cost of Goods Sold			
Cost of goods sold	XXX	Adjusting entry for estimated customer returns	XXX

Dual Nature of Merchandise Transactions

Each merchandising transaction affects a buyer and a seller. In the illustration shown in Exhibit 10, the same transactions for a seller and buyer are recorded. In Exhibit 10, the seller is Scully Company and the buyer is Burton Co.

Sales Taxes and Trade Discounts

Sales of merchandise often involve sales taxes. Also, the seller may offer buyers trade discounts.

Sales Taxes Almost all states levy a tax on sales of merchandise.[12] The liability for the sales tax is incurred when the sale is made.

At the time of a cash sale, the seller collects the sales tax. When a sale is made on account, the seller charges the tax to the buyer by debiting Accounts Receivable. The seller credits the sales account for the amount of the sale and credits the tax to Sales Tax Payable. For example, the seller would record a sale of $100 on account, subject to a tax of 6%, as follows:

Aug.	12	Accounts Receivable—Lemon Co.		106	
		Sales			100
		Sales Tax Payable			6
		Invoice No. 339.			

$$A = L + E$$
$$+ \quad + \quad + \quad \text{Rev}$$

---

[12] Businesses that purchase merchandise for resale to others are normally exempt from paying sales taxes on their purchases. Only final buyers of merchandise normally pay sales taxes.

Exhibit 10 Illustration of Inventory Transactions for Seller and Buyer

Transaction	Scully Company (Seller)		Burton Co. (Buyer)	
July 1. Scully Company sold merchandise on account to Burton Co., $7,500, terms FOB shipping point, n/45. The cost of the goods sold was $4,500.	Accounts Receivable—Burton Co. ... 7,500 Sales........................ Cost of Goods Sold .... 4,500 Inventory	7,500 4,500	Inventory .... 7,500 Accounts Payable—Scully Co. ...	7,500
July 2. Burton Co. paid freight of $150 on July 1 purchase from Scully Company.	No journal entry.		Inventory .... 150 Cash...........................	150
July 3. Scully Company sold merchandise on account to Burton Co., $5,000, terms FOB destination, n/15. The cost of the goods sold was $3,500.	Accounts Receivable—Burton Co. ... 5,000 Sales........................ Cost of Goods Sold .... 3,500 Inventory	5,000 3,500	Inventory .... 5,000 Accounts Payable—Scully Co. ...	5,000
July 7. Scully Company paid freight of $250 for delivery of merchandise sold to Burton Co. on July 5.	Delivery Expense .... 250 Cash...........................	250	No journal entry.	
July 17. Scully Company received payment from Burton Co. for purchase of July 3.	Cash .... 5,000 Accounts Receivable—Burton Co.	5,000	Accounts Payable—Scully Co. .... 5,000 Cash...........................	5,000
July 18. Scully Company sold merchandise on account to Burton Co., $12,000, terms FOB shipping point, 2/10, n/eom. Scully Company prepaid freight of $500, which was added to the invoice. The cost of the goods sold was $7,200.	Accounts Receivable—Burton Co. ... 11,760 Sales........................ Accounts Receivable—Burton Co. ... 500 Cash........................... Cost of Goods Sold .... 7,200 Inventory	11,760 500 7,200	Inventory .... 12,260 Accounts Payable—Scully Co. ...	12,260
July 22. Scully Company paid Burton Co. a refund of $750 for merchandise damaged in the July 3 purchase. Burton kept the merchandise.	Customer Refunds Payable .... 750 Cash...........................	750	Cash .... 750 Inventory	750
July 28. Scully Company received payment from Burton Co. for purchase of July 18.	Cash .... 12,260 Accounts Receivable—Burton Co. .	12,260	Accounts Payable—Scully Co. .... 12,260 Cash...........................	12,260
July 31. Scully Company granted a customer allowance (credit memo) to Burton Co. for $2,500 for merchandise returned from July 1 purchase. The cost of the merchandise returned was $1,500.	Customer Refunds Payable .... 2,500 Accounts Receivable—Burton Co. . Inventory .... 1,500 Estimated Returns Inventory....	2,500 1,500	Accounts Payable—Scully Co..... 2,500 Inventory......................	2,500

On a regular basis, the seller pays to the taxing authority (state) the amount of the sales tax collected. The seller records such a payment as follows:

Sept.	15	Sales Tax Payable	2,900	
		Cash		2,900
		Payment for sales taxes collected during August.		

$$A \;=\; \underline{L} \;+\; \underline{E}$$
$$\underline{}$$

Trade Discounts Wholesalers are companies that sell merchandise to other businesses rather than to the public, called B2B transactions. Wholesalers may offer special discounts off list prices to government agencies or businesses that order large quantities. Such discounts are called **trade discounts**.

Sellers and buyers do not normally record the list prices of merchandise and trade discounts in their accounts. For example, assume that an item has a list price of $1,000 and a 40% trade discount. The seller records the sale of the item at $600 [$1,000 less the trade discount of $400 ($1,000 × 40%)]. Likewise, the buyer records the purchase at $600.

The Adjusting Process

Objective 3
Describe and illustrate the adjusting process for a retail business.

The chart of accounts (Exhibit 2) and the recording of transactions for a retail business (Net-Solutions) have been described and illustrated. Next, the adjusting process for a retail business is described and illustrated. This discussion focuses on the following adjusting entries that differ from those of a service business:

- Inventory Shrinkage
- Customer Returns and Allowances

Adjusting Entry for Inventory Shrinkage

Under the perpetual inventory system, the inventory account is continually updated for purchase and sales transactions. As a result, the balance of the inventory account is the amount of merchandise available for sale at that point in time. However, retailers normally experience some loss of inventory due to shoplifting, employee theft, or errors. Thus, the physical inventory on hand at the end of the accounting period is usually less than the balance of Inventory. This difference is called **inventory shrinkage** or **inventory shortage**.

Why It Matters

E-commerce Shopping Carts

When you shop on an e-commerce site, you will often select items that fill out a shopping cart form that identifies the items to be purchased and their prices. This illustration is from **Apple's (AAPL)** shopping cart. The shopping cart has a set of Apple EarPods at a price of $29. When checking out, the e-commerce site will automatically record the sales transaction for this purchase at a sales price of $29, plus appropriate sales tax and shipping. In addition, completing the checkout will record the reduction of EarPod inventory by one unit and record the appropriate cost of goods sold. Thus, all the merchandising transactions are generated from the shopping cart checkout process.

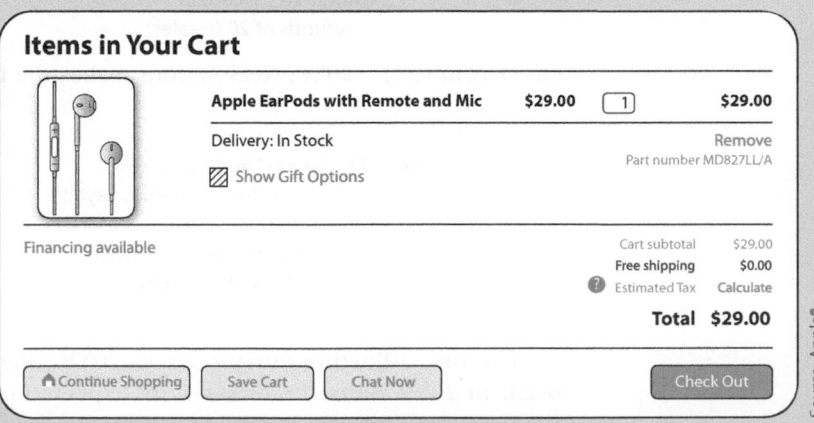

Items in Your Cart

| | **Apple EarPods with Remote and Mic** | $29.00 | 1 | $29.00 |

Delivery: In Stock — Remove
Part number MD827LL/A
Show Gift Options

Financing available

Cart subtotal $29.00
Free shipping $0.00
Estimated Tax Calculate

Total $29.00

Continue Shopping | Save Cart | Chat Now | Check Out

Source: Apple®

To illustrate, **NetSolutions**' inventory on December 31, 20Y8, is as follows:

Account balance of Inventory	$63,950
Physical inventory on hand	62,150
Inventory shrinkage	$ 1,800

At the end of the accounting period, inventory shrinkage is recorded by the following adjusting entry:

		Adjusting Entry		
Dec.	31	Cost of Goods Sold	1,800	
		Inventory		1,800
		Inventory shrinkage ($63,950 − $62,150).		

After the preceding entry is recorded, the balance of Inventory agrees with the physical inventory on hand at the end of the period. Since inventory shrinkage cannot be totally eliminated, it is considered a normal cost of operations. If, however, the amount of the shrinkage is unusually large, it may be disclosed separately on the income statement. In such cases, the shrinkage may be recorded in a separate account, such as Loss from Inventory Shrinkage.

Adjusting Entries for Customer Refunds, Allowances, and Returns

Sellers are required to estimate returns and allowances at the end of an accounting period and prepare two adjusting entries:

1. The first adjusting entry reduces the sales account and creates a customer refund liability account for the estimated refunds and allowances that will be granted to customers in the future.
2. The second adjusting entry creates an estimated returns inventory account for the cost of merchandise that is expected to be returned and reduces Cost of Goods Sold.

To illustrate, assume the following for **NetSolutions** on December 31, 20Y8, before any adjustments:

	Unadjusted Balances December 31, 20Y8	
	Debit	Credit
Sales		$715,409
Cost of Goods Sold	$523,505	
Estimated Returns Inventory	300	
Customer Refunds Payable		800
Estimated cost of merchandise returned for 20Y8 sales	$5,000	
Estimated percent of refunds of 20Y8 sales	1%	

On December 31, 20Y8, NetSolutions makes the following two adjusting entries:[13]

Dec.	31	Sales (1% × $715,409)	7,154	
		Customer Refunds Payable		7,154
	31	Estimated Returns Inventory	5,000	
		Cost of Goods Sold		5,000

The first adjusting entry reduces 20Y8 sales by the amount of estimated refunds that may occur in 20Y9. Since 1% of sales are expected to be refunded, Sales is debited for $7,154 (1% × $715,409). In addition, a liability is recorded for $7,154 by crediting Customer Refunds Payable for the estimated customer refunds in 20Y9.

[13] The accounting illustrated is based upon *Revenue from Contracts with Customers*, Topic 606, *FASB Accounting Standards Update*, Financial Accounting Standards Board, Norwalk, CT, May 2014.

The second adjusting entry debits the asset Estimated Returns Inventory and reduces Cost of Goods Sold for the cost of merchandise that is expected to be returned in 20Y9 of $5,000. Estimated Returns Inventory is debited rather than Inventory because the type of merchandise returned will not be known until the returns actually occur.

After the adjusting entries are posted to the ledger, Estimated Returns Inventory will have an adjusted balance of $5,300 ($300 + $5,000). Estimated returns inventory of $5,300 is reported on the balance sheet as a current asset following Inventory. Customer Refunds Payable will have a balance of $7,954 ($800 + $7,154). Customer refunds payable of $7,954 is reported as a current liability.

Adjusted Trial Balance

After the adjusted entries are posted to the ledger, an adjusted trial balance is prepared. The adjusted trial balance for **NetSolutions** as of December 31, 20Y8, is shown in Exhibit 11.

NetSolutions Adjusted Trial Balance December 31, 20Y8	Account No.	Debit Balances	Credit Balances
Cash	110	52,650	
Accounts Receivable	112	91,080	
Inventory	115	62,150	
Estimated Returns Inventory	116	5,300	
Office Supplies	117	480	
Prepaid Insurance	118	2,650	
Land	120	20,000	
Store Equipment	123	27,100	
Accumulated Depreciation—Store Equipment	124		5,700
Office Equipment	125	15,570	
Accumulated Depreciation—Office Equipment	126		4,720
Accounts Payable	210		14,466
Salaries Payable	211		1,140
Unearned Rent	212		1,800
Customer Refunds Payable	213		7,954
Notes Payable	215		25,000
Common Stock	310		30,000
Retained Earnings	311		123,800
Dividends	312	18,000	
Sales	410		708,255
Cost of Goods Sold	510	520,305	
Sales Salaries Expense	520	53,430	
Advertising Expense	521	10,860	
Depreciation Expense—Store Equipment	522	3,100	
Delivery Expense	523	2,800	
Miscellaneous Selling Expense	529	630	
Office Salaries Expense	530	21,020	
Rent Expense	531	8,100	
Depreciation Expense—Office Equipment	532	2,490	
Insurance Expense	533	1,910	
Office Supplies Expense	534	610	
Miscellaneous Admininstrative Expense	539	760	
Rent Revenue	610		600
Interest Expense	710	2,440	
		923,435	923,435

Exhibit 11

Adjusted Trial Balance

Objective 4

Describe and illustrate the financial statements and closing entries for a retail business.

Financial Statements and Closing Entries for a Retail Business

Although merchandising transactions affect the balance sheet in reporting inventory, they primarily affect the income statement. An income statement for a retail business is normally prepared using either a *multiple-step* or *single-step* format.

The financial statements for **NetSolutions** are illustrated in Exhibits 12–14. These financial statements were prepared from the adjusted trial balance shown in Exhibit 11.

Multiple-Step Income Statement

The 20Y8 income statement for **NetSolutions** is shown in Exhibit 12. This form of income statement, called a **multiple-step income statement**, contains several sections, subsections, and subtotals.

Exhibit 12

Multiple-Step Income Statement

NetSolutions Income Statement For the Year Ended December 31, 20Y8			
Sales...			$ 708,255
Cost of goods sold			(520,305)
Gross profit......................................			$ 187,950
Operating expenses:			
Selling expenses:			
Sales salaries expense	$53,430		
Advertising expense......................	10,860		
Depreciation expense—store equipment .	3,100		
Delivery expense.........................	2,800		
Miscellaneous selling expense	630		
Total selling expenses		$70,820	
Administrative expenses:			
Office salaries expense	$21,020		
Rent expense	8,100		
Depreciation expense—office equipment.	2,490		
Insurance expense	1,910		
Office supplies expense	610		
Miscellaneous administrative expense....	760		
Total administrative expenses.........		34,890	
Total operating expenses			(105,710)
Operating income			$ 82,240
Other revenue and expense:			
Rent revenue		$ 600	
Interest expense		(2,440)	(1,840)
Net income......................................			$ 80,400

Sales The total amount of sales to customers for cash and on account is reported in this section. **NetSolutions** reported sales of $708,255 for the year ended December 31, 20Y8.

Cost of Goods Sold As shown in Exhibit 12, **NetSolutions** reported cost of goods sold of $520,305 during 20Y8. This amount is the cost of goods sold to customers. Cost of goods sold may also be reported as *cost of merchandise sold* or *cost of sales*.

Gross Profit The excess of sales over cost of goods sold is gross profit. As shown in Exhibit 12, **NetSolutions** reported gross profit of $187,950 in 20Y8.

Operating Income **Operating income**, sometimes called **income from operations**, is determined by subtracting operating expenses from gross profit. Operating expenses are normally classified as either selling expenses or administrative expenses.

Selling expenses are incurred directly in the selling of merchandise. Examples of selling expenses include sales salaries, store supplies used, depreciation of store equipment, delivery expense, and advertising.

Administrative expenses, sometimes called **general expenses**, are incurred in the administration or general operations of the business. Examples of administrative expenses include office salaries, depreciation of office equipment, and office supplies used.

Each selling and administrative expense may be reported separately as shown in Exhibit 12. However, many companies report selling, administrative, and operating expenses as single line items, as follows for **NetSolutions**:

Gross profit		$ 187,950
Operating expenses:		
Selling expenses	$70,820	
Administrative expenses	34,890	
Total operating expenses		(105,710)
Operating income		$ 82,240

IFRS
See Appendix C for more information.

Other Revenue and Expense Other revenue and expense items are not related to the primary operations of the business. **Other revenue** is revenue from sources other than the primary operating activity of a business. Examples of other revenue include income from interest, rent, and gains resulting from the sale of fixed assets. **Other expense** is an expense that cannot be traced directly to the normal operations of the business. Examples of other expenses include interest expense and losses from disposing of fixed assets.

Other revenue and other expense are offset against each other on the income statement. If the total of other revenue exceeds the total of other expense, the difference is added to operating income to determine net income. If the reverse is true, the difference is subtracted from operating income. The other revenue and expense items of **NetSolutions** are reported as follows and in Exhibit 12:

Operating income		$82,240
Other revenue and expense:		
Rent revenue	$ 600	
Interest expense	(2,440)	(1,840)
Net income		$80,400

Dollar Tree reports its income using the multiple-step income statement format.

Link to Dollar Tree

Check Up Corner 5-3 Multiple-Step Income Statement

The following account balances were taken from the adjusted trial balance for Laser-Tek Company for the fiscal year ended December 31, 20Y2:

Advertising Expense	$ 32,500	Miscellaneous Selling Expense	$ 4,320
Cost of Goods Sold	512,400	Office Salaries Expense	82,400
Depreciation Expense—Office Equipment	20,000	Office Supplies Expense	1,650
Interest Revenue	1,425	Sales	912,500
Miscellaneous Administrative Expense	1,200	Sales Salaries Expense	160,000

Prepare a multiple-step income statement for Laser-Tek Company.

Solution:

Laser-Tek Company
Income Statement
For the Year Ended December 31, 20Y2

Sales			$ 912,500
Cost of goods sold			(512,400)
Gross profit			$ 400,100
Operating expenses:			
Selling expenses:			
Sales salaries expense	$160,000		
Advertising expense	32,500		
Miscellaneous selling expense	4,320		
Total selling expenses		$196,820	
Administrative expenses:			
Office salaries expense	$ 82,400		
Depreciation expense—office equipment	20,000		
Office supplies expense	1,650		
Miscellaneous administrative expense	1,200		
Total administrative expenses		105,250	
Total operating expenses			(302,070)
Operating income			$ 98,030
Other revenue and expense:			
Interest revenue			1,425
Net income			$ 99,455

Gross profit is the excess of sales over the cost of goods sold.

Operating income is computed by subtracting operating expenses from gross profit.

Other revenue and expense items are not related to the company's primary business.

Check Up Corner

Single-Step Income Statement

An alternate form of income statement is the **single-step income statement.** As shown in Exhibit 13, the income statement for **NetSolutions** deducts the total of all expenses *in one step* from the total of all revenues.

The single-step form emphasizes total revenues and total expenses in determining net income. A criticism of the single-step form is that gross profit and operating income are not reported.

Exhibit 13

Single-Step Income Statement

NetSolutions
Income Statement
For the Year Ended December 31, 20Y8

Revenues:		
Sales		$ 708,255
Rent revenue		600
Total revenues		$ 708,855
Expenses:		
Cost of goods sold	$520,305	
Selling expenses	70,820	
Administrative expenses	34,890	
Interest expense	2,440	
Total expenses		(628,455)
Net income		$ 80,400

Statement of Stockholders' Equity

The statement of stockholders' equity for **NetSolutions** is shown in Exhibit 14. This statement assumes that NetSolutions issued $5,000 of additional common stock in 20Y8. The net income of $80,400 is taken from the income statement, while the dividends of $18,000 is taken from the adjusted trial balance, shown in Exhibit 11.

		NetSolutions Statement of Stockholders' Equity For the Year Ended December 31, 20Y8			

	Common Stock	Retained Earnings	Total
Balances, January 1, 20Y8	$25,000	$123,800	$148,800
Issued common stock...................	5,000		5,000
Net income		80,400	80,400
Dividends		(18,000)	(18,000)
Balances, December 31, 20Y8	$30,000	$186,200	$216,200

Exhibit 14

Statement of Stockholders' Equity for Retail Business

Balance Sheet

The balance sheet for **NetSolutions** is shown in Exhibit 15. Inventory and estimated returns inventory are reported as current assets. In addition, customer refunds payable and the current portion of the note payable of $5,000 are reported as current liabilities.

	NetSolutions Balance Sheet December 31, 20Y8		

Exhibit 15

Balance Sheet for Retail Business

Assets

Current assets:

Cash..		$ 52,650	
Accounts receivable		91,080	
Inventory		62,150	
Estimated returns inventory		5,300	
Office supplies		480	
Prepaid insurance...........................		2,650	
Total current assets			$214,310

Property, plant, and equipment:

Land..		$ 20,000	
Store equipment	$27,100		
Accumulated depreciation	(5,700)		
Book value................................		21,400	
Office equipment...........................	$15,570		
Accumulated depreciation	(4,720)		
Book value		10,850	
Total property, plant, and equipment			52,250
Total assets			$266,560

Liabilities

Current liabilities:

Accounts payable...........................		$ 14,466	
Customer refunds payable....................		7,954	
Note payable (current portion)		5,000	
Salaries payable		1,140	
Unearned rent..............................		1,800	
Total current liabilities			$ 30,360

Long-term liabilities:

Note payable (long-term portion)			20,000
Total liabilities			$ 50,360

Stockholders' Equity

Common stock		$ 30,000	
Retained earnings...........................		186,200	
Total stockholders' equity......................			216,200
Total liabilities and stockholders' equity...........			$266,560

Ethics: Don't Do It!

The Cost of Employee Theft

One survey reported that the 25 largest U.S. retail store chains have lost more than $6 billion to shoplifting and employee theft. The stores apprehended over 1 million shoplifters and dishonest employees and recovered more than $200 million from these thieves. Approximately 1 out of every 38 employees was apprehended for theft from his or her employer. Each dishonest employee stole approximately 6 times the amount stolen by shoplifters ($734.16 versus $128.86).

Source: Jack L. Hayes International, Inc., *28th Annual Retail Theft Survey*, 2016.

The Closing Process

The closing entries for a retail business are similar to those for a service business. The two closing entries for a retail business are as follows:

Closing Entry 1. Debit each revenue account for its balance, credit each expense account for its balance, and credit the retained earnings account for net income. Debit the retained earnings account for a net loss. Cost of Goods Sold is a temporary account and is closed like an expense account.

Closing Entry 2. Debit the retained earnings account for the balance of the dividends account and credit the dividends account.

The two closing entries for **NetSolutions** are as follows:

Date		Item	Post. Ref.	Debit	Credit
		Journal			*Page 29*
		Closing Entries			
20Y8 Dec.	31	Sales	410	708,255	
		Rent Revenue	610	600	
		Cost of Goods Sold	510		520,305
		Sales Salaries Expense	520		53,430
		Advertising Expense	521		10,860
		Depr. Expense—Store Equipment	522		3,100
		Delivery Expense	523		2,800
		Miscellaneous Selling Expense	529		630
		Office Salaries Expense	530		21,020
		Rent Expense	531		8,100
		Depr. Expense—Office Equipment	532		2,490
		Insurance Expense	533		1,910
		Office Supplies Expense	534		610
		Misc. Administrative Expense	539		760
		Interest Expense	710		2,440
		Retained Earnings	311		80,400
	31	Retained Earnings	311	18,000	
		Dividends	312		18,000

After the closing entries are posted to the accounts, a post-closing trial balance is prepared. The only accounts that appear on the post-closing trial balance are the asset, contra asset, liability, and stockholders' equity accounts with balances. These are the same accounts that appear on the end-of-period balance sheet. If the two totals of the trial balance columns are not equal, an error has occurred that must be found and corrected. The post-closing trial balance for NetSolutions is shown in Exhibit 16.

NetSolutions Post-Closing Trial Balance December 31, 20Y8			
	Account No.	**Debit Balances**	**Credit Balances**
Cash	110	52,650	
Accounts Receivable	112	91,080	
Inventory	115	62,150	
Estimated Returns Inventory	116	5,300	
Office Supplies	117	480	
Prepaid Insurance	118	2,650	
Land	120	20,000	
Store Equipment	123	27,100	
Accumulated Depreciation—Store Equipment	124		5,700
Office Equipment	125	15,570	
Accumulated Depreciation—Office Equipment	126		4,720
Accounts Payable	210		14,466
Salaries Payable	211		1,140
Unearned Rent	212		1,800
Customer Refunds Payable	213		7,954
Notes Payable	215		25,000
Common Stock	310		30,000
Retained Earnings	311		186,200
		276,980	276,980

Exhibit 16

Post-Closing
Trial Balance

Analysis for Decision Making

Asset Turnover Ratio

The **asset turnover ratio** measures how effectively a business is using its assets to generate sales. A high ratio indicates an effective use of assets.

The asset turnover ratio is computed as follows:

$$\text{Asset Turnover Ratio} = \frac{\text{Sales}}{\text{Average Total Assets}}$$

The denominator is the average of the total assets at the beginning and end of the year. To illustrate the use of this ratio, the following data (in millions) were taken from recent annual reports of **Dollar Tree, Inc. (DLTR)**:

	Year 2	Year 1
Total sales	$15,498	$8,602
Total assets:		
Beginning of year	3,493	2,772
End of year	15,901	3,493

Objective 5

Describe and illustrate the use of the asset turnover ratio in evaluating a company's operating performance.

The asset turnover ratio for each year is as follows:

	Year 2	Year 1
Asset turnover ratio*	1.60	2.75
	{$15,498 ÷ [($3,493 + $15,901) ÷ 2]}	{$8,602 ÷ [($2,772 + $3,493) ÷ 2]}

*Rounded to two decimal places.

Dollar Tree's asset turnover ratio decreased from 2.75 in Year 1 to 1.60 in Year 2. Thus, Dollar Tree had a significant decline in the use of its assets to generate sales in Year 2. This decline is likely due to Dollar Tree's acquisition of Family Dollar Stores in Year 2. The acquisition increased Dollar Tree's number of stores (and related assets) by more than 8,200 stores. As Dollar Tree reduces the duplication of assets from the acquisition and increases its sales, the asset turnover ratio is expected to increase in coming years.

Using the asset turnover ratio for comparisons to competitors and with industry averages could also be beneficial in interpreting Dollar Tree's use of its assets (see MAD 5-2).

Make a Decision

Asset Turnover Ratio

Analyze and compare Amazon.com and NetFlix (MAD 5-1)
(Continuing company analysis)

Analyze Dollar General (MAD 5-2)

Compare Dollar Tree and Dollar General (MAD 5-3)

Analyze and compare CSX, Union Pacific, and YRC Worldwide (MAD 5-4)

Analyze Home Depot (MAD 5-5)

Analyze and compare Kroger and Tiffany (MAD 5-6)

Analyze J. C. Penney (MAD 5-7)

Make a Decision

Appendix 1 Gross Method of Recording Sales Discounts

Objective App 1
Describe and illustrate the gross method of recording sales discounts.

In this chapter, sales discounts for early payment of an invoice were recorded using the net method. Under the *net method*, an invoice is recorded net of any discounts for early payment. This appendix illustrates the gross method of recording sales discounts.

Transactions

Under the **gross method**, a sales invoice with credit terms granting a discount for early payment is recorded at the gross amount of the invoice. If the customer pays within the discount period, Cash is debited for the amount received, the discount is recorded as a debit to Sales, and Accounts Receivable is credited for the invoice amount.

To illustrate, assume that **NetSolutions** uses the perpetual inventory system and sold $18,000 of merchandise to Digital Technologies on March 10, 20Y8, with credit terms of 2/10, n/30. The cost of the merchandise sold was $10,800. The sale would be recorded under the gross method as follows:

20Y8				
Mar.	10	Accounts Receivable—Digital Technologies	18,000	
		Sales		18,000
	10	Cost of Goods Sold	10,800	
		Inventory		18,000

Assuming that Digital Technologies pays within the discount period on March 19, the payment would be recorded as follows:

Mar.	19	Cash	17,640	
		Sales	360	
		Accounts Receivable—Digital Technologies		18,000

Cash is debited for the amount received of $17,640, which is the invoice amount of $18,000 less the sales discount of $360 ($18,000 × 2%). Generally accepted accounting principles (GAAP) require that revenue (sales) be recognized in the amount of consideration received for the sale.[14] Since cash of $17,640 was received, Sales must be decreased (debited) for the sales discount of $360. The customer's account receivable is credited for its balance of $18,000.

Instead of paying within the discount period, assume that Digital Technologies pays the gross amount of $18,000 on April 9. The payment would be recorded as follows:

Apr.	9	Cash	18,000	
		Accounts Receivable—Digital Technologies		18,000

Since $18,000 was received, the revenue (sales) is $18,000; the amount recorded on March 10.

Adjusting Entry

Since GAAP requires that revenue (sales) be recorded in the amount mostly likely to be received, the gross method requires an adjusting entry at the end of the accounting period. The adjusting entry reduces Sales for the estimated sales discounts related to the current period's sales that are expected to be taken in the next period.

To illustrate, assume the following data for **NetSolutions** on December 31, 20Y8:

NetSolutions should record the following adjusting entry on December 31, 20Y8:

	Dec. 31, 20Y8 Balances	
	Debit	**Credit**
Sales		$709,955
Accounts Receivable	$92,880	
Allowance for Sales Discounts		100
Estimated sales discounts that will be taken in 20Y9…..	$ 1,700	

---

[14] *Revenue from Contracts with Customers, Topic 606, FASB Accounting Standards Update,* Financial Accounting Standards Board, Norwalk, CT, May 2014.

The preceding adjusting entry debits Sales for $1,700 and credits Allowance for Sales Discounts.

	20Y8				
	Dec.	31	Sales	1,700	
			Allowance for Sales Discounts		1,700

Allowance for Sales Discounts is a contra asset account similar to the contra asset account Accumulated Depreciation. Just as Accumulated Depreciation is a contra account to a fixed asset account, Allowance for Sales Discounts is a contra account to Accounts Receivable.

After the adjusting entry is posted, Allowance for Sales Discounts will have a credit balance of $1,800 ($100 + $1,700) and would be reported on the balance sheet as follows:

Accounts receivable	$92,880
Allowance for sales discounts	(1,800)
Net accounts receivable	91,080

NetSolutions would report Sales of $708,255 ($709,955 − $1,700) on its income statement for the year ending December 31, 20Y8.

Subsequent Period

Customers with outstanding accounts receivable balances on December 31, 20Y8, will pay their balances in 20Y9. If a customer pays within the discount period, Allowance for Sales Discounts is debited instead of Sales. To illustrate, assume that Jay Smith pays his December 31, 20Y8, account receivable of $2,000 on January 4, 20Y9, and takes a 2/10 sales discount. The payment would be recorded as follows:

	20Y9				
	Jan.	4	Cash	1,960	
			Allowance for Sales Discounts	40	
			Accounts Receivable—Jay Smith		2,000

Assume instead that Jay Smith pays on January 20 and does not take the sales discount. The payment would be recorded as follows:

	20Y9				
	Jan.	20	Cash	2,000	
			Accounts Receivable—Jay Smith		2,000

At the end of 20Y9, Allowance for Sales Discounts will be adjusted for expected sales discounts related to 20Y9 sales that will be taken in the next year.

Comparison with the Net Method

Both the gross method and the net method are acceptable under GAAP. However, the gross method is more complex in that it requires an adjusting entry and a contra asset account. Exhibit 17 shows a comparison of the gross and net methods using the **NetSolutions** sale of $18,000 illustrated earlier.

Exhibit 17 Gross Method Versus Net Method

		Gross Method		Net Method	
Sale:					
20Y8 Mar.10	Accounts Receivable—Digital Technologies..............	18,000		17,640	
	Sales..		18,000		17,640
10	Cost of Goods Sold..	10,800		10,800	
	Inventory..		10,800		10,800
Discount Taken:					
Mar.19	Cash	17,640		17,640	
	Sales...	360			
	Accounts Receivable—Digital Technologies		18,000		17,640
Discount Not Taken:					
Apr. 9	Cash	18,000		18,000	
	Sales...				360
	Accounts Receivable—Digital Technologies		18,000		17,640
Adjusting Entry:					
20Y8 Dec. 31	Sales..	1,700		No entry[15]	
	Allowance for Sales Discounts		1,700		
	No journal entry required				

Appendix 2 The Periodic Inventory System

Objective App 2
Describe and illustrate the periodic system of accounting for merchandise transactions.

Throughout this chapter, the perpetual inventory system was used to record purchases and sales of merchandise. Not all retail businesses, however, use the perpetual inventory system. For example, small retail businesses, such as a local hardware store, may use a manual accounting system. A manual perpetual inventory system is time consuming and costly to maintain. In this case, the periodic inventory system may be used.

Under the periodic inventory system, purchases are normally recorded at their invoice amount as a debit to Purchases. If the invoice is paid within the discount period, the discount is recorded as a credit in a separate account called Purchases Discounts. Likewise, purchases returns are recorded as a credit in a separate account called Purchases Returns and Allowances.

Chart of Accounts Under the Periodic Inventory System

The chart of accounts for **NetSolutions** under a periodic inventory system is shown in Exhibit 18. The accounts used to record transactions under the periodic inventory system are highlighted in blue in Exhibit 18.

[15] Customers with accounts receivable balances at the end of the period may have credit terms such as 2/10, n/30. We assume that the amount of consideration expected to be received from these receivables is the "most likely amount," which is net of the discount. However, the discount period for a customer's account receivable may have expired by the end of the period and, thus, a customer may pay more than the net amount. Any such missed discounts are likely to be insignificant (immaterial). Therefore, we assume no adjusting entry is required under the net method.

Exhibit 18
Chart of Accounts Under the Periodic Inventory System

Balance Sheet Accounts	**Income Statement Accounts**
100 Assets	400 Revenues
110 Cash	410 Sales
111 Notes Receivable	500 Costs and Expenses
112 Accounts Receivable	510 Purchases
115 Inventory	511 Purchases Returns and
116 Estimated Returns Inventory	Allowances
117 Office Supplies	512 Purchases Discounts
118 Prepaid Insurance	513 Freight In
120 Land	520 Sales Salaries Expense
123 Store Equipment	521 Advertising Expense
124 Accumulated Depreciation—	522 Depreciation Expense—
Store Equipment	Store Equipment
125 Office Equipment	523 Delivery Expense
126 Accumulated Depreciation—	529 Miscellaneous Selling Expense
Office Equipment	530 Office Salaries Expense
	531 Rent Expense
200 Liabilities	532 Depreciation Expense—
210 Accounts Payable	Office Equipment
211 Salaries Payable	533 Insurance Expense
212 Unearned Rent	534 Office Supplies Expense
213 Customer Refunds Payable	539 Misc. Administrative Expense
215 Notes Payable	
	600 Other Revenue
300 Stockholders' Equity	610 Rent Revenue
310 Common Stock	700 Other Expense
311 Retained Earnings	710 Interest Expense
312 Dividends	

Recording Merchandise Transactions Under the Periodic Inventory System

Using the periodic inventory system, purchases of inventory are not recorded in the inventory account. Instead, purchases, purchases discounts, and purchases returns and allowances accounts are used. In addition, the sales of merchandise are not recorded in the inventory account. Thus, there is no detailed record of the amount of inventory on hand at any given time. At the end of the period, a physical count of inventory on hand is taken. This physical count is used to determine the cost of goods sold as will be illustrated later.

The use of purchases, purchases discounts, purchases returns and allowances, and freight in accounts are described in this section.

Purchases Purchases of inventory are recorded in a purchases account rather than in the inventory account. Purchases is debited for the invoice amount of a purchase.

Purchases Discounts Purchases discounts are normally recorded in a separate purchases discounts account. The balance of the purchases discounts account is reported as a deduction from Purchases for the period. Thus, Purchases Discounts is a contra (or offsetting) account to Purchases.

Purchases Returns and Allowances Purchases returns and allowances are recorded in a similar manner as purchases discounts. A separate purchases returns and allowances account is used to record returns and allowances. Purchases returns and allowances are reported as a deduction from Purchases for the period. Thus, Purchases Returns and Allowances is a contra (or offsetting) account to Purchases.

Freight In When merchandise is purchased FOB shipping point, the buyer pays for the freight. Under the periodic inventory system, freight paid when purchasing merchandise FOB shipping point is debited to Freight In, Transportation In, or a similar account.

The preceding periodic inventory accounts and their effect on the cost of merchandise purchased are summarized as follows:

Account	Entry to Increase	Normal Balance	Effect on Cost of Merchandise Purchased
Purchases	Debit	Debit	Increases
Purchases Discounts	Credit	Credit	Decreases
Purchases Returns and Allowances	Credit	Credit	Decreases
Freight In	Debit	Debit	Increases

Exhibit 19 illustrates the recording of merchandise transactions using the periodic system.

Transaction	Periodic Inventory System	
June 5. Purchased $30,000 of merchandise on account, terms 2/10, n/30.	Purchases .... 30,000 Accounts Payable	 30,000

June 8. Returned merchandise purchased on account on June 5, $500.	Accounts Payable 500
	    Purchases Returns and
	       Allowances ....
		
		500

June 15. Paid for purchase of June 5, less return of $500 and discount of $590 [($30,000 – $500) × 2%].	Accounts Payable 29,500
	    Cash ....
	    Purchases Discounts ......
		
		28,910
		590

June 18. Sold merchandise on account, $12,500, 1/10, n/30. The cost of the goods sold was $9,000.	Accounts Receivable 12,375
	    Sales ....
	    [$12,500 – ($12,500 × 1%)].
		
		12,375

June 22. Purchased merchandise, $15,000, terms FOB shipping point, 2/15, n/30, with prepaid freight of $750 added to the invoice.	Purchases .... 15,000 Freight In .... 750 Accounts Payable	 15,750
June 28. Received payment on account from June 18 sale.	Cash .... 12,375 Accounts Receivable	 12,375
June 29. Received $19,600 from cash sales. The cost of the goods sold was $13,800.	Cash .... 19,600 Sales	 19,600

Exhibit 19

Transactions Using the Periodic Inventory System

Adjusting Process Under the Periodic Inventory System

The adjusting process is the same under the periodic and perpetual inventory systems except for the inventory shrinkage adjustment and customer refunds and allowances. The ending inventory is determined by a physical count under both systems.

Under the perpetual inventory system, the ending inventory physical count is compared to the balance of Inventory. The difference is the amount of inventory shrinkage. The inventory shrinkage is then recorded as a debit to Cost of Goods Sold and a credit to Inventory.

Under the periodic inventory system, the inventory account is not kept up to date for purchases and sales. As a result, the inventory shrinkage cannot be directly determined. Instead, any inventory shrinkage is included indirectly in the computation of the cost of goods sold as shown in Exhibit 20. This is a major disadvantage of the periodic inventory system. That is, inventory shrinkage is not separately determined.

Like the perpetual inventory system, the periodic system records the same adjusting entry debiting Sales and crediting Customer Refunds Payable for estimated customer refunds and allowances of $7,154. No entry, however, is made for estimated returns inventory. Instead, cost of goods sold is reduced by the cost of the estimated returns inventory for the current year. The estimated cost of the returns for **NetSolutions**' 20Y9 sales is $5,000. This amount is subtracted from the cost of goods sold before estimated returns of $525,305 to yield cost of goods sold of $520,305, as shown in Exhibit 20.

Financial Statements Under the Periodic Inventory System

The financial statements are similar under the perpetual and periodic inventory systems. When the multiple-step format of income statement is used, the cost of goods sold may be reported as shown in Exhibit 20.

Exhibit 20

Determining Cost of Goods Sold Using the Periodic System

Inventory, January 1, 20Y8		$ 59,700
Cost of merchandise purchased:		
Purchases	$521,980	
Purchases returns and allowances	(9,100)	
Purchases discounts	(2,525)	
Net purchases	$510,355	
Freight in	17,400	
Total cost of merchandise purchased		527,755
Inventory available for sale		$587,455
Inventory, December 31, 20Y8		(62,150)
Cost of goods sold before estimated returns		$525,305
Increase in estimated returns inventory		(5,000)
Cost of goods sold		$520,305

Closing Entries Under the Periodic Inventory System

The closing entries differ in the periodic inventory system in that there is no cost of goods sold account to close. Instead, the purchases, purchases discounts, purchases returns and allowances, and freight in accounts are closed. In addition, the inventory account is adjusted to the end-of-period physical inventory count during the closing process. The estimated returns inventory account is also adjusted for the estimated returns from the current period's sales.

The two closing entries under the periodic inventory system are as follows:

1. a. Debit Inventory for its end-of-period balance based on the physical inventory.
    b. Debit Estimated Returns Inventory for the cost of the future estimated returns of the current period's sales.
    c. Debit each revenue account and the following temporary periodic inventory accounts for their balances.
        ■ Purchases Discounts
        ■ Purchases Returns and Allowances
    d. Credit Inventory for its balance as of the beginning of the period.

e. Credit each expense account and the following temporary periodic inventory accounts for their balances.
  - Purchases
  - Freight In
f. Credit the retained earnings account for the net income, or debit the retained earnings account for a net loss.

2. Debit the retained earnings account and credit the dividends account for its balance.

The two closing entries for **NetSolutions** under the periodic inventory system are shown in Exhibit 21.

	Journal				
			Post.		
Date	**Item**		**Ref.**	**Debit**	**Credit**
	Closing Entries				
20Y8					
Dec. 31	Inventory		115	62,150	
	Estimated Returns Inventory		116	5,000	
	Sales		410	708,255	
	Purchases Returns and Allowances		511	9,100	
	Purchases Discounts		512	2,525	
	Rent Revenue		610	600	
	Inventory		115		59,700
	Purchases		510		521,980
	Freight In		513		17,400
	Sales Salaries Expense		520		53,430
	Advertising Expense		521		10,860
	Depreciation Expense—Store Equipment		522		3,100
	Delivery Expense		523		2,800
	Miscellaneous Selling Expense		529		630
	Office Salaries Expense		530		21,020
	Rent Expense		531		8,100
	Depreciation Expense—Office Equipment		532		2,490
	Insurance Expense		533		1,910
	Office Supplies Expense		534		610
	Miscellaneous Administrative Expense		539		760
	Interest Expense		710		2,440
	Retained Earnings		311		80,400
31	Retained Earnings		311	18,000	
	Dividends		312		18,000

Exhibit 21

Closing Entries for Periodic Inventory System

In the first closing entry, Inventory is debited for $62,150. This is the ending physical inventory count on December 31, 20Y8. In addition, the cost of the estimated merchandise returns from 20Y8 sales is debited to Estimated Returns Inventory for $5,000. Inventory is credited for its January 1, 20Y8, balance of $59,700. In this way, the closing entries reflect the effects of the beginning and ending inventory in determining the cost of goods sold, as shown in Exhibit 20. After the closing entries are posted, inventory will have a balance of $62,150 and Estimated Returns Inventory will have a balance of $5,300, which are the amounts reported on the December 31, 20Y8, balance sheet.

In Exhibit 21, the periodic inventory accounts are highlighted. Under the perpetual inventory system, the highlighted periodic inventory accounts are replaced by the cost of goods sold account.

Let's Review

Chapter Summary

1. Retail businesses purchase merchandise for selling to customers. On a retail business's income statement, revenue from selling merchandise is reported as sales. The cost of the goods sold is subtracted from sales to arrive at gross profit. The operating expenses are subtracted from gross profit to arrive at operating income. Inventory, which is merchandise not sold, is reported as a current asset on the balance sheet. The chart of accounts for a retail business (NetSolutions) is shown in Exhibit 2.

2. Purchases of merchandise for cash or on account are recorded as inventory. Discounts for early payment of purchases on account are purchases discounts. Purchases of inventory subject to purchases discounts are recorded net of the discount. Price adjustments or returned merchandise are purchases returns. Price adjustments or returned merchandise are recorded net of any purchase discount.

   Sales of merchandise for cash or on account are recorded as sales. The cost of goods sold and the reduction in inventory are also recorded at the time of sale.

   A seller may grant customers a variety of discounts, called customer discounts. A sales discount encourages customers to pay their invoices early. Sales subject to a sales discount are recorded net of the discount.

   A seller may pay a customer a refund or grant a price allowance for returned or damaged merchandise, called customer returns and allowances. When a customer doesn't return merchandise but is granted an allowance, Customer Refunds Payable is debited and either Cash, if the customer has already paid for the merchandise, or Accounts Receivable is credited. When merchandise is returned for a refund, Customer Refunds Payable is debited and Cash is credited for the amount of the refund. The returned merchandise is recorded as a debit to Inventory and a credit to Estimated Returns Inventory.

   When merchandise is shipped FOB shipping point, the buyer pays the freight and debits Inventory. When merchandise is shipped FOB destination, the seller pays the freight and debits Delivery Expense or Freight Out.

   Inventory transactions can be summarized in T account form as shown in Exhibit 9. Each merchandising transaction affects a buyer and a seller. The liability for sales tax is incurred when the sale is made and is recorded by the seller as a credit to the sales tax payable account. Trade discounts are discounts off the list price of merchandise.

3. At the end of the accounting period, a retail business must record several adjusting entries that differ from those of a service business. An adjusting entry to reconcile the physical inventory and the balance of the perpetual inventory account is made. The normal adjusting entry for when the inventory account is greater than the physical inventory, called inventory shrinkage, is to debit Cost of Goods Sold and credit Inventory. A seller must also record two adjusting entries for expected returns and allowances. The first adjusting entry debits Sales and credits Customer Refunds Payable. The second entry debits Estimated Returns Inventory and credits Cost of Goods Sold.

4. The multiple-step income statement of a retailer reports sales. The cost of the goods sold is subtracted from sales to determine the gross profit. Operating income is determined by subtracting selling and administrative expenses from gross profit. Net income is determined by adding or subtracting the net of other revenue and expense. The income statement may also be reported in a single-step form. The statement of stockholders' equity is similar to that for a service business. The balance sheet reports inventory and estimated returns inventory as current assets. Customer refunds payable is reported as a current liability. The closing entries for a retail business are similar to those for a service business except that Cost of Goods Sold is also closed.

5. The asset turnover ratio measures how effectively a business is using its assets to generate sales. A high ratio indicates an effective use of assets. The asset turnover ratio is computed by dividing sales by average total assets.

Key Terms

accounts payable subsidiary ledger (237)

accounts receivable subsidiary ledger (237)

administrative expenses (general expenses) (255)

asset turnover ratio (259)

cash refund (244)

controlling account (237)

cost of goods sold (235)

credit memorandum (credit memo) (244)

credit period (238)

credit terms (238)

customer allowance (244)

customer discounts (243)

Customer Refunds Payable (244)

debit memorandum (debit memo) (240)

Estimated Returns Inventory (245)

FOB (free on board) destination (247)

FOB (free on board) shipping point (247)

Practice

Multiple-Choice Questions

1. If merchandise purchased on account is returned, the buyer may inform the seller of the details by issuing a(n):
   a. debit memo.
   b. credit memo.
   c. invoice.
   d. bill.

2. If merchandise is sold on account to a customer for $1,000, terms FOB shipping point, 1/10, n/30, and the seller prepays $50 in freight, the amount of the discount for early payment would be:
   a. $0.
   b. $5.00.
   c. $10.00.
   d. $10.50.

3. The income statement in which the total of all expenses is deducted from the total of all revenues is termed the:
   a. multiple-step form.
   b. single-step form.
   c. account form.
   d. report form.

4. On a multiple-step income statement, the excess of sales over the cost of goods sold is called:
   a. operating income.
   b. income from operations.
   c. gross profit.
   d. net income.

5. Which of the following expenses would normally be classified as other expense on a multiple-step income statement?
   a. Depreciation expense—office equipment
   b. Sales salaries expense
   c. Insurance expense
   d. Interest expense

Answers provided after Problem. Need more practice? Find additional multiple-choice questions, exercises, and problems in CengageNOWv2.

Exercises

1. Gross profit
Obj. 1

During the current year, merchandise is sold for $615,000 cash and $4,110,000 on account. The cost of the goods sold is $2,835,000. What is the amount of the gross profit?

2. Purchases transactions
Obj. 2

Halibut Company purchased merchandise on account from a supplier for $18,600, terms 2/10, n/30. Halibut returned merchandise with an invoice amount of $5,000 and received full credit.

a. If Halibut Company pays the invoice within the discount period, what is the amount of cash required for the payment?

b. What account is credited by Halibut Company to record the return?

3. Sales transactions
Obj. 2

Journalize the following merchandise transactions:

a. Sold merchandise on account, $72,500 with terms 2/10, n/30. The cost of the goods sold was $43,500.
b. Received payment less the discount.
c. Refunded $1,000 to customer for defective merchandise that was not returned.

4. Freight terms
Obj. 2

Determine the amount to be paid in full settlement of each of two invoices, (a) and (b), assuming that credit for returns and allowances was received prior to payment and that all invoices were paid within the discount period.

	Merchandise	Freight Paid by Seller	Freight Terms	Returns and Allowances
a.	$ 90,000	$1,000	FOB shipping point, 1/10, n/30	$15,000
b.	110,000	1,575	FOB destination, 2/10, n/30	8,500

5. Transactions for buyer and seller
Obj. 2

Sather Co. sold merchandise to Boone Co. on account, $31,800, terms 2/15, n/30. The cost of the goods sold is $19,000. Journalize the entries for Sather Co. and Boone Co. for the sale, purchase, and payment of amount due.

6. Adjusting entries
Obj. 3

Castle Furnishings Company uses a perpetual inventory system. Journalize the November 30 adjusting entries based upon the following:

a. The inventory account has a balance of $675,400, while physical inventory indicates that $663,800 of merchandise is on hand. Assume any shrinkage is a normal amount.
b. Sales returns of $40,000 and merchandise returns of $15,000 are estimated for the current year's sales.

7. Asset turnover ratio
Obj. 5

Financial statement data for the years ended December 31, 20Y7 and 20Y6, for Latchkey Company follow:

	20Y7	20Y6
Sales	$1,734,000	$1,645,000
Total assets:		
Beginning of year	480,000	460,000
End of year	540,000	480,000

a. Determine the asset turnover ratio for 20Y7 and 20Y6. Round to one decimal place.
b. ▬▬▬▬▬ Is the change in the asset turnover from 20Y6 to 20Y7 favorable or unfavorable?

Answers provided after Problem. Need more practice? Find additional multiple-choice questions, exercises, and problems in CengageNOWv2.

Problem

The following transactions were completed by Montrose Company during May of the current year. Montrose uses a perpetual inventory system.

May 3. Purchased merchandise on account from Floyd Co., $4,000, terms FOB shipping point, 2/10, n/30, with pre-paid freight of $120 added to the invoice.

5. Purchased merchandise on account from Kramer Co., $8,500, terms FOB destination, 1/10, n/30.

6. Sold merchandise on account to C. F. Howell Co., list price $4,000, trade discount 30%, terms 2/10, n/30. The cost of the goods sold was $1,125.

8. Purchased office supplies for cash, $150.

10. Returned merchandise purchased on May 5 from Kramer Co., with an invoice amount of $1,300.

13. Paid Floyd Co. on account for purchase of May 3.

14. Purchased merchandise for cash, $10,500.

15. Paid Kramer Co. on account for purchase of May 5, less return of May 10.

May 16. Received cash on account from sale of May 6 to C. F. Howell Co.

19. Sold merchandise on MasterCard credit cards, $2,450. The cost of the goods sold was $980.

22. Sold merchandise for cash to Comer Co., $3,480. The cost of the goods sold was $1,400.

24. Sold merchandise on account to Smith Co., $4,350. The cost of the goods sold was $1,750.

25. Refunded Comer Co. $1,480 for returned merchandise from sale on May 22. The cost of the returned merchandise was $600.

31. Paid a service processing fee of $140 for MasterCard sales.

Instructions

1. Journalize the preceding transactions.

2. Journalize the adjusting entry for inventory shrinkage, $3,750.

3. Journalize the adjusting entries for estimated customer refunds and returns. Assume that sales of $3,000 are estimated to be refunded and inventory costing $1,800 is estimated to be returned.

Need more practice? Find additional multiple-choice questions, exercises, and problems in CengageNOWv2.

Answers

Multiple-Choice Questions

1. **a** A debit memo (answer a), issued by the buyer, indicates the amount the buyer proposes to debit to the accounts payable account. A credit memo (answer b), issued by the seller, indicates the amount the seller proposes to credit to the accounts receivable account. An invoice (answer c) or a bill (answer d), issued by the seller, indicates the amount and terms of the sale.

2. **c** The amount of discount for early payment is $10 (answer c), or 1% of $1,000. Although the $50 of freight paid by the seller is debited to the customer's account, the customer is not entitled to a discount on that amount.

3. **b** The single-step form of income statement (answer b) is so named because the total of all expenses is deducted in one step from the total of all revenues. The multiple-step form (answer a) includes numerous sections and subsections with several subtotals. The account form (answer c) and the report form (answer d) are two common forms of the balance sheet.

4. **c** Gross profit (answer c) is the excess of sales over the cost of goods sold. Operating income (answer a) or income from operations (answer b) is the excess of gross profit over operating expenses. Net income (answer d) is the final figure on the income statement after all revenues and expenses have been reported.

5. **d** Expenses such as interest expense (answer d) that cannot be associated directly with operations are identified as other expense or nonoperating expense. Depreciation expense— office equipment (answer a) is an administrative expense. Sales salaries expense (answer b) is a selling expense. Insurance expense (answer c) is a mixed expense with elements of both selling expense and administrative expense. For small businesses, insurance expense is usually reported as an administrative expense.

Exercises

1. $1,890,000 ($615,000 + $4,110,000 − $2,835,000)
2. a. $13,328. Purchase of $18,228 [$18,600 − ($18,600 × 2%)] less the return of $4,900 [$5,000 − ($5,000 × 2%)]
   b. Inventory

3. a.

Accounts Receivable	71,050	
Sales		71,050
[$72,500 − ($72,500 × 2%)].		

Cost of Goods Sold	43,500	
Inventory		43,500

b.

Cash	71,050	
Accounts Receivable		71,050

c.

Customer Refunds Payable	1,000	
Cash		1,000

4. a. $75,250. Purchase of $89,100 [$90,000 ($90,000 × 1%)] less return of $14,850 [$15,000 − ($15,000 × 1%)] plus $1,000 of shipping

   b. $99,470. Purchase of $107,800 [$110,000 − ($110,000 × 2%)] less return of $8,330 [$8,500 − ($8,500 × 2%)]

5.
Sather Co. journal entries:

Accounts Receivable—Boone Co.	31,164	
Sales		31,164
[$31,800 − ($31,800 × 2%)].		

Cost of Goods Sold	19,000	
Inventory		19,000

Cash	31,164	
Accounts Receivable—Boone Co.		31,164

Boone Co. journal entries:

Inventory [$31,800 − ($31,800 × 2%)]	31,164	
Accounts Payable—Sather Co.		31,164

Accounts Payable—Sather Co.	31,164	
Cash		31,164

6. a.

Nov.	30 Cost of Goods Sold	11,600	
	Inventory		11,600
	($675,400 − $663,800).		

   b.

Sales	40,000	
Customer Refunds Payable		40,000

Estimated Returns Inventory	15,000	
Cost of Goods Sold		15,000

7. a.

	20Y7	20Y6
Asset turnover	3.4	3.5
	{$1,734,000 ÷ [($480,000 + $540,000) ÷ 2]}	{$1,645,000 ÷ [($460,000 + $480,000) ÷ 2]}

   b. The decrease from 3.5 to 3.4 indicates an unfavorable change in using assets to generate sales.

Need more help? Watch step-by-step videos of how to compute answers to these Exercises in CengageNOWv2.

Problem

1.	May 3	Inventory [$4,000 − ($4,000 × 2%)] + $120	4,040	
		Accounts Payable—Floyd Co.		4,040
	5	Inventory [$8,500 − ($8,500 × 1%)]	8,415	
		Accounts Payable—Kramer Co.		8,415
	6	Accounts Receivable—C. F. Howell Co.	2,744	
		Sales		2,744
		{[$4,000 − (30% × $4,000)] = $2,800; [$2,800 − ($2,800 × 2%)] = $2,744}.		
	6	Cost of Goods Sold	1,125	
		Inventory		1,125
	8	Office Supplies	150	
		Cash		150
	10	Accounts Payable—Kramer Co. [$1,300 − ($1,300 × 1%)]	1,287	
		Inventory		1,287
	13	Accounts Payable—Floyd Co.	4,040	
		Cash		4,040
	14	Inventory	10,500	
		Cash		10,500
	15	Accounts Payable—Kramer Co. ($8,415 − $1,287)	7,128	
		Cash		7,128
	16	Cash	2,744	
		Accounts Receivable—C. F. Howell Co.		2,744
	19	Cash	2,450	
		Sales		2,450
	19	Cost of Goods Sold	980	
		Inventory		980
	22	Cash	3,480	
		Sales		3,480
	22	Cost of Goods Sold	1,400	
		Inventory		1,400
	24	Accounts Receivable—Smith Co.	4,350	
		Sales		4,350
	24	Cost of Goods Sold	1,750	
		Inventory		1,750
	25	Customer Refunds Payable	1,480	
		Cash		1,480
	25	Inventory	600	
		Estimated Returns Inventory		600
	31	Credit Card Expense	140	
		Cash		140
2.	May 31	Cost of Goods Sold	3,750	
		Inventory		3,750
3.	May 31	Sales	3,000	
		Customer Refunds Payable		3,000
	31	Estimated Returns Inventory	1,800	
		Cost of Goods Sold		1,800

Discussion Questions

1. What distinguishes a retail business from a service business?

2. Can a business earn a gross profit but incur a net loss? Explain.

3. The credit period during which the buyer of merchandise is allowed to pay usually begins with what date?

4. What is the meaning of (a) 1/15, n/60; (b) n/30; (c) n/eom?

5. How are sales to customers using MasterCard and VISA recorded?

6. What is the nature of (a) a credit memo issued by the seller of merchandise, (b) a debit memo issued by the buyer of merchandise?

7. Who is responsible for freight when the terms of sale are (a) FOB shipping point, (b) FOB destination?

8. Name three accounts that would normally appear in the chart of accounts of a retail business but would not appear in the chart of accounts of a service business.

9. Audio Outfitter Inc., which uses a perpetual inventory system, experienced a normal inventory shrinkage of $13,675. What accounts would be debited and credited to record the adjustment for the inventory shrinkage at the end of the accounting period?

10. Assume that Audio Outfitter Inc. in Discussion Question 9 experienced an abnormal inventory shrinkage of $98,600. Audio Outfitter has decided to record the abnormal inventory shrinkage so that it would be separately disclosed on the income statement. What account would be debited for the abnormal inventory shrinkage?

Basic Exercises

SHOW ME HOW

BE 5-1   Gross profit   Obj. 1

During the current year, merchandise is sold for $95,500 cash and $1,315,000 on account. The cost of the goods sold is $848,500. What is the amount of the gross profit?

SHOW ME HOW

BE 5-2   Purchases transactions   Obj. 2

Elkhorn Company purchased merchandise on account from Springhill Company for $42,000, terms 2/10, n/30. Elkhorn returned merchandise with an invoice amount of $8,000 and received full credit.

a. If Elkhorn Company pays the invoice within the discount period, what is the amount of cash required for the payment?

b. What account is debited by Elkhorn Company to record the return?

BE 5-3   Sales transactions   Obj. 2

Journalize the following merchandise transactions:

a. Sold merchandise on account, $18,000 with terms 1/10, n/30. The cost of the goods sold was $10,800.

b. Received payment less the discount.

c. Refunded $600 to customer for defective merchandise that was not returned.

SHOW ME HOW

BE 5-4   Freight terms   Obj. 2

Determine the amount to be paid in full settlement of each of two invoices, (a) and (b), assuming that credit for returns and allowances was received prior to payment and that all invoices were paid within the discount period.

	Merchandise (Invoice Amount)	Freight Paid by Seller	Freight Terms	Returns and Allowances (Invoice Amount)
a.	$24,000	$300	FOB destination, 1/10, n/30	$2,000
b.	31,500	250	FOB shipping point, 2/10, n/30	2,500

BE 5-5 Transactions for buyer and seller
Obj. 2

Shore Co. sold merchandise to Blue Star Co. on account, $112,000, terms FOB shipping point, 2/10, n/30. The cost of the goods sold is $67,200. Shore paid freight of $1,800. Journalize the entries for Shore and Blue Star for the sale, purchase, and payment of amount due.

BE 5-6 Adjusting entries
Obj. 3

Hahn Flooring Company uses a perpetual inventory system. Journalize the December 31 adjusting entries based upon the following:

a. The inventory account has a balance of $1,333,150, while physical inventory indicates that $1,309,900 of merchandise is on hand. Assume any shrinkage is a normal amount.

b. Sales returns of $125,000 and merchandise returns of $80,000 are estimated for the current year's sales.

BE 5-7 Asset turnover ratio
Obj. 5

Financial statement data for years ended December 31, 20Y3 and 20Y2, for Edison Company follow:

	20Y3	20Y2
Sales	$1,884,000	$1,562,000
Total assets:		
Beginning of year	770,000	650,000
End of year	800,000	770,000

a. Determine the asset turnover ratio for 20Y3 and 20Y2.

b. ➤ Is the change in the asset turnover ratio from 20Y2 to 20Y3 favorable or unfavorable?

Exercises

EX 5-1 Determining gross profit
Obj. 1

During the current year, merchandise is sold for $8,100,000. The cost of the goods sold is $4,698,000.

a. What is the amount of the gross profit?

b. Compute the gross profit percentage (gross profit divided by sales).

c. ➤ Will the income statement always report an operating income? Explain.

EX 5-2 Determining cost of goods sold
Obj. 1

For a recent year, **Best Buy (BBY)** reported sales of $39,528 million. Its gross profit was $9,191 million. What was the amount of Best Buy's cost of goods sold?

EX 5-3 Chart of accounts

Obj. 2

Monet Paints Co. is a newly organized retail business with a list of accounts arranged in alphabetical order, as follows:

Accounts Payable	Land
Accounts Receivable	Miscellaneous Administrative
Accumulated Depreciation—Office Equipment	Expense
Accumulated Depreciation—Store Equipment	Miscellaneous Selling Expense
Advertising Expense	Notes Payable
Cash	Office Equipment
Common Stock	Office Salaries Expense
Cost of Goods Sold	Office Supplies
Customer Refunds Payable	Office Supplies Expense
Delivery Expense	Prepaid Insurance
Depreciation Expense—Office Equipment	Rent Expense
Depreciation Expense—Store Equipment	Retained Earnings
Dividends	Salaries Payable
Estimated Returns Inventory	Sales
Insurance Expense	Sales Salaries Expense
Interest Expense	Store Equipment
Interest Revenue	Store Supplies
Inventory	Store Supplies Expense

Construct a chart of accounts, assigning account numbers and arranging the accounts in balance sheet and income statement order, as illustrated in Exhibit 2. Each account number is three digits: the first digit is to indicate the major classification (1 for assets, and so on); the second digit is to indicate the subclassification (11 for current assets, and so on); and the third digit is to identify the specific account (110 for Cash, 112 for Accounts Receivable, 114 for Inventory, 115 for Estimated Returns Inventory, and so on).

SHOW ME HOW

EX 5-4 Purchase-related transactions

Obj. 2

The Stationery Company purchased merchandise on account from a supplier for $14,500, terms 2/10, n/30. The Stationery Company returned merchandise with an invoice amount of $3,500 and received full credit.

a. What is the amount of cash required for the payment?

b. Under a perpetual inventory system, what account is credited by The Stationery Company to record the return?

EX 5-5 Purchase-related transactions

Obj. 2

A retailer is considering the purchase of 1,000 units of a specific item from either of two suppliers. Their offers are as follows:

Supplier One: $34.80 a unit, 1/10, n/30, no charge for freight.

Supplier Two: $35.00 a unit, 2/10, n/30, plus freight of $200.

Which of the two offers, Supplier One or Supplier Two, yields the lower price?

EX 5-6 Purchase-related transactions

Obj. 2

The debits and credits from four related transactions, (1) through (4), are presented in the following T accounts. Assume that the freight terms were FOB shipping point and that the credit terms were 1/10, n/30.

Cash				Accounts Payable			
		(2)	150	(3)	1,980	(1)	13,860
		(4)	11,880	(4)	11,880		

Inventory			
(1)	13,860	(3)	1,980
(2)	150		

a. ⟹ Describe each transaction.

b. Determine the invoice amount of the merchandise that was returned in (3).

✔ (c) Cash, cr. $39,690

SHOW ME HOW

EX 5-7 Purchase-related transactions

Obj. 2

Stylon Co., a women's clothing store, purchased $48,000 of merchandise from a supplier on account, terms FOB destination, 2/10, n/30. Stylon returned merchandise with an invoice amount of $7,500, receiving a credit memo. Journalize Stylon's entries to record (a) the purchase, (b) the merchandise return, (c) the payment within the discount period of 10 days, and (d) the payment beyond the discount period of 10 days.

✔ (e) Cash, dr. $3,910

SHOW ME HOW

EX 5-8 Purchase-related transactions

Obj. 2

Journalize entries for the following related transactions of Lilly Heating & Air Company:

a. Purchased $36,000 of merchandise from Schell Co. on account, terms 1/10, n/30.

b. Paid the amount owed on the invoice within the discount period.

c. Discovered that merchandise with an invoice amount of $9,000 purchased in (a) was defective and returned items, receiving credit.

d. Purchased $5,000 of merchandise from Schell Co. on account, terms n/30.

e. Received a refund from Schell Co. for return in (c) less the purchase in (d).

SHOW ME HOW

EX 5-9 Sales-related transactions, including the use of credit cards

Obj. 2

Journalize the entries for the following transactions:

a. Sold merchandise for cash, $25,000. The cost of the goods sold was $17,500.

b. Sold merchandise on account, $98,000. The cost of the goods sold was $58,800.

c. Sold merchandise to customers who used MasterCard and VISA, $475,000. The cost of the goods sold was $280,000.

d. Sold merchandise to customers who used American Express, $63,000. The cost of the goods sold was $39,000.

e. Received an invoice from National Clearing House Credit Co. for $13,450 representing a service fee paid for processing MasterCard, VISA, and American Express sales.

EX 5-10 Customer refund

Obj. 2

Senger Company sold merchandise of $15,500, terms 2/10, n/30, to Burris Inc. on April 23. Burris paid Senger for the merchandise on May 2. On May 12, Senger paid Burris $650 for costs incurred by Burris to repair defective merchandise. (a) Journalize the entry by Senger Company to record the customer refund to Burris Inc. (b) Assume that instead of paying Burris cash, Senger issued a credit memo to Burris to be used against Burris's outstanding account receivable balance. Journalize the entry by Senger Company to record the issuance of the credit memo.

EX 5-11 Customer return and refund

Obj. 2

On December 28, 20Y3, Silverman Enterprises sold $18,500 of merchandise to Beasley Co. with terms 2/10, n/30. The cost of the goods sold was $11,200. On December 31, 20Y3, Silverman prepared its adjusting entries, yearly financial statements, and closing entries. On January 3, 20Y4, Silverman Enterprises issued Beasley Co. a credit memo for returned merchandise. The invoice amount of the returned merchandise was $4,000 and the merchandise originally cost Silverman Enterprises $2,350. (a) Journalize the entries by Silverman Enterprises to record the December 28, 20Y3, sale. (b) Journalize the entries by Silverman Enterprises to record the merchandise returned by Beasley Co. on January 3, 20Y4. (c) Journalize the entry to record the receipt of the amount due by Beasley Co. on January 7, 20Y4.

SHOW ME HOW

EX 5-12 Sales-related transactions

Obj. 2

After the amount due on a sale of $28,000, terms 2/10, n/eom, is received from a customer within the discount period, the seller consents to the return of the entire shipment for a cash refund. The cost of the merchandise returned is $16,800. (a) What is the amount of the refund owed to the customer? (b) Journalize the entries made by the seller to record the return and the refund.

EX 5-13 Sales-related transactions

Obj. 2

The debits and credits for five related transactions, (1) through (5), are presented in the following T accounts. Assume the credit terms were 2/10, n/30.

Cash					Sales		
(5)	10,290					(1)	11,760

Accounts Receivable					Cost of Goods Sold		
(1)	11,760	(3)	1,470		(2)	7,000	
		(5)	10,290				

Inventory			
(4)	900	(2)	7,000

Estimated Returns Inventory			
		(4)	900

Customer Refunds Payable			
(3)	1,470		

a. ➡ Describe each transaction.

b. What was the invoice amount of the merchandise that was returned?

SHOW ME HOW

EX 5-14 Sales-related transactions

Obj. 2

Sayers Co. sold merchandise on account to a customer for $80,000 terms 2/10, n/30. The cost of the goods sold was $58,000. Journalize Sayers' entries to record (a) the sale, (b) the receipt of payment within the discount period, and (c) the receipt of payment beyond the discount period of 10 days.

✔ a. $30,400

EX 5-15 Determining amounts to be paid on invoices

Obj. 2

Determine the amount to be paid in full settlement of each of the following invoices, assuming that credit for returns and allowances was received prior to payment and that all invoices were paid within the discount period:

SHOW ME HOW

	Merchandise Invoice Amount	Freight Paid by Seller		Customer Returns and Allowances
a.	$32,000	—	FOB destination, n/30	$1,600
b.	12,800	$300	FOB shipping point, 2/10, n/30	2,500
c.	21,000	—	FOB shipping point, 1/10, n/30	4,000
d.	9,000	175	FOB shipping point, 2/10, n/30	1,000
e.	77,400	—	FOB destination, 1/10, n/30	—

EX 5-16 Sales-related transactions

Obj. 2

Showcase Co., a furniture wholesaler, sells merchandise to Balboa Co. on account, $254,500, terms n/30. The cost of the goods sold is $152,700. Showcase Co. issues a credit memo for $30,000 for merchandise returned prior to Balboa Co. paying the original invoice. The cost of the merchandise returned is $17,500. Journalize Showcase Co.'s entries for (a) the sale, including the cost of the goods sold, (b) the credit memo, including the cost of the returned merchandise, and (c) the receipt of the check for the amount due from Balboa Co.

SHOW ME HOW

EX 5-17 Purchase-related transactions

Obj. 2

Based on the data presented in Exercise 5-16, journalize Balboa Co.'s entries for (a) the purchase, (b) the return of the merchandise for credit, and (c) the payment of the invoice.

EX 5-18 Sales tax

Obj. 2

✔ c. $38,880

A sale of merchandise on account for $36,000 is subject to an 8% sales tax. (a) Should the sales tax be recorded at the time of sale or when payment is received? (b) What is the amount credited to Sales? (c) What is the amount debited to Accounts Receivable? (d) What is the account to which the $2,880 ($36,000 × 8%) is credited?

SHOW ME HOW

EX 5-19 Sales tax transactions
Obj. 2

Journalize the entries to record the following selected transactions:

a. Sold $640,000 of merchandise on account, subject to a sales tax of 7%. The cost of the goods sold was $385,000.

b. Paid $61,750 to the state sales tax department for taxes collected.

EX 5-20 Normal balances of accounts for retail business
Obj. 2

What is the normal balance of the following accounts: (a) Cost of Goods Sold, (b) Customer Refunds Payable, (c) Delivery Expense, (d) Estimated Returns Inventory, (e) Inventory, (f) Sales, (g) Sales Tax Payable.

EX 5-21 Income statement and accounts for retail business
Obj. 4

For the fiscal year, sales were $46,680,000 and the cost of goods sold was $28,000,000.

a. What was the amount of gross profit?

b. If total operating expenses were $5,000,000, could you determine net income?

c. Is Customer Refunds Payable an asset, liability, or stockholders' equity account, and what is its normal balance?

d. Is Estimated Returns Inventory an asset, liability, or stockholders' equity account, and what is its normal balance?

EX 5-22 Adjusting entry for inventory shrinkage
Obj. 3

Omega Tire Co.'s perpetual inventory records indicate that $3,145,000 of merchandise should be on hand on August 31, 20Y4. The physical inventory indicates that $3,113,500 of merchandise is actually on hand. Journalize the adjusting entry for the inventory shrinkage for Omega Tire Co. for the fiscal year ended August 31, 20Y4.

EX 5-23 Adjusting entry for customer refunds, allowances, and returns
Obj. 3

Scott Company had sales of $12,350,000 and related cost of goods sold of $7,500,000 for the year ending December 31, 20Y8. Scott provides customers a refund for any returned or damaged merchandise. Scott Company estimates that customers will request refunds for 0.8% of sales and estimates that merchandise costing $48,000 will be returned in 20Y9. Journalize the adjusting entries on December 31, 20Y8, to record the expected customer returns.

EX 5-24 Adjusting entry for customer refunds, allowances, and returns
Obj. 3

Statz Company had sales of $1,800,000 and related cost of goods sold of $1,150,000 for its first year of operations ending December 31, 20Y1. Statz provides customers a refund for any returned or damaged merchandise. At the end of 20Y1, Statz Company estimates that customers will request refunds for 1.5% of sales and estimates that merchandise costing $16,000 will be returned. Assume that on February 3, 20Y2, Buck Co. returned merchandise with an invoice amount of $5,000 for a cash refund. The returned merchandise originally cost Statz Company $3,100. (a) Journalize the adjusting entries on December 31, 20Y1, to record the expected customer returns. (b) Journalize the entries to record the returned merchandise and cash refund to Buck Co. on February 3, 20Y2.

EX 5-25 Income statement for retail business
Obj. 4

The following expenses were incurred by a retail business during the year. In which expense section of the income statement should each be reported: (a) selling, (b) administrative, or (c) other?

1. Advertising expense
2. Depreciation expense on store equipment
3. Insurance expense on office equipment
4. Interest expense on notes payable
5. Rent expense on office building
6. Salaries of office personnel
7. Salary of sales manager
8. Sales supplies used

SHOW ME HOW

EX 5-26   Determining amounts for items omitted from income statement   Obj. 4

One item is omitted in each of the following four lists of income statement data. Determine the amounts of the missing items, identifying them by letter.

	Chase Company	Jessup Inc.	Osterman Company	Snyder Co.
Sales	$735,000	(b)	$8,220,000	(d)
Cost of goods sold	(a)	$157,850	(c)	$44,500
Gross profit	110,000	42,150	2,300,000	15,500

✔ a. Net income:
$1,720,000

SHOW ME HOW   EXCEL TEMPLATE

EX 5-27   Multiple-step income statement   Obj. 4

On March 31, 20Y9, the balances of the accounts appearing in the ledger of Royal Furnishings Company, a furniture store, are as follows:

Accounts Receivable	$ 170,000	Inventory	$ 980,000
Accumulated Depreciation—Building	750,000	Notes Payable	250,000
Administrative Expenses	435,000	Office Supplies	20,000
Building	3,500,000	Retained Earnings	1,987,000
Cash	80,000	Salaries Payable	8,000
Common Stock	300,000	Sales	8,245,000
Cost of Goods Sold	5,500,000	Selling Expenses	575,000
Dividends	175,000	Store Supplies	90,000
Interest Expense	15,000		

a. Prepare a multiple-step income statement for the fiscal year ended March 31, 20Y9.

b. ⬤▬▬▶ Compare the major advantages and disadvantages of the multiple and single-step forms of income statements.

EX 5-28   Multiple-step income statement   Obj. 4

✔ b. Net income:
$730,000

The following income statement for Curbstone Company was prepared for the year ended August 31, 20Y5:

Curbstone Company
Income Statement
For the Year Ended August 31, 20Y5

Sales		$ 8,595,000
Cost of goods sold..		(6,110,000)
Operating income..		$ 2,485,000
Expenses:		
Selling expenses......................................	$800,000	
Administrative expenses	575,000	
Delivery expense	425,000	
Total expenses		(1,800,000)
		$ 685,000
Other expense:		
Interest revenue.......................................		45,000
Gross profit		$ 640,000

a. Identify the errors in the income statement.

b. Prepare a corrected income statement.

EX 5-29   Single-step income statement   Obj. 4

✔ Net income:
$1,277,500

Summary operating data for Custom Wire & Tubing Company during the year ended April 30, 20Y2, are as follows: cost of goods sold, $6,100,000; administrative expenses, $740,000; interest expense, $25,000; rent revenue, $60,000; sales, $9,332,500; and selling expenses, $1,250,000. Prepare a single-step income statement.

SHOW ME HOW

EX 5-30 Closing the accounts of a retail business
Obj. 4

From the following list, identify the accounts that should be closed at the end of the fiscal year under a perpetual inventory system: (a) Accounts Payable, (b) Advertising Expense, (c) Cost of Goods Sold, (d) Office Equipment, (e) Inventory, (f) Sales, (g) Supplies, (h) Supplies Expense, (i) Wages Payable.

EX 5-31 Closing entries; net income
Obj. 4

Based on the data presented in Exercise 5-27, journalize the closing entries.

EX 5-32 Closing entries
Obj. 4

On July 31, the close of the fiscal year, the balances of the accounts appearing in the ledger of Serbian Interiors Company, a furniture retailer, are as follows:

Accumulated Depr.—Building	$365,000	Inventory	$ 115,000
Administrative Expenses	440,000	Notes Payable	100,000
Building	810,000	Retained Earnings	455,000
Cash	78,000	Sales	1,437,000
Common Stock	75,000	Sales Tax Payable	4,500
Cost of Goods Sold	775,000	Selling Expenses	160,000
Dividends	15,000	Store Supplies	16,000
Interest Expense	6,000	Store Supplies Expense	21,500

Prepare the July 31 closing entries for Serbian Interiors Company.

Appendix 1
EX 5-33 Gross method for sales discounts
Obj. 4

Schofield Co. sold merchandise on account to Bernard Retail Inc. for $15,000, terms 2/10, n/30. The cost of the merchandise sold was $8,000. Assuming Schofield Co. uses the gross method of recording sales discounts, journalize the entries to record (a) the sale, (b) the receipt of payment assuming it is made within the discount period, and (c) the receipt of payment assuming it is made beyond the discount period.

Appendix 1
EX 5-34 Gross method for sales discounts
Obj. 4

The following were selected from among the transactions completed by Essex Company during March of the current year:

Mar. 2. Sold merchandise on account to Parsley Co., $32,000, terms 1/10, n/30. The cost of the merchandise sold was $18,500.

8. Sold merchandise on account to Tabor Co., $24,000, terms 2/10, n/30. The cost of the merchandise sold was $14,400.

11. Received payment on account for the sale of March 2 less the discount.

20. Received payment on account for the sale of March 8.

Journalize the March transactions using the gross method of recording sales discounts.

Appendix 1
EX 5-35 Adjusting entry for gross method
Obj. 4

The following data were extracted from the accounting records of Sacajawea Mercantile Co. for the year ended June 30, 20Y4:

	June 30, 20Y4 Balances	
	Debit	Credit
Sales		$10,000,000
Accounts Receivable	$850,000	
Allowance for Sales Discounts		400
Estimated sales discounts that will be taken in fiscal year ending June 30, 20Y4......	$ 7,000	

a. Journalize the June 30, 20Y4, adjusting entry for estimated sales discounts.

b. How would sales and accounts receivable be reported on the financial statements for the year ending June 30, 20Y4?

Appendix 1

EX 5-36   Discount taken in next fiscal year   Obj. 4

Using the data for Sacajawea Mercantile Co. in Exercise 5-35, assume that Mark Bishop pays his June 30, 20Y4, account receivable of $1,500 on July 6, 20Y4, and takes a 2% sales discount. Journalize the entry to record the payment on account from Mark Bishop.

Appendix 1

EX 5-37   Gross and net methods for sales discounts   Obj. 4

The following were selected from among the transactions completed by Strong Retail Group during August of the current year:

Aug. 5. Sold merchandise on account to M. Quinn, $7,500, terms 2/10, n/30. The cost of the merchandise sold was $4,200.

  9. Sold merchandise on account to R. Busch., $4,000, terms 1/10, n/30. The cost of the merchandise sold was $2,100.

  15. Received payment on account for the sale of August 5 less the discount.

  20. Sold merchandise on account to S. Mooney, $6,000, terms n/eom. The cost of the merchandise sold was $3,300.

  25. Received payment on account for the sale of August 9.

  31. Received payment on account for the sale of August 20.

a. Journalize the August transactions using the gross method of recording sales discounts.

b. Journalize the August transactions using the net method of recording sales discounts.

c. What is the total sales for August under each method?

d. Which method of recording sales discounts requires an end-of-period adjusting entry?

Appendix 2

EX 5-38   Rules of debit and credit for periodic inventory accounts

Complete the following table by indicating for (a) through (g) whether the proper answer is debit or credit:

Account	Increase	Decrease	Normal Balance
Purchases	debit	(a)	(b)
Purchases Discounts	credit	(c)	credit
Purchases Returns and Allowances	(d)	(e)	(f)
Freight In	debit	(g)	debit

Appendix 2

EX 5-39   Journal entries using the periodic inventory system

The following selected transactions were completed by Air Systems Company during January of the current year. Air Systems uses the periodic inventory system.

Jan. 2. Purchased $18,200 of merchandise on account, FOB shipping point, terms 2/15, n/30.

  5. Paid freight of $190 on the January 2 purchase.

  6. Returned $2,750 of the merchandise purchased on January 2.

  13. Sold merchandise on account, $37,300, FOB destination, 1/10, n/30. The cost of goods sold was $22,400.

  15. Paid freight of $215 for the merchandise sold on January 13.

  17. Paid for the purchase of January 2 less the return and discount.

  23. Received payment on account for the sale of January 13 less the discount.

Journalize the entries to record the transactions of Air Systems Company.

Appendix 2

EX 5-40   Identify items missing in determining cost of goods sold

For (a) through (e), identify the items designated by X and Y.

a. Purchases − (X + Y) = Net purchases

b. Net purchases + X = Cost of inventory purchased

c. Inventory (beginning) + Cost of inventory purchased = X

d. Inventory available for sale − X = Cost of inventory before estimated returns

e. Cost of goods sold before estimated returns − X = Cost of goods sold

Appendix

EX 5-41 Cost of goods sold and related items

✔ a. Cost of goods sold, $3,540,000

The following data were extracted from the accounting records of Harkins Company for the year ended April 30, 20Y8:

Estimated returns of current year sales	$ 11,600
Inventory, May 1, 20Y7	380,000
Inventory, April 30, 20Y8	415,000
Purchases	3,800,000
Purchases returns and allowances	150,000
Purchases discounts	80,000
Sales	5,850,000
Freight in	16,600

a. Prepare the "Cost of goods sold" section of the income statement for the year ended April 30, 20Y8, using the periodic inventory system.

b. Determine the gross profit to be reported on the income statement for the year ended April 30, 20Y8.

c. ━━━▶ Would gross profit be different if the perpetual inventory system was used instead of the periodic inventory system?

Appendix 2

EX 5-42 Cost of goods sold

Based on the following data, determine the cost of goods sold for November:

Estimated returns of November sales	$ 14,500
Inventory, November 1	28,000
Inventory, November 30	31,500
Purchases	475,000
Purchases returns and allowances	15,000
Purchases discounts	9,000
Freight in	7,000

Appendix 2

EX 5-43 Cost of goods sold

Based on the following data, determine the cost of goods sold for July:

Estimated returns of July sales	$ 34,900
Inventory, July 1	190,850
Inventory, July 31	160,450
Purchases	1,126,000
Purchases returns and allowances	46,000
Purchases discounts	23,000
Freight in	17,500

Appendix 2

EX 5-44 Cost of goods sold

✔ Correct cost of goods sold, $990,000

Identify the errors in the following schedule of the cost of goods sold for the year ended May 31, 20Y5:

Cost of goods sold:		
Inventory, May 31, 20Y5		$ 105,000
Cost of merchandise purchased:		
Purchases	$ 1,110,000	
Purchases returns and allowances	55,000	
Purchases discounts.....................................	30,000	
Freight in...	(22,000)	
Total cost of merchandise purchased.................		1,173,000
Inventory available for sale		$ 1,278,000
Inventory, June 1, 20Y4.......................................		(91,300)
Cost of goods sold before estimated returns		$ 1,186,700
Estimated returns of this year's sales		43,300
Cost of goods sold		$1,230,000

Appendix 2

EX 5-45   Closing entries using periodic inventory system

United Rug Company is a small rug retailer owned and operated by Pat Kirwan. After the accounts have been adjusted on December 31, the following selected account balances were taken from the ledger:

Advertising Expense...	$ 36,000
Depreciation Expense	13,000
Dividends	65,000
Freight In..	17,000
Inventory, December 1...	375,000
Inventory, December 31	460,000
Miscellaneous Expense	9,000
Purchases..	1,760,000
Purchases Discounts..	35,000
Purchases Returns and Allowances	45,000
Salaries Expense	375,000
Sales	2,220,000

The estimated cost of merchandise returns from December sales is $20,000. Journalize the closing entries.

Problems: Series A

PR 5-1A   Purchase-related transactions using perpetual inventory system   **Obj. 2**

The following selected transactions were completed by Betz Company during July of the current year:

July 1. Purchased merchandise from Sabol Imports Co., $20,500, terms FOB destination, n/30.
       3. Purchased merchandise from Saxon Co., $12,000, terms FOB shipping point, 2/10, n/eom. Prepaid freight of $75 was added to the invoice.
       5. Purchased merchandise from Schnee Co., $8,000, terms FOB destination, 2/10, n/30.
       6. Issued debit memo to Schnee Co. for merchandise with an invoice amount of $1,500 returned from purchase on July 5.
      13. Paid Saxon Co. for invoice of July 3.
      14. Paid Schnee Co. for invoice of July 5, less debit memo of July 6.
      19. Purchased merchandise from Southmont Co., $18,900, terms FOB shipping point, n/eom.
      19. Paid freight of $140 on July 19 purchase from Southmont Co.
      20. Purchased merchandise from Stevens Co., $33,000, terms FOB destination, 1/10, n/30.
      30. Paid Stevens Co. for invoice of July 20.
      31. Paid Sabol Imports Co. for invoice of July 1.
      31. Paid Southmont Co. for invoice of July 19.

Instructions

Journalize the entries to record the transactions of Betz Company for July.

SHOW ME HOW   EXCEL TEMPLATE

PR 5-2A   Sales-related transactions using perpetual inventory system   **Obj. 2**

The following selected transactions were completed by Amsterdam Supply Co., which sells office supplies primarily to other businesses and occasionally to retail customers:

Mar. 2. Sold merchandise on account to Equinox Co., $18,900, terms FOB destination, 1/10, n/30. The cost of the goods sold was $13,300.
       3. Sold merchandise for $11,350 plus 6% sales tax to retail cash customers. The cost of the goods sold was $7,000.
       4. Sold merchandise on account to Empire Co., $55,400, terms FOB shipping point, n/eom. The cost of the goods sold was $33,200.
       5. Sold merchandise for $30,000 plus 6% sales tax to retail customers who used MasterCard. The cost of the goods sold was $19,400.
      12. Received check for amount due from Equinox Co. for sale on March 2.

Mar. 14. Sold merchandise to customers who used American Express cards, $13,700. The cost of the goods sold was $8,350.

16. Sold merchandise on account to Targhee Co., $27,500, terms FOB shipping point, 1/10, n/30. The cost of the goods sold was $16,000.

18. Issued credit memo to Targhee Co. for merchandise with an invoice amount of $4,800 returned from sale on March 16. The cost of the merchandise returned was $2,900.

19. Sold merchandise on account to Vista Co., $8,250, terms FOB shipping point, 2/10, n/30. Added $75 to the invoice for prepaid freight. The cost of the goods sold was $5,000.

26. Received check for amount due from Targhee Co. for sale on March 16 less credit memo of March 18.

28. Received check for amount due from Vista Co. for sale of March 19.

31. Received check for amount due from Empire Co. for sale of March 4.

31. Paid Fleetwood Delivery Service $5,600 for merchandise delivered during March to customers under shipping terms of FOB destination.

Apr. 3. Paid City Bank $940 for service fees for handling MasterCard and American Express sales during March.

15. Paid $6,544 to state sales tax division for taxes owed on sales.

Instructions

Journalize the entries to record the transactions of Amsterdam Supply Co.

SHOW ME HOW

PR 5-3A Sales and purchase-related transactions using perpetual inventory system
Obj. 2

The following were selected from among the transactions completed by Babcock Company during November of the current year:

Nov. 3. Purchased merchandise on account from Moonlight Co., list price $85,000, trade discount 25%, terms FOB destination, 2/10, n/30.

4. Sold merchandise for cash, $37,680. The cost of the goods sold was $22,600.

5. Purchased merchandise on account from Papoose Creek Co., $47,500, terms FOB shipping point, 2/10, n/30, with prepaid freight of $810 added to the invoice.

6. Returned merchandise with an invoice amount of $13,500 ($18,000 list price less trade discount of 25%) purchased on November 3 from Moonlight Co.

8. Sold merchandise on account to Quinn Co., $15,600 with terms n/15. The cost of the goods sold was $9,400.

13. Paid Moonlight Co. on account for purchase of November 3, less return of November 6.

14. Sold merchandise on VISA, $236,000. The cost of the goods sold was $140,000.

15. Paid Papoose Creek Co. on account for purchase of November 5.

23. Received cash on account from sale of November 8 to Quinn Co.

24. Sold merchandise on account to Rabel Co., $56,900, terms 1/10, n/30. The cost of the goods sold was $34,000.

28. Paid VISA service fee of $3,540.

30. Paid Quinn Co. a cash refund of $6,000 for returned merchandise from sale of November 8. The cost of the returned merchandise was $3,300.

Instructions

Journalize the transactions.

PR 5-4A Sales and purchase-related transactions for seller and buyer using perpetual inventory system
Obj. 2

The following selected transactions were completed during August between Summit Company and Beartooth Co.:

Aug. 1. Summit Company sold merchandise on account to Beartooth Co., $48,000, terms FOB destination, 2/15, n/eom. The cost of the goods sold was $28,800.

2. Summit Company paid freight of $1,150 for delivery of merchandise sold to Beartooth Co. on August 1.

5. Summit Company sold merchandise on account to Beartooth Co., $66,000, terms FOB shipping point, n/eom. The cost of the goods sold was $40,000.

9. Beartooth Co. paid freight of $2,300 on August 5 purchase from Summit Company.

15. Summit Company sold merchandise on account to Beartooth Co., $58,700, terms FOB shipping point, n/45. Summit paid freight of $1,675, which was added to the invoice. The cost of the goods sold was $35,000.

16. Beartooth Co. paid Summit Company for purchase of August 1.

(Continued)

Aug. 20. Summit Company paid Beartooth Co. a cash refund of $1,000 for defective merchandise purchased on August 1. Beartooth Co. kept the merchandise.

31. Beartooth Co. paid Summit Company on account for purchase of August 5.

31. Summit Company issued Beartooth Co. a credit memo for merchandise with an invoice amount of $4,000 that was returned from the August 15 sale. The cost of the merchandise returned was $2,500.

Instructions

Journalize the August transactions for (1) Summit Company and (2) Beartooth Co.

PR 5-5A   Multiple-step income statement and balance sheet   Obj. 4

✔ 1. Net income
$943,400

EXCEL TEMPLATE

The following selected accounts and their current balances appear in the ledger of Clairemont Co. for the fiscal year ended May 31, 20Y2:

Cash	$ 240,000	Retained Earnings	$ 2,949,100
Accounts Receivable	966,000	Dividends	100,000
Inventory	1,690,000	Sales	11,343,000
Estimated Returns Inventory	22,500	Cost of Goods Sold	7,850,000
Office Supplies	13,500	Sales Salaries Expense	916,000
Prepaid Insurance	8,000	Advertising Expense	550,000
Office Equipment	830,000	Depreciation Expense—	
Accumulated Depreciation—		Store Equipment	140,000
Office Equipment	550,000	Miscellaneous Selling Expense	38,000
Store Equipment	3,600,000	Office Salaries Expense	650,000
Accumulated Depreciation—		Rent Expense	94,000
Store Equipment	1,820,000	Depreciation Expense—	
Accounts Payable	326,000	Office Equipment	50,000
Customer Refunds Payable	40,000	Insurance Expense	48,000
Salaries Payable	41,500	Office Supplies Expense	28,100
Note Payable		Miscellaneous Administrative Exp.	14,500
(final payment due in 6 years)	300,000	Interest Expense	21,000
Common Stock	500,000		

Instructions

1. Prepare a multiple-step income statement.

2. Prepare a statement of stockholders' equity. Additional common stock of $75,000 was issued during the year ended May 31, 20Y2.

3. Prepare a balance sheet, assuming that the current portion of the note payable is $50,000.

4. ➡ Briefly explain how multiple and single-step income statements differ.

PR 5-6A   Single-step income statement and balance sheet   Obj. 4

✔ 3. Total assets:
$5,000,000

EXCEL TEMPLATE

Selected accounts and related amounts for Clairemont Co. for the fiscal year ended May 31, 20Y2, are presented in Problem 5-5A.

Instructions

1. Prepare a single-step income statement in the format shown in Exhibit 13.

2. Prepare a statement of stockholders' equity.

3. Prepare a balance sheet, assuming that the current portion of the note payable is $50,000.

4. Prepare closing entries as of May 31, 20Y2.

Appendix 2
PR 5-7A   Purchase-related transactions using periodic inventory system

Selected transactions for Betz Company during July of the current year are listed in Problem 5-1A.

Instructions

Journalize the entries to record the transactions of Betz Company for July using the periodic inventory system.

Appendix 2
PR 5-8A   Sales and purchase-related transactions using periodic inventory system

Selected transactions for Babcock Company during November of the current year are listed in Problem 5-3A.

Instructions

Journalize the entries to record the transactions of Babcock Company for November using the periodic inventory system.

Appendix 2
PR 5-9A   Sales and purchase-related transactions for buyer and seller using periodic inventory system

Selected transactions during August between Summit Company and Beartooth Co. are listed in Problem 5-4A.

Instructions

Journalize the entries to record the transactions for (1) Summit Company and (2) Beartooth Co., assuming that both companies use the periodic inventory system.

Appendix 2
PR 5-10A   Periodic inventory accounts, multiple-step income statement, closing entries

✔ 2. Net income,
$185,000

EXCEL TEMPLATE

On December 31, 20Y5, the balances of the accounts appearing in the ledger of Wyman Company are as follows:

Cash	$ 13,500	Dividends	$ 25,000
Accounts Receivable	72,000	Sales	3,280,000
Inventory, January 1, 20Y5	257,000	Purchases	2,650,000
Estimated Returns Inventory,		Purchases Returns and Allowances	93,000
January 1, 20Y5	35,000	Purchases Discounts	37,000
Office Supplies	3,000	Freight In	48,000
Prepaid Insurance	4,500	Sales Salaries Expense	300,000
Land	150,000	Advertising Expense	45,000
Store Equipment	270,000	Delivery Expense	9,000
Accumulated Depreciation—		Depreciation Expense—	
Store Equipment	55,900	Store Equipment	6,000
Office Equipment	78,500	Miscellaneous Selling Expense	12,000
Accumulated Depreciation—		Office Salaries Expense	175,000
Office Equipment	16,000	Rent Expense	28,000
Accounts Payable	77,800	Insurance Expense	3,000
Salaries Payable	3,000	Office Supplies Expense	2,000
Customer Refunds Payable	50,000	Depreciation Expense—	
Unearned Rent	8,300	Office Equipment	1,500
Notes Payable	50,000	Miscellaneous Administrative Expense	3,500
Common Stock	150,000	Rent Revenue	7,000
Retained Earnings	365,600	Interest Expense	2,000

Instructions

1. ➡ Does Wyman Company use a periodic or perpetual inventory system? Explain.

2. Prepare a multiple-step income statement for Wyman Company for the year ended December 31, 20Y5. The inventory as of December 31, 20Y5, was $305,000. The estimated cost of customer returns inventory for December 31, 20Y5, is estimated to increase to $40,000.

3. Prepare the closing entries for Wyman Company as of December 31, 20Y5.

4. What would be the net income if the perpetual inventory system had been used?

Problems: Series B

PR 5-1B Purchase-related transactions using perpetual inventory system Obj. 2

The following selected transactions were completed by Niles Co. during March of the current year:

Mar. 1. Purchased merchandise from Haas Co., $43,250, terms FOB shipping point, 2/10, n/eom. Prepaid freight of $650 was added to the invoice.

5. Purchased merchandise from Whitman Co., $19,175, terms FOB destination, n/30.

10. Paid Haas Co. for invoice of March 1.

13. Purchased merchandise from Jost Co., $15,550, terms FOB destination, 2/10, n/30.

14. Issued debit memo to Jost Co. for merchandise with an invoice amount of $3,750 returned from purchase on March 13.

18. Purchased merchandise from Fairhurst Company, $13,560, terms FOB shipping point, n/eom.

18. Paid freight of $140 on March 18 purchase from Fairhurst Company.

19. Purchased merchandise from Bickle Co., $6,500, terms FOB destination, 2/10, n/30.

23. Paid Jost Co. for invoice of March 13, less debit memo of March 14.

29. Paid Bickle Co. for invoice of March 19.

31. Paid Fairhurst Company for invoice of March 18.

31. Paid Whitman Co. for invoice of March 5.

Instructions

Journalize the entries to record the transactions of Niles Co. for March.

SHOW ME HOW EXCEL TEMPLATE

PR 5-2B Sales-related transactions using perpetual inventory system Obj. 2

The following selected transactions were completed by Green Lawn Supplies Co., which sells irrigation supplies primarily to other businesses and occasionally to retail customers:

July 1. Sold merchandise on account to Landscapes Co., $33,450, terms FOB shipping point, n/eom. The cost of the goods sold was $20,000.

2. Sold merchandise for $86,000 plus 8% sales tax to retail cash customers. The cost of the goods sold was $51,600.

5. Sold merchandise on account to Peacock Company, $17,500, terms FOB destination, 1/10, n/30. The cost of the goods sold was $10,000.

8. Sold merchandise for $112,000 plus 8% sales tax to retail customers who used VISA cards. The cost of the goods sold was $67,200.

13. Sold merchandise to customers who used MasterCard cards, $96,000. The cost of the goods sold was $57,600.

14. Sold merchandise on account to Loeb Co., $16,000, terms FOB shipping point, 1/10, n/30. The cost of the goods sold was $9,000.

15. Received check for amount due from Peacock Company for sale on July 5.

16. Issued credit memo to Loeb Co. for merchandise with an invoice amount of $3,000 returned from the sale on July 14. The cost of the merchandise returned was $1,800.

18. Sold merchandise on account to Jennings Company, $11,350, terms FOB shipping point, 2/10, n/30. Paid $475 for freight and added it to the invoice. The cost of the goods sold was $6,800.

24. Received check for amount due from Loeb Co. for sale on July 14 less credit memo of July 16.

28. Received check for amount due from Jennings Company for sale of July 18.

31. Paid Black Lab Delivery Service $8,550 for merchandise delivered during July to customers under shipping terms of FOB destination.

31. Received check for amount due from Landscapes Co. for sale of July 1.

Aug. 3. Paid Hays Federal Bank $3,770 for service fees for handling MasterCard and VISA sales during July.

10. Paid $41,260 to state sales tax division for taxes owed on sales.

Instructions

Journalize the entries to record the transactions of Green Lawn Supplies Co.

SHOW ME HOW

PR 5-3B Sales and purchase-related transactions using perpetual inventory system

Obj. 2

The following were selected from among the transactions completed by Essex Company during July of the current year:

July 3. Purchased merchandise on account from Hamling Co., list price $72,000, trade discount 15%, terms FOB shipping point, 2/10, n/30, with prepaid freight of $1,450 added to the invoice.

5. Purchased merchandise on account from Kester Co., $33,450, terms FOB destination, 2/10, n/30.

6. Sold merchandise on account to Parsley Co., $36,000, terms n/15. The cost of the goods sold was $25,000.

7. Returned merchandise with an invoice amount of $6,850 purchased on July 5 from Kester Co.

13. Paid Hamling Co. on account for purchase of July 3.

15. Paid Kester Co. on account for purchase of July 5, less return of July 7.

21. Received cash on account from sale of July 6 to Parsley Co.

21. Sold merchandise on MasterCard, $108,000. The cost of the goods sold was $64,800.

22. Sold merchandise on account to Tabor Co., $16,650, terms 2/10, n/30. The cost of the goods sold was $10,000.

23. Sold merchandise for cash, $91,200. The cost of the goods sold was $55,000.

28. Paid Parsley Co. a cash refund of $7,150 for returned merchandise from sale of July 6. The cost of the returned merchandise was $4,250.

31. Paid MasterCard service fee of $1,650.

Instructions
Journalize the transactions.

PR 5-4B Sales and purchase-related transactions for seller and buyer using perpetual inventory system

Obj. 2

The following selected transactions were completed during April between Swan Company and Bird Company:

Apr. 2. Swan Company sold merchandise on account to Bird Company, $32,000, terms FOB shipping point, 2/10, n/30. Swan paid freight of $330, which was added to the invoice. The cost of the goods sold was $19,200.

8. Swan Company sold merchandise on account to Bird Company, $49,500, terms FOB destination, 1/15, n/eom. The cost of the goods sold was $29,700.

8. Swan Company paid freight of $710 for delivery of merchandise sold to Bird Company on April 8.

12. Bird Company paid Swan Company for purchase of April 2.

23. Bird Company paid Swan Company for purchase of April 8.

24. Swan Company sold merchandise on account to Bird Company, $67,350, terms FOB shipping point, n/eom. The cost of the goods sold was $40,400.

25. Swan Company paid Bird Company a cash refund of $1,200 for damaged merchandise in the April 8 sale. Bird Company kept the merchandise.

26. Bird Company paid freight of $875 on April 24 purchase from Swan Company.

30. Bird Company paid Swan Company on account for purchase of April 24.

Instructions
Journalize the April transactions for (1) Swan Company and (2) Bird Company.

PR 5-5B Multiple-step income statement and balance sheet

Obj. 4

✔ 1. Net income: $1,340,000

EXCEL TEMPLATE

The following selected accounts and their current balances appear in the ledger of Kanpur Co. for the fiscal year ended June 30, 20Y7:

Cash	$ 92,000	Retained Earnings	$ 381,000
Accounts Receivable	450,000	Dividends	300,000
Inventory	370,000	Sales	8,925,000
Estimated Returns Inventory	5,000	Cost of Goods Sold	5,620,000
Office Supplies	10,000	Sales Salaries Expense	850,000
Prepaid Insurance	12,000	Advertising Expense	420,000
Office Equipment	220,000	Depreciation Expense—	
Accumulated Depreciation—		Store Equipment	33,000
Office Equipment	58,000	Miscellaneous Selling Expense	18,000

(Continued)

Store Equipment	$650,000	Office Salaries Expense	$540,000
Accumulated Depreciation—		Rent Expense	48,000
Store Equipment	87,500	Insurance Expense	24,000
Accounts Payable	38,500	Depreciation Expense—	
Customers Refunds Payable	10,000	Office Equipment	10,000
Salaries Payable	4,000	Office Supplies Expense	4,000
Note Payable		Miscellaneous Administrative	
(final payment due in 20 years)	140,000	Expense	6,000
Common Stock	50,000	Interest Expense	12,000

Instructions

1. Prepare a multiple-step income statement.

2. Prepare a statement of stockholders' equity. Additional common stock of $7,500 was issued during the year ended June 30, 20Y7.

3. Prepare a balance sheet, assuming that the current portion of the note payable is $7,000.

4. ━━━▶ Briefly explain how multiple and single-step income statements differ.

✔ 3. Total assets:
$1,663,500

EXCEL TEMPLATE

PR 5-6B   Single-step income statement and balance sheet   Obj. 4

Selected accounts and related amounts for Kanpur Co. for the fiscal year ended June 30, 20Y7, are presented in Problem 5-5B.

Instructions

1. Prepare a single-step income statement in the format shown in Exhibit 13.

2. Prepare a statement of stockholders' equity. Additional common stock of $7,500 was issued during the year ended June 30, 20Y7.

3. Prepare a balance sheet, assuming that the current portion of the note payable is $7,000.

4. Prepare closing entries as of June 30, 20Y7.

Appendix 2
PR 5-7B   Purchase-related transactions using periodic inventory system

Selected transactions for Niles Co. during March of the current year are listed in Problem 5-1B.

Instructions

Journalize the entries to record the transactions of Niles Co. for March using the periodic inventory system.

Appendix 2
PR 5-8B   Sales and purchase-related transactions using periodic inventory system

Selected transactions for Essex Company during July of the current year are listed in Problem 5-3B.

Instructions

Journalize the entries to record the transactions of Essex Company for July using the periodic inventory system.

Appendix 2
PR 5-9B   Sales and purchase-related transactions for buyer and seller using periodic inventory system

Selected transactions during April between Swan Company and Bird Company are listed in Problem 5-4B.

Instructions

Journalize the entries to record the transactions for (1) Swan Company and (2) Bird Company assuming that both companies use the periodic inventory system.

Appendix 2

PR 5-10B   Periodic inventory accounts, multiple-step income statement, closing entries

On June 30, 20Y9, the balances of the accounts appearing in the ledger of Simkins Company are as follows:

✔ 2. Net income,
$1,208,000

EXCEL TEMPLATE

Cash	$125,000	Dividends	$ 275,000
Accounts Receivable	340,000	Sales	6,590,000
Inventory, July 1, 20Y8	415,000	Purchases	4,100,000
Estimated Returns Inventory,		Purchases Returns and Allowances	32,000
July 1, 20Y8	25,000	Purchases Discounts	13,000
Office Supplies	9,000	Freight In	45,000
Prepaid Insurance	18,000	Sales Salaries Expense	580,000
Land	300,000	Advertising Expense	315,000
Store Equipment	550,000	Delivery Expense	18,000
Accumulated Depreciation—		Depreciation Expense—	
Store Equipment	190,000	Store Equipment	12,000
Office Equipment	250,000	Miscellaneous Selling Expense	28,000
Accumulated Depreciation—		Office Salaries Expense	375,000
Office Equipment	110,000	Rent Expense	43,000
Accounts Payable	85,000	Insurance Expense	17,000
Customer Refunds Payable	30,000	Office Supplies Expense	5,000
Salaries Payable	9,000	Depreciation Expense—	
Unearned Rent	6,000	Office Equipment	4,000
Notes Payable	50,000	Miscellaneous Administrative Expense	16,000
Common Stock	300,000	Rent Revenue	32,500
Retained Earnings	520,000	Interest Expense	2,500

Instructions

1. ▬▬▬► Does Simkins Company use a periodic or perpetual inventory system? Explain.

2. Prepare a multiple-step income statement for Simkins Company for the year ended June 30, 20Y9. The inventory as of June 30, 20Y9, was $508,000. The estimated cost of customer returns inventory for June 30, 20Y9, is estimated to increase to $33,000.

3. Prepare the closing entries for Simkins Company as of June 30, 20Y9.

4. What would be the net income if the perpetual inventory system had been used?

Comprehensive Problem 2

✔ 8. Net income:
$741,855

Palisade Creek Co. is a retail business that uses the perpetual inventory system. The account balances for Palisade Creek as of May 1, 20Y6 (unless otherwise indicated), are as follows:

110	Cash	$ 83,600		312	Dividends	$ 135,000
112	Accounts Receivable	233,900		410	Sales	5,069,000
115	Inventory	624,400		510	Cost of Goods Sold	2,823,000
116	Estimated Returns Inventory	28,000		520	Sales Salaries Expense	664,800
117	Prepaid Insurance	16,800		521	Advertising Expense	281,000
118	Store Supplies	11,400		522	Depreciation Expense	—
123	Store Equipment	569,500		523	Store Supplies Expense	—
124	Accumulated Depreciation—			529	Miscellaneous Selling Expense	12,600
	Store Equipment	56,700		530	Office Salaries Expense	382,100
210	Accounts Payable	96,600		531	Rent Expense	83,700
211	Salaries Payable	—		532	Insurance Expense	—
212	Customers Refunds Payable	50,000		539	Miscellaneous Administrative	
310	Common Stock	100,000			Expense	7,800
311	Retained Earnings	585,300				

During May, the last month of the fiscal year, the following transactions were completed:

May   1.   Paid rent for May, $5,000.

3.   Purchased merchandise on account from Martin Co., terms 2/10, n/30, FOB shipping point, $36,000.

(Continued)

May 4. Paid freight on purchase of May 3, $600.
 6. Sold merchandise on account to Korman Co., terms 2/10, n/30, FOB shipping point, $68,500. The cost of the goods sold was $41,000.
 7. Received $22,300 cash from Halstad Co. on account.
 10. Sold merchandise for cash, $54,000. The cost of the goods sold was $32,000.
 13. Paid for merchandise purchased on May 3.
 15. Paid advertising expense for last half of May, $11,000.
 16. Received cash from sale of May 6.
 19. Purchased merchandise for cash, $18,700.
 19. Paid $33,450 to Buttons Co. on account.
 20. Paid Korman Co. a cash refund of $13,230 for returned merchandise from sale of May 6. The invoice amount of the returned merchandise was $13,500 and the cost of the returned merchandise was $8,000.

Record the following transactions on Page 21 of the journal:

May 20. Sold merchandise on account to Crescent Co., terms 1/10, n/30, FOB shipping point, $110,000. The cost of the goods sold was $70,000.
 21. For the convenience of Crescent Co., paid freight on sale of May 20, $2,300.
 21. Received $42,900 cash from Gee Co. on account.
 21. Purchased merchandise on account from Osterman Co., terms 1/10, n/30, FOB destination, $88,000.
 24. Returned damaged merchandise purchased on May 21, receiving a credit memo from the seller for $5,000.
 26. Refunded cash on sales made for cash, $7,500. The cost of the merchandise returned was $4,800.
 28. Paid sales salaries of $56,000 and office salaries of $29,000.
 29. Purchased store supplies for cash, $2,400.
 30. Sold merchandise on account to Turner Co., terms 2/10, n/30, FOB shipping point, $78,750. The cost of the goods sold was $47,000.
 30. Received cash from sale of May 20 plus freight paid on May 21.
 31. Paid for purchase of May 21, less return of May 24.

Instructions

1. Enter the balances of each of the accounts in the appropriate balance column of a four-column account. Write *Balance* in the item section, and place a check mark (✓) in the Posting Reference column. Journalize the transactions for May, starting on Page 20 of the journal.

2. Post the journal to the general ledger, extending the month-end balances to the appropriate balance columns after all posting is completed. In this problem, you are not required to update or post to the accounts receivable and accounts payable subsidiary ledgers.

3. Prepare an unadjusted trial balance.

4. At the end of May, the following adjustment data were assembled. Analyze and use these data to complete (5) and (6).

a.	Inventory on May 31		$570,000
b.	Insurance expired during the year		12,000
c.	Store supplies on hand on May 31		4,000
d.	Depreciation for the current year		14,000
e.	Accrued salaries on May 31:		
	Sales salaries	$7,000	
	Office salaries	6,600	13,600

   f. The adjustment for customer returns and allowances is $60,000 for sales and $35,000 for cost of goods sold.

5. *(Optional)* Enter the unadjusted trial balance on a 10-column end-of-period spreadsheet (work sheet), and complete the spreadsheet.

6. Journalize and post the adjusting entries. Record the adjusting entries on Page 22 of the journal.

7. Prepare an adjusted trial balance.

8. Prepare an income statement, a statement of stockholders' equity, and a balance sheet. Assume that additional common stock of $10,000 was issued in January 20Y6.

9. Prepare and post the closing entries. Record the closing entries on Page 23 of the journal. Indicate closed accounts by inserting a line in both the Balance columns opposite the closing entry. Insert the new balance in the retained earnings account.

10. Prepare a post-closing trial balance.

Make a Decision
Asset Turnover Ratio

REAL WORLD

MAD 5-1 Analyze and compare Amazon.com and Netflix Obj. 5

Amazon.com, Inc. (AMZN) is one of the largest Internet retailers in the world. **Netflix, Inc. (NFLX)** provides digital streaming and DVD rentals in the United States. Amazon and Netflix compete in streaming and digital services; however, Amazon also sells many other products through the Internet. The sales and total assets (in millions) from recent financial statements were reported as follows for both companies:

	Amazon	Netflix
Total revenues (sales)	$135,987	$ 8,831
Total assets:		
Beginning of year	64,747	10,203
End of year	83,402	13,587

a. Based on your knowledge of each company, identify three major assets used by each company in generating revenue.

b. Compute the asset turnover ratio for each company. Round to two decimal places.

c. ━━━▶ Which company generates sales from total assets more efficiently?

REAL WORLD

MAD 5-2 Analyze Dollar General Obj. 5

Dollar General Corporation (DG) is a discount retailer with more than 12,000 stores. It offers a wide range of merchandise normally for $10 or less. The following data (in millions) were taken from recent financial statements of Dollar General:

	Year 2	Year 1
Total sales	$21,987	$20,369
Total assets:		
Beginning of year	11,258	11,209
End of year	11,672	11,258

a. Compute the asset turnover ratio for Year 2 and Year 1. Round to two decimal places.

b. ━━━▶ Interpret the change in the asset turnover ratio from Year 1 to Year 2.

REAL WORLD

MAD 5-3 Compare Dollar Tree and Dollar General Obj. 5

The asset turnover ratios for two recent years for **Dollar Tree, Inc. (DLTR)** are shown in the Analysis for Decision Making section of this chapter.

━━━▶ Using your results from MAD 5-2, compare and interpret the asset turnover ratios for Dollar Tree and **Dollar General (DG)**.

REAL WORLD

MAD 5-4 Analyze and compare CSX, Union Pacific, and YRC Worldwide Obj. 5

CSX Corporation (CSX) and **Union Pacific Corporation (UNP)** are major railroads, operating primarily in the eastern and western portion of the United States, respectively. **YRC Worldwide Inc. (YRCW)** is one of the largest trucking companies in the United States.

The sales and total assets (in millions) for a recent year for each company are as follows:

	CSX	Union Pacific	YRC
Total sales	$11,069	$19,941	$4,698
Total assets:			
Beginning of year	34,745	54,600	1,879
End of year	35,414	55,718	1,770

a. Compute the asset turnover ratio for each company. Round to two decimal places.

b. ━━━▶ Which of the two railroad companies is more efficient in generating revenues from its assets?

c. ━━━▶ How does YRC's asset turnover ratio compare to the two railroads? Why?

SHOW ME HOW   REAL WORLD

MAD 5-5   Analyze Home Depot   Obj. 5

The Home Depot (HD) reported the following data (in millions) in its recent financial statements:

	Year 2	Year 1
Total sales	$95,595	$88,519
Total assets:		
Beginning of year	41,973	39,946
End of year	42,966	41,973

a. Determine the asset turnover ratio for Home Depot for Year 2 and Year 1. Round to two decimal places.

b. ➤ What conclusions can be drawn from these ratios concerning the change in the ability of Home Depot to effectively use its assets to generate sales?

REAL WORLD

MAD 5-6   Analyze and compare Kroger and Tiffany   Obj. 5

The Kroger Company (KR), a national supermarket chain, reported the following data (in millions) in its financial statements for a recent year:

Total sales	$115,337
Total assets:	
Beginning of year	33,897
End of year	36,505

a. Compute the asset turnover ratio. Round to two decimal places.

b. ➤ **Tiffany & Co. (TIF)** is a large North American retailer of jewelry. Tiffany's asset turnover ratio is 0.78. Why would Tiffany's asset turnover ratio be lower than that of Kroger?

REAL WORLD

MAD 5-7   Analyze J. C. Penney   Obj. 5

J. C. Penney Company, Inc. (JCP) is a large general merchandise retailer in the United States. The following data (in millions) were obtained from its financial statements for four recent years:

	Year 4	Year 3	Year 2	Year 1
Total sales	$12,547	$12,625	$12,257	$11,859
Total assets:				
Beginning of year	9,442	10,404	11,801	9,781
End of year	9,314	9,442	10,404	11,801

a. Compute the asset turnover ratio for each year. Round to two decimal places.

b. Plot the asset turnover ratio on a line chart with the year on the horizontal axis.

c. ➤ Interpret the trend in this ratio over the four years.

Take It Further

ETHICS

TIF 5-1   Inventory shrinkage adjustment

Margie Johnson is a staff accountant at ToolEx Company, a manufacturer of tools and equipment. The company is under pressure from investors to increase earnings, and the president of the company expects the Accounting Department to "make this happen." Margie's boss, who has been a mentor to her, is concerned that if earnings do not increase, he will be terminated.

Shortly after the end of the fiscal year, the company performs a physical count of the inventory. When Margie compares the physical count to the balance in the inventory account, she finds a significant amount of inventory shrinkage. The amount is so large that it will result in a significant drop in earnings this period. Margie's boss asks her not to make the adjusting entry for shrinkage this period. He assures her that they will get "caught up" on shrinkage in the next period, after the pressure is off to reach this period's earnings goal. Margie's boss asks her to do this as a personal favor to him.

What should Margie do in this situation? Why?

ETHICS

TIF 5-2   Purchases discount

On April 18, 20Y7, Bontanica Company, a garden retailer, purchased $9,800 of seed, terms 2/10, n/30, from Whitetail Seed Co. Even though the discount period had expired, Shelby Davey subtracted the discount of $196 when he processed the documents for payment on May 1, 20Y7.

Discuss whether Shelby Davey behaved in a professional manner by subtracting the discount even though the discount period had expired.

TEAM ACTIVITY   REAL WORLD

TIF 5-3   Real-world annual report

In teams, select a public company that interests you. Obtain the company's most recent annual report on Form 10-K. The Form 10-K is a company's annually required filing with the Securities and Exchange Commission (SEC). It includes the company's financial statements and accompanying notes. The Form 10-K can be obtained either (a) from the investor relations section of the company's website or (b) by using the company search feature of the SEC's EDGAR database service found at www.sec.gov/edgar/searchedgar/companysearch.html.

1. Based on the information in the company's most recent annual report, determine each of the following:
    a. Gross profit for each year reported.
    b. Gross profit rate (Gross profit ÷ Sales) for each year reported. Round to one decimal place.
    c. Operating income for each year reported.
    d. Percentage change in operating income for the most recent year. Round to one decimal place.
    e. Net income for each year reported.
    f. Percentage change in net income for the most recent year. Round to one decimal place.
2. Based solely on your responses to item 1, has the company's performance improved, remained constant, or deteriorated over the periods presented? Briefly explain your answer.

TEAM ACTIVITY

TIF 5-4   Shopping for a television

Assume that you are planning to purchase a 55-inch LED, LCD flat-screen television. In groups of three or four, determine the lowest cost for the television, considering the available alternatives and the advantages and disadvantages of each alternative. For example, you could purchase from a local store, through mail order, or through an Internet shopping service. Consider such factors as delivery charges, interest-free financing, discounts, coupons, and availability of warranty services. Prepare a report for presentation to the class.

COMMUNICATION

TIF 5-5   Effect of sales discounts

Suzi Nomro operates Watercraft Supply Company, an online boat parts distributorship that is in its third year of operation. The following income statement was prepared for the year ended October 31, 20Y3.

Watercraft Supply Company
Income Statement
For the Year Ended October 31, 20Y3

Revenues:		
Sales		$ 1,350,000
Interest		15,000
Total revenues		$ 1,365,000
Expenses:		
Cost of goods sold	$810,000	
Selling expenses	140,000	
Administrative expenses	90,000	
Interest expense	4,000	
Total expenses		(1,044,000)
Net income		$ 321,000

(Continued)

Suzi is considering a proposal to increase net income by offering sales discounts of 2/15, n/30 and by shipping all merchandise FOB shipping point. Currently, no sales discounts are allowed and merchandise is shipped FOB destination. It is estimated that the new terms will increase sales by 10%. The ratio of the cost of goods sold to sales is expected to be 60%. All selling and administrative expenses are expected to remain unchanged, except for store supplies and miscellaneous selling expenses, which are expected to increase proportionately with increased sales. The amounts of these items for the year ended October 31, 20Y3, were as follows:

Store supplies expense	$12,000
Miscellaneous selling expenses	6,000

The interest revenue and expense items will remain unchanged. The shipment of all merchandise FOB shipping point will eliminate all delivery expenses, which for the year ended October 31, 20Y3, were $12,000.

➤ Write a brief memo to Suzi discussing the potential benefits and limitations of this proposal. Include a determination of the net income that Watercraft Supply could generate next year, under the new proposal, assuming that all sales are collected within the discount period.

TIF 5-6   Purchases Discounts and Accounts Payable

Rustic Furniture Co. is owned and operated by Cam Pfeifer. The following is an excerpt from a conversation between Cam Pfeifer and Mitzi Wheeler, the chief accountant for Rustic Furniture Co.:

Cam: Mitzi, I've got a question about this recent balance sheet.

Mitzi: Sure, what's your question?

Cam: Well, as you know, I'm applying for a bank loan to finance our new store in Garden Grove, and I noticed that the accounts payable are listed as $320,000.

Mitzi: That's right. Approximately $275,000 of that represents amounts due our suppliers, and the remainder is miscellaneous payables to creditors for utilities, office equipment, supplies, etc.

Cam: That's what I thought. But as you know, we normally receive a 2% discount from our suppliers for earlier payment, and we always try to take the discount.

Mitzi: That's right. I can't remember the last time we missed a discount.

Cam: Well, in that case, it seems to me the accounts payable should be listed minus the 2% discount. Let's list the accounts payable due suppliers as $314,500 rather than $320,000. Every little bit helps. You never know. It might make the difference between getting and not getting the loan.

➤ How would you respond to Cam Pfeifer's request?

TIF 5-7   Determining the Cost of a Purchase

The following is an excerpt from a conversation between Mark Loomis and Krista Huff. Mark is debating whether to buy a stereo system from Tru-Sound Systems, a locally owned electronics store, or Wholesale Stereo, an online electronics company.

Mark: Krista, I don't know what to do about buying my new stereo.

Krista: What's the problem?

Mark: Well, I can buy it locally at Tru-Sound Systems for $1,175.00. However, Wholesale Stereo has the same system listed for $1,200.00.

Krista: What's the big deal? Buy it from Tru-Sound Systems.

Mark: It's not quite that simple. Wholesale Stereo charges $49.99 for shipping and handling. If I have Wholesale Stereo send it next-day air, it'll cost $89.99 for shipping and handling.

Krista: So?

Mark: But, that's not all. Tru-Sound Systems will give an additional 2% discount if I pay cash. Otherwise, they will let me use my VISA, or I can pay it off in three monthly installments. In addition, if I buy it from Tru-Sound Systems, I have to pay 9% sales tax. I won't have to pay sales tax if I buy it from Wholesale Stereo, since they are out of state.

Krista: Anything else???

Mark: Well . . . Wholesale Stereo says I have to charge it on my VISA. They don't accept checks.

Krista: I am not surprised. Many online stores don't accept checks.

Mark: I give up. What would you do?

1. Assuming that Wholesale Stereo doesn't charge sales tax on the sale to Mark, which company is offering the best buy?

2. ➤ What might be some considerations other than price that influence Mark's decision on where to buy the stereo system?

Pathways Challenge

This is Accounting!

Information/Consequences

Because placing an order does not create an asset or a liability, accounting standards do not require a company to increase Inventory or Accounts Payable when entering into a purchase contract (commitment). Instead, the purchase transaction is recorded only upon the delivery of the coffee. However, because the purchase commitment provides relevant information to users, **Starbucks (SBUX)** is required to disclose commitments in the notes to its financial statements. For the commitments where the price is to be determined, Starbucks is required to provide its best estimate of the amount that will be paid once the coffee is delivered.

For purchase contracts (commitments) in which the market price falls below the fixed purchase price, Starbucks is required to make an adjusting entry to record an accrued loss. The recording of the loss prior to the purchase (delivery) of the coffee is consistent with accrual accounting in that the loss is recorded in the period that it occurs. That is, the loss is recorded in the period that the price declined.

For purchase contracts (commitments) in which the market price rises above the fixed purchase price, Starbucks would not record a gain. Instead, it would record the delivery of the inventory at the lower fixed purchase price.

Suggested Answer

6 Inventories

STATEMENT OF STOCKHOLDERS' EQUITY
For the Year Ended December 31, 20Y5

	Common Stock	Retained Earnings	Total
Balances, Jan. 1, 20Y5	$XXX	$ XXX	$ XXX
Issued common stock	XXX		XXX
Net income		XXX	XXX
Dividends		(XXX)	(XXX)
Balances, Dec. 31, 20Y5	$XXX	$ XXX	$ XXX

STATEMENT OF CASH FLOWS
For the Year Ended December 31, 20Y5

Cash flows from (used for) operating activities	$XXX
Cash flows from (used for) investing activities	XXX
Cash flows from (used for) financing activities	XXX
Net increase (decrease) in cash	$XXX
Cash balance, January 1, 20Y5	XXX
Cash balance, December 31, 20Y5	$XXX

INCOME STATEMENT
For the Year Ended December 31, 20Y5

Sales		$ XXX
Cost of goods sold		(XXX)
Gross profit		$ XXX
Operating expenses:		
Wages expense	$XXX	
Advertising expense	XXX	
Utilities expense	XXX	
Depreciation expense	XXX	
…	XXX	
Total operating expenses		(XXX)
Operating income		$ XXX
Other revenue and expense		XXX
Net income		$ XXX

BALANCE SHEET
December 31, 20Y5

Assets		
Current assets:		
Cash	$XXX	
Accounts receivable	XXX	
Inventory	XXX	
Total current assets		$XXX
Property, plant, and equipment		XXX
Total assets		$XXX
Liabilities		
Current liabilities	$XXX	
Long-term liabilities	XXX	
Total liabilities		$XXX
Stockholders' Equity		
Common stock	$XXX	
Retained earnings	XXX	
Total stockholders' equity		XXX
Total liabilities and stockholders' equity		$XXX

Best Buy

Assume that in September you purchased a Sony HDTV from **Best Buy (BBY)**. At the same time, you purchased a Denon surround sound system for $599.99. You liked your surround sound so well that in November you purchased an identical Denon system on sale for $549.99 for your bedroom TV. Over the holidays, you moved to a new apartment and in the process of unpacking discovered that one of the Denon surround sound systems was missing. Luckily, your renters or homeowners insurance policy will cover the theft; but the insurance company needs to know the cost of the system that was stolen.

The Denon systems were identical. However, to respond to the insurance company, you will need to identify which system was stolen. Was it the first system, which cost $599.99, or was it the second system, which cost $549.99? Whichever assumption you make may determine the amount that you receive from the insurance company.

Businesses such as Best Buy make similar assumptions when identical merchandise is purchased at different costs. For example, Best Buy may have purchased thousands of Denon surround sound systems over the past year at different costs. At the end of a period, some of the Denon systems will still be in inventory, and some will have been sold. But which costs relate to the sold systems, and which costs relate to the Denon systems still in inventory? Best Buy's assumption about inventory costs can involve large dollar amounts and, thus, can have a significant impact on the financial statements. For example, Best Buy reported $5,051 million of inventory and net income of $897 million for a recent year.

This chapter discusses such issues as how to determine the cost of merchandise in inventory and the cost of goods sold. However, this chapter begins by discussing the importance of control over inventory.

©RICHARD LEVINE/ALAMY STOCK PHOTO

What's Covered

Inventories

Nature of Inventory	**Perpetual Inventory System**	**Periodic Inventory System**	**Valuing Inventory**
■ Safeguarding Inventory (Obj. 1)	■ First-In, First-Out Method (Obj. 3)	■ First-In, First-Out Method (Obj. 4)	■ Comparing FIFO, LIFO, and Weighted Average Methods (Obj. 5)
■ Cost Flow Overview (Obj. 2)	■ Last-In, First-Out Method (Obj. 3)	■ Last-In, First-Out Method (Obj. 4)	■ Lower of Cost or Market (Obj. 6)
	■ Weighted Average Cost Method (Obj. 3)	■ Weighted Average Cost Method (Obj. 4)	■ Balance Sheet (Obj. 6)
			■ Effect of Errors (Obj. 6)

Learning Objectives

Obj. 1 Describe the importance of control over inventory.

Obj. 2 Describe three inventory cost flow assumptions and how they impact the income statement and balance sheet.

Obj. 3 Determine the cost of inventory under the perpetual inventory system, using the FIFO, LIFO, and weighted average cost methods.

Obj. 4 Determine the cost of inventory under the periodic inventory system, using the FIFO, LIFO, and weighted average cost methods.

Obj. 5 Compare and contrast the use of the three inventory costing methods.

Obj. 6 Describe and illustrate the reporting of inventory in the financial statements.

Analysis for Decision Making

Obj. 7   Describe and illustrate the inventory turnover and the number of days' sales in inventory in analyzing the efficiency and effectiveness of inventory management.

Obj. App Describe and illustrate the estimation of inventory using the retail inventory and gross profit methods of inventory costing.

Objective 1
Describe the importance of control over inventory.

Control of Inventory

Two primary objectives of control over inventory are as follows:[1]

■ Safeguarding the inventory from damage or theft.
■ Reporting inventory in the financial statements.

Safeguarding Inventory

Controls for safeguarding inventory begin as soon as the inventory is ordered. The following documents are often used for inventory control:

■ Purchase order
■ Receiving report
■ Vendor's invoice

The **purchase order** authorizes the purchase of the inventory from an approved vendor. As soon as the inventory is received, a receiving report is completed. The **receiving report** establishes an initial record of the receipt of the inventory. To make sure the inventory received is what was ordered, the receiving report is compared with the purchase order. The price, quantity, and description of the item on the purchase order and receiving report are then compared to the vendor's invoice. If the receiving report, purchase order, and vendor's invoice agree, the inventory is recorded in the accounting records. If any differences exist, they should be investigated and reconciled.

Recording inventory using a perpetual inventory system is also an effective means of control. The amount of inventory is always available in the **subsidiary inventory ledger**. This helps keep inventory quantities at proper levels. For example, comparing inventory quantities with maximum and minimum levels allows for the timely reordering of inventory and prevents ordering excess inventory.

---

[1] Additional controls used by businesses are described and illustrated in Chapter 7, "Internal Control and Cash."

Finally, controls for safeguarding inventory should include security measures to prevent damage and customer or employee theft. Some examples of security measures include the following:

- Storing inventory in areas that are restricted to only authorized employees
- Locking high-priced inventory in cabinets
- Using two-way mirrors, cameras, security tags, and guards

Best Buy uses scanners to screen customers as they leave the store for merchandise that has not been purchased. In addition, Best Buy stations greeters at the store's entrance to keep customers from bringing in bags that can be used to shoplift merchandise.

Link to Best Buy

Reporting Inventory

A **physical inventory** or *count of inventory* should be taken near year-end to make sure that the quantity of inventory reported in the financial statements is accurate. After the quantity of inventory on hand is determined, the cost of the inventory is assigned for reporting in the financial statements. Most companies assign costs to inventory using one of three inventory cost flow assumptions. If a physical count is not possible or inventory records are not available, the inventory cost may be estimated as described in the appendix at the end of this chapter.

Best Buy conducts ongoing physical counts of inventory throughout the year as a basis for monitoring and predicting loss adjustments for theft.

Link to Best Buy

Inventory Cost Flow Assumptions

Objective 2
Describe three inventory cost flow assumptions and how they impact the income statement and balance sheet.

An accounting issue arises when identical units of merchandise are acquired at different unit costs during a period. In such cases, when an item is sold, it is necessary to determine its cost using a cost flow assumption and related inventory costing method. Three common cost flow assumptions and related inventory costing methods are shown in Exhibit 1.

Exhibit 1 Cost Flow Assumptions

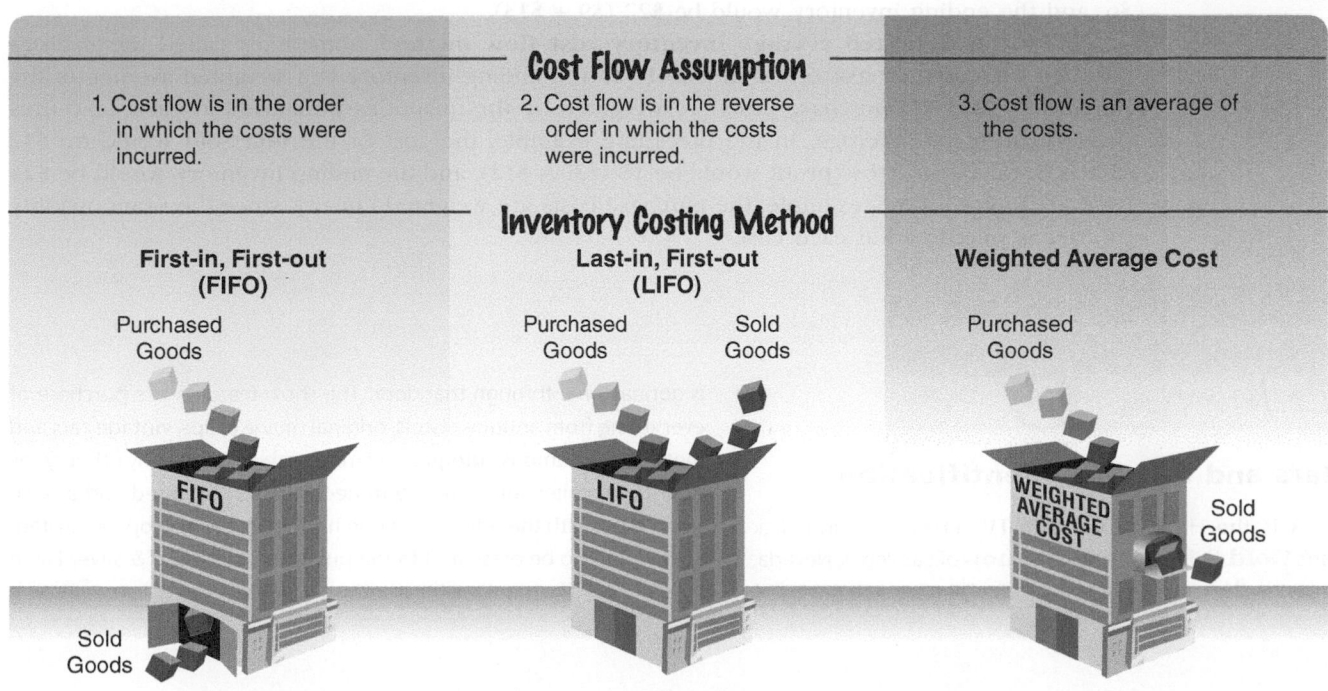

Cost Flow Assumption		
1. Cost flow is in the order in which the costs were incurred.	2. Cost flow is in the reverse order in which the costs were incurred.	3. Cost flow is an average of the costs.

Inventory Costing Method		
First-in, First-out (FIFO)	**Last-in, First-out (LIFO)**	**Weighted Average Cost**

To illustrate, assume that three identical units of merchandise are purchased during May, as follows:

			Units	Cost
May	10	Purchase	1	$ 9
	18	Purchase	1	13
	24	Purchase	1	14
Total			3	$36

Average cost per unit: $12 ($36 ÷ 3 units)

Assume that one unit is sold on May 30 for $20. Depending upon which unit was sold, the gross profit varies from $11 to $6, computed as follows:

	May 10 Unit Sold	May 18 Unit Sold	May 24 Unit Sold
Sales	$20	$ 20	$ 20
Cost of goods sold	(9)	(13)	(14)
Gross profit	$11	$ 7	$ 6
Ending inventory	$27	$ 23	$ 22
	($13 + $14)	($9 + $14)	($9 + $13)

Under the **specific identification inventory cost flow method**, the unit sold is identified with a specific purchase. The ending inventory is made up of the remaining units on hand. Thus, the gross profit, cost of goods sold, and ending inventory can vary as illustrated. For example, if the May 18 unit was sold, the cost of goods sold is $13, the gross profit is $7, and the ending inventory is $23.

The specific identification method is not practical unless each inventory unit can be separately identified. For example, an automobile dealer may use the specific identification method because each automobile has a unique serial number. However, most businesses cannot identify each inventory unit separately. In such cases, one of the following three inventory cost flow methods is used.

Under the **first-in, first-out (FIFO) inventory cost flow method**, the first units purchased are assumed to be sold and the ending inventory is made up of the most recent purchases. In the preceding example, the May 10 unit would be assumed to have been sold. Thus, the gross profit would be $11, and the ending inventory would be $27 ($13 + $14).

Under the **last-in, first-out (LIFO) inventory cost flow method**, the last units purchased are assumed to be sold and the ending inventory is made up of the first purchases. In the preceding example, the May 24 unit would be assumed to have been sold. Thus, the gross profit would be $6, and the ending inventory would be $22 ($9 + $13).

Under the **weighted average inventory cost flow method**, sometimes called the *average cost flow method*, the cost of the units sold and in ending inventory is a weighted average of the purchase costs. The purchase costs are weighted by the quantities purchased at each cost, thus the term *weighted average*. In the preceding example, the cost of the unit sold would be $12 ($36 ÷ 3 units), the gross profit would be $8 ($20 − $12), and the ending inventory would be $24 ($12 × 2 units). In this example, the purchase costs are weighted equally, since the same quantity (one) was purchased at each cost.

Why It Matters ▶

CONCEPT CLIP

Pawn Stars and Specific Identification

*P*awn Stars is the History Channel's TV series featuring Rick Harrison's **Gold & Silver Pawn Shop** of Las Vegas, Nevada. As Rick says in the opening of every show, "you never know what is gonna come through that door." The show features the purchase of everything from antique pistols, original movie props, vintage cars and motorcycles, famous autographed memorabilia, and many other types of unusual collectibles. Each item needs to be appraised and a price negotiated with the seller. Once purchased, the pawn shop has an item of inventory to be presented to the public for sale. Gold & Silver Pawn uses the specific identification method for valuing inventory.

Best Buy uses the weighted average cost method for its inventory.

Link to Best Buy

The three inventory cost flow methods, FIFO, LIFO, and weighted average, are shown in Exhibit 2.

Exhibit 2 Inventory Costing Methods

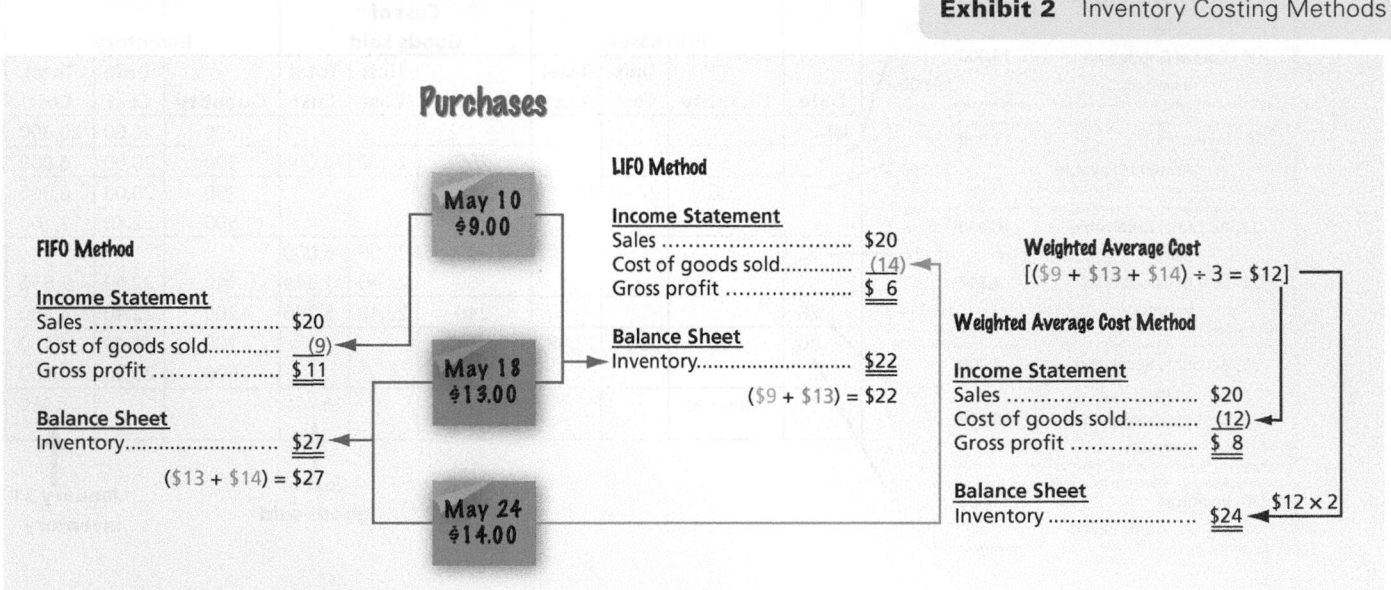

Inventory Costing Methods Under a Perpetual Inventory System

Objective 3
Determine the cost of inventory under the perpetual inventory system, using the FIFO, LIFO, and weighted average cost methods.

As illustrated in the prior section, when identical units of an item are purchased at different unit costs, an inventory cost flow method must be used. This is true regardless of whether the perpetual or periodic inventory system is used.

In this section, the FIFO, LIFO, and weighted average cost methods are illustrated under a perpetual inventory system. For purposes of illustration, the following data for **Item 127B** are used:

	Item 127B	Units	Cost
Jan. 1	Inventory	1,000	$20.00
4	Sale at $30 per unit	700	
10	Purchase	500	22.40
22	Sale at $30 per unit	360	
28	Sale at $30 per unit	240	
30	Purchase	600	23.30

First-In, First-Out Method

When the FIFO method is used, costs are included in the cost of goods sold in the order in which they were purchased. This is often the same as the physical flow of the goods. Thus, the FIFO method often provides results that are about the same as those that would have been obtained using the specific identification method. For example, grocery stores shelve milk and other perishable products by expiration dates. Products with early expiration dates are stocked in front. In this way, the oldest products (earliest purchases) are sold first.

To illustrate, Exhibit 3 shows the use of FIFO under a perpetual inventory system for **Item 127B**.

Exhibit 3   Entries and Perpetual Inventory Account (FIFO)

Jan. 4	Accounts Receivable	21,000	
	Sales		21,000
4	Cost of Goods Sold	14,000	
	Inventory		14,000

10	Inventory	11,200	
	Accounts Payable		11,200

22	Accounts Receivable	10,800	
	Sales		10,800
22	Cost of Goods Sold	7,344	
	Inventory		7,344

28	Accounts Receivable	7,200	
	Sales		7,200
28	Cost of Goods Sold	5,376	
	Inventory		5,376

30	Inventory	13,980	
	Accounts Payable		13,980

Item 127B

		Purchases			Cost of Goods Sold			Inventory		
Date	Quantity	Unit Cost	Total Cost	Quantity	Unit Cost	Total Cost	Quantity	Unit Cost	Total Cost
Jan. 1							1,000	20.00	20,000
4				700	20.00	14,000	300	20.00	6,000
10	500	22.40	11,200				300	20.00	6,000
							500	22.40	11,200
22				300	20.00	6,000			
				60	22.40	1,344	440	22.40	9,856
28				240	22.40	5,376	200	22.40	4,480
30	600	23.30	13,980				200	22.40	4,480
							600	23.30	13,980
31	Balances					26,720			18,460

Cost of goods sold

January 31 inventory

The journal entries and the subsidiary inventory ledger for Item 127B are shown in Exhibit 3 as follows:

1. The beginning balance on January 1 is $20,000 (1,000 units at a unit cost of $20.00).
2. On January 4, 700 units were sold at a price of $30 each for sales of $21,000 (700 units at a selling price of $30 per unit). The cost of goods sold is $14,000 (700 units at a unit cost of $20). After the sale, there remains $6,000 of inventory (300 units at a unit cost of $20).
3. On January 10, $11,200 is purchased (500 units at a unit cost of $22.40). After the purchase, the inventory is reported on two lines, $6,000 (300 units at a unit cost of $20.00) from the beginning inventory and $11,200 (500 units at a unit cost of $22.40) from the January 10 purchase.
4. On January 22, 360 units are sold at a price of $30 each for sales of $10,800 (360 units at a selling price of $30 per unit). Using FIFO, the cost of goods sold of $7,344 consists of $6,000 (300 units at a unit cost of $20.00) from the beginning inventory plus $1,344 (60 units at a unit cost of $22.40) from the January 10 purchase. After the sale, there remains $9,856 of inventory (440 units at a unit cost of $22.40) from the January 10 purchase.
5. The January 28 sale and January 30 purchase are recorded in a similar manner.
6. The ending balance on January 31 is $18,460. This balance is made up of two layers of inventory as follows:

	Date of Purchase	Quantity	Unit Cost	Total Cost
Layer 1:	Jan. 10	200	$22.40	$ 4,480
Layer 2:	Jan. 30	600	23.30	13,980
Total		800		$18,460

Last-In, First-Out Method

When the LIFO method is used, the cost of the units sold is the cost of the most recent purchases. The LIFO method was originally used in those rare cases where the units sold were taken from the most recently purchased units. However, for tax purposes, LIFO is now widely used even when it does not represent the physical flow of units. The tax impact of LIFO is discussed later in this chapter.

To illustrate, Exhibit 4 shows the use of LIFO under a perpetual inventory system for **Item 127B**.

Exhibit 4 Entries and Perpetual Inventory Account (LIFO)

Jan. 4 Accounts Receivable	21,000	
Sales		21,000
4 Cost of Goods Sold	14,000	
Inventory		14,000

10 Inventory	11,200	
Accounts Payable		11,200

22 Accounts Receivable	10,800	
Sales		10,800
22 Cost of Goods Sold	8,064	
Inventory		8,064

28 Accounts Receivable	7,200	
Sales		7,200
28 Cost of Goods Sold	5,136	
Inventory		5,136

30 Inventory	13,980	
Accounts Payable		13,980

Item 127B

	Purchases			Cost of Goods Sold			Inventory		
Date	Quantity	Unit Cost	Total Cost	Quantity	Unit Cost	Total Cost	Quantity	Unit Cost	Total Cost
Jan. 1							1,000	20.00	20,000
4				700	20.00	14,000	300	20.00	6,000
10	500	22.40	11,200				300	20.00	6,000
							500	22.40	11,200
22				360	22.40	8,064	300	20.00	6,000
							140	22.40	3,136
28				140	22.40	3,136	200	20.00	4,000
				100	20.00	2,000			
30	600	23.30	13,980				200	20.00	4,000
							600	23.30	13,980
31	Balances					27,200			17,980

Cost of goods sold

January 31 inventory

The journal entries and the subsidiary inventory ledger for Item 127B are shown in Exhibit 4 as follows:

1. The beginning balance on January 1 is $20,000 (1,000 units at a unit of cost of $20.00).

2. On January 4, 700 units were sold at a price of $30 each for sales of $21,000 (700 units at a selling price of $30 per unit). The cost of goods sold is $14,000 (700 units at a unit cost of $20). After the sale, there remains $6,000 of inventory (300 units at a unit cost of $20).

3. On January 10, $11,200 is purchased (500 units at a unit cost of $22.40). After the purchase, the inventory is reported on two lines, $6,000 (300 units at a unit cost of $20.00) from the beginning inventory and $11,200 (500 units at a unit cost of $22.40) from the January 10 purchase.

IFRS

See Appendix C for more information.

4. On January 22, 360 units are sold at a price of $30 each for sales of $10,800 (360 units at a selling price of $30 per unit). Using LIFO, the cost of goods sold is $8,064 (360 units at unit cost of $22.40) from the January 10 purchase. After the sale, there remains $9,136 of inventory consisting of $6,000 (300 units at a unit cost of $20.00) from the beginning inventory and $3,136 (140 units at a unit cost of $22.40) from the January 10 purchase.

5. The January 28 sale and January 30 purchase are recorded in a similar manner.

6. The ending balance on January 31 is $17,980. This balance is made up of two layers of inventory as follows:

	Date of Purchase	Quantity	Unit Cost	Total Cost
Layer 1:	Beg. inv. (Jan. 1)	200	$20.00	$ 4,000
Layer 2:	Jan. 30	600	23.30	13,980
Total		800		$17,980

When the LIFO method is used, the subsidiary inventory ledger is sometimes maintained in units only. The units are converted to dollars when the financial statements are prepared at the end of the period.

Check Up Corner 6-1   Perpetual Inventory: FIFO and LIFO Methods

The beginning inventory, purchases, and sales of Item QX3 for the month of January are as follows:

Jan.	1	Inventory	40 units at $5
	9	Sale	30 units
	18	Purchase	70 units at $7
	22	Sale	36 units

The company uses the perpetual inventory system. Determine (1) the cost of goods sold for January and (2) the January 31 inventory balance using the:

a. first-in, first-out (FIFO) method.

b. last-in, first-out (LIFO) method.

Solution:

a. Under the FIFO method, costs are included in the cost of goods sold in the order in which they are purchased.

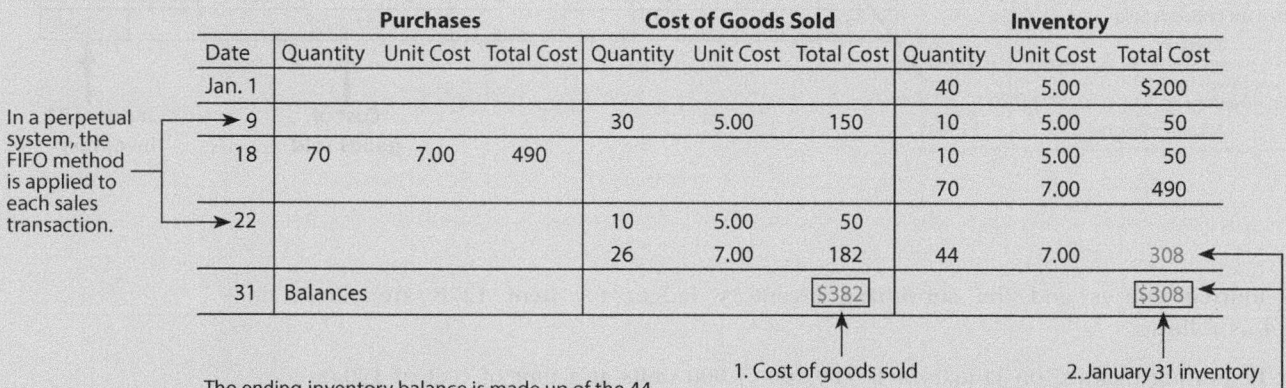

		Purchases			Cost of Goods Sold			Inventory		
Date	Quantity	Unit Cost	Total Cost	Quantity	Unit Cost	Total Cost	Quantity	Unit Cost	Total Cost
Jan. 1							40	5.00	$200
9				30	5.00	150	10	5.00	50
18	70	7.00	490				10	5.00	50
							70	7.00	490
22				10	5.00	50			
				26	7.00	182	44	7.00	308
31	Balances					$382			$308

In a perpetual system, the FIFO method is applied to each sales transaction.

1. Cost of goods sold

2. January 31 inventory

The ending inventory balance is made up of the 44 remaining (unsold) units at the most recent purchase price ($7 per unit).

b. Under the LIFO method, the costs of the most recent purchases are included in the cost of goods sold.

The ending inventory balance is made up of two layers: 10 units at the beginning inventory unit cost ($5 per unit), and 34 units at the Jan. 18 purchase price ($7 per unit).

		Purchases			Cost of Goods Sold			Inventory		
Date	Quantity	Unit Cost	Total Cost	Quantity	Unit Cost	Total Cost	Quantity	Unit Cost	Total Cost
Jan. 1							40	5.00	$200
9				30	5.00	150	10	5.00	50
18	70	7.00	490				10	5.00	50
							70	7.00	490
22				36	7.00	252	10	5.00	50
							34	7.00	238
31	Balances					$402			$288

In a perpetual system, the LIFO method is applied to each sales transaction.

1. Cost of goods sold

2. January 31 inventory

Check Up Corner

International Connection

IFRS International Financial Reporting Standards (IFRS)

IFRS permit the first-in, first-out and weighted average cost methods but prohibit the last-in, first-out (LIFO) method for determining inventory costs. Since LIFO is used in the United States, adoption of IFRS could have a significant impact on many U.S. companies. One estimate is that the elimination of LIFO would increase net income of U.S. companies by over $250 billion and raise approximately $76 billion in taxes.*

*Differences between U.S. GAAP and IFRS are further discussed and illustrated in Appendix C.

Weighted Average Cost Method

When the weighted average cost method is used in a perpetual inventory system, a weighted average unit cost for each item is computed each time a purchase is made. This unit cost is used to determine the cost of each sale until another purchase is made and a new average is computed. This technique is called a *moving average*.

To illustrate, Exhibit 5 shows the use of weighted average under a perpetual inventory system for **Item 127B**.

Exhibit 5 Entries and Perpetual Inventory Account (Weighted Average)

Jan. 4	Accounts Receivable	21,000	
	Sales		21,000
4	Cost of Goods Sold	14,000	
	Inventory		14,000
10	Inventory	11,200	
	Accounts Payable		11,200
22	Accounts Receivable	10,800	
	Sales		10,800
22	Cost of Goods Sold	7,740	
	Inventory		7,740
28	Accounts Receivable	7,200	
	Sales		7,200
28	Cost of Goods Sold	5,160	
	Inventory		5,160
30	Inventory	13,980	
	Accounts Payable		13,980

Item 127B

	Purchases			Cost of Goods Sold			Inventory		
Date	Quantity	Unit Cost	Total Cost	Quantity	Unit Cost	Total Cost	Quantity	Unit Cost	Total Cost
Jan. 1							1,000	20.00	20,000
4				700	20.00	14,000	300	20.00	6,000
10	500	22.40	11,200				800	21.50	17,200
22				360	21.50	7,740	440	21.50	9,460
28				240	21.50	5,160	200	21.50	4,300
30	600	23.30	13,980				800	22.85	18,280
31	Balances					26,900	800	22.85	18,280

Cost of goods sold ↑

January 31 inventory ↑

The journal entries and the subsidiary inventory ledger for Item 127B are shown in Exhibit 5 as follows:

1. The beginning balance on January 1 is $20,000 (1,000 units at a unit cost of $20.00).

2. On January 4, 700 units were sold at a price of $30 each for sales of $21,000 (700 units at a selling price of $30 per unit). The cost of goods sold is $14,000 (700 units at a unit cost of $20). After the sale, there remains $6,000 of inventory (300 units at a unit cost of $20).

3. On January 10, $11,200 is purchased (500 units at a unit cost of $22.40). After the purchase, the weighted average unit cost of $21.50 is determined by dividing the total cost of the inventory on hand of $17,200 ($6,000 + $11,200) by the total quantity of inventory on hand of 800 (300 + 500) units. Thus, after the purchase, the inventory consists of 800 units at $21.50 per unit for a total cost of $17,200.

4. On January 22, 360 units are sold at a price of $30 each for sales of $10,800 (360 units at a selling price of $30 per unit). Using weighted average, the cost of goods sold is $7,740 (360 units × $21.50 per unit). After the sale, there remains $9,460 of inventory (440 units × $21.50 per unit).

5. The January 28 sale and January 30 purchase are recorded in a similar manner.

6. The ending balance on January 31 is $18,280 (800 units × $22.85 per unit).

Check Up Corner 6-2   Perpetual Inventory: Weighted Average Method

The beginning inventory, purchases, and sales of Item QX3 for the month of January are as follows:

Jan.	1	Inventory	40 units at $5
	9	Sale	30 units
	18	Purchase	70 units at $7
	22	Sale	36 units

The company uses the perpetual inventory system. Determine (1) the cost of goods sold for January and (2) the January 31 inventory balance using the weighted average cost method.

Solution:

Under the weighted average cost method, a weighted average unit cost for each item is computed each time a purchase is made and used to determine the cost of each sale until another purchase is made.

	Purchases			Cost of Goods Sold			Inventory		
Date	Quantity	Unit Cost	Total Cost	Quantity	Unit Cost	Total Cost	Quantity	Unit Cost	Total Cost
Jan. 1							40	5.00	$200
9				30	5.00	150	10	5.00	50
18	70	7.00	490				80	6.75 *	540
22				36	6.75	243	44	6.75	297
31	Balances					$393			$297

* ($50 + $490) ÷ 80 units

1. Cost of goods sold

2. January 31 inventory

The weighted average unit cost may change with each new inventory purchase.

There are no cost layers of inventory like in FIFO and LIFO; instead, the inventory balance is the quantity times the weighted average unit cost.

Check Up Corner

Why It Matters

Computerized Perpetual Inventory Systems

Your purchases are scanned when you go through the checkout line at **Best Buy (BBY)**. The scanned data are used to identify the price and adjust the inventory levels. Computerized perpetual inventory systems are used like this when there are many inventory transactions and a manual system is simply not feasible.

Computerized perpetual inventory systems are useful to managers in controlling and managing inventory. For example, if Best Buy has fast-selling items, they can be reordered before the stock runs out. Sales patterns can also be analyzed to determine when to mark down merchandise or when to restock seasonal merchandise. Finally, computerized inventory data can be used to evaluate the effectiveness of advertising campaigns and promotions.

Inventory Costing Methods Under a Periodic Inventory System

Objective 4
Determine the cost of inventory under the periodic inventory system, using the FIFO, LIFO, and weighted average cost methods.

When the periodic inventory system is used, only revenue is recorded each time a sale is made. No entry is made at the time of the sale to record the cost of the goods sold. At the end of the accounting period, a physical inventory is taken to determine the cost of the inventory and the cost of the goods sold.[2]

Like the perpetual inventory system, a cost flow assumption must be made when identical units are acquired at different unit costs during a period. In such cases, the FIFO, LIFO, or weighted average cost method is used.

First-In, First-Out Method

To illustrate the use of the FIFO method in a periodic inventory system, we use the same data for **Item 127B** as in the perpetual inventory example. The beginning inventory and purchases of Item 127B in January are as follows:

Jan. 1	Inventory	1,000 units at	$20.00	$20,000
10	Purchase	500 units at	22.40	11,200
30	Purchase	600 units at	23.30	13,980
Available for sale during month		2,100		$45,180

The physical count on January 31 shows that 800 units are on hand. Using the FIFO method, the cost of the goods on hand at the end of the period is made up of the most recent costs. The cost of the 800 units in the ending inventory on January 31 is determined as follows:

Most recent costs, January 30 purchase	600 units at	$23.30	$13,980
Next most recent costs, January 10 purchase	200 units at	22.40	4,480
Inventory, January 31	800 units		$18,460

Deducting the cost of the January 31 inventory of $18,460 from the cost of goods available for sale of $45,180 yields the cost of goods sold of $26,720, computed as follows:

Beginning inventory, January 1	$ 20,000
Purchases ($11,200 + $13,980)	25,180
Cost of goods available for sale in January	$ 45,180
Ending inventory, January 31	(18,460)
Cost of goods sold	$ 26,720

The $18,460 cost of the ending inventory on January 31 is made up of the most recent costs. The $26,720 cost of goods sold is made up of the beginning inventory and the earliest costs. Exhibit 6 shows the relationship of the cost of goods sold for January and the ending inventory on January 31.

Last-In, First-Out Method

When the LIFO method is used, the cost of goods on hand at the end of the period is made up of the earliest costs. Based on the same data for **Item 127B** as in the FIFO example, the cost of the 800 units in ending inventory on January 31 is $16,000, which consists of 800 units from the beginning inventory at a cost of $20.00 per unit.

IFRS
See Appendix C for more information.

Deducting the cost of the January 31 inventory of $16,000 from the cost of goods available for sale of $45,180 yields the cost of goods sold of $29,180, computed as follows:

Beginning inventory, January 1	$ 20,000
Purchases ($11,200 + $13,980)	25,180
Cost of goods available for sale in January	$ 45,180
Ending inventory, January 31	(16,000)
Cost of goods sold	$ 29,180

The $16,000 cost of the ending inventory on January 31 is made up of the earliest costs. The $29,180 cost of goods sold is made up of the most recent costs. Exhibit 7 shows the relationship of the cost of goods sold for January and the ending inventory on January 31.

---

[2] Determining the cost of goods sold using the periodic system was illustrated in Appendix 2 to Chapter 5.

Exhibit 6

First-In, First-Out Flow of Costs with Periodic Inventory

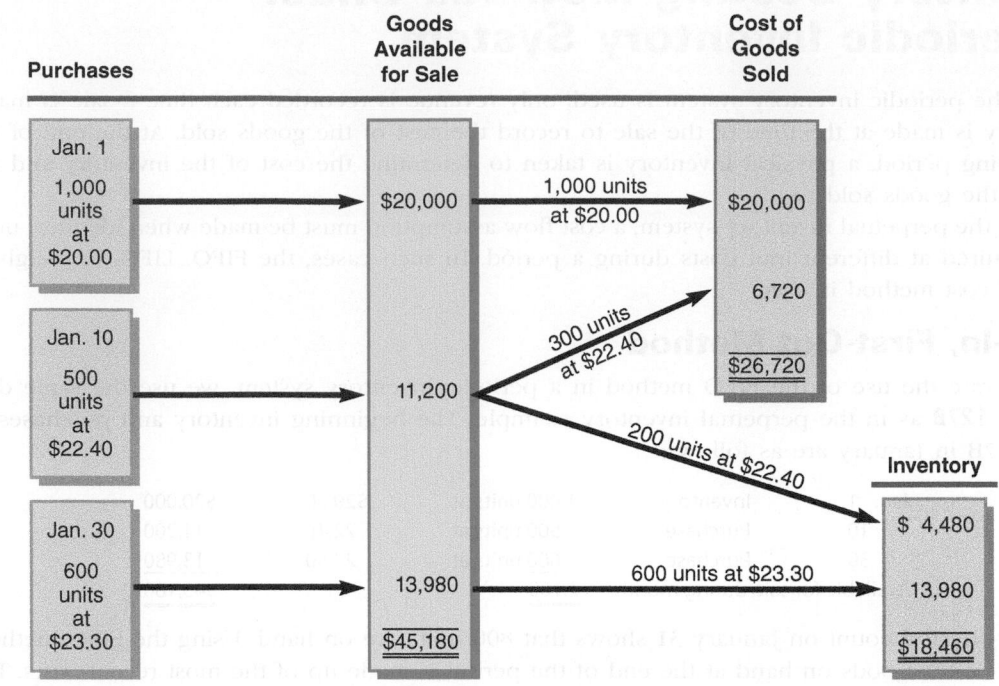

Exhibit 7

Last-In, First-Out Flow of Costs with Periodic Inventory

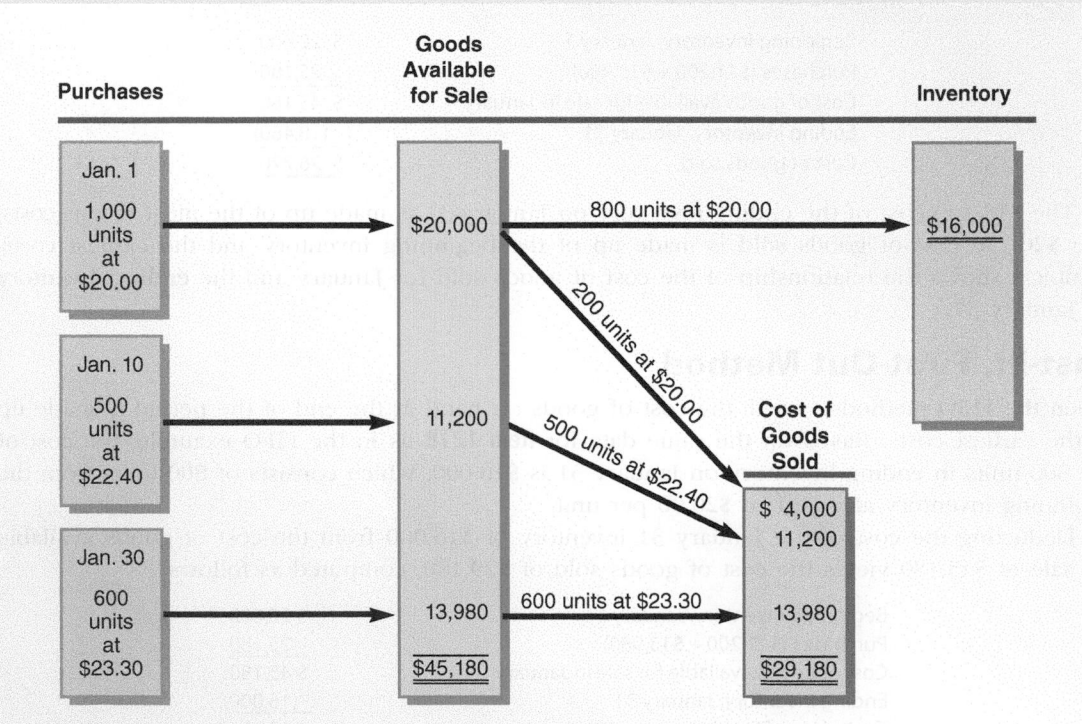

Weighted Average Cost Method

The weighted average cost method uses the weighted average unit cost for determining the cost of goods sold and the ending inventory. If purchases are relatively uniform during a period, the weighted average cost method provides results that are similar to the physical flow of goods.

The weighted average unit cost is determined as follows:

$$\text{Weighted Average Unit Cost} = \frac{\text{Total Cost of Units Available for Sale}}{\text{Units Available for Sale}}$$

To illustrate, the data for **Item 127B** are used as follows:

$$\text{Weighted Average Unit Cost} = \frac{\text{Total Cost of Units Available for Sale}}{\text{Units Available for Sale}} = \frac{\$45,180}{2,100 \text{ units}}$$

$$= \$21.51 \text{ per unit (rounded)}$$

The cost of the January 31 ending inventory is as follows:

Inventory, January 31: $17,208 (800 units × $21.51)

Deducting the cost of the January 31 inventory of $17,208 from the cost of goods available for sale of $45,180 yields the cost of goods sold of $27,972, computed as follows:

Beginning inventory, January 1	$ 20,000
Purchases ($11,200 + $13,980)	25,180
Cost of goods available for sale in January	$ 45,180
Ending inventory, January 31	(17,208)
Cost of goods sold	$ 27,972

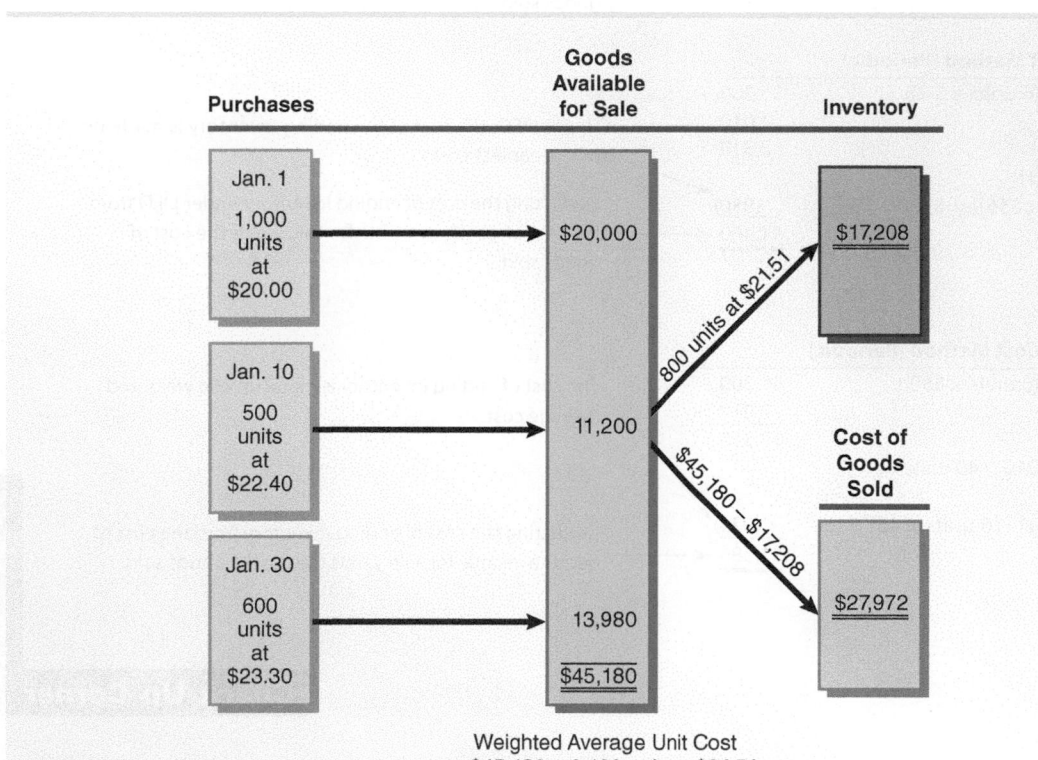

Exhibit 8
Weighted Average
Flow of Costs with
Periodic Inventory

Check Up Corner 6-3   Periodic Inventory

The beginning inventory, purchases, and sales of Item PEAR4 for a recent year are as follows:

Jan.	1	Inventory	6 units at $50	$ 300
Mar.	20	Purchase	14 units at $55	770
Oct.	30	Purchase	20 units at $62	1,240
		Available for sale	40 units	$2,310

There are 16 units of the item in the physical inventory at December 31, the end of the fiscal year. The company uses the periodic inventory system. Determine (1) the December 31 inventory balance and (2) the cost of goods sold for the year, using the:

a.   first-in, first-out (FIFO) method.

b.   last-in, first-out (LIFO) method.

c.   weighted average cost method.

Solution:

Under the periodic system, the LIFO and FIFO methods are applied at the end of the accounting period.

a.

First-In, First-Out Method (Periodic)

Beginning inventory, January 1 (6 units × $50)	$ 300
Purchases ($770 + $1,240)	2,010
Cost of goods available for sale	$2,310
1. Ending inventory, December 31 (16 units × $62)	(992)
2. Cost of goods sold	$1,318

Under FIFO, the cost of the ending inventory is made up of the most recent costs.

Deducting the cost of ending inventory under FIFO from the cost of goods available for sale yields the cost of goods sold.

b.

Last-In, Last-Out Method (Periodic)

Beginning inventory, January 1 (6 units × $50)	$ 300
Purchases ($770 + $1,240)	2,010
Cost of goods available for sale	$2,310
1. Ending inventory, December 31:	
[(6 units × $50) + (10 units × $55)] = $300 + $550	(850)
2. Cost of goods sold	$1,460

Under LIFO, the cost of the ending inventory is made up of the earliest costs.

Deducting the cost of ending inventory under LIFO from the cost of goods available for sale yields the cost of goods sold.

c.

Weighted Average Cost Method (Periodic)

Beginning inventory, January 1 (6 units × $50)	$ 300
Purchases ($770 + $1,240)	2,010
Cost of goods available for sale	$2,310
Weighted average unit cost ($2,310 ÷ 40 units = $57.75 per unit)	
1. Ending inventory, December 31 (16 units × $57.75)	(924)
2. Cost of goods sold	$1,386

The cost of ending inventory is made up of a weighted average cost.

Deducting the cost of ending inventory from the cost of goods available for sale yields the cost of goods sold.

Check Up Corner

Comparing Inventory Costing Methods

A different cost flow is assumed for the FIFO, LIFO, and weighted average inventory cost flow methods. As a result, the three methods normally yield different amounts for the following:

- Cost of goods sold
- Gross profit
- Net income
- Ending inventory

Using the perpetual inventory system illustration with sales of $39,000 (1,300 units × $30), the following differences are apparent:[3]

IFRS
See Appendix C for more information.

Partial Income Statements

	First-In, First-Out	Weighted Average Cost	Last-In, First-Out
Sales	$ 39,000	$ 39,000	$ 39,000
Cost of goods sold	(26,720)	(26,900)	(27,200)
Gross profit	$ 12,280	$ 12,100	$ 11,800
Inventory, Jan. 31	$ 18,460	$ 18,280	$ 17,980

The preceding differences show the effect of increasing costs (prices). If costs (prices) remain the same, all three methods would yield the same results. However, costs (prices) normally do change. The effects of changing costs (prices) on the FIFO and LIFO methods are summarized in Exhibit 9. The weighted average cost method will always yield results between those of FIFO and LIFO.

FIFO reports higher gross profit and net income than the LIFO method when costs (prices) are increasing, as shown in Exhibit 9. However, in periods of rapidly rising costs, the inventory that is sold must be replaced at increasingly higher costs. In such cases, the larger FIFO gross profit and net income are sometimes called *inventory profits* or *illusory profits*.

During a period of increasing costs, LIFO matches more recent costs against sales on the income statement. Thus, it can be argued that the LIFO method more nearly matches current costs with current revenues. LIFO also offers an income tax savings during periods of increasing costs. This is because LIFO reports the lowest amount of gross profit and, thus, taxable net income.[4] However, under LIFO, the ending inventory on the balance sheet may be quite different from its current replacement cost. In such cases, the financial statements normally include a note that estimates what the inventory would have been if FIFO had been used.

The weighted average cost method is, in a sense, a compromise between FIFO and LIFO. The effect of cost (price) trends is averaged in determining the cost of goods sold and the ending inventory.

	+ Increasing Costs (Prices)		− Decreasing Costs (Prices)	
	↑ Highest Amount	↓ Lowest Amount	↑ Highest Amount	↓ Lowest Amount
Cost of goods sold	LIFO	FIFO	FIFO	LIFO
Gross profit	FIFO	LIFO	LIFO	FIFO
Net income	FIFO	LIFO	LIFO	FIFO
Ending inventory	FIFO	LIFO	LIFO	FIFO

Exhibit 9
Effects of Changing Costs (Prices): FIFO and LIFO Cost Methods

---

[3] Similar results would also occur when comparing inventory costing methods under a periodic inventory system.
[4] A proposal currently exists to not allow the use of LIFO for tax purposes.

Objective 6
Describe and illustrate the reporting of inventory in the financial statements.

Reporting Inventory in the Financial Statements

Cost is the primary basis for valuing and reporting inventories in the financial statements. However, inventory may be valued at other than cost in the following cases:

- The cost of replacing items in inventory is below the recorded cost.
- The inventory cannot be sold at normal prices due to imperfections, style changes, spoilage, damage, obsolescence, or other causes.

Valuation at Lower of Cost or Market

IFRS
See Appendix C for more information.

If the market is lower than the purchase cost, the **lower-of-cost-or-market (LCM) method** is used to value the inventory. *Market,* as used in *lower of cost or market,* is the **net realizable value** of the inventory.[5] Net realizable value is determined as follows:

Net Realizable Value = Estimated Selling Price – Direct Costs of Disposal

Direct costs of disposal include selling expenses such as special advertising or sales commissions. To illustrate, assume the following data about an item of damaged inventory:

Original cost	$1,000
Estimated selling price	800
Estimated selling expenses	150

In applying LCM, the market value of the inventory is $650, computed as follows:

Market Value (Net Realizable Value) = $800 – $150 = $650

Thus, the inventory would be valued at $650, which is the lower of its cost of $1,000 and its market value of $650.

The lower-of-cost-or-market method can be applied in one of three ways. The cost, market price, and any declines could be determined for the following:

1. Each item in the inventory
2. Each major class or category of inventory
3. Total inventory as a whole

The amount of any price decline is included in the cost of goods sold. This, in turn, reduces gross profit and net income in the period in which the price declines occur. This matching of price declines to the period in which they occur is the primary advantage of using the lower-of-cost-or-market method.

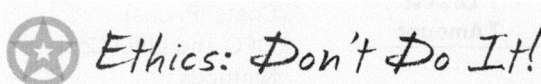
Link to Best Buy

Best Buy values its inventory at lower of cost or market based upon cost and the amount it expects to realize from the sale.

Ethics: Don't Do It!

Where's the Bonus?

Managers are often given bonuses based on reported earnings numbers. This can create a conflict. For example, LIFO can improve the value of the company through lower taxes. However, using LIFO also lowers management bonuses that are based on reported income. Thus, a manager might use FIFO to maximize his or her bonus even though LIFO is better for the company.

[5] The discussion in this section applies to companies that use the FIFO or weighted average cost methods and follows the guidance in Accounting Standards Update, *Inventory (Topic 330): Simplifying the Measurement of Inventory,* July 2015, FASB. For companies that use LIFO, market value is defined as replacement cost.

To illustrate, assume the following data for 400 identical units of Item A in inventory on December 31:

Cost per unit	$10.25
Market value (net realizable value) per unit	9.50

Since the market value of Item A is $9.50 per unit, $9.50 is used under the lower-of-cost-or-market method.

Exhibit 10 illustrates applying the lower-of-cost-or-market method to (1) each inventory item (Echo, Foxtrot, Sierra, Tango), (2) each major class of inventory (Class 1, Class 2), and (3) inventory in total. As applied on an item-by-item basis, the total lower-of-cost-or-market is $15,070, which is a market decline of $450 ($15,520 − $15,070). As applied to each class of inventory, the inventory would be valued at $15,412, which is a market decline of $108 ($15,520 − $15,412). Finally, if the lower-of-cost-or-market method is applied to the total inventory, the inventory would be valued at $15,472, which is a market decline of $48 ($15,520 − $15,472). The market declines under each approach ($450, $108, or $48) would be included in cost of goods sold.

Applying the lower-of-cost-or-market method on an item-by-item basis always gives the lowest value for inventory. Conversely, applying the lower-of-cost-or-market method to the total inventory always gives the highest value for inventory.

Exhibit 10
Determining Inventory at Lower of Cost or Market (LCM)

Item	Inventory Quantity	Cost per Unit	Market Value per Unit (Net Realizable Value)	Cost	Market	Lower of Cost or Market (LCM)	
Echo	400	$10.25	$ 9.50	$ 4,100	$ 3,800	$ 3,800	**(1)**
Foxtrot	120	22.50	24.10	2,700	2,892	2,700	**Applied**
Sierra	600	8.00	7.75	4,800	4,650	4,650	**Individual Item**
Tango	280	14.00	14.75	3,920	4,130	3,920	**by Item**
Total				$15,520	$15,472	**$15,070**	
Class 1:							
Echo	400	$10.25	$ 9.50	$ 4,100	$ 3,800		
Foxtrot	120	22.50	24.10	2,700	2,892		
Subtotal				$ 6,800	$ 6,692	$ 6,692	**(2)**
							Applied Class
Class 2:							**by Class**
Sierra	600	8.00	7.75	$ 4,800	$ 4,650		
Tango	280	14.00	14.75	3,920	4,130		
Subtotal				$ 8,720	$ 8,780	8,720	
Total				$15,520	$15,472	**$15,412**	
Echo	400	$10.25	$ 9.50	$ 4,100	$ 3,800		**(3)**
Foxtrot	120	22.50	24.10	2,700	2,892		**Applied in**
Sierra	600	8.00	7.75	4,800	4,650		**Total**
Tango	280	14.00	14.75	3,920	4,130		
Total				$15,520	$15,472	**$15,472**	

The excess of cost over the amount **Best Buy** expects to receive from the sale of an item is called a markdown.

Link to
Best Buy

Check Up Corner 6-4 Lower of Cost or Market

JJ's Electronics Company has three products in inventory (PCs, tablets, and smartphones). Each product's quantity, cost per unit, and market value per unit are as follows:

Item	Inventory Quantity	Cost per Unit	Market Value per Unit (Net Realizable Value)
PC	10	$175	$168
Tablet	12	132	150
Smartphone	8	199	187

Apply the lower-of-cost-or-market method to each inventory item in a form similar to Exhibit 10.

Solution:

The cost of each item is determined by multiplying the inventory quantity by the cost per unit.

The market value of each item is determined by multiplying the inventory quantity by the market value per unit.

	A	B	C	D	E	F	G	
1				Market Value				
2		Inventory	Cost per	per Unit				
3	Item	Quantity	Unit	(Net Realizable Value)	Cost	Market	LCM	
4	PC	10	$175	$168	$1,750	$1,680	$1,680	When applying
5	Tablet	12	132	150	1,584	1,800	1,584	the LCM method
6	Smartphone	8	199	187	1,592	1,496	1,496	to each inventory item,
7	Total				$4,926	$4,976	$4,760	the lower of the cost or
8								market is selected.

The total inventory value is the sum of the lower of the cost or market value for each item in inventory.

Check Up Corner

Inventory on the Balance Sheet

IFRS
See Appendix C for more information.

Inventory is usually reported in the Current assets section of the balance sheet. In addition to this amount, the following are reported on the balance sheet or in the accompanying notes:

- The method of determining the cost of the inventory (FIFO, LIFO, or weighted average)
- The method of valuing the inventory (cost or the lower of cost or market)

The presentation for inventory for **Best Buy (BBY)** within the Current assets section of the balance sheet and accompanying notes is as follows:

Link to Best Buy

Best Buy Co., Inc.
Balance Sheet
January 30
(in millions)

Assets

Current assets:

Cash and cash equivalents...		$1,976
Short-term investments		1,305
Accounts receivable	$1,211	
Allowance for doubtful accounts.....................................	(49)	
Accounts receivable, net		1,162
Merchandise inventories		5,051
Other current assets		392
Total current assets		$9,886

Notes to Financial Statements:

Merchandise Inventories

Merchandise inventories are recorded at the lower of cost, using the average cost, or market.

Source: Adapted from Best Buy Co., Inc., *Form 10-K for the Fiscal Year Ended January 30, 2016.*

It is not unusual for a large business to use different costing methods for segments of its inventories. Also, a business may change its inventory costing method. In such cases, the effect of the change and the reason for the change are disclosed in the notes to the financial statements.

Effect of Inventory Errors on the Financial Statements

Any errors in inventory will affect the balance sheet and income statement. Some reasons that inventory errors may occur include the following:

- Physical inventory on hand was miscounted.
- Costs were incorrectly assigned to inventory. For example, the FIFO, LIFO, or weighted average cost method was incorrectly applied.
- Inventory in transit was incorrectly included or excluded from inventory.
- Consigned inventory was incorrectly included or excluded from inventory.

Inventory errors often arise from merchandise that is in transit at year-end. As discussed in Chapter 5, shipping terms determine when the title to merchandise passes. When goods are purchased or sold *FOB shipping point*, title passes to the buyer when the goods are shipped. When the terms are *FOB destination*, title passes to the buyer when the goods are received.

To illustrate, assume that SysExpress ordered the following merchandise from American Products:

Date ordered:	December 27, 20Y6
Amount:	$10,000
Terms:	FOB shipping point, 2/10, n/30
Date shipped by seller:	December 30, 20Y6
Date delivered:	January 3, 20Y7

When SysExpress counts its physical inventory on December 31, 20Y6, the merchandise is still in transit. In such cases, it would be easy for SysExpress to not include the $10,000 of merchandise in its December 31 physical inventory. However, since the merchandise was purchased *FOB shipping point*, SysExpress owns the merchandise. Thus, it should be included in the December 31

Pathways Challenge

This is Accounting!

Economic Activity

Tyson Foods (TSN), one of the world's largest food companies, operates a chicken production process that begins with the hatching of chicks and ends with packaged chicken for sale at your local grocery market. The most desirable chickens are maintained as breeding stock for laying eggs and producing chicks. Once a chick is hatched, it is transported to a growing farm. At the farm, the chicken is housed and fed corn, soybean, and other feed. Once the chicken reaches maturity, it is transported to a processing plant where it is converted into a finished product and packaged for delivery to your local grocery store.

Critical Thinking/Judgment

How should Tyson account for the transportation, boarding, and feed costs related to chickens sent to the processing plant?
Can you think of any other costs related to chickens raised for processing?
Should the costs of the breeder flock be included in inventory?

Suggested answer at end of chapter.

inventory, even though it is not on hand. Likewise, any merchandise *sold* by SysExpress *FOB destination* is still SysExpress's inventory, even if it is in transit to the buyer on December 31.

Inventory errors often arise from **consigned inventory**. Manufacturers sometimes ship merchandise to retailers who act as the manufacturer's selling agent. The manufacturer, called the **consignor**, retains title until the goods are sold. Such merchandise is said to be shipped *on consignment* to the retailer, called the **consignee**. Any unsold merchandise at year-end is a part of the manufacturer's (consignor's) inventory, even though the merchandise is in the hands of the retailer (consignee). At year-end, it would be easy for the retailer (consignee) to incorrectly include the consigned merchandise in its physical inventory. Likewise, the manufacturer (consignor) should include consigned inventory in its physical inventory, even though the inventory is not on hand.

Income Statement Effects Inventory errors will misstate the income statement amounts for cost of goods sold, gross profit, and net income. The effects of inventory errors on the current period's income statement are summarized in Exhibit 11.

Exhibit 11

Effect of Inventory Errors on Current Period's Income Statement

	Income Statement Effect		
Inventory Error	**Cost of Goods Sold**	**Gross Profit**	**Net Income**
Beginning inventory is:			
↓ Understated	↓ Understated	↑ Overstated	↑ Overstated
↑ Overstated	↑ Overstated	↓ Understated	↓ Understated
Ending inventory is:			
↓ Understated	↑ Overstated	↓ Understated	↓ Understated
↑ Overstated	↓ Understated	↑ Overstated	↑ Overstated

To illustrate, the income statements of SysExpress shown in Exhibit 12 are used.[6] On December 31, 20Y6, assume that SysExpress incorrectly records its physical inventory as $50,000 instead of the correct amount of $60,000. Thus, the December 31, 20Y6, inventory is understated by $10,000 ($60,000 – $50,000). As a result, the cost of goods sold is overstated by $10,000. The gross profit and the net income for the year will also be understated by $10,000.

The December 31, 20Y6, inventory becomes the January 1, 20Y7, inventory. Thus, the beginning inventory for 20Y7 is understated by $10,000. As a result, the cost of goods sold is understated by $10,000 for 20Y7. The gross profit and net income for 20Y7 will be overstated by $10,000.

As shown in Exhibit 12, because the ending inventory of one period is the beginning inventory of the next period, the effects of inventory errors carry forward to the next period. Specifically, if uncorrected, the effects of inventory errors reverse themselves in the next period. In Exhibit 12, the combined net income for the two years of $525,000 is correct, even though the 20Y6 and 20Y7 income statements were incorrect.

Balance Sheet Effects Inventory errors misstate the inventory, current assets, total assets, and stockholders' equity on the balance sheet. The effects of inventory errors on the current period's balance sheet are summarized in Exhibit 13.

For the SysExpress illustration shown in Exhibit 12, the December 31, 20Y6, ending inventory was understated by $10,000. As a result, the inventory, current assets, and total assets would be understated by $10,000 on the December 31, 20Y6, balance sheet. Because the ending physical inventory is understated, the cost of goods sold for 20Y6 will be overstated by $10,000. Thus, the gross profit and the net income for 20Y6 are understated by $10,000. Because the net income is closed to Retained Earnings at the end of the period, the stockholders' equity on the December 31, 20Y6, balance sheet is also understated by $10,000.

[6] The effect of inventory errors will be illustrated using the periodic system. This is because it is easier to see the impact of inventory errors on the income statement using the periodic system. The effect of inventory errors would be the same under the perpetual inventory system.

Exhibit 12 Effects of Inventory Errors on Two Years' Income Statements

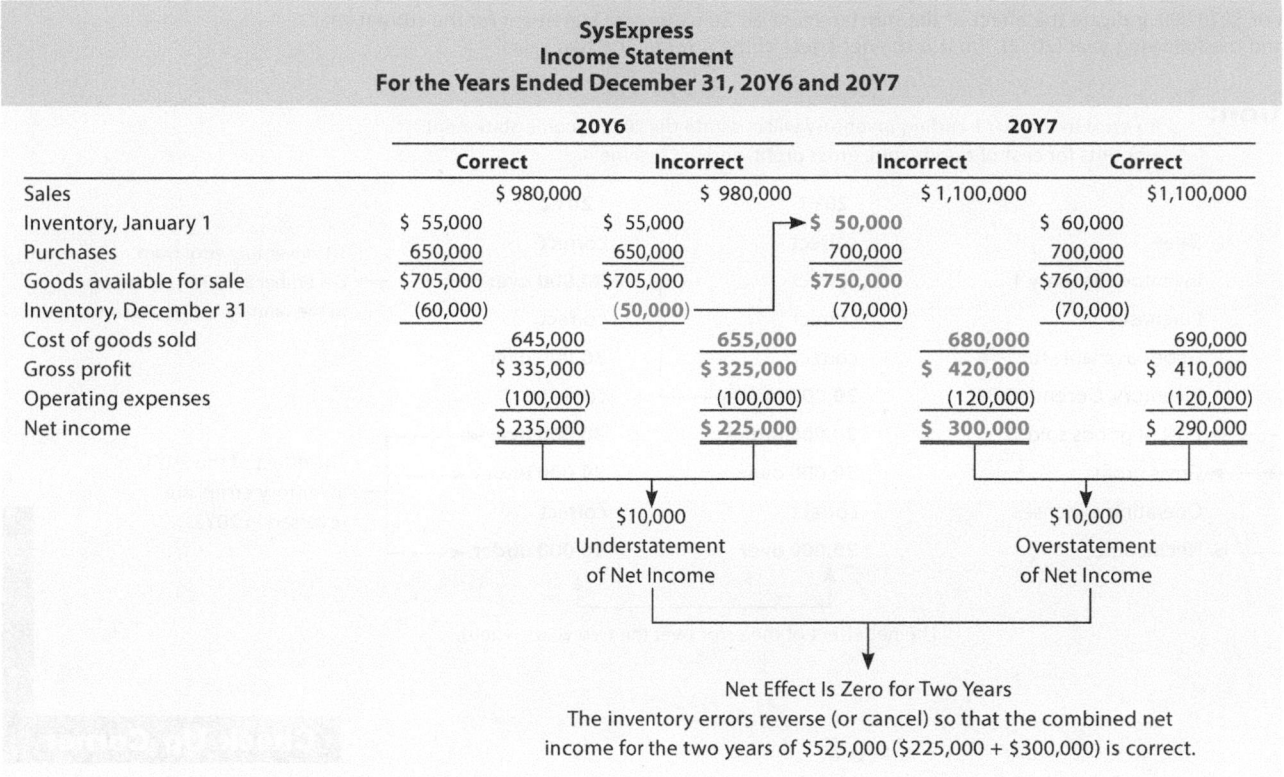

	20Y6		20Y7	
	Correct	**Incorrect**	**Incorrect**	**Correct**
Sales	$ 980,000	$ 980,000	$ 1,100,000	$1,100,000
Inventory, January 1	$ 55,000	$ 55,000	$ 50,000	$ 60,000
Purchases	650,000	650,000	700,000	700,000
Goods available for sale	$705,000	$705,000	$750,000	$760,000
Inventory, December 31	(60,000)	(50,000)	(70,000)	(70,000)
Cost of goods sold	645,000	655,000	680,000	690,000
Gross profit	$ 335,000	$ 325,000	$ 420,000	$ 410,000
Operating expenses	(100,000)	(100,000)	(120,000)	(120,000)
Net income	$ 235,000	$ 225,000	$ 300,000	$ 290,000

$10,000
Understatement
of Net Income

$10,000
Overstatement
of Net Income

Net Effect Is Zero for Two Years
The inventory errors reverse (or cancel) so that the combined net
income for the two years of $525,000 ($225,000 + $300,000) is correct.

Inventory errors reverse themselves within two years. As a result, the balance sheet will be correct as of December 31, 20Y7. Using the SysExpress illustration from Exhibit 12, these effects are summarized as follows:

	Amount of Misstatement	
Balance Sheet:	**December 31, 20Y6**	**December 31, 20Y7**
Inventory overstated (understated)	$(10,000)	Correct
Current assets overstated (understated)	(10,000)	Correct
Total assets overstated (understated)	(10,000)	Correct
Stockholders' equity overstated (understated)	(10,000)	Correct
Income Statement:	**20Y6**	**20Y7**
Cost of goods sold overstated (understated)	$ 10,000	$(10,000)
Gross profit overstated (understated)	(10,000)	10,000
Net income overstated (understated)	(10,000)	10,000

		Balance Sheet Effect		
Ending Inventory Error	**Inventory**	**Current Assets**	**Total Assets**	**Stockholders' Equity (Retained Earnings)**
↓ Understated	↓ Understated	↓ Understated	↓ Understated	↓ Understated
↑ Overstated	↑ Overstated	↑ Overstated	↑ Overstated	↑ Overstated

Exhibit 13

Effect of Inventory Errors on Current Period's Balance Sheet

Check Up Corner 6-5   Effects of Inventory Errors

Zulu Industries incorrectly counted its December 31, 20Y1, inventory at $250,000 instead of the correct amount of $220,000. Indicate the effect of the misstatement on Zulu's income statement for the current year (20Y1) and the following year (20Y2). What is the net effect of the error for the two years?

Solution:

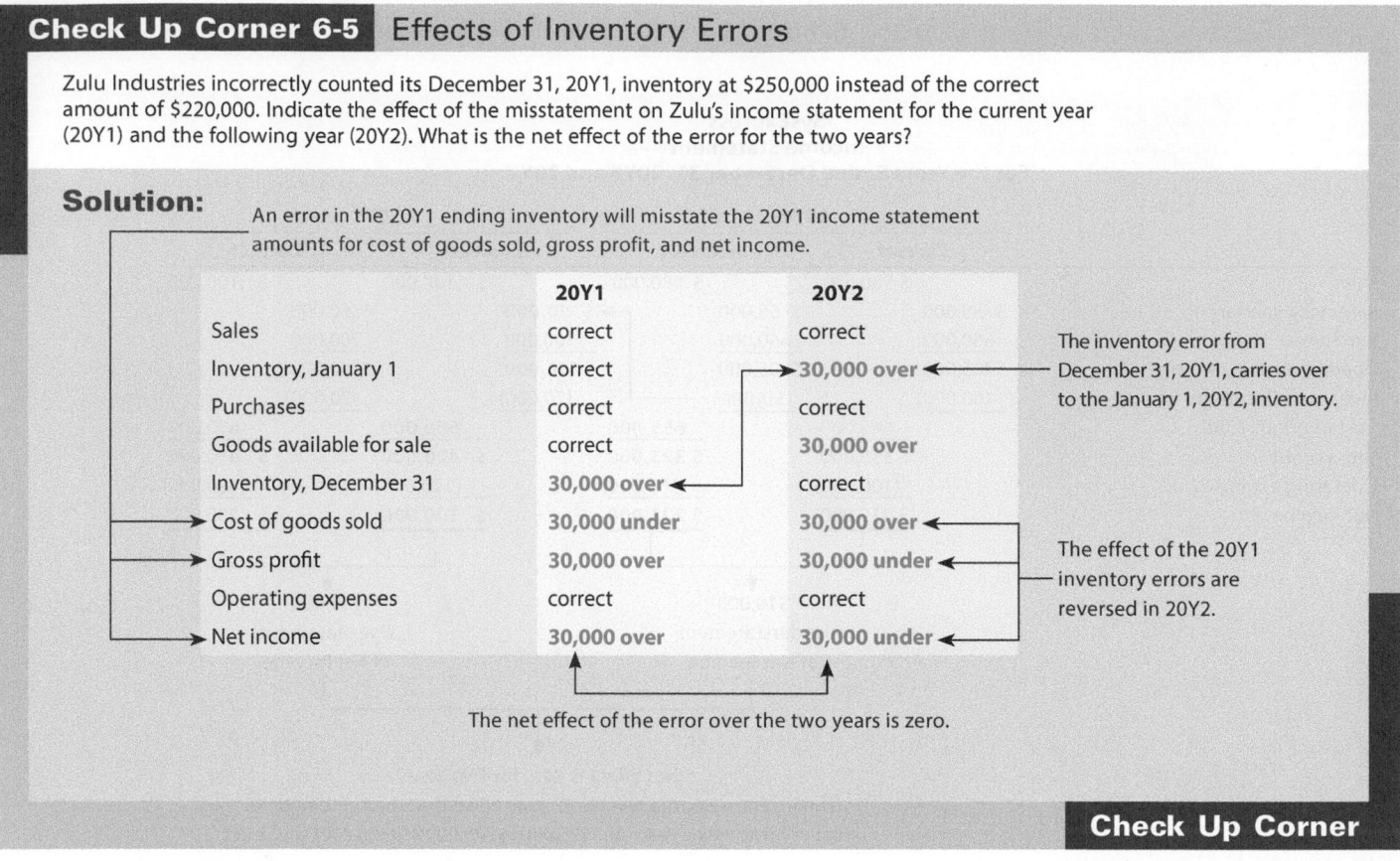

An error in the 20Y1 ending inventory will misstate the 20Y1 income statement amounts for cost of goods sold, gross profit, and net income.

	20Y1	20Y2	
Sales	correct	correct	
Inventory, January 1	correct	30,000 over	The inventory error from December 31, 20Y1, carries over to the January 1, 20Y2, inventory.
Purchases	correct	correct	
Goods available for sale	correct	30,000 over	
Inventory, December 31	30,000 over	correct	
Cost of goods sold	30,000 under	30,000 over	
Gross profit	30,000 over	30,000 under	The effect of the 20Y1 inventory errors are reversed in 20Y2.
Operating expenses	correct	correct	
Net income	30,000 over	30,000 under	

The net effect of the error over the two years is zero.

Check Up Corner

Analysis for Decision Making

Objective 7

Describe and illustrate the inventory turnover and the number of days' sales in inventory in analyzing the efficiency and effectiveness of inventory management.

Inventory Turnover and Number of Days' Sales in Inventory

A merchandising business should keep enough inventory on hand to meet its customers' needs. A failure to do so may result in lost sales. However, too much inventory ties up funds that could be used to improve operations. Also, excess inventory increases expenses such as storage and property taxes. Finally, excess inventory increases the risk of losses due to price decreases, damage, or changes in customer tastes.

Two measures to analyze inventory management are:

- inventory turnover and
- number of days' sales in inventory.

Inventory turnover measures the relationship between the cost of goods sold and the amount of inventory carried during the period. It measures the number of times inventory is turned into sold goods during the year. It is computed as follows:

$$\text{Inventory Turnover} = \frac{\text{Cost of Goods Sold}}{\text{Average Inventory}}$$

To illustrate, inventory turnover for **Best Buy (BBY)** is computed from the following data (in millions) from two recent annual reports:

	Year 3	Year 2	Year 1
Cost of goods sold	$30,334	$31,292	$31,212
Inventories:			
Beginning of year	$5,174	$5,376	$6,781
End of year	$5,051	$5,174	$5,376
Average inventory:*			
($5,174 + $5,051) ÷ 2	$5,112.5		
($5,376 + $5,174) ÷ 2		$5,275.0	
($6,781 + $5,376) ÷ 2			$6,078.5
Inventory turnover:*			
$30,334 ÷ $5,112.5	5.9		
$31,292 ÷ $5,275.0		5.9	
$31,212 ÷ $6,078.5			5.1

* Rounded to one decimal place.

Generally, the larger the inventory turnover, the more efficient and effective the company is in managing inventory. In the preceding example, inventory turnover increased slightly from 5.1 to 5.9 during Year 2; thus, Best Buy's inventory management improved during Year 2. Between Year 2 and Year 3, inventory turnover remained stable.

The **number of days' sales in inventory** measures the length of time it takes to acquire, sell, and replace the inventory. It is computed as follows:[7]

$$\text{Number of Days' Sales in Inventory} = \frac{\text{Average Inventory}}{\text{Average Daily Cost of Goods Sold}}$$

The average daily cost of goods sold is determined by dividing the cost of goods sold by 365.[8] Based upon the preceding data, the number of days' sales in inventory for **Best Buy** is computed as follows:

	Year 3	Year 2	Year 1
Cost of goods sold	$30,334	$31,292	$31,212
Average daily cost of goods sold:*			
$30,334 ÷ 365 days	83.1		
$31,292 ÷ 365 days		85.7	
$31,212 ÷ 365 days			85.5
Average inventory:*			
($5,174 + $5,051) ÷ 2	$5,112.5		
($5,376 + $5,174) ÷ 2		$5,275.0	
($6,781 + $5,376) ÷ 2			$6,078.5
Number of days' sales in inventory:*			
$5,112.5 ÷ $83.1	61.5 days		
$5,275.0 ÷ $85.7		61.6 days	
$6,078.5 ÷ $85.5			71.1 days

* Rounded to one decimal place.

Generally, the lower the number of days' sales in inventory, the more efficient and effective the company is in managing inventory. The number of days' sales in inventory decreased from 71.1 days in Year 1 to 61.5 days in Year 3; thus, Best Buy's inventory management improved. This is consistent with the increase in inventory turnover during the year.

As with most financial ratios, differences exist among industries. To illustrate, **Whole Foods Market (WFM), Inc.** is a leading retailer of organic and natural foods in the United States. Because food is perishable, it will sell more rapidly than Best Buy's consumer electronics. Thus, Whole Foods' inventory management should be significantly more efficient than Best Buy's. For a recent year, this is confirmed as follows:

	Best Buy	Whole Foods
Inventory turnover	5.9	21.2
Number of days' sales in inventory	61.5 days	17.2 days

[7] Number of days' sales in inventory may also be computed as 365 days divided by the inventory turnover.

[8] We use 365 days for all computations involving real-world companies and data. We do this to highlight differences among companies and because computations using real-world data normally require rounding.

Make a Decision   Inventory Turnover and Number of Days' Sales in Inventory

Analyze and compare Amazon.com to Target (MAD 6-1)
(Continuing company analysis)

Analyze and compare Darden Restaurants to Panera Bread (MAD 6-2)

Analyze and compare Costco, Wal-Mart, and Nordstrom (MAD 6-3)

Analyze and compare Monster Beverage and Brown-Forman (MAD 6-4)

Make a Decision

Objective App

Describe and illustrate the estimation of inventory using the retail and gross profit methods of inventory costing.

Appendix Estimating Inventory Cost

A business may need to estimate the amount of inventory for the following reasons:

- Perpetual inventory records are not maintained.
- A disaster such as a fire or flood has destroyed the inventory records and the inventory.
- Monthly or quarterly financial statements are needed, but a physical inventory is taken only once a year.

This appendix describes and illustrates two widely used methods of estimating inventory cost.

Retail Method of Inventory Costing

The **retail inventory method** of estimating inventory cost requires costs and retail prices to be maintained for the merchandise available for sale. A ratio of cost to retail price is then used to convert ending inventory at retail to estimate the ending inventory cost.

The retail inventory method is applied as follows:

- Step 1. Determine the total merchandise available for sale at cost and retail.

- Step 2. Determine the ratio of the cost to retail of the merchandise available for sale.

- Step 3. Determine the ending inventory at retail by deducting the sales from the merchandise available for sale at retail.

- Step 4. Estimate the ending inventory cost by multiplying the ending inventory at retail by the cost to retail ratio.

Exhibit 14 illustrates the retail inventory method.

Exhibit 14

Determining Inventory by the Retail Method

	A	B	C
1		Cost	Retail
2	Inventory, January 1	$19,400	$ 36,000
3	Purchases in January (net)	42,600	64,000
Step 1 → 4	Merchandise available for sale	$62,000	$100,000
Step 2 → 5	Ratio of cost to retail price: $\dfrac{\$62,000}{\$100,000} = 62\%$		
6	Sales for January		70,000
Step 3 → 7	Inventory, January 31, at retail		$ 30,000
Step 4 → 8	Inventory, January 31, at estimated cost		
9	($30,000 × 62%)		$ 18,600
10			

When estimating the cost to retail ratio, the mix of items in the ending inventory is assumed to be the same as the merchandise available for sale. If the ending inventory is made up of different classes of merchandise, cost to retail ratios may be developed for each class of inventory.

An advantage of the retail method is that it provides inventory figures for preparing monthly statements. Department stores and similar retailers often determine gross profit and operating income each month but may take a physical inventory only once or twice a year. Thus, the retail method allows management to monitor operations more closely.

The retail method may also be used as an aid in taking a physical inventory. In this case, the items are counted and recorded at their retail (selling) prices instead of their costs. The physical inventory at retail is then converted to cost by using the cost to retail ratio.

Gross Profit Method of Inventory Costing

The **gross profit method** uses the estimated gross profit for the period to estimate the inventory at the end of the period. The gross profit is estimated from the preceding year, adjusted for any current-period changes in the cost and sales prices.

The gross profit method is applied as follows:

- Step 1. Determine the merchandise available for sale at cost.

- Step 2. Determine the estimated gross profit by multiplying the sales by the gross profit percentage, assumed to be 30% in this illustration.

- Step 3. Determine the estimated cost of goods sold by deducting the estimated gross profit from the sales.

- Step 4. Estimate the ending inventory cost by deducting the estimated cost of goods sold from the merchandise available for sale.

Exhibit 15 illustrates the gross profit method.

	A	B	C
1			**Cost**
2	Inventory, January 1		$ 57,000
3	Purchases in January (net)		180,000
Step 1 → 4	Merchandise available for sale		$ 237,000
5	Sales for January	$250,000	
Step 2 → 6	Estimated gross profit ($250,000 × 30%)	(75,000)	
Step 3 → 7	Estimated cost of goods sold		(175,000)
Step 4 → 8	Estimated inventory, January 31		$ 62,000
9			

Exhibit 15
Estimating Inventory by Gross Profit Method

The gross profit method is useful for estimating inventories for monthly or quarterly financial statements. It is also useful in estimating the cost of inventory destroyed by fire or other disasters.

Let's Review

Chapter Summary

1. Two objectives of inventory control are safeguarding the inventory and properly reporting it in the financial statements. The perpetual inventory system and physical count enhance control over inventory.

2. The three common inventory cost flow assumptions used in business are the (1) first-in, first-out method (FIFO); (2) last-in, first-out method (LIFO); and (3) weighted average cost method. The cost flow assumption affects the income statement and balance sheet.

3. In a perpetual inventory system, the number of units and the cost of each type of merchandise are recorded in a subsidiary inventory ledger, with a separate account for each type of merchandise.

4. In a periodic inventory system, a physical inventory is taken to determine the cost of the inventory and the cost of goods sold.

5. The three inventory costing methods will normally yield different amounts for (1) the ending inventory, (2) the cost of goods sold for the period, and (3) the gross profit (and net income) for the period.

6. The lower-of-cost-or-market (LCM) method is used to value inventory. The market value is the net realizable value of the merchandise. Inventory is usually presented in the Current assets section of the balance sheet, following receivables. The methods of determining the cost and valuing the inventory are reported. Errors in reporting inventory will affect the balance sheet and income statement.

7. Inventory turnover measures the number of times inventory is turned into sold goods during the period. It is computed as Cost of Goods Sold ÷ Average Inventory. The number of days' sales in inventory measures the length of time it takes to acquire, sell, and replace the inventory. It is computed as Average Inventory ÷ Average Daily Cost of Goods Sold. Generally, the larger the inventory turnover and the lower the number of days' sales in inventory, the more efficient and effective the company is in managing inventory.

Key Terms

consigned inventory (318)

consignee (318)

consignor (318)

first-in, first-out (FIFO) inventory cost flow method (302)

gross profit method (323)

inventory turnover (320)

last-in, first-out (LIFO) inventory cost flow method (302)

lower-of-cost-or-market (LCM) method (314)

net realizable value (314)

number of days' sales in inventory (321)

physical inventory (301)

purchase order (300)

receiving report (300)

retail inventory method (322)

specific identification inventory cost flow method (302)

subsidiary inventory ledger (300)

weighted average inventory cost flow method (302)

Practice

Multiple-Choice Questions

1. The inventory costing method that is based on the assumption that costs should be charged against revenue in the order in which they were incurred is:
   a. FIFO.
   b. LIFO.
   c. weighted average cost.
   d. perpetual inventory.

2. The following units of a particular item were purchased and sold during the period:

Beginning inventory	40 units at $20
First purchase	50 units at $21
Second purchase	50 units at $22
First sale	110 units
Third purchase	50 units at $23
Second sale	45 units

What is the cost of the 35 units on hand at the end of the period as determined under the perpetual inventory system by the LIFO costing method?

a. $715 c. $700
b. $705 d. $805

3. The following units of a particular item were available for sale during the period:

Beginning inventory	40 units at $20
First purchase	50 units at $21
Second purchase	50 units at $22
Third purchase	50 units at $23

What is the unit cost of the 35 units on hand at the end of the period as determined under the periodic inventory system by the FIFO costing method?

a. $20 c. $22
b. $21 d. $23

4. If inventory is being valued at cost and the price level is steadily rising, the method of costing that will yield the highest net income is:

a. LIFO. c. average.
b. FIFO. d. periodic.

5. If the inventory at the end of the year is understated by $7,500, the error will cause an:

a. understatement of cost of goods sold for the year by $7,500.
b. overstatement of gross profit for the year by $7,500.
c. overstatement of beginning inventory for the following year by $7,500.
d. understatement of net income for the year by $7,500.

Answers provided after Problem. Need more practice? Find additional multiple-choice questions, exercises, and problems in CengageNOWv2.

Exercises

1. Cost flow methods

Obj. 2

The following three identical units of Item BZ1810 are purchased during November:

Item BZ1810		Units	Cost
Nov.	2	Purchase	1	$ 55
	14	Purchase	1	57
	28	Purchase	1	62
	Total	3	$174
	Average cost per unit		$ 58 ($174 ÷ 3 units)

Assume that one unit is sold on November 30 for $90.

Determine the gross profit for November and ending inventory on November 30 using the (a) first-in, first-out (FIFO); (b) last-in, first-out (LIFO); and (c) weighted average cost methods.

2. Perpetual inventory using FIFO

Obj. 3

Beginning inventory, purchases, and sales for Item ProX2 are as follows:

Jan.	1	Inventory	60 units at $100
	9	Sale	35 units
	13	Purchase	50 units at $110
	25	Sale	48 units

Assuming a perpetual inventory system and using the first-in, first-out (FIFO) method, determine (a) the cost of goods sold on January 25 and (b) the inventory on January 31.

3. Perpetual inventory using LIFO

Obj. 3

Beginning inventory, purchases, and sales for Item Zebra 9x are as follows:

Apr.	1	Inventory	420 units at $8
	10	Sale	300 units
	18	Purchase	280 units at $9
	27	Sale	250 units

Assuming a perpetual inventory system and using the last-in, first-out (LIFO) method, determine (a) the cost of goods sold on April 27 and (b) the inventory on April 30.

4. Perpetual inventory using weighted average   Obj. 3

Beginning inventory, purchases, and sales for 30xT are as follows:

May	1	Inventory	50 units at $80
	12	Sale	35 units
	23	Purchase	60 units at $90
	26	Sale	55 units

Assuming a perpetual inventory system and using the weighted average method, determine the (a) weighted average unit cost after the May 23 purchase, (b) cost of goods sold on May 26, and (c) inventory on May 31.

5. Periodic inventory using FIFO, LIFO, and weighted average cost methods   Obj. 4

The units of an item available for sale during the year were as follows:

Jan.	1	Inventory	12 units at $5,400	$ 64,800
Aug.	7	Purchase	18 units at $6,000	108,000
Dec.	11	Purchase	15 units at $6,480	97,200
		Available for sale	45 units	$270,000

There are 14 units of the item in the physical inventory at December 31. The periodic inventory system is used. Determine the inventory cost using the (a) first-in, first-out (FIFO) method; (b) last-in, first-out (LIFO) method; and (c) weighted average cost method.

6. Lower-of-cost-or-market method   Obj. 6

On the basis of the following data, determine the value of the inventory at the lower of cost or market. Apply lower of cost or market to each inventory item, as shown in Exhibit 10.

Item	Inventory Quantity	Cost per Unit	Market Value per Unit (Net Realizable Value)
Raven 10	1,200	$115	$112
Dove 23	6,500	17	22

7. Effect of inventory errors   Obj. 6

During the taking of its physical inventory on August 31, 20Y4, Kate Interiors Company incorrectly counted its inventory as $366,900 instead of the correct amount of $378,500. Indicate the effect of the misstatement on Kate Interiors' August 31, 20Y4, balance sheet and income statement for the year ended August 31, 20Y4.

8. Inventory turnover and number of days' sales in inventory   Obj. 7

Financial statement data for two years ending December 31 for Holland Company follow:

	20Y4	20Y3
Cost of goods sold	$4,504,500	$3,715,200
Inventories:		
Beginning of year	788,000	760,000
End of year	850,000	788,000

a. Determine the inventory turnover for 20Y4 and 20Y3.

b. Determine the number of days' sales in inventory for 20Y4 and 20Y3. Use 365 days and round to one decimal place.

c. Are the changes in the inventory turnover and number of days' sales in inventory from 20Y3 to 20Y4 favorable or unfavorable?

Answers provided after Problem. Need more practice? Find additional multiple-choice questions, exercises, and problems in CengageNOWv2.

Problem

Stewart Co.'s beginning inventory and purchases during the year ended December 31, 20Y2, were as follows:

		Unit	Unit Cost	Total Cost
January 1	Inventory	1,000	$50.00	$ 50,000
March 10	Purchase	3,000	52.00	156,000
June 25	Sold 1,600 units			
August 30	Purchase	2,600	55.00	143,000
October 5	Sold 4,000 units			
November 26	Purchase	1,000	57.68	57,680
December 31	Sold 800 units			
Total		7,600		$406,680

Instructions

1. Determine the cost of inventory on December 31, 20Y2, using the perpetual inventory system and each of the following inventory costing methods:
   a. first-in, first-out
   b. last-in, first-out
   c. weighted average (round weighted average cost per unit to two decimal places)

2. Determine the cost of inventory on December 31, 20Y2, using the periodic inventory system and each of the following inventory costing methods:
   a. first-in, first-out
   b. last-in, first-out
   c. weighted average cost (round weighted average cost per unit to two decimal places)

3. (*Appendix*) Assume that during the fiscal year ended December 31, 20Y2, sales were $530,000 and the estimated gross profit rate was 36%. Estimate the ending inventory at December 31, 20Y2, using the gross profit method.

Need more practice? Find additional multiple-choice questions, exercises, and problems in CengageNOWv2.

Answers

Multiple-Choice Questions

1. **a** The FIFO method (answer a) is based on the assumption that costs are charged against revenue in the order in which they were incurred. The LIFO method (answer b) charges the most recent costs incurred against revenue, and the weighted average cost method (answer c) charges a weighted average of unit costs of items sold against revenue. The perpetual inventory system (answer d) is a system and not a method of costing.

2. **a** The LIFO method of costing is based on the assumption that costs should be charged against revenue in the reverse order in which costs were incurred. Thus, the oldest costs are assigned to ending inventory. Thirty of the 35 units would be assigned a unit cost of $20 (since 10 of the beginning inventory units were sold on the first sale), and the remaining 5 units would be assigned a cost of $23, for a total of $715 (answer a).

3. **d** The FIFO method of costing is based on the assumption that costs should be charged against revenue in the order in which they were incurred (first-in, first-out). Thus, the most recent costs are assigned to inventory. The 35 units would be assigned a unit cost of $23 (answer d).

4. **b** When the price level is steadily rising, the earlier unit costs are lower than recent unit costs. Under the FIFO method (answer b), these earlier costs are matched against revenue to yield the highest possible net income. The periodic inventory system (answer d) is a system and not a method of costing.

5. **d** The understatement of inventory by $7,500 at the end of the year will cause the cost of goods sold for the year to be overstated by $7,500, the gross profit for the year to be understated by $7,500, next year's beginning inventory to be understated by $7,500, and the net income for the year to be understated by $7,500 (answer d).

Exercises

1.

		Gross Profit November	Ending Inventory November 30
a.	First-in, first-out (FIFO)	$35 ($90 – $55)	$119 ($57 + $62)
b.	Last-in, first-out (LIFO)	$28 ($90 – $62)	$112 ($55 + $57)
c.	Weighted average cost	$32 ($90 – $58)	$116 ($58 × 2)

2. a. Cost of goods sold (January 25):

      25 units @ $100 $2,500
      <u>23</u> units @ $110 <u> 2,530</u>
      <u>48</u> $5,030

    b. Inventory, January 31: $2,970 = 27 units × $110

3. a. Cost of goods sold (April 27): $2,250 = 250 units × $9
    b. Inventory, April 30:

      120 units @ $8 $ 960
      <u> 30</u> units @ $ 9 <u> 270</u>
      <u>150</u> $1,230

4. a. Weighted average unit cost: $88
    Inventory total cost after purchase on May 23:

      15 units @ $80 $1,200
      <u>60</u> units @ $90 <u> 5,400</u>
      <u>75</u> $6,600

    Weighted average unit cost = $88 ($6,600 ÷ 75 units)
    b. Cost of goods sold (May 26): $4,840 (55 units × $88)
    c. Inventory, May 31: $1,760 = 20 units × $88

5. a. First-in, first-out (FIFO) method: $90,720 = 14 units × $6,480
    b. Last-in, first-out (LIFO) method: $76,800 = [(12 units × $5,400) + (2 units × $6,000)]
    c. Weighted average cost method: $84,000 (14 units × $6,000),
       where average cost = $6,000 = $270,000 ÷ 45 units

6.

Commodity	Inventory Quantity	Cost per Unit	Market Value per Unit (Net Realizable Value)	Total Cost	Total Market	Total LCM
Raven 10	1,200	$115	$112	$138,000	$134,400	$134,400
Dove 23	6,500	17	22	110,500	143,000	110,500
Total				$248,500	$277,400	$244,900

7.

	Amount of Misstatement Overstatement (Understatement)
Balance Sheet:	
Inventory understated*	$(11,600)
Current assets understated	(11,600)
Total assets understated	(11,600)
Stockholders' equity understated	(11,600)
Income Statement:	
Cost of goods sold overstated	$ 11,600
Gross profit understated	(11,600)
Net income understated	(11,600)

* $378,500 − $366,900 = $11,600

8. a.

Inventory Turnover	20Y4	20Y3
Cost of goods sold	$4,504,500	$3,715,200
Inventories:		
Beginning of year	$788,000	$760,000
End of year	$850,000	$788,000
Average inventory	$819,000	$774,000
	[($788,000 + $850,000) ÷ 2]	[($760,000 + $788,000) ÷ 2]
Inventory turnover	5.5	4.8
	($4,504,500 ÷ $819,000)	($3,715,200 ÷ $774,000)

b.

Number of Days' Sales in Inventory	20Y4	20Y3
Cost of goods sold	$4,504,500	$3,715,200
Average daily cost of goods sold	$12,341.1	$10,178.6
	($4,504,500 ÷ 365 days)	($3,715,200 ÷ 365 days)
Average inventory	$819,000	$774,000
	[($788,000 + $850,000) ÷ 2]	[($760,000 + $788,000) ÷ 2]
Number of days' sales in inventory	66.4 days	76.0 days
	($819,000 ÷ $12,341.1)	($774,000 ÷ $10,178.6)

c. The increase in the inventory turnover from 4.8 to 5.5 and the decrease in the number of days' sales in inventory from 76.0 days to 66.4 days indicate favorable changes in managing inventory.

Need more help? Watch step-by-step videos of how to compute answers to these Exercises in CengageNOWv2.

Problem

1. a.   First-in, first-out method: $68,680 ($11,000 + $57,680)

Date	Purchases			Cost of Goods Sold			Inventory		
	Quantity	Unit Cost	Total Cost	Quantity	Unit Cost	Total Cost	Quantity	Unit Cost	Total Cost
20Y2									
Jan. 1							1,000	50.00	50,000
Mar. 10	3,000	52.00	156,000				1,000	50.00	50,000
							3,000	52.00	156,000
June 25				1,000	50.00	50,000	2,400	52.00	124,800
				600	52.00	31,200			
Aug. 30	2,600	55.00	143,000				2,400	52.00	124,800
							2,600	55.00	143,000
Oct. 5				2,400	52.00	124,800	1,000	55.00	55,000
				1,600	55.00	88,000			
Nov. 26	1,000	57.68	57,680				1,000	55.00	55,000
							1,000	57.68	57,680
Dec. 31				800	55.00	44,000	200	55.00	11,000
							1,000	57.68	57,680
31	Balances					338,000			68,680

b.   Last-in, first-out method: $61,536 ($50,000 + $11,536)

Date	Purchases			Cost of Goods Sold			Inventory		
	Quantity	Unit Cost	Total Cost	Quantity	Unit Cost	Total Cost	Quantity	Unit Cost	Total Cost
20Y2									
Jan. 1							1,000	50.00	50,000
Mar. 10	3,000	52.00	156,000				1,000	50.00	50,000
							3,000	52.00	156,000
June 25				1,600	52.00	83,200	1,000	50.00	50,000
							1,400	52.00	72,800
Aug. 30	2,600	55.00	143,000				1,000	50.00	50,000
							1,400	52.00	72,800
							2,600	55.00	143,000
Oct. 5				2,600	55.00	143,000	1,000	50.00	50,000
				1,400	52.00	72,800			
Nov. 26	1,000	57.68	57,680				1,000	50.00	50,000
							1,000	57.68	57,680
Dec. 31				800	57.68	46,144	1,000	50.00	50,000
							200	57.68	11,536
31	Balances					345,144			61,536

c.   Weighted average cost method: $66,600 (1,200 units × $55.50)

Date	Purchases			Cost of Goods Sold			Inventory		
	Quantity	Unit Cost	Total Cost	Quantity	Unit Cost	Total Cost	Quantity	Unit Cost	Total Cost
20Y2									
Jan. 1							1,000	50.00	50,000
Mar. 10	3,000	52.00	156,000				4,000	51.50	206,000
June 25				1,600	51.50	82,400	2,400	51.50	123,600
Aug. 30	2,600	55.00	143,000				5,000	53.32	266,600
Oct. 5				4,000	53.32	213,280	1,000	53.32	53,320
Nov. 26	1,000	57.68	57,680				2,000	55.50	111,000
Dec. 31				800	55.50	44,400	1,200	55.50	66,600
31	Balances					340,080	1,200	55.50	66,600

2. a. First-in, first-out method:

1,000 units at $57.68	$57,680
200 units at $55.00	11,000
1,200 units	$68,680

b. Last-in, first-out method:

1,000 units at $50.00	$50,000
200 units at $52.00	10,400
1,200 units	$60,400

c. Weighted average cost method:

Weighted average cost per unit: $406,680 ÷ 7,600 units = $53.51 (rounded)

Inventory, December 31, 20Y2: 1,200 units × $53.51 = $64,212

3. (*Appendix*)

		Cost
Inventory, January 1, 20Y2		$ 50,000
Purchases (net)		356,680
Merchandise available for sale		$ 406,680
Sales	$530,000	
Estimated gross profit ($530,000 × 36%)	190,800	
Estimated cost of goods sold		(339,200)
Estimated inventory, December 31, 20Y2		$ 67,480

Discussion Questions

1. Before inventory purchases are recorded, the receiving report should be reconciled to what documents?

2. Why is it important to periodically take a physical inventory when using a perpetual inventory system?

3. Do the terms *FIFO, LIFO,* and *weighted average* refer to techniques used in determining quantities of the various classes of inventory on hand? Explain.

4. If inventory is being valued at cost and the price level is decreasing, which of the three methods of costing—FIFO, LIFO, or weighted average cost—will yield (a) the highest inventory cost, (b) the lowest inventory cost, (c) the highest gross profit, and (d) the lowest gross profit?

5. Which of the three methods of inventory costing—FIFO, LIFO, or weighted average cost—will in general yield an inventory cost most nearly approximating current replacement cost?

6. If inventory is being valued at cost and the price level is steadily rising, which of the three methods of costing—FIFO, LIFO, or weighted average cost—will yield the lowest annual income tax expense? Explain.

7. Using the following data, how should the inventory be valued under lower of cost or market?

Original cost	$1,350
Estimated selling price	1,475
Selling expenses	180

8. The inventory at the end of the year was understated by $14,750. (a) Did the error cause an overstatement or an understatement of the gross profit for the year? (b) Which items on the balance sheet at the end of the year were overstated or understated as a result of the error?

9. Hutch Co. sold merchandise to Bibbins Company on May 31, FOB shipping point. If the merchandise is in transit on May 31, the end of the fiscal year, which company would report it in its financial statements? Explain.

10. A manufacturer shipped merchandise to a retailer on a consignment basis. If the merchandise is unsold at the end of the period, in whose inventory should the merchandise be included?

Basic Exercises

SHOW ME HOW

BE 6-1   Cost flow methods   Obj. 2

The following three identical units of Item P401C are purchased during April:

		Item Beta	Units	Cost
Apr.	2	Purchase	1	$100
	15	Purchase	1	120
	20	Purchase	1	140
		Total	3	$360
		Average cost per unit		$120 ($360 ÷ 3 units)

Assume that one unit is sold on April 27 for $300.

Determine the gross profit for April and ending inventory on April 30 using the (a) first-in, first-out (FIFO); (b) last-in, first-out (LIFO); and (c) weighted average cost methods.

SHOW ME HOW

BE 6-2   Perpetual inventory using FIFO   Obj. 3

Beginning inventory, purchases, and sales for Item Zeta9 are as follows:

Oct.	1	Inventory	200 units at $30
	7	Sale	160 units
	15	Purchase	180 units at $33
	24	Sale	150 units

Assuming a perpetual inventory system and using the first-in, first-out (FIFO) method, determine (a) the cost of goods sold on October 24 and (b) the inventory on October 31.

SHOW ME HOW

BE 6-3   Perpetual inventory using LIFO   Obj. 3

Beginning inventory, purchases, and sales for Item 88-HX are as follows:

July	1	Inventory	90 units at $52
	8	Sale	75 units
	15	Purchase	125 units at $58
	27	Sale	100 units

Assuming a perpetual inventory system and using the last-in, first-out (LIFO) method, determine (a) the cost of goods sold on July 27 and (b) the inventory on July 31.

SHOW ME HOW

BE 6-4   Perpetual inventory using weighted average   Obj. 3

Beginning inventory, purchases, and sales for WCS12 are as follows:

Oct.	1	Inventory	320 units at $10
	13	Sale	180 units
	22	Purchase	360 units at $12
	29	Sale	300 units

Assuming a perpetual inventory system and using the weighted average method, determine (a) the weighted average unit cost after the October 22 purchase, (b) the cost of goods sold on October 29, and (c) the inventory on October 31.

SHOW ME HOW

BE 6-5   Periodic inventory using FIFO, LIFO, and weighted average cost methods   Obj. 4

The units of an item available for sale during the year were as follows:

Jan.	1	Inventory	40 units at $165	$ 6,600
Aug.	13	Purchase	200 units at $180	36,000
Nov.	30	Purchase	60 units at $200	12,000
		Available for sale	300 units	$54,600

There are 75 units of the item in the physical inventory at December 31. The periodic inventory system is used. Determine the inventory cost using the (a) first-in, first-out (FIFO) method; (b) last-in, first-out (LIFO) method; and (c) weighted average cost method.

SHOW ME HOW

BE 6-6 Lower-of-cost-or-market method

Obj. 6

On the basis of the following data, determine the value of the inventory at the lower of cost or market. Apply lower of cost or market to each inventory item, as shown in Exhibit 10.

Item	Inventory Quantity	Cost per Unit	Market Value per Unit (Net Realizable Value)
JFW1	6,330	$10	$11
SAW9	1,140	36	34

SHOW ME HOW

BE 6-7 Effect of inventory errors

Obj. 6

During the taking of its physical inventory on December 31, 20Y3, Waterjet Bath Company incorrectly counted its inventory as $728,660 instead of the correct amount of $719,880. Indicate the effect of the misstatement on Waterjet Bath's December 31, 20Y3, balance sheet and income statement for the year ended December 31, 20Y3.

SHOW ME HOW

BE 6-8 Inventory turnover and number of days' sales in inventory

Obj. 7

Financial statement data for years ending December 31 for Tango Company follow:

	20Y7	20Y6
Cost of goods sold	$3,864,000	$4,001,500
Inventories:		
Beginning of year	770,000	740,000
End of year	840,000	770,000

a. Determine the inventory turnover for 20Y7 and 20Y6.

b. Determine the number of days' sales in inventory for 20Y7 and 20Y6. Use 365 days and round to one decimal place.

c. ➤ Are the changes in inventory turnover and the number of days' sales in inventory from 20Y6 to 20Y7 favorable or unfavorable?

Exercises

EX 6-1 Control of inventories

Obj. 1

Triple Creek Hardware Store currently uses a periodic inventory system. Kevin Carlton, the owner and sole stockholder, is considering the purchase of a computer system that would make it feasible to switch to a perpetual inventory system.

Kevin is unhappy with the periodic inventory system because it does not provide timely information on inventory levels. Kevin has noticed on several occasions that the store runs out of good-selling items, while too many poor-selling items are on hand.

Kevin is also concerned about lost sales while a physical inventory is being taken. Triple Creek currently takes a physical inventory twice a year. To minimize distractions, the store is closed on the day inventory is taken. Kevin believes that closing the store is the only way to get an accurate inventory count.

➤ Will switching to a perpetual inventory system strengthen Triple Creek Hardware's control over inventory items? Will switching to a perpetual inventory system eliminate the need for a physical inventory count? Explain.

EX 6-2 Control of inventories

Obj. 1

Hardcase Luggage Shop is a small retail establishment located in a large shopping mall. This shop has implemented the following procedures regarding inventory items:

a. Because the shop carries mostly high-quality, designer luggage, all inventory items are tagged with a control device that activates an alarm if a tagged item is removed from the store.

b. Because the display area of the store is limited, only a sample of each piece of luggage is kept on the selling floor. Whenever a customer selects a piece of luggage, the salesclerk gets

(Continued)

the appropriate piece from the store's stockroom. Because all salesclerks need access to the stockroom, it is not locked. The stockroom is adjacent to the break room used by all mall employees.

c. Whenever Hardcase receives a shipment of new inventory, the items are taken directly to the stockroom. Hardcase's accountant uses the vendor's invoice to record the amount of inventory received.

State whether each of these procedures is appropriate or inappropriate. If it is inappropriate, state why.

EX 6-3 Perpetual inventory using FIFO

Obj. 2, 3

✔ Inventory balance, November 30, $7,480

SHOW ME HOW

Beginning inventory, purchases, and sales data for DVD players are as follows:

Nov.	1	Inventory	120 units at $39
	10	Sale	90 units
	15	Purchase	140 units at $40
	20	Sale	110 units
	24	Sale	45 units
	30	Purchase	160 units at $43

The business maintains a perpetual inventory system, costing by the first-in, first-out method.

a. Determine the cost of goods sold for each sale and the inventory balance after each sale, presenting the data in the form illustrated in Exhibit 3.

b. Based upon the preceding data, would you expect the inventory to be higher or lower using the last-in, first-out method?

EX 6-4 Perpetual inventory using LIFO

Obj. 2, 3

✔ Inventory balance, November 30, $7,465

SHOW ME HOW   EXCEL TEMPLATE

Assume that the business in Exercise 6-3 maintains a perpetual inventory system, costing by the last-in, first-out method. Determine the cost of goods sold for each sale and the inventory balance after each sale, presenting the data in the form illustrated in Exhibit 4.

EX 6-5 Perpetual inventory using LIFO

Obj. 2, 3

✔ Inventory balance, December 31, $8,064

SHOW ME HOW   EXCEL TEMPLATE

Beginning inventory, purchases, and sales data for prepaid cell phones for December are as follows:

Inventory		Purchases		Sales	
Dec. 1	310 units at $88	Dec. 10	144 units at $90	Dec. 12	240 units
		20	240 units at $96	14	166 units
				31	200 units

a. Assuming that the perpetual inventory system is used, costing by the LIFO method, determine the cost of goods sold for each sale and the inventory balance after each sale, presenting the data in the form illustrated in Exhibit 4.

b. Based upon the preceding data, would you expect the inventory to be higher or lower using the first-in, first-out method?

EX 6-6 Perpetual inventory using FIFO

Obj. 2, 3

✔ Inventory balance, December 31, $8,448

SHOW ME HOW   EXCEL TEMPLATE

Assume that the business in Exercise 6-5 maintains a perpetual inventory system, costing by the first-in, first-out method. Determine the cost of goods sold for each sale and the inventory balance after each sale, presenting the data in the form illustrated in Exhibit 3.

EX 6-7 FIFO and LIFO costs under perpetual inventory system

Obj. 2, 3

✔ b. $1,258,000

SHOW ME HOW

The following units of an item were available for sale during the year:

Beginning inventory	8,100 units at $180
Sale	5,300 units at $300
First purchase	15,000 units at $185
Sale	13,000 units at $300
Second purchase	16,000 units at $192
Sale	14,000 units at $300

The firm uses the perpetual inventory system, and there are 6,800 units of the item on hand at the end of the year. What is the total cost of the ending inventory according to (a) FIFO and (b) LIFO?

✔ Total Cost of goods
sold, $1,758,750

SHOW ME HOW

EX 6-8 Weighted average cost flow method under perpetual inventory system   Obj. 3

The following units of a particular item were available for sale during the calendar year:

Jan.	1	Inventory	10,000 units at $75.00
Mar.	18	Sale	8,000 units
May	2	Purchase	18,000 units at $77.50
Aug.	9	Sale	15,000 units
Oct.	20	Purchase	7,000 units at $80.25

The firm uses the weighted average cost method with a perpetual inventory system. Determine the cost of goods sold for each sale and the inventory balance after each sale. Present the data in the form illustrated in Exhibit 5.

✔ Total Cost of goods
sold, $315,000

EX 6-9 Weighted average cost flow method under perpetual inventory system   Obj. 3

The following units of a particular item were available for sale during the calendar year:

Jan.	1	Inventory	4,000 units at $40
Apr.	19	Sale	2,500 units
June	30	Purchase	4,500 units at $44
Sept.	2	Sale	5,000 units
Nov.	15	Purchase	2,000 units at $46

The firm uses the weighted average cost method with a perpetual inventory system. Determine the cost of goods sold for each sale and the inventory balance after each sale. Present the data in the form illustrated in Exhibit 5.

✔ Total Cost of goods
sold, $314,000

EX 6-10 Perpetual inventory using FIFO   Obj. 3

Assume that the business in Exercise 6-9 maintains a perpetual inventory system. Determine the cost of goods sold for each sale and the inventory balance after each sale, assuming the first-in, first-out method. Present the data in the form illustrated in Exhibit 3.

✔ Total Cost of goods
sold, $318,000

EX 6-11 Perpetual inventory using LIFO   Obj. 3

Assume that the business in Exercise 6-9 maintains a perpetual inventory system. Determine the cost of goods sold for each sale and the inventory balance after each sale, assuming the last-in, first-out method. Present the data in the form illustrated in Exhibit 4.

✔ b. $7,500

SHOW ME HOW

EX 6-12 Periodic inventory by three methods   Obj. 2, 4

The units of an item available for sale during the year were as follows:

Jan.	1	Inventory	2,500 units at $5
Feb.	17	Purchase	3,300 units at $6
July	21	Purchase	3,000 units at $7
Nov.	23	Purchase	1,200 units at $8

There are 1,500 units of the item in the physical inventory at December 31. The periodic inventory system is used. Determine the inventory cost by the (a) first-in, first-out method, (b) last-in, first-out method, and (c) weighted average cost method.

✔ a. Inventory,
$24,912

SHOW ME HOW

EX 6-13 Periodic inventory by three methods; cost of goods sold   Obj. 2, 4

The units of an item available for sale during the year were as follows:

Jan.	1	Inventory	180 units at $108
Mar.	10	Purchase	224 units at $110
Aug.	30	Purchase	200 units at $116
Dec.	12	Purchase	196 units at $120

(Continued)

There are 208 units of the item in the physical inventory at December 31. The periodic inventory system is used. Determine the ending inventory cost and the cost of goods sold by three methods, presenting your answers in the following form:

Inventory Method	Ending Inventory	Cost of Goods Sold
a. First-in, first-out	$	$
b. Last-in, first-out		
c. Weighted average cost		

EX 6-14 Comparing inventory methods — Obj. 5

Assume that a firm separately determined inventory under FIFO and LIFO and then compared the results.

a. In each space that follows, place the correct sign [less than (<), greater than (>), or equal (=)] for each comparison, assuming periods of rising prices.

1. FIFO inventory	_____	LIFO inventory
2. FIFO cost of goods sold	_____	LIFO cost of goods sold
3. FIFO net income	_____	LIFO net income
4. FIFO income taxes	_____	LIFO income taxes

b. ▬▬▶ Why would management prefer to use LIFO over FIFO in periods of rising prices?

SHOW ME HOW   EXCEL TEMPLATE

EX 6-15 Lower-of-cost-or-market inventory — Obj. 6

On the basis of the following data, determine the value of the inventory at the lower of cost or market applied to (a) each item in the inventory, (b) each class of inventory, and (c) total inventory. Assemble the data in the form illustrated in Exhibit 10.

Product	Inventory Quantity	Cost per Unit	Market Value per Unit (Net Realizable Value)
Class 1:			
Model A	300	$140	$125
Model B	500	90	112
Model C	150	60	59
Class 2:			
Model D	800	120	115
Model E	400	140	145

EX 6-16 Inventory on the balance sheet — Obj. 6

Based on the data in Exercise 6-15 part (a) and assuming that cost was determined by the FIFO method, show how the inventory would appear on the balance sheet.

EX 6-17 Effect of errors in physical inventory — Obj. 6

Madison River Supply Co. sells canoes, kayaks, whitewater rafts, and other boating supplies. During the taking of its physical inventory on December 31, 20Y8, Madison incorrectly counted its inventory as $545,000 instead of the correct amount of $555,400.

a. State the effects of the error on the December 31, 20Y8, balance sheet of Madison River Supply.

b. State the effects of the error on the income statement of Madison River Supply for the year ended December 31, 20Y8.

c. If uncorrected, what would be the effects of the error on the 20Y9 income statement?

d. If uncorrected, what would be the effects of the error on the December 31, 20Y9, balance sheet?

EX 6-18   Effect of errors in physical inventory   Obj. 6

Fonda Motorcycle Shop sells motorcycles, ATVs, and other related supplies and accessories. During the taking of its physical inventory on December 31, 20Y1, Fonda incorrectly counted its inventory as $452,500 instead of the correct amount of $425,500.

a. State the effects of the error on the December 31, 20Y1, balance sheet of Fonda Motorcycle Shop.

b. State the effects of the error on the income statement of Fonda Motorcycle Shop for the year ended December 31, 20Y1.

c. If uncorrected, what would be the effects of the error on the 20Y2 income statement?

d. If uncorrected, what would be the effects of the error on the December 31, 20Y2, balance sheet?

EX 6-19   Error in inventory   Obj. 6

During 20Y5, the accountant discovered that the physical inventory at the end of 20Y4 had been understated by $42,750. Instead of correcting the error, however, the accountant assumed that the error would balance out (correct itself) in 20Y5.

▬▬▬▶ Are there any flaws in the accountant's assumption? Explain.

**Appendix
EX 6-20   Retail method**

A business using the retail method of inventory costing determines that inventory at retail is $1,235,000. If the ratio of cost to retail price is 54%, what is the amount of inventory to be reported on the financial statements?

**Appendix
EX 6-21   Retail method**

A business using the retail method of inventory costing determines that inventory at retail is $396,400. If the ratio of cost to retail price is 61%, what is the amount of inventory to be reported on the financial statements?

**Appendix
EX 6-22   Retail method**

A business using the retail method of inventory costing determines that inventory at retail is $775,000. If the ratio of cost to retail price is 66%, what is the amount of inventory to be reported on the financial statements?

EXCEL TEMPLATE

**Appendix
EX 6-23   Retail method**

On the basis of the following data, estimate the cost of the inventory at June 30 by the retail method:

		Cost	Retail
June 1	Inventory	$ 165,000	$ 275,000
June 1–30	Purchases (net)	2,361,500	3,800,000
June 1–30	Sales		3,550,000

✔ a. Inventory
destroyed: $414,000

**Appendix
EX 6-24   Gross profit method**

The inventory was destroyed by fire on December 31. The following data were obtained from the accounting records:

Jan. 1	Inventory	$ 350,000
Jan. 1–Dec. 31	Purchases (net)	2,950,000
	Sales	4,440,000
	Estimated gross profit rate	35%

a. Estimate the cost of the inventory destroyed.

b. ▬▬▬▶ Briefly describe the situations in which the gross profit method is useful.

Appendix
EX 6-25   Gross profit method
Based on the following data, estimate the cost of the ending inventory:

Sales	$9,250,000
Estimated gross profit rate	36%
Beginning inventory	$ 180,000
Purchases (net)	5,945,000
Merchandise available for sale	$6,125,000

Appendix
EX 6-26   Gross profit method
Based on the following data, estimate the cost of the ending inventory:

Sales	$1,450,000
Estimated gross profit rate	42%
Beginning inventory	$ 100,000
Purchases (net)	860,000
Merchandise available for sale	$ 960,000

Problems: Series A

PR 6-1A   FIFO perpetual inventory   Obj. 2, 3

✔ 3. $8,983,125

The beginning inventory at Midnight Supplies and data on purchases and sales for a three-month period ending March 31 are as follows:

SHOW ME HOW   EXCEL TEMPLATE

Date		Transaction	Number of Units	Per Unit	Total
Jan.	1	Inventory	7,500	$ 75.00	$ 562,500
	10	Purchase	22,500	85.00	1,912,500
	28	Sale	11,250	150.00	1,687,500
	30	Sale	3,750	150.00	562,500
Feb.	5	Sale	1,500	150.00	225,000
	10	Purchase	54,000	87.50	4,725,000
	16	Sale	27,000	160.00	4,320,000
	28	Sale	25,500	160.00	4,080,000
Mar.	5	Purchase	45,000	89.50	4,027,500
	14	Sale	30,000	160.00	4,800,000
	25	Purchase	7,500	90.00	675,000
	30	Sale	26,250	160.00	4,200,000

Instructions

1. Record the inventory, purchases, and cost of goods sold data in a perpetual inventory record similar to the one illustrated in Exhibit 3, using the first-in, first-out method.

2. Determine the total sales and the total cost of goods sold for the period. Journalize the entries in the sales and cost of goods sold accounts. Assume that all sales were on account.

3. Determine the gross profit from sales for the period.

4. Determine the ending inventory cost as of March 31.

5. Based upon the preceding data, would you expect the ending inventory using the last-in, first-out method to be higher or lower?

✔ 2. Gross profit, $8,853,750

SHOW ME HOW   EXCEL TEMPLATE

PR 6-2A   LIFO perpetual inventory   Obj. 2, 3

The beginning inventory at Midnight Supplies and data on purchases and sales for a three-month period are shown in Problem 6-1A.

Instructions

1. Record the inventory, purchases, and cost of goods sold data in a perpetual inventory record similar to the one illustrated in Exhibit 4, using the last-in, first-out method.

2. Determine the total sales, the total cost of goods sold, and the gross profit from sales for the period.

3. Determine the ending inventory cost as of March 31.

✔ 2. Gross profit, $8,973,750

PR 6-3A   Weighted average cost method with perpetual inventory   Obj. 2, 3

The beginning inventory for Midnight Supplies and data on purchases and sales for a three-month period are shown in Problem 6-1A.

Instructions

1. Record the inventory, purchases, and cost of goods sold data in a perpetual inventory record similar to the one illustrated in Exhibit 5, using the weighted average cost method.

2. Determine the total sales, the total cost of goods sold, and the gross profit from sales for the period.

3. Determine the ending inventory cost as of March 31.

✔ 2. Inventory, $881,250

PR 6-4A   Periodic inventory by three methods   Obj. 2, 3

The beginning inventory for Midnight Supplies and data on purchases and sales for a three-month period are shown in Problem 6-1A.

Instructions

1. Determine the inventory on March 31 and the cost of goods sold for the three-month period, using the first-in, first-out method and the periodic inventory system.

2. Determine the inventory on March 31 and the cost of goods sold for the three-month period, using the last-in, first-out method and the periodic inventory system.

3. Determine the inventory on March 31 and the cost of goods sold for the three-month period, using the weighted average cost method and the periodic inventory system. Round the weighted average unit cost to the nearest cent.

4. Compare the gross profit and the March 31 inventories, using the following column headings:

	FIFO	LIFO	Weighted Average
Sales			
Cost of goods sold			
Gross profit			
Inventory, March 31			

✔ 1. $10,700

SHOW ME HOW   EXCEL TEMPLATE

PR 6-5A   Periodic inventory by three methods   Obj. 2, 4

Dymac Appliances uses the periodic inventory system. Details regarding the inventory of appliances at January 1, purchases invoices during the next 12 months, and the inventory count at December 31 are summarized as follows:

Model	Inventory, January 1	Purchases Invoices 1st	Purchases Invoices 2nd	Purchases Invoices 3rd	Inventory Count, December 31
A10	—	4 at $ 64	4 at $ 70	4 at $ 76	6
B15	8 at $176	4 at 158	3 at 170	6 at 184	8
E60	3 at 75	3 at 65	15 at 68	9 at 70	5
G83	7 at 242	6 at 250	5 at 260	10 at 259	9
J34	12 at 240	10 at 246	16 at 267	16 at 270	15
M90	2 at 108	2 at 110	3 at 128	3 at 130	5
Q70	5 at 160	4 at 170	4 at 175	7 at 180	8

(Continued)

Instructions

1. Determine the cost of the inventory on December 31 by the first-in, first-out method. Present data in columnar form, using the following headings:

Model	Quantity	Unit Cost	Total Cost

If the inventory of a particular model comprises one entire purchase plus a portion of another purchase acquired at a different unit cost, use a separate line for each purchase.

2. Determine the cost of the inventory on December 31 by the last-in, first-out method, following the procedures indicated in (1).

3. Determine the cost of the inventory on December 31 by the weighted average cost method, using the columnar headings indicated in (1).

4. ➤ Discuss which method (FIFO or LIFO) would be preferred for income tax purposes in periods of (a) rising prices and (b) declining prices.

PR 6-6A   Lower-of-cost-or-market inventory   **Obj. 6**

✔ Total LCM, $39,873   Data on the physical inventory of Ashwood Products Company as of December 31 follow:

Description	Inventory Quantity	Market Value per Unit (Net Realizable Value)
B12	38	$ 57
E41	18	180
G19	33	126
L88	18	550
N94	400	7
P24	90	18
R66	8	250
T33	140	20
Z16	15	752

Quantity and cost data from the last purchases invoice of the year and the next-to-the-last purchases invoice are summarized as follows:

Description	Last Purchases Invoice Quantity Purchased	Last Purchases Invoice Unit Cost	Next-to-the-Last Purchases Invoice Quantity Purchased	Next-to-the-Last Purchases Invoice Unit Cost
B12	30	$ 60	30	$ 59
E41	35	178	20	180
G19	20	128	25	129
L88	10	563	10	560
N94	500	8	500	7
P24	80	22	50	21
R66	5	248	4	260
T33	100	21	100	19
Z16	10	750	9	745

Instructions

Determine the inventory at cost and also at the lower of cost or market applied on an item-by-item basis, using the first-in, first-out method. Record the appropriate unit costs on the inventory sheet, and complete the pricing of the inventory. When there are two different unit costs applicable to an item, proceed as follows:

1. Draw a line through the quantity, and insert the quantity and unit cost of the last purchase.

2. On the following line, insert the quantity and unit cost of the next-to-the-last purchase.

3. Total the cost and market columns and insert the lower of the two totals in the LCM column. The first item on the inventory sheet has been completed as an example.

Inventory Sheet
December 31

Description	Inventory Quantity	Cost per Unit	Market Value per Unit (Net Realizable Value)	Total Cost	Total Market	LCM
B12	~~38~~ 30	$60	$57	$1,800	$1,710	
	8	59	57	472	456	
				$2,272	$2,166	$2,166

Appendix
PR 6-7A   Retail method; gross profit method

✔ 1. $306,900

Selected data on inventory, purchases, and sales for Celebrity Tan Co. and Ranchworks Co. are as follows:

	Cost	Retail
Celebrity Tan Co.		
Inventory, August 1	$ 300,000	$ 575,000
Transactions during August:		
Purchases (net)	2,021,900	3,170,000
Sales		3,250,000
Ranchworks Co.		
Inventory, March 1	$ 880,000	
Transactions during March through November:		
Purchases (net)	9,500,000	
Sales	15,800,000	
Estimated gross profit rate	38%	

Instructions

1. Determine the estimated cost of the inventory of Celebrity Tan Co. on August 31 by the retail method, presenting details of the computations.

2. a. Estimate the cost of the inventory of Ranchworks Co. on November 30 by the gross profit method, presenting details of the computations.

   b. Assume that Ranchworks Co. took a physical inventory on November 30 and discovered that $369,750 of inventory was on hand. What was the estimated loss of inventory due to theft or damage during March through November?

Problems: Series B

PR 6-1B   FIFO perpetual inventory

Obj. 2, 3

✔ 3. $214,474

The beginning inventory at Dunne Co. and data on purchases and sales for a three-month period ending June 30 are as follows:

SHOW ME HOW   EXCEL TEMPLATE

Date		Transaction	Number of Units	Per Unit	Total
Apr.	3	Inventory	25	$1,200	$ 30,000
	8	Purchase	75	1,240	93,000
	11	Sale	40	2,000	80,000
	30	Sale	30	2,000	60,000
May	8	Purchase	60	1,260	75,600
	10	Sale	50	2,000	100,000
	19	Sale	20	2,000	40,000
	28	Purchase	80	1,260	100,800

(Continued)

Date		Transaction	Number of Units	Per Unit	Total
June	5	Sale	40	2,250	$90,000
	16	Sale	25	2,250	56,250
	21	Purchase	35	1,264	44,240
	28	Sale	44	2,250	99,000

Instructions

1. Record the inventory, purchases, and cost of goods sold data in a perpetual inventory record similar to the one illustrated in Exhibit 3, using the first-in, first-out method.

2. Determine the total sales and the total cost of goods sold for the period. Journalize the entries in the sales and cost of goods sold accounts. Assume that all sales were on account.

3. Determine the gross profit from sales for the period.

4. Determine the ending inventory cost on June 30.

5. Based upon the preceding data, would you expect the ending inventory using the last-in, first-out method to be higher or lower?

PR 6-2B LIFO perpetual inventory   Obj. 2, 3

✔ 2. Gross profit, $213,170

SHOW ME HOW   EXCEL TEMPLATE

The beginning inventory for Dunne Co. and data on purchases and sales for a three-month period are shown in Problem 6-1B.

Instructions

1. Record the inventory, purchases, and cost of goods sold data in a perpetual inventory record similar to the one illustrated in Exhibit 4, using the last-in, first-out method.

2. Determine the total sales, the total cost of goods sold, and the gross profit from sales for the period.

3. Determine the ending inventory cost on June 30.

PR 6-3B Weighted average cost method with perpetual inventory   Obj. 2, 3

✔ 2. Gross profit, $214,396

The beginning inventory for Dunne Co. and data on purchases and sales for a three-month period are shown in Problem 6-1B.

Instructions

1. Record the inventory, purchases, and cost of goods sold data in a perpetual inventory record similar to the one illustrated in Exhibit 5, using the weighted average cost method.

2. Determine the total sales, the total cost of goods sold, and the gross profit from sales for the period.

3. Determine the ending inventory cost on June 30.

PR 6-4B Periodic inventory by three methods   Obj. 2, 3

✔ 2. Inventory, $31,240

The beginning inventory for Dunne Co. and data on purchases and sales for a three-month period are shown in Problem 6-1B.

Instructions

1. Determine the inventory on June 30 and the cost of goods sold for the three-month period, using the first-in, first-out method and the periodic inventory system.

2. Determine the inventory on June 30 and the cost of goods sold for the three-month period, using the last-in, first-out method and the periodic inventory system.

3. Determine the inventory on June 30 and the cost of goods sold for the three-month period, using the weighted average cost method and the periodic inventory system. Round the weighted average unit cost to the dollar.

4. Compare the gross profit and June 30 inventories using the following column headings:

	FIFO	LIFO	Weighted Average
Sales			
Cost of goods sold			
Gross profit			
Inventory, June 30			

PR 6-5B Periodic inventory by three methods

Obj. 2, 4

✔ 1. $18,545

SHOW ME HOW

EXCEL TEMPLATE

Pappa's Appliances uses the periodic inventory system. Details regarding the inventory of appliances at January 1, purchases invoices during the year, and the inventory count at December 31 are summarized as follows:

		Purchases Invoices			
Model	Inventory, January 1	1st	2nd	3rd	Inventory Count, December 31
C55	3 at $1,040	3 at $1,054	3 at $1,060	3 at $1,070	4
D11	9 at 639	7 at 645	6 at 666	6 at 675	11
F32	5 at 240	3 at 260	1 at 260	1 at 280	2
H29	6 at 305	3 at 310	3 at 316	4 at 317	4
K47	6 at 520	8 at 531	4 at 549	6 at 542	8
S33	—	4 at 222	4 at 232	—	2
X74	4 at 35	6 at 36	8 at 37	7 at 39	7

Instructions

1. Determine the cost of the inventory on December 31 by the first-in, first-out method. Present data in columnar form, using the following headings:

Model	Quantity	Unit Cost	Total Cost

If the inventory of a particular model comprises one entire purchase plus a portion of another purchase acquired at a different unit cost, use a separate line for each purchase.

2. Determine the cost of the inventory on December 31 by the last-in, first-out method, following the procedures indicated in (1).

3. Determine the cost of the inventory on December 31 by the weighted average cost method, using the columnar headings indicated in (1).

4. ➤ Discuss which method (FIFO or LIFO) would be preferred for income tax purposes in periods of (a) rising prices and (b) declining prices.

PR 6-6B Lower-of-cost-or-market inventory

Obj. 6

✔ Total LCM, $41,873

Data on the physical inventory of Katus Products Co. as of December 31 follows:

Description	Inventory Quantity	Market Value per Unit (Net Realizable Value)
A54	37	$ 56
C77	24	178
F66	30	132
H83	21	545
K12	375	5
Q58	90	18
S36	8	235
V97	140	20
Y88	17	744

Quantity and cost data from the last purchases invoice of the year and the next-to-the-last purchases invoice are summarized as follows:

	Last Purchases Invoice		Next-to-the-Last Purchases Invoice	
Description	Quantity Purchased	Unit Cost	Quantity Purchased	Unit Cost
A54	30	$ 60	40	$ 58
C77	25	174	15	180
F66	20	130	15	128
H83	6	547	15	540
K12	500	6	500	7
Q58	75	25	80	26
S36	5	256	4	260
V97	100	17	115	16
Y88	10	750	8	740

(Continued)

Instructions

Determine the inventory at cost and also at the lower of cost or market applied on an item-by-item basis, using the first-in, first-out method. Record the appropriate unit costs on the inventory sheet, and complete the pricing of the inventory. When there are two different unit costs applicable to an item, proceed as follows:

1. Draw a line through the quantity, and insert the quantity and unit cost of the last purchase.
2. On the following line, insert the quantity and unit cost of the next-to-the-last purchase.
3. Total the cost and market columns and insert the lower of the two totals in the LCM column. The first item on the inventory sheet has been completed as an example.

Inventory Sheet

December 31

Description	Inventory Quantity	Cost per Unit	Market Value per Unit (Net Realizable Value)	Cost	Market	LCM
A54	37 30	$60	$56	$1,800	$1,680	
	7	58	56	406	392	
				$2,206	$2,072	$2,072

Appendix

PR 6-7B   Retail method; gross profit method

✔ 1. $630,000   Selected data on inventory, purchases, and sales for Jaffe Co. and Coronado Co. are as follows:

	Cost	Retail
Jaffe Co.		
Inventory, February 1	$ 400,000	$ 615,000
Transactions during February:		
Purchases (net)	4,055,000	5,325,000
Sales		5,100,000
Coronado Co.		
Inventory, May 1	$ 400,000	
Transactions during May thru October:		
Purchases (net)	3,150,000	
Sales	4,750,000	
Estimated gross profit rate	35%	

Instructions

1. Determine the estimated cost of the inventory of Jaffe Co. on February 28 by the retail method, presenting details of the computations.

2. a. Estimate the cost of the inventory of Coronado Co. on October 31 by the gross profit method, presenting details of the computations.

   b. Assume that Coronado Co. took a physical inventory on October 31 and discovered that $366,500 of inventory was on hand. What was the estimated loss of inventory due to theft or damage during May through October?

Make a Decision
Inventory Turnover and Number of Days' Sales in Inventory

REAL WORLD

MAD 6-1 Analyze and compare Amazon.com to Target   Obj. 7

Amazon.com, Inc. (AMZN) is one of the largest Internet retailers in the world. **Target Corporation (TGT)** is one of the largest value-priced general merchandisers operating in the United States. Target sells through nearly 1,800 brick-and-mortar stores and through the Internet. Amazon and Target compete for customers across a wide variety of products, including media, general merchandise, apparel, and consumer electronics. Cost of goods sold and inventory information from a recent annual report are provided for both companies as follows (in millions):

	Amazon	Target
Cost of goods sold	$71,651	$51,997
Inventories:		
Beginning of year	8,299	8,282
End of year	10,243	8,601

a. Compute the inventory turnover for both companies. Round all calculations to one decimal place.

b. Compute the number of days' sales in inventory for both companies. Use 365 days and round all calculations to one decimal place.

c. ⟶ Which company has the better inventory efficiency?

d. ⟶ What might explain the difference in inventory efficiency between the two companies?

REAL WORLD

MAD 6-2 Analyze and compare Darden Restaurants to Panera Bread   Obj. 7

Darden Restaurants, Inc. (DRI) is the largest full-service restaurant company in the world. It operates over 2,200 restaurants under a variety of brand names, including Olive Garden, Bahama Breeze, and LongHorn Steakhouse. **Panera Bread Company (PNRA)** operates over 1,800 bakery-café locations across North America. It is one of the largest food service companies in the United States. The cost of food, beverage, and packaging and the beginning and ending inventory balances from recent annual reports for Darden and Panera are as follows (in millions):

	Darden	Panera
Cost of goods sold (food, beverage, and packaging)	$2,039.7	$715.5
Inventories:		
Beginning of year	163.9	22.8
End of year	175.4	22.5

a. Compute the inventory turnover for both companies. Round calculations to one decimal place.

b. Compute the number of days' sales in inventory for both companies. Round calculations to one decimal place.

c. ⟶ Which company is more efficient in managing inventory?

d. ⟶ What might explain the difference in the inventory management efficiency of the two companies?

REAL WORLD

MAD 6-3 Analyze and compare Costco, Wal-Mart, and Nordstrom   Obj. 7

The general merchandise retail industry has a number of segments represented by the following companies:

Company Name	Merchandise Concept
Costco Wholesale Corporation (COST)	Membership warehouse
Wal-Mart Stores, Inc. (WMT)	Discount general merchandise
Nordstrom, Inc. (JWN)	Fashion department store

(Continued)

For a recent year, the following cost of goods sold and beginning and ending inventories are provided from corporate annual reports (in millions) for these three companies:

	Costco	Wal-Mart	Nordstrom
Cost of goods sold	$102,901	$360,984	$9,168
Inventories:			
Beginning of year	8,908	45,141	1,733
End of year	8,969	44,469	1,945

a. Determine the inventory turnover ratio for all three companies. Round all calculations to one decimal place.

b. Determine the number of days' sales in inventory for all three companies. Use 365 days and round all calculations to one decimal place.

c. ➤ Interpret these results based on each company's merchandising concept.

REAL WORLD

MAD 6-4   Analyze and compare Monster Beverage and Brown-Forman   Obj. 7

Monster Beverage Corporation (MNST) develops, markets, and sells energy and other alternative beverage brands. **Brown-Forman Corporation (BF.B)** manufactures and sells a wide variety of spirit and wine beverages, such as Jack Daniel's®. The cost of goods sold and inventory were obtained from a recent annual report for both companies as follows (in millions):

	Monster Beverage	Brown-Forman
Cost of goods sold	$1,090	$ 945
Inventories:		
Beginning of year	175	953
End of year	156	1,054

a. Determine the inventory turnover for both companies. Round all calculations to one decimal place.

b. Determine the number of days' sales in inventory for both companies. Use 365 days and round all calculations to one decimal place.

c. ➤ Interpret the difference in inventory efficiency based on the companies' respective product types.

Take It Further

ETHICS

TIF 6-1   Lower of cost or market

Sizemo Elektroniks sells semiconductors that are used in games and small toys. The company has been extremely successful in recent years, recording an increase in earnings each of the past six quarters. At the end of the current quarter, Jay Shulz, the company's staff accountant, calculated the ending inventory for the semiconductors and was surprised to find that the quantity of the Hayden X537 model had not changed during the quarter. Jay confirmed his calculation with the inventory control manager, who indicated that sales of the Hayden 537X had stopped when the Hayden 637X semiconductor was released early in the quarter. Jay researched the issue further and found that the Hayden 637X semiconductor has the same applications as the Hayden 537X, but has more computing power and a lower cost than the 537X. Jay emailed this information to Tina Vereen, the chief financial officer, and recommended that the company apply the lower-of-cost-or-market method to the Hayden 537X semiconductors in inventory. Later that day, Tina emailed Jay back instructing him not to apply the lower-of-cost-or-market method to the 537X inventory because "the company is under considerable pressure to maintain its track record of earnings growth, and a lower-of-cost-or-market adjustment would result in a significant decline in earnings this quarter." Reluctantly, Jay followed Tina's instructions.

Evaluate the decision not to apply the lower-of-cost-or-market method in the current quarter.

1. ▬▬▶ Who benefits from this decision?

2. ▬▬▶ Who is harmed by this decision?

3. ▬▬▶ Are Jay and Tina acting in an ethical manner? Explain.

TIF 6-2 Shipping terms

Anstead Co. is experiencing a decrease in sales and operating income for the fiscal year ending October 31. Ryan Frazier, controller of Anstead Co., has suggested that all orders received before the end of the fiscal year be shipped by midnight, October 31, even if the Shipping Department must work overtime. Because Anstead Co. ships all merchandise FOB shipping point, it would record all such shipments as sales for the year ending October 31, thereby offsetting some of the decreases in sales and operating income.

▬▬▶ Discuss whether Ryan Frazier is behaving in a professional manner.

TEAM ACTIVITY   REAL WORLD

TIF 6-3 Real-world annual report

In teams, select a public company that interests you and is a business that requires inventory. Obtain the company's most recent annual report on Form 10-K. The Form 10-K is a company's annually required filing with the Securities and Exchange Commission (SEC). It includes the company's financial statements and accompanying notes. The Form 10-K can be obtained either (a) from the investor relations section of the company's website or (b) by using the company search feature of the SEC's EDGAR database service found at www.sec.gov/edgar/searchedgar/companysearch.html.

1. Based on the information in the company's most recent annual report, answer the following questions:

   a. What types of items are included in the company's inventory?

   b. What inventory costing method or methods does the company use to determine the inventory amount reported on its balance sheet?

   c. How much inventory does the company have at the end of the most recent year?

   d. What percentage of total current assets is inventory during the two years presented? Has this percentage increased, decreased, or remained the same during this period?

   e. How much cost of goods sold does the company report for the most recent year?

2. ▬▬▶ Using the information presented in the company's annual report, calculate the company's inventory turnover for the current and previous years. Based on this information, has the company's performance improved? Briefly explain your answer.

TIF 6-4 Inventory cost flow methods

COMMUNICATION

Golden Eagle Company began operations on April 1 by selling a single product. Data on purchases and sales for the year are as follows:

Purchases:

Date	Units Purchased	Unit Cost	Total Cost
April 6	31,000	$36.60	$1,134,600
May 18	33,000	39.00	1,287,000
June 6	40,000	39.60	1,584,000
July 10	40,000	42.00	1,680,000
August 10	27,200	42.75	1,162,800
October 25	12,800	43.50	556,800
November 4	8,000	44.85	358,800
December 10	8,000	48.00	384,000
	200,000		$8,148,000

(Continued)

Sales:

April	16,000 units
May	16,000
June	20,000
July	24,000
August	28,000
September	28,000
October	18,000
November	10,000
December	8,000
Total units	168,000
Total sales	$10,000,000

The president of the company, Connie Kilmer, has asked for your advice on which inventory cost flow method should be used for the 32,000-unit physical inventory that was taken on December 31. The company plans to expand its product line in the future and uses the periodic inventory system.

➤ Write a brief memo to Ms. Kilmer comparing and contrasting the LIFO and FIFO inventory cost flow methods and their potential impacts on the company's financial statements.

Pathways Challenge

This is Accounting!

Information/Consequences

All of **Tyson**'s costs related to raising chickens for sale are accounted for as inventory. Thus, the transportation, boarding, and feed costs are included in the cost of chicken inventory.

Other costs that should be included as part of chicken inventory include the labor costs of raising the chickens held for sale. In addition, depreciation on the farm buildings and equipment should be allocated to chicken inventory.

The breeding stock is not held for sale, but instead is an operating asset used in the production of chickens. In other words, the breeding stock is a fixed asset. As with any fixed asset, the cost is depreciated over its useful life. Theoretically, this depreciation should be allocated to the costs of raising the chickens for sale and, thus, is also an inventory cost.

Suggested Answer

STATEMENT OF STOCKHOLDERS' EQUITY
For the Year Ended December 31, 20Y5

	Common Stock	Retained Earnings	Total
Balances, Jan. 1, 20Y5	$XXX	$ XXX	$ XXX
Issued common stock	XXX		XXX
Net income		XXX	XXX
Dividends		(XXX)	(XXX)
Balances, Dec. 31, 20Y5	$XXX	$ XXX	$ XXX

STATEMENT OF CASH FLOWS
For the Year Ended December 31, 20Y5

Cash flows from (used for) operating activities	$XXX
Cash flows from (used for) investing activities	XXX
Cash flows from (used for) financing activities	XXX
Net increase (decrease) in cash	$XXX
Cash balance, January 1, 20Y5	XXX
Cash balance, December 31, 20Y5	$XXX

INCOME STATEMENT
For the Year Ended December 31, 20Y5

Sales		$ XXX
Cost of goods sold		(XXX)
Gross profit		$ XXX
Operating expenses:		
Wages expense	$XXX	
Advertising expense	XXX	
Utilities expense	XXX	
Depreciation expense	XXX	
…	XXX	
Total operating expenses		(XXX)
Operating income		$ XXX
Other revenue and expense		XXX
Net income		$ XXX

BALANCE SHEET
December 31, 20Y5

Assets		
Current assets:		
Cash	$XXX	
Accounts receivable	XXX	
Inventory	XXX	
Total current assets		$XXX
Property, plant, and equipment		XXX
Total assets		$XXX
Liabilities		
Current liabilities	$XXX	
Long-term liabilities	XXX	
Total liabilities		$XXX
Stockholders' Equity		
Common stock	$XXX	
Retained earnings	XXX	
Total stockholders' equity		XXX
Total liabilities and stockholders' equity		$XXX

eBay Inc.

Controls are a part of your everyday life. At one extreme, laws are used to limit your behavior. For example, speed limits are designed to control your driving for traffic safety. In addition, you may also use many nonlegal controls. For example, you can keep credit card receipts in order to compare your transactions to the monthly credit card statement. Comparing receipts to the monthly statement is a control designed to catch mistakes made by the credit card company. In addition, banks give you a personal identification number (PIN) as a control against unauthorized access to your cash if you lose your automated teller machine (ATM) card. Dairies use freshness dating on their milk containers as a control to prevent the purchase or sale of soured milk. As you can see, you use and encounter controls every day.

Just as there are many examples of controls throughout society, businesses must also implement controls to help guide the behavior of their managers, employees, and customers. For example, **eBay Inc. (EBAY)** maintains an Internet-based marketplace for the sale of goods and services. Using eBay's online platform, buyers and sellers can browse, buy, and sell a wide variety of items including antiques and used cars. However, in order to maintain the integrity and trust of its buyers and sellers, eBay must have controls to ensure that buyers pay for their items and sellers don't misrepresent their items or fail to deliver sales. One such control eBay uses is a feedback forum that establishes buyer and seller reputations. A prospective buyer or seller can view the member's reputation and feedback comments before completing a transaction. Dishonest or unfair trading can lead to a negative reputation and even suspension or cancellation of the member's ability to trade on eBay.

This chapter discusses controls that can be included in accounting systems to provide reasonable assurance that the financial statements are reliable. Controls to discover and prevent errors to a bank account are also discussed. This chapter begins by discussing the Sarbanes-Oxley Act and its impact on controls and financial reporting.

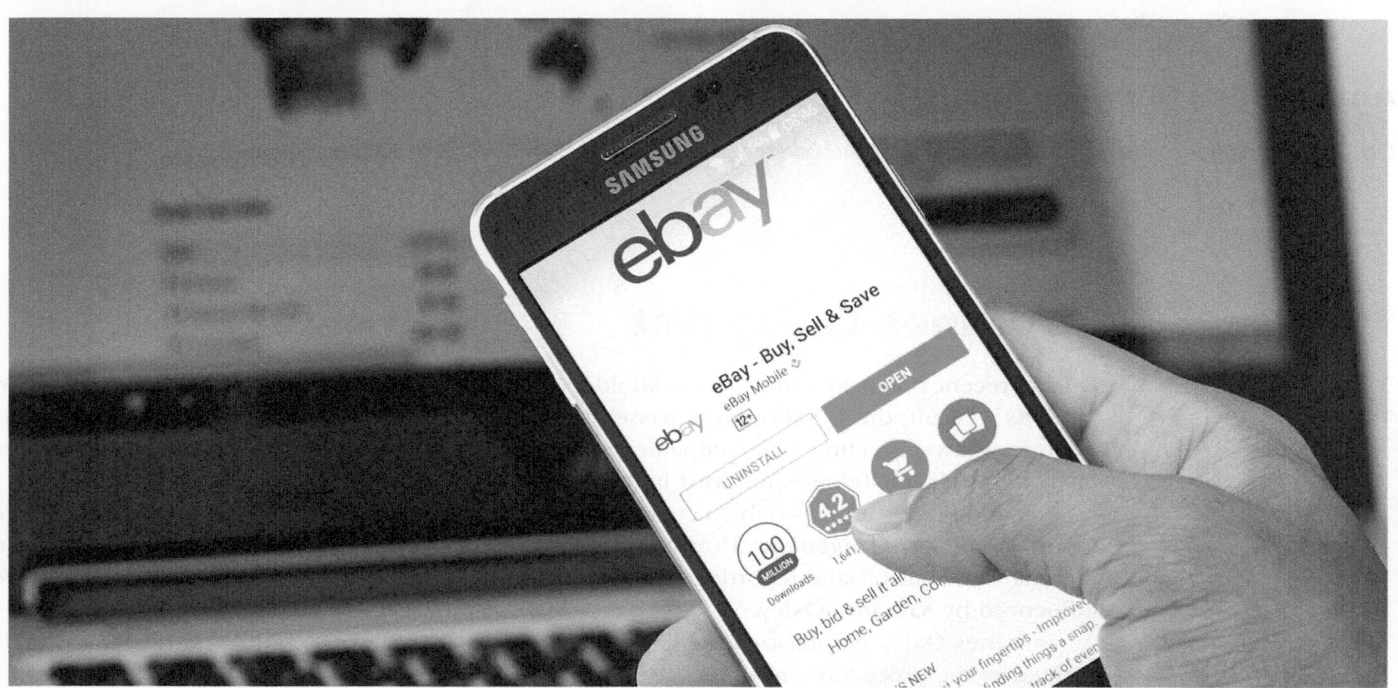

©CHONLACHAI/SHUTTERSTOCK.COM

What's Covered

Internal Control and Cash

Internal Controls	Cash Receipts and Payments	Bank Accounts	Special-Purpose Cash Funds	Reporting Cash
■ Sarbanes-Oxley Act (Obj. 1)	■ Control of Cash Receipts (Obj. 3)	■ Bank Statement (Obj. 4)	■ Petty Cash (Obj. 6)	■ Balance Sheet (Obj. 7)
■ Elements (Obj. 2)	■ Control of Cash Payments (Obj. 3)	■ Bank Reconciliation (Obj. 5)		
■ Limitations (Obj. 2)				

Learning Objectives

Obj. 1 Describe the Sarbanes-Oxley Act and its impact on internal controls and financial reporting.

Obj. 2 Describe and illustrate the objectives and elements of internal control.

Obj. 3 Describe and illustrate the application of internal controls to cash.

Obj. 4 Describe the nature of a bank account and its use in controlling cash.

Obj. 5 Describe and illustrate the use of a bank reconciliation in controlling cash.

Obj. 6 Describe the accounting for special-purpose cash funds.

Obj. 7 Describe and illustrate the reporting of cash and cash equivalents in the financial statements.

Analysis for Decision Making

Obj. 8 Describe and illustrate the use of days' cash on hand to assess a company's ability to meet its cash commitments.

Objective 1

Describe the Sarbanes-Oxley Act and its impact on internal controls and financial reporting.

Sarbanes-Oxley Act

During recent financial scandals, stockholders, creditors, and other investors lost billions of dollars.[1] As a result, the U.S. Congress passed the **Sarbanes-Oxley Act**. This act is one of the most important laws affecting U.S. companies in recent history. The purpose of Sarbanes-Oxley is to maintain public confidence and trust in the financial reporting of companies.

Sarbanes-Oxley applies only to companies whose stock is traded on public exchanges, referred to as *publicly held companies*. However, Sarbanes-Oxley highlighted the importance of assessing the financial controls and reporting of all companies. As a result, companies of all sizes have been influenced by Sarbanes-Oxley.

Sarbanes-Oxley emphasizes the importance of effective internal control.[2] **Internal control** is defined as the procedures and processes used by a company to:

■ Safeguard its assets.

■ Process information accurately.

■ Ensure compliance with laws and regulations.

Sarbanes-Oxley requires companies to maintain effective internal controls over the recording of transactions and the preparing of financial statements. Such controls are important because they deter fraud and prevent misleading financial statements as shown in Exhibit 1.

---

[1] Exhibit 2 in Chapter 1 briefly summarizes these scandals.

[2] Sarbanes-Oxley also has important implications for corporate governance and the regulation of the public accounting profession. This chapter, however, focuses on the internal control implications of Sarbanes-Oxley.

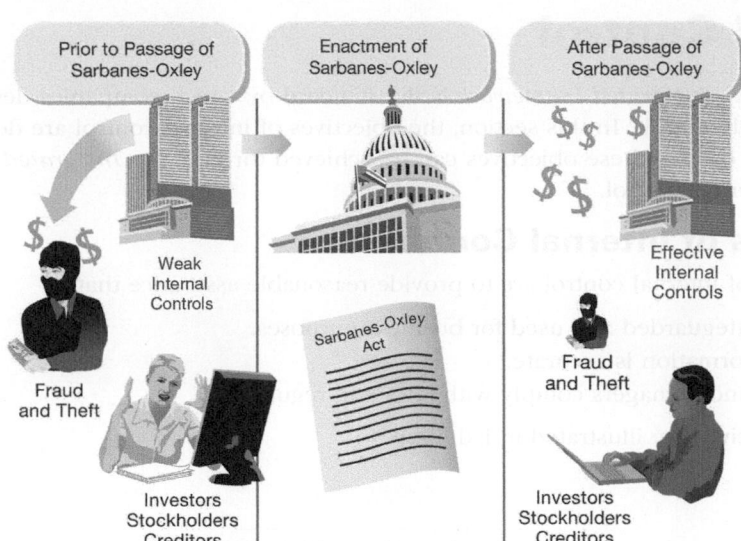

Exhibit 1
Effect of
Sarbanes-Oxley

Sarbanes-Oxley also requires companies and their independent accountants to report on the effectiveness of the company's internal controls.[3] These reports are required to be filed with the company's annual 10-K report with the Securities and Exchange Commission. Companies are also encouraged to include these reports in their annual reports to stockholders. An example of such a report by the management of **eBay** is shown in Exhibit 2.

Management's Annual Report on Internal Control Over Financial Reporting

Our management is responsible for establishing and maintaining adequate internal control over financial reporting. Our management, including our principal executive officer and principal financial officer, conducted an evaluation of the effectiveness of our internal control over financial reporting based on the framework in Internal Control—Integrated Framework (2013) issued by the Committee of Sponsoring Organizations of the Treadway Commission. Based on its evaluation under the framework in Internal Control—Integrated Framework, our management concluded that our internal control over financial reporting was effective as of December 31, ...

Source: eBay, Form 10-K, For the Fiscal Year Ended December 31, 2015.

Exhibit 2
eBay's Report of
Compliance with
Sarbanes-Oxley

Exhibit 2 is taken from the annual (10-K) report of **eBay**.

Link to eBay

Exhibit 2 indicates that the evaluation of internal controls is based on *Internal Control—Integrated Framework*, which was issued by the Committee of Sponsoring Organizations (COSO) of the Treadway Commission. This framework is the standard by which companies design, analyze, and evaluate internal controls. For this reason, this framework is used as the basis for discussing internal controls.[4]

---

[3] These reporting requirements are required under Section 404 of the act. As a result, these requirements and reports are often referred to as 404 requirements and 404 reports.

[4] Additional information on *Internal Control—Integrated Framework* can be found on COSO's website at www.coso.org.

Objective 2

Describe and illustrate the objectives and elements of internal control.

Internal Control

Internal Control—Integrated Framework is the standard by which companies design, analyze, and evaluate internal control.[5] In this section, the objectives of internal control are described, followed by a discussion of how these objectives can be achieved through the *Integrated Framework's* five elements of internal control.

Objectives of Internal Control

The objectives of internal control are to provide reasonable assurance that:

- Assets are safeguarded and used for business purposes.
- Business information is accurate.
- Employees and managers comply with laws and regulations.

These objectives are illustrated in Exhibit 3.

Exhibit 3

Objectives of Internal Control

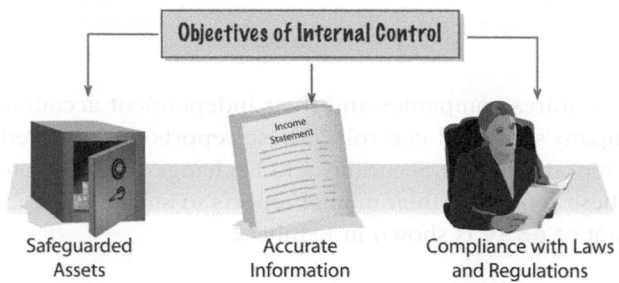

| Safeguarded Assets | Accurate Information | Compliance with Laws and Regulations |

Internal control can safeguard assets by preventing theft, fraud, misuse, or misplacement. A serious concern of internal control is preventing employee fraud. **Employee fraud** is the intentional act of deceiving an employer for personal gain. Such fraud may range from minor overstating of a travel expense report to stealing millions of dollars. Employees stealing from a business often adjust the accounting records in order to hide their fraud. Thus, employee fraud usually affects the accuracy of business information.

Accurate information is necessary to successfully operate a business. Businesses must also comply with laws, regulations, and financial reporting standards. Examples of such standards include environmental regulations, safety regulations, and generally accepted accounting principles (GAAP).

Why It Matters

Employee Fraud

The Association of Fraud Examiners estimates that 5% of annual revenues worldwide or more than $6.3 billion is lost to employee fraud. A common *cash receipts* employee fraud can occur when employees accept cash payments from customers, do not record the sale, and then pocket the cash. A common *cash payments* employee fraud can occur when employees bill their employer for false services or personal items.

Source: 2016 *ACFE Report to the Nations on Occupational Fraud and Abuse,* Association of Fraud Examiners.

Elements of Internal Control

The three internal control objectives can be achieved by applying the five **elements of internal control** set forth by the *Integrated Framework.*[6] These elements are as follows:

- Control environment
- Risk assessment
- Control procedures

[5] *Internal Control—Integrated Framework* by the Committee of Sponsoring Organizations of the Treadway Commission, 2013.
[6] Ibid., pp. 12–14.

- Monitoring
- Information and communication

The elements of internal control are illustrated in Exhibit 4.

Exhibit 4
Elements of Internal Control

In Exhibit 4, the elements of internal control form an umbrella over the business to protect it from control threats. The control environment is the size of the umbrella. Risk assessment, control procedures, and monitoring are the fabric of the umbrella, which keep it from leaking. Information and communication connect the umbrella to management and the business.

As technology changes, **eBay** must continually monitor and strengthen its controls over its e-commerce transactions.

Link to eBay

Control Environment

The **control environment** is the overall attitude of management and employees about the importance of controls. Three factors influencing a company's control environment include the following, as shown in Exhibit 5:

- Management's philosophy and operating style
- The company's organizational structure
- The company's personnel policies

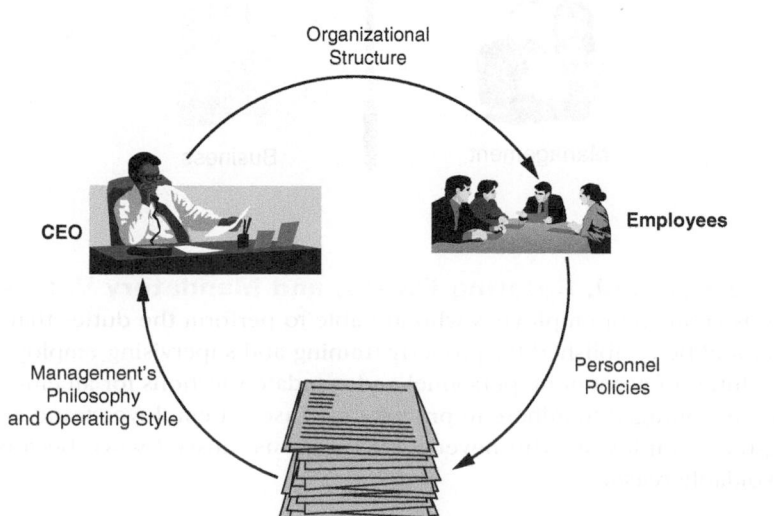

Exhibit 5
Control Environment

Management's philosophy and operating style relate to whether management emphasizes the importance of internal controls. An emphasis on controls and adherence to control policies creates an effective control environment. In contrast, overemphasizing operating goals and tolerating deviations from control policies creates an ineffective control environment.

The business's organizational structure is the framework for planning and controlling operations. For example, a retail store chain might organize each of its stores as separate business units. Each store manager has full authority over pricing and other operating activities. In such a structure, each store manager has the responsibility for establishing an effective control environment.

The business's personnel policies involve the hiring, training, evaluation, compensation, and promotion of employees. In addition, job descriptions, employee codes of ethics, and conflict-of-interest policies are part of the personnel policies. Such policies can enhance the internal control environment if they provide reasonable assurance that only competent, honest employees are hired and retained.

Risk Assessment

All businesses face risks such as changes in customer requirements, competitive threats, regulatory changes, and changes in economic factors. Management should identify such risks, analyze their significance, assess their likelihood of occurring, and take any necessary actions to minimize them.

Control Procedures

Control procedures provide reasonable assurance that business goals will be achieved, including the prevention of fraud. Control procedures, which constitute one of the most important elements of internal control, include the following as shown in Exhibit 6:

- Competent personnel, rotating duties, and mandatory vacations
- Separating responsibilities for related operations
- Separating operations, custody of assets, and accounting
- Proofs and security measures

Exhibit 6
Internal Control
Procedures

Control Threats

Control Procedures
Competent personnel, rotating duties, and
mandatory vacations
Separating responsibilities for related operations
Separating operations, custody of assets, and accounting
Proofs and security measures

Management   Business

Competent Personnel, Rotating Duties, and Mandatory Vacations A successful company needs competent employees who are able to perform the duties that they are assigned. Procedures should be established for properly training and supervising employees. It is also advisable to rotate duties of accounting personnel and mandate vacations for all employees. In this way, employees are encouraged to adhere to procedures. Cases of employee fraud are often discovered when a long-term employee, who never took vacations, missed work because of an illness or another unavoidable reason.

Separating Responsibilities for Related Operations The responsibility for related operations should be divided among two or more people. This decreases the possibility of errors and fraud. For example, if the same person orders supplies, verifies the receipt of the supplies, and pays the supplier, the following abuses may occur:

- Orders may be placed on the basis of friendship with a supplier, rather than on price, quality, and other objective factors.
- The quantity and quality of supplies received may not be verified; thus, the company may pay for supplies not received or that are of poor quality.
- Supplies may be stolen by the employee.
- The validity and accuracy of invoices may not be verified; hence, the company may pay false or inaccurate invoices.

For the preceding reasons, the responsibilities for purchasing, receiving, and paying for supplies should be divided among three persons or departments.

Separating Operations, Custody of Assets, and Accounting The responsibilities for operations, custody of assets, and accounting should be separated. In this way, the accounting records serve as an independent check on the operating managers and the employees who have custody of assets.

To illustrate, employees who handle cash receipts should not record cash receipts in the accounting records. To do so would allow employees to borrow or steal cash and hide the theft in the accounting records. Likewise, operating managers should not also record the results of operations. To do so would allow the managers to distort the accounting reports to show favorable results, which might allow them to receive larger bonuses.

Proofs and Security Measures Proofs and security measures are used to safeguard assets and ensure reliable accounting data. Proofs involve procedures such as authorization, approval, and reconciliation. For example, an employee planning to travel on company business may be required to complete a "travel request" form for a manager's authorization and approval.

Documents used for authorization and approval should be prenumbered, accounted for, and safeguarded. Prenumbering of documents helps prevent transactions from being recorded more than once or not at all. In addition, accounting for and safeguarding prenumbered documents helps prevent fraudulent transactions from being recorded. For example, blank checks are prenumbered and safeguarded. Once a payment has been properly authorized and approved, the checks are filled out and issued.

Reconciliations are also an important control. Later in this chapter, the use of bank reconciliations as an aid in controlling cash is described and illustrated.

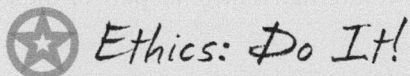 *Ethics: Do It!*

Tips on Preventing Employee Fraud in Small Companies

- Do not have the same employee write company checks and keep the books. Look for payments to vendors you don't know or payments to vendors whose names appear to be misspelled.
- If your business has a computer system, restrict access to accounting files as much as possible. Also, keep a backup copy of your accounting files and store it at an off-site location.
- Be wary of anybody working in finance who declines to take vacations. They may be afraid that a replacement will uncover fraud.

- Require and monitor supporting documentation (such as vendor invoices) before signing checks.
- Track the number of credit card bills you sign monthly.
- Limit and monitor access to important documents and supplies, such as blank checks and signature stamps.
- Check W-2 forms against your payroll annually to make sure you're not carrying any fictitious employees.
- Rely on yourself, not on your accountant, to spot fraud.

Source: Steve Kaufman, "Embezzlement Common at Small Companies," Knight-Ridder Newspapers, reported in *Athens Daily News/Athens Banner-Herald*, March 10, 1996, p. 4D.

Security measures involve measures to safeguard assets. For example, cash on hand should be kept in a cash register or safe. Inventory not on display should be stored in a locked storeroom or warehouse. Accounting records such as the accounts receivable subsidiary ledger should also be safeguarded to prevent their loss. For example, electronically maintained accounting records should be safeguarded with access codes and backed up so that any lost or damaged files could be recovered if necessary.

Monitoring

Monitoring the internal control system is used to locate weaknesses and improve controls. Monitoring often includes observing employee behavior and the accounting system for indicators of control problems. Some such indicators are shown in Exhibit 7.[7]

Exhibit 7 Warning Signs of Internal Control Problems

Warning signs with regard to people

- Abrupt change in lifestyle (without winning the lottery).
- Close social relationships with suppliers.
- Refusing to take a vacation.
- Frequent borrowing from other employees.
- Excessive use of alcohol or drugs.

Warning signs from the accounting system

- Missing documents or gaps in transaction numbers (could mean documents are being used for fraudulent transactions).
- An unusual increase in customer refunds (refunds may be phony).
- Differences between daily cash receipts and bank deposits (could mean receipts are being pocketed before being deposited).
- Sudden increase in slow payments (employee may be pocketing the payments).
- Backlog in recording transactions (possibly an attempt to delay detection of fraud).

Evaluations of controls are often performed when there are major changes in strategy, senior management, business structure, or operations. Internal auditors, who are independent of operations, usually perform such evaluations. Internal auditors are also responsible for day-to-day monitoring of controls. External auditors also evaluate and report on internal control as part of their annual financial statement audit.

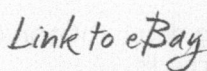 **eBay** reduces fraudulent activities by restricting or suspending buyers and sellers with questionable transaction histories.

Information and Communication

Information and communication is an essential element of internal control. Information about the control environment, risk assessment, control procedures, and monitoring is used by management for guiding operations and ensuring compliance with reporting, legal, and regulatory requirements. Management also uses external information to assess events and conditions that impact decision making and external reporting. For example, management uses pronouncements of the Financial Accounting Standards Board (FASB) to assess the impact of changes in reporting standards on the financial statements.

---

[7] Edwin C. Bliss, "Employee Theft," *Boardroom Reports*, July 15, 1994, pp. 5–6.

Check Up Corner 7-1 Internal Controls

Identify the control procedure violated in each of the following scenarios:

a. Todd Leone is the accounting clerk for Home Chic, a small boutique retail store that is owned and operated by Al Dente. Al does not care much for the accounting side of the business and allows Todd to make all payments to the company's suppliers. Todd pays all invoices that Home Chic receives. Al does not review the payments Todd makes.

b. Jose Muldoon's Mobile Foods is a food truck with two trusted employees. One employee stocks the food truck each day, prepares the orders, and cleans up the kitchen at the end of the day. The other employee takes orders, collects payment from customers, counts the cash at the end of the day, records the cash receipts, and deposits the cash in the night depository slot at the bank.

c. Tad is the treasurer and chief financial officer of a local bank in Wisteria, California. Tad was born and raised in the community and has never had a desire to travel. As a result, he has not taken a vacation or a day off of work in over six years.

Solution:

a. Separating operations, custody of assets, and accounting. The responsibility for maintaining the accounting records, operations, and custody of assets should be separated. This is a violation of this control procedure because the payments do not require approval by an independent party.

b. Separating operations, custody of assets, and accounting. The responsibility for maintaining the accounting records, operations, and custody of assets should be separated. This is a violation of this control procedure because the same employee collects the cash (operations and custody of assets), records the cash receipts (accounting records), and deposits the cash (custody of assets).

c. Competent personnel, rotating duties, and mandatory vacations. Procedures should be established to rotate duties of accounting personnel and mandate vacations for all employees. This is a violation of this control procedure.

Check Up Corner

Limitations of Internal Control

Internal control systems can provide only reasonable assurance for safeguarding assets, processing accurate information, and compliance with laws and regulations. In other words, internal controls are not a guarantee. This is due to the following factors:

- The human element of controls
- Cost-benefit considerations

The *human element* recognizes that controls are applied and used by humans. As a result, human errors can occur because of fatigue, carelessness, confusion, or misjudgment. For example, an employee may unintentionally shortchange a customer or miscount the amount of inventory received from a supplier. In addition, two or more employees may collude together to defeat or circumvent internal controls. This latter case often involves fraud and the theft of assets. For example, the cashier and the accounts receivable clerk might collude to steal customer payments on account.

Cost-benefit considerations recognize that the cost of internal controls should not exceed their benefits. For example, retail stores could eliminate shoplifting by searching all customers before they leave the store. However, such a control procedure would upset customers and result in lost sales. Instead, retailers use cameras or signs saying, "*We prosecute all shoplifters.*"

The auditor's report for **eBay** includes the statement: . . . internal control over financial reporting is a process designed to provide reasonable assurance regarding the reliability of financial reporting . . .

Link to eBay

Objective 3

Describe and illustrate the application of internal controls to cash.

Cash Controls over Receipts and Payments

Cash includes coins, currency (paper money), checks, and money orders. Money on deposit with a bank or other financial institution that is available for withdrawal is also considered cash. Normally, you can think of cash as anything that a bank would accept for deposit in your account. For example, a check made payable to you could normally be deposited in a bank and, thus, is considered cash.

Businesses usually have several bank accounts. For example, a business might have one bank account for general cash payments and another for payroll. A separate ledger account is normally used for each bank account. For example, a bank account at City Bank could be identified in the ledger as *Cash in Bank—City Bank*. To simplify, this chapter assumes that a company has only *one* bank account, which is identified in the ledger as *Cash*.

Cash is the asset most likely to be stolen or used improperly in a business. For this reason, businesses must carefully control cash and cash transactions.

Control of Cash Receipts

To protect cash from theft and misuse, a business must control cash from the time it is received until it is deposited in a bank. Businesses normally receive cash from two main sources.

- Customers purchasing products or services
- Customers making payments on account

Cash Received from Cash Sales An important control to protect cash received in over-the-counter sales is a cash register. The use of a cash register to control cash is shown in Exhibit 8.

Exhibit 8

Cash Register as a Control

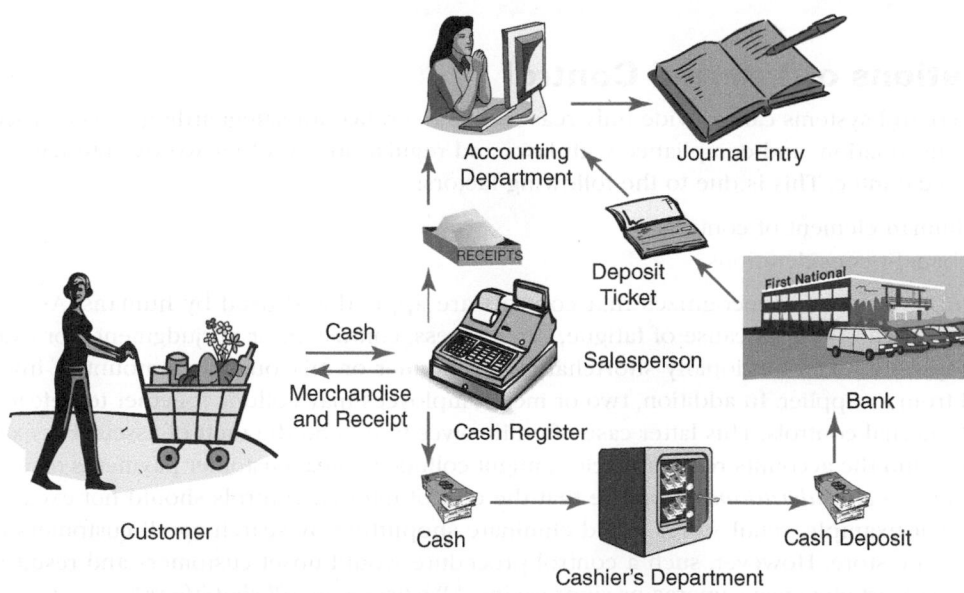

A cash register controls cash as follows:

1. At the beginning of every work shift, each cash register clerk is given a cash drawer containing a predetermined amount of cash. This amount is used for making change for customers and is sometimes called a *change fund*.
2. When a salesperson enters the amount of a sale, the cash register displays the amount to the customer. This allows the customer to verify that the clerk has charged the correct amount. The customer also receives a cash receipt.
3. At the end of the shift, the clerk and the supervisor count the cash in the clerk's cash drawer. The amount of cash in each drawer should equal the beginning amount of cash plus the cash sales for the day.

4. The supervisor takes the cash to the Cashier's Department where it is placed in a safe.

5. The supervisor forwards the clerk's cash register receipts to the Accounting Department.

6. The cashier prepares a bank deposit ticket.

7. The cashier deposits the cash in the bank, or the cash is picked up by an armored car service, such as **Wells Fargo (WFC)**.

8. The Accounting Department summarizes the cash receipts and records the day's cash sales.

9. When cash is deposited in the bank, the bank normally stamps a duplicate copy of the deposit ticket with the amount received. This bank receipt is returned to the Accounting Department, where it is compared to the total amount that should have been deposited. This control helps ensure that all the cash is deposited and that no cash is lost or stolen on the way to the bank. Any shortages are thus promptly detected.

Salespersons may make errors in making change for customers or in ringing up cash sales. As a result, the amount of cash on hand may differ from the amount of cash sales. Such differences are recorded in a **cash short and over account**.

To illustrate, assume the following cash register data for May 3:

Cash register total for cash sales	$35,690
Cash receipts from cash sales	35,668

The cash sales, receipts, and shortage of $22 ($35,690 − $35,668) would be journalized as follows:

May 3	Cash	35,668	
	Cash Short and Over	22	
	Sales		35,690

$$A = L + E$$
$$+ \qquad + \text{Rev}$$
$$- \text{Exp}$$

If there had been cash over, Cash Short and Over would have been credited for the overage. At the end of the accounting period, a debit balance in Cash Short and Over is included in miscellaneous expenses on the income statement. A credit balance is included in the "Other revenue" section. If a salesperson consistently has large cash short and over amounts, the supervisor may require the clerk to take additional training.

Cash Received in the Mail Cash is received in the mail when customers pay their bills. This cash is usually in the form of checks and money orders. Most companies design their invoices so that customers return a portion of the invoice, called a *remittance advice*, with their payment. Remittance advices may be used to control cash received in the mail as follows:

1. An employee opens the incoming mail and compares the amount of cash received with the amount shown on the remittance advice. If a customer does not return a remittance advice, the employee prepares one. The remittance advice serves as a record of the cash initially received. It also helps ensure that the posting to the customer's account is for the amount of cash received.

2. The employee opening the mail stamps checks and money orders "For Deposit Only" in the bank account of the business.

3. The remittance advices and their summary totals are delivered to the Accounting Department.

4. All cash and money orders are delivered to the Cashier's Department.

5. The cashier prepares a bank deposit ticket.

6. The cashier deposits the cash in the bank, or the cash is picked up by an armored car service, such as **Brinks (BCO)**.

7. An accounting clerk records the cash received and posts the amounts to the customer accounts.

8. When cash is deposited in the bank, the bank normally stamps a duplicate copy of the deposit ticket with the amount received. This bank receipt is returned to the Accounting Department, where it is compared to the total amount that should have been deposited. This control helps ensure that all cash is deposited and that no cash is lost or stolen on the way to the bank. Any shortages are thus promptly detected.

Separating the duties of the Cashier's Department, which handles cash, and the Accounting Department, which records cash, is a control. If Accounting Department employees both handle and record cash, an employee could steal cash and change the accounting records to hide the theft.

Cash Received by EFT Cash may also be received from customers through **electronic funds transfer (EFT)**. For example, customers may authorize automatic electronic transfers from their checking accounts to pay monthly bills for such items as cell phone, Internet, and electric services. In such cases, the company sends the customer's bank a signed form from the customer authorizing the monthly electronic transfers. Each month, the company notifies the customer's bank of the amount of the transfer and the date the transfer should take place. On the due date, the company records the electronic transfer as a receipt of cash to its bank account and posts the amount paid to the customer's account.

Companies encourage customers to use EFT for the following reasons:

- EFTs cost less than receiving cash payments through the mail.
- EFTs enhance internal controls over cash, since the cash is received directly by the bank without any employees handling cash.
- EFTs reduce late payments from customers and speed up the processing of cash receipts.

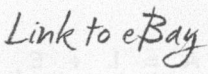 In a recent year, **eBay** generated $2.8 billion in cash from operations.

Control of Cash Payments

The control of cash payments should provide reasonable assurance that:

- Payments are made for only authorized transactions.
- Cash is used effectively and efficiently. For example, controls should ensure that all available purchase discounts are taken.

In a small business, an owner/manager may authorize payments based on personal knowledge. In a large business, however, purchasing goods, inspecting the goods received, and verifying the invoices are usually performed by different employees. These duties must be coordinated to ensure that proper payments are made to creditors. One system used for this purpose is the voucher system.

Voucher System A **voucher system** is a set of procedures for authorizing and recording liabilities and cash payments. A **voucher** is any document that serves as proof of authority to pay cash or issue an electronic funds transfer. An invoice that has been approved for payment could be considered a voucher. In many businesses, however, a voucher is a special form used to record data about a liability and the details of its payment.

In a manual system, a voucher is normally prepared after all necessary supporting documents have been received. For the purchase of goods, a voucher is supported by the supplier's invoice, a purchase order, and a receiving report. After a voucher is prepared, it is submitted for approval. Once approved, the voucher is recorded in the accounts and filed by due date. Upon payment, the voucher is recorded in the same manner as the payment of an account payable.

In a computerized system, data from the supporting documents (such as purchase orders, receiving reports, and suppliers' invoices) are entered directly into computer files. At the due date, the checks are automatically generated and mailed to creditors. At that time, the voucher is electronically transferred to a paid voucher file.

Cash Paid by EFT Cash can also be paid by electronic funds transfer (EFT) systems. For example, you can withdraw cash from your bank account using an ATM machine. Your withdrawal is a type of EFT transfer.

Companies also use EFT transfers. For example, many companies pay their employees via EFT. Under such a system, employees authorize the deposit of their payroll checks directly into their checking accounts. Each pay period, the company transfers the employees' net pay to their checking accounts through the use of EFT. Many companies also use EFT systems to pay their suppliers and other vendors.

Bank Accounts

Objective 4

Describe the nature of a bank account and its use in controlling cash.

A major reason that companies use bank accounts is for internal control. Some of the control advantages of using bank accounts are as follows:

- Bank accounts reduce the amount of cash on hand.
- Bank accounts provide an independent recording of cash transactions. Reconciling the balance of the cash account in the company's records with the cash balance according to the bank is an important control.
- Use of bank accounts facilitates the transfer of funds using EFT systems.

Bank Statement

Banks maintain a record of all checking account transactions. A summary of all transactions, called a **bank statement**, is mailed, usually each month, to the company (depositor) or made available online. The bank statement shows the beginning balance, additions, deductions, and the ending balance. A typical bank statement is shown in Exhibit 9 for **Power Networking**.

Checks or copies of the checks listed in the order that they were paid by the bank may accompany the bank statement. If paid checks are returned, they are stamped "Paid," together with the date of payment. Many banks no longer return checks or check copies. Instead, the check payment information is available online.

The company's checking account balance *in the bank records* is a liability. Thus, in the bank's records, the company's account has a credit balance. Because the bank statement is prepared from the bank's point of view, a credit memo entry on the bank statement indicates an increase (a credit) to the company's account. Likewise, a debit memo entry on the bank statement indicates a decrease (a debit) in the company's account. This relationship is shown in Exhibit 10.

Exhibit 9
Bank Statement

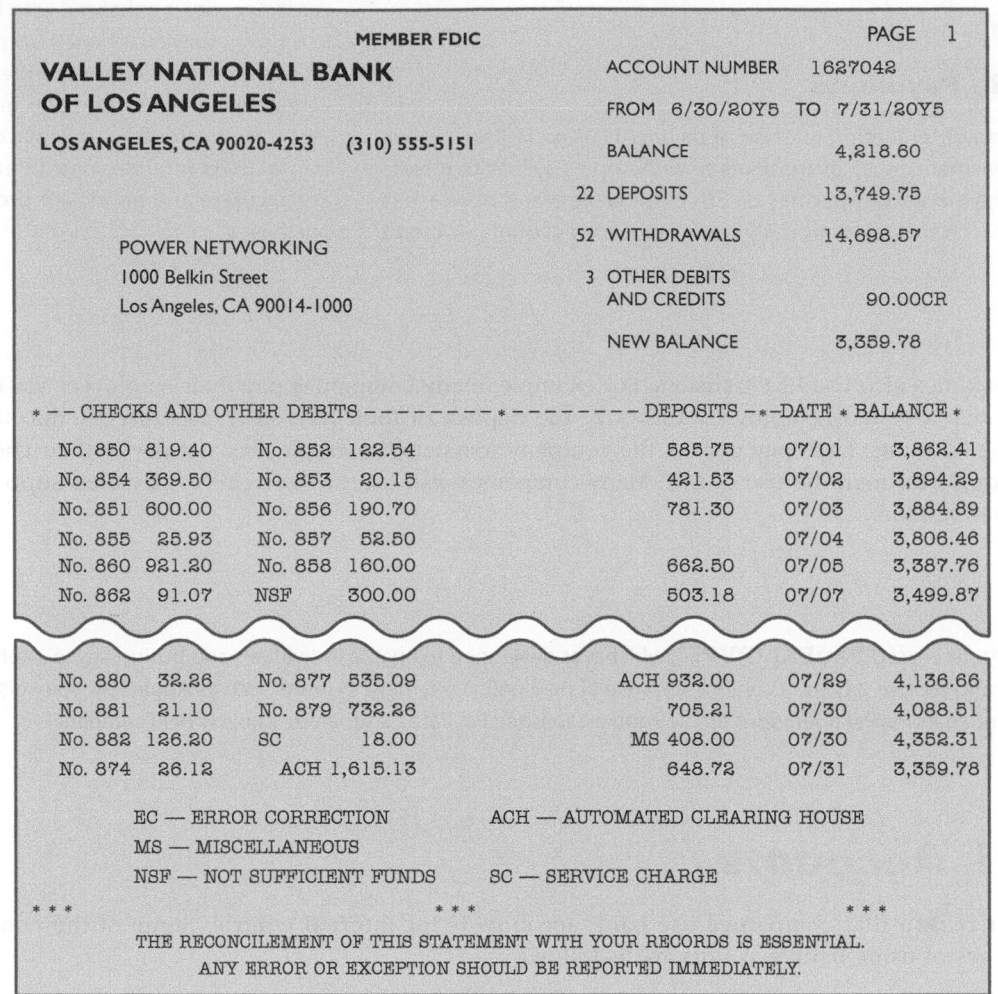

Exhibit 10   Checking Account: Company and Bank Perspectives

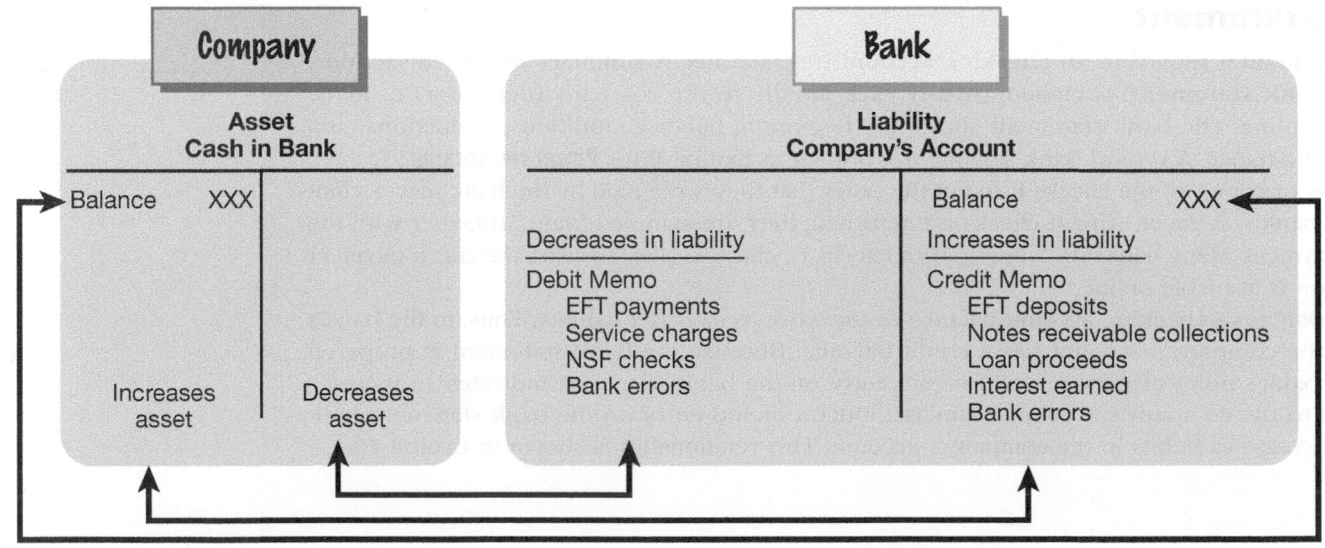

A bank makes credit entries (issues credit memos) for the following:

- Deposits made by electronic funds transfer (EFT)
- Collections of notes receivable for the company
- Proceeds for a loan made to the company by the bank
- Interest earned on the company's account
- Correction (if any) of bank errors

A bank makes debit entries (issues debit memos) for the following:

- Payments made by electronic funds transfer (EFT)
- Service charges
- Customer checks returned for not sufficient funds
- Correction (if any) of bank errors

Customers' checks returned for not sufficient funds, called *NSF checks*, are customer checks that were initially deposited but were not paid by the customer's bank. Because the company's bank credited the customer's check to the company's account when it was deposited, the bank debits the company's account (issues a debit memo) when the check is returned without payment.

The reason for a credit or debit memo entry is indicated on the bank statement. Exhibit 9 identifies the following types of credit and debit memo entries:

- EC: Error correction to correct bank error
- NSF: Not sufficient funds check
- SC: Service charge
- ACH: Automated clearing house entry for electronic funds transfer
- MS: Miscellaneous item such as collection of a note receivable on behalf of the company or receipt of a loan by the company from the bank

The preceding list includes the notation "ACH" for electronic funds transfers. ACH is a network for clearing electronic funds transfers among individuals, companies, and banks.[8] Because electronic funds transfers may be either deposits or payments, ACH entries may indicate either a debit or credit entry to the company's account. Likewise, entries to correct bank errors and miscellaneous items may indicate a debit or credit entry to the company's account.

Why It Matters

Bank Error in Your Favor (or Maybe Not)

A New Zealand couple expected a $100,000 deposit into their checking account, but discovered the bank accidentally deposited $10,000,000. The couple immediately transferred the $10,000,000 to another account and left the country, hoping to cash in on this supposed windfall. Not surprisingly, they were found, arrested, and prosecuted for fraud. So, if you find a bank error in your favor, it really isn't like getting a Monopoly card. You cannot keep the cash, but must return it to the bank. Banks typically have a long time to correct such errors, and if it can be reasonably determined that you knew of the error, but failed to report it, you could be prosecuted for bank fraud.

Source: Nickel, "Bank Error in Your Favor?," *Forbes.com*, May 2012 (www.forbes.com/sites/moneybuilder/2012/05/24/bank-error-in-your-favor/).

Using the Bank Statement as a Control over Cash

The bank statement is a primary control that a company uses over cash. A company uses the bank's statement by comparing the company's record of cash transactions to those recorded by the bank.

The cash balance shown by a bank statement is usually different from the company's cash balance, as shown in Exhibit 11 for **Power Networking**.

---

[8] For further information on ACH, go to www.nacha.org/. Click on "NACHA and the ACH Network" and then click on "ACH Network: How It Works."

Exhibit 11

Power Networking's Bank Statement and Records

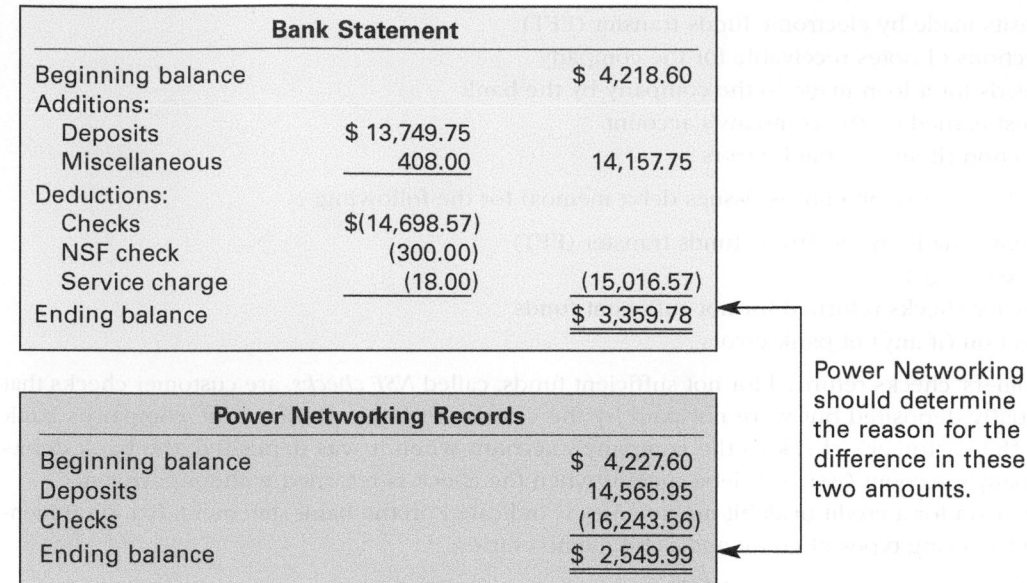

Bank Statement		
Beginning balance		$ 4,218.60
Additions:		
Deposits	$ 13,749.75	
Miscellaneous	408.00	14,157.75
Deductions:		
Checks	$(14,698.57)	
NSF check	(300.00)	
Service charge	(18.00)	(15,016.57)
Ending balance		$ 3,359.78

Power Networking should determine the reason for the difference in these two amounts.

Power Networking Records	
Beginning balance	$ 4,227.60
Deposits	14,565.95
Checks	(16,243.56)
Ending balance	$ 2,549.99

Differences between the company balance and bank balance may arise because of a delay by either the company or bank in recording transactions. For example, there is normally a time lag of one or more days between the date a check is written and the date that it is paid by the bank. Likewise, there is normally a time lag between when the company mails a deposit to the bank (or uses the night depository) and when the bank receives and records the deposit.

Differences may also arise because the bank has debited or credited the company's account for transactions that the company will not know about until the bank statement is received. Finally, differences may arise from errors made by either the company or the bank. For example, the company may incorrectly post to Cash a check written for $4,500 as $450. Likewise, a bank may incorrectly record the amount of a check.

Objective 5

Describe and illustrate the use of a bank reconciliation in controlling cash.

Bank Reconciliation

A **bank reconciliation** is an analysis of the items and amounts creating the difference between the cash balance reported in the bank statement and the balance of the cash account in the ledger. The adjusted cash balance determined in the bank reconciliation is reported on the balance sheet.

A bank reconciliation is usually divided into two sections as follows:

1. The *bank section* begins with the cash balance according to the bank statement and ends with the *adjusted balance*.

2. The *company section* begins with the cash balance according to the company's records and ends with the *adjusted balance*.

The *adjusted balance* from bank and company sections must be equal. The format of the bank reconciliation follows:

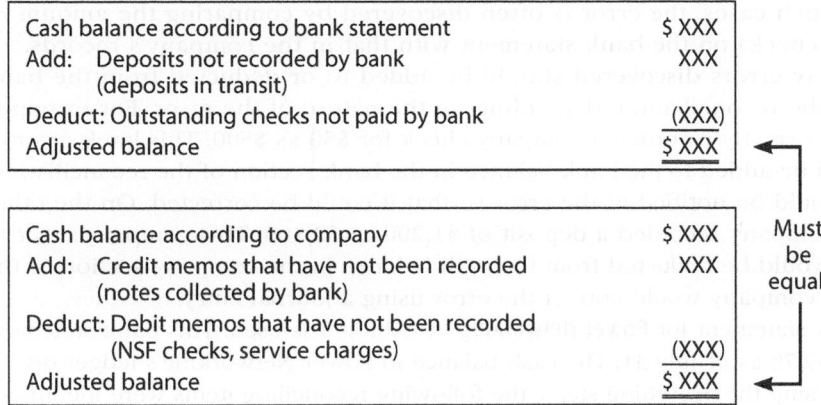

Cash balance according to bank statement	$ XXX
Add: Deposits not recorded by bank (deposits in transit)	XXX
Deduct: Outstanding checks not paid by bank	(XXX)
Adjusted balance	$ XXX

Must be equal.

Cash balance according to company	$ XXX
Add: Credit memos that have not been recorded (notes collected by bank)	XXX
Deduct: Debit memos that have not been recorded (NSF checks, service charges)	(XXX)
Adjusted balance	$ XXX

A bank reconciliation is prepared using steps illustrated in Exhibit 12.

Exhibit 12

How to Prepare a Bank Reconcilation

Bank Section of Reconciliation

■ Step 1. Enter the *Cash balance according to bank* from the ending cash balance according to the bank statement.

■ Step 2. *Add deposits not recorded by the bank.*
Identify deposits not recorded by the bank by comparing each deposit listed on the bank statement with unrecorded deposits appearing in the preceding period's reconciliation and with the current period's deposits.
Examples: Deposits in transit at the end of the period.

■ Step 3. *Deduct outstanding checks that have not been paid by the bank.*
Identify outstanding checks by comparing paid checks with outstanding checks appearing on the preceding period's reconciliation and with recorded checks.
Examples: Outstanding checks at the end of the period.

■ Step 4. Determine the *Adjusted balance* by adding Step 2 and deducting Step 3.

Company Section of Reconciliation

■ Step 5. Enter the *Cash balance according to company* from the ending cash balance in the ledger.

■ Step 6. *Add credit memos that have not been recorded.*
Identify the bank credit memos that have not been recorded by comparing the bank statement credit memos to entries in the journal.
Examples: A note receivable and interest that the bank has collected for the company.

■ Step 7. *Deduct debit memos that have not been recorded.*
Identify the bank debit memos that have not been recorded by comparing the bank statement debit memos to entries in the journal.
Examples: Customers' not sufficient funds (NSF) checks; bank service charges.

■ Step 8. Determine the *Adjusted balance* by adding Step 6 and deducting Step 7.

Verify That Adjusted Balances Are Equal

■ Step 9. Verify that the adjusted balances determined in Steps 4 and 8 are equal.

The adjusted balances in the bank and company sections of the reconciliation must be equal. If the balances are not equal, an item has been overlooked and must be found.

Sometimes, the adjusted balances are not equal because either the company or the bank has made an error. In such cases, the error is often discovered by comparing the amount of each item (deposit and check) on the bank statement with that in the company's records.

Any bank or company errors discovered should be added to or deducted from the bank or company section of the reconciliation, depending on the nature of the error. For example, assume that the bank incorrectly recorded a company check for $50 as $500. This bank error of $450 ($500 – $50) would be added to the bank balance in the bank section of the reconciliation. In addition, the bank would be notified of the error so that it could be corrected. On the other hand, assume that the company recorded a deposit of $1,200 as $2,100. This company error of $900 ($2,100 – $1,200) would be deducted from the cash balance in the company section of the bank reconciliation. The company would correct the error using a journal entry.

To illustrate, the bank statement for **Power Networking** in Exhibit 9 is used. This bank statement shows a balance of $3,359.78 as of July 31. The cash balance in Power Networking's ledger on the same date is $2,549.99. Using the preceding steps, the following reconciling items were identified:

- Step 2. Deposit of July 31, not recorded on bank statement: $816.20
- Step 3. Outstanding checks:

Check No. 812	$1,061.00
Check No. 878	435.39
Check No. 883	48.60
Total	$1,544.99

- Step 6. Note receivable of $400 plus interest of $8 collected by bank not recorded in the journal as indicated by a credit memo of $408.
- Step 7. Check from customer (Thomas Ivey) for $300 returned by bank because of insufficient funds (NSF) as indicated by a debit memo of $300.00.
  Bank service charges of $18, not recorded in the journal as indicated by a debit memo of $18.00.

In addition, an error of $9 was discovered. This error occurred when Check No. 879 for $732.26 to Taylor Co., on account, was recorded in the company's journal as $723.26.

The bank reconciliation, based on the Exhibit 9 bank statement and the preceding reconciling items, is shown in Exhibit 13 for Power Networking.

Exhibit 13   Bank Reconciliation for Power Networking

Power Networking
Bank Reconciliation
July 31, 20Y5

Step 1 →	Cash balance according to bank statement		$ 3,359.78
Step 2 →	Add: Deposit in transit on July 31		816.20
Step 3 →	Deduct: Outstanding Check No. 812	$1,061.00	
	Outstanding Check No. 878	435.39	
	Outstanding Check No. 883	48.60	
	Total deductions		(1,544.99)
Step 4 →	Adjusted balance		$ 2,630.99
Step 5 →	Cash balance according to Power Networking		$ 2,549.99
Step 6 →	Add: Note and interest collected by bank		408.00
Step 7 →	Deduct: Check returned because of insufficient funds	$ 300.00	
	Bank service charge	18.00	
	Error in recording Check No. 879	9.00	
	Total deductions		(327.00)
Step 8 →	Adjusted balance		$ 2,630.99

Step 9

The company's records do not need to be updated for any items in the *bank section* of the reconciliation. This section begins with the cash balance according to the bank statement. However, the bank should be notified of any errors that need to be corrected.

The company's records must be updated for any items in the *company section* of the bank reconciliation. The company's records are updated using journal entries. For example, journal entries should be made for any unrecorded bank memos and any company errors.

The journal entries for Power Networking, based on the bank reconciliation shown in Exhibit 13, are as follows:

July 31	Cash	408	
	Notes Receivable		400
	Interest Revenue		8
31	Accounts Receivable—Thomas Ivey	300	
	Miscellaneous Expense	18	
	Accounts Payable—Taylor Co.	9	
	Cash		327

A = L + E
+ −   + Rev

A = L + E
+ −   −   − Exp

Check Up Corner 7-2 Bank Reconciliation

The following data related to the bank account of Apex Company were gathered on December 31, 20Y9, the end of the fiscal year:

Balance per bank account	$14,500
Balance per company records	13,875

The following additional information was provided to help reconcile the company's bank account:

Bank service charges	$ 75
Deposit in transit	3,750
Check from Dave Hilman returned for insufficient funds (NSF)	800
Outstanding checks	5,250

Prepare a bank reconciliation for Apex Company on December 31, 20Y9.

Solution:

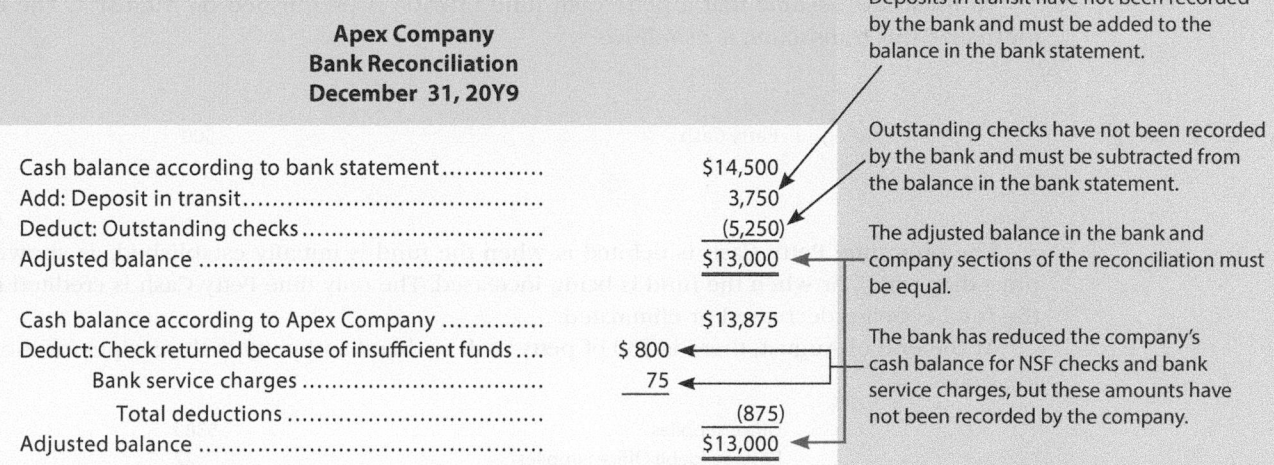

Apex Company
Bank Reconciliation
December 31, 20Y9

Cash balance according to bank statement..............		$14,500
Add: Deposit in transit...		3,750
Deduct: Outstanding checks.................................		(5,250)
Adjusted balance		$13,000
Cash balance according to Apex Company		$13,875
Deduct: Check returned because of insufficient funds	$ 800	
Bank service charges	75	
Total deductions		(875)
Adjusted balance		$13,000

Deposits in transit have not been recorded by the bank and must be added to the balance in the bank statement.

Outstanding checks have not been recorded by the bank and must be subtracted from the balance in the bank statement.

The adjusted balance in the bank and company sections of the reconciliation must be equal.

The bank has reduced the company's cash balance for NSF checks and bank service charges, but these amounts have not been recorded by the company.

Check Up Corner

After the preceding journal entries are recorded and posted, the cash account will have a debit balance of $2,630.99. This cash balance agrees with the adjusted balance shown on the bank reconciliation. This is the amount of cash on July 31 and is the amount that is reported on Power Networking's July 31 balance sheet.

Businesses may reconcile their bank accounts in a slightly different format from that shown in Exhibit 13. Regardless, the objective is to control cash by reconciling the company's records with the bank statement. In doing so, any errors or misuse of cash may be detected.

To enhance internal control, the bank reconciliation should be prepared by an employee who does not take part in or record cash transactions. Otherwise, mistakes may occur, and it is more likely that cash will be stolen or misapplied. For example, an employee who handles cash and also reconciles the bank statement could steal a cash deposit, omit the deposit from the accounts, and omit it from the reconciliation.

Bank reconciliations are also an important part of computerized systems where deposits and checks are stored in electronic files and records. Some systems use computer software to determine the difference between the bank statement and company cash balances. The software then adjusts for deposits in transit and outstanding checks. Any remaining differences are reported for further analysis.

Objective 6

Describe the accounting for special-purpose cash funds.

Special-Purpose Cash Funds

A company often has to pay small amounts for such items as postage, office supplies, or minor repairs. Although small, such payments may occur often enough to total a significant amount. Thus, it is desirable to control such payments. However, writing a check for each small payment is not practical. Instead, a special cash fund, called a **petty cash fund**, is used.

A petty cash fund is established by estimating the amount of payments needed from the fund during a period, such as a week or a month. A check is then written and cashed for this amount. The money obtained from cashing the check is then given to an employee, called the *petty cash custodian*. The petty cash custodian disburses monies from the fund as needed. For control purposes, the company may place restrictions on the maximum amount and the types of payments that can be made from the fund. Each time money is paid from petty cash, the custodian records the details on a petty cash receipts form.

The petty cash fund is normally replenished at periodic intervals, when it is depleted, or when it reaches a minimum amount. When a petty cash fund is replenished, the accounts debited are determined by summarizing the petty cash receipts. A check is then written for this amount, payable to Petty Cash.

To illustrate, assume that a petty cash fund of $500 is established on August 1. The entry to journalize this transaction is as follows:

A = L + E
+ −

Aug. 1 Petty Cash	500	
Cash		500

The only time Petty Cash is debited is when the fund is initially established, as shown in the preceding entry, or when the fund is being increased. The only time Petty Cash is credited is when the fund is being decreased or eliminated.

At the end of August, there is $30 of petty cash on hand and petty cash receipts for the following items:

Office supplies	$380
Postage (debit Office Supplies)	22
Store supplies	35
Miscellaneous administrative expense	30
Total	$467

If the amount to replenish the petty cash fund does not equal the total of the petty cash receipts, the difference is recorded as Cash Short and Over. In the preceding example, $470 ($500 less cash on hand of $30) is needed to replenish the petty cash fund. Since the total of the petty cash receipts is $467, Cash Short and Over is debited for $3, as shown in the following entry to replenish the petty cash fund.

Aug. 31	Office Supplies	402	
	Store Supplies	35	
	Miscellaneous Administrative Expense	30	
	Cash Short and Over	3	
	Cash		470

$$\begin{array}{ccccc} A & = & L & + & E \\ +\,- & & & & -\,\text{Exp} \end{array}$$

Petty Cash is not debited or credited when the petty cash fund is replenished. Instead, only the accounts affected by the petty cash receipts and any Cash Short and Over are recorded, as shown in the preceding entry. Replenishing the petty cash fund restores the fund to its original cash on hand of $500.

Companies often use other cash funds for special needs, such as payroll or travel expenses. Such funds are called **special-purpose funds**. For example, each salesperson might be given $1,000 for travel-related expenses. Periodically, each salesperson submits an expense report, and the fund is replenished. Special-purpose funds are established and controlled in a manner similar to that of the petty cash fund.

Financial Statement Reporting of Cash

Objective 7

Describe and illustrate the reporting of cash and cash equivalents in the financial statements.

Cash is normally listed as the first asset in the "Current assets" section of the balance sheet. Most companies present only a single cash amount on the balance sheet by combining all their bank and cash fund accounts.

A company may temporarily have excess cash. In such cases, the company normally invests in highly liquid investments in order to earn interest. These investments are called **cash equivalents**.[9] Examples of cash equivalents include U.S. Treasury bills, notes issued by major corporations (referred to as *commercial paper*), and money market funds. In such cases, companies usually report *Cash and cash equivalents* as one amount on the balance sheet with an accompanying note on cash equivalents.

The balance sheet presentation for cash for **eBay** follows:

Link to eBay

eBay Inc. Balance Sheet December 31 (in millions)

Assets	
Current assets:	
Cash and cash equivalents...	$1,816

Notes to Financial Statements:

Cash and cash equivalents

Cash and cash equivalents are short-term, highly liquid investments with original maturities of three months or less when purchased and are primarily comprised of bank deposits, certificates of deposit and commercial paper.

Source: eBay, *Form 10-K,* For the Fiscal Year Ended December 31, 2015.

---

[9] To be classified as a cash equivalent, according to FASB *Accounting Standards Codification,* Section 305.10, the investment is expected to be converted to cash within three months.

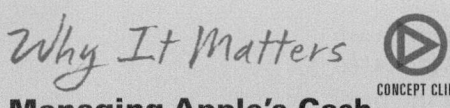

Managing Apple's Cash

Apple Inc. (AAPL) has investments and cash that total over $67 billion. This represents over 62% of Apple's total assets, and thus requires significant management attention. How does Apple manage these assets? Apple owns **Braeburn Capital**, a Nevada-based asset management company. Braeburn was established in 2006 for one purpose: to manage Apple's cash and investments. Braeburn operates under a veil of secrecy, and little is known about the firm. It is simply described as "Braeburn Capital Inc. is the asset management arm of Apple Inc. The firm invests in the public equity markets." Apple's financial statement footnotes provide some detail describing its holdings. More than $20 billion is incuded as cash or cash equivalents, such as money market funds. The remainder is divided between short- and long-term investments.

Source: Apple Inc. annual report, *Form 10-K*, For the Year Ended September 24, 2016.

Banks may require that companies maintain minimum cash balances in their bank accounts. Such a balance is called a **compensating balance**. This is often required by the bank as part of a loan agreement or line of credit. A *line of credit* is a preapproved amount the bank is willing to lend to a customer upon request. Compensating balance requirements are normally disclosed in notes to the financial statements.

Pathways Challenge

This is Accounting!

Economic Activity

Bitcoin is a type of digital currency, called a cryptocurrency, that has gained acceptance from a number of investors, businesses, and consumers. Like the U.S. dollar, bitcoins are a medium of exchange, but unlike the U.S. dollar, they do not possess physical form, are not legal tender, and are not backed by a government. **Overstock.com, Inc. (OSTK)** is an online retailer based in Midvale, Utah, that accepts bitcoins as a form of payment.

Critical Thinking/Judgment

How should Overstock.com report its bitcoin holdings in its financial statements?
How should Overstock.com value its bitcoin holdings?

Suggested answer at end of chapter.

Analysis for Decision Making

Objective 8

Describe and illustrate the use of days' cash on hand to assess a company's ability to meet its cash commitments.

Days' Cash on Hand

Days' cash on hand measures how long a company could survive if its sources of revenue were to decline significantly. A higher number of days implies a higher liquidity and is viewed favorably by creditors. However, a number of days' cash on hand that is too high may indicate that the company has not invested cash back into the business or returned profits back to the owners. Days' cash on hand greater than 50 days would be considered adequate for businesses. Days' cash on hand is calculated as follows:

$$\text{Days' Cash on Hand} = \frac{\text{Cash and Short-Term Investments}}{\text{Daily Cash Operating Expenses}}$$

The cash and short-term investments are taken from the year-end balance sheet and represent the most liquid assets. The daily cash operating expenses are computed from income statement information, as follows:

Daily Cash Operating Expenses = (Operating Expenses – Depreciation Expense) ÷ 365 Days

Depreciation expense is subtracted from the operating expenses because it is a noncash expense. The net amount is divided by 365 days in order to convert the annual cash operating expense amount into a daily amount.

Days' cash on hand is the number of days the daily cash operating expenses can be supported by cash and near-cash balances. It is a popular measure used by nonprofits whose revenues are based on contributions. It reveals how long the nonprofit could survive if contributions dropped significantly. It is also used by start-up companies to measure how long cash is available to support operations until revenues begin to be earned. The measure can be used to estimate how long a business could survive a catastrophic event, such as a software virus for an Internet company or a national health emergency for an airline.

To illustrate, the following information is provided from three recent annual financial statements for **eBay** (in millions):

	Year 3	Year 2	Year 1
Cash (end of year)	$1,816	$1,832	$4,105
Short-term investments (end of year)	5,333	4,299	3,730
Operating expenses	4,647	4,624	4,651
Depreciation expense	682	687	682

The days' cash on hand for all three years is computed as follows:

	Year 3	Year 2	Year 1
Cash and short-term investments:			
$1,816 + $5,333	$7,149		
$1,832 + $4,299		$6,131	
$4,105 + $3,730			$7,835
Daily cash operating expenses:*			
($4,647 − $682) ÷ 365 days	$ 10.9		
($4,624 − $687) ÷ 365 days		$ 10.8	
($4,651 − $682) ÷ 365 days			$ 10.9
Days' cash on hand:*			
$7,149 ÷ $10.9	655.9		
$6,131 ÷ $10.8		567.7	
$7,835 ÷ $10.9			718.8

*Rounded to one decimal place

As can be seen, eBay's days' cash on hand varied from a high of 718.8 days in Year 1 to a low of 567.7 days in Year 2. However, the days' cash on hand exceeds 550 days for all three years. Thus, the change in days' cash on hand is not a concern. This high number of days suggests that a catastrophic event would not threaten eBay's survival. eBay appears to have sufficient liquidity to support operations and business growth.

Make a Decision Days' Cash on Hand

Analyze and compare Amazon.com to Netflix (MAD 7-1)
(Continuing company analysis)

Analyze and compare J. C. Penny and Macy's (MAD 7-2)

Analyze Apache Corporation (MAD 7-3)

Analyze and compare Krispy Kreme and Dunkin' Brands (MAD 7-4)

Analyze and compare Nike, lululemon, and Under Armour (MAD 7-5)

Make a Decision

Let's Review

Chapter Summary

1. Sarbanes-Oxley requires companies to maintain strong and effective internal controls and to report on the effectiveness of the internal controls.

2. The objectives of internal control are to provide reasonable assurance that (1) assets are safeguarded and used for business purposes, (2) business information is accurate, and (3) the company is complying with laws and regulations. The elements of internal control are the control environment, risk assessment, control procedures, monitoring, and information and communication.

3. A cash register is a control for protecting cash received in over-the-counter sales. A remittance advice is a control for cash received through the mail. Separating the duties of handling cash and recording cash is also a control. A voucher system is a control system for cash payments. Many companies use electronic funds transfers for cash receipts and cash payments.

4. Bank accounts control cash by reducing the amount of cash on hand and facilitating the transfer of cash between businesses and locations. In addition, the bank statement allows a business to reconcile the cash transactions recorded in the accounting records to those recorded by the bank.

5. A bank reconciliation is prepared using the nine steps as summarized in Exhibit 12. The items in the company section of a bank reconciliation must be journalized on the company's records.

6. Special-purpose cash funds, such as a petty cash fund or a travel fund, are used by businesses to meet specific needs. Each fund is established by cashing a check for the amount of cash needed. At periodic intervals, the fund is replenished and the disbursements recorded.

7. Cash is listed as the first asset in the "Current assets" section of the balance sheet. Companies that have invested excess cash in highly liquid investments usually report *Cash and cash equivalents* on the balance sheet.

8. Days' cash on hand is the number of days the daily cash operating expenses can be supported by cash and near-cash balances. A higher number of days implies a higher liquidity and is viewed favorably by creditors. However, a number of days' cash on hand that is too high may indicate that a company has not invested cash back into the business or returned profits back to the owners.

Key Terms

bank reconciliation (366)
bank statement (363)
cash (360)
cash equivalents (371)
cash short and over account (361)
compensating balance (372)

control environment (355)
days' cash on hand (372)
electronic funds transfer (EFT) (362)
elements of internal control (354)
employee fraud (354)
internal control (352)

petty cash fund (370)
Sarbanes-Oxley Act (352)
special-purpose funds (371)
voucher (362)
voucher system (362)

Practice

Multiple-Choice Questions

1. Which of the following is *not* an element of internal control?
   a. Control environment
   b. Monitoring
   c. Compliance with laws and regulations
   d. Control procedures

2. The bank erroneously charged Tropical Services' account for $450.50 for a check that was correctly written and recorded by Tropical Services as $540.50. To reconcile the bank account of Tropical Services at the end of the month, you would:
   a. add $90 to the cash balance according to the bank statement.
   b. add $90 to the cash balance according to Tropical Services' records.
   c. deduct $90 from the cash balance according to the bank statement.
   d. deduct $90 from the cash balance according to Tropical Services' records.

3. In preparing a bank reconciliation, the amount of checks outstanding would be:
   a. added to the cash balance according to the bank statement.
   b. deducted from the cash balance according to the bank statement.
   c. added to the cash balance according to the company's records.
   d. deducted from the cash balance according to the company's records.

4. Journal entries based on the bank reconciliation are required for:
   a. additions to the cash balance according to the company's records.
   b. deductions from the cash balance according to the company's records.
   c. both (a) and (b).
   d. neither (a) nor (b).

5. A petty cash fund is:
   a. used to pay relatively small amounts.
   b. established by estimating the amount of cash needed for disbursements of relatively small amounts during a specified period.
   c. reimbursed when the amount of money in the fund is reduced to a predetermined minimum amount.
   d. all of the above.

Answers provided after Problem. Need more practice? Find additional multiple-choice questions, exercises, and problems in CengageNOWv2.

Exercises

1. Internal control elements
Obj. 2

Identify each of the following as relating to (a) the control environment, (b) control procedures, or (c) information and communication:

1. Organizational structure
2. Report of company's conformity with environmental laws and regulations
3. Proofs and security measures

2. Items on company's bank statement
Obj. 4

The following items may appear on a bank statement:

1. Bank correction of an error from recording a $6,200 deposit as $2,600
2. EFT payment
3. Note collected for company
4. Service charge

Using the following format, indicate whether each item would appear as a debit or credit memo on the bank statement and whether the item would increase or decrease the balance of the company's account:

Item No.	Appears on the Bank Statement as a Debit or Credit Memo	Increases or Decreases the Balance of the Company's Bank Account

3. Bank reconciliation
Obj. 5

The following data were gathered to use in reconciling the bank account of Eves Company:

Balance per bank	$9,350
Balance per company records	8,510
Bank service charges	35
Deposit in transit	2,350
NSF check	1,875
Outstanding checks	5,100

a. What is the adjusted balance on the bank reconciliation?

b. Journalize any necessary entries for Eves Company based on the bank reconciliation.

---

4. Petty cash fund

Obj. 6

Prepare journal entries for each of the following:

a. Issued a check to establish a petty cash fund of $750.

b. The amount of cash in the petty cash fund is $115. Issued a check to replenish the fund, based on the following summary of petty cash receipts: repair expense, $515 and miscellaneous selling expense, $88. Record any missing funds in the cash short and over account.

---

5. Days' cash on hand

Obj. 8

Financial statement data for years ended December 31 for Holland Company follow:

	20Y3	20Y2
Cash and short-term investments (end of year)	$ 8,900	$ 7,920
Operating expenses	10,400	11,800
Depreciation expense	1,200	1,350

Determine the days' cash on hand for 20Y2 and 20Y3. Round all calculations to one decimal place.

Answers provided after Problem. Need more practice? Find additional multiple-choice questions, exercises, and problems in CengageNOWv2.

Problem

The bank statement for Urethane Company for June 30, 20Y2, indicates a balance of $9,293.11. All cash receipts are deposited each evening in a night depository, after banking hours. The accounting records indicate the following summary data for cash receipts and payments for June:

Cash balance as of June 1	$ 3,943.50
Total cash receipts for June	28,971.60
Total amount of checks issued in June	28,388.85

Comparing the bank statement and the accompanying canceled checks and memos with the records reveals the following reconciling items:

a. The bank had collected for Urethane Company $1,030 on a note left for collection. The face amount of the note was $1,000.

b. A deposit of $1,852.21, representing receipts of June 30, had been made too late to appear on the bank statement.

c. Checks outstanding totaled $5,265.27.

d. A check drawn for $139 had been incorrectly charged by the bank as $157.

e. A check for $370 returned with the statement had been recorded in the company's records as $730. The check was for the payment of an obligation to Avery Equipment Company for the purchase of office supplies on account.

f. Bank service charges for June amounted to $18.20.

Instructions

1. Prepare a bank reconciliation for June.

2. Journalize the entries that should be made by Urethane Company.

Need more practice? Find additional multiple-choice questions, exercises, and problems in CengageNOWv2.

Answers

Multiple-Choice Questions

1. **c** Compliance with laws and regulations (answer c) is an objective, not an element, of internal control. The control environment (answer a), monitoring (answer b), control procedures (answer d), risk assessment, and information and communication are the five elements of internal control.

2. **c** The error was made by the bank, so the cash balance according to the bank statement needs to be adjusted. Since the bank deducted $90 ($540.50 − $450.50) too little, the error of $90 should be deducted from the cash balance according to the bank statement (answer c).

3. **b** On any specific date, the cash account in a company's ledger may not agree with the account in the bank's ledger because of delays and/or errors by either party in recording transactions. The purpose of a bank reconciliation is to determine the reasons for any differences between the two account balances. All errors should then be corrected by the company or the bank, as appropriate. In arriving at the adjusted cash balance according to the bank statement, outstanding checks must be deducted (answer b) to adjust for checks that have been written by the company but that have not yet been presented to the bank for payment.

4. **c** All reconciling items that are added to and deducted from the cash balance according to the company's records on the bank reconciliation (answer c) require that journal entries be made by the company to correct errors made in recording transactions or to bring the cash account up to date for delays in recording transactions.

5. **d** To avoid the delay, annoyance, and expense that is associated with paying all obligations by check, relatively small amounts (answer a) are paid from a petty cash fund. The fund is established by estimating the amount of cash needed to pay these small amounts during a specified period (answer b), and it is then reimbursed when the amount of money in the fund is reduced to a predetermined minimum amount (answer c).

Exercises

1. 1. (a) the control environment
   2. (c) information and communication
   3. (b) control procedures

2.

Item No.	Appears on the Bank Statement as a Debit or Credit Memo	Increases or Decreases the Balance of the Company's Bank Account
1	credit memo	increases
2	debit memo	decreases
3	credit memo	increases
4	debit memo	decreases

3. a. $6,600, determined as follows:
   Bank section of reconciliation: $9,350 + $2,350 − $5,100 = $6,600
   Company section of reconciliation: $8,510 − $35 − $1,875 = $6,600

   b.

Accounts Receivable	1,875	
Miscellaneous Expense	35	
Cash		1,910

4. a.

Petty Cash	750	
Cash		750

b.

Repairs Expense	515	
Miscellaneous Selling Expense	88	
Cash Short and Over	32	
Cash		635

5.

	20Y3	20Y2
Daily cash operating expenses:		
($10,400 − $1,200) ÷ 365	$25.2	
($11,800 − $1,350) ÷ 365		$28.6
Days' cash on hand:		
$8,900 ÷ $25.2	353.2	
$7,920 ÷ $28.6		276.9

Need more help? Watch step-by-step videos of how to compute answers to these Exercises in CengageNOWv2.

Problem

1.

Urethane Company Bank Reconciliation June 30, 20Y2		
Cash balance according to bank statement		$ 9,293.11
Add: Deposit in transit on June 30..	$1,852.21	
Bank error in charging check as $157 instead of $139...............	18.00	
Total additions..		1,870.21
Deduct: Outstanding checks...		(5,265.27)
Adjusted balance		$ 5,898.05
Cash balance according to company's records		$ 4,526.25*
Add: Note collected by bank, including $30 interest	$1,030.00	
Error in recording check..	360.00	
Total additions		1,390.00
Deduct: Bank service charges..		(18.20)
Adjusted balance		$ 5,898.05

*$3,943.50 + $28,971.60 − $28,388.85

2.

June	30	Cash	1,390.00	
		Notes Receivable		1,000.00
		Interest Revenue		30.00
		Accounts Payable—Avery Equipment Company		360.00
	30	Miscellaneous Administrative Expense	18.20	
		Cash		18.20

Discussion Questions

1. (a) Name and describe the five elements of internal control. (b) Is any one element of internal control more important than another?

2. Why should the employee who handles cash receipts not have the responsibility for maintaining the accounts receivable records? Explain.

3. The ticket seller at a movie theater doubles as a ticket taker for a few minutes each day while the ticket taker is on a break. Which control procedure of a business's system of internal control is violated in this situation?

4. Why should the responsibility for maintaining the accounting records be separated from the responsibility for operations? Explain.

5. Assume that Brooke Miles, accounts payable clerk for West Coast Design Inc., stole $48,350 by paying fictitious invoices for goods that were never received. The clerk set up accounts in the names of the fictitious companies and cashed the checks at a local bank. Describe a control procedure that would have prevented or detected the fraud.

6. Before a voucher for the purchase of merchandise is approved for payment, supporting documents should be compared to verify the accuracy of the liability. Give an example of supporting documents for the purchase of merchandise.

7. The balance of Cash is likely to differ from the bank statement balance. What two factors are likely to be responsible for the difference?

8. What is the purpose of preparing a bank reconciliation?

9. Knott Inc. has a petty cash fund of $750. (a) Since the petty cash fund is only $750, should Knott implement controls over petty cash? (b) What controls, if any, could be used for the petty cash fund?

10. (a) How are cash equivalents reported in the financial statements? (b) What are some examples of cash equivalents?

Basic Exercises

SHOW ME HOW

BE 7-1 Internal control elements   Obj. 2

Identify each of the following as relating to (a) the control environment, (b) control procedures, or (c) monitoring:

1. Hiring of external auditors to review the adequacy of controls
2. Personnel policies
3. Safeguarding inventory in a locked warehouse

SHOW ME HOW

BE 7-2 Items on company's bank statement   Obj. 4

The following items may appear on a bank statement:

1. Bank correction of an error from posting another customer's check (disbursement) to the company's account
2. EFT deposit
3. Loan proceeds
4. NSF check

Using the following format, indicate whether each item would appear as a debit or credit memo on the bank statement and whether the item would increase or decrease the balance of the company's account:

Item No.	Appears on the Bank Statement as a Debit or Credit Memo	Increases or Decreases the Balance of the Company's Bank Account

BE 7-3 Bank reconciliation
Obj. 5

The following data were gathered to use in reconciling the bank account of Reddan Company:

Balance per bank	$25,750
Balance per company records	19,140
Bank service charges	45
Deposit in transit	2,300
Note collected by bank with $200 interest	5,200
Outstanding checks	3,755

a. What is the adjusted balance on the bank reconciliation?

b. Journalize any necessary entries for Reddan Company based on the bank reconciliation.

BE 7-4 Petty cash fund
Obj. 6

Prepare journal entries for each of the following:

a. Issued a check to establish a petty cash fund of $500.

b. The amount of cash in the petty cash fund is $85. Issued a check to replenish the fund, based on the following summary of petty cash receipts: store supplies, $360, and miscellaneous selling expense, $40. Record any missing funds in the cash short and over account.

BE 7-5 Days' cash on hand
Obj. 8

Financial statement data for years ending December 31 for Newton Company follow:

	20Y9	20Y8
Cash (end of year)	$25,500	$24,250
Short-term investments (end of year)	8,270	9,460
Operating expenses	60,135	63,780
Depreciation expense	13,225	11,400

Determine the days' cash on hand for 20Y8 and 20Y9. Round all calculations to one decimal place.

Exercises

EX 7-1 Sarbanes-Oxley internal control report
Obj. 1

Using Wikipedia (www.wikipedia.com), look up the entry for Sarbanes-Oxley Act. Look over the table of contents and find the section that describes Section 404.

➤ What does Section 404 require of management's internal control report?

EX 7-2 Internal controls
Obj. 2, 3

Faith Cassen has recently been hired as the manager of Gibraltar Coffee Shop. Gibraltar Coffee Shop is a national chain of franchised coffee shops. During her first month as store manager, Faith encountered the following internal control situations:

a. Faith caught an employee putting a case of 1,000 single-serving tea bags in his car. Not wanting to create a scene, Faith smiled and said, "I don't think you're putting those tea bags on the right shelf. Don't they belong inside the coffee shop?" The employee returned the tea bags to the stockroom.

b. Gibraltar Coffee Shop has one cash register. Prior to Faith's joining the coffee shop, each employee working on a shift would take a customer order, accept payment, and then prepare the order. Faith made one employee on each shift responsible for taking orders and accepting the customer's payment. Other employees prepare the orders.

c. Because only one employee uses the cash register, that employee is responsible for counting the cash at the end of the shift and verifying that the cash in the drawer matches the amount of cash sales recorded by the cash register. Faith expects each cashier to balance the drawer to the penny *every* time—no exceptions.

➤ State whether you agree or disagree with Faith's method of handling each situation and explain your answer.

EX 7-3 Internal controls

Obj. 2, 3

Ramona's Clothing is a retail store specializing in women's clothing. The store has established a liberal return policy for the holiday season in order to encourage gift purchases. Any item purchased during November and December may be returned through January 31, with a receipt, for cash or exchange. If the customer does not have a receipt, cash will still be refunded for any item under $75. If the item is more than $75, a check is mailed to the customer.

Whenever an item is returned, a store clerk completes a return slip, which the customer signs. The return slip is placed in a special box. The store manager visits the return counter approximately once every two hours to authorize the return slips. Clerks are instructed to place the returned merchandise on the proper rack on the selling floor as soon as possible.

This year, returns at Ramona's have reached an all-time high. There are a large number of returns under $75 without receipts.

a. ▶ How can sales clerks employed at Ramona's Clothing use the store's return policy to steal money from the cash register?

b. ▶ What internal control weaknesses do you see in the return policy that make cash thefts easier?

c. ▶ Would issuing a store credit in place of a cash refund for all merchandise returned without a receipt reduce the possibility of theft? List some advantages and disadvantages of issuing a store credit in place of a cash refund.

d. ▶ Assume that Ramona's Clothing is committed to the current policy of issuing cash refunds without a receipt. What changes could be made in the store's procedures regarding customer refunds in order to improve internal control?

EX 7-4 Internal controls for bank lending

Obj. 2, 3

Pacific Bank provides loans to businesses in the community through its Commercial Lending Department. Small loans (less than $100,000) may be approved by an individual loan officer, while larger loans (greater than $100,000) must be approved by a board of loan officers. Once a loan is approved, the funds are made available to the loan applicant under agreed-upon terms. Pacific Bank has instituted a policy whereby its president has the individual authority to approve loans up to $5,000,000. The president believes that this policy will allow flexibility to approve loans to valued clients much quicker than under the previous policy.

▶ As an internal auditor of Pacific Bank, how would you respond to this change in policy?

REAL WORLD

EX 7-5 Internal controls

Obj. 2, 3

One of the largest losses in history from unauthorized securities trading involved a securities trader for the French bank, **Societe Generale (SCGLY)**. The trader was able to circumvent internal controls and create more than $7 billion in trading losses in six months. The trader apparently escaped detection by using knowledge of the bank's internal control systems learned from a previous back-office monitoring job. Much of this monitoring involved the use of software to monitor trades. In addition, traders were usually kept to tight trading limits. Apparently, these controls failed in this case.

▶ What general weaknesses in Societe Generale's internal controls contributed to the occurrence and size of the losses?

REAL WORLD

EX 7-6 Internal controls

Obj. 2, 3

An employee of **JHT Holdings, Inc.**, a private trucking company, was responsible for resolving roadway accident claims under $25,000. The employee created fake accident claims and wrote settlement checks of between $5,000 and $25,000 to friends or acquaintances acting as phony "victims." One friend recruited subordinates at his place of work to cash some of the checks. Beyond this, the JHT employee also recruited lawyers, whom he paid to represent both the trucking company and the fake victims in the bogus accident settlements. When the lawyers cashed the checks, they allegedly split the money with the corrupt JHT employee. This fraud went undetected for two years.

▶ Why would it take so long to discover such a fraud?

EX 7-7   Internal controls   Obj. 2, 3

All-Around Sound Co. discovered a fraud whereby one of its front office administrative employees used company funds to purchase goods, such as computers, digital cameras, and other electronic items for her own use. The fraud was discovered when employees noticed an increase in delivery frequency from vendors and the use of unusual vendors. After some investigation, it was discovered that the employee would alter the description or change the quantity on an invoice in order to explain the cost on the bill.

➤ What general internal control weaknesses contributed to this fraud?

EX 7-8   Financial statement fraud   Obj. 2, 3

REAL WORLD

A former chairman, CFO, and controller of **Donnkenny, Inc.**, an apparel company that makes sportswear for Pierre Cardin and Victoria Jones, pleaded guilty to financial statement fraud. These managers used false journal entries to record fictitious sales, hid inventory in public warehouses so that it could be recorded as "sold," and required sales orders to be backdated so that the sale could be moved back to an earlier period. The combined effect of these actions caused $25 million out of $40 million in quarterly sales to be phony.

a. ➤ Why might control procedures listed in this chapter be insufficient in stopping this type of fraud?

b. ➤ How could this type of fraud be stopped?

EX 7-9   Internal control of cash receipts   Obj. 2, 3

The procedures used for over-the-counter receipts are as follows. At the close of each day's business, the sales clerks count the cash in their respective cash drawers, after which they determine the amount recorded by the cash register and prepare the memo cash form, noting any discrepancies. An employee from the cashier's office counts the cash, compares the total with the memo, and takes the cash to the cashier's office.

a. ➤ Indicate the weak link in internal control.

b. ➤ How can the weakness be corrected?

EX 7-10   Internal control of cash receipts   Obj. 2, 3

Sergio Flores works at the drive-through window of Big & Bad Burgers. Occasionally, when a drive-through customer orders, Sergio fills the order and pockets the customer's money. He does not ring up the order on the cash register.

➤ Identify the internal control weaknesses that exist at Big & Bad Burgers, and discuss what can be done to prevent this theft.

EX 7-11   Internal control of cash receipts   Obj. 2, 3

The mailroom employees send all remittances and remittance advices to the cashier. The cashier deposits the cash in the bank and forwards the remittance advices and duplicate deposit slips to the Accounting Department.

a. ➤ Indicate the weak link in internal control in the handling of cash receipts.

b. ➤ How can the weakness be corrected?

SHOW ME HOW

EX 7-12   Entry for cash sales; cash short   Obj. 3

The actual cash received from cash sales was $83,452, and the amount indicated by the cash register total was $83,480. Journalize the entry to record the cash receipts and cash sales.

SHOW ME HOW

EX 7-13   Entry for cash sales; cash over   Obj. 3

The actual cash received from cash sales was $315,280, and the amount indicated by the cash register total was $315,150. Journalize the entry to record the cash receipts and cash sales.

EX 7-14   Internal control of cash payments   Obj. 3

Abbe Co. is a small merchandising company with a manual accounting system. An investigation revealed that in spite of a sufficient bank balance, a significant amount of available cash discounts had been lost because of failure to make timely payments. In addition, it was discovered that the invoices for several purchases had been paid twice.

➤ Outline procedures for the payment of vendors' invoices so that the possibilities of losing available cash discounts and of paying an invoice a second time will be minimized.

EX 7-15　Internal control of cash payments

Obj. 2, 3

Paragon Tech Company, a communications equipment manufacturer, recently fell victim to a fraud scheme developed by one of its employees. To understand the scheme, it is necessary to review Paragon's procedures for the purchase of services.

The purchasing agent is responsible for ordering services (such as repairs to a photocopy machine or office cleaning) after receiving a service requisition from an authorized manager. However, because no tangible goods are delivered, a receiving report is not prepared. When the Accounting Department receives an invoice billing Paragon Tech for a service call, the accounts payable clerk calls the manager who requested the service in order to verify that it was performed.

The fraud scheme involves Mae Jansma, the manager of plant and facilities. Mae arranged for her uncle's company, Radiate Systems, to be placed on Paragon's approved vendor list. Mae did not disclose the family relationship.

On several occasions, Mae would submit a requisition for services to be provided by Radiate. However, the service requested was really not needed, and it was never performed. Radiate would bill Paragon for the service and then split the cash payment with Mae.

➤Explain what changes should be made to Paragon Tech Company's procedures for ordering and paying for services in order to prevent such occurrences in the future.

EX 7-16　Bank reconciliation

Obj. 5

Identify each of the following reconciling items as: (a) an addition to the cash balance according to the bank statement, (b) a deduction from the cash balance according to the bank statement, (c) an addition to the cash balance according to the company's records, or (d) a deduction from the cash balance according to the company's records. (None of the transactions reported by bank debit and credit memos have been recorded by the company.)

1. Bank service charges, $50.
2. Check of a customer returned by bank to company because of insufficient funds, $520.
3. Check for $345 incorrectly recorded by the company as $435.
4. Check for $200 incorrectly charged by bank as $2,000.
5. Deposit in transit, $4,250.
6. Outstanding checks, $5,420.
7. Note collected by bank, $5,300.

EX 7-17　Entries based on bank reconciliation

Obj. 5

Which of the reconciling items listed in Exercise 7-16 require an entry in the company's accounts?

EX 7-18　Bank reconciliation

Obj. 5

✔ Adjusted balance: $44,235

SHOW ME HOW

The following data were accumulated for use in reconciling the bank account of Creative Design Co. for August 20Y6:

1. Cash balance according to the company's records at August 31, $42,920.
2. Cash balance according to the bank statement at August 31, $56,300.
3. Checks outstanding, $25,390.
4. Deposit in transit not recorded by bank, $13,325.
5. A check for $150 in payment of an account was erroneously recorded in the check register as $1,500.
6. Bank debit memo for service charges, $35.

a. Prepare a bank reconciliation, using the format shown in Exhibit 13.

b. If the balance sheet were prepared for Creative Design Co. on August 31, what amount should be reported for cash?

c. ➤ Must a bank reconciliation always balance (reconcile)?

EX 7-19　Entries for bank reconciliation

Obj. 5

SHOW ME HOW

Using the data presented in Exercise 7-18, journalize the entry or entries that should be made by the company.

EX 7-20 Entries for note collected by bank

Obj. 5

Accompanying a bank statement for Borden Company is a credit memo for $21,200 representing the principal ($20,000) and interest ($1,200) on a note that had been collected by the bank. The company had been notified by the bank at the time of the collection but had made no entries. Journalize the entry that should be made by the company to bring the accounting records up to date.

EX 7-21 Bank reconciliation

Obj. 5

An accounting clerk for Chesner Co. prepared the following bank reconciliation:

Chesner Co.
Bank Reconciliation
July 31, 20Y4

Cash balance according to company's records		$18,520
Adjustments:		
Outstanding checks	$ 4,780	
Error by Chesner Co. in recording Check		
No. 1056 as $875 instead of $785	90	
Note for $15,000 collected by bank, including interest	15,600	
Deposit in transit on July 31	(11,300)	
Bank service charges	(45)	
Total adjustments		9,125
Cash balance according to bank statement		$27,645

a. From the data in this bank reconciliation, prepare a new bank reconciliation for Chesner Co., using the format shown in the Let's Review section.

b. If a balance sheet were prepared for Chesner Co. on July 31, 20Y4, what amount should be reported for cash?

EX 7-22 Bank reconciliation

Obj. 5

✔ Corrected adjusted balance: $19,780

The following bank reconciliation was prepared as of June 30, 20Y7:

Poway Co.
Bank Reconciliation
For the Month Ended June 30, 20Y7

Cash balance according to bank statement		$16,185
Add: Outstanding Check No. 1067	$ 575	
Outstanding Check No. 1106	470	
Outstanding Check No. 1110	1,050	
Outstanding Check No. 1113	910	
Total additions		3,005
Deduct: Deposit of June 30 not recorded by bank		(6,600)
Adjusted balance		$12,590
Cash balance according to company's records		$ 8,985
Add: Proceeds of note collected by bank: Face value	$6,000	
Proceeds of note collected by bank: Interest	300	
Service charges	15	
Total additions		6,315
Deduct: Check returned because of insufficient funds	$ 890	
Error in recording June 17 deposit of $7,150 as $1,750	5,400	
Total deductions		(6,290)
Adjusted balance		$ 9,010

a. Identify the errors in the bank reconciliation.

b. Prepare a corrected bank reconciliation.

EX 7-23 Using bank reconciliation to determine cash receipts stolen Obj. 2, 3, 5

Alaska Impressions Co. records all cash receipts on the basis of its cash register tapes. Alaska Impressions discovered during October 20Y3 that one of its sales clerks had stolen an undetermined amount of cash receipts by taking the daily deposits to the bank. The following data have been gathered for October:

Cash in bank according to the general ledger	$11,680
Cash according to the October 31, 20Y3, bank statement	13,275
Outstanding checks as of October 31, 20Y3	3,670
Bank service charge for October	40
Note receivable, including interest collected by bank in October	2,100

No deposits were in transit on October 31.

a. Determine the amount of cash receipts stolen by the sales clerk.

b. ➤ What accounting controls would have prevented or detected this theft?

EX 7-24 Petty cash fund entries Obj. 6

Journalize the entries to record the following:

a. Check No. 12-375 is issued to establish a petty cash fund of $500.

b. The amount of cash in the petty cash fund is now $40. Check No. 12-476 is issued to replenish the fund, based on the following summary of petty cash receipts: office supplies, $212; miscellaneous selling expense, $156; miscellaneous administrative expense, $61. (Because the amount of the check to replenish the fund plus the balance in the fund do not equal $500, record the discrepancy in the cash short and over account.)

Problems: Series A

PR 7-1A Evaluating internal control of cash Obj. 2, 3

The following procedures were recently installed by Raspberry Creek Company:

a. After necessary approvals have been obtained for the payment of a voucher, the treasurer signs and mails the check. The treasurer then stamps the voucher and supporting documentation as paid and returns the voucher and supporting documentation to the accounts payable clerk for filing.

b. The accounts payable clerk prepares a voucher for each disbursement. The voucher along with the supporting documentation is forwarded to the treasurer's office for approval.

c. Along with petty cash expense receipts for postage, office supplies, etc., several postdated employee checks are in the petty cash fund.

d. At the end of the day, cash register clerks are required to use their own funds to make up any cash shortages in their registers.

e. At the end of each day, all cash receipts are placed in the bank's night depository.

f. At the end of each day, an accounting clerk compares the duplicate copy of the daily cash deposit slip with the deposit receipt obtained from the bank.

g. All mail is opened by the mail clerk, who forwards all cash remittances to the cashier. The cashier prepares a listing of the cash receipts and forwards a copy of the list to the accounts receivable clerk for recording in the accounts.

h. The bank reconciliation is prepared by the cashier, who works under the supervision of the treasurer.

Instructions

➤ Indicate whether each of the procedures of internal control over cash represents (1) a strength or (2) a weakness. For each weakness, indicate why it exists.

SHOW ME HOW   EXCEL TEMPLATE

PR 7-2A   Transactions for petty cash, cash short and over

Obj. 3, 6

Wyoming Restoration Company completed the following selected transactions during July 20Y1:

July   1.   Established a petty cash fund of $1,100.

     12.   The cash sales for the day, according to the cash register records, totaled $8,192. The actual cash received from cash sales was $8,220.

     31.   Petty cash on hand was $47. Replenished the petty cash fund for the following disbursements, each evidenced by a petty cash receipt:

       July   3.   Store supplies, $580.

           7.   Express charges on merchandise sold, $90 (Delivery Expense).

           9.   Office supplies, $30.

         13.   Office supplies, $35.

         19.   Postage stamps, $50 (Office Supplies).

         21.   Repair to office file cabinet lock, $60 (Miscellaneous Administrative Expense).

         22.   Postage due on special delivery letter, $28 (Miscellaneous Administrative Expense).

         24.   Express charges on merchandise sold, $135 (Delivery Expense).

         30.   Office supplies, $25.

     31.   The cash sales for the day, according to the cash register records, totaled $10,241. The actual cash received from cash sales was $10,232.

     31.   Decreased the petty cash fund by $150.

Instructions

Journalize the transactions.

PR 7-3A   Bank reconciliation and entries

Obj. 5

✔ 1. Adjusted balance: $189,281

SHOW ME HOW   EXCEL TEMPLATE

The cash account for Pala Medical Co. at June 30, 20Y1, indicated a balance of $166,436. The bank statement indicated a balance of $195,688 on June 30, 20Y1. Comparing the bank statement and the accompanying canceled checks and memos with the records revealed the following reconciling items:

a.   Checks outstanding totaled $19,427.

b.   A deposit of $12,300, representing receipts of June 30, had been made too late to appear on the bank statement.

c.   The bank collected $26,500 on a $25,000 note, including interest of $1,500.

d.   A check for $4,000 returned with the statement had been incorrectly recorded by Pala Medical Co. as $400. The check was for the payment of an obligation to Skyline Supply Co. for a purchase on account.

e.   A check drawn for $195 had been erroneously charged by the bank as $915.

f.   Bank service charges for June amounted to $55.

Instructions

1.   Prepare a bank reconciliation.

2.   Journalize the necessary entries.

3.   If a balance sheet were prepared for Pala Medical Co. on June 30, 20Y1, what amount should be reported as cash?

PR 7-4A   Bank reconciliation and entries

Obj. 5

✔ 1. Adjusted balance: $4,830

SHOW ME HOW   EXCEL TEMPLATE

The cash account for Coastal Bike Co. at October 1, 20Y9, indicated a balance of $5,140. During October, the total cash deposited was $39,175, and checks written totaled $40,520. The bank statement indicated a balance of $8,980 on October 31, 20Y9. Comparing the bank statement, the canceled checks, and the accompanying memos with the records revealed the following reconciling items:

a.   Checks outstanding totaled $5,560.

b.   A deposit of $1,050 representing receipts of October 31 had been made too late to appear on the bank statement.

c.   The bank had collected for Coastal Bike Co. $2,120 on a note left for collection. The face of the note was $2,000.

d.   A check for $370 returned with the statement had been incorrectly charged by the bank as $730.

e. A check for $310 returned with the statement had been recorded by Coastal Bike Co. as $130. The check was for the payment of an obligation to Rack Pro Co. on account.

f. Bank service charges for October amounted to $25.

g. A check for $880 from Bay View Condos was returned by the bank due to insufficient funds.

Instructions

1. Prepare a bank reconciliation as of October 31, 20Y9.

2. Journalize the necessary entries.

3. If a balance sheet were prepared for Coastal Bike Co. on October 31, 20Y9, what amount should be reported as cash?

PR 7-5A   Bank reconciliation and entries   Obj. 5

✔ 1. Adjusted balance: $13,216

EXCEL TEMPLATE

Beeler Furniture Company deposits all cash receipts each Wednesday and Friday in a night depository, after banking hours. The data required to reconcile the bank statement as of June 30, 20Y2, have been taken from various documents and records and are reproduced as follows. The sources of the data are printed in capital letters. All checks were written for payments on account.

CASH ACCOUNT:

Balance as of June 1	$9,317.40
CASH RECEIPTS FOR MONTH OF JUNE	9,223.76

DUPLICATE DEPOSIT TICKETS:

Date and amount of each deposit in June:

Date	Amount	Date	Amount	Date	Amount
June 1	$1,080.50	June 10	$ 996.61	June 22	$ 897.34
3	854.17	15	882.95	24	947.21
8	840.50	17	1,606.74	30	1,117.74

CHECKS WRITTEN:

Number and amount of each check issued in June:

Check No.	Amount	Check No.	Amount	Check No.	Amount
740	$237.50	747	Void	754	$ 449.75
741	495.15	748	$450.90	755	272.75
742	501.90	749	640.13	756	113.95
743	761.30	750	276.77	757	407.95
744	506.88	751	299.37	758	259.60
745	117.25	752	537.01	759	901.50
746	298.66	753	380.95	760	486.39
	Total amount of checks issued in June				$8,395.66

BANK RECONCILIATION FOR PRECEDING MONTH:

Beeler Furniture Company
Bank Reconciliation
May 31, 20Y2

Cash balance according to bank statement..........................		$9,447.20
Add: Deposit in transit on May 31.....................................		690.25
Deduct: Outstanding Check No. 731	$162.15	
Outstanding Check No. 736	345.95	
Outstanding Check No. 738	251.40	
Outstanding Check No. 739	60.55	
Total deductions		(820.05)
Adjusted balance..		$9,317.40
Cash balance according to company's records		$9,352.50
Deduct: Bank service charges		(35.10)
Adjusted balance..		$9,317.40

(Continued)

JUNE BANK STATEMENT:

			MEMBER FDIC		PAGE 1

AMERICAN NATIONAL BANK OF CHICAGO

CHICAGO, IL 60603   (312) 441-1239

ACCOUNT NUMBER

FROM 6/01/20Y2   TO 6/30/20Y2

BALANCE   9,447.20

9 DEPOSITS   8,691.77

20 WITHDRAWALS   7,599.26

BEELER FURNITURE COMPANY

4 OTHER DEBITS
   AND CREDITS   3,085.00CR

NEW BALANCE   13,624.71

* - - CHECKS AND OTHER DEBITS - - - *				* - DEPOSITS - - *	- DATE - *	- - BALANCE- - *
No. 731	162.15	No. 736	345.95	690.25	6/01	9,629.35
No. 739	60.55	No. 740	237.50	1,080.50	6/02	10,411.80
No. 741	495.15	No. 742	501.90	854.17	6/04	10,268.92
No. 743	671.30	No. 744	506.88	840.50	6/09	9,931.24
No. 745	117.25	No. 746	298.66	MS 3,500.00	6/09	13,015.33
No. 748	450.90	No. 749	640.13	MS 210.00	6/09	12,134.30
No. 750	276.77	No. 751	299.37	896.61	6/11	12,454.77
No. 752	537.01	No. 753	380.95	882.95	6/16	12,419.76
No. 754	449.75	No. 755	272.75	1,606.74	6/18	13,304.00
No. 757	407.95	No. 760	486.39	897.34	6/23	13,307.00
				942.71	6/25	14,249.71
		NSF	550.00		6/28	13,699.71
		SC	75.00		6/30	13,624.71

EC — ERROR CORRECTION   OD — OVERDRAFT
MS — MISCELLANEOUS   PS — PAYMENT STOPPED
NSF — NOT SUFFICIENT FUNDS   SC — SERVICE CHARGE

* * *   * * *   * * *

THE RECONCILEMENT OF THIS STATEMENT WITH YOUR RECORDS IS ESSENTIAL.
ANY ERROR OR EXCEPTION SHOULD BE REPORTED IMMEDIATELY.

Instructions

1. Prepare a bank reconciliation as of June 30, 20Y2. If errors in recording deposits or checks are discovered, assume that the errors were made by the company. Assume that all deposits are from cash sales. All checks are written to satisfy accounts payable.

2. Journalize the necessary entries.

3. What is the amount of cash that should appear on the balance sheet as of June 30, 20Y2?

4. ➤ Assume that a canceled check for $390 has been incorrectly recorded by the bank as $930. Briefly explain how the error would be included in a bank reconciliation and how it should be corrected.

Problems: Series B

PR 7-1B   Evaluating internal control of cash   Obj. 2, 3

The following procedures were recently installed by The China Shop:

a.   All sales are rung up on the cash register, and a receipt is given to the customer. All sales are recorded on a record locked inside the cash register.

b.   Each cashier is assigned a separate cash register drawer to which no other cashier has access.

c.   At the end of a shift, each cashier counts the cash in his or her cash register, unlocks the cash register record, and compares the amount of cash with the amount on the record to determine cash shortages and overages.

d.   Checks received through the mail are given daily to the accounts receivable clerk for recording collections on account and for depositing in the bank.

e.   Vouchers and all supporting documents are perforated with a PAID designation after being paid by the treasurer.

f.   Disbursements are made from the petty cash fund only after a petty cash receipt has been completed and signed by the payee.

g.   The bank reconciliation is prepared by the cashier.

Instructions

━━━► Indicate whether each of the procedures of internal control over cash represents (1) a strength or (2) a weakness. For each weakness, indicate why it exists.

SHOW ME HOW   EXCEL TEMPLATE

PR 7-2B   Transactions for petty cash, cash short and over   Obj. 3, 6

Cedar Springs Company completed the following selected transactions during June 20Y3:

June 1.   Established a petty cash fund of $1,000.

12.   The cash sales for the day, according to the cash register records, totaled $9,440. The actual cash received from cash sales was $9,506.

30.   Petty cash on hand was $46. Replenished the petty cash fund for the following disbursements, each evidenced by a petty cash receipt:

June 2.   Store supplies, $375.

10.   Express charges on merchandise purchased, $105 (Inventory).

14.   Office supplies, $85.

15.   Office supplies, $90.

18.   Postage stamps, $33 (Office Supplies).

20.   Repair to fax, $100 (Miscellaneous Administrative Expense).

21.   Repair to office door lock, $25 (Miscellaneous Administrative Expense).

22.   Postage due on special delivery letter, $9 (Miscellaneous Administrative Expense).

28.   Express charges on merchandise purchased, $110 (Inventory).

30.   The cash sales for the day, according to the cash register records, totaled $13,390. The actual cash received from cash sales was $13,350.

30.   Increased the petty cash fund by $200.

Instructions

Journalize the transactions.

✔ 1. Adjusted balance:
       $24,305

SHOW ME HOW   EXCEL TEMPLATE

PR 7-3B   Bank reconciliation and entries   Obj. 5

The cash account for Stone Systems at July 31, 20Y5, indicated a balance of $17,750. The bank statement indicated a balance of $33,650 on July 31, 20Y5. Comparing the bank statement and the accompanying canceled checks and memos with the records reveals the following reconciling items:

a.   Checks outstanding totaled $17,865.

b.   A deposit of $9,150, representing receipts of July 31, had been made too late to appear on the bank statement.

c.   The bank had collected $6,095 on a note left for collection. The face of the note was $5,750.

d.   A check for $390 returned with the statement had been incorrectly recorded by Stone Systems as $930. The check was for the payment of an obligation to Holland Co. for the purchase of office supplies on account.

e.   A check drawn for $1,810 had been incorrectly charged by the bank as $1,180.

f.   Bank service charges for July amounted to $80.

(Continued)

Instructions

1. Prepare a bank reconciliation.

2. Journalize the necessary entries.

3. If a balance sheet were prepared for Stone Systems on July 31, 20Y5, what amount should be reported as cash?

PR 7-4B Bank reconciliation and entries　　　　　　　　　　　　　　　　　　　**Obj. 5**

✔ **1. Adjusted balance: $78,535**

SHOW ME HOW　EXCEL TEMPLATE

The cash account for Collegiate Sports Co. on November 1, 20Y9, indicated a balance of $81,145. During November, the total cash deposited was $293,150, and checks written totaled $307,360. The bank statement indicated a balance of $112,675 on November 30, 20Y9. Comparing the bank statement, the canceled checks, and the accompanying memos with the records revealed the following reconciling items:

a. Checks outstanding totaled $41,840.

b. A deposit of $12,200, representing receipts of November 30, had been made too late to appear on the bank statement.

c. A check for $7,250 had been incorrectly charged by the bank as $2,750.

d. A check for $760 returned with the statement had been recorded by Collegiate Sports Co. as $7,600. The check was for the payment of an obligation to Ramirez Co. on account.

e. The bank had collected for Collegiate Sports Co. $7,385 on a note left for collection. The face of the note was $7,000.

f. Bank service charges for November amounted to $125.

g. A check for $2,500 from Hallen Academy was returned by the bank because of insufficient funds.

Instructions

1. Prepare a bank reconciliation as of November 30, 20Y9.

2. Journalize the necessary entries.

3. If a balance sheet were prepared for Collegiate Sports Co. on November 30, 20Y9, what amount should be reported as cash?

PR 7-5B Bank reconciliation and entries　　　　　　　　　　　　　　　　　　　**Obj. 5**

✔ **1. Adjusted balance: $11,494**

EXCEL TEMPLATE

Sunshine Interiors deposits all cash receipts each Wednesday and Friday in a night depository, after banking hours. The data required to reconcile the bank statement as of July 31, 20Y0, have been taken from various documents and records and are reproduced as follows. The sources of the data are printed in capital letters. All checks were written for payments on account.

CASH ACCOUNT:

Balance as of July 1	$9,578.00
CASH RECEIPTS FOR MONTH OF JULY	6,465.42

DUPLICATE DEPOSIT TICKETS:

Date and amount of each deposit in July:

Date	Amount	Date	Amount	Date	Amount
July 2	$569.50	July 12	$580.70	July 23	$ 713.45
5	701.80	16	600.10	26	601.50
9	819.24	19	701.26	31	1,177.87

CHECKS WRITTEN:

Number and amount of each check issued in July:

Check No.	Amount	Check No.	Amount	Check No.	Amount
614	$243.50	621	$309.50	628	$ 837.70
615	350.10	622	Void	629	329.90
616	279.90	623	Void	630	882.80
617	395.50	624	707.01	631	1,081.56
618	435.40	625	158.63	632	325.40
619	320.10	626	550.03	633	310.08
620	238.87	627	381.73	634	241.71
Total amount of checks issued in July					$8,379.42

BANK RECONCILIATION FOR PRECEDING MONTH:

Sunshine Interiors
Bank Reconciliation
June 30, 20Y0

Cash balance according to bank statement..........................		$9,422.80
Add: Deposit of June 30 not recorded by bank.......................		780.80
Deduct: Outstanding Check No. 580	$310.10	
Outstanding Check No. 602	85.50	
Outstanding Check No. 612	92.50	
Outstanding Check No. 613	137.50	
Total deductions		(625.60)
Adjusted balance..		$9,578.00
Cash balance according to company's records		$9,605.70
Deduct: Bank service charges		(27.70)
Adjusted balance...		$9,578.00

JULY BANK STATEMENT:

MEMBER FDIC	PAGE 1

**A
N
B
AMERICAN NATIONAL BANK
OF DETROIT**

DETROIT, MI 48201-2500   (313) 933-8547

ACCOUNT NUMBER

FROM	7/01/20Y0	TO 7/31/20Y0
BALANCE		9,422.80
9 DEPOSITS		6,086.35
20 WITHDRAWALS		7,656.74
4 OTHER DEBITS AND CREDITS		3,749.00CR
NEW BALANCE		11,601.41

SUNSHINE INTERIORS

----- CHECKS AND OTHER DEBITS ------ DEPOSITS -*- DATE -*- BALANCE-*

No. 580	310.10	No. 612	92.50		780.80	07/01	9,801.00
No. 602	85.50	No. 614	243.50		569.50	07/03	10,041.50
No. 615	350.10	No. 616	279.90		701.80	07/06	10,113.30
No. 617	395.50	No. 618	435.40		819.24	07/11	10,101.64
No. 619	320.10	No. 620	238.87		580.70	07/13	10,123.37
No. 621	309.50	No. 624	707.01	MS 4,000.00		07/14	13,106.86
No. 625	158.63	No. 626	550.03	MS	160.00	07/14	12,558.20
No. 627	318.73	No. 629	329.90		600.10	07/17	12,509.67
No. 630	882.80	No. 631	1,081.56	NSF 375.00		07/20	10,170.31
No. 632	325.40	No. 634	241.71		701.26	07/21	10,304.46
					731.45	07/24	11,035.91
					601.50	07/28	11,637.41
		SC	36.00			07/31	11,601.41

EC — ERROR CORRECTION   OD — OVERDRAFT

MS — MISCELLANEOUS   PS — PAYMENT STOPPED

NSF — NOT SUFFICIENT FUNDS   SC — SERVICE CHARGE

* * *   * * *   * * *

THE RECONCILEMENT OF THIS STATEMENT WITH YOUR RECORDS IS ESSENTIAL.
ANY ERROR OR EXCEPTION SHOULD BE REPORTED IMMEDIATELY.

(Continued)

Instructions

1. Prepare a bank reconciliation as of July 31, 20Y0. If errors in recording deposits or checks are discovered, assume that the errors were made by the company. Assume that all deposits are from cash sales. All checks are written to satisfy accounts payable.

2. Journalize the necessary entries.

3. What is the amount of cash that should appear on the balance sheet as of July 31, 20Y0?

4. ➤ Assume that a canceled check for $180 has been incorrectly recorded by the bank as $1,800. Briefly explain how the error would be included in a bank reconciliation and how it should be corrected.

Make a Decision
Days' Cash on Hand

REAL WORLD

MAD 7-1   Analyze and compare Amazon.com to Netflix   Obj. 8

Amazon.com, Inc. (AMZN) is one of the largest Internet retailers in the world. **Netflix, Inc. (NFLX)** provides digital streaming and DVD rentals in the United States. Amazon and Netflix compete in streaming and digital services; however, Amazon also sells many other products online. The cash, temporary investments, operating expenses, and depreciation expense from recent financial statements were reported as follows for both companies (in millions):

	Amazon	Netflix
Balance sheet, end of year:		
Cash	$ 19,334	$1,468
Short-term investments	6,647	266
Income statement:		
Operating expenses	131,801	8,451
Depreciation expense	8,116	4,925

a. Determine the days' cash on hand for Amazon and Netflix. Round all calculations to one decimal place.

b. ➤ Interpret the results.

REAL WORLD

MAD 7-2   Analyze and compare J. C. Penney and Macy's   Obj. 8

J. C. Penney Company, Inc. (JCP) and **Macy's, Inc. (M)** are large department store chains in the United States. Information from recent annual reports for both companies is as follows (in millions):

	J. C. Penney	Macy's
Cash (end of year)	$ 119	$1,109
Short-term investments (end of year)	781	—
Operating expenses	4,640	8,256
Depreciation expense	616	1,061

a. Determine the days' cash on hand for each company. Round to one decimal place.

b. ➤ Which company has the better liquidity position?

REAL WORLD

MAD 7-3   Analyze Apache Corporation   Obj. 8

Apache Corporation (APA) is an independent energy company that explores, develops, and produces oil and gas products. Apache operates worldwide, including in the United States, Canada, and the North Sea. The profitability of the oil and gas business is highly influenced by the price of crude oil and natural gas, and by the success in finding oil and gas. Selected financial information for Apache for three recent years follows (in millions):

	Year 3	Year 2	Year 1
Balance sheet, end of year:			
Cash	$1,377	$ 1,467	$ 769
Income statement:			
Operating expenses	7,036	19,058	18,302
Depreciation expense	2,618	3,300	4,526

a. Determine the days' cash on hand for each year. Round all calculations to one decimal place.

b. ▬▬▬▶ Interpret the results.

c. ▬▬▬▶ What are some ways a company can respond to a liquidity squeeze?

REAL WORLD

MAD 7-4 Analyze and compare Krispy Kreme and Dunkin' Brands   **Obj. 8**

Krispy Kreme Doughnuts, Inc. (KKD) is a leading retailer and wholesaler of doughnuts. Krispy Kreme owns or franchises more than 1,100 stores where the "hot" light tells you if doughnuts are cooking. **Dunkin' Brands Group, Inc. (DNKN)** is a leading franchisor of doughnut (Dunkin' Donuts) and ice cream (Baskin-Robbins) shops with more than 20,000 stores worldwide. Selected financial statement information for a recent year for both companies follows (in thousands):

	Krispy Kreme	Dunkin' Brands
Operating expenses	$466,616	$438,108
Depreciation expense	16,199	20,458
Cash (end-of-year balance)	50,785	361,425

a. Determine the days' cash on hand for each company. Round all calculations to one decimal place.

b. ▬▬▬▶ Which company appears to have the stronger cash liquidity position?

REAL WORLD

MAD 7-5 Analyze and compare Nike, lululemon, and Under Armour   **Obj. 8**

Three companies that compete in the athletic and activewear market segment are **Nike, Inc. (NKE)**, **lululemon athletica inc. (LULU)**, and **Under Armour, Inc. (UAA)**. Nike is the largest designer and seller of athletic footwear and apparel in the world. Lululemon designs and sells technical athletic apparel featuring yoga, fitness, and dance-inspired wear. Under Armour designs and sells athletic apparel featuring high-performance fabrics for men and women around the world. Selected financial information for a recent year follows (in millions):

	Nike	lululemon	Under Armour
Balance sheet:			
Cash	$ 3,138	$ 501	$ 250
Temporary investments	2,319		
Income statement:			
Operating expenses	10,469	628	1,823
Depreciation expense	649	73	145
Total revenues	32,376	2,061	4,825

a. ▬▬▬▶ How does the size of these companies, as represented by total revenues, compare to each other?

b. Compute the days' cash on hand for all three companies. Round all calculations to one decimal place.

c. ▬▬▬▶ Comment on the cash sufficiency for these three companies.

d. Which company appears to have the greatest cash liquidity?

e. ▬▬▬▶ Why is a ratio used to compare cash sufficiency across the three companies rather than just the companies' cash balances?

Take It Further

ETHICS

TIF 7-1   Expense reimbursement

Tehra Dactyl is an accountant for Skeds, Inc., a footwear and apparel company. The company's revenue and net income have increased by more than 100% over the past three years. During the same period, Tehra and her colleagues in the Accounting Department have not received a raise or salary increase. Frustrated by not receiving a raise while the company has thrived, Tehra has begun submitting expense reimbursements for personal purchases. Tehra has a good relationship with her supervisor, and he simply "signs off" on Tehra's expense reimbursements. Tehra suspects that he knows that she is submitting personal expenses for reimbursement and is "looking the other way" because Tehra has not received a raise in the past three years.

➡ Are Tehra and her supervisor acting in an ethical manner? Why?

ETHICS

TIF 7-2   Bank error

During the preparation of the bank reconciliation for Building Concepts Co., Joel Knolls, the assistant controller, discovered that Lone Peak National Bank incorrectly recorded a $3,290 check written by Building Concepts Co. as $329. Joel has decided not to notify the bank but wait for the bank to detect the error. Joel plans to record the $2,961 error as "Other revenue" if the bank fails to detect the error within the next three months.

➡ Discuss whether Joel is behaving in a professional manner.

TEAM ACTIVITY   REAL WORLD

TIF 7-3   Real-world annual report

In teams, select a public company that interests you. Obtain the company's most recent annual report on Form 10-K. The Form 10-K is a company's annually required filing with the Securities and Exchange Commission (SEC). It includes the company's financial statements and accompanying notes. The Form 10-K can be obtained either (a) from the investor relations section of the company's website or (b) by using the company search feature of the SEC's EDGAR database service found at www.sec.gov/edgar/searchedgar/companysearch.html.

1. Based on the information in the company's most recent annual report, answer the following questions:
   a. How much cash does the company have at the end of the most recent year?
   b. What percentage of total current assets is cash during the most recent two years presented? Has this percentage increased, decreased, or remained the same during this period?

2. Review Management's Annual Report on Internal Control Over Financial Reporting. Based on this information, answer the following questions:
   a. Who has responsibility for establishing and maintaining adequate internal controls over a company's financial reporting?
   b. How is "internal control over financial reporting" defined in this report?
   c. What is a material weakness?
   d. Were any material weaknesses identified?

COMMUNICATION

TIF 7-4   Control procedures for self-checkout lanes

Wholesome and Happy Foods is a farm-to-family grocery store located in the Pacific Northwest. The company recently installed four self-checkout lanes that allow customers to scan their own groceries and pay for their purchases using an automated checkout kiosk. The kiosks are monitored by a single attendant. In recent weeks, management has become concerned that some customers are not scanning all of the items that they bring through the self-checkout lanes.

➡ Write a brief memo to your instructor suggesting features and capabilities for the kiosks that would serve as control procedures, ensuring that all items brought through the self-checkout lanes are properly scanned and purchased.

TIF 7-5 Internal controls—merchandise returns

The following is an excerpt from a conversation between two sales clerks, Jean Moen and Sara Cheney. Jean and Sara are employed by Turpin Meadows Electronics, a locally owned and operated electronics retail store.

Jean: Did you hear the news?

Sara: What news?

Jean: Neal and Linda were both arrested this morning.

Sara: What? Arrested? You're putting me on!

Jean: No, really! The police arrested them first thing this morning. Put them in handcuffs, read them their rights—the whole works. It was unreal!

Sara: What did they do?

Jean: Well, apparently they were filling out merchandise refund forms for fictitious customers and then taking the cash.

Sara: I guess I never thought of that. How did they catch them?

Jean: The store manager noticed that returns were twice that of last year and seemed to be increasing. When he confronted Neal, he became flustered and admitted to taking the cash, apparently more than $9,000 in just three months. They're going over the transactions of the last six months to try to determine how much Linda stole. She apparently started stealing first.

➤ Suggest appropriate control procedures that would have prevented or detected the theft of cash.

Pathways Challenge

This is Accounting!

Information/Consequences

The Financial Accounting Standards Board (FASB) has not issued any specific guidance on the proper accounting and reporting of bitcoins. Thus, there is considerable debate and variation in practice. Some companies consider bitcoins as equivalent to cash, while others consider bitcoins as an investment or a pre-paid asset. **Overstock.com (OSTK)** accounts for bitcoins as a prepaid asset and includes its bitcoin holdings as a current asset on its balance sheet.

Overstock.com values its bitcoin holdings using lower of cost or market. Decreases in the value of the bitcoin holdings are reported as a loss on the income statement. Increases in the value are reported as a gain, but only to the extent of the prior write-downs (decreases).

As the use of bitcoins and other cryptocurrencies grow, the FASB will face increasing pressure to issue guidance in this area.

Suggested Answer

Receivables

STATEMENT OF STOCKHOLDERS' EQUITY
For the Year Ended December 31, 20Y5

	Common Stock	Retained Earnings	Total
Balances, Jan. 1, 20Y5	$XXX	$ XXX	$ XXX
Issued common stock	XXX		XXX
Net income		XXX	XXX
Dividends		(XXX)	(XXX)
Balances, Dec. 31, 20Y5	$XXX	$ XXX	$ XXX

STATEMENT OF CASH FLOWS
For the Year Ended December 31, 20Y5

Cash flows from (used for) operating activities	$XXX
Cash flows from (used for) investing activities	XXX
Cash flows from (used for) financing activities	XXX
Net increase (decrease) in cash	$XXX
Cash balance, January 1, 20Y5	XXX
Cash balance, December 31, 20Y5	$XXX

INCOME STATEMENT
For the Year Ended December 31, 20Y5

Sales		$ XXX
Cost of goods sold		(XXX)
Gross profit		$ XXX
Operating expenses:		
Wages expense	$XXX	
Advertising expense	XXX	
Utilities expense	XXX	
Depreciation expense	XXX	
Bad debt expense	XXX	
…	XXX	
Total operating expenses		(XXX)
Operating income		$ XXX
Other revenue and expense:		
Interest revenue		XXX
Net income		$ XXX

BALANCE SHEET
December 31, 20Y5

Assets		
Current assets:		
Cash		$XXX
Accounts receivable	$ XXX	
Allowance for doubtful accounts	(XXX)	
Net accounts receivable		XXX
Notes receivable		XXX
Inventory		XXX
Total current assets		$XXX
Property, plant, and equipment		XXX
Total assets		$XXX
Liabilities		
Current liabilities		$XXX
Long-term liabilities		XXX
Total liabilities		$XXX
Stockholders' Equity		
Common stock		$XXX
Retained earnings		XXX
Total stockholders' equity		XXX
Total liabilities and stockholders' equity		$XXX

Under Armour, Inc.

A company generates revenues by providing goods or services to customers. For example, **Under Armour, Inc. (UAA)** sells performance apparel, footwear, and other accessories to national, regional, and specialty retailers. Under Armour also sells directly to consumers through its brand and factory house stores and website.

If you were to purchase an athletic shirt from the Under Armour website, you would use a credit card to complete the purchase. In this case, Under Armour would record the transaction as a cash sale. However, Under Armour allows its business customers to purchase its products "on account." Sales on account create accounts receivable with credit terms requiring payment within the credit period.

Unlike cash sales, not all credit sales will generate cash. That is, some customers will not pay their account receivable and the company will have to record a bad debt expense. Companies like Under Armour try to reduce uncollectible accounts by reviewing customer credit rating and payment history prior to a sale. Even with such procedures, however, companies will experience bad debts.

This chapter describes common classifications of receivables, including notes receivable. In addition, methods of accounting for and estimating uncollectible accounts are described and illustrated. Finally, the reporting of receivables, the allowance for uncollectible accounts, and bad debt expense in the financial statements is described and illustrated.

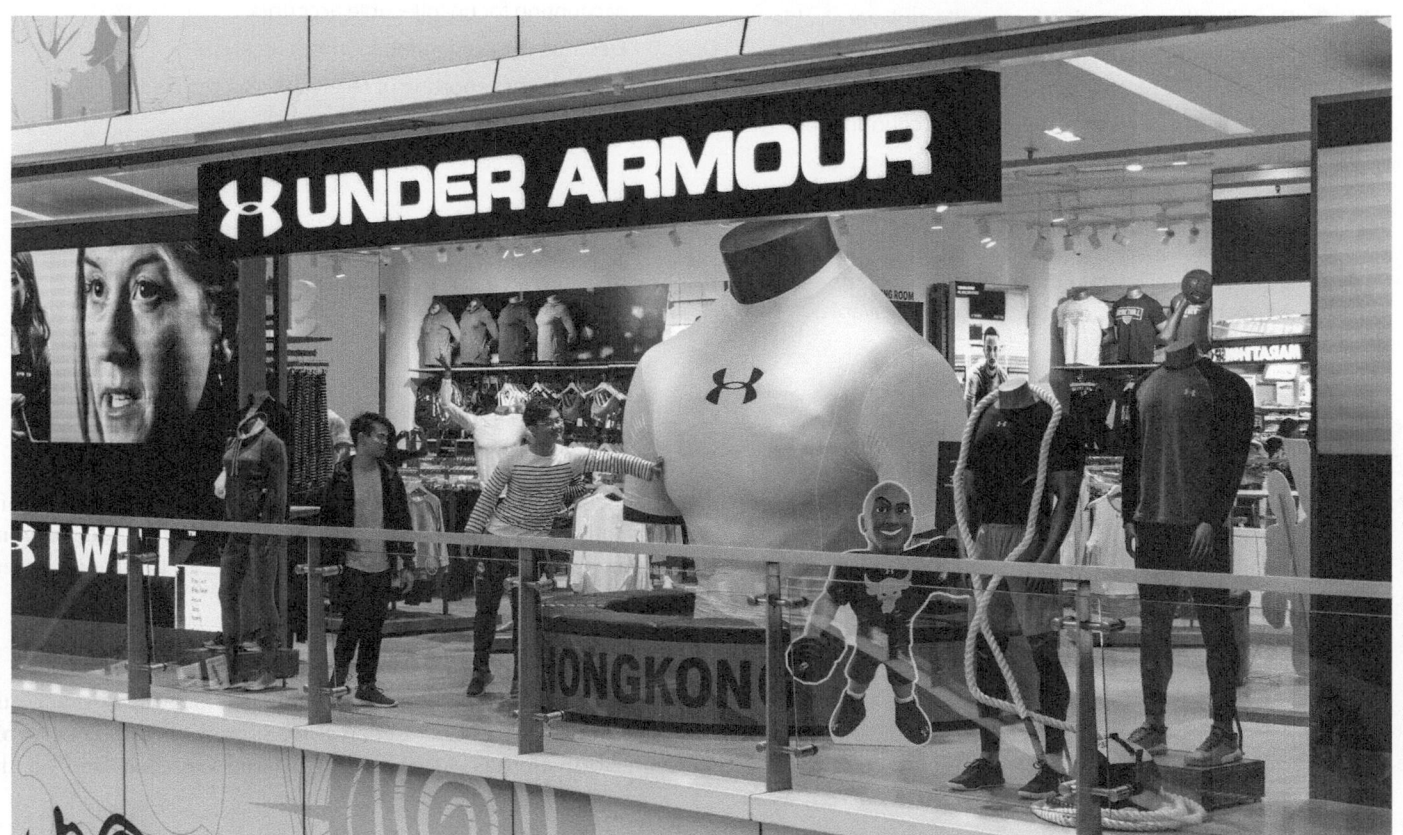

©RaymondAsiaPhotography/Alamy Stock Photo

What's Covered

Receivables

Accounts Receivable	Uncollectible Receivables	Notes Receivable	Reporting Receivables
■ Accounts Receivable (Obj. 1)	■ Uncollectible Receivables (Obj. 2)	■ Characteristics of Notes Receivable (Obj. 6)	■ Balance Sheet (Obj. 7)
■ Notes Receivable (Obj. 1)	■ The Direct Write-Off Method (Obj. 3)	■ Accounting for Notes Receivable (Obj. 6)	
■ Other Receivables (Obj. 1)	■ The Allowance Method (Obj. 4)		
	■ Estimating Uncollectibles (Obj. 4)		
	■ Comparing Methods (Obj. 5)		

Learning Objectives

Obj. 1 Describe the common classes of receivables.

Obj. 2 Describe the accounting for uncollectible receivables.

Obj. 3 Describe the direct write-off method of accounting for uncollectible receivables.

Obj. 4 Describe the allowance method of accounting for uncollectible receivables.

Obj. 5 Compare the direct write-off and allowance methods of accounting for uncollectible accounts.

Obj. 6 Describe the accounting for notes receivable.

Obj. 7 Describe the reporting of receivables on the balance sheet.

Analysis for Decision Making

Obj. 8 Describe and illustrate the use of the accounts receivable turnover and number of days' sales in receivables to evaluate a company's efficiency in collecting its receivables.

Objective 1
Describe the common classes of receivables.

Classification of Receivables

The receivables that result from sales on account are normally accounts receivable or notes receivable. The term **receivables** includes all money claims against other entities, including people, companies, and other organizations. Receivables are usually a significant portion of the total current assets.

Accounts Receivable

The most common transaction creating a receivable is selling merchandise or services on account (on credit). The receivable is recorded as a debit to Accounts Receivable. Such **accounts receivable** are normally collected within a short period, such as 30 or 60 days. They are classified on the balance sheet as a current asset.

Link to Under Armour

In a recent annual report, **Under Armour** reported accounts receivable of $622.7 million, with approximately $99.6 million due from its largest customer, **Dick's Sporting Goods, Inc. (DKS)**.

Notes Receivable

Notes receivable are amounts that customers owe for which a formal, written instrument of credit has been issued. If notes receivable are expected to be collected within a year, they are classified on the balance sheet as a current asset.

Notes are often used for credit periods of more than 60 days. For example, an automobile dealer may require a down payment at the time of sale and accept a note or a series of notes for the remainder. Such notes usually provide for monthly payments.

Notes may also be used to settle a customer's account receivable. Notes and accounts receivable that result from sales transactions are sometimes called *trade receivables*. In this chapter, all notes and accounts receivable are from sales transactions.

Other Receivables

Other receivables include interest receivable, taxes receivable, and receivables from officers or employees. Other receivables are normally reported separately on the balance sheet. If they are expected to be collected within one year, they are classified as current assets. If collection is expected beyond one year, they are classified as noncurrent assets and reported under the caption *Investments*.

Uncollectible Receivables

Objective 2
Describe the accounting for uncollectible receivables.

In prior chapters, the accounting for sales of merchandise or services on account (on credit) was described and illustrated. A major issue that has not yet been discussed is that some customers will not pay their accounts. That is, some accounts receivable will be uncollectible.

Companies may shift the risk of uncollectible receivables to other companies. For example, some retailers do not accept sales on account but will only accept cash or credit cards. Such policies shift the risk to the credit card companies.

Companies may also sell their receivables. This is often the case when a company issues its own credit card. For example, **Macy's, Inc. (M)** and **J. C. Penney Company, Inc. (JCP)** issue their own credit cards. Selling receivables is called *factoring* the receivables. The buyer of the receivables is called a *factor*. An advantage of factoring is that the company selling its receivables immediately receives cash for operating and other needs. Also, depending on the factoring agreement, some of the risk of uncollectible accounts is shifted to the factor.

Regardless of how careful a company is in granting credit, some credit sales will be uncollectible. The operating expense recorded from uncollectible receivables is called **bad debt expense**, *uncollectible accounts expense*, or *doubtful accounts expense*.

There is no general rule for when an account becomes uncollectible. Some indications that an account may be uncollectible include the following:

- The receivable is past due.
- The customer does not respond to the company's attempts to collect.
- The customer files for bankruptcy.
- The customer closes its business.
- The company cannot locate the customer.

If a customer doesn't pay, a company may turn the account over to a collection agency. After the collection agency attempts to collect payment, any remaining balance in the account is considered worthless.

The two methods of accounting for uncollectible receivables are as follows:

- The **direct write-off method** records bad debt expense only when an account is determined to be worthless.
- The **allowance method** records bad debt expense by estimating uncollectible accounts at the end of the accounting period.

> **Under Armour** uses the allowance method and estimates uncollectible accounts based upon historical experience, significant economic developments, and specific customer risk, such as a customer who is experiencing financial difficulties.

Link to Under Armour

Why It Matters

Warning Signs   CONCEPT CLIP

A business must manage the risk of extending credit. The following early warning signs can be used to signal the need to monitor future sales and accelerate collection efforts:

- You're only receiving partial payments.
- The customer's ordering pattern has declined dramatically, or the customer has stopped buying from you.

- The customer requests frequent changes in the payment schedule.
- You are repeatedly told that late payments are in the mail.
- The customer refuses to make payment, claiming dissatisfaction with the product.
- You can't reach your customer, or the customer refuses to acknowledge you.

Source: BMO Harris Bank website, Small Business Learning Center, "7 Steps for Extending Customer Credit," 2015, https://yourfinanciallife.bmoharris.com/articles/extend-customer-credit-550169/.

The direct write-off method is often used by small companies and companies with few receivables.[1] Generally accepted accounting principles (GAAP), however, require companies with a large amount of receivables to use the allowance method. As a result, most well-known companies such as **General Electric (GE)**, **PepsiCo (PEP)**, **Intel (INTC)**, and **FedEx (FDX)** use the allowance method.

Direct Write-Off Method for Uncollectible Accounts

Objective 3

Describe the direct write-off method of accounting for uncollectible receivables.

Under the direct write-off method, Bad Debt Expense is not recorded until the customer's account is determined to be worthless. At that time, the customer's account receivable is written off.

To illustrate, assume that a $4,200 account receivable from D. L. Ross has been determined to be uncollectible. The entry to write off the account is as follows:

A = L + E
−   − Exp

May 10	Bad Debt Expense	4,200	
	Accounts Receivable—D. L. Ross		4,200

An account receivable that has been written off may be collected later. In such cases, the account is reinstated by an entry that reverses the write-off entry. The cash received in payment is then recorded as a receipt on account.

To illustrate, assume that the D. L. Ross account of $4,200 written off on May 10 is later collected on November 21. The reinstatement and receipt of cash is journalized as follows:

A = L + E
+   + Exp

A = L + E
+ −

Nov. 21	Accounts Receivable—D. L. Ross	4,200	
	Bad Debt Expense		4,200
21	Cash	4,200	
	Accounts Receivable—D. L. Ross		4,200

The direct write-off method is used by businesses that sell most of their goods or services for cash or through the acceptance of **MasterCard (MA)** or **VISA (V)**, which are recorded as cash sales. In such cases, receivables are a small part of the current assets and any bad debt expense is small. Examples of such businesses are a restaurant, a convenience store, and a small retail store.

Allowance Method for Uncollectible Accounts

Objective 4

Describe the allowance method of accounting for uncollectible receivables.

The allowance method estimates the uncollectible accounts receivable at the end of the accounting period. Based on this estimate, Bad Debt Expense is recorded by an adjusting entry.

Why It Matters

Failure to Collect

When customers fail to pay their accounts, a business has the option of seeking payment through a variety of means. The easiest recourse is to simply inquire about the cause of non-payment and adjust terms to maximize the potential for collection. For large amounts, the cost and time of legal remedies may be appropriate. However, for smaller amounts, most businesses wish to minimize the time, effort, and cost of collecting amounts past due. Thus, after exhausting their internal efforts to collect, it is typical to use the services of a collection agency to collect overdue accounts. Such services must abide by a number of consumer protection laws in collecting overdue accounts. The final amount collected will often be less than the full amount due, of which the collection agency will often keep 25–45% as a fee. Thus, the collection agency is often the last resort before a final write-off.

[1] The direct write-off method is also required for federal income tax purposes.

To illustrate, assume that **ExTone Company** began operations August 1, 20Y1. As of the end of its accounting period on December 31, ExTone has an accounts receivable balance of $200,000. This balance includes some past due accounts. Based on industry averages, ExTone estimates that $30,000 of the December 31, 20Y1, accounts receivable will be uncollectible. However, on December 31, 20Y1, ExTone doesn't know which customer accounts will be uncollectible. Thus, specific customer accounts cannot be decreased or credited. Instead, a contra asset account, **Allowance for Doubtful Accounts**, is credited for the estimated bad debts.

Using the $30,000 estimate, the following adjusting entry is made on December 31, 20Y1:

20Y1			
Dec. 31	Bad Debt Expense	30,000	
	Allowance for Doubtful Accounts		30,000
	Uncollectible accounts estimate.		

A = L + E
−   − Exp

The preceding adjusting entry affects the income statement and balance sheet. On the income statement, the $30,000 of Bad Debt Expense will be matched against the related revenues of the period. On the balance sheet, the value of the receivables is reduced to the amount that is expected to be collected or realized. This amount, $170,000 ($200,000 − $30,000), is called the **net realizable value** of the receivables.

After the preceding adjusting entry is recorded, Accounts Receivable still has a debit balance of $200,000. This balance is the total amount owed by customers on account on December 31, 20Y1, as supported by the accounts receivable subsidiary ledger. The accounts receivable contra account, Allowance for Doubtful Accounts, has a credit balance of $30,000.

note:
The adjusting entry reduces receivables to their net realizable value and matches the uncollectible expense with revenues.

Write-Offs to the Allowance Account

When a customer's account is identified as uncollectible, it is written off against the allowance account. This requires the company to remove the specific accounts receivable and an equal amount from the allowance account.

To illustrate, on January 21, 20Y2, John Parker's account of $6,000 with **ExTone Company** is written off as follows:

20Y2			
Jan. 21	Allowance for Doubtful Accounts	6,000	
	Accounts Receivable—John Parker		6,000

A = L + E
+ −

At the end of a period, Allowance for Doubtful Accounts will normally have a balance. This is because Allowance for Doubtful Accounts is based on an estimate. As a result, the total write-offs to the allowance account during the period will rarely equal the balance of the account at the beginning of the period. The allowance account will have a credit balance at the end of the period if

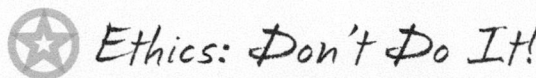 **Ethics: Don't Do It!**

Collecting Past Due Accounts

Companies should make reasonable attempts (steps) to collect past due accounts, as we discussed in the previous Why It Matters. Many companies first send a collection reminder as a first step. As a second step, a company may send a collection letter which offers options such as a willingness to negotiate a schedule for future payments. The next step is normally to turn the past due amount over to a collection agency or to file action in court. However, in no case should a company employee harass or misrepresent themselves as an attorney, collection agent, or agent of the court to the customer.

the write-offs during the period are less than the beginning balance. It will have a debit balance if the write-offs exceed the beginning balance.

Exhibit 1 illustrates the allowance method where the adjusting entry increases the Allowance for Doubtful Accounts (fills the bucket) while writing off accounts decreases the Allowance for Doubtful Accounts (empties the bucket).

Exhibit 1
The Allowance Method

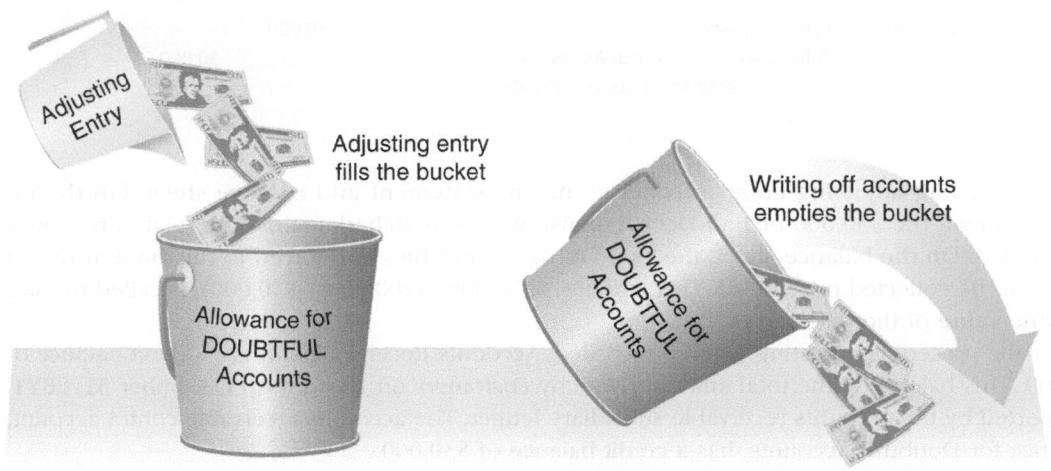

To illustrate, assume that during 20Y2, **ExTone Company** writes off $26,750 of uncollectible accounts, including the $6,000 account of John Parker recorded on January 21, 20Y2. Allowance for Doubtful Accounts will have a credit balance of $3,250 ($30,000 – $26,750), computed as follows:

Allowance for Doubtful Accounts

	Jan.	21	6,000	Jan. 1, 20Y2	Balance	30,000
Total accounts	Feb.	2	3,900			
written off in 20Y2 $26,750	⋮		⋮			
				Dec. 31, 20Y2	Unadjusted balance	3,250

If ExTone had written off $32,100 in accounts receivable during the second year, Allowance for Doubtful Accounts would have a debit balance of $2,100, computed as follows:

Allowance for Doubtful Accounts

	Jan.	21	6,000	Jan. 1, 20Y2	Balance	30,000
Total accounts	Feb.	2	3,900			
written off in 20Y2 $32,100	⋮		⋮			
Dec. 31, 20Y2	Unadjusted balance		2,100			

The allowance account balances (credit balance of $3,250 and debit balance of $2,100) in the preceding illustrations are *before* the end-of-period adjusting entry. After the end-of-period adjusting entry is recorded, Allowance for Doubtful Accounts should always have a credit balance.

An account receivable that has been written off against the allowance account may be collected later. Like the direct write-off method, the account is reinstated by an entry that reverses the write-off entry. The cash received in payment is then recorded as a receipt on account.

To illustrate, assume that Nancy Smith's account of $5,000, which was written off on April 2, 20Y2, is collected later on June 10. **ExTone Company** journalizes the reinstatement and the collection as follows:

20Y2					
June	10	Accounts Receivable—Nancy Smith	5,000		A = L + E
		Allowance for Doubtful Accounts		5,000	+ −
	10	Cash	5,000		A = L + E
		Accounts Receivable—Nancy Smith		5,000	+ −

Estimating Uncollectibles

The allowance method requires an estimate of uncollectible accounts at the end of the period. This estimate is normally based on past experience, industry averages, and forecasts of the future.

The two methods used to estimate uncollectible accounts are as follows:

- Percent of sales method.
- Analysis of receivables method.

Percent of Sales Method Since accounts receivable are created by credit sales, uncollectible accounts can be estimated as a percent of credit sales. If the portion of credit sales to sales is relatively constant, the percent may be applied to total sales.

To illustrate, assume the following data for **ExTone Company** on December 31, 20Y2, before any adjustments:

Balance of Accounts Receivable	$ 240,000
Balance of Allowance for Doubtful Accounts	3,250 (Cr.)
Total credit sales	3,000,000
Bad debt as a percent of credit sales	¾%

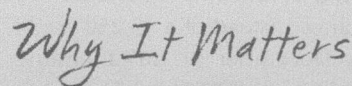

Allowance Percentages Across Companies

The percent of the allowance for doubtful accounts to total accounts receivable will vary across companies and industries. For example, the following percentages were computed from recent annual reports:

Company	Industry	Percent of Allowance for Doubtful Accounts to Total Accounts Receivable
The Coca-Cola Company (KO)	Beverages	10.8%
DuPont (DD)	Chemicals	7.4%
HCA Healthcare Inc. (HCA)	Health services	46.1%
Nike, Inc. (NKE)	Apparel	1.3%
Union Pacific Corporation (UNP)	Transportation services	0.3%
Wynn Resorts, Limited (WYNN)	Casino gaming	25.5%

Coca-Cola had an unusual increase in its estimated bad debts stemming from collection issues regarding its Venezuelan bottling partner. HCA's higher percentage is due in part because of charity care and collection challenges with deductibles and copays. Wynn Resorts' high percentage is typical for casinos, representing the challenges in collecting gambling debts.

Bad Debt Expense of $22,500 is estimated as follows:

Bad Debt Expense = Credit Sales × Bad Debt as a Percent of Credit Sales
Bad Debt Expense = $3,000,000 × ¾% = $22,500

The adjusting entry for uncollectible accounts on December 31, 20Y2, is as follows:

A = L + E
–   – Exp

20Y2				
Dec.	31	Bad Debt Expense	22,500	
		Allowance for Doubtful Accounts		22,500
		Uncollectible accounts estimate		
		($3,000,000 × ¾% = $22,500).		

After the adjusting entry is posted to the ledger, Bad Debt Expense will have an adjusted balance of $22,500. Allowance for Doubtful Accounts will have an adjusted balance of $25,750 ($3,250 + $22,500). Both T accounts follow:

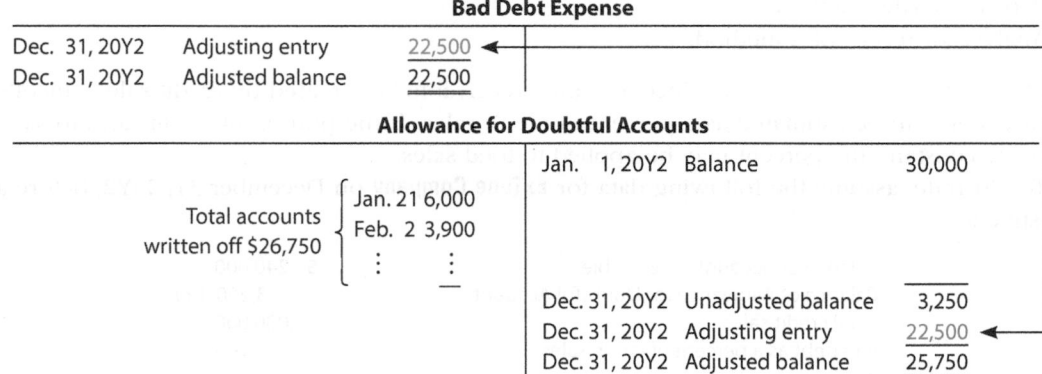

Bad Debt Expense

| Dec. 31, 20Y2 | Adjusting entry | 22,500 |
| Dec. 31, 20Y2 | Adjusted balance | 22,500 |

Allowance for Doubtful Accounts

	Jan. 1, 20Y2	Balance	30,000
Total accounts written off $26,750	Jan. 21 6,000		
	Feb. 2 3,900		
	⋮ ⋮		
	Dec. 31, 20Y2	Unadjusted balance	3,250
	Dec. 31, 20Y2	Adjusting entry	22,500
	Dec. 31, 20Y2	Adjusted balance	25,750

Under the percent of sales method, the amount of the adjusting entry is the amount estimated for Bad Debt Expense. This estimate is credited to whatever the unadjusted balance is for Allowance for Doubtful Accounts.

To illustrate, assume that in the preceding example the unadjusted balance of Allowance for Doubtful Accounts on December 31, 20Y2, had been a $2,100 debit balance instead of a $3,250 credit balance. The adjustment would still have been $22,500. However, the December 31, 20Y2, ending adjusted balance of Allowance for Doubtful Accounts would have been $20,400 ($22,500 – $2,100).

note:

The estimate based on sales is added to any balance in Allowance for Doubtful Accounts.

Check Up Corner 8-1 Percent of Sales Method

At the end of the current year, ARS Industries has the following account balances before making an adjusting entry for uncollectible accounts:

Accounts Receivable	$800,000 debit
Allowance for Doubtful Accounts	7,500 credit

The company recorded $3,500,000 of credit sales during the year. The company uses the percent of sales method and estimates that ½ of 1% of credit sales for the year will be uncollectible.

a. Determine the bad debt expense for the period, and journalize the adjusting entry.

b. Determine the adjusted balances of Allowance for Doubtful Accounts and Accounts Receivable.

c. Determine the net realizable value of accounts receivable at the end of the period.

Solution:

a. Bad Debt Expense = Credit Sales × Bad Debt as a Percent of Credit Sales
     $17,500 = $3,500,000 × 0.5%

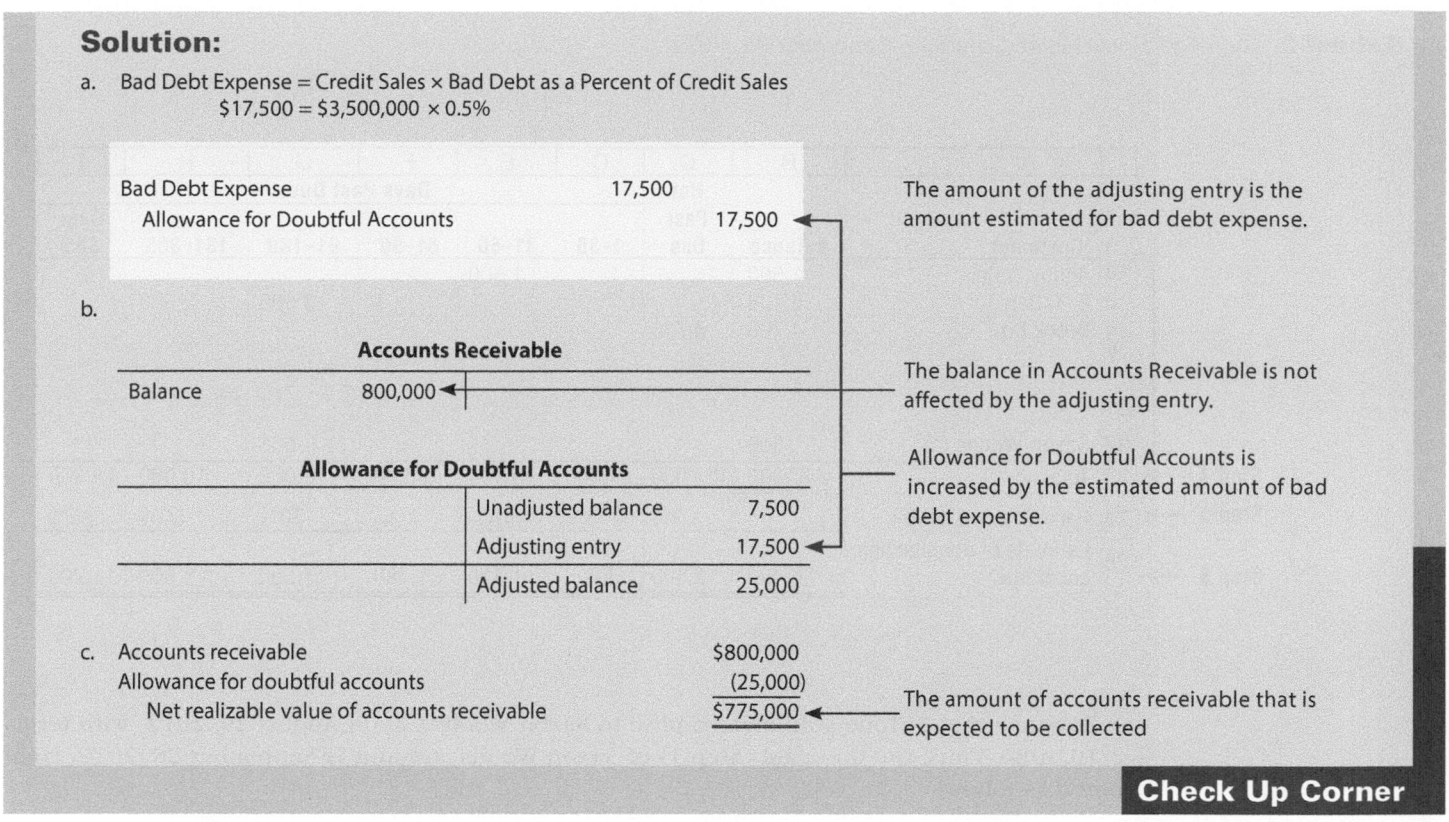

| Bad Debt Expense | 17,500 | | The amount of the adjusting entry is the amount estimated for bad debt expense. |
| Allowance for Doubtful Accounts | | 17,500 | |

b.

Accounts Receivable

| Balance | 800,000 | | The balance in Accounts Receivable is not affected by the adjusting entry. |

Allowance for Doubtful Accounts

	Unadjusted balance	7,500	Allowance for Doubtful Accounts is increased by the estimated amount of bad debt expense.
	Adjusting entry	17,500	
	Adjusted balance	25,000	

c.
Accounts receivable	$800,000	
Allowance for doubtful accounts	(25,000)	
Net realizable value of accounts receivable	$775,000	The amount of accounts receivable that is expected to be collected

Check Up Corner

Analysis of Receivables Method The analysis of receivables method is based on the assumption that the longer an account receivable is outstanding, the less likely that it will be collected. The analysis of receivables method is applied as follows:

- Step 1. The due date of each account receivable is determined.
- Step 2. The number of days each account is past due is determined. This is the number of days between the due date of the account and the date of the analysis.
- Step 3. Each account is placed in an aged class according to its days past due. Typical aged classes include the following:

| Days Past Due |
| Not past due |
| 1–30 |
| 31–60 |
| 61–90 |
| 91–180 |
| 181–365 |
| Over 365 |

- Step 4. The totals for each aged class are determined.
- Step 5. The total for each aged class is multiplied by an estimated percentage of uncollectible accounts for that class.
- Step 6. The estimated total of uncollectible accounts is determined as the sum of the uncollectible accounts for each aged class.

The preceding steps are summarized in an aging schedule, and this overall process is called **aging the receivables**.

To illustrate, assume that **ExTone Company** uses the analysis of receivables method instead of the percent of sales method. ExTone prepared an aging schedule for its accounts receivable of $240,000 as of December 31, 20Y2, as shown in Exhibit 2.

Exhibit 2   Aging of Receivables Schedule, December 31, 20Y2

	A	B	C	D	E	F	G	H	I
1			Not			Days Past Due			
2			Past						Over
3	Customer	Balance	Due	1–30	31–60	61–90	91–180	181–365	365
4	Ashby & Co.	1,500			1,500				
5	B. T. Barr	6,100					3,500	2,600	
6	Brock Co.	4,700	4,700						
7									
21									
22	Saxon Woods Co.	600					600		
23	Total	240,000	125,000	64,000	13,100	8,900	5,000	10,000	14,000
24	Percent uncollectible		2%	5%	10%	20%	30%	50%	80%
25	Estimate of uncollectible accounts	26,490	2,500	3,200	1,310	1,780	1,500	5,000	11,200

Steps 1–3

Step 4 → 23

Step 5 → 24

Step 6 → 25

Assume that ExTone sold merchandise to Saxon Woods Co. on August 29, 20Y2, with terms 2/10, n/30. Thus, the due date (Step 1) of Saxon Woods' account is September 28, 20Y2, computed as follows:

Credit terms, net	30 days
Less: Aug. 30 and Aug. 31	(2) days
Days in September	28 days

As of December 31, 20Y2, Saxon Woods' account is 94 days past due (Step 2), computed as follows:

Number of days past due in September	2 days (30 – 28)
Number of days past due in October	31 days
Number of days past due in November	30 days
Number of days past due in December	31 days
Total number of days past due	94 days

Exhibit 2 shows that the $600 account receivable for Saxon Woods Co. was placed in the 91–180 days past due class (Step 3).

The total for each of the aged classes is determined (Step 4). Exhibit 2 shows that $125,000 of the accounts receivable are not past due, while $64,000 are 1–30 days past due. ExTone applies a different estimated percentage of uncollectible accounts to the totals of each of the aged classes (Step 5). As shown in Exhibit 2, the percent is 2% for accounts not past due, while the percent is 80% for accounts over 365 days past due.

The sum of the estimated uncollectible accounts for each aged class (Step 6) is the estimated uncollectible accounts on December 31, 20Y2. This is the desired adjusted balance for Allowance for Doubtful Accounts. For ExTone, this amount is $26,490, as shown in Exhibit 2.

Comparing the estimate of $26,490 with the unadjusted balance of the allowance account determines the amount of the adjustment for Bad Debt Expense. For ExTone, the unadjusted balance of the allowance account is a credit balance of $3,250. The amount to be added to this balance is therefore $23,240 ($26,490 – $3,250). The adjusting entry is as follows:

note:

The estimate based on receivables is compared to the balance in the allowance account to determine the amount of the adjusting entry.

A = L + E
−   − Exp

20Y2			
Dec. 31	Bad Debt Expense	23,240	
	Allowance for Doubtful Accounts		23,240
	Uncollectible accounts estimate		
	($26,490 – $3,250).		

After the preceding adjusting entry is posted to the ledger, Bad Debt Expense will have an adjusted balance of $23,240. Allowance for Doubtful Accounts will have an adjusted balance of $26,490, and the net realizable value of the receivables is $213,510 ($240,000 − $26,490). Both T accounts follow:

Bad Debt Expense

Dec. 31, 20Y2	Adjusting entry	23,240 ◄	
Dec. 31, 20Y2	Adjusted balance	23,240	

Allowance for Doubtful Accounts

	Dec. 31, 20Y2	Unadjusted balance	3,250
	Dec. 31, 20Y2	Adjusting entry	23,240 ◄
	Dec. 31, 20Y2	Adjusted balance	26,490

Under the analysis of receivables method, the amount of the adjusting entry is the amount that will yield an adjusted balance for Allowance for Doubtful Accounts equal to that estimated by the aging schedule.

To illustrate, if the unadjusted balance of the allowance account had been a debit balance of $2,100, the amount of the adjustment would have been $28,590 ($26,490 + $2,100). In this case, Bad Debt Expense would have an adjusted balance of $28,590. However, the adjusted balance of Allowance for Doubtful Accounts would still have been $26,490. After the adjusting entry is posted, both T accounts follow:

Bad Debt Expense

Dec. 31, 20Y2	Adjusting entry	28,590 ◄	
Dec. 31, 20Y2	Adjusted balance	28,590	

Allowance for Doubtful Accounts

Dec. 31, 20Y2	Unadjusted balance	2,100	
	Dec. 31, 20Y2	Adjusting entry	28,590 ◄
	Dec. 31, 20Y2	Adjusted balance	26,490

Check Up Corner 8-2 | Analysis of Receivables Method

At the end of the current year, ARS Industries has the following account balances before making an adjusting entry for uncollectible accounts:

Accounts Receivable	$800,000 debit
Allowance for Doubtful Accounts	7,500 credit

The company recorded $3,500,000 of credit sales during the year. An aging of the company's accounts receivable on December 31 and a historical analysis of the percentage of uncollectible accounts in each age class follow:

Age Class	Balance	Percent Uncollectible
Not past due	$658,000	1%
1–30 days	69,000	6
31–90 days	47,000	14
Over 90 days	26,000	20
	$800,000	

The company estimates the allowance for doubtful accounts based on the analysis of receivables method.

a. Determine the bad debt expense for the period, and journalize the adjusting entry.

b. Determine the adjusted balances of Allowance for Doubtful Accounts and Accounts Receivable.

c. Determine the net realizable value of accounts receivable at the end of the period.

(Continued)

Solution:

a.

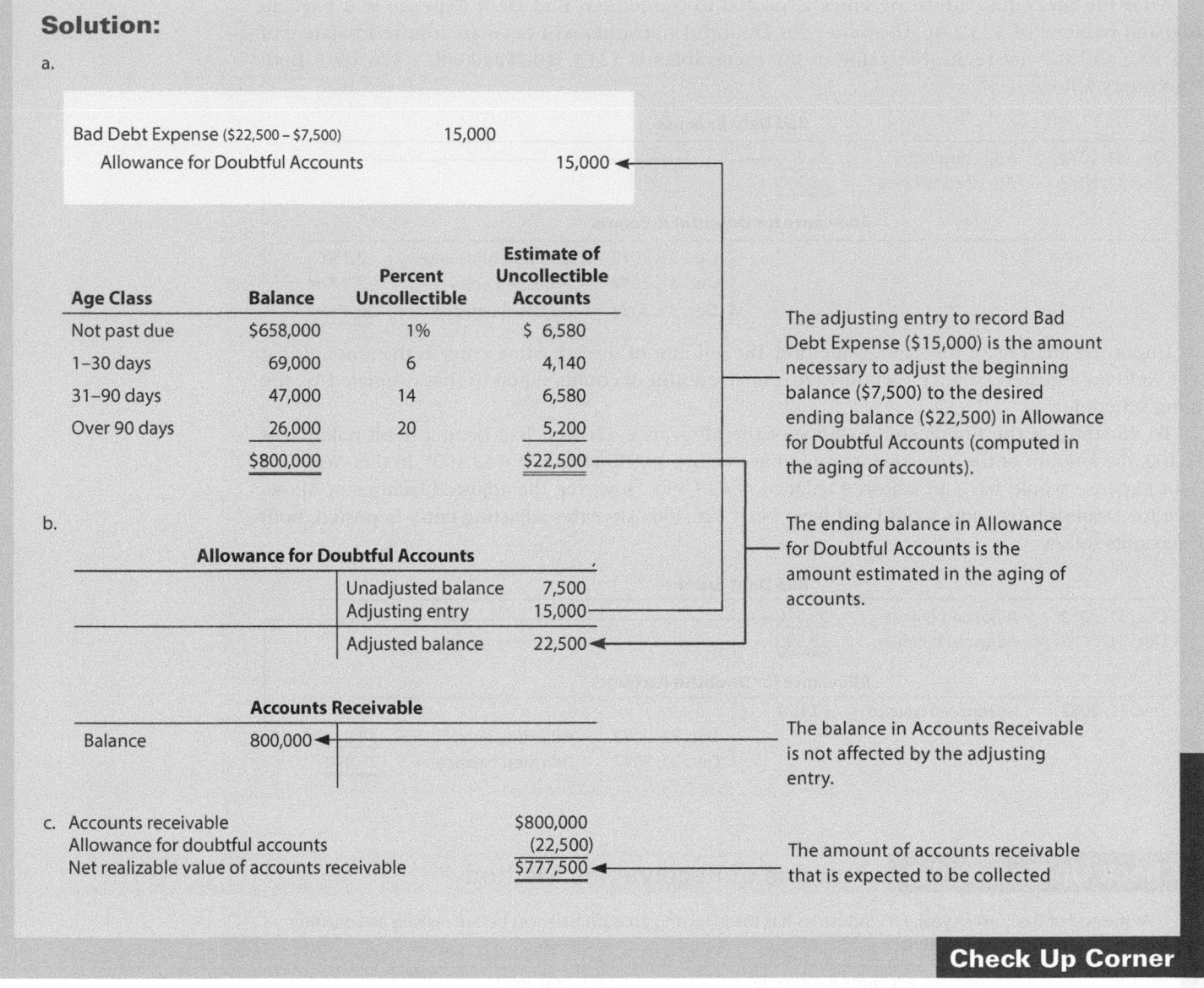

Bad Debt Expense ($22,500 – $7,500)	15,000	
Allowance for Doubtful Accounts		15,000

Age Class	Balance	Percent Uncollectible	Estimate of Uncollectible Accounts
Not past due	$658,000	1%	$ 6,580
1–30 days	69,000	6	4,140
31–90 days	47,000	14	6,580
Over 90 days	26,000	20	5,200
	$800,000		$22,500

The adjusting entry to record Bad Debt Expense ($15,000) is the amount necessary to adjust the beginning balance ($7,500) to the desired ending balance ($22,500) in Allowance for Doubtful Accounts (computed in the aging of accounts).

b.

Allowance for Doubtful Accounts

	Unadjusted balance	7,500
	Adjusting entry	15,000
	Adjusted balance	22,500

The ending balance in Allowance for Doubtful Accounts is the amount estimated in the aging of accounts.

Accounts Receivable

Balance	800,000

The balance in Accounts Receivable is not affected by the adjusting entry.

c.
Accounts receivable	$800,000
Allowance for doubtful accounts	(22,500)
Net realizable value of accounts receivable	$777,500

The amount of accounts receivable that is expected to be collected

Check Up Corner

Comparing Estimation Methods Both the percent of sales and analysis of receivables methods estimate uncollectible accounts. However, each method has a slightly different focus and financial statement emphasis.

Under the percent of sales method, Bad Debt Expense is the focus of the estimation process. The percent of sales method places more emphasis on matching revenues and expenses and, thus, emphasizes the income statement. That is, the amount of the adjusting entry is based on the estimate of Bad Debt Expense for the period. Allowance for Doubtful Accounts is then credited for this amount.

Under the analysis of receivables method, Allowance for Doubtful Accounts is the focus of the estimation process. The analysis of receivables method places more emphasis on the net realizable value of the receivables and, thus, emphasizes the balance sheet. That is, the amount of the adjusting entry is the amount that will yield an adjusted balance for Allowance for Doubtful Accounts equal to that estimated by the aging schedule. Bad Debt Expense is then debited for this amount.

Exhibit 3 summarizes these differences between the percent of sales and the analysis of receivables methods. Exhibit 3 also shows the results of the **ExTone Company** illustration for the percent of sales and analysis of receivables methods. The amounts shown in Exhibit 3 assume an unadjusted credit balance

Exhibit 3
Difference Between
Estimation Methods

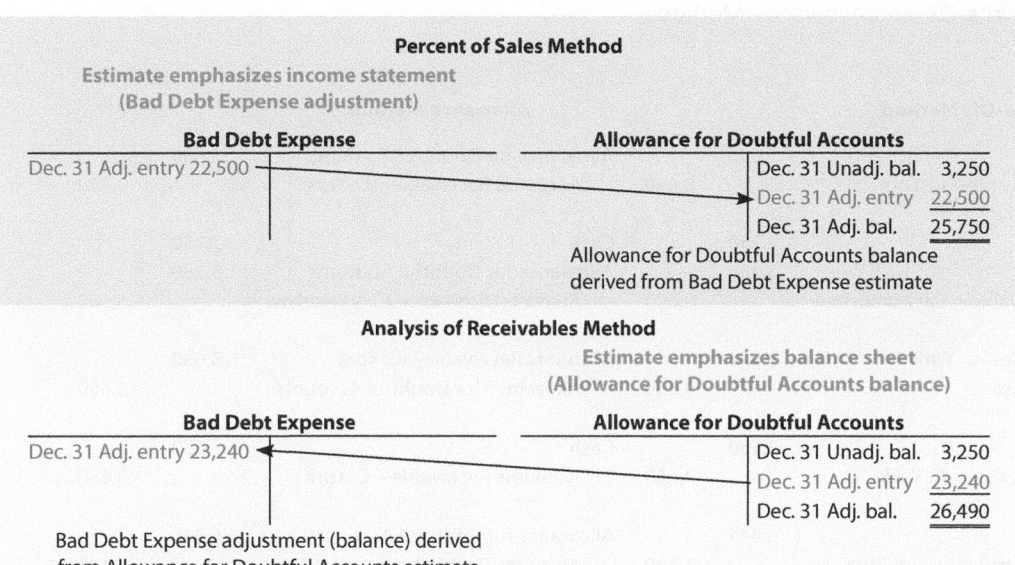

Percent of Sales Method

Estimate emphasizes income statement
(Bad Debt Expense adjustment)

Bad Debt Expense	Allowance for Doubtful Accounts
Dec. 31 Adj. entry 22,500	Dec. 31 Unadj. bal. 3,250
	Dec. 31 Adj. entry 22,500
	Dec. 31 Adj. bal. 25,750

Allowance for Doubtful Accounts balance
derived from Bad Debt Expense estimate

Analysis of Receivables Method

Estimate emphasizes balance sheet
(Allowance for Doubtful Accounts balance)

Bad Debt Expense	Allowance for Doubtful Accounts
Dec. 31 Adj. entry 23,240	Dec. 31 Unadj. bal. 3,250
	Dec. 31 Adj. entry 23,240
	Dec. 31 Adj. bal. 26,490

Bad Debt Expense adjustment (balance) derived
from Allowance for Doubtful Accounts estimate

of $3,250 for Allowance for Doubtful Accounts. While the methods normally yield different amounts for any one period, over several periods the amounts should be similar.

In a recent balance sheet, **Under Armour** reported net receivables of $622,685,000 and an allowance for uncollectible accounts of $11,341,000.

Link to Under Armour

Comparing Direct Write-Off and Allowance Methods

Journal entries for the direct write-off and allowance methods are illustrated and compared in this section. As a basis for illustration, the following transactions, taken from the records of Hobbs Company for the year ending December 31, 20Y6, are used:

Mar.   1. Wrote off account of C. York, $3,650.

Apr. 12. Received $2,250 as partial payment on the $5,500 account of Cary Bradshaw. Wrote off the remaining balance as uncollectible.

June 22. Received the $3,650 from C. York, which had been written off on March 1. Reinstated the account and recorded the cash receipt.

Sept.   7. Wrote off the following accounts as uncollectible (record as one journal entry):

Jason Bigg	$1,100
Steve Bradey	2,220
Samantha Neeley	775
Stanford Noonan	1,360
Aiden Wyman	990

Dec. 31. Hobbs Company uses the percent of credit sales method of estimating uncollectible expenses. Based on past history and industry averages, 1.25% of credit sales are expected to be uncollectible. Hobbs recorded $3,400,000 of credit sales during the year.

Exhibit 4 illustrates the journal entries for Hobbs using the direct write-off and allowance methods. Using the direct write-off method, there is no adjusting entry on December 31 for uncollectible accounts. In contrast, the allowance method records an adjusting entry for estimated uncollectible accounts of $42,500.

Exhibit 4 Comparing Direct Write-Off and Allowance Methods

		Direct Write-Off Method			Allowance Method		
20Y6							
Mar.	1	Bad Debt Expense	3,650		Allowance for Doubtful Accounts	3,650	
		Accounts Receivable—C. York		3,650	Accounts Receivable—C. York		3,650
Apr.	12	Cash	2,250		Cash	2,250	
		Bad Debt Expense	3,250		Allowance for Doubtful Accounts	3,250	
		Accounts Receivable—Cary Bradshaw		5,500	Accounts Receivable—Cary Bradshaw		5,500
June	22	Accounts Receivable—C. York	3,650		Accounts Receivable—C. York	3,650	
		Bad Debt Expense		3,650	Allowance for Doubtful Accounts		3,650
	22	Cash	3,650		Cash	3,650	
		Accounts Receivable—C. York		3,650	Accounts Receivable—C. York		3,650
Sept.	7	Bad Debt Expense	6,445		Allowance for Doubtful Accounts	6,445	
		Accounts Receivable—Jason Bigg		1,100	Accounts Receivable—Jason Bigg		1,100
		Accounts Receivable—Steve Bradey		2,220	Accounts Receivable—Steve Bradey		2,220
		Accounts Receivable—Samantha Neeley		775	Accounts Receivable—Samantha Neeley		775
		Accounts Receivable—Stanford Noonan		1,360	Accounts Receivable—Stanford Noonan		1,360
		Accounts Receivable—Aiden Wyman		990	Accounts Receivable—Aiden Wyman		990
Dec.	31	No Entry			Bad Debt Expense	42,500	
					Allowance for Doubtful Accounts		42,500
					Uncollectible accounts estimate ($3,400,000 × 0.0125 = $42,500).		

The primary differences between the direct write-off and allowance methods are summarized in Exhibit 5.

Exhibit 5
Direct Write-Off and Allowance Methods

	Direct Write-Off Method	Allowance Method
Bad debt expense is recorded	When the specific customer accounts are determined to be uncollectible.	Using an estimate based on: (1) a percent of sales or (2) an analysis of receivables.
Allowance account	No allowance account is used.	The allowance account is used.
Primary users	Small companies and companies with few receivables.	Large companies and those with a large amount of receivables.

Objective 6
Describe the accounting for notes receivable.

Notes Receivable

A note has some advantages over an account receivable. By signing a note, the debtor recognizes the debt and agrees to pay it according to its terms. Thus, a note is a stronger legal claim.

Characteristics of Notes Receivable

A promissory note is a written promise to pay the face amount, usually with interest, on demand or at a date in the future.[2] Characteristics of a promissory note are as follows:

1. The *maker* is the party making the promise to pay.
2. The *payee* is the party to whom the note is payable.

[2] You may see references to non-interest-bearing notes. Such notes are not widely used and carry an assumed or implicit interest rate.

3. The *face amount* is the amount for which the note is written on its face.

4. The *issuance date* is the date a note is issued.

5. The *due date* or *maturity date* is the date the note is to be paid.

6. The *term* of a note is the amount of time between the issuance and due dates.

7. The *interest rate* is that rate of interest that must be paid on the face amount for the term of the note.

Exhibit 6 illustrates a promissory note.

Exhibit 6 Promissory Note

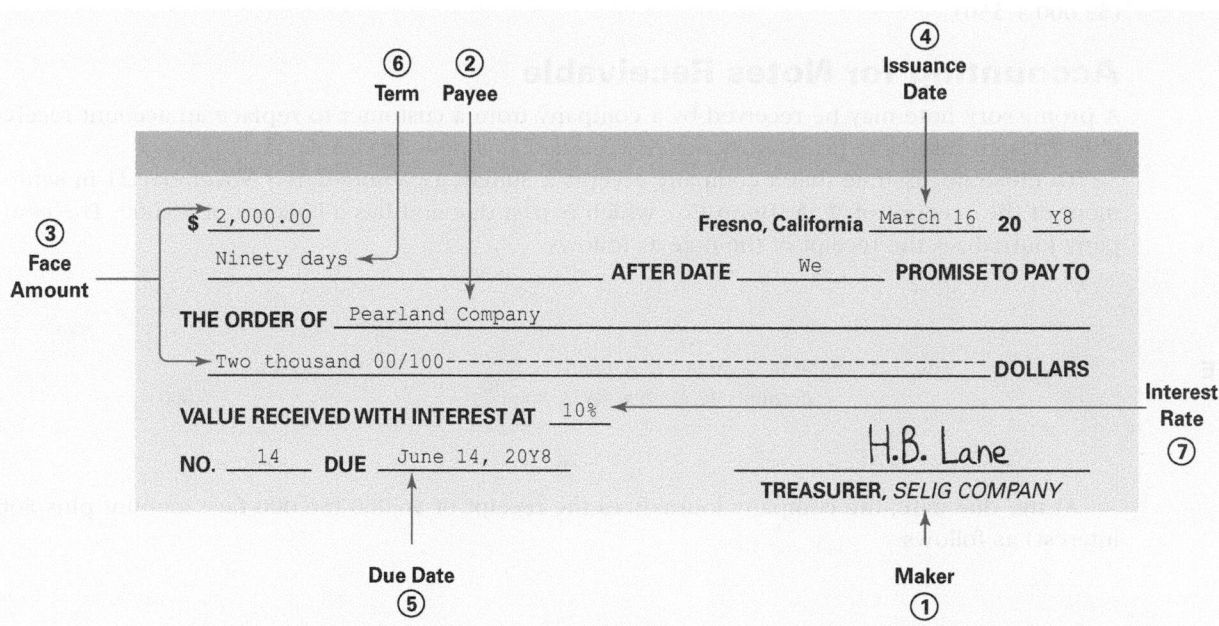

The maker of the note is Selig Company, and the payee is Pearland Company. The face value of the note is $2,000, the interest rate is 10%, and the issuance date is March 16, 20Y8. The term of the note is 90 days, which results in a due date of June 14, 20Y8, computed as follows and shown in Exhibit 7:

Days in March	31 days
Minus issuance date of note	(16)
Days remaining in March	15 days
Add days in April	30
Add days in May	31
Add days in June (due date of June 14)	14
Term of note	90 days

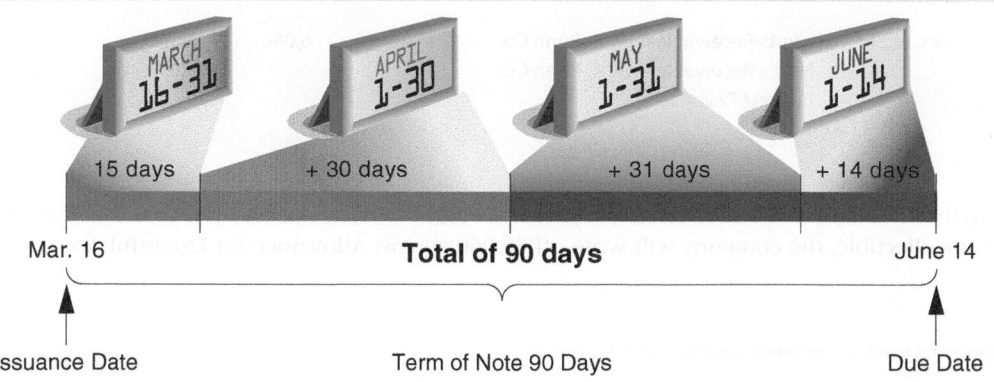

Exhibit 7
Determining Due Date of Promissory Note

The interest on a note is computed as follows:

$$\text{Interest} = \text{Face Amount} \times \text{Interest Rate} \times (\text{Term} \div 360 \text{ days})$$

The interest rate is stated on an annual (yearly) basis, while the term is expressed as days. Thus, the interest on the note in Exhibit 6 is computed as follows:

$$\text{Interest} = \$2,000 \times 10\% \times (90 \div 360) = \$50$$

To simplify, 360 days per year will be used. In practice, companies such as banks and mortgage companies use the exact number of days in a year, 365.

The **maturity value** is the amount that must be paid at the due date of the note, which is the sum of the face amount and the interest. The maturity value of the note in Exhibit 6 is $2,050 ($2,000 + $50).

Accounting for Notes Receivable

A promissory note may be received by a company from a customer to replace an account receivable. In such cases, the promissory note is recorded as a note receivable.[3]

To illustrate, assume that a company accepts a 30-day, 12% note dated November 21 in settlement of the account of W. A. Bunn Co., which is past due and has a balance of $6,000. The company journalizes the receipt of the note as follows:

A = L + E
+ –

Nov.	21	Notes Receivable—W. A. Bunn Co.	6,000	
		Accounts Receivable—W. A. Bunn Co.		6,000

At the due date, the company journalizes the receipt of $6,060 ($6,000 face amount plus $60 interest) as follows:

A = L + E
+ –   + Rev

Dec.	21	Cash	6,060	
		Notes Receivable—W. A. Bunn Co.		6,000
		Interest Revenue		60
		[$6,060 = $6,000 + ($6,000 × 12% × 30 ÷ 360)].		

If the maker of a note fails to pay the note on the due date, the note is a **dishonored note receivable**. A company that holds a dishonored note transfers the face amount of the note plus any interest due back to an accounts receivable account. For example, assume that the $6,000, 30-day, 12% note received from W. A. Bunn Co. and recorded on November 21 is dishonored. The company holding the note transfers the note and interest back to the customer's account as follows:

A = L + E
+ –   + Rev

Dec.	21	Accounts Receivable—W. A. Bunn Co.	6,060	
		Notes Receivable—W. A. Bunn Co.		6,000
		Interest Revenue		60

The company has earned the interest of $60, even though the note is dishonored. If the account receivable is uncollectible, the company will write off $6,060 against Allowance for Doubtful Accounts.

---

[3] The accounting for notes payable is described and illustrated in Chapter 10.

A company receiving a note should record an adjusting entry for any accrued interest at the end of the period. For example, assume that Crawford Company issues a $4,000, 90-day, 12% note dated December 1, 20Y3, to settle its account receivable. If the accounting period ends on December 31, 20Y3, the company receiving the note would journalize the following entries:

20Y3				
Dec.	1	Notes Receivable—Crawford Company	4,000	
		Accounts Receivable—Crawford Company		4,000
	31	Interest Receivable	40	
		Interest Revenue		40
		Accrued interest		
		($4,000 × 12% × 30 ÷ 360).		

A = L + E
+ –

A = L + E
+   + **Rev**

The receipt of the maturity value of the note on its due date of March 1, 20Y4, is recorded as follows:

20Y4				
Mar.	1	Cash	4,120	
		Notes Receivable—Crawford Company		4,000
		Interest Receivable		40
		Interest Revenue		80
		Total interest of $120		
		($4,000 × 12% × 90 ÷ 360).		

A = L + E
+ –   + **Rev**

The interest revenue account is closed at the end of each accounting period. The amount of interest revenue is normally reported in the "Other revenue and expense" section of the income statement.

Pathways Challenge

This is Accounting!

Economic Activity

When a company sells goods or services on credit, it is exposed to credit risk—the risk that the account will be uncollectible and, thus, the company will not receive what it is owed. Some types of accounts receivable are more susceptible to credit risk than others. For example, **Wynn Resorts (WYNN)** operates resorts and casinos located in Las Vegas, Nevada, and Macau, China. Casino revenue represents over 70% of its total revenue. A major portion of its casino accounts receivable comes from international customers.

Critical Thinking/Judgment

On its balance sheet, should Wynn Resorts report casino accounts receivable separately from its other business-related accounts receivable?

Do you think accounts receivable from international casino customers are riskier than local casino customers? If so, why?

What percent of Wynn Resorts' casino accounts receivable would you estimate to be uncollectible?

What percent of Wynn Resorts' other business-related accounts receivable would you estimate to be uncollectible?

Suggested answer at end of chapter.

Check Up Corner 8-3 | Notes Receivable

Icebreaker Company receives a 120-day, 6% note for $40,000, dated May 14, in settlement of a $40,000 account that is past due.

a. Determine the due date of the note.

b. Determine the maturity value of the note.

c. Prepare the journal entries to record the (1) receipt of the note and (2) collection at maturity.

Solution:

a. The due date of the note is September 11, determined as follows:

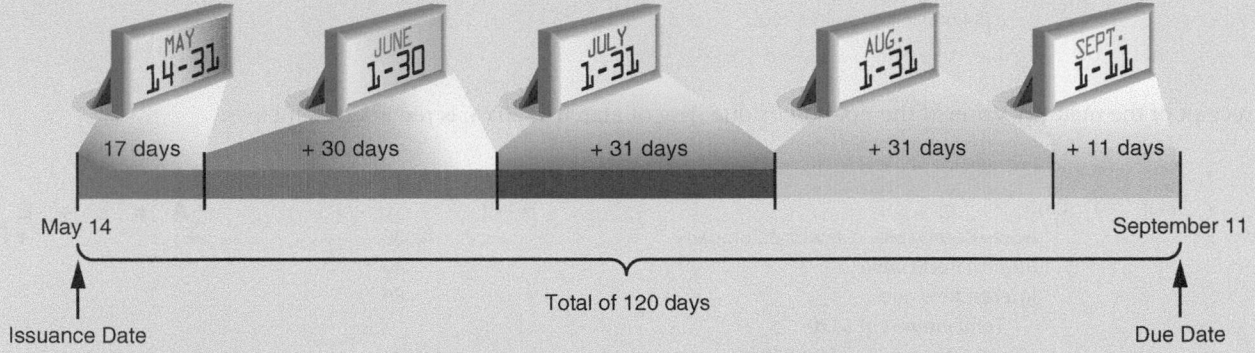

b. The maturity value of the note is the sum of the face amount and interest. The interest is computed as follows:

$$\text{Interest} = \text{Face Amount} \times \text{Interest Rate} \times (\text{Term} \div 360 \text{ days})$$
$$= \$40,000 \times 6\% \times 120 \div 360$$
$$= \$800$$

Face amount	$40,000
Interest	800
Maturity value of the note	$40,800

The maturity value is the amount that must be collected at the due date of the note.

c. The journal entries to record the (1) receipt of the note and (2) collection at maturity are as follows:

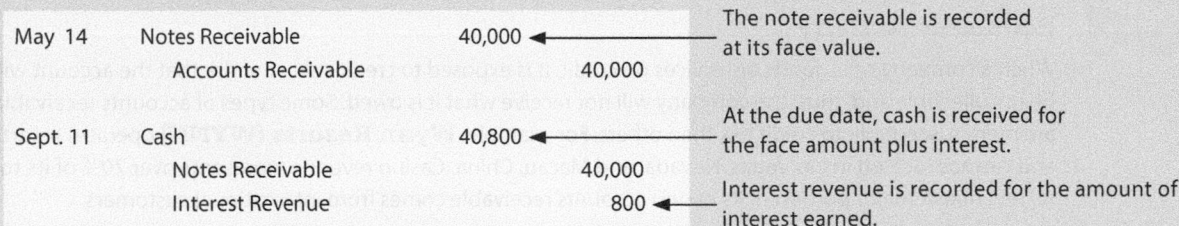

May 14	Notes Receivable	40,000	
	Accounts Receivable		40,000

The note receivable is recorded at its face value.

Sept. 11	Cash	40,800	
	Notes Receivable		40,000
	Interest Revenue		800

At the due date, cash is received for the face amount plus interest.

Interest revenue is recorded for the amount of interest earned.

Check Up Corner

Objective 7

Describe the reporting of receivables on the balance sheet.

Reporting Receivables on the Balance Sheet

All receivables that are expected to be realized in cash within a year are reported in the "Current assets" section of the balance sheet. Current assets are normally reported in the order of their liquidity, beginning with cash and cash equivalents.

The balance sheet presentation for receivables for **Under Armour (UAA)** follows:

Under Armour, Inc. Balance Sheet December 31 (in thousands)	
Assets	
Current assets:	
Cash and cash equivalents...	$250,470
Accounts receivable, net	622,685

Notes to Financial Statements:

Allowance for Doubtful Accounts

We make ongoing estimates related to the collectability of accounts receivable and maintain an allowance for estimated losses resulting from the inability of our customers to make required payments. ... As of December 31, the allowance for doubtful accounts was $11.3 million.

Source: Adapted from the 2016 10-K of Under Armour's annual report.

Link to Under Armour

In Under Armour's financial statements, accounts receivable is reported at the net realizable value on the balance sheet with a note showing the amount of the allowance for doubtful accounts. A company may choose to subtract the allowance for doubtful accounts from accounts receivable on the balance sheet to report the net realizable value of receivables.

Other disclosures, such as unusual credit risks within the receivables, are reported in the financial statement notes. For example, if the majority of the receivables are due from one customer or are due from customers located in one area of the country or one industry, these facts are disclosed.[4]

Analysis for Decision Making

Accounts Receivable Turnover and Number of Days' Sales in Receivables

Two financial measures that are useful in evaluating efficiency in collecting receivables are the following:

- accounts receivable turnover
- number of days' sales in receivables

The **accounts receivable turnover** measures how frequently during the year the accounts receivable are being converted to cash. For example, with credit terms of n/30, the accounts receivable should turn over about 12 times per year.

The accounts receivable turnover is computed as follows:[5]

$$\text{Accounts Receivable Turnover} = \frac{\text{Sales}}{\text{Average Accounts Receivable}}$$

Objective 8
Describe and illustrate the use of the accounts receivable turnover and number of days' sales in receivables to evaluate a company's efficiency in collecting its receivables.

[4] *FASB Accounting Standards Codification*, Section 210-10-50.

[5] If known, credit sales can be used in the numerator. However, because credit sales are not normally disclosed to external users, most analysts use sales in the numerator.

The average accounts receivable can be determined by adding the beginning and ending accounts receivable balances and dividing by 2. For example, consider the following financial data (in millions) for **Under Armour, Inc. (UAA)**:

	Year 2	Year 1
Sales	$4,825	$3,963
Accounts receivable:		
Beginning of year	434	280
End of year	623	434

The accounts receivable turnover for Years 1 and 2 can be computed as follows (rounding to one decimal place):

$$\text{Accounts Receivable Turnover, Year 1} = \frac{\$3,963}{(\$280 + \$434) \div 2}$$

$$= \frac{\$3,963}{\$357} = 11.1$$

$$\text{Accounts Receivable Turnover, Year 2} = \frac{\$4,825}{(\$434 + \$623) \div 2}$$

$$= \frac{\$4,825}{\$528.5} = 9.1$$

The accounts receivable turnover has declined in Year 2. This suggests that Under Armour is allowing customers to take longer to pay their accounts.

The **number of days' sales in receivables** is an estimate of the length of time the accounts receivable have been outstanding. With credit terms of n/30, the number of days' sales in receivables should be about 30 days. It is computed as follows:[6]

$$\text{Number of Days' Sales in Receivables} = \frac{\text{Average Accounts Receivable}}{\text{Average Daily Sales}}$$

Average daily sales are determined by dividing sales by 365 days.[7] For example, using the preceding data for Under Armour, the number of days' sales in receivables for Years 1 and 2 is computed as follows (rounding all calculations to one decimal place):

$$\text{Number of Days' Sales in Receivables, Year 1} = \frac{\$357}{\$3,963 \div 365}$$

$$= \frac{\$357}{\$10.9} = 32.8$$

$$\text{Number of Days' Sales in Receivables, Year 2} = \frac{\$528.5}{\$4,825 \div 365}$$

$$= \frac{\$528.5}{\$13.2} = 40.0$$

The number of days' sales in receivables confirms that Under Armour's efficiency in collecting accounts receivable declined from Year 1 to Year 2. Lengthening the credit terms or selling in markets where longer credit terms are standard could cause this decline. The efficiency in collecting accounts receivable has declined when the accounts receivable turnover decreases or the number of days' sales in receivables increases.

[6] The number of days' sales in receivables can also be computed as 365 days ÷ Accounts Receivable Turnover.

[7] We use 365 days for all computations involving real-world companies and data. We do this to highlight differences among companies and because computations using real-world data normally require rounding.

The efficiency in collecting accounts receivable can be compared across companies in similar industries. For example, the accounts receivable turnover and number of days' sales in receivables for Under Armour can be compared to a competitor, such as **Columbia Sportswear Company (COLM)**, as shown in Exhibit 8.

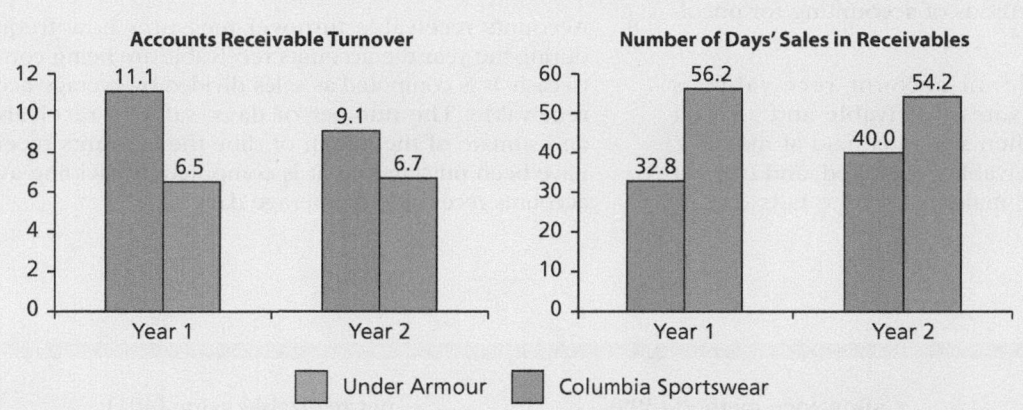

Exhibit 8

Accounts Receivable Turnover and Number of Days' Sales in Receivables for Under Armour and Columbia Sportswear

In this analysis, Under Armour is more efficient in collecting accounts receivable than is Columbia Sportswear.

Make a Decision	**Accounts Receivable Turnover and Number of Days' Sales in Receivables**

Analyze and compare Amazon.com to Best Buy (MAD 8-1) (Continuing company analysis)

Analyze Ralph Lauren (MAD 8-2)

Analyze L Brands (MAD 8-3)

Compare Ralph Lauren and L Brands (MAD 8-4)

Analyze DISH Network (MAD 8-5)

Make a Decision

Let's Review

Chapter Summary

1. *Receivables* include all money claims against other entities. Receivables are normally classified as accounts receivable, notes receivable, or other receivables.

2. The operating expense recorded from uncollectible receivables is called *bad debt expense*. The two methods of accounting for uncollectible receivables are the direct write-off method and the allowance method.

3. Under the direct write-off method, the entry to write off an account debits Bad Debt Expense and credits Accounts Receivable. Neither an allowance account nor an adjusting entry is needed at the end of the period.

4. Under the allowance method, an adjusting entry is made for uncollectible accounts. When an account is determined to be uncollectible, it is written off against

the allowance account. The allowance account is a contra asset account that normally has a credit balance after the adjusting entry has been posted. The estimate of uncollectibles may be based on a percent of sales or an analysis of receivables. Exhibit 3 compares and contrasts these two methods.

5. Exhibit 4 illustrates the differences between the direct write-off and allowance methods of accounting for uncollectible accounts.

6. A note received to settle an account receivable is journalized as a debit to Notes Receivable and a credit to Accounts Receivable. When a note is paid at maturity, Cash is debited, Notes Receivable is credited, and Interest Revenue is credited. If the maker of a note fails to pay, the dishonored note is journalized by debiting an account receivable for the amount due from the maker of the note.

7. All receivables that are expected to be realized in cash within a year are reported in the "Current assets" section of the balance sheet. In addition to the allowance for doubtful accounts, additional receivable disclosures include the market (fair) value and unusual credit risks.

8. Accounts receivable turnover measures how frequently during the year the accounts receivable are being converted to cash. It is computed as sales divided by average accounts receivable. The number of days' sales in receivables is an estimate of the length of time the accounts receivable have been outstanding. It is computed by dividing average accounts receivable by average daily sales.

Key Terms

accounts receivable (398)
accounts receivable turnover (415)
aging the receivables (405)
Allowance for Doubtful
   Accounts (401)

allowance method (399)
bad debt expense (399)
direct write-off method (399)
dishonored note receivable (412)
maturity value (412)

net realizable value (401)
notes receivable (398)
number of days' sales in
   receivables (416)
receivables (398)

Practice

Multiple-Choice Questions

1. At the end of the fiscal year, before the accounts are adjusted, Accounts Receivable has a balance of $200,000 and Allowance for Doubtful Accounts has a credit balance of $2,500. If the estimate of uncollectible accounts determined by aging the receivables is $8,500, the amount of bad debt expense is:
   a. $2,500
   b. $6,000
   c. $8,500
   d. $11,000

2. At the end of the fiscal year, Accounts Receivable has a balance of $100,000 and Allowance for Doubtful Accounts has a balance of $7,000. The expected net realizable value of the accounts receivable is:
   a. $7,000
   b. $93,000
   c. $100,000
   d. $107,000

3. What is the maturity value of a 90-day, 12% note for $10,000?
   a. $8,800
   b. $10,000
   c. $10,300
   d. $11,200

4. What is the due date of a $12,000, 90-day, 8% note receivable dated August 5?
   a. October 31
   b. November 2
   c. November 3
   d. November 4

5. When a note receivable is dishonored, Accounts Receivable is debited for what amount?
   a. The face value of the note
   b. The maturity value of the note
   c. The maturity value of the note less accrued interest
   d. The maturity value of the note plus accrued interest

Answers provided after Problem. Need more practice? Find additional multiple-choice questions, exercises, and problems in CengageNOWv2.

Exercises

1. Direct write-off method   Obj. 3

Journalize the following transactions, using the direct write-off method of accounting for uncollectible receivables:

June 2. Received $1,200 from Melissa Crone and wrote off the remainder owed of $4,000 as uncollectible.

Oct. 9. Reinstated the account of Melissa Crone and received $4,000 cash in full payment.

2. Allowance method   Obj. 4

Journalize the following transactions, using the allowance method of accounting for uncollectible receivables:

June 2. Received $1,200 from Melissa Crone and wrote off the remainder owed of $4,000 as uncollectible.

Oct. 9. Reinstated the account of Melissa Crone and received $4,000 cash in full payment.

3. Percent of sales method   Obj. 4

At the end of the current year, Accounts Receivable has a balance of $1,975,000; Allowance for Doubtful Accounts has a credit balance of $19,670; and sales for the year total $28,550,000. Bad debt expense is estimated at ¾ of 1% of sales.

Determine (a) the amount of the adjusting entry for uncollectible accounts; (b) the adjusted balances of Accounts Receivable, Allowance for Doubtful Accounts, and Bad Debt Expense; and (c) the net realizable value of accounts receivable.

4. Analysis of receivables method   Obj. 4

At the end of the current year, Accounts Receivable has a balance of $1,975,000; Allowance for Doubtful Accounts has a credit balance of $19,670; and sales for the year total $28,550,000. Using the aging method, the balance of Allowance for Doubtful Accounts is estimated as $225,000.

Determine (a) the amount of the adjusting entry for uncollectible accounts; (b) the adjusted balances of Accounts Receivable, Allowance for Doubtful Accounts, and Bad Debt Expense; and (c) the net realizable value of accounts receivable.

5. Note receivable   Obj. 6

Guzman Company received a 60-day, 5% note for $54,000 dated July 12 from a customer on account.

a. Determine the due date of the note.

b. Determine the maturity value of the note.

c. Journalize the entry to record the receipt of the payment of the note at maturity.

6. Accounts receivable turnover and day's sales in receivables   Obj. 8

Chiro-Solutions Company reported the following for two recent years:

	20Y2	20Y1
Sales	$2,912,000	$2,958,000
Accounts receivable:		
Beginning of year	300,000	280,000
End of year	340,000	300,000

a. Determine the accounts receivable turnover for 20Y2 and 20Y1. Round answers to one decimal place.

b. Determine the days' sales in receivables for 20Y2 and 20Y1. Use 365 days and round all calculations to one decimal place.

c. Are the changes in the accounts receivable turnover and days' sales in receivables from 20Y1 to 20Y2 favorable or unfavorable?

Answers provided after Problem. Need more practice? Find additional multiple-choice questions, exercises, and problems in CengageNOWv2.

Problem

Ditzler Company, a construction supply company, uses the allowance method of accounting for uncollectible accounts receivable. Selected transactions completed by Ditzler are as follows:

Feb. 1. Sold merchandise on account to Ames Co., $8,000. The cost of the goods sold was $4,500.

Mar. 15. Accepted a 60-day, 12% note for $8,000 from Ames Co. on account.

Apr. 9. Wrote off a $2,500 account from Dorset Co. as uncollectible.

21. Loaned $7,500 cash to Jill Klein, receiving a 90-day, 14% note.

May 14. Received the interest due from Ames Co. and a new 90-day, 14% note as a renewal of the loan. (Record both the debit and the credit to the notes receivable account.)

June 13. Reinstated the account of Dorset Co., written off on April 9, and received $2,500 in full payment.

July 20. Jill Klein dishonored her note.

Aug. 12. Received from Ames Co. the amount due on its note of May 14.

19. Received from Jill Klein the amount owed on the dishonored note, plus interest for 30 days at 15%, computed on the maturity value of the note. Round to the nearest cent.

Dec. 16. Accepted a 60-day, 12% note for $12,000 from Global Company on account.

31. It is estimated that 3% of the credit sales of $1,375,000 for the year ended December 31 will be uncollectible.

Instructions

1. Journalize the transactions.

2. Journalize the adjusting entry to record the accrued interest on December 31 on the Global Company note.

Need more practice? Find additional multiple-choice questions, exercises, and problems in CengageNOWv2.

Answers

Multiple-Choice Questions

1. **b** The estimate of uncollectible accounts, $8,500 (answer c), is the amount of the desired balance of Allowance for Doubtful Accounts after adjustment. The amount of the current provision to be made for uncollectible accounts expense is thus $6,000 (answer b), which is the amount that must be added to the Allowance for Doubtful Accounts credit balance of $2,500 (answer a) so that the account will have the desired balance of $8,500.

2. **b** The amount expected to be realized from accounts receivable is the balance of Accounts Receivable, $100,000, less the balance of Allowance for Doubtful Accounts, $7,000, or $93,000 (answer b).

3. **c** Maturity value is the amount that is due at the maturity or due date. The maturity value of $10,300 (answer c) is determined as follows:

Face amount of note	$10,000
Plus interest ($10,000 × 0.12 × 90 ÷ 360)	300
Maturity value of note	$10,300

4. **c** November 3 is the due date of a $12,000, 90-day, 8% note receivable dated August 5 [26 days in August (31 days – 5 days) + 30 days in September + 31 days in October + 3 days in November].

5. **b** If a note is dishonored, Accounts Receivable is debited for the maturity value of the note (answer b). The maturity value of the note is its face value (answer a) plus the accrued interest. The maturity value of the note less accrued interest (answer c) is equal to the face value of the note. The maturity value of the note plus accrued interest (answer d) is incorrect, since the interest would be added twice.

Exercises

1.

June 2	Cash	1,200	
	Bad Debt Expense	4,000	
	Accounts Receivable—Melissa Crone		5,200

| Oct. 9 | Accounts Receivable—Melissa Crone | 4,000 | |
| | Bad Debt Expense | | 4,000 |

| 9 | Cash | 4,000 | |
| | Accounts Receivable—Melissa Crone | | 4,000 |

2.

June 2	Cash	1,200	
	Allowance for Doubtful Accounts	4,000	
	Accounts Receivable—Melissa Crone		5,200

| Oct. 9 | Accounts Receivable—Melissa Crone | 4,000 | |
| | Allowance for Doubtful Accounts | | 4,000 |

| 9 | Cash | 4,000 | |
| | Accounts Receivable—Melissa Crone | | 4,000 |

3. a. $214,125 [$28,550,000 × (3/4 × 1%)]

b.

	Adjusted Balances
Accounts Receivable	$1,975,000
Allowance for Doubtful Accounts ($19,670 + $214,125)	233,795
Bad Debt Expense	214,125

c. $1,741,205 ($1,975,000 – $233,795)

4. a. $205,330 ($225,000 – $19,670)

b.

	Adjusted Balances
Accounts Receivable	$1,975,000
Allowance for Doubtful Accounts	225,000
Bad Debt Expense	205,330

c. $1,750,000 ($1,975,000 – $225,000)

5. a. The due date for the note is September 10, determined as follows:

July	19 days (31 – 12)
August	31
September	10
Total	60 days

b. $54,450 [$54,000 + ($54,000 × 5% × 60 ÷ 360)]

c.

Sept. 10	Cash	54,450	
	Notes Receivable		54,000
	Interest Revenue		450

6. a.

Turnover	20Y2	20Y1
Sales	$2,912,000	$2,958,000
Accounts receivable:		
Beginning of year	$ 300,000	$ 280,000
End of year	$ 340,000	$ 300,000
Average accts. receivable	$ 320,000	$ 290,000
	[($300,000 + $340,000) ÷ 2]	[($280,000 + $300,000) ÷ 2]
Accts. receivable turnover	9.1	10.2
	($2,912,000 ÷ $320,000)	($2,958,000 ÷ $290,000)

b.

Days' Sales in Receivables	20Y2	20Y1
Sales	$2,912,000	$2,958,000
Average daily sales	$ 7,978.1	$ 8,104.1
	($2,912,000 ÷ 365 days)	($2,958,000 ÷ 365 days)
Average accts. receivable	$ 320,000	$ 290,000
	[($300,000 + $340,000) ÷ 2]	[($280,000 + $300,000) ÷ 2]
Days' sales in receivables	40.1 days	35.8 days
	($320,000 ÷ $7,978.1)	($290,000 ÷ $8,104.1)

c. The decrease in the accounts receivable turnover from 10.2 to 9.1 and the increase in the days' sales in receivables from 35.8 days to 40.1 days indicate unfavorable changes in the efficiency of collecting receivables.

Need more help? Watch step-by-step videos of how to compute answers to these Exercises in CengageNOWv2.

Problem

1.

Feb.	1	Accounts Receivable—Ames Co.		8,000.00	
		Sales			8,000.00
	1	Cost of Goods Sold		4,500.00	
		Inventory			4,500.00
Mar.	15	Notes Receivable—Ames Co.		8,000.00	
		Accounts Receivable—Ames Co.			8,000.00
Apr.	9	Allowance for Doubtful Accounts		2,500.00	
		Accounts Receivable—Dorset Co.			2,500.00
	21	Notes Receivable—Jill Klein		7,500.00	
		Cash			7,500.00
May	14	Notes Receivable—Ames Co.		8,000.00	
		Cash		160.00	
		Notes Receivable—Ames Co.			8,000.00
		Interest Revenue			160.00
		($8,000 × 12% × 60 ÷ 360 = $160).			
June	13	Accounts Receivable—Dorset Co.		2,500.00	
		Allowance for Doubtful Accounts			2,500.00
	13	Cash		2,500.00	
		Accounts Receivable—Dorset Co.			2,500.00
July	20	Accounts Receivable—Jill Klein		7,762.50	
		Notes Receivable—Jill Klein			7,500.00
		Interest Revenue			262.50
		($7,500 × 14% × 90 ÷ 360 = $262.50).			

Aug.	12	Cash	8,280.00		
		Notes Receivable—Ames Co.		8,000.00	
		Interest Revenue		280.00	
		($8,000 × 14% × 90 ÷ 360 = $280).			
	19	Cash	7,859.53		
		Accounts Receivable—Jill Klein		7,762.50	
		Interest Revenue		97.03	
		($7,762.50 × 15% × 30 ÷ 360 = $97.03).			
Dec.	16	Notes Receivable—Global Company	12,000.00		
		Accounts Receivable—Global Company		12,000.00	
	31	Bad Debt Expense	41,250.00		
		Allowance for Doubtful Accounts		41,250.00	
		Uncollectible accounts estimate			
		($1,375,000 × 3%).			

2. | | | | | | |
|---|---|---|---|---|---|
| | Dec. | 31 | Interest Receivable | 60.00 | |
| | | | Interest Revenue | | 60.00 |
| | | | Accrued interest | | |
| | | | ($12,000 × 12% × 15 ÷ 360). | | |

Discussion Questions

1. What are the three classifications of receivables?

2. Dan's Hardware is a small hardware store in the rural township of Twin Bridges. It rarely extends credit to its customers in the form of an account receivable. The few customers who are allowed to carry accounts receivable are long-time residents of Twin Bridges with a history of doing business at Dan's Hardware. What method of accounting for uncollectible receivables should Dan's Hardware use? Why?

3. What kind of an account (asset, liability, etc.) is Allowance for Doubtful Accounts, and is its normal balance a debit or a credit?

4. After the accounts are adjusted and closed at the end of the fiscal year, Accounts Receivable has a balance of $673,400, and Allowance for Doubtful Accounts has a balance of $11,900. Describe how the accounts receivable and the allowance for doubtful accounts are reported on the balance sheet.

5. A firm has consistently adjusted its allowance account at the end of the fiscal year by adding a fixed percent of the period's sales on account. After seven years, the balance in Allowance for Doubtful Accounts has become very large in relationship to the balance in Accounts Receivable. Give two possible explanations.

6. Which of the two methods of estimating uncollectibles provides for the most accurate estimate of the current net realizable value of the receivables?

7. Neptune Company issued a note receivable to Sailfish Company. (a) Who is the payee? (b) What is the title of the account used by Sailfish Company in recording the note?

8. If a note provides for payment of principal of $85,000 and interest at the rate of 6%, will the interest amount to $5,100? Explain.

9. The maker of a $240,000, 6%, 90-day note receivable failed to pay the note on the due date of November 30. What accounts should be debited and credited by the payee to record the dishonored note receivable?

10. The note receivable dishonored in Discussion Question 9 is paid on December 30 by the maker, plus interest for 30 days at 9%. What entry should be made to record the receipt of the payment?

Basic Exercises

SHOW ME HOW

BE 8-1   Direct write-off method   Obj. 3

Journalize the following transactions, using the direct write-off method of accounting for uncollectible receivables:

Mar.   17. Received $275 from Shawn McNeely and wrote off the remainder owed of $1,000 as uncollectible.

July   29. Reinstated the account of Shawn McNeely and received $1,000 cash in full payment.

SHOW ME HOW

BE 8-2   Allowance method   Obj. 4

Journalize the following transactions, using the allowance method of accounting for uncollectible receivables:

Mar.   17. Received $275 from Shawn McNeely and wrote off the remainder owed of $1,000 as uncollectible.

July   29. Reinstated the account of Shawn McNeely and received $1,000 cash in full payment.

SHOW ME HOW

BE 8-3   Percent of sales method   Obj. 4

At the end of the current year, Accounts Receivable has a balance of $4,375,000; Allowance for Doubtful Accounts has a debit balance of $21,300; and sales for the year total $102,480,000. Bad debt expense is estimated at ¼ of 1% of sales.

Determine (a) the amount of the adjusting entry for uncollectible accounts; (b) the adjusted balances of Accounts Receivable, Allowance for Doubtful Accounts, and Bad Debt Expense; and (c) the net realizable value of accounts receivable.

SHOW ME HOW

BE 8-4   Analysis of receivables method   Obj. 4

At the end of the current year, Accounts Receivable has a balance of $4,375,000; Allowance for Doubtful Accounts has a debit balance of $21,300; and sales for the year total $102,480,000. Using the aging method, the balance of Allowance for Doubtful Accounts is estimated as $205,000.

Determine (a) the amount of the adjusting entry for uncollectible accounts; (b) the adjusted balances of Accounts Receivable, Allowance for Doubtful Accounts, and Bad Debt Expense; and (c) the net realizable value of accounts receivable.

SHOW ME HOW

BE 8-5   Note receivable   Obj. 6

Prefix Supply Company received a 120-day, 8% note for $450,000, dated April 9 from a customer on account.

a. Determine the due date of the note.

b. Determine the maturity value of the note.

c. Journalize the entry to record the receipt of the payment of the note at maturity.

SHOW ME HOW

BE 8-6   Accounts receivable turnover and days' sales in receivables   Obj. 8

For two recent years, Robinhood Company reported the following:

	20Y9	20Y8
Sales	$7,906,000	$6,726,000
Accounts receivable:		
Beginning of year	600,000	540,000
End of year	580,000	600,000

a. Determine the accounts receivable turnover for 20Y9 and 20Y8. Round answers to one decimal place.

b. Determine the days' sales in receivables for 20Y9 and 20Y8. Use 365 days and round all calculations to one decimal place.

c. Are the changes in the accounts receivable turnover and days' sales in receivables from 20Y8 to 20Y9 favorable or unfavorable?

Exercises

REAL WORLD

EX 8-1 Classifications of receivables
Obj. 1

The Boeing Company (BA) is one of the world's major aerospace firms with operations involving commercial aircraft, military aircraft, missiles, satellite systems, and information and battle management systems. As of a recent year, Boeing had $4,639 million of receivables involving U.S. government contracts and $2,432 million of receivables involving commercial aircraft customers, such as **Delta Air Lines (DAL)** and **United Airlines (UAL)**.

➤ Should Boeing report these receivables separately in the financial statements or combine them into one overall accounts receivable amount? Explain.

✔ a. 15.7%

SHOW ME HOW REAL WORLD

EX 8-2 Nature of uncollectible accounts
Obj. 2

MGM Resorts International (MGM) owns and operates hotels and casinos including the MGM Grand and the Bellagio in Las Vegas, Nevada. As of a recent year, MGM reported accounts receivable of $570,348,000 and allowance for doubtful accounts of $89,789,000. **Johnson & Johnson (JNJ)** manufactures and sells a wide range of healthcare products including Band-Aids and Tylenol. As of a recent year, J&J reported accounts receivable of $11,002,000,000 and allowance for doubtful accounts of $268,000,000.

a. Compute the percentage of the allowance for doubtful accounts to the accounts receivable for MGM. Round to one decimal place.

b. Compute the percentage of the allowance for doubtful accounts to the accounts receivable for J&J. Round to one decimal place.

c. ➤ Discuss possible reasons for the difference in the two ratios computed in (a) and (b).

SHOW ME HOW

EX 8-3 Entries for uncollectible accounts, using direct write-off method
Obj. 3

Journalize the following transactions in the accounts of Canyon River Medical Co., a medical equipment company that uses the direct write-off method of accounting for uncollectible receivables:

Jan.   19. Sold merchandise on account to Dr. Kyle Norby, $6,400. The cost of goods sold was $3,000.

June   2. Received $500 from Dr. Kyle Norby and wrote off the remainder owed on the sale of January 19 as uncollectible.

Oct.   23. Reinstated the account of Dr. Kyle Norby that had been written off on June 2 and received $5,900 cash in full payment.

SHOW ME HOW

EX 8-4 Entries for uncollectible receivables, using allowance method
Obj. 4

Journalize the following transactions in the accounts of Zippy Interiors Company, a restaurant supply company that uses the allowance method of accounting for uncollectible receivables:

May   24. Sold merchandise on account to Old Town Cafe, $24,450. The cost of goods sold was $14,500.

Sept.   30. Received $9,000 from Old Town Cafe and wrote off the remainder owed on the sale of May 24 as uncollectible.

Dec.   7. Reinstated the account of Old Town Cafe that had been written off on September 30 and received $15,450 cash in full payment.

EX 8-5 Entries to write off accounts receivable
Obj. 3, 4

Creative Solutions Company, a computer consulting firm, has decided to write off the $13,780 balance of an account owed by a customer, Wil Treadwell. Journalize the entry to record the write-off, assuming that (a) the direct write-off method is used and (b) the allowance method is used.

EX 8-6   Providing for doubtful accounts   Obj. 4

At the end of the current year, the accounts receivable account has a debit balance of $1,835,000 and sales for the year total $25,690,000. Determine the amount of the adjusting entry to provide for doubtful accounts under each of the following assumptions:

a. The allowance account before adjustment has a debit balance of $12,500. Bad debt expense is estimated at ½ of 1% of sales.

b. The allowance account before adjustment has a debit balance of $12,500. An aging of the accounts in the customer ledger indicates estimated doubtful accounts of $162,000.

c. The allowance account before adjustment has a credit balance of $26,810. Bad debt expense is estimated at ¾ of 1% of sales.

d. The allowance account before adjustment has a credit balance of $26,810. An aging of the accounts in the customer ledger indicates estimated doubtful accounts of $171,200.

EX 8-7   Number of days past due   Obj. 4

Toot Auto Supply distributes new and used automobile parts to local dealers throughout the Midwest. Toot's credit terms are n/30. As of the end of business on October 31, the following accounts receivable were past due:

Account	Due Date	Amount
Avalanche Auto	August 15	$12,000
Bales Auto	October 4	2,400
Derby Auto Repair	June 26	3,900
Lucky's Auto Repair	September 10	6,600
Pit Stop Auto	September 24	1,100
Reliable Auto Repair	July 2	9,750
Trident Auto	August 25	1,800
Valley Repair & Tow	May 23	4,000

Determine the number of days each account is past due as of October 31.

EX 8-8   Aging of receivables schedule   Obj. 4

The accounts receivable clerk for Evers Industries prepared the following partially completed aging of receivables schedule as of the end of business on July 31:

	A	B	C	D	E	F	G
1			Not		Days Past Due		
2			Past				Over
3	Customer	Balance	Due	1–30	31–60	61–90	90
4	Acme Industries Inc.	3,000	3,000				
5	Alliance Company	4,500		4,500			
21	Zollinger Company	5,000			5,000		
22	Subtotals	1,050,000	600,000	220,000	115,000	85,000	30,000

The following accounts were unintentionally omitted from the aging schedule and not included in the preceding subtotals:

Customer	Balance	Due Date
Boyd Industries	$36,000	April 7
Hodges Company	11,500	May 29
Kent Creek Inc.	6,600	June 8
Lockwood Company	7,400	August 10
Van Epps Company	13,000	July 2

a. Determine the number of days past due for each of the preceding accounts as of July 31.

b. Complete the aging of receivables schedule by adding the omitted accounts to the bottom of the schedule and updating the totals.

✔ Allowance for
doubtful accounts,
$106,106

SHOW ME HOW EXCEL TEMPLATE

EX 8-9   Estimating allowance for doubtful accounts

Obj. 4

Evers Industries has a past history of uncollectible accounts, as follows. Estimate the allowance for doubtful accounts, based on the aging of receivables schedule you completed in Exercise 8-8.

Age Class	Percent Uncollectible
Not past due	1%
1–30 days past due	3
31–60 days past due	12
61–90 days past due	30
Over 90 days past due	75

SHOW ME HOW

EX 8-10   Adjustment for uncollectible accounts

Obj. 4

Using data in Exercise 8-9, assume that the allowance for doubtful accounts for Evers Industries has a credit balance of $8,240 before adjustment on July 31. Journalize the adjusting entry for uncollectible accounts as of July 31.

SHOW ME HOW

EX 8-11   Estimating doubtful accounts

Obj. 4

Outlaw Bike Co. is a wholesaler of motorcycle supplies. An aging of the company's accounts receivable on December 31 and a historical analysis of the percentage of uncollectible accounts in each age category are as follows:

Age Class	Balance	Percent Uncollectible
Not past due	$ 892,000	¾%
1–30 days past due	285,000	1
31–60 days past due	101,000	8
61–90 days past due	63,000	16
91–180 days past due	43,100	50
Over 180 days past due	17,700	80
	$1,401,800	

Estimate what the proper balance of the allowance for doubtful accounts should be as of December 31.

SHOW ME HOW

EX 8-12   Entry for uncollectible accounts

Obj. 4

Using the data in Exercise 8-11, assume that the allowance for doubtful accounts for Outlaw Bike Co. had a debit balance of $5,140 as of December 31.

Journalize the adjusting entry for uncollectible accounts as of December 31.

✔ c. $8,225 higher

SHOW ME HOW

EX 8-13   Entries for bad debt expense under the direct write-off and allowance methods

Obj. 5

The following selected transactions were taken from the records of Shipway Company for the first year of its operations ending December 31:

Apr. 13. Wrote off account of Dean Sheppard, $8,450.

May 15. Received $500 as partial payment on the $7,100 account of Dan Pyle. Wrote off the remaining balance as uncollectible.

July 27. Received $8,450 from Dean Sheppard, whose account had been written off on April 13. Reinstated the account and recorded the cash receipt.

Dec. 31. Wrote off the following accounts as uncollectible (record as one journal entry):

Paul Chapman	$2,225
Duane DeRosa	3,550
Teresa Galloway	4,770
Ernie Klatt	1,275
Marty Richey	1,690

31. If necessary, record the year-end adjusting entry for uncollectible accounts.

a. Journalize the transactions under the direct write-off method.

b. Journalize the transactions under the allowance method. Shipway Company uses the percent of credit sales method of estimating uncollectible accounts expense. Based on past

(Continued)

history and industry averages, ¾% of credit sales are expected to be uncollectible. Shipway recorded $3,778,000 of credit sales during the year.

c. How much higher (lower) would Shipway Company's net income have been under the direct write-off method than under the allowance method?

EX 8-14 Entries for bad debt expense under the direct write-off and allowance methods
Obj. 5

✔ c. $11,090 higher

SHOW ME HOW EXCEL TEMPLATE

The following selected transactions were taken from the records of Rustic Tables Company for the year ending December 31:

June 8. Wrote off account of Kathy Quantel, $8,440.

Aug. 14. Received $3,000 as partial payment on the $12,500 account of Rosalie Oakes. Wrote off the remaining balance as uncollectible.

Oct. 16. Received the $8,440 from Kathy Quantel, whose account had been written off on June 8. Reinstated the account and recorded the cash receipt.

Dec. 31. Wrote off the following accounts as uncollectible (record as one journal entry):

Wade Dolan	$4,600
Greg Gagne	3,600
Amber Kisko	7,150
Shannon Poole	2,975
Niki Spence	6,630

31. If necessary, record the year-end adjusting entry for uncollectible accounts.

a. Journalize the transactions under the direct write-off method.

b. Journalize the transactions under the allowance method, assuming that the allowance account had a beginning balance of $36,000 at the beginning of the year and the company uses the analysis of receivables method. Rustic Tables Company prepared the following aging schedule for its accounts receivable:

Aging Class (Number of Days Past Due)	Receivables Balance on December 31	Estimated Percent of Uncollectible Accounts
0–30 days	$320,000	1%
31–60 days	110,000	3
61–90 days	24,000	10
91–120 days	18,000	33
More than 120 days	43,000	75
Total receivables	$515,000	

c. How much higher (lower) would Rustic Tables' net income have been under the direct write-off method than under the allowance method?

EX 8-15 Effect of doubtful accounts on net income
Obj. 5

During its first year of operations, Mack's Plumbing Supply Co. had sales of $6,740,000, wrote off $48,600 of accounts as uncollectible using the direct write-off method, and reported net income of $712,500. Determine what the net income would have been if the allowance method had been used and the company estimated that 1% of sales would be uncollectible.

EX 8-16 Effect of doubtful accounts on net income
Obj. 5

✔ b. $41,300 credit balance

Using the data in Exercise 8-15, assume that during the second year of operations Mack's Plumbing Supply Co. had sales of $7,450,000, wrote off $52,000 of accounts as uncollectible using the direct write-off method, and reported net income of $800,000.

a. Determine what net income would have been in the second year if the allowance method (using 1% of sales) had been used in both the first and second years.

b. Determine what the balance of the allowance for doubtful accounts would have been at the end of the second year if the allowance method had been used in both the first and second years.

EX 8-17   Entries for bad debt expense under the direct write-off and allowance methods   Obj. 5

Casebolt Company wrote off the following accounts receivable as uncollectible for the first year of its operations ending December 31:

Customer	Amount
Shawn Brooke	$ 4,650
Eve Denton	5,180
Art Malloy	11,050
Cassie Yost	9,120
Total	$30,000

a. Journalize the write-offs under the direct write-off method.

b. Journalize the write-offs under the allowance method. Also, journalize the adjusting entry for uncollectible accounts. The company recorded $5,250,000 of credit sales during the year. Based on past history and industry averages, ¾% of credit sales are expected to be uncollectible.

c. How much higher (lower) would Casebolt Company's net income have been under the direct write-off method than under the allowance method?

EX 8-18   Entries for bad debt expense under the direct write-off and allowance methods   Obj. 5

Seaforth International wrote off the following accounts receivable as uncollectible for the year ending December 31:

Customer	Amount
Kim Abel	$ 24,300
Lee Drake	31,195
Jenny Green	29,715
Mike Lamb	17,890
Total	$103,100

The company prepared the following aging schedule for its accounts receivable on December 31:

Aging Class (Number of Days Past Due)	Receivables Balance on December 31	Estimated Percent of Uncollectible Accounts
0–30 days	$ 735,000	1%
31–60 days	290,000	2
61–90 days	111,000	15
91–120 days	70,000	30
More than 120 days	94,000	60
Total receivables	$1,300,000	

a. Journalize the write-offs under the direct write-off method.

b. Journalize the write-offs and the year-end adjusting entry under the allowance method, assuming that the allowance account had a beginning balance of $89,000 and the company uses the analysis of receivables method.

c. How much higher (lower) would Seaforth International's net income have been under the allowance method than under the direct write-off method?

✔ a. May 4, $1,800

SHOW ME HOW   EXCEL TEMPLATE

EX 8-19   Determine due date and interest on notes

Obj. 6

Determine the due date and the amount of interest due at maturity on the following notes:

	Date of Note	Face Amount	Interest Rate	Term of Note
a.	January 5 *	$90,000	6%	120 days
b.	February 15 *	21,000	4	30 days
c.	May 19	68,000	8	45 days
d.	August 20	34,400	5	90 days
e.	October 19	50,000	7	90 days

* Assume a leap year in which February has 29 days.

✔ b. $81,600

SHOW ME HOW

EX 8-20   Entries for notes receivable

Obj. 6

Valley Designs issued a 120-day, 6% note for $80,000 dated April 20 to Bork Furniture Company on account.

a. Determine the due date of the note.

b. Determine the maturity value of the note.

c. Journalize the entries to record the following: (1) receipt of the note by Bork Furniture and (2) receipt of payment of the note at maturity.

EX 8-21   Entries for notes receivable

Obj. 6

The series of five transactions, (a) through (e), recorded in the following T accounts were related to a sale to a customer on account and the receipt of the amount owed. Briefly describe each transaction.

Cash	
(e) 76,500	

Notes Receivable	
(c) 75,000	(d) 75,000

Accounts Receivable	
(a) 75,000	(c) 75,000
(d) 75,400	(e) 75,400

Cost of Goods Sold	
(b) 45,000	

Inventory	
	(b) 45,000

Interest Revenue	
	(d) 400
	(e) 1,100

Sales	
	(a) 75,000

SHOW ME HOW

EX 8-22   Entries for notes receivable, including year-end entries

Obj. 6

The following selected transactions were completed by Interlocking Devices Co., a supplier of zippers for clothing:

20Y7
Dec.   7. Received from Unitarian Clothing & Bags Co., on account, a $75,000, 60-day, 3% note dated December 7.

31. Recorded an adjusting entry for accrued interest on the note of December 7.

31. Recorded the closing entry for interest revenue.

20Y8
Feb.   5. Received payment of note and interest from Unitarian Clothing & Bags Co.

Journalize the entries to record the transactions.

EX 8-23   Entries for receipt and dishonor of note receivable

Obj. 6

Journalize the following transactions of Trapper Jon's Productions:

June 23. Received a $48,000, 90-day, 8% note dated June 23 from Radon Express Co. on account.

Sept. 21. The note is dishonored by Radon Express Co.

Oct. 21. Received the amount due on the dishonored note plus interest for 30 days at 10% on the total amount charged to Radon Express Co. on September 21.

SHOW ME HOW

EX 8-24 Entries for receipt and dishonor of notes receivable

Obj. 4, 6

Journalize the following transactions in the accounts of Missouri Gaming Co., which operates a riverboat casino:

Mar. 29. Received a $30,000, 60-day, 5% note dated March 29 from Karie Platt on account.

Apr. 30. Received a $24,000, 60-day, 8% note dated April 30 from Jon Kelly on account.

May 28. The note dated March 29 from Karie Platt is dishonored, and the customer's account is charged for the note, including interest.

June 29. The note dated April 30 from Jon Kelly is dishonored, and the customer's account is charged for the note, including interest.

Aug. 26. Cash is received for the amount due on the dishonored note dated March 29 plus interest for 90 days at 8% on the total amount debited to Karie Platt on May 28.

Oct. 22. Wrote off against the allowance account the amount charged to Jon Kelly on June 29 for the dishonored note dated April 30.

EX 8-25 Receivables on the balance sheet

Obj. 7

List any errors you can find in the following partial balance sheet:

Napa Vino Company
Balance Sheet
December 31, 20Y6

Assets		
Current assets:		
Cash		$ 78,500
Notes receivable	$ 300,000	
Interest receivable	(4,500)	
Notes receivable, net		295,500
Accounts receivable	$1,200,000	
Allowance for doubtful accounts	11,500	
Accounts receivable, net		1,211,500

Problems: Series A

✔ 3. $1,749,300

SHOW ME HOW

PR 8-1A Allowance method entries

Obj. 4

The following transactions were completed by Irvine Company during the current fiscal year ended December 31:

Feb. 8. Received 40% of the $18,000 balance owed by DeCoy Co., a bankrupt business, and wrote off the remainder as uncollectible.

May 27. Reinstated the account of Seth Nelsen, which had been written off in the preceding year as uncollectible. Journalized the receipt of $7,350 cash in full payment of Seth's account.

Aug. 13. Wrote off the $6,400 balance owed by Kat Tracks Co., which has no assets.

Oct. 31. Reinstated the account of Crawford Co., which had been written off in the preceding year as uncollectible. Journalized the receipt of $3,880 cash in full payment of the account.

Dec. 31. Wrote off the following accounts as uncollectible (compound entry): Newbauer Co., $7,190; Bonneville Co., $5,500; Crow Distributors, $9,400; Fiber Optics, $1,110.

31. Based on an analysis of the $1,785,000 of accounts receivable, it was estimated that $35,700 will be uncollectible. Journalized the adjusting entry.

Instructions

1. Record the January 1 credit balance of $26,000 in a T account for Allowance for Doubtful Accounts.

2. Journalize the transactions. Post each entry that affects the following selected T accounts and determine the new balances:

Allowance for Doubtful Accounts
Bad Debt Expense

(Continued)

3. Determine the expected net realizable value of the accounts receivable as of December 31.

4. Assuming that instead of basing the provision for uncollectible accounts on an analysis of receivables, the adjusting entry on December 31 had been based on an estimated expense of ¼ of 1% of the sales of $18,200,000 for the year, determine the following:

   a. Bad debt expense for the year.

   b. Balance in the allowance account after the adjustment of December 31.

   c. Expected net realizable value of the accounts receivable as of December 31.

✔ 3. $121,000

EXCEL TEMPLATE

PR 8-2A Aging of receivables; estimating allowance for doubtful accounts   Obj. 4

Trophy Fish Company supplies flies and fishing gear to sporting goods stores and outfitters throughout the western United States. The accounts receivable clerk for Trophy Fish prepared the following partially completed aging of receivables schedule as of the end of business on December 31, 20Y4:

	A	B	C	D	E	F	G	H
1			Not		Days Past Due			
2			Past					Over
3	Customer	Balance	Due	1–30	31–60	61–90	91–120	120
4	AAA Outfitters	20,000	20,000					
5	Brown Trout Fly Shop	7,500			7,500			
30	Zigs Fish Adventures	4,000		4,000				
31	Subtotals	1,300,000	750,000	290,000	120,000	40,000	20,000	80,000

The following accounts were unintentionally omitted from the aging schedule. Assume all due dates are for the current year except for Wolfe Sports, which is due in the next year.

Customer	Due Date	Balance
Adams Sports & Flies	May 22	$5,000
Blue Dun Flies	Oct. 10	4,900
Cicada Fish Co.	Sept. 29	8,400
Deschutes Sports	Oct. 20	7,000
Green River Sports	Nov. 7	3,500
Smith River Co.	Nov. 28	2,400
Western Trout Company	Dec. 7	6,800
Wolfe Sports	Jan. 20	4,400

Trophy Fish has a past history of uncollectible accounts by age category, as follows:

Age Class	Percent Uncollectible
Not past due	1%
1–30 days past due	2
31–60 days past due	10
61–90 days past due	30
91–120 days past due	40
Over 120 days past due	80

Instructions

1. Determine the number of days past due for each of the preceding accounts.

2. Complete the aging of receivables schedule by adding the omitted accounts to the bottom of the schedule and updating the totals.

3. Estimate the allowance for doubtful accounts, based on the aging of receivables schedule.

4. Assume that the allowance for doubtful accounts for Trophy Fish Company has a debit balance of $3,600 before adjustment on December 31. Journalize the adjusting entry for uncollectible accounts.

5. ▬▬▶ Assume that the adjusting entry in (4) was inadvertently omitted, how would the omission affect the balance sheet and income statement?

✔ 1. Year 4: Balance of allowance account, end of year, $15,050

PR 8-3A Compare two methods of accounting for uncollectible receivables Obj. 3, 4, 5

Call Systems Company, a telephone service and supply company, has just completed its fourth year of operations. The direct write-off method of recording bad debt expense has been used during the entire period. Because of substantial increases in sales volume and the amount of uncollectible accounts, the company is considering changing to the allowance method. Information is requested as to the effect that an annual provision of 1% of sales would have had on the amount of bad debt expense reported for each of the past four years. It is also considered desirable to know what the balance of Allowance for Doubtful Accounts would have been at the end of each year. The following data have been obtained from the accounts:

| | | | Year of Origin of Accounts Receivable Written Off as Uncollectible | | | |
Year	Sales	Uncollectible Accounts Written Off	1	2	3	4
1	$ 900,000	$ 4,500	$4,500			
2	1,250,000	9,600	3,000	$6,600		
3	1,500,000	12,800	1,000	3,700	$8,100	
4	2,200,000	16,550		1,500	4,300	$10,750

Instructions

1. Assemble the desired data, using the following column headings:

| | Bad Debt Expense | | | |
Year	Expense Actually Reported	Expense Based on Estimate	Increase (Decrease) in Amount of Expense	Balance of Allowance Account, End of Year

2. Experience during the first four years of operations indicated that the receivables were either collected within two years or had to be written off as uncollectible. Does the estimate of 1% of sales appear to be reasonably close to the actual experience with uncollectible accounts originating during the first two years? Explain.

PR 8-4A Details of notes receivable and related entries Obj. 6

✔ 1. Note 2: Due date, May 22; Interest due at maturity, $300

SHOW ME HOW

Water Closet Co. wholesales bathroom fixtures. During the current year ending December 31, Water Closet received the following notes:

	Date	Face Amount	Term	Interest Rate
1.	Mar. 6	$75,000	60 days	4%
2.	Apr. 7	40,000	45 days	6
3.	Aug. 12	36,000	120 days	5
4.	Oct. 22	27,000	30 days	8
5.	Nov. 19	48,000	90 days	3
6.	Dec. 15	72,000	45 days	5

Instructions

1. Determine for each note (a) the due date and (b) the amount of interest due at maturity, identifying each note by number.
2. Journalize the entry to record the dishonor of Note (3) on its due date.
3. Journalize the adjusting entry to record the accrued interest on Notes (5) and (6) on December 31.
4. Journalize the entries to record the receipt of the amounts due on Notes (5) and (6) in January and February.

PR 8-5A Notes receivable entries Obj. 6

The following data relate to notes receivable and interest for CGH Cable Co., a cable manufacturer and supplier. (All notes are dated as of the day they are received.)

Apr. 10. Received a $144,000, 5%, 60-day note on account.
May 15. Received a $270,000, 7%, 120-day note on account.
June 9. Received $145,200 on note of April 10.
Aug. 22. Received a $150,000, 4%, 45-day note on account.

(Continued)

Sept. 12. Received $276,300 on note of May 15.

    30. Received a $210,000, 8%, 60-day note on account.

Oct. 6. Received $150,750 on note of August 22.

    18. Received a 120,000, 5%, 60-day note on account.

Nov. 29. Received $212,800 on note of September 30.

Dec. 17. Received $121,000 on note of October 18.

Instructions

Journalize the entries to record the transactions.

PR 8-6A   Sales and notes receivable transactions   Obj. 6

The following were selected from among the transactions completed by Caldemeyer Co. during the current year. Caldemeyer sells and installs home and business security systems.

Jan. 3. Loaned $18,000 cash to Trina Gelhaus, receiving a 90-day, 8% note.

Feb. 10. Sold merchandise on account to Bradford & Co., $24,000. The cost of goods sold was $14,400.

    13. Sold merchandise on account to Dry Creek Co., $60,000. The cost of goods sold was $54,000.

Mar. 12. Accepted a 60-day, 7% note for $24,000 from Bradford & Co. on account.

    14. Accepted a 60-day, 9% note for $60,000 from Dry Creek Co. on account.

Apr. 3. Received the interest due from Trina Gelhaus and a new 120-day, 9% note as a renewal of the loan of January 3. (Record both the debit and the credit to the notes receivable account.)

May 11. Received from Bradford & Co. the amount due on the note of March 12.

    13. Dry Creek Co. dishonored its note dated March 14.

July 12. Received from Dry Creek Co. the amount owed on the dishonored note, plus interest for 60 days at 12% computed on the maturity value of the note.

Aug. 1. Received from Trina Gelhaus the amount due on her note of April 3.

Oct. 5. Sold merchandise on account, terms 2/10, n/30, to Halloran Co., $13,500. Record the sale net of the 2% discount. The cost of goods sold was $8,100.

    15. Received from Halloran Co. the amount of the invoice of October 5, less 2% discount.

Instructions

Journalize the entries to record the transactions.

Problems: Series B

PR 8-1B   Allowance method entries   Obj. 4

✔ 3. $2,290,000

SHOW ME HOW

The following transactions were completed by Wild Trout Gallery during the current fiscal year ended December 31:

Jan. 19. Reinstated the account of Arlene Gurley, which had been written off in the preceding year as uncollectible. Journalized the receipt of $2,660 cash in full payment of Arlene's account.

Apr. 3. Wrote off the $12,750 balance owed by Premier GS Co., which is bankrupt.

July 16. Received 25% of the $22,000 balance owed by Hayden Co., a bankrupt business, and wrote off the remainder as uncollectible.

Nov. 23. Reinstated the account of Harry Carr, which had been written off two years earlier as uncollectible. Recorded the receipt of $4,000 cash in full payment.

Dec. 31. Wrote off the following accounts as uncollectible (compound entry): Cavey Co., $3,300; Fogle Co., $8,100; Lake Furniture, $11,400; Melinda Shryer, $1,200.

    31. Based on an analysis of the $2,350,000 of accounts receivable, it was estimated that $60,000 will be uncollectible. Journalized the adjusting entry.

Instructions

1. Record the January 1 credit balance of $50,000 in a T account for Allowance for Doubtful Accounts.

2. Journalize the transactions. Post each entry that affects the following selected T accounts and determine the new balances:

Allowance for Doubtful Accounts
Bad Debt Expense

3. Determine the expected net realizable value of the accounts receivable as of December 31.

4. Assuming that instead of basing the provision for uncollectible accounts on an analysis of receivables, the adjusting entry on December 31 had been based on an estimated expense of ½ of 1% of the sales of $15,800,000 for the year, determine the following:

   a. Bad debt expense for the year.

   b. Balance in the allowance account after the adjustment of December 31.

   c. Expected net realizable value of the accounts receivable as of December 31.

PR 8-2B   Aging of receivables; estimating allowance for doubtful accounts   **Obj. 4**

✔ **3. $123,235**

EXCEL TEMPLATE

Wig Creations Company supplies wigs and hair care products to beauty salons throughout Texas and the Southwest. The accounts receivable clerk for Wig Creations prepared the following partially completed aging of receivables schedule as of the end of business on December 31, 20Y7:

	A	B	C	D	E	F	G	H
1			Not			Days Past Due		
2			Past					Over
3	Customer	Balance	Due	1–30	31–60	61–90	91–120	120
4	ABC Beauty	15,000	15,000					
5	Angel Wigs	8,000			8,000			
30	Zodiac Beauty	3,000		3,000				
31	Subtotals	875,000	415,000	210,000	112,000	55,000	18,000	65,000

The following accounts were unintentionally omitted from the aging schedule. Assume all due dates are for the current year except for Visions Hair & Nail, which is due in the next year.

Customer	Due Date	Balance
Arcade Beauty	Aug. 17	$10,000
Creative Images	Oct. 30	8,500
Excel Hair Products	July 3	7,500
First Class Hair Care	Sept. 8	6,600
Golden Images	Nov. 23	3,600
Oh That Hair	Nov. 29	1,400
One Stop Hair Designs	Dec. 7	4,000
Visions Hair & Nail	Jan. 11	9,000

Wig Creations has a past history of uncollectible accounts by age category, as follows:

Age Class	Percent Uncollectible
Not past due	1%
1–30 days past due	4
31–60 days past due	16
61–90 days past due	25
91–120 days past due	40
Over 120 days past due	80

Instructions

1. Determine the number of days past due for each of the preceding accounts.

2. Complete the aging of receivables schedule by adding the omitted accounts to the bottom of the schedule and updating the totals.

3. Estimate the allowance for doubtful accounts, based on the aging of receivables schedule.

4. Assume that the allowance for doubtful accounts for Wig Creations has a credit balance of $7,375 before adjustment on December 31. Journalize the adjustment for uncollectible accounts.

5. ────▶ Assume that the adjusting entry in (4) was inadvertently omitted, how would the omission affect the balance sheet and income statement?

✔ 1. Year 4: Balance of
allowance account, end
of year, $32,550

PR 8-3B   Compare two methods of accounting for uncollectible receivables   Obj. 3, 4, 5

Digital Depot Company, which operates a chain of 40 electronics supply stores, has just completed its fourth year of operations. The direct write-off method of recording bad debt expense has been used during the entire period. Because of substantial increases in sales volume and the amount of uncollectible accounts, the firm is considering changing to the allowance method. Information is requested as to the effect that an annual provision of ¼% of sales would have had on the amount of bad debt expense reported for each of the past four years. It is also considered desirable to know what the balance of Allowance for Doubtful Accounts would have been at the end of each year. The following data have been obtained from the accounts:

| | | | Year of Origin of Accounts Receivable Written Off as Uncollectible | | | |
| | | | | | | |
Year	Sales	Uncollectible Accounts Written Off	1	2	3	4
1	$12,500,000	$18,000	$18,000			
2	14,800,000	30,200	9,000	$21,200		
3	18,000,000	39,900	3,600	9,300	$27,000	
4	24,000,000	52,600		5,100	12,500	$35,000

Instructions

1. Assemble the desired data, using the following column headings:

| | Bad Debt Expense | | | |
| | | | | |
Year	Expense Actually Reported	Expense Based on Estimate	Increase (Decrease) in Amount of Expense	Balance of Allowance Account, End of Year

2. ━━▶ Experience during the first four years of operations indicated that the receivables were either collected within two years or had to be written off as uncollectible. Does the estimate of ¼% of sales appear to be reasonably close to the actual experience with uncollectible accounts originating during the first two years? Explain.

PR 8-4B   Details of notes receivable and related entries   Obj. 6

✔ 1. Note 1: Due date,
Feb. 13; Interest due at
maturity, $110

Gen-X Ads Co. produces advertising videos. During the current year ending December 31, Gen-X Ads received the following notes:

SHOW ME HOW

	Date	Face Amount	Term	Interest Rate
1.	Jan. 14	$33,000	30 days	4%
2.	Mar. 9	60,000	45 days	7
3.	July 12	48,000	90 days	5
4.	Aug. 23	16,000	75 days	6
5.	Nov. 15	36,000	60 days	8
6.	Dec. 10	24,000	60 days	6

Instructions

1. Determine for each note (a) the due date and (b) the amount of interest due at maturity, identifying each note by number.

2. Journalize the entry to record the dishonor of Note (3) on its due date.

3. Journalize the adjusting entry to record the accrued interest on Notes (5) and (6) on December 31.

4. Journalize the entries to record the receipt of the amounts due on Notes (5) and (6) in January and February.

PR 8-5B   Notes receivable entries   Obj. 6

The following data relate to notes receivable and interest for Owens Co., a financial services company. (All notes are dated as of the day they are received.)

Mar.   8. Received a $33,000, 5%, 60-day note on account.

    31. Received an $80,000, 7%, 90-day note on account.

May 7. Received $33,275 on note of March 8.

16. Received a $72,000, 7%, 90-day note on account.

June 11. Received a $36,000, 6%, 45-day note on account.

29. Received $81,400 on note of March 31.

July 26. Received $36,270 on note of June 11.

Aug. 4. Received a $48,000, 9%, 120-day note on account.

14. Received $73,260 on note of May 16.

Dec. 2. Received $49,440 on note of August 4.

Instructions

Journalize the entries to record the transactions.

PR 8-6B Sales and notes receivable transactions

Obj. 6

The following were selected from among the transactions completed during the current year by Danix Co., an appliance wholesale company:

Jan. 21. Sold merchandise on account to Black Tie Co., $28,000. The cost of goods sold was $16,800.

Mar. 18. Accepted a 60-day, 6% note for $28,000 from Black Tie Co. on account.

May 17. Received from Black Tie Co. the amount due on the note of March 18.

June 15. Sold merchandise on account, terms 1/10, n/30, to Pioneer Co. for $17,700. Record the sale net of the discount. The cost of goods sold was $10,600.

21. Loaned $18,000 cash to JR Stutts, receiving a 30-day, 8% note.

25. Received from Pioneer Co. the amount due on the invoice of June 15, less 1% discount.

July 21. Received the interest due from JR Stutts and a new 60-day, 9% note as a renewal of the loan of June 21. (Record both the debit and the credit to the notes receivable account.)

Sept. 19. Received from JR Stutts the amount due on her note of July 21.

22. Sold merchandise on account to Wycoff Co., $20,000. The cost of goods sold was $12,000.

Oct. 14. Accepted a 30-day, 6% note for $20,000 from Wycoff Co. on account.

Nov. 13. Wycoff Co. dishonored the note dated October 14.

Dec. 28. Received from Wycoff Co. the amount owed on the dishonored note, plus interest for 45 days at 8% computed on the maturity value of the note.

Instructions

Journalize the entries to record the transactions.

Make a Decision
Accounts Receivable Turnover and Number of Days' Sales in Receivables

REAL WORLD

MAD 8-1 Analyze and compare Amazon.com to Best Buy

Obj. 8

Amazon.com, Inc. (AMZN) is one of the largest Internet retailers in the world. **Best Buy, Inc. (BBY)** is a leading retailer of consumer electronics and media products in the United States. Amazon and Best Buy compete in similar markets; however, Best Buy sells through both traditional retail stores and the Internet, while Amazon sells only through the Internet. Sales and accounts receivable information for both companies for a recent period follows (in millions):

	Amazon	Best Buy
Sales	$135,987	$39,528
Accounts receivable:		
Beginning of year	5,654	1,280
End of year	8,339	1,162

(Continued)

a. Determine the accounts receivable turnover for each company. Round all calculations to one decimal place.

b. Determine the number of days' sales in receivables for each company. Round all calculations to one decimal place.

c. ━━━━▶ Evaluate the relative efficiency in collecting accounts receivables between the two companies.

d. ━━━━▶ What might explain this difference?

SHOW ME HOW   REAL WORLD

MAD 8-2   Analyze Ralph Lauren   Obj. 8

Ralph Lauren Corporation (RL) designs, markets, and distributes a variety of apparel, home décor, accessory, and fragrance products. The company's products include such brands as Ralph Lauren, Polo by Ralph Lauren, and Chaps. For two recent years, the company reported the following (in millions):

	Year 2	Year 1
Sales	$7,230	$7,451
Accounts receivable (end of year)	517	655

The accounts receivable at the beginning of Year 1 was $588 million.

a. Compute the accounts receivable turnover for Year 1 and Year 2. Round to one decimal place.

b. Compute the number of days' sales in receivables for Year 1 and Year 2. Use 365 days and round all calculations to one decimal place.

c. ━━━━▶ What conclusions can be drawn from these analyses regarding Ralph Lauren's efficiency in collecting receivables?

REAL WORLD

MAD 8-3   Analyze L Brands   Obj. 8

L Brands, Inc. (LB) sells women's clothing and personal health care products through specialty retail stores including Victoria's Secret and Bath & Body Works stores. L Brands reported the following (in millions) for two recent years:

	Year 2	Year 1
Sales	$12,154	$11,454
Accounts receivable:		
Beginning of year	252	244
End of year	261	252

a. Determine the accounts receivable turnover for Year 1 and Year 2. Round all calculations to one decimal place.

b. Compute the number of days' sales in receivables for Year 1 and Year 2. Use 365 days and round all calculations to one decimal place.

c. ━━━━▶ What conclusions can be drawn from these analyses regarding L Brands' efficiency in collecting receivables?

REAL WORLD

MAD 8-4   Compare Ralph Lauren and L Brands   Obj. 8

Use the data in MAD 8-2 and MAD 8-3 to analyze the accounts receivable turnover ratios of **Ralph Lauren Corporation** and **L Brands, Inc.**

a. Compute the accounts receivable turnover ratios for Ralph Lauren and L Brands for the years shown in MAD 8-2 and MAD 8-3. Average the accounts receivable turnover ratio for the two years. Round all calculations to one decimal place.

b. Does L Brands or Ralph Lauren have the higher average accounts receivable turnover ratio?

c. ━━━━▶ What might explain the difference in the average accounts receivable turnover ratios between the two companies?

REAL WORLD

MAD 8-5 Analyze DISH Network

Obj. 8

DISH Network Corporation (DISH) provides satellite-based entertainment services to residential and business customers. Services are billed and collected on a monthly basis. DISH Network reported the following (in millions) for two recent years:

	20Y4	20Y3
Sales	$15,034	$15,069
Accounts receivable:		
Beginning of year	864	951
End of year	753	864

a. Determine the accounts receivable turnover for 20Y3 and 20Y4. Round all calculations to one decimal place.

b. Compute the number of days' sales in receivables for 20Y3 and 20Y4. Use 365 days and round all calculations to one decimal place.

c. ▬▬► What conclusions can be drawn from these analyses regarding DISH Network's efficiency in collecting receivables?

Take It Further

ETHICS

TIF 8-1 Uncollectible accounts receivable

Bud Lighting Co. is a retailer of commercial and residential lighting products. Gowen Geter, the company's chief accountant, is in the process of making year-end adjusting entries for uncollectible accounts receivable. In recent years, the company has experienced an increase in accounts that have become uncollectible. As a result, Gowen believes that the company should increase the percentage used for estimating doubtful accounts from 2% to 4% of credit sales. This change will significantly increase bad debt expense, resulting in a drop in earnings for the first time in company history. The company president, Tim Burr, is under considerable pressure to meet earnings goals. He suggests that this is "not the right time" to change the estimate. He instructs Gowen to keep the estimate at 2%. Gowen is confident that 2% is too low, but he follows Tim's instructions.

▬▬► Evaluate the decision to use the lower percentage to improve earnings. Are Tim and Gowen acting in an ethical manner?

ETHICS

TIF 8-2 Interest computations

Bev Wynn, vice president of operations for Dillon County Bank, has instructed the bank's computer programmer to use a 365-day year to compute interest on depository accounts (liabilities). Bev also instructed the programmer to use a 360-day year to compute interest on loans (assets).

▬▬► Discuss whether Bev is behaving in a professional manner.

TEAM ACTIVITY   REAL WORLD

TIF 8-3 Real-world annual report

In teams, select a public company that interests you and is a business that has accounts receivable. Obtain the company's most recent annual report on Form 10-K. The Form 10-K is a company's annually required filing with the Securities and Exchange Commission (SEC). It includes the company's financial statements and accompanying notes. The Form 10-K can be obtained either (a) from the investor relations section of the company's website or (b) by using the company search feature of the SEC's EDGAR database service found at www.sec.gov/edgar/searchedgar/companysearch.html.

1. Based on the information in the company's most recent annual report, answer the following questions:

a. What amount of accounts receivable did the company report at the end of the most recent year?

b. What is the balance in the company's Allowance for Uncollectible Accounts at the end of the most recent year?

(Continued)

c. What percentage of total current assets is accounts receivable at the end of each of the two years presented? Has this percentage increased, decreased, or remained the same during this period?

d. How much bad debt expense did the company report for the most recent year?

2. ➡ Using the information presented in the company's annual report, compute the company's accounts receivable turnover for the current and previous years. Based on this information, has the company's management of accounts receivable improved? Briefly explain your answer.

COMMUNICATION

TIF 8-4 Uncollectible accounts receivable

On January 1, Xtreme Co. began offering credit with terms of n/30. Uncollectible accounts are estimated to be 1% of credit sales, which is the average for the industry. The CEO, Todd Hurley, has no background in accounting and is struggling to understand the allowance method.

➡ Write a brief memo to Todd explaining the allowance method and how this information is reported in the financial statements.

CRITICAL
THINKING

TIF 8-5 Allowance for doubtful accounts

For several years, Xtreme Co.'s sales have been on a "cash only" basis. On January 1, 20Y4, however, Xtreme Co. began offering credit on terms of n/30. The amount of the adjusting entry to record the estimated uncollectible receivables at the end of each year has been ½ of 1% of credit sales, which is the rate reported as the average for the industry. Credit sales and the year-end credit balances in Allowance for Doubtful Accounts for the past four years are as follows:

Year	Credit Sales	Allowance for Doubtful Accounts
20Y4	$4,000,000	$ 5,000
20Y5	4,400,000	8,250
20Y6	4,800,000	10,200
20Y7	5,100,000	14,400

Laurie Jones, president of Xtreme Co., is concerned that the method used to account for and write off uncollectible receivables is unsatisfactory. She has asked for your advice in the analysis of past operations in this area and for recommendations for change.

1. Determine the amount of (a) the addition to Allowance for Doubtful Accounts and (b) the accounts written off for each of the four years.

2. a. ➡ Advise Laurie Jones as to whether the estimate of ½ of 1% of credit sales appears reasonable.

   b. ➡ Assume that after discussing (a) with Laurie Jones, she asked you what action might be taken to determine what the balance of Allowance for Doubtful Accounts should be at December 31, 20Y7, and what possible changes, if any, you might recommend in accounting for uncollectible receivables. How would you respond?

Pathways Challenge

This is Accounting!

Information/Consequences

Generally accepted accounting principles do not require companies like **Wynn Resorts (WYNN)** to report casino accounts receivable separately on their balance sheets. However, Wynn Resorts chooses to disclose the percentage of its accounts receivable generated from casino operations in the notes to its financial statements.

Casino accounts receivable from international customers are generally considered riskier than those of U.S. customers. One obvious reason is the logistics of collecting a foreign debt. In addition, some countries do not recognize the enforceability of gaming-related debt.

Notes to a recent financial statement of Wynn Resorts estimate casino doubtful accounts receivable at 25.5%.

Notes to a recent financial statement of Wynn Resorts estimate doubtful accounts receivable from other (non-casino) business at 1.4%.

Suggested Answer

9 Long-Term Assets: Fixed and Intangible

STATEMENT OF STOCKHOLDERS' EQUITY
For the Year Ended December 31, 20Y5

	Common Stock	Retained Earnings	Total
Balances, Jan. 1, 20Y5	$XXX	$ XXX	$ XXX
Issued common stock	XXX		XXX
Net income		XXX	XXX
Dividends		(XXX)	(XXX)
Balances, Dec. 31, 20Y5	$XXX	$ XXX	$ XXX

STATEMENT OF CASH FLOWS
For the Year Ended December 31, 20Y5

Cash flows from (used for) operating activities	$XXX
Cash flows from (used for) investing activities	XXX
Cash flows from (used for) financing activities	XXX
Net increase (decrease) in cash	$XXX
Cash balance, January 1, 20Y5	XXX
Cash balance, December 31, 20Y5	$XXX

INCOME STATEMENT
For the Year Ended December 31, 20Y5

Sales		$ XXX
Cost of goods sold		(XXX)
Gross profit		$ XXX
Operating expenses:		
Wages expense	$XXX	
Advertising expense	XXX	
Utilities expense	XXX	
Depreciation expense	XXX	
Amortization expense	XXX	
Depletion expense	XXX	
...	XXX	
Total operating expenses		(XXX)
Operating income		$ XXX
Other revenue and expense		XXX
Net income		$ XXX

BALANCE SHEET
December 31, 20Y5

Assets		
Current assets:		
Cash	$XXX	
Accounts receivable	XXX	
Inventory	XXX	
Total current assets		$XXX
Long-term assets:		
Property, plant, and equipment	$ XXX	
Accumulated depreciation	(XXX)	
Book value	$XXX	
Natural resources	$ XXX	
Accumulated depletion	(XXX)	
Net natural resources	XXX	
Intangible assets	XXX	
Total long-term assets		XXX
Total assets		$XXX
Liabilities		
Current liabilities	$XXX	
Long-term liabilities	XXX	
Total liabilities		$XXX
Stockholders' Equity		
Common stock	$XXX	
Retained earnings	XXX	
Total stockholders' equity		XXX
Total liabilities and stockholders' equity		$XXX

McDonald's

McDonald's (MCD) began in 1940 in San Bernardino, California, as a Bar-B-Q restaurant operated by two brothers, Dick and Mac McDonald. In 1954, Ray Kroc visited the restaurant and convinced the McDonald brothers to let him franchise its operations nationwide. Ray Kroc opened his first McDonald's in Des Plaines, Illinois, in 1955, with its distinguishing Golden Arches. Today, McDonald's operates in more than 100 countries, has more than 30,000 restaurants, employs approximately 375,000 people, has sold billions of hamburgers, and generates yearly revenues over $20 billion.

Would you like to own and operate a McDonald's restaurant? McDonald's grants 20-year franchises to individuals who want to become owner/operators of a restaurant. Individuals may purchase either an existing or a new restaurant. When opening a new restaurant, the owner must invest in the store equipment, signs, seating, and décor. The company normally owns the land and the building. McDonald's also provides training for its owner/operators. In return, the company is paid a monthly service charge, which is either a fixed amount or a percent of sales. The total cost of opening a new restaurant may exceed several million dollars.

Obviously, the decision to open a McDonald's restaurant is a major commitment with long-lasting implications. This chapter discusses the accounting for investments in long-term, fixed assets such as a new restaurant. This accounting addresses such issues as how much of the investment should be recorded as an asset, how much should be written off as an expense each year, and how the disposal of a fixed asset should be recorded. Finally, accounting for natural resources, such as mineral deposits, and intangible assets, such as patents and copyrights, is discussed.

Source: www.aboutmcdonalds.com

©SORBIS/SHUTTERSTOCK.COM

What's Covered

Long-Term Assets: Fixed and Intangible

Fixed Assets	**Natural Resources**	**Intangible Assets**	**Reporting Long-Term Assets**
■ Cost (Obj. 1)	■ Cost (Obj. 4)	■ Patents, Copyrights, Trademarks, and Goodwill (Obj. 5)	
■ Depreciation (Obj. 2)	■ Depletion (Obj. 4)		■ Income Statement (Obj. 6)
■ Repairs and Improvements (Obj. 2)		■ Amortization and Impairment (Obj. 5)	■ Balance Sheet (Obj. 6)
■ Disposal (Obj. 3)			

Learning Objectives

Obj. 1 Define, classify, and account for the cost of fixed assets.

Obj. 2 Compute depreciation using the following methods: straight-line, units-of-activity, and double-declining-balance.

Obj. 3 Journalize the disposal of fixed assets.

Obj. 4 Describe the accounting for natural resources, including the journal entry for depletion.

Obj. 5 Describe the accounting for intangible assets, such as patents, copyrights, and goodwill.

Obj. 6 Describe how depreciation expense is reported on an income statement and prepare a balance sheet that includes fixed assets and intangible assets.

Analysis for Decision Making

Obj. 7 Describe and illustrate the fixed asset turnover ratio to assess the efficiency of a company's use of its fixed assets.

Obj. App Describe and illustrate the accounting for the exchange of similar fixed assets.

Objective 1
Define, classify, and account for the cost of fixed assets.

Nature of Fixed Assets

Fixed assets are long-term or relatively permanent assets such as equipment, machinery, buildings, and land. Other descriptive titles for fixed assets are *plant assets* or *property, plant, and equipment*. Fixed assets have the following characteristics:

- They exist physically and, thus, are *tangible* assets.
- They are owned and used by the company in its normal operations.
- They are not offered for sale as part of normal operations.

Fixed assets are critical to the success of many businesses. For example, computers and Internet servers are critical fixed assets for a business that provides online retail or technology services.

Classifying Costs

IFRS
See Appendix C for more information.

A cost that has been incurred may be classified as a fixed asset, an investment, or an expense. Exhibit 1 shows how to determine the proper classification of a cost and how it should be recorded.

Exhibit 1
Classifying Costs

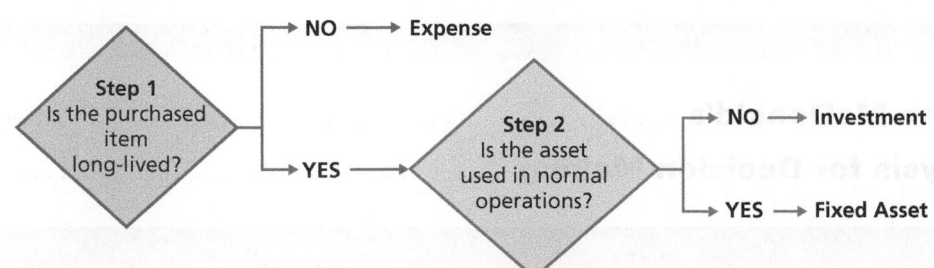

As shown in Exhibit 1, classifying a cost involves the following steps:

■ Step 1. Is the purchased item long-lived?

If *yes*, the item is recorded as an asset on the balance sheet, either as a fixed asset or an investment. Proceed to Step 2.

If *no*, the item is classified and recorded as an *expense*.

■ Step 2. Is the asset used in normal operations?

If *yes*, the asset is classified and recorded as a *fixed asset*.

If *no*, the asset is classified and recorded as an *investment*.

Items that are classified and recorded as fixed assets include land, buildings, or equipment. Such assets normally last more than a year and are used in the normal operations of the business. However, standby equipment for use during peak periods or when other equipment breaks down is still classified as a fixed asset, even though it is not used very often. In contrast, fixed assets that have been abandoned or are no longer used in operations are not classified as fixed assets.

In a recent financial statement, **McDonald's** reported total property, plant, and equipment of over $34 billion, which consists of land, buildings, and equipment.

Link to McDonald's

Why It Matters

CONCEPT CLIP

Fixed Assets

Fixed assets often represent a significant portion of a company's total assets. The table that follows shows the fixed assets as a percent of total assets for some select companies across a variety of industries. As can be seen, the type of industry will impact the proportion of fixed assets to total assets. Retail has the highest percent of fixed assets to total assets, while social media and software are on the lower end of the scale. High-tech service companies often use fewer fixed assets to deliver their services than will companies that use stores, equipment, planes, cell towers, or theme parks.

Company	Industry	Percent of Fixed Assets to Total Assets
McDonald's Corporation (MCD)	Food Retail	69%
Target Corporation (TGT)	Merchandise Retail	63%
Delta Air Lines, Inc. (DAL)	Transportation	48%
Verizon Communications Inc. (VZ)	Communications	35%
The Walt Disney Company (DIS)	Entertainment	30%
Facebook, Inc. (FB)	Social Media	13%
Microsoft Corporation (MSFT)	Software	9%

Fixed assets have important properties that require management attention:

■ Fixed assets require a long-term commitment. Mistakes in acquiring fixed assets can be very costly and difficult to reverse; thus, managers must take special care in acquiring fixed assets.

■ Fixed assets wear out over time and need to be replaced. Managers must monitor fixed assets and know when to replace fixed assets due to wear and tear or obsolescence.

■ Fixed assets need to be maintained during use. Managers need to develop maintenance programs to keep the investment in fixed assets productive.

■ Fixed assets often require significant funds to purchase. Managers must acquire funding internally or by other sources to finance the purchase of fixed assets.

Although fixed assets may be sold, they should not be offered for sale as part of normal operations. For example, cars and trucks offered for sale by an automotive dealership are not fixed assets of the dealership. On the other hand, a tow truck used in the normal operations of the dealership is a fixed asset of the dealership.

Investments are long-lived assets that are not used in the normal operations and are held for future resale. Such assets are reported on the balance sheet in a section entitled *Investments*. For example, undeveloped land acquired for future resale would be classified and reported as an investment, not land.

The Cost of Fixed Assets

In addition to purchase price, the costs of acquiring fixed assets include all amounts spent getting the asset in place and ready for use. For example, freight costs and the costs of installing equipment are part of the asset's total cost.

Exhibit 2 summarizes some of the common costs of acquiring fixed assets. These costs are recorded by debiting the related fixed asset account, such as Building, Machinery and Equipment, Land,[1] and Land Improvements.

Exhibit 2 Costs of Acquiring Fixed Assets

Building

- Architects' fees
- Engineers' fees
- Insurance costs incurred during construction
- Interest on money borrowed to finance construction
- Sales taxes
- Repairs (purchase of existing building)
- Reconditioning (purchase of existing building)
- Modifying for use
- Permits from government agencies

Machinery & Equipment

- Sales taxes
- Freight
- Installation
- Repairs (purchase of used equipment)
- Reconditioning (purchase of used equipment)
- Insurance while in transit
- Assembly
- Modifying for use
- Testing for use
- Permits from government agencies

Land

- Purchase price
- Sales taxes
- Permits from government agencies
- Broker's commissions
- Title fees
- Surveying fees
- Delinquent real estate taxes
- Removing unwanted building less any salvage
- Grading and leveling

Land Improvements

- Trees and shrubs
- Fences
- Outdoor lighting
- Paved parking areas or walkways

Only costs necessary for preparing the fixed asset for use are included as a cost of the asset. Unnecessary costs that do not increase the asset's usefulness are recorded as an expense. For example, the following costs are included as an expense:

- Vandalism
- Mistakes in installation

[1] As discussed here, land is assumed to be used only as a location or site and not for its mineral deposits or other natural resources.

- Uninsured theft
- Damage during unpacking and installing
- Fines for not obtaining proper permits from governmental agencies

To illustrate, assume Kimble Inc. purchased equipment for $12,000. Freight costs of $600 were incurred to transport the equipment to the installation site. On site, installation costs of $1,500 were incurred, including $500 due to an error in installation. The journal entry to record the equipment is as follows:

Equipment ($12,000 + $600 + $1,500 − $500)	13,600	
Cash		13,600

A = L + E
+ −

The cost of the error in installing the equipment of $500 is not included in the cost of the equipment, but instead is recorded as an expense.

A company may incur costs associated with constructing a fixed asset such as a new building. The direct costs incurred in the construction, such as labor and materials, should be capitalized as a debit to an account entitled *Construction in Progress*. When the construction is complete, the costs are reclassified by crediting Construction in Progress and debiting the proper fixed asset account such as Building.

Leasing Fixed Assets

A *lease* is a contract for the use of an asset for a period of time. Leases are often used in business. For example, automobiles, computers, medical equipment, buildings, and airplanes are often leased.

The two parties to a lease contract are as follows:

- The *lessor* is the party who owns the asset.
- The *lessee* is the party to whom the rights to use the asset are granted by the lessor.

Under a lease contract, the lessee pays rent on a periodic basis for the lease term. An advantage of leasing an asset is that the lessee has access to an asset without having to spend funds or obtain financing to buy the asset. In addition, expenses such as maintenance and repair costs may be the responsibility of the lessor. Finally, the risk of incurring additional cost because the asset becomes obsolete before the end of its useful life can be mitigated by leasing an asset.

McDonald's recently reported that it is the lessee in over 14,700 locations. The leases are normally for 20 years with an option to renew.

Link to McDonald's

The Financial Accounting Standards Board (FASB) and the International Accounting Standards Board (IASB) recently completed a project to merge U.S. and international standards on leasing.[2] The new FASB standard distinguishes between finance leases and operating leases. Under both finance and operating leases, the lessee records an asset and liability similar to having purchased the asset. However, the amount of depreciation expense and interest expense will differ for each type of lease. For short-term leases (the lease term is 12 months or less), the lessee records lease payments by debiting Rent Expense and crediting Cash. In some cases, like those illustrated in earlier chapters, Prepaid Rent is initially recorded with an adjusting entry at the end of the period to record Rent Expense. For purposes of this text, we assume that all leases are short-term leases.

Regardless of the type of lease, lease terms should be disclosed in the notes to the financial statements. These disclosures should include such items as the length of the lease, termination rights, and renewal options.

IFRS
See Appendix C for more information.

---

[2] Accounting Standards Update, *Leases (Topic 842)*, February 2016, FASB (Norwalk, CT).

Objective 2

Compute depreciation using the following methods: straight-line, units-of-activity, and double-declining-balance.

Accounting for Depreciation

Over time, fixed assets, with the exception of land, lose their ability to provide services. Thus, the costs of fixed assets such as equipment and buildings should be recorded as an expense over their useful lives. Recording the cost of fixed assets as an expense is called **depreciation**. Because land has an unlimited life, it is not depreciated.

Depreciation can be caused by physical or functional factors.

■ *Physical depreciation* factors include wear and tear during use or from exposure to weather.
■ *Functional depreciation* factors include obsolescence and changes in customer needs that cause the asset to no longer provide services for which it was intended. For example, equipment may become obsolete due to changing technology.

Two common misunderstandings that exist about depreciation as used in accounting include:

■ Depreciation does not measure a decline in the market value of a fixed asset. Instead, depreciation is an allocation of a fixed asset's cost to expense over the asset's useful life. Thus, the **book value** of a fixed asset (cost less accumulated depreciation) usually does not agree with the asset's market value. This is justified in accounting because a fixed asset is for use in a company's operations rather than for resale.
■ Depreciation does not provide cash to replace fixed assets as they wear out. This misunderstanding may occur because depreciation, unlike most expenses, does not require an outlay of cash when it is recorded.

Factors in Computing Depreciation Expense

The three factors that determine the depreciation expense for a fixed asset are as follows:

■ The asset's initial cost
■ The asset's expected useful life
■ The asset's estimated residual value

The **initial cost** of a fixed asset is the purchase price of the asset plus all costs to obtain and ready it for use. This initial cost is determined using the concepts discussed and illustrated earlier in this chapter.

The **expected useful life** of a fixed asset is the estimated length of time the asset will be used in normal operations. It is estimated at the time the asset is placed into service. Estimates of expected useful lives are available from industry trade associations. The Internal Revenue Service also publishes guidelines for useful lives, which may be helpful for financial reporting purposes. However, it is not uncommon for different companies to use a different useful life for similar assets.

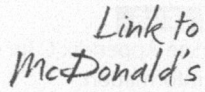

Link to McDonald's

McDonald's uses a useful life of up to 40 years for its buildings and from 3–12 years for its equipment.

The **residual value** of a fixed asset is the estimated value of the asset at the end of its useful life. It is estimated at the time the asset is placed into service. Residual value is sometimes referred to as *scrap value, salvage value,* or *trade-in value*.

The difference between a fixed asset's initial cost and its residual value is called the asset's **depreciable cost**. This is the asset's cost that is allocated over its useful life as depreciation expense. If a fixed asset has no residual value, then its entire cost should be allocated to depreciation.

To illustrate depreciation methods, assume **Exeter Company** purchased a new forklift on January 1 as follows:

Initial cost	$24,000
Expected useful life	5 years
Estimated residual value	$2,000

Exhibit 3 shows the relationship between depreciation expense and the forklift's initial cost, expected useful life, and estimated residual value.

Exhibit 3 Depreciation Expense

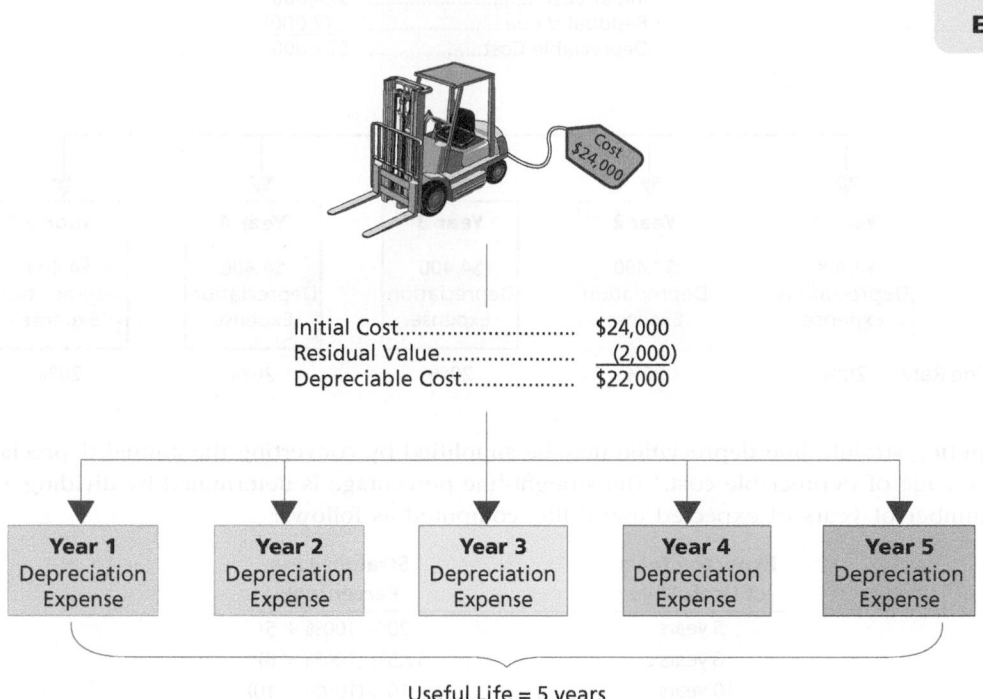

The three depreciation methods used most often are as follows:[3]

- Straight-line depreciation
- Units-of-activity depreciation
- Double-declining-balance depreciation

It is not necessary for a company to use only one method of computing depreciation for all of its fixed assets. For example, a company may use one method for depreciating equipment and another method for depreciating buildings.

Straight-Line Method

The **straight-line method** provides for the same amount of depreciation expense for each year of the asset's useful life. The annual straight-line depreciation for **Exeter**'s forklift is $4,400, computed as follows:

$$\text{Annual Depreciation} = \frac{\text{Cost} - \text{Residual Value}}{\text{Useful Life}} = \frac{\$24,000 - \$2,000}{5 \text{ Years}} = \$4,400$$

The straight-line method reports the same amount of depreciation expense each year, as illustrated in Exhibit 4.

---

[3] Another method not often used today, called the *sum-of-the-years-digits method*, is described and illustrated in an online appendix located at www.cengage.com.

Exhibit 4   Straight-Line Method

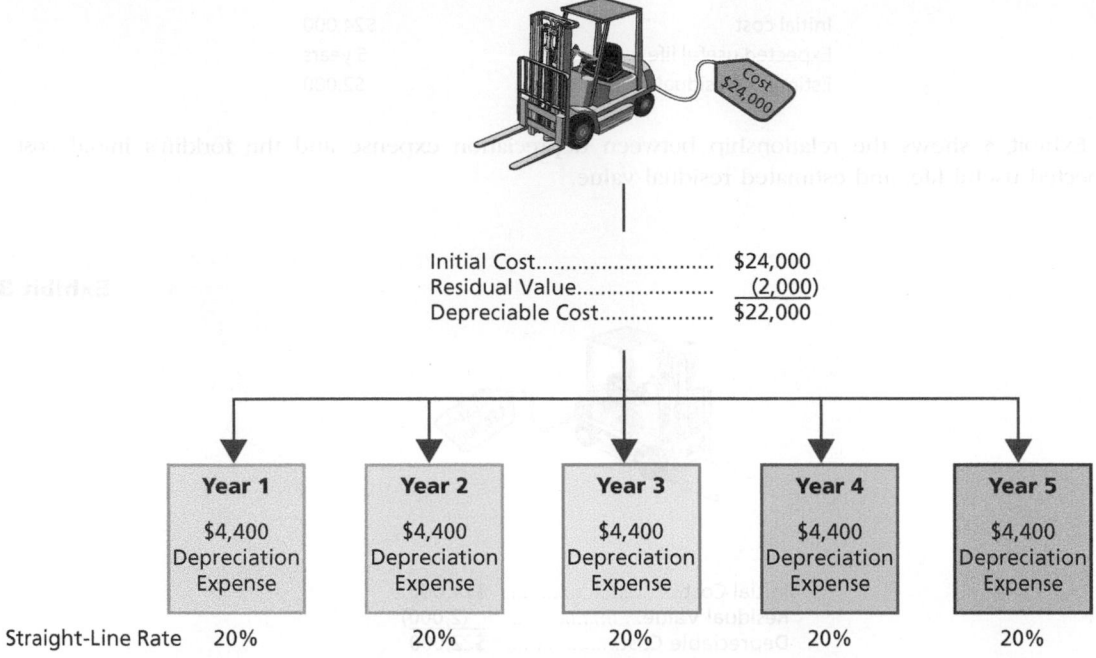

Computing straight-line depreciation may be simplified by converting the annual depreciation to a percentage of depreciable cost.[4] The straight-line percentage is determined by dividing 100% by the number of years of expected useful life, computed as follows:

Expected Years of Useful Life	Straight-Line Percentage
5 years	20% (100% ÷ 5)
8 years	12.5% (100% ÷ 8)
10 years	10% (100% ÷ 10)
20 years	5% (100% ÷ 20)
25 years	4% (100% ÷ 25)

For the preceding equipment, the annual depreciation of $4,400 can be computed by multiplying the depreciable cost of $22,000 by 20% (100% ÷ 5).

Depreciation of the forklift for the first year using the straight-line method is recorded as follows:

A   =   L   +   E
–   – Exp

| | Dec. 31 | Depreciation Expense—Forklift | 4,400 | |
| | | Accumulated Depreciation—Forklift | | 4,400 |

Accumulated depreciation accounts are called *contra accounts*, or *contra asset accounts*. This is because accumulated depreciation accounts are deducted from their related fixed asset accounts on the balance sheet. The difference between the fixed asset account and its related accumulated depreciation account is called the asset's book value or *net book value of the asset*.

[4] The depreciation rate may also be expressed as a fraction. For example, the annual straight-line rate for an asset with a three-year useful life is 1/3.

The book value of the forklift at the end of the first year is $19,600. It would be reported on the balance sheet as follows:

Equipment	$24,000
Accumulated depreciation	(4,400)
Book value	$19,600

As shown in Exhibit 5, as depreciation expense is recorded each year, the book value of the forklift will decrease.

Exhibit 5 Straight-Line Method: Depreciation Expense and Book Value

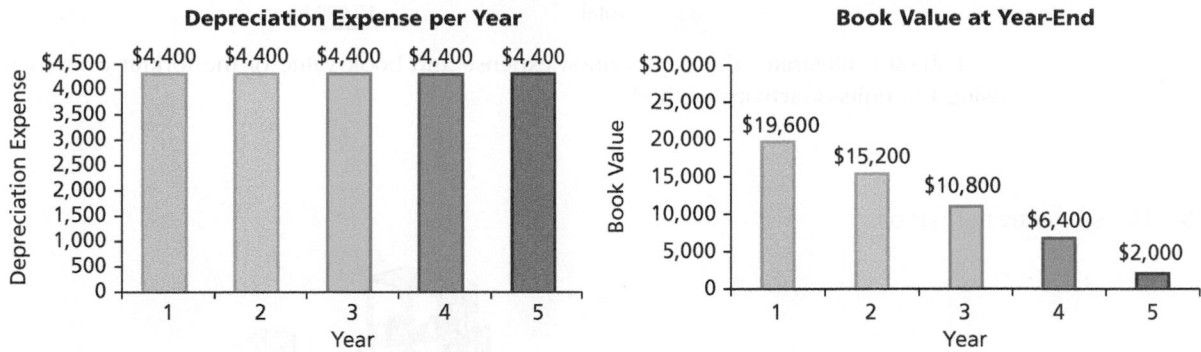

The straight-line method is simple to use. When an asset's revenues are about the same from period to period, straight-line depreciation provides a good matching of depreciation expense with the asset's revenues.

Units-of-Activity Method

The **units-of-activity method** provides the same amount of depreciation expense for each unit of activity of the asset. Depending on the asset, the units of activity can be expressed in terms of hours, miles driven, or quantity produced. For example, the unit of activity for a truck is normally expressed in miles driven. For manufacturing assets, the units of activity are often expressed as units of product. In this case, the units-of-activity method may be called the *units-of-production method* or *units-of-output method*.

The units-of-activity method is applied in the following two steps:

■ Step 1. Determine the depreciation per unit as follows:

$$\text{Depreciation per Unit} = \frac{\text{Cost} - \text{Residual Value}}{\text{Total Estimated Units of Activity}}$$

■ Step 2. Compute the depreciation expense as follows:

$$\text{Depreciation Expense} = \text{Depreciation per Unit} \times \text{Units of Activity for Period}$$

To illustrate, assume that **Exeter**'s forklift is estimated to have a useful life of 10,000 operating hours over the life of the asset. During the first year, the forklift was operated 2,100 hours. The units-of-activity depreciation for the year is $4,620, computed as follows:

■ Step 1. Determine the depreciation per hour as follows:

$$\text{Depreciation per Hour} = \frac{\text{Cost} - \text{Residual Value}}{\text{Total Estimated Units of Activity}} = \frac{\$24,000 - \$2,000}{10,000 \text{ Hours}} = \$2.20 \text{ per Hour}$$

■ Step 2. Compute the depreciation expense as follows:

$$\text{Depreciation Expense} = \text{Depreciation per Unit} \times \text{Units of Activity for Period}$$
$$= \$2.20 \text{ per Hour} \times 2,100 \text{ Hours} = \$4,620$$

Depreciation for the first year using the units-of-activity method is recorded as follows:

$$\underset{-}{\underline{A}} = L + \underset{- \text{ Exp}}{\underline{E}}$$

Dec. 31	Depreciation Expense—Forklift		4,620	
	Accumulated Depreciation—Forklift			4,620

Assume that during its five-year life, the forklift was used as follows:

Year 1	2,100 hours
Year 2	1,500
Year 3	2,600
Year 4	1,800
Year 5	2,000
Total	10,000 hours

Exhibit 6 illustrates the depreciation expense and book value of the forklift over its five-year life using the units-of-activity method.

Exhibit 6 Units-of-Activity Method

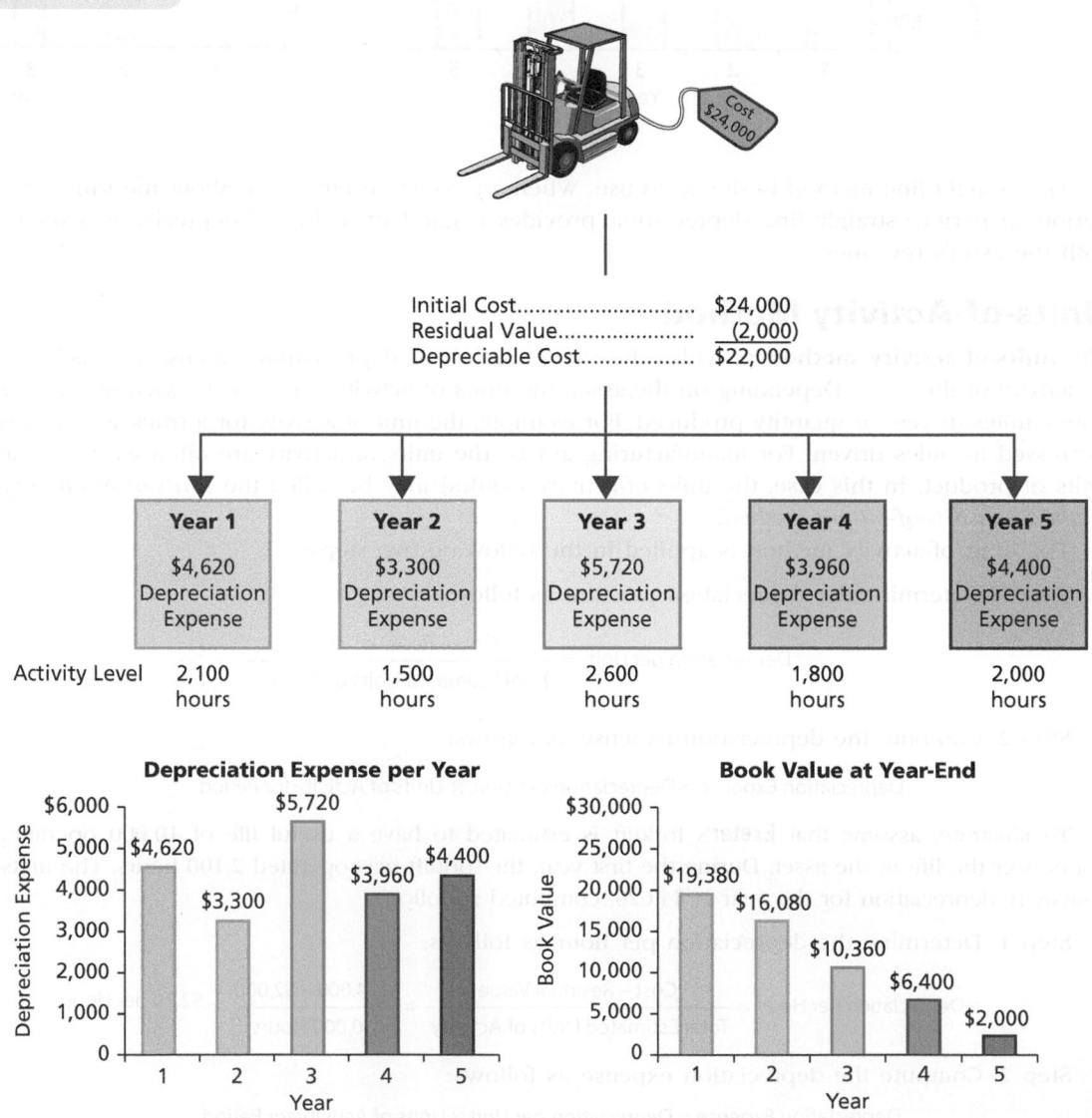

As shown in Exhibit 6, depreciation expense and book value vary each year depending on the hours the forklift is operated.

The units-of-activity method is often used when a fixed asset's use varies from year to year. In such cases, the units-of-activity method matches depreciation expense with the asset's revenues.

Double-Declining-Balance Method

The **double-declining-balance method** provides for a declining periodic expense over the expected useful life of the asset. The double-declining-balance method is applied in the following three steps:

- Step 1. Determine the straight-line percentage, using the expected useful life.
- Step 2. Determine the double-declining-balance rate by multiplying the straight-line rate (from Step 1) by 2.
- Step 3. Compute the depreciation expense by multiplying the double-declining-balance rate (from Step 2) times the book value of the asset.

To illustrate, the purchase of **Exeter**'s forklift is used to compute double-declining-balance depreciation. For the first year, the depreciation is $9,600, computed as follows:

- Step 1. Straight-line percentage = 20% (100% ÷ 5)
- Step 2. Double-declining-balance rate = 40% (20% × 2)
- Step 3. Depreciation expense = $9,600 ($24,000 × 40%)

Depreciation of the forklift for the first year using the double-declining-balance method is recorded as follows:

| Dec. 31 | Depreciation Expense—Forklift | 9,600 | |
| | Accumulated Depreciation—Forklift | | 9,600 |

A = L + E
− − Exp

At the beginning of the first year, the book value of the equipment is its initial cost of $24,000. After the first year, the book value declines, and thus, the depreciation also declines. The double-declining-balance depreciation for the full five-year life of the forklift is as follows:

Year	Cost	Acc. Dep. at Beginning of Year	Book Value at Beginning of Year	Double-Declining-Balance Rate	Depreciation for Year	Book Value at End of Year
1	$24,000		$24,000.00 ×	40%	$9,600.00	$14,400.00
2	24,000	$ 9,600.00	14,400.00 ×	40%	5,760.00	8,640.00
3	24,000	15,360.00	8,640.00 ×	40%	3,456.00	5,184.00
4	24,000	18,816.00	5,184.00 ×	40%	2,073.60	3,110.40
5	24,000	20,889.60	3,110.40	—	1,110.40	2,000.00

When the double-declining-balance method is used, the estimated residual value is *not* considered. However, the asset should not be depreciated below its estimated residual value. In the preceding example, the estimated residual value was $2,000. Therefore, the depreciation for the fifth year is $1,110.40 ($3,110.40 − $2,000.00) instead of $1,244.16 (40% × $3,110.40).

Exhibit 7 illustrates the depreciation expense and book value of the forklift over its five-year life using the double-declining-balance method. As shown in Exhibit 7, the double-declining-balance method has higher depreciation in the first year of the asset's life, followed by declining depreciation amounts. For this reason, the double-declining-balance method is called an **accelerated depreciation method**.

Exhibit 7 Double-Declining-Balance Method

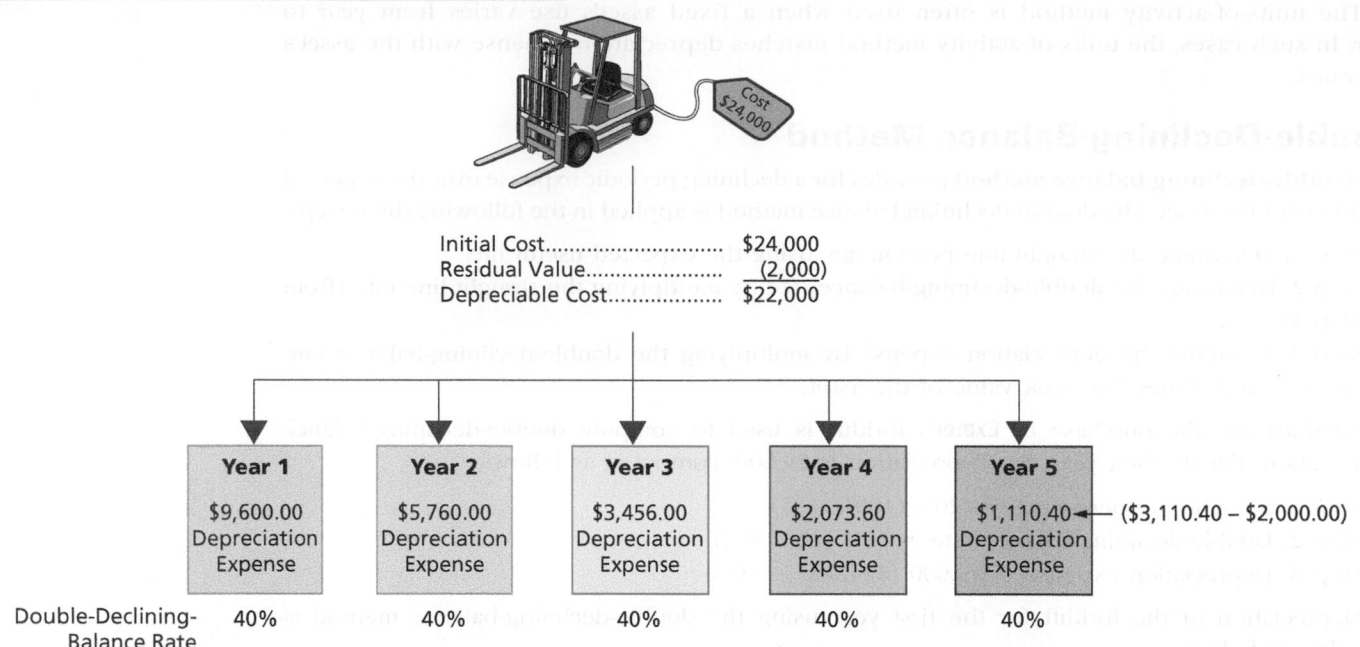

Initial Cost.............................. $24,000
Residual Value..................... (2,000)
Depreciable Cost.................. $22,000

Year 1	Year 2	Year 3	Year 4	Year 5
$9,600.00 Depreciation Expense	$5,760.00 Depreciation Expense	$3,456.00 Depreciation Expense	$2,073.60 Depreciation Expense	$1,110.40 ◄— ($3,110.40 – $2,000.00) Depreciation Expense

Double-Declining-
Balance Rate   40%   40%   40%   40%   40%

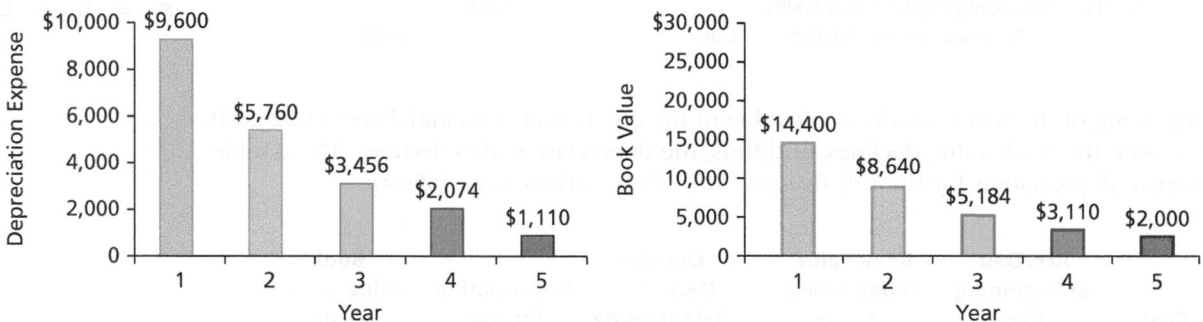

Revenues generated by an asset are often greater in the early years of its use than in later years. In such cases, the double-declining-balance method provides a good matching of depreciation expense with the asset's revenues.

Comparing Depreciation Methods

The three depreciation methods are summarized in Exhibit 8. All three methods allocate a portion of the total cost of an asset to an accounting period, while never depreciating an asset below its residual value.

Exhibit 8	Method	Useful Life	Depreciable Cost	Depreciation Rate	Depreciation Expense
Summary of Depreciation Methods	Straight-line	Years	Cost less residual value	Straight-line rate*	Constant
	Units-of-activity	Units of activity	Cost less residual value	$\dfrac{\text{Cost} - \text{Residual value}}{\text{Total units of activity}}$	Variable
	Double-declining-balance	Years	Declining book value, but not below residual value	Straight-line rate* × 2	Declining

*Straight-line rate = (100% ÷ Useful life)

The straight-line method provides for the same periodic amounts of depreciation expense over the life of the asset. The units-of-activity method provides for periodic amounts of depreciation expense that vary, depending on the amount the asset is used. The double-declining-balance method provides for a higher depreciation amount in the first year of the asset's use, followed by declining amounts.

Exhibit 9 illustrates depreciation expense for each depreciation method over the five-year life of the forklift.

	Depreciation Expense			**Exhibit 9**
Year	**Straight-Line Method**	**Units-of-Activity Method**	**Double-Declining-Balance Method**	Comparing Depreciation Methods
1	$ 4,400*	$ 4,620 ($2.20 × 2,100 hrs.)	$ 9,600.00 ($24,000 × 40%)	
2	4,400	3,300 ($2.20 × 1,500 hrs.)	5,760.00 ($14,400 × 40%)	
3	4,400	5,720 ($2.20 × 2,600 hrs.)	3,456.00 ($8,640 × 40%)	
4	4,400	3,960 ($2.20 × 1,800 hrs.)	2,073.60 ($5,184 × 40%)	
5	4,400	4,400 ($2.20 × 2,000 hrs.)	1,110.40**	
Total	$22,000	$22,000	$22,000.00	

*$4,400 = ($24,000 – $2,000) ÷ 5 years

**$3,110.40 – $2,000.00 because the equipment cannot be depreciated below its residual value of $2,000.

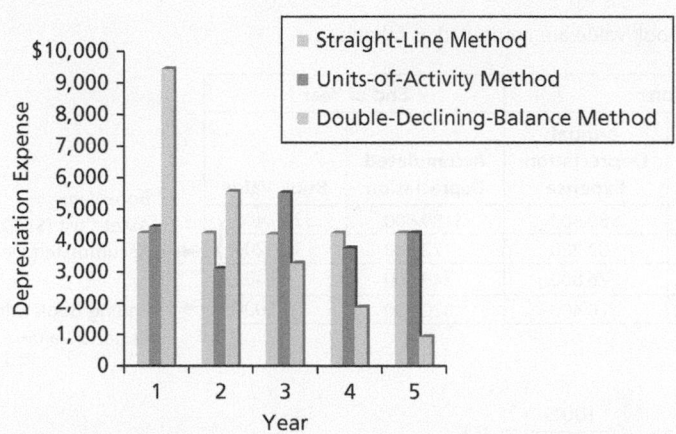

Check Up Corner 9-1 Fixed Assets: Depreciation

On the first day of the year, Firefall Company acquired equipment for use in operations at a cost of $340,000. The equipment was expected to have a useful life of four years or 1,000 hours, and a residual value of $20,000. The equipment was used for 280 hours during the first year, 260 hours during the second year, 240 hours during the third year, and 220 hours during the fourth year.

Determine the annual depreciation expense in each year and the book value of the equipment at the end of each year under the:

1. straight-line method

2. units-of-activity method

3. double-declining-balance method

Solution:

1. Straight-Line Method:

$$\text{Annual Depreciation Expense} = \frac{\text{Cost} - \text{Residual Value}}{\text{Useful Life}} = \frac{\$340,000 - \$20,000}{4 \text{ Years}} = \$80,000$$

(Continued)

The straight-line percentage is computed as follows:

$$\text{Straight-Line Percentage} = \frac{100\%}{4 \text{ Years}} = 25\%$$

Annual depreciation expense and end-of-year book value are computed as follows:

Year	Straight-Line Percentage	x	Depreciable Cost	=	Annual Depreciation Expense	Accumulated Depreciation	Book Value
			Calculation of Depreciation			**End of Year**	
1	25%	x	$320,000	=	$80,000	$ 80,000	$260,000
2	25%	x	320,000	=	80,000	160,000	180,000
3	25%	x	320,000	=	80,000	240,000	100,000
4	25%	x	320,000	=	80,000	320,000	20,000

Book Value =
Asset Cost ($340,000) –
Accumulated Depreciation

Ending Book Value =
Residual Value

2. Units-of-Activity Method:

$$\frac{\text{Depreciation per}}{\text{Hour of Use}} = \frac{\text{Cost} - \text{Residual Value}}{\text{Total Number of Hours}} = \frac{\$340,000 - \$20,000}{1,000 \text{ Hours}} = \$320 \text{ per Hour}$$

Annual depreciation expense and end-of-year book value are computed as follows:

Year	Depreciation per Hour of Use	x	Total Hours of Activity Used	=	Annual Depreciation Expense	Accumulated Depreciation	Book Value
			Calculation of Depreciation			**End of Year**	
1	$320	x	280	=	$89,600	$ 89,600	$250,400
2	320	x	260	=	83,200	172,800	167,200
3	320	x	240	=	76,800	249,600	90,400
4	320	x	220	=	70,400	320,000	20,000

Book Value =
Asset Cost ($340,000) –
Accumulated Depreciation

Ending Book Value =
Residual Value

3. Double-Declining-Balance Method:

$$\text{Straight-Line Percentage} = \frac{100\%}{4 \text{ Years}} = 25\%$$

$$\text{Double-Declining-Balance Rate} = 2 \times 25\% = 50\%$$

Annual depreciation expense and end-of-year book value are computed as follows:

Year	Book Value at Beginning of Year	x	Double-Declining-Balance Rate	=	Annual Depreciation Expense	Accumulated Depreciation	Book Value
			Calculation of Depreciation			**End of Year**	
1	$340,000	x	50%	=	$170,000	$170,000	$170,000
2	170,000	x	50%	=	85,000	255,000	85,000
3	85,000	x	50%	=	42,500	297,500	42,500
4	42,500		not applicable		22,500	320,000	20,000

Book Value =
Asset Cost ($340,000) –
Accumulated Depreciation

Ending Book Value =
Residual Value

Final Year Depreciation Expense = Book Value at Beginning of
Final Year – Residual Value
= $42,500 – $20,000

Check Up Corner

Partial-Year Depreciation

A fixed asset may be purchased and placed in service other than the first month of an accounting period. In such cases, depreciation is prorated based on the month the asset is placed in service. For example, assume an asset is placed in service on March 1. For an accounting period ending December 31, depreciation would be computed (prorated) for 10 months (March 1 to December 31).

Assets may also be placed in service other than the first day of a month. In such cases, assets placed in service during the first half of a month are normally treated as having been purchased on the first day of *that* month. Likewise, asset purchases during the second half of a month are treated as having been purchased on the first day of the *next* month.

Straight-Line Method Under the straight-line method, depreciation is prorated based on the number of months the asset is in service. To illustrate, assume that **Exeter Company** purchased the forklift on October 1 instead of January 1. The first-year depreciation would be based upon three months (October, November, December). First-year depreciation would be $1,100, computed as follows:

Annual Depreciation = ($24,000 – $2,000) ÷ 5 years = $4,400

First-Year Depreciation = $4,400 × (3 ÷ 12) = $1,100

Units-of-Activity Method The units-of-activity method computes depreciation expense using an activity rate and the activity level for the period. To illustrate, assume that **Exeter** purchased the forklift on October 1 instead of January 1. Assume that during October 1 to December 31, the forklift was used for 400 hours. First-year depreciation would be $880, computed as follows:

Depreciation per Hour = ($24,000 – $2,000) ÷ 10,000 Hours = $2.20 per Hour

First-Year Depreciation = $2.20 per Hour × 400 Hours = $880

Double-Declining-Balance Method Like straight-line depreciation, if an asset is used for only part of a year, the annual double-declining-balance depreciation is prorated based on the number of months the asset is in service. To illustrate, assume that **Exeter**'s forklift was purchased and placed into service on October 1 instead of January 1. First-year depreciation would be based upon three months (October, November, December). First-year depreciation would be $2,400, computed as follows:

Double-Declining-Balance Rate = (100 ÷ 5) × 2 = 40%

First-Year Annual Depreciation = $24,000 × 40% = $9,600

First-Year Partial Depreciation = $9,600 × (3 ÷ 12) = $2,400

The second-year depreciation would be computed by multiplying the book value on January 1 of the second year by the double-declining-balance rate. To illustrate, assume that Exeter purchased the forklift on October 1 and that $2,400 partial depreciation was recorded on December 31. The book value on January 1 of the second year is $21,600 ($24,000 – $2,400). The second-year depreciation would then be $8,640, computed as follows:

Second-Year Annual Depreciation = $21,600 × 40% = $8,640

Revising Depreciation Estimates

Estimates of residual values and useful lives of fixed assets may change due to abnormal wear and tear or obsolescence. When new estimates are made by management, they are used to determine the depreciation expense in future periods. The depreciation expense recorded in earlier years is not affected.[5]

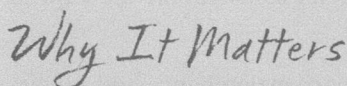

Tax Return Depreciation

The Internal Revenue Code uses the Modified Cost Recovery System (MACRS) to compute depreciation for tax purposes. Depreciation under MACRS is similar to that computed under the double-declining-balance method. MACRS is beneficial for tax purposes since depreciation is accelerated, thus creating faster tax deductions. Therefore, most companies use straight-line depreciation for their financial statements and MACRS for their tax accounting. This is a major reason for accounting and tax income to differ.

[5] *FASB Accounting Standards Codification*, Section 250-10-05.

To illustrate, assume the following data for a machine that was purchased on January 1:

Initial machine cost	$140,000
Expected useful life	5 years
Estimated residual value	$10,000
Annual depreciation using the straight-line method	
[($140,000 – $10,000) ÷ 5 years]	$26,000

At the end of the second year, the machine's book value (undepreciated cost) is $88,000, computed as follows:

Initial machine cost	$140,000
Accumulated depreciation ($26,000 per year × 2 years)	(52,000)
Book value (undepreciated cost), end of second year	$ 88,000

At the beginning of the third year, the company estimates that the machine's remaining useful life is eight years (instead of three) and that its residual value is $8,000 (instead of $10,000). The depreciation expense for each of the remaining eight years is $10,000, computed as follows:

$$\text{Revised Depreciation Expense} = \frac{\text{Book Value} - \text{Revised Residual Value}}{\text{Revised Remaining Useful Life}} = \frac{\$88,000 - \$8,000}{8\,\text{Years}} = \$10,000$$

Exhibit 10 shows the book value of the asset over its original and revised lives. After the depreciation is revised at the end of the second year, book value declines at a slower rate. At the end of the tenth year, the book value reaches the revised residual value of $8,000.

Exhibit 10

Book Value of Asset with Change in Estimate

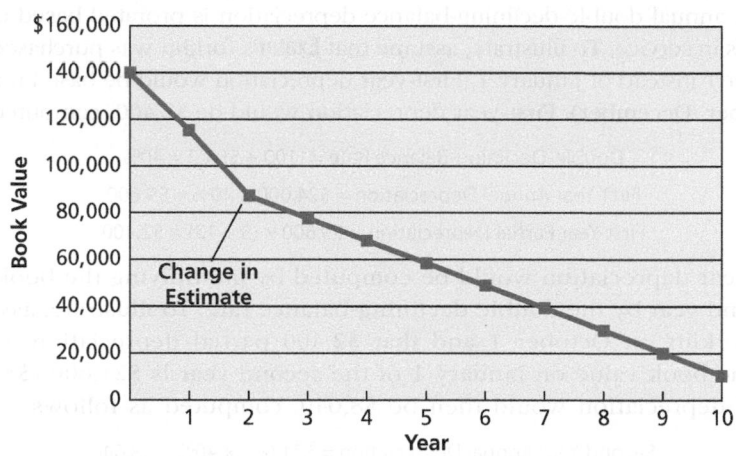

Repair and Improvements

IFRS

See Appendix C for more information.

Once a fixed asset has been acquired and placed into service, costs may be incurred for ordinary maintenance and repairs. In addition, costs may be incurred for improving an asset or for extraordinary repairs that extend the asset's useful life. Costs that benefit only the current period are called **revenue expenditures**. Costs that improve the asset or extend its useful life are **capital expenditures**.

Ordinary Maintenance and Repairs Costs related to the ordinary maintenance and repairs of a fixed asset are recorded as an expense of the current period. Such expenditures are *revenue expenditures* and are recorded as increases to Repairs and Maintenance Expense. For example, $300 paid for a tune-up of a delivery truck is recorded as follows:

A = L + E
–   – Exp

Repairs and Maintenance Expense	300	
Cash		300

Extraordinary Repairs After a fixed asset has been placed into service, costs may be incurred to extend the asset's useful life. For example, the engine of a forklift that is near the end of its useful life may be overhauled at a cost of $4,500, extending its useful life by eight years. Such costs are *capital expenditures* and are recorded as a decrease in an accumulated depreciation account. In the case of the forklift, the expenditure is recorded as follows:

Accumulated Depreciation—Forklift	4,500	
Cash		4,500

A = L + E
+ −

Because the forklift's remaining useful life has changed, depreciation for the forklift will also change based on the new book value and useful life of the forklift.

Asset Improvements After a fixed asset has been placed into service, costs may be incurred to improve the asset. For example, the service value of a delivery truck might be improved by adding a $5,500 hydraulic lift to allow for easier and quicker loading of cargo. Such costs are *capital expenditures* and are recorded as increases to the fixed asset account. In the case of the hydraulic lift, the expenditure is recorded as follows:

Delivery Truck	5,500	
Cash		5,500

A = L + E
+ −

Because the cost of the delivery truck has increased, depreciation for the truck will also change over its remaining useful life.

The accounting for revenue and capital expenditures is summarized in Exhibit 11.

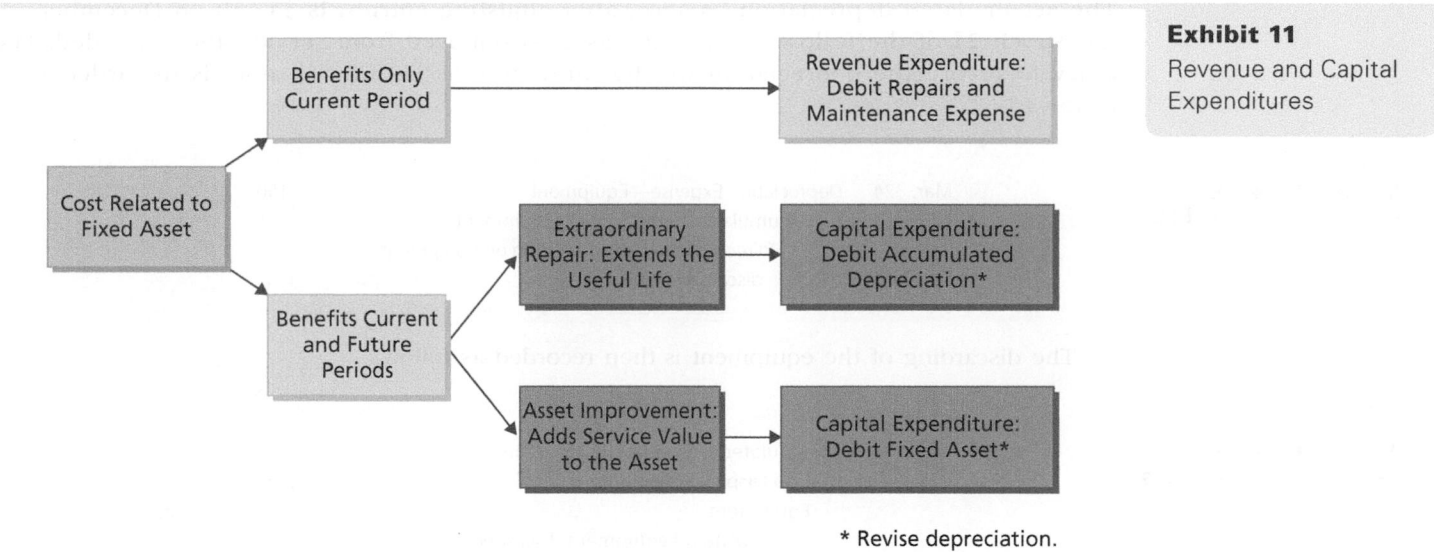

Exhibit 11
Revenue and Capital Expenditures

* Revise depreciation.

Capital Crime

One of the largest accounting frauds in history involved the improper accounting for maintenance expenditures. World-Com, the second largest telecommunications company in the United States at the time, improperly treated maintenance expenditures on its telecommunications network as capital expenditures. As a result, the company had to restate its prior years' earnings downward by nearly $4 billion to correct this error. The company declared bankruptcy within months of disclosing the error, and the CEO was sentenced to 25 years in prison.

Objective 3

Journalize the disposal of fixed assets.

Disposal of Fixed Assets

Fixed assets that are no longer useful may be discarded or sold.[6] In such cases, the fixed asset is removed from the accounts. Just because a fixed asset is fully depreciated, however, does not mean that it should be removed from the accounts.

If a fixed asset is still being used, its cost and accumulated depreciation should remain in the ledger even if the asset is fully depreciated. If the asset was removed from the ledger, the accounts would contain no evidence of their continued existence. In addition, cost and accumulated depreciation data on such assets are often needed for property tax and income tax reports.

Discarding Fixed Assets

If a fixed asset is no longer used and has no residual value, it is discarded. For example, assume that a fixed asset is fully depreciated, has no residual value, and is discarded. The discarded asset and its accumulated depreciation are removed from the accounts and ledger.

To illustrate, assume that equipment acquired at a cost of $25,000 is fully depreciated. On February 14, the equipment is discarded. The entry to record the discard is as follows:

A = L + E
+ –

Feb. 14	Accumulated Depreciation—Equipment	25,000	
	Equipment		25,000
	To write off equipment discarded.		

If an asset has not been fully depreciated, depreciation should be recorded before removing the asset from the accounting records. To illustrate, assume that equipment costing $6,000 with no estimated residual value is depreciated at a straight-line rate of 10%. The accumulated depreciation balance, after adjusting entries, is $4,650 on December 31. On March 24 of the following year, the asset is removed from service and discarded. The entry to record the depreciation for the three months before the asset is discarded is as follows:

A = L + E
–   – Exp

Mar. 24	Depreciation Expense—Equipment	150	
	Accumulated Depreciation—Equipment		150
	To record current depreciation on equipment		
	discarded ($600 × 3/12).		

The discarding of the equipment is then recorded as follows:

A = L + E
+ –   – Loss

Mar. 24	Accumulated Depreciation—Equipment	4,800	
	Loss on Disposal of Equipment	1,200	
	Equipment		6,000
	To write off equipment discarded.		

The loss of $1,200 is recorded because the book value of the asset ($6,000 – $4,800) is greater than the amount received for the asset ($0). Losses on the discarding of fixed assets are reported on the income statement.

---

[6] The accounting for the exchange of fixed assets is described and illustrated in the appendix at the end of this chapter.

Selling Fixed Assets

The entry to record the sale of a fixed asset is similar to the entry for discarding an asset. The only difference is that the receipt of cash is also recorded. If the selling price is more than the book value of the asset, a gain is recorded. If the selling price is less than the book value, a loss is recorded.

To illustrate, assume that equipment is purchased at a cost of $10,000 with no estimated residual value and is depreciated at a straight-line rate of 10%. The equipment is sold for cash on October 12 of the eighth year of its use. The balance of the accumulated depreciation account as of the preceding December 31 is $7,000. The entry to update the depreciation for the nine months of the current year is as follows:

Oct. 12	Depreciation Expense—Equipment	750	
	Accumulated Depreciation—Equipment		750
	To record current depreciation on		
	equipment sold ($10,000 × $9/12$ × 10%).		

$$A = L + E$$
$$- \qquad - \text{Exp}$$

After the current depreciation is recorded, the book value of the asset is $2,250 ($10,000 − $7,750). The entries to record the sale, assuming three different selling prices, are as follows:

Sold at book value, for $2,250. No gain or loss.

Oct. 12	Cash	2,250	
	Accumulated Depreciation—Equipment	7,750	
	Equipment		10,000

$$A = L + E$$
$$+ -$$

Sold below book value, for $1,000. Loss of $1,250.

Oct. 12	Cash	1,000	
	Accumulated Depreciation—Equipment	7,750	
	Loss on Sale of Equipment	1,250	
	Equipment		10,000

$$A = L + E$$
$$+ - \qquad - \text{Loss}$$

Sold above book value, for $2,800. Gain of $550.

Oct. 12	Cash	2,800	
	Accumulated Depreciation—Equipment	7,750	
	Equipment		10,000
	Gain on Sale of Equipment		550

$$A = L + E$$
$$+ - \qquad + \text{Gain}$$

Why It Matters

Downsizing

Management may decide to sell a fixed asset when it is perceived to no longer meet business objectives. This can happen when the strategy of the business changes or the business is downsizing operations. For example, over a recent three-year period, **Ruby Tuesday (RT)**, a national restaurant chain, sold stores and equipment at a book value of $30 million for cash proceeds of $34 million, resulting in a $4 million gain. These fixed assets were sold in order to focus on more profitable restaurants.

Check Up Corner 9-2 | Selling Fixed Assets

On the first day of the year, Firefall Company purchased equipment at a cost of $340,000. The equipment was expected to have a useful life of four years, a residual value of $20,000, and is depreciated at a straight-line rate of 25%. Firefall sold the equipment at the beginning of the fourth year when the balance in the accumulated depreciation account was $240,000. Journalize the entry to record the sale if the equipment was sold for:

a. $95,000

b. $105,000

Solution:

a. Equipment sold for $95,000:

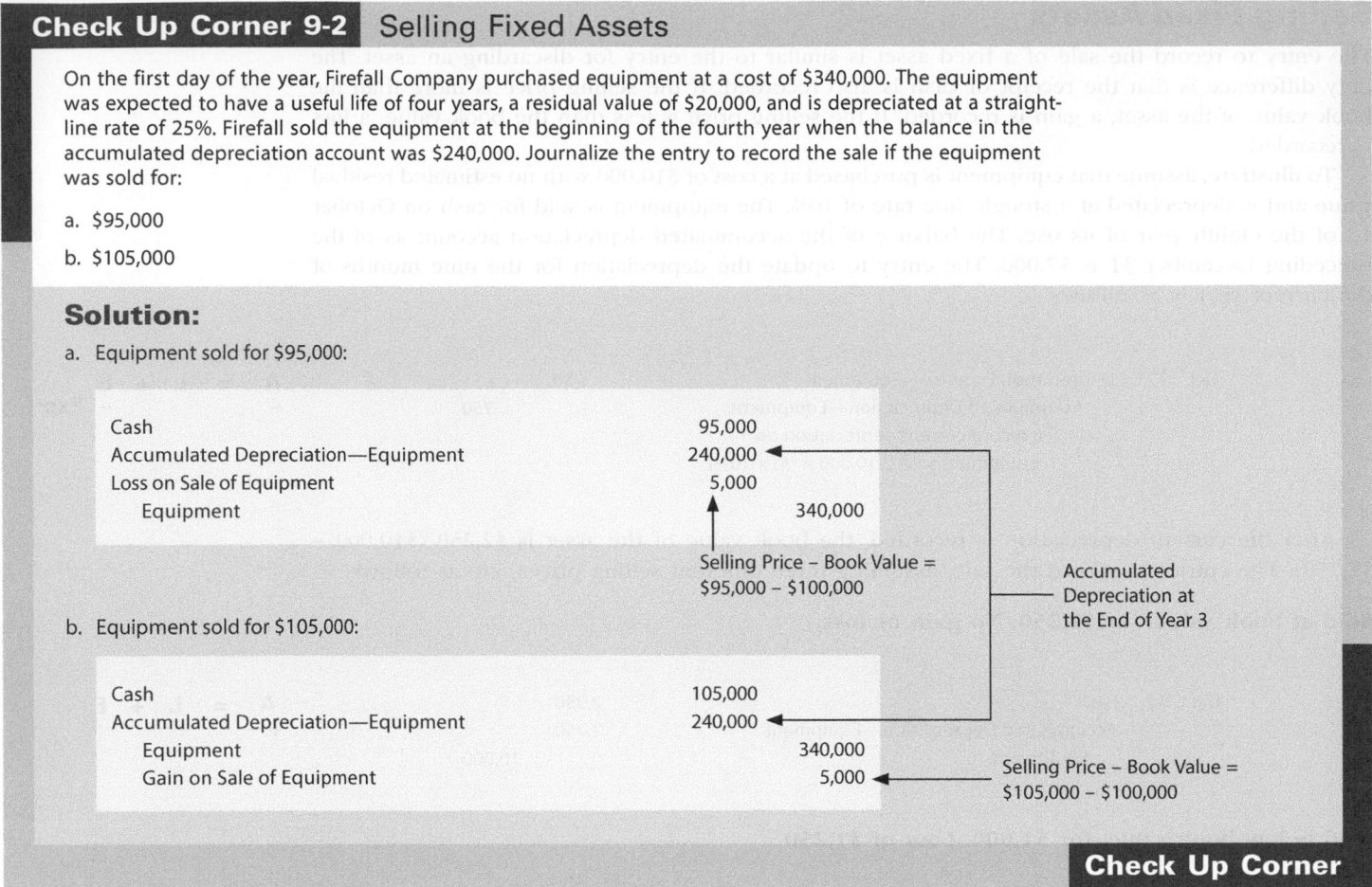

Cash	95,000	
Accumulated Depreciation—Equipment	240,000	
Loss on Sale of Equipment	5,000	
Equipment		340,000

Selling Price – Book Value =
$95,000 – $100,000

Accumulated Depreciation at the End of Year 3

b. Equipment sold for $105,000:

Cash	105,000	
Accumulated Depreciation—Equipment	240,000	
Equipment		340,000
Gain on Sale of Equipment		5,000

Selling Price – Book Value =
$105,000 – $100,000

Check Up Corner

Objective 4

Describe the accounting for natural resources, including the journal entry for depletion.

Natural Resources

Some businesses own natural resources such as timber, minerals, or oil. The characteristics of natural resources are as follows:

- **Naturally Occurring:** An asset that is created through natural growth or naturally through the passage of time. For example, timber is a natural resource that naturally grows over time.
- **Removed for Sale:** The asset is consumed by removing it from its land source. For example, timber is removed for use when it is harvested, and minerals are removed when they are mined.
- **Removed and Sold over More Than One Year:** The natural resource is removed and sold over a period of more than one year.

Natural resources are classified as a type of fixed asset. The cost of a natural resource includes the cost of obtaining and preparing it for use. For example, legal fees incurred in purchasing a natural resource are included as part of its cost.

As natural resources are harvested or mined and then sold, a portion of their cost is debited to an expense account called **Depletion Expense**.

Depletion is determined as follows:[7]

■ Step 1. Determine the depletion rate as follows:

$$\text{Depletion Rate} = \frac{\text{Cost of Resource}}{\text{Estimated Total Units of Resource}}$$

■ Step 2. Multiply the depletion rate by the quantity removed from the resource during the period.

$$\text{Depletion Expense} = \text{Depletion Rate} \times \text{Quantity Removed}$$

To illustrate, assume that Karst Company purchased mining rights as follows:

Cost of mineral deposit	$400,000
Estimated total units of resource	1,000,000 tons
Tons mined during year	90,000 tons

The depletion expense of $36,000 for the year is computed as follows:

$$\text{Step 1. Depletion Rate} = \frac{\text{Cost of Resource}}{\text{Estimated Total Units of Resource}} = \frac{\$400,000}{1,000,000 \text{ Tons}} = \$0.40 \text{ per Ton}$$

Step 2. Depletion Expense = $0.40 per Ton × 90,000 Tons = $36,000

The adjusting entry to record the depletion is as follows:

Dec. 31	Depletion Expense	36,000	
	Accumulated Depletion		36,000
	Depletion of mineral deposit.		

$$\begin{array}{l} A = L + E \\ - \qquad\qquad - \text{Exp} \end{array}$$

Like the accumulated depreciation account, Accumulated Depletion is a contra asset account. It is reported on the balance sheet as a deduction from the cost of the mineral deposit.

Check Up Corner 9-3 Natural Resources

Caldwell Mining Co. acquired mineral rights for $126,000,000. The mineral deposit is estimated at 42,000,000 tons. During the current year, 3,800,000 tons were mined and sold.

a. What is the depletion rate per ton?

b. Determine the amount of depletion expense for the current year.

c. Journalize the adjusting entry to recognize depletion expense at the end of the year.

Solution:

a. $$\text{Depletion Rate} = \frac{\text{Cost of Resource}}{\text{Estimated Total Units of Resource}} = \frac{\$126,000,000}{42,000,000 \text{ Tons}} = \$3.00 \text{ per Ton}$$

b. Depletion Expense = Depletion Rate × Quantity Removed
   = $3.00 per Ton × 3,800,000 Tons
   = $11,400,000

c.

Depletion Expense	11,400,000	
Accumulated Depletion		11,400,000

Check Up Corner

---

[7] We assume that there is no significant residual value after all the natural resource is removed.

Objective 5

Describe the accounting for intangible assets, such as patents, copyrights, and goodwill.

IFRS

See Appendix C for more information.

Intangible Assets

Long-term assets that are used in the operations of the business, but do not exist physically, are called intangible assets. **Intangible assets** may be acquired through innovative, creative activities or from purchasing the rights from another company. Examples of intangible assets include patents, copyrights, trademarks, and goodwill.

The accounting for intangible assets is similar to that for fixed assets. The major issues are:

- Determining the initial cost.
- Determining the **amortization**, which is the amount of cost to transfer to expense.

Amortization results from the passage of time or a decline in the usefulness of the intangible asset.

Patents

Manufacturers may acquire exclusive rights to produce and sell goods with one or more unique features. Such rights are granted by **patents**, which the federal government issues to inventors. These rights continue in effect for 20 years. A business may purchase patent rights from others, or it may obtain patents developed by its own research and development.

The initial cost of a purchased patent, including any legal fees, is debited to an asset account. This cost is written off, or amortized, over the years of the patent's expected useful life. The expected useful life of a patent may be less than its legal life. For example, a patent may become worthless due to changing technology or consumer tastes.

Patent amortization is normally computed using the straight-line method. The amortization is recorded by debiting an amortization expense account and crediting the patents account. A separate contra asset account is usually *not* used for intangible assets.

To illustrate, assume that at the beginning of its fiscal year, a company acquires patent rights for $100,000. Although the patent will not expire for 14 years, its remaining useful life is estimated as five years. The adjusting entry to amortize the patent at the end of the year is as follows:

A = L + E
−   − Exp

Dec.	31	Amortization Expense—Patents	20,000	
		Patents		20,000
		Patent amortization ($100,000 ÷ 5).		

Some companies develop their own patents through research and development. In such cases, any *research and development costs* are recorded as current operating expenses in the period in which they are incurred. This accounting for research and development costs is justified on the basis that any future benefits from current research and development are highly uncertain.

Why It Matters

Facebook Value

The market value of **Facebook, Inc. (FB)** can be determined by multiplying the common stock outstanding by the market price per share. The market value of Facebook at the end of a recent year was $270.8 billion. The book value of stockholders' equity (net assets) of Facebook on the same date was $59.2 billion. The difference of $211.6 billion is largely due to the unrecognized intangible assets of Facebook. Intangible assets that are recognized for accounting purposes are only those that are supported by a business transaction. For Facebook, these include acquired goodwill, patents, technology, and trade name, which total only $20.7 billion. Technology companies, such as Facebook, will typically have large unrecognized intangible value beyond that recorded for accounting purposes.

Copyrights and Trademarks

The exclusive right to publish and sell a literary, artistic, or musical composition is granted by a **copyright**. Copyrights are issued by the federal government and extend for 70 years beyond the author's death. The costs of a copyright include all costs of creating the work plus any other costs of obtaining the copyright. A copyright that is purchased is recorded at the price paid for it. Copyrights are amortized over their estimated useful lives.

A **trademark** is a name, term, or symbol used to identify a business and its products. Under federal law, businesses can protect their trademarks by registering them for 10 years and renewing the registration for 10-year periods. Like a copyright, the legal costs of registering a trademark are recorded as an asset. Most businesses identify their registered trademarks with ® in their advertisements and on their products.

If a trademark is purchased from another business, its cost is recorded as an asset. In such cases, the cost of the trademark is considered to have an indefinite useful life. Thus, trademarks are not amortized. Instead, trademarks are reviewed periodically for impaired value. When a trademark is impaired, the trademark should be written down and a loss recognized.

McDonald's Corporation owns trademarks on "McDonald's" and the Golden Arches logo.

Link to McDonald's

Goodwill

Goodwill refers to an intangible asset of a business that is created from such favorable factors as location, product quality, reputation, and managerial skill. Goodwill allows a business to earn a greater rate of return than normal.

Generally accepted accounting principles (GAAP) allow goodwill to be recorded only if it is objectively determined by a transaction. An example of such a transaction is the purchase of a business at a price in excess of the fair value of its net assets (assets less liabilities). The excess is recorded as goodwill and reported as an intangible asset.

On a recent balance sheet, **McDonald's** reported goodwill of $2.3 billion. Most of McDonald's goodwill arises when it purchases existing restaurants from franchisees.

Link to McDonald's

International Connection

IFRS International Financial Reporting Standards (IFRS)

IFRS allow certain research and development (R&D) costs to be recorded as assets when incurred. Typically, R&D costs are classified as either research costs or development costs. If certain criteria are met, research costs can be recorded as an expense, while development costs can be recorded as an asset. This criterion includes such considerations as the company's intent to use or to sell the intangible asset. For example, **Volkswagen AG (VOW3)** reported capitalized development costs of €5 billion in a recent statement of financial position (balance sheet), where € represents the euro, the common currency of the European Economic Union.*

*Differences between U.S. GAAP and IFRS are further discussed and illustrated in Appendix C.

Unlike patents and copyrights, goodwill is not amortized. However, a loss should be recorded if the future prospects of the purchased firm become impaired. This loss would normally be disclosed in the "Other expense" section of the income statement.

To illustrate, assume that on December 31 FaceCard Company has determined that $250,000 of the goodwill created from the purchase of Electronic Systems is impaired. The entry to record the impairment is as follows:

A = L + E
− − Loss

Dec. 31	Loss from Impaired Goodwill	250,000	
	Goodwill		250,000
	Impaired goodwill.		

Link to McDonald's

McDonald's compares fair value to book (carrying) value to determine whether goodwill is impaired. In a recent annual report, McDonald's reported $39.9 million of losses from impaired goodwill related to its global restructuring activities.

Exhibit 12 shows common intangible asset disclosures for 500 large firms. Goodwill is the most often reported intangible asset. This is because goodwill arises from merger transactions, which are common.

Exhibit 12

Frequency of Intangible Asset Disclosures for 500 Firms

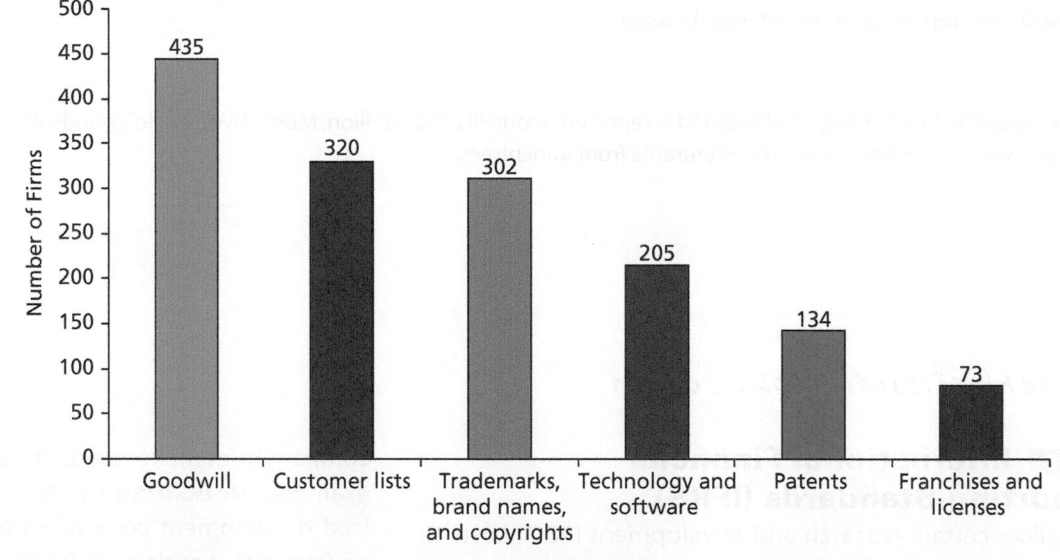

Note: Some firms have multiple disclosures.
Source: *Accounting Trends & Techniques,* 66th ed., American Institute of Certified Public Accountants, New York, 2012.

Exhibit 13 summarizes the characteristics of intangible assets.

Exhibit 13
Comparison of
Intangible Assets

Intangible Asset	Description	Amortization Period	Periodic Expense
Patent	Exclusive right to benefit from an innovation	Estimated useful life not to exceed legal life	Amortization expense
Copyright	Exclusive right to benefit from a literary, artistic, or musical composition	Estimated useful life not to exceed legal life	Amortization expense
Trademark	Exclusive use of a name, term, or symbol	None	Impairment loss if fair value less than carrying value (impaired)
Goodwill	Excess of purchase price of a business over the fair value of its net assets (assets – liabilities)	None	Impairment loss if fair value less than carrying value (impaired)

Pathways Challenge

This is Accounting!

Economic Activity

Verizon Communications Inc. (VZ) is the largest wireless service provider in the United States with over 114 million retail subscribers. To deliver its products and services, Verizon must have access to spectrum—the radio frequencies that carry sound, data, and video to wireless devices. However, spectrum is a limited resource that the Federal Communications Commission (FCC) licenses to businesses for a period of 10 years, subject to renewal. In a recent year, Verizon acquired almost $10 billion in wireless licenses.

Critical Thinking/Judgment

How should Verizon account for its acquisition of wireless licenses?
What is the useful life of a wireless license?
Should Verizon expense (amortize) the cost of its wireless licenses?

Suggested answer at end of chapter.

Check Up Corner 9-4 | Intangible Assets

Hollis Company acquired patents for $125,000 on July 1 of the current year. The technology supported by these patents was expected to have a 10-year life. In addition, goodwill from acquiring Logan Company in a prior year was impaired by $30,000 due to new competitive technologies.

a. Journalize the acquisition of the patent on July 1.

b. Journalize the adjusting entry for the amortization of the patent on December 31.

c. Journalize the adjusting entry for the impairment of goodwill on December 31.

Solution:

a.	July 1	Patents	125,000	
		Cash		125,000
b.	Dec. 31	Amortization Expense—Patents	6,250	
		Patents [($125,000 ÷ 10 years) × 1/2]		6,250
c.	Dec. 31	Loss from Impaired Goodwill	30,000	
		Goodwill		30,000

Amortization is normally computed using the straight-line method.

Check Up Corner

Objective 6

Describe how depreciation expense is reported on an income statement and prepare a balance sheet that includes fixed assets and intangible assets.

Financial Reporting for Long-Term Assets: Fixed and Intangible

On the income statement, depreciation and amortization expense should be reported separately or disclosed in a note. A description of the methods used in computing depreciation should also be reported.

On the balance sheet, each class of fixed assets should be disclosed on the face of the statement or in the notes. The related accumulated depreciation should also be disclosed, either by class or in total. The fixed assets may be shown at their *book value* (cost less accumulated depreciation), which can also be described as their *net* amount.

If there are many classes of fixed assets, a single amount may be presented on the balance sheet, supported by a note with a separate listing. Fixed assets may be reported under the more descriptive caption of property, plant, and equipment.

Intangible assets are usually reported on the balance sheet in a separate section following fixed assets. The balance of each class of intangible assets should be disclosed net of any amortization.

The balance sheet and note presentation for **McDonald's** fixed and intangible assets follow:

McDonald's Corporation
Balance Sheet
December 31
(in millions)

Assets

Property and equipment...	$ 34,443.4	
Accumulated depreciation..	(13,185.8)	
Net property and equipment..................................		21,257.6
Goodwill...		2,336.5
Note to Financial Statements:		
Land..		$ 5,465.0
Buildings and improvements...................................		25,207.1
Equipment and other...		3,771.3
Total cost..		$34,443.4

Source: Adapted from McDonald's Corporation's 2016 annual report.

Link to McDonald's

The cost and related accumulated depletion of mineral rights are normally shown as part of the "Fixed assets" section of the balance sheet. The mineral rights may be shown net of depletion on the face of the balance sheet. In such cases, a supporting note discloses the accumulated depletion.

Analysis for Decision Making

Fixed Asset Turnover Ratio

The **fixed asset turnover ratio** measures the number of sales dollars earned per dollar of fixed assets. The higher the ratio, the more efficiently a company is using its fixed assets in generating sales. The ratio is computed as follows:

$$\text{Fixed Asset Turnover Ratio} = \frac{\text{Sales}}{\text{Average Book Value of Fixed Assets}}$$

To illustrate, the following data (in millions) were taken from a recent financial statement of **McDonald's Corporation (MCD)**:

Sales	$24,621.9
Fixed assets (net):	
Beginning of year	21,257.6
End of year	23,117.6

McDonald's fixed asset turnover ratio for the year is computed as follows (rounded to one decimal place):

$$\text{Fixed Asset Turnover Ratio} = \frac{\text{Sales}}{\text{Average Book Value of Fixed Assets}}$$

$$= \frac{\$24,621.9}{(\$21,257.6 + \$23,117.6) \div 2}$$

$$= \frac{\$24,621.9}{\$22,187.6} = 1.1$$

Is 1.1 efficient? To answer this question, McDonald's fixed asset turnover ratio can be compared to other quick-service restaurant companies, as shown in Exhibit 14. **Yum! Brands (YUM)** operates KFC, Pizza Hut, and Taco Bell quick-service restaurants. The other restaurants are likely familiar by name.

Objective 7
Describe and illustrate the fixed asset turnover ratio to assess the efficiency of a company's use of its fixed assets.

Exhibit 14

Fixed Asset
Turnover: Selected
Quick-Service
Restaurants

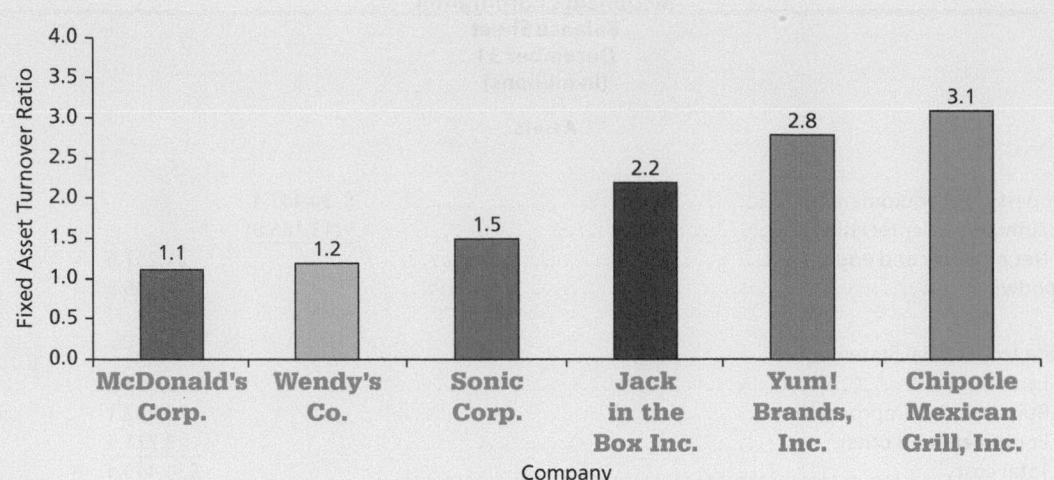

Differences in the fixed asset turnover between these companies can be due to a number of factors, including differences in both the average fixed asset book value and sales per restaurant. Explaining McDonald's low fixed asset turnover ratio relative to the other restaurants would require a deeper analysis into these factors.

Comparing companies within industries is useful because the fixed asset turnover ratio should be comparable within an industry. However, the fixed asset turnover ratio will vary across industries because of differences in how industries use fixed assets. For example, the fixed asset turnover ratio for selected companies in different industries is shown in Exhibit 15.

Exhibit 15

Fixed Asset
Turnover Ratio:
Various Industries

Company (Industry)	Fixed Asset Turnover Ratio
Disney (DIS) (entertainment)	2.1
ExxonMobil (XOM) (petrochemical)	0.9
Macy's (M) (retail)	3.5
ManpowerGroup (MAN) (temporary employment)	133.5
McDonald's (MCD) (quick-service restaurant)	1.1
Union Pacific (UNP) (railroad)	0.4

The smaller fixed asset turnover ratios are associated with industries that require large fixed asset investments to generate revenues. The larger fixed asset turnover ratios are associated with industries that require smaller fixed asset investments to generate revenues. Thus, for example, the difference in the fixed asset turnover ratio between Union Pacific and ManpowerGroup is due to the difference in the way fixed assets are used in their respective industries. Railroads require extensive investments in track, engines, and railcars, while temporary employment agencies require few investments in fixed assets.

Make a Decision	Fixed Asset Turnover Ratio

Analyze and compare Amazon.com to Netflix (MAD 9-1)
(Continuing company analysis)

Analyze and compare Alaska Air, Delta Air Lines, and Southwest Airlines (MAD 9-2)

Analyze Verizon (MAD 9-3)

Analyze and compare FedEx and UPS (MAD 9-4)

Analyze and compare Comcast, Alphabet, and Wal-Mart (MAD 9-5)

Make a Decision

Appendix Exchanging Similar Fixed Assets

Objective App

Describe and illustrate the accounting for the exchange of similar fixed assets.

Old equipment is often traded in for new equipment having a similar use. In such cases, the seller allows the buyer an amount for the old equipment traded in. This amount, called the **trade-in allowance**, may be either greater or less than the book value of the old equipment. The remaining balance—the amount owed—is either paid in cash or recorded as a liability. It is normally called **boot**, which is its tax name.

Accounting for the exchange of similar assets depends on whether the transaction has *commercial substance*.[8] An exchange has commercial substance if future cash flows change as a result of the exchange. If an exchange of similar assets has commercial substance, a gain or loss is recognized. In such cases, the exchange is accounted for similar to that of a sale of a fixed asset. The gain or loss is determined as the difference between the fair market value (trade-in allowance) of the asset given up (exchanged) and its book value. Alternatively, the gain or loss can be determined as the difference between the fair market value of the new asset received and the assets given up in the exchange (cash and book value of the old asset).

Gain on Exchange

To illustrate a gain on an exchange of similar assets, assume the following:

Similar equipment acquired (new):

Price (fair market value) of new equipment	$ 5,000
Trade-in allowance on old equipment	(1,100)
Cash paid at June 19, date of exchange	$ 3,900

Equipment traded in (old):

Cost of old equipment	$ 4,000
Accumulated depreciation at date of exchange	(3,200)
Book value at June 19, date of exchange	$ 800

The entry to record this exchange and payment of cash is as follows:

June 19	Accumulated Depreciation—Equipment	3,200	
	Equipment (new equipment)	5,000	
	Equipment (old equipment)		4,000
	Cash		3,900
	Gain on Exchange of Equipment		300

$$A = L + E$$
$$+ - \qquad + \text{ Gain}$$

[8] *FASB Accounting Standards Codification*, Section 360-10-30.

The gain on the exchange, $300, is the difference between the fair market value (trade-in allowance) of the asset given up (exchanged) of $1,100 and its book value of $800, computed as follows:

Fair market value (trade-in allowance) of old equipment	$1,100
Book value of old equipment	(800)
Gain on exchange of assets	$ 300

The gain on the exchange, $300, can also be determined as the difference between the fair market value of the new asset of $5,000 and the book value of the old asset traded in of $800 plus the cash paid of $3,900, computed as follows:

Price (fair market value) of new equipment		$ 5,000
Assets given up in exchange:		
Book value of old equipment ($4,000 – $3,200)	$ 800	
Cash paid on the exchange	3,900	(4,700)
Gain on exchange of assets		$ 300

Loss on Exchange

To illustrate a loss on an exchange of similar assets, assume that instead of a trade-in allowance of $1,100, a trade-in allowance of only $675 was allowed in the preceding example. In this case, the cash paid on the exchange is $4,325, computed as follows:

Price (fair market value) of new equipment	$5,000
Trade-in allowance of old equipment	(675)
Cash paid at June 19, date of exchange	$4,325

The entry to record this exchange and payment of cash is as follows:

A = L + E
+ –   – Loss

June 19	Accumulated Depreciation—Equipment	3,200	
	Equipment (new equipment)	5,000	
	Loss on Exchange of Equipment	125	
	Equipment (old equipment)		4,000
	Cash		4,325

The loss on the exchange, $125, is the difference between the fair market value (trade-in allowance) of the asset given up (exchanged) of $675 and its book value of $800, computed as follows:

Fair market value (trade-in allowance) of old equipment	$ 675
Book value of old equipment	(800)
Loss on exchange of assets	$(125)

The loss on the exchange, $125, can also be determined as the difference between the fair market value of the new asset of $5,000 and the book value of the old asset traded in of $800 plus the cash paid of $4,325, computed as follows:

Price (fair market value) of new equipment		$ 5,000
Assets given up in exchange:		
Book value of old equipment ($4,000 – $3,200)	$ 800	
Cash paid on the exchange	4,325	(5,125)
Loss on exchange of assets		$ (125)

In those cases where an asset exchange *lacks commercial substance*, no gain is recognized on the exchange. Instead, the cost of the new asset is reduced by any gain. For example, in the first illustration, the gain of $300 would be subtracted from the purchase price of $5,000 and the new asset would be recorded at $4,700. Accounting for the exchange of assets that lack commercial substance is discussed in more advanced accounting texts.[9]

---

[9] The exchange of similar assets also involves complex tax issues which are discussed in advanced accounting courses.

Let's Review

Chapter Summary

1. Fixed assets are long-term tangible assets used in the normal operations of the business such as machinery and equipment, buildings, land, and land improvements. The initial cost of a fixed asset includes all amounts spent to get the asset in place and ready for use.

2. All fixed assets except land should be depreciated over time. Three factors are considered in determining depreciation: (1) the fixed asset's initial cost, (2) the useful life of the asset, and (3) the residual value of the asset. Depreciation may be determined using the straight-line, units-of-activity, and double-declining-balance methods. Depreciation may be revised into the future for changes in an asset's useful life or residual value. Revenue expenditures include ordinary repairs and maintenance. Capital expenditures include asset improvements and extraordinary repairs.

3. When discarding a fixed asset, any depreciation for the current period is recorded, and the book value of the asset is then removed from the accounts. When a fixed asset is sold, the book value is removed, and the cash or other asset received is recorded. If the selling price is more than the book value of the asset, the transaction results in a gain. If the selling price is less than the book value, there is a loss.

4. The amount of periodic depletion is computed by multiplying the quantity of minerals extracted during the period by a depletion rate. The depletion rate is computed by dividing the cost of the mineral deposit by its estimated total units of resource. The entry to record depletion debits a depletion expense account and credits an accumulated depletion account.

5. Long-term assets such as patents, copyrights, trademarks, and goodwill are intangible assets. The cost of patents and copyrights should be amortized over the years of the asset's expected usefulness by debiting an expense account and crediting the intangible asset account. Trademarks and goodwill are not amortized but are written down only upon impairment.

6. The amount of depreciation expense and the depreciation methods used should be disclosed in the financial statements. Each major class of fixed assets should be disclosed, along with the related accumulated depreciation. Intangible assets are usually presented in a separate section following fixed assets. Each major class of intangible assets should be disclosed net of the amortization recorded to date.

7. The fixed asset turnover ratio measures the number of sales dollars earned per dollar of fixed assets. It is computed as sales divided by the average book value of fixed assets. The higher the ratio, the more efficiently a company is using its fixed assets in generating sales.

Key Terms

accelerated depreciation method (453)
amortization (464)
book value (448)
boot (471)
capital expenditures (458)
copyright (465)
depletion expense (462)
depreciable cost (448)

depreciation (448)
double-declining-balance method (453)
expected useful life (448)
fixed asset turnover ratio (469)
fixed assets (444)
goodwill (465)
initial cost (448)
intangible assets (464)

patents (464)
residual value (448)
revenue expenditures (458)
straight-line method (449)
trade-in allowance (471)
trademark (465)
units-of-activity method (451)

Practice

Multiple-Choice Questions

1. Which of the following expenditures incurred in connection with acquiring machinery is a proper charge to the asset account?
   a. Freight
   b. Installation costs
   c. Both (a) and (b)
   d. Neither (a) nor (b)

2. What is the amount of depreciation, using the double-declining-balance method for the second year of use for equipment costing $9,000, with an estimated residual value of $600 and an estimated life of three years?
   a. $6,000
   b. $3,000
   c. $2,000
   d. $400

3. An example of an accelerated depreciation method is:
   a. straight-line.
   b. double-declining-balance.
   c. units-of-activity.
   d. depletion.

4. Equipment purchased on January 3 for $80,000 was depreciated using the straight-line method based upon a five-year life and $7,500 residual value. The equipment was sold three years later on December 31 for $40,000. What is the gain on the sale of the equipment?
   a. $3,500
   b. $14,500
   c. $36,500
   d. $43,500

5. Which of the following is an example of an intangible asset?
   a. Patents
   b. Goodwill
   c. Copyrights
   d. All of these

Answers provided after Problem. Need more practice? Find additional multiple-choice questions, exercises, and problems in CengageNOWv2.

Exercises

1. Straight-line depreciation
Obj. 2

Equipment acquired at the beginning of the year at a cost of $340,000 has an estimated residual value of $45,000 and an estimated useful life of 10 years. Determine (a) the depreciable cost, (b) the straight-line rate, and (c) the annual straight-line depreciation.

2. Units-of-activity depreciation
Obj. 2

A tractor acquired at a cost of $420,000 has an estimated residual value of $30,000, has an estimated useful life of 25,000 hours, and was operated 1,850 hours during the year. Determine (a) the depreciable cost, (b) the depreciation rate, and (c) the units-of-activity depreciation for the year.

3. Double-declining-balance depreciation
Obj. 2

Equipment acquired at the beginning of the year at a cost of $175,000 has an estimated residual value of $12,000 and an estimated useful life of 10 years. Determine (a) the double-declining-balance rate and (b) the double-declining-balance depreciation for the first year.

4. Revision of depreciation
Obj. 2

A truck with a cost of $82,000 has an estimated residual value of $16,000, has an estimated useful life of 12 years, and is depreciated by the straight-line method. (a) Determine the amount of the annual depreciation. (b) Determine the book value at the end of the seventh year of use. (c) Assuming that at the start of the eighth year the remaining life is estimated to be six years and the residual value is estimated to be $12,000, determine the depreciation expense for each of the remaining six years.

5. Capital and revenue expenditures   Obj. 2

On August 7, Green River Inflatables Co. paid $1,675 to install a hydraulic lift and $40 for an air filter for one of its delivery trucks. Journalize the entries for the new lift and air filter expenditures.

6. Sale of equipment   Obj. 3

Equipment was acquired at the beginning of the year at a cost of $465,000. The equipment was depreciated using the straight-line method based on an estimated useful life of 15 years and an estimated residual value of $45,000.

a. What was the depreciation for the first year?

b. Assuming the equipment was sold at the end of the eighth year for $235,000, determine the gain or loss on the sale of the equipment.

c. Journalize the entry to record the sale.

7. Depletion   Obj. 4

Caldwell Mining Co. acquired mineral rights for $127,500,000. The mineral deposit is estimated at 425,000,000 tons. During the current year, 42,000,000 tons were mined and sold.

a. Determine the depletion rate.

b. Determine the amount of depletion expense for the current year.

c. Journalize the adjusting entry on December 31 to recognize the depletion expense.

8. Impaired goodwill and amortization of patent   Obj. 5

On December 31, it was estimated that goodwill of $4,000,000 was impaired. In addition, a patent with an estimated useful economic life of 15 years was acquired for $900,000 on August 1.

a. Journalize the adjusting entry on December 31 for the impaired goodwill.

b. Journalize the adjusting entry on December 31 for the amortization of the patent rights.

9. Fixed asset turnover ratio   Obj. 7

Select financial statement data for two recent years for DePuy Company are as follows:

	20Y8	20Y7
Sales	$5,510,000	$4,880,000
Fixed assets:		
Beginning of year	1,600,000	1,450,000
End of year	2,200,000	1,600,000

a. Determine the fixed asset turnover ratio for 20Y7 and 20Y8.

b. Does the change in the fixed asset turnover ratio from 20Y7 to 20Y8 indicate a favorable or an unfavorable change?

Answers provided after Problem. Need more practice? Find additional multiple-choice questions, exercises, and problems in CengageNOWv2.

Problem

McCollum Company, a furniture wholesaler, acquired new equipment at a cost of $150,000 at the beginning of the fiscal year. The equipment has an estimated life of five years and an estimated residual value of $12,000. Ellen McCollum, the president, has requested information regarding alternative depreciation methods.

Instructions

1. Determine the annual depreciation for each of the five years of estimated useful life of the equipment, the accumulated depreciation at the end of each year, and the book value of the equipment at the end of each year by (a) the straight-line method and (b) the double-declining-balance method.

2. Assume that the equipment was depreciated under the double-declining-balance method. In the first week of the fifth year, the equipment was sold for $10,000. Journalize the entry to record the sale.

Need more practice? Find additional multiple-choice questions, exercises, and problems in CengageNOWv2.

Answers

Multiple-Choice Questions

1. **c** All amounts spent to get a fixed asset (such as machinery) in place and ready for use are proper charges to the asset account. In the case of machinery acquired, the freight (answer a) and the installation costs (answer b) are both (answer c) proper charges to the machinery account.

2. **c** The periodic charge for depreciation under the double-declining-balance method for the second year is determined as follows:

    Step 1: Determine the straight-line percentage, using the expected useful life.

    $$\text{Straight-line percentage} = 100\% \div 3 \text{ years}$$
    $$= 33.333\%$$

    Step 2: Determine the double-declining-balance rate by multiplying the straight-line rate from Step 1 by 2.

    $$\text{Double-declining-balance rate} = 33.333\% \times 2$$
    $$= 66.666\%$$

    Step 3: Compute the depreciation expense by multiplying the double-declining-balance rate from Step 2 times the book value of the asset.

    $$\text{First-Year Depreciation} = 66.666\% \times \$9,000$$
    $$= \$6,000 \qquad \text{(answer a)}$$

    $$\text{Book Value at End of Year 1} = \$9,000 - \$6,000$$
    $$= \$3,000$$

    $$\text{Second-Year Depreciation} = \$3,000 \times 66.666\%$$
    $$= \$2,000 \qquad \text{(answer c)}$$

    $$\text{Third-Year Depreciation} = (\$3,000 - \$2,000) \times 66.666\%$$
    $$= \$667$$

    The equipment cannot be depreciated below its residual value of $600; thus, the third-year depreciation is $400 ($1,000 − $600) (answer d).

3. **b** A depreciation method that provides for a higher depreciation amount in the first year of the use of an asset and a gradually declining periodic amount thereafter is called an accelerated depreciation method. The double-declining-balance method (answer b) is an example of such a method.

4. **a** A gain of $3,500 is recognized on the sale of the equipment, computed as follows:

Annual depreciation [($80,000 − $7,500) ÷ 5 years]	$14,500
Cost of equipment	$80,000
Accumulated depreciation on December 31 ($14,500 × 3)	(43,500)
Book value of equipment on December 31	$36,500
Selling price	$40,000
Book value of equipment on December 31	(36,500)
Gain on sale of equipment	$ 3,500

5. **d** Long-lived assets that are useful in operations, not held for sale, and without physical qualities are called intangible assets. Patents, goodwill, and copyrights are examples of intangible assets (answer d).

Exercises

1. a. $295,000 ($340,000 − $45,000)
   b. 10.0% = (1 ÷ 10)
   c. $29,500 ($295,000 × 10.0%), or ($295,000 ÷ 10 years)

2. a. $390,000 ($420,000 − $30,000)
   b. $15.60 per hour ($390,000 ÷ 25,000 hours)
   c. $28,860 (1,850 hours × $15.60)

3. a. 20.0% = [(1 ÷ 10) × 2]
   b. $35,000 ($175,000 × 20.0%)

4. a. $5,500 [($82,000 − $16,000) ÷ 12]
   b. $43,500 [$82,000 − ($5,500 × 7)]
   c. $5,250 [($43,500 − $12,000) ÷ 6]

5.

Aug. 7	Delivery Truck	1,675	
	Cash		1,675
7	Repairs and Maintenance Expense	40	
	Cash		40

6. a. $28,000 [($465,000 − $45,000) ÷ 15]
   b. $6,000 loss {235,000 − [$465,000 − ($28,000 × 8)]}
   c.

Cash	235,000	
Accumulated Depreciation—Equipment	224,000	
Loss on Sale of Equipment	6,000	
Equipment		465,000

7. a. $0.30 per ton = $127,500,000 ÷ 425,000,000 tons
   b. $12,600,000 = 42,000,000 tons × $0.30 per ton
   c.

Dec. 31	Depletion Expense	12,600,000	
	Accumulated Depletion		12,600,000
	Depletion of mineral deposit.		

8. a.

Dec. 31	Loss from Impaired Goodwill	4,000,000	
	Goodwill		4,000,000
	Impaired goodwill.		

   b.

Dec. 31	Amortization Expense—Patents	25,000	
	Patents		25,000
	Amortized patent rights		
	[($900,000 ÷ 15) × 5/12].		

9. a. $$\text{Fixed Asset Turnover Ratio} = \frac{\text{Sales}}{\text{Average Book Value of Fixed Assets}}$$

   $$20Y7: \frac{\$4,880,000}{(\$1,450,000 + \$1,600,000) \div 2} = \frac{\$4,880,000}{\$1,525,000} = 3.2$$

   $$20Y8: \frac{\$5,510,000}{(\$1,600,000 + \$2,200,000) \div 2} = \frac{\$5,510,000}{\$1,900,000} = 2.9$$

   b. The decrease in the fixed asset turnover ratio from 3.2 to 2.9 indicates an unfavorable change in the efficiency of using fixed assets to generate sales.

Need more help? Watch step-by-step videos of how to compute answers to these Exercises in CengageNOWv2.

Problem

1.

Year	Depreciation Expense	Accumulated Depreciation, End of Year	Book Value, End of Year
a. 1	$27,600*	$ 27,600	$122,400
2	27,600	55,200	94,800
3	27,600	82,800	67,200
4	27,600	110,400	39,600
5	27,600	138,000	12,000

*$27,600 = ($150,000 − $12,000) ÷ 5

Year	Depreciation Expense	Accumulated Depreciation, End of Year	Book Value, End of Year
b. 1	$60,000**	$ 60,000	$ 90,000
2	36,000	96,000	54,000
3	21,600	117,600	32,400
4	12,960	130,560	19,440
5	7,440***	138,000	12,000

**$60,000 = $150,000 × 40%, where 40% = (100% ÷ 5) × 2
***The asset is not depreciated below the estimated residual value of $12,000.
   $7,440 = $150,000 − $130,560 − $12,000

2.

Cash	10,000	
Accumulated Depreciation—Equipment	130,560	
Loss on Sale of Equipment	9,440	
Equipment		150,000

Discussion Questions

1. O'Neil Office Supplies has a fleet of automobiles and trucks for use by salespersons and for delivery of office supplies and equipment. Collins Auto Sales Co. has automobiles and trucks for sale. Under what caption would the automobiles and trucks be reported in the balance sheet of (a) O'Neil Office Supplies and (b) Collins Auto Sales Co.?

2. Bullwinkle Co. acquired an adjacent vacant lot with the hope of selling it in the future at a gain. The lot is not intended to be used in Bullwinkle's business operations. Where should such real estate be listed on the balance sheet?

3. Alpine Company solicited bids from several contractors to construct an addition to its office building. The lowest bid received was for $1,200,000. Alpine decided to construct the addition itself at a cost of $1,100,000. What amount should be recorded in the building account?

4. Distinguish between the accounting for capital expenditures and revenue expenditures.

5. Immediately after a used truck is acquired, a new motor is installed at a total cost of $3,850. Is this a capital expenditure or a revenue expenditure?

6. Keyser Company purchased a machine that has a manufacturer's suggested life of 20 years. The company plans to use the machine on a special project that will last 12 years. At the completion of the project, the machine will be sold. Over how many years should the machine be depreciated?

7. Is it necessary for a business to use the same method of computing depreciation (a) for all classes of its depreciable assets and (b) for financial statement purposes and in determining income taxes?

8. a. Under what conditions is the use of an accelerated depreciation method most appropriate?
   b. Why is an accelerated depreciation method often used for income tax purposes?

9. For some of the fixed assets of a business, the balance in Accumulated Depreciation is exactly equal to the cost of the asset. (a) Is it permissible to record additional depreciation on the assets if they are still useful to the business? Explain. (b) When should an entry be made to remove the cost and the accumulated depreciation from the accounts?

10. a. Over what period of time should the cost of a patent acquired by purchase be amortized?
    b. In general, what is the required accounting treatment for research and development costs?
    c. How should goodwill be amortized?

Basic Exercises

SHOW ME HOW

BE 9-1   Straight-line depreciation   Obj. 2
A building acquired at the beginning of the year at a cost of $2,200,000 has an estimated residual value of $400,000 and an estimated useful life of 20 years. Determine (a) the depreciable cost, (b) the straight-line rate, and (c) the annual straight-line depreciation.

SHOW ME HOW

BE 9-2   Units-of-activity depreciation   Obj. 2
A truck acquired at a cost of $80,000 has an estimated residual value of $8,000, has an estimated useful life of 200,000 miles, and was driven 18,000 miles during the year. Determine (a) the depreciable cost, (b) the depreciation rate, and (c) the units-of-activity depreciation for the year.

SHOW ME HOW

BE 9-3   Double-declining-balance depreciation   Obj. 2
A building acquired at the beginning of the year at a cost of $3,585,000 has an estimated residual value of $125,000 and an estimated useful life of 50 years. Determine (a) the double-declining-balance rate and (b) the double-declining-balance depreciation for the first year.

SHOW ME HOW

BE 9-4   Revision of depreciation   Obj. 2
Equipment with a cost of $240,000 has an estimated residual value of $18,600, has an estimated useful life of 12 years, and is depreciated by the straight-line method. (a) Determine the amount of the annual depreciation. (b) Determine the book value at the end of the tenth year of use. (c) Assuming that at the start of the eleventh year the remaining life is estimated to be four years and the residual value is estimated to be $4,800, determine the depreciation expense for each of the remaining four years.

SHOW ME HOW

BE 9-5   Capital and revenue expenditures   Obj. 2
On February 14, Garcia Associates Co. paid $2,300 to repair the transmission on one of its delivery vans. In addition, Garcia paid $450 to install a GPS system in its van. Journalize the entries for the transmission and GPS system.

SHOW ME HOW

BE 9-6   Sale of equipment   Obj. 3
Equipment was acquired at the beginning of the year at a cost of $600,000. The equipment was depreciated using the double-declining-balance method based on an estimated useful life of 16 years and an estimated residual value of $60,000.
a. What was the depreciation for the first year?
b. Assuming the equipment was sold at the end of the second year for $480,000, determine the gain or loss on the sale of the equipment.
c. Journalize the entry on December 31 to record the sale.

SHOW ME HOW

BE 9-7   Depletion   Obj. 4
Glacier Mining Co. acquired mineral rights for $494,000,000. The mineral deposit is estimated at 475,000,000 tons. During the current year, 31,500,000 tons were mined and sold.
a. Determine the depletion rate.
b. Determine the amount of depletion expense for the current year.
c. Journalize the adjusting entry on December 31 to recognize the depletion expense.

SHOW ME HOW

BE 9-8   Impaired goodwill and amortization of patent   Obj. 5
On April 1, a patent with an estimated useful economic life of 12 years was acquired for $1,500,000. In addition, on December 31, it was estimated that goodwill of $6,000,000 was impaired.
a. Record the acquisition of patent.
b. Journalize the adjusting entry on December 31 for the amortization of the patent rights.
c. Journalize the adjusting entry on December 31 for the impaired goodwill.

BE 9-9   Fixed asset turnover ratio   Obj. 7

Select financial statement data for two recent years for Davenport Company are as follows:

	20Y5	20Y4
Sales	$1,668,000	$1,125,000
Fixed assets:		
Beginning of year	670,000	580,000
End of year	720,000	670,000

a. Determine the fixed asset turnover ratio for 20Y4 and 20Y5.

b. ➤ Does the change in the fixed asset turnover ratio from 20Y4 to 20Y5 indicate a favorable or an unfavorable change?

Exercises

EX 9-1   Costs of acquiring fixed assets   Obj. 1

Melinda Stoffers owns and operates ABC Print Co. During February, ABC incurred the following costs in acquiring two printing presses. One printing press was new, and the other was purchased from a business that recently filed for bankruptcy.

Costs related to new printing press:

1. Fee paid to factory representative for installation
2. Freight
3. Insurance while in transit
4. New parts to replace those damaged in unloading
5. Sales tax on purchase price
6. Special foundation

Costs related to used printing press:

7. Fees paid to attorney to review purchase agreement
8. Freight
9. Installation
10. Repair of damage incurred in reconditioning the press
11. Replacement of worn-out parts
12. Vandalism repairs during installation

a. Indicate which costs incurred in acquiring the new printing press should be debited to the asset account.

b. Indicate which costs incurred in acquiring the used printing press should be debited to the asset account.

EX 9-2   Determining cost of land   Obj. 1, 2

Bridger Ski Co. has developed a tract of land into a ski resort. The company has cut the trees, cleared and graded the land and hills, and constructed ski lifts.

➤ (a) Should the tree cutting, land clearing, and grading costs of constructing the ski slopes be debited to the land account? (b) If such costs are debited to Land, should they be depreciated? Explain.

EX 9-3   Determining cost of land   Obj. 1

On-Time Delivery Company acquired an adjacent lot to construct a new warehouse, paying $90,000 in cash and giving a short-term note for $50,000. Legal fees paid were $1,750, delinquent taxes assumed were $25,000, and fees paid to remove an old building from the land were $9,000. Materials salvaged from the demolition of the building were sold for $1,000. A contractor was paid $415,000 to construct a new warehouse. Determine the cost of the land to be reported on the balance sheet.

EX 9-4   Nature of depreciation   Obj. 2

Tri-City Ironworks Co. reported $65,500,000 for equipment and $33,415,000 for accumulated depreciation—equipment on its balance sheet.

➤ Does this mean (a) that the replacement cost of the equipment is $65,500,000 and (b) that $33,415,000 is set aside in a special fund for the replacement of the equipment? Explain.

EX 9-5 Straight-line depreciation rates
Obj. 2

✔ c. 10%

Convert each of the following estimates of useful life to a straight-line depreciation rate, stated as a percentage: (a) 4 years, (b) 8 years, (c) 10 years, (d) 16 years, (e) 25 years, (f) 40 years, (g) 50 years.

EX 9-6 Straight-line depreciation
Obj. 2

SHOW ME HOW

A refrigerator used by a wholesale warehouse has a cost of $82,000, an estimated residual value of $6,200, and an estimated useful life of 8 years. What is the amount of the annual depreciation computed by the straight-line method?

EX 9-7 Depreciation by units-of-activity method
Obj. 2

SHOW ME HOW

A diesel-powered tractor with a cost of $120,000 and an estimated residual value of $16,400 is expected to have a useful operating life of 28,000 hours. During April, the tractor was operated 150 hours. Determine the depreciation for the month.

EX 9-8 Depreciation by units-of-activity method
Obj. 2

✔ a. Truck #1, credit to Accumulated Depreciation, $5,460

Prior to adjustment at the end of the year, the balance in Trucks is $296,900 and the balance in Accumulated Depreciation—Trucks is $99,740. Details of the subsidiary ledger are as follows:

SHOW ME HOW

Truck No.	Cost	Estimated Residual Value	Estimated Useful Life	Accumulated Depreciation at Beginning of Year	Miles Operated During Year
1	$80,000	$15,000	250,000 miles	—	21,000 miles
2	54,000	6,000	300,000	$14,400	33,500
3	72,900	10,900	200,000	60,140	8,000
4	90,000	22,800	240,000	25,200	22,500

a. Determine the depreciation rates per mile and the amount to be credited to the accumulated depreciation section of each of the subsidiary accounts for the miles operated during the current year.

b. Journalize the entry on December 31 to record depreciation for the year.

EX 9-9 Depreciation by two methods
Obj. 2

✔ a. $8,500

A Kubota tractor acquired on January 8 at a cost of $85,000 has an estimated useful life of 10 years. Assuming that it will have no residual value, determine the depreciation for each of the first two years (a) by the straight-line method and (b) by the double-declining-balance method.

SHOW ME HOW

EX 9-10 Depreciation by two methods
Obj. 2

✔ a. $3,120

A storage tank acquired at the beginning of the fiscal year at a cost of $90,000 has an estimated residual value of $12,000 and an estimated useful life of 25 years. Determine the following: (a) the amount of annual depreciation by the straight-line method and (b) the amount of depreciation for the first and second years computed by the double-declining-balance method.

SHOW ME HOW

EX 9-11 Partial-year depreciation
Obj. 2

✔ a. First year, $6,200

Equipment acquired at a cost of $105,000 has an estimated residual value of $12,000 and an estimated useful life of 10 years. It was placed into service on May 1 of the current fiscal year, which ends on December 31. Determine the depreciation for the current fiscal year and for the following fiscal year by (a) the straight-line method and (b) the double-declining-balance method.

SHOW ME HOW

EX 9-12 Revision of depreciation
Obj. 2

✔ a. $41,875

A building with a cost of $1,800,000 has an estimated residual value of $125,000, has an estimated useful life of 40 years, and is depreciated by the straight-line method. (a) What is the amount of the annual depreciation? (b) What is the book value at the end of the twenty-eighth year of use? (c) If at the start of the twenty-ninth year it is estimated that the remaining life is 5 years and that the residual value is $80,000, what is the depreciation expense for each of the remaining 5 years?

SHOW ME HOW

EX 9-13 Capital and revenue expenditures
Obj. 2

Warner Freight Lines Co. incurred the following costs related to trucks and vans used in operating its delivery service:

1. Changed the oil and greased the joints of all the trucks and vans.
2. Changed the radiator fluid on a truck that had been in service for the past four years.
3. Installed a hydraulic lift to a van.
4. Installed security systems on four of the newer trucks.
5. Overhauled the engine on one of the trucks purchased three years ago.
6. Rebuilt the transmission on one of the vans that had been driven 40,000 miles. The van was no longer under warranty.
7. Removed a two-way radio from one of the trucks and installed a new radio with a greater range of communication.
8. Repaired a flat tire on one of the vans.
9. Replaced a truck's suspension system with a new suspension system that allows for the delivery of heavier loads.
10. Tinted the back and side windows of one of the vans to discourage theft of contents.

Classify each of the costs as a capital expenditure or a revenue expenditure.

EX 9-14 Capital and revenue expenditures
Obj. 2

Jackie Fox owns and operates Platinum Transport Co. During the past year, Jackie incurred the following costs related to an 18-wheel truck:

1. Changed engine oil.
2. Installed a television in the sleeping compartment of the truck.
3. Installed a wind deflector on top of the cab to increase fuel mileage.
4. Modified the factory-installed turbo charger with a special-order kit designed to add 50 more horsepower to the engine performance.
5. Replaced a headlight that had burned out.
6. Replaced a shock absorber that had worn out.
7. Replaced fog and cab light bulbs.
8. Replaced the hydraulic brake system that had begun to fail during his latest trip through the Rocky Mountains.
9. Removed the old radio and replaced it with a new communications module.
10. Replaced the old radar detector with a newer model that is fastened to the truck with a locking device that prevents its removal.

Classify each of the costs as a capital expenditure or a revenue expenditure.

EX 9-15 Capital and revenue expenditures
Obj. 1, 2

SHOW ME HOW

Quality Move Company made the following expenditures on one of its delivery trucks:

Mar. 20. Replaced the transmission at a cost of $1,890.
June 11. Paid $1,350 for installation of a hydraulic lift.
Nov. 30. Paid $55 to change the oil and air filter.

Prepare journal entries for each expenditure.

EX 9-16 Capital expenditure and depreciation
Obj. 1, 2

✔ b. Depreciation Expense, $800

Willow Creek Company purchased and installed carpet in its new general offices on April 30 for a total cost of $18,000. The carpet is estimated to have a 15-year useful life and no residual value.

a. Prepare the journal entry necessary for recording the purchase of the new carpet.

b. Record the December 31 adjusting entry for the partial-year depreciation expense for the carpet, assuming that Willow Creek uses the straight-line method.

SHOW ME HOW

EX 9-17 Entries for sale of fixed asset

Obj. 3

Equipment acquired on January 8 at a cost of $212,000 has an estimated useful life of 15 years, has an estimated residual value of $14,000, and is depreciated by the straight-line method.

a. What was the book value of the equipment at December 31 the end of the fifth year?

b. Assuming that the equipment was sold on April 1 of the sixth year for $105,800, journalize the entries to record (1) depreciation for the three months until the sale date, and (2) the sale of the equipment.

✔ b. $322,500

SHOW ME HOW

EX 9-18 Disposal of fixed asset

Obj. 3

Equipment acquired on January 6 at a cost of $375,000 has an estimated useful life of 20 years and an estimated residual value of $25,000.

a. What was the annual amount of depreciation for Years 1–3 using the straight-line method of depreciation?

b. What was the book value of the equipment on January 1 of Year 4?

c. Assuming that the equipment was sold on January 3 of Year 4 for $300,000, journalize the entry to record the sale.

d. Assuming that the equipment had been sold on January 3 of Year 4 for $325,000 instead of $300,000, journalize the entry to record the sale.

✔ a. $9,000,000

SHOW ME HOW

EX 9-19 Depletion entries

Obj. 4

Alaska Mining Co. acquired mineral rights for $67,500,000. The mineral deposit is estimated at 30,000,000 tons. During the current year, 4,000,000 tons were mined and sold.

a. Determine the amount of depletion expense for the current year.

b. Journalize the adjusting entry on December 31 to recognize the depletion expense.

✔ a. $357,600

SHOW ME HOW

EX 9-20 Amortization entries

Obj. 5

Kleen Company acquired patent rights on January 10 of Year 1 for $2,800,000. The patent has a useful life equal to its legal life of eight years. On January 7 of Year 4, Kleen successfully defended the patent in a lawsuit at a cost of $38,000.

a. Determine the patent amortization expense for Year 4 ended December 31.

b. Journalize the adjusting entry on December 31 of Year 4 to recognize the amortization.

REAL WORLD

EX 9-21 Book value of fixed assets

Obj. 6

Apple Inc. (AAPL) designs, manufactures, and markets personal computers and related software. Apple also manufactures and distributes music players (iPod), mobile phones (iPhone), and smartwatches (Apple Watch) along with related accessories and services, including online distribution of third-party music, videos, and applications. The following information was taken from a recent annual report of Apple:

Property, plant, and equipment (in millions):

	Current Year	Preceding Year
Land and buildings	$ 10,185	$ 6,956
Machinery, equipment, and internal-use software	44,543	37,038
Other fixed assets	6,517	5,263
Accumulated depreciation and amortization	(34,235)	(26,786)

a. Compute the book value of the fixed assets for the current year and the preceding year and explain the differences, if any.

b. ⟶ Would you normally expect Apple's book value of fixed assets to increase or decrease during the year? Why?

EX 9-22 Balance sheet presentation

Obj. 6

List the errors you find in the following partial balance sheet:

Burnt Red Company
Balance Sheet
December 31, 20Y2

Assets

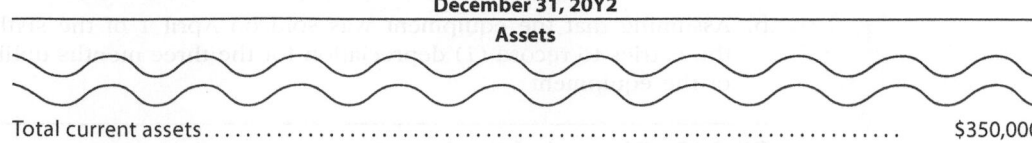

Total current assets. $350,000

	Replacement Cost	Accumulated Depreciation	Book Value
Property, plant, and equipment:			
Land.	$ 250,000	$ 50,000	$200,000
Buildings.	450,000	160,000	290,000
Factory equipment	375,000	140,000	235,000
Office equipment.	125,000	60,000	65,000
Patents	90,000	—	90,000
Goodwill.	60,000	10,000	50,000
Total property, plant, and equipment	$1,350,000	$420,000	$930,000

Appendix
EX 9-23 Asset traded for similar asset

✔ a. $185,000

A printing press priced at a fair market value of $275,000 is acquired in a transaction that has commercial substance by trading in a similar press and paying cash for the difference between the trade-in allowance and the price of the new press.

a. Assuming that the trade-in allowance is $90,000, what is the amount of cash given?

b. Assuming that the book value of the press traded in is $68,000, what is the gain or loss on the exchange?

Appendix
EX 9-24 Asset traded for similar asset

✔ b. $18,500 loss

Assume the same facts as in Exercise 9-23, except that the book value of the press traded in is $108,500. (a) What is the amount of cash given? (b) What is the gain or loss on the exchange?

Appendix
EX 9-25 Entries for trade of fixed asset

On July 1, Twin Pines Co., a water distiller, acquired new bottling equipment with a list price (fair market value) of $220,000. Twin Pines received a trade-in allowance (fair market value) of $45,000 on the old equipment of a similar type and paid cash of $175,000. The following information about the old equipment is obtained from the account in the equipment ledger: cost, $180,000; accumulated depreciation on December 31, the end of the preceding fiscal year, $120,000; annual depreciation, $12,000. Assuming the exchange has commercial substance, journalize the entries to record (a) the current depreciation of the old equipment to the date of trade-in and (b) the exchange transaction on July 1.

Appendix
EX 9-26 Entries for trade of fixed asset

On October 1, Bentley Delivery Services acquired a new truck with a list price (fair market value) of $75,000. Bentley Delivery received a trade-in allowance (fair market value) of $24,000 on an old truck of similar type and paid cash of $51,000. The following information about the old truck is obtained from the account in the equipment ledger: cost, $56,000; accumulated depreciation on December 31, the end of the preceding fiscal year, $35,000; annual depreciation, $7,000. Assuming the exchange has commercial substance, journalize the entries to record (a) the current depreciation of the old truck to the date of trade-in and (b) the transaction on October 1.

Problems: Series A

PR 9-1A Allocating payments and receipts to fixed asset accounts

Obj. 1

✔ Land, $400,000

The following payments and receipts are related to land, land improvements, and buildings acquired for use in a wholesale ceramic business. The receipts are identified by an asterisk.

a.	Fee paid to attorney for title search	$ 2,500
b.	Cost of real estate acquired as a plant site: Land..................................	285,000
	Building (to be demolished)...........	55,000
c.	Delinquent real estate taxes on property, assumed by purchaser	15,500
d.	Cost of razing and removing building acquired in (b)	5,000
e.	Proceeds from sale of salvage materials from old building	4,000*
f.	Special assessment paid to city for extension of water main to the property........	29,000
g.	Architect's and engineer's fees for plans and supervision	60,000
h.	Premium on one-year insurance policy during construction......................	6,000
i.	Cost of filling and grading land	12,000
j.	Money borrowed to pay building contractor.....................................	900,000*
k.	Cost of repairing windstorm damage during construction	5,500
l.	Cost of paving parking lot to be used by customers	32,000
m.	Cost of trees and shrubbery planted	11,000
n.	Cost of floodlights installed on parking lot......................................	2,000
o.	Cost of repairing vandalism damage during construction........................	2,500
p.	Proceeds from insurance company for windstorm and vandalism damage	7,500*
q.	Payment to building contractor for new building................................	800,000
r.	Interest incurred on building loan during construction	34,500
s.	Refund of premium on insurance policy (h) canceled after 11 months	500*

Instructions

1. Assign each payment and receipt to Land (unlimited life), Land Improvements (limited life), Building, or Other Accounts. Indicate receipts by an asterisk. Identify each item by letter and list the amounts in columnar form, as follows:

Item	Land	Land Improvements	Building	Other Accounts

2. Determine the amount debited to Land, Land Improvements, and Building.

3. ━━━▶ The costs assigned to the land, which is used as a plant site, will not be depreciated, while the costs assigned to land improvements will be depreciated. Explain this seemingly contradictory application of the concept of depreciation.

4. What would be the effect on the income statement and balance sheet if the cost of filling and grading land of $12,000 [payment (i)] was incorrectly classified as Land Improvements rather than Land? Assume Land Improvements are depreciated over a 20-year life using the double-declining-balance method.

PR 9-2A Comparing three depreciation methods

Obj. 2

✔ 1. a. Year 1: straight-line depreciation, $22,500

SHOW ME HOW   EXCEL TEMPLATE

Dexter Industries purchased packaging equipment on January 8 for $72,000. The equipment was expected to have a useful life of three years, or 18,000 operating hours, and a residual value of $4,500. The equipment was used for 7,600 hours during Year 1, 6,000 hours in Year 2, and 4,400 hours in Year 3.

Instructions

1. Determine the amount of depreciation expense for the three years ending December 31, by (a) the straight-line method, (b) the units-of-activity method, and (c) the double-declining-balance method. Also determine the total depreciation expense for the three years by each

(Continued)

method. The following columnar headings are suggested for recording the depreciation expense amounts:

	Depreciation Expense		
Year	Straight-Line Method	Units-of-Activity Method	Double-Declining-Balance Method

2. What method yields the highest depreciation expense for Year 1?

3. What method yields the most depreciation over the three-year life of the equipment?

PR 9-3A   Depreciation by three methods; partial years　　　　　　　　　　Obj. 2

✔ a. Year 1: $65,250

EXCEL TEMPLATE

Perdue Company purchased equipment on April 1 for $270,000. The equipment was expected to have a useful life of three years or 18,000 operating hours, and a residual value of $9,000. The equipment was used for 7,500 hours during Year 1, 5,500 hours in Year 2, 4,000 hours in Year 3, and 1,000 hours in Year 4.

Instructions

Determine the amount of depreciation expense for the years ended December 31, Year 1, Year 2, Year 3, and Year 4, by (a) the straight-line method, (b) the units-of-activity method, and (c) the double-declining-balance method.

PR 9-4A   Depreciation by two methods; sale of fixed asset　　　　　　Obj. 2, 3

✔ 1. b. Year 1: $320,000 depreciation expense

EXCEL TEMPLATE

New lithographic equipment, acquired at a cost of $800,000 on March 1 at the beginning of a fiscal year, has an estimated useful life of five years and an estimated residual value of $90,000. The manager requested information regarding the effect of alternative methods on the amount of depreciation expense each year.

　　In the first week of the fifth year, on March 4, the equipment was sold for $135,000.

Instructions

1. Determine the annual depreciation expense for each of the estimated five years of use, the accumulated depreciation at the end of each year, and the book value of the equipment at the end of each year by (a) the straight-line method and (b) the double-declining-balance method. The following columnar headings are suggested for each schedule:

Year	Depreciation Expense	Accumulated Depreciation, End of Year	Book Value, End of Year

2. Journalize the entry to record the sale assuming the manager chose the double-declining-balance method.

3. Journalize the entry to record the sale in (2), assuming that the equipment was sold for $88,750 instead of $135,000.

PR 9-5A   Transactions for fixed assets, including sale　　　　　　　　Obj. 1, 2, 3

The following transactions and adjusting entries were completed by Legacy Furniture Co. during a three-year period. All are related to the use of delivery equipment. The double-declining-balance method of depreciation is used.

Year 1

Jan. 4.   Purchased a used delivery truck for $26,000, paying cash.

Nov. 2.   Paid garage $825 for miscellaneous repairs to the truck.

Dec. 31.   Recorded depreciation on the truck for the year. The estimated useful life of the truck is four years, with a residual value of $2,000 for the truck.

Year 2

Jan. 6. Purchased a new truck for $60,000, paying cash.

Apr. 1. Sold the used truck for $14,000. (Record depreciation to date in Year 2 for the truck.)

June 11. Paid garage $280 for miscellaneous repairs to the truck.

Dec. 31. Record depreciation for the new truck. It has an estimated residual value of $7,000 and an estimated life of five years.

Year 3

July 1. Purchased a new truck for $65,000, paying cash.

Oct. 2. Sold the truck purchased January 6, Year 2, for $19,520. (Record depreciation to date for Year 3 for the truck.)

Dec. 31. Recorded depreciation on the remaining truck. It has an estimated residual value of $6,000 and an estimated useful life of eight years.

Instructions

Journalize the transactions and the adjusting entries.

✔ 1. a. $352,000

PR 9-6A Amortization and depletion entries   Obj. 4, 5

Data related to the acquisition of timber rights and intangible assets during the current year ended December 31 are as follows:

a. Timber rights on a tract of land were purchased for $1,600,000 on February 22. The stand of timber is estimated at 5,000,000 board feet. During the current year, 1,100,000 board feet of timber were cut and sold.

b. On December 31, the company determined that $3,750,000 of goodwill was impaired.

c. Governmental and legal costs of $6,600,000 were incurred on April 3 in obtaining a patent with an estimated economic life of 12 years. Amortization is to be for three-fourths of a year.

Instructions

1. Determine the amount of the amortization, depletion, or impairment for the current year for each of the foregoing items.

2. Journalize the adjusting entries required to record the amortization, depletion, or impairment for each item.

Problems: Series B

PR 9-1B Allocating payments and receipts to fixed asset accounts   Obj. 1

✔ Land, $860,000

The following payments and receipts are related to land, land improvements, and buildings acquired for use in a wholesale apparel business. The receipts are identified by an asterisk.

a.	Fee paid to attorney for title search	$ 3,600
b.	Cost of real estate acquired as a plant site: Land	720,000
	Building (to be demolished)	60,000
c.	Finder's fee paid to real estate agency	23,400
d.	Delinquent real estate taxes on property, assumed by purchaser	15,000
e.	Architect's and engineer's fees for plans for new building	75,000
f.	Cost of removing building purchased with land in (b)	10,000
g.	Proceeds from sale of salvage materials from old building	3,400*
h.	Cost of filling and grading land	18,000
i.	Premium on one-year insurance policy during construction	8,400
j.	Money borrowed to pay building contractor	800,000*
k.	Special assessment paid to city for extension of water main to the property	13,400
l.	Cost of repairing windstorm damage during construction	3,000
m.	Cost of repairing vandalism damage during construction	2,000
n.	Cost of trees and shrubbery planted	14,000
o.	Cost of paving parking lot to be used by customers	21,600
p.	Interest incurred on building loan during construction	40,000
q.	Proceeds from insurance company for windstorm and vandalism damage	4,500*
r.	Payment to building contractor for new building	800,000
s.	Refund of premium on insurance policy (i) canceled after 10 months	1,400*

(Continued)

Instructions

1. Assign each payment and receipt to Land (unlimited life), Land Improvements (limited life), Building, or Other Accounts. Indicate receipts by an asterisk. Identify each item by letter and list the amounts in columnar form, as follows:

Item	Land	Land Improvements	Building	Other Accounts

2. Determine the amount debited to Land, Land Improvements, and Building.

3. ⟶ The costs assigned to the land, which is used as a plant site, will not be depreciated, while the costs assigned to land improvements will be depreciated. Explain this seemingly contradictory application of the concept of depreciation.

4. What would be the effect on the income statement and balance sheet if the cost of paving the parking lot of $21,600 [payment (o)] was incorrectly classified as Land rather than Land Improvements? Assume Land Improvements are depreciated over a 10-year life using the double-declining-balance method.

PR 9-2B Comparing three depreciation methods   Obj. 2

✔ 1. a. Year 1: straight-line depreciation, $71,250

SHOW ME HOW   EXCEL TEMPLATE

Waylander Coatings Company purchased waterproofing equipment on January 6 for $320,000. The equipment was expected to have a useful life of four years, or 20,000 operating hours, and a residual value of $35,000. The equipment was used for 7,200 hours during Year 1, 6,400 hours in Year 2, 4,400 hours in Year 3, and 2,000 hours in Year 4.

Instructions

1. Determine the amount of depreciation expense for the years ended December 31, Year 1, Year 2, Year 3, and Year 4, by (a) the straight-line method, (b) the units-of-activity method, and (c) the double-declining-balance method. Also determine the total depreciation expense for the four years by each method. The following columnar headings are suggested for recording the depreciation expense amounts:

	Depreciation Expense		
Year	Straight-Line Method	Units-of-Activity Method	Double-Declining-Balance Method

2. What method yields the highest depreciation expense for Year 1?

3. What method yields the most depreciation over the four-year life of the equipment?

PR 9-3B Depreciation by three methods; partial years   Obj. 2

✔ a. Year 1, $8,400

EXCEL TEMPLATE

Layton Company purchased tool sharpening equipment on October 1 for $108,000. The equipment was expected to have a useful life of three years or 12,000 operating hours, and a residual value of $7,200. The equipment was used for 1,350 hours during Year 1, 4,200 hours in Year 2, 3,650 hours in Year 3, and 2,800 hours in Year 4.

Instructions

Determine the amount of depreciation expense for the years ended December 31, Year 1, Year 2, Year 3, and Year 4, by (a) the straight-line method, (b) the units-of-activity method, and (c) the double-declining-balance method.

PR 9-4B Depreciation by two methods; sale of fixed asset   Obj. 2, 3

✔ 1. b. Year 1, $55,000 depreciation expense

EXCEL TEMPLATE

New tire retreading equipment, acquired at a cost of $110,000 on September 1 at the beginning of a fiscal year, has an estimated useful life of four years and an estimated residual value of $7,500. The manager requested information regarding the effect of alternative methods on the amount of depreciation expense each year. On the basis of the data presented to the manager, the double-declining-balance method was selected.

In the first week of the fourth year, on September 6, the equipment was sold for $18,000.

Instructions

1. Determine the annual depreciation expense for each of the estimated four years of use, the accumulated depreciation at the end of each year, and the book value of the equipment at the end of each year by (a) the straight-line method and (b) the double-declining-balance method. The following columnar headings are suggested for each schedule:

Year	Depreciation Expense	Accumulated Depreciation, End of Year	Book Value, End of Year

2. Journalize the entry to record the sale.

3. Journalize the entry to record the sale, assuming that the equipment sold for $10,500 instead of $18,000.

PR 9-5B Transactions for fixed assets, including sale Obj. 1, 2, 3

The following transactions and adjusting entries were completed by Robinson Furniture Co. during a three-year period. All are related to the use of delivery equipment. The double-declining-balance method of depreciation is used.

Year 1

Jan. 8. Purchased a used delivery truck for $24,000, paying cash.

Mar. 7. Paid garage $900 for changing the oil, replacing the oil filter, and tuning the engine on the delivery truck.

Dec. 31. Recorded depreciation on the truck for the fiscal year. The estimated useful life of the truck is four years, with a residual value of $4,000 for the truck.

Year 2

Jan. 9. Purchased a new truck for $50,000, paying cash.

Feb. 28. Paid garage $250 to tune the engine and make other minor repairs on the used truck.

Apr. 30. Sold the used truck for $9,500. (Record depreciation to date in Year 2 for the truck.)

Dec. 31. Record depreciation for the new truck. It has an estimated residual value of $12,000 and an estimated life of eight years.

Year 3

Sept. 1. Purchased a new truck for $58,500, paying cash.

4. Sold the truck purchased January 9, Year 2, for $36,000. (Record depreciation to date for Year 3 for the truck.)

Dec. 31. Recorded depreciation on the remaining truck. It has an estimated residual value of $16,000 and an estimated useful life of 10 years.

Instructions

Journalize the transactions and the adjusting entries.

✔ b. $150,000

PR 9-6B Amortization and depletion entries Obj. 4, 5

Data related to the acquisition of timber rights and intangible assets during the current year ended December 31 are as follows:

a. On December 31, the company determined that $3,400,000 of goodwill was impaired.

b. Governmental and legal costs of $4,800,000 were incurred on September 30 in obtaining a patent with an estimated economic life of eight years. Amortization is to be for one-fourth of a year.

c. Timber rights on a tract of land were purchased for $2,975,000 on February 4. The stand of timber is estimated at 12,500,000 board feet. During the current year, 4,150,000 board feet of timber were cut and sold.

Instructions

1. Determine the amount of the amortization, depletion, or impairment for the current year for each of the foregoing items.

2. Journalize the adjusting entries to record the amortization, depletion, or impairment for each item.

Make a Decision
Fixed Asset Turnover Ratio

REAL WORLD

MAD 9-1   Compare Amazon.com to Netflix
Obj. 7

Amazon.com, Inc. (AMZN) is the world's leading Internet retailer of merchandise and media. Amazon also designs and sells electronic products, such as e-readers. **Netflix, Inc. (NFLX)** is one of the world's leading Internet television networks. Both companies compete in the digital media and streaming space. However, Netflix is more narrowly focused in the digital streaming business than is Amazon.

Sales and average book value of fixed assets information (in millions) are provided for Amazon and Netflix for a recent year as follows:

	Amazon.com	Netflix
Sales	$135,987	$8,830
Average book value of fixed assets	25,476	212

a. Compute the fixed asset turnover ratio for each company. Round to one decimal place.

b. ➡ Which company is more efficient in generating sales from fixed assets?

c. ➡ Interpret your results.

REAL WORLD

MAD 9-2   Compare Alaska Air, Delta Air Lines, and Southwest Airlines
Obj. 7

Alaska Air Group (ALK), **Delta Air Lines (DAL)**, and **Southwest Airlines (LUV)** reported the following financial information (in millions) in a recent year:

	Alaska Air Group	Delta Air Lines	Southwest Airlines
Sales	$5,931	$39,639	$20,425
Average book value of fixed assets	5,234	23,707	16,323

a. Determine the fixed asset turnover ratio for each airline. Round to one decimal place.

b. ➡ Based on the fixed asset turnover ratio, which airline appears to be the most efficient in the use of its fixed assets?

c. ➡ The most important fixed asset to an airline is the aircraft. Given this, what factors might influence the efficient use of fixed assets for an airline?

REAL WORLD

MAD 9-3   Analyze Verizon
Obj. 7

Verizon Communications Inc. (VZ) is a major telecommunications company in the United States. Two recent balance sheets for Verizon disclosed the following information regarding fixed assets:

	End of Year (in millions)	Beginning of Year (in millions)
Property, plant, and equipment	$232,215	$220,163
Accumulated depreciation	(147,464)	(136,622)
Property, plant, and equipment (net)	$ 84,751	$ 83,541

Verizon's revenue for the year was $125,980 million. Assume the fixed asset turnover ratio for the telecommunications industry averages approximately 1.1.

a. Determine Verizon's fixed asset turnover ratio. Round to one decimal place.

b. ➡ Interpret this ratio with respect to the industry average.

REAL WORLD

MAD 9-4 Compare FedEx and UPS

Obj. 7

FedEx Corporation (FDX) and **United Parcel Service, Inc. (UPS)** compete in the package delivery business. The major fixed assets for each business include aircraft, sorting and handling facilities, delivery vehicles, and information technology. The sales and average book value of fixed assets reported on recent financial statements for each company were as follows:

	FedEx	UPS
Sales (in millions)	$50,365	$60,906
Average book value of fixed assets (in millions)	22,580	18,576

a. Compute the fixed asset turnover ratio for each company. Round to one decimal place.
b. Which company appears more efficient in using fixed assets?
c. ➤ Interpret the meaning of the ratio for the more efficient company.

REAL WORLD

MAD 9-5 Compare Comcast, Alphabet, and Wal-Mart

Obj. 7

The following table shows the sales and average book value of fixed assets for three different companies from three different industries for a recent year:

Company (Industry)	Sales (in millions)	Average Book Value of Fixed Assets (in millions)
Comcast Corporation (CMCSA) (communications)	$ 80,403	$ 34,959
Alphabet Inc. (GOOGL) (Internet)	90,272	31,625
Wal-Mart Stores, Inc. (WMT) (retail)	482,130	112,226

a. For each company, determine the fixed asset turnover ratio. Round to one decimal place.
b. ➤ Explain Comcast's fixed asset turnover ratio relative to the other two companies.

Take It Further

ETHICS

TIF 9-1 Revising depreciation estimates

Hard Bodies Co. is a fitness chain that has just completed its second year of operations. At the beginning of its first fiscal year, the company purchased fitness equipment at a cost of $600,000 and estimated that the equipment would have a useful life of five years and no residual value. The company uses the straight-line depreciation method. The company reported net income for the first two years of operations as follows:

Year	Net Income (Loss)
1	$50,000
2	(2,000)

Mike Gambit, the company's chief financial officer (CFO), has recently run financial models to predict future net income, and he expects net losses to continue at $(2,000) per year for the next three years. James Steed, the president of Hard Bodies, is concerned about these predictions, as he is under pressure from the company's owner to return the company to Year 1 net income levels. If the company does not meet these goals, both he and Mike will likely be fired. Mike suggests that the company change the estimated useful life of the fitness equipment to 10 years and increase the equipment's estimated residual value to $50,000. This will reduce depreciation expense and increase net income.

1. ➤ Evaluate the decision to change the equipment's estimated useful life and estimated residual value to improve earnings. How does this change impact the usefulness of the company's net income for external decision makers?
2. ➤ If Mike and James make the change, are they acting in an ethical manner? Explain.

TIF 9-2   Real-world annual report

In teams, select a public company that interests you. Obtain the company's most recent annual report on Form 10-K. The Form 10-K is a company's annually required filing with the Securities and Exchange Commission (SEC). It includes the company's financial statements and accompanying notes. The Form 10-K can be obtained either (a) from the investor relations section of the company's website or (b) by using the company search feature of the SEC's EDGAR database service found at www.sec.gov/edgar/searchedgar/companysearch.html.

1. Based on the information in the company's most recent annual report, answer the following questions:

   a. What depreciation methods does the company use to compute depreciation expense?

   b. How much depreciation expense does the company report on its income statement?

   c. What is the initial cost of the company's fixed assets?

   d. What is the book value of the company's fixed assets?

   e. What types of intangible assets, if any, does the company report on its balance sheet?

2. ➡ Does the book value of the company's fixed assets reflect their current market value? Explain your answer.

TIF 9-3   Improvements and repairs

Godwin Co. owns three delivery trucks. Details for each truck at the end of the most recent year follow:

	Age	Expected Useful Life	Initial Cost	Accumulated Depreciation
Truck 1	3	6	$22,500	$11,250
Truck 2	5	6	26,250	21,875
Truck 3	2	6	28,500	9,500

- At the beginning of the year, a hydraulic lift is added to Truck 1 at a cost of $4,500. The addition of the hydraulic lift will allow the company to deliver much larger objects than could previously be delivered.

- At the beginning of the year, the engine of Truck 2 is overhauled at a cost of $5,000. The engine overhaul will extend the truck's useful life by three years.

➡ Write a short memo to Godwin's chief financial officer explaining the financial statement effects of the expenditures associated with Trucks 1 and 2.

TIF 9-4   Financial statement versus tax depreciation

The following is an excerpt from a conversation between two employees of WXT Technologies, Nolan Sears and Stacy Mays. Nolan is the accounts payable clerk, and Stacy is the cashier.

Nolan: Stacy, could I get your opinion on something?

Stacy: Sure, Nolan.

Nolan: Do you know Rita, the fixed assets clerk?

Stacy: I know who she is, but I don't know her very well. Why?

Nolan: Well, I was talking to her at lunch last Monday about how she liked her job. You know, the usual; and she mentioned something about having to keep two sets of books—one for taxes and one for the financial statements. That can't be good accounting, can it? What do you think?

Stacy: Two sets of books? It doesn't sound right.

Nolan: It doesn't seem right to me either. I was always taught that you had to use generally accepted accounting principles. How can there be two sets of books? What can be the difference between the two?

➡ How would you respond to Nolan and Stacy if you were Rita?

Pathways Challenge

This is Accounting!

Information/Consequences

Because a wireless license does not exist physically, **Verizon**'s **(VZ)** wireless licenses are intangible assets. All of the costs of acquiring a wireless license should be recorded as an asset. In a recent year, Verizon reported almost $87 billion of wireless licenses, representing 35% of its total assets.

Even though the FCC license is granted for a 10-year period, Verizon considers this license to have an indefinite useful life. This is because the license is subject to renewal at a low cost and, historically, the FCC has renewed Verizon's licenses.

Verizon does not expense (amortize) the cost of its wireless licenses. Instead, the licenses are reviewed for any impaired value.

Suggested Answer

10 Liabilities: Current, Installment Notes, and Contingencies

STATEMENT OF STOCKHOLDERS' EQUITY
For the Year Ended December 31, 20Y5

	Common Stock	Retained Earnings	Total
Balances, Jan. 1, 20Y5	$XXX	$ XXX	$ XXX
Issued common stock	XXX		XXX
Net income		XXX	XXX
Dividends		(XXX)	(XXX)
Balances, Dec. 31, 20Y5	$XXX	$ XXX	$ XXX

STATEMENT OF CASH FLOWS
For the Year Ended December 31, 20Y5

Cash flows from (used for) operating activities	$XXX
Cash flows from (used for) investing activities	XXX
Cash flows from (used for) financing activities	XXX
Net increase (decrease) in cash	$XXX
Cash balance, January 1, 20Y5	XXX
Cash balance, December 31, 20Y5	$XXX

INCOME STATEMENT
For the Year Ended December 31, 20Y5

Sales		$ XXX
Cost of goods sold		(XXX)
Gross profit		$ XXX
Operating expenses:		
Wages expense	$XXX	
Advertising expense	XXX	
Utilities expense	XXX	
Depreciation expense	XXX	
…	XXX	
Total operating expenses		(XXX)
Operating income		$ XXX
Other revenue and expense:		
Interest expense		(XXX)
Net income		$ XXX

BALANCE SHEET
December 31, 20Y5

Assets

Current assets:		
Cash	$XXX	
Accounts receivable	XXX	
Inventory	XXX	
Total current assets		$XXX
Property, plant, and equipment		XXX
Total assets		$XXX

Liabilities

Current liabilities:		
Accounts payable	$XXX	
Payroll liabilities	XXX	
Notes payable	XXX	
Interest payable	XXX	
Total current liabilities		$XXX
Long-term liabilities		XXX
Total liabilities		$XXX

Stockholders' Equity

Common stock	$XXX	
Retained earnings	XXX	
Total stockholders' equity		XXX
Total liabilities and stockholders' equity		$XXX

Starbucks Corporation

Buying goods on credit is essential for businesses to run efficiently. The use of credit makes transactions more convenient and improves buying power. For individuals, the most common form of short-term credit is a credit card. Credit cards allow individuals to purchase items before they are paid for, while removing the need for individuals to carry large amounts of cash. They also provide documentation of purchases through a monthly credit card statement.

Short-term credit is used by *businesses* to make purchasing items more convenient. It also gives the business control over the payment for goods and services. When **Starbucks Corporation (SBUX)** opened its first coffee shop in 1971,

it relied on short-term trade credit, or accounts payable, to purchase ingredients for its coffee shop in Seattle's historic Pike Place Market. Today, Starbucks still relies on accounts payable and short-term trade credit, which also gives it control over cash payments by separating the purchase function from the payment function. Thus, the employee responsible for purchasing the ingredients is separated from the employee responsible for paying for the purchase. This separation of duties can help prevent unauthorized purchases or payments.

In addition to accounts payable, Starbucks has liabilities related to payroll, notes, and contingencies. This chapter describes and illustrates the accounting for each of these liabilities.

©ROBERT MULLAN/GETTY IMAGES

What's Covered

Liabilities: Current, Installment Notes, Contingencies

Current Liabilities	Installment Notes	Contingent Liabilities	Reporting Liabilities
■ Accounts Payable and Accruals (Obj. 1) ■ Notes Payable (Obj. 1) ■ Current Portion of Long-Term Debt (Obj. 1) ■ Payroll (Obj. 2) ■ Fringe Benefits (Obj. 3)	■ Issuance (Obj. 4) ■ Periodic Payments (Obj. 4)	■ Probable Estimable (Obj. 5) ■ Probable Not Estimable (Obj. 5) ■ Reasonably Possible (Obj. 5) ■ Remote (Obj. 5)	■ Balance Sheet (Obj. 6)

Learning Objectives

Obj. 1 Describe and illustrate current liabilities, including those related to accounts payable, accruals, notes payable, and the current portion of long-term debt.

Obj. 2 Describe and illustrate the accounting for payroll liabilities.

Obj. 3 Describe and illustrate the accounting for employee fringe benefits, including vacation pay and pensions.

Obj. 4 Describe and illustrate the accounting for installment notes.

Obj. 5 Describe and illustrate the accounting for contingent liabilities, including product warranties.

Obj. 6 Describe the reporting of liabilities on the balance sheet.

Analysis for Decision Making

Obj. 7 Describe and illustrate the use of the quick ratio in analyzing a company's ability to pay its current liabilities.

Objective 1

Describe and illustrate current liabilities, including those related to accounts payable, accruals, notes payable, and the current portion of long-term debt.

Current Liabilities

When a company or a bank advances *credit*, it is making a loan. The company or bank is called a *creditor* (or *lender*). The individuals or companies receiving the loan are called *debtors* (or *borrowers*).

Debt is recorded as a liability by the debtor. *Long-term liabilities* are debts due beyond one year. Thus, a 30-year mortgage used to purchase property is a long-term liability. *Current liabilities* are debts that will be paid out of current assets and are due within one year.

Types of current liabilities discussed in this section include the following:

■ Accounts payable and accruals
■ Short-term notes payable
■ Current portion of long-term debt

Accounts Payable and Accruals

Accounts payable transactions have been described and illustrated in earlier chapters. These transactions involve a variety of purchases on account, including the purchase of merchandise and supplies.

Accruals have also been described and illustrated in earlier chapters. Accrued liabilities reflect an obligation to pay current assets in the future. Accrued liabilities are normally recorded at the end of an accounting period as part of the adjustment process. For example, wages due employees at the end of the period are recorded as an expense (Wages Expense) and an accrued liability (Wages Payable).

For most companies, accounts payable and accrued liabilities are the largest portion of current liabilities.

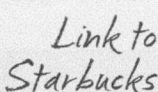
Link to Starbucks

On a recent balance sheet, **Starbucks** reported $730.6 million of accounts payable and $1,999.1 million of accrued liabilities, which make up 60% of its current liabilities.

Short-Term Notes Payable

Notes may be issued to purchase merchandise or other assets. Notes may also be issued to creditors to satisfy an account payable created earlier.[1]

To illustrate, assume that Nature's Sunshine Company issued a 90-day, 12% note for $1,000, dated August 1, to Murray Co. for a $1,000 overdue account. The entry to record the issuance of the note is as follows:

Aug. 1	Accounts Payable—Murray Co.	1,000
	Notes Payable		1,000
	Issued a 90-day, 12% note on account.	

$$A = L + E$$
$$+-$$

When the note matures, the entry to record the payment of $1,000 plus $30 interest ($1,000 \times 12\% \times 90 \div 360$[2]) is as follows:

Oct. 30	Notes Payable	1,000
	Interest Expense	30
	Cash		1,030
	Paid principal and interest due on note.	

$$A = L + E$$
$$- \quad - \quad - Exp$$

The interest expense is reported in the "Other expense" section of the income statement for the year ended December 31. The interest expense account is closed at December 31.

Each note transaction affects a debtor (borrower) and creditor (lender). Exhibit 1 shows how the same transactions are recorded by the debtor and creditor. In Exhibit 1, the debtor (borrower) is Bowden Co., and the creditor (lender) is Coker Co.

Exhibit 1 Note Transactions: Borrower and Creditor

	Bowden Co. (Borrower)		Coker Co. (Creditor)	
May 1. Bowden Co. purchased merchandise on account from Coker Co., $10,000, n/30. The merchandise cost Coker Co. $7,500.	Inventory 10,000		Accounts Receivable 10,000	
	Accounts Payable	10,000	Sales	10,000
			Cost of Goods Sold 7,500	
			Inventory	7,500
May 31. Bowden Co. issued a 60-day, 12% note for $10,000 to Coker Co. on account.	Accounts Payable 10,000		Notes Receivable 10,000	
	Notes Payable	10,000	Accounts Receivable	10,000
July 30. Bowden Co. paid Coker Co. the amount due on the note of May 31. Interest: $10,000 × 12% × 60 ÷ 360.	Notes Payable 10,000		Cash 10,200	
	Interest Expense 200		Interest Revenue	200
	Cash	10,200	Notes Receivable	10,000

A company may also borrow from a bank by issuing a note. To illustrate, assume that on September 19, Iceburg Company borrowed cash from First National Bank by issuing a $4,000, 90-day, 8% note to the bank. The entry to record the issuance of the note and the cash proceeds is as follows:

Sept. 19	Cash	4,000
	Notes Payable		4,000
	Issued a 90-day, 8% note	
	to First National Bank.	

$$A = L + E$$
$$+ \quad +$$

[1] The accounting for notes received to satisfy an account receivable was described and illustrated in Chapter 8, *Receivables*.

[2] To simplify computations and rounding, 360 days per year are used. In practice, companies use 365 days.

On the due date of the note (December 18), Iceburg Company owes First National Bank $4,000 plus interest of $80 ($4,000 × 8% × 90 ÷ 360). The entry to record the payment of the note is as follows:

A = L + E
−   −   − Exp

Dec. 18	Notes Payable	4,000	
	Interest Expense	80	
	Cash		4,080
	Paid principal and interest due on note.		

In some cases, a *discounted note* may be issued rather than an interest-bearing note. A discounted note has the following characteristics:

- The interest rate on the note is called the *discount rate*.
- The amount of interest on the note, called the *discount*, is computed by multiplying the discount rate times the face amount of the note.
- The debtor (borrower) receives the face amount of the note less the discount, called the *proceeds*.
- The debtor must repay the face amount of the note on the due date.

To illustrate, assume that on August 10, Cary Company issues a $20,000, 90-day discounted note to Western National Bank. The discount rate is 9%, and the amount of the discount is $450 ($20,000 × 9% × 90 ÷ 360). Thus, the proceeds received by Cary are $19,550. The entry by Cary is as follows:

A = L + E
+   +   − Exp

Aug. 10	Cash	19,550	
	Interest Expense	450	
	Notes Payable		20,000
	Issued a 90-day discounted note to Western		
	National Bank at a 9% discount rate.		

The entry when Cary pays the discounted note on November 8 is as follows:[3]

A = L + E
−   −   −

Nov. 8	Notes Payable	20,000	
	Cash		20,000
	Paid note due.		

Current Portion of Long-Term Debt

The current portions of long-term debt, such as the current portion of installment notes, are reported on the balance sheet as a current liability. An **installment note** is a debt that requires the borrower to make equal periodic payments to the lender for the term of the note. Installment notes are often used to purchase property, plant, and equipment. The accounting for installment notes is described and illustrated later in this chapter.

 *Link to Starbucks*   On a recent balance sheet, **Starbucks** reported $400 million of currently maturing long-term debt.

Check Up Corner 10-1   Short-Term Notes Payable

On October 3, Bering Industries Inc. is considering two alternatives for a short-term loan from Community Bank: (1) issue a $60,000, 60-day, 5% note or (2) issue a $60,000, 60-day note that the bank discounts at 5%.

a. Journalize the entries to record the issuance and repayment of the note, assuming the company selects the $60,000, 60-day, 5% note.

b. Journalize the entries to record the issuance and repayment of the note, assuming the company selects the $60,000, 60-day note that the bank discounts at 5%.

[3] If the accounting period ends before a discounted note is paid, an adjusting entry should record the prepaid (deferred) interest that is not yet an expense. This deferred interest would be deducted from Notes Payable in the "Current liabilities" section of the balance sheet.

Solution:

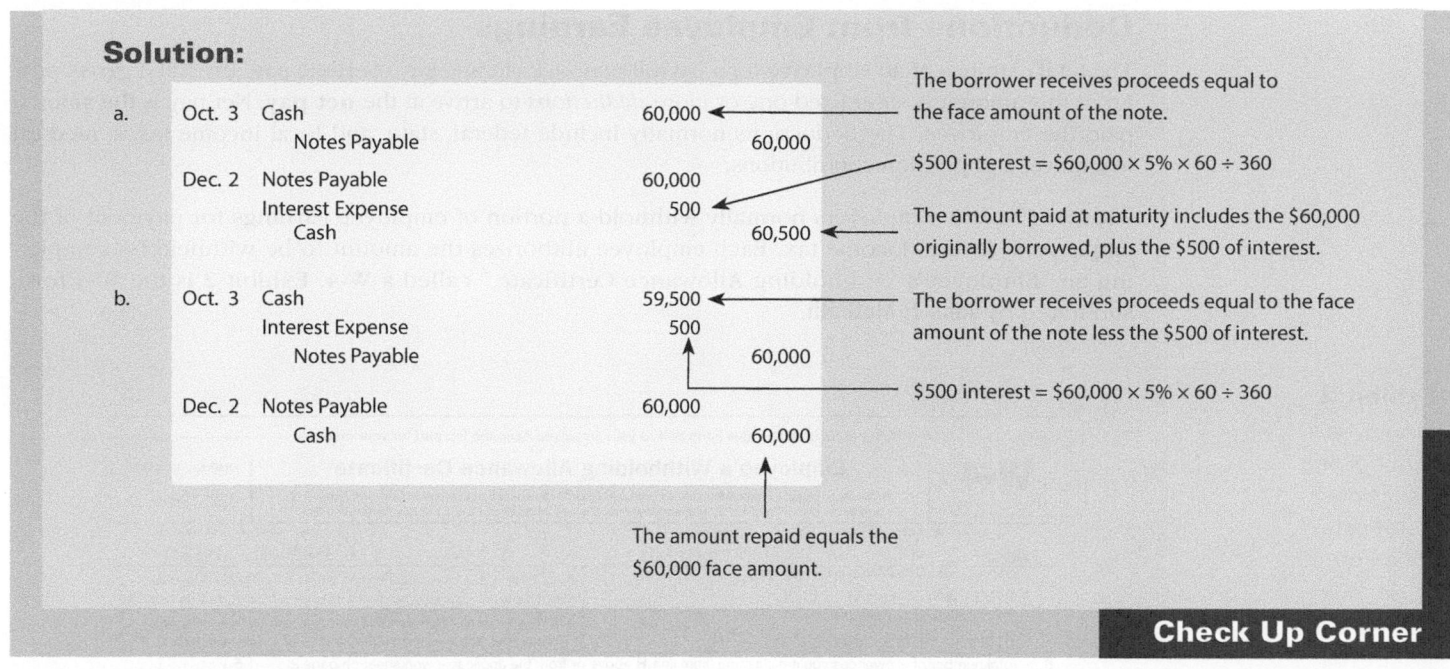

a. Oct. 3 Cash   60,000 ← The borrower receives proceeds equal to the face amount of the note.
        Notes Payable   60,000

   Dec. 2 Notes Payable   60,000
        Interest Expense   500 ← $500 interest = $60,000 × 5% × 60 ÷ 360
        Cash   60,500 ← The amount paid at maturity includes the $60,000 originally borrowed, plus the $500 of interest.

b. Oct. 3 Cash   59,500 ← The borrower receives proceeds equal to the face amount of the note less the $500 of interest.
        Interest Expense   500
        Notes Payable   60,000

   Dec. 2 Notes Payable   60,000 ← $500 interest = $60,000 × 5% × 60 ÷ 360
        Cash   60,000

The amount repaid equals the $60,000 face amount.

Check Up Corner

Payroll Liabilities

Objective 2
Describe and illustrate the accounting for payroll liabilities.

In accounting, **payroll** refers to the amount paid to employees for services they provided during the period. A company's payroll is important for the following reasons:

- Payroll and related payroll taxes significantly affect the net income of most companies.
- Payroll is subject to federal and state regulations.
- Good employee morale requires payroll to be paid timely and accurately.

Liability for Employee Earnings

Salary usually refers to payment for managerial and administrative services. Salary is normally expressed in terms of a month or a year. *Wages* usually refers to payment for employee manual labor. The rate of wages is normally stated on an hourly or a weekly basis. The salary or wage of an employee may be increased by bonuses, commissions, profit sharing, or cost-of-living adjustments.

Companies engaged in interstate commerce must follow the Fair Labor Standards Act. This act, sometimes called the Federal Wage and Hour Law, requires employers to pay a minimum rate of 1½ times the regular rate for all hours worked in excess of 40 hours per week. Exemptions are provided for executive, administrative, and some supervisory positions. Increased rates for working overtime, nights, or holidays are common, even when not required by law. These rates may be as much as twice the regular rate.

To illustrate computing an employee's earnings, assume that **John T. McGrath** is a salesperson employed by **McDermott Supply Co.** McGrath's regular rate is $34 per hour, and any hours worked in excess of 40 hours per week are paid at 1½ times the regular rate. McGrath worked 42 hours for the week ended December 27. His earnings of $1,462 for the week are computed as follows:

Earnings at regular rate (40 hrs. × $34)	$1,360
Earnings at overtime rate [2 hrs. × ($34 × 1½)]	102
Total earnings	$1,462

Deductions from Employee Earnings

The total earnings of an employee for a payroll period, including any overtime pay, are called **gross pay**. From this amount is subtracted one or more *deductions* to arrive at the **net pay**. Net pay is the amount paid the employee. The deductions normally include federal, state, and local income taxes, medical insurance, and pension contributions.

Income Taxes Employers normally withhold a portion of employee earnings for payment of the employees' federal income tax. Each employee authorizes the amount to be withheld by completing an "Employee's Withholding Allowance Certificate," called a W-4. Exhibit 2 is the W-4 form submitted by **John T. McGrath**.

Exhibit 2 Employee's Withholding Allowance Certificate (W-4 Form)

Separate here and give Form W-4 to your employer. Keep the top part for your records.

Form **W-4** Department of the Treasury Internal Revenue Service

Employee's Withholding Allowance Certificate

▶ Whether you are entitled to claim a certain number of allowances or exemption from withholding is subject to review by the IRS. Your employer may be required to send a copy of this form to the IRS.

OMB No. 1545-0074 **20--**

1 Your first name and middle initial: John T. | Last name: McGrath | 2 Your social security number: 381 48 9120

Home address (number and street or rural route): 1830 4th Street

3 ☒ Single ☐ Married ☐ Married, but withhold at higher Single rate.
Note. If married, but legally separated, or spouse is a nonresident alien, check the "Single" box.

City or town, state, and ZIP code: Clinton, Iowa 52732-6142

4 If your last name differs from that shown on your social security card, check here. You must call 1-800-772-1213 for a replacement card. ▶ ☐

5 Total number of allowances you are claiming (from line **H** above **or** from the applicable worksheet on page 2) . . . 5 | 1
6 Additional amount, if any, you want withheld from each paycheck . . . 6 | $
7 I claim exemption from withholding for 20--, and I certify that I meet **both** of the following conditions for exemption.
• Last year I had a right to a refund of **all** federal income tax withheld because I had **no** tax liability, **and**
• This year I expect a refund of **all** federal income tax withheld because I expect to have **no** tax liability.
If you meet both conditions, write "Exempt" here . . . ▶ 7

Under penalties of perjury, I declare that I have examined this certificate and, to the best of my knowledge and belief, it is true, correct, and complete.

Employee's signature (This form is not valid unless you sign it.) ▶ *John T. McGrath* Date ▶ June 2, 20--

8 Employer's name and address (Employer: Complete lines 8 and 10 only if sending to the IRS.) | 9 Office code (optional) | 10 Employer identification number (EIN)

For Privacy Act and Paperwork Reduction Act Notice, see page 2. Cat. No. 10220Q Form **W-4** (20--)

On the W-4, an employee indicates marital status and the number of withholding allowances. A single employee may claim one withholding allowance. A married employee may claim an additional allowance for a spouse. An employee may also claim an allowance for each dependent other than a spouse. Each allowance reduces the federal income tax withheld from the employee's pay. Exhibit 2 indicates that McGrath is single and, thus, claimed one withholding allowance.

The federal income tax withheld depends on each employee's gross pay and W-4 allowance. Withholding tables issued by the Internal Revenue Service (IRS) are used to determine amounts to withhold.

FICA Tax Employers are required by the Federal Insurance Contributions Act (FICA) to withhold a portion of the earnings of each employee. The **FICA tax** withheld contributes to the following two federal programs:

- *Social security*, which provides payments for retirees, survivors, and disability insurance.
- *Medicare*, which provides health insurance for senior citizens.

The amount withheld from each employee is based on the employee's earnings *paid* in the *calendar* year. The withholding tax rates and maximum earnings subject to tax are often revised by Congress.[4] To simplify, this chapter assumes the following rates and earnings subject to tax:

- Social security: 6% on all earnings
- Medicare: 1.5% on all earnings

[4] For 2017, the social security tax rate was 6.2% and the Medicare tax rate was 1.45%. Earnings subject to the social security tax are limited to an annual threshold amount. To simplify, we assume all earnings are subject to social security taxes.

To illustrate, assume that **John T. McGrath**'s earnings for the week ending December 27 are $1,462 and the total FICA tax to be withheld is $109.65, computed as follows:

Earnings subject to 6% social security tax	$1,462
Social security tax rate	× 6%
Social security tax	$ 87.72
Earnings subject to 1.5% Medicare tax	$1,462
Medicare tax rate	× 1.5%
Medicare tax	21.93
Total FICA tax	$109.65

Other Deductions Employees may choose to have additional amounts deducted from their gross pay. For example, an employee may authorize deductions for retirement savings, charitable contributions, or life insurance. A union contract may also require the deduction of union dues.

Computing Employee Net Pay

Gross earnings less payroll deductions equals *net pay*, sometimes called *take-home pay*. Assume that **John T. McGrath** authorized weekly deductions of $20 for retirement savings and $5 for a United Fund contribution. Assuming that $257.95 of federal income tax is withheld, McGrath's net pay for the week ended December 27 is $1,069.40, computed as follows:

Gross earnings for the week		$1,462.00
Deductions:		
Social security tax	$ 87.72	
Medicare tax	21.93	
Federal income tax	257.95	
Retirement savings	20.00	
United Fund	5.00	
Total deductions		(392.60)
Net pay		$1,069.40

In the Notes to the financial statements, **Starbucks** recently reported payroll-related liabilities of $510.8 million.

Link to Starbucks

Employer's Payroll Taxes

Employers are subject to the following payroll taxes for amounts paid their employees:

- *FICA Tax:* Employers must match the employee's FICA tax contribution.
- *Federal Unemployment Compensation Tax (FUTA):* This employer tax provides for temporary payments to those who become unemployed. The tax collected by the federal government is allocated among the states for use in state programs rather than paid directly to employees. Congress often revises the FUTA tax rate and maximum earnings subject to tax.

Why It Matters

The Most You Will Ever Pay

In 1936, the Social Security Board described how the tax was expected to affect a worker's pay, as follows:

The taxes called for in this law will be paid both by your employer and by you. For the next 3 years, you will pay maybe 15 cents a week, maybe 25 cents a week, maybe 30 cents or more, according to what you earn. That is to say, during the next 3 years, beginning January 1, 1937, you will pay 1 cent for every dollar you earn, and at the same time, your employer will pay 1 cent for every dollar you earn, up to $3,000 a year. . . .

. . . Beginning in 1940 you will pay, and your employer will pay, 1½ cents for each dollar you earn, up to $3,000 a year . . . and then

beginning in 1943, you will pay 2 cents, and so will your employer, for every dollar you earn for the next three years. After that, you and your employer will each pay half a cent more for 3 years, and finally, beginning in 1949, . . . you and your employer will each pay 3 cents on each dollar you earn, up to $3,000 a year. That is the most you will ever pay.

The rate on January 1, 2017, was 7.65 cents per dollar earned (7.65%). The social security portion was 6.20% on the first $127,200 of earnings. The Medicare portion was 1.45% on all earnings. In addition, there is an additional Medicare tax of 0.9% on wages in excess of $200,000 for the calendar year.

Source: Arthur Lodge, "That Is the Most You Will Ever Pay," *Journal of Accountancy,* October 1985, p. 44.

■ *State Unemployment Compensation Tax (SUTA):* This employer tax also provides temporary payments to those who become unemployed. The FUTA and SUTA programs are closely coordinated, with the states distributing the unemployment checks.[5] SUTA tax rates and earnings subject to tax vary by state.[6]

The preceding employer taxes are an operating expense of the company. Exhibit 3 summarizes the responsibility for employee and employer payroll taxes.

Exhibit 3

Responsibility for Tax Payments

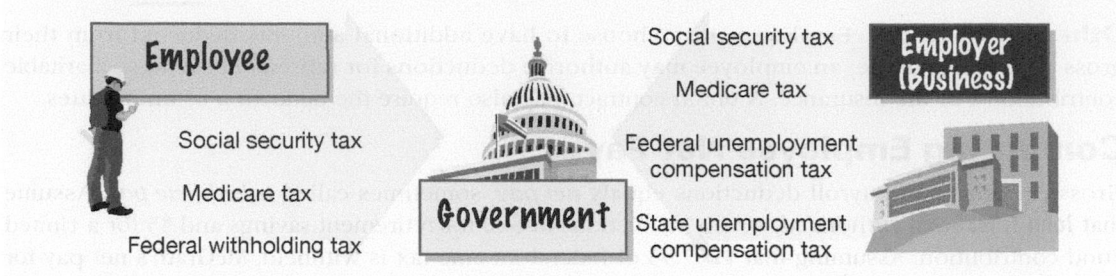

Recording Payroll

The payroll liabilities are normally recorded at the end of each payroll period. To illustrate, the following data for **McDermott Supply** for its payroll period ending March 21 are used.

Payroll:	
Sales salaries	$20,000
Office salaries	5,000
Total payroll	$25,000
Salaries subject to payroll taxes:	
Social security and Medicare	$25,000
State and federal unemployment tax	10,000
Payroll tax rates:	
Social security tax	6.0%
Medicare tax	1.5
State unemployment compensation tax	5.4
Federal unemployment compensation tax	0.8
Employee deductions:	
Federal income tax withholdings	$2,100
State income tax withholdings	550
Retirement contributions	1,200
Charitable contributions	250

The journal entry to record the March 21 payroll is as follows:

A = L + E
    +   – Exp

Mar. 21	Sales Salaries Expense	20,000	
	Office Salaries Expense	5,000	
	Social Security Tax Payable ($25,000 × 6%)		1,500
	Medicare Tax Payable ($25,000 × 1.5%)		375
	Employees Federal Income Tax Payable		2,100
	Employees State Income Tax Payable		550
	Retirement Contributions Payable		1,200
	Charitable Contributions Payable		250
	Salaries Payable		19,025

[5] This rate may be reduced to 0.8% for credits for state unemployment compensation tax.
[6] For 2017, the maximum state rate credited against the federal unemployment rate was 5.4% of the first $7,000 of each employee's earnings during a calendar year.

Employers must match the employees' social security and Medicare taxes. In addition, an employer must pay state and federal unemployment compensation taxes.

The employer's payroll taxes of $2,495 for the March 21 payroll are as follows:

Social security tax ($25,000 × 6%)	$1,500
Medicare tax ($25,000 × 1.5%)	375
State unemployment tax ($10,000 × 5.4%)	540
Federal unemployment tax ($10,000 × 0.8%)	80
Total payroll taxes	$2,495

The journal entry to record the payroll tax expense is as follows:

Mar. 21	Payroll Tax Expense	2,495	
	Social Security Tax Payable		1,500
	Medicare Tax Payable		375
	State Unemployment Tax Payable		540
	Federal Unemployment Tax Payable		80

$$A = L + E$$
$$+ \quad - \text{Exp}$$

When the preceding liabilities are paid, a journal entry is recorded debiting the liability accounts and crediting Cash.

Check Up Corner 10-2 Payroll Entries

Wildcat Company had gross wages of $180,000 for the week ended March 20. All $180,000 of wages are subject to social security and Medicare taxes, while $30,000 of wages are subject to federal and state unemployment taxes. Tax rates are as follows:

Social security tax	6.0%
Medicare tax	1.5
State unemployment compensation tax	5.4
Federal unemployment compensation tax	0.8

The total amount withheld from employee wages for federal taxes was $38,500.

a. Journalize the entry to record the payroll for the week of March 20.

b. Journalize the entry to record the employer's payroll tax expense incurred for the week of March 20.

Solution:

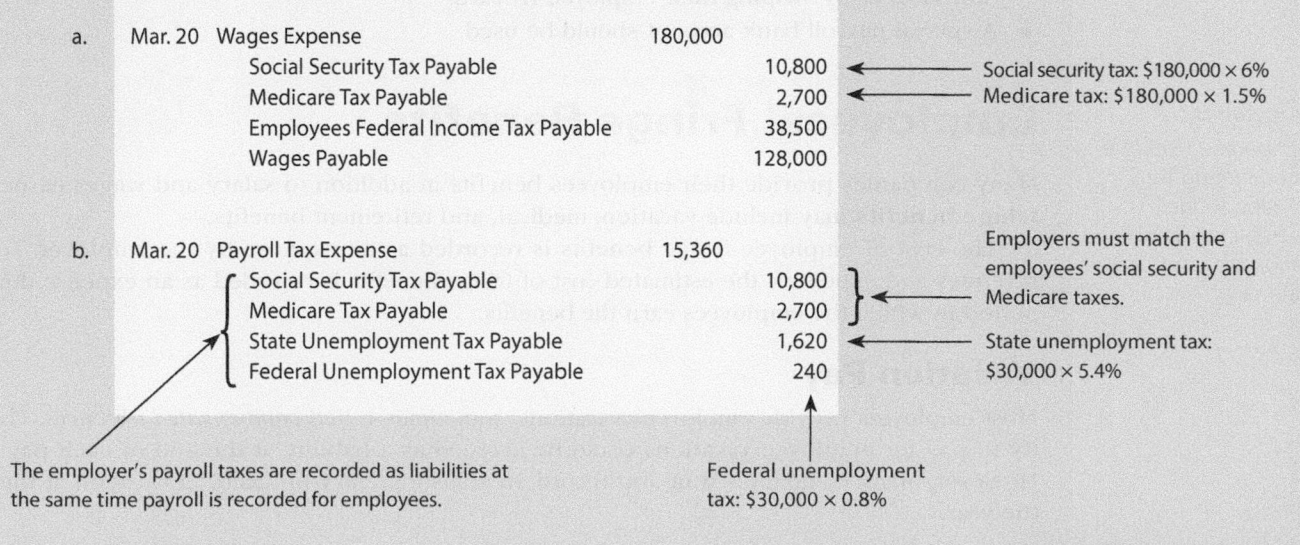

a. Mar. 20 Wages Expense — 180,000
Social Security Tax Payable — 10,800 ← Social security tax: $180,000 × 6%
Medicare Tax Payable — 2,700 ← Medicare tax: $180,000 × 1.5%
Employees Federal Income Tax Payable — 38,500
Wages Payable — 128,000

b. Mar. 20 Payroll Tax Expense — 15,360
Social Security Tax Payable — 10,800
Medicare Tax Payable — 2,700 ← Employers must match the employees' social security and Medicare taxes.
State Unemployment Tax Payable — 1,620 ← State unemployment tax: $30,000 × 5.4%
Federal Unemployment Tax Payable — 240

The employer's payroll taxes are recorded as liabilities at the same time payroll is recorded for employees.

Federal unemployment tax: $30,000 × 0.8%

Check Up Corner

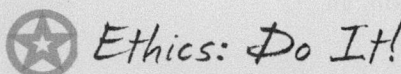

Ethics: Do It!

$8 Million for 18 Minutes of Work

Computer system controls can be very important in issuing payroll checks. In one case, a Detroit schoolteacher was paid $4,015,625 after deducting $3,884,375 in payroll deductions for 18 minutes of overtime work. The error was caused by a computer glitch when the teacher's employee identification number was substituted incorrectly in the "hourly wage"

field and wasn't caught by the payroll software. After six days, the error was discovered, and the money was returned. "One of the things that came with (the software) is a fail-safe that prevents that. It doesn't work," a financial officer said. The district has since installed a program to flag any paycheck exceeding $10,000.

Source: Associated Press, September 27, 2002.

Paying Payroll

Companies pay employees either by electronic funds transfer or by issuing *payroll checks*. With electronic funds transfers, the employee's net pay is electronically deposited into their bank account each period. The employees receive a payroll statement summarizing how the net pay was computed.

Most companies use a special payroll bank account for payroll. In such cases, payroll is processed as follows:

1. The total net pay for the period is determined.
2. The company authorizes an electronic funds transfer (EFT) from its regular bank account to the special payroll bank account for the total net pay.
3. Individual EFTs or payroll checks are disbursed from the payroll account.

An advantage of using a separate payroll bank account is that reconciling the bank statements is simplified.

Internal Controls for Payroll

The controls described in Chapter 7 also apply to payrolls. Some examples of payroll controls include the following:

- The hiring and firing of employees should be properly authorized and approved in writing.
- All changes in pay rates should be properly authorized and approved in writing.
- Employees should be observed when arriving for work to verify that employees are "checking in" for work only once and only for themselves. Employees may "check in" for work by using a time card or by swiping their employee ID card.
- A special payroll bank account should be used.

Objective 3

Describe and illustrate the accounting for employee fringe benefits, including vacation pay and pensions.

Employees' Fringe Benefits

Many companies provide their employees benefits in addition to salary and wages earned. Such **fringe benefits** may include vacation, medical, and retirement benefits.

The cost of employee fringe benefits is recorded as an expense by the employer. To match revenues and expenses, the estimated cost of fringe benefits is recorded as an expense during the period in which the employees earn the benefits.

Vacation Pay

Most employers provide employees vacations, sometimes called *compensated absences*. The liability to pay for employee vacations could be accrued as a liability at the end of each pay period. However, many companies wait and record an adjusting entry for accrued vacation at the end of the year.

To illustrate, assume that employees earn one day of vacation for each month worked. The estimated vacation pay for the year ending December 31 is $325,000. The adjusting entry for the accrued vacation is as follows:

Dec. 31	Vacation Pay Expense	325,000	
	Vacation Pay Payable		325,000
	Accrued vacation pay for the year.		

$$A = L + E$$
$$+ \quad - \text{Exp}$$

Employees may be required to take all their vacation time within one year. In such cases, any accrued vacation pay will be paid within one year. Thus, the vacation pay payable is reported as a current liability on the balance sheet. If employees are allowed to accumulate their vacation pay, the estimated vacation pay payable that will *not* be taken within a year is reported as a long-term liability.

When employees take vacations, the liability for vacation pay is decreased by debiting Vacation Pay Payable. Salaries or Wages Payable and the other related payroll accounts for taxes and withholdings are credited.

Pensions

A **pension** is a cash payment to retired employees. Pension rights are accrued by employees as they work, based on the employer's pension plan. Two basic types of pension plans are defined contribution and defined benefit plans.[7]

Defined Contribution Plans In a **defined contribution plan**, the company invests contributions on behalf of the employee during the employee's working years. Normally, the employee and employer contribute to the plan. The employee's pension depends on the total contributions and the investment returns earned on those contributions.

One of the more popular defined contribution plans is the 401k plan. Under this plan, employees contribute a portion of their gross pay to investments, such as mutual funds. A 401k plan offers employees two advantages.

- The employee contribution is deducted before taxes.
- The contributions and related earnings are not taxed until withdrawn at retirement.

In most cases, the employer matches some portion of the employee's contribution. The employer's cost is debited to *Pension Expense*. To illustrate, assume that Heaven Scent Perfumes Company contributes 10% of employee monthly salaries to an employee 401k plan. Assuming $500,000 of monthly salaries, the journal entry to record the monthly contribution is as follows:

Dec. 31	Pension Expense	50,000	
	Cash		50,000
	Contributed 10% of monthly salaries		
	to pension plan.		

$$A = L + E$$
$$- \qquad - \text{Exp}$$

In a recent year, **Starbucks** disclosed that it made matching contributions of $86.2 million to its defined contribution plan.

Link to Starbucks

Defined Benefit Plans In a **defined benefit plan**, the company pays the employee a fixed annual pension based on a formula. The formula is normally based on such factors as the employee's years of service, age, and past salary.

In a defined benefit plan, the employer is obligated to pay for (fund) the employee's future pension benefits. As a result, many companies are replacing their defined benefit plans with defined contribution plans.

[7] The accounting for pensions is complex due to the uncertainties of estimating future pension liabilities. These estimates depend on such factors as employee life expectancies, employee turnover, expected employee compensation levels, and investment income on pension contributions. Additional accounting and disclosures related to pensions are covered in advanced accounting courses.

The pension cost of a defined benefit plan is debited to *Pension Expense*. Cash is credited for the amount contributed (funded) by the employer. Any unfunded amount is credited to *Unfunded Pension Liability*.

To illustrate, assume that the defined benefit plan of Hinkle Co. requires an annual pension cost of $80,000. This annual contribution is based on estimates of Hinkle's future pension liabilities. On December 31, Hinkle pays $60,000 to the pension fund. The entry to record the payment and the unfunded liability is as follows:

A = L + E
–   +   – Exp

	Dec. 31	Pension Expense	80,000	
		Cash		60,000
		Unfunded Pension Liability		20,000
		Annual pension cost and contribution.		

If the unfunded pension liability is to be paid within one year, it is reported as a current liability on the balance sheet. Any portion of the unfunded pension liability that will be paid beyond one year is a long-term liability.

Postretirement Benefits Other than Pensions

Employees may earn rights to other postretirement benefits from their employer. Such benefits may include dental care, eye care, medical care, life insurance, tuition assistance, tax services, and legal services.

Why It Matters

State Pension Obligations

E ach state has a pension plan for its employees. The plan is determined by the state legislature through the normal political process. The funding of each state's plan relative to the outstanding obligation differs across the states, again according to political decisions regarding the funding level. Some states are well funded, while others face significant pension shortfalls. Only 13 out of 50 states have pension assets greater than 80% of their pension obligations, which is considered a healthy funding ratio. The U.S. Census Bureau provides an annual survey on the status of state pension plans. According to a recent survey, the top and bottom five states by the percent of pension obligations funded are as follows:

Rank	State	Percent of Pension Funded	Pension Contributions as a Percent of State Payroll	Pension Liability per State Resident
1	Wisconsin	102%	12.6%	$ 0
2	North Carolina	95	12.7	407
3	New York	93	15.7	877
4	South Dakota	93	13.3	730
5	Tennessee	89	15.1	693
46	New Jersey	55	16.4	6,447
47	Alaska	53	31.6	11,028
48	Kentucky	50	21.6	5,907
49	Connecticut	49	25.7	7,027
50	Illinois	47	31.9	7,636

As can be seen, the states with the most severe underfunding are also the states making the largest contributions to their pension plans as a percent of the state's governmental payroll. This is likely an attempt to "catch up" to their obligations, but is coming at a high cost to the state's taxpayers.

The accounting for other postretirement benefits is similar to that of defined benefit pension plans. The estimate of the annual benefits expense is recorded by debiting *Postretirement Benefits Expense*. If the benefits are fully funded, Cash is credited for the same amount. If the benefits are not fully funded, a postretirement benefits plan liability account is also credited.

The financial statements should disclose the nature of the postretirement benefits liabilities. These disclosures are usually included as notes to the financial statements. Additional accounting and disclosures for postretirement benefits are covered in advanced accounting courses.

Installment Notes

Objective 4
Describe and illustrate the accounting for installment notes.

An installment note is a debt that requires the borrower to make equal periodic payments to the lender for the term of the note. Each note payment includes the following:

- Payment of a portion of the amount initially borrowed, called the *principal*
- Payment of interest on the outstanding balance

At the end of the note's term, the principal will have been repaid in full.

Installment notes are often used to purchase specific assets such as equipment, and are often secured by the purchased asset. If the borrower fails to pay the note, the lender has the right to take possession of the pledged asset and sell it to pay off the debt. Installment notes that are secured by purchased assets are sometimes called *mortgage notes*.

Issuance

When an installment note is issued, an entry is recorded debiting Cash and crediting Notes Payable. To illustrate, assume that on January 1 of Year 1 Lewis Company issues the following installment note to City National Bank:

Principal amount of note	$24,000
Interest rate	6%
Term of note	5 years
Annual payments	$5,698[8]

The entry to record the issuance of the note is as follows:

Year 1			
Jan. 1	Cash	24,000	
	Notes Payable		24,000
	Issued installment note for cash.		

$$A = L + E$$
$$+ \quad +$$

In a recent financial statement, **Starbucks** reported $3,202 of long-term notes payable.

Link to Starbucks

Periodic Payments

The preceding note payable requires Lewis Company to repay the principal and interest in equal payments of $5,698 beginning December 31 of Year 1 for each of the next five years. Each installment note payment includes an interest and principal component.

The interest portion of an installment note payment is computed by multiplying the interest rate by the carrying amount (book value) of the note at the beginning of the period. The principal portion of the payment is then computed as the difference between the total installment note payment (cash paid) and the interest component. These computations are illustrated in Exhibit 4 (rounded to the nearest dollar).

[8] The annual payment is computed using present value concepts that are discussed in advanced accounting courses.

Exhibit 4 Allocation of Periodic Payments

For the Year Ending December 31	A January 1 Carrying Amount	B Note Payment (cash paid)	C Interest Expense (6% of January 1 Note Carrying Amount)	D Decrease in Notes Payable (B – C)	E December 31 Carrying Amount (A – D)
Year 1	$24,000	$ 5,698	$ 1,440 (6% of $24,000)	$ 4,258	$19,742
Year 2	19,742	5,698	1,185 (6% of $19,742)	4,513	15,229
Year 3	15,229	5,698	914 (6% of $15,229)	4,784	10,445
Year 4	10,445	5,698	627 (6% of $10,445)	5,071	5,374
Year 5	5,374	5,698	324* (6% of $5,374)	5,374	0
		$28,490	$4,490	$24,000	

*Rounded ($5,698 – $5,374).

1. The January 1 carrying value (Column A) for Year 1 equals the amount borrowed from the bank. The January 1 balance in the following years equals the December 31 balance from the prior year.

2. The note payment (Column B) remains constant at $5,698, the annual cash payment required by the bank.

3. The interest expense (Column C) is computed at 6% of the installment note carrying amount at the beginning of each year. As a result, the interest expense decreases each year.

4. Notes payable decreases each year by the amount of the principal repayment (Column D). The principal repayment is computed by subtracting the interest expense (Column C) from the total payment (Column B). The principal repayment (Column D) increases each year as the interest expense decreases (Column C).

5. The carrying amount on December 31 (Column E) of the note decreases from $24,000, the initial amount borrowed, to $0 at the end of Year 5.

The entry to record the first payment on December 31 of Year 1 is as follows:

A = L + E
–   –   – Exp

Year 1			
Dec. 31	Interest Expense	1,440	
	Notes Payable	4,258	
	Cash		5,698
	Paid principal and interest on installment note.		

The entry to record the second payment on December 31 of Year 2 is as follows:

A = L + E
–   –   – Exp

Year 2			
Dec. 31	Interest Expense	1,185	
	Notes Payable	4,513	
	Cash		5,698
	Paid principal and interest on installment note.		

As the preceding entries show, the cash payment of $5,698 is the same in each year. The interest and principal repayment, however, change each year. This is because the carrying amount (book value) of the note decreases each year as principal is repaid, which decreases the interest component the next period.

The entry to record the final payment on December 31 of Year 5 is as follows:

A = L + E
–   –   – Exp

Year 5			
Dec. 31	Interest Expense	324	
	Notes Payable	5,374	
	Cash		5,698
	Paid principal and interest on installment note.		

After the final payment, the carrying amount on the note is zero, indicating that the note has been paid in full. Any assets that secure the note would then be released by the bank.

| **Check Up Corner 10-3** | Installment Notes |

On January 1, the first day of the fiscal year, Anchor Company issues a $30,000, 10%, five-year installment note that has annual payments of $7,914.

a. Journalize the annual note payment at the end of Year 1 and Year 2.

b. Determine the carrying amount of the note at the end of Year 1 and Year 2.

Solution:

For the Year Ending December 31	January 1 Carrying Amount	Note Payment	Interest Expense	Decrease in Notes Payable	December 31 Carrying Amount
Year 1	$30,000	$7,914	$3,000 (10% × $30,000)	$4,914	$25,086
Year 2	25,086	7,914	2,509 (10% × $25,086)	5,405	19,681

a. Year 1

Dec. 31	Interest Expense	3,000		← Payment of interest on the original $30,000 balance
	Notes Payable	4,914		← Payment of a portion of the amount
	Cash		7,914	initially borrowed

Year 2

Dec. 31	Interest Expense	2,509		← Payment of interest on the December 31, Year 1, balance
	Notes Payable	5,405		← Payment of a portion of the
	Cash		7,914	amount initially borrowed

b. December 31, Year 1 $25,086   ← The remaining balance on the installment note at the end of
    December 31, Year 2   19,681   each year (see table)

Check Up Corner

Why It Matters

CONCEPT CLIP

Installment Credit

The type of loan most often obtained by a consumer for large purchases such as an automobile or a home is the installment loan. The installment payments consist of both principal and interest. The interest portion starts large at the beginning of the installment period and gets smaller toward the end of an installment period. For example, the payment for a 30-year, $150,000 mortgage at 5% interest would be $805. At the beginning of the 30-year period, 76% or $610 would go toward interest, with the remainder going toward principal reduction. At the end of the 30-year period, nearly all of the $805 payment would go toward principal reduction. The reason for this pattern is because the principal balance is large at the beginning of the installment period, and gradually reduces as payments are made. Thus, the amount of interest paid per period is trending with the declining loan balance.

Objective 5
Describe and illustrate the accounting for contingent liabilities, including product warranties.

Contingent Liabilities

Some liabilities may arise from past transactions only if certain events occur in the future. These *potential* liabilities are called **contingent liabilities**.

The accounting for contingent liabilities depends on the following two factors:

- *Likelihood of occurring*
- *Measurement*

The likelihood of occurring is classified as *probable*, *reasonably possible*, or *remote*. The ability to measure the potential liability is classified as *estimable* or *not estimable*.

Probable and Estimable

If a contingent liability is *probable* and the amount of the liability can be *reasonably estimated*, it is recorded and disclosed. The liability is recorded by debiting an expense and crediting a liability.

To illustrate, assume that during June a company sold a product for $60,000 that includes a 36-month warranty for repairs.[9] The average cost of repairs over the warranty period is estimated at 5% of the sales price. The entry to record the estimated product warranty expense for June is as follows:

A = L + E
+   – Exp

June 30	Product Warranty Expense	3,000	
	Product Warranty Payable		3,000
	Warranty expense for June (5% × $60,000).		

The preceding entry records warranty expense in the same period in which the sale is recorded. In this way, warranty expense is matched with the related revenue (sales).

If the product is repaired under warranty, the repair costs are recorded by debiting *Product Warranty Payable* and crediting *Cash, Supplies, Wages Payable*, or other appropriate accounts. Thus, if a $200 part is replaced under warranty on August 16, the entry is as follows:

A = L + E
–   –

Aug. 16	Product Warranty Payable	200	
	Supplies		200
	Replaced defective part under warranty.		

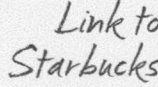

Link to Starbucks

In 2011, **Starbucks** terminated a contract with **Kraft Foods** that allowed Kraft to sell bagged Starbucks coffee in grocery stores. The early termination resulted in litigation between Kraft and Starbucks. After an arbitrator found in Kraft's favor, Starbucks recorded a contingent liability for $2.8 billion.

Probable and Not Estimable

A contingent liability may be probable, but cannot be estimated. In this case, the contingent liability is disclosed in the notes to the financial statements. For example, a company may have accidentally polluted a local river by dumping waste products. At the end of the period, the cost of the cleanup and any fines may not be able to be estimated.

---

[9] This discussion is limited to warranties that provide assurance that a product will work as promised (assurance-type warranties). A more detailed discussion of the different types of warranties is provided in intermediate accounting texts.

Reasonably Possible

A contingent liability may be only possible. For example, a company may have lost a lawsuit for infringing on another company's patent rights. However, the verdict is under appeal and the company's lawyers feel that the verdict will be reversed or significantly reduced. In this case, the contingent liability is disclosed in the notes to the financial statements.

Remote

A contingent liability may be remote. For example, a ski resort may be sued for injuries incurred by skiers. In most cases, the courts have found that a skier accepts the risk of injury when participating in the activity. Thus, unless the ski resort is grossly negligent, the resort will not incur a liability for ski injuries. In such cases, no disclosure needs to be made in the notes to the financial statements. The accounting treatment of contingent liabilities is summarized in Exhibit 5.

Exhibit 5 Accounting Treatment of Contingent Liabilities

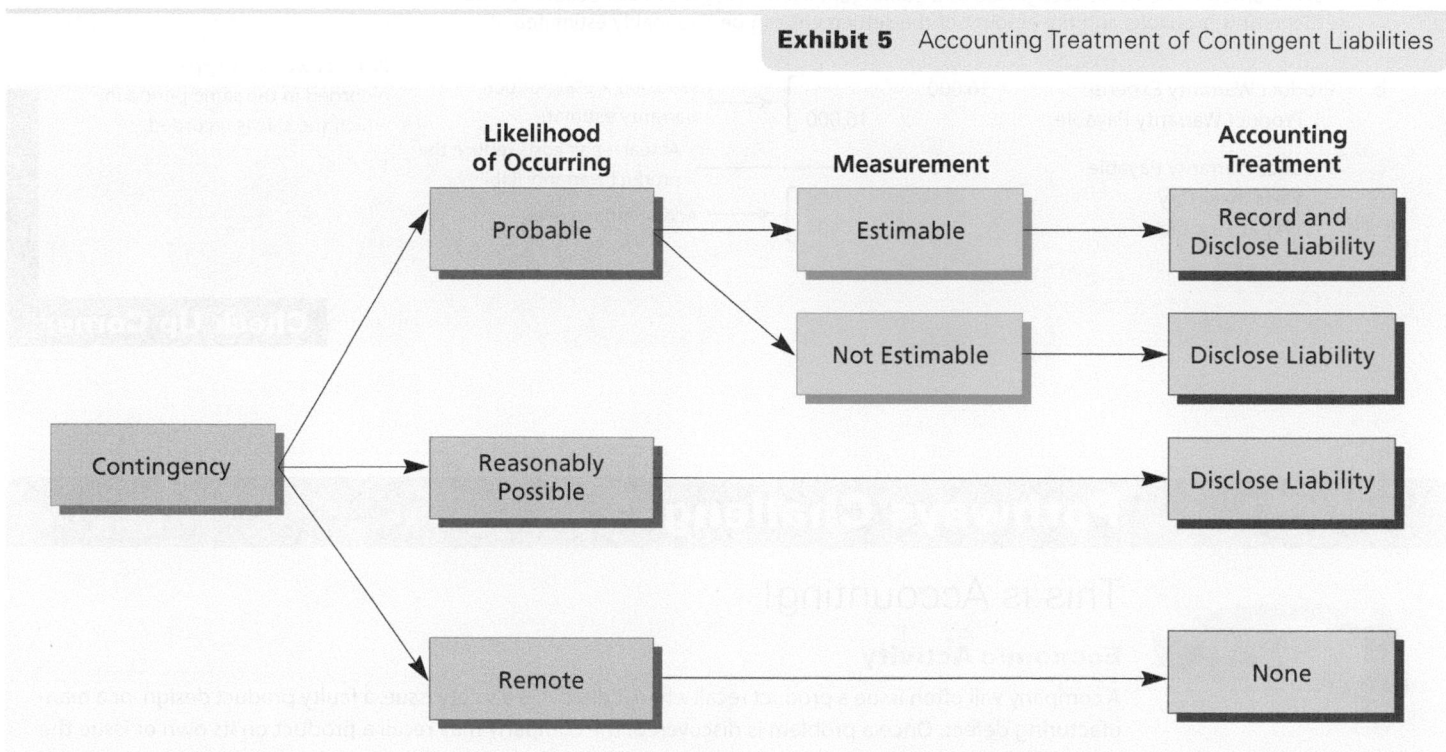

Common examples of contingent liabilities disclosed in notes to the financial statements are litigation, environmental matters, guarantees, and contingencies from the sale of receivables.

Professional judgment is necessary in distinguishing between classes of contingent liabilities. This is especially the case when distinguishing between probable and reasonably possible contingent liabilities.

In a recent annual report, **Starbucks** reported that in its normal course of business, it is party to a variety of legal actions. However, the management of Starbucks believes none of these actions will have a material effect on its financial statements.

Link to Starbucks

Check Up Corner 10-4 | Contingent Liabilities

Scooter General Inc. is in its first year of manufacturing and selling high-end scooters. The company warrants its products for one year and estimates product warranty costs at 2% of sales. During January, a customer sued the company for false advertising. The company's legal counsel has been in negotiations with the customer's attorney and believes that it is probable the company will reach an out-of-court settlement for $85,000 in the coming weeks. The lawsuit will not impact the company's warranty cost estimate.

a. Should the company journalize the contingent liability associated with the lawsuit?

b. Journalize the adjusting entry required at the end of January to record the estimated product warranty costs. Sales were $800,000 during January.

c. In February, the company made warranty repairs requiring $900 of replacement parts and $400 of labor costs. Journalize the entry to record the warranty work provided in February.

Solution:

a. Yes. The amount should be recognized as a contingent liability. Legal counsel believes an out-of-court settlement is probable, and the amount of the settlement can be reasonably estimated.

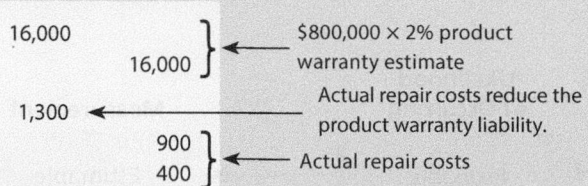

b.	Product Warranty Expense	16,000	
	Product Warranty Payable		16,000
c.	Product Warranty Payable	1,300	
	Parts Inventory		900
	Wages Payable		400

$800,000 × 2% product warranty estimate

Actual repair costs reduce the product warranty liability.

Actual repair costs

Product warranty expense is recorded in the same period in which the sale is recorded.

Check Up Corner

Pathways Challenge

This is Accounting!

Economic Activity

A company will often issue a product recall when it discovers a safety issue, a faulty product design, or a manufacturing defect. Once a problem is discovered, the company may recall a product on its own or issue the recall in response to a regulatory agency's demands.

When a customer returns a product that has been recalled, the company will fix the issue, replace the product, or provide a refund. Several high-profile companies have recently issued product recalls. For example, **Samsung (SSNLS)** voluntarily recalled approximately 2.5 million of its Galaxy Note 7 phones due to battery failures that led to the device catching on fire. In addition, numerous automakers [e.g., **Toyota (TM)**, **General Motors (GM)**, **Nissan (NSANY)**] recently issued recalls due to faulty air bags.

Critical Thinking/Judgment

Is a warranty the same thing as a product recall?
What is the accounting for the estimated costs of a product recall?

Suggested answer at end of chapter.

Reporting Liabilities

Objective 6
Describe the reporting of liabilities on the balance sheet.

Accounts payable, accruals, notes payable, the current portion of installment notes payable, and any other debts that are due within one year are reported as current liabilities on the balance sheet. Any remaining installment notes payable or other debts are reported as long-term liabilities.

The reporting of **Starbucks Corporation**'s current liabilities and long-term debt is as follows:

Link to Starbucks

Starbucks Corporation Balance Sheet October 2 (in millions)		
Current liabilities:		
Accounts payable......................................	$ 730.6	
Accrued liabilities.....................................	1,999.1	
Insurance reserves....................................	246.0	
Stored value card liability	1,171.2	
Current portion of long-term debt	400.0	
Total current liabilities		$4,546.9
Long-term debt		3,202.2
Other long-term liabilities............................		689.7
Total current liabilities		$8,438.8

Source: Adapted from a recent Starbucks annual report.

Analysis for Decision Making

Quick Ratio

Objective 7
Describe and illustrate the use of the quick ratio in analyzing a company's ability to pay its current liabilities.

Current position analysis helps creditors evaluate a company's ability to pay its current liabilities. This analysis is based on the following three measures:

- Working capital
- Current ratio
- Quick ratio

Working capital and the current ratio were discussed in Chapter 4 and are computed as follows:

$$\text{Working Capital} = \text{Current Assets} - \text{Current Liabilities}$$

$$\text{Current Ratio} = \frac{\text{Current Assets}}{\text{Current Liabilities}}$$

While these two measures can be used to weigh a company's ability to pay its current liabilities, they do not show the company's ability to pay these liabilities within a short period of time. This is because some current assets, such as inventory, cannot be converted into cash as quickly as other current assets, such as cash and accounts receivable.

The **quick ratio** overcomes this limitation by measuring the "instant" debt-paying ability of a company and is computed as follows:

$$\text{Quick Ratio} = \frac{\text{Quick Assets}}{\text{Current Liabilities}}$$

Quick assets are cash and other current assets that can be easily converted to cash, such as temporary investments and accounts receivable. Temporary investments include securities that can be easily sold and turned into cash. The other current assets are not included as part of quick assets because they often include prepaid expenses or other deferred assets that are not easily converted to cash.

The current and quick ratios are particularly useful in making comparisons across companies. To illustrate, the following selected balance sheet data (excluding ratios) were taken from recent financial statements of **Panera Bread Company (PNRA)** and **Starbucks Corporation (SBUX)** (in thousands):

	Panera	Starbucks
Current assets:		
Cash and cash equivalents	$ 105,529	$2,128,800
Temporary investments	—	134,400
Accounts receivable	112,923	768,800
Inventory..	23,775	1,378,500
Other current assets	69,194	350,000
Total current assets	$ 311,421	$4,760,500
Current liabilities:		
Accounts payable..	$ 22,455	$ 730,600
Other current liabilities	425,866	3,816,300
Total current liabilities	$ 448,321	$4,546,900
Working capital (current assets – current liabilities).....................	$(136,900)	$ 213,600
Current ratio (current assets ÷ current liabilities)	0.69	1.05
Quick ratio (quick assets ÷ current liabilities)*	0.49	0.67

*The quick ratio for each company is computed as follows:
Panera: ($105,529 + $112,923) ÷ $448,321 = 0.49
Starbucks: ($2,128,800 + $134,400 + $768,800) ÷ $4,546,900 = 0.67

Source: Panera Bread Company, *Form 10-K for the Fiscal Year Ended Dec. 31, 2016*, and Starbucks Corporation, *Form 10-K for the Fiscal Year Ended Oct. 2, 2016*.

Starbucks is significantly larger than Panera and has much greater working capital. Such size differences make working capital comparisons between companies difficult. In contrast, current and quick ratios provide more meaningful comparisons across companies. In this example, Starbucks has higher current and quick ratios than Panera. The higher current ratio is mostly due to the larger relative inventory held by Starbucks. Both companies have quick ratios below 1.0, indicating that quick assets do not fully cover current liabilities. This is not a concern, because inventory turns into cash quickly for these two food companies.

Make a Decision Quick Ratio

Analyze and compare Amazon.com to Best Buy (MAD 10-1)
(Continuing company analysis)

Analyze and compare Abercrombie & Fitch and The Gap (MAD 10-2)

Analyze Hershey (MAD 10-3)

Analyze and compare Neiman Marcus and Kohl's (MAD 10-4)

Analyze and compare Cabela's and Dick's Sporting Goods (MAD 10-5)

Make a Decision

Let's Review

Chapter Summary

1. Current liabilities are obligations that are to be paid out of current assets and are due within a short time, usually within one year. The primary types of current liabilities are accounts payable, accruals, notes payable, and the current portion of long-term debt.

2. Payroll liabilities include those for employee earnings and employer's payroll taxes. An employer's liability for employee earnings is determined from employee total earnings, including overtime pay. From this amount, employee deductions are subtracted to arrive at the net pay to be paid to each employee. Employers also incur liabilities for payroll taxes, such as social security tax, Medicare tax, federal unemployment compensation tax, and state unemployment compensation tax.

3. Fringe benefits are expenses of the period in which the employees earn the benefits. Fringe benefits are recorded by debiting an expense account and crediting a liability account.

4. An installment note requires the borrower to make equal periodic payments to the lender for the term of the note. Each payment consists of principal and interest. The

journal entry for the payment debits Interest Expense and Notes Payable and credits Cash for the amount of the payment. After the final payment, the carrying amount on the note is zero.

5. A contingent liability is a potential obligation that results from a past transaction but depends on a future event. The accounting for contingent liabilities is summarized in Exhibit 5.

6. Accounts payable, accruals, notes payable, the current portion of installment notes payable, and any other debts that are due within one year are reported as current liabilities on the balance sheet. Any remaining installment notes payable or other debts are reported as long-term liabilities.

7. Current position analysis helps creditors evaluate a company's ability to pay its current liabilities. The quick ratio shows a company's ability to pay these liabilities within a short period of time. It is computed as quick assets ÷ current liabilities. Quick assets are cash and other current assets that can be easily converted to cash, such as temporary investments and accounts receivable.

Key Terms

contingent liabilities (510)
defined benefit plan (505)
defined contribution plan (505)
FICA tax (500)

fringe benefits (504)
gross pay (500)
installment note (498)
net pay (500)

payroll (499)
pension (505)
quick assets (514)
quick ratio (513)

Practice

Multiple-Choice Questions

1. A business issued a $5,000, 60-day, 12% note to the bank. The amount due at maturity is:
   a. $4,900
   b. $5,000
   c. $5,100
   d. $5,600

2. A business issued a $5,000, 60-day note to a supplier, which discounted the note at 12%. The proceeds are:
   a. $4,400
   b. $4,900
   c. $5,000
   d. $5,100

3. Which of the following taxes are employers usually not required to withhold from employees?
   a. Federal income tax
   b. Federal unemployment compensation tax
   c. Medicare tax
   d. State and local income tax

4. An employee's rate of pay is $36 per hour, with time and a half for all hours worked in excess of 40 during a week. The employee worked 45 hours during the week. The amount of the employee's gross pay for the week is:

a. $1,440
b. $1,620
c. $1,710
d. $1,800

5. Which of the following is the journal entry to record a periodic payment on an installment note?

a. Debit Notes Payable; credit Cash

b. Debit Interest Expense; credit Cash

c. Debit Interest Expense; debit Notes Payable; credit Cash

d. Debit Interest Expense; credit Notes Payable; credit Cash

Answers provided after Problem. Need more practice? Find additional multiple-choice questions, exercises, and problems in CengageNOWv2.

Exercises

1. Proceeds from notes payable
Obj. 1

On October 12, Belleville Co. borrowed cash from Texas Bank by issuing a 30-day note with a face amount of $70,000.

a. Determine the proceeds of the note, assuming the note carries an interest rate of 6%.

b. Determine the proceeds of the note, assuming the note is discounted at 6%.

2. Employee net pay
Obj. 2

Lily Flower's weekly gross earnings for the week ended October 20 were $2,500, and her federal income tax withholding was $517.24. Assuming the social security rate is 6% and Medicare is 1.5% of all earnings, what is Flower's net pay?

3. Journalize period payroll
Obj. 2

The payroll register of Konrath Co. indicates $13,200 of social security withheld and $3,300 of Medicare tax withheld on total salaries of $220,000 for the period. Federal withholding for the period totaled $43,560.

Journalize the entry to record the period's payroll.

4. Journalize payroll tax
Obj. 2

The payroll register of Konrath Co. indicates $13,200 of social security withheld and $3,300 of Medicare tax withheld on total salaries of $220,000 for the period. Earnings of $35,000 are subject to state and federal unemployment compensation taxes at the federal rate of 0.8% and the state rate of 5.4%.

Journalize the entry to record the payroll tax expense for the period.

5. Vacation pay and pension benefits
Obj. 3

Fukushima Company provides its employees with vacation benefits and a defined contribution pension plan. Employees earned vacation pay of $19,500 for the period. The pension plan requires a contribution to the plan administrator equal to 6% of employee salaries. Salaries were $260,000 during the period, and the full amount due was contributed to the pension plan administrator.

Journalize the entry to record the (a) vacation pay and (b) pension benefit.

6. Journalizing installment notes
Obj. 4

On the first day of the fiscal year, a company issues $65,000, 6%, five-year installment notes that have annual payments of $15,431. The first note payment consists of $3,900 of interest and $11,531 of principal repayment.

a. Journalize the entry to record the issuance of the installment notes.

b. Journalize the first annual note payment.

7. Estimated warranty liability

Obj. 5

Chloe Co. sold $300,000 of equipment during January under a one-year warranty. The cost to repair defects under the warranty is estimated at 5% of the sales price. On June 20, a customer required a $90 part replacement plus $42 of labor under the warranty.

Journalize the entry to record (a) the estimated warranty expense on January 31 for January sales, and (b) the June 20 warranty work.

8. Quick ratio

Obj. 7

Nabors Company reported the following current assets and current liabilities for two recent years:

	Dec. 31, 20Y8	Dec. 31, 20Y7
Cash	$ 650	$ 680
Temporary investments	1,500	1,550
Accounts receivable	700	770
Inventory	1,250	1,400
Accounts payable	2,375	2,000

a. Compute the quick ratio on December 31 for each year. Round to one decimal place.

b. Interpret the company's quick ratio. Is the quick ratio improving or declining?

Answers provided after Problem. Need more practice? Find additional multiple-choice questions, exercises, and problems in CengageNOWv2.

Problem

Selected transactions of Taylor Company, completed during the fiscal year ended December 31, are as follows:

Mar. 1.	Purchased merchandise on account from Kelvin Co., $20,000.
Apr. 10.	Issued a 60-day, 12% note for $20,000 to Kelvin Co. on account.
June 9.	Paid Kelvin Co. the amount owed on the note of April 10.
Aug. 1.	Issued a $50,000, 90-day note to Harold Co. in exchange for a building. Harold Co. discounted the note at 15%.
Oct. 30.	Paid Harold Co. the amount due on the note of August 1.
Dec. 27.	Journalized the entry to record the biweekly payroll. A summary of the payroll record follows:

Salary distribution:

Sales	$63,400	
Officers	36,600	
Office	10,000	$110,000

Deductions:

Social security tax	$ 6,600	
Medicare tax	1,650	
Federal income tax withheld	17,600	
State income tax withheld	4,950	
Savings bond deductions	850	
Medical insurance deductions	1,120	(32,770)
Net amount		$ 77,230

27.	Journalized the entry to record payroll taxes for social security and Medicare from the biweekly payroll.
30.	Issued a check in payment of liabilities for employees' federal income tax of $17,600, social security tax of $13,200, and Medicare tax of $3,300.

Dec. 31.   Issued a check for $9,500 to the pension fund trustee to fully fund the pension cost for December.

31.   Journalized an entry to record the employees' accrued vacation pay, $36,100.

31.   Journalized an entry to record the estimated accrued product warranty liability, $37,240.

Instructions
Journalize the preceding transactions.

Need more practice? Find additional multiple-choice questions, exercises, and problems in CengageNOWv2.

Answers

Multiple-Choice Questions

1. **c** The maturity value is $5,100, determined as follows:

Face amount of note	$5,000
Interest ($5,000 × 12% × 60 ÷ 360)	100
Maturity value	$5,100

2. **b** The net amount available to a borrower from discounting a note payable is called the proceeds. The proceeds of $4,900 (answer b) is determined as follows:

Face amount of note	$5,000
Discount ($5,000 × 12% × 60 ÷ 360)	(100)
Proceeds	$4,900

3. **b** Employers are usually required to withhold a portion of their employees' earnings for payment of federal income taxes (answer a), Medicare tax (answer c), and state and local income taxes (answer d). Generally, federal unemployment compensation taxes (answer b) are levied against the employer only and thus are not deducted from employee earnings.

4. **c** The amount of gross pay of $1,710 (answer c) is determined as follows:
   $1,710 = (40 \text{ hours} \times \$36) + [(45 \text{ hrs.} - 40 \text{ hrs.}) \times (\$36 \times 1.5)]$
   $1,710 = \$1,440 + (5 \text{ hrs.} \times \$54) = \$1,440 + \$270$

5. **c** The journal entry to record a periodic payment on an installment note debits Interest Expense, debits Notes Payable, and credits Cash (answer c).

Exercises

1. a. $70,000

   b. $69,650 [$70,000 − ($70,000 × 30 ÷ 360 × 6%)]

2.
Total wage payment		$2,500.00
Deductions:		
Federal income tax	$(517.24)	
Social security tax ($2,500 × 6%)	(150.00)	
Medicare tax ($2,500 × 1.5%)	(37.50)	
Total deductions		(704.74)
Net pay		$1,795.26

3.
Salaries Expense	220,000	
Social Security Tax Payable		13,200
Medicare Tax Payable		3,300
Employees Federal Income Tax Payable		43,560
Salaries Payable		159,940

4.
Payroll Tax Expense	18,670	
Social Security Tax Payable		13,200
Medicare Tax Payable		3,300
State Unemployment Tax Payable*		1,890
Federal Unemployment Tax Payable**		280

*$35,000 × 5.4%
**$35,000 × 0.8%

5. a.
Vacation Pay Expense	19,500	
Vacation Pay Payable		19,500
Vacation pay accrued for the period.		

b.
Pension Expense	15,600	
Cash		15,600
To record pension contribution		
(6% × $260,000).		

6. a.
Cash	65,000	
Notes Payable		65,000
Issued installment notes for cash.		

b.
Interest Expense	3,900	
Notes Payable	11,531	
Cash		15,431
Paid principal and interest on installment notes.		

7. a.
Jan.	31 Product Warranty Expense	15,000	
	Product Warranty Payable		15,000
	To record warranty expense for		
	February (5% × $300,000).		

b.
June	20 Product Warranty Payable	132	
	Supplies		90
	Wages Payable		42

8. a.

$$\text{Quick Ratio} = \frac{\text{Quick Assets}}{\text{Current Liabilities}}$$

20Y7: $\dfrac{\$680 + \$1,550 + \$770}{\$2,000} = 1.5$

20Y8: $\dfrac{\$650 + \$1,500 + \$700}{\$2,375} = 1.2$

b. The quick ratio of Nabors Company has declined from 1.5 in 20Y7 to 1.2 in 20Y8. This decrease is the result of a large increase in accounts payable compared to decreases in the three types of quick assets (cash, temporary investments, and accounts receivable).

Need more help? Watch step-by-step videos of how to compute answers to these Exercises in CengageNOWv2.

Problem

Mar.	1	Inventory	20,000	
		Accounts Payable—Kelvin Co.		20,000
Apr.	10	Accounts Payable—Kelvin Co.	20,000	
		Notes Payable		20,000
June	9	Notes Payable	20,000	
		Interest Expense ($20,000 × 12% × 60 ÷ 360)	400	
		Cash		20,400
Aug.	1	Building	48,125	
		Interest Expense ($50,000 × 15% × 90 ÷ 360)	1,875	
		Notes Payable		50,000
Oct.	30	Notes Payable	50,000	
		Cash		50,000
Dec.	27	Sales Salaries Expense	63,400	
		Officers Salaries Expense	36,600	
		Office Salaries Expense	10,000	
		Social Security Tax Payable		6,600
		Medicare Tax Payable		1,650
		Employees Federal Income Tax Payable		17,600
		Employees State Income Tax Payable		4,950
		Bond Deductions Payable		850
		Medical Insurance Payable		1,120
		Salaries Payable		77,230
	27	Payroll Tax Expense	8,250	
		Social Security Tax Payable		6,600
		Medicare Tax Payable		1,650
	30	Employees Federal Income Tax Payable	17,600	
		Social Security Tax Payable	13,200	
		Medicare Tax Payable	3,300	
		Cash		34,100
	31	Pension Expense	9,500	
		Cash		9,500
		Fund pension cost.		
	31	Vacation Pay Expense	36,100	
		Vacation Pay Payable		36,100
		Accrue vacation pay.		
	31	Product Warranty Expense	37,240	
		Product Warranty Payable		37,240
		Accrue warranty expense.		

Discussion Questions

1. Does a discounted note payable provide credit without interest? Discuss.

2. Employees are subject to taxes withheld from their paychecks.
   a. List the federal taxes withheld from most employee paychecks.
   b. Give the title of the accounts credited by amounts withheld.

3. Why are deductions from employees' earnings classified as liabilities for the employer?

4. For each of the following payroll-related taxes, indicate whether they generally apply to (a) employees only, (b) employers only, or (c) both employees and employers:
   1. Federal income tax
   2. Medicare tax
   3. Social security tax
   4. Federal unemployment compensation tax
   5. State unemployment compensation tax

5. What are the principal reasons for using a special payroll bank account?

6. To match revenues and expenses properly, should the expense for employee vacation pay be recorded in the period during which the vacation privilege is earned or during the period in which the vacation is taken? Discuss.

7. Explain how a defined contribution pension plan works.

8. Installment notes require equal periodic payments.
   a. What is included in each periodic payment?
   b. Does the periodic interest expense on an installment note increase or decrease over the life of the note?

9. When should the liability associated with a product warranty be recorded? Discuss.

10.  **General Motors Corporation (GM)** reported $2.6 billion of product warranties in the "Current liabilities" section of a recent balance sheet. How would costs of repairing a defective product be recorded?

Basic Exercises

SHOW ME HOW

BE 10-1 Proceeds from notes payable Obj. 1

On January 26, Nyree Co. borrowed cash from Conrad Bank by issuing a 45-day note with a face amount of $225,000.
a. Determine the proceeds of the note, assuming the note carries an interest rate of 8%.
b. Determine the proceeds of the note, assuming the note is discounted at 8%.

SHOW ME HOW

BE 10-2 Employee net pay Obj. 2

Lindsey Vater's weekly gross earnings for the week ended March 9 were $800, and her federal income tax withholding was $128.96. Assuming the social security tax rate is 6% and Medicare tax is 1.5% of all earnings, what is Lindsey's net pay?

SHOW ME HOW

BE 10-3 Journalize period payroll Obj. 2

The payroll register of Heritage Co. indicates $4,200 of social security withheld and $1,050 of Medicare tax withheld on total salaries of $70,000 for the period. Federal withholding for the period totaled $15,350. Retirement savings withheld from employee paychecks were $2,800 for the period.
   Journalize the entry to record the period's payroll.

SHOW ME HOW

BE 10-4 Journalize payroll tax Obj. 2

The payroll register of Heritage Co. indicates $4,200 of social security withheld and $1,050 of Medicare tax withheld on total salaries of $70,000 for the period. Earnings of $12,000 are subject to state and federal unemployment compensation taxes at the federal rate of 0.8% and the state rate of 5.4%.
   Journalize the entry to record the payroll tax expense for the period.

SHOW ME HOW

BE 10-5 Vacation pay and pension benefits
Obj. 3

Regling Company provides its employees vacation benefits and a defined benefit pension plan. Employees earned vacation pay of $40,000 for the period. The pension formula calculated a pension cost of $222,750. Only $185,000 was contributed to the pension plan administrator.

Journalize the entry to record the (a) vacation pay and (b) pension benefit.

SHOW ME HOW

BE 10-6 Journalizing installment notes
Obj. 4

On the first day of the fiscal year, a company issues $45,000, 8%, six-year installment notes that have annual payments of $9,734. The first note payment consists of $3,600 of interest and $6,134 of principal repayment.

a. Journalize the entry to record the issuance of the installment notes.

b. Journalize the first annual note payment.

SHOW ME HOW

BE 10-7 Estimated warranty liability
Obj. 5

Quantas Industries sold $325,000 of consumer electronics during July under a nine-month warranty. The cost to repair defects under the warranty is estimated at 4.5% of the sales price. On November 11, a customer was given $220 cash under terms of the warranty.

Journalize the entry to record (a) the estimated warranty expense on July 31 for July sales, and (b) the November 11 cash payment.

SHOW ME HOW

BE 10-8 Quick ratio
Obj. 7

Adieu Company reported the following current assets and current liabilities for two recent years:

	Dec. 31, 20Y4	Dec. 31, 20Y3
Cash	$1,000	$1,140
Temporary investments	1,200	1,400
Accounts receivable	800	910
Inventory	2,200	2,600
Accounts payable	1,875	2,300

a. Compute the quick ratio on December 31 for each year. Round to one decimal place.

b. Interpret the company's quick ratio. Is the quick ratio improving or declining?

Exercises

✔ **Total current liabilities, $2,750,500**

SHOW ME HOW

EX 10-1 Current liabilities
Obj. 1

Bon Nebo Co. sold 30,000 annual subscriptions of *Bjorn* for $105 during December 20Y5. These new subscribers will receive monthly issues, beginning in January 20Y6. In addition, the business had taxable income of $970,000 during the first calendar quarter of 20Y6. The federal tax rate is 40%. A quarterly tax payment will be made on April 12, 20Y6.

Prepare the "Current liabilities" section of the balance sheet for Bon Nebo Co. on March 31, 20Y6.

SHOW ME HOW

EX 10-2 Entries for notes payable
Obj. 1

Bennett Enterprises issues a $400,000, 90-day, 5% note to Spectrum Industries for merchandise inventory.

a. Journalize Bennett Enterprises' entries to record:

1. the issuance of the note.

2. the payment of the note at maturity.

b. Journalize Spectrum Industries' entries to record:

1. the receipt of the note.

2. the receipt of the payment of the note at maturity.

SHOW ME HOW

EX 10-3 Evaluating alternative notes
Obj. 1

A borrower has two alternatives for a loan: (1) issue a $150,000, 45-day, 4% note or (2) issue a $150,000, 45-day note that the creditor discounts at 4%.

a. Calculate the amount of the interest expense for each option.

b. Determine the proceeds received by the borrower in each situation.

c. ➤ Which alternative is more favorable to the borrower? Explain.

SHOW ME HOW

EX 10-4 Entries for notes payable
Obj. 1

A business issued a 120-day, 5% note for $60,000 to a creditor on account. Journalize the entries to record (a) the issuance of the note and (b) the payment of the note at maturity, including interest.

SHOW ME HOW

EX 10-5 Entries for discounted note payable
Obj. 1

A business issued a 60-day note for $60,000 to a bank. The note was discounted at 8%. Journalize the entries to record (a) the issuance of the note and (b) the payment of the note at maturity.

SHOW ME HOW

EX 10-6 Fixed asset purchases with note
Obj. 1

On June 30, Collins Management Company purchased land for $400,000 and a building for $560,000, paying $360,000 cash and issuing a 5% note for the balance, secured by a mortgage on the property. The terms of the note provide for 20 semiannual payments of $30,000 on the principal plus the interest accrued from the date of the preceding payment. Journalize the entry to record (a) the transaction on June 30, (b) the payment of the first installment on December 31, and (c) the payment of the second installment the following June 30.

REAL WORLD

EX 10-7 Current portion of long-term debt
Obj. 1

PepsiCo, Inc. (PEP) reported the following information about its long-term debt in the notes to a recent financial statement (in millions):

Long-term debt consists of the following:

| | December 31 | |
	Current Year	Prior Year
Total long-term debt	$27,917	$26,557
Current portion	(4,096)	(2,224)
Long-term debt	$23,821	$24,333

a. How much of the long-term debt was disclosed as a current liability on the current year's December 31 balance sheet?

b. How much did the total current liabilities change between the preceding year and the current year as a result of the current portion of long-term debt?

c. If PepsiCo did not issue additional long-term debt next year, what would be the total long-term debt on December 31 of the upcoming year?

✔ b. Net pay, $1,397.75

EX 10-8 Calculate payroll
Obj. 2

An employee earns $30 per hour and 1.5 times that rate for all hours in excess of 40 hours per week. If the employee worked 54 hours during the week, determine the employee's (a) gross pay and (b) net pay for the week. Assume that the social security tax rate is 6.0%, the Medicare tax rate is 1.5%, and the employee's federal income tax withheld is $295.

SHOW ME HOW

✔ Consultant net pay, $3,475.00

EX 10-9 Calculate payroll
Obj. 2

K. Mello Company has three employees—a consultant, a computer programmer, and an administrator. The following payroll information is available for each employee:

	Consultant	Computer Programmer	Administrator
Regular earnings rate	$5,000 per week	$50 per hour	$60 per hour
Overtime earnings rate	Not applicable	2 times hourly rate	1.5 times hourly rate
Federal income tax withheld	$1,150	$428	$572

For hourly employees, overtime is paid for hours worked in excess of 40 hours per week.

SHOW ME HOW

(Continued)

For the current pay period, the computer programmer worked 48 hours and the administrator worked 51 hours. Assume that the social security tax rate was 6.0%, and the Medicare tax rate was 1.5%.

Determine the gross pay and the net pay for each of the three employees for the current pay period.

✔ a. (3) Total earnings, $540,000

EXCEL TEMPLATE

EX 10-10 Summary payroll data   Obj. 2

In the following summary of data for a payroll period, some amounts have been intentionally omitted:

Earnings:	
1. At regular rate	$?
2. At overtime rate	80,000
3. Total earnings	$?
Deductions:	
4. Social security tax	$ (32,400)
5. Medicare tax	(8,100)
6. Income tax withheld	(135,000)
7. Medical insurance	(18,900)
8. Union dues	?
9. Total deductions	$(201,150)
10. Net amount paid	$ 338,850
Accounts debited:	
11. Factory Wages	$ 285,000
12. Sales Salaries	?
13. Office Salaries	120,000

a. Calculate the amounts omitted in lines (1), (3), (8), and (12).

b. Journalize the entry to record the payroll accrual.

c. Journalize the entry to record the payment of the payroll.

✔ a. $9,800

SHOW ME HOW   EXCEL TEMPLATE

EX 10-11 Payroll tax entries   Obj. 2

According to a summary of the payroll of Mountain Streaming Co., $110,000 was subject to the 6.0% social security tax and the 1.5% Medicare tax. Also, $25,000 was subject to state and federal unemployment taxes.

a. Calculate the employer's payroll taxes, using the following rates: state unemployment, 5.4%; federal unemployment, 0.8%.

b. Journalize the entry to record the accrual of payroll taxes.

SHOW ME HOW

EX 10-12 Payroll entries   Obj. 2

The payroll register for D. Salah Company for the week ended May 18 indicated the following:

Salaries	$615,000
Federal income tax withheld	165,000

The salaries were all subject to the 6.0% social security tax and the 1.5% Medicare tax. In addition, state and federal unemployment taxes were calculated at the rate of 5.4% and 0.8%, respectively, on $45,000 of salaries.

a. Journalize the entry to record the payroll for the week of May 18.

b. Journalize the entry to record the payroll tax expense incurred for the week of May 18.

SHOW ME HOW

EX 10-13 Payroll entries
Obj. 2

Widmer Company had gross wages of $320,000 during the week ended June 17. The amount of wages subject to social security tax was $320,000, while the amount of wages subject to federal and state unemployment taxes was $48,000. Tax rates are as follows:

Social security	6.0%
Medicare	1.5%
State unemployment	5.4%
Federal unemployment	0.8%

The total amount withheld from employee wages for federal taxes was $64,000.

a. Journalize the entry to record the payroll for the week of June 17.

b. Journalize the entry to record the payroll tax expense incurred for the week of June 17.

EX 10-14 Payroll internal control procedures
Obj. 2

Big Howie's Hot Dog Stand is a fast-food restaurant specializing in hot dogs and hamburgers. The store employs 8 full-time and 12 part-time workers. The store's weekly payroll averages $5,600 for all 20 workers.

Big Howie's uses a personal computer to assist in preparing paychecks. Each week, the store's accountant collects employee time cards and enters the hours worked into the payroll program. The payroll program calculates each employee's pay and prints a paycheck. The accountant uses a check-signing machine to sign the paychecks. Next, the restaurant's owner/manager authorizes the transfer of funds from the restaurant's regular bank account to the payroll account.

For the week of May 12, the accountant accidentally recorded 100 hours worked instead of 40 hours for one of the full-time employees.

Does Big Howie's Hot Dog Stand have internal controls in place to catch this error? If so, how will this error be detected?

EX 10-15 Internal control procedures
Obj. 2

Dave's Scooters is a small manufacturer of specialty scooters. The company employs 14 production workers and four administrative persons. The following procedures are used to process the company's weekly payroll:

a. Whenever an employee receives a pay raise, the supervisor must fill out a wage adjustment form, which is signed by the company president. This form is used to change the employee's wage rate in the payroll system.

b. All employees are required to record their hours worked by clocking in and out on a time clock. Employees must clock out for lunch break. Due to congestion around the time clock area at lunch time, management has not objected to having one employee clock their entire department in and out.

c. Whenever a salaried employee is terminated, Personnel authorizes Payroll to remove the employee from the payroll system. However, this procedure is not required when an hourly worker is fired. Hourly employees only receive a paycheck if their time cards show hours worked. The computer automatically drops an employee from the payroll system when that employee has six consecutive weeks with no hours worked.

d. Paychecks are signed by using a check-signing machine. This machine is located in the main office so that it can be easily accessed by anyone needing a check signed.

e. Dave's Scooters maintains a separate checking account for payroll checks. Each week, the total net pay for all employees is transferred from the company's regular bank account to the payroll account.

State whether each of the procedures is appropriate or inappropriate, after considering the principles of internal control. If a procedure is inappropriate, describe the appropriate procedure.

EX 10-16 Accrued vacation pay
Obj. 3

A business provides its employees with varying amounts of vacation per year, depending on the length of employment. The estimated amount of the current year's vacation pay is $42,000.

a. Journalize the adjusting entry required on January 31, the end of the first month of the current year, to record the accrued vacation pay.

b. How is the vacation pay reported on the company's balance sheet? When is this amount removed from the company's balance sheet?

EX 10-17 Pension plan entries
Obj. 3

Yuri Co. operates a chain of gift shops. The company maintains a defined contribution pension plan for its employees. The plan requires quarterly installments to be paid to the funding agent, Whims Funds, by the fifteenth of the month following the end of each quarter. Assume that the pension cost is $365,000 for the quarter ended December 31.

a. Journalize the entries to record the accrued pension liability on December 31 and the payment to the funding agent on January 15.

b.  How does a defined contribution plan differ from a defined benefit plan?

EX 10-18 Defined benefit pension plan terms
Obj. 3

In a recent year's financial statements, **Procter & Gamble (PG)** showed an unfunded pension liability of $5,955 million and a periodic pension cost of $432 million.

Explain the meaning of the $5,955 million unfunded pension liability and the $432 million periodic pension cost.

EX 10-19 Entries for installment note transactions
Obj. 4

On the first day of the fiscal year, Shiller Company borrowed $85,000 by giving a seven-year, 7% installment note to Soros Bank. The note requires annual payments of $15,772, with the first payment occurring on the last day of the fiscal year. The first payment consists of interest of $5,950 and principal repayment of $9,822.

a. Journalize the entries to record the following:

1. Issued the installment note for cash on the first day of the fiscal year.

2. Paid the first annual payment on the note.

b. Explain how the notes payable would be reported on the balance sheet at the end of the first year.

EX 10-20 Entries for installment note transactions
Obj. 4

On January 1, 20Y2, Hebron Company issued a $175,000, five-year, 8% installment note to Ventsam Bank. The note requires annual payments of $43,830, beginning on December 31, 20Y2. Journalize the entries to record the following:

20Y2

Jan. 1. Issued the note for cash at its face amount.

Dec. 31. Paid the annual payment on the note, which consisted of interest of $14,000 and principal of $29,830.

20Y5

Dec. 31. Paid the annual payment on the note, included $6,253 of interest. The remainder of the payment reduced the principal balance on the note.

EX 10-21 Entries for installment note transactions
Obj. 4

On January 1 of Year 1, Bryson Company obtained a $147,750, four-year, 7% installment note from Campbell Bank. The note requires annual payments of $43,620, beginning on December 31 of Year 1.

a. Prepare a table for this installment note, similar to the one presented in Exhibit 4. Round to the nearest dollar.

b. Journalize the entries for the issuance of the note and the four annual note payments.

c. Describe how the annual note payment would be reported on the Year 1 income statement.

EX 10-22 Accrued product warranty
Obj. 5

Fosters Manufacturing Co. warrants its products for one year. The estimated product warranty is 2% of sales. Assume that sales were $1,500,000 for January. On February 7, a customer received warranty repairs requiring $325 of parts and $120 of labor.

a. Journalize the adjusting entry required at January 31, the end of the first month of the current fiscal year, to record the accrued product warranty.

b. Journalize the entry to record the warranty work provided in February.

REAL WORLD

EX 10-23 Accrued product warranty

Obj. 5

General Motors Company (GM) disclosed estimated product warranty payable for comparative years as follows:

	(in millions)	
	Current Year	Prior Year
Current estimated product warranty payable	$3,517	$3,487
Noncurrent estimated product warranty payable	6,184	5,792
Total	$9,701	$9,279

Assume that GM's sales were $166,380 million in the current year and that the total paid on warranty claims during the current year was $3,710 million.

a. ━━━━▶ Why are short- and long-term estimated warranty liabilities separately disclosed?

b. Provide the journal entry for the current year product warranty expense.

c. What two conditions must be met in order for a product warranty liability to be reported in the financial statements?

EX 10-24 Contingent liabilities

Obj. 6

Several months ago, Ayers Industries Inc. experienced a hazardous materials spill at one of its plants. As a result, the Environmental Protection Agency (EPA) fined the company $240,000. The company is contesting the fine. In addition, an employee is seeking $220,000 in damages related to the spill. Lastly, a homeowner has sued the company for $310,000. The homeowner lives 35 miles from the plant but believes that the incident has reduced the home's resale value by $310,000.

Ayers' legal counsel believes that it is probable that the EPA fine will stand. In addition, counsel indicates that an out-of-court settlement of $125,000 has recently been reached with the employee. The final papers will be signed next week. Counsel believes that the homeowner's case is much weaker and will be decided in favor of Ayers. Other litigation related to the spill is possible, but the damage amounts are uncertain.

a. Journalize the contingent liabilities associated with the hazardous materials spill. Use the account "Damage Awards and Fines" to recognize the expense for the period.

b. ━━━━▶ Prepare a note disclosure relating to this incident.

Problems: Series A

SHOW ME HOW

PR 10-1A Liability transactions

Obj. 1, 5

The following items were selected from among the transactions completed by Sherwood Co. during the current year:

Mar. 1. Purchased merchandise on account from Kirkwood Co., $225,000, terms n/30.

31. Issued a 30-day, 8% note for $225,000 to Kirkwood Co., on account.

Apr. 30. Paid Kirkwood Co. the amount owed on the note of March 31.

June 1. Borrowed $600,000 from Triple Creek Bank, issuing a 45-day, 6% note.

July 1. Purchased tools by issuing a $50,000, 60-day note to Poulin Co., which discounted the note at the rate of 6%.

16. Paid Triple Creek Bank the interest due on the note of June 1 and renewed the loan by issuing a new 30-day, 7% note for $600,000. (Journalize both the debit and credit to the notes payable account.)

Aug. 15. Paid Triple Creek Bank the amount due on the note of July 16.

30. Paid Poulin Co. the amount due on the note of July 1.

Dec. 1. Purchased equipment from Greenwood Co. for $280,000, paying $80,000 cash and issuing a series of ten 9% notes for $20,000 each, coming due at 30-day intervals.

22. Settled a product liability lawsuit with a customer for $40,000, payable in January. Accrued the loss in a litigation claims payable account.

31. Paid the amount due to Greenwood Co. on the first note in the series issued on December 1.

(Continued)

Instructions

1. Journalize the transactions.
2. Journalize the adjusting entry for each of the following accrued expenses at the end of the current year:

   a. Product warranty cost, $65,000.

   b. Interest on the nine remaining notes owed to Greenwood Co.

PR 10-2A   Entries for payroll and payroll taxes   **Obj. 2**

✔ 1. (b) Dr. Payroll Tax Expense, $61,476

The following information about the payroll for the week ended December 30 was obtained from the records of Boltz Co.:

Salaries:		Deductions:	
Sales salaries	$540,000	Income tax withheld	$160,000
Warehouse salaries	155,000	U.S. savings bonds	10,500
Office salaries	85,000	Group insurance	9,000
	$780,000		

Tax rates assumed:

Social security, 6%	State unemployment (employer only), 5.4%
Medicare, 1.5%	Federal unemployment (employer only), 0.8%

Instructions

1. Assuming that the payroll for the last week of the year is to be paid on December 31, journalize the following entries:

   a. December 30, to record the payroll.

   b. December 30, to record the employer's payroll taxes on the payroll to be paid on December 31. Of the total payroll for the last week of the year, $48,000 is subject to unemployment compensation taxes.

2. Assuming that the payroll for the last week of the year is to be paid on January 5 of the following fiscal year, journalize the following entries:

   a. December 30, to record the payroll.

   b. January 5, to record the employer's payroll taxes on the payroll to be paid on January 5. Since it is a new fiscal year, all $780,000 in salaries is subject to unemployment compensation taxes.

PR 10-3A   Wage and tax statement data on employer FICA tax   **Obj. 2**

✔ 2. (e) $29,847.15

EXCEL TEMPLATE

Ehrlich Co. began business on January 2. Salaries were paid to employees on the last day of each month, and social security tax, Medicare tax, and federal income tax were withheld in the required amounts. An employee who is hired in the middle of the month receives half the monthly salary for that month. All required payroll tax reports were filed, and the correct amount of payroll taxes was remitted by the company for the calendar year. Early in the following year, before the Wage and Tax Statements (Form W-2) could be prepared for distribution to employees and for filing with the Social Security Administration, the employees' earnings records were inadvertently destroyed.

None of the employees resigned or were discharged during the year, and there were no changes in salary rates. The social security tax was withheld at the rate of 6.0% and Medicare tax at the rate of 1.5% on salary. Data on dates of employment, salary rates, and employees' income taxes withheld, which are summarized as follows, were obtained from personnel records and payroll records:

Employee	Date First Employed	Monthly Salary	Monthly Income Tax Withheld
Arnett	Nov. 16	$ 6,000	$1,132
Cruz	Jan. 2	4,600	798
Edwards	Oct. 1	8,200	1,632
Harvin	Dec. 1	5,900	1,052
Nicks	Feb. 1	12,000	2,820
Shiancoe	Mar. 1	11,300	2,533
Ward	Nov. 16	4,700	788

Instructions

1. Compute the amounts to be reported for the year on each employee's Wage and Tax Statement (Form W-2), arranging the data as follows. Round all amounts to the nearest cent.

Employee	Gross Earnings	Federal Income Tax Withheld	Social Security Tax Withheld	Medicare Tax Withheld

2. Compute the following employer payroll taxes for the year: (a) social security, (b) Medicare, (c) state unemployment compensation at 5.4% on the first $10,000 of each employee's earnings, (d) federal unemployment compensation at 0.8% on the first $10,000 of each employee's earnings, and (e) total. Round all amounts to the nearest cent.

PR 10-4A Payroll summary

Obj. 2

✔ 1. Total net pay
$15,424.12

EXCEL TEMPLATE

The following data for Throwback Industries Inc. relate to the payroll for the week ended December 9.

Employee	Hours Worked	Hourly Rate	Weekly Salary	Federal Income Tax	U.S. Savings Bonds
Aaron	46	$68.00		$750.20	$100
Cobb	41	62.00		537.68	110
Clemente	48	70.00		832.64	120
DiMaggio	35	56.00		366.04	0
Griffey, Jr.	45	62.00		641.84	130
Mantle			$1,800	342.45	120
Robinson	36	54.00		382.56	130
Williams			2,000	398.24	125
Vaughn	42	62.00		584.72	50

Employees Mantle and Williams are office staff, and all of the other employees are sales personnel. All sales personnel are paid 1½ times the regular rate for all hours in excess of 40 hours per week. The social security tax rate is 6.0%, and Medicare tax is 1.5% of each employee's annual earnings. The next payroll check to be used is No. 901.

Instructions

1. Prepare a payroll summary for Throwback Industries Inc. for the week ended December 9. Use the following columns: Employee, Total Hours, Regular Earnings, Overtime Earnings, Total Earnings, Social Security Tax, Medicare Tax, Federal Income Tax, U.S. Savings Bonds, Total Deductions, Net Pay, Ck. No., Sales Salaries Expense, and Office Salaries Expense.

2. Journalize the entry to record the payroll for the week.

PR 10-5A Payroll accounts and year-end entries

Obj. 2, 3

The following accounts, with the balances indicated, appear in the ledger of Garcon Co. on December 1 of the current year:

211	Salaries Payable	—	218	Bond Deductions Payable	$ 3,400
212	Social Security Tax Payable	$ 9,273	219	Medical Insurance Payable	27,000
213	Medicare Tax Payable	2,318	411	Operations Salaries Expense	950,000
214	Employees Federal Income Tax Payable	15,455	511	Officers Salaries Expense	600,000
215	Employees State Income Tax Payable	13,909	512	Office Salaries Expense	150,000
216	State Unemployment Tax Payable	1,400	519	Payroll Tax Expense	137,951
217	Federal Unemployment Tax Payable	500			

The following transactions relating to payroll, payroll deductions, and payroll taxes occurred during December:

Dec. 2. Issued Check No. 410 for $3,400 to Jay Bank to purchase U.S. savings bonds for employees.

   2. Issued Check No. 411 to Jay Bank for $27,046 in payment of $9,273 of social security tax, $2,318 of Medicare tax, and $15,455 of employees' federal income tax due.

(Continued)

Dec. 13. Journalized the entry to record the biweekly payroll. A summary of the payroll record follows:

Salary distribution:		
Operations	$43,200	
Officers	27,200	
Office	6,800	$ 77,200
Deductions:		
Social security tax	$ 4,632	
Medicare tax	1,158	
Federal income tax withheld	15,440	
State income tax withheld	3,474	
Savings bond deductions	1,700	
Medical insurance deductions	4,500	(30,904)
Net amount		$ 46,296

13. Issued Check No. 420 in payment of the net amount of the biweekly payroll.

13. Journalized the entry to record payroll taxes on employees' earnings of December 13: social security tax, $4,632; Medicare tax, $1,158; state unemployment tax, $350; federal unemployment tax, $125.

16. Issued Check No. 424 to Jay Bank for $27,020, in payment of $9,264 of social security tax, $2,316 of Medicare tax, and $15,440 of employees' federal income tax due.

19. Issued Check No. 429 to Sims-Walker Insurance Company for $31,500 in payment of the semiannual premium on the group medical insurance policy.

27. Journalized the entry to record the biweekly payroll. A summary of the payroll record follows:

Salary distribution:		
Operations	$ 42,800	
Officers	28,000	
Office	7,000	$ 77,800
Deductions:		
Social security tax	$ 4,668	
Medicare tax	1,167	
Federal income tax withheld	15,404	
State income tax withheld	3,501	
Savings bond deductions	1,700	(26,440)
Net amount		$ 51,360

27. Issued Check No. 541 in payment of the net amount of the biweekly payroll.

27. Journalized the entry to record payroll taxes on employees' earnings of December 27: social security tax, $4,668; Medicare tax, $1,167; state unemployment tax, $225; federal unemployment tax, $75.

27. Issued Check No. 543 for $20,884 to State Department of Revenue in payment of employees' state income tax due on December 31.

31. Issued Check No. 545 to Jay Bank for $3,400 to purchase U.S. savings bonds for employees.

31. Paid $45,000 to the employee pension plan. The annual pension cost is $60,000. (Record both the payment and unfunded pension liability.)

Instructions

1. Journalize the transactions.

2. Journalize the following adjusting entries on December 31:

   a. Salaries accrued: operations salaries, $8,560; officers salaries, $5,600; office salaries, $1,400. The payroll taxes are immaterial and are not accrued.

   b. Vacation pay, $15,000.

Problems: Series B

SHOW ME HOW

PR 10-1B Liability transactions

Obj. 1, 5

The following items were selected from among the transactions completed by Aston Martin Inc. during the current year:

Apr. 15. Borrowed $225,000 from Audi Company, issuing a 30-day, 6% note for that amount.

May 1. Purchased equipment by issuing a $320,000, 180-day note to Spyder Manufacturing Co., which discounted the note at the rate of 6%.

15. Paid Audi Company the interest due on the note of April 15 and renewed the loan by issuing a new 60-day, 8% note for $225,000. (Record both the debit and credit to the notes payable account.)

July 14. Paid Audi Company the amount due on the note of May 15.

Aug. 16. Purchased merchandise on account from Exige Co., $90,000, terms, n/30.

Sept. 15. Issued a 45-day, 6% note for $90,000 to Exige Co., on account.

Oct. 28. Paid Spyder Manufacturing Co. the amount due on the note of May 1.

30. Paid Exige Co. the amount owed on the note of September 15.

Nov. 16. Purchased store equipment from Gallardo Co. for $450,000, paying $50,000 and issuing a series of twenty 9% notes for $20,000 each, coming due at 30-day intervals.

Dec. 16. Paid the amount due Gallardo Co. on the first note in the series issued on November 16.

28. Settled a personal injury lawsuit with a customer for $87,500, to be paid in January. Aston Martin Inc. accrued the loss in a litigation claims payable account.

Instructions

1. Journalize the transactions.

2. Journalize the adjusting entry for each of the following accrued expenses at the end of the current year:

   a. Product warranty cost, $26,800.

   b. Interest on the 19 remaining notes owed to Gallardo Co.

PR 10-2B Entries for payroll and payroll taxes

Obj. 2

✔ 1. (b) Dr. Payroll Tax Expense, $90,735

The following information about the payroll for the week ended December 30 was obtained from the records of Saine Co.:

Salaries:		Deductions:	
Sales salaries	$ 625,000	Income tax withheld	$232,260
Warehouse salaries	240,000	U.S. savings bonds	35,500
Office salaries	320,000	Group insurance	53,325
	$1,185,000		

Tax rates assumed:
   Social security, 6%
   Medicare, 1.5%
   State unemployment (employer only), 5.4%
   Federal unemployment (employer only), 0.8%

Instructions

1. Assuming that the payroll for the last week of the year is to be paid on December 31, journalize the following entries:

   a. December 30, to record the payroll.

   b. December 30, to record the employer's payroll taxes on the payroll to be paid on December 31. Of the total payroll for the last week of the year, $30,000 is subject to unemployment compensation taxes.

2. Assuming that the payroll for the last week of the year is to be paid on January 4 of the following fiscal year, journalize the following entries:

   a. December 30, to record the payroll.

   b. January 4, to record the employer's payroll taxes on the payroll to be paid on January 4. Because it is a new fiscal year, all $1,185,000 in salaries is subject to unemployment compensation taxes.

PR 10-3B Wage and tax statement data and employer FICA tax   Obj. 2

✔ 2. (e) $25,136.13

EXCEL TEMPLATE

Jocame Inc. began business on January 2. Salaries were paid to employees on the last day of each month, and social security tax, Medicare tax, and federal income tax were withheld in the required amounts. An employee who is hired in the middle of the month receives half the monthly salary for that month. All required payroll tax reports were filed, and the correct amount of payroll taxes was remitted by the company for the calendar year. Early in the following year, before the Wage and Tax Statements (Form W-2) could be prepared for distribution to employees and for filing with the Social Security Administration, the employees' earnings records were inadvertently destroyed.

None of the employees resigned or were discharged during the year, and there were no changes in salary rates. The social security tax was withheld at the rate of 6.0% and Medicare tax at the rate of 1.5% on salary. Data on dates of employment, salary rates, and employees' income taxes withheld, which are summarized as follows, were obtained from personnel records and payroll records:

Employee	Date First Employed	Monthly Salary	Monthly Income Tax Withheld
Addai	July 16	$ 8,160	$1,704
Kasay	June 1	3,600	533
McGahee	Feb. 16	6,420	1,238
Moss	Jan. 1	4,600	783
Stewart	Dec. 1	4,500	758
Tolbert	Nov. 16	3,250	446
Wells	May 1	10,500	2,359

Instructions

1. Compute the amounts to be reported for the year on each employee's Wage and Tax Statement (Form W-2), arranging the data as follows. Round all amounts to the nearest cent.

Employee	Gross Earnings	Federal Income Tax Withheld	Social Security Tax Withheld	Medicare Tax Withheld

2. Compute the following employer payroll taxes for the year: (a) social security, (b) Medicare, (c) state unemployment compensation at 5.4% on the first $10,000 of each employee's earnings, (d) federal unemployment compensation at 0.8% on the first $10,000 of each employee's earnings, and (e) total. Round all amounts to the nearest cent.

PR 10-4B Payroll summary   Obj. 2

✔ 1. Total net pay, $16,592.58

EXCEL TEMPLATE

The following data for Flexco Inc. relate to the payroll for the week ended December 9:

Employee	Hours Worked	Hourly Rate	Weekly Salary	Federal Income Tax	U.S. Savings Bonds
Carlton	52	$50.00		$667.00	$ 60
Grove			$4,000	860.00	100
Johnson	36	52.00		355.68	0
Koufax	45	58.00		578.55	44
Maddux	37	45.00		349.65	62
Seaver			3,200	768.00	120
Spahn	46	52.00		382.20	0
Winn	48	50.00		572.00	75
Young	43	54.00		480.60	80

Employees Grove and Seaver are office staff, and all of the other employees are sales personnel. All sales personnel are paid 1½ times the regular rate for all hours in excess of 40 hours per week. The social security tax rate is 6.0% of each employee's annual earnings, and Medicare tax is 1.5% of each employee's annual earnings. The next payroll check to be used is No. 328.

Instructions

1. Prepare a payroll summary for Flexco Inc. for the week ended December 9. Use the following columns: Employee, Total Hours, Regular Earnings, Overtime Earnings, Total Earnings, Social Security Tax, Medicare Tax, Federal Income Tax, U.S. Savings Bonds, Total Deductions, Net Pay, Ck. No., Sales Salaries Expense, and Office Salaries Expense. Round to the nearest cent.

2. Journalize the entry to record the payroll for the week.

PR 10-5B   Payroll accounts and year-end entries

Obj. 2, 3

The following accounts, with the balances indicated, appear in the ledger of Codigo Co. on December 1 of the current year:

101 Salaries Payable	—	
102 Social Security Tax Payable	$2,913	
103 Medicare Tax Payable	728	
104 Employees Federal Income Tax Payable	4,490	
105 Employees State Income Tax Payable	4,078	
106 State Unemployment Tax Payable	1,260	
107 Federal Unemployment Tax Payable	360	

108 Bond Deductions Payable	$ 2,300
109 Medical Insurance Payable	2,520
201 Sales Salaries Expense	700,000
301 Officers Salaries Expense	340,000
401 Office Salaries Expense	125,000
408 Payroll Tax Expense	59,491

The following transactions relating to payroll, payroll deductions, and payroll taxes occurred during December:

Dec.   1. Issued Check No. 815 to Aberderas Insurance Company for $2,520, in payment of the semiannual premium on the group medical insurance policy.

1. Issued Check No. 816 to Alvarez Bank for $8,131, in payment for $2,913 of social security tax, $728 of Medicare tax, and $4,490 of employees' federal income tax due.

2. Issued Check No. 817 for $2,300 to Alvarez Bank to purchase U.S. savings bonds for employees.

12. Journalized the entry to record the biweekly payroll. A summary of the payroll record follows:

Salary distribution:		
Sales	$14,500	
Officers	7,100	
Office	2,600	$24,200
Deductions:		
Social security tax	$ 1,452	
Medicare tax	363	
Federal income tax withheld	4,308	
State income tax withheld	1,089	
Savings bond deductions	1,150	
Medical insurance deductions	420	(8,782)
Net amount		$15,418

12. Issued Check No. 822 in payment of the net amount of the biweekly payroll.

12. Journalized the entry to record payroll taxes on employees' earnings of December 12: social security tax, $1,452; Medicare tax, $363; state unemployment tax, $315; federal unemployment tax, $90.

15. Issued Check No. 830 to Alvarez Bank for $7,938, in payment of $2,904 of social security tax, $726 of Medicare tax, and $4,308 of employees' federal income tax due.

26. Journalized the entry to record the biweekly payroll. A summary of the payroll record follows:

Salary distribution:		
Sales	$14,250	
Officers	7,250	
Office	2,750	$24,250
Deductions:		
Social security tax	$ 1,455	
Medicare tax	364	
Federal income tax withheld	4,317	
State income tax withheld	1,091	
Savings bond deductions	1,150	(8,377)
Net amount		$15,873

26. Issued Check No. 840 for the net amount of the biweekly payroll.

26. Journalized the entry to record payroll taxes on employees' earnings of December 26: social security tax, $1,455; Medicare tax, $364; state unemployment tax, $150; federal unemployment tax, $40.

30. Issued Check No. 851 for $6,258 to State Department of Revenue, in payment of employees' state income tax due on December 31.

(Continued)

Dec. 30. Issued Check No. 852 to Alvarez Bank for $2,300 to purchase U.S. savings bonds for employees.

31. Paid $55,400 to the employee pension plan. The annual pension cost is $65,500. (Record both the payment and the unfunded pension liability.)

Instructions

1. Journalize the transactions.
2. Journalize the following adjusting entries on December 31:

   a. Salaries accrued: sales salaries, $4,275; officers salaries, $2,175; office salaries, $825. The payroll taxes are immaterial and are not accrued.

   b. Vacation pay, $13,350.

Comprehensive Problem 3

✔ 5. Total assets, $3,569,300

Selected transactions completed by Kornett Company during its first fiscal year ended December 31, 20Y5, were as follows:

Jan. 3. Issued a check to establish a petty cash fund of $4,500.

Feb. 26. Replenished the petty cash fund, based on the following summary of petty cash receipts: office supplies, $1,680; miscellaneous selling expense, $570; miscellaneous administrative expense, $880.

Apr. 14. Purchased $31,300 of merchandise on account, terms n/30. The perpetual inventory system is used to account for inventory.

May 13. Paid the invoice of April 14.

17. Received cash from daily cash sales for $21,200. The amount indicated by the cash register was $21,240.

June 2. Received a 60-day, 8% note for $180,000 on the Ryanair account.

Aug. 1. Received amount owed on June 2 note, plus interest at the maturity date.

24. Received $7,600 on the Finley account and wrote off the remainder owed on a $9,000 accounts receivable balance. (The allowance method is used in accounting for uncollectible receivables.)

Sept. 15. Reinstated the Finley account written off on August 24 and received $1,400 cash in full payment.

15. Purchased land by issuing a $670,000, 90-day note to Zahorik Co., which discounted it at 9%.

Oct. 17. Sold office equipment in exchange for $135,000 cash plus receipt of a $100,000, 90-day, 9% note. The equipment had a cost of $320,000 and accumulated depreciation of $64,000 as of October 17.

Nov. 30. Journalized the monthly payroll for November, based on the following data:

Salaries		Deductions	
Sales salaries	$135,000	Income tax withheld	$39,266
Office salaries	77,250	Social security tax withheld	12,735
	$212,250	Medicare tax withheld	3,184

Unemployment tax rates:	
State unemployment	5.4%
Federal unemployment	0.8%
Amount subject to unemployment taxes:	
State unemployment	$5,000
Federal unemployment	5,000

30. Journalized the employer's payroll taxes on the payroll.

Dec. 14. Journalized the payment of the September 15 note at maturity.

31. The pension cost for the year was $190,400, of which $139,700 was paid to the pension plan trustee.

Instructions

1. Journalize the selected transactions.
2. Based on the following data, prepare a bank reconciliation for December of the current year:

   • Balance according to the bank statement at December 31, $283,000.

   • Balance according to the ledger at December 31, $245,410.

- Checks outstanding at December 31, $68,540.
- Deposit in transit, not recorded by bank, $29,500.
- Bank debit memo for service charges, $750.
- A check for $12,700 in payment of an invoice was incorrectly recorded in the accounts as $12,000.

3. Based on the bank reconciliation prepared in (2), journalize the entry or entries to be made by Kornett Company. Use the Miscellaneous Administrative Expense account to record bank service charges.

4. Based on the following selected data, journalize the adjusting entries as of December 31 of the current year:

   a. Estimated uncollectible accounts at December 31, $16,000, based on an aging of accounts receivable. The balance of Allowance for Doubtful Accounts at December 31 was $2,000 (debit).

   b. The physical inventory on December 31 indicated an inventory shrinkage of $3,300.

   c. Prepaid insurance expired during the year, $22,820.

   d. Office supplies used during the year, $3,920.

   e. Depreciation is computed as follows:

Asset	Cost	Residual Value	Acquisition Date	Useful Life in Years	Depreciation Method Used
Buildings	$900,000	$ 0	January 2	50	Double-declining-balance
Office Equip.	246,000	26,000	January 3	5	Straight-line
Store Equip.	112,000	12,000	July 1	10	Straight-line

   f. A patent costing $48,000 when acquired on January 2 has a remaining legal life of 10 years and is expected to have value for 8 years.

   g. The cost of mineral rights was $546,000. Of the estimated deposit of 910,000 tons of ore, 50,000 tons were mined and sold during the year.

   h. Vacation pay expense for December, $10,500.

   i. A product warranty was granted beginning December 1 and covering a one-year period. The estimated cost is 4% of sales, which totaled $1,900,000 in December.

   j. Interest was accrued on the note receivable received on October 17.

5. Based on the following information and the post-closing trial balance that follows, prepare a balance sheet in report form at December 31 of the current year:

   The merchandise inventory is stated at cost by the LIFO method.
   The product warranty payable is a current liability.

   Vacation pay payable:
   Current liability $7,140
   Long-term liability   3,360

   The unfunded pension liability is a long-term liability.

   Notes payable:
   Current liability $ 70,000
   Long-term liability   630,000

(Continued)

Kornett Company
Post-Closing Trial Balance
December 31, 20Y5

	Debit Balances	Credit Balances
Petty Cash	4,500	
Cash	243,960	
Notes Receivable	100,000	
Accounts Receivable	470,000	
Allowance for Doubtful Accounts		16,000
Inventory	320,000	
Interest Receivable	1,875	
Prepaid Insurance	45,640	
Office Supplies	13,400	
Land	654,925	
Buildings	900,000	
Accumulated Depreciation—Buildings		36,000
Office Equipment	246,000	
Accumulated Depreciation—Office Equipment		44,000
Store Equipment	112,000	
Accumulated Depreciation—Store Equipment		5,000
Mineral Rights	546,000	
Accumulated Depletion		30,000
Patents	42,000	
Social Security Tax Payable		25,470
Medicare Tax Payable		4,710
Employees Federal Income Tax Payable		40,000
State Unemployment Tax Payable		270
Federal Unemployment Tax Payable		40
Salaries Payable		157,000
Accounts Payable		131,600
Interest Payable		28,000
Product Warranty Payable		76,000
Vacation Pay Payable		10,500
Unfunded Pension Liability		50,700
Notes Payable		700,000
Common Stock		500,000
Retained Earnings		1,845,010
	3,700,300	3,700,300

Make a Decision
Short-Term Liquidity Analysis

REAL WORLD

MAD 10-1   Analyze and compare Amazon.com to Best Buy   Obj. 7

Amazon.com, Inc. (AMZN) is one of the largest Internet retailers in the world. **Best Buy, Co. Inc. (BBY)** is a leading retailer of consumer electronics and media products in the United States. Amazon and Best Buy compete in similar markets; however, Best Buy sells through both traditional retail stores and the Internet, while Amazon sells only through the Internet. Current asset and current liability information from recent financial statements are as follows (in millions):

	Amazon	Best Buy
Current assets:		
Cash	$19,334	$ 1,976
Short-term investments	6,647	1,305
Accounts receivable	8,339	1,162
Inventories	11,461	5,051
Other current assets	—	392
Total current assets	$45,781	$ 9,886
Current liabilities:		
Accounts payable	$25,309	$ 4,450
Other current liabilities	18,507	2,475
Total current liabilities	$43,816	$ 6,925

a. Compute working capital for each company

b. Compute the current ratio for each company. Round to one decimal place.

c. Compute the quick ratio for each company. Round to one decimal place.

d.  Can the working capital be usefully compared between the two companies? Explain.

e. Which company has the greater debt-paying ability according to the current ratio?

f. Which company has the greater short-term debt-paying ability according to the quick ratio?

g.  Why are the results different between (e) and (f)? (*Hint:* Perform a vertical analysis of the current assets.)

REAL WORLD

MAD 10-2   Analyze and compare Abercrombie & Fitch and The Gap   Obj. 7

Abercrombie & Fitch Co. (ANF) and **The Gap, Inc. (GPS)** are two U.S. apparel retailers. The current assets and current liabilities for each company from recent balance sheets are as follows (in thousands):

	Abercrombie & Fitch	The Gap
Current assets:		
Cash	$ 547,189	$1,783,000
Accounts receivable	93,384	—
Inventories	399,795	1,830,000
Other current assets	98,932	702,000
Total current assets	$1,139,300	$4,315,000
Current liabilities:		
Accounts payable	$ 187,017	$1,243,000
Other current liabilities	298,983	1,210,000
Total current liabilities	$ 486,000	$2,453,000

a. Compute the working capital for each company.

b. Compute the current ratio for each company. Round to one decimal place.

c. Compute the quick ratio for each company. Round to one decimal place.

d.  Which company appears to have the greater short-term liquidity? Why?

REAL WORLD

MAD 10-3 Analyze Hershey
Obj. 7

The Hershey Company (HSY) is the largest producer of chocolate in North America under the Hershey's and Reese's brand names. The following balance sheet information is provided at the end of three recent years (in thousands):

	Year 3	Year 2	Year 1
Current assets:			
Cash	$ 296,967	$ 346,529	$ 374,854
Short-term investments....................	—	—	97,131
Accounts receivable	581,381	599,073	596,940
Inventories................................	745,678	750,970	801,036
Other current assets	192,752	152,026	377,086
Total current assets....................	$1,816,778	$1,848,598	$2,247,047
Current liabilities:			
Accounts payable.........................	$ 522,536	$ 474,266	$ 482,017
Other current liabilities	1,386,907	1,743,646	1,453,630
Total current liabilities.................	$1,909,443	$2,217,912	$1,935,647

a. Compute the working capital for the three years.

b. Compute the current ratio for the three years. Round to one decimal place.

c. Compute the quick ratio for the three years. Round to one decimal place.

d. ▬▬▶ Interpret the short-term liquidity for the three years from (c).

e. ▬▬▶ Are the other two measures in (a) and (b) consistent with your analysis in (d)?

REAL WORLD

MAD 10-4 Analyze and compare Neiman Marcus and Kohl's
Obj. 7

Neiman Marcus Group (NMG) is one of the largest luxury fashion retailers in the world. **Kohl's Corporation (KSS)** sells moderately priced private and national branded products through more than 1,100 department stores located throughout the United States. The current assets and current liabilities at the end of a recent year for both companies are as follows (in millions):

	Neiman Marcus	Kohl's
Current assets:		
Cash	$ 62	$1,074
Inventories...............................	1,125	3,795
Other current assets	147	378
Total current assets....................	$1,334	$5,247
Current liabilities:		
Accounts payable.........................	$ 318	$1,507
Other current liabilities	522	1,467
Total current liabilities.................	$ 840	$2,974

a. ▬▬▶ Would an analysis of working capital between the two companies be meaningful? Explain.

b. Compute the quick ratio for both companies. Round to one decimal place.

c. ▬▬▶ Interpret your results.

REAL WORLD

MAD 10-5 Analyze and compare Cabela's and Dick's Sporting Goods
Obj. 7

Cabela's Incorporated (CAB) is a leading specialty retailer of outdoor sports merchandise. **Dick's Sporting Goods, Inc. (DKS)** is a leading full-line retailer of sporting equipment and apparel. The current assets and current liabilities of both companies are provided as follows from recent financial statements (in millions):

	Cabela's	Dick's
Current assets:		
Cash	$ 313	$ 165
Accounts receivable	76	75
Credit card loans	5,580	—
Inventories	860	1,639
Other current assets	208	117
Total current assets	$7,037	$1,996
Current liabilities:		
Accounts payable	$ 348	$ 756
Gift cards	388	—
Other current liabilities	1,954	641
Total current liabilities	$2,690	$1,397

Cabela's has a branded credit card that is the basis for its financial services business. "Credit card loans" in Cabela's current assets represent the amounts due from Cabela's CLUB® Visa credit card customers. The credit card loans represent 2,064,517 active accounts with an average balance of $2,480. The credit card holders have a median FICO score of 793, which denotes highly creditworthy customers. Cabela's other current liabilities include, among other items, short-term funding to support credit card purchases from its CLUB members.

a. ▆▆▆▶ What do the "gift cards" listed under Cabela's current liabilities represent?
b. ▆▆▆▶ Should the "credit card loans" be considered part of quick assets for Cabela's computation of the quick ratio? Explain.
c. Compute the current ratio for Cabela's and Dick's Sporting Goods. Round to one decimal place.
d. Compute the quick ratio for Cabela's and Dick's Sporting Goods. Round to one decimal place.
e. ▆▆▆▶ Compare the two companies using the computations in (c) and (d).

Take It Further

ETHICS

TIF 10-1 Payroll: Bonus

Tonya Latirno is a staff accountant for Cannally and Kennedy, a local CPA firm. For the past 10 years, the firm has given employees a year-end bonus equal to two weeks' salary. On November 15, the firm's management team announced that there would be no annual bonus this year. Because of the firm's long history of giving a year-end bonus, Tonya and her co-workers had come to expect the bonus and felt that Cannally and Kennedy had breached an implicit agreement by discontinuing the bonus. As a result, Tonya decided that she would make up for the lost bonus by working an extra six hours of overtime per week for the rest of the year. Cannally and Kennedy's policy is to pay overtime at 150% of straight time.

Tonya's supervisor was surprised to see overtime being reported, because there are generally very little additional or unusual client service demands at the end of the calendar year. However, the overtime was not questioned, because employees are on the "honor system" in reporting their work hours.

1. ▆▆▆▶ Is Cannally and Kennedy acting in an ethical manner by eliminating the bonus? Explain your answer.
2. ▆▆▆▶ Is Tonya behaving ethically by making up the bonus with unnecessary overtime? Why?

ETHICS

TIF 10-2 Payroll—Cash payments

Marvin Turner was discussing summer employment with Tina Song, president of Motown Construction Service:

Tina: I'm glad you're thinking about joining us for the summer. We certainly can use the help.

Marvin: Sounds good. I enjoy outdoor work, and I could use the money to help with next year's school expenses.

Tina: I've got a plan that can help you out on that. As you know, I'll pay you $14 per hour, but in addition, I'd like to pay you with cash. Since you're only working for the summer, it really doesn't make sense for me to go to the trouble of formally putting you on our payroll system. In fact, I do some jobs for my clients on a strictly cash basis, so it would be easy just to pay you that way.

Marvin: Well, that's a bit unusual, but I guess money is money.

Tina: Yeah, not only that, it's tax-free!

Marvin: What do you mean?

Tina: Didn't you know? Any money that you receive in cash is not reported to the IRS on a W-2 form; therefore, the IRS doesn't know about the income—hence, it's the same as tax-free earnings.

1. ➡ Why does Tina Song want to conduct business transactions using cash (not check or credit card)?

2. ➡ How should Marvin respond to Tina's suggestion?

TEAM ACTIVITY   REAL WORLD

TIF 10-3 Real-world annual report

In teams, select a public company that interests you. Obtain the company's most recent annual report on Form 10-K. The Form 10-K is a company's annually required filing with the Securities and Exchange Commission (SEC). It includes the company's financial statements and accompanying notes. The Form 10-K can be obtained either (a) from the investor relations section of the company's website or (b) by using the company search feature of the SEC's EDGAR database service found at www.sec.gov/edgar/searchedgar/companysearch.html.

Based on the information in the company's annual report, answer the following questions:

1. What amount of current liabilities does the company report on its balance sheet at the end of the most recent year? What types of current liabilities does the company report?

2. Have current liabilities increased or decreased from the prior year? By what amount?

3. Does the company disclose any contingent liabilities in the notes to the financial statements? If so, briefly describe the nature of these contingent liabilities.

4. How much of the company's long-term debt will come due in the coming year?

COMMUNICATION

TIF 10-4 Contingent liability

WBM Motorworks is a manufacturer of high-end touring and off-road motorcycles. On November 30, the company was sued by a customer who was injured when the front shock absorber on the WBM Series 3 motorcycle cracked during use. The company conducted a preliminary investigation into the matter during December and found evidence of a manufacturing defect in the shock absorber. While it is uncertain whether the manufacturing defect is the source of the product failure, the company has voluntarily recalled the front shock absorbers on the Series 3 motorcycles. The company is uncertain how the lawsuit will be resolved. Similar lawsuits against other manufacturers have been settled for approximately $2,000,000.

➡ Write a brief memo to the president of WBM Motorworks, U. D. Mach III, discussing how the lawsuit might be reported in the financial statements.

TIF 10-5 Pension expense

The annual examination of Felton Company's financial statements by its external public accounting firm (auditors) is nearing completion. The following conversation took place between the controller of Felton Company (Francie) and the audit manager from the public accounting firm (Sumana):

Sumana: You know, Francie, we are about to wrap up our audit for this fiscal year. Yet, there is one item still to be resolved.

Francie: What's that?

Sumana: Well, as you know, at the beginning of the year, Felton began a defined benefit pension plan. This plan promises your employees an annual payment when they retire, using a formula based on their salaries at retirement and their years of service. I believe that a pension expense should be recognized this year, equal to the amount of pension earned by your employees.

Francie: Wait a minute. I think you have it all wrong. The company doesn't have a pension expense until it actually pays the pension in cash when the employee retires. After all, some of these employees may not reach retirement, and if they don't, the company doesn't owe them anything.

Sumana: You're not really seeing this the right way. The pension is earned by your employees during their working years. You actually make the payment much later—when they retire. It's like one long accrual—much like incurring wages in one period and paying them in the next. Thus, I think you should recognize the expense in the period the pension is earned by the employees.

Francie: Let me see if I've got this straight. I should recognize an expense this period for something that may or may not be paid to the employees in 20 or 30 years, when they finally retire. How am I supposed to determine what the expense is for the current year? The amount of the final retirement depends on many uncertainties: salary levels, employee longevity, mortality rates, and interest earned on investments to fund the pension. I don't think an amount can be determined even if I accepted your arguments.

⟹ Evaluate Sumana's position. Is she right, or is Francie correct?

Pathways Challenge

This is Accounting!

Information/Consequences

A warranty is not the same as a product recall. A warranty is a seller's promise, made at the time of sale, that a product will perform as intended. This promise creates an obligation for the company to repair or replace the product. When issued by a seller, a warranty is a contingent liability. If warranty costs are probable and the amount can be reasonably estimated, it is recorded at the time of sale as a debit to a warranty expense and a credit to a related warranty liability. In contrast, a product recall is issued when a product is determined to be potentially unsafe. Thus, a contingent liability is not recorded until the recall is issued, which may be in a period other than the period the sale is made.

When a product recall is issued, the estimated costs of the recall should be recorded if they can be reasonably estimated. These estimated costs are recorded as a recall expense and related recall liability. **Samsung**'s **(SSNLS)** recall of its Galaxy Note 7 phones is estimated to cost approximately $5.3 billion.

Suggested Answer

STATEMENT OF STOCKHOLDERS' EQUITY
For the Year Ended December 31, 20Y5

	Common Stock	Retained Earnings	Total
Balances, Jan. 1, 20Y5	$XXX	$ XXX	$ XXX
Issued common stock	XXX		XXX
Net income		XXX	XXX
Dividends		(XXX)	(XXX)
Balances, Dec. 31, 20Y5	$XXX	$ XXX	$ XXX

STATEMENT OF CASH FLOWS
For the Year Ended December 31, 20Y5

Cash flows from (used for) operating activities	$XXX
Cash flows from (used for) investing activities	XXX
Cash flows from (used for) financing activities	XXX
Net increase (decrease) in cash	$XXX
Cash balance, January 1, 20Y5	XXX
Cash balance, December 31, 20Y5	$XXX

INCOME STATEMENT
For the Year Ended December 31, 20Y5

Sales		$ XXX
Cost of goods sold		(XXX)
Gross profit		$ XXX
Operating expenses:		
Wages expense	$XXX	
Advertising expense	XXX	
Utilities expense	XXX	
Depreciation expense	XXX	
...	XXX	
Total operating expenses		(XXX)
Operating income		$ XXX
Other revenue and expense:		
Interest expense		(XXX)
Net income		$ XXX

BALANCE SHEET
December 31, 20Y5

Assets		
Current assets:		
Cash	$XXX	
Accounts receivable	XXX	
Inventory	XXX	
Total current assets		$XXX
Property, plant, and equipment		XXX
Total assets		$XXX
Liabilities		
Current liabilities		$XXX
Long-term liabilities:		
Bonds payable		XXX
Total liabilities		$XXX
Stockholders' Equity		
Common stock	$XXX	
Retained earnings	XXX	
Total stockholders' equity		XXX
Total liabilities and stockholders' equity		$XXX

PepsiCo, Inc.

PepsiCo, Inc. (PEP) is best known for its beverages, which include Pepsi, Diet Pepsi, Gatorade, Mountain Dew, Diet Mountain Dew, Tropicana fruit juices, and Aquafina water.* However, PepsiCo also produces a variety of foods, which include Lay's potato chips, Fritos corn chips, Doritos, Cheetos, Quaker oatmeal, Aunt Jemima mixes and syrups, and Cap'n Crunch cereal. PepsiCo produces, distributes, and sells its products in over 200 countries.

PepsiCo uses a variety of methods to finance its operations, including long-term debt and stock. A recent balance sheet revealed that almost 85% of its total assets are financed with liabilities, and 66% of these liabilities are long-term. Included in PepsiCo's long-term liabilities are a variety of notes and bonds. For example, PepsiCo has $18,558 million of bonds maturing throughout 2022–2046 with interest rates of 3.7% and 3.9%. In this chapter, we will discuss the accounting and reporting of bonds payable.

* The brands listed here are trademarked by PepsiCo.

©B CHRISTOPHER/ALAMY STOCK PHOTO

Link to PepsiCo . . . . Pages 545, 548, 550, 554

Analysis for Decision Making . . . . Page 555

What's Covered

Liabilities: Bonds Payable

Nature of Bonds Payable	Accounting for Bonds Payable	Reporting Bonds Payable
■ Characteristics (Obj. 1)	■ Nature of Bonds (Obj. 2)	■ Balance Sheet (Obj. 3)
■ Terminology (Obj. 1)	■ Bonds Issued at Par (Obj. 2)	
■ Proceeds from Issuing Bonds (Obj. 1)	■ Bonds Issued at Discount (Obj. 2)	
	■ Amortizing Bond Discount (Obj. 2)	
	■ Bonds Issued at Premium (Obj. 2)	
	■ Amortizing Bond Premium (Obj. 2)	
	■ Bond Redemption (Obj. 2)	

Learning Objectives

Obj. 1 Describe the characteristics and terminology of bonds payable.

Obj. 2 Describe and illustrate the accounting for bonds payable.

Obj. 3 Describe and illustrate the reporting of bonds payable.

Analysis for Decision Making

Obj. 4 Describe and illustrate how the times interest earned ratio is used to evaluate a company's financial condition.

Appendices 1 and 2

Obj. App 1 Determine the selling price of a bond payable using present value concepts.

Obj. App 2 Describe and illustrate the effective interest rate method of amortizing bond discounts and premiums.

Objective 1

Describe the characteristics and terminology of bonds payable.

Nature of Bonds Payable

A **bond** is a form of interest-bearing note. Like a note, a bond requires periodic interest payments, with the face amount to be repaid at the maturity date. For example, a 12% bond requires the company issuing the bond to pay 12% interest on the face amount of the bonds every year. As creditors of the corporation, bondholder claims on the corporation's assets rank ahead of stockholders.

Corporate bonds normally differ in face amount, interest rates, interest payment dates, and maturity dates. Bonds also differ in other ways such as whether corporate assets are pledged in support of the bonds.

Bond Characteristics and Terminology

A bond issue is normally divided into a number of individual bonds. The face amount of each bond is called the *principal*. This is the amount that must be repaid on the dates the bonds mature. The principal is usually $1,000, or a multiple of $1,000. The interest on bonds may be payable annually, semiannually, or quarterly. Most bonds pay interest semiannually.

The underlying contract between the company issuing bonds and the bondholders is called a **bond indenture**. This contract can be written in different ways, depending on the financing needs of the company. The two most common types of bonds are term bonds and serial bonds. When all bonds of an issue mature at the same time, they are called *term bonds*. If the bonds mature over several dates, they are called *serial bonds*. For example, one-tenth of an issue of $1,000,000 bonds, or $100,000, may mature 16 years from the issue date, another $100,000 in the 17th year, and so on.

There are also a variety of more complicated bond structures. For example, *convertible bonds* may be exchanged for shares of common stock, and *callable bonds* may be redeemed by the corporation prior to maturity.

Proceeds from Issuing Bonds

When a corporation issues bonds, the proceeds received for the bonds depend on:

- The face amount of the bonds, which is the amount due at the maturity date.
- The interest rate on the bonds.
- The market rate of interest for similar bonds.

The face amount and the interest rate on the bonds are identified in the bond indenture. The interest rate to be paid on the face amount of the bond is called the **contract rate** or *coupon rate*.

The **market rate of interest**, sometimes called the **effective rate of interest**, is the rate determined from sales and purchases of similar bonds. The market rate of interest is affected by a variety of factors, including investors' expectations of current and future economic conditions.

By comparing the market and contract rates of interest, it can be determined whether the bonds will sell for more than, less than, or at their face amount, as shown in Exhibit 1.

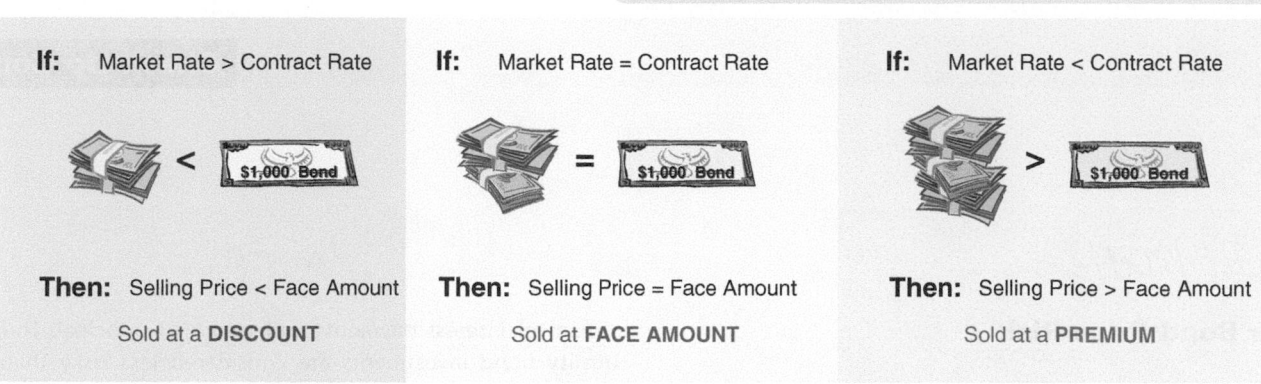

Exhibit 1
Issuing Bonds at a Discount, at Face Amount, and at a Premium

If the market rate equals the contract rate, bonds will sell at the **face amount**. If the market rate is greater than the contract rate, the bonds will sell for less than their face value. The face amount of the bonds less the selling price is called a **discount**. A bond sells at a discount because buyers are not willing to pay the full face amount for bonds with a contract rate that is lower than the market rate.

PepsiCo's 2.75% bonds maturing in 2025 were recently selling for less than their face value.   *Link to PepsiCo*

If the market rate is less than the contract rate, the bonds will sell for more than their face value. The selling price of the bonds less the face amount is called a **premium**. A bond sells at a premium because buyers are willing to pay more than the face amount for bonds with a contract rate that is higher than the market rate.

PepsiCo's 4.45% bonds maturing in 2046 were recently selling for more than their face value.   *Link to PepsiCo*

The price of a bond is quoted as a percentage of the bond's face value. For example, a $1,000 bond quoted at 98 could be purchased or sold for $980 ($1,000 × 0.98). Likewise, bonds quoted at 109 could be purchased or sold for $1,090 ($1,000 × 1.09).

Check Up Corner 11-1 Nature of Bonds Payable

Match the bond terminology in the left column to the correct definition from the right column.

Bond Terminology	Definitions
1. Contract rate of interest	a. The amount due at the maturity date
2. Discount	b. The interest rate to be paid on the face amount of the bond
3. Face amount	c. The interest rate determined from sales and purchases of similar bonds
4. Market rate of interest	d. When bonds sell for less than their face value
5. Premium	e. When bonds sell for more than their face value

Solution:

1. b
2. d
3. a
4. c
5. e

Check Up Corner

Why It Matters

Investor Bond Price Risk

Corporate bonds are purchased as investments by individuals and institutions, such as pension funds. Bonds issued by financially strong issuers provide the investor a contracted stream of interest payments and return of principal. Thus, high-quality bond investments are considered less risky than equity investments. However, this does not mean the investor has no price risk. Bond prices move opposite to changes in market interest rates, as follows:

Market Rate of Interest	Market Price of Bonds
Increase	Decrease
Decrease	Increase

In addition, the magnitude of the change in a bond's price will be a function of its maturity. Short-term bond market prices fluctuate minimally in response to changes in market interest rates, whereas a change in market interest rates will lead to a greater fluctuation in the market price of long-term bonds. This is illustrated in the following table:

Bond Term	Contract Rate	Estimated Price of $1,000 Par Value Bond if Market Interest Rate Doubles	Estimated Price of $1,000 Par Value Bond if Market Interest Rate Halves
1 year	0.5%	$995	$1,002
5 years	1.5%	931	1,037
10 years	2.0%	836	1,095
30 years	3.0%	585	1,361

This table shows that the price of the bond is much more variable, and hence riskier, to changes in the market interest rate as the term of the bond gets longer. This relationship is one of the reasons long-term bonds often have higher coupon rates than do shorter-term bonds. The bond's term must be considered in managing the risk versus return of a bond investment.

Accounting for Bonds Payable

Objective 2

Describe and illustrate the accounting for bonds payable.

Bonds may be issued at their face amount, a discount, or a premium. When bonds are issued at less or more than their face amount, the discount or premium must be amortized over the life of the bonds. At the maturity date, the face amount must be repaid. In some situations, a corporation may redeem bonds before their maturity date by repurchasing them from investors.

Bonds Issued at Face Amount

If the market rate of interest is equal to the contract rate of interest, the bonds will sell for their face amount or at a price of 100. To illustrate, assume that on January 1, 20Y5, Eastern Montana Communications Inc. issued the following bonds:

Face amount	$100,000
Contract rate of interest	12%
Interest paid semiannually on June 30 and December 31.	
Term of bonds	5 years
Market rate of interest	12%

Since the contract rate of interest and the market rate of interest are the same, the bonds will sell at their face amount. The entry to record the issuance of the bonds is as follows:

20Y5					
Jan. 1	Cash		100,000		
	Bonds Payable			100,000	
	Issued $100,000 bonds payable at face amount.				

$$A = L + E$$
$$+ \quad +$$

Every six months (on June 30 and December 31) after the bonds are issued, interest of $6,000 ($100,000 × 12% × ½ year) is paid. The first interest payment on June 30, 20Y5, is recorded as follows:

20Y5				
June 30	Interest Expense		6,000	
	Cash			6,000
	Paid six months' interest on bonds.			

$$A = L + E$$
$$- \qquad\quad - \text{ Exp}$$

At the maturity date, the payment of the principal of $100,000 is recorded as follows:

20Y9				
Dec. 31	Bonds Payable		100,000	
	Cash			100,000
	Paid bond principal at maturity date.			

$$A = L + E$$
$$- \quad -$$

Bonds Issued at a Discount

If the market rate of interest is greater than the contract rate of interest, the bonds will sell for less than their face amount. This is because investors are not willing to pay the full face amount for bonds that pay a lower contract rate of interest than the rate they could earn on similar bonds (market rate). The difference between the face amount and the selling price of the bonds is the bond discount.[1]

To illustrate, assume that on January 1, 20Y1, Western Wyoming Distribution Inc. issued the following bonds:

note:

Bonds will sell at a discount when the market rate of interest is higher than the contract rate.

Face amount	$100,000
Contract rate of interest	12%
Interest paid semiannually on June 30 and December 31.	
Term of bonds...................................	5 years
Market rate of interest	13%

[1] The price that investors are willing to pay for the bonds depends on present value concepts. Present value concepts, including the computation of bond prices, are described and illustrated in Appendix 1 at the end of this chapter.

Because the contract rate of interest is less than the market rate of interest, the bonds will sell at less than their face amount. Assuming the bonds sell for $96,406, the entry to record the issuance of the bonds is as follows:

$$A = L + E$$
$$+ \quad + $$

20Y1			
Jan. 1	Cash	96,406	
	Discount on Bonds Payable	3,594	
	Bonds Payable		100,000
	Issued $100,000 bonds at discount.		

The $96,406 is the amount investors are willing to pay for bonds that have a lower contract rate of interest (12%) than the market rate (13%). The discount is the market's way of adjusting the contract rate of interest to the higher market rate of interest.

Link to PepsiCo **PepsiCo**'s 3.45% bonds maturing in 2046 were selling for 90.4% of their face value, which implies that the market rate of interest for equivalent bonds is more than 3.45%.

The account, Discount on Bonds Payable, is a contra account to Bonds Payable and has a normal debit balance. It is subtracted from Bonds Payable to determine the carrying amount (or book value) of the bonds payable. The **carrying amount** of bonds payable is the face amount of the bonds less any unamortized discount or plus any unamortized premium. Thus, after the preceding entry, the carrying amount of the bonds payable is $96,406 ($100,000 − $3,594).

Amortizing a Bond Discount

Every period, a portion of the bond discount must be reduced and added to interest expense to reflect the passage of time. This process, called **amortization**, increases the contract rate of interest on a bond to the market rate of interest that existed on the date the bonds were issued. The entry to amortize a bond discount is as follows:

Interest Expense	XXX	
Discount on Bonds Payable		XXX

Why It Matters

U.S. Government Debt

Like many corporations, the U.S. government issues debt to finance its operations. Currently, debt provides approximately 24% of the total annual funding needs of the U.S. government.

The remainder comes from taxes. The debt is issued by the U.S. Treasury Department in the form of U.S. Treasury bills, notes, and bonds. An individual investor can purchase these as an investment through the TreasuryDirect® website or through a broker. Treasury securities have the following characteristics:

	Issued at	Interest Paid	Term
U.S. Treasury bills	Discount	None	1 year or less
U.S. Treasury notes	Face value	Semiannual	1 to 10 years
U.S. Treasury bonds	Face value	Semiannual	30 years

The interest rate for government securities will normally be lowest for Treasury bills and largest for Treasury bonds. For example, recently U.S. Treasury bills maturing in 3 months had a rate of 1.02%, 5-year Treasury notes had a rate of 1.87%, and 30-year Treasury bonds had a rate of 2.92%.

The preceding entry may be made annually as an adjusting entry, or it may be combined with the semiannual interest payment. In the latter case, the entry would be as follows:

Interest Expense	XXX	
Discount on Bonds Payable		XXX
Cash (amount of semiannual interest)		XXX

The two methods of computing the amortization of a bond discount are:

- *Straight-line method*
- *Effective interest rate method,* sometimes called the *interest method*

The **effective interest rate method** is required by generally accepted accounting principles. However, the straight-line method may be used if the results do not differ significantly from the interest method. The straight-line method is used in this chapter. The effective interest rate method is described and illustrated in Appendix 2 at the end of this chapter.

The **straight-line method of amortization** provides equal amounts of discount (or premium) to be written off to interest expense each period. To illustrate, amortization of the Western Wyoming Distribution bond discount of $3,594 is computed as follows:

Discount on bonds payable	$3,594
Term of bonds	5 years
Semiannual amortization	$359.40 ($3,594 ÷ 10 periods)

The combined entry to record the first interest payment and the amortization of the discount is as follows:

20Y1				
June 30	Interest Expense		6,359.40	
	Discount on Bonds Payable			359.40
	Cash			6,000.00
	Paid semiannual interest and amortized ¹/₁₀ of bond discount.			

$$A = L + E$$
$$- \quad + \quad - \quad \text{Exp}$$

The preceding entry is made on each interest payment date. Thus, the amount of the semiannual interest expense on the bonds ($6,359.40) remains the same over the life of the bonds.

The effect of the discount amortization is to increase the interest expense from $6,000.00 to $6,359.40 on every semiannual interest payment date. In effect, this increases the contract rate of interest from 12% to a rate of interest that approximates the market rate of 13%. In addition, as the discount is amortized, the carrying amount of the bonds increases until it equals the face amount of the bonds on the maturity date.

Check Up Corner 11-2 Bonds Issued at a Discount

On January 1, the first day of the fiscal year, Nickson Company issues a $1,000,000, 6%, five-year bond, receiving cash of $936,420. The bond pays interest semiannually on June 30 and December 31, and is amortized semiannually using the straight-line method.

a. Journalize the issuance of the bond on January 1.

b. Journalize the semiannual interest payments on June 30 and December 31 of the first year. The bond discount amortization is combined with the semiannual interest payment.

c. Determine the carrying amount of the bond at the end of the first year.

(Continued)

Solution:

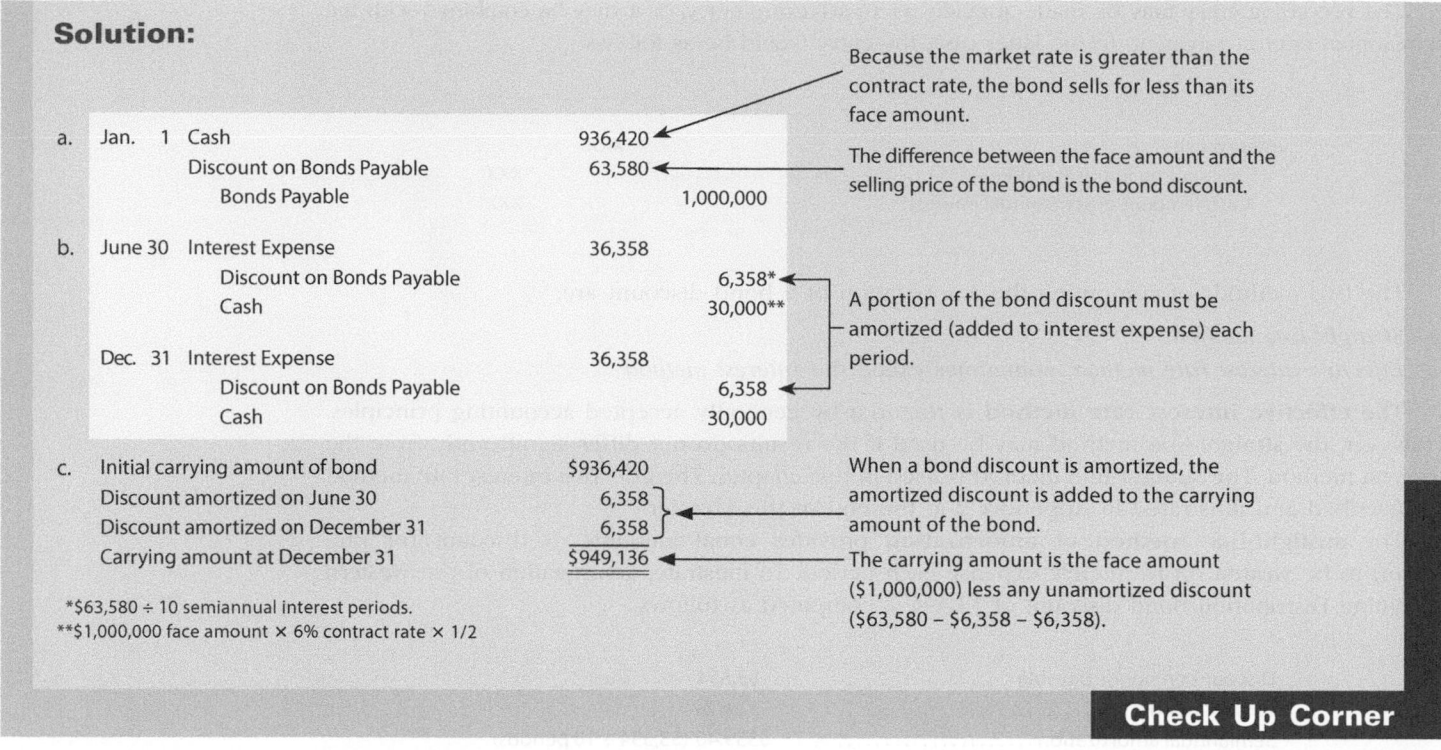

Because the market rate is greater than the contract rate, the bond sells for less than its face amount.

a. Jan. 1 Cash — 936,420
Discount on Bonds Payable — 63,580
Bonds Payable — 1,000,000

The difference between the face amount and the selling price of the bond is the bond discount.

b. June 30 Interest Expense — 36,358
Discount on Bonds Payable — 6,358*
Cash — 30,000**

Dec. 31 Interest Expense — 36,358
Discount on Bonds Payable — 6,358
Cash — 30,000

A portion of the bond discount must be amortized (added to interest expense) each period.

c. Initial carrying amount of bond — $936,420
Discount amortized on June 30 — 6,358
Discount amortized on December 31 — 6,358
Carrying amount at December 31 — $949,136

When a bond discount is amortized, the amortized discount is added to the carrying amount of the bond.

The carrying amount is the face amount ($1,000,000) less any unamortized discount ($63,580 − $6,358 − $6,358).

*$63,580 ÷ 10 semiannual interest periods.
**$1,000,000 face amount × 6% contract rate × 1/2

Check Up Corner

Bonds Issued at a Premium

If the market rate of interest is less than the contract rate of interest, the bonds will sell for more than their face amount. This is because investors are willing to pay more for bonds that pay a higher contract rate of interest than the rate they could earn on similar bonds (market rate).

To illustrate, assume that on January 1, 20Y3, Northern Idaho Transportation Inc. issued the following bonds:

Face amount	$100,000
Contract rate of interest	12%
Interest paid semiannually on June 30 and December 31.	
Term of bonds	5 years
Market rate of interest	11%

Because the contract rate of interest is more than the market rate of interest, the bonds will sell for more than their face amount. Assuming the bonds sell for $103,769, the entry to record the issuance of the bonds is as follows:

A = L + E
+ +

20Y3
Jan. 1 Cash — 103,769
Bonds Payable — 100,000
Premium on Bonds Payable — 3,769
Issued $100,000 bonds at a premium.

The $3,769 premium is the extra amount investors are willing to pay for bonds that have a higher contract rate of interest (12%) than the market rate (11%). The premium is the market's way of adjusting the contract rate of interest to the lower market rate of interest.

Link to PepsiCo

PepsiCo's 5.5% bonds maturing in 2040 were selling for approximately 120% of their face value, which implies that the market rate of interest for equivalent bonds is less than 5.5%.

The account, Premium on Bonds Payable, has a normal credit balance. It is added to Bonds Payable to determine the carrying amount (or book value) of the bonds payable. Thus, after the preceding entry, the carrying amount of the bonds payable is $103,769 ($100,000 + $3,769).

Amortizing a Bond Premium

Like bond discounts, a bond premium must be amortized over the life of the bond. The amortization of a bond premium decreases the contract rate of interest on a bond to the market rate of interest that existed on the date the bonds were issued. The amortization can be computed using either the straight-line or the effective interest rate method. The entry to amortize a bond premium is as follows:

Premium on Bonds Payable	XXX
Interest Expense	XXX

The preceding entry may be made annually as an adjusting entry, or it may be combined with the semiannual interest payment. In the latter case, it would be:

Interest Expense	XXX	
Premium on Bonds Payable	XXX	
Cash (amount of semiannual interest)		XXX

To illustrate, amortization of the preceding premium of $3,769 is computed as follows using the straight-line method:

Premium on bonds payable..................	$3,769
Term of bonds...............................	5 years
Semiannual amortization....................	$376.90 ($3,769 ÷ 10 periods)

The combined entry to record the first interest payment and the amortization of the premium is as follows:

20Y3			
June 30	Interest Expense	5,623.10	
	Premium on Bonds Payable	376.90	
	Cash		6,000.00
	Paid semiannual interest and		
	amortized $^{1}/_{10}$ of bond premium.		

$A = L + E$
$-\quad-\quad- \text{Exp}$

The preceding entry is made on each interest payment date. Thus, the amount of the semiannual interest expense ($5,623.10) on the bonds remains the same over the life of the bonds.

The effect of the premium amortization is to decrease the interest expense from $6,000.00 to $5,623.10. In effect, this decreases the rate of interest from 12% to a rate of interest that approximates the market rate of 11%. In addition, as the premium is amortized, the carrying amount of the bonds decreases until it equals the face amount of bonds on the maturity date.

Why It Matters ▶

CONCEPT CLIP

Bond Ratings

When purchasing bonds, investors are very interested in the likelihood that the bond issuer will not be able to repay bond principal and associated interest. This is termed the *likelihood of default*. To help them assess the likelihood of default, independent rating agencies review and grade the financial condition of companies that issue bonds. For example, the **Standard & Poor's (S&P)** rating agency rates bonds on a scale from D (lowest) to AAA (highest). Bonds with a rating of BBB– or higher are called *investment grade* (or *IG*) bonds because they are issued by companies who are unlikely to default. Bonds issued by companies in weaker financial condition receive ratings below BBB–, reflecting the higher potential for default. These lesser-quality bonds are referred to as *noninvestment grade* or *high-yield* (or *HY*) bonds. Noninvestment grade bonds have a higher yield to compensate investors for their higher risk of default.

Check Up Corner 11-3   Bonds Issued at a Premium

On January 1, the first day of the fiscal year, Johnson Company issues a $2,000,000, 8%, five-year bond, receiving cash of $2,170,600. The bond pays interest semiannually on June 30 and December 31 and is amortized semiannually using the straight-line method.

a. Journalize the issuance of the bond on January 1.

b. Journalize the semiannual interest payments on June 30 and December 31 of the first year. The bond premium amortization is combined with the semiannual interest payment.

c. Determine the carrying amount of the bond at the end of the first year.

Solution:

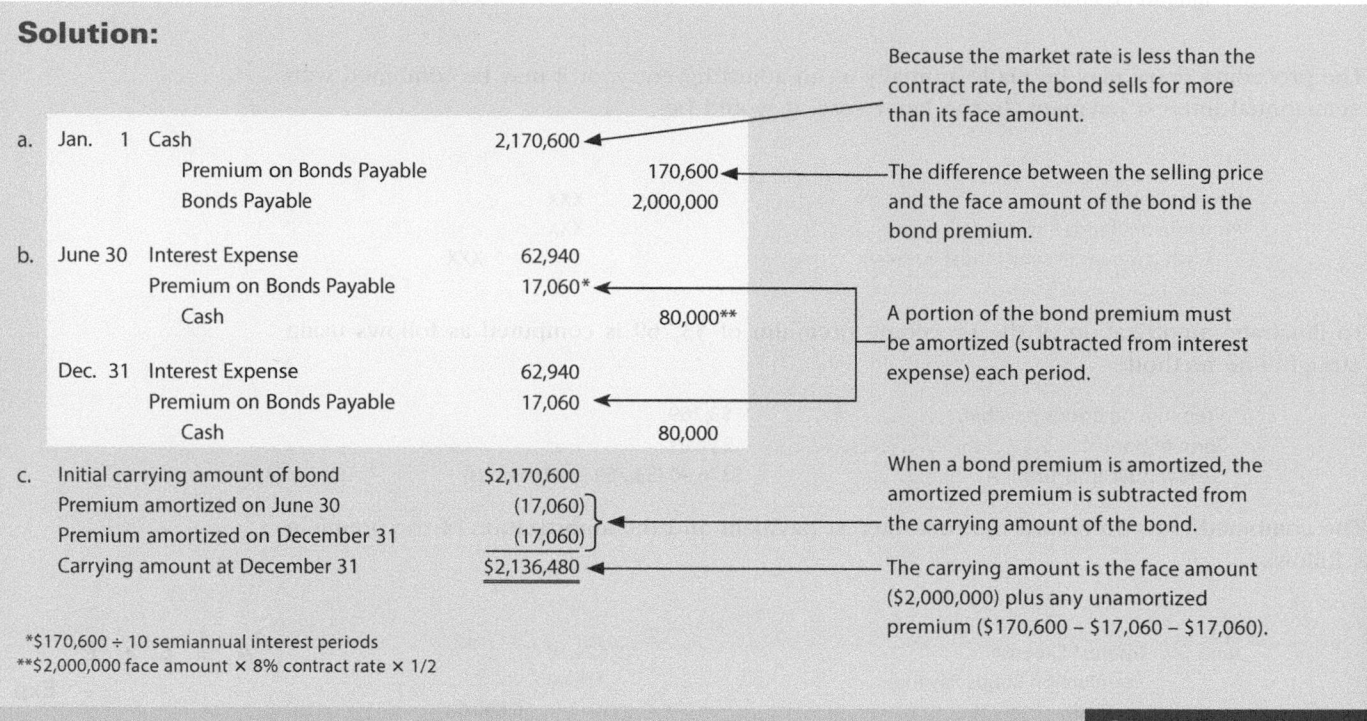

Because the market rate is less than the contract rate, the bond sells for more than its face amount.

a.	Jan.	1	Cash	2,170,600	
			Premium on Bonds Payable		170,600
			Bonds Payable		2,000,000

The difference between the selling price and the face amount of the bond is the bond premium.

b.	June 30	Interest Expense	62,940	
		Premium on Bonds Payable	17,060*	
		Cash		80,000**
	Dec. 31	Interest Expense	62,940	
		Premium on Bonds Payable	17,060	
		Cash		80,000

A portion of the bond premium must be amortized (subtracted from interest expense) each period.

c.	Initial carrying amount of bond	$2,170,600
	Premium amortized on June 30	(17,060)
	Premium amortized on December 31	(17,060)
	Carrying amount at December 31	$2,136,480

When a bond premium is amortized, the amortized premium is subtracted from the carrying amount of the bond.

The carrying amount is the face amount ($2,000,000) plus any unamortized premium ($170,600 − $17,060 − $17,060).

*$170,600 ÷ 10 semiannual interest periods
**$2,000,000 face amount × 8% contract rate × 1/2

Check Up Corner

Bond Redemption

A corporation may redeem or call bonds before they mature. This is often done when the market rate of interest declines below the contract rate of interest. In such cases, the corporation may issue new bonds at a lower interest rate and use the proceeds to redeem the original bond issue.

Callable bonds can be redeemed by the issuing corporation within the period of time and at the price stated in the bond indenture. Normally, the call price is above the face value. A corporation may also redeem its bonds by purchasing them on the open market.[2]

A corporation usually redeems its bonds at a price different from the carrying amount (or book value) of the bonds. A gain or loss may be realized on a bond redemption as follows:

- A *gain* is recorded if the price paid for redemption is below the bond carrying amount.
- A *loss* is recorded if the price paid for the redemption is above the carrying amount.

Gains and losses on the redemption of bonds are reported in the *Other revenue (expense)* section of the income statement.

To illustrate, assume that on June 30, a corporation has the following bond issue:

| Face amount of bonds | $100,000 |
| Premium on bonds payable | 4,000 |

---

[2] Some bond indentures require the corporation issuing the bonds to transfer cash to a special cash fund, called a *sinking fund,* over the life of the bond. Such funds help assure investors that there will be adequate cash to pay the bonds at their maturity date.

On June 30, the corporation redeemed one-fourth ($25,000) of these bonds in the market for $24,000. The entry to record the redemption is as follows:

June 30	Bonds Payable	25,000	
	Premium on Bonds Payable	1,000	
	Cash		24,000
	Gain on Redemption of Bonds		2,000
	Redeemed bonds for $24,000.		

$$A = L + E$$
$$- \quad - \quad + \text{Gain}$$

In the preceding entry, only the portion of the premium related to the redeemed bonds ($4,000 × 25% = $1,000) is written off. The difference between the carrying amount of the bonds redeemed, $26,000 ($25,000 + $1,000), and the redemption price, $24,000, is recorded as a gain.

Assume that the corporation calls the remaining $75,000 of outstanding bonds, which are held by a private investor, for $79,500 on July 1. The entry to record the redemption is as follows:

July 1	Bonds Payable	75,000	
	Premium on Bonds Payable	3,000	
	Loss on Redemption of Bonds	1,500	
	Cash		79,500
	Redeemed bonds for $79,500.		

$$A = L + E$$
$$- \quad - \quad - \text{Loss}$$

The difference between the carrying amount of the bonds redeemed of $78,000 ($75,000 + $3,000) and the redemption price of $79,500 is recorded as a loss of $1,500 ($79,500 − $78,000).

 Ethics: Don't Do It!

The Ratings Game

In February 2013, the United States Justice Department filed a lawsuit against **Standard & Poor's (S&P)** for inflating its ratings on high-risk bond issuances between 2004 and 2007. During this time period, Standard & Poor's gave its highest rating (AAA) to debt securities that were, in fact, highly risky. During the financial crisis of 2008, most of these bonds experienced significant drops in value, leaving investors with huge losses. The Justice Department lawsuit alleged that Standard & Poor's was aware of the high risks associated with these bonds but inflated its ratings because of the large fee it received for providing a rating on these bonds. In 2015, Standard & Poor's settled this and related lawsuits for $1.5 billion.

Source: "U.S. vs. S&P: The Rating Game," *The Chicago Tribune*, February 6, 2013. "S&P Reaches $1.5 Billion Deal with U.S., States over Crisis-Era Ratings," Reuters, Business News, February 3, 2015.

Pathways Challenge

This is Accounting!

Economic Activity

Advanced Micro Devices, Inc. (AMD) is a leading manufacturer of semiconductors. It recently issued $805 million of convertible bonds payable that pay interest of 2.125% annually. Each $1,000 bond can be converted into cash or shares of AMD's common stock. For each bond converted, AMD has the option to deliver to the bondholder cash, shares of common stock, or a combination of cash and shares.

Critical Thinking/Judgment

Should AMD's convertible bonds be reported as debt, equity, or some combination?

Suggested answer at end of chapter.

Objective 3

Describe and illustrate the reporting of bonds payable.

Reporting Bonds Payable

Bonds payable are reported as liabilities on the balance sheet. As illustrated in Chapter 10 with notes payable, any portion of the bonds that is due within one year is reported as a current liability. Any remaining bonds are reported as a long-term liability. Any unamortized premium is reported as an addition to the face amount of the bonds. Any unamortized discount is reported as a deduction from the face amount of the bonds. A description of the bonds should also be reported either on the face of the financial statements or in the accompanying notes.

The reporting of bonds payable for **PepsiCo** follows:

Link to PepsiCo

PepsiCo, Inc.
Balance Sheet
December 31
(in millions)

Liabilities

Current liabilities:

Accounts payable and other current liabilities	$14,243
Current maturities of long-term debt obligations	4,401
Other debt obligations	2,491
Total current liabilities	$21,135
Long-term debt obligations	30,053
Other liabilities	6,669
Deferred income taxes	5,073
Total liabilities	$62,930

Notes to Financial Statements:

Note 8 – Debt Obligations

The following table summarizes the Company's debt obligations:

Long-term debt obligations

Due 2017 (1.4% and 1.2%)	$ 4,398
Due 2018 (2.3% and 3.6%)	2,561
Due 2019 (1.7% and 3.7%)	2,837
Due 2020 (2.6% and 2.4%)	3,816
Due 2021 (2.4% and 3.0%)	2,249
Due 2022–2046 (3.7% and 3.9%)	18,558
Other, due 2017–2026 (1.4% and 4.3%)	35
	$34,454
Less: Current maturities of long-term debt obligations	(4,401)
Total	$30,053

Source: PepsiCo, Inc., *Form 10-K for the Fiscal Year Ended December 31, 2016* (adapted).

Analysis for Decision Making

Times Interest Earned

Objective 4
Describe and illustrate how the times interest earned ratio is used to evaluate a company's financial condition.

As we have discussed, the assets of a company are subject to (1) the claims of creditors and (2) the rights of owners. As creditors, bondholders are primarily concerned with the company's ability to make its periodic interest payments and repay the face amount of the bonds at maturity.

Analysts assess the risk that bondholders will not receive their interest payments by computing the **times interest earned** ratio during the year as follows:

$$\text{Times Interest Earned} = \frac{\text{Income Before Income Tax Expense} + \text{Interest Expense}}{\text{Interest Expense}}$$

This ratio computes the number of times interest payments could be paid out of current-period earnings. Because interest payments reduce income tax expense, the ratio is computed using income before tax. High values of this ratio are considered favorable. In contrast, low values are considered unfavorable. Values of this ratio less than 1.0 suggest that the firm is unable to cover interest payments from income before tax. Such a situation could eventually lead to loan defaults.

To illustrate, the following data were taken from recent annual reports of four companies in the soft drink beverage industry—**PepsiCo, Inc. (PEP)**, **The Coca-Cola Company (KO)**, **Dr Pepper Snapple Group, Inc. (DPS)**, and **Monster Beverage Corporation (MNST)** (in thousands):

	PepsiCo	Coca-Cola	Dr Pepper Snapple	Monster
Interest expense	$1,342,000	$ 733,000	$ 147,000	$ 68
Income before income tax expense	8,553,000	8,136,000	1,283,000	1,079,685

The times interest earned is computed as follows for all four companies:

	PepsiCo	Coca-Cola	Dr Pepper Snapple	Monster
Interest expense	$1,342,000	$ 733,000	$ 147,000	$ 68
Income before income tax expense	8,553,000	8,136,000	1,283,000	1,079,685
Income before income tax expense + Interest expense	$9,895,000	$8,869,000	$1,430,000	$1,079,753
Times interest earned	7.4	12.1	9.7	15,878.7
	($9,895,000 ÷ $1,342,000)	($8,869,000 ÷ $733,000)	($1,430,000 ÷ $147,000)	($1,079,753 ÷ $68)

Monster is much smaller than the other three beverage companies. However, it has a times interest earned ratio of 15,878.7, which is much greater than the other three companies. This is because Monster has no long-term debt and only a small amount of short-term bank loans. Among the other three beverage companies, Coca-Cola has greater interest coverage than PepsiCo and Dr Pepper Snapple. Since all of the ratios are in excess of 7, all of the companies generate enough income before tax to pay (cover) their interest payments. As a result, bondholders of these companies have extremely good protection in the event of an earnings decline.

Make a Decision | **Times Interest Earned**

Analyze and compare Amazon.com and Wal-Mart (MAD 11-1)
(Continuing company analysis)

Analyze and compare Clorox and Procter & Gamble (MAD 11-2)

Analyze Aeropostale (MAD 11-3)

Analyze and compare Hilton and Marriott (MAD 11-4)

Make a Decision

Objective App 1

Determine the selling price of a bond payable using present value concepts.

Appendix 1 Present Value Concepts and Pricing Bonds Payable

When a corporation issues bonds, the price that investors are willing to pay for the bonds depends on the following:

- The face amount of the bonds, which is the amount due at the maturity date.
- The periodic interest to be paid on the bonds.
- The market rate of interest.

An investor determines how much to pay for the bonds by computing the present value of the bond's future cash receipts, using the market rate of interest. A bond's future cash receipts include its face value at maturity and the periodic interest payments.

Present Value Concepts

The concept of present value is based on the time value of money. The *time value of money concept* recognizes that cash received today is worth more than the same amount of cash to be received in the future.

To illustrate, what would you rather have: $1,000 today or $1,000 one year from now? You would rather have the $1,000 today because it could be invested to earn interest. For example, if the $1,000 could be invested to earn 10% per year, the $1,000 will accumulate to $1,100 ($1,000 plus $100 interest) in one year. In this sense, you can think of the $1,000 in hand today as the **present value** of $1,100 to be received a year from today. This present value is illustrated in Exhibit 2.

Exhibit 2

Present Value and Future Value

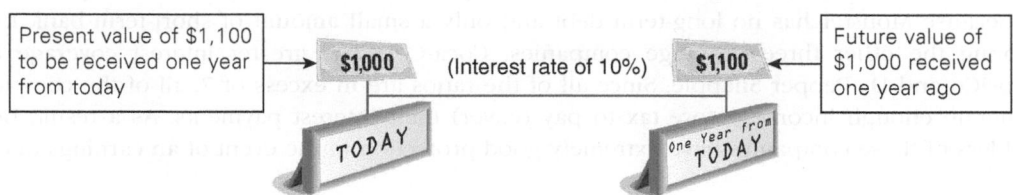

A related concept to present value is **future value**. Using the preceding example, the $1,100 to be received one year from today is the *future value* of $1,000 today, assuming an interest rate of 10%. This future value is illustrated in Exhibit 2.

Present Value of an Amount To illustrate the present value of an amount, assume that $1,000 is to be received in one year. If the market rate of interest is 10%, the present value of the $1,000 is $909.09 ($1,000 ÷ 1.10). This present value is illustrated in Exhibit 3.

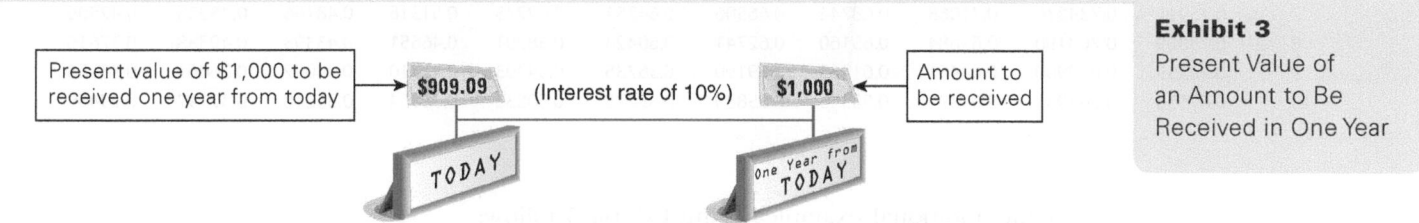

Exhibit 3

Present Value of an Amount to Be Received in One Year

If the $1,000 is to be received in two years, with interest of 10% compounded at the end of the first year, the present value is $826.45 ($909.09 ÷ 1.10).[3] This present value is illustrated in Exhibit 4.

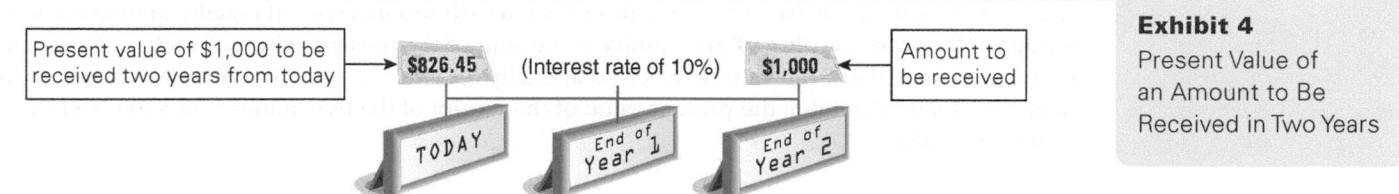

Exhibit 4

Present Value of an Amount to Be Received in Two Years

As illustrated, the present value of an amount to be received in the future can be determined by a series of divisions. In practice, however, it is easier to use a table of present values.

The *present value of $1* table is used to find the present value factor for $1 to be received after a number of periods in the future. The amount to be received is then multiplied by this factor to determine its present value.

To illustrate, Exhibit 5 is a partial table of the present value of $1.[4] Exhibit 5 indicates that the present value of $1 to be received in two years with a market rate of interest of 10% a year is 0.82645. Multiplying $1,000 to be received in two years by 0.82645 yields $826.45 ($1,000 × 0.82645). This amount is the same amount computed in Exhibit 4.

In Exhibit 5, the Periods column represents the number of compounding periods, and the percentage columns represent the compound interest rate per period. Thus, the present value factor from Exhibit 5 for 12% for five years is 0.56743. If the interest is compounded semiannually, the interest rate is 6% (12% ÷ 2), and the number of periods is 10 (5 years × 2 times per year). Thus, the present value factor from Exhibit 5 for 6% and 10 periods is 0.55839.

---

[3] Note that the future value of $826.45 in two years, at an interest rate of 10% compounded annually, is $1,000.
[4] To simplify the illustrations and homework assignments, the tables presented in this chapter are limited to 10 periods for a small number of interest rates, and the amounts are carried to only five decimal places. Computer programs can be used to determine present values for any number of interest rates, decimal places, or periods. More complete interest tables are presented in Appendix A of the text.

Exhibit 5 Present Value of $1 at Compound Interest

Periods	4%	4½%	5%	5½%	6%	6½%	7%	10%	11%	12%	13%
1	0.96154	0.956940	0.95238	0.94787	0.94340	0.93897	0.93458	0.90909	0.90090	0.89286	0.88496
2	0.92456	0.915730	0.90703	0.89845	0.89000	0.88166	0.87344	0.82645	0.81162	0.79719	0.78315
3	0.88900	0.876300	0.86384	0.85161	0.83962	0.82785	0.81630	0.75131	0.73119	0.71178	0.69305
4	0.85480	0.838560	0.82270	0.80722	0.79209	0.77732	0.76290	0.68301	0.65873	0.63552	0.61332
5	0.82193	0.802450	0.78353	0.76513	0.74726	0.72988	0.71299	0.62092	0.59345	0.56743	0.54276
6	0.79031	0.767900	0.74622	0.72525	0.70496	0.68533	0.66634	0.56447	0.53464	0.50663	0.48032
7	0.75992	0.734830	0.71068	0.68744	0.66506	0.64351	0.62275	0.51316	0.48166	0.45235	0.42506
8	0.73069	0.703190	0.67684	0.65160	0.62741	0.60423	0.58201	0.46651	0.43393	0.40388	0.37616
9	0.70259	0.672900	0.64461	0.61763	0.59190	0.56735	0.54393	0.42410	0.39092	0.36061	0.33288
10	0.67556	0.643930	0.61391	0.58543	0.55839	0.53273	0.50835	0.38554	0.35218	0.32197	0.29459

Some additional examples using Exhibit 5 follow:

	Interest Rate	Number of Periods	Present Value of $1 Factor from Exhibit 5
10% for *two* years compounded *annually*	10%	2	0.82645
10% for *two* years compounded *semiannually*	5%	4	0.82270
10% for *three* years compounded *semiannually*	5%	6	0.74622
12% for *five* years compounded *semiannually*	6%	10	0.55839

Present Value of an Annuity A series of equal cash receipts spaced equally in time is called an **annuity**. The **present value of an annuity** is the sum of the present values of each cash receipt. To illustrate, assume that $100 is to be received annually for two years and that the market rate of interest is 10%. Using Exhibit 5, the present value of the receipt of the two amounts of $100 is $173.55, as shown in Exhibit 6.

Exhibit 6

Present Value of an Annuity

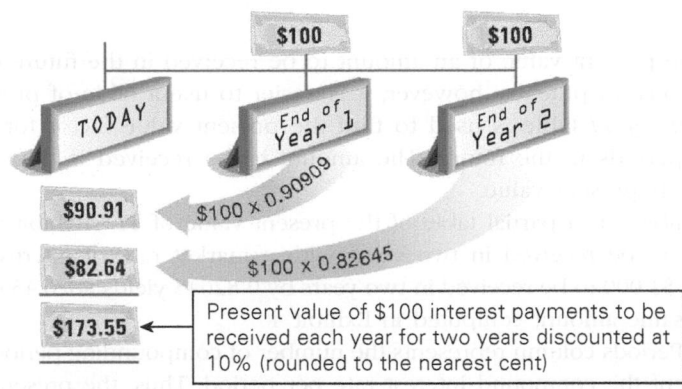

Instead of using present value of $1 tables to determine the present value of each cash flow separately, such as in Exhibit 5, the present value of an annuity can be computed in a single step. Using a value from the *present value of an annuity of $1* table in Exhibit 7, the present value of the entire annuity can be calculated by multiplying the equal cash payment times the appropriate present value of an annuity of $1.

To illustrate, the present value of $100 to be received at the end of each of the next two years at 10% compound interest per period is $173.55 ($100 × 1.73554). This amount is the same amount computed previously using the present value of $1.

Exhibit 7   Present Value of an Annuity of $1 at Compound Interest

Periods	4%	4½%	5%	5½%	6%	6½%	7%	10%	11%	12%	13%
1	0.96154	0.95694	0.95238	0.94787	0.94340	0.93897	0.93458	0.90909	0.90090	0.89286	0.88496
2	1.88609	1.87267	1.85941	1.84632	1.83339	1.82063	1.80802	1.73554	1.71252	1.69005	1.66810
3	2.77509	2.74896	2.72325	2.69793	2.67301	2.64848	2.62432	2.48685	2.44371	2.40183	2.36115
4	3.62990	3.58753	3.54595	3.50515	3.46511	3.42580	3.38721	3.16987	3.10245	3.03735	2.97447
5	4.45182	4.38998	4.32948	4.27028	4.21236	4.15568	4.10020	3.79079	3.69590	3.60478	3.51723
6	5.24214	5.15787	5.07569	4.99553	4.91732	4.84101	4.76654	4.35526	4.23054	4.11141	3.99755
7	6.00205	5.89270	5.78637	5.68297	5.58238	5.48452	5.38929	4.86842	4.71220	4.56376	4.42261
8	6.73274	6.59589	6.46321	6.33457	6.20979	6.08875	5.97130	5.33493	5.14612	4.96764	4.79677
9	7.43533	7.26879	7.10782	6.95220	6.80169	6.65610	6.51523	5.75902	5.53705	5.32825	5.13166
10	8.11090	7.91272	7.72173	7.53763	7.36009	7.18883	7.02358	6.14457	5.88923	5.65022	5.42624

Pricing Bonds

The selling price of a bond is the sum of the present values of:

- The face amount of the bonds due at the maturity date
- The periodic interest to be paid on the bonds

The market rate of interest is used to compute the present value of both the face amount and the periodic interest.

To illustrate the pricing of bonds, assume that Southern Utah Communications Inc. issued the following bond on January 1:

Face amount	$100,000
Contract rate of interest	12%
Interest paid semiannually on June 30 and December 31.	
Term of bonds	5 years

Market Rate of Interest of 12% Assuming a market rate of interest of 12%, the bonds would sell for their face amount. As shown by the following present value computations, the bonds would sell for $100,000:

Present value of face amount of $100,000 due in five years,
   at 12% compounded semiannually: $100,000 × 0.55839
   (present value of $1 for 10 periods at 6% from Exhibit 5) .... $ 55,839
Present value of 10 semiannual interest payments of $6,000,
   at 12% compounded semiannually: $6,000 × 7.36009
   (present value of an annuity of $1 for 10 periods at 6% from Exhibit 7)   44,161
Total present value of bonds $100,000

Market Rate of Interest of 13% Assuming a market rate of interest of 13%, the bonds would sell at a discount. As shown by the following present value computations, the bonds would sell for $96,406:[5]

Present value of face amount of $100,000 due in five years,
   at 13% compounded semiannually: $100,000 × 0.53273
   (present value of $1 for 10 periods at 6½% from Exhibit 5) .... $ 53,273
Present value of 10 semiannual interest payments of $6,000,
   at 13% compounded semiannually: $6,000 × 7.18883
   (present value of an annuity of $1 for 10 periods at 6½% from Exhibit 7)   43,133
Total present value of bonds .... $ 96,406

[5] Some corporations issue bonds called *zero-coupon bonds* that provide for only the payment of the face amount at maturity. Such bonds sell for large discounts. In this example, such a bond would sell for $53,273, which is the present value of the face amount.

Market Rate of Interest of 11% Assuming a market rate of interest of 11%, the bonds would sell at a premium. As shown by the following present value computations, the bonds would sell for $103,769:

Present value of face amount of $100,000 due in five years, at 11% compounded semiannually: $100,000 × 0.58543 (present value of $1 for 10 periods at 5½% from Exhibit 5)	$ 58,543
Present value of 10 semiannual interest payments of $6,000, at 11% compounded semiannually: $6,000 × 7.53763 (present value of an annuity of $1 for 10 periods at 5½% from Exhibit 7)	45,226
Total present value of bonds	$103,769

As shown, the selling price of the bond varies with the present value of the bond's face amount at maturity, the interest payments, and the market rate of interest.

Computing Present Values

Instead of using the present value tables as shown in Exhibits 5 and 7, present values can be computed directly using a financial calculator or a spreadsheet program such as Excel. For example, the formula for the present value of a cash amount (labeled C) to be received in n periods at compound interest rate of i% is computed as follows:

$$\text{Present value of } C \text{ at compound interest} = C \times \frac{1}{(1+i)^n} = \frac{C}{(1+i)^n}$$

Where: C is the cash to be received at the end of period n
i% is the interest rate
n is the number of periods

To illustrate, the present value of $1,000 to be received in two periods with a market rate of interest of 10% is computed as follows:

$$\text{Present value of \$1 at compound interest} = \frac{C}{(1+i)^n} = \frac{\$1,000}{(1+0.10)^2} = \frac{\$1,000}{(1.10)^2} = \frac{\$1,000}{1.21} = \$826.46280\ldots$$

This is the same amount, $826.45 (rounded to nearest cent), shown in Exhibit 4 and computed using the present value table shown in Exhibit 5.

The present value of an annuity of C dollars to be received for n periods at compound interest rate of i% can also be computed directly as follows:

$$\text{Present value of an annuity of \$1 at compound interest} = C \times \frac{\left(1 - \frac{1}{(1+i)^n}\right)}{i}$$

Where: C is the cash to be received at the end of each period for n periods
i% is the interest rate
n is the number of periods

The online appendix, *Computing Present Values*, contains examples of Excel spreadsheets for computing these present values and pricing bonds.

Appendix 2 Effective Interest Rate Method of Amortization

Objective App 2

Describe and illustrate the effective interest rate method of amortizing bond discounts and premiums.

The effective interest rate method of amortization provides for a constant *rate* of interest over the life of the bonds. As the discount or premium is amortized, the carrying amount of the bonds changes. As a result, interest expense also changes each period. This is in contrast to the straight-line method, which provides for a constant *amount* of interest expense each period.

The interest rate used in the effective interest rate method of amortization, sometimes called the *interest method*, is the market rate on the date the bonds are issued. The carrying amount of the bonds is multiplied by this interest rate to determine the interest expense for the period. The difference between the interest expense and the interest payment is the amount of discount or premium to be amortized for the period.

Amortization of Discount by the Interest Method

To illustrate, the following data taken from the chapter illustration of issuing bonds at a discount on January 1, 20Y1, are used:

Face value of 12%, five-year bonds, interest compounded semiannually....................	$100,000
Present value of bonds at effective (market) rate of interest of 13%	(96,406)
Discount on bonds payable...	$ 3,594

Exhibit 8 illustrates the interest method for the preceding bonds. Exhibit 8 begins with six columns. The first column is the interest payment date. The remaining columns are lettered A through E. The exhibit was then prepared as follows:

- Step 1. List the interest payment dates in the first column, which for the preceding bond are 10 interest payment dates (semiannual interest over five years). Also, list on the first line the initial amount of discount in Column D and the initial carrying amount (selling price) of the bonds in Column E.
- Step 2. List in Column A the semiannual interest payments, which for the preceding bond are $6,000 ($100,000 × 6%).

Exhibit 8 Amortization of Discount on Bonds Payable

Interest Payment Date	A Interest Paid (6% of Face Amount)	B Interest Expense (6½% of Bond Carrying Amount)	C Discount Amortization (B – A)	D Unamortized Discount (D – C)	E Bond Carrying Amount ($100,000 – D)
				$3,594	$ 96,406
June 30, 20Y1	$6,000	$6,266 (6½% of $96,406)	$266	3,328	96,672
Dec. 31, 20Y1	6,000	6,284 (6½% of $96,672)	284	3,044	96,956
June 30, 20Y2	6,000	6,302 (6½% of $96,956)	302	2,742	97,258
Dec. 31, 20Y2	6,000	6,322 (6½% of $97,258)	322	2,420	97,580
June 30, 20Y3	6,000	6,343 (6½% of $97,580)	343	2,077	97,923
Dec. 31, 20Y3	6,000	6,365 (6½% of $97,923)	365	1,712	98,288
June 30, 20Y4	6,000	6,389 (6½% of $98,288)	389	1,323	98,677
Dec. 31, 20Y4	6,000	6,414 (6½% of $98,677)	414	909	99,091
June 30, 20Y5	6,000	6,441 (6½% of $99,091)	441	468	99,532
Dec. 31, 20Y5	6,000	6,470 (6½% of $99,532)	468*	—	100,000

*Cannot exceed unamortized discount.

- Step 3. Compute the interest expense in Column B by multiplying the bond carrying amount at the beginning of each period times 6½%, which is the semiannual effective interest (market) rate (13% ÷ 2).
- Step 4. In Column C, compute the discount to be amortized each period by subtracting the interest payment in Column A ($6,000) from the interest expense for the period shown in Column B.
- Step 5. Compute the remaining unamortized discount by subtracting the amortized discount in Column C for the period from the unamortized discount at the beginning of the period in Column D.
- Step 6. Compute the bond carrying amount at the end of the period by subtracting the unamortized discount at the end of the period in Column D from the face amount of the bonds ($100,000).

Steps 3–6 are repeated for each interest payment.

As shown in Exhibit 8, the interest expense increases each period as the carrying amount of the bond increases. Also, the unamortized discount decreases each period to zero at the maturity date. Finally, the carrying amount of the bonds increases from $96,406 to $100,000 (the face amount) at maturity.

The entry to record the first interest payment on June 30, 20Y1, and the related discount amortization is as follows:

A = L + E
−   +   − Exp

20Y1			
June 30	Interest Expense	6,266	
	Discount on Bonds Payable		266
	Cash		6,000
	Paid semiannual interest and amortized		
	bond discount for ½ year.		

If the amortization is recorded only at the end of the year, the amount of the discount amortized on December 31, 20Y1, would be $550. This is the sum of the first two semiannual amortization amounts ($266 and $284) from Exhibit 8.

Amortization of Premium by the Interest Method

To illustrate, the following data taken from the chapter illustration of issuing bonds at a premium on January 1, 20Y3, are used:

Present value of bonds at effective (market) rate of interest of 11%.	$ 103,769
Face value of 12%, five-year bonds, interest compounded semiannually.	(100,000)
Premium on bonds payable.	$ 3,769

Exhibit 9 illustrates the interest method for the preceding bonds. Exhibit 9 begins with six columns. The first column is the interest payment date. The remaining columns are lettered A through E. The exhibit was then prepared as follows:

- Step 1. List the number of interest payments in the first column, which for the preceding bond are 10 interest payments (semiannual interest over five years). Also, list on the first line the initial amount of premium in Column D and the initial carrying amount of the bonds in Column E.
- Step 2. List in Column A the semiannual interest payments, which for the preceding bond are $6,000 ($100,000 × 6%).
- Step 3. Compute the interest expense in Column B by multiplying the bond carrying amount at the beginning of each period times 5½%, which is the semiannual effective interest (market) rate (11% ÷ 2).

Exhibit 9 Amortization of Premium on Bonds Payable

Interest Payment Date	A Interest Paid (6% of Face Amount)	B Interest Expense (5½% of Bond Carrying Amount)	C Premium Amortization (A – B)	D Unamortized Premium (D – C)	E Bond Carrying Amount ($100,000 + D)
				$3,769	$103,769
June 30, 20Y3	$6,000	$5,707 (5½% of $103,769)	$293	3,476	103,476
Dec. 31, 20Y3	6,000	5,691 (5½% of $103,476)	309	3,167	103,167
June 30, 20Y4	6,000	5,674 (5½% of $103,167)	326	2,841	102,841
Dec. 31, 20Y4	6,000	5,656 (5½% of $102,841)	344	2,497	102,497
June 30, 20Y5	6,000	5,637 (5½% of $102,497)	363	2,134	102,134
Dec. 31, 20Y5	6,000	5,617 (5½% of $102,134)	383	1,751	101,751
June 30, 20Y6	6,000	5,596 (5½% of $101,751)	404	1,347	101,347
Dec. 31, 20Y6	6,000	5,574 (5½% of $101,347)	426	921	100,921
June 30, 20Y7	6,000	5,551 (5½% of $100,921)	449	472	100,472
Dec. 31, 20Y7	6,000	5,526 (5½% of $100,472)	472*	—	100,000

*Cannot exceed unamortized premium.

- Step 4. In Column C, compute the premium to be amortized each period by subtracting the interest expense for the period shown in Column B from the interest payment in Column A ($6,000).
- Step 5. Compute the remaining unamortized premium by subtracting the amortized premium in Column C for the period from the unamortized premium at the beginning of the period in Column D.
- Step 6. Compute the bond carrying amount at the end of the period by adding the unamortized premium at the end of the period in Column D to the face amount of the bonds ($100,000).

Steps 3–6 are repeated for each interest payment.

As shown in Exhibit 9, the interest expense decreases each period as the carrying amount of the bond decreases. Also, the unamortized premium decreases each period to zero at the maturity date. Finally, the carrying amount of the bonds decreases from $103,769 to $100,000 (the face amount) at maturity.

The entry to record the first interest payment on June 30, 20Y3, and the related premium amortization is as follows:

20Y3				
June 30	Interest Expense		5,707	
	Premium on Bonds Payable		293	
	Cash			6,000
	Paid semiannual interest and amortized bond premium for ½ year.			

A = L + E
– – – Exp

If the amortization is recorded only at the end of the year, the amount of the premium amortized on December 31, 20Y3, would be $602. This is the sum of the first two semiannual amortization amounts ($293 and $309) from Exhibit 9.

Let's Review

Chapter Summary

1. The face amount of a bond is called the principal, and the underlying contract is called a bond indenture. When all the bonds of an issue mature at the same time, they are called term bonds. If the bonds mature over several dates, they are called serial bonds. Convertible bonds may be exchanged with common stock, while callable bonds may be redeemed prior to maturity.

   When a corporation issues bonds, the price that buyers are willing to pay for the bonds depends on (1) the face amount of the bonds, (2) the contract rate of interest to be paid on the bonds, and (3) the market rate of interest. If the contract rate of interest equals the market rate of interest, the bonds will sell at their face amount. If the contract rate of interest is less than the market rate of interest, the bonds will sell at a discount. If the contract rate of interest is more than the market rate of interest, the bonds will sell at a premium.

2. The journal entry for issuing bonds payable debits Cash and credits Bonds Payable. Any difference between the face amount of the bonds and the selling price is debited to Discount on Bonds Payable or credited to Premium on Bonds Payable when the bonds are issued. Any discount or premium on bonds payable is amortized to interest expense over the life of the bonds. At the maturity date, the entry to record the repayment of the face value of a bond is a debit to Bonds Payable and a credit to Cash.

   When a corporation redeems bonds before they mature, Bonds Payable is debited for the face amount of the bonds, Premium (Discount) on Bonds Payable is debited (credited) for its unamortized balance, Cash is credited, and any gain or loss on the redemption is recorded.

3. Bonds payable are usually reported as long-term liabilities. If the bonds are due within one year of the balance sheet date, they are reported as current liabilities. A discount on bonds is reported as a deduction from the related bonds payable. A premium on bonds is reported as an addition to the related bonds payable.

4. Analysts assess the risk that bondholders will not receive their interest payments by computing the times interest earned ratio, which is the number of times interest payments could be paid out of current-period earnings. High values of this ratio are considered favorable. In contrast, values of this ratio less than 1.0 suggest that the firm is unable to cover interest payments from current-period income before tax.

Key Terms

amortization (548)	discount (545)	premium (545)
annuity (558)	effective interest rate method (549)	present value (556)
bond (544)	effective rate of interest (545)	present value of annuity (558)
bond indenture (544)	face amount (545)	straight-line method of
carrying amount (548)	future value (557)	amortization (549)
contract rate (545)	market rate of interest (545)	times interest earned (555)

Practice

Multiple-Choice Questions

1. The proceeds received from issuing bonds depends on which of the following?
   a. Coupon rate of interest
   b. Market rate of interest
   c. Principal
   d. All of these

2. If a corporation plans to issue $1,000,000 of 5% bonds at a time when the market rate for similar bonds is 4%, the bonds can be expected to sell at:
   a. their face amount.
   b. a premium.
   c. a discount.
   d. a premium or discount.

3. If the bonds payable account has a balance of $900,000 and the discount on bonds payable account has a balance of $72,000, what is the carrying amount of the bonds?
   a. $828,000
   b. $900,000
   c. $972,000
   d. $580,000

4. Which of the following is the entry to amortize a discount on bonds?
   a. Debit Discount on Bonds Payable; credit Interest Expense; credit Cash
   b. Debit Bonds Payable; credit Discount on Bonds Payable; credit Cash
   c. Debit Interest Expense; credit Discount on Bonds Payable; credit Cash
   d. Debit Premium on Bonds Payable; credit Interest Expense; credit Cash

5. The balance in the discount on bonds payable account would usually be reported on the balance sheet in the:
   a. "Current assets" section.
   b. "Current liabilities" section.
   c. "Long-term liabilities" section.
   d. "Investments" section.

Answers provided after Problem. Need more practice? Find additional multiple-choice questions, exercises, and problems in CengageNOWv2.

Exercises

---

1. Issuing bonds at face amount   Obj. 2
On January 1, the first day of the fiscal year, a company issues a $500,000, 5%, 10-year bond that pays semiannual interest of $12,500 ($500,000 × 5% × ½ year), receiving cash of $500,000. Journalize the entries to record (a) the issuance of the bonds, (b) the first interest payment on June 30, and (c) the payment of the principal on the maturity date.

---

2. Issuing bonds at a discount   Obj. 2
On the first day of the fiscal year, a company issues a $1,200,000, 9%, five-year bond that pays semiannual interest of $54,000 ($1,200,000 × 9% × ½), receiving cash of $1,153,670. Journalize the bond issuance.

---

3. Discount amortization   Obj. 2
Using the bond from Exercise 2, journalize the first interest payment and the amortization of the related bond discount. Round to the nearest dollar.

---

4. Issuing bonds at a premium   Obj. 2
On the first day of the fiscal year, a company issues a $2,000,000, 8%, five-year bond that pays semiannual interest of $80,000 ($2,000,000 × 8% × ½), receiving cash of $2,170,604. Journalize the bond issuance.

---

5. Premium amortization   Obj. 2
Using the bond from Exercise 4, journalize the first interest payment and the amortization of the related bond premium. Round to the nearest dollar.

---

6. Redemption of bonds payable   Obj. 2
A $1,500,000 bond issue on which there is an unamortized discount of $70,100 is redeemed for $1,455,000. Journalize the redemption of the bonds.

---

7. Times interest earned   Obj. 4
Berry Company reported the following on the company's income statement in two recent years:

	20Y5	20Y4
Interest expense	$ 320,000	$ 300,000
Income before income tax expense	3,200,000	3,600,000

a. Determine the times interest earned ratio for 20Y4 and 20Y5. Round to one decimal place.
b. Is the change in the times interest earned ratio favorable or unfavorable?

Answers provided after Problem. Need more practice? Find additional multiple-choice questions, exercises, and problems in CengageNOWv2.

Problem

The fiscal year of Russell Inc., a manufacturer of acoustical supplies, ends December 31. Selected transactions for the period 20Y1 through 20Y6 involving bonds payable issued by Russell Inc. are as follows:

20Y1

June 30. Issued $2,000,000 of 25-year, 7% callable bonds dated June 30, 20Y1, for cash of $1,920,000. Interest is payable semiannually on June 30 and December 31.

Dec. 31. Paid the semiannual interest on the bonds.

20Y2

June 30. Paid the semiannual interest on the bonds.

Dec. 31. Paid the semiannual interest on the bonds.

20Y6

June 30. Recorded the redemption of the bonds, which were called at 101.5. The balance in the bond discount account is $57,600 after the payment of interest and amortization of discount have been recorded. (Record the redemption only.)

Instructions

1. Journalize entries to record the preceding transactions.

2. Determine the amount of interest expense for 20Y1 and 20Y2.

3. Determine the carrying amount of the bonds as of December 31, 20Y2.

Need more practice? Find additional multiple-choice questions, exercises, and problems in CengageNOWv2.

Answers

Multiple-Choice Questions

1. **d** The proceeds received from issuing bonds depends upon the coupon rate of interest (answer a), the market rate of interest (answer b), and the principal (answer c).

2. **b** Since the contract rate on the bonds is higher than the prevailing market rate, a rational investor would be willing to pay more than the face amount, or a premium (answer b), for the bonds. If the contract rate and the market rate were equal, the bonds could be expected to sell at their face amount (answer a). Likewise, if the market rate is higher than the contract rate, the bonds would sell at a discount (answer c).

3. **a** The bond carrying amount is the face amount plus any unamortized premium or less any unamortized discount. For this question, the carrying amount is $900,000 less $72,000, or $828,000 (answer a).

4. **c** The entry to amortize a discount on bonds payable debits Interest Expense, credits Discount on Bonds Payable, and credits Cash (answer c). The entry to amortize a premium on bonds payable debits Premium on Bonds Payable, credits Interest Expense, and credits Cash (answer d).

5. **c** The balance of Discount on Bonds Payable is usually reported as a deduction from Bonds Payable in the "Long-term liabilities" section (answer c) of the balance sheet. Likewise, a balance in Premium on Bonds Payable would be reported as an addition to Bonds Payable in the "Long-term liabilities" section of the balance sheet.

Exercises

1. **a.**

Cash	500,000	
Bonds Payable		500,000

b.

Interest Expense	12,500	
Cash		12,500

c.

Bonds Payable	500,000	
Cash		500,000

2.

Cash	1,153,670	
Discount on Bonds Payable	46,330	
Bonds Payable		1,200,000

3.

Interest Expense	58,633	
Discount on Bonds Payable		4,633
Cash		54,000

Discount on Bonds Payable = $46,330 ÷ 10 semiannual payments

4.

Cash	2,170,604	
Premium on Bonds Payable		170,604
Bonds Payable		2,000,000

5.

Interest Expense	62,940	
Premium on Bonds Payable	17,060	
Cash		80,000

Premium on Bonds Payable = $170,604 ÷ 10 semiannual payments

6.

Bonds Payable	1,500,000	
Loss on Redemption of Bonds	25,100	
Discount on Bonds Payable		70,100
Cash		1,455,000

7. **a.**

20Y4:

Times interest earned: $\dfrac{\$3,600,000 + \$300,000}{\$300,000} = 13.0$

20Y5:

Times interest earned: $\dfrac{\$3,200,000 + \$320,000}{\$320,000} = 11.0$

b. The times interest earned ratio has decreased from 13.0 in 20Y4 to 11.0 in 20Y5. Although the company has adequate earnings to pay interest, the decline in this ratio is unfavorable and may cause concern among debtholders.

Need more help? Watch step-by-step videos of how to compute answers to these Exercises in CengageNOWv2.

Problem

1.

20Y1				
June 30	Cash		1,920,000	
	Discount on Bonds Payable		80,000	
	Bonds Payable			2,000,000
Dec. 31	Interest Expense		71,600	
	Discount on Bonds Payable			1,600
	Cash			70,000
20Y2				
June 30	Interest Expense		71,600	
	Discount on Bonds Payable			1,600
	Cash			70,000
Dec. 31	Interest Expense		71,600	
	Discount on Bonds Payable			1,600
	Cash			70,000
20Y6				
June 30	Bonds Payable		2,000,000	
	Loss on Redemption of Bonds Payable		87,600	
	Discount on Bonds Payable			57,600
	Cash			2,030,000

2. 20Y1: $71,600 = $70,000 + $1,600
   20Y2: $143,200 = $71,600 + $71,600

3.

Initial carrying amount of bonds	$1,920,000
Discount amortized on December 31, 20Y1	1,600
Discount amortized on December 31, 20Y2	3,200
Carrying amount of bonds, December 31, 20Y2	$1,924,800

Discussion Questions

1. Describe the two distinct obligations incurred by a corporation when issuing bonds.

2. Explain the meaning of each of the following terms as they relate to a bond issue: (a) convertible and (b) callable.

3. If you asked your broker to purchase for you a 11% bond when the market interest rate for such bonds was 12%, would you expect to pay more or less than the face amount for the bond? Explain.

4. A corporation issues $26,000,000 of 9% bonds to yield interest at the rate of 7%. (a) Was the amount of cash received from the sale of the bonds greater or less than $26,000,000? (b) Identify the following amounts as they relate to the bond issue: (1) face amount, (2) market or effective rate of interest, (3) contract rate of interest, and (4) maturity amount.

5. If bonds issued by a corporation are sold at a discount, is the market rate of interest greater or less than the contract rate?

6. The following data relate to a $2,000,000, 8% bond issued for a selected semiannual interest period:

Bond carrying amount at beginning of period	$2,125,000
Interest paid during period	160,000
Interest expense allocable to the period	148,750

(a) Were the bonds issued at a discount or at a premium? (b) What is the unamortized amount of the discount or premium account at the beginning of the period? (c) What account was debited to amortize the discount or premium?

7. Bonds Payable has a balance of $5,000,000 and Discount on Bonds Payable has a balance of $150,000. If the issu-ing corporation redeems the bonds at 98, is there a gain or loss on the bond redemption?

8. Fleeson Company needs additional funds to purchase equipment for a new production facility and is consider-ing either issuing bonds payable or borrowing the money from a local bank in the form of an installment note. How does an installment note differ from a bond payable?

9. In what section of the balance sheet would a bond pay-able be reported if (a) it is payable within one year and (b) it is payable beyond one year?

Basic Exercises

SHOW ME HOW

BE 11-1 Issuing bonds at face amount   **Obj. 2**

On January 1, the first day of the fiscal year, Designer Fabric Inc. issues a $3,000,000, 8%, 10-year bond that pays semiannual interest of $120,000 ($3,000,000 × 8% × ½ year), receiving cash of $3,000,000. Journalize the entries to record (a) the issuance of the bonds, (b) the first interest payment on June 30, and (c) the payment of the principal on the maturity date.

SHOW ME HOW

BE 11-2 Issuing bonds at a discount   **Obj. 2**

On the first day of the fiscal year, a company issues a $3,500,000, 6% five-year bond that pays semiannual interest of $105,000 ($3,500,000 × 6% × ½), receiving cash of $3,350,000. Journalize the bond issuance.

SHOW ME HOW

BE 11-3 Discount amortization   **Obj. 2**

Using the bond from Basic Exercise 11-2, journalize the first interest payment and the amortiza-tion of the related bond discount.

SHOW ME HOW

BE 11-4 Issuing bonds at a premium   **Obj. 2**

On the first day of the fiscal year, a company issues a $5,000,000, 7%, five-year bond that pays semiannual interest of $175,000 ($5,000,000 × 7% × ½), receiving cash of $5,400,000. Journalize the bond issuance.

SHOW ME HOW

BE 11-5 Premium amortization   **Obj. 2**

Using the bond from Basic Exercise 11-4, journalize the first interest payment and the amortiza-tion of the related bond premium.

SHOW ME HOW

BE 11-6 Redemption of bonds payable   **Obj. 2**

An $800,000 bond issue on which there is an unamortized premium of $57,000 is redeemed for $785,000. Journalize the redemption of the bonds.

BE 11-7 Times interest earned   **Obj. 4**

Averill Products Inc. reported the following on the company's income statement in 20Y8 and 20Y9:

SHOW ME HOW

	20Y9	20Y8
Interest expense	$ 440,000	$ 400,000
Income before income tax expense	5,544,000	4,400,000

a. Determine the times interest earned ratio for 20Y8 and 20Y9. Round to one decimal place.

b. Is the change in the times interest earned ratio favorable or unfavorable?

Exercises

REAL WORLD

EX 11-1   Bond price   Obj. 1

United States Steel Corporation's **(X)** 7.5% bonds due in 2022 were reported as selling for 103.2. ➤ Were the bonds selling at a premium or at a discount? Why is United States Steel able to sell its bonds at this price?

SHOW ME HOW

EX 11-2   Entries for issuing bonds   Obj. 2

Thomson Co. produces and distributes semiconductors for use by computer manufacturers. Thomson issued $800,000 of 10-year, 6% bonds on May 1 of the current year at face value, with interest payable on May 1 and November 1. The fiscal year of the company is the calendar year. Journalize the entries to record the following selected transactions for the current year:

May   1.   Issued the bonds for cash at their face amount.
Nov.   1.   Paid the interest on the bonds.
Dec. 31.   Recorded accrued interest for two months.

✔ b. $781,118

SHOW ME HOW

EX 11-3   Entries for issuing bonds and amortizing discount by straight-line method   Obj. 2

On the first day of its fiscal year, Chin Company issued $10,000,000 of five-year, 7% bonds to finance its operations of producing and selling home improvement products. Interest is payable semiannually. The bonds were issued at a market (effective) interest rate of 8%, resulting in Chin receiving cash of $9,594,415.

a. Journalize the entries to record the following:

1. Issuance of the bonds.

2. First semiannual interest payment. The bond discount is combined with the semiannual interest payment. Round to the nearest dollar.

3. Second semiannual interest payment. The bond discount is combined with the semiannual interest payment. Round to the nearest dollar.

b. Determine the amount of the bond interest expense for the first year.

c. ➤ Explain why the company was able to issue the bonds for only $9,594,415 rather than for the face amount of $10,000,000.

SHOW ME HOW

EX 11-4   Entries for issuing bonds and amortizing premium by straight-line method   Obj. 2

Smiley Corporation wholesales repair products to equipment manufacturers. On April 1, 20Y1, Smiley issued $20,000,000 of five-year, 9% bonds at a market (effective) interest rate of 8%, receiving cash of $20,811,010. Interest is payable semiannually on April 1 and October 1. Journalize the entries to record the following:

a. Issuance of bonds on April 1, 20Y1.

b. First interest payment on October 1, 20Y1, and amortization of bond premium for six months, using the straight-line method.

c. ➤ Explain why the company was able to issue the bonds for $20,811,010 rather than for the face amount of $20,000,000.

SHOW ME HOW

EX 11-5   Entries for issuing and calling bonds; loss   Obj. 2

Hoover Corp., a wholesaler of music equipment, issued $20,000,000 of 20-year, 6% callable bonds on March 1, 20Y2, at their face amount, with interest payable on March 1 and September 1. The fiscal year of the company is the calendar year. Journalize the entries to record the following selected transactions:

20Y2
Mar.   1.   Issued the bonds for cash at their face amount.
Sept. 1.   Paid the interest on the bonds.

20Y4
Sept. 1.   Called the bond issue at 102, the rate provided in the bond indenture. (Omit entry for payment of interest.)

SHOW ME HOW

EX 11-6 Entries for issuing and calling bonds; gain

Obj. 2

Mia Breen Corp. produces and sells wind-energy-driven engines. To finance its operations, Mia Breen issued $22,000,000 of 20-year, 4% callable bonds on May 1, 20Y5, at their face amount, with interest payable on May 1 and November 1. The fiscal year of the company is the calendar year. Journalize the entries to record the following selected transactions:

20Y5

May 1. Issued the bonds for cash at their face amount.

Nov. 1. Paid the interest on the bonds.

20Y9

Nov. 1. Called the bond issue at 97, the rate provided in the bond indenture. (Omit entry for payment of interest.)

EX 11-7 Reporting bonds

Obj. 3

At the beginning of the current year, two bond issues (Simmons Industries 7%, 20-year bonds and Hunter Corporation 8%, 10-year bonds) were outstanding. During the year, the Simmons Industries bonds were redeemed and a significant loss on the redemption of bonds was reported on the income statement. At the end of the year, the Hunter bonds were reported as a noncurrent liability. The maturity date on the Hunter bonds was early in the following year.

Identify the flaws in the reporting practices related to the two bond issues.

Appendix 1

EX 11-8 Present value of amounts due

Assume that you are going to receive $50,000 in 10 years. The current market rate of interest is 4%.

a. Using the present value of $1 table in Exhibit 5, determine the present value of this amount compounded annually.

b. Why is the present value less than the $50,000 to be received in the future?

Appendix 1

EX 11-9 Present value of an annuity

Determine the present value of $200,000 to be received at the end of each of four years, using an interest rate of 7%, compounded annually, as follows:

a. By successive computations, using the present value of $1 table in Exhibit 5.

b. By using the present value of an annuity of $1 table in Exhibit 7.

c. Why is the present value of the four $200,000 cash receipts less than the $800,000 to be received in the future?

Appendix 1

EX 11-10 Present value of an annuity

On January 1, you win $50,000,000 in the state lottery. The $50,000,000 prize will be paid in equal installments of $6,250,000 over eight years. The payments will be made on December 31 of each year, beginning on December 31 of this year. If the current interest rate is 5%, determine the present value of your winnings. Use the present value tables in Appendix A.

Appendix 1

EX 11-11 Present value of an annuity

Assume the same data as in Exercise 11-10, except that the current interest rate is 12%.

Will the present value of your winnings using an interest rate of 12% be more than the present value of your winnings using an interest rate of 5%? Why or why not?

Appendix 1

EX 11-12 Present value of bonds payable; discount

Pinder Co. produces and sells high-quality video equipment. To finance its operations, Pinder issued $25,000,000 of five-year, 7% bonds, with interest payable semiannually, at a market (effective)

(Continued)

interest rate of 9%. Determine the present value of the bonds payable, using the present value tables in Exhibits 5 and 7. Round to the nearest dollar.

Appendix 1

EX 11-13 Present value of bonds payable; premium

Moss Co. issued $42,000,000 of five-year, 11% bonds, with interest payable semiannually, at a market (effective) interest rate of 9%. Determine the present value of the bonds payable using the present value tables in Exhibits 5 and 7. Round to the nearest dollar.

Appendix 2

EX 11-14 Amortize discount by interest method

✔ b. $3,923,959   On the first day of its fiscal year, Ebert Company issued $50,000,000 of 10-year, 7% bonds to finance its operations. Interest is payable semiannually. The bonds were issued at a market (effective) interest rate of 9%, resulting in Ebert receiving cash of $43,495,895. The company uses the interest method.

a. Journalize the entries to record the following:

     1. Sale of the bonds.

     2. First semiannual interest payment, including amortization of discount. Round to the nearest dollar.

     3. Second semiannual interest payment, including amortization of discount. Round to the nearest dollar.

b. Compute the amount of the bond interest expense for the first year.

c. ▬▬▶ Explain why the company was able to issue the bonds for only $43,495,895 rather than for the face amount of $50,000,000.

Appendix 2

EX 11-15 Amortize premium by interest method

✔ b. $2,586,545   Shunda Corporation wholesales parts to appliance manufacturers. On January 1, Shunda issued $30,000,000 of five-year, 10% bonds at a market (effective) interest rate of 8%, receiving cash of $32,433,150. Interest is payable semiannually. Shunda's fiscal year begins on January 1. The company uses the interest method.

a. Journalize the entries to record the following:

     1. Sale of the bonds.

     2. First semiannual interest payment, including amortization of premium. Round to the nearest dollar.

     3. Second semiannual interest payment, including amortization of premium. Round to the nearest dollar.

b. Determine the bond interest expense for the first year.

c. ▬▬▶ Explain why the company was able to issue the bonds for $32,433,150 rather than for the face amount of $30,000,000.

Appendix 1 and Appendix 2

EX 11-16 Compute bond proceeds, amortizing premium by interest method, and interest expense

✔ a. $37,702,483   Ware Co. produces and sells motorcycle parts. On the first day of its fiscal year, Ware issued
✔ c. $225,620 $35,000,000 of five-year, 12% bonds at a market (effective) interest rate of 10%, with interest payable semiannually. Compute the following, presenting figures used in your computations:

a. The amount of cash proceeds from the sale of the bonds. Use the tables of present values in Exhibits 5 and 7. Round to the nearest dollar.

b. The amount of premium to be amortized for the first semiannual interest payment period, using the interest method. Round to the nearest dollar.

   c. The amount of premium to be amortized for the second semiannual interest payment period, using the interest method. Round to the nearest dollar.

   d. The amount of the bond interest expense for the first year.

Appendix 1 and Appendix 2

EX 11-17 Compute bond proceeds, amortizing discount by interest method, and interest expense

✔ a. $71,167,524
✔ b. $670,051

Boyd Co. produces and sells aviation equipment. On the first day of its fiscal year, Boyd issued $80,000,000 of five-year, 9% bonds at a market (effective) interest rate of 12%, with interest payable semiannually. Compute the following, presenting figures used in your computations:

   a. The amount of cash proceeds from the sale of the bonds. Use the tables of present values in Exhibits 5 and 7. Round to the nearest dollar.

   b. The amount of discount to be amortized for the first semiannual interest payment period, using the interest method. Round to the nearest dollar.

   c. The amount of discount to be amortized for the second semiannual interest payment period, using the interest method. Round to the nearest dollar.

   d. The amount of the bond interest expense for the first year.

Problems: Series A

PR 11-1A Bond discount, entries for bonds payable transactions   **Obj. 2**

✔ 3. $2,311,554

On July 1, 20Y1, Danzer Industries Inc. issued $50,000,000 of 10-year, 8% bonds at a market (effective) interest rate of 10%, receiving cash of $43,768,920. Interest on the bonds is payable semiannually on December 31 and June 30. The fiscal year of the company is the calendar year.

SHOW ME HOW

Instructions

1. Journalize the entry to record the amount of cash proceeds from the issuance of the bonds on July 1, 20Y1.

2. Journalize the entries to record the following:

   a. The first semiannual interest payment on December 31, 20Y1, and the amortization of the bond discount, using the straight-line method. Round to the nearest dollar.

   b. The interest payment on June 30, 20Y2, and the amortization of the bond discount, using the straight-line method. Round to the nearest dollar.

3. Determine the total interest expense for 20Y1.

4. Will the bond proceeds always be less than the face amount of the bonds when the contract rate is less than the market rate of interest?

5. *(Appendix 1)* Compute the price of $43,768,920 received for the bonds by using the present value tables in Appendix A at the end of the text. Round to the nearest dollar.

PR 11-2A Bond premium, entries for bonds payable transactions   **Obj. 2**

✔ 3. $1,402,444

Campbell Inc. produces and sells outdoor equipment. On July 1, 20Y1, Campbell issued $30,000,000 of 10-year, 10% bonds at a market (effective) interest rate of 9%, receiving cash of $31,951,110. Interest on the bonds is payable semiannually on December 31 and June 30. The fiscal year of the company is the calendar year.

Instructions

1. Journalize the entry to record the amount of cash proceeds from the issuance of the bonds on July 1, 20Y1.

(Continued)

2. Journalize the entries to record the following:

   a. The first semiannual interest payment on December 31, 20Y1, and the amortization of the bond premium, using the straight-line method. Round to the nearest dollar.

   b. The interest payment on June 30, 20Y2, and the amortization of the bond premium, using the straight-line method. Round to the nearest dollar.

3. Determine the total interest expense for 20Y1.

4. Will the bond proceeds always be greater than the face amount of the bonds when the contract rate is greater than the market rate of interest?

5. *(Appendix 1)* Compute the price of $31,951,110 received for the bonds by using the present value tables in Appendix A at the end of the text. Round to the nearest dollar.

PR 11-3A   Entries for bonds payable, including bond redemption   Obj. 2

✔ 3. $64,317,346

SHOW ME HOW   EXCEL TEMPLATE

The following transactions were completed by Winklevoss Inc., whose fiscal year is the calendar year:

20Y1

July   1. Issued $74,000,000 of 20-year, 11% callable bonds dated July 1, 20Y1, at a market (effective) rate of 13%, receiving cash of $63,532,267. Interest is payable semiannually on December 31 and June 30.

Dec. 31. Paid the semiannual interest on the bonds. The bond discount amortization of $261,693 is combined with the semiannual interest payment.

20Y2

June 30. Paid the semiannual interest on the bonds. The bond discount amortization of $261,693 is combined with the semiannual interest payment.

Dec. 31. Paid the semiannual interest on the bonds. The bond discount amortization of $261,693 is combined with the semiannual interest payment.

20Y3

June 30. Recorded the redemption of the bonds, which were called at 98. The balance in the bond discount account is $9,420,961 after payment of interest and amortization of discount have been recorded. (Record the redemption only.)

Instructions

1. Journalize the entries to record the transactions. Round all amounts to the nearest dollar.

2. Indicate the amount of the interest expense in (a) 20Y1 and (b) 20Y2.

3. Determine the carrying amount of the bonds as of December 31, 20Y2.

Appendix 1 and Appendix 2
PR 11-4A   Bond discount, entries for bonds payable transactions, interest method of amortizing bond discount

✔ 3. $1,491,282

On July 1, 20Y1, Danzer Industries Inc. issued $40,000,000 of 10-year, 7% bonds at a market (effective) interest rate of 8%, receiving cash of $37,282,062. Interest on the bonds is payable semiannually on December 31 and June 30. The fiscal year of the company is the calendar year.

Instructions

1. Journalize the entry to record the amount of cash proceeds from the issuance of the bonds.

2. Journalize the entries to record the following:

   a. The first semiannual interest payment on December 31, 20Y1, and the amortization of the bond discount, using the interest method. Round to the nearest dollar.

   b. The interest payment on June 30, 20Y2, and the amortization of the bond discount, using the interest method. Round to the nearest dollar.

3. Determine the total interest expense for 20Y1.

Appendix 1 and Appendix 2
PR 11-5A   Bond premium, entries for bonds payable transactions, interest method of amortizing bond premium

✔ 3. $1,437,800

Campbell, Inc. produces and sells outdoor equipment. On July 1, 20Y1. Campbell issued $30,000,000 of 10-year, 10% bonds at a market (effective) interest rate of 9%, receiving cash of $31,951,110.

Interest on the bonds is payable semiannually on December 31 and June 30. The fiscal year of the company is the calendar year.

Instructions

1. Journalize the entry to record the amount of cash proceeds from the issuance of the bonds.

2. Journalize the entries to record the following:

a. The first semiannual interest payment on December 31, 20Y1, and the amortization of the bond premium, using the interest method. Round to the nearest dollar.

b. The interest payment on June 30, 20Y2, and the amortization of the bond premium, using the interest method. Round to the nearest dollar.

3. Determine the total interest expense for 20Y1.

Problems: Series B

PR 11-1B   Bond discount, entries for bonds payable transactions   **Obj. 2**

✔ 3. $2,392,269

SHOW ME HOW

On July 1, 20Y1, Livingston Corporation, a wholesaler of manufacturing equipment, issued $46,000,000 of 20-year, 10% bonds at a market (effective) interest rate of 11%, receiving cash of $42,309,236. Interest on the bonds is payable semiannually on December 31 and June 30. The fiscal year of the company is the calendar year.

Instructions

1. Journalize the entry to record the amount of cash proceeds from the issuance of the bonds on July 1, 20Y1.

2. Journalize the entries to record the following:

a. The first semiannual interest payment on December 31, 20Y1, and the amortization of the bond discount, using the straight-line method. Round to the nearest dollar.

b. The interest payment on June 30, 20Y2, and the amortization of the bond discount, using the straight-line method. Round to the nearest dollar.

3. Determine the total interest expense for 20Y1.

4. Will the bond proceeds always be less than the face amount of the bonds when the contract rate is less than the market rate of interest?

5. *(Appendix 1)* Compute the price of $42,309,236 received for the bonds by using the present value tables in Appendix A at the end of the text. Round to the nearest dollar.

PR 11-2B   Bond premium, entries for bonds payable transactions   **Obj. 2**

✔ 3. $3,494,977

Rodgers Corporation produces and sells football equipment. On July 1, 20Y1, Rodgers issued $65,000,000 of 10-year, 12% bonds at a market (effective) interest rate of 10%, receiving cash of $73,100,469. Interest on the bonds is payable semiannually on December 31 and June 30. The fiscal year of the company is the calendar year.

Instructions

1. Journalize the entry to record the amount of cash proceeds from the issuance of the bonds on July 1, 20Y1.

2. Journalize the entries to record the following:

a. The first semiannual interest payment on December 31, 20Y1, and the amortization of the bond premium, using the straight-line method. Round to the nearest dollar.

b. The interest payment on June 30, 20Y2, and the amortization of the bond premium, using the straight-line method. Round to the nearest dollar.

3. Determine the total interest expense for 20Y1.

4. Will the bond proceeds always be greater than the face amount of the bonds when the contract rate is greater than the market rate of interest?

5. *(Appendix 1)* Compute the price of $73,100,469 received for the bonds by using the present value tables in Appendix A at the end of the text. Round to the nearest dollar.

PR 11-3B **Entries for bonds payable, including bond redemption** Obj. 2

✔ 3. $61,644,484

SHOW ME HOW EXCEL TEMPLATE

The following transactions were completed by Montague Inc., whose fiscal year is the calendar year:

20Y1

July 1. Issued $55,000,000 of 10-year, 9% callable bonds dated July 1, 20Y1, at a market (effective) rate of 7%, receiving cash of $62,817,040. Interest is payable semiannually on December 31 and June 30.

Dec. 31. Paid the semiannual interest on the bonds. The bond premium amortization of $390,852 is combined with the semiannual interest payment.

20Y2

June 30. Paid the semiannual interest on the bonds. The bond premium amortization of $390,852 is combined with the semiannual interest payment.

Dec. 31. Paid the semiannual interest on the bonds. The bond premium amortization of $390,852 is combined with the semiannual interest payment.

20Y3

June 30. Recorded the redemption of the bonds, which were called at 103. The balance in the bond premium account is $6,253,632 after payment of interest and amortization of premium have been recorded. (Record the redemption only.)

Instructions

1. Journalize the entries to record the foregoing transactions.

2. Indicate the amount of the interest expense in (a) 20Y1 and (b) 20Y2.

3. Determine the carrying amount of the bonds as of December 31, 20Y2.

Appendix 1 and Appendix 2
PR 11-4B **Bond discount, entries for bonds payable transactions, interest method of amortizing bond discount**

✔ 3. $2,327,008

On July 1, 20Y1, Livingston Corporation, a wholesaler of manufacturing equipment, issued $46,000,000 of 20-year, 10% bonds at a market (effective) interest rate of 11%, receiving cash of $42,309,236. Interest on the bonds is payable semiannually on December 31 and June 30. The fiscal year of the company is the calendar year.

Instructions

1. Journalize the entry to record the amount of cash proceeds from the issuance of the bonds.

2. Journalize the entries to record the following:

   a. The first semiannual interest payment on December 31, 20Y1, and the amortization of the bond discount, using the interest method. Round to the nearest dollar.

   b. The interest payment on June 30, 20Y2, and the amortization of the bond discount, using the interest method. Round to the nearest dollar.

3. Determine the total interest expense for 20Y1.

Appendix 1 and Appendix 2
PR 11-5B **Bond premium, entries for bonds payable transactions, interest method of amortizing bond premium**

✔ 3. $3,655,023

Rodgers Corporation produces and sells football equipment. On July 1, 20Y1, Rodgers issued $65,000,000 of 10-year, 12% bonds at a market (effective) interest rate of 10%, receiving cash of $73,100,469. Interest on the bonds is payable semiannually on December 31 and June 30. The fiscal year of the company is the calendar year.

Instructions

1. Journalize the entry to record the amount of cash proceeds from the issuance of the bonds.

2. Journalize the entries to record the following:

   a. The first semiannual interest payment on December 31, 20Y1, and the amortization of the bond premium, using the interest method. Round to the nearest dollar.

   b. The interest payment on June 30, 20Y2, and the amortization of the bond premium, using the interest method. Round to the nearest dollar.

3. Determine the total interest expense for 20Y1.

Make a Decision
Times Interest Earned

REAL WORLD

MAD 11-1   Analyze and compare Amazon.com and Wal-Mart   Obj. 4

Amazon.com, Inc. (AMZN) is one of the largest Internet retailers in the world. **Wal-Mart Stores, Inc. (WMT)** is the largest retailer in the United States. Amazon and Wal-Mart compete in similar markets; however, Wal-Mart sells through both traditional retail stores and the Internet, while Amazon sells only through the Internet. Interest expense and income before income tax expense from the financial statements of both companies for two recent years follow (in millions):

	Amazon		Wal-Mart	
	Year 2	Year 1	Year 2	Year 1
Interest expense	$ 484	$ 459	$ 2,548	$ 2,461
Income (loss) before income tax expense	3,892	1,568	21,638	24,799

a. Compute the times interest earned ratio for both companies for the two years. Round to one decimal place.

b. ➤ Interpret Amazon's interest coverage from Year 1 to Year 2.

c. ➤ Does a times interest earned ratio less than 1.0 mean that creditors will not get paid interest?

d. ➤ Interpret Wal-Mart's interest coverage from Year 1 to Year 2.

e. ➤ Which company appears to have the greater protection for creditors?

MAD 11-2   Analyze and compare Clorox and Procter & Gamble   Obj. 4

REAL WORLD

The Clorox Company (CLX) and **The Procter & Gamble Company (PG)** produce and sell packaged consumer products around the world. Income and interest expense information from financial statements for a recent year follows (in millions):

	Clorox	Procter & Gamble
Interest expense	$ 88	$ 579
Income before income tax expense	983	13,369

a. Compute the times interest earned for each company. Round to one decimal place.

b. ➤ If you were a lender to these two companies, which one appears to have the greater coverage of interest expense and thus the greater protection for your loan interest?

MAD 11-3   Analyze Aeropostale   Obj. 4

REAL WORLD

Aeropostale, Inc. (ARO) is a specialty fashion retailer targeting young adults. The income before income tax expense and interest expense for four recent years follow (in millions):

	Year 4	Year 3	Year 2	Year 1
Income (loss) before income tax expense	$(132.3)	$(221.9)	$(186.1)	$59.0
Interest expense	12.9	8.8	0.9	0.5

a. Compute the times interest earned ratio for each year. Round to one decimal place.

b. Plot the four points on a graph with the year numbers on the horizontal axis, beginning with Year 1.

c. ➤ Interpret the trend in the ratio from your graph.

d. ➤ What happened to interest expense in Year 4? What might be the cause?

REAL WORLD

MAD 11-4 **Analyze and compare Hilton and Marriott**   Obj. 4

Hilton Worldwide Holdings, Inc. (HLT) and **Marriott International, Inc. (MAR)** are two of the largest hotel operators in the world. Selected financial information from recent income statements for both companies follows (in millions):

	Hilton	Marriott
Operating income	$1,861	$1,368
Interest expense	(587)	(234)
Other income (expense) items	(19)	50
Income before income tax expense	$1,255	$1,184
Income tax expense	(891)	(404)
Net income	$ 364	$ 780

a. Compute the times interest earned ratio for each company. Round to one decimal place.

b. ━━━▶ Which company appears to better protect creditor interest? Why?

Take It Further

ETHICS

TIF 11-1 **Debt issuance and risk**

CEG Capital Inc. is a large holding company that uses long-term debt extensively to fund its operations. At December 31, the company reported total assets of $100 million, total debt of $55 million, and total equity of $45 million. In January, the company issued $11 billion in long-term bonds to investors at par value. This was the largest debt issuance in the company's history, and it significantly increased the company's ratio of total debt to total equity. Five days after the debt issuance, CEG filed legal documents to prepare for an additional $50 billion long-term bond issue. As a result of this filing, the price of the $11 billion in bonds that the company issued earlier in the week dropped to 94 because of the increased risk associated with the company's debt. The investors in the original $11 billion bond issuance were not informed of the company's plans to issue additional debt so quickly after the initial bond issue.

━━━▶ Did CEG Capital act unethically by not disclosing to initial bond investors its immediate plans to issue an additional $50 billion debt offering?

TEAM ACTIVITY

REAL WORLD

TIF 11-2 **Real-world annual report**

In teams, select a public company that interests you. Obtain the company's most recent annual report on Form 10-K. The Form 10-K is a company's annually required filing with the Securities and Exchange Commission (SEC). It includes the company's financial statements and accompanying notes. The Form 10-K can be obtained either (a) from the investor relations section of the company's website or (b) by using the company search feature of the SEC's EDGAR database service found at www.sec.gov/edgar/searchedgar/companysearch.html.

1. Based on the information in the company's most recent annual report, answer the following questions:

a. How much long-term debt does the company report at the end of the most recent year presented?

b. Does the company have any bonds outstanding at the end of the most recent year? If so, read the supporting notes to the financial statements and determine:

   (1) The contract rate of interest on the bond issue(s).

   (2) The discount or premium on the bond issue(s).

(3) The due date of the bond issue(s).

(4) The total amount of any bonds that will mature within one year of the balance sheet date.

2. ━━━▶ Based on your answers to the questions in requirement 1, evaluate the company's debt position.

COMMUNICATION

TIF 11-3 Bond redemption

Nordbock Inc. reports the following outstanding bond issue on its December 31, 20Y1, balance sheet:

$1,000,000, 7%, 10-year bonds that pay interest semiannually.

The bonds have been outstanding for five years and were originally issued at face amount. The company is considering redeeming these bonds on January 1, 20Y2, at 103 and issuing new $1,000,000, 5%, five-year bonds at their face amount. These bonds would pay interest semiannually on June 30 and December 31.

━━━▶ Write a brief memo to Liz Nolan, the chief financial officer, discussing the costs of redeeming the existing bonds, the proceeds from issuing the new bonds, and whether this is a good financial decision.

TIF 11-4 Present values

Alex Kelton recently won the jackpot in the Colorado lottery while he was visiting his parents. When he arrived at the lottery office to collect his winnings, he was offered the following three payout options:

a. Receive $100,000,000 in cash today.

b. Receive $25,000,000 today and $9,000,000 per year for eight years, with the first payment being received one year from today.

c. Receive $15,000,000 per year for 10 years, with the first payment being received one year from today.

━━━▶ Assuming that the effective rate of interest is 7%, which payout option should Alex select? Use the present value tables in Appendix 1. Explain your answer and provide any necessary supporting calculations.

Pathways Challenge

This is Accounting!

Information/Consequences

The convertible bonds payable consist of two financial instruments—a debt instrument (bonds payable) and an equity instrument (a conversion option). Because the conversion option can be settled in cash or some combination of cash and stock, generally accepted accounting principles (GAAP) require that the amount received be allocated to debt and equity.

At the end of a recent year, **AMD** reported the $805 million in bonds as follows (amounts in millions):

Long-term debt:

Principal	$ 805
Unamortized discount	(308)
Total	$ 497

Equity:

Additional paid-in capital	$ 305

Suggested Answer

12 Corporations: Organization, Stock Transactions, and Dividends

STATEMENT OF STOCKHOLDERS' EQUITY
For the Year Ended December 31, 20Y5

	Common Stock	Retained Earnings	Total
Balances, Jan. 1, 20Y5	$XXX	$ XXX	$ XXX
Issued common stock	XXX		XXX
Net income		XXX	XXX
Dividends		(XXX)	(XXX)
Balances, Dec. 31, 20Y5	$XXX	$ XXX	$ XXX

STATEMENT OF CASH FLOWS
For the Year Ended December 31, 20Y5

Cash flows from (used for) operating activities	$XXX
Cash flows from (used for) investing activities	XXX
Cash flows from (used for) financing activities	XXX
Net increase (decrease) in cash	$XXX
Cash balance, January 1, 20Y5	XXX
Cash balance, December 31, 20Y5	$XXX

INCOME STATEMENT
For the Year Ended December 31, 20Y5

Sales		$ XXX
Cost of goods sold		(XXX)
Gross profit		$ XXX
Operating expenses:		
Wages expense	$XXX	
Advertising expense	XXX	
Utilities expense	XXX	
Depreciation expense	XXX	
…	XXX	
Total operating expenses		(XXX)
Operating income		$ XXX
Other revenue and expense		XXX
Net income		$ XXX

BALANCE SHEET
December 31, 20Y5

Assets		
Current assets:		
Cash	$ XXX	
Accounts receivable	XXX	
Inventory	XXX	
Total current assets		$XXX
Property, plant, and equipment		XXX
Total assets		$XXX
Liabilities		
Current liabilities	$ XXX	
Long-term liabilities	XXX	
Total liabilities		$XXX
Stockholders' Equity		
Common stock	$ XXX	
Preferred stock	XXX	
Additional paid-in capital	XXX	
Retained earnings	XXX	
Treasury stock	(XXX)	
Total stockholders' equity		XXX
Total liabilities and stockholders' equity		$XXX

Alphabet Inc.

If you purchase a share of stock from **Alphabet Inc. (GOOG)**, you own a small interest in a company that includes businesses such as Google, Android, and YouTube. You may request an Alphabet stock certificate as an indication of your ownership.

Alphabet's largest segment, Google, is one of the most visible names on the Internet. Many of us cannot visit the Web without using Google to power a search or to retrieve our e-mail using Google's Gmail. Yet Google's Internet tools are free to online browsers. The Google segment generates 99% of Alphabet's revenues, with most of this revenue coming from online advertising.

Purchasing a share of stock from Alphabet may be a great gift idea for the "hard-to-shop-for person." However, a stock certificate represents more than just a picture that you can frame. In fact, the stock certificate is a document that reflects legal ownership of the future financial prospects of Alphabet.

In addition, as a shareholder, it represents your claim against the assets and earnings of the corporation.

If you are purchasing Alphabet stock as an investment, you should analyze Alphabet's financial statements and management's plans for the future. For example, Alphabet first offered its stock to the public on August 19, 2004, for $100 per share. Alphabet's stock has sold for more than $1,000 per share, even though it pays no dividends. In addition, Alphabet recently expanded into developing and offering free software platforms for mobile devices such as cell phones. For example, your cell phone may use the Android™ operating system. So, should you purchase Alphabet stock?

This chapter describes and illustrates the nature of corporations, including the accounting for stock and dividends. This discussion will aid you in making decisions such as whether or not to buy stock in a company.

© SILICONVALLEYSTOCK/ALAMY STOCK PHOTO

What's Covered

Corporations: Organization, Stock Transactions, and Dividends

Corporations	Classes of Stock	Dividends and Stock Splits	Treasury Stock	Reporting Stockholders' Equity
■ Characteristics (Obj. 1) ■ Forming a Corporation (Obj. 1)	■ Common Stock (Obj. 2) ■ Preferred Stock (Obj. 2) ■ Paid-In Capital (Obj. 2)	■ Cash Dividends (Obj. 3) ■ Stock Dividends (Obj. 3) ■ Stock Splits (Obj. 4)	■ Purchasing (Obj. 5) ■ Selling (Obj. 5)	■ Common Stock (Obj. 6) ■ Preferred Stock (Obj. 6) ■ Paid-In Capital (Obj. 6) ■ Retained Earnings (Obj. 6)

Learning Objectives

Obj. 1 Describe the nature of the corporate form of organization.

Obj. 2 Describe and illustrate the characteristics of stock, classes of stock, and entries for issuing stock.

Obj. 3 Describe and illustrate the accounting for cash dividends and stock dividends.

Obj. 4 Describe the effect of stock splits on stockholders' equity.

Obj. 5 Describe and illustrate the accounting for treasury stock transactions.

Obj. 6 Describe and illustrate the reporting of stockholders' equity.

Analysis for Decision Making

Obj. 7 Describe and illustrate the use of earnings per share in evaluating a company's profitability.

Objective 1
Describe the nature of the corporate form of organization.

Nature of a Corporation

Most large businesses are organized as corporations. As a result, corporations generate more than 90% of the total business dollars in the United States. In contrast, most small businesses are organized as proprietorships, partnerships, or limited liability companies.

Characteristics of a Corporation

A *corporation* is a legal entity, distinct and separate from the individuals who create and operate it. As a legal entity, a corporation may acquire, own, and dispose of property in its own name. It may also incur liabilities and enter into contracts. Most importantly, it can sell shares of ownership, called **stock**. This characteristic gives corporations the ability to raise large amounts of capital.

The **stockholders** or *shareholders* who own the stock own the corporation. They can buy and sell stock without affecting the corporation's operations or continued existence. Corporations whose shares of stock are traded in public markets are called *public corporations*. Corporations whose shares are not traded publicly are usually owned by a small group of investors and are called *nonpublic* or *private corporations*.

The stockholders of a corporation have *limited liability*. This means that creditors usually may not go beyond the assets of the corporation to satisfy their claims. Thus, the financial loss that a stockholder may suffer is limited to the amount invested.

The stockholders control a corporation by electing a *board of directors*. This board meets periodically to establish corporate policies. It also selects the chief executive officer (CEO) and other major officers to manage the corporation's day-to-day affairs. Exhibit 1 shows the organizational structure of a corporation.

note:
Corporations have a separate legal existence, transferable units of ownership, and limited stockholder liability.

As a separate entity, a corporation is subject to taxes. For example, corporations must pay federal income taxes on their income.[1] Thus, corporate income that is distributed to stockholders in the form of *dividends* has already been taxed. In turn, stockholders must pay income taxes on the dividends they receive. This *double taxation* of corporate earnings is a major disadvantage of the corporate form. The advantages and disadvantages of the corporate form are listed in Exhibit 2.

---

[1] A majority of states also require corporations to pay income taxes.

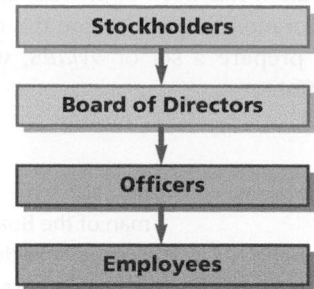

Exhibit 1

Organizational Structure of a Corporation

Exhibit 2 Advantages and Disadvantages of the Corporate Form

Advantages	Explanation
Separate legal existence	A corporation exists separately from its owners.
Continuous life	A corporation's life is separate from its owners; therefore, it exists indefinitely.
Raising large amounts of capital	The corporate form is suited for raising large amounts of money from shareholders.
Ownership rights are easily transferable	A corporation sells shares of ownership, called *stock*. The stockholders of a public company can transfer their shares of stock to other stockholders through stock markets, such as the New York Stock Exchange.
Limited liability	A corporation's creditors usually may not go beyond the assets of the corporation to satisfy their claims. Thus, the financial loss that a stockholder may suffer is limited to the amount invested.

Disadvantages	Explanation
Owner is separate from management	Stockholders control management through a board of directors. The board of directors should represent shareholder interests; however, the board is often more closely tied to management than to shareholders. As a result, the board of directors and management may not always behave in the best interests of stockholders.
Double taxation of dividends	As a separate legal entity, a corporation is subject to taxation. Thus, net income distributed as dividends will be taxed once at the corporation level, and then again at the individual level.
Regulatory costs	Corporations must satisfy many requirements, such as those required by the Sarbanes-Oxley Act.

Forming a Corporation

The first step in forming a corporation is to file an *application of incorporation* with the state. State incorporation laws differ, and corporations often organize in those states with the more favorable laws. For this reason, more than half of the largest companies are incorporated in Delaware. Exhibit 3 lists some corporations, their states of incorporation, and the location of their headquarters.

Corporation	State of Incorporation	Headquarters
Caterpillar Inc. (CAT)	Delaware	Peoria, IL
Delta Air Lines, Inc. (DAL)	Delaware	Atlanta, GA
The Dow Chemical Company (DOW)	Delaware	Midland, MI
Alphabet Inc. (GOOG)	Delaware	Mountain View, CA
General Electric Company (GE)	New York	Fairfield, CT
The Home Depot (HD)	Delaware	Atlanta, GA
Kellogg Company (K)	Delaware	Battle Creek, MI
Reynolds American Inc. (RAI)	Delaware	Winston-Salem, NC
Starbucks Corporation (SBUX)	Washington	Seattle, WA
3M Company (MMM)	Delaware	St. Paul, MN
Walt Disney Company (DIS)	Delaware	Burbank, CA
Whirlpool Corporation (WHR)	Delaware	Benton Harbor, MI

Exhibit 3

Examples of Corporations and Their States of Incorporation

After the application of incorporation has been approved, the state grants a *charter* or *articles of incorporation*. The articles of incorporation formally create the corporation.[2] The corporate management and board of directors then prepare a set of *bylaws*, which are the rules and procedures for conducting the corporation's affairs.

Link to Alphabet

Some excepts from **Alphabet**'s bylaws follow:

ARTICLE I—CORPORATE OFFICES

1.1 REGISTERED OFFICE.
The registered office of Alphabet Inc. shall be fixed in the corporation's certificate of incorporation. …

1.2 OTHER OFFICES.
The corporation's Board of Directors (the "Board") may at any time establish other offices at any place or places where the corporation is qualified to do business.

ARTICLE II—MEETINGS OF STOCKHOLDERS

2.2 ANNUAL MEETING.
The annual meeting of stockholders shall be held each year on a date and at a time designated by the Board. At the annual meeting, directors shall be elected and any other proper business may be transacted.

2.4 NOTICE OF STOCKHOLDERS' MEETINGS.
All notices of meetings of stockholders shall be sent … not less than ten (10) nor more than sixty (60) days before the date of the meeting to each stockholder entitled to vote at such meeting. … The notice shall specify the place, if any, date and hour of the meeting, the means of remote communication, if any, by which stockholders and proxy holders may be deemed to be present in person and vote at such meeting. …

2.8 ADMINISTRATION OF THE MEETING.
Meetings of stockholders shall be presided over by the chairman of the Board. …

ARTICLE V—OFFICERS

5.1 OFFICERS.
The officers of the corporation shall be a chief executive officer and a secretary. The corporation

may also have, at the discretion of the Board, a chairman of the Board, a vice chairman of the Board, one or more presidents, a chief financial officer, a treasurer, one or more vice presidents, one or more assistant vice presidents, one or more assistant treasurers, one or more assistant secretaries, and any such other officers as may be appointed in accordance with the provisions of these bylaws.

5.6 CHAIRMAN OF THE BOARD.
The chairman of the Board shall be a member of the Board and, if present, preside at meetings of the Board. …

5.7 CHIEF EXECUTIVE OFFICER.
Subject to the control of the Board, … the chief executive officer shall have general supervision, direction, and control of the business and affairs of the corporation. … The chief executive officer shall … preside at all meetings of the stockholders.

5.11 CHIEF FINANCIAL OFFICER.
The chief financial officer shall keep and maintain … adequate and correct books and records of accounts of the properties and business transactions of the corporation, including accounts of its assets, liabilities, receipts, disbursements, gains, losses, capital, retained earnings and shares. …

5.12 TREASURER.
The treasurer shall deposit all moneys and other valuables in the name and to the credit of the corporation. …

Source: https://abc.xyz/investor/other/bylaws.html

Costs may be incurred in organizing a corporation. These costs include legal fees, taxes, state incorporation fees, license fees, and promotional costs. Such costs are debited to an expense account entitled *Organizational Expenses*.

To illustrate, a corporation's organizing costs of $8,500 on January 5 are recorded as follows:

A = L + E
–   – Exp

Jan. 5	Organizational Expenses	8,500	
	Cash		8,500
	Paid costs of organizing the corporation.		

---

[2] The articles of incorporation may also restrict a corporation's activities in certain areas, such as owning certain types of real estate, conducting certain types of business activities, or purchasing its own stock.

Paid-In Capital from Stock

Objective 2
Describe and illustrate the characteristics of stock, classes of stock, and entries for issuing stock.

The two main sources of stockholders' equity are paid-in capital (or contributed capital) and retained earnings. The main source of paid-in capital is from issuing stock.

Characteristics of Stock

The number of shares of stock that a corporation is *authorized* to issue is stated in its charter. The term *issued* refers to the shares issued to the stockholders. A corporation may reacquire some of the stock that it has issued. The stock remaining in the hands of stockholders is then called **outstanding stock**. The relationship between authorized, issued, and outstanding stock is shown in Exhibit 4.

Exhibit 4
Authorized, Issued, and Outstanding Stock

Authorized
Issued
Outstanding

Number of shares authorized, issued, and outstanding

Upon request, corporations may issue stock certificates to stockholders to document their ownership. Printed on a stock certificate is the name of the company, the name of the stockholder, and the number of shares owned. The stock certificate may also indicate a dollar amount assigned to each share of stock, called **par value**. Stock may be issued without par, in which case it is called *no-par stock*. In some states, the board of directors of a corporation is required to assign a *stated value* to no-par stock.

The par value of **Alphabet's** stock is $0.001 per share.

Link to Alphabet

Why It Matters

Red Tape and Starting a Business

The ease of starting a business varies around the world depending upon the number of regulatory procedures, time, cost, and minimum capital requirements imposed by governments.

Countries that maintain minimum barriers to starting a business allow for creativity to be more easily expressed in the marketplace by entrepreneurs. The World Bank Group provides an annual survey of the ease of starting a business by country. Some of their recent selected findings are as follows:

Country	Ease of Starting a Business World Rank	Country	Ease of Starting a Business World Rank
New Zealand	1	Japan	81
Canada	3	Germany	107
Singapore	10	China	136
United Kingdom	17	India	155
Russia	41	Libya	158
United States	49	Haiti	188
Mexico	65		

Source: *Doing Business 2016*, World Bank Group.

Corporations have limited liability, and thus, creditors have no claim against stockholders' personal assets. To protect creditors, however, some states require corporations to maintain a minimum amount of paid-in capital. This minimum amount, called *legal capital,* usually includes the par or stated value of the shares issued.

The major rights that accompany ownership of a share of stock are as follows:

- The right to vote in matters concerning the corporation.
- The right to share in distributions of earnings.
- The right to share in assets upon liquidation.

These stock rights normally vary with the class of stock.

note:

The two primary classes of paid-in capital are common stock and preferred stock.

Types of Stock

When only one class of stock is issued, it is called **common stock**. Each share of common stock has equal rights. Recently, many public companies have begun issuing different classes of common stock with different rights.

Link to Alphabet

Alphabet has three classes of common stock outstanding. Class A has one vote per share; Class B has ten votes per share; and Class C has no voting rights. The current executive chairman and the two original founders control over 56% of the voting power through their ownership of Class B stock.

A corporation may also issue one or more classes of stock with various preference rights such as a preference to dividends. Such a stock is called a **preferred stock**. The dividend rights of preferred stock are stated either as dollars per share or as a percent of par. For example, a $50 par value preferred stock with a $4 per share dividend may be described as either:[3]

preferred $4 stock, $50 par

or

preferred 8% stock, $50 par

As shown in Exhibit 5, preferred stockholders have first rights (preference) to any dividends, and thus, they have a greater chance of receiving dividends than common stockholders. However, since dividends are normally based on earnings, a corporation cannot guarantee dividends even to preferred stockholders.

Why It Matters

▷ CONCEPT CLIP

You Have No Vote

An emerging trend in technology companies is using multiple classes of stock to concentrate voting control of the company to the founders. For example, Mark Zuckerberg, the founder and CEO of **Facebook (FB)**, owns Class B shares of Facebook. The public owns Class A shares. The Class B shares have ten votes for every one vote in the Class A shares. As a result, Zuckerberg owns 18% of the stock, but 57% of the voting rights of Facebook. Other companies using multiple classes of stock in this way include **Alphabet (GOOG)**, **Groupon (GRPN)**, **Zynga (ZNGA)**, and **Yelp! (YELP)**. While becoming prevalent among new technology companies, using multiple classes of stock is not a new idea. **The Hershey Company (HSY)** has had two classes of stock since becoming a public company in 1927. The Hershey Trust Company, which oversees the Hershey School for orphans, has 80% of the voting control of The Hershey Company by controlling super voting shares. The argument in favor of super voting rights is that the founders can concentrate on the long-term goals of the company without concern for possibly more short-term goals of public shareholders. The argument in opposition is that concentrating control among the founders can eliminate or reduce the public shareholders' ability to hold management accountable.

[3] In some cases, preferred stock may receive additional dividends if certain conditions are met. Such stock, called *participating preferred stock,* is not often issued.

Exhibit 5
Dividend Preferences

Alphabet has 100,000,000 shares of authorized preferred stock with a par of $0.001, which are convertible to common stock. However, there are no shares of preferred stock issued or outstanding.

Link to Alphabet

The payment of dividends is authorized by the corporation's board of directors. When authorized, the directors are said to have *declared* a dividend.

Cumulative preferred stock has a right to receive regular dividends that were not declared (paid) in prior years. Noncumulative preferred stock does not have this right.

Cumulative preferred stock dividends that have not been paid in prior years are said to be **in arrears**. Any preferred dividends in arrears must be paid before any common stock dividends are paid. In addition, any dividends in arrears are normally disclosed in notes to the financial statements.

To illustrate, assume that a corporation has issued the following preferred and common stock:

1,000 shares of cumulative preferred $4 stock, $50 par
4,000 shares of common stock, $15 par

The corporation was organized on January 1 of 20Y1 and paid no dividends in 20Y1 and 20Y2. In 20Y3, the corporation paid $22,000 in dividends, of which $12,000 was paid to preferred stockholders and $10,000 was paid to common stockholders, computed as shown in Exhibit 6.

Total dividends paid		$ 22,000
Preferred stockholders:		
20Y1 dividends in arrears (1,000 shares × $4)	$4,000	
20Y2 dividends in arrears (1,000 shares × $4)	4,000	
20Y3 dividend (1,000 shares × $4)	4,000	
Total preferred dividends paid		(12,000)
Dividends available to common stockholders		$ 10,000

Exhibit 6
Preferred Dividends
in Arrears

As a result, preferred stockholders received $12.00 per share ($12,000 ÷ 1,000 shares) in dividends, while common stockholders received $2.50 per share ($10,000 ÷ 4,000 shares).

In addition to dividend preference, preferred stock may be given preferences to assets if the corporation goes out of business and is liquidated. However, claims of creditors must be satisfied first. Preferred stockholders are then next in line to receive any remaining assets, followed by the common stockholders.

Issuing Stock

A separate account is used for recording the amount of each class of stock issued to investors in a corporation. For example, assume that a corporation is authorized to issue 10,000 shares of $100 par preferred stock and 100,000 shares of $20 par common stock. The corporation issued 5,000 shares of preferred stock and 50,000 shares of common stock at par for cash. The corporation's entry to record the stock issue is as follows:[4]

A = L + E
+   +

Cash	1,500,000	
Preferred Stock		500,000
Common Stock		1,000,000
Issued preferred stock and common stock at par for cash.		

Stock is often issued by a corporation at a price other than its par. The price at which stock is sold depends on a variety of factors, such as the following:

- The financial condition, earnings record, and dividend record of the corporation.
- Investor expectations of the corporation's potential earning power.
- General business and economic conditions and expectations.

If stock is issued (sold) for a price that is more than its par, the stock has been sold at a **premium**. For example, if common stock with a par of $50 is sold for $60 per share, the stock has sold at a premium of $10.

If stock is issued (sold) for a price that is less than its par, the stock has been sold at a **discount**. For example, if common stock with a par of $50 is sold for $45 per share, the stock has sold at a discount of $5. Many states do not permit stock to be sold at a discount. In other states, stock may be sold at a discount in only unusual cases. Because stock is rarely sold at a discount, it is not illustrated.

In order to distribute dividends, financial statements, and other reports, a corporation must keep track of its stockholders. Large public corporations normally use a financial institution, such as a bank, for this purpose.[5] In such cases, the financial institution is referred to as a *transfer agent* or *registrar*.

Pathways Challenge

This is Accounting!

Economic Activity

As part of its financing strategy, **Extended Stay America, Inc. (STAY)** issued 21,202 shares of 8% preferred stock valued at $21.2 million. While the preferred stockholders have a preference with regard to the 8% dividend, this stock has a unique feature. Specifically, Extended Stay America is *required* to buy back the stock in November 2020 at $1,000 per share plus any unpaid dividends.

Critical Thinking/Judgment

Is Extended Stay America's security (preferred stock) equity or debt?

Suggested answer at end of chapter.

---

[4] The accounting for investments in stocks from the point of view of the investor is discussed in Appendix D.

Premium on Stock

When stock is issued at a premium, Cash is debited for the amount received. Common Stock or Preferred Stock is credited for the par amount. The excess of the amount paid over par is part of the paid-in capital. An account entitled *Paid-In Capital in Excess of Par* is credited for this amount.

Alphabet recently reported paid-in capital of over $36 billion.

Link to Alphabet

To illustrate, assume that Caldwell Company issues 2,000 shares of $50 par preferred stock for cash at $55. The entry to record this transaction is as follows:

Cash	110,000	
Preferred Stock		100,000
Paid-In Capital in Excess of Par—Preferred Stock		10,000
Issued $50 par preferred stock at $55.		

$$A = L + E$$
$$+ \quad\quad +$$

When stock is issued in exchange for assets other than cash, such as land, buildings, and equipment, the assets acquired are recorded at their fair market value. If this value cannot be determined, the fair market price of the stock issued is used.

To illustrate, assume that a corporation acquired land with a fair market value that cannot be determined. In exchange, the corporation issued 10,000 shares of its $10 par common stock. If the stock has a market price of $12 per share, the transaction is recorded as follows:

Land	120,000	
Common Stock		100,000
Paid-In Capital in Excess of Par		20,000
Issued $10 par common stock, valued		
at $12 per share, for land.		

$$A = L + E$$
$$+ \quad\quad +$$

Why It Matters

Buying and Selling Stock

A company will issue stock as part of an IPO, or initial public offering. This event creates the accounting entries for issuing stock. Once the stock is issued, it will trade publicly between buyers and sellers of the stock. These transactions are not recorded on the company's books, unless the company is repurchasing its own stock. Public trading of stock occurs on the New York Stock Exchange (NYSE) and NASDAQ markets. For example, **General Electric (GE)** trades on the NYSE and **Facebook (FB)** trades on the NASDAQ.

---

[5] Small corporations may use a subsidiary ledger, called a *stockholders ledger*. in this case, the stock accounts (Preferred Stock and Common Stock) are controlling accounts for the subsidiary ledger.

No-Par Stock

In most states, no-par preferred and common stock may be issued. When no-par stock is issued, Cash is debited and Common Stock is credited for the proceeds. As no-par stock is issued over time, this entry is the same even if the issuing price varies.

To illustrate, assume that on January 9, a corporation issues 10,000 shares of no-par common stock at $40 a share. On June 27, the corporation issues an additional 1,000 shares at $36. The entries to record these issuances of the no-par stock are as follows:

A = L + E		Jan. 9	Cash	400,000	
+	+		Common Stock		400,000
			Issued 10,000 shares of no-par		
			common stock at $40.		

A = L + E		June 27	Cash	36,000	
+	+		Common Stock		36,000
			Issued 1,000 shares of no-par		
			common stock at $36.		

In some states, no-par stock may be assigned a *stated value per share.* The stated value is recorded like a par value. Any excess of the proceeds over the stated value is credited to *Paid-In Capital in Excess of Stated Value.*

To illustrate, assume that in the preceding example the no-par common stock is assigned a stated value of $25. The issuance of the stock on January 9 and June 27 is recorded as follows:

A = L + E		Jan. 9	Cash	400,000	
+	+		Common Stock		250,000
			Paid-In Capital in Excess of Stated Value		150,000
			Issued 10,000 shares of no-par common stock		
			at $40; stated value, $25.		

A = L + E		June 27	Cash	36,000	
+	+		Common Stock		25,000
			Paid-In Capital in Excess of Stated Value		11,000
			Issued 1,000 shares of no-par common stock		
			at $36; stated value, $25.		

Check Up Corner 12-1 Classes of Stock

On January 1, 20Y1, DeFrance Corporation issued for cash 40,000 shares of $10 par common stock at $24.
On March 30, 20Y1, DeFrance issued 6,000 shares of cumulative preferred 3% stock of $100 par at $142.
The following amounts were distributed as dividends on December 31 of each year:

20Y1	$ 6,000
20Y2	46,000
20Y3	80,000

a. Journalize the entries to record the January 1 and March 30, 20Y1, transactions.

b. Determine the dividends per share for preferred and common stock for 20Y1, 20Y2, and 20Y3.

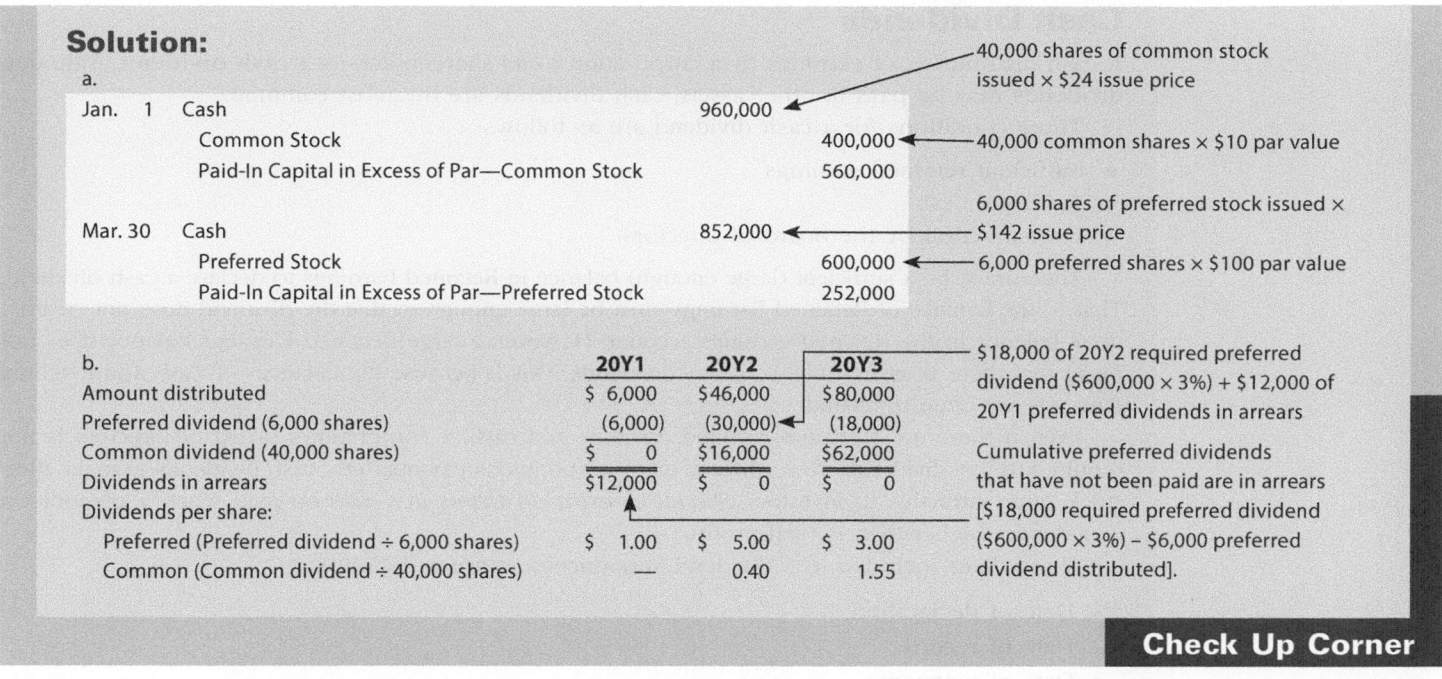

Solution:

a.

Jan. 1	Cash	960,000	
	Common Stock		400,000
	Paid-In Capital in Excess of Par—Common Stock		560,000
Mar. 30	Cash	852,000	
	Preferred Stock		600,000
	Paid-In Capital in Excess of Par—Preferred Stock		252,000

- 40,000 shares of common stock issued × $24 issue price
- 40,000 common shares × $10 par value
- 6,000 shares of preferred stock issued × $142 issue price
- 6,000 preferred shares × $100 par value

b.

	20Y1	20Y2	20Y3
Amount distributed	$ 6,000	$46,000	$ 80,000
Preferred dividend (6,000 shares)	(6,000)	(30,000)	(18,000)
Common dividend (40,000 shares)	$ 0	$16,000	$62,000
Dividends in arrears	$12,000	$ 0	$ 0
Dividends per share:			
Preferred (Preferred dividend ÷ 6,000 shares)	$ 1.00	$ 5.00	$ 3.00
Common (Common dividend ÷ 40,000 shares)	—	0.40	1.55

- $18,000 of 20Y2 required preferred dividend ($600,000 × 3%) + $12,000 of 20Y1 preferred dividends in arrears
- Cumulative preferred dividends that have not been paid are in arrears [$18,000 required preferred dividend ($600,000 × 3%) − $6,000 preferred dividend distributed].

Check Up Corner

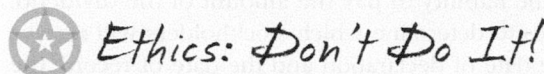 **Ethics: Don't Do It!**

The Professor Who Knew Too Much

A major Midwestern university released a quarterly "American Customer Satisfaction Index" based on its research of customers of popular U.S. products and services. Before the release of the index to the public, the professor in charge of the research bought and sold stocks of some of the companies in the report. The professor was quoted as saying that he thought it was important to test his theories of customer satisfaction with "real" [his own] money.

Is this proper or ethical? Apparently, the dean of the Business School didn't think so. In a statement to the press, the dean stated: "I have instructed anyone affiliated with the (index) not to make personal use of information gathered in the course of producing the quarterly index, prior to the index's release to the general public, and they [the researchers] have agreed."

Sources: Jon E. Hilsenrath and Dan Morse, "Researcher Uses Index to Buy, Short Stocks," *The Wall Street Journal*, February 18, 2003; and Jon E. Hilsenrath, "Satisfaction Theory: Mixed Results," *The Wall Street Journal*, February 19, 2003.

Accounting for Dividends

When a board of directors declares a cash dividend, it authorizes the distribution of cash to stockholders. When a board of directors declares a stock dividend, it authorizes the distribution of its stock. In both cases, declaring a dividend reduces the retained earnings of the corporation.[6]

Objective 3

Describe and illustrate the accounting for cash dividends and stock dividends.

Alphabet has never paid a cash dividend and has no intention of doing so in the foreseeable future.

Link to Alphabet

---

[6] In rare cases, when a corporation is reducing its operations or going out of business, a dividend may be a distribution of paid-in capital. Such a dividend is called a *liquidating dividend*.

Cash Dividends

A cash distribution of earnings by a corporation to its shareholders is a **cash dividend**. Although dividends may be paid in other assets, cash dividends are the most common.

Three conditions for a cash dividend are as follows:

- Sufficient retained earnings
- Sufficient cash
- Formal action by the board of directors

There must be a sufficient (large enough) balance in Retained Earnings to declare a cash dividend. That is, the balance of Retained Earnings must be large enough so that the dividend does not create a debit balance in the retained earnings account. However, a large Retained Earnings balance does not mean that there is cash available to pay dividends. This is because the balances of Cash and Retained Earnings are often unrelated.

Even if there are sufficient retained earnings and cash, a corporation's board of directors is not required to pay dividends. Nevertheless, many corporations pay quarterly cash dividends to make their stock more attractive to investors. *Special* or *extra dividends* may also be paid when a corporation experiences higher than normal profits.

Three dates included in a dividend announcement are as follows:

1. Date of declaration
2. Date of record
3. Date of payment

The *date of declaration* is the date the board of directors formally authorizes the payment of the dividend. On this date, the corporation incurs the liability to pay the amount of the dividend.

The *date of record* is the date the corporation uses to determine which stockholders will receive the dividend. During the period of time between the date of declaration and the date of record, the stock price is quoted as selling *with-dividends*. This means that any investors purchasing the stock before the date of record will receive the dividend.

The *date of payment* is the date the corporation will pay the dividend to the stockholders who owned the stock on the date of record. During the period of time between the record date and the payment date, the stock price is quoted as selling *ex-dividends*. This means that since the date of record has passed, any new investors will not receive the dividend.

To illustrate, assume that on October 1, Hiber Corporation declares the following cash dividends with a date of record of November 10 and a date of payment of December 2:

	Dividend per Share	Total Dividends
Preferred stock, $100 par, 5,000 shares outstanding........................	$2.50	$12,500
Common stock, $10 par, 100,000 shares outstanding	$0.30	30,000
Total		$42,500

Declaration Date   On October 1, the declaration date, Hiber Corporation records the following entry:

$$A = L + E$$
$$+ \quad - \text{Div}$$

Oct. 1	Cash Dividends	42,500	
	Cash Dividends Payable		42,500
	Declared cash dividends.		

Date of Record   On November 10, the date of record, no entry is necessary. This date merely determines which stockholders will receive the dividends.

Date of Payment   On December 2, the date of payment, Hiber Corporation records the payment of the dividends as follows:

$$A = L + E$$
$$- \quad -$$

Dec. 2	Cash Dividends Payable	42,500	
	Cash		42,500
	Paid cash dividends.		

At the end of the accounting period, the balance in Cash Dividends will be transferred to Retained Earnings as part of the closing process. This closing entry debits Retained Earnings and credits Cash Dividends for the balance of the cash dividends account. If the cash dividends have not been paid by the end of the period, Cash Dividends Payable will be reported on the balance sheet as a current liability.

Stock Dividends

A **stock dividend** is a distribution of shares of stock to stockholders. Stock dividends are normally declared only on common stock and issued to common stockholders.

A stock dividend affects only stockholders' equity. Specifically, the amount of the stock dividend is transferred from Retained Earnings to Paid-In Capital. The amount transferred is normally the fair value (market price) of the shares issued in the stock dividend.[7]

To illustrate, assume that the stockholders' equity accounts of Hendrix Corporation as of December 15 are as follows:

Common Stock, $20 par (2,000,000 shares issued)	$40,000,000
Paid-In Capital in Excess of Par—Common Stock	9,000,000
Retained Earnings	26,600,000

On December 15, Hendrix Corporation declares a stock dividend of 5% or 100,000 shares (2,000,000 shares × 5%) to be issued on January 10 to stockholders of record on December 31. The market price of the stock on December 15 (the date of declaration) is $31 per share.

The entry to record the stock dividend is as follows:

Dec. 15	Stock Dividends	3,100,000		A = L + E
	Stock Dividends Distributable		2,000,000	+ –
	Paid-In Capital in Excess of Par—Common Stock		1,100,000	
	Declared 5% (100,000 shares) stock			
	dividend on $20 par common stock			
	with a market price of $31 per share.			

After the preceding entry is recorded, Stock Dividends will have a debit balance of $3,100,000. Like cash dividends, the stock dividends account is closed to Retained Earnings at the end of the accounting period. This closing entry debits Retained Earnings and credits Stock Dividends.

At the end of the period, the *stock dividends distributable* and *paid-in capital in excess of par—common stock* accounts are reported in the "Paid-in capital" section of the balance sheet. Thus, the effect of the preceding stock dividend is to transfer $3,100,000 of retained earnings to paid-in capital.

On January 10, the stock dividend is distributed to stockholders by issuing 100,000 shares of common stock. The issuance of the stock is recorded by the following entry:

Jan. 10	Stock Dividends Distributable	2,000,000		A = L + E
	Common Stock		2,000,000	+ –
	Issued stock as stock dividend.			

A stock dividend does not change the assets, liabilities, or total stockholders' equity of a corporation. Likewise, a stock dividend does not change an individual stockholder's proportionate interest (equity) in the corporation.

To illustrate, assume a stockholder owns 1,000 of a corporation's 10,000 shares outstanding. If the corporation declares a 6% stock dividend, the stockholder's proportionate interest will not change, computed as follows:

	Before **Stock Dividend**	*After* **Stock Dividend**
Total shares issued	10,000	10,600 [10,000 + (10,000 × 6%)]
Number of shares owned	1,000	1,060 [1,000 + (1,000 × 6%)]
Proportionate ownership	10% (1,000 ÷ 10,000)	10% (1,060 ÷ 10,600)

---

[7] The use of fair market value is justified as long as the number of shares issued for the stock dividend is small (less than 25% of the shares outstanding). The accounting for large stock dividends is discussed in advanced accounting texts.

Check Up Corner 12-2 Dividends

Borzilova Company has 150,000 shares of $20 par common stock outstanding on January 1. During the year, the company had the following dividend transactions:

a. On April 7, the company declared a cash dividend of $0.06 per share on common stock to shareholders of record on April 28. The cash dividend is paid on March 10.

b. On August 30, the company declared a 2% stock dividend to stockholders of record on October 20. The stock certificates for the stock dividend are distributed on October 31.

The market price of the company's stock was $60 on August 30, $64 on October 20, and $67 on October 31. Journalize the entries required on each date.

Solution:

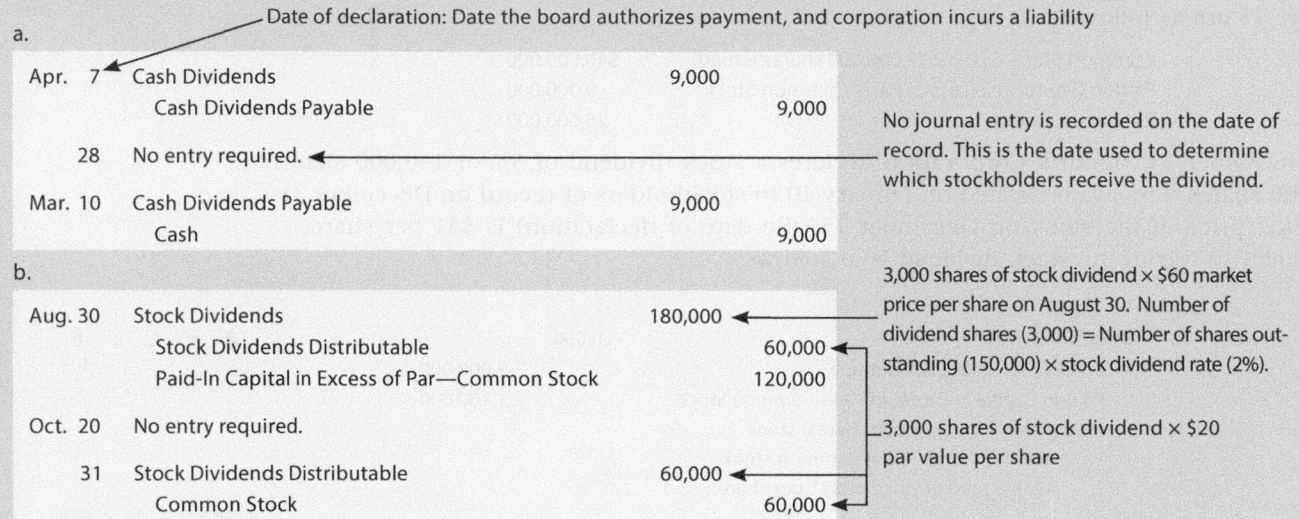

a.   Date of declaration: Date the board authorizes payment, and corporation incurs a liability

Apr.	7	Cash Dividends	9,000	
		Cash Dividends Payable		9,000
	28	No entry required.		
Mar.	10	Cash Dividends Payable	9,000	
		Cash		9,000

No journal entry is recorded on the date of record. This is the date used to determine which stockholders receive the dividend.

b.

Aug.	30	Stock Dividends	180,000	
		Stock Dividends Distributable		60,000
		Paid-In Capital in Excess of Par—Common Stock		120,000
Oct.	20	No entry required.		
	31	Stock Dividends Distributable	60,000	
		Common Stock		60,000

3,000 shares of stock dividend × $60 market price per share on August 30. Number of dividend shares (3,000) = Number of shares outstanding (150,000) × stock dividend rate (2%).

3,000 shares of stock dividend × $20 par value per share

Check Up Corner

Objective 4

Describe the effect of stock splits on stockholders' equity.

Stock Splits

A **stock split** is a process by which a corporation reduces the par or stated value of its common stock and issues a proportionate number of additional shares. A stock split applies to all common shares including the unissued and issued shares.

A major objective of a stock split is to reduce the market price per share of the stock. This attracts more investors and broadens the types and numbers of stockholders.

To illustrate, assume that Rojek Corporation has 10,000 shares of $100 par common stock outstanding with a current market price of $150 per share. The board of directors declares the following stock split:

1. Each common shareholder will receive 5 shares for each share held. This is called a 5-for-1 stock split. As a result, 50,000 shares (10,000 shares × 5) will be outstanding.
2. The par of each share of common stock will be reduced to $20 ($100 ÷ 5).

The par value of the common stock outstanding is $1,000,000 both before and after the stock split as shown in Exhibit 7 and computed as follows:

	Before Split	After Split
Number of shares	10,000	50,000
Par value per share	× $100	× $20
Total	$1,000,000	$1,000,000

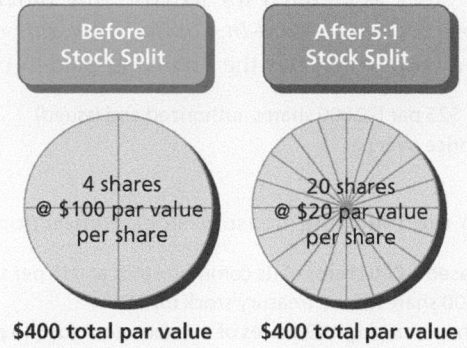

Exhibit 7

Stock Split:
Before and After

In addition, each Rojek Corporation shareholder owns the same total par amount of stock before and after the stock split. For example, a stockholder who owned 4 shares of $100 par stock before the split (total par of $400) would own 20 shares of $20 par stock after the split (total par of $400). Only the number of shares and the par value per share have changed.

Because there are more shares outstanding after the stock split, the market price of the stock should decrease. For example, in the preceding example, there would be 5 times as many shares outstanding after the split. Thus, the market price of the stock would be expected to fall from $150 to about $30 ($150 ÷ 5).

Stock splits do not require a journal entry because only the par (or stated) value and number of shares outstanding have changed. However, the details of stock splits are normally disclosed in the notes to the financial statements.

note:
A stock split does not require a journal entry.

In 2014, **Alphabet** implemented a 2-for-1 stock split through the issue of Class C common stock.

Link to Alphabet

Why It Matters

Buffett on Stock Splits

Warren E. Buffett, chief executive officer of **Berkshire Hathaway Inc. (BRK.A)**, opposes stock splits on the basis that they add no value to the company. Since its inception, Berkshire Hathaway has never declared a stock split on its primary (Class A) common stock. As a result, Berkshire Hathaway's Class A common stock sells well above $200,000 per share, which is the most expensive stock on the New York Stock Exchange. Such a high price doesn't bother Buffet because he believes that high stock prices attract more sophisticated and long-term investors and discourage stock speculators and short-term investors.

In contrast, **Microsoft Corporation (MSFT)** has split its stock nine times since it went public in 1986. As a result, one share of Microsoft purchased in 1986 is equivalent to 288 shares today.

Treasury Stock Transactions

Objective 5
Describe and illustrate the accounting for treasury stock transactions.

Treasury stock is stock that a corporation has issued and then reacquired. A corporation may reacquire (purchase) its own stock for a variety of reasons, including the following:

- To provide shares for resale to employees
- To reissue as bonuses to employees, or
- To support the market price of the stock

The *cost method* is normally used for recording the purchase and resale of treasury stock.[8] Using the cost method, *Treasury Stock* is debited for the cost (purchase price) of the stock. When

---

[8] Another method that is infrequently used, called the *par value method*, is discussed in advanced accounting texts.

the stock is resold, Treasury Stock is credited for its cost. Any difference between the cost and the selling price is debited or credited to *Paid-In Capital from Sale of Treasury Stock*.

To illustrate, assume that a corporation has the following paid-in capital on January 1:

Common stock, $25 par (20,000 shares authorized and issued)	$500,000
Excess of issue price over par	150,000
	$650,000

The corporation entered into the following treasury stock transactions:

Feb. 13. Purchased 1,000 shares of its common stock at $45 per share.
Apr. 29. Sold 600 shares of the treasury stock for $60.
Oct. 4. Sold the remaining 400 shares of treasury stock for $40 per share.

The journal entries to record the preceding transactions are shown in Exhibit 8.

Exhibit 8

Treasury Stock Transactions

Feb. 13	Treasury Stock		45,000		A = L + E
	Cash			45,000	− −
	Purchased 1,000 shares of treasury stock at $45.				
Apr. 29	Cash		36,000		A = L + E
	Treasury Stock			27,000	+ +
	Paid-In Capital from Sale of Treasury Stock			9,000	
	Sold 600 shares of treasury stock at $60.				
Oct. 4	Cash		16,000		A = L + E
	Paid-In Capital from Sale of Treasury Stock		2,000		+ +
	Treasury Stock			18,000	
	Sold 400 shares of treasury stock at $40.				

The October 4 entry in Exhibit 8 decreases paid-in capital by $2,000. Because Paid-In Capital from Sale of Treasury Stock has a credit balance of $9,000, the entire $2,000 was debited to Paid-In Capital from Sale of Treasury Stock. If the credit balance in Paid-In Capital from Sale of Treasury Stock on October 4 had been $1,500 instead of $9,000, Retained Earnings would have been debited for $500 ($2,000 − $1,500). This is because Paid-In Capital from Sale of Treasury Stock cannot have a debit balance.

No dividends (cash or stock) are paid on the shares of treasury stock. To do so would result in the corporation earning dividend revenue from itself.

Check Up Corner 12-3 Treasury Stock Transactions

The following transactions were completed by Grayson Inc. during the current fiscal year ended December 31:

Apr. 19. Reacquired 10,000 shares of its own $10 par common stock at $30 per share.
Aug. 30. Sold 6,000 of the reacquired shares at $36 per share.
Nov. 10. Sold 2,000 of the reacquired shares at $34 per share.

a. Journalize the transactions of April 19, August 30, and November 10.

b. What is the balance of Paid-In Capital from Sale of Treasury Stock on December 31 of the current year?

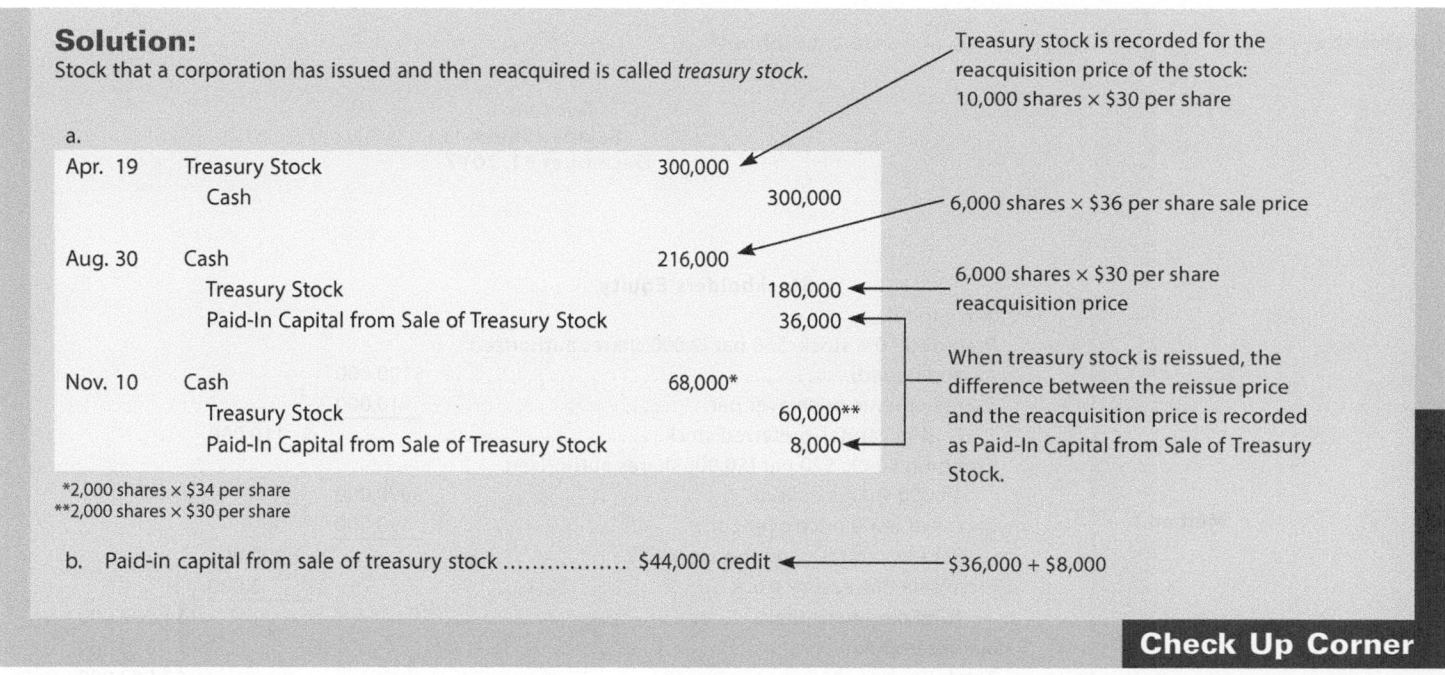

Solution:

Stock that a corporation has issued and then reacquired is called *treasury stock*.

Treasury stock is recorded for the reacquisition price of the stock:
10,000 shares × $30 per share

a.

Apr. 19	Treasury Stock	300,000	
	Cash		300,000

6,000 shares × $36 per share sale price

Aug. 30	Cash	216,000	
	Treasury Stock		180,000
	Paid-In Capital from Sale of Treasury Stock		36,000

6,000 shares × $30 per share reacquisition price

Nov. 10	Cash	68,000*	
	Treasury Stock		60,000**
	Paid-In Capital from Sale of Treasury Stock		8,000

When treasury stock is reissued, the difference between the reissue price and the reacquisition price is recorded as Paid-In Capital from Sale of Treasury Stock.

*2,000 shares × $34 per share
**2,000 shares × $30 per share

b. Paid-in capital from sale of treasury stock .... $44,000 credit ← $36,000 + $8,000

Check Up Corner

Why It Matters

Treasury Stock vs. Dividends

A company has two major ways to return cash to shareholders: cash dividends and stock repurchases. A shareholder preferring a current cash income may prefer to receive a steady cash dividend. A shareholder preferring share price appreciation may prefer stock repurchases. This is because when a company purchases treasury stock, the amount of shares outstanding will decline, and the market value per share should increase. Another consideration is that cash dividends are currently taxed at 15%, while the gains on share price increases are tax-deferred until sold. A company may prefer returning cash through stock repurchases because it provides management greater flexibility in managing the company's cash flows. It is considered more difficult to decrease a cash dividend than it is to reduce share repurchases over time. So, overall, the answer to the question depends on circumstances. This is likely why many companies do both.

Reporting Stockholders' Equity

Objective 6
Describe and illustrate the reporting of stockholders' equity.

As with other sections of the balance sheet, alternative terms and formats may be used in reporting stockholders' equity. Also, changes in retained earnings and paid-in capital may be reported in separate statements or notes to the financial statements.

Stockholders' Equity on the Balance Sheet

Exhibit 9 shows two methods for reporting stockholders' equity for the December 31, 20Y7, balance sheet for Telex Inc.

■ Method 1. Each class of stock is reported, followed by its related paid-in capital accounts. Retained earnings is then reported followed by a deduction for treasury stock.

■ Method 2. The stock accounts are reported, followed by the paid-in capital reported as a single item, additional paid-in capital. Retained earnings is then reported followed by a deduction for treasury stock.

Exhibit 9 "Stockholders' Equity" Section of a Balance Sheet

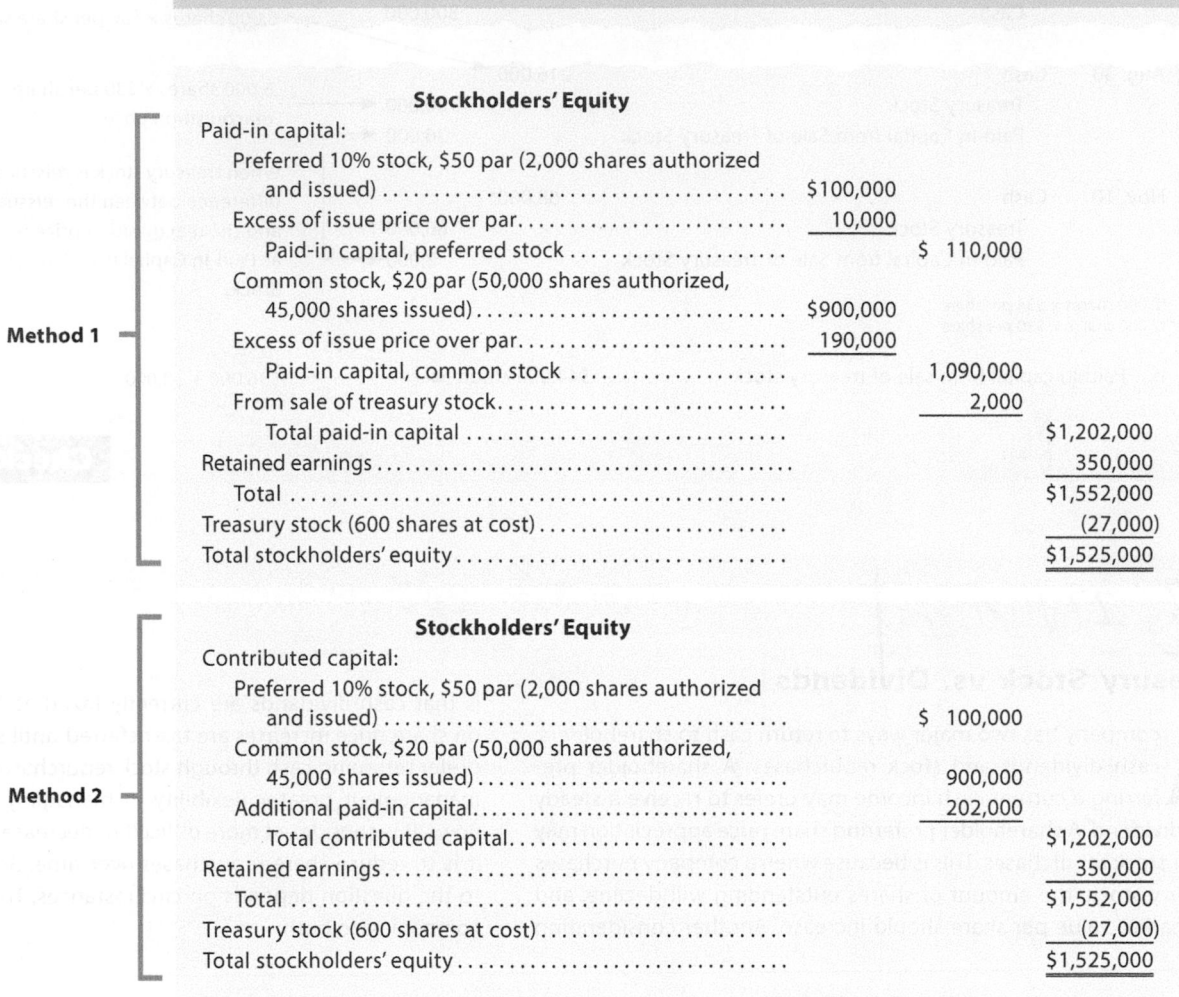

Telex Inc.
Balance Sheet
December 31, 20Y7

Stockholders' Equity

Method 1

Paid-in capital:
Preferred 10% stock, $50 par (2,000 shares authorized and issued)	$100,000		
Excess of issue price over par	10,000		
Paid-in capital, preferred stock		$ 110,000	
Common stock, $20 par (50,000 shares authorized, 45,000 shares issued)	$900,000		
Excess of issue price over par	190,000		
Paid-in capital, common stock		1,090,000	
From sale of treasury stock		2,000	
Total paid-in capital			$1,202,000
Retained earnings			350,000
Total			$1,552,000
Treasury stock (600 shares at cost)			(27,000)
Total stockholders' equity			$1,525,000

Stockholders' Equity

Method 2

Contributed capital:
Preferred 10% stock, $50 par (2,000 shares authorized and issued)	$ 100,000	
Common stock, $20 par (50,000 shares authorized, 45,000 shares issued)	900,000	
Additional paid-in capital	202,000	
Total contributed capital		$1,202,000
Retained earnings		350,000
Total		$1,552,000
Treasury stock (600 shares at cost)		(27,000)
Total stockholders' equity		$1,525,000

Link to Alphabet **Alphabet** has 691,293,000 shares of common stock outstanding as follows: Class A, 296,992,000 shares; Class B, 47,437,000 shares; and Class C, 346,864,000 shares.

Significant changes in stockholders' equity during a period may also be presented in a statement of stockholders' equity or in the notes to the financial statements. The statement of stockholders' equity was introduced in Chapter 1 and is illustrated later in this section.

Relevant rights and privileges of the various classes of stock outstanding should also be reported.[9] Examples include dividend and liquidation preferences, conversion rights, and redemption rights. Such information may be disclosed on the face of the balance sheet or in the notes to the financial statements.

Reporting Retained Earnings

Changes in retained earnings may be reported using one of the following:

- Separate retained earnings statement
- Combined income and retained earnings statement
- Statement of stockholders' equity

[9] *FASB Accounting Standards Codification,* Section 505-10-50.

When a separate **retained earnings statement** is prepared, the beginning balance of retained earnings is reported. The net income is then added (or net loss is subtracted) and any dividends are subtracted to arrive at the ending retained earnings for the period.

At the end of a recent year, **Alphabet** reported retained earnings of $105,131,000,000.   *Link to Alphabet*

To illustrate, a retained earnings statement for Telex Inc. is shown in Exhibit 10.

Exhibit 10   Retained Earnings Statement

Telex Inc. Retained Earnings Statement For the Year Ended December 31, 20Y7			
Retained earnings, January 1, 20Y7			$245,000
Net income		$180,000	
Dividends:			
Preferred stock dividends	$(10,000)		
Common stock dividends	(65,000)	(75,000)	
Change in retained earnings			105,000
Retained earnings, December 31, 20Y7..................			$350,000

Changes in retained earnings may also be reported in combination with the income statement. This format emphasizes net income as the connecting link between the income statement and ending retained earnings. Because this format is not often used, it is not illustrated. Changes in retained earnings may also be reported in a statement of stockholders' equity. An example of reporting changes in retained earnings in a statement of stockholders' equity for Telex Inc. is shown later.

Alphabet does not report a separate retained earnings statement but instead reports changes in retained earnings in its statement of stockholders' equity.   *Link to Alphabet*

Restrictions The use of retained earnings for payment of dividends may be restricted by action of a corporation's board of directors. Such **restrictions**, sometimes called *appropriations*, remain part of the retained earnings.

Restrictions of retained earnings are classified as:

- *Legal*. State laws may require a restriction of retained earnings.

   Example: States may restrict retained earnings by the amount of treasury stock purchased. In this way, legal capital cannot be used for dividends.

- *Contractual*. A corporation may enter into contracts that require restrictions of retained earnings.

   Example: A bank loan may restrict retained earnings so that money for repaying the loan cannot be used for dividends.

- *Discretionary*. A corporation's board of directors may restrict retained earnings voluntarily.

   Example: The board may restrict retained earnings and, thus, limit dividend distributions so that more money is available for expanding the business.

Restrictions of retained earnings must be disclosed in the financial statements. Such disclosures are usually included in the notes to the financial statements.

Prior Period Adjustments An error may arise from a mathematical mistake or from a mistake in applying accounting principles. Such errors may not be discovered within the same period in which they occur. In such cases, the effect of the error should not affect the current period's net income. Instead, the correction of the error, called a **prior period adjustment**, is reported as an adjustment to the beginning balance of retained earnings.[10]

Statement of Stockholders' Equity

When a corporation has changes in stock and paid-in capital accounts as well as retained earnings, a **statement of stockholders' equity** is normally prepared. A statement of stockholders' equity is prepared in a columnar format where each column is a major stockholders' equity classification. Changes in each classification are then described in the left-hand column.

Exhibit 11 illustrates a statement of stockholders' equity for Telex Inc.

Exhibit 11 Statement of Stockholders' Equity

Telex Inc. Statement of Stockholders' Equity For the Year Ended December 31, 20Y7						
	Preferred Stock	Common Stock	Additional Paid-In Capital	Retained Earnings	Treasury Stock	Total
Balances, January 1, 20Y7	$100,000	$850,000	$177,000	$245,000	$(17,000)	$1,355,000
Net income				180,000		180,000
Dividends on preferred stock				(10,000)		(10,000)
Dividends on common stock				(65,000)		(65,000)
Issuance of additional common stock . . .		50,000	25,000			75,000
Purchase of treasury stock					(10,000)	(10,000)
Balances, December 31, 20Y7	$100,000	$900,000	$202,000	$350,000	$(27,000)	$1,525,000

Link to Alphabet **Alphabet** reports a separate statement of stockholders' equity.

International Connection

IFRS **IFRS for SMEs**

In 2010, the International Accounting Standards Board (IASB) issued a set of accounting standards specifically designed for small- and medium-sized enterprises (SMEs) called International Financial Reporting Standards (IFRS) for SMEs. SMEs in the United States are private companies and such small corporations that they do not report to the Securities and Exchange Commission (SEC). IFRS for SMEs consist of only 230 pages, compared to 2,700 pages for full IFRS. These standards are designed to be cost effective for SMEs. Thus, IFRS for SMEs require fewer disclosures and contain no industry-specific standards or exceptions.

The American Institute of CPAs (AICPA) has accepted IFRS for SMEs as part of U.S. generally accepted accounting principles (GAAP) for private companies not reporting to the SEC. If users, such as bankers and investors, accept these financial statements, IFRS for SMEs may become popular in the United States.*

*Differences between U.S. GAAP and IFRS are further discussed and illustrated in Appendix C.

[10] Prior period adjustments are illustrated in advanced accounting texts.

Reporting Stockholders' Equity for Alphabet

Alphabet reports stockholders' equity in its balance sheet. It also includes a statement of stockholders' equity in its financial statements.

The "Stockholders' Equity" section of Alphabet's balance sheet as of December 31 of a recent year follows:

Link to Alphabet

Alphabet Inc.
Balance Sheet
December 31
(in millions)

Stockholders' Equity

Class A, B, and C common stock, $0.001 par value.........................	$ 691	
Additional paid-in capital..	35,616	
Total contributed capital		$ 36,307
Accumulated other comprehensive loss.................................		(2,402)
Retained earnings...		105,131
Total stockholders' equity...		$139,036

Source: Alphabet Inc., *Form 10-K for the Fiscal Year Ended December 31, 2016* (adapted).

The statement of stockholders' equity for Alphabet follows:

Link to Alphabet

Alphabet Inc.
Statement of Stockholders' Equity
For the Year Ended December 31
(in millions)

	Common Stock and Additional Paid-In Capital	Accumulated Other Comprehensive Loss	Retained Earnings	Total
Balances, January 1..................	$32,982	$(1,874)	$ 89,223	$120,331
Common stock issued	298			298
Repurchases of common stock	(256)		(3,437)	(3,693)
Net income........................			19,478	19,478
Other*.............................	3,283	(528)	(133)	2,622
Balances, December 31	$36,307	$(2,402)	$105,131	$139,036

*The "Other" category includes topics, such as other comprehensive income (loss) and the effect of an accounting change, that are discussed in advanced accounting courses.

Source: Alphabet Inc., *Form 10-K for the Fiscal Year Ended December 31, 2016* (adapted).

Analysis for Decision Making

Objective 7
Describe and illustrate the use of earnings per share in evaluating a company's profitability.

Earnings per Share

Net income is often used by investors and creditors in evaluating a company's profitability. However, net income by itself is difficult to use in comparing companies of different sizes. Also, trends in net income may be difficult to evaluate if there have been significant changes in the company's stockholders' equity. One ratio used for analyzing profitability is the earnings per share of common stock outstanding during a period. This ratio is called **earnings per common share (EPS)**, or sometimes *basic earnings per share*.[11]

Corporations whose stock is traded in a public market must report earnings per common share on their income statements. Stockholders in these corporations measure the value of their shareholdings by the market price per share as quoted by a stock exchange. Generally, changes in the market price per share will be related to changes in the earnings per share of the stock. Thus, shareholders actively monitor the earnings per share because of this relationship.

Earnings per share is computed as follows:

$$\text{Earnings per Share} = \frac{\text{Net Income} - \text{Preferred Dividends}}{\text{Average Number of Common Shares Outstanding}}$$

Any preferred dividends are subtracted from net income because the numerator represents only those earnings available to the common shareholders.

To illustrate, the following data (in millions, except per-share amounts) were taken from recent financial statements of **Facebook (FB)**:

	Recent Year	Prior Year
Net income...............................	$10,188	$3,669
Average number of common shares outstanding	2,863 shares	2,803 shares
Earnings per share........................	$3.56	$1.31
	($10,188 ÷ 2,863 shares)	($3,669 ÷ 2,803 shares)

Facebook had no preferred stock outstanding; thus, no preferred dividends were subtracted in computing earnings per share. As illustrated, Facebook's earnings per share increased from $1.31 in the prior year to $3.56 in the recent year. An increase in earnings per share is generally considered a favorable trend.

Make a Decision

Earnings per Share

**Analyze and compare Amazon.com and Wal-Mart (MAD 12-1)
(Continuing company analysis)**

Analyze and compare Bank of America and Wells Fargo (MAD 12-2)

Analyze Pacific Gas and Electric Company (MAD 12-3)

Analyze Caterpillar (MAD 12-4)

Analyze and compare BB&T and Regions Financial (MAD 12-5)

Make a Decision

---

[11] For complex capital structures, including securities such as convertible bonds or executive stock options, earnings per share assuming dilution may also be reported.

Let's Review

Chapter Summary

1. Corporations have a separate legal existence, transferable units of stock, unlimited life, and limited stockholders' liability. The advantages and disadvantages of the corporate form are summarized in Exhibit 2. Costs incurred in organizing a corporation are debited to Organizational Expenses.

2. The main source of paid-in capital is from issuing common and preferred stock. Stock issued at par is recorded by debiting Cash and crediting the class of stock issued for its par amount. Stock issued for more than par is recorded by debiting Cash, crediting the class of stock for its par, and crediting Paid-In Capital in Excess of Par for the difference. When no-par stock is issued, the entire proceeds are credited to the stock account. No-par stock may be assigned a stated value per share, and the excess of the proceeds over the stated value may be credited to Paid-In Capital in Excess of Stated Value.

3. The entry to record a declaration of cash dividends debits Dividends and credits Dividends Payable. When a stock dividend is declared, Stock Dividends is debited for the fair value of the stock to be issued. Stock Dividends Distributable is credited for the par or stated value of the common stock to be issued. The difference between the fair value of the stock and its par or stated value is credited to Paid-In Capital in Excess of Par—Common Stock. When the stock is issued on the date of payment, Stock Dividends Distributable is debited and Common Stock is credited for the par or stated value of the stock issued.

4. When a corporation reduces the par or stated value of its common stock and issues a proportionate number of additional shares, a stock split has occurred. There are no changes in the balances of any accounts, and no entry is required for a stock split.

5. When a corporation buys its own stock, the cost method of accounting is normally used. Treasury Stock is debited for its cost, and Cash is credited. If the stock is resold, Treasury Stock is credited for its cost and any difference between the cost and the selling price is normally debited or credited to Paid-In Capital from Sale of Treasury Stock.

6. Two alternatives for reporting stockholders' equity are shown in Exhibit 9. Changes in retained earnings are reported in either a retained earnings statement (Exhibit 10) or a statement of stockholders' equity (Exhibit 11). Restrictions to retained earnings should be disclosed. Any prior period adjustments are reported as an adjustment to the beginning balance of retained earnings.

7. Earnings per common share (EPS) is used for evaluating a company's profitability. EPS is particularly useful when comparing companies of different sizes or evaluating trends in net income if there have been significant changes to a company's stockholders' equity.

Key Terms

cash dividend (592)
common stock (586)
cumulative preferred stock (587)
discount (588)
earnings per common share (EPS) (602)
in arrears (587)

outstanding stock (585)
par value (585)
preferred stock (586)
premium (588)
prior period adjustment (600)
restrictions (599)
retained earnings statement (599)

statement of stockholders' equity (600)
stock (582)
stock dividend (593)
stock split (594)
stockholders (582)
treasury stock (595)

Practice

Multiple-Choice Questions

1. Which of the following is a disadvantage of the corporate form of organization?
   a. Limited liability
   b. Continuous life
   c. Owner is separate from management
   d. Ability to raise capital

2. Paid-in capital for a corporation may arise from which of the following sources?
   a. Issuing preferred stock
   b. Issuing common stock
   c. Selling the corporation's treasury stock
   d. All of the above

3. The "Stockholders' Equity" section of the balance sheet may include:
   a. common stock.
   b. stock dividends distributable.
   c. preferred stock.
   d. all of the above.

4. If a corporation reacquires its own stock, the stock is listed on the balance sheet in the:
   a. "Current assets" section.
   b. "Long-term liabilities" section.
   c. "Stockholders' Equity" section.
   d. "Investments" section.

5. A corporation has issued 25,000 shares of $100 par common stock and holds 3,000 of these shares as treasury stock. If the corporation declares a $2 per share cash dividend, what amount will be recorded as cash dividends?
   a. $22,000
   b. $25,000
   c. $44,000
   d. $50,000

Answers provided after Problem. Need more practice? Find additional multiple-choice questions, exercises, and problems in CengageNOWv2.

Exercises

1. Dividends per share   Obj. 2

National Furniture Company has 25,000 shares of cumulative preferred 2% stock, $75 par and 200,000 shares of $10 par common stock. The following amounts were distributed as dividends:

20Y1	$25,000
20Y2	88,000
20Y3	95,500

Determine the dividends per share for preferred and common stock for each year.

2. Entries for issuing stock   Obj. 2

On August 26, Mountain Realty Inc. issued for cash 120,000 shares of no-par common stock (with a stated value of $5) at $8. On October 1, Mountain Realty issued at par value 40,000 shares of preferred 1% stock, $10 par for cash. On November 30, Mountain Realty issued for cash 18,000 shares of preferred 1% stock, $10 par at $13.

Journalize the entries to record the August 26, October 1, and November 30 transactions.

3. Entries for cash dividends   Obj. 3

The declaration, record, and payment dates in connection with a cash dividend of $710,000 on a corporation's common stock are June 15, August 10, and September 15. Journalize the entries required on each date.

4. Entries for stock dividends   Obj. 3

Olde Wine Corporation has 250,000 shares of $40 par common stock outstanding. On February 15, Olde Wine declared a 2% stock dividend to be issued May 2 to stockholders of record on March 27. The market price of the stock was $52 per share on February 15.

Journalize the entries required on February 15, March 27, and May 2.

5. Entries for treasury stock   Obj. 5

On January 31, Wilderness Resorts Inc. reacquired 22,500 shares of its common stock at $31 per share. On April 20, Wilderness Resorts sold 12,800 of the reacquired shares at $40 per share. On October 4, Wilderness Resorts sold the remaining shares at $28 per share.

Journalize the transactions of January 31, April 20, and October 4.

6. Reporting stockholders' equity

Obj. 6

Using the following accounts and balances, prepare the "Stockholders' Equity" section of the balance sheet. Two hundred fifty thousand shares of common stock are authorized, and 17,500 shares have been reacquired.

Common Stock, $60 par	$12,000,000
Paid-In Capital from Sale of Treasury Stock	320,000
Paid-In Capital in Excess of Par—Common Stock	3,200,000
Retained Earnings	18,500,000
Treasury Stock	1,137,500

7. Statement of stockholders' equity

Obj. 6

Rockwell Inc. began the month of June with the following balances: Common Stock, $50,000; Additional Paid-In Capital, $2,000,000; and Retained Earnings, $3,900,000. During June, Rockwell issued for cash 10,000 shares of common stock (with a stated value of $1) at $10 per share. Rockwell reported the following results for the month ended June 30:

Net income	$714,000
Cash dividends declared	150,000

Prepare a statement of stockholders' equity for the month ended June 30.

8. Earnings per share

Obj. 7

Financial statement data for the years 20Y2 and 20Y3 for Dovetail Corporation follow:

	20Y3	20Y2
Net income	$448,750	$376,000
Preferred dividends	$40,000	$40,000
Average number of common shares outstanding	75,000 shares	60,000 shares

a. Determine the earnings per share for 20Y2 and 20Y3.

b. Is the change in the earnings per share from 20Y2 to 20Y3 favorable or unfavorable?

Answers provided after Problem. Need more practice? Find additional multiple-choice questions, exercises, and problems in CengageNOWv2.

Problem

Altenburg Inc. is a lighting fixture wholesaler located in Arizona. During its current fiscal year, ended December 31, Altenburg completed the following selected transactions:

Feb.   3.   Purchased 2,500 shares of its own common stock at $26, recording the stock at cost. (Prior to the purchase, there were 40,000 shares of $20 par common stock outstanding.)

May   1.   Declared a semiannual dividend of $1 on the 10,000 shares of preferred stock and a $0.30 dividend on the common stock to stockholders of record on May 31, payable on June 15.

June   15.   Paid the cash dividends.

Sept.   23.   Sold 1,000 shares of treasury stock at $28, receiving cash.

Nov.   1.   Declared semiannual dividends of $1 on the preferred stock and $0.30 on the common stock. In addition, a 5% common stock dividend was declared on the common stock outstanding, to be capitalized at the fair market value of the common stock, which is estimated at $30.

Dec.   1.   Paid the cash dividends and issued the certificates for the common stock dividend.

Instructions

Journalize the entries to record the transactions for Altenburg Inc.

Need more practice? Find additional multiple-choice questions, exercises, and problems in CengageNOWv2.

Answers

Multiple-Choice Questions

1. **c** The separation of the owner from management (answer c) is a disadvantage of the corporate form of organization. This is because management may not always behave in the best interests of the owners. Limited liability (answer a), continuous life (answer b), and the ability to raise capital (answer d) are all advantages of the corporate form of organization.

2. **d** Paid-in capital is one of the two major subdivisions of the stockholders' equity of a corporation. It may result from many sources, including the issuance of preferred stock (answer a), the issuance of common stock (answer b), or the sale of a corporation's treasury stock (answer c).

3. **d** The "Stockholders' Equity" section of corporate balance sheets is divided into two principal subsections: (1) investments contributed by the stockholders and others and (2) net income retained in the business. Included as part of the investments by stockholders and others is the par of common stock (answer a), stock dividends distributable (answer b), and the par of preferred stock (answer c).

4. **c** Reacquired stock, known as treasury stock, should be listed in the "Stockholders' Equity" section (answer c) of the balance sheet. The price paid for the treasury stock is deducted from the total of all the stockholders' equity accounts.

5. **c** If a corporation that holds treasury stock declares a cash dividend, the dividends are not paid on the treasury shares. To do so would place the corporation in the position of earning income through dealing with itself. Thus, the corporation will record $44,000 (answer c) as cash dividends [(25,000 shares issued less 3,000 shares held as treasury stock) × $2 per share dividend].

Exercises

1.

	20Y1	20Y2	20Y3
Amount distributed	$ 25,000	$ 88,000	$ 95,500
Preferred dividend (25,000 shares)	(25,000)	(50,000)*	(37,500)
Common dividend (200,000 shares)	$ 0	$ 38,000	$ 58,000

*$12,500 + $37,500

Dividends per share:			
Preferred stock	$1.00	$2.00	$1.50
Common stock	None	$0.19	$0.29

2.

Aug. 26	Cash (120,000 shares × $8)	960,000	
	Common Stock (120,000 shares × $5)		600,000
	Paid-In Capital in Excess of Stated Value—		
	Common Stock [120,000 shares × ($8 – $5)]		360,000
Oct. 1	Cash	400,000	
	Preferred Stock (40,000 shares × $10)		400,000
Nov. 30	Cash (18,000 shares × $13)	234,000	
	Preferred Stock (18,000 shares × $10)		180,000
	Paid-In Capital in Excess of Par—		
	Preferred Stock [18,000 shares × ($13 – $10)]		54,000

3.

June 15	Cash Dividends	710,000	
	Cash Dividends Payable		710,000
Aug. 10	No entry required.		
Sept. 15	Cash Dividends Payable	710,000	
	Cash		710,000

4.

Feb. 15	Stock Dividends (250,000 shares × 2% × $52)	260,000	
	Stock Dividends Distributable		
	(5,000 shares × $40)		200,000
	Paid-In Capital in Excess of Par—		
	Common Stock [5,000 shares × ($52 – $40)]		60,000
Mar. 27	No entry required.		
May 2	Stock Dividends Distributable	200,000	
	Common Stock		200,000

5.

Jan. 31	Treasury Stock (22,500 shares × $31)	697,500	
	Cash		697,500
Apr. 20	Cash (12,800 shares × $40)	512,000	
	Treasury Stock (12,800 shares × $31)		396,800
	Paid-In Capital from Sale of		
	Treasury Stock [12,800 shares × ($40 – $31)]		115,200
Oct. 4	Cash (9,700 shares × $28)	271,600	
	Paid-In Capital from Sale of		
	Treasury Stock [9,700 shares × ($31 – $28)]	29,100	
	Treasury Stock (9,700 shares × $31)		300,700

6.

Stockholders' Equity		
Paid-in capital:		
Common stock, $60 par (250,000 shares authorized, 200,000 shares issued)	$12,000,000	
Excess of issue price over par	3,200,000	
Paid-in capital, common stock		$15,200,000
From sale of treasury stock		320,000
Total paid-in capital		$15,520,000
Retained earnings		18,500,000
Total		$34,020,000
Treasury stock (17,500 shares at cost)		(1,137,500)
Total stockholders' equity		$32,882,500

7.

Rockwell Inc.
Statement of Stockholders' Equity
For the Month Ended June 30

	Common Stock	Additional Paid-In Capital	Retained Earnings	Total
Balances, June 1	$50,000	$2,000,000	$3,900,000	$5,950,000
Issued common stock	10,000	90,000		100,000
Net income			714,000	714,000
Dividends			(150,000)	(150,000)
Balances, June 30	$60,000	$2,090,000	$4,464,000	$6,614,000

8. a.

$$\text{20Y2: Earnings per Share} = \frac{\text{Net Income} - \text{Preferred Dividends}}{\text{Average Number of Common Shares Outstanding}}$$

$$= \frac{\$376,000 - \$40,000}{60,000 \text{ shares}}$$

$$= \frac{\$336,000}{60,000 \text{ shares}} = \$5.60$$

$$\text{20Y3: Earnings per Share} = \frac{\text{Net Income} - \text{Preferred Dividends}}{\text{Average Number of Common Shares Outstanding}}$$

$$= \frac{\$448,750 - \$40,000}{75,000 \text{ shares}}$$

$$= \frac{\$408,750}{75,000 \text{ shares}} = \$5.45$$

b. The decrease in the earnings per share from $5.60 to $5.45 indicates an unfavorable change in the company's profitability.

Need more help? Watch step-by-step videos of how to compute answers to these Exercises in CengageNOWv2.

Problem

Feb.	3	Treasury Stock	65,000	
		Cash		65,000
May	1	Cash Dividends	21,250	
		Cash Dividends Payable		21,250
		(10,000 × $1) + [(40,000 − 2,500) × $0.30].		
June	15	Cash Dividends Payable	21,250	
		Cash		21,250
Sept.	23	Cash	28,000	
		Treasury Stock		26,000
		Paid-In Capital from Sale of Treasury Stock		2,000
Nov.	1	Cash Dividends	21,550	
		Cash Dividends Payable		21,550
		(10,000 × $1) + [(40,000 − 1,500) × $0.30].		
	1	Stock Dividends	57,750*	
		Stock Dividends Distributable		38,500
		Paid-In Capital in Excess of		
		Par—Common Stock		19,250
		*(40,000 − 1,500) × 5% × $30.		
Dec.	1	Cash Dividends Payable	21,550	
		Stock Dividends Distributable	38,500	
		Cash		21,550
		Common Stock		38,500

Discussion Questions

1. Of two corporations organized at approximately the same time and engaged in competing businesses, one issued $80 par common stock, and the other issued $1 par common stock. Do the par designations provide any indication as to which stock is preferable as an investment? Explain.

2. A stockbroker advises a client to buy preferred stock, saying "With that type of stock, you will never have to worry about losing the dividends." Is the broker right?

3. A corporation with both preferred stock and common stock outstanding has a substantial credit balance in its retained earnings account at the beginning of the current fiscal year. Although net income for the current year is sufficient to pay the preferred dividend of $150,000 each quarter and a common dividend of $90,000 each quarter, the board of directors declares dividends only on the preferred stock. Suggest possible reasons for not paying dividends on the common stock.

4. An owner of 2,500 shares of Simmons Company common stock receives a stock dividend of 50 shares.

   a. What is the effect of the stock dividend on the stockholder's proportionate interest (equity) in the corporation?

   b. How does the total equity of 2,550 shares compare with the total equity of 2,500 shares before the stock dividend?

5. a. Where should a declared but unpaid cash dividend be reported on the balance sheet?

   b. Where should a declared but unissued stock dividend be reported on the balance sheet?

6. What is the primary purpose of a stock split?

7. A corporation reacquires 60,000 shares of its own $10 par common stock for $3,000,000, recording it at cost.

   a. What effect does this transaction have on revenue or expense of the period?

   b. What effect does it have on stockholders' equity?

8. The treasury stock in Discussion Question 7 is resold for $3,750,000.

   a. What is the effect on the corporation's revenue of the period?

   b. What is the effect on stockholders' equity?

9. What are the three classifications of restrictions of retained earnings, and how are such restrictions normally reported on the financial statements?

10. Indicate how prior period adjustments would be reported on the financial statements presented only for the current period.

Basic Exercises

SHOW ME HOW

BE 12-1 Dividends per share Obj. 2

Zero Calories Company has 15,000 shares of cumulative preferred 1% stock, $50 par and 100,000 shares of $10 par common stock. The following amounts were distributed as dividends:

20Y1	$ 28,500
20Y2	6,000
20Y3	110,000

Determine the dividends per share for preferred and common stock for each year.

SHOW ME HOW

BE 12-2 Entries for issuing stock Obj. 2

On January 22, Zentric Corporation issued for cash 160,000 shares of no-par common stock at $8. On February 14, Zentric issued at par value 45,000 shares of preferred 2% stock, $50 par for cash. On August 30, Zentric issued for cash 10,000 shares of preferred 2% stock, $50 par at $56.

Journalize the entries to record the January 22, February 14, and August 30 transactions.

SHOW ME HOW

BE 12-3 Entries for cash dividends Obj. 3

The declaration, record, and payment dates in connection with a cash dividend of $375,000 on a corporation's common stock are October 1, November 7, and December 15. Journalize the entries required on each date.

SHOW ME HOW

BE 12-4 Entries for stock dividends
Obj. 3

Alpine Energy Corporation has 1,500,000 shares of $10 par common stock outstanding. On August 2, Alpine Energy declared a 5% stock dividend to be issued October 8 to stockholders of record on September 15. The market price of the stock was $60 per share on August 2.

Journalize the entries required on August 2, September 15, and October 8.

SHOW ME HOW

BE 12-5 Entries for treasury stock
Obj. 5

On May 27, Hydro Clothing Inc. reacquired 65,000 shares of its common stock at $6 per share. On August 3, Hydro Clothing sold 48,000 of the reacquired shares at $9 per share. On November 14, Hydro Clothing sold the remaining shares at $5 per share.

Journalize the transactions of May 27, August 3, and November 14.

SHOW ME HOW

BE 12-6 Reporting stockholders' equity
Obj. 6

Using the following accounts and balances, prepare the "Stockholders' Equity" section of the balance sheet. Five hundred thousand shares of common stock are authorized, and 40,000 shares have been reacquired.

Common Stock, $120 par	$48,000,000
Paid-In Capital from Sale of Treasury Stock	4,500,000
Paid-In Capital in Excess of Par—Common Stock	6,400,000
Retained Earnings	63,680,000
Treasury Stock	5,200,000

SHOW ME HOW

BE 12-7 Statement of stockholders' equity
Obj. 6

Noric Cruises Inc. began the month of October with the following balances: Common Stock, $150,000; Additional Paid-In Capital, $3,225,000; and Retained Earnings, $12,400,000. During June, Noric issued for cash 50,000 shares of common stock (with a stated value of $1) at $16 per share. Noric reported the following results for the month ended October 31:

Net income	$2,350,000
Cash dividends declared	475,000

Prepare a statement of stockholders' equity for the month ended October 31.

SHOW ME HOW

BE 12-8 Earnings per share
Obj. 7

Financial statement data for the years 20Y5 and 20Y6 for Black Bull Inc. follow:

	20Y6	**20Y5**
Net income	$2,485,700	$1,538,000
Preferred dividends	$50,000	$50,000
Average number of common shares outstanding	115,000 shares	80,000 shares

a. Determine the earnings per share for 20Y5 and 20Y6.

b. Is the change in the earnings per share from 20Y5 to 20Y6 favorable or unfavorable?

Exercises

✔ Preferred stock,
1st year: $0.85

SHOW ME HOW

EXCEL TEMPLATE

EX 12-1 Dividends per share
Obj. 2

Seventy-Two Inc., a developer of radiology equipment, has stock outstanding as follows: 60,000 shares of cumulative preferred 2% stock, $60 par and 300,000 shares of $20 par common. During its first four years of operations, the following amounts were distributed as dividends: first year, $51,000; second year, $105,000; third year, $81,000; fourth year, $120,000. Determine the dividends per share on each class of stock for each of the four years.

✔ Preferred stock,
1st year: $0.90

EX 12-2 Dividends per share
Obj. 2

Lightfoot Inc., a software development firm, has stock outstanding as follows: 40,000 shares of cumulative preferred 1% stock, $125 par and 100,000 shares of $150 par common. During its first four years of operations, the following amounts were distributed as dividends: first year, $36,000;

second year, $58,000; third year, $75,000; fourth year, $124,000. Determine the dividends per share on each class of stock for each of the four years.

SHOW ME HOW

EX 12-3   Entries for issuing par stock

Obj. 2

On January 22, Jefferson County Rocks Inc., a marble contractor, issued for cash 210,000 shares of $30 par common stock at $34, and on February 27, it issued for cash 15,000 shares of preferred stock, $9 par at $12.

a. Journalize the entries for January 22 and February 27.

b. What is the total amount invested (total paid-in capital) by all stockholders as of February 27?

SHOW ME HOW

EX 12-4   Entries for issuing no-par stock

Obj. 2

On May 15, Helena Carpet Inc., a carpet wholesaler, issued for cash 750,000 shares of no-par common stock (with a stated value of $1.50) at $4, and on June 30, it issued for cash 17,500 shares of preferred stock, $50 par at $60.

a. Journalize the entries for May 15 and June 30, assuming that the common stock is to be credited with the stated value.

b. What is the total amount invested (total paid-in capital) by all stockholders as of June 30?

SHOW ME HOW

EX 12-5   Issuing stock for assets other than cash

Obj. 2

On November 23, Elder Lift Corporation, a wholesaler of hydraulic lifts, acquired land in exchange for 14,200 shares of $25 par common stock with a current market price of $34. Journalize the entry to record the transaction.

EX 12-6   Selected stock transactions

Obj. 2

Alpha Sounds Corp., an electric guitar retailer, was organized by Michele Kirby, Paul Glenn, and Gretchen Northway. The charter authorized 1,000,000 shares of common stock with a par of $1. The following transactions affecting stockholders' equity were completed during the first year of operations:

a. Issued 100,000 shares of stock at par to Paul Glenn for cash.

b. Issued 3,000 shares of stock at par to Michele Kirby for promotional services provided in connection with the organization of the corporation, and issued 45,000 shares of stock at par to Michele Kirby for cash.

c. Purchased land and a building from Gretchen Northway in exchange for stock issued at par. The building is mortgaged for $180,000 for 20 years at 6%, and there is accrued interest of $5,200 on the mortgage note at the time of the purchase. The corporation agreed to assume responsibility for paying the mortgage note and accrued interest. It is agreed that the land is to be valued at $60,000 and the building at $225,000 and that Gretchen Northway will be issued stock at par.

Journalize the entries to record the transactions.

EX 12-7   Issuing stock

Obj. 2

Willow Creek Nursery, with an authorization of 75,000 shares of preferred stock and 200,000 shares of common stock, completed several transactions involving its stock on October 1, the first day of operations. The trial balance at the close of the day follows:

Cash	3,780,000	
Land	840,000	
Buildings	2,380,000	
Preferred 1% Stock, $80 par		2,800,000
Paid-In Capital in Excess of Par—Preferred Stock		420,000
Common Stock, $30 par		3,600,000
Paid-In Capital in Excess of Par—Common Stock		180,000
	7,000,000	7,000,000

All shares within each class of stock were sold at the same price. The preferred stock was issued in exchange for the land and buildings.

Journalize the two entries to record the transactions summarized in the trial balance.

SHOW ME HOW

EX 12-8 Issuing stock
Obj. 2

Professional Products Inc., a wholesaler of office products, was organized on February 5 of the current year, with an authorization of 50,000 shares of preferred 2% stock, $60 par and 1,000,000 shares of $8 par common stock. The following selected transactions were completed during the first year of operations:

Feb. 5. Issued 700,000 shares of common stock at par for cash.

5. Issued 1,200 shares of common stock at par to an attorney in payment of legal fees for organizing the corporation.

Apr. 9. Issued 40,000 shares of common stock in exchange for land, buildings, and equipment with fair market prices of $120,000, $280,000, and $80,000, respectively.

June 14. Issued 25,000 shares of preferred stock at $82 for cash.

Journalize the transactions.

SHOW ME HOW

EX 12-9 Entries for cash dividends
Obj. 3

The declaration, record, and payment dates in connection with a cash dividend of $1,425,000 on a corporation's common stock are July 9, August 31, and October 1. Journalize the entries required on each date.

✔ b. (1) $42,000,000
(3) $131,550,000

SHOW ME HOW

EX 12-10 Entries for stock dividends
Obj. 3

Healthy Life Co. is an HMO for businesses in the Fresno area. The following account balances appear on Healthy Life's balance sheet: Common stock (3,000,000 shares authorized; 2,200,000 shares issued), $15 par, $33,000,000; Paid-in capital in excess of par—common stock, $9,000,000; and Retained earnings, $89,550,000. The board of directors declared a 5% stock dividend when the market price of the stock was $18 a share. Healthy Life reported no income or loss for the current year.

a. Journalize the entries to record (1) the declaration of the dividend, capitalizing an amount equal to market value, and (2) the issuance of the stock certificates.

b. Determine the following amounts before the stock dividend was declared: (1) total paid-in capital, (2) total retained earnings, and (3) total stockholders' equity.

c. Determine the following amounts after the stock dividend was declared and closing entries were recorded at the end of the year: (1) total paid-in capital, (2) total retained earnings, and (3) total stockholders' equity.

SHOW ME HOW

EX 12-11 Effect of stock split
Obj. 4

Willey's Grill & Restaurant Corporation wholesales ovens and ranges to restaurants throughout the Southwest. Willey's Grill & Restaurant, which had 325,000 shares of common stock outstanding, declared a 3-for-1 stock split.

a. What will be the number of shares outstanding after the split?

b. If the common stock had a market price of $450 per share before the stock split, what would be an approximate market price per share after the split?

EX 12-12 Effect of cash dividend and stock split
Obj. 3, 4

Indicate whether the following actions would (+) increase, (–) decrease, or (0) not affect Indigo Inc.'s total assets, liabilities, and stockholders' equity:

	Assets	Liabilities	Stockholders' Equity
a. Authorizing and issuing stock certificates in a stock split			
b. Declaring a stock dividend			
c. Issuing stock certificates for the stock dividend declared in (b)			
d. Declaring a cash dividend			
e. Paying the cash dividend declared in (d)			

EX 12-13 Selected dividend transactions, stock split
Obj. 3, 4

Selected transactions completed by Canyon Ferry Boating Corporation during the current fiscal year are as follows:

Jan. 8. Split the common stock 2 for 1 and reduced the par from $100 to $50 per share. After the split, there were 300,000 common shares outstanding.

Apr. 30. Declared semiannual dividends of $0.60 per share on 16,000 shares of preferred stock and $0.22 per share on the common stock payable on July 1.

July 1. Paid the cash dividends.

Oct. 31. Declared semiannual dividends of $0.60 per share on the preferred stock and $0.11 per share on the common stock (before the stock dividend). In addition, a 5% common stock dividend was declared on the common stock outstanding. The fair market value of the common stock is estimated at $56.

Dec. 31. Paid the cash dividends and issued the certificates for the common stock dividend.

Journalize the transactions.

EX 12-14 Treasury stock transactions   Obj. 5

✔ b. $375,000 credit

SHOW ME HOW

Mystic Lake Inc. bottles and distributes spring water. On July 9 of the current year, Mystic Lake reacquired 60,000 shares of its common stock at $42 per share. On September 22, Mystic Lake sold 45,000 of the reacquired shares at $51 per share. The remaining 15,000 shares were sold at $40 per share on November 23.

a. Journalize the transactions of July 9, September 22, and November 23.

b. What is the balance in Paid-In Capital from Sale of Treasury Stock on December 31 of the current year?

c. ➤ For what reasons might Mystic Lake Inc. have purchased the treasury stock?

EX 12-15 Treasury stock transactions   Obj. 5, 6

✔ b. $454,500 credit

SHOW ME HOW

SprayCo Inc. develops and produces spraying equipment for lawn maintenance and industrial uses. On March 9 of the current year, SprayCo reacquired 62,000 shares of its common stock at $51 per share. On June 9, 48,000 of the reacquired shares were sold at $60 per share, and on November 13, 7,500 of the reacquired shares were sold at $54.

a. Journalize the transactions of March 9, June 9, and November 13.

b. What is the balance in Paid-In Capital from Sale of Treasury Stock on December 31 of the current year?

c. What is the balance in Treasury Stock on December 31 of the current year?

d. How will the balance in Treasury Stock be reported on the balance sheet?

EX 12-16 Treasury stock transactions   Obj. 5, 6

✔ b. $55,500 credit

Biscayne Bay Water Inc. bottles and distributes spring water. On May 14 of the current year, Biscayne Bay Water reacquired 23,500 shares of its common stock at $75 per share. On September 6, Biscayne Bay Water sold 14,000 of the reacquired shares at $81 per share. The remaining 9,500 shares were sold at $72 per share on November 30.

a. Journalize the transactions of May 14, September 6, and November 30.

b. What is the balance in Paid-In Capital from Sale of Treasury Stock on December 31 of the current year?

c. Where will the balance in Paid-In Capital from Sale of Treasury Stock be reported on the balance sheet?

d. ➤ For what reasons might Biscayne Bay Water Inc. have purchased the treasury stock?

EX 12-17 Reporting paid-in capital   Obj. 6

✔ Total paid-in capital, $13,615,000

The following accounts and their balances were selected from the adjusted trial balance of Point Loma Group Inc., a freight forwarder, at October 31, the end of the current fiscal year:

Common Stock, no par, $14 stated value	$ 4,480,000
Paid-In Capital from Sale of Treasury Stock	45,000
Paid-In Capital in Excess of Par—Preferred Stock	210,000
Paid-In Capital in Excess of Stated Value—Common Stock	480,000
Preferred 2% Stock, $120 par	8,400,000
Retained Earnings	39,500,000

Prepare the Paid-in capital portion of the "Stockholders' Equity" section of the balance sheet using Method 1 of Exhibit 9. There are 375,000 shares of common stock authorized and 85,000 shares of preferred stock authorized.

EX 12-18 "Stockholders' Equity" section of balance sheet

Obj. 6

✔ Total stockholders' equity, $23,676,000

The following accounts and their balances appear in the ledger of Goodale Properties Inc. on June 30 of the current year:

Common Stock, $45 par	$ 3,060,000
Paid-In Capital from Sale of Treasury Stock	115,000
Paid-In Capital in Excess of Par—Common Stock	272,000
Retained Earnings	20,553,000
Treasury Stock	324,000

Prepare the "Stockholders' Equity" section of the balance sheet as of June 30. Eighty thousand shares of common stock are authorized, and 9,000 shares have been reacquired.

EX 12-19 "Stockholders' Equity" section of balance sheet

Obj. 6

✔ Total stockholders' equity, $89,100,000

Specialty Auto Racing Inc. retails racing products for BMWs, Porsches, and Ferraris. The following accounts and their balances appear in the ledger of Specialty Auto Racing on July 31, the end of the current year:

Common Stock, $36 par	$10,080,000
Paid-In Capital from Sale of Treasury Stock—Common	340,000
Paid-In Capital in Excess of Par—Common Stock	420,000
Paid-In Capital in Excess of Par—Preferred Stock	384,000
Preferred 1% Stock, $150 par	7,200,000
Retained Earnings	71,684,000
Treasury Stock—Common	1,008,000

Fifty thousand shares of preferred and 300,000 shares of common stock are authorized. There are 24,000 shares of common stock held as treasury stock.

Prepare the "Stockholders' Equity" section of the balance sheet as of July 31, the end of the current year, using Method 1 of Exhibit 9.

EX 12-20 Retained earnings statement

Obj. 6

✔ Retained earnings, December 31, $64,210,000

SHOW ME HOW

Sumter Pumps Corporation, a manufacturer of industrial pumps, reports the following results for the year ended December 31, 20Y3:

Retained earnings, January 1, 20Y3	$59,650,000
Net income	8,160,000
Cash dividends declared	1,000,000
Stock dividends declared	2,600,000

Prepare a retained earnings statement for the year ended December 31, 20Y3.

EX 12-21 "Stockholders' Equity" section of balance sheet

Obj. 6

✔ Corrected total stockholders' equity, $122,800,000

List the errors in the following "Stockholders' Equity" section of the balance sheet prepared as of the end of the current year:

Stockholders' Equity

Paid-in capital:		
Preferred 2% stock, $80 par (125,000 shares authorized and issued)	$10,000,000	
Excess of issue price over par	500,000	
Paid-in capital, preferred stock		$ 10,500,000
Retained earnings		96,700,000
Treasury stock (75,000 shares at cost)		1,755,000
Dividends payable		430,000
Total paid-in capital		$ 109,385,000
Common stock, $20 par (1,000,000 shares authorized, 825,000 shares issued)		17,655,000
Organizing costs		300,000
Total stockholders' equity		$127,340,000

EX 12-22 Statement of stockholders' equity

Obj. 6

✔ Total stockholders' equity, Dec. 31, $21,587,000

EXCEL TEMPLATE

The stockholders' equity T accounts of I-Cards Inc. for the year ended December 31, 20Y9, are as follows. Prepare a statement of stockholders' equity for the year ended December 31, 20Y9.

Common Stock

	Jan. 1	Balance	4,800,000
	Apr. 14	Issued	
		30,000 shares	1,200,000
	Dec. 31	Balance	6,000,000

Paid-In Capital in Excess of Par

	Jan. 1	Balance	960,000
	Apr. 14	Issued	
		30,000 shares	300,000
	Dec. 31	Balance	1,260,000

Treasury Stock

Aug. 7	Purchased		
	12,000 shares	552,000	

Retained Earnings

Mar. 31	Dividend	69,000	Jan. 1	Balance	11,375,000
June 30	Dividend	69,000	Dec. 31	Closing	
Sept. 30	Dividend	69,000		(net income)	3,780,000
Dec. 31	Dividend	69,000			
			Dec. 31	Balance	14,879,000

Problems: Series A

PR 12-1A Dividends on preferred and common stock

Obj. 2

✔ 1. Common dividends in 20Y3: $20,000

SHOW ME HOW

EXCEL TEMPLATE

Pecan Theatre Inc. owns and operates movie theaters throughout Florida and Georgia. Pecan Theatre has declared the following annual dividends over a six-year period: 20Y1, $80,000; 20Y2, $90,000; 20Y3, $150,000; 20Y4, $150,000; 20Y5, $160,000; and 20Y6, $180,000. During the entire period ended December 31 of each year, the outstanding stock of the company was composed of 250,000 shares of cumulative, preferred 2% stock, $20 par, and 500,000 shares of common stock, $15 par.

Instructions

1. Determine the total dividends and the per-share dividends declared on each class of stock for each of the six years. There were no dividends in arrears at the beginning of 20Y1. Summarize the data in tabular form, using the following column headings:

Year	Total Dividends	Preferred Dividends Total	Preferred Dividends Per Share	Common Dividends Total	Common Dividends Per Share
20Y1	$ 80,000				
20Y2	90,000				
20Y3	150,000				
20Y4	150,000				
20Y5	160,000				
20Y6	180,000				

2. Determine the average annual dividend per share for each class of stock for the six-year period.

3. Assuming a market price per share of $25.00 for the preferred stock and $17.50 for the common stock, determine the average annual percentage return on initial shareholders' investment, based on the average annual dividend per share (a) for preferred stock and (b) for common stock.

PR 12-2A   Stock transactions for corporate expansion

Obj. 2

On December 1 of the current year, the following accounts and their balances appear in the ledger of Latte Corp., a coffee processor:

Preferred 2% Stock, $50 par (250,000 shares authorized, 80,000 shares issued)	$ 4,000,000
Paid-In Capital in Excess of Par—Preferred Stock	560,000
Common Stock, $35 par (1,000,000 shares authorized, 400,000 shares issued)........	14,000,000
Paid-In Capital in Excess of Par—Common Stock	1,200,000
Retained Earnings...	180,000,000

At the annual stockholders' meeting on March 31, the board of directors presented a plan for modernizing and expanding plant operations at a cost of approximately $11,000,000. The plan provided (a) that a building, valued at $3,375,000, and the land on which it is located, valued at $1,500,000, be acquired in accordance with preliminary negotiations by the issuance of 125,000 shares of common stock, (b) that 40,000 shares of the unissued preferred stock be issued through an underwriter, and (c) that the corporation borrow $4,000,000. The plan was approved by the stockholders and accomplished by the following transactions:

May 11.   Issued 125,000 shares of common stock in exchange for land and a building, according to the plan.
   20.   Issued 40,000 shares of preferred stock, receiving $52 per share in cash.
   31.   Borrowed $4,000,000 from Laurel National, giving a 5% mortgage note.

Instructions

Journalize the entries to record the May transactions.

PR 12-3A   Selected stock transactions

Obj. 2, 3, 5

✔ f. Cash dividends, $443,200

SHOW ME HOW

The following selected accounts appear in the ledger of Parks Construction Inc. at the beginning of the current year:

Preferred 2% Stock, $100 par (100,000 shares authorized, 80,000 shares issued).......	$ 8,000,000
Paid-In Capital in Excess of Par—Preferred Stock.....................................	440,000
Common Stock, $5 par (5,000,000 shares authorized, 4,000,000 shares issued)........	20,000,000
Paid-In Capital in Excess of Par—Common Stock.....................................	2,280,000
Retained Earnings	115,400,000

During the year, the corporation completed a number of transactions affecting the stockholders' equity. They are summarized as follows:

a.   Issued 200,000 shares of common stock at $12, receiving cash.
b.   Issued 8,000 shares of preferred 2% stock at $115.
c.   Purchased 175,000 shares of treasury common for $10 per share.
d.   Sold 110,000 shares of treasury common for $14 per share.
e.   Sold 30,000 shares of treasury common for $8 per share.
f.   Declared cash dividends of $1.25 per share on preferred stock and $0.08 per share on common stock.
g.   Paid the cash dividends.

Instructions

Journalize the entries to record the transactions. Identify each entry by letter.

PR 12-4A   Entries for selected corporate transactions

Obj. 2, 3, 4, 6

✔ 4. Total stockholders' equity, $44,436,200

EXCEL TEMPLATE

Morrow Enterprises Inc. manufactures bathroom fixtures. Morrow Enterprises' stockholders' equity accounts, with balances on January 1, 20Y6, are as follows:

Common Stock, $20 stated value (500,000 shares authorized, 375,000 shares issued)......	$ 7,500,000
Paid-In Capital in Excess of Stated Value—Common Stock..............................	825,000
Retained Earnings	33,600,000
Treasury Stock (25,000 shares, at cost)	450,000

The following selected transactions occurred during the year:

Jan. 22.   Paid cash dividends of $0.08 per share on the common stock. The dividend had been properly recorded when declared on December 1 of the preceding fiscal year for $28,000.
Apr. 10.   Issued 75,000 shares of common stock for $24 per share.
June 6.   Sold all of the treasury stock for $26 per share.
July 5.   Declared a 4% stock dividend on common stock, to be capitalized at the market price of the stock, which is $25 per share.

Aug. 15. Issued shares of stock for the stock dividend declared on July 5.

Nov. 23. Purchased 30,000 shares of treasury stock for $19 per share.

Dec. 28. Declared a $0.10-per-share dividend on common stock.

  31. Closed the two dividends accounts to Retained Earnings.

Instructions

1. Enter the January 1 balances in T accounts for the stockholders' equity accounts listed. Also prepare T accounts for the following: Paid-In Capital from Sale of Treasury Stock; Stock Dividends Distributable; Stock Dividends; Cash Dividends.

2. Journalize the entries to record the transactions, and post to the eight selected accounts. Assume that the closing entry for revenues and expenses has been made and post net income of $1,125,000 to the retained earnings account.

3. Prepare a statement of stockholders' equity for the year ended December 31, 20Y6. Assume that net income was $1,125,000 for the year ended December 31, 20Y6.

4. Prepare the "Stockholders' Equity" section of the December 31, 20Y6, balance sheet.

PR 12-5A Entries for selected corporate transactions   Obj. 2, 3, 4, 5

✔ Oct. 1, cash dividends, $202,800

Selected transactions completed by Primo Discount Corporation during the current fiscal year are as follows:

Jan. 9. Split the common stock 3 for 1 and reduced the par from $75 to $25 per share. After the split, there were 1,200,000 common shares outstanding.

Feb. 28. Purchased 40,000 shares of the corporation's own common stock at $28, recording the stock at cost.

May 1. Declared semiannual dividends of $0.80 per share on 75,000 shares of preferred stock and $0.12 per share on the common stock to stockholders of record on June 1, payable on July 10.

July 10. Paid the cash dividends.

Sept. 7. Sold 30,000 shares of treasury stock at $34, receiving cash.

Oct. 1. Declared semiannual dividends of $0.80 per share on the preferred stock and $0.12 per share on the common stock (before the stock dividend). In addition, a 2% common stock dividend was declared on the common stock outstanding. The fair market value of the common stock is estimated at $36.

Dec. 1. Paid the cash dividends and issued the certificates for the common stock dividend.

Instructions

Journalize the transactions.

Problems: Series B

PR 12-1B Dividends on preferred and common stock   Obj. 2

✔ 1. Common dividends in 20Y3: $25,000

SHOW ME HOW   EXCEL TEMPLATE

Yosemite Bike Corp. manufactures mountain bikes and distributes them through retail outlets in California, Oregon, and Washington. Yosemite Bike has declared the following annual dividends over a six-year period ended December 31 of each year: 20Y1, $24,000; 20Y2, $10,000; 20Y3, $126,000; 20Y4, $100,000; 20Y5, $125,000; and 20Y6, $125,000. During the entire period, the outstanding stock of the company was composed of 25,000 shares of cumulative preferred 2% stock, $90 par, and 100,000 shares of common stock, $4 par.

Instructions

1. Determine the total dividends and the per-share dividends declared on each class of stock for each of the six years. There were no dividends in arrears at the beginning of 20Y1. Summarize the data in tabular form, using the following column headings:

Year	Total Dividends	Preferred Dividends Total	Per Share	Common Dividends Total	Per Share
20Y1	$ 24,000				
20Y2	10,000				
20Y3	126,000				
20Y4	100,000				
20Y5	125,000				
20Y6	125,000				

(Continued)

2. Determine the average annual dividend per share for each class of stock for the six-year period.

3. Assuming a market price of $100 for the preferred stock and $5 for the common stock, determine the average annual percentage return on initial shareholders' investment, based on the average annual dividend per share (a) for preferred stock and (b) for common stock.

PR 12-2B   Stock transaction for corporate expansion

Obj. 2

Pulsar Optics produces medical lasers for use in hospitals. The accounts and their balances appear in the ledger of Pulsar Optics on April 30 of the current year as follows:

Preferred 1% Stock, $120 par (300,000 shares authorized, 36,000 shares issued)	$ 4,320,000
Paid-In Capital in Excess of Par—Preferred Stock	180,000
Common Stock, $15 par (2,000,000 shares authorized, 1,400,000 shares issued)	21,000,000
Paid-In Capital in Excess of Par—Common Stock	3,500,000
Retained Earnings	78,000,000

At the annual stockholders' meeting on August 5, the board of directors presented a plan for modernizing and expanding plant operations at a cost of approximately $9,000,000. The plan provided (a) that the corporation borrow $1,500,000, (b) that 20,000 shares of the unissued preferred stock be issued through an underwriter, and (c) that a building, valued at $4,150,000, and the land on which it is located, valued at $800,000, be acquired in accordance with preliminary negotiations by the issuance of 300,000 shares of common stock. The plan was approved by the stockholders and accomplished by the following transactions:

Oct. 9.   Borrowed $1,500,000 from St. Peter City Bank, giving a 4% mortgage note.

17.   Issued 20,000 shares of preferred stock, receiving $126 per share in cash.

28.   Issued 300,000 shares of common stock in exchange for land and a building, according to the plan.

Instructions

Journalize the entries to record the October transactions.

✔ f. Cash dividends,
$234,775

SHOW ME HOW

PR 12-3B   Selected stock transactions

Obj. 2, 3, 5

Diamondback Welding & Fabrication Corporation sells and services pipe welding equipment in Illinois. The following selected accounts appear in the ledger of Diamondback Welding & Fabrication at the beginning of the current year:

Preferred 2% Stock, $80 par (100,000 shares authorized, 60,000 shares issued)	$ 4,800,000
Paid-In Capital in Excess of Par—Preferred Stock	210,000
Common Stock, $9 par (3,000,000 shares authorized, 1,750,000 shares issued)	15,750,000
Paid-In Capital in Excess of Par—Common Stock	1,400,000
Retained Earnings	52,840,000

During the year, the corporation completed a number of transactions affecting the stockholders' equity. They are summarized as follows:

a.   Purchased 87,500 shares of treasury common for $8 per share.

b.   Sold 55,000 shares of treasury common for $11 per share.

c.   Issued 20,000 shares of preferred 2% stock at $84.

d.   Issued 400,000 shares of common stock at $13, receiving cash.

e.   Sold 18,000 shares of treasury common for $7.50 per share.

f.   Declared cash dividends of $1.60 per share on preferred stock and $0.05 per share on common stock.

g.   Paid the cash dividends.

Instructions

Journalize the entries to record the transactions. Identify each entry by letter.

✔ 4. Total
stockholders' equity,
$11,262,432

EXCEL TEMPLATE

PR 12-4B   Entries for selected corporate transactions

Obj. 2, 3, 4, 6

Nav-Go Enterprises Inc. produces aeronautical navigation equipment. Navo-Go Enterprises' stockholders' equity accounts, with balances on January 1, 20Y1, are as follows:

Common Stock, $5 stated value (900,000 shares authorized, 620,000 shares issued)	$3,100,000
Paid-In Capital in Excess of Stated Value—Common Stock	1,240,000
Retained Earnings	4,875,000
Treasury Stock (48,000 shares, at cost)	288,000

The following selected transactions occurred during the year:

Jan. 15. Paid cash dividends of $0.06 per share on the common stock. The dividend had been properly recorded when declared on December 1 of the preceding fiscal year for $34,320.

Mar. 15. Sold all of the treasury stock for $6.75 per share.

Apr. 13. Issued 200,000 shares of common stock for $8 per share.

June 14. Declared a 3% stock dividend on common stock, to be capitalized at the market price of the stock, which is $7.50 per share.

July 16. Issued stock for stock dividend declared on June 14.

Oct. 30. Purchased 50,000 shares of treasury stock for $6 per share.

Dec. 30. Declared an $0.08-per-share dividend on common stock.

　31. Closed the two dividends accounts to Retained Earnings.

Instructions

1. Enter the January 1 balances in T accounts for the stockholders' equity accounts listed. Also prepare T accounts for the following: Paid-In Capital from Sale of Treasury Stock; Stock Dividends Distributable; Stock Dividends; Cash Dividends.

2. Journalize the entries to record the transactions, and post to the eight selected accounts. Assume that the closing entry for revenues and expenses has been made and post net income of $775,000 to the retained earnings account.

3. Prepare a statement of stockholders' equity for the year ended December 31, 20Y1. Assume that net income was $775,000 for the year ended December 31, 20Y1.

4. Prepare the "Stockholders' Equity" section of the December 31, 20Y1, balance sheet.

PR 12-5B　Entries for selected corporate transactions　　　　　　　Obj. 2, 3, 4, 5

✔ Sept. 1, Cash dividends, $95,200

West Yellowstone Outfitters Corporation manufactures and distributes leisure clothing. Selected transactions completed by West Yellowstone Outfitters during the current fiscal year are as follows:

Jan. 15. Split the common stock 4 for 1 and reduced the par from $120 to $30 per share. After the split, there were 800,000 common shares outstanding.

Mar. 1. Declared semiannual dividends of $0.25 per share on 100,000 shares of preferred stock and $0.07 per share on the 800,000 shares of $30 par common stock to stockholders of record on March 31, payable on April 30.

Apr. 30. Paid the cash dividends.

May 31. Purchased 60,000 shares of the corporation's own common stock at $32, recording the stock at cost.

Aug. 17. Sold 40,000 shares of treasury stock at $38, receiving cash.

Sept. 1. Declared semiannual dividends of $0.25 per share on the preferred stock and $0.09 per share on the common stock (before the stock dividend). In addition, a 1% common stock dividend was declared on the common stock outstanding, to be capitalized at the fair market value of the common stock, which is estimated at $40.

Oct. 31. Paid the cash dividends and issued the certificates for the common stock dividend.

Instructions

Journalize the transactions.

Comprehensive Problem 4

✔ 2. c. Total assets, $13,500,000

Selected transactions completed by Equinox Products Inc. during the fiscal year ended December 31, 20Y8, were as follows:

a. Issued 15,000 shares of $20 par common stock at $30, receiving cash.

b. Issued 4,000 shares of $80 par preferred 5% stock at $100, receiving cash.

c. Issued $500,000 of 10-year, 5% bonds at 104, with interest payable semiannually.

d. Declared a quarterly dividend of $0.50 per share on common stock and $1.00 per share on preferred stock. On the date of record, 100,000 shares of common stock were outstanding, no treasury shares were held, and 20,000 shares of preferred stock were outstanding.

e. Paid the cash dividends declared in (d).

f. Purchased 8,000 shares of treasury common stock at $33 per share.

g. Declared a $1.00 quarterly cash dividend per share on preferred stock. On the date of record, 20,000 shares of preferred stock had been issued.

(Continued)

h. Paid the cash dividends to the preferred stockholders.

i. Sold, at $38 per share, 2,600 shares of treasury common stock purchased in (f).

j. Recorded the payment of semiannual interest on the bonds issued in (c) and the amortization of the premium for six months. The amortization is determined using the straight-line method.

Instructions

1. Journalize the selected transactions.

2. The data that follow were taken from the records of Equinox Products Inc. Unless otherwise stated, assume a December 31 balance after adjusting entries.

Income statement data:	
Advertising expense	$ 150,000
Cost of goods sold	3,700,000
Delivery expense	30,000
Depreciation expense—office buildings and equipment	30,000
Depreciation expense—store buildings and equipment	100,000
Income tax expense	140,500
Interest expense	21,000
Interest revenue	30,000
Miscellaneous administrative expense	7,500
Miscellaneous selling expense	14,000
Office rent expense	50,000
Office salaries expense	170,000
Office supplies expense	10,000
Sales	5,313,000
Sales commissions	185,000
Sales salaries expense	385,000
Store supplies expense	21,000

Retained earnings and balance sheet data:	
Accounts payable	$ 194,300
Accounts receivable	545,000
Accumulated depreciation—office buildings and equipment	1,580,000
Accumulated depreciation—store buildings and equipment	4,126,000
Allowance for doubtful accounts	8,450
Bonds payable, 5%, due in 10 years	500,000
Cash	282,850
Common stock, $20 par (400,000 shares authorized; 85,000 shares issued, 94,600 outstanding), January 1, 20Y8	1,700,000
Dividends:	
Cash dividends for common stock	155,120
Cash dividends for preferred stock	100,000
Goodwill	700,000
Income tax payable	44,000
Interest receivable	1,200
Inventory (December 31, 20Y8), at lower of cost (FIFO) or market	778,000
Office buildings and equipment	4,320,000
Paid-in capital from sale of treasury stock, January 1, 20Y8	0
Paid-in capital in excess of par—common stock, January 1, 20Y8	736,800
Paid-in capital in excess of par—preferred stock, January 1, 20Y8	70,000
Preferred 5% stock, $80 par (30,000 shares authorized; 16,000 shares issued), January 1, 20Y8	1,280,000
Premium on bonds payable	19,000
Prepaid expenses	27,400
Retained earnings, January 1, 20Y8	8,197,220
Store buildings and equipment	12,560,000
Treasury stock, January 1, 20Y8	0

a. Prepare a multiple-step income statement for the year ended December 31, 20Y8.

b. Prepare a statement of stockholders' equity for the year ended December 31, 20Y8.

c. Prepare a balance sheet in report form as of December 31, 20Y8.

Make a Decision
Earnings per Share

REAL WORLD

MAD 12-1 Analyze and compare Amazon.com and Wal-Mart   Obj. 7

Amazon.com, Inc. (AMZN) is one of the largest Internet retailers in the world. **Wal-Mart (WMT)** is the largest retailer in the United States. Amazon and Wal-Mart compete in similar markets; however, Wal-Mart sells through both traditional retail stores and the Internet, while Amazon sells only through the Internet. Earnings and common stock outstanding information was obtained from recent financial statements for both companies as follows (in millions):

	Amazon	Wal-Mart
Net income	$2,371	$14,694
Average number of common shares outstanding	474	3,207

a. Determine the earnings per share for each company. Neither company had preferred stock outstanding. Round to the nearest cent.

b. ━━━━▶ Which company appears more profitable from an earnings-per-share perspective?

c. ━━━━▶ The market price of Amazon common stock was $750 per share at a time when Wal-Mart's was $69 per share. How would you explain this difference in market price given the earnings per share computed in (a) for both companies?

REAL WORLD

MAD 12-2 Analyze and compare Bank of America and Wells Fargo   Obj. 7

Bank of America Corporation (BAC) and **Wells Fargo & Company (WFC)** are two large financial services companies. The following data (in millions) were taken from a recent year's financial statements for both companies:

	Bank of America	Wells Fargo
Net income	$17,906	$ 21,938
Preferred dividends	$1,662	$1,565
Average number of common shares outstanding	10,284	5,052.8

a. Compute the earnings per share for both companies. Round to the nearest cent.

b. ━━━━▶ Which company appears to be more profitable on an earnings-per-share basis?

c. ━━━━▶ Which company would you expect to have the larger quoted market price?

REAL WORLD

MAD 12-3 Analyze Pacific Gas and Electric Company   Obj. 7

Pacific Gas and Electric Company (PCG) is a large gas and electric utility operating in northern and central California. Three recent years of financial data for Pacific Gas and Electric are as follows (in millions):

	Year 3	Year 2	Year 1
Net income	$1,407	$888	$1,450
Preferred dividends	$14	$14	$14
Average number of common shares outstanding	499	484	468

a. Determine the earnings per share for Years 1–3. Round to the nearest cent.

b. ━━━━▶ Interpret the trend in earnings per share using horizontal analysis for the three years in terms of the change in earnings and average shares outstanding.

REAL WORLD

MAD 12-4 Analyze Caterpillar   Obj. 7

Caterpillar Inc. (CAT) is the world's leading manufacturer of construction and mining equipment. In addition, **Birinyi Associates** identified Caterpillar as one of the top five companies

(Continued)

to repurchase its own shares in a recent year.[12] Three recent years of earnings and average common shares outstanding data for Caterpillar are as follows (in millions):

	Year 3	Year 2	Year 1
Net income	$2,102	$3,695	$3,789
Average number of common shares outstanding	594.3	617.2	645.2

a. Determine the earnings per share for Years 1–3. Caterpillar had no preferred stock outstanding. Round to the nearest cent.

b. ➡ Interpret the trend in earnings per share using horizontal analysis for the three years in terms of the change in earnings and average shares outstanding.

[12] Laura Lorenzetti, "5 Biggest Share Buybacks of 2014," *Fortune*, May 29, 2014 (online edition).

REAL WORLD

MAD 12-5 Analyze and compare BB&T and Regions Financial Obj. 7

BB&T Corporation (BBT) and **Regions Financial Corporation (RF)** are large regional banking companies. The net income and average common shares outstanding for both companies were reported in recent financial reports as follows (in millions):

	BB&T	Regions Financial
Net income	$2,458	$1,158
Preferred dividends	$167	$64
Average number of common shares outstanding	815	1,255

a. Determine the earnings per share for each company. Round to the nearest cent.

b. ➡ Which company appears more profitable from a total net income perspective?

c. ➡ Which company appears more profitable from an earnings-per-share perspective?

d. ➡ From a stockholder's perspective, is net income or earnings per share the better relative earnings measure between the two banks?

Take It Further

ETHICS

TIF 12-1 Employee purchases of stock

Tommy Gunn is a division manager for K-Cern Inc., a small pharmaceutical company. Tommy's division has been working on a new drug that has the potential to revolutionize the treatment of skin cancer. Once the drug is proven to be effective in clinical trials, it will be approved for sale by the government and patented by the company. Because of the potential market for this drug, it is highly likely that the company's revenues and net income will increase significantly when it is approved. Tommy recently saw an internal company memo indicating that the drug passed its final clinical trial and that the company has received government approval to sell the drug. The company will issue a press release announcing this news in the next two days, and this announcement is expected to result in a dramatic increase in the company's stock price. Tommy knows that there is "free money" to be made if he invests in the stock before the announcement is made. However, K-Cern has a strict policy against employee purchases of company stock outside of established employee stock purchase plans. To get around this rule, Tommy asks his father to purchase the stock for him. The next morning, Tommy's father purchases the stock with the understanding that he will split the profits with Tommy.

➡ Is Tommy behaving ethically? Why or why not?

ETHICS

TIF 12-2 Issuing stock

Lou Hoskins and Shirley Crothers are organizing Red Lodge Metals Unlimited Inc. to under-take a high-risk gold mining venture in Canada. Lou and Shirley tentatively plan to request authorization for 400,000,000 shares of common stock to be sold to the general public. Lou and Shirley have decided to establish par of $0.03 per share in order to appeal to a wide variety of potential investors. Lou and Shirley believe that investors would be more willing to invest in the company if they received a large quantity of shares for what might appear to be a "bargain" price.

 Discuss whether Lou and Shirley are behaving in a professional manner.

TEAM ACTIVITY   REAL WORLD

TIF 12-3 Real-world annual report

In teams, select a public company that interests you. Obtain the company's most recent annual report on Form 10-K. The Form 10-K is a company's annually required filing with the Securities and Exchange Commission (SEC). It includes the company's financial statements and accompany-ing notes. The Form 10-K can be obtained either (a) from the investor relations section of the company's website or (b) by using the company search feature of the SEC's EDGAR database service found at www.sec.gov/edgar/searchedgar/companysearch.html.

Based on the information in the company's most recent annual report, determine the following:

1. Name of the corporation
2. State of incorporation
3. Nature of its operations
4. Total assets reported on the most recent balance sheet
5. Total liabilities reported on the most recent balance sheet
6. Total stockholders' equity reported on the most recent balance sheet
7. Total revenues reported on the most recent income statement
8. Net income reported on the most recent income statement
9. The number of shares of common stock authorized, issued, and outstanding
10. The par value per share of each class of stock
11. Market price of the stock outstanding
12. High and low closing price of the stock for the past year
13. Cash dividends paid for each share of stock during the past year

COMMUNICATION

TIF 12-4 Cash dividend

Motion Designs Inc. has paid quarterly cash dividends since 20Y7. These dividends have steadily increased from $0.05 per share to the latest dividend declaration of $0.50 per share. The board of directors would like to continue this trend and is hesitant to suspend or decrease the amount of quarterly dividends. Unfortunately, sales dropped sharply in the fourth quarter of 20Y8 due to worsening economic conditions and increased competition. As a result, the board is uncertain as to whether it should declare a dividend for the last quarter of 20Y8.

On October 1, 20Y8, Motion Designs Inc. borrowed $4,000,000 from Valley National Bank to use in modernizing its retail stores and to expand its product line in response to changes in its industry. The terms of the 10-year, 6% loan require Motion Designs to:

- Pay monthly interest on the last day of the month.
- Pay $400,000 of the principal each October 1, beginning in 20Y9.
- Maintain a current ratio (current assets ÷ current liabilities) of 2.
- Maintain a minimum balance (a compensating balance) of $100,000 in its Valley National Bank account.

(Continued)

On December 31, 20Y8, $1,000,000 of the $4,000,000 loan had been disbursed in modernization of the retail stores and in expansion of the product line. Motion Designs Inc.'s balance sheet as of December 31, 20Y8, follows:

Motion Designs Inc. Balance Sheet December 31, 20Y8		
Assets		
Current assets:		
Cash..		$ 250,000
Marketable securities...........................		3,000,000
Accounts reveivable...........................	$ 800,000	
Allowance for doubtful accounts..............	(50,000)	
Accounts receivable, net		750,000
Inventory......................................		2,980,000
Prepaid expenses		20,000
Total current assets		$ 7,000,000
Property, plant, and equipment:		
Land		$1,500,000
Buildings	$ 5,050,000	
Accumulated depreciation—buildings............	(1,140,000)	
Buildings, book value		3,910,000
Equipment....................................	$ 3,320,000	
Accumulated depreciation equipment	(730,000)	
Equipment, book value		2,590,000
Total property, plant, and equipment....		8,000,000
Total assets		$15,000,000
Liabilities		
Current liabilities:		
Accounts payable	$ 1,590,000	
Notes payable (Valley National Bank)..........	400,000	
Salaries payable..............................	10,000	
Total current liabilities.....................		$2,000,000
Long-term liabilities:		
Notes payable (Valley National Bank).........		3,600,000
Total liabilities...................................		$ 5,600,000
Stockholders' Equity		
Paid-in capital:		
Common stock, $25 par (200,000 shares authorized, 180,000 shares issued)..........	$ 4,500,000	
Excess of issue price over par.................	270,000	
Total paid-in capital.......................		$4,770,000
Retained earnings................................		4,630,000
Total stockholders' equity........................		9,400,000
Total liabilities and stockholders' equity		$15,000,000

The board of directors is scheduled to meet January 10, 20Y9, to discuss the results of operations for 20Y8 and to consider the declaration of dividends for the fourth quarter of 20Y8. The chairman of the board, Lord Matt Cengage, has asked for your advice on the declaration of dividends.

Write a brief memo to the chairman of the board, outlining the factors that the board should consider in deciding whether to declare a cash dividend.

Pathways Challenge

This is Accounting!

Information/Consequences

The mandatory redemption feature, including any unpaid dividends, makes **Extended Stay America's (STAY)** preferred stock similar to debt (a bond). Even though the security is called "preferred stock," it represents an obligation that meets the definition of a liability. Thus, Extended Stay America reports this preferred stock as a liability on its balance sheet as follows (in thousands):

Liabilities:

Accounts payable and accrued liabilities	$ 193,303
Term loan payable	1,274,756
Senior notes payable	1,265,518
Mandatorily redeemable preferred stock	21,202
Other	48,286
Total liabilities	$2,803,065

Suggested Answer

13 Statement of Cash Flows

STATEMENT OF STOCKHOLDERS' EQUITY
For the Year Ended December 31, 20Y5

	Common Stock	Retained Earnings	Total
Balances, Jan. 1, 20Y5	$XXX	$ XXX	$ XXX
Issued common stock	XXX		XXX
Net income		XXX	XXX
Dividends		(XXX)	(XXX)
Balances, Dec. 31, 20Y5	$XXX	$ XXX	$ XXX

STATEMENT OF CASH FLOWS
For the Year Ended December 31, 20Y5

Cash flows from (used for) operating activities	$XXX
Cash flows from (used for) investing activities	XXX
Cash flows from (used for) financing activities	XXX
Net increase (decrease) in cash	$XXX
Cash balance, January 1, 20Y5	XXX
Cash balance, December 31, 20Y5	$XXX

INCOME STATEMENT
For the Year Ended December 31, 20Y5

Sales		$ XXX
Cost of goods sold		(XXX)
Gross profit		$ XXX
Operating expenses:		
Wages expense	$XXX	
Advertising expense	XXX	
Utilities expense	XXX	
Depreciation expense	XXX	
…	XXX	
Total operating expenses		(XXX)
Operating income		$ XXX
Other revenue and expense		XXX
Net income		$ XXX

BALANCE SHEET
December 31, 20Y5

Assets		
Current assets:		
Cash	$XXX	
Accounts receivable	XXX	
Inventory	XXX	
Total current assets		$XXX
Property, plant, and equipment		XXX
Total assets		$XXX
Liabilities		
Current liabilities	$XXX	
Long-term liabilities	XXX	
Total liabilities		$XXX
Stockholders' Equity		
Retained earnings	$XXX	
Common stock	XXX	
Total stockholders' equity		XXX
Total liabilities and stockholders' equity		$XXX

National Beverage Corp.

Suppose you were to receive $100 from an event. Would it make a difference what the event was? Yes, it would! If you received $100 for your birthday, then it's a gift. If you received $100 as a result of working part time for a week, then it's the result of your effort. If you received $100 as a loan, then it's money that you will have to pay back in the future. If you received the $100 as a result of selling your iPod, then it's the result of selling an asset. Thus, the $100 received can be associated with different types of events, and these events have different meanings to you and different implications for your future. You would much rather receive a $100 gift than take out a $100 loan. Likewise, company stakeholders view inflows and outflows of cash differently, depending on their source.

Companies are required to report information about the events causing a change in cash over a period of time. This information is reported on the statement of cash flows. One such company is **National Beverage Corp. (FIZZ)**, which is an alternative beverage company, known for its innovative soft drinks, enhanced juices and waters, and fortified powders and supplements. You have probably seen the company's Shasta and Faygo soft drinks, or LaCroix, Everfresh, and Crystal Bay drinks at your local grocery or convenience store. As with any company, cash is important to National Beverage. Without cash, National Beverage would be unable to expand its brands, distribute its products, support extreme sports, or provide a return for its owners. Thus, its managers are concerned about the sources and uses of cash.

In previous chapters, we have used the income statement, balance sheet, statement of stockholders' equity, and other information to analyze the effects of management decisions on a business's financial position and operating performance. In this chapter, we focus on the events causing a change in cash by presenting the preparation and use of the statement of cash flows.

© RICHARD LEVINE/ALAMY STOCK PHOTO

What's Covered

Statement of Cash Flows

Cash Flows	**Operating Activities— Indirect Method**	**Investing Activities**	**Financing Activities**	**Reporting Cash Flows**
■ Types of Cash Flows (Obj. 1) ■ Direct Method (Obj. 1) ■ Indirect Method (Obj. 1) ■ Noncash Transactions (Obj. 1)	■ Net Income (Obj. 2) ■ Noncash Expenses (Obj. 2) ■ Gains and Losses (Obj. 2) ■ Current Assets and Liabilities (Obj. 2)	■ Land (Obj. 3) ■ Buildings (Obj. 3)	■ Bonds Payable (Obj. 4) ■ Common Stock (Obj. 4) ■ Dividends and Dividends Payable (Obj. 4)	■ Preparing the Statement of Cash Flows (Obj. 5)

Learning Objectives

Obj. 1 Describe the cash flow activities reported on the statement of cash flows.

Obj. 2 Prepare the "Cash flows from operating activities" section of the statement of cash flows using the indirect method.

Obj. 3 Prepare the "Cash flows from investing activities" section of the statement of cash flows.

Obj. 4 Prepare the "Cash flows from financing activities" section of the statement of cash flows.

Obj. 5 Prepare a statement of cash flows.

Analysis for Decision Making

Obj. 6 Describe and illustrate the use of free cash flow in evaluating a company's cash flow.

Appendices 1 and 2

Obj. App 1 Use a spreadsheet to prepare the statement of cash flows under the indirect method.

Obj. App 2 Prepare a statement of cash flows under the direct method.

Objective 1
Describe the cash flow activities reported on the statement of cash flows.

Reporting Cash Flows

The **statement of cash flows** reports a company's cash inflows and outflows for a period.[1] The statement of cash flows provides useful information about a company's ability to do the following:

■ Generate cash from operations
■ Maintain and expand its operating capacity
■ Meet its financial obligations
■ Pay dividends

The statement of cash flows is used by managers in evaluating past operations and in planning future investing and financing activities. It is also used by external users such as investors and creditors to assess a company's profit potential and ability to pay its debt and pay dividends.

The statement of cash flows reports three types of cash flow activities, as follows:

note:

The statement of cash flows reports cash flows from operating, investing, and financing activities.

1. **Cash flows from operating activities** are the cash flows from transactions that affect the net income of the company.

   Example: Purchase and sale of merchandise by a retailer.

2. **Cash flows from investing activities** are the cash flows from transactions that affect investments in the noncurrent assets of the company.

   Example: Purchase and sale of fixed assets, such as equipment and buildings.

---

[1] As used in this chapter, *cash* refers to cash and cash equivalents. Examples of cash equivalents include short-term, highly liquid investments, such as money market accounts, bank certificates of deposit, and U.S. Treasury bills.

3. **Cash flows from financing activities** are the cash flows from transactions that affect the debt and equity of the company.

Example: Issuing or retiring equity and debt securities.

The cash flows are reported on the statement of cash flows as follows:

Cash flows from operating activities	$XXX
Cash flows from investing activities	XXX
Cash flows from financing activities	XXX
Net increase (decrease) in cash	$XXX
Cash at the beginning of the period	XXX
Cash at the end of the period	$XXX

The ending cash on the statement of cash flows equals the cash reported on the company's balance sheet at the end of the year.

Exhibit 1 illustrates the sources (increases) and uses (decreases) of cash by each of the three cash flow activities. A *source* of cash causes the cash flow to increase and is called a *cash inflow*. A *use* of cash causes cash flow to decrease and is called a *cash outflow*.

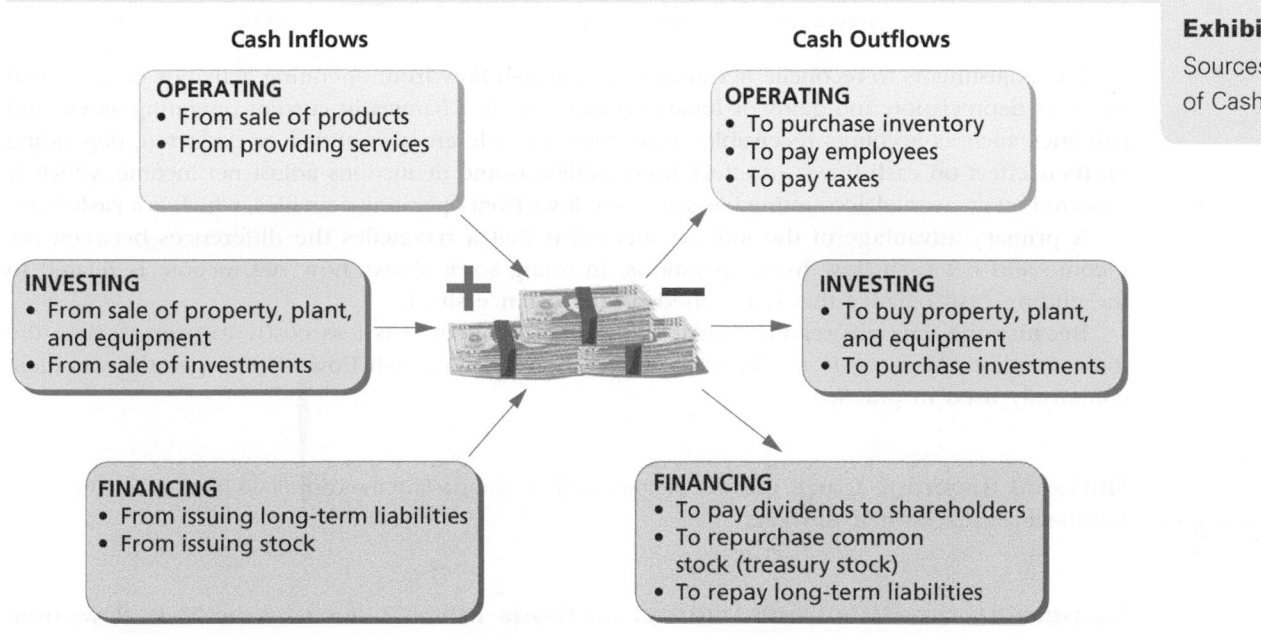

Exhibit 1

Sources and Uses of Cash

Cash Flows from Operating Activities

Cash flows from operating activities report the cash inflows and outflows from a company's day-to-day operations. Companies may select one of two alternative methods for reporting cash flows from operating activities on the statement of cash flows:

- The direct method
- The indirect method

Both methods result in the same amount of cash flows from operating activities. They differ in the way they report cash flows from operating activities.

The Direct Method The **direct method** reports operating cash inflows (receipts) and cash outflows (payments) as follows:

Cash flows from (used for) operating activities:	
Cash received from customers	$ XXX
Cash payments for merchandise	(XXX)
Cash payments for operating expenses	(XXX)
Cash payments for interest	(XXX)
Cash payments for income taxes	(XXX)
Net cash flow from operating activities	$XXX

The primary operating cash inflow is cash received from customers. The primary operating cash outflows are cash payments for merchandise, operating expenses, interest, and income tax payments. The cash received from operating activities less the cash payments for operating activities is the net cash flow from operating activities.

The primary advantage of the direct method is that it *directly* reports cash receipts and cash payments on the statement of cash flows. Its primary disadvantage is that these data may not be readily available in the accounting records. Thus, the direct method is normally more costly to prepare and, as a result, is used infrequently in practice. For this reason, the direct method is described and illustrated in Appendix 2 following this chapter.

The Indirect Method The **indirect method** reports cash flows from operating activities by beginning with net income and adjusting it for revenues and expenses that do not involve the receipt or payment of cash, as follows:

Cash flows from (used for) operating activities:		
Net income	$XXX	
Adjustments to reconcile net income to net cash flow from operating activities	XXX	
Net cash flow from operating activities		$XXX

The adjustments to reconcile net income to net cash flow from operating activities include such items as depreciation and gains or losses on fixed assets. Changes in current operating assets and liabilities such as accounts receivable or accounts payable are also added or deducted, depending on their effect on cash flows. In effect, these additions and deductions adjust net income, which is reported on an accrual accounting basis, to cash flows from operating activities, which is a cash basis.

A primary advantage of the indirect method is that it reconciles the differences between net income and net cash flow from operations. In doing so, it shows how net income is related to the ending cash balance that is reported on the balance sheet.

Because the data are readily available, the indirect method is less costly to prepare than the direct method. As a result, the indirect method of reporting cash flows from operations is most commonly used in practice.

Link to National Beverage **National Beverage Corp.** uses the indirect method of reporting the cash flows from operating activities in its statement of cash flows.

Comparing the Direct and Indirect Methods Exhibit 2 illustrates the "Cash flows from operating activities" section of the statement of cash flows for **NetSolutions**. It shows the direct and indirect methods using the NetSolutions data from Chapter 1. As Exhibit 2 illustrates, both methods report the same amount of net cash flow from operating activities of $2,900.

Exhibit 2 Cash Flows from Operations: Direct and Indirect Methods—NetSolutions

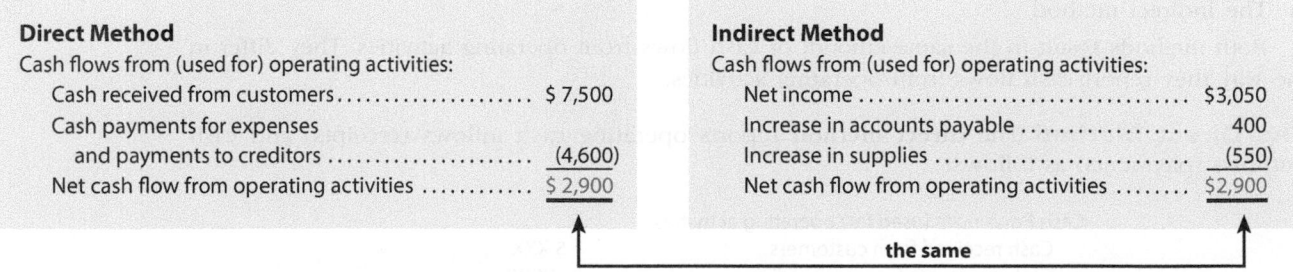

Direct Method

Cash flows from (used for) operating activities:	
Cash received from customers	$ 7,500
Cash payments for expenses and payments to creditors	(4,600)
Net cash flow from operating activities	$ 2,900

Indirect Method

Cash flows from (used for) operating activities:	
Net income	$3,050
Increase in accounts payable	400
Increase in supplies	(550)
Net cash flow from operating activities	$2,900

the same

Link to National Beverage For a recent year, **National Beverage Corp.** reported net cash provided by operating activities of $78,955,000.

Cash Crunch!

	Year 3	Year 2	Year 1
Cash provided (used for) operating activities	$(17,589)	$(26,191)	$61,900

The Wet Seal, Inc. (WTSL), a young women's clothing retailer, recently filed for bankruptcy protection. The cash flows from operating activities for the three years prior to bankruptcy (in thousands) follow:

As can be seen, cash flows from operating activities trended into negative territory during the two years prior to the firm's bankruptcy. Thus, when cash flows from operating activities are negative, it can lead to financial distress.

Cash Flows from Investing Activities

Cash flows from investing activities show the cash inflows and outflows related to changes in a company's long-term assets. Cash flows from investing activities are reported on the statement of cash flows as follows:

Cash flows from (used for) investing activities:		
Cash inflows from investing activities	$ XXX	
Cash used for investing activities	(XXX)	
Net cash flow from investing activities		$XXX

Cash inflows from investing activities normally arise from selling fixed assets, investments, and intangible assets. Cash outflows normally include payments to purchase fixed assets, investments, and intangible assets.

For a recent year, **National Beverage Corp.** reported net cash used for investing activities of $12,024,000.

Link to National Beverage

Cash Flows from Financing Activities

Cash flows from financing activities show the cash inflows and outflows related to changes in a company's long-term liabilities and stockholders' equity. Cash flows from financing activities are reported on the statement of cash flows as follows:

Cash flows from (used for) financing activities:		
Cash inflows from financing activities	$ XXX	
Cash used for financing activities	(XXX)	
Net cash flow from financing activities		$XXX

Cash inflows from financing activities normally arise from issuing long-term debt or equity securities. For example, issuing bonds, notes payable, preferred stock, and common stock creates cash inflows from financing activities. Cash outflows from financing activities include paying cash dividends, repaying long-term debt, and acquiring treasury stock.

For a recent year, **National Beverage Corp.** reported net cash used for financing activities of $13,810,000.

Link to National Beverage

Why It Matters

Growing Pains

Twitter, Inc. (TWTR) is a global social media platform used for real-time self-expression and conversation within the limits of 140-character tweets. The cash flows from operating, investing, and financing activities for Twitter's first four years as a public company (in thousands) are as follows:

Cash provided by (used for)

	Operating activities	Investing activities	Financing activities	Net change for year
Year 1	$ 1,398	$(1,306,066)	$1,942,176	$637,508
Year 2	81,796	(1,097,272)	1,691,722	676,246
Year 3	383,066	(902,421)	(62,998)	(582,353)
Year 4	763,055	(598,008)	(83,975)	81,072

Twitter significantly improved its cash flows from operations from Year 1 to Year 4. Twitter made significant investments in order to expand. This is shown by the cash flows used in investing activities for Years 1 through 4. Since the cash flows from operations were insufficient to fund this growth, the company obtained cash from financing activities. For example, Twitter received cash from stockholders in Year 1 and from creditors in Year 2, which was used to expand and provide future flexibility.

Noncash Investing and Financing Activities

A company may enter into transactions involving investing and financing activities that do not *directly* affect cash. For example, a company may issue common stock to retire long-term debt. Although this transaction does not directly affect cash, it does eliminate future cash payments for interest and for paying the bonds when they mature. Because such transactions *indirectly* affect cash flows, they are reported in a separate section of the statement of cash flows. This section usually appears at the bottom of the statement of cash flows.

Format of the Statement of Cash Flows

The statement of cash flows presents the cash flows generated from, or used for, the three activities previously discussed: operating, investing, and financing. These three activities are always reported in the same order, as shown in Exhibit 3.

Exhibit 3

Order of Reporting Statement of Cash Flows

Rundell Inc.
Statement of Cash Flows
For the Year Ended 20Y8

Cash flows from (used for) operating activities:		
(List of items, as illustrated in Exhibit 1)	$XXX	
Net cash flow from operating activities		$XXX
Cash flows from (used for) investing activities:		
(List of items, as illustrated in Exhibit 1)	$XXX	
Net cash flow from (used for) investing activities		XXX
Cash flows from (used for) financing activities:		
(List of items, as illustrated in Exhibit 1)	$XXX	
Net cash flow from (used for) financing activities		XXX
Net increase (decrease) in cash		$XXX
Cash at the beginning of the period		XXX
Cash at the end of the period		$XXX
Noncash investing and financing activities		$XXX

No Cash Flow per Share

Cash flow per share is sometimes reported in the financial press. As reported, cash flow per share is normally computed as *cash flow from operations divided by the number of common shares outstanding*. However, such reporting may be misleading because of the following:

■ Users may misinterpret cash flow per share as the per-share amount available for dividends. This would not be the case if the cash generated by operations is required for repaying loans or for reinvesting in the business.

■ Users may misinterpret cash flow per share as equivalent to (or better than) earnings per share.

For these reasons, the financial statements, including the statement of cash flows, should not report cash flow per share.

Check Up Corner 13-1 Classifications of Cash Flows

During its first month of operations, Templeton Company had the following cash transactions:

a. Issued 30,000 shares of common stock.

b. Purchased a new piece of equipment.

c. Sold merchandise to customers.

d. Paid employees' wages.

e. Paid a dividend.

Identify whether each of these transactions would be reported as an operating, investing, or financing activity on the statement of cash flows.

Solution:

a. Financing	Issued 30,000 shares of common stock.	Operating activities show the cash inflows and outflows from a company's day-to-day operations.
b. Investing	Purchased a new piece of equipment.	
c. Operating	Sold merchandise to customers.	Investing activities show the cash inflows and outflows related to changes in a company's long-term assets.
d. Operating	Paid employees' wages.	
e. Financing	Paid a dividend.	Financing activities show the cash inflows and outflows related to changes in a company's long-term liabilities and stockholders' equity.

Check Up Corner

Cash Flows from Operating Activities— The Indirect Method

Objective 2
Prepare the "Cash flows from operating activities" section of the statement of cash flows using the indirect method.

The indirect method of reporting cash flows from operating activities uses the logic that a change in any balance sheet account (including cash) can be analyzed in terms of changes in the other balance sheet accounts. Thus, by analyzing changes in noncash balance sheet accounts, any change in the cash account can be *indirectly* determined.

To illustrate, the accounting equation can be solved for cash as follows:

$$\text{Assets} = \text{Liabilities} + \text{Stockholders' Equity}$$
$$\text{Cash} + \text{Noncash Assets} = \text{Liabilities} + \text{Stockholders' Equity}$$
$$\text{Cash} = \text{Liabilities} + \text{Stockholders' Equity} - \text{Noncash Assets}$$

Therefore, any change in the cash account can be determined by analyzing changes in the liability, stockholders' equity, and noncash asset accounts as follows:

$$\text{\textit{Change} in Cash} = \text{\textit{Change} in Liabilities} + \text{\textit{Change} in Stockholders' Equity} - \text{\textit{Change} in Noncash Assets}$$

Under the indirect method, there is no order in which the balance sheet accounts must be analyzed. However, net income (or net loss) is the first amount reported on the statement of cash flows. Because net income (or net loss) is a component of any change in Retained Earnings, the first account normally analyzed is Retained Earnings.

To illustrate the indirect method, the income statement and comparative balance sheets for **Rundell Inc.**, shown in Exhibit 4, are used. Ledger accounts and other data supporting the income statement and balance sheet are presented as needed.[2]

Exhibit 4

Income Statement and Comparative Balance Sheet

Rundell Inc. Income Statement For the Year Ended December 31, 20Y8			
Sales			$1,180,000
Cost of goods sold			(790,000)
Gross profit			$ 390,000
Operating expenses:			
Depreciation expense		$ 7,000	
Other operating expenses		196,000	
Total operating expenses			(203,000)
Operating income			$ 187,000
Other revenue and expense:			
Gain on sale of land		$ 12,000	
Interest expense		(8,000)	4,000
Income before income tax			$ 191,000
Income tax expense			(83,000)
Net income			$ 108,000

Rundell Inc. Comparative Balance Sheet December 31, 20Y8 and 20Y7			
	20Y8	**20Y7**	**Increase (Decrease)**
Assets			
Cash	$ 97,500	$ 26,000	$ 71,500
Accounts receivable (net)	74,000	65,000	9,000
Inventories	172,000	180,000	(8,000)
Land	80,000	125,000	(45,000)
Building	260,000	200,000	60,000
Accumulated depreciation—building	(65,300)	(58,300)	(7,000)*
Total assets	$618,200	$537,700	$ 80,500
Liabilities			
Accounts payable (merchandise creditors)	$ 43,500	$ 46,700	$ (3,200)
Accrued expenses payable (operating expenses)	26,500	24,300	2,200
Income taxes payable	7,900	8,400	(500)
Dividends payable	14,000	10,000	4,000
Bonds payable	100,000	150,000	(50,000)
Total liabilities	$191,900	$239,400	$(47,500)
Stockholders' Equity			
Common stock, $2 par	$ 24,000	$ 16,000	$ 8,000
Paid-in capital in excess of par	120,000	80,000	40,000
Retained earnings	282,300	202,300	80,000
Total stockholders' equity	$426,300	$298,300	$128,000
Total liabilities and stockholders' equity	$618,200	$537,700	$ 80,500

*There is a $7,000 increase to Accumulated Depreciation—Building, which is a contra asset account. As a result, the $7,000 increase in this account must be subtracted in summing to the increase in total assets of $80,500.

---

[2] An appendix that discusses using a spreadsheet (work sheet) as an aid in assembling data for the statement of cash flows is presented at the end of this chapter. This appendix illustrates the use of this spreadsheet in reporting cash flows from operating activities using the indirect method.

Net Income

Rundell Inc.'s net income for 20Y8 is $108,000 as shown in the income statement in Exhibit 4. Since net income is closed to Retained Earnings, net income also helps explain the change in retained earnings during the year. The retained earnings account for Rundell is as follows:

Account Retained Earnings				Account No.	
				Balance	
Date	**Item**	**Debit**	**Credit**	**Debit**	**Credit**
20Y8					
Jan. 1	Balance				202,300
June 30	Dividends declared	14,000			188,300
Dec. 31	Net income		108,000		296,300
31	Dividends declared	14,000			282,300

The retained earnings account indicates that the $80,000 ($282,300 − $202,300) change resulted from net income of $108,000 and cash dividends of $28,000 ($14,000 + $14,000). The net income of $108,000 is the first amount reported in the "Cash flows from operating activities" section. The impact of the dividends of $28,000 on cash flows will be included as part of financing activities.

Adjustments to Net Income

The net income of $108,000 reported by **Rundell Inc.** does not equal the cash flows from operating activities for the period. This is because net income is determined using the accrual method of accounting.

Under the accrual method of accounting, revenues and expenses are recorded at different times from when cash is received or paid. For example, merchandise may be sold on account and the cash received at a later date. Likewise, insurance premiums may be paid in the current period but expensed in a following period.

Thus, under the indirect method, adjustments to net income must be made to determine cash flows from operating activities. The typical adjustments to net income are shown in Exhibit 5.[3]

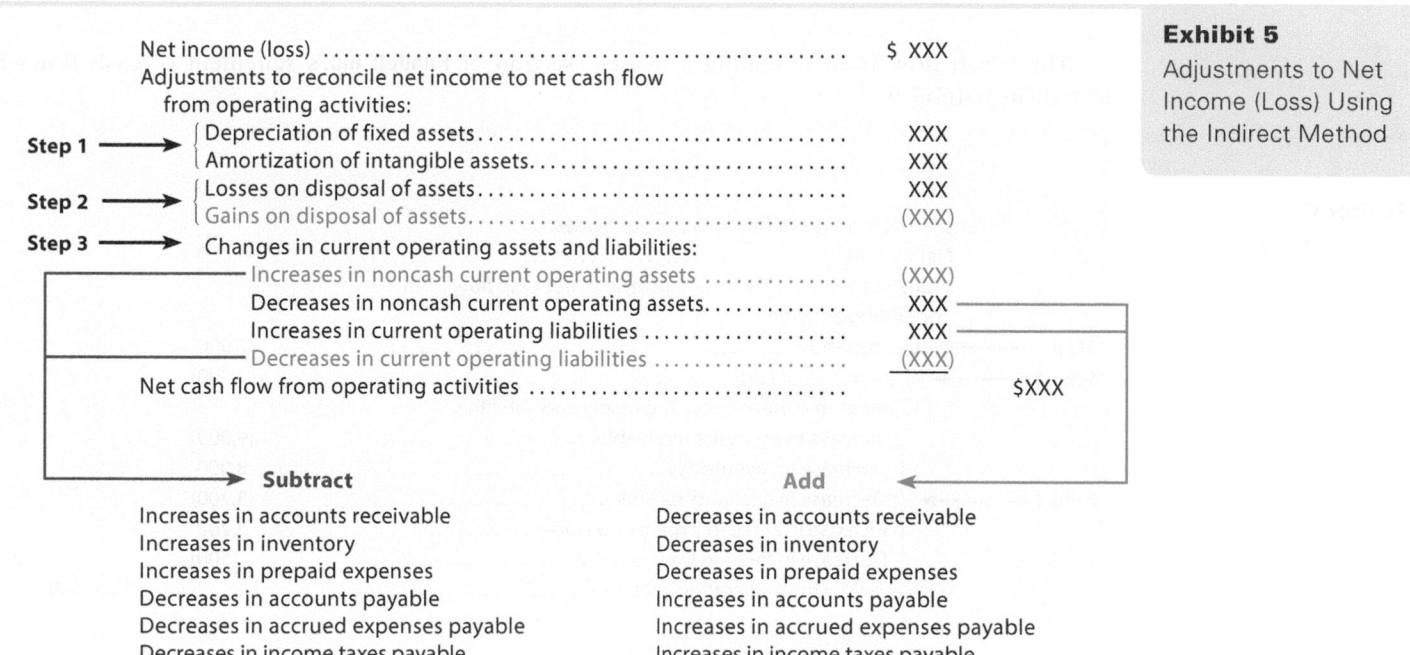

Exhibit 5

Adjustments to Net Income (Loss) Using the Indirect Method

[3] Other items that also require adjustments to net income to obtain cash flows from operating activities include amortization of bonds payable discounts (add), losses on debt retirement (add), amortization of bonds payable premiums (deduct), and gains on retirement of debt (deduct). These topics are covered in advanced accounting courses.

Net income is normally adjusted to cash flows from operating activities, using the following steps:

- Step 1. Expenses that do not affect cash are added. Such expenses decrease net income but do not involve cash payments.

  Example: Depreciation of fixed assets and amortization of intangible assets are added to net income.

- Step 2. Losses on the disposal of assets are added and gains on the disposal of assets are deducted. The disposal (sale) of assets is an investing activity rather than an operating activity. However, such losses and gains are reported as part of net income. As a result, any *losses* on disposal of assets are *added* back to net income. Likewise, any *gains* on disposal of assets are *deducted* from net income.

  Example: Land costing $100,000 is sold for $90,000. The loss of $10,000 is added back to net income.

- Step 3. Changes in current operating assets and liabilities are added or deducted as follows:

  - Increases in noncash current operating assets are deducted.
  - Decreases in noncash current operating assets are added.
  - Increases in current operating liabilities are added.
  - Decreases in current operating liabilities are deducted.

  Example: A sale of $10,000 on account increases sales, accounts receivable, and net income by $10,000. However, cash is not affected. Thus, the $10,000 increase in accounts receivable is deducted. Similar adjustments are required for the changes in the other current asset and liability accounts, such as inventory, prepaid expenses, accounts payable, accrued expenses payable, and income taxes payable, as shown in Exhibit 5.

Link to National Beverage In a recent statement of cash flows, **National Beverage Corp.** reported changes in current asset and liability accounts for accounts receivable, inventories, accounts payable, and accrued liabilities.

The "Cash flow from operating activities" section of **Rundell Inc.**'s statement of cash flows is shown in Exhibit 6.

Exhibit 6

Net Cash Flow from Operating Activities— Indirect Method

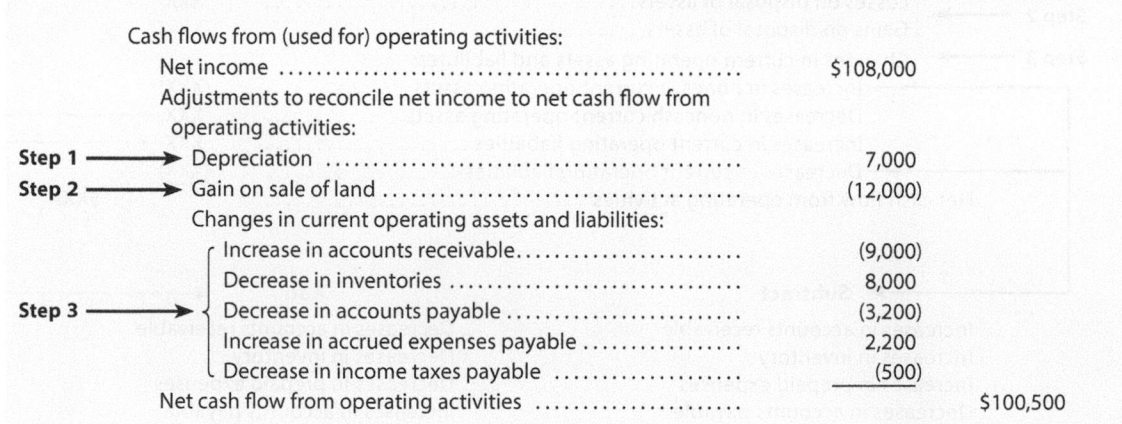

Cash flows from (used for) operating activities:	
Net income	$108,000
Adjustments to reconcile net income to net cash flow from operating activities:	
Step 1 → Depreciation	7,000
Step 2 → Gain on sale of land	(12,000)
Changes in current operating assets and liabilities:	
Increase in accounts receivable	(9,000)
Decrease in inventories	8,000
Step 3 → Decrease in accounts payable	(3,200)
Increase in accrued expenses payable	2,200
Decrease in income taxes payable	(500)
Net cash flow from operating activities	$100,500

Rundell's net income of $108,000 is converted to cash flows from operating activities of $100,500 as follows:

- Step 1. Add depreciation of $7,000.

    Analysis: The comparative balance sheet in Exhibit 4 indicates that Accumulated Depreciation—Building increased by $7,000. The following account indicates that depreciation for the year was $7,000 for the building:

Account *Accumulated Depreciation—Building*					Account No.	
					Balance	
Date	**Item**	**Debit**	**Credit**	**Debit**	**Credit**	
20Y8						
Jan. 1	Balance				58,300	
Dec. 31	Depreciation for year		7,000		65,300	

- Step 2. Deduct the gain on the sale of land of $12,000.

    Analysis: The income statement in Exhibit 4 reports a gain of $12,000 from the sale of land. The proceeds, which include the gain, are reported in the investing section of the statement of cash flows.[4] Thus, the gain of $12,000 is deducted from net income in determining cash flows from operating activities.

- Step 3. Add and deduct changes in current operating assets and liabilities excluding cash.

    Analysis: The increases and decreases in the current operating asset and current liability accounts excluding cash are as follows:

	December 31		**Increase**
Accounts	**20Y8**	**20Y7**	**(Decrease)**
Accounts Receivable (net)	$ 74,000	$ 65,000	$ 9,000
Inventories	172,000	180,000	(8,000)
Accounts Payable (merchandise creditors)	43,500	46,700	(3,200)
Accrued Expenses Payable (operating expenses)	26,500	24,300	2,200
Income Taxes Payable	7,900	8,400	(500)

Accounts receivable (net): The $9,000 increase is deducted from net income. This is because the $9,000 increase in accounts receivable indicates that sales on account were $9,000 more than the cash received from customers. Thus, sales (and net income) includes $9,000 that was not received in cash during the year.

Inventories: The $8,000 decrease is added to net income. This is because the $8,000 decrease in inventories indicates that the cost of goods *sold* exceeds the cost of the merchandise *purchased* during the year by $8,000. In other words, the cost of goods sold includes $8,000 of merchandise from inventory that was not purchased (used cash) during the year.

Accounts payable (merchandise creditors): The $3,200 decrease is deducted from net income. This is because a decrease in accounts payable indicates that the cash *payments* to merchandise creditors exceed the merchandise *purchased on account* by $3,200. Therefore, the cost of goods sold is $3,200 less than the cash paid to merchandise creditors during the year.

Accrued expenses payable (operating expenses): The $2,200 increase is added to net income. This is because an increase in accrued expenses payable indicates that operating expenses exceed the cash payments for operating expenses by $2,200. In other words, operating expenses reported on the income statement include $2,200 that did not require a cash outflow during the year.

Income taxes payable: The $500 decrease is deducted from net income. This is because a decrease in income taxes payable indicates that taxes paid exceed the amount of taxes incurred during the year by $500. In other words, the amount reported on the income statement for income tax expense is less than the amount paid by $500.

---

[4] The reporting of the proceeds (cash flows) from the sale of land as part of investing activities is discussed later in this chapter.

Check Up Corner 13-2 Cash Flows from Operating Activities

Omicron Inc. reported net income of $120,000 for 20Y2. In addition, the income statement reported $12,000 of depreciation expense and a $15,000 loss on the disposal of equipment. The current operating assets and liabilities from the company's comparative balance sheet are as follows:

	12/31/20Y2	12/31/20Y1	Increase (Decrease)
Accounts receivable	$18,240	$13,240	$ 5,000
Accounts payable	11,200	13,200	(2,000)

Prepare the "Cash flows from operating activities" section of the statement of cash flows, using the indirect method.

Solution:

Cash flows from (used for) operating activities:	
Net income......................................	$120,000
Adjustments to reconcile net income to cash flow	
from operating activities:	
Depreciation expense.......................	12,000
Loss on disposal of equipment	15,000
Changes in current operating assets and liabilities:	
Increase in accounts receivable	(5,000)
Decrease in accounts payable...........	(2,000)
Net cash flow from operating activities	$140,000

Expenses that decrease net income but do not involve cash payments, such as depreciation, are added to net income.

Losses on the disposal of assets are added to and gains on the disposal of assets are deducted from net income.

Increases (decreases) in noncash current operating assets are deducted (added) from net income.

Increases (decreases) in current operating liabilities are added (subtracted) to net income.

Check Up Corner

Cash Flows from Investing Activities

Cash flows from investing activities report the cash inflows and outflows related to changes in a company's long-term assets. **Rundell Inc.**'s comparative balance sheet in Exhibit 4 lists land, building, and accumulated depreciation—building as long-term assets. Similar to preparing the "Cash flows from operating activities" section, each change in each long-term asset account is analyzed for its effect on cash flows from investing activities.

Land

The $45,000 decline in the land account of **Rundell Inc.** was from two transactions, as follows:

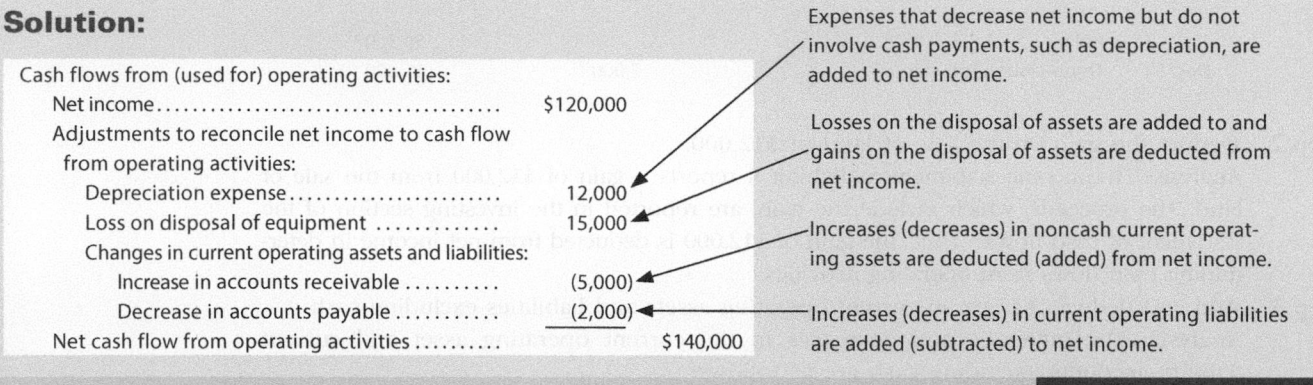

				Balance	
Account Land					Account No.
Date	Item	Debit	Credit	Debit	Credit
20Y8					
Jan. 1	Balance			125,000	
June 8	Sold for $72,000 cash		60,000	65,000	
Oct. 12	Purchased for $15,000 cash	15,000		80,000	

The June 8 transaction is the sale of land with a cost of $60,000 for $72,000 in cash. The $72,000 proceeds from the sale are reported in the "Cash flows from investing activities" section as follows:

Cash flows from investing activities:

Cash received from sale of land $72,000

The proceeds of $72,000 include the $12,000 gain on the sale of land and the $60,000 cost (book value) of the land. As shown in Exhibit 6, the $12,000 gain in deducted from net income in the "Cash flows from operating activities" section. This is so that the $12,000 cash inflow related to the gain is not included twice as a cash inflow.

The October 12 transaction is the purchase of land for cash of $15,000. This transaction is reported as an outflow of cash in the investing activities section as follows:

Cash flows from investing activities:

Cash paid for purchase of land .... $(15,000)

Building and Accumulated Depreciation—Building

The building account of **Rundell Inc.** increased by $60,000 ($260,000 − $200,000), and the accumulated depreciation—building account increased by $7,000 ($65,300 − $58,300), as follows:

Account Building				Account No.	
				Balance	
Date	Item	Debit	Credit	Debit	Credit
20Y8					
Jan. 1	Balance			200,000	
Dec. 27	Purchased for cash	60,000		260,000	

Account Accumulated Depreciation—Building				Account No.	
				Balance	
Date	Item	Debit	Credit	Debit	Credit
20Y8					
Jan. 1	Balance				58,300
Dec. 31	Depreciation for the year		7,000		65,300

The purchase of a building for cash of $60,000 is reported as an outflow of cash in the "Cash flows from investing activities" section as follows:

Cash flows from investing activities:

Cash paid for purchase of building .... $(60,000)

The credit in the accumulated depreciation—building account represents depreciation expense for the year. This depreciation expense of $7,000 on the building was added to net income in determining cash flows from operating activities, as reported in Exhibit 6.

In a recent statement of cash flows, **National Beverage Corp.** reported cash used for purchases of property, plant, and equipment of $12,140,000 and cash received for selling property, plant, and equipment of $116,0000 resulting in net cash used for investing activities of $12,024,000.

Link to National Beverage

Check Up Corner 13-3   Cash Flows from Investing Activities

Mercury Inc. reported net income of $100,000 for 20Y2. In addition, the income statement reported $20,000 of depreciation expense and a $10,000 gain on the sale of land. The noncurrent assets from the company's comparative balance sheet are as follows:

	12/31/20Y2	12/31/20Y1	Increase (Decrease)
Land	$ 125,000	$ 225,000	$(100,000)
Equipment	500,000	400,000	100,000
Accumulated depreciation—equipment	(120,000)	(100,000)	20,000

There were no disposals of equipment, and all purchases of equipment were for cash.
Prepare the "Cash flows from investing activities" section of the statement of cash flows.

(Continued)

Solution:

Cash flows from (used for) investing activities:	
Cash received from sale of land.................	$ 110,000
Cash paid for purchase of equipment	(100,000)
Net cash flow from investing activities	$10,000

Land was sold for $110,000 ($100,000 decrease in land account + $10,000 gain on the sale). This is the amount of cash received from the sale of land.

The increase in the balance of the equipment account comes from the purchase of equipment for cash.

Note: The increase in Accumulated Depreciation—Equipment is from 20Y2 depreciation expense, which is included in the "Cash flows from operating activities" section.

Check Up Corner

Objective 4
Prepare the "Cash flows from financing activities" section of the statement of cash flows.

Cash Flows from Financing Activities

Cash flows from financing activities reports the cash inflows and outflows related to changes in a company's long-term liabilities and stockholders' equity. **Rundell Inc.**'s comparative balance sheet in Exhibit 4 reports changes in bonds payable, common stock, and paid-in capital in excess of par. In addition, dividends payable has changed, which impacts retained earnings. Each change must be analyzed to determine its effect on cash flows from financing activities.

Bonds Payable

The bonds payable account of **Rundell Inc.** decreased by $50,000 ($100,000 − $150,000), as follows:

Account Bonds Payable					Account No.	
					Balance	
Date	**Item**	**Debit**	**Credit**	**Debit**	**Credit**	
20Y8						
Jan. 1	Balance				150,000	
June 1	Retired by payment of cash at face					
	amount	50,000			100,000	

This decrease is from retiring the bonds by a cash payment for their face amount. This cash outflow is reported in the financing activities section as follows:

Cash flows from (used for) financing activities:

Cash paid to retire bonds payable.................. $(50,000)

Common Stock

The common stock account of **Rundell Inc.** increased by $8,000 ($24,000 − $16,000), and the paid-in capital in excess of par—common stock account increased by $40,000 ($120,000 − $80,000), as follows:

Account Common Stock					Account No.	
					Balance	
Date	**Item**	**Debit**	**Credit**	**Debit**	**Credit**	
20Y8						
Jan. 1	Balance				16,000	
Nov. 1	4,000 shares issued for cash		8,000		24,000	

Account *Paid-In Capital in Excess of Par—Common Stock*				Account No.	
				Balance	
Date	Item	Debit	Credit	Debit	Credit
20Y8					
Jan. 1	Balance				80,000
Nov. 1	4,000 shares issued for cash		40,000		120,000

These increases were from issuing 4,000 shares of common stock for $12 per share. This cash inflow is reported in the financing activities section as follows:

Cash flows from financing activities:

Cash received from sale of common stock $48,000

Dividends and Dividends Payable

The retained earnings account of **Rundell Inc.** indicates cash dividends of $28,000 ($14,000 + $14,000) were declared during the year. However, the following dividends payable account indicates that only $24,000 ($10,000 + $14,000) of dividends were paid during the year:

Account *Dividends Payable*				Account No.	
				Balance	
Date	Item	Debit	Credit	Debit	Credit
20Y8					
Jan. 1	Balance				10,000
10	Cash paid	10,000		—	—
June 30	Dividends declared		14,000		14,000
July 10	Cash paid	14,000		—	—
Dec. 31	Dividends declared		14,000		14,000

Cash dividends paid during the year can also be computed by adjusting the dividends declared during the year for the change in the dividends payable account as follows:

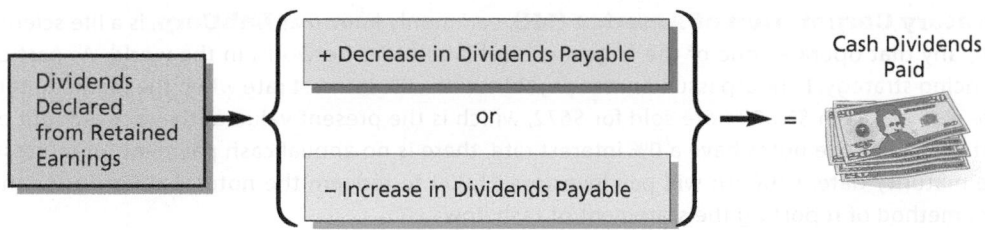

The cash dividends paid by Rundell Inc. during 20Y8 are $24,000, computed as follows:

Dividends declared ($14,000 + $14,000)	$28,000
Increase in Dividends Payable	(4,000)
Cash dividends paid	$24,000

Because dividend payments are a financing activity, the cash dividends paid of $24,000 are reported in the financing activities section of the statement of cash flows, as follows:

Cash flows from financing activities:

Cash paid for dividends . . . . $(24,000)

In a recent statement of cash flows, **National Beverage Corp.** reported cash used for dividends of $186,000; cash used for payment of debt of $10,000,000; and cash used for redeeming preferred stock of $6,000,000.

Link to National Beverage

Check Up Corner 13-4   Cash Flows from Financing Activities

Mohroman Inc. reported net income of $80,000 for 20Y2. The liability and equity accounts from the company's comparative balance sheet are as follows:

	12/31/20Y2	12/31/20Y1	Increase (Decrease)
Accounts payable	$ 42,680	$ 41,500	$ 1,180
Dividends payable	10,000	8,000	2,000
Bonds payable	210,000	300,000	(90,000)
Common stock, $10 par value	120,000	100,000	20,000
Paid-in capital in excess of par—common stock	300,000	200,000	100,000
Retained earnings	240,000	180,000	60,000

During the year, the company retired bonds payable at their face amount, declared dividends of $20,000, and issued 2,000 shares of common stock for $60 per share. Prepare the "Cash flows from financing activities" section of the statement of cash flows.

Solution:

Cash flows from (used for) financing activities:		
Cash paid to retire bonds	$ (90,000)	
Cash received from issuing common stock	120,000	
Cash paid for dividends	(18,000)	
Net cash flow from financing activities		$12,000

Bonds payable with a $90,000 face amount were retired. This is a cash outflow from financing activities.

$120,000 in cash was received from the issuance of common stock (2,000 shares × $60 per share).

$20,000 in dividends declared less the $2,000 increase in dividends payable

Pathways Challenge

This is Accounting!

Economic Activity

Laboratory Corporation of America (LH), commonly known as **LabCorp**, is a life sciences company that operates one of the largest clinical laboratory networks in the world. As part of its financing strategy, LabCorp issued notes payable with a 0% interest rate when the market interest rate was 2%. Each $1,000 note sold for $672, which is the present value of the face amount of the note. Because the notes have a 0% interest rate, there is no annual cash payment for interest. On the maturity date, LabCorp will pay investors $1,000 to redeem the notes. LabCorp uses the indirect method of reporting the statement of cash flows.

Critical Thinking/Judgment

Would the statement of cash flows report a yearly "cash outflow" for interest expense?
How would LabCorp report the redemption of each $1,000 note at maturity on the statement of cash flows?

Suggested answer at end of chapter.

Objective 5

Prepare a statement of cash flows.

Preparing the Statement of Cash Flows

The statement of cash flows for **Rundell Inc.**, using the indirect method, is shown in Exhibit 7. The statement of cash flows indicates that cash increased by $71,500 during the year. The most significant increase in net cash flows ($100,500) was from operating activities. The most

Rundell Inc.
Statement of Cash Flows
For the Year Ended December 31, 20Y8

Cash flows from (used for) operating activities:		
Net income.	$108,000	
Adjustments to reconcile net income to net cash flow		
from operating activities:		
Depreciation	7,000	
Gain on sale of land.	(12,000)	
Changes in current operating assets and liabilities:		
Increase in accounts receivable	(9,000)	
Decrease in inventories.	8,000	
Decrease in accounts payable	(3,200)	
Increase in accrued expenses payable.	2,200	
Decrease in income taxes payable	(500)	
Net cash flow from operating activities.		$100,500
Cash flows from (used for) investing activities:		
Cash received from sale of land	$ 72,000	
Cash paid for purchase of land.	(15,000)	
Cash paid for purchase of building	(60,000)	
Net cash flow used for investing activities		(3,000)
Cash flows from (used for) financing activities:		
Cash received from sale of common stock	$ 48,000	
Cash paid to retire bonds payable.	(50,000)	
Cash paid for dividends	(24,000)	
Net cash flow used for financing activities		(26,000)
Net increase in cash.		$ 71,500
Cash balance, January 1, 20Y8		26,000
Cash balance, December 31, 20Y8.		$ 97,500

significant use of cash ($26,000) was for financing activities. The ending balance of cash on December 31, 20Y8, is $97,500. This ending cash balance is also reported on the December 31, 20Y8, balance sheet shown in Exhibit 4.

In a recent statement of cash flows, **National Beverage Corp.** reported net cash provided by operating activities of $78,955,000; net cash used for investing activities of $12,024,000; and net cash used for financing activities of $13,810,000 for a net increase in cash of $53,121,000 for the year.

Link to National Beverage

International Connection

IFRS

IFRS for Statement of Cash Flows

The statement of cash flows is required under International Financial Reporting Standards (IFRS). The statement of cash flows under IFRS is similar to that reported under U.S. GAAP in that the statement has separate sections for operating, investing, and financing activities. Like U.S. GAAP, IFRS also allow the use of either the indirect or direct method of reporting cash flows from operating activities. IFRS differ from U.S. GAAP in some minor areas, including:

■ Interest paid can be reported as either an operating or a financing activity, while interest received can be reported as either an operating or an investing activity. In contrast, U.S. GAAP reports interest paid or received as an operating activity.

■ Dividends paid can be reported as either an operating or a financing activity, while dividends received can be reported as either an operating or an investing activity. In contrast, U.S. GAAP reports dividends paid as a financing activity and dividends received as an operating activity.

■ Cash flows to pay taxes are reported as a separate line in the operating activities, in contrast to U.S. GAAP, which does not require a separate line disclosure.

*IFRS are further discussed and illustrated in Appendix C.

Analysis for Decision Making

Objective 6

Describe and illustrate the use of free cash flow in evaluating a company's cash flow.

Free Cash Flow

A valuable tool for evaluating the profitability of a business is free cash flow. **Free cash flow** measures the operating cash flow available to a company after it purchases the property, plant, and equipment (PP&E) necessary to maintain its current operations. Since the investments in PP&E necessary to maintain current operations cannot often be determined from financial statements, analysts estimate this amount using the cash used to purchase PP&E, as shown in the statement of cash flows. Thus, free cash flow is computed as follows:

Cash flows from operating activities	XXX
Cash used to purchase property, plant, and equipment	(XXX)
Free cash flow	XXX

The free cash flow can be expressed as a percentage of sales in order to provide a measure that can be compared over time or to other companies. This ratio is computed as follows:

$$\text{Ratio of Free Cash Flow to Sales} = \frac{\text{Free Cash Flow}}{\text{Sales}}$$

Positive free cash flow is considered favorable. A company that has free cash flow is able to fund growth and acquisitions, retire debt, purchase treasury stock, and pay dividends. A company with no free cash flow may have limited financial flexibility, potentially leading to liquidity problems. As one analyst notes, "Free cash flow gives the company firepower to reduce debt and ultimately generate consistent, actual income."

To illustrate, information from the annual reports of **National Beverage Corp. (FIZZ)** for three recent years is as follows (in thousands):

	Year 3	Year 2	Year 1
Cash flows from operating activities	$ 78,955	$ 58,020	$ 52,382
Cash used to purchase property, plant, and equipment	12,140	11,630	12,124
Sales	704,785	645,825	641,135

The free cash flow is computed for the three years as follows:

	Year 3	Year 2	Year 1
Cash flows from operating activities	$ 78,955	$ 58,020	$ 52,382
Cash used to purchase property, plant, and equipment	(12,140)	(11,630)	(12,124)
Free cash flow	$ 66,815	$ 46,390	$ 40,258

As can be seen, free cash flow has increased across the three years. In Year 3, it is nearly 66% higher than in Year 1 [($66,815 − $40,258) ÷ $40,258]. The ratio of free cash flow to sales is as follows (rounded to one decimal place):

	Year 3	Year 2	Year 1
Ratio of free cash flow to sales	9.4%	7.2%	6.3%
	($66,185 ÷	($46,390 ÷	($40,258 ÷
	$704,785)	$645,825)	$641,135)

The ratio of free cash flow to sales has also increased across these three years, from 6.3% in Year 1 to 9.4% in Year 3, which is a 49% increase [(9.4% − 6.3%) ÷ 6.3%].

| Make a Decision | Free Cash Flow |

Analyze and compare Amazon.com, Best Buy, and Wal-Mart (MAD 13-1)
(Continuing company analysis)

Analyze and compare Apple, Coca-Cola, and Verizon (MAD 13-2)

Analyze Aeropostale (MAD 13-3)

Analyze and compare AT&T and Facebook (MAD 13-4)

Analyze Priceline (MAD 13-5)

Make a Decision

Why It Matters

Twenty Years After

The S&P 500 is made up of the 500 largest publicly traded companies in the United States. **Deutsche Bank**, one of the world's largest financial institutions, aggregated the free cash flow performance of today's S&P 500 companies and the S&P 500 companies from 20 years ago, as follows:

S&P 500 in aggregate (in billions, except ratio)	20 Years Ago	Currently
Free cash flow	$148	$958
Ratio of free cash flow to sales	6%	8%
Cash paid for dividends...................................	$58	$426
Cash paid for treasury stock purchases	30	475
Total...	$88	$901

As can be seen, the free cash flow has grown over six-fold, while the ratio of free cash flow to sales has improved from 6% 20 years ago to 8% currently. Twenty years ago, $88 billion of free cash flow, or nearly 60% of free cash flow ($88 ÷ $148), was used to pay dividends and treasury stock. Currently, $901 billion of free cash flow, or 94% of free cash flow ($901 ÷ $958), is used to pay dividends and treasury stock. Compared to twenty years ago, companies are using a much greater portion of their free cash flow to return cash to stockholders. This suggests companies are seeing fewer opportunities for internal investment than 20 years ago.

Appendix 1 Spreadsheet (Work Sheet) for Statement of Cash Flows—The Indirect Method

Objective App 1
Use a spreadsheet to prepare the statement of cash flows under the indirect method.

A spreadsheet (work sheet) may be used in preparing the statement of cash flows. However, whether or not a spreadsheet (work sheet) is used, the concepts presented in this chapter are not affected.

The data for **Rundell Inc.**, presented in Exhibit 4, are used as a basis for illustrating the spreadsheet (work sheet) for the indirect method. The steps in preparing this spreadsheet (work sheet), shown in Exhibit 8, are as follows:

- Step 1. List the title of each balance sheet account in the Accounts column.
- Step 2. For each balance sheet account, enter its balance as of December 31, 20Y7, in the first column and its balance as of December 31, 20Y8, in the last column. Place the credit balances in parentheses.
- Step 3. Add the December 31, 20Y7 and 20Y8 column totals, which should total to zero.
- Step 4. Analyze the change during the year in each noncash account to determine its net increase (decrease) and classify the change as affecting cash flows from operating activities, investing activities, financing activities, or noncash investing and financing activities.

Exhibit 8 End-of-Period Spreadsheet (Work Sheet) for Statement of Cash Flows—Indirect Method

Step 2

	A	B	C	D	E	F	G
		Rundell Inc.					
1							
2		End-of-Period Spreadsheet (Work Sheet) for Statement of Cash Flows					
3		For the Year Ended December 31, 20Y8					
4	Accounts	Balance,	Transactions				Balance,
5		Dec. 31, 20Y7		Debit		Credit	Dec. 31, 20Y8
6	Cash	26,000	(o)	71,500			97,500
7	Accounts receivable (net)	65,000	(n)	9,000			74,000
8	Inventories	180,000			(m)	8,000	172,000
9	Land	125,000	(k)	15,000	(l)	60,000	80,000
10	Building	200,000	(j)	60,000			260,000
11	Accumulated depreciation—building	(58,300)			(i)	7,000	(65,300)
12	Accounts payable (merchandise creditors)	(46,700)	(h)	3,200			(43,500)
13	Accrued expenses payable (operating expenses)	(24,300)			(g)	2,200	(26,500)
14	Income taxes payable	(8,400)	(f)	500			(7,900)
15	Dividends payable	(10,000)			(e)	4,000	(14,000)
16	Bonds payable	(150,000)	(d)	50,000			(100,000)
17	Common stock	(16,000)			(c)	8,000	(24,000)
18	Paid-in capital in excess of par	(80,000)			(c)	40,000	(120,000)
19	Retained earnings	(202,300)	(b)	28,000	(a)	108,000	(282,300)
20	Totals Step 3 →	0		237,200		237,200	0 ← Step 3
21	Operating activities:						
22	Net income		(a)	108,000			
23	Depreciation of building		(i)	7,000			
24	Gain on sale of land				(l)	12,000	
25	Increase in accounts receivable				(n)	9,000	
26	Decrease in inventories		(m)	8,000			
27	Decrease in accounts payable				(h)	3,200	
28	Increase in accrued expenses payable		(g)	2,200			
29	Decrease in income taxes payable				(f)	500	
30	Investing activities:						
31	Sale of land		(l)	72,000			
32	Purchase of land				(k)	15,000	
33	Purchase of building				(j)	60,000	
34	Financing activities:						
35	Issued common stock		(c)	48,000			
36	Retired bonds payable				(d)	50,000	
37	Declared cash dividends				(b)	28,000	
38	Increase in dividends payable		(e)	4,000			
39	Net increase in cash				(o)	71,500	
40	Totals			249,200		249,200	
41							

Steps 4–7

- Step 5. Indicate the effect of the change on cash flows by making entries in the Transactions columns.
- Step 6. After all noncash accounts have been analyzed, enter the net increase (decrease) in cash during the period.
- Step 7. Add the Debit and Credit Transactions columns. The totals should be equal.

Analyzing Accounts

In analyzing the noncash accounts (Step 4), try to determine the type of cash flow activity (operating, investing, or financing) that led to the change in the account. As each noncash account is analyzed, an entry (Step 5) is made on the spreadsheet (work sheet) for the type of cash flow activity that caused the change. After all noncash accounts have been analyzed, an entry (Step 6) is made for the increase (decrease) in cash during the period.

The entries made on the spreadsheet are not posted to the ledger. They are only used in preparing and summarizing the data on the spreadsheet.

The order in which the accounts are analyzed is not important. However, it is more efficient to begin with Retained Earnings and proceed upward in the account listing.

Retained Earnings

The spreadsheet (work sheet) shows a Retained Earnings balance of $202,300 at December 31, 20Y7, and $282,300 at December 31, 20Y8. Thus, Retained Earnings increased $80,000 during the year. This increase is from the following:

- Net income of $108,000
- Declaring cash dividends of $28,000

To identify the cash flows from these activities, two entries are made on the spreadsheet.

The $108,000 is reported on the statement of cash flows as part of cash flows from operating activities. Thus, an entry is made in the Transactions columns on the spreadsheet, as follows:

(a)	Operating Activities—Net Income	108,000	
	Retained Earnings		108,000

The preceding entry accounts for the net income portion of the change to Retained Earnings. It also identifies the cash flow in the bottom portion of the spreadsheet as related to operating activities.

The $28,000 of dividends is reported as a financing activity on the statement of cash flows. Thus, an entry is made in the Transactions columns on the spreadsheet, as follows:

(b)	Retained Earnings	28,000	
	Financing Activities—Declared Cash Dividends		28,000

The preceding entry accounts for the dividends portion of the change to Retained Earnings. It also identifies the cash flow in the bottom portion of the spreadsheet as related to financing activities. The $28,000 of declared dividends will be adjusted later for the actual amount of cash dividends paid during the year.

Other Accounts

The entries for the other noncash accounts are made in the spreadsheet in a manner similar to entries (a) and (b). A summary of these entries follows:

(c)	Financing Activities—Issued Common Stock	48,000	
	Common Stock		8,000
	Paid-In Capital in Excess of Par—Common Stock		40,000
(d)	Bonds Payable	50,000	
	Financing Activities—Retired Bonds Payable		50,000
(e)	Financing Activities—Increase in Dividends Payable	4,000	
	Dividends Payable		4,000
(f)	Income Taxes Payable	500	
	Operating Activities—Decrease in Income Taxes Payable		500
(g)	Operating Activities—Increase in Accrued Expenses Payable	2,200	
	Accrued Expenses Payable		2,200
(h)	Accounts Payable	3,200	
	Operating Activities—Decrease in Accounts Payable		3,200
(i)	Operating Activities—Depreciation of Building	7,000	
	Accumulated Depreciation—Building		7,000
(j)	Building	60,000	
	Investing Activities—Purchase of Building		60,000

(k)	Land	15,000	
	Investing Activities—Purchase of Land		15,000
(l)	Investing Activities—Sale of Land	72,000	
	Operating Activities—Gain on Sale of Land		12,000
	Land		60,000
(m)	Operating Activities—Decrease in Inventories	8,000	
	Inventories		8,000
(n)	Accounts Receivable	9,000	
	Operating Activities—Increase in Accounts Receivable		9,000
(o)	Cash	71,500	
	Net Increase in Cash		71,500

After all the balance sheet accounts are analyzed and the entries made on the spreadsheet (work sheet), all the operating, investing, and financing activities are identified in the bottom portion of the spreadsheet. The accuracy of the entries is verified by totaling the Debit and Credit Transactions columns. The totals of the columns should be equal.

Preparing the Statement of Cash Flows

The statement of cash flows prepared from the spreadsheet is identical to the statement in Exhibit 7. The data for the three sections of the statement are obtained from the bottom portion of the spreadsheet.

Objective App 2

Prepare a statement of cash flows under the direct method.

Appendix 2 Preparing the Statement of Cash Flows—The Direct Method

The direct method reports cash flows from operating activities as follows:

Cash flows from (used for) operating activities:	
Cash received from customers	$ XXX
Cash payments for merchandise	(XXX)
Cash payments for operating expenses	(XXX)
Cash payments for interest	(XXX)
Cash payments for income taxes	(XXX)
Net cash flow from operating activities	$XXX

The "Cash flows from investing activities" and "Cash flows from financing activities" sections of the statement of cash flows are exactly the same under both the direct and indirect methods. The amount of net cash flow from operating activities is also the same, but the manner in which it is reported is different.

Under the direct method, the income statement is adjusted to cash flows from operating activities as shown in Exhibit 9.

Exhibit 9

Converting Income Statement to Cash Flows from Operating Activities Using the Direct Method

Income Statement	Adjusted to	Cash Flows from Operating Activities
Sales	→	Cash received from customers
Cost of goods sold	→	Cash payments for merchandise
Operating expenses:		
Depreciation expense*	n/a	n/a
Other operating expenses	→	Cash payments for operating expenses
Gain (loss) on sale of land**	n/a	n/a
Interest expense	→	Cash payments for interest
Income tax expense	→	Cash payments for income taxes
Net income	→	Net cash flow from operating activities

* Depreciation does not affect cash and, thus, is not considered in the direct method.
** Gains (Losses) on sales of property, plant, and equipment are reported as part of investing activities.

As shown in Exhibit 9, depreciation expense is not adjusted or reported as part of cash flows from operating activities. This is because depreciation expense does not involve a cash outflow. The gain on the sale of the land is also not adjusted and is not reported as part of cash flows from operating activities. This is because the cash flow from operating activities is determined directly, rather than by reconciling net income. The cash proceeds from the sale of the land are reported as an investing activity.

To illustrate the direct method, the income statement and comparative balance sheet for **Rundell Inc.**, shown in Exhibit 4, are used.

Cash Received from Customers

The income statement (shown in Exhibit 4) of **Rundell Inc.** reports sales of $1,180,000. To determine the cash received from customers, the $1,180,000 is adjusted for any increase or decrease in accounts receivable. The adjustment is summarized in Exhibit 10.

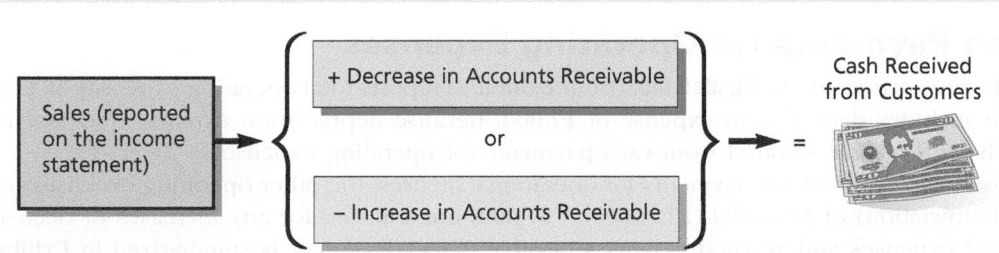

Exhibit 10

Determining the Cash Received from Customers

The cash received from customers is $1,171,000, computed as follows:

Sales	$1,180,000
Increase in accounts receivable	(9,000)
Cash received from customers	$1,171,000

The increase of $9,000 in accounts receivable (shown in Exhibit 4) during 20Y8 indicates that sales on account exceeded cash received from customers by $9,000. In other words, sales include $9,000 that did not result in a cash inflow during the year. Thus, $9,000 is deducted from sales to determine the cash received from customers.

Cash Payments for Merchandise

The income statement (shown in Exhibit 4) for **Rundell Inc.** reports cost of goods sold of $790,000. To determine the cash payments for merchandise, the $790,000 is adjusted for any increases or decreases in inventories and accounts payable. Assuming the accounts payable are owed to merchandise suppliers, the adjustment is summarized in Exhibit 11.

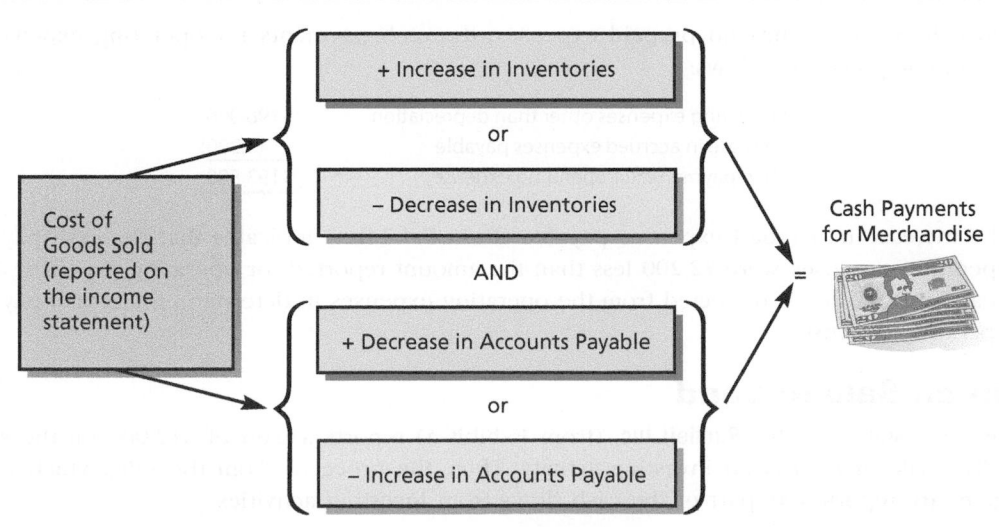

Exhibit 11

Determining the Cash Payments for Merchandise

The cash payments for merchandise are $785,200, computed as follows:

Cost of goods sold	$790,000
Decrease in inventories	(8,000)
Decrease in accounts payable	3,200
Cash payments for merchandise	$785,200

The $8,000 decrease in inventories (from Exhibit 4) indicates that the merchandise sold exceeded the cost of the merchandise purchased by $8,000. In other words, the cost of goods sold includes $8,000 of merchandise sold from inventory that did not require a cash outflow during the year. Thus, $8,000 is deducted from the cost of goods sold in determining the cash payments for merchandise.

The $3,200 decrease in accounts payable (from Exhibit 4) indicates that cash payments for merchandise were $3,200 more than the purchases on account during 20Y8. Therefore, $3,200 is added to the cost of goods sold in determining the cash payments for merchandise.

Cash Payments for Operating Expenses

The income statement for **Rundell Inc.** (from Exhibit 4) reports total operating expenses of $203,000, which includes depreciation expense of $7,000. Because depreciation expense does not require a cash outflow, it is omitted from cash payments for operating expenses.

To determine the cash payments for operating expenses, the other operating expenses (excluding depreciation) of $196,000 ($203,000 − $7,000) are adjusted for any increases or decreases in prepaid expenses and accrued expenses payable. This adjustment is summarized in Exhibit 12.

Exhibit 12

Determining the Cash Payments for Operating Expenses

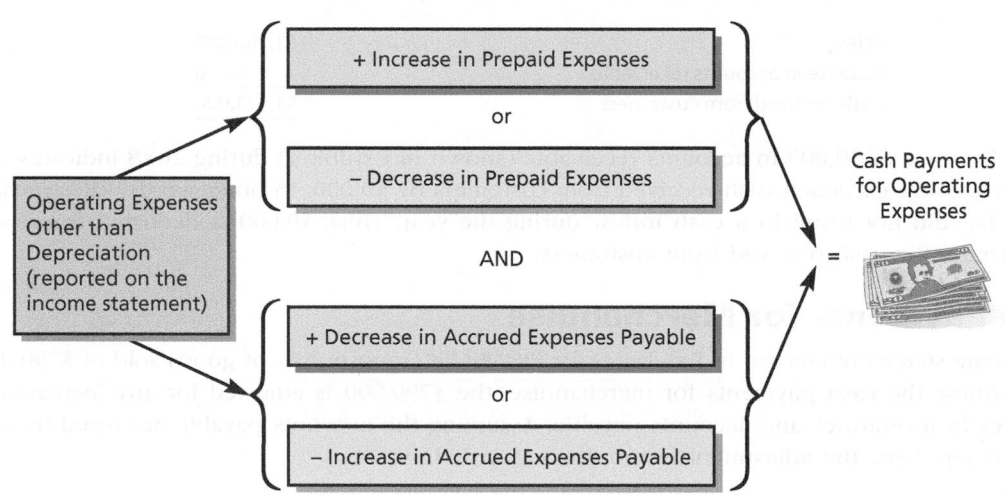

Since Rundell Inc. has no prepaid expenses, the cash payments for operating expenses are $193,800, computed as follows:

Operating expenses other than depreciation	$196,000
Increase in accrued expenses payable	(2,200)
Cash payments for operating expenses	$193,800

The increase in accrued expenses payable (from Exhibit 4) indicates that the cash payments for operating expenses were $2,200 less than the amount reported for operating expenses during the year. Thus, $2,200 is deducted from the operating expenses in determining the cash payments for operating expenses.

Gain on Sale of Land

The income statement for **Rundell Inc.** (from Exhibit 4) reports a gain of $12,000 on the sale of land. The sale of land is an investing activity. Thus, the proceeds from the sale, which include the gain, are reported as part of the cash flows from investing activities.

Interest Expense

The income statement for **Rundell Inc.** (from Exhibit 4) reports interest expense of $8,000. To determine the cash payments for interest, the $8,000 is adjusted for any increases or decreases in interest payable. The adjustment is summarized in Exhibit 13.

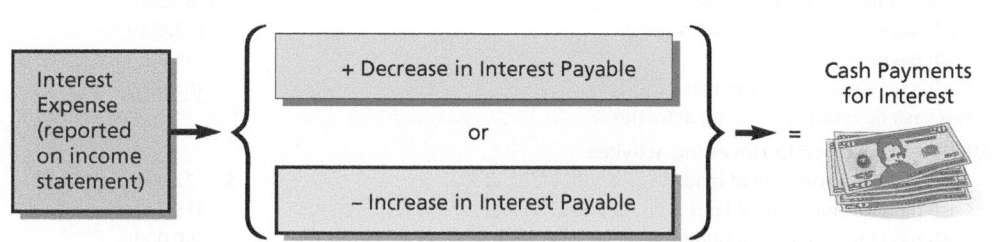

Exhibit 13
Determining the Cash Payments for Interest

The comparative balance sheet of Rundell in Exhibit 4 indicates no interest payable. This is because the interest expense on the bonds payable is paid on June 1 and December 31. Because there is no interest payable, no adjustment of the interest expense of $8,000 is necessary.

Cash Payments for Income Taxes

The income statement for **Rundell Inc.** (from Exhibit 4) reports income tax expense of $83,000. To determine the cash payments for income taxes, the $83,000 is adjusted for any increases or decreases in income taxes payable. The adjustment is summarized in Exhibit 14.

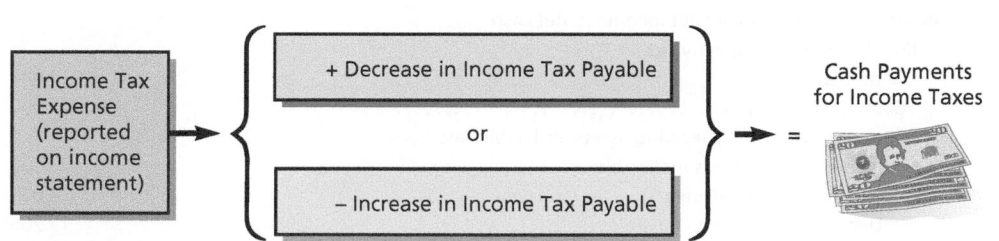

Exhibit 14
Determining the Cash Payments for Income Taxes

The cash payments for income taxes are $83,500, computed as follows:

Income tax expense	$83,000
Decrease in income taxes payable	500
Cash payments for income taxes	$83,500

The $500 decrease in income taxes payable (from Exhibit 4) indicates that the cash payments for income taxes were $500 more than the amount reported for income tax expense during 20Y8. Thus, $500 is added to the income tax expense in determining the cash payments for income taxes.

Reporting Cash Flows from Operating Activities—Direct Method

The statement of cash flows for **Rundell Inc.**, using the direct method for reporting cash flows from operating activities, is shown in Exhibit 15. The portions of the statement that differ from those prepared under the indirect method are highlighted.

Exhibit 15 also includes the separate schedule reconciling net income and net cash flow from operating activities. This schedule is included as part of the statement of cash flows when the direct method is used. This schedule is similar to the "Cash flows from operating activities" section prepared under the indirect method.

Exhibit 15

Statement of Cash Flows—Direct Method

Rundell Inc.
Statement of Cash Flows
For the Year Ended December 31, 20Y8

Cash flows from (used for) operating activities:

Cash received from customers	$1,171,000	
Cash payments for merchandise	(785,200)	
Cash payments for operating expenses	(193,800)	
Cash payments for interest	(8,000)	
Cash payments for income taxes	(83,500)	
Net cash flow from operating activities		$100,500

Cash flows from (used for) investing activities:

Cash received from sale of land	$ 72,000	
Cash paid for purchase of land	(15,000)	
Cash paid for purchase of building	(60,000)	
Net cash flow used for investing activities		(3,000)

Cash flows from (used for) financing activities:

Cash received from sale of common stock	$ 48,000	
Cash paid to retire bonds payable	(50,000)	
Cash paid for dividends	(24,000)	
Net cash flow used for financing activities		(26,000)
Net increase in cash		$ 71,500
Cash balance, January 1, 20Y8		26,000
Cash balance, December 31, 20Y8		$ 97,500

Schedule Reconciling Net Income with Cash
Flows from Operating Activities:

Cash flows from (used for) operating activities:

Net income		$108,000
Adjustments to reconcile net income to net cash flow from operating activities:		
Depreciation		7,000
Gain on sale of land		(12,000)
Changes in current operating assets and liabilities:		
Increase in accounts receivable		(9,000)
Decrease in inventories		8,000
Decrease in accounts payable		(3,200)
Increase in accrued expenses payable		2,200
Decrease in income taxes payable		(500)
Net cash flow from operating activities		$100,500

Let's Review

Chapter Summary

1. The statement of cash flows reports cash receipts and cash payments by three types of activities: operating activities, investing activities, and financing activities. Cash flows from operating activities reports the cash inflows and outflows from a company's day-to-day operations. Cash flows from investing activities reports the cash inflows and outflows related to changes in a company's long-term assets. Cash flows from financing activities reports the cash inflows and outflows related to changes in a company's long-term liabilities and stockholders' equity. Investing and financing for a business may be affected by transactions that do not involve cash. The effect of such transactions should be reported in a separate schedule accompanying the statement of cash flows.

2. The indirect method reports cash flows from operating activities by adjusting net income for revenues and expenses that do not involve the receipt or payment of cash. Noncash expenses such as depreciation are added back to net income. Gains and losses on the disposal of assets are added to or deducted from net income. Changes in current operating assets and liabilities are added to or subtracted from net income, depending on their effect on cash.

3. Cash flows from investing activities are reported below cash flows from operating activities on the statement of cash flows. Cash flows from investing activities reports the cash inflows and outflows related to changes in a company's long-term assets.

4. Cash flows from financing activities are reported below cash flows from operating activities on the statement of cash flows. Cash flows from financing activities reports the cash inflows and outflows related to changes in a company's long-term liabilities and stockholders' equity.

5. The statement of cash flows reports cash flows from operating activities followed by cash flows from investing and financing activities. The result of adding the net cash flows from operating, investing, and financing activities is the net increase or decrease in cash for the period. Cash at the beginning of the year is added to determine the cash at the end of the period. This ending cash amount must agree with cash reported on the end-of-period balance sheet.

6. Free cash flow measures the operating cash flow available to a company after it purchases the property, plant, and equipment necessary to maintain its current operations. It is computed as cash flows from operating activities minus cash used to purchase property, plant, and equipment. Free cash flow can be expressed as a percentage of sales in order to provide a relative measure that can be compared over time or to other companies. Positive free cash flow is considered favorable.

Key Terms

cash flow per share (633)
cash flows from financing activities (629)
cash flows from investing activities (628)

cash flows from operating activities (628)
direct method (629)

free cash flow (644)
indirect method (630)
statement of cash flows (628)

Practice

Multiple-Choice Questions

1. An example of a cash flow from an operating activity is:
   a. receipt of cash from the sale of stock.
   b. receipt of cash from the sale of bonds.
   c. payment of cash for dividends.
   d. receipt of cash from customers on account.

2. An example of a cash flow from an investing activity is:
   a. receipt of cash from the sale of equipment.
   b. receipt of cash from the sale of stock.
   c. payment of cash for dividends.
   d. payment of cash to acquire treasury stock.

3. An example of a cash flow from a financing activity is:
   a. receipt of cash from customers on account.
   b. receipt of cash from the sale of equipment.
   c. payment of cash for dividends.
   d. payment of cash to acquire land.

4. Which of the following methods of reporting cash flows from operating activities adjusts net income for revenues and expenses not involving the receipt or payment of cash?
   a. Direct method
   b. Purchase method
   c. Reciprocal method
   d. Indirect method

5. The net income reported on the income statement for the year was $55,000, and depreciation of fixed assets for the year was $22,000. The balances of the current asset and current liability accounts at the beginning and end of the year are as follows:

	End of Year	Beginning of Year
Cash	$ 65,000	$ 70,000
Accounts receivable	100,000	90,000
Inventories	145,000	150,000
Prepaid expenses	7,500	8,000
Accounts payable (merchandise creditors)	51,000	58,000

   The total amount reported for cash flows from operating activities on the statement of cash flows using the indirect method is:
   a. $33,000.
   b. $55,000.
   c. $65,500.
   d. $77,000.

Answers provided after Problem. Need more practice? Find additional multiple-choice questions, exercises, and problems in CengageNOWv2.

Exercises

1. Classifying cash flows   Obj. 1

Identify whether each of the following would be reported as an operating, investing, or financing activity on the statement of cash flows:

a. Repurchase of common stock

b. Cash received from customers

c. Payment of accounts payable

d. Retirement of bonds payable

e. Purchase of equipment

f. Purchase of inventory for cash

2. Adjustments to net income—indirect method
Obj. 2

Pearl Corporation's accumulated depreciation—furniture account increased by $8,400, while $3,080 of patent amortization was recognized between balance sheet dates. There were no purchases or sales of depreciable or intangible assets during the year. In addition, the income statement showed a loss of $4,480 from the sale of land. Reconcile a net income of $120,400 to net cash flow from operating activities.

3. Changes in current operating assets and liabilities—indirect method
Obj. 2

Alpenrose Corporation's comparative balance sheet for current assets and liabilities was as follows:

	Dec. 31, 20Y2	Dec. 31, 20Y1
Accounts receivable	$27,000	$32,400
Inventory	18,000	15,480
Accounts payable	16,200	14,220
Dividends payable	49,500	53,100

Adjust net income of $207,000 for changes in operating assets and liabilities to arrive at net cash flow from operating activities.

4. Cash flows from operating activities—indirect method
Obj. 2

Pettygrove Inc. reported the following data:

Net income	$405,000
Depreciation expense	45,000
Gain on disposal of equipment	36,900
Decrease in accounts receivable	25,200
Decrease in accounts payable	6,480

Prepare the "Cash flows from operating activities" section of the statement of cash flows, using the indirect method.

5. Land transactions on the statement of cash flows
Obj. 3

Milo Corporation purchased land for $540,000. Later in the year, the company sold a different piece of land with a book value of $270,000 for $180,000. How are the effects of these transactions reported on the statement of cash flows?

6. Common stock transactions on the statement of cash flows
Obj. 4

Wright Inc. received $1,200,000 from issuing shares of its common stock. During the year, Wright Inc. paid $500,000 to retire bonds and paid dividends of $250,000. How are the effects of these transactions reported on the statement of cash flows?

7. Free cash flow
Obj. 6

McMahon Inc. reported the following on the company's statement of cash flows in 20Y8 and 20Y7:

	20Y8	20Y7
Net cash flow from operating activities	$ 294,000	$ 280,000
Net cash flow used for investing activities	(224,000)	(252,000)
Net cash flow used for financing activities	(63,000)	(42,000)

Seventy percent of the net cash flow used for investing activities was for the purchase of property, plant, and equipment.

a. Determine McMahon's free cash flow for both years.

b. Has McMahon's free cash flow improved or declined from 20Y7 to 20Y8?

Answers provided after Problem. Need more practice? Find additional multiple-choice questions, exercises, and problems in CengageNOWv2.

Problem

The comparative balance sheet of Dowling Company for December 31, 20Y5 and 20Y4, is as follows:

Dowling Company Comparative Balance Sheet December 31, 20Y5 and 20Y4	20Y5	20Y4
Assets		
Cash	$ 140,350	$ 95,900
Accounts receivable (net)	95,300	102,300
Inventories	165,200	157,900
Prepaid expenses	6,240	5,860
Investments (long-term)	35,700	84,700
Land	75,000	90,000
Buildings	375,000	260,000
Accumulated depreciation—buildings	(71,300)	(58,300)
Machinery and equipment	428,300	428,300
Accumulated depreciation—machinery and equipment	(148,500)	(138,000)
Patents	58,000	65,000
Total assets	$1,159,290	$1,093,660
Liabilities and Stockholders' Equity		
Accounts payable (merchandise creditors)	$ 43,500	$ 46,700
Accrued expenses payable (operating expenses)	14,000	12,500
Income taxes payable	7,900	8,400
Dividends payable	14,000	10,000
Mortgage note payable, due in 10 years	40,000	0
Bonds payable	150,000	250,000
Common stock, $30 par	450,000	375,000
Paid-in capital in excess of par—common stock	66,250	41,250
Retained earnings	373,640	349,810
Total liabilities and stockholders' equity	$1,159,290	$1,093,660

The income statement for Dowling Company follows:

Dowling Company Income Statement For the Year Ended December 31, 20Y5		
Sales		$1,100,000
Cost of goods sold		(710,000)
Gross profit		$ 390,000
Operating expenses:		
Depreciation expense	$ 23,500	
Patent amortization	7,000	
Other operating expenses	196,000	
Total operating expenses		(226,500)
Operating income		$ 163,500
Other revenue and expense:		
Gain on sale of investments	$ 11,000	
Interest expense	(26,000)	(15,000)
Income before income tax		$ 148,500
Income tax expense		(50,000)
Net income		$ 98,500

An examination of the accounting records revealed the following additional information applicable to 20Y5:

a. Land costing $15,000 was sold for $15,000.
b. A mortgage note was issued for $40,000.
c. A building costing $115,000 was constructed.

   d. 2,500 shares of common stock were issued at $40 in exchange for the bonds payable.

   e. Cash dividends declared were $74,670.

Instructions

1. Prepare a statement of cash flows, using the indirect method of reporting cash flows from operating activities.

2. (*Appendix 2*) Prepare a statement of cash flows, using the direct method of reporting cash flows from operating activities.

Need more practice? Find additional multiple-choice questions, exercises, and problems in CengageNOWv2.

Answers

Multiple-Choice Questions

1. **d** Cash flows from operating activities affect transactions that enter into the determination of net income, such as the receipt of cash from customers on account (answer d). Receipts of cash from the sale of stock (answer a) and the sale of bonds (answer b) and payments of cash for dividends (answer c) are cash flows from financing activities.

2. **a** Cash flows from investing activities include receipts from the sale of noncurrent assets, such as equipment (answer a), and payments to acquire noncurrent assets. Receipts of cash from the sale of stock (answer b) and payments of cash for dividends (answer c) and to acquire treasury stock (answer d) are cash flows from financing activities.

3. **c** Payment of cash for dividends (answer c) is an example of a financing activity. The receipt of cash from customers on account (answer a) is an operating activity. The receipt of cash from the sale of equipment (answer b) and the payment of cash to acquire land (answer d) are examples of investing activities.

4. **d** The indirect method (answer d) reports cash flows from operating activities by beginning with net income and adjusting it for revenues and expenses not involving the receipt or payment of cash.

5. **c** The "Cash flows from operating activities" section of the statement of cash flows would report net cash flow from operating activities of $65,500, determined as follows:

Cash flow from (used for) operating activities:		
Net income...	$ 55,000	
Adjustments to reconcile net income to net cash flow from operating activities:		
Depreciation expense	22,000	
Changes in current operating assets and liabilities:		
Increase in accounts receivable......................	(10,000)	
Decrease in inventories................................	5,000	
Decrease in prepaid expenses	500	
Decrease in accounts payable........................	(7,000)	
Net cash flow from operating activities		$65,500

Exercises

1.	a.	Financing	d.	Financing
	b.	Operating	e.	Investing
	c.	Operating	f.	Operating

2. Net income $120,400

    Adjustments to reconcile net income to net cash flow from
      operating activities:

        Depreciation   8,400

        Amortization of patents   3,080

        Loss from sale of land..   <u>4,480</u>

    Net cash flow from operating activities $136,360

3. Net income $207,000

    Changes in current operating assets and liabilities:

      Decrease in accounts receivable   5,400

      Increase in inventory...   (2,520)

      Increase in accounts payable ....   <u>1,980</u>

    Net cash flow from operating activities $211,860

Note: The change in dividends payable impacts the cash paid for dividends, which is disclosed under financing activities.

4. Cash flows from operating activities:

    Net income $405,000

    Adjustments to reconcile net income to net cash flow from
      operating activities:

        Depreciation   45,000

        Gain on disposal of equipment ....   (36,900)

      Changes in current operating assets and liabilities:

        Decrease in accounts receivable..................................   25,200

        Decrease in accounts payable.......................................   <u>(6,480)</u>

    Net cash flow from operating activities $431,820

5. The loss on the sale of land is added to net income in the "Cash flows from operating activities" section.

    Loss on sale of land $90,000

    The purchase and sale of land are reported as part of cash flows from investing activities as follows:

    Cash received from sale of land .... $ 180,000

    Cash paid for purchase of land ....   (540,000)

6. Cash flows from (used for) financing activities:

    Cash received from issuing common stock $1,200,000

    Cash paid to retire bonds...   (500,000)

    Cash paid for dividends ....   <u>(250,000)</u>

    Net cash flow from financing activities.................................... $ 450,000

7. a.

	20Y8	20Y7
Net cash flow from operating activities	$ 294,000	$ 280,000
Cash used to purchase property, plant, and equipment	(156,800)*	(176,400)**
Free cash flow	$ 137,200	$ 103,600

      *70% × $224,000

      **70% × $252,000

    b. The change in free cash flow from $103,600 to $137,200 represents an improvement.

Need more help? Watch step-by-step videos of how to compute answers to these Exercises in CengageNOWv2.

Problem

1.

Dowling Company **Statement of Cash Flows—Indirect Method** **For the Year Ended December 31, 20Y5**		
Cash flows from (used for) operating activities:		
Net income...	$ 98,500	
Adjustments to reconcile net income to net cash flow from operating activities:		
Depreciation....................................	23,500	
Amortization of patents.........................	7,000	
Gain on sale of investments	(11,000)	
Changes in current operating assets and liabilities:		
Decrease in accounts receivable..............	7,000	
Increase in inventories.......................	(7,300)	
Increase in prepaid expenses.................	(380)	
Decrease in accounts payable	(3,200)	
Increase in accrued expenses payable	1,500	
Decrease in income taxes payable	(500)	
Net cash flow from operating activities		$115,120
Cash flows from (used for) investing activities:		
Cash received from sale of investments	$ 60,000[1]	
Cash received from sale of land	15,000	
Cash paid for construction of building.................	(115,000)	
Net cash flow used for investing activities.............		(40,000)
Cash flows from (used for) financing activities:		
Cash received from issuing mortgage note payable.....	$ 40,000	
Cash paid for dividends.............................	(70,670)[2]	
Net cash flow used for financing activities		(30,670)
Net increase in cash		$ 44,450
Cash balance, January 1, 20Y5..............................		95,900
Cash balance, December 31, 20Y5		$140,350
Schedule of Noncash Investing and Financing Activities:		
Issued common stock to retire bonds payable..........		$100,000

[1] $60,000 = $11,000 gain + $49,000 (decrease in investments)
[2] $70,670 = $74,670 – $4,000 (increase in dividends)

2.

Dowling Company **Statement of Cash Flows—Direct Method** **For the Year Ended December 31, 20Y5**		
Cash flows from (used for) operating activities:		
Cash received from customers[1].......................	$1,107,000	
Cash paid for merchandise[2]...........................	(720,500)	
Cash paid for operating expenses[3].....................	(194,880)	
Cash paid for interest expense	(26,000)	
Cash paid for income tax[4].............................	(50,500)	
Net cash flow from operating activities		$115,120
Cash flows from (used for) investing activities:		
Cash received from sale of investments	$ 60,000[5]	
Cash received from sale of land	15,000	
Cash paid for construction of building.................	(115,000)	
Net cash flow used for investing activities.............		(40,000)

(Continued)

Cash flows from (used for) financing activities:

Cash received from issuing mortgage note payable.............	$ 40,000	
Cash paid for dividends[6].....................................	(70,670)	
Net cash flow used for financing activities		(30,670)
Net increase in cash		$ 44,450
Cash balance, January 1, 20Y5..................................		95,900
Cash balance, December 31, 20Y5		$140,350

Schedule of Noncash Investing and Financing Activities:

Issued common stock to retire bonds payable.................	$100,000

Schedule Reconciling Net Income with Cash Flows from Operating Activities[7]

Computations:

[1]$1,100,000 + $7,000 = $1,107,000

[2]$710,000 + $3,200 + $7,300 = $720,500

[3]$196,000 + $380 – $1,500 = $194,880

[4]$50,000 + $500 = $50,500

[5]$60,000 = $11,000 gain + $49,000 (decrease in investments)

[6]$74,670 + $10,000 – $14,000 = $70,670

[7]The content of this schedule is the same as the "Cash flows from operating activities" section of part (1) of this solution and is not reproduced here for the sake of brevity.

Discussion Questions

1. What is the principal disadvantage of the direct method of reporting cash flows from operating activities?

2. What are the major advantages of the indirect method of reporting cash flows from operating activities?

3. A corporation issued $2,000,000 of common stock in exchange for $2,000,000 of fixed assets. Where would this transaction be reported on the statement of cash flows?

4. A retail business, using the accrual method of accounting, owed merchandise creditors (accounts payable) $320,000 at the beginning of the year and $350,000 at the end of the year. How would the $30,000 increase be used to adjust net income in determining the amount of cash flows from operating activities by the indirect method? Explain.

5. If salaries payable was $100,000 at the beginning of the year and $75,000 at the end of the year, should the $25,000 decrease be added to or deducted from income to determine the amount of cash flows from operating activities by the indirect method? Explain.

6. A long-term investment in bonds with a cost of $500,000 was sold for $600,000 cash. (a) What was the gain or loss on the sale? (b) What was the effect of the transaction on cash flows? (c) How should the transaction be reported on the statement of cash flows if cash flows from operating activities are reported by the indirect method?

7. A corporation issued $2,000,000 of 20-year bonds for cash at 98. How would the transaction be reported on the statement of cash flows?

8. Fully depreciated equipment costing $50,000 was discarded. What was the effect of the transaction on cash flows if (a) $15,000 cash is received for the equipment, and (b) no cash is received for the equipment?

9. For the current year, Packers Company decided to switch from the indirect method to the direct method for reporting cash flows from operating activities on the statement of cash flows. Will the change cause the amount of net cash flow from operating activities to be larger, smaller, or the same as if the indirect method had been used? Explain.

10. Name five common major classes of operating cash receipts or operating cash payments presented on the statement of cash flows when the cash flows from operating activities are reported by the direct method.

Basic Exercises

SHOW ME HOW

BE 13-1 Classifying cash flows
Obj. 1

Identify whether each of the following would be reported as an operating, investing, or financing activity on the statement of cash flows:

a. Purchase of investments

b. Disposal of equipment

c. Payment for selling expenses

d. Collection of accounts receivable

e. Cash sales

f. Issuance of bonds payable

SHOW ME HOW

BE 13-2 Adjustments to net income—indirect method
Obj. 2

Ripley Corporation's accumulated depreciation—equipment account increased by $15,325 while $3,800 of patent amortization was recognized between balance sheet dates. There were no purchases or sales of depreciable or intangible assets during the year. In addition, the income statement showed a gain of $22,420 from the sale of investments. Reconcile a net income of $286,900 to net cash flow from operating activities.

SHOW ME HOW

BE 13-3 Changes in current operating assets and liabilities—indirect method
Obj. 2

Huluduey Corporation's comparative balance sheet for current assets and liabilities was as follows:

	Dec. 31, 20Y2	Dec. 31, 20Y1
Accounts receivable	$17,500	$12,500
Inventory	51,650	44,200
Accounts payable	8,480	5,100
Dividends payable	9,480	6,100

Adjust net income of $75,800 for changes in operating assets and liabilities to arrive at net cash flow from operating activities.

SHOW ME HOW

BE 13-4 Cash flows from operating activities—indirect method
Obj. 2

Staley Inc. reported the following data:

Net income	$396,200
Depreciation expense	61,250
Loss on disposal of equipment	27,600
Increase in accounts receivable	9,000
Increase in accounts payable	3,350

Prepare the "Cash flows from operating activities" section of the statement of cash flows, using the indirect method.

SHOW ME HOW

BE 13-5 Land transactions on the statement of cash flows
Obj. 3

IZ Corporation purchased land for $500,000. Later in the year, the company sold a different piece of land with a book value of $250,000 for $280,000. How are the effects of these transactions reported on the statement of cash flows?

SHOW ME HOW

BE 13-6 Common stock transactions on the statement of cash flows
Obj. 4

Jones Industries received $600,000 from issuing shares of its common stock and $400,000 from issuing bonds. During the year, Jones Industries also paid dividends of $60,000. How are the effects of these transactions reported on the statement of cash flows?

SHOW ME HOW

BE 13-7 Free cash flow
Obj. 6

Dillin Inc. reported the following on the company's statement of cash flows in 20Y2 and 20Y1:

(Continued)

	20Y2	20Y1
Net cash flow from operating activities	$ 476,000	$ 455,000
Net cash flow used for investing activities	(427,000)	(378,000)
Net cash flow used for financing activities	(42,000)	(58,800)

Eighty percent of the net cash flow used for investing activities was used for the purchase of property, plant, and equipment.

a. Determine Dillin's free cash flow for both years.

b. Has Dillin's free cash flow improved or declined from 20Y1 to 20Y2?

SHOW ME HOW

Appendix 2
BE 13-8   Cash received from customers—direct method
Sales reported on the income statement were $225,000. The accounts receivable balance decreased $14,300 over the year. Determine the amount of cash received from customers.

SHOW ME HOW

Appendix 2
BE 13-9   Cash payments for merchandise—direct method
The cost of goods sold reported on the income statement was $185,000. The accounts payable balance increased $8,000, and the inventory balance increased by $11,100 over the year. Determine the amount of cash paid for merchandise.

Exercises

REAL WORLD

EX 13-1   Cash flows from operating activities—net loss   Obj. 1
In a prior year, **United Continental Holdings, Inc. (UAL)**, the parent company of **United Airlines**, reported a net *loss* of $723 million from operations. However, on its statement of cash flows, it reported $935 million of cash flows from operating activities.

➤ Explain this apparent contradiction between the loss and the positive cash flows.

EX 13-2   Effect of transactions on cash flows   Obj. 1

✔ b. Cash receipt, $600,000

State the effect (cash receipt or cash payment and amount) of each of the following transactions, considered individually, on cash flows:

a. Retired $500,000 of bonds, on which there was $4,000 of unamortized discount, for $510,000.

b. Sold 20,000 shares of $5 par common stock for $30 per share.

c. Sold equipment with a book value of $68,900 for $72,400.

d. Purchased land for $825,000 cash.

e. Purchased a building by paying $30,000 cash and issuing a $570,000 mortgage note payable.

f. Sold a new issue of $400,000 of bonds at 98.

g. Purchased 10,000 shares of $10 par common stock as treasury stock at $22.50 per share.

h. Paid dividends of $1.25 per share. There were 1,000,000 shares issued and 180,000 shares of treasury stock.

EX 13-3   Classifying cash flows   Obj. 1
Identify the type of cash flow activity for each of the following events (operating, investing, or financing):

a. Net income

b. Paid cash dividends

c. Issued common stock

d. Issued bonds

e. Redeemed bonds

f. Sold long-term investments

g. Purchased treasury stock

h. Sold equipment

i. Issued preferred stock

j. Purchased buildings

k. Purchased patents

EX 13-4 Cash flows from operating activities—indirect method **Obj. 2**

Indicate whether each of the following would be added to or deducted from net income in determining net cash flow from operating activities by the indirect method:

a. Decrease in inventory

b. Increase in accounts receivable

c. Increase in accounts payable

d. Loss on retirement of long-term debt

e. Depreciation of fixed assets

f. Decrease in notes receivable due in 60 days from customers

g. Increase in salaries payable

h. Decrease in prepaid expenses

i. Amortization of patent

j. Increase in notes payable due in 120 days to vendors

k. Gain on disposal of fixed assets

EX 13-5 Cash flows from operating activities—indirect method **Obj. 1, 2**

✔ Net cash flow from operating activities, $128,550

SHOW ME HOW

The net income reported on the income statement for the current year was $93,700. Depreciation recorded on store equipment for the year amounted to $31,200. Balances of the current asset and current liability accounts at the beginning and end of the year are as follows:

	End of Year	Beginning of Year
Cash	$24,100	$19,700
Accounts receivable (net)	65,000	56,000
Inventories	47,200	50,000
Prepaid expenses	3,250	8,000
Accounts payable (merchandise creditors)	23,400	17,200
Wages payable	5,300	6,400

a. Prepare the "Cash flows from operating activities" section of the statement of cash flows, using the indirect method.

b. ➤ Briefly explain why net cash flow from operating activities is different than net income.

EX 13-6 Cash flows from operating activities—indirect method **Obj. 1, 2**

✔ Net cash flow from operating activities, $296,900

SHOW ME HOW

The net income reported on the income statement for the current year was $214,000. Depreciation recorded on equipment and a building amounted to $99,300 for the year. Balances of the current asset and current liability accounts at the beginning and end of the year are as follows:

	End of Year	Beginning of Year
Cash	$ 75,900	$ 86,150
Accounts receivable (net)	82,150	88,750
Inventories	181,600	178,000
Prepaid expenses	4,800	5,100
Accounts payable (merchandise creditors)	93,700	115,000
Salaries payable	6,500	4,900

a. Prepare the "Cash flows from operating activities" section of the statement of cash flows, using the indirect method.

b. ➤ If the direct method had been used, would the net cash flow from operating activities have been the same? Explain.

EX 13-7 Cash flows from operating activities—indirect method **Obj. 1, 2**

✔ Net cash flow from operating activities, $525,410

SHOW ME HOW

The income statement disclosed the following items for the year:

Depreciation expense	$ 57,600
Gain on disposal of equipment	33,600
Net income	508,000

(Continued)

The changes in the current asset and liability accounts for the year are as follows:

	Increase (Decrease)
Accounts receivable	$ 8,960
Inventory	(5,120)
Prepaid insurance	(1,920)
Accounts payable	(6,080)
Income taxes payable	1,410
Dividends payable	2,200

a. Prepare the "Cash flows from operating activities" section of the statement of cash flows, using the indirect method.

b. ➡ Briefly explain why net cash flow from operating activities is different than net income.

EX 13-8 Reporting changes in equipment on statement of cash flows   Obj. 3
An analysis of the general ledger accounts indicates that office equipment, which cost $245,000 and on which accumulated depreciation totaled $112,500 on the date of sale, was sold for $105,900 during the year. Using this information, indicate the items to be reported on the statement of cash flows.

EX 13-9 Reporting changes in equipment on statement of cash flows   Obj. 3
An analysis of the general ledger accounts indicates that delivery equipment, which cost $75,000 and on which accumulated depreciation totaled $58,000 on the date of sale, was sold for $20,200 during the year. Using this information, indicate the items to be reported on the statement of cash flows.

EX 13-10 Reporting land transactions on statement of cash flows   Obj. 3
On the basis of the details of the following fixed asset account, indicate the items to be reported on the statement of cash flows:

ACCOUNT *Land*					ACCOUNT NO.	
					Balance	
Date		Item	Debit	Credit	Debit	Credit
Jan.	1	Balance			925,000	
Mar.	12	Purchased for cash	134,300		1,059,300	
Oct.	4	Sold for $106,800		89,400	969,900	

EX 13-11 Determining cash payments to stockholders   Obj. 4
The board of directors declared cash dividends totaling $1,200,000 during the current year. The comparative balance sheet indicates dividends payable of $250,000 at the beginning of the year and $100,000 at the end of the year. What was the amount of cash payments to stockholders during the year?

EX 13-12 Reporting stockholders' equity items on statement of cash flows   Obj. 4
On the basis of the following stockholders' equity accounts, indicate the items, exclusive of net income, to be reported on the statement of cash flows. There were no unpaid dividends at either the beginning or the end of the year.

ACCOUNT *Common Stock, $40 par* ACCOUNT NO.

Date		Item	Debit	Credit	Balance Debit	Balance Credit
Jan.	1	Balance, 120,000 shares				4,800,000
Apr.	2	30,000 shares issued for cash		1,200,000		6,000,000
June	30	5% stock dividend		300,000		6,300,000

ACCOUNT *Paid-In Capital in Excess of Par—Common Stock* ACCOUNT NO.

Date		Item	Debit	Credit	Balance Debit	Balance Credit
Jan.	1	Balance				360,000
Apr.	2	30,000 shares issued for cash		720,000		1,080,000
June	30	Stock dividend		150,000		1,230,000

ACCOUNT *Retained Earnings* ACCOUNT NO.

Date		Item	Debit	Credit	Balance Debit	Balance Credit
Jan.	1	Balance				2,000,000
June	30	Stock dividend	450,000			1,550,000
Dec.	30	Cash dividend	315,000			1,235,000
	31	Net income		1,000,000		2,235,000

**EX 13-13   Reporting land acquisition for cash and mortgage note on statement of   Obj. 3, 4
cash flows**
On the basis of the details of the following fixed asset account, indicate the items to be reported on the statement of cash flows:

ACCOUNT *Land* ACCOUNT NO.

Date		Item	Debit	Credit	Balance Debit	Balance Credit
Jan.	1	Balance			156,000	
Feb.	10	Purchased for cash	246,000		402,000	
Nov.	20	Purchased with long-term mortgage note	324,000		726,000	

EX 13-14   Reporting issuance and retirement of long-term debt   Obj. 4
On the basis of the details of the following bonds payable and related discount accounts, indicate the items to be reported in the "Cash flows from financing activities" section of the statement of cash flows, assuming no gain or loss on retiring the bonds:

ACCOUNT *Bonds Payable* ACCOUNT NO.

Date		Item	Debit	Credit	Balance Debit	Balance Credit
Jan.	1	Balance				750,000
	2	Retire bonds	150,000			600,000
June	30	Issue bonds		450,000		1,050,000

(Continued)

ACCOUNT *Discount on Bonds Payable*					ACCOUNT NO.	
					Balance	
Date		Item	Debit	Credit	Debit	Credit
Jan.	1	Balance			33,750	
	2	Retire bonds		12,000	21,750	
June	30	Issue bonds	30,000		51,750	
Dec.	31	Amortize discount		2,625	49,125	

EX 13-15 Determining net income from net cash flow from operating activities

Obj. 2, 3, 4

✔ Net income, $341,770

SHOW ME HOW

Curwen Inc. reported net cash flow from operating activities of $357,500 on its statement of cash flows for the year ended December 31. The following information was reported in the "Cash flows from operating activities" section of the statement of cash flows, using the indirect method:

Decrease in income taxes payable	$ 7,700
Decrease in inventories	19,140
Depreciation	29,480
Gain on sale of investments	13,200
Increase in accounts payable	5,280
Increase in prepaid expenses	2,970
Increase in accounts receivable	14,300

a. Determine the net income reported by Curwen Inc. for the year ended December 31.

b. ▬▬▶ Briefly explain why Curwen's net income is different than net cash flow from operating activities.

EX 13-16 Cash flows from operating activities—indirect method

Obj. 2

✔ Net cash flow from operating activities, $58,020

EXCEL TEMPLATE   REAL WORLD

Selected data (in thousands) derived from the income statement and balance sheet of **National Beverage Corp.** for a recent year are as follows:

Income statement data:	
Net income	$49,311
Gain on disposal of property	1,188
Depreciation expense	11,580
Other items involving noncash expenses	1,383
Balance sheet data:	
Increase in accounts receivable	1,746
Decrease in inventory	990
Increase in prepaid expenses	605
Decrease in accounts payable	710
Decrease in accrued and other current liabilities	995

a. Prepare the "Cash flows from operating activities" section of the statement of cash flows, using the indirect method for National Beverage Corp.

b. ▬▬▶ Interpret your results in part (a).

EX 13-17 Statement of cash flows—indirect method

Obj. 2, 3, 4, 5

✔ Net cash flow from operating activities, $38

SHOW ME HOW   EXCEL TEMPLATE

The comparative balance sheet of Olson-Jones Industries Inc. for December 31, 20Y2 and 20Y1, is as follows:

	Dec. 31, 20Y2	Dec. 31, 20Y1
Assets		
Cash	$183	$ 14
Accounts receivable (net)	55	49
Inventories	117	99
Land	250	330
Equipment	205	175
Accumulated depreciation—equipment	(68)	(42)
Total assets	$742	$625
Liabilities and Stockholders' Equity		
Accounts payable (merchandise creditors)	$ 51	$ 37
Dividends payable	5	—
Common stock, $1 par	125	80
Paid-in capital in excess of par—common stock	85	70
Retained earnings	476	438
Total liabilities and stockholders' equity	$742	$625

The following additional information is taken from the records:

a. Land was sold for $120.

b. Equipment was acquired for cash.

c. There were no disposals of equipment during the year.

d. The common stock was issued for cash.

e. There was a $62 credit to Retained Earnings for net income.

f. There was a $24 debit to Retained Earnings for cash dividends declared.

a. Prepare a statement of cash flows, using the indirect method of presenting cash flows from operating activities.

b. ▬▬▶ Was Olson-Jones's net cash flow from operations more or less than net income? What is the source of this difference?

EX 13-18 Statement of cash flows—indirect method

Obj. 2, 3, 4, 5

List the errors you find in the following statement of cash flows. The cash balance at the beginning of the year was $240,000. All other amounts are correct, except the cash balance at the end of the year.

Shasta Inc.
Statement of Cash Flows
For the Year Ended December 31, 20Y9

Cash flows from (used for) operating activities:		
Net income	$ 360,000	
Adjustments to reconcile net income to net cash flow from operating activities:		
Depreciation	100,800	
Gain on sale of investments	17,280	
Changes in current operating assets and liabilities:		
Increase in accounts receivable	27,360	
Increase in inventories	(36,000)	
Increase in accounts payable	(3,600)	
Decrease in accrued expenses payable	(2,400)	
Net cash flow from operating activities		$ 463,440
Cash flows from (used for) investing activities:		
Cash received from sale of investments	$ 240,000	
Cash paid for purchase of land	(259,200)	
Cash paid for purchase of equipment	(432,000)	
Net cash flow used for investing activities		(415,200)

(Continued)

Cash flows from (used for) financing activities:		
Cash received from sale of common stock..................	$312,000	
Cash paid for dividends.....................................	(132,000)	
Net cash flow from financing activities....................		180,000
Net increase in cash		$ 47,760
Cash balance, December 31, 20Y9		192,240
Cash balance, January 1, 20Y9...............................		$240,000

Appendix 2

EX 13-19   Cash flows from operating activities—direct method

✔ a. $801,900   The cash flows from operating activities are reported by the direct method on the statement of cash flows. Determine the following:

a. If sales for the current year were $753,500 and accounts receivable decreased by $48,400 during the year, what was the amount of cash received from customers?

b. If income tax expense for the current year was $50,600 and income tax payable decreased by $5,500 during the year, what was the amount of cash payments for income taxes?

c. ➤ Briefly explain why the cash received from customers in (a) is different than sales.

Appendix 2

EX 13-20   Determining selected amounts for cash flows from operating activities—direct method

✔ a. $1,025,800   Selected data taken from the accounting records of Ginis Inc. for the current year ended December 31 are as follows:

	Balance, December 31	Balance, January 1
Accrued expenses payable (operating expenses)	$ 12,650	$ 14,030
Accounts payable (merchandise creditors)	96,140	105,800
Inventories	178,020	193,430
Prepaid expenses	7,360	8,970

During the current year, the cost of goods sold was $1,031,550, and the operating expenses other than depreciation were $179,400. The direct method is used for presenting the cash flows from operating activities on the statement of cash flows.

Determine the amount reported on the statement of cash flows for (a) cash payments for merchandise and (b) cash payments for operating expenses.

Appendix 2

EX 13-21   Cash flows from operating activities—direct method

✔ Net cash flow from operating activities, $96,040

The income statement of Booker T Industries Inc. for the current year ended June 30 is as follows:

Sales		$ 511,000
Cost of goods sold..		(290,500)
Gross profit		$ 220,500
Operating expenses:		
Depreciation expense	$ 39,200	
Other operating expenses	105,000	
Total operating expenses		(144,200)
Income before income tax		$ 76,300
Income tax expense		(21,700)
Net income		$ 54,600

Changes in the balances of selected accounts from the beginning to the end of the current year are as follows:

	Increase (Decrease)
Accounts receivable (net)	$(11,760)
Inventories	3,920
Prepaid expenses	(3,780)
Accounts payable (merchandise creditors)	(7,980)
Accrued expenses payable (operating expenses)	1,260
Income tax payable...	(2,660)

a. Prepare the "Cash flows from operating activities" section of the statement of cash flows, using the direct method.

b. ➤ What does the direct method show about a company's cash flows from operating activities that is not shown using the indirect method?

Appendix 2
EX 13-22 Cash flows from operating activities—direct method

✔ Net cash flow from operating activities, $123,860

The income statement for Rhino Company for the current year ended June 30 and balances of selected accounts at the beginning and the end of the year are as follows:

Sales	$ 445,500
Cost of goods sold..	(154,000)
Gross profit...	$ 291,500
Operating expenses:	
Depreciation expense	$ 38,500
Other operating expenses	115,280
Total operating expenses	(153,780)
Income before income tax	$ 137,720
Income tax expense	(39,600)
Net income	$ 98,120

	End of Year	Beginning of Year
Accounts receivable (net)	$36,300	$31,240
Inventories	92,400	80,300
Prepaid expenses	14,520	15,840
Accounts payable (merchandise creditors)	67,540	62,700
Accrued expenses payable (operating expenses)	19,140	20,900
Income tax payable..	4,400	4,400

Prepare the "Cash flows from operating activities" section of the statement of cash flows, using the direct method.

Problems: Series A

✔ Net cash flow from operating activities, $490,000

PR 13-1A   Statement of cash flows—indirect method   Obj. 2, 3, 4, 5

The comparative balance sheet of Livers Inc. for December 31, 20Y3 and 20Y2, is shown as follows:

SHOW ME HOW   EXCEL TEMPLATE

	Dec. 31, 20Y3	Dec. 31, 20Y2
Assets		
Cash	$ 155,000	$ 150,000
Accounts receivable (net)	450,000	400,000
Inventories	770,000	750,000
Investments	0	100,000
Land	500,000	0
Equipment	1,400,000	1,200,000
Accumulated depreciation—equipment	(600,000)	(500,000)
Total assets	$2,675,000	$2,100,000
Liabilities and Stockholders' Equity		
Accounts payable (merchandise creditors)	$ 340,000	$ 300,000
Accrued expenses payable (operating expenses)	45,000	50,000
Dividends payable	30,000	25,000
Common stock, $4 par	700,000	600,000
Paid-in capital in excess of par—common stock	200,000	175,000
Retained earnings	1,360,000	950,000
Total liabilities and stockholders' equity	$2,675,000	$2,100,000

Additional data obtained from an examination of the accounts in the ledger for 20Y3 are as follows:

a. The investments were sold for $175,000 cash.

b. Equipment and land were acquired for cash.

c. There were no disposals of equipment during the year.

d. The common stock was issued for cash.

e. There was a $500,000 credit to Retained Earnings for net income.

f. There was a $90,000 debit to Retained Earnings for cash dividends declared.

Instructions

Prepare a statement of cash flows, using the indirect method of presenting cash flows from operating activities.

✔ Net cash flow from operating activities, $350,000

PR 13-2A   Statement of cash flows—indirect method   Obj. 2, 3, 4, 5

The comparative balance sheet of Yellow Dog Enterprises Inc. at December 31, 20Y8 and 20Y7, is as follows:

SHOW ME HOW   EXCEL TEMPLATE

	Dec. 31, 20Y8	Dec. 31, 20Y7
Assets		
Cash	$ 95,000	$ 110,000
Accounts receivable (net)	260,000	280,000
Inventories	520,000	450,000
Prepaid expenses	15,000	5,000
Equipment	1,130,000	800,000
Accumulated depreciation—equipment	(235,000)	(190,000)
Total assets	$1,785,000	$1,455,000
Liabilities and Stockholders' Equity		
Accounts payable (merchandise creditors)	$ 100,000	$ 75,000
Mortgage note payable	0	500,000
Common stock, $10 par	500,000	200,000
Paid-in capital in excess of par—common stock	400,000	100,000
Retained earnings	785,000	580,000
Total liabilities and stockholders' equity	$1,785,000	$1,455,000

Additional data obtained from the income statement and from an examination of the accounts in the ledger for 20Y8 are as follows:

a. Net income, $250,000.

b. Depreciation reported on the income statement, $135,000.

c. Equipment was purchased at a cost of $420,000 and fully depreciated equipment costing $90,000 was discarded, with no salvage realized.

d. The mortgage note payable was not due for six years, but the terms permitted earlier payment without penalty.

e. 30,000 shares of common stock were issued at $20 for cash.

f. Cash dividends declared and paid, $45,000.

Instructions

Prepare a statement of cash flows, using the indirect method of presenting cash flows from operating activities.

PR 13-3A Statement of cash flows—indirect method

Obj. 2, 3, 4, 5

✔ Net cash flow used for operating activities, $(169,600)

EXCEL TEMPLATE

The comparative balance sheet of Whitman Co. at December 31, 20Y2 and 20Y1, is as follows:

	Dec. 31, 20Y2	Dec. 31, 20Y1
Assets		
Cash	$ 918,000	$ 964,800
Accounts receivable (net)	828,900	761,940
Inventories	1,268,460	1,162,980
Prepaid expenses	29,340	35,100
Land	315,900	479,700
Buildings	1,462,500	900,900
Accumulated depreciation—buildings	(408,600)	(382,320)
Equipment	512,280	454,680
Accumulated depreciation—equipment	(141,300)	(158,760)
Total assets	$4,785,480	$4,219,020
Liabilities and Stockholders' Equity		
Accounts payable (merchandise creditors)	$ 922,500	$ 958,320
Bonds payable	270,000	0
Common stock, $25 par	317,000	117,000
Paid-in capital in excess of par—common stock	758,000	558,000
Retained earnings	2,517,980	2,585,700
Total liabilities and stockholders' equity	$4,785,480	$4,219,020

The noncurrent asset, noncurrent liability, and stockholders' equity accounts for 20Y2 are as follows:

ACCOUNT *Land*   **ACCOUNT NO.**

Date		Item	Debit	Credit	Balance Debit	Balance Credit
20Y2						
Jan.	1	Balance			479,700	
Apr.	20	Realized $151,200 cash from sale		163,800	315,900	

ACCOUNT *Buildings*   **ACCOUNT NO.**

Date		Item	Debit	Credit	Balance Debit	Balance Credit
20Y2						
Jan.	1	Balance			900,900	
Apr.	20	Acquired for cash	561,600		1,462,500	

(Continued)

ACCOUNT *Accumulated Depreciation—Buildings*　　　　　**ACCOUNT NO.**

					Balance	
Date		Item	Debit	Credit	Debit	Credit
20Y2						
Jan.	1	Balance				382,320
Dec.	31	Depreciation for year		26,280		408,600

ACCOUNT *Equipment*　　　　　**ACCOUNT NO.**

					Balance	
Date		Item	Debit	Credit	Debit	Credit
20Y2						
Jan.	1	Balance			454,680	
	26	Discarded, no salvage		46,800	407,880	
Aug.	11	Purchased for cash	104,400		512,280	

ACCOUNT *Accumulated Depreciation—Equipment*　　　　　**ACCOUNT NO.**

					Balance	
Date		Item	Debit	Credit	Debit	Credit
20Y2						
Jan.	1	Balance				158,760
	26	Equipment discarded	46,800			111,960
Dec.	31	Depreciation for year		29,340		141,300

ACCOUNT *Bonds Payable*　　　　　**ACCOUNT NO.**

					Balance	
Date		Item	Debit	Credit	Debit	Credit
20Y2						
May	1	Issued 20-year bonds		270,000		270,000

ACCOUNT *Common Stock, $25 par*　　　　　**ACCOUNT NO.**

					Balance	
Date		Item	Debit	Credit	Debit	Credit
20Y2						
Jan.	1	Balance				117,000
Dec.	7	Issued 8,000 shares of common stock for $50 per share		200,000		317,000

ACCOUNT *Paid-In Capital in Excess of Par—Common Stock*　　　　　**ACCOUNT NO.**

					Balance	
Date		Item	Debit	Credit	Debit	Credit
20Y2						
Jan.	1	Balance				558,000
Dec.	7	Issued 8,000 shares of common stock for $50 per share		200,000		758,000

ACCOUNT *Retained Earnings*   **ACCOUNT NO.**

Date		Item	Debit	Credit	Balance Debit	Balance Credit
20Y2						
Jan.	1	Balance				2,585,700
Dec.	31	Net loss	35,320			2,550,380
	31	Cash dividends	32,400			2,517,980

Instructions

Prepare a statement of cash flows, using the indirect method of presenting cash flows from operating activities.

Appendix 2
PR 13-4A Statement of cash flows—direct method

✔ Net cash flow from operating activities, $293,600

SHOW ME HOW   EXCEL TEMPLATE

The comparative balance sheet of Canace Products Inc. for December 31, 20Y6 and 20Y5, is as follows:

	Dec. 31, 20Y6	Dec. 31, 20Y5
Assets		
Cash	$ 643,400	$ 679,400
Accounts receivable (net)	566,800	547,400
Inventories	1,011,000	982,800
Investments	0	240,000
Land	520,000	0
Equipment	880,000	680,000
Accumulated depreciation	(244,400)	(200,400)
Total assets	$3,376,800	$2,929,200
Liabilities and Stockholders' Equity		
Accounts payable (merchandise creditors)	$ 771,800	$ 748,400
Accrued expenses payable (operating expenses)	63,400	70,800
Dividends payable	8,800	6,400
Common stock, $2 par	56,000	32,000
Paid-in capital in excess of par—common stock	408,000	192,000
Retained earnings	2,068,800	1,879,600
Total liabilities and stockholders' equity	$3,376,800	$2,929,200

The income statement for the year ended December 31, 20Y6, is as follows:

Sales		$ 5,980,000
Cost of goods sold		(2,452,000)
Gross profit		$ 3,528,000
Operating expenses:		
Depreciation expense	$ 44,000	
Other operating expenses	3,100,000	
Total operating expenses		(3,144,000)
Operating income		$ 384,000
Other expense:		
Loss on sale of investments		(64,000)
Income before income tax		$ 320,000
Income tax expense		(102,800)
Net income		$ 217,200

Additional data obtained from an examination of the accounts in the ledger for 20Y6 are as follows:

a. Equipment and land were acquired for cash.

b. There were no disposals of equipment during the year.

(Continued)

c. The investments were sold for $176,000 cash.

d. The common stock was issued for cash.

e. There was a $28,000 debit to Retained Earnings for cash dividends declared.

Instructions

Prepare a statement of cash flows, using the direct method of presenting cash flows from operating activities.

Appendix 2

PR 13-5A   Statement of cash flows—direct method applied to PR 13-1A

✔ Net cash flow from operating activities, $490,000

EXCEL TEMPLATE

The comparative balance sheet of Livers Inc. for December 31, 20Y3 and 20Y2, is as follows:

	Dec. 31, 20Y3	Dec. 31, 20Y2
Assets		
Cash	$ 155,000	$ 150,000
Accounts receivable (net)	450,000	400,000
Inventories	770,000	750,000
Investments	0	100,000
Land	500,000	0
Equipment...	1,400,000	1,200,000
Accumulated depreciation—equipment	(600,000)	(500,000)
Total assets	$2,675,000	$2,100,000
Liabilities and Stockholders' Equity		
Accounts payable (merchandise creditors)	$ 340,000	$ 300,000
Accrued expenses payable (operating expenses)	45,000	50,000
Dividends payable...	30,000	25,000
Common stock, $4 par...	700,000	600,000
Paid-in capital in excess of par—common stock	200,000	175,000
Retained earnings...	1,360,000	950,000
Total liabilities and stockholders' equity.......................	$2,675,000	$2,100,000

The income statement for the year ended December 31, 20Y3, is as follows:

Sales		$ 3,000,000
Cost of goods sold..		(1,400,000)
Gross profit		$ 1,600,000
Operating expenses:		
Depreciation expense	$100,000	
Other operating expenses	950,000	
Total operating expenses		(1,050,000)
Operating income...		$ 550,000
Other revenue:		
Gain on sale of investments................................		75,000
Income before income tax		$ 625,000
Income tax expense		(125,000)
Net income		$ 500,000

Additional data obtained from an examination of the accounts in the ledger for 20Y3 are as follows:

a. The investments were sold for $175,000 cash.

b. Equipment and land were acquired for cash.

c. There were no disposals of equipment during the year.

d. The common stock was issued for cash.

e. There was a $90,000 debit to Retained Earnings for cash dividends declared.

Instructions

Prepare a statement of cash flows, using the direct method of presenting cash flows from operating activities.

Problems: Series B

PR 13-1B   Statement of cash flows—indirect method

Obj. 2, 3, 4, 5

The comparative balance sheet of Merrick Equipment Co. for December 31, 20Y9 and 20Y8, is as follows:

	Dec. 31, 20Y9	Dec. 31, 20Y8
Assets		
Cash	$ 70,720	$ 47,940
Accounts receivable (net)	207,230	188,190
Inventories	298,520	289,850
Investments	0	102,000
Land	295,800	0
Equipment..	438,600	358,020
Accumulated depreciation—equipment	(99,110)	(84,320)
Total assets	$1,211,760	$901,680
Liabilities and Stockholders' Equity		
Accounts payable (merchandise creditors)	$ 205,700	$194,140
Accrued expenses payable (operating expenses)	30,600	26,860
Dividends payable...	25,500	20,400
Common stock, $1 par...	202,000	102,000
Paid-in capital in excess of par—common stock..................	354,000	204,000
Retained earnings...	393,960	354,280
Total liabilities and stockholders' equity.......................	$1,211,760	$901,680

Additional data obtained from an examination of the accounts in the ledger for 20Y9 are as follows:

a. Equipment and land were acquired for cash.

b. There were no disposals of equipment during the year.

c. The investments were sold for $91,800 cash.

d. The common stock was issued for cash.

e. There was a $141,680 credit to Retained Earnings for net income.

f. There was a $102,000 debit to Retained Earnings for cash dividends declared.

Instructions

Prepare a statement of cash flows, using the indirect method of presenting cash flows from operating activities.

PR 13-2B   Statement of cash flows—indirect method

Obj. 2, 3, 4, 5

The comparative balance sheet of Harris Industries Inc. at December 31, 20Y4 and 20Y3, is as follows:

	Dec. 31, 20Y4	Dec. 31, 20Y3
Assets		
Cash	$ 443,240	$ 360,920
Accounts receivable (net)	665,280	592,200
Inventories	887,880	1,022,560
Prepaid expenses	31,640	25,200
Land	302,400	302,400
Buildings	1,713,600	1,134,000
Accumulated depreciation—buildings......................	(466,200)	(414,540)
Machinery and equipment......................................	781,200	781,200
Accumulated depreciation—machinery and equipment.....	(214,200)	(191,520)
Patents..	106,960	112,000
Total assets	$4,251,800	$3,724,420

(Continued)

Liabilities and Stockholders' Equity

Accounts payable (merchandise creditors)	$ 837,480	$ 927,080
Dividends payable	32,760	25,200
Salaries payable	78,960	87,080
Mortgage note payable, due in nine years	224,000	0
Bonds payable	0	390,000
Common stock, $5 par	200,400	50,400
Paid-in capital in excess of par—common stock	366,000	126,000
Retained earnings	2,512,200	2,118,660
Total liabilities and stockholders' equity	$4,251,800	$3,724,420

An examination of the income statement and the accounting records revealed the following additional information applicable to 20Y4:

a. Net income, $524,580.

b. Depreciation expense reported on the income statement: buildings, $51,660; machinery and equipment, $22,680.

c. Patent amortization reported on the income statement, $5,040.

d. A building was constructed for $579,600.

e. A mortgage note for $224,000 was issued for cash.

f. 30,000 shares of common stock were issued at $13 in exchange for the bonds payable.

g. Cash dividends declared, $131,040.

Instructions

Prepare a statement of cash flows, using the indirect method of presenting cash flows from operating activities.

PR 13-3B   Statement of cash flows—indirect method   Obj. 2, 3, 4, 5

✔ Net cash flow from
operating activities,
$162,800

EXCEL TEMPLATE

The comparative balance sheet of Coulson, Inc. at December 31, 20Y2 and 20Y1, is as follows:

	Dec. 31, 20Y2	Dec. 31, 20Y1
Assets		
Cash	$ 300,600	$ 337,800
Accounts receivable (net)	704,400	609,600
Inventories	918,600	865,800
Prepaid expenses	18,600	26,400
Land	990,000	1,386,000
Buildings	1,980,000	990,000
Accumulated depreciation—buildings	(397,200)	(366,000)
Equipment	660,600	529,800
Accumulated depreciation—equipment	(133,200)	(162,000)
Total assets	$5,042,400	$4,217,400
Liabilities and Stockholders' Equity		
Accounts payable (merchandise creditors)	$ 594,000	$ 631,200
Income taxes payable	26,400	21,600
Bonds payable	330,000	0
Common stock, $20 par	320,000	180,000
Paid-in capital in excess of par—common stock	950,000	810,000
Retained earnings	2,822,000	2,574,600
Total liabilities and stockholders' equity	$5,042,400	$4,217,400

The noncurrent asset, noncurrent liability, and stockholders' equity accounts for 20Y2 are as follows:

ACCOUNT *Land*   ACCOUNT NO.

Date		Item	Debit	Credit	Balance Debit	Balance Credit
20Y2						
Jan.	1	Balance			1,386,000	
Apr.	20	Realized $456,000 cash from sale		396,000	990,000	

ACCOUNT *Buildings*   ACCOUNT NO.

Date		Item	Debit	Credit	Balance Debit	Balance Credit
20Y2						
Jan.	1	Balance			990,000	
Apr.	20	Acquired for cash	990,000		1,980,000	

ACCOUNT *Accumulated Depreciation—Buildings*   ACCOUNT NO.

Date		Item	Debit	Credit	Balance Debit	Balance Credit
20Y2						
Jan.	1	Balance				366,000
Dec.	31	Depreciation for year		31,200		397,200

ACCOUNT *Equipment*   ACCOUNT NO.

Date		Item	Debit	Credit	Balance Debit	Balance Credit
20Y2						
Jan.	1	Balance			529,800	
	26	Discarded, no salvage		66,000	463,800	
Aug.	11	Purchased for cash	196,800		660,600	

ACCOUNT *Accumulated Depreciation—Equipment*   ACCOUNT NO.

Date		Item	Debit	Credit	Balance Debit	Balance Credit
20Y2						
Jan.	1	Balance				162,000
	26	Equipment discarded	66,000			96,000
Dec.	31	Depreciation for year		37,200		133,200

ACCOUNT *Bonds Payable*   ACCOUNT NO.

Date		Item	Debit	Credit	Balance Debit	Balance Credit
20Y2						
May	1	Issued 20-year bonds		330,000		330,000

(Continued)

ACCOUNT *Common Stock, $20 par*   ACCOUNT NO.

Date		Item	Debit	Credit	Balance Debit	Balance Credit
20Y2						
Jan.	1	Balance				180,000
Dec.	7	Issued 7,000 shares of common stock for $40 per share		140,000		320,000

ACCOUNT *Paid-In Capital in Excess of Par—Common Stock*   ACCOUNT NO.

Date		Item	Debit	Credit	Balance Debit	Balance Credit
20Y2						
Jan.	1	Balance				810,000
Dec.	7	Issued 7,000 shares of common stock for $40 per share		140,000		950,000

ACCOUNT *Retained Earnings*   ACCOUNT NO.

Date		Item	Debit	Credit	Balance Debit	Balance Credit
20Y2						
Jan.	1	Balance				2,574,600
Dec.	31	Net income		326,600		2,901,200
	31	Cash dividends	79,200			2,822,000

Instructions

Prepare a statement of cash flows, using the indirect method of presenting cash flows from operating activities.

Appendix 2
PR 13-4B   Statement of cash flows—direct method

✔ Net cash flow from operating activities, $509,220

The comparative balance sheet of Martinez Inc. for December 31, 20Y4 and 20Y3, is as follows:

SHOW ME HOW   EXCEL TEMPLATE

	Dec. 31, 20Y4	Dec. 31, 20Y3
Assets		
Cash	$ 661,920	$ 683,100
Accounts receivable (net)	992,640	914,400
Inventories	1,394,400	1,363,800
Investments	0	432,000
Land	960,000	0
Equipment..	1,224,000	984,000
Accumulated depreciation—equipment	(481,500)	(368,400)
Total assets	$4,751,460	$4,008,900
Liabilities and Stockholders' Equity		
Accounts payable (merchandise creditors)	$1,080,000	$ 966,600
Accrued expenses payable (operating expenses)	67,800	79,200
Dividends payable..	100,800	91,200
Common stock, $5 par	130,000	30,000
Paid-in capital in excess of par—common stock................	950,000	450,000
Retained earnings..	2,422,860	2,391,900
Total liabilities and stockholders' equity....................	$4,751,460	$4,008,900

The income statement for the year ended December 31, 20Y3, is as follows:

Sales		$ 4,512,000
Cost of goods sold		(2,352,000)
Gross profit		$ 2,160,000
Operating expenses:		
Depreciation expense	$ 113,100	
Other operating expenses	1,344,840	
Total operating expenses		(1,457,940)
Operating income		$ 702,060
Other revenue:		
Gain on sale of investments		156,000
Income before income tax		$ 858,060
Income tax expense		(299,100)
Net income		$ 558,960

Additional data obtained from an examination of the accounts in the ledger for 20Y3 are as follows:

a. Equipment and land were acquired for cash.

b. There were no disposals of equipment during the year.

c. The investments were sold for $588,000 cash.

d. The common stock was issued for cash.

e. There was a $528,000 debit to Retained Earnings for cash dividends declared.

Instructions

Prepare a statement of cash flows, using the direct method of presenting cash flows from operating activities.

Appendix 2
PR 13-5B   Statement of cash flows—direct method applied to PR 13-1B

✔ Net cash flow from operating activities, $154,260

EXCEL TEMPLATE

The comparative balance sheet of Merrick Equipment Co. for Dec. 31, 20Y9 and 20Y8, is:

	Dec. 31, 20Y9	Dec. 31, 20Y8
Assets		
Cash	$ 70,720	$ 47,940
Accounts receivable (net)	207,230	188,190
Inventories	298,520	289,850
Investments	0	102,000
Land	295,800	0
Equipment	438,600	358,020
Accumulated depreciation—equipment	(99,110)	(84,320)
Total assets	$1,211,760	$ 901,680
Liabilities and Stockholders' Equity		
Accounts payable (merchandise creditors)	$ 205,700	$ 194,140
Accrued expenses payable (operating expenses)	30,600	26,860
Dividends payable	25,500	20,400
Common stock, $1 par	202,000	102,000
Paid-in capital in excess of par—common stock	354,000	204,000
Retained earnings	393,960	354,280
Total liabilities and stockholders' equity	$1,211,760	$ 901,680

(Continued)

The income statement for the year ended December 31, 20Y9, is as follows:

Sales		$ 2,023,898
Cost of goods sold		(1,245,476)
Gross profit		$ 778,422
Operating expenses:		
Depreciation expense	$ 14,790	
Other operating expenses	517,299	
Total operating expenses		(532,089)
Operating income		$ 246,333
Other expenses:		
Loss on sale of investments		(10,200)
Income before income tax		$ 236,133
Income tax expense		(94,453)
Net income		$ 141,680

Additional data obtained from an examination of the accounts in the ledger for 20Y9 are as follows:

a. Equipment and land were acquired for cash.

b. There were no disposals of equipment during the year.

c. The investments were sold for $91,800 cash.

d. The common stock was issued for cash.

e. There was a $102,000 debit to Retained Earnings for cash dividends declared.

Instructions

Prepare a statement of cash flows, using the direct method of presenting cash flows from operating activities.

Make a Decision
Free Cash Flow

REAL WORLD

MAD 13-1 Analyze and compare Amazon.com, Best Buy, and Wal-Mart Obj. 6

Amazon.com, Inc. (AMZN) is one of the largest Internet retailers in the world. **Best Buy Co., Inc. (BBY)** is a leading retailer of consumer electronics and media products in the United States, while **Wal-Mart Stores, Inc. (WMT)** is the leading retailer in the United States. Amazon, Best Buy, and Wal-Mart compete in similar markets. Best Buy and Wal-Mart sell through both traditional retail stores and the Internet, while Amazon sells only through the Internet. Sales and cash flow information from recent annual reports for all three companies is as follows (in millions):

	Amazon	Best Buy	Wal-Mart
Sales	$135,987	$39,403	$485,873
Cash flows from operating activities	16,443	2,545	31,530
Purchases of property, plant, and equipment	(6,737)	(582)	(10,619)

a. Determine the free cash flow for all three companies.

b. Compute the ratio of free cash flow to sales for all three companies. Round percentages to one decimal place.

c. ➡ How does Amazon compare to the other two companies with respect to generating free cash flow?

REAL WORLD

MAD 13-2 Analyze and compare Apple, Coca-Cola, and Verizon   Obj. 6

Financial information for **Apple Inc. (AAPL)**, **The Coca-Cola Company (KO)**, and **Verizon Communications (VZ)** follows (in millions):

	Apple	Coca-Cola	Verizon
Sales	$215,639	$41,863	$125,980
Cash flows from operating activities	65,824	8,796	22,715
Cash used to purchase property, plant, and equipment	(12,734)	(2,262)	(17,059)

a. Compute the free cash flow for each company.

b. Compute the ratio of free cash flow to sales for each company. Round to one decimal place.

c. ➤ Which company has the greatest free cash flow?

d. ➤ How does Verizon differ from the other two companies?

REAL WORLD

MAD 13-3 Analyze Aeropostale   Obj. 6

Aeropostale, Inc. (AROPQ) is a specialty retailer of casual apparel and accessories for teens. Recently, the company declared bankruptcy to provide financial protection while attempting to reorganize its operations. Annual report information for the three most recent years prior to the bankruptcy are as follows (in millions):

	Year 3	Year 2	Year 1
Cash flows from operating activities	$ (68)	$ (56)	$ (38)
Cash used to purchase property, plant, and equipment	(16)	(24)	(84)
Sales	1,507	1,839	2,091

a. Determine the free cash flow.

b. Determine the ratio of free cash flow to sales. Round percentages to one decimal place.

c. ➤ Did the free cash flow information indicate financial stress? Explain.

REAL WORLD

MAD 13-4 Analyze and compare AT&T and Facebook   Obj. 6

AT&T Inc. (T) is a leading global provider of telecommunication services. **Facebook, Inc. (FB)** is a major worldwide social media company. AT&T has a lengthy history and was founded by Alexander Graham Bell. Facebook has a short history and was founded by Mark Zuckerberg. Facebook uses telecommunication networks, like those of AT&T, to deliver social content to its users. Free cash flow and revenue information for both companies for three recent years is as follows (in millions):

AT&T
Information from the statement of cash flows:

	Year 3	Year 2	Year 1
Cash flows from operating activities	$ 39,344	$ 35,880	$ 31,338
Cash used to purchase property, plant, and equipment	(22,408)	(20,015)	(21,433)

Information from the income statement:

	Year 3	Year 2	Year 1
Revenue	$163,786	$146,801	$132,447

(Continued)

Facebook
Information from the statement of cash flows:

	Year 3	Year 2	Year 1
Cash flows from operating activities	$ 16,108	$ 10,320	$ 7,326
Cash used to purchase property, plant, and equipment	(4,491)	(2,523)	(1,831)

Information from the income statement:

	Year 3	Year 2	Year 1
Revenue	$27,638	$17,928	$12,466

a. Using total revenue, which company appears to be the larger at the end of Year 3?

b. Using total revenue, which company appears to be growing faster across the three years?

c. Compute the cash used to purchase property, plant, and equipment (PP&E) as a percent of the cash flows from operating activities for all three years for each company. Round to the nearest whole percent.

d. ━━━━▶ Using the computations in (c), which company appears to require more cash to purchase PP&E, and what impact does this have on free cash flow?

e. Compute the ratio of free cash flow to revenue for all three years for each company, and plot the data on a line chart with the years on the horizontal axis.

f. ━━━━▶ Interpret the chart.

REAL WORLD

MAD 13-5   Analyze Priceline   Obj. 6

The Priceline Group Inc. (PCLN) is a leading provider of online travel reservation services, including brand names Priceline, KAYAK, and OpenTable. Selected cash flow information from the statement of cash flows for three recent years is as follows (in millions):

	Year 3	Year 2	Year 1
Net cash provided by operating activities	$ 3,925	$ 3,102	$ 2,914
Net cash used for investing activities	(3,333)	(3,895)	(2,358)
Net cash provided by (used for) financing activities	58	(730)	1,429
Additions to property, plant, and equipment	(220)	(174)	(132)
Repurchase common stock	(1,014)	(3,089)	(750)
Acquisitions and investments	(8)	(140)	(2,496)

a. Determine the net change in cash for each year.

b. Determine the free cash flow for each year.

c. ━━━━▶ How is the free cash flow being used based on the data provided?

d. ━━━━▶ Which is better for measuring the cash flow available for investment, dividends, debt repayments, and stock repurchases: the change in cash for the period or the free cash flow? Explain.

Take It Further

ETHICS

TIF 13-1   Cash flow per share

Head Donuts Inc. is a retailer of designer headphones, earphones, and hands-free audio devices. Polly Ester, the company president, is reviewing the company's financial statements after the close of the fiscal year and is troubled that earnings decreased by 10%. She shares her concerns with the company's chief accountant, Lucas Simmons, who points out that the drop in earnings was balanced by a 20% increase in cash flows, from operating activities. Polly is encouraged by the increase in cash flows from operating activities, but is worried that investors might miss this information because it is "buried" in the statement of cash flows. To make it easier for investors to find this information, she instructs Lucas to include an operating cash flow per share number on the face of the income statement, directly below earnings per share. While Lucas is concerned about using such an unconventional financial reporting tactic, he agrees to include the information on the income statement.

Is Lucas behaving in an ethical and professional manner? Explain your answer.

TEAM ACTIVITY   REAL WORLD

TIF 13-2   Real-world annual report

In teams, select a public company that interests you. Obtain the company's most recent annual report on Form 10-K. The Form 10-K is a company's annually required filing with the Securities and Exchange Commission (SEC). It includes the company's financial statements and accompanying notes. The Form 10-K can be obtained either (a) from the investor relations section of the company's website or (b) by using the company search feature of the SEC's EDGAR database service found at www.sec.gov/edgar/searchedgar/companysearch.html.

1. Based on the information in the company's most recent annual report, answer the following questions:

   a. What is the net cash flows from operating activities reported by the company at the end of the most recent year?

   b. What is the net cash flows from investing activities reported by the company at the end of the most recent year?

   c. What is the net cash flows from financing activities reported by the company at the end of the most recent year?

   d. What was the net increase (or decrease) in cash during the year?

2. Evaluate the company's cash inflows and outflows.

COMMUNICATION

TIF 13-3   Financial condition

Tidewater Inc., a retailer, provided the following financial information for its most recent fiscal year:

Net income..	$945,000
Return on invested capital	8%
Cash flows used for operating activities	$(1,428,000)
Cash flows from investing activities	$600,000
Cash flows from financing activities......................................	$900,000

The company's "Cash flows from operating activities" section is as follows:

Net income..	$ 945,000
Depreciation..	210,000
Increase in accounts receivable	(1,134,000)
Increase in inventory...	(1,260,000)
Decrease in accounts payable..	(189,000)
Net cash flow used for operating activities	$ (1,428,000)

(Continued)

An examination of the financial statements revealed the following additional information:

■ Revenues increased during the year as a result of an aggressive marketing campaign aimed at increasing the number of new "Tidewater Card" credit card customers. This is the company's branded credit card, which can only be used at Tidewater stores. The credit card balances are accounts receivable on Tidewater's balance sheet.

■ Some suppliers have made their merchandise available at a deep discount. As a result, the company purchased large quantities of these goods in an attempt to improve the company's profitability.

■ In recent years, the company has struggled to pay its accounts payable on time. The company has improved on this during the past year and is nearly caught up on overdue payables balances.

■ The company reported net losses in each of the two prior years.

━━━► Write a brief memo to your instructor evaluating the financial condition of Tidewater Inc.

TIF 13-4 Using the statement of cash flows

You are considering an investment in a new start-up company, Giraffe Inc., an Internet service provider. A review of the company's financial statements reveals a negative retained earnings. In addition, it appears as though the company has been running a negative cash flow from operating activities since the company's inception.

━━━► How is the company staying in business under these circumstances? Could this be a good investment?

Pathways Challenge

This is Accounting!

Information/Consequences

The statement of cash flows would not report a yearly "cash outflow" for interest expense. However, the discount on the note payable of $328 ($1,000 − $672) must be amortized to interest expense each year, even though no cash is paid. The related interest expense is reported on the income statement as an expense. Since no cash is paid for interest, the interest expense must be added back to net income under the indirect method in the operating activities section of the statement of cash flows.

The payment on each note payable of $1,000 at the maturity date includes a payment for principal ($672) and interest ($328). The amount related to the principal of $672 is reported as a cash outflow in the financing activities section, while the interest portion of $328 is reported as a cash outflow in the operating activities section. Note that as described in the preceding paragraph, the amortized discount in the year of maturity is also reported in the operating activities section as an addition to net income under the indirect method.

Suggested Answer

Financial Statement Analysis

STATEMENT OF STOCKHOLDERS' EQUITY
For the Year Ended December 31, 20Y5

	Common Stock	Retained Earnings	Total
Balances, Jan. 1, 20Y5	$XXX	$ XXX	$ XXX
Issued common stock	XXX		XXX
Net income		XXX	XXX
Dividends		(XXX)	(XXX)
Balances, Dec. 31, 20Y5	$XXX	$ XXX	$ XXX

STATEMENT OF CASH FLOWS
For the Year Ended December 31, 20Y5

Cash flows from (used for) operating activities	$XXX
Cash flows from (used for) investing activities	XXX
Cash flows from (used for) financing activities	XXX
Net increase (decrease) in cash	$XXX
Cash balance, January 1, 20Y5	XXX
Cash balance, December 31, 20Y5	$XXX

INCOME STATEMENT
For the Year Ended December 31, 20Y5

Sales		$ XXX
Cost of goods sold		(XXX)
Gross profit		$ XXX
Operating expenses:		
Advertising expense	$XXX	
Depreciation expense	XXX	
Amortization expense	XXX	
Depletion expense	XXX	
...	XXX	
Total operating expenses		(XXX)
Operating income		$ XXX
Other revenue and expense		XXX
Net income		$ XXX

BALANCE SHEET
December 31, 20Y5

Assets		
Current assets:		
Cash	$XXX	
Accounts receivable	XXX	
Inventory	XXX	
Total current assets		$XXX
Property, plant, and equipment		XXX
Total assets		$XXX
Liabilities		
Current liabilities	$XXX	
Long-term liabilities	XXX	
Total liabilities		$XXX
Stockholders' Equity		
Common stock	$XXX	
Retained earnings	XXX	
Total stockholders' equity		XXX
Total liabilities and stockholders' equity		$XXX

Nike, Inc.

"Just do it." These three words identify one of the most recognizable brands in the world, **Nike, Inc. (NKE)**. While this phrase inspires athletes to "compete and achieve their potential," it also defines the company.

Nike began in 1964 as a partnership between University of Oregon track coach Bill Bowerman and one of his former student-athletes, Phil Knight. The two began by selling shoes imported from Japan out of the back of Knight's car to athletes at track-and-field events. As sales grew, the company opened retail outlets, calling itself **Blue Ribbon Sports**. The company also began to develop its own shoes. In 1971, the company commissioned a graphic design student at Portland State University to develop the swoosh logo for a fee of $35. In 1978, the company changed its name to Nike, and in 1980, it sold its first shares of stock to the public.

Nike would have been a great company to invest in at the time. If you had invested in Nike's common stock back in 1990, you would have paid $5 per share. As of November 2015, Nike's stock was worth over $130 per share. Unfortunately, you can't invest using hindsight.

How can you select companies in which to invest? Like any significant purchase, you should do some research to guide your investment decision. If you were buying a car, for example, you might go to **Edmunds.com** to obtain reviews, ratings, prices, specifications, options, and fuel economies to evaluate different vehicles. In selecting companies in which to invest, you can use financial analysis to gain insight into a company's past performance and future prospects. This chapter describes and illustrates common financial data that can be analyzed to assist you in making investment decisions such as whether or not to invest in Nike's stock.

Source: www.nikebiz.com/.

©JOSHUA RAINEY PHOTOGRAPHY/SHUTTERSTOCK.COM

Link to Nike . . . . Pages 690, 691, 692, 693, 695, 698, 700, 701, 704, 706, 707, 709, 712

What's Covered

Financial Statement Analysis

Analyzing and Interpreting Financial Statements	Analytical Methods	Liquidity	Solvency	Profitability	Corpoate Annual Reports
■ Value of Financial Statement Information (Obj. 1) ■ Techniques (Obj. 1)	■ Horizontal Analysis (Obj. 2) ■ Vertical Analysis (Obj. 2) ■ Common-Sized Statements (Obj. 2)	■ Current Position (Obj. 3) ■ Accounts Receivable (Obj. 3) ■ Inventory (Obj. 3)	■ Fixed Assets to Long-Term Liabilities (Obj. 4) ■ Liabilities to Stockholders' Equity (Obj. 4) ■ Times Interest Earned (Obj. 4)	■ Asset Turnover (Obj. 5) ■ Rates of Return (Obj. 5) ■ Earnings per Share (Obj. 5) ■ Price to Earnings (Obj. 5) ■ Dividend Measures (Obj. 5)	■ Management Discussion (Obj. 6) ■ Internal Control (Obj. 6) ■ Audit Report (Obj. 6)

Learning Objectives

Obj. 1 Describe the techniques and tools used to analyze financial statement information.

Obj. 2 Describe and illustrate basic financial statement analytical methods.

Obj. 3 Describe and illustrate how to use financial statement analysis to assess liquidity.

Obj. 4 Describe and illustrate how to use financial statement analysis to assess solvency.

Obj. 5 Describe and illustrate how to use financial statement analysis to assess profitability.

Obj. 6 Describe the contents of corporate annual reports.

Appendices 1 and 2

Obj. App 1 Describe the reporting of unusual items on the income statement.

Obj. App 2 Describe the concepts of fair value and comprehensive income.

Objective 1
Describe the techniques and tools used to analyze financial statement information.

Analyzing and Interpreting Financial Statements

The objective of accounting is to provide relevant and timely information to support the decision-making needs of financial statement users. Bankers, creditors, and investors all rely on financial statements to provide insight into a company's financial condition and performance. This chapter discusses the value of financial statement information, techniques used to evaluate financial statements, and the impact of that information on decision making.

The Value of Financial Statement Information

General-purpose financial statements are distributed to a wide range of potential users, providing each group with valuable information about a company's economic performance and financial condition. Users typically evaluate this information along three dimensions: liquidity, solvency, and profitability.

Liquidity Short-term creditors such as banks and financial institutions are primarily concerned with whether a company will be able to repay short-term borrowings such as loans and notes. As such, they are most interested in evaluating a company's ability to convert assets into cash, which is called **liquidity**.

Solvency Long-term creditors, such as bondholders, loan money for long periods of time. Thus, they are interested in evaluating a company's ability to make its periodic interest payments and repay the face amount of debt at maturity, which is called **solvency**.

Profitability Investors, such as stockholders, are the owners of the company. They benefit from increases in the price of a company's shares and are interested in evaluating the potential for the price of the company's stock to increase. The price of a company's stock depends on a variety of factors, including the company's current and potential future earnings. As such, investors focus on evaluating a company's ability to generate earnings, which is called **profitability**.

Techniques for Analyzing Financial Statements

Financial statement users rely on the following techniques to analyze and interpret a company's financial performance and condition:

- **Analytical methods** examine changes in the amount and percentage of financial statement items within and across periods.
- **Ratios** express a financial statement item or set of financial statement items as a percentage of another financial statement item, in order to measure an important economic relationship as a single number.

Both analytical methods and ratios can be used to compare a company's financial performance over time or to another company.

- *Comparisons Over Time:* The comparison of a financial statement item or ratio with the same item or ratio from a prior period often helps the user identify trends in a company's economic performance, financial condition, liquidity, solvency, and profitability.
- *Comparisons Among Companies:* The comparison of a financial statement item or ratio to other companies in the same industry can provide insight into a company's economic performance and financial condition relative to its competitors.

Analytical Methods

Users analyze a company's financial statements using a variety of analytical methods. Three such methods are:

- Horizontal analysis
- Vertical analysis
- Common-sized statements

Objective 2
Describe and illustrate basic financial statement analytical methods.

Horizontal Analysis

The analysis of increases and decreases in the amount and percentage of comparative financial statement items is called **horizontal analysis**. Each item on the most recent statement is compared with the same item on one or more earlier statements in terms of the following:

- *Amount* of increase or decrease
- *Percent* of increase or decrease

When comparing statements, the earlier statement is normally used as the base year for computing increases and decreases.

Exhibit 1 illustrates horizontal analysis for the December 31, 20Y6 and 20Y5 balance sheets of **Lincoln Company**. In Exhibit 1, the December 31, 20Y5, balance sheet (the earliest year presented) is used as the base year.

Exhibit 1 indicates that total assets decreased by $91,000 (7.4%), liabilities decreased by $133,000 (30.0%), and stockholders' equity increased by $42,000 (5.3%). Since the long-term investments account decreased by $82,500, it appears that most of the decrease in long-term liabilities of $100,000 was achieved through the sale of long-term investments.

Exhibit 1

Comparative Balance Sheet—Horizontal Analysis

	Lincoln Company Comparative Balance Sheet December 31, 20Y6 and 20Y5			
	Dec. 31, 20Y6	Dec. 31, 20Y5	Increase/(Decrease) Amount	Percent
Assets				
Current assets....................................	$ 550,000	$ 533,000	$ 17,000	3.2%
Long-term investments..............................	95,000	177,500	(82,500)	(46.5%)
Property, plant, and equipment (net)	444,500	470,000	(25,500)	(5.4%)
Intangible assets	50,000	50,000	—	—
Total assets	$1,139,500	$1,230,500	$ (91,000)	(7.4%)
Liabilities				
Current liabilities.....................................	$ 210,000	$ 243,000	$ (33,000)	(13.6%)
Long-term liabilities	100,000	200,000	(100,000)	(50.0%)
Total liabilities	$ 310,000	$ 443,000	$(133,000)	(30.0%)
Stockholders' Equity				
Preferred 6% stock, $100 par	$ 150,000	$ 150,000	—	—
Common stock, $10 par................................	500,000	500,000	—	—
Retained earnings....................................	179,500	137,500	$ 42,000	30.5%
Total stockholders' equity............................	$ 829,500	$ 787,500	$ 42,000	5.3%
Total liabilities and stockholders' equity...............	$1,139,500	$1,230,500	$ (91,000)	(7.4%)

Link to Nike For a recent year, **Nike**'s current liabilities decreased by 15.4%.

The balance sheets in Exhibit 1 may be expanded or supported by a separate schedule that includes the individual asset and liability accounts. For example, Exhibit 2 is a supporting schedule of **Lincoln Company**'s current asset accounts.

Exhibit 2

Comparative Schedule of Current Assets—Horizontal Analysis

	Lincoln Company Comparative Schedule of Current Assets December 31, 20Y6 and 20Y5			
	Dec. 31, 20Y6	Dec. 31, 20Y5	Increase/(Decrease) Amount	Percent
Cash	$ 90,500	$ 64,700	$ 25,800	39.9%
Temporary investments................................	75,000	60,000	15,000	25.0%
Accounts receivable, net................................	115,000	120,000	(5,000)	(4.2%)
Inventories	264,000	283,000	(19,000)	(6.7%)
Prepaid expenses	5,500	5,300	200	3.8%
Total current assets....................................	$550,000	$533,000	$ 17,000	3.2%

Exhibit 2 indicates that while cash and temporary investments increased, accounts receivable and inventories decreased. The decrease in accounts receivable could be caused by improved collection policies, which would increase cash. The decrease in inventories could be caused by increased sales.

Exhibit 3 illustrates horizontal analysis for the 20Y6 and 20Y5 income statements of **Lincoln Company**. Exhibit 3 indicates an increase in sales of $298,000, or 24.8%. However, the percentage increase in sales of 24.8% was accompanied by an even greater percentage increase in the cost of goods sold of 27.2%. Thus, gross profit increased by only 19.7% rather than by the 24.8% increase in sales.

Exhibit 3 also indicates that selling expenses increased by 29.9%. Thus, the 24.8% increase in sales could have been caused by an advertising campaign, which increased selling expenses.

Lincoln Company Comparative Income Statement For the Years Ended December 31, 20Y6 and 20Y5			Increase/(Decrease)	
	20Y6	**20Y5**	**Amount**	**Percent**
Sales	$ 1,498,000	$ 1,200,000	$298,000	24.8%
Cost of goods sold......................................	(1,043,000)	(820,000)	223,000	27.2%
Gross profit	$ 455,000	$ 380,000	$ 75,000	19.7%
Selling expenses	$ (191,000)	$ (147,000)	$ 44,000	29.9%
Administrative expenses................................	(104,000)	(97,400)	6,600	6.8%
Total operating expenses	$ (295,000)	$ (244,400)	$ 50,600	20.7%
Operating income.......................................	$ 160,000	$ 135,600	$ 24,400	18.0%
Other revenue and expense:				
Other revenue	8,500	11,000	(2,500)	(22.7%)
Other expense (interest)..............................	(6,000)	(12,000)	(6,000)	(50.0%)
Income before income tax expense......................	$ 162,500	$ 134,600	$ 27,900	20.7%
Income tax expense	(71,500)	(58,100)	13,400	23.1%
Net income	$ 91,000	$ 76,500	$ 14,500	19.0%

Exhibit 3

Comparative Income Statement—Horizontal Analysis

Administrative expenses increased by only 6.8%, total operating expenses increased by 20.7%, and operating income increased by 18.0%. Interest expense decreased by 50.0%. This decrease was probably caused by the 50.0% decrease in long-term liabilities (Exhibit 1). Overall, net income increased by 19.0%, a favorable result.

For a recent year, **Nike**'s net income increased by 14.9%.   *Link to Nike*

The comparative balance sheet in Exhibit 1 shows no change in the preferred stock or common stock accounts for 20Y5 and 20Y6. For this reason, a comparative statement of stockholders' equity is not shown. Instead, a comparative retained earnings statement is shown in Exhibit 4. Exhibit 4 indicates that retained earnings increased by 30.5% for the year. The increase is due to net income of $91,000 for the year, less dividends of $49,000.

Lincoln Company Comparative Retained Earnings Statement For the Years Ended December 31, 20Y6 and 20Y5			Increase/(Decrease)	
	20Y6	**20Y5**	**Amount**	**Percent**
Retained earnings, January 1........................	$137,500	$100,000	$ 37,500	37.5%
Net income	91,000	76,500	14,500	19.0%
Dividends:				
On preferred stock	(9,000)	(9,000)	—	—
On common stock...............................	(40,000)	(30,000)	(10,000)	33.3%
Retained earnings, December 31	$179,500	$137,500	$ 42,000	30.5%

Exhibit 4

Comparative Retained Earnings Statement— Horizontal Analysis

Vertical Analysis

The percentage analysis of the relationship of each component in a financial statement to a total within the statement is called **vertical analysis**. Although vertical analysis is applied to a single statement, it may be applied on the same statement over time. This enhances the analysis by showing how the percentages of each item have changed over time.

In vertical analysis of the balance sheet, the percentages are computed as follows:

- Each asset item is stated as a percent of the total assets.
- Each liability and stockholders' equity item is stated as a percent of the total liabilities and stockholders' equity.

Exhibit 5 illustrates the vertical analysis of the December 31, 20Y6 and 20Y5 balance sheets of **Lincoln Company**. Exhibit 5 indicates that current assets have increased from 43.3% to 48.3% of total assets. Long-term investments decreased from 14.4% to 8.3% of total assets. Stockholders' equity increased from 64.0% to 72.8%, with a comparable decrease in liabilities.

Exhibit 5

Comparative Balance Sheet—Vertical Analysis

Lincoln Company Comparative Balance Sheet December 31, 20Y6 and 20Y5				
	Dec. 31, 20Y6		**Dec. 31, 20Y5**	
	Amount	**Percent**	**Amount**	**Percent**
Assets				
Current assets....................................	$ 550,000	48.3%	$ 533,000	43.3%
Long-term investments..........................	95,000	8.3	177,500	14.4
Property, plant, and equipment (net)	444,500	39.0	470,000	38.2
Intangible assets	50,000	4.4	50,000	4.1
Total assets	$1,139,500	100.0%	$1,230,500	100.0%
Liabilities				
Current liabilities................................	$ 210,000	18.4%	$ 243,000	19.7%
Long-term liabilities	100,000	8.8	200,000	16.3
Total liabilities	$ 310,000	27.2%	$ 443,000	36.0%
Stockholders' Equity				
Preferred 6% stock, $100 par	$ 150,000	13.2%	$ 150,000	12.2%
Common stock, $10 par..........................	500,000	43.9	500,000	40.6
Retained earnings...............................	179,500	15.7	137,500	11.2
Total stockholders' equity.......................	$ 829,500	72.8%	$ 787,500	64.0%
Total liabilities and stockholders' equity..........	$1,139,500	100.0%	$1,230,500	100.0%

Link to Nike For a recent year, **Nike**'s current assets were 70.2% of total assets.

In a vertical analysis of the income statement, each item is stated as a percent of sales. Exhibit 6 illustrates the vertical analysis of the 20Y6 and 20Y5 income statements of **Lincoln Company**.

Exhibit 6

Comparative Income Statement—Vertical Analysis

Lincoln Company Comparative Income Statement For the Years Ended December 31, 20Y6 and 20Y5				
	20Y6		**20Y5**	
	Amount	**Percent**	**Amount**	**Percent**
Sales	$ 1,498,000	100.0%	$1,200,000	100.0%
Cost of goods sold................................	(1,043,000)	(69.6)	(820,000)	(68.3)
Gross profit	$ 455,000	30.4%	$ 380,000	31.7%
Selling expenses	$ (191,000)	(12.8)%	$ (147,000)	(12.3)%
Administrative expenses..........................	(104,000)	(6.9)	(97,400)	(8.1)
Total operating expenses	$ (295,000)	(19.7)%	$ (244,400)	(20.4)%
Operating income................................	$ 160,000	10.7%	$ 135,600	11.3%
Other revenue and expense:				
Other revenue	8,500	0.6	11,000	0.9
Other expense (interest)......................	(6,000)	(0.4)	(12,000)	(1.0)
Income before income tax expense................	$ 162,500	10.9%	$ 134,600	11.2%
Income tax expense	(71,500)	(4.8)	(58,100)	(4.8)
Net income	$ 91,000	6.1%	$ 76,500	6.4%

Exhibit 6 indicates a decrease in the gross profit rate from 31.7% in 20Y5 to 30.4% in 20Y6. Although this is only a 1.3 percentage point (31.7% – 30.4%) decrease, in dollars of potential gross profit, it represents a decrease of $19,474 (1.3% × $1,498,000) based on 20Y6 sales. Thus, a small percentage decrease can have a large dollar effect.

For a recent year, **Nike**'s net income was 11.6% of sales.

Link to Nike

Common-Sized Statements

In a **common-sized statement**, all items are expressed as percentages, with no dollar amounts shown. Common-sized statements are often useful for comparing one company with another or for comparing a company with industry averages.

Exhibit 7 illustrates common-sized income statements for **Lincoln Company** and Madison Corporation. Exhibit 7 indicates that Lincoln has a slightly higher gross profit percentage (30.4%) than Madison (30.0%). However, Lincoln has a higher percentage of selling expenses (12.8%) and administrative expenses (6.9%) than does Madison (11.5% and 4.1%). As a result, the operating income as a percentage of sales of Lincoln (10.7%) is less than that of Madison (14.4%).

	Lincoln Company	Madison Corporation
Sales	100.0%	100.0%
Cost of goods sold	(69.6)	(70.6)
Gross profit	30.4%	30.0%
Selling expenses	(12.8)%	(11.5)%
Administrative expenses	(6.9)	(4.1)
Total operating expenses	(19.7)%	(15.6)%
Operating income	10.7%	14.4%
Other revenue and expense:		
Other revenue	0.6	0.6
Other expense (interest)	(0.4)	(0.5)
Income before income tax expense	10.9%	14.5%
Income tax expense	(4.8)	(5.5)
Net income	6.1%	9.0%

Exhibit 7
Common-Sized Income Statements

The unfavorable difference of 3.7 (14.4% – 10.7%) percentage points in operating income would concern the managers and other stakeholders of Lincoln. The underlying causes of the difference should be investigated and possibly corrected. For example, Lincoln may decide to outsource some of its administrative duties so that its administrative expenses are more comparative to that of Madison.

Check Up Corner 14-1 | Horizontal and Vertical Analyses

Select income statement data for Bukasy Company for two recent years ended December 31 are as follows:

	20Y2	20Y1
Sales	$ 2,200,000	$ 2,000,000
Cost of goods sold	(1,337,500)	(1,250,000)
Gross profit	$ 862,500	$ 750,000
Selling, general, and administrative expenses	(440,000)	(400,000)
Operating income	$ 422,500	$ 350,000

Prepare horizontal and vertical analyses of Bukasy's income statement. Round percentages to one decimal place.

Solution:

Horizontal Analysis

	20Y2	20Y1	Increase/(Decrease) Amount	Percent
Sales	$ 2,200,000	$ 2,000,000	$200,000	10.0%
Cost of goods sold	(1,337,500)	(1,250,000)	87,500	7.0%
Gross profit	$ 862,500	$ 750,000	$112,500	15.0%
Selling, general, and administrative expenses	(440,000)	(400,000)	40,000	10.0%
Operating income	$ 422,500	$ 350,000	$ 72,500	20.7%

Horizontal analysis shows increases and decreases in the amount and percentage of financial statement items. The amount and percentage of each item on the most recent statement is compared with the same item on one or more earlier statements.

Vertical Analysis

	20Y2 Amount	Percent	20Y1 Amount	Percent
Sales	$ 2,200,000	100.0%	$ 2,000,000	100.0%
Cost of goods sold	(1,337,500)	(60.8)	(1,250,000)	(62.5)
Gross profit	$ 862,500	39.2%	$ 750,000	37.5%
Selling, general, and administrative expenses	(440,000)	(20.0)	(400,000)	(20.0)
Operating income	$ 422,500	19.2%	$ 350,000	17.5%

Vertical analysis compares each component in a financial statement to a total within the statement. It can be applied to a single statement or to the same statement over time.

Check Up Corner

Analyzing Liquidity

Objective 3
Describe and illustrate how to use financial statement analysis to assess liquidity.

Liquidity analysis evaluates the ability of a company to convert current assets into cash. Banks and other short-term creditors rely heavily on liquidity analysis, because they are interested in evaluating a company's ability to repay loans and short-term notes. Exhibit 8 shows three categories of measures used to evaluate a company's liquidity. These ratios and measures focus upon a company's current position (current assets and liabilities), accounts receivable, and inventory.

Exhibit 8
Liquidity Ratios and Measures

Current Position Analysis	Accounts Receivable Analysis	Inventory Analysis
Working Capital	Accounts Receivable Turnover	Inventory Turnover
Current Ratio	Number of Days' Sales in Receivables	Number of Days' Sales in Inventory
Quick Ratio		

Current Position Analysis

Current position analysis evaluates a company's ability to pay its current liabilities. This information helps short-term creditors determine how quickly they will be repaid. This analysis includes:

- Working capital
- Current ratio
- Quick ratio

Working Capital A company's **working capital** is computed as follows:

$$\text{Working Capital} = \text{Current Assets} - \text{Current Liabilities}$$

To illustrate, the working capital for **Lincoln Company** for 20Y6 and 20Y5 is computed as follows:

	20Y6	20Y5
Current assets	$ 550,000	$ 533,000
Current liabilities	(210,000)	(243,000)
Working capital	$ 340,000	$ 290,000

The working capital is used to evaluate a company's ability to pay current liabilities. A company's working capital is often monitored monthly, quarterly, or yearly by creditors and other debtors. However, it is difficult to use working capital to compare companies of different sizes. For example, working capital of $250,000 may be adequate for a local sporting goods store, but it would be inadequate for **Nike**.

Current Ratio The **current ratio**, sometimes called the *working capital ratio*, is computed as follows:

$$\text{Current Ratio} = \frac{\text{Current Assets}}{\text{Current Liabilities}}$$

To illustrate, the current ratio for **Lincoln Company** is computed as follows:

	20Y6	20Y5
Current assets	$550,000	$533,000
Current liabilities	$210,000	$243,000
Current ratio	2.6 ($550,000 ÷ $210,000)	2.2 ($533,000 ÷ $243,000)

The current ratio is a more reliable indicator of a company's ability to pay its current liabilities than is working capital, and it is much easier to compare across companies. To illustrate, assume that as of December 31, 20Y6, the working capital of a competitor is much greater than Lincoln's $340,000, but its current ratio is only 1.3. Considering these facts alone, Lincoln is in a more favorable position to obtain short-term credit than the competitor because it has a higher current ratio.

For a recent five-year period, **Nike**'s average current ratio was 2.9.   *Link to Nike*

Quick Ratio One limitation of working capital and the current ratio is that they do not consider the types of current assets a company has and how easily they can be turned into cash. Because of this, two companies may have the same working capital and current ratios but differ significantly in their ability to pay their current liabilities.

To illustrate, the current assets and liabilities for **Lincoln Company** and Jefferson Company as of December 31, 20Y6, are as follows:

	Lincoln Company	Jefferson Company
Current assets:		
Cash	$ 90,500	$ 45,500
Temporary investments	75,000	25,000
Accounts receivable (net)	115,000	90,000
Inventories	264,000	380,000
Prepaid expenses	5,500	9,500
Total current assets	$ 550,000	$ 550,000
Current assets	$ 550,000	$ 550,000
Current liabilities	(210,000)	(210,000)
Working capital	$ 340,000	$ 340,000
Current ratio (Current assets ÷ Current liabilities)	2.6	2.6

Lincoln and Jefferson both have a working capital of $340,000 and current ratios of 2.6. Jefferson, however, has more of its current assets in inventories. These inventories must be sold and the receivables collected before all the current liabilities can be paid. This takes time. In addition, if the market for its product declines, Jefferson may have difficulty selling its inventory. This, in turn, could impair its ability to pay its current liabilities.

In contrast, Lincoln's current assets contain more cash, temporary investments, and accounts receivable, which can easily be converted to cash. Thus, Lincoln is in a stronger current position than Jefferson to pay its current liabilities.

A ratio that captures this difference and measures the "instant" debt-paying ability of a company is the **quick ratio**, sometimes called the *acid-test ratio*. The quick ratio is computed as follows:

$$\text{Quick Ratio} = \frac{\text{Quick Assets}}{\text{Current Liabilities}}$$

Quick assets are cash and other current assets that can be easily converted to cash. Quick assets normally include cash, temporary investments, and receivables but exclude inventories and prepaid assets.

To illustrate, the quick ratios for **Lincoln Company** and Jefferson Company are computed as follows:

	Lincoln Company	Jefferson Company
Quick assets:		
Cash	$ 90,500	$ 45,500
Temporary investments	75,000	25,000
Accounts receivable (net)	115,000	90,000
Total quick assets	$280,500	$160,500
Current liabilities	$210,000	$210,000
Quick ratio	1.3 ($280,500 ÷ $210,000)	0.8 ($160,500 ÷ $210,000)

Accounts Receivable Analysis

A company's ability to collect its accounts receivable is called **accounts receivable analysis**. It includes the computation and analysis of the following:

- Accounts receivable turnover
- Number of days' sales in receivables

Collecting accounts receivable as quickly as possible improves a company's liquidity. In addition, the cash collected from receivables may be used to improve or expand operations. Quick collection of receivables also reduces the risk of uncollectible accounts.

Accounts Receivable Turnover The **accounts receivable turnover** is computed as follows:

$$\text{Accounts Receivable Turnover} = \frac{\text{Sales}^1}{\text{Average Accounts Receivable}}$$

[1] If known, *credit* sales should be used in the numerator. Because credit sales are not normally known by external users, we use sales in the numerator.

To illustrate, the accounts receivable turnover for **Lincoln Company** for 20Y6 and 20Y5 is computed as follows. Lincoln's accounts receivable balance at the beginning of 20Y5 is $140,000.

	20Y6	**20Y5**
Sales	$1,498,000	$1,200,000
Accounts receivable (net):		
Beginning of year	$ 120,000	$ 140,000
End of year	115,000	120,000
Total	$ 235,000	$ 260,000
Average accounts receivable	$117,500 ($235,000 ÷ 2)	$130,000 ($260,000 ÷ 2)
Accounts receivable turnover	12.7 ($1,498,000 ÷ $117,500)	9.2 ($1,200,000 ÷ $130,000)

The increase in Lincoln's accounts receivable turnover from 9.2 to 12.7 indicates that the collection of receivables has improved during 20Y6. This may be due to a change in how credit is granted, collection practices, or both.

For Lincoln, the average accounts receivable was computed using the accounts receivable balance at the beginning and the end of the year. When sales are seasonal and, thus, vary throughout the year, monthly balances of receivables are often used. Also, if sales on account include notes receivable as well as accounts receivable, notes and accounts receivable are normally combined for analysis.

Number of Days' Sales in Receivables The **number of days' sales in receivables** is computed as follows:

$$\text{Number of Days' Sales in Receivables} = \frac{\text{Average Accounts Receivable}}{\text{Average Daily Sales}}$$

where

$$\text{Average Daily Sales} = \frac{\text{Sales}}{365 \text{ days}}$$

To illustrate, the number of days' sales in receivables for **Lincoln Company** is computed as follows:

	20Y6	**20Y5**
Average accounts receivable	$117,500 ($235,000 ÷ 2)	$130,000 ($260,000 ÷ 2)
Average daily sales	$4,104 ($1,498,000 ÷ 365)	$3,288 ($1,200,000 ÷ 365)
Number of days' sales in receivables	28.6 ($117,500 ÷ $4,104)	39.5 ($130,000 ÷ $3,288)

The number of days' sales in receivables is an estimate of the time (in days) that the accounts receivable have been outstanding. The number of days' sales in receivables is often compared with a company's credit terms to evaluate the efficiency of the collection of receivables.

To illustrate, if Lincoln's credit terms are 2/10, n/30, then Lincoln was very *inefficient* in collecting receivables in 20Y5. In other words, receivables should have been collected in 30 days or less but were being collected in 39.5 days. Although collections improved during 20Y6 to 28.6 days, there is probably still room for improvement. On the other hand, if Lincoln's credit terms are n/45, then there is probably little room for improving collections.

Inventory Analysis

A company's ability to manage its inventory effectively is evaluated using **inventory analysis**. It includes the computation and analysis of the following:

- Inventory turnover
- Number of days' sales in inventory

Excess inventory decreases liquidity by tying up funds (cash) in inventory. In addition, excess inventory increases insurance expense, property taxes, storage costs, and other related expenses. These expenses further reduce funds that could be used elsewhere to improve or expand operations.

Why It Matters

Flying Off the Shelves

Two companies with a fast inventory turnover relative to their industries are **Apple Inc. (AAPL)** and **Costco Wholesale Corporation (COST)**:

	Inventory Turnover	Industry	Industry Average
Apple	52.3	Technology	21.0
Costco	11.4	Retail	7.1

Apple turns over its inventory approximately every week. There are two primary reasons for this performance. First, Apple does not manufacture its products, but contracts their manufacture by others. Thus, Apple has no inventory related to manufacturing. Second, the Apple Store inventory moves very quickly due to the popularity of its products. Costco is one of the most effective companies within the retail industry for inventory turns. This is because Costco employs a club warehouse model that stocks a minimum variety of highly popular products. Products that don't sell quickly are removed from its offerings.

Excess inventory also increases the risk of losses because of price declines or obsolescence of the inventory. On the other hand, a company should keep enough inventory in stock so that it doesn't lose sales because of lack of inventory.

Inventory Turnover The **inventory turnover** is computed as follows:

$$\text{Inventory Turnover} = \frac{\text{Cost of Goods Sold}}{\text{Average Inventory}}$$

To illustrate, the inventory turnover for **Lincoln Company** for 20Y6 and 20Y5 is computed as follows. Lincoln's inventory balance at the beginning of 20Y5 is $311,000.

	20Y6	20Y5
Cost of goods sold	$1,043,000	$820,000
Inventories:		
Beginning of year	$ 283,000	$311,000
End of year	264,000	283,000
Total	$ 547,000	$594,000
Average inventory	$273,500 ($547,000 ÷ 2)	$297,000 ($594,000 ÷ 2)
Inventory turnover	3.8 ($1,043,000 ÷ $273,500)	2.8 ($820,000 ÷ $297,000)

The increase in Lincoln's inventory turnover from 2.8 to 3.8 indicates that the management of inventory has improved in 20Y6. The inventory turnover improved because of an increase in the cost of goods sold, which indicates more sales and a decrease in the average inventories.

What is considered a good inventory turnover varies by type of inventory, company, and industry. For example, grocery stores have a higher inventory turnover than jewelers or furniture stores. Likewise, within a grocery store, perishable foods have a higher turnover than the soaps and cleansers.

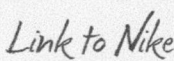 *Link to Nike* For a recent five-year period, **Nike**'s average inventory turnover was 4.1.

Number of Days' Sales in Inventory The **number of days' sales in inventory** is computed as follows:

$$\text{Number of Days' Sales in Inventory} = \frac{\text{Average Inventory}}{\text{Average Daily Cost of Goods Sold}}$$

where

$$\text{Average Daily Cost of Goods Sold} = \frac{\text{Cost of Goods Sold}}{365 \text{ days}}$$

To illustrate, the number of days' sales in inventory for **Lincoln Company** is computed as follows:

	20Y6	20Y5
Average inventory	$273,500 ($547,000 ÷ 2)	$297,000 ($594,000 ÷ 2)
Average daily cost of goods sold	$2,858 ($1,043,000 ÷ 365)	$2,247 ($820,000 ÷ 365)
Number of days' sales in inventory	95.7 ($273,500 ÷ $2,858)	132.2 ($297,000 ÷ $2,247)

The number of days' sales in inventory is a rough measure of the length of time it takes to purchase, sell, and replace the inventory. Lincoln's number of days' sales in inventory improved from 132.2 days to 95.7 days during 20Y6. This is a major improvement in managing inventory.

Check Up Corner 14-2 Liquidity Analysis

Select financial statement data for OM&M Inc. for two recent years follows:

	20Y2	20Y1
Select income statement information:		
Sales	$1,800,000	$1,740,000
Cost of goods sold	1,200,000	1,120,000
Select balance sheet information:		
Cash	$ 300,000	$ 290,000
Temporary investments	100,000	100,000
Accounts receivable (net)	200,000	160,000
Inventory	160,000	140,000
Accounts payable	400,000	350,000

Based on these data, calculate the following liquidity measures for 20Y2:

a. Current ratio
b. Quick ratio
c. Accounts receivable turnover
d. Inventory turnover

Solution:

a.

$$\text{Current Ratio} = \frac{\text{Current Assets}}{\text{Current Liabilities}} = \frac{\$300,000 + \$100,000 + \$200,000 + \$160,000}{\$400,000} = \frac{\$760,000}{\$400,000} = 1.9$$

The current ratio is used to evaluate a company's ability to pay current liabilities.

b.

$$\text{Quick Ratio} = \frac{\text{Quick Assets}}{\text{Current Liabilities}} = \frac{\$300,000 + \$100,000 + \$200,000}{\$400,000} = \frac{\$600,000}{\$400,000} = 1.5$$

The quick ratio measures the "instant" debt-paying ability of a company. Quick assets are cash and other current assets that can be easily converted to cash.

c.

$$\text{Accounts Receivable Turnover} = \frac{\text{Sales}}{\text{Average Accounts Receivable}} = \frac{\$1,800,000}{(\$200,000 + \$160,000) \div 2} = \frac{\$1,800,000}{\$180,000} = 10.0$$

Accounts receivable turnover measures the speed with which a company collects its accounts receivable.

d.

$$\text{Inventory Turnover} = \frac{\text{Cost of Goods Sold}}{\text{Average Inventory}} = \frac{\$1,200,000}{(\$160,000 + \$140,000) \div 2} = \frac{\$1,200,000}{\$150,000} = 8.0$$

Inventory turnover measures the number of times each year that a company sells its inventory.

Check Up Corner

Objective 4
Describe and illustrate how to use financial statement analysis to assess solvency.

Analyzing Solvency

Solvency analysis evaluates a company's ability to pay its long-term debts. Bondholders and other long-term creditors use solvency analysis to evaluate a company's ability to (i) repay the face amount of debt at maturity and (ii) make periodic interest payments. Three common solvency ratios are shown in Exhibit 9.

Exhibit 9

Solvency Ratios

Solvency Ratios		
Ratio of Fixed Assets to Long-Term Liabilities	Ratio of Liabilities to Stockholders' Equity	Times Interest Earned

Ratio of Fixed Assets to Long-Term Liabilities

Fixed assets are often pledged as security for long-term notes and bonds. The **ratio of fixed assets to long-term liabilities** provides a measure of how much fixed assets a company has to support its long-term debt. This measures a company's ability to repay the face amount of debt at maturity and is computed as follows:

$$\text{Ratio of Fixed Assets to Long-Term Liabilities} = \frac{\text{Fixed Assets (net)}}{\text{Long-Term Liabilities}}$$

To illustrate, the ratio of fixed assets to long-term liabilities for **Lincoln Company** is computed as follows:

	20Y6	20Y5
Fixed assets (net)	$444,500	$470,000
Long-term liabilities	$100,000	$200,000
Ratio of fixed assets to long-term liabilities	4.4 ($444,500 ÷ $100,000)	2.4 ($470,000 ÷ $200,000)

During 20Y6, Lincoln's ratio of fixed assets to long-term liabilities increased from 2.4 to 4.4. This increase was due primarily to Lincoln paying off one-half of its long-term liabilities in 20Y6.

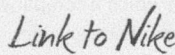 *Link to Nike* For a recent year, **Nike**'s ratio of fixed assets to long-term liabilities was 0.9.

Ratio of Liabilities to Stockholders' Equity

The **ratio of liabilities to stockholders' equity** measures how much of the company is financed by debt and equity. It is computed as follows:

$$\text{Ratio of Liabilities to Stockholders' Equity} = \frac{\text{Total Liabilities}}{\text{Total Stockholders' Equity}}$$

To illustrate, the ratio of liabilities to stockholders' equity for **Lincoln Company** is computed as follows:

	20Y6	20Y5
Total liabilities	$310,000	$443,000
Total stockholders' equity	$829,500	$787,500
Ratio of liabilities to stockholders' equity	0.4 ($310,000 ÷ $829,500)	0.6 ($443,000 ÷ $787,500)

Lincoln's ratio of liabilities to stockholders' equity decreased from 0.6 to 0.4 during 20Y6. The lower ratio indicates that the proportion of Lincoln's liabilities and equity that is made up of liabilities is decreasing. This is an improvement and indicates that the margin of safety for Lincoln's creditors is improving.

> For a recent five-year period, **Nike**'s average ratio of liabilities to stockholders' equity was 0.7.
> *Link to Nike*

Times Interest Earned

The **times interest earned**, sometimes called the *coverage ratio*, measures the risk that interest payments will not be made if earnings decrease. It is computed as follows:

$$\text{Times Interest Earned} = \frac{\text{Income Before Income Tax Expense} + \text{Interest Expense}}{\text{Interest Expense}}$$

Interest expense is paid before income taxes. In other words, interest expense is deducted in determining taxable income and, thus, income tax. For this reason, income *before taxes* is used in computing the times interest earned.

The *higher* the ratio, the more likely interest payments will be paid if earnings decrease. To illustrate, the times interest earned for **Lincoln Company** is computed as follows:

	20Y6	20Y5
Income before income tax expense	$162,500	$134,600
Interest expense	6,000	12,000
Amount available to pay interest	$168,500	$146,600
Times interest earned	28.1 ($168,500 ÷ $6,000)	12.2 ($146,600 ÷ $12,000)

The times interest earned improved from 12.2 to 28.1 during 20Y6. The higher ratio indicates that the relationship between the amount of income available to pay interest and the amount of interest expense has improved. Lincoln has more than enough earnings (28 times) to make its interest payments.

> For a recent year, **Nike**'s times interest earned ratio was 12 1/2 times higher than the industry average.
> *Link to Nike*

Why It Matters

Liquidity Crunch

RadioShack Corporation, an electronics retailer, filed for bankruptcy protection. Information on the company's liquidity and solvency for the three years prior to bankruptcy follows:

	Year 3	Year 2	Year 1
Liquidity measures:			
Working capital (in thousands)	$748,400	$1,003,700	$1,176,700
Current ratio	2.3	2.0	2.9
Quick ratio	0.7	1.0	1.5
Solvency measures:			
Ratio of liabilities to			
stockholders' equity	6.7	2.8	1.9
Ratio of fixed assets to			
long-term liabilities	0.2	0.3	0.3

The data show that the company's liquidity and solvency measures deteriorated in the years prior to the firm's bankruptcy. All three of the company's liquidity measures declined significantly during the three-year period, indicating a growing risk that the company would not be able to repay its current liabilities. The ratio of liabilities to stockholders' equity also increased significantly during this period, indicating that the company might not be able to repay its long-term debts. Finally, the ratio of fixed assets to long-term liabilities began to deteriorate in Year 3, indicating that fewer assets would be available to secure the company's long-term liabilities.

Check Up Corner 14-3   Solvency Analysis

The following are select balance sheet and income statement data for Wilton Strand Inc. for the year ended December 31, 20Y3:

	Dec. 31, 20Y3
Assets	
Current assets	$ 560,000
Property, plant, and equipment (net)	1,400,000
Total assets	$1,960,000
Liabilities	
Current liabilities	$ 160,000
Long-term liabilities	400,000
Total liabilities	$ 560,000
Stockholders' Equity	
Common stock, $5 par......................	$ 200,000
Retained earnings	1,200,000
Total stockholders' equity...................	$1,400,000
Total liabilities and stockholders' equity	$1,960,000
Select income statement information:	
Interest expense.............................	$ 100,000
Income before income tax expense..........	260,000

Based on these data, calculate the following solvency measures:

a.   Ratio of fixed assets to long-term liabilities
b.   Ratio of liabilities to stockholders' equity
c.   Times interest earned

Solution:

a.

$$\text{Ratio of Fixed Assets to Long-Term Liabilities} = \frac{\text{Fixed Assets (net)}}{\text{Long-Term Liabilities}} = \frac{\$1,400,000}{\$400,000} = 3.5$$

Because fixed assets are often pledged as security for long-term notes and bonds, the ratio of fixed assets to long-term liabilities provides a measure of whether noteholders or bondholders will be paid.

b.

$$\text{Ratio of Liabilities to Stockholders' Equity} = \frac{\text{Total Liabilities}}{\text{Total Stockholders' Equity}} = \frac{\$560,000}{\$1,400,000} = 0.4$$

The ratio of liabilities to stockholders' equity measures how much of the company is financed by debt and equity.

c.

$$\text{Times Interest Earned} = \frac{\text{Income Before Income Tax Expense} + \text{Interest Expense}}{\text{Interest Expense}} = \frac{\$260,000 + \$100,000}{\$100,000} = \frac{\$360,000}{\$100,000} = 3.6$$

Times interest earned measures the risk that interest payments will not be made if earnings decrease.

Check Up Corner

Objective 5

Describe and illustrate how to use financial statement analysis to assess profitability.

Analyzing Profitability

Profitability analysis evaluates the ability of a company to generate future earnings. This ability depends on the relationship between the company's operating results and the assets the company has available for use in its operations. Thus, the relationships between income statement and balance sheet items are used to evaluate profitability.

Common profitability ratios are shown in Exhibit 10.

Profitability Ratios		
Asset Turnover	Return on Stockholders' Equity	Price-Earnings Ratio
Return on Total Assets	Return on Common Stockholders' Equity	Dividends per Share
	Earnings per Share on Common Stock	Dividend Yield

Exhibit 10
Profitability Ratios

Asset Turnover

The **asset turnover** ratio measures how effectively a company uses its assets. It is computed as follows:

$$\text{Asset Turnover} = \frac{\text{Sales}}{\text{Average Total Assets (excluding long-term investments)}}$$

Note that long-term investments are excluded in computing asset turnover. This is because long-term investments are unrelated to normal operations and sales.

To illustrate, the asset turnover for **Lincoln Company** is computed as follows. Total assets (excluding long-term investments) are $1,010,000 at the beginning of 20Y5.

	20Y6	20Y5
Sales	$1,498,000	$1,200,000
Total assets (excluding long-term investments):		
Beginning of year	$1,053,000*	$1,010,000
End of year	1,044,500**	1,053,000*
Total	$2,097,500	$2,063,000
Average total assets	$1,048,750 ($2,097,500 ÷ 2)	$1,031,500 ($2,063,000 ÷ 2)
Asset turnover	1.4 ($1,498,000 ÷ $1,048,750)	1.2 ($1,200,000 ÷ $1,031,500)

*($1,230,500 total assets – $177,500 long-term investments)
**($1,139,500 total assets – $95,000 long-term investments)

For Lincoln, the average total assets was computed using total assets (excluding long-term investments) at the beginning and end of the year. The average total assets could also be based on monthly or quarterly averages.

The asset turnover ratio indicates that Lincoln's use of its operating assets has improved in 20Y6. This was primarily due to the increase in sales in 20Y6.

Return on Total Assets

The **return on total assets** measures the profitability of total assets, without considering how the assets are financed. In other words, this ratio is not affected by the portion of assets financed by creditors or stockholders. It is computed as follows:

$$\text{Return on Total Assets} = \frac{\text{Net Income} + \text{Interest Expense}}{\text{Average Total Assets}}$$

The return on total assets is computed by adding interest expense to net income. By adding interest expense to net income, the effect of whether the assets are financed by creditors (debt) or stockholders (equity) is eliminated. Because net income includes any income earned from long-term investments, the average total assets includes long-term investments as well as the net operating assets.

To illustrate, the return on total assets by **Lincoln Company** is computed as follows. Total assets are $1,187,500 at the beginning of 20Y5.

	20Y6	**20Y5**
Net income	$ 91,000	$ 76,500
Interest expense	6,000	12,000
	$ 97,000	$ 88,500
Total assets:		
Beginning of year	$1,230,500	$1,187,500
End of year	1,139,500	1,230,500
Total	$2,370,000	$2,418,000
Average total assets	$1,185,000 ($2,370,000 ÷ 2)	$1,209,000 ($2,418,000 ÷ 2)
Return on total assets	8.2% ($97,000 ÷ $1,185,000)	7.3% ($88,500 ÷ $1,209,000)

The return on total assets improved from 7.3% to 8.2% during 20Y6.

The *return on operating assets* is sometimes computed when there are large amounts of non-operating income and expense. It is computed as follows:

$$\text{Return on Operating Assets} = \frac{\text{Operating Income}}{\text{Average Operating Assets}}$$

Because Lincoln does not have a significant amount of nonoperating income and expense, the return on operating assets is not illustrated.

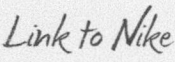 **Link to Nike**   For a recent five-year period, **Nike**'s average return on total assets was 15.8%.

Return on Stockholders' Equity

The **return on stockholders' equity** measures the rate of income earned on the amount invested by the stockholders. It is computed as follows:

$$\text{Return on Stockholders' Equity} = \frac{\text{Net Income}}{\text{Average Total Stockholders' Equity}}$$

To illustrate, the return on stockholders' equity for **Lincoln Company** is computed as follows. Total stockholders' equity is $750,000 at the beginning of 20Y5.

	20Y6	**20Y5**
Net income	$ 91,000	$ 76,500
Total stockholders' equity:		
Beginning of year	$ 787,500	$ 750,000
End of year	829,500	787,500
Total	$1,617,000	$1,537,500
Average total stockholders' equity	$808,500 ($1,617,000 ÷ 2)	$768,750 ($1,537,500 ÷ 2)
Return on stockholders' equity	11.3% ($91,000 ÷ $808,500)	10.0% ($76,500 ÷ $768,750)

The return on stockholders' equity improved from 10.0% to 11.3% during 20Y6.

Leverage involves using debt to increase the return on an investment. The return on stockholders' equity is normally higher than the return on total assets. This is because of the effect of leverage. For **Lincoln Company**, the effect of leverage for 20Y6 is 3.1% and for 20Y5 is 2.7% computed as follows:

	20Y6	**20Y5**
Return on stockholders' equity	11.3%	10.0%
Return on total assets	(8.2)	(7.3)
Effect of leverage	3.1%	2.7%

Exhibit 11 shows the 20Y6 and 20Y5 effects of leverage for Lincoln.

The Accounting Equation

Another term for leverage is "financial gearing." **Exxon Mobil Corporation (XOM)**, a worldwide-integrated energy company, is an example of a company that uses leverage for financial advantage. Exxon had a return on total assets of 2.5% for a recent year, while its return on stockholders' equity was 5%. Thus, Exxon is "geared" 2:1 by using debt on its balance sheet. Exxon is very profitable; thus, leverage is beneficial. In contrast, **Chesapeake Energy Corporation (CHK)**, an oil and gas exploration company, had return on assets of –12.5% for a recent 12-month period, and return on stockholders' equity of –135%. In this case, the almost 11:1 leverage (135% ÷ 12.5%) creates a financial disadvantage because the company is experiencing losses.

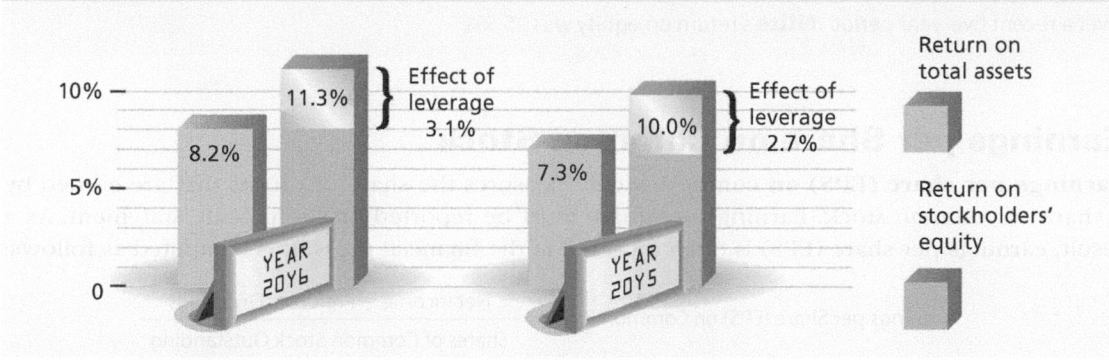

Exhibit 11
Effect of Leverage

Return on Common Stockholders' Equity

The **return on common stockholders' equity** measures the rate of profits earned on the amount invested by the common stockholders. It is computed as follows:

$$\text{Return on Common Stockholders' Equity} = \frac{\text{Net Income} - \text{Preferred Dividends}}{\text{Average Common Stockholders' Equity}}$$

Because preferred stockholders rank ahead of the common stockholders in their claim on earnings, any preferred dividends are subtracted from net income in computing the return on common stockholders' equity.

Lincoln Company had $150,000 par value of 6% preferred stock outstanding on December 31, 20Y6 and 20Y5. Thus, preferred dividends of $9,000 ($150,000 × 6%) are deducted from net income. Lincoln's common stockholders' equity is determined as follows:

	December 31		
	20Y6	**20Y5**	**20Y4**
Common stock, $10 par	$500,000	$500,000	$500,000
Retained earnings	179,500	137,500	100,000
Common stockholders' equity	$679,500	$637,500	$600,000

The retained earnings on December 31, 20Y4, of $100,000 is the same as the retained earnings on January 1, 20Y5, as shown in Lincoln's retained earnings statement in Exhibit 4.

Using this information, the return on common stockholders' equity for Lincoln is computed as follows:

	20Y6	**20Y5**
Net income	$ 91,000	$ 76,500
Preferred dividends	(9,000)	(9,000)
Total	$ 82,000	$ 67,500
Common stockholders' equity:		
Beginning of year	$ 637,500	$ 600,000
End of year	679,500*	637,500**
Total	$1,317,000	$1,237,500
Average common stockholders' equity	$658,500 ($1,317,000 ÷ 2)	$618,750 ($1,237,500 ÷ 2)
Return on common stockholders' equity	12.5% ($82,000 ÷ $658,500)	10.9% ($67,500 ÷ $618,750)

*($829,500 total stockholders' equity – $150,000 preferred 6% stock)
**($787,500 total stockholders' equity – $150,000 preferred 6% stock)

Lincoln's return on common stockholders' equity improved from 10.9% to 12.5% in 20Y6. This return differs from Lincoln's returns on total assets and stockholders' equity, which follow:

	20Y6	20Y5
Return on total assets	8.2%	7.3%
Return on stockholders' equity	11.3%	10.0%
Return on common stockholders' equity	12.5%	10.9%

These returns differ because of leverage, as discussed in the preceding section.

Earnings per Share on Common Stock

Earnings per share (EPS) on common stock measures the share of profits that are earned by a share of common stock. Earnings per share must be reported on the income statement. As a result, earnings per share (EPS) is often reported in the financial press. It is computed as follows:

$$\text{Earnings per Share (EPS) on Common Stock} = \frac{\text{Net Income} - \text{Preferred Dividends}}{\text{Shares of Common Stock Outstanding}}$$

When preferred and common stock are outstanding, preferred dividends are subtracted from net income to determine the income related to the common shares.

To illustrate, the earnings per share (EPS) of common stock for **Lincoln Company** is computed as follows:

	20Y6	20Y5
Net income	$91,000	$76,500
Preferred dividends	(9,000)	(9,000)
Total	$82,000	$67,500
Shares of common stock outstanding	50,000	50,000
Earnings per share on common stock	$1.64 ($82,000 ÷ 50,000)	$1.35 ($67,500 ÷ 50,000)

Lincoln had $150,000 par value of 6% preferred stock outstanding on December 31, 20Y6 and 20Y5. Thus, preferred dividends of $9,000 ($150,000 × 6%) are deducted from net income in computing earnings per share on common stock.

Lincoln did not issue any additional shares of common stock in 20Y6. If Lincoln had issued additional shares in 20Y6, a weighted average of common shares outstanding during the year would have been used.

Lincoln's earnings per share (EPS) on common stock improved from $1.35 to $1.64 during 20Y6.

Lincoln has a simple capital structure with only common stock and preferred stock outstanding. Many corporations, however, have complex capital structures with various types of equity securities outstanding, such as convertible preferred stock, stock options, and stock warrants. In such cases, the possible effects of such securities on the shares of common stock outstanding are considered in reporting earnings per share. These possible effects are reported separately as *earnings per common share assuming dilution* or *diluted earnings per share*. This topic is described and illustrated in advanced accounting courses and textbooks.

Pathways Challenge

This is Accounting!

Economic Activity

PayPal Holdings, Inc. (PYPL) is a leading provider of digital payments. In a recent annual report, PayPal reported the following information (in millions):

	From the Income Statement	Adjusted Amounts
Operating income	$1,586	$2,174
Net income	1,401	1,825

The adjusted amounts exclude expenses related to stock options and the amortization of some intangible assets. PayPal management excluded these expenses from the adjusted amounts because they felt these expenses did not reflect its "ongoing operations."

Critical Thinking/Judgment

Are the operating income and net income reported on the income statement in the annual report based on GAAP?

Should companies report adjusted (non-GAAP) amounts in their annual reports?

How would the adjusted (non-GAAP) amounts for PayPal affect the return on total assets, return on stockholders' equity, and earnings per share?

Can adjusted (non-GAAP) amounts provide better information about a company's operations than GAAP amounts?

Suggested answer at end of chapter.

Price-Earnings Ratio

The **price-earnings (P/E) ratio** on common stock measures a company's future earnings prospects. It is often quoted in the financial press and is computed as follows:

$$\text{Price-Earnings (P/E) Ratio} = \frac{\text{Market Price per Share of Common Stock}}{\text{Earnings per Share on Common Stock}}$$

To illustrate, the price-earnings (P/E) ratio for **Lincoln Company** is computed as follows:

	20Y6	20Y5
Market price per share of common stock	$41.00	$27.00
Earnings per share on common stock	$1.64	$1.35
Price-earnings ratio on common stock	25 ($41 ÷ $1.64)	20 ($27 ÷ $1.35)

The price-earnings ratio improved from 20 to 25 during 20Y6. In other words, a share of common stock of Lincoln was selling for 20 times earnings per share at the end of 20Y5. At the end of 20Y6, the common stock was selling for 25 times earnings per share. This indicates that the market expects Lincoln to experience favorable earnings in the future.

For a recent five-year period, **Nike**'s price-earnings ratio was 25.

Link to Nike

Dividends per Share

Dividends per share measures the extent to which earnings are being distributed to common shareholders. It is computed as follows:

$$\text{Dividends per Share} = \frac{\text{Dividends on Common Stock}}{\text{Shares of Common Stock Outstanding}}$$

To illustrate, the dividends per share for **Lincoln Company** are computed as follows:

	20Y6	20Y5
Dividends on common stock	$40,000	$30,000
Shares of common stock outstanding	50,000	50,000
Dividends per share of common stock	$0.80 ($40,000 ÷ 50,000)	$0.60 ($30,000 ÷ 50,000)

The dividends per share of common stock increased from $0.60 to $0.80 during 20Y6.

Dividends per share are often reported with earnings per share. Comparing the two per-share amounts indicates the extent to which earnings are being retained for use in operations. To illustrate, the dividends and earnings per share for **Lincoln Company** are shown in Exhibit 12.

Exhibit 12
Dividends and Earnings per Share of Common Stock

Dividend Yield

The **dividend yield** on common stock measures the rate of return to common stockholders from cash dividends. It is of special interest to investors whose objective is to earn revenue (dividends) from their investment. It is computed as follows:

$$\text{Dividend Yield} = \frac{\text{Dividends per Share of Common Stock}}{\text{Market Price per Share of Common Stock}}$$

To illustrate, the dividend yield for **Lincoln Company** is computed as follows:

	20Y6	**20Y5**
Dividends per share of common stock	$0.80	$0.60
Market price per share of common stock	$41.00	$27.00
Dividend yield on common stock	2.0% ($0.80 ÷ $41)	2.2% ($0.60 ÷ $27)

The dividend yield declined slightly from 2.2% to 2.0% in 20Y6. This decline was primarily due to the increase in the market price of Lincoln's common stock.

For a recent five-year period, **Nike**'s average dividend yield was 1.3%.

Link to Nike

Check Up Corner 14-4 Profitability Analysis

The following data were taken from the financial statements of French Broad Steel Works Inc. for a recent year:

Shares of common stock outstanding	20,000
Sales	$2,400,000
Interest expense	40,000
Net income	250,000
Market price per share of common stock at year-end	120.00
Dividends per share of common stock	3.00
Average total assets (excluding long-term investments)	1,600,000
Average total assets	2,000,000
Average total stockholders' equity	1,000,000

Based on these data, determine the following profitability measures:

a. Asset turnover
b. Return on total assets
c. Return on stockholders' equity
d. Earnings per share
e. Price-earnings ratio
f. Dividend yield

Solution:

a.

$$\text{Asset Turnover} = \frac{\text{Sales}}{\text{Average Total Assets (excluding long-term investments)}} = \frac{\$2,400,000}{\$1,600,000} = 1.5$$

The asset turnover measures how effectively a company uses its assets.

b.

$$\text{Return on Total Assets} = \frac{\text{Net Income + Interest Expense}}{\text{Average Total Assets}} = \frac{\$250,000 + \$40,000}{\$2,000,000} = \frac{\$290,000}{\$2,000,000} = 14.5\%$$

The return on total assets measures the profitability of total assets, without considering how the assets are financed.

c.

$$\text{Return on Stockholders' Equity} = \frac{\text{Net Income}}{\text{Average Total Stockholders' Equity}} = \frac{\$250,000}{\$1,000,000} = 25.0\%$$

The return on stockholders' equity measures the return on the amount invested by stockholders.

d.

$$\text{Earnings per Share} = \frac{\text{Net Income - Preferred Dividends}}{\text{Shares of Common Stock Outstanding}} = \frac{\$250,000 - \$0}{20,000} = \$12.50$$

Earnings per share (EPS) measures the share of profits earned by each share of common stock.

e.

$$\text{Price-Earnings Ratio} = \frac{\text{Market Price per Share of Common Stock}}{\text{Earnings per Share on Common Stock}} = \frac{\$120.00}{\$12.50} = 9.6$$

The price-earnings (P/E) ratio measures a company's future earnings prospects.

f.

$$\text{Dividend Yield} = \frac{\text{Dividends per Share of Common Stock}}{\text{Market Price per Share of Common Stock}} = \frac{\$3.00}{\$120.00} = 2.5\%$$

The dividend yield measures the return to common stockholders from cash dividends.

Check Up Corner

Summary of Analytical Measures

Exhibit 13 shows a summary of the solvency and profitability measures discussed in this chapter. The type of industry and the company's operations usually affect which measures are used. In many cases, additional measures are used for a specific industry. For example, airlines use *revenue per passenger mile* and *cost per available seat* as profitability measures. Likewise, hotels use *occupancy rates* as a profitability measure.

The analytical measures shown in Exhibit 13 are a useful starting point for analyzing a company's liquidity, solvency and profitability. However, they are not a substitute for sound judgment. The general economic and business environment should always be considered in analyzing a company's future prospects. In addition, any trends and interrelationships among the measures should be carefully studied.

Exhibit 13 Summary of Analytical Measures

Liquidity Measures

	Method of Computation	Use
Working Capital	Current Assets – Current Liabilities	Measures the company's ability to pay current liabilities.
Current Ratio	$\dfrac{\text{Current Assets}}{\text{Current Liabilities}}$	
Quick Ratio	$\dfrac{\text{Quick Assets}}{\text{Current Liabilities}}$	Measures the company's instant debt-paying ability.
Accounts Receivable Turnover	$\dfrac{\text{Sales}}{\text{Average Accounts Receivable}}$	Measures the company's efficiency in collecting receivables and in the management of credit.
Numbers of Days' Sales in Receivables	$\dfrac{\text{Average Accounts Receivable}}{\text{Average Daily Sales}}$	
Inventory Turnover	$\dfrac{\text{Cost of Goods Sold}}{\text{Average Inventory}}$	Measures the company's efficiency in managing inventory.
Number of Days' Sales in Inventory	$\dfrac{\text{Average Inventory}}{\text{Average Daily Cost of Goods Sold}}$	

Solvency Measures

Ratio of Fixed Assets to Long-Term Liabilities	$\dfrac{\text{Fixed Assets (net)}}{\text{Long-Term Liabilities}}$	Measures the margin of safety available to long-term creditors.
Ratio of Liabilities to Stockholders' Equity	$\dfrac{\text{Total Liabilities}}{\text{Total Stockholders' Equity}}$	Measures how much of the company is financed by debt and equity.
Times Interest Earned	$\dfrac{\text{Income Before Income Tax Expense + Interest Expense}}{\text{Interest Expense}}$	Measures the risk that interest payments will not be made if earnings decrease.

Exhibit 13 Summary of Analytical Measures *(Concluded)*

Profitability Measures

	Method of Computation	Use
Asset Turnover	$$\frac{Sales}{\text{Average Total Assets (excluding long-term investments)}}$$	Measures how effectively a company uses its assets.
Return on Total Assets	$$\frac{\text{Net Income + Interest Expense}}{\text{Average Total Assets}}$$	Measures the profitability of a company's assets.
Return on Stockholders' Equity	$$\frac{\text{Net Income}}{\text{Average Total Stockholders' Equity}}$$	Measures the profitability of the investment by stockholders.
Return on Common Stockholders' Equity	$$\frac{\text{Net Income − Preferred Dividends}}{\text{Average Common Stockholders' Equity}}$$	Measures the profitability of the investment by common stockholders.
Earnings per Share (EPS) on Common Stock	$$\frac{\text{Net Income − Preferred Dividends}}{\text{Shares of Common Stock Outstanding}}$$	
Price-Earnings (P/E) Ratio	$$\frac{\text{Market Price per Share of Common Stock}}{\text{Earnings per Share on Common Stock}}$$	Measures future earnings prospects, based on the relationship between market value of common stock and earnings.
Dividends per Share	$$\frac{\text{Dividends on Common Stock}}{\text{Shares of Common Stock Outstanding}}$$	Measures the extent to which earnings are being distributed to common stockholders.
Dividend Yield	$$\frac{\text{Dividends per Share of Common Stock}}{\text{Market Price per Share of Common Stock}}$$	Measures the rate of return to common stockholders in terms of dividends.

Corporate Annual Reports

> **Objective 6**
> Describe the contents of corporate annual reports.
>
> **IFRS**
> See Appendix C for more information.

Public corporations issue annual reports summarizing their operating activities for the past year and plans for the future. Such annual reports include the financial statements and the accompanying notes. In addition, annual reports normally include the following sections:

- Management discussion and analysis
- Report on internal control
- Report on fairness of the financial statements

Management Discussion and Analysis

Management's Discussion and Analysis (MD&A) is required in annual reports filed with the Securities and Exchange Commission. It includes management's analysis of current operations and its plans for the future. Typical items included in the MD&A are as follows:

- Management's analysis and explanations of any significant changes between the current and prior years' financial statements.
- Important accounting principles or policies that could affect interpretation of the financial statements, including the effect of changes in accounting principles or the adoption of new accounting principles.
- Management's assessment of the company's liquidity and the availability of capital to the company.
- Significant risk exposures that might affect the company.
- Any "off-balance-sheet" arrangements such as leases not included in the financial statements. Such arrangements are discussed in advanced accounting courses and textbooks.

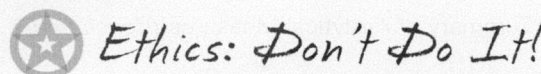 *Ethics: Don't Do It!*

Characteristics of Financial Statement Fraud

Each year the Association of Certified Fraud Examiners conducts a worldwide survey examining the characteristics of corporate fraud. The most recent study found that:

- 39.1% of frauds were detected by a tip from an employee or someone close to the company;
- Frauds committed by owners and executives tended to be much larger than those caused by employees;

Source: *2016 Report to the Nations*, Association of Certified Fraud Examiners, 2016.

- Most people who are caught committing fraud are first-time offenders with clean employment histories; and
- In 78.9% of the cases, the person committing the fraud displayed one or more behavioral red flags, such as living beyond their means, financial difficulties, and excessive control issues.

Fraud examiners can use these trends to help them narrow their focus when searching for fraud.

Report on Internal Control

The Sarbanes-Oxley Act of 2002 requires a report on internal control by management. The report states management's responsibility for establishing and maintaining internal control. In addition, management's assessment of the effectiveness of internal controls over financial reporting is included in the report.

Sarbanes-Oxley also requires a public accounting firm to verify management's conclusions on internal control. Thus, two reports on internal control, one by management and one by a public accounting firm, are included in the annual report. In some situations, these may be combined into a single report on internal control.

Report on Fairness of the Financial Statements

All publicly held corporations are required to have an independent audit (examination) of their financial statements. The Certified Public Accounting (CPA) firm that conducts the audit renders an opinion, called the *Report of Independent Registered Public Accounting Firm*, on the fairness of the statements.

An opinion stating that the financial statements present fairly the financial position, results of operations, and cash flows of the company is said to be an *unmodified opinion*, sometimes called a *clean opinion*. Any report other than an unmodified opinion raises a "red flag" for financial statement users and requires further investigation as to its cause. The types and nature of audit opinions are covered in more detail in advanced courses on auditing.

Link to Nike   **Nike**'s annual report (shown in Appendix E) includes Management Discussion and Analysis, a Report on Internal Control, and a Report of Independent Registered Public Accounting Firm.

Make a Decision

Analyze and compare Amazon.com, Best Buy, and Wal-Mart (MAD 14-1) (Continuing company analysis)

Analyze and compare Alphabet, PepsiCo, and Caterpillar (MAD 14-2)

Analyze Deere & Company (MAD 14-3)

Analyze and compare Marriott and Hyatt (MAD 14-4)

Make a Decision

Appendix 1 Unusual Items on the Income Statement

Generally accepted accounting principles require that unusual items be reported separately on the income statement. This is because such items do not occur frequently and are typically unrelated to current operations. Without separate reporting of these items, users of the financial statements might be misled about current and future operations.

Unusual items on the income statement are classified as one of the following:

- Affecting the *current period* income statement
- Affecting a *prior period* income statement

Unusual Items Affecting the Current Period's Income Statement

Discontinued operations are an unusual item that affects the current period's:

- Income statement presentation
- Earnings per share presentation

Discontinued operations are reported separately on the income statement for any period in which they occur.

Income Statement Presentation A company may discontinue a component of its operations by selling or abandoning the component's operations. For example, a retailer might decide to sell its product only online and, thus, discontinue selling its merchandise at its retail outlets (stores).

If the discontinued component is (1) the result of a strategic shift and (2) has a major effect on the entity's operations and financial results, any gain or loss on discontinued operations is reported on the income statement as a *Gain (or loss) from discontinued operations*. It is reported immediately following *Income from continuing operations*.

To illustrate, assume that Jones Corporation produces and sells electrical products, hardware supplies, and lawn equipment. Because of a lack of profits, Jones discontinues its electrical products operation and sells the remaining inventory and other assets at a loss of $100,000. Exhibit 14 illustrates the reporting of the loss on discontinued operations.[2]

Jones Corporation Income Statement For the Year Ended December 31, 20Y2	
Sales	$12,350,000
Cost of goods sold	(5,800,000)
Gross profit	$ 6,550,000
Selling and administrative expenses	(5,240,000)
Income from continuing operations before income tax expense	$ 1,310,000
Income tax expense	(620,000)
Income from continuing operations	$ 690,000
Loss on discontinued operations	(100,000)
Net income	$ 590,000

Exhibit 14
Unusual Items in the Income Statement

[2] The gain or loss on discontinued operations is reported net of any tax effects. To simplify, the tax effects are not specifically identified in Exhibit 14.

In addition, a note to the financial statements should describe the operations sold, including the date operations were discontinued, and details about the assets, liabilities, income, and expenses of the discontinued component.

Earnings per Share Presentation Earnings per common share should be reported separately for discontinued operations. To illustrate, a partial income statement for Jones Corporation is shown in Exhibit 15. The company has 200,000 shares of common stock outstanding.

Exhibit 15
Income Statement with
Earnings per Share

| Jones Corporation |
| Income Statement |
| For the Year Ended December 31, 20Y2 |

Earnings per common share:	
Income from continuing operations..	$ 3.45
Loss on discontinued operations..	(0.50)
Net income..	$ 2.95

Exhibit 15 reports earnings per common share for income from continuing operations, discontinued operations, and net income. However, only earnings per share for income from continuing operations and net income are required by generally accepted accounting principles. The other per-share amounts may be presented in the notes to the financial statements.

Unusual Items Affecting the Prior Period's Income Statement

An unusual item may occur that affects a prior period's income statement. Two such items are as follows:

- Errors in applying generally accepted accounting principles
- Changes from one generally accepted accounting principle to another

If an error is discovered in a prior period's financial statement, the prior-period statement and all following statements are restated and thus corrected.

A company may change from one generally accepted accounting principle to another. In this case, the prior-period financial statements are restated as if the new accounting principle had always been used.[3]

For both of the preceding items, the current-period earnings are not affected. That is, only the earnings reported in prior periods are restated. However, because the prior earnings are restated, the beginning balance of Retained Earnings may also have to be restated. This, in turn, may cause the restatement of other balance sheet accounts. Illustrations of these types of adjustments and restatements are provided in advanced accounting courses.

Objective App 2
Describe the concepts
of fair value and
comprehensive income.

Appendix 2 Fair Value and Comprehensive Income

In previous chapters, assets have been reported on the balance sheet using the cost basis. Many companies, however, acquire assets that are required by GAAP to be reported on the balance sheet at a different measurement basis called fair value. When a company reports assets at fair value, the financial reporting becomes complex. In the following sections, the concepts of fair value and comprehensive income are introduced. A detailed discussion of these concepts is provided in intermediate and advanced accounting texts.

[3] Changes from one acceptable depreciation method to another acceptable depreciation method are an exception to this general rule and are to be treated prospectively as a change in estimate, as discussed in Chapter 9.

Fair Value

Fair value is the price that could be received for an asset if it were sold today. This differs from historical cost, in that the amount reported on the balance sheet changes each period to reflect the asset's fair (current) value at the balance sheet date. The change in an asset's fair value from one period to the next is recorded in the financial statements as either:

- a gain or loss on the income statement, or
- an increase or decrease in stockholders' equity reported as other comprehensive income.

Comprehensive Income

When a change in an asset's fair value is not recorded as a gain or loss on the income statement, it is recorded as an element of **other comprehensive income.**[4] These include changes in the fair value of certain investment securities, foreign currency exposures, and pension assets.

The elements of other comprehensive income are included in the computation of **comprehensive income**, which is defined as all changes in stockholders' equity during a period, except those resulting from dividends and stockholders' investments. Comprehensive income is determined by adding or subtracting *other comprehensive income* elements to (from) net income, as follows:

Net income	$XXX
Other comprehensive income	XXX
Comprehensive income	$XXX

Companies must report comprehensive income in the financial statements either:

- on the income statement, directly below net income, or
- in a separate statement of comprehensive income.

Reporting Comprehensive Income on the Income Statement Bart Company purchased investment securities during the year that had an increase of $2,600 in fair value. Because of the accounting methods selected by Bart Company, this increase in fair value is recorded as an element of other comprehensive income and is called an **unrealized gain**. If Bart Company elects to report other comprehensive income on the income statement, the elements of other comprehensive income are added to or subtracted from net income at the bottom of the income statement as follows:

Bart Company Income Statement For the Year Ended December 31, 20Y2	
Sales	$1,200,000
Cost of goods sold	(960,000)
Gross profit	$ 240,000
Operating expenses	(144,500)
Operating income	$ 95,500
Income tax expense	(36,290)
Net income	$ 59,210
Other comprehensive income	2,600
Comprehensive income	$ 61,810

Reporting Comprehensive Income on the Statement of Comprehensive Income As an alternative to reporting comprehensive income on the income statement, companies may elect to report comprehensive income on a separate statement of comprehensive income.

[4] Fair value accounting is discussed in greater detail in intermediate and advanced accounting texts. A discussion of fair value accounting is also included in Appendix D.

This statement should immediately follow the income statement. Using the Bart Company example, the income statement and statement of comprehensive income would be presented as follows:

Bart Company Income Statement For the Year Ended December 31, 20Y2	
Sales	$1,200,000
Cost of goods sold	(960,000)
Gross profit	$ 240,000
Operating expenses	(144,500)
Operating income	$ 95,500
Income tax expense	(36,290)
Net income	$ 59,210

Bart Company Statement of Comprehensive Income For the Year Ended December 31, 20Y2	
Net income	$59,210
Other comprehensive income	2,600
Comprehensive income	$61,810

Reporting Accumulated Other Comprehensive Income on the Balance Sheet

The *cumulative* effect of the elements of other comprehensive income is reported on the balance sheet as **accumulated other comprehensive income**.

Continuing the Bart Company example, the unrealized gain of $2,600 would be reported as accumulated other comprehensive income in the "Stockholders' Equity" section of the balance sheet, as follows:

Bart Company Balance Sheet December 31, 20Y2	
Stockholders' Equity	
Common stock	$ 20,000
Paid-in capital in excess of par	300,000
Retained earnings	250,000
Accumulated other comprehensive income	2,600
Total stockholders' equity	$572,600

Let's Review

Chapter Summary

1. The basic financial statements provide important information that users rely on to make economic decisions. Financial statement users typically evaluate this information along three dimensions: liquidity, solvency, and profitability. Two common techniques are used to analyze a company's financial performance and condition: analytical methods and ratios. Both analytical methods and ratios can be used to compare a company's financial performance over time or to another company.

2. Analytical methods are used to compare items on a current financial statement with related items on earlier statements or to examine relationships within a financial statement. Horizontal analysis is the analysis of percentage increases and decreases in related items in comparative financial statements. The analysis of the relationship of each component in a financial statement to a significant total within the statement is called vertical analysis. In a common-sized statement, all items are expressed as percentages with no dollar amounts shown.

3. Liquidity analysis evaluates a company's ability to convert current assets into cash. Short-term creditors use liquidity analysis to evaluate a company's ability to repay short-term debts by focusing on a company's current position, accounts receivable, and inventory. The measures and ratios used to evaluate a company's liquidity include: (1) working capital, (2) current ratio, (3) quick ratio, (4) accounts receivable turnover, (5) number of days' sales in receivables, (6) inventory turnover, and (7) number of days' sales in inventory.

4. Solvency analysis evaluates the ability of a company to pay its long-term debts. Long-term creditors use solvency analysis to evaluate a company's ability to make its periodic interest payments and repay the face amount of bonds at maturity. Solvency is normally assessed by examining (1) the ratio of fixed assets to long-term liabilities, (2) the ratio of liabilities to stockholders' equity, and (3) the times interest earned ratio.

5. Profitability analysis focuses on the relationship between operating results (income statement) and assets (balance sheet). Profitability analyses include (1) the asset turnover ratio, (2) the return on total assets, (3) the return on stockholders' equity, (4) the return on common stockholders' equity, (5) earnings per share on common stock, (6) the price-earnings ratio, (7) dividends per share, and (8) dividend yield.

6. Public corporations issue annual reports summarizing their operating activities for the past year and plans for the future. In addition to the financial statements and accompanying notes, annual reports include management discussion and analysis (MD&A), a report on internal control, and a report on fairness of the financial statements. Management discussion and analysis includes management's analysis of current operations and its plans for the future. The report on internal control states management's responsibility for establishing and maintaining internal controls. The report on fairness of the financial statements provides the CPA firm's opinion on whether the financial statements fairly present the financial position, results of operations, and cash flows of the company.

Key Terms

accounts receivable analysis (696)

accounts receivable turnover (696)

accumulated other comprehensive income (716)

analytical methods (689)

asset turnover (703)

common-sized statement (693)

comprehensive income (715)

current position analysis (695)

current ratio (695)

dividend yield (708)

dividends per share (708)

earnings per share (EPS) on common stock (706)

fair value (715)

horizontal analysis (689)

inventory analysis (697)

inventory turnover (698)

leverage (704)

liquidity (688)

Management's Discussion and Analysis (MD&A) (711)

number of days' sales in inventory (698)

number of days' sales in receivables (697)

other comprehensive income (715)

price-earnings (P/E) ratio (707)

profitability (689)

quick assets (696)

quick ratio (696)

ratio of fixed assets to long-term liabilities (700)

ratio of liabilities to stockholders' equity (700)

ratios (689)

return on common stockholders' equity (705)

return on stockholders' equity (704)

return on total assets (703)

solvency (689)

times interest earned (701)

unrealized gain (715)

vertical analysis (691)

working capital (695)

Practice

Multiple-Choice Questions

1. What type of analysis is indicated by the following?

	Amount	Percent
Current assets	$100,000	20%
Property, plant, and equipment	400,000	80%
Total assets	$500,000	100%

   a.   Vertical analysis   c.   Liquidity analysis
   b.   Horizontal analysis   d.   Profitability analysis

2. The ability of a company to pay its debts is called:
   a.   earnings per share.   c.   profitability.
   b.   liquidity.   d.   solvency.

3. The ratio that measures how much of a company is financed by debt and equity is the:
   a.   current ratio.   c.   ratio of liabilities to stockholders'
   b.   ratio of fixed assets to long-term   equity.
       liabilities.   d.   price-earnings ratio.

4. The ratio that measures the "instant" debt-paying ability of a firm, by focusing on current assets that can be easily converted to cash, is the:
   a.   working capital.   c.   number of days' sales in inventory.
   b.   quick ratio.   d.   ratio of fixed assets to long-term
                                        liabilities.

5. A measure useful in evaluating efficiency in the management of inventories is the:
   a.   working capital.   c.   number of days' sales in inventory.
   b.   quick ratio.   d.   ratio of fixed assets to long-term
                                        liabilities.

Answers provided after Problem. Need more practice? Find additional multiple-choice questions, exercises, and problems in CengageNOWv2.

Exercises

1. Horizontal analysis
Obj. 2

The comparative temporary investments and inventory balances of a company follow.

	Current Year	Previous Year
Temporary investments	$59,280	$52,000
Inventory	70,680	76,000

Based on this information, what is the amount and percentage of increase or decrease that would be shown on a balance sheet with horizontal analysis?

2. Vertical analysis
Obj. 2

Income statement information for Axiom Corporation follows:

Sales	$725,000
Cost of goods sold	391,500
Gross profit	333,500

Prepare a vertical analysis of the income statement for Axiom Corporation.

3. Current position analysis

Obj. 3

The following items are reported on a company's balance sheet:

Cash	$160,000
Marketable securities	75,000
Accounts receivable (net)	65,000
Inventory	140,000
Accounts payable	200,000

Determine (a) the current ratio and (b) the quick ratio. Round to one decimal place.

4. Accounts receivable analysis

Obj. 3

A company reports the following:

Sales	$832,000
Average accounts receivable (net)	80,000

Determine (a) the accounts receivable turnover and (b) the number of days' sales in receivables. Round to one decimal place.

5. Inventory analysis

Obj. 3

A company reports the following:

Cost of goods sold	$630,000
Average inventory	90,000

Determine (a) the inventory turnover and (b) the number of days' sales in inventory. Round to one decimal place.

6. Long-term solvency analysis

Obj. 4

The following information was taken from Kellman Company's balance sheet:

Fixed assets (net)	$ 960,000
Long-term liabilities	800,000
Total liabilities	1,000,000
Total stockholders' equity	625,000

Determine the company's (a) ratio of fixed assets to long-term liabilities and (b) ratio of liabilities to stockholders' equity. Round to one decimal place.

7. Times interest earned

Obj. 4

A company reports the following:

Income before income tax expense	$4,000,000
Interest expense	400,000

Determine the times interest earned ratio. Round to one decimal place.

8. Asset turnover

Obj. 5

A company reports the following:

Sales	$1,800,000
Average total assets (excluding long-term investments)	1,125,000

Determine the asset turnover ratio. Round to one decimal place.

9. Return on total assets

Obj. 5

A company reports the following income statement and balance sheet information for the current year:

Net income	$ 250,000
Interest expense	100,000
Average total assets	2,500,000

Determine the return on total assets. Round to one decimal place.

10. Common stockholders' profitability analysis

Obj. 5

A company reports the following:

Net income	$ 375,000
Preferred dividends	75,000
Average stockholders' equity	2,500,000
Average common stockholders' equity	1,875,000

Determine (a) the return on stockholders' equity and (b) the return on common stockholders' equity. Round to one decimal place.

11. Earnings per share and price-earnings ratio

Obj. 5

A company reports the following:

Net income	$185,000
Preferred dividends	$25,000
Shares of common stock outstanding	100,000
Market price per share of common stock	$20

a. Determine the company's earnings per share on common stock.

b. Determine the company's price-earnings ratio. Round to one decimal place.

Answers provided after Problem. Need more practice? Find additional multiple-choice questions, exercises, and problems in CengageNOWv2.

Problem

Rainbow Paint Co.'s comparative financial statements for the years ending December 31, 20Y9 and 20Y8, are as follows. The market price of Rainbow Paint's common stock was $25 on December 31, 20Y9, and $30 on December 31, 20Y8.

Rainbow Paint Co.
Comparative Income Statement
For the Years Ended December 31, 20Y9 and 20Y8

	20Y9	20Y8
Sales	$ 5,000,000	$ 3,200,000
Cost of goods sold	(3,400,000)	(2,080,000)
Gross profit	$ 1,600,000	$ 1,120,000
Selling expenses	$ (650,000)	$ (464,000)
Administrative expenses	(325,000)	(224,000)
Total operating expenses	$ (975,000)	$ (688,000)
Operating income	$ 625,000	$ 432,000
Other revenue and expense:		
Other revenue	25,000	19,200
Other expense (interest)	(105,000)	(64,000)
Income before income tax expense	$ 545,000	$ 387,200
Income tax expense	(300,000)	(176,000)
Net income	$ 245,000	$ 211,200

Rainbow Paint Co.
Comparative Retained Earnings Statement
For the Years Ended December 31, 20Y9 and 20Y8

	20Y9	20Y8
Retained earnings, January 1	$723,000	$581,800
Net income	245,000	211,200
Dividends:		
On preferred stock	(40,000)	(40,000)
On common stock	(45,000)	(30,000)
Retained earnings, December 31	$883,000	$723,000

Rainbow Paint Co.		
Comparative Balance Sheet		
December 31, 20Y9 and 20Y8		

	20Y9	20Y8
Assets		
Current assets:		
Cash	$ 175,000	$ 125,000
Temporary investments	150,000	50,000
Accounts receivable (net)	425,000	325,000
Inventories	720,000	480,000
Prepaid expenses	30,000	20,000
Total current assets	$1,500,000	$1,000,000
Long-term investments	250,000	225,000
Property, plant, and equipment (net)	2,093,000	1,948,000
Total assets	$3,843,000	$3,173,000
Liabilities		
Current liabilities	$ 750,000	$ 650,000
Long-term liabilities:		
Mortgage note payable, 10%, due in five years	$ 410,000	—
Bonds payable, 8%, due in fifteen years	800,000	$ 800,000
Total long-term liabilities	$1,210,000	$ 800,000
Total liabilities	$1,960,000	$1,450,000
Stockholders' Equity		
Preferred 8% stock, $100 par	$ 500,000	$ 500,000
Common stock, $10 par	500,000	500,000
Retained earnings	883,000	723,000
Total stockholders' equity	$1,883,000	$1,723,000
Total liabilities and stockholders' equity	$3,843,000	$3,173,000

Instructions

Determine the following measures for 20Y9. Round percentages and ratios other than per-share amounts to one decimal place.

1. Working capital
2. Current ratio
3. Quick ratio
4. Accounts receivable turnover
5. Number of days' sales in receivables
6. Inventory turnover
7. Number of days' sales in inventory
8. Ratio of fixed assets to long-term liabilities
9. Ratio of liabilities to stockholders' equity
10. Times interest earned
11. Asset turnover
12. Return on total assets
13. Return on stockholders' equity
14. Return on common stockholders' equity
15. Earnings per share on common stock
16. Price-earnings ratio
17. Dividends per share
18. Dividend yield

Need more practice? Find additional multiple-choice questions, exercises, and problems in CengageNOWv2.

Answers

Multiple-Choice Questions

1. **a** Vertical analysis compares each component in a financial statement to a total within the statement. Horizontal analysis (answer b) compares the amount and percentage of each item on the most recent statement to the same item on an earlier statement. Liquidity analysis (answer c) evaluates the ability of a company to convert current assets into cash. Profitability analysis (answer d) focuses on the ability of a company to earn profits by examining the relationship between operating results and the resources available.

2. **d** Solvency is a company's ability to pay its debts. Earnings per share (answer a) measures the share of profits that are earned by a share of common stock. Liquidity (answer b) is the ability of a company to convert current assets into cash. Profitability (answer c) focuses on the ability of a company to earn profits by examining the relationship between operating results and the resources available.

3. **c** The ratio of liabilities to stockholders' equity measures the relationship between debt and equity, which measures how much of the company is financed with debt and equity. The current ratio (answer a) measures a company's ability to pay its current liabilities. The ratio of fixed assets to long-term liabilities (answer b) provides a measure of whether noteholders or bondholders will be paid. The price-earnings ratio (answer d) measures a company's future earnings prospects.

4. **b** The quick ratio measures the "instant" debt-paying ability of a company. Working capital (answer a) is the difference between current assets and current liabilities. The number of days' sales in inventory (answer c) is a measure of the length of time it takes to purchase, sell, and replace the inventory. The ratio of fixed assets to long-term liabilities (answer d) provides a measure of whether noteholders or bondholders will be paid.

5. **c** The number of days' sales in inventory is a measure of the length of time it takes to purchase, sell, and replace the inventory. Working capital (answer a) is the difference between current assets and current liabilities. The quick ratio (answer b) measures the "instant" debt-paying ability of a company. The ratio of fixed assets to long-term liabilities (answer d) provides a measure of whether noteholders or bondholders will be paid.

Exercises

1. Temporary investments.................... $7,280 increase ($59,280 – $52,000), or 14%

   Inventory .... $5,320 decrease ($70,680 – $76,000), or –7%

2.

	Amount	Percentage	
Sales...	$ 725,000	100%	($725,000 ÷ $725,000)
Cost of goods sold.........................	(391,500)	(54)%	($391,500 ÷ $725,000)
Gross profit..................................	$ 333,500	46%	($333,500 ÷ $725,000)

3. a. Current Ratio = Current Assets ÷ Current Liabilities

   $$= (\$160,000 + \$75,000 + \$65,000 + \$140,000) \div \$200,000$$

   $$= 2.2$$

   b. Quick Ratio = Quick Assets ÷ Current Liabilities

   $$= (\$160,000 + \$75,000 + \$65,000) \div \$200,000$$

   $$= 1.5$$

4. a. Accounts Receivable Turnover = Sales ÷ Average Accounts Receivable

   $$= \$832,000 \div \$80,000$$

   $$= 10.4$$

b. Number of Days' Sales in Receivables = $\dfrac{\text{Average Accounts Receivable}}{\text{Average Daily Sales}}$

$$= \$80,000 \div (\$832,000 \div 365)$$

$$= \$80,000 \div \$2,279$$

$$= 35.1 \text{ days}$$

5. a. Inventory Turnover = Cost of Goods Sold ÷ Average Inventory

$$= \$630,000 \div \$90,000$$

$$= 7.0$$

b. Number of Days' Sales in Inventory = $\dfrac{\text{Average Inventory}}{\text{Average Daily Cost of Goods Sold}}$

$$= \$90,000 \div (\$630,000 \div 365)$$

$$= \$90,000 \div \$1,726$$

$$= 52.1 \text{ days}$$

6. a. Ratio of Fixed Assets to Long-Term Liabilities = $\dfrac{\text{Fixed Assets}}{\text{Long-Term Liabilities}}$

$$= \$960,000 \div \$800,000$$

$$= 1.2$$

b. Ratio of Liabilities to Stockholders' Equity = $\dfrac{\text{Total Liabilities}}{\text{Total Stockholders' Equity}}$

$$= \$1,000,000 \div \$625,000$$

$$= 1.6$$

7. Times Interest Earned = $\dfrac{\text{Income Before Income Tax Expense} + \text{Interest Expense}}{\text{Interest Expense}}$

$$= \dfrac{\$4,000,000 + \$400,000}{\$400,000}$$

$$= 11.0$$

8. Asset Turnover = Sales ÷ Average Total Assets

$$= \$1,800,000 \div \$1,125,000$$

$$= 1.6$$

9. Return on Total Assets = $\dfrac{\text{Net Income} + \text{Interest Expense}}{\text{Average Total Assets}}$

$$= \dfrac{\$250,000 + \$100,000}{\$2,500,000}$$

$$= \dfrac{\$350,000}{\$2,500,000}$$

$$= 14.0\%$$

10. a. Return on Stockholders' Equity = $\dfrac{\text{Net Income}}{\text{Average Stockholders' Equity}}$

$$= \$375,000 \div \$2,500,000$$

$$= 15.0\%$$

b. Return on Common Stockholders' Equity $= \dfrac{\text{Net Income} - \text{Preferred Dividends}}{\text{Average Common Stockholders' Equity}}$

$$= \dfrac{\$375,000 - \$75,000}{\$1,875,000}$$

$$= 16.0\%$$

11. a. Earnings per Share on Common Stock $= \dfrac{\text{Net Income} - \text{Preferred Dividends}}{\text{Shares of Common Stock Outstanding}}$

$$= (\$185,000 - \$25,000) \div 100,000$$

$$= \$1.60$$

b. Price-Earnings Ratio $= \dfrac{\text{Market Price per Share of Common Stock}}{\text{Earnings per Share on Common Stock}}$

$$= \$20.00 \div \$1.60$$

$$= 12.5$$

Need more help? Watch step-by-step videos of how to compute answers to these Exercises in CengageNOWv2.

Problem

Ratios are rounded to one decimal place.

1. Working capital: $750,000

    $1,500,000 – $750,000

2. Current ratio: 2.0

    $1,500,000 ÷ $750,000

3. Quick ratio: 1.0

    $750,000 ÷ $750,000

4. Accounts receivable turnover: 13.3

    $5,000,000 ÷ [($425,000 + $325,000) ÷ 2]

5. Number of days' sales in receivables: 27.4 days

    $5,000,000 ÷ 365 days = $13,699

    $375,000 ÷ $13,699

6. Inventory turnover: 5.7

    $3,400,000 ÷ [($720,000 + $480,000) ÷ 2]

7. Number of days' sales in inventory: 64.4 days

    $3,400,000 ÷ 365 days = $9,315

    $600,000 ÷ $9,315

8. Ratio of fixed assets to long-term liabilities: 1.7

    $2,093,000 ÷ $1,210,000

9. Ratio of liabilities to stockholders' equity: 1.0

    $1,960,000 ÷ $1,883,000

10. Times interest earned: 6.2

    ($545,000 + $105,000) ÷ $105,000

11. Asset turnover: 1.5

    $5,000,000 ÷ [($3,593,000 + $2,948,000) ÷ 2]

12. Return on total assets: 10.0%

    ($245,000 + $105,000) ÷ [($3,843,000 + $3,173,000) ÷ 2]

13. Return on stockholders' equity: 13.6%

   $245,000 ÷ [($1,883,000 + $1,723,000) ÷ 2]

14. Return on common stockholders' equity: 15.7%

   ($245,000 − $40,000) ÷ [($1,383,000 + $1,223,000) ÷ 2]

15. Earnings per share on common stock: $4.10

   ($245,000 − $40,000) ÷ 50,000 shares

16. Price-earnings ratio: 6.1

   $25 ÷ $4.10

17. Dividends per share: $0.90

   $45,000 ÷ 50,000 shares

18. Dividend yield: 3.6%

   $0.90 ÷ $25

Discussion Questions

1. Briefly explain the difference between liquidity, solvency, and profitability analysis.

2. What is the advantage of using comparative statements for financial analysis rather than statements for a single date or period?

3. A company's current year net income (after income tax) is 25% larger than that of the preceding year. Does this indicate improved operating performance? Why?

4. How would the current and quick ratios of a service business compare?

5. a. Why is a high inventory turnover considered to be a positive indicator?

   b. Is it possible to have a high inventory turnover and a high number of days' sales in inventory? Why?

6. What do the following data, taken from a comparative balance sheet, indicate about the company's ability to borrow additional long-term debt in the current year as compared to the preceding year?

	Current Year	Preceding Year
Fixed assets (net)	$1,260,000	$1,360,000
Total long-term liabilities	300,000	400,000

7. a. How does the return on total assets differ from the return on stockholders' equity?

   b. Which ratio is normally higher? Why?

8.  **The Kroger Company (KR),** a grocery store chain, recently had a price-earnings ratio of 13.7, while the average price-earnings ratio in the grocery store industry was 22.5. What might explain this difference?

9.  The dividend yield of **Suburban Propane Partners, L.P. (SPH)** was 7.7% in a recent year, and the dividend yield of **Alphabet Inc. (GOOG)** was 0% in the same year. What might explain the difference between these ratios?

10. Describe two reports provided by independent auditors in the annual report to shareholders.

Basic Exercises

SHOW ME HOW

BE 14-1 Horizontal analysis   Obj. 2

The comparative accounts payable and long-term debt balances for a company follow.

	Current Year	Previous Year
Accounts payable	$114,240	$102,000
Long-term debt	127,200	120,000

Based on this information, what is the amount and percentage of increase or decrease that would be shown on a balance sheet with horizontal analysis?

SHOW ME HOW

BE 14-2 Vertical analysis

Obj. 2

Income statement information for Einsworth Corporation follows:

Sales	$1,500,000
Cost of goods sold	900,000
Gross profit	600,000

Prepare a vertical analysis of the income statement for Einsworth Corporation.

SHOW ME HOW

BE 14-3 Current position analysis

Obj. 3

The following items are reported on a company's balance sheet:

Cash	$225,000
Marketable securities	115,000
Accounts receivable (net)	112,000
Inventory	158,000
Accounts payable	244,000

Determine (a) the current ratio and (b) the quick ratio. Round to one decimal place.

SHOW ME HOW

BE 14-4 Accounts receivable analysis

Obj. 3

A company reports the following:

Sales	$4,560,000
Average accounts receivable (net)	380,000

Determine (a) the accounts receivable turnover and (b) the number of days' sales in receivables. Round to one decimal place.

SHOW ME HOW

BE 14-5 Inventory analysis

Obj. 3

A company reports the following:

Cost of goods sold	$500,000
Average inventory	62,500

Determine (a) the inventory turnover and (b) the number of days' sales in inventory. Round to one decimal place.

SHOW ME HOW

BE 14-6 Long-term solvency analysis

Obj. 4

The following information was taken from Charu Company's balance sheet:

Fixed assets (net)	$910,000
Long-term liabilities	260,000
Total liabilities	800,000
Total stockholders' equity	320,000

Determine the company's (a) ratio of fixed assets to long-term liabilities and (b) ratio of liabilities to stockholders' equity. Round to one decimal place.

SHOW ME HOW

BE 14-7 Times interest earned

Obj. 4

A company reports the following:

Income before income tax expense	$9,100,000
Interest expense	650,000

Determine the times interest earned. Round to one decimal place.

BE 14-8   Asset turnover   **Obj. 5**

A company reports the following:

Sales	$6,750,000
Average total assets (excluding long-term investments)	2,500,000

Determine the asset turnover ratio. Round to one decimal place.

BE 14-9   Return on total assets   **Obj. 5**

A company reports the following income statement and balance sheet information for the current year:

Net income	$ 424,000
Interest expense	80,000
Average total assets	4,200,000

Determine the return on total assets. Round percentage to one decimal place.

BE 14-10   Common stockholders' profitability analysis   **Obj. 5**

A company reports the following:

Net income	$1,225,000
Preferred dividends	47,800
Average stockholders' equity	8,750,000
Average common stockholders' equity	5,400,000

Determine (a) the return on stockholders' equity and (b) the return on common stockholders' equity. Round percentages to one decimal place.

BE 14-11   Earnings per share and price-earnings ratio   **Obj. 5**

A company reports the following:

Net income	$562,000
Preferred dividends	$50,000
Shares of common stock outstanding	80,000
Market price per share of common stock	$32

a. Determine the company's earnings per share on common stock.

b. Determine the company's price-earnings ratio. Round to one decimal place.

Exercises

✔ a. Current year net
income: $360,000; 9%
of sales

EX 14-1   Vertical analysis of income statement   **Obj. 2**

Revenue and expense data for Innovation Quarter Inc. for two recent years are as follows:

	Current Year	Previous Year
Sales	$4,000,000	$3,600,000
Cost of goods sold	2,280,000	1,872,000
Selling expenses	600,000	648,000
Administrative expenses	520,000	360,000
Income tax expense	240,000	216,000

a. Prepare an income statement in comparative form, stating each item for both years as a percent of sales. Round to the nearest whole percentage.

b. ▬▬▬ Comment on the significant changes disclosed by the comparative income statement.

EX 14-2 Vertical analysis of income statement

Obj. 2

The following comparative income statement (in thousands of dollars) for two recent fiscal years was adapted from the annual report of **Speedway Motorsports, Inc. (TRK)**, owner and operator of several major motor speedways, such as the Atlanta, Texas, and Las Vegas Motor Speedways.

	Current Year	Previous Year
Revenues:		
Admissions	$ 90,639	$ 100,694
Event-related revenue	136,900	146,980
NASCAR broadcasting revenue	224,227	217,469
Other operating revenue	60,390	31,320
Total revenues	$ 512,156	$ 496,463
Expenses and other:		
Direct expense of events	$ (102,786)	$ (104,303)
NASCAR event management fees	(137,727)	(133,682)
Other direct expenses	(43,784)	(19,541)
General and administrative	(166,663)	(285,166)
Total expenses and other	$ (450,960)	$ (542,692)
Income from continuing operations	$ 61,196	$ (46,229)

a. Prepare a comparative income statement for these two years in vertical form, stating each item as a percent of revenues. Round percentages to one decimal place.

b. ➡ Comment on the significant changes.

EX 14-3 Common-sized income statement

Obj. 2

Revenue and expense data for the current calendar year for Tannenhill Company and for the electronics industry are as follows. Tannenhill's data are expressed in dollars. The electronics industry averages are expressed in percentages.

	Tannenhill Company	Electronics Industry Average
Sales	$ 4,000,000	100.0%
Cost of goods sold	(2,120,000)	(60.0)
Gross profit	$ 1,880,000	40.0%
Selling expenses	$ (1,080,000)	(24.0)%
Administrative expenses	(640,000)	(14.0)
Total operating expenses	$ (1,720,000)	(38.0)%
Operating income	$ 160,000	2.0%
Other revenue and expense:		
Other revenue	120,000	3.0
Other expense	(80,000)	(2.0)
Income before income tax expense	$ 200,000	3.0%
Income tax expense	(80,000)	(2.0)
Net income	$ 120,000	1.0%

a. Prepare a common-sized income statement comparing the results of operations for Tannenhill Company with the industry average. Round to the nearest whole percentage.

b. ➡ As far as the data permit, comment on significant relationships revealed by the comparisons.

EX 14-4   Vertical analysis of balance sheet

Obj. 2

✔ Retained earnings, current year, 36.8%

SHOW ME HOW   EXCEL TEMPLATE

Balance sheet data for Alvarez Company on December 31, the end of two recent fiscal years, follow:

	Current Year	Previous Year
Current assets	$2,500,000	$1,840,000
Property, plant, and equipment	5,600,000	6,072,000
Intangible assets	1,900,000	1,288,000
Current liabilities	2,000,000	1,380,000
Long-term liabilities	3,400,000	3,680,000
Common stock	920,000	920,000
Retained earnings	3,680,000	3,220,000

Prepare a comparative balance sheet for both years, stating each asset as a percent of total assets and each liability and stockholders' equity item as a percent of the total liabilities and stockholders' equity. Round percentages to one decimal place.

EX 14-5   Horizontal analysis of the income statement

Obj. 2

✔ a. Net income increase, 78.0%

SHOW ME HOW   EXCEL TEMPLATE

Income statement data for Winthrop Company for two recent years ended December 31 are as follows:

	Current Year	Previous Year
Sales	$ 2,240,000	$ 2,000,000
Cost of goods sold	(1,925,000)	(1,750,000)
Gross profit	$ 315,000	$ 250,000
Selling expenses	$ (152,500)	$ (125,000)
Administrative expenses	(118,000)	(100,000)
Total operating expenses	$ (270,500)	$ (225,000)
Income before income tax expense	$ 44,500	$ 25,000
Income tax expense	(17,800)	(10,000)
Net income	$ 26,700	$ 15,000

a.   Prepare a comparative income statement with horizontal analysis, indicating the increase (decrease) for the current year when compared with the previous year. Round percentages to one decimal place.

b.   ➤ What conclusions can be drawn from the horizontal analysis?

EX 14-6   Current position analysis

Obj. 3

✔ a. (1) Current year working capital, $1,090,000

SHOW ME HOW

The following data were taken from the balance sheet of Nilo Company at the end of two recent fiscal years:

	Current Year	Previous Year
Current assets:		
Cash	$ 391,000	$ 300,000
Marketable securities	515,000	354,000
Accounts and notes receivable (net)	634,000	426,000
Inventories	368,000	222,000
Prepaid expenses	182,000	138,000
Total current assets	$ 2,090,000	$1,440,000
Current liabilities:		
Accounts and notes payable (short-term)	$ 725,000	$ 600,000
Accrued liabilities	275,000	300,000
Total current liabilities	$1,000,000	$ 900,000

a.   Determine for each year (1) the working capital, (2) the current ratio, and (3) the quick ratio. Round ratios to one decimal place.

b.   ➤ What conclusions can be drawn from these data as to the company's ability to meet its currently maturing debts?

EX 14-7 Current position analysis

Obj. 3

PepsiCo, Inc. (PEP), the parent company of Frito-Lay snack foods and Pepsi beverages, had the following current assets and current liabilities at the end of two recent years:

	Current Year (in millions)	Previous Year (in millions)
Cash and cash equivalents	$ 9,158	$ 9,096
Short-term investments, at cost	6,967	2,913
Accounts and notes receivable, net	6,694	6,437
Inventories	2,723	2,720
Prepaid expenses and other current assets	1,547	1,865
Short-term obligations	6,892	4,071
Accounts payable	14,243	13,507

a. Determine the (1) current ratio and (2) quick ratio for both years. Round to one decimal place.

b. ➤ What conclusions can you draw from these data about PepsiCo's liquidity?

EX 14-8 Current position analysis

Obj. 3

The bond indenture for the 10-year, 9% debenture bonds issued January 2, 20Y5, required working capital of $100,000, a current ratio of 1.5, and a quick ratio of 1.0 at the end of each calendar year until the bonds mature. At December 31, 20Y6, the three measures were computed as follows:

1.	Current assets:		
	Cash..	$102,000	
	Temporary investments	48,000	
	Accounts and notes receivable (net)...........	120,000	
	Inventories.................................	36,000	
	Prepaid expenses............................	24,000	
	Intangible assets	124,800	
	Property, plant, and equipment...............	55,200	
	Total current assets (net)		$ 510,000
	Current liabilities:		
	Accounts and short-term notes payable	$ 96,000	
	Accrued liabilities...........................	204,000	
	Total current liabilities		(300,000)
	Working capital		$ 210,000
2.	Current ratio	1.7	$ 510,000 ÷ $300,000
3.	Quick ratio....................................	1.2	$ 115,200 ÷ $ 96,000

a. List the errors in the determination of the three measures of current position analysis.

b. ➤ Is the company satisfying the terms of the bond indenture?

EX 14-9 Accounts receivable analysis

Obj. 3

The following data are taken from the financial statements of Sigmon Inc. Terms of all sales are 2/10, n/45.

	20Y3	20Y2	20Y1
Accounts receivable, end of year	$ 725,000	$ 650,000	$600,000
Sales on account	5,637,500	4,687,500	

a. For 20Y2 and 20Y3, determine (1) the accounts receivable turnover and (2) the number of days' sales in receivables. Round to the nearest dollar and one decimal place.

b. ➤ What conclusions can be drawn from these data concerning accounts receivable and credit policies?

EX 14-10 Accounts receivable analysis

Obj. 3

Xavier Stores Company and Lestrade Stores Inc. are large retail department stores. Both companies offer credit to their customers through their own credit card operations. Information from the financial statements for both companies for two recent years is as follows (in millions):

	Xavier	Lestrade
Sales	$8,500,000	$4,585,000
Credit card receivables—beginning	820,000	600,000
Credit card receivables—ending	880,000	710,000

a. Determine the (1) accounts receivable turnover and (2) the number of days' sales in receivables for both companies. Round to one decimal place.

b. ➤ Compare the two companies with regard to their credit card policies.

EX 14-11 Inventory analysis

Obj. 3

✔ a. (1) Inventory turnover, current year, 9.0

SHOW ME HOW

The following data were extracted from the income statement of Keever Inc.:

	Current Year	Previous Year
Sales	$18,500,000	$20,000,000
Beginning inventories	940,000	860,000
Cost of goods sold	9,270,000	10,800,000
Ending inventories	1,120,000	940,000

a. Determine for each year (1) the inventory turnover and (2) the number of days' sales in inventory. Round to the nearest dollar and one decimal place.

b. ➤ What conclusions can be drawn from these data concerning the inventories?

EX 14-12 Inventory analysis

Obj. 3

✔ a. (1) QT inventory turnover, 32.1

QT, Inc. and Elppa Computers, Inc. compete with each other in the personal computer market. QT assembles computers to customer orders, building and delivering a computer within four days of a customer entering an order online. Elppa, on the other hand, builds computers for inventory prior to receiving an order. These computers are sold from inventory once an order is received. Selected financial information for both companies from recent financial statements follows (in millions):

	QT	Elppa
Sales	$56,940	$120,357
Cost of goods sold	44,754	92,385
Inventory, beginning of period	1,382	6,317
Inventory, end of period	1,404	7,490

a. Determine for both companies (1) the inventory turnover and (2) the number of days' sales in inventory. Round to one decimal place.

b. ➤ Interpret the inventory ratios in the context of both companies' operating strategies.

EX 14-13 Ratio of liabilities to stockholders' equity and times interest earned

Obj. 4

✔ a. Ratio of liabilities to stockholders' equity, current year, 0.9

The following data were taken from the financial statements of Hunter Inc. for December 31 of two recent years:

	Current Year	Previous Year
Accounts payable	$ 924,000	$ 800,000
Current maturities of serial bonds payable	200,000	200,000
Serial bonds payable, 10%	1,000,000	1,200,000
Common stock, $10 par value	250,000	250,000
Paid-in capital in excess of par	1,250,000	1,250,000
Retained earnings	860,000	500,000

The income before income tax expense was $480,000 and $420,000 for the current and previous years, respectively.

a. Determine the ratio of liabilities to stockholders' equity at the end of each year. Round to one decimal place.

b. Determine the times interest earned ratio for both years. Round to one decimal place.

c. ➤ What conclusions can be drawn from these data as to the company's ability to meet its currently maturing debts?

EX 14-14 Ratio of liabilities to stockholders' equity and times interest earned Obj. 4

Hasbro, Inc. (HAS), and **Mattel, Inc. (MAT)**, are the two largest toy companies in North America. Condensed liabilities and stockholders' equity from a recent balance sheet are shown for each company as follows (in thousands):

	Hasbro	Mattel
Liabilities:		
Current liabilities	$1,617,859	$1,505,573
Long-term debt	1,588,067	2,580,439
Total liabilities	$3,205,926	$4,086,012
Total stockholders' equity	$1,862,736	$2,407,782
Total liabilities and stockholders' equity	$5,068,662	$6,493,794

The operating income and interest expense from the income statement for each company were as follows (in thousands):

	Hasbro	Mattel
Operating income (before income tax expense)	$692,489	$409,472
Interest expense	97,405	95,118

a. Determine the ratio of liabilities to stockholders' equity for both companies. Round to one decimal place.

b. Determine the times interest earned ratio for both companies. Round to one decimal place.

c. ⬤▬▬▶ Interpret the ratio differences between the two companies.

EX 14-15 Ratio of liabilities to stockholders' equity and ratio of fixed assets to long-term liabilities Obj. 4

Recent balance sheet information for two companies in the food industry, **Mondelez International, Inc. (MDLZ)**, and **The Hershey Company (HSY)**, is as follows (in thousands):

	Mondelez	Hershey
Net property, plant, and equipment	$ 8,229,000	$2,177,248
Current liabilities	14,417,000	1,909,443
Long-term debt	13,217,000	2,347,455
Other long-term liabilities	8,689,000	439,748
Stockholders' equity	25,215,000	827,687

a. Determine the ratio of liabilities to stockholders' equity for both companies. Round to one decimal place.

b. Determine the ratio of fixed assets to long-term liabilities for both companies. Round to one decimal place.

c. ⬤▬▬▶ Interpret the ratio differences between the two companies.

EX 14-16 Asset turnover Obj. 5

Three major segments of the transportation industry are motor carriers, such as **YRC Worldwide (YRCW)**; railroads, such as **Union Pacific (UNP)**; and transportation logistics services, such as **C.H. Robinson Worldwide, Inc. (CHRW)**. Financial statement information for these three companies follows (in thousands):

	YRC	Union Pacific	C.H. Robinson
Sales	$4,697,500	$19,941,000	$13,144,413
Average total assets	1,824,700	55,159,000	3,436,058

a. Determine the asset turnover for all three companies. Round to one decimal place.

b. ⬤▬▬▶ Assume that the asset turnover for each company represents their respective industry segment. Interpret the differences in the asset turnover in terms of the operating characteristics of each of the respective segments.

EX 14-17 Profitability ratios Obj. 5

✔ a. Return on total assets, 20Y7, 12.0%

SHOW ME HOW

The following selected data were taken from the financial statements of Vidahill Inc. for December 31, 20Y7, 20Y6, and 20Y5:

	20Y7	20Y6	20Y5
Total assets	$4,800,000	$4,400,000	$4,000,000
Notes payable (8% interest)	2,250,000	2,250,000	2,250,000
Common stock......................................	250,000	250,000	250,000
Preferred 4% stock, $100 par (no change during year)..	500,000	500,000	500,000
Retained earnings...................................	1,574,000	1,222,000	750,000

The 20Y7 net income was $372,000, and the 20Y6 net income was $492,000. No dividends on common stock were declared between 20Y5 and 20Y7. Preferred dividends were declared and paid in full in 20Y6 and 20Y7.

a. Determine the return on total assets, the return on stockholders' equity, and the return on common stockholders' equity for the years 20Y6 and 20Y7. Round percentages to one decimal place.

b. ▬▬▬➤ What conclusions can be drawn from these data as to the company's profitability?

EX 14-18 Profitability ratios Obj. 5

✔ a. Year 3 return on total assets, 6.8%

REAL WORLD

Ralph Lauren Corporation (RL) sells apparel through company-owned retail stores. Financial information for Ralph Lauren follows (in thousands):

	Fiscal Year 3	Fiscal Year 2	
Net income	$396,400	$702,200	
Interest expense	21,000	16,700	
	Fiscal Year 3	Fiscal Year 2	Fiscal Year 1
Total assets (at end of fiscal year)	$6,213,100	$6,106,000	$6,088,000
Total stockholders' equity (at end of fiscal year)	3,743,500	3,891,000	4,034,000

Assume the apparel industry average return on total assets is 8.0%, and the average return on stockholders' equity is 15.0% for the year ended April 2, Year 3.

a. Determine the return on total assets for Ralph Lauren for fiscal Years 2 and 3. Round percentages to one decimal place.

b. Determine the return on stockholders' equity for Ralph Lauren for fiscal Years 2 and 3. Round percentages to one decimal place.

c. ▬▬▬➤ Evaluate the two-year trend for the profitability ratios determined in (a) and (b).

d. ▬▬▬➤ Evaluate Ralph Lauren's profit performance relative to the industry.

EX 14-19 Six measures of solvency or profitability Obj. 4, 5

✔ c. Asset turnover, 4.2

The following data were taken from the financial statements of Gates Inc. for the current fiscal year.

Property, plant, and equipment (net)		$ 3,200,000
Liabilities:		
Current liabilities......................................	$1,000,000	
Note payable, 6%, due in 15 years	2,000,000	
Total liabilities		$ 3,000,000
Stockholders' equity:		
Preferred $10 stock, $100 par (no change during year) ...		$ 1,000,000
Common stock, $10 par (no change during year)		2,000,000
Retained earnings:		
Balance, beginning of year...........................	$1,570,000	
Net income...	930,000	
Preferred dividends	(100,000)	
Common dividends	(400,000)	
Balance, end of year.................................		2,000,000
Total stockholders' equity..............................		$ 5,000,000
Sales		$18,900,000
Interest expense		$ 120,000

Assuming that long-term investments totaled $3,000,000 throughout the year and that total assets were $7,000,000 at the beginning of the current fiscal year, determine the following: (a) ratio of

(Continued)

fixed assets to long-term liabilities, (b) ratio of liabilities to stockholders' equity, (c) asset turnover, (d) return on total assets, (e) return on stockholders' equity, and (f) return on common stockholders' equity. Round ratios and percentages to one decimal place as appropriate.

EX 14-20   Five measures of solvency or profitability Obj. 4, 5

✔ c. Price-earnings ratio, 10.0

The balance sheet for Garcon Inc. at the end of the current fiscal year indicated the following:

Bonds payable, 8%	$5,000,000
Preferred $4 stock, $50 par	2,500,000
Common stock, $10 par	5,000,000

Income before income tax expense was $3,000,000, and income taxes were $1,200,000 for the current year. Cash dividends paid on common stock during the current year totaled $1,200,000. The common stock was selling for $32 per share at the end of the year. Determine each of the following: (a) times interest earned ratio (b) earnings per share on common stock, (c) price-earnings ratio, (d) dividends per share of common stock, and (e) dividend yield. Round ratios and percentages to one decimal place, except for per-share amounts.

EX 14-21   Earnings per share, price-earnings ratio, dividend yield Obj. 5

✔ b. Price-earnings ratio, 15.0

The following information was taken from the financial statements of Tolbert Inc. for December 31 of the current fiscal year:

SHOW ME HOW

Common stock, $20 par (no change during the year)	$10,000,000
Preferred $4 stock, $40 par (no change during the year)	2,500,000

The net income was $1,750,000 and the declared dividends on the common stock were $1,125,000 for the current year. The market price of the common stock is $45 per share.

For the common stock, determine (a) the earnings per share, (b) the price-earnings ratio, (c) the dividends per share, and (d) the dividend yield. Round ratios and percentages to one decimal place, except for per-share amounts.

EX 14-22   Price-earnings ratio; dividend yield Obj. 5

✔ a. Alphabet, 37.9

The table that follows shows the stock price, earnings per share, and dividends per share for three companies for a recent year:

REAL WORLD

	Price	Earnings per Share	Dividends per Share
Deere & Company (DE)	$103.04	$ 4.83	$2.40
Alphabet (GOOG)	792.45	20.91	0.00
The Coca-Cola Company (KO)	178.85	1.51	1.40

a. Determine the price-earnings ratio and dividend yield for the three companies. Round ratios and percentages to one decimal place as appropriate.

b. Explain the differences in these ratios across the three companies.

Appendix 1
EX 14-23   Earnings per share, discontinued operations

✔ b. Earnings per share on common stock, $7.60

The net income reported on the income statement of Cutler Co. was $4,000,000. There were 500,000 shares of $10 par common stock and 100,000 shares of $2 preferred stock outstanding throughout the current year. The income statement included a gain on discontinued operations of $400,000 after applicable income tax. Determine the per-share figures for common stock for (a) income before discontinued operations and (b) net income.

Appendix 1
EX 14-24   Income statement and earnings per share for discontinued operations

Apex Inc. reports the following for a recent year:

Income from continuing operations before income tax expense	$1,000,000
Loss from discontinued operations	$240,000*
Weighted average number of shares outstanding	20,000
Applicable tax rate	40%
*Net of any tax effect.	

a. Prepare a partial income statement for Apex Inc., beginning with income from continuing operations before income tax expense.

b. Determine the earnings per common share for Apex Inc., including per-share amounts for unusual items.

Appendix 1
EX 14-25 Unusual items

Explain whether Colston Company correctly reported the following items in the financial statements:

a. In a recent year, the company discovered a clerical error in the prior year's accounting records. As a result, the reported net income for the previous year was overstated by $45,000. The company corrected this error by restating the prior-year financial statements.

b. In a recent year, the company voluntarily changed its method of accounting for long-term construction contracts from the percentage of completion method to the completed contract method. Both methods are acceptable under generally acceptable accounting principles. The cumulative effect of this change was reported as a separate component of income in the current period income statement.

Appendix 2
EX 14-26 Comprehensive income

Anson Industries, Inc., reported the following information on its 20Y1 income statement:

Sales	$4,000,000
Cost of goods sold	2,300,000
Operating expenses	1,000,000
Income tax expense	280,000
Other comprehensive income	450,000

Prepare the following for Anson Industries, Inc.:

a. Income statement, including comprehensive income.

b. Income statement and a separate statement of comprehensive income.

Problems: Series A

PR 14-1A Horizontal analysis of income statement   Obj. 2

✔ 1. Sales, 12.0% increase

SHOW ME HOW   EXCEL TEMPLATE

For 20Y2, McDade Company reported a decline in net income. At the end of the year, T. Burrows, the president, is presented with the following condensed comparative income statement:

McDade Company
Comparative Income Statement
For the Years Ended December 31, 20Y2 and 20Y1

	20Y2	20Y1
Sales	$ 16,800,000	$ 15,000,000
Cost of goods sold	(11,500,000)	(10,000,000)
Gross profit	$ 5,300,000	$ 5,000,000
Selling expenses	$ (1,770,000)	$ (1,500,000)
Administrative expenses	(1,220,000)	(1,000,000)
Total operating expenses	$ (2,990,000)	$ (2,500,000)
Operating income	$ 2,310,000	$ 2,500,000
Other revenue	256,950	225,000
Income before income tax expense	$ 2,566,950	$ 2,725,000
Income tax expense	(1,413,000)	(1,500,000)
Net income	$ 1,153,950	$ 1,225,000

Instructions

1. Prepare a comparative income statement with horizontal analysis for the two-year period, using 20Y1 as the base year. Round percentages to one decimal place.

2. To the extent the data permit, comment on the significant relationships revealed by the horizontal analysis prepared in (1).

✔ 1. Net income, 20Y2, 10.0%

EXCEL TEMPLATE

PR 14-2A Vertical analysis of income statement

Obj. 2

For 20Y2, Tri-Comic Company initiated a sales promotion campaign that included the expenditure of an additional $50,000 for advertising. At the end of the year, Lumi Neer, the president, is presented with the following condensed comparative income statement:

Tri-Comic Company
Comparative Income Statement
For the Years Ended December 31, 20Y2 and 20Y1

	20Y2	20Y1
Sales	$1,500,000	$1,250,000
Cost of goods sold	(510,000)	(475,000)
Gross profit	$ 990,000	$ 775,000
Selling expenses	$ (270,000)	$ (200,000)
Administrative expenses	(180,000)	(156,250)
Total operating expenses	$ (450,000)	$ (356,250)
Operating income	$ 540,000	$ 418,750
Other revenue	60,000	50,000
Income before income tax expense	$ 600,000	$ 468,750
Income tax expense	(450,000)	(375,000)
Net income	$ 150,000	$ 93,750

Instructions

1. Prepare a comparative income statement for the two-year period, presenting an analysis of each item in relationship to sales for each of the years. Round percentages to one decimal place.

2. ➤ To the extent the data permit, comment on the significant relationships revealed by the vertical analysis prepared in (1).

PR 14-3A Effect of transactions on current position analysis

Obj. 3

✔ 2. c. Current ratio, 2.0

Data pertaining to the current position of Forte Company follow:

Cash	$412,500
Marketable securities	187,500
Accounts and notes receivable (net)	300,000
Inventories	700,000
Prepaid expenses	50,000
Accounts payable	200,000
Notes payable (short-term)	250,000
Accrued expenses	300,000

EXCEL TEMPLATE

Instructions

1. Compute (a) the working capital, (b) the current ratio, and (c) the quick ratio. Round to one decimal place.

2. List the following captions on a sheet of paper:

Transaction	Working Capital	Current Ratio	Quick Ratio

Compute the working capital, the current ratio, and the quick ratio after each of the following transactions, and record the results in the appropriate columns. *Consider each transaction separately* and assume that only that transaction affects the data given. Round to one decimal place.

a. Sold marketable securities at no gain or loss, $70,000.
b. Paid accounts payable, $125,000.
c. Purchased goods on account, $110,000.
d. Paid notes payable, $100,000.
e. Declared a cash dividend, $150,000.
f. Declared a common stock dividend on common stock, $50,000.
g. Borrowed cash from bank on a long-term note, $225,000.
h. Received cash on account, $125,000.
i. Issued additional shares of stock for cash, $600,000.
j. Paid cash for prepaid expenses, $10,000.

PR 14-4A   Measures of liquidity, solvency, and profitability   Obj. 3, 4, 5

✔ 5. Number of days' sales in receivables, 18.3

EXCEL TEMPLATE

The comparative financial statements of Marshall Inc. are as follows. The market price of Marshall common stock was $82.60 on December 31, 20Y2.

Marshall Inc.
Comparative Retained Earnings Statement
For the Years Ended December 31, 20Y2 and 20Y1

	20Y2	20Y1
Retained earnings, January 1	$3,704,000	$3,264,000
Net income	$ 600,000	$ 550,000
Dividends:		
On preferred stock	(10,000)	(10,000)
On common stock	(100,000)	(100,000)
Increase in retained earnings	$ 490,000	$ 440,000
Retained earnings, December 31	$4,194,000	$3,704,000

Marshall Inc.
Comparative Income Statement
For the Years Ended December 31, 20Y2 and 20Y1

	20Y2	20Y1
Sales	$ 10,850,000	$10,000,000
Cost of goods sold	(6,000,000)	(5,450,000)
Gross profit	$ 4,850,000	$ 4,550,000
Selling expenses	$ (2,170,000)	$ (2,000,000)
Administrative expenses	(1,627,500)	(1,500,000)
Total operating expenses	$(3,797,500)	$ (3,500,000)
Operating income	$ 1,052,500	$ 1,050,000
Other revenue and expense:		
Other revenue	99,500	20,000
Other expense (interest)	(132,000)	(120,000)
Income before income tax expense	$ 1,020,000	$ 950,000
Income tax expense	(420,000)	(400,000)
Net income	$ 600,000	$ 550,000

Marshall Inc.
Comparative Balance Sheet
December 31, 20Y2 and 20Y1

	20Y2	20Y1
Assets		
Current assets:		
Cash	$1,050,000	$ 950,000
Marketable securities	301,000	420,000
Accounts receivable (net)	585,000	500,000
Inventories	420,000	380,000
Prepaid expenses	108,000	20,000
Total current assets	$ 2,464,000	$2,270,000
Long-term investments	800,000	800,000
Property, plant, and equipment (net)	5,760,000	5,184,000
Total assets	$ 9,024,000	$8,254,000
Liabilities		
Current liabilities	$ 880,000	$ 800,000
Long-term liabilities:		
Mortgage note payable, 6%,	$ 200,000	$ 0
Bonds payable, 4%,	3,000,000	3,000,000
Total long-term liabilities	$ 3,200,000	$3,000,000
Total liabilities	$ 4,080,000	$3,800,000
Stockholders' Equity		
Preferred 4% stock, $5 par	$ 250,000	$ 250,000
Common stock, $5 par	500,000	500,000
Retained earnings	4,194,000	3,704,000
Total stockholders' equity	$ 4,944,000	$4,454,000
Total liabilities and stockholders' equity	$ 9,024,000	$8,254,000

(Continued)

Instructions

Determine the following measures for 20Y2. Round to one decimal place, including percentages, except for per-share amounts, which should be rounded to the nearest cent.

1. Working capital
2. Current ratio
3. Quick ratio
4. Accounts receivable turnover
5. Number of days' sales in receivables
6. Inventory turnover
7. Number of days' sales in inventory
8. Ratio of fixed assets to long-term liabilities
9. Ratio of liabilities to stockholders' equity
10. Times interest earned
11. Asset turnover
12. Return on total assets
13. Return on stockholders' equity
14. Return on common stockholders' equity
15. Earnings per share on common stock
16. Price-earnings ratio
17. Dividends per share of common stock
18. Dividend yield

PR 14-5A   Solvency and profitability trend analysis   Obj. 4, 5

✔ 1. b. 20Y7, 11.3%   Addai Company has provided the following comparative information:

	20Y8	20Y7	20Y6	20Y5	20Y4
Net income	$ 273,406	$ 367,976	$ 631,176	$ 884,000	$ 800,000
Interest expense	616,047	572,003	528,165	495,000	440,000
Income tax expense	31,749	53,560	106,720	160,000	200,000
Total assets (ending balance)	4,417,178	4,124,350	3,732,443	3,338,500	2,750,000
Total stockholders' equity (ending balance)	3,706,557	3,433,152	3,065,176	2,434,000	1,550,000
Average total assets	4,270,764	3,928,397	3,535,472	3,044,250	2,475,000
Average total stockholders' equity	3,569,855	3,249,164	2,749,588	1,992,000	1,150,000

You have been asked to evaluate the historical performance of the company over the last five years.

Selected industry ratios have remained relatively steady at the following levels for the last five years:

	20Y4–20Y8
Return on total assets	28%
Return on stockholders' equity	18%
Times interest earned	2.7
Ratio of liabilities to stockholders' equity	0.4

Instructions

1. Prepare four line graphs with the ratio on the vertical axis and the years on the horizontal axis for the following four ratios (round to one decimal place):

   a. Return on total assets

   b. Return on stockholders' equity

   c. Times interest earned

   d. Ratio of liabilities to stockholders' equity

   Display both the company ratio and the industry benchmark on each graph. That is, each graph should have two lines.

2. ⬤⬤⬤▶ Prepare an analysis of the graphs in (1).

Problems: Series B

PR 14-1B Horizontal analysis of income statement

Obj. 2

SHOW ME HOW   EXCEL TEMPLATE

✔ 1. Sales, 30.0% increase

For 20Y2, Macklin Inc. reported a significant increase in net income. At the end of the year, John Mayer, the president, is presented with the following condensed comparative income statement:

Macklin Inc.
Comparative Income Statement
For the Years Ended December 31, 20Y2 and 20Y1

	20Y2	20Y1
Sales	$ 910,000	$ 700,000
Cost of goods sold	(441,000)	(350,000)
Gross profit	$ 469,000	$ 350,000
Selling expenses	$ (139,150)	$ (115,000)
Administrative expenses	(99,450)	(85,000)
Total operating expenses	$ (238,600)	$ (200,000)
Operating income	$ 230,400	$ 150,000
Other revenue	65,000	50,000
Income before income tax expense	$ 295,400	$ 200,000
Income tax expense	(65,000)	(50,000)
Net income	$ 230,400	$ 150,000

Instructions

1. Prepare a comparative income statement with horizontal analysis for the two-year period, using 20Y1 as the base year. Round percentages to one decimal place.

2. ➡ To the extent the data permit, comment on the significant relationships revealed by the horizontal analysis prepared in (1).

PR 14-2B Vertical analysis of income statement

Obj. 2

✔ 1. Net income, 20Y1, 14.0%

EXCEL TEMPLATE

For 20Y2, Fielder Industries Inc. initiated a sales promotion campaign that included the expenditure of an additional $40,000 for advertising. At the end of the year, Leif Grando, the president, is presented with the following condensed comparative income statement:

Fielder Industries Inc.
Comparative Income Statement
For the Years Ended December 31, 20Y2 and 20Y1

	20Y2	20Y1
Sales	$1,300,000	$1,180,000
Cost of goods sold	(682,500)	(613,600)
Gross profit	$ 617,500	$ 566,400
Selling expenses	$ (260,000)	$ (188,800)
Adminstrative expenses	(169,000)	(177,000)
Total operating expenses	$ (429,000)	$ (365,800)
Operating income	$ 188,500	$ 200,600
Other revenue	78,000	70,800
Income before income tax expense	$ 266,500	$ 271,400
Income tax expense	(117,000)	(106,200)
Net income	$ 149,500	$ 165,200

Instructions

1. Prepare a comparative income statement for the two-year period, presenting an analysis of each item in relationship to sales for each of the years. Round percentages to one decimal place.

2. ➡ To the extent the data permit, comment on the significant relationships revealed by the vertical analysis prepared in (1).

PR 14-3B   Effect of transactions on current position analysis   Obj. 3

Data pertaining to the current position of Lucroy Industries Inc. follows:

Cash	$ 800,000
Marketable securities	550,000
Accounts and notes receivable (net)	850,000
Inventories	700,000
Prepaid expenses	300,000
Accounts payable	1,200,000
Notes payable (short-term)	700,000
Accrued expenses	100,000

Instructions

1. Compute (a) the working capital, (b) the current ratio, and (c) the quick ratio. Round to one decimal place.

2. List the following captions on a sheet of paper:

Transaction	Working Capital	Current Ratio	Quick Ratio

Compute the working capital, the current ratio, and the quick ratio after each of the following transactions, and record the results in the appropriate columns. *Consider each transaction separately* and assume that only that transaction affects the data given. Round to one decimal place.

a. Sold marketable securities at no gain or loss, $500,000.
b. Paid accounts payable, $287,500.
c. Purchased goods on account, $400,000.
d. Paid notes payable, $125,000.
e. Declared a cash dividend, $325,000.
f. Declared a common stock dividend on common stock, $150,000.
g. Borrowed cash from bank on a long-term note, $1,000,000.
h. Received cash on account, $75,000.
i. Issued additional shares of stock for cash, $2,000,000.
j. Paid cash for prepaid expenses, $200,000.

PR 14-4B   Measures of liquidity, solvency and profitability   Obj. 3, 4, 5

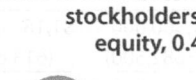

The comparative financial statements of Stargel Inc. are as follows. The market price of Stargel common stock was $119.70 on December 31, 20Y2.

Stargel Inc.
Comparative Retained Earnings Statement
For the Years Ended December 31, 20Y2 and 20Y1

	20Y2	20Y1
Retained earnings, January 1	$5,375,000	$4,545,000
Net income	$ 900,000	$ 925,000
Dividends:		
On preferred stock	(45,000)	(45,000)
On common stock	(50,000)	(50,000)
Increase in retained earnings	$ 805,000	$ 830,000
Retained earnings, December 31	$6,180,000	$5,375,000

Stargel Inc.
Comparative Income Statement
For the Years Ended December 31, 20Y2 and 20Y1

	20Y2	20Y1
Sales	$ 10,000,000	$ 9,400,000
Cost of goods sold	(5,350,000)	(4,950,000)
Gross profit	$ 4,650,000	$ 4,450,000
Selling expenses	$ (2,000,000)	$ (1,880,000)
Administrative expenses	(1,500,000)	(1,410,000)
Total operating expenses	$ (3,500,000)	$ (3,290,000)
Operating income	$ 1,150,000	$ 1,160,000
Other revenue and expense:		
Other revenue	150,000	140,000
Other expense (interest)	(170,000)	(150,000)
Income before income tax expense:	$ 1,130,000	$ 1,150,000
Income tax expense	(230,000)	(225,000)
Net income	$ 900,000	$ 925,000

Stargel Inc.
Comparative Balance Sheet
December 31, 20Y2 and 20Y1

	20Y2	20Y1
Assets		
Current assets:		
Cash	$ 500,000	$ 400,000
Marketable securities	1,010,000	1,000,000
Accounts receivable (net)	740,000	510,000
Inventories	1,190,000	950,000
Prepaid expenses	250,000	229,000
Total current assets	$3,690,000	$3,089,000
Long-term investments	2,350,000	2,300,000
Property, plant, and equipment (net)	3,740,000	3,366,000
Total assets	$9,780,000	$8,755,000
Liabilities		
Current liabilities	$ 900,000	$ 880,000
Long-term liabilities:		
Mortgage note payable, 10%	$ 200,000	$ 0
Bonds payable, 10%	1,500,000	1,500,000
Total long-term liabilities	$1,700,000	$1,500,000
Total liabilities	$2,600,000	$2,380,000
Stockholders' Equity		
Preferred $0.90 stock, $10 par	$ 500,000	$ 500,000
Common stock, $5 par	500,000	500,000
Retained earnings	6,180,000	5,375,000
Total stockholders' equity	$7,180,000	$6,375,000
Total liabilities and stockholders' equity	$9,780,000	$8,755,000

Instructions

Determine the following measures for 20Y2. Round to one decimal place including percentages, except for per-share amounts, which should be rounded to the nearest cent.

1. Working capital

2. Current ratio

3. Quick ratio

4. Accounts receivable turnover

5. Number of days' sales in receivables

6. Inventory turnover

7. Number of days' sales in inventory

(Continued)

8. Ratio of fixed assets to long-term liabilities
9. Ratio of liabilities to stockholders' equity
10. Times interest earned
11. Asset turnover
12. Return on total assets
13. Return on stockholders' equity
14. Return on common stockholders' equity
15. Earnings per share on common stock
16. Price-earnings ratio
17. Dividends per share of common stock
18. Dividend yield

PR 14-5B   Solvency and profitability trend analysis   Obj. 4, 5

✔ 1. b. 20Y7, 32.9%   Crosby Company has provided the following comparative information:

	20Y8	20Y7	20Y6	20Y5	20Y4
Net income	$ 5,571,720	$ 3,714,480	$ 2,772,000	$ 1,848,000	$ 1,400,000
Interest expense	1,052,060	891,576	768,600	610,000	500,000
Income tax expense	1,225,572	845,222	640,320	441,600	320,000
Total assets (ending balance)	29,378,491	22,598,839	17,120,333	12,588,480	10,152,000
Total stockholders' equity (ending balance)	18,706,200	13,134,480	9,420,000	6,648,000	4,800,000
Average total assets	25,988,665	19,859,586	14,854,406	11,370,240	8,676,000
Average total stockholders' equity	15,920,340	11,277,240	8,034,000	5,724,000	4,100,000

You have been asked to evaluate the historical performance of the company over the last five years.
   Selected industry ratios have remained relatively steady at the following levels for the last five years:

	20Y4–20Y8
Return on total assets	19%
Return on stockholders' equity	26%
Times interest earned	3.4
Ratio of liabilities to stockholders' equity	1.4

Instructions

1. Prepare four line graphs with the ratio on the vertical axis and the years on the horizontal axis for the following four ratios. Round ratios and percentages to one decimal place.

   a. Return on total assets

   b. Return on stockholders' equity

   c. Times interest earned

   d. Ratio of liabilities to stockholders' equity

   Display both the company ratio and the industry benchmark on each graph. That is, each graph should have two lines.

2. ━━━━▶ Prepare an analysis of the graphs in (1).

Make a Decision
Financial Statement Analysis

REAL WORLD

MAD 14-1 Analyze and compare Amazon.com, Best Buy, and Wal-Mart Obj. 2

The condensed income statements through operating income for **Amazon.com, Inc. (AMZN)**, **Best Buy Co., Inc. (BBY)**, and **Wal-Mart Stores, Inc. (WMT)**, for a recent fiscal year follow (in millions):

	Amazon	Best Buy	Wal-Mart
Sales	$135,987	$ 39,403	$ 485,873
Cost of sales	(88,265)	(29,963)	(361,256)
Gross profit	$ 47,722	$ 9,440	$ 124,617
Selling, general, and administrative expenses	(43,369)	(7,547)	(101,853)
Operating expenses	(167)	(39)	0
Operating income	$ 4,186	$ 1,854	$ 22,764

1. Prepare comparative common-sized income statements for each company. Round percentages to one decimal place.

2. ━━━▶ Use the common-sized analysis to compare the financial performance of the three companies.

REAL WORLD

MAD 14-2 Analyze and compare Alphabet, PepsiCo, and Caterpillar Obj. 5

The following table shows the stock price, earnings per share, and dividends per share for **Alphabet Inc. (GOOG)**, **PepsiCo, Inc. (PEP)**, and **Caterpillar Inc. (CAT)** for a recent year:

	Alphabet	PepsiCo	Caterpillar
Market price of common stock at year-end	$778.01	$99.92	$67.96
Earnings per share	22.84	3.71	4.23
Dividends per share	0.00	2.76	3.01

1. For each company, determine the:
   a. Price-earnings ratio. Round to the nearest cent.
   b. Dividend yield. Round to one decimal place.

2. ━━━▶ Based on the information available, which company would you expect to have the best potential for future common stock price appreciation? Why?

REAL WORLD

MAD 14-3 Analyze Deere & Company Obj. 5

Deere & Company (DE) manufactures and distributes farm and construction machinery that it sells around the world. In addition to its manufacturing operations, Deere's credit division loans money to customers to finance the purchase of their farm and construction equipment.

The following information is available for three recent years (in millions except per-share amounts):

	Year 3	Year 2	Year 1
Net income (loss)	$1,523.9	$1,940.0	$3,161.7
Preferred dividends	$0.00	$0.00	$0.00
Interest expense	$763.7	$680.0	$664.0
Shares outstanding for computing earnings per share	315	334	363
Cash dividend per share	$2.40	$2.40	$2.22
Average total assets	$57,965	$59,642	$60,429
Average stockholders' equity	$6,644	$7,912	$9,667
Average stock price per share	$92.03	$81.10	$85.58

1. Calculate the following ratios for each year. Round ratios and percentages to one decimal place, except for per-share amounts, which should be rounded to the nearest cent.
   a. Return on total assets
   b. Return on stockholders' equity

(Continued)

c. Earnings per share

d. Dividend yield

e. Price-earnings ratio

2. ➤ Based on these data, evaluate Deere's profitability.

REAL WORLD

MAD 14-4 Analyze and compare Marriott and Hyatt

Obj. 4, 5

Marriott International, Inc. (MAR), and **Hyatt Hotels Corporation (H)** are two major owners and managers of lodging and resort properties in the United States. Abstracted income statement information for the two companies is as follows for a recent year (in millions):

	Marriott	Hyatt
Operating profit before other revenue and interest	$1,368	$299
Other revenue (expense)	50	66
Interest expense	(234)	(76)
Income before income tax expense	$1,184	$289
Income tax expense	(404)	(85)
Net income	$ 780	$204

Balance sheet information is as follows:

	Marriott	Hyatt
Total liabilities	$18,783	$3,841
Total stockholders' equity	5,357	3,908
Total liabilities and stockholders' equity	$24,140	$7,749

The average liabilities, average stockholders' equity, and average total assets are as follows:

	Marriott	Hyatt
Average total liabilities	$14,228	$3,719
Average total stockholders' equity	883	3,951
Average total assets	15,111	7,670

1. Determine the following ratios for both companies. Round ratios and percentages to one decimal place.

a. Return on total assets

b. Return on stockholders' equity

c. Times interest earned

d. Ratio of total liabilities to stockholders' equity

2. ➤ Based on the information in (1), analyze and compare the two companies' solvency and profitability.

Take It Further

ETHICS

TIF 14-1 Internal control

Rodgers Industries Inc. completed its fiscal year on December 31. Near the end of the fiscal year, the company's internal audit department determined that an important internal control procedure had not been functioning properly. The head of internal audit, Dash Riprock, reported the internal control failure to the company's chief accountant, Todd Barleywine. Todd reported the failure to the company's chief financial officer, Josh McCoy. After discussing the issue, Josh instructed Todd not to inform the external auditors of the internal control failure and to fix the problem quietly after the end of the fiscal year. The external auditors did not discover the internal control failure during their audit. In March, after the audit was complete, the company released its annual report, including associated reports by management. As chief financial officer, Josh authorized the release of Management's Report on Internal Control, which stated that the management team believed that the company's internal controls were effective during the period covered by the annual report.

▬▬▶ Did Josh behave ethically in this situation? Explain your answer.

REAL WORLD

TIF 14-2 Real-world annual report

The financial statements for **Nike, Inc. (NKE)**, are presented in Appendix E at the end of the text. The following additional information is available (in thousands):

Accounts receivable at May 31, 2015	$ 3,358
Inventories at May 31, 2015	4,337
Total assets at May 31, 2015	21,597
Stockholders' equity at May 31, 2015	12,707

Instructions

1. Determine the following measures for the fiscal years ended May 31, 2017, and May 31, 2016. Round ratios and percentages to one decimal place.

   a. Working capital

   b. Current ratio

   c. Quick ratio

   d. Accounts receivable turnover

   e. Number of days' sales in receivables

   f. Inventory turnover

   g. Number of days' sales in inventory

   h. Ratio of liabilities to stockholders' equity

   i. Asset turnover

   j. Return on total assets, assuming interest expense is $82 million for the year ending May 31, 2017, and $33 million for the year ending May 31, 2016.

   k. Return on common stockholders' equity

   l. Price-earnings ratio, assuming that the market price was $52.81 per share on May 31, 2017, and $54.35 per share on May 31, 2016.

   m. Percentage relationship of net income to sales

2. ▬▬▶ What conclusions can be drawn from these analyses?

COMMUNICATION

TIF 14-3 Debt versus equity financing

The president of Freeman Industries Inc. made the following statement in the annual report to shareholders: "The founding family and majority shareholders of the company do not believe in using debt to finance future growth. The founding family learned from hard experience during Prohibition and the Great Depression that debt can cause loss of flexibility and eventual loss of corporate control. The company will not place itself at such risk again. As such, all future growth will be financed either by stock sales to the public or by internally generated resources."

▬▬▶ Write a brief memo to the company's president, Boss Freeman, outlining the errors in his logic.

Pathways Challenge

This is Accounting!

Information/Consequences

Yes, the operating income and net income reported on the income statement in the annual report are based on GAAP.

Companies are allowed to report adjusted (non-GAAP) amounts in their annual reports. However, the adjusted amounts must be labeled as non-GAAP and a reconciliation to the GAAP amounts must be provided. Adjusted (non-GAAP) amounts are often reported when companies feel that GAAP reporting does not accurately reflect their operations, as was the case for **PayPal (PYPL)**.

Because the adjusted (non-GAAP) amounts are higher than the GAAP amounts, return on assets, return on stockholders' equity, and earnings per share will be higher.

Whether adjusted (non-GAAP) amounts provide better information than GAAP amounts is an area of current research. One study[5] concluded that GAAP earnings are more useful than adjusted earnings that exclude expenses related to stock options. However, it is still uncertain whether adjusted (non-GAAP) amounts, combined with GAAP amounts, provide more useful information than the GAAP amounts alone.

Suggested Answer

---

[5] Mary E. Barth, Ian D. Gow, and Daniel Taylor, "Why Do Pro Forma and Street Earnings Not Reflect Changes in GAAP? Evidence from SFAS 123R," *Review of Accounting Studies* (September 2012): 526–562.

Appendices

Appendix A

Interest Tables

Present Value of $1 at Compound Interest Due in n Periods $= \dfrac{1}{(1+i)^n}$

Periods	4.0%	4.5%	5%	5.5%	6%	6.5%	7%
1	0.96154	0.95694	0.95238	0.94787	0.94340	0.93897	0.93458
2	0.92456	0.91573	0.90703	0.89845	0.89000	0.88166	0.87344
3	0.88900	0.87630	0.86384	0.85161	0.83962	0.82785	0.81630
4	0.85480	0.83856	0.82270	0.80722	0.79209	0.77732	0.76290
5	0.82193	0.80245	0.78353	0.76513	0.74726	0.72988	0.71299
6	0.79031	0.76790	0.74622	0.72525	0.70496	0.68533	0.66634
7	0.75992	0.73483	0.71068	0.68744	0.66506	0.64351	0.62275
8	0.73069	0.70319	0.67684	0.65160	0.62741	0.60423	0.58201
9	0.70259	0.67290	0.64461	0.61763	0.59190	0.56735	0.54393
10	0.67556	0.64393	0.61391	0.58543	0.55839	0.53273	0.50835
11	0.64958	0.61620	0.58468	0.55491	0.52679	0.50021	0.47509
12	0.62460	0.58966	0.55684	0.52598	0.49697	0.46968	0.44401
13	0.60057	0.56427	0.53032	0.49856	0.46884	0.44102	0.41496
14	0.57748	0.53997	0.50507	0.47257	0.44230	0.41410	0.38782
15	0.55526	0.51672	0.48102	0.44793	0.41727	0.38883	0.36245
16	0.53391	0.49447	0.45811	0.42458	0.39365	0.36510	0.33873
17	0.51337	0.47318	0.43630	0.40245	0.37136	0.34281	0.31657
18	0.49363	0.45280	0.41552	0.38147	0.35034	0.32189	0.29586
19	0.47464	0.43330	0.39573	0.36158	0.33051	0.30224	0.27651
20	0.45639	0.41464	0.37689	0.34273	0.31180	0.28380	0.25842
21	0.43883	0.39679	0.35894	0.32486	0.29416	0.26648	0.24151
22	0.42196	0.37970	0.34185	0.30793	0.27751	0.25021	0.22571
23	0.40573	0.36335	0.32557	0.29187	0.26180	0.23494	0.21095
24	0.39012	0.34770	0.31007	0.27666	0.24698	0.22060	0.19715
25	0.37512	0.33273	0.29530	0.26223	0.23300	0.20714	0.18425
26	0.36069	0.31840	0.28124	0.24856	0.21981	0.19450	0.17220
27	0.34682	0.30469	0.26785	0.23560	0.20737	0.18263	0.16093
28	0.33348	0.29157	0.25509	0.22332	0.19563	0.17148	0.15040
29	0.32065	0.27902	0.24295	0.21168	0.18456	0.16101	0.14056
30	0.30832	0.26700	0.23138	0.20064	0.17411	0.15119	0.13137
31	0.29646	0.25550	0.22036	0.19018	0.16425	0.14196	0.12277
32	0.28506	0.24450	0.20987	0.18027	0.15496	0.13329	0.11474
33	0.27409	0.23397	0.19987	0.17087	0.14619	0.12516	0.10723
34	0.26355	0.22390	0.19035	0.16196	0.13791	0.11752	0.10022
35	0.25342	0.21425	0.18129	0.15352	0.13011	0.11035	0.09366
40	0.20829	0.17193	0.14205	0.11746	0.09722	0.08054	0.06678
45	0.17120	0.13796	0.11130	0.08988	0.07265	0.05879	0.04761
50	0.14071	0.11071	0.08720	0.06877	0.05429	0.04291	0.03395

Present Value of \$1 at Compound Interest Due in *n* Periods $= \dfrac{1}{(1+i)^n}$

Periods	8%	9%	10%	11%	12%	13%	14%
1	0.92593	0.91743	0.90909	0.90090	0.89286	0.88496	0.87719
2	0.85734	0.84168	0.82645	0.81162	0.79719	0.78315	0.76947
3	0.79383	0.77218	0.75131	0.73119	0.71178	0.69305	0.67497
4	0.73503	0.70843	0.68301	0.65873	0.63552	0.61332	0.59208
5	0.68058	0.64993	0.62092	0.59345	0.56743	0.54276	0.51937
6	0.63017	0.59627	0.56447	0.53464	0.50663	0.48032	0.45559
7	0.58349	0.54703	0.51316	0.48166	0.45235	0.42506	0.39964
8	0.54027	0.50187	0.46651	0.43393	0.40388	0.37616	0.35056
9	0.50025	0.46043	0.42410	0.39092	0.36061	0.33288	0.30751
10	0.46319	0.42241	0.38554	0.35218	0.32197	0.29459	0.26974
11	0.42888	0.38753	0.35049	0.31728	0.28748	0.26070	0.23662
12	0.39711	0.35553	0.31863	0.28584	0.25668	0.23071	0.20756
13	0.36770	0.32618	0.28966	0.25751	0.22917	0.20416	0.18207
14	0.34046	0.29925	0.26333	0.23199	0.20462	0.18068	0.15971
15	0.31524	0.27454	0.23939	0.20900	0.18270	0.15989	0.14010
16	0.29189	0.25187	0.21763	0.18829	0.16312	0.14150	0.12289
17	0.27027	0.23107	0.19784	0.16963	0.14564	0.12522	0.10780
18	0.25025	0.21199	0.17986	0.15282	0.13004	0.11081	0.09456
19	0.23171	0.19449	0.16351	0.13768	0.11611	0.09806	0.08295
20	0.21455	0.17843	0.14864	0.12403	0.10367	0.08678	0.07276
21	0.19866	0.16370	0.13513	0.11174	0.09256	0.07680	0.06383
22	0.18394	0.15018	0.12285	0.10067	0.08264	0.06796	0.05599
23	0.17032	0.13778	0.11168	0.09069	0.07379	0.06014	0.04911
24	0.15770	0.12640	0.10153	0.08170	0.06588	0.05323	0.04308
25	0.14602	0.11597	0.09230	0.07361	0.05882	0.04710	0.03779
26	0.13520	0.10639	0.08391	0.06631	0.05252	0.04168	0.03315
27	0.12519	0.09761	0.07628	0.05974	0.04689	0.03689	0.02908
28	0.11591	0.08955	0.06934	0.05382	0.04187	0.03264	0.02551
29	0.10733	0.08215	0.06304	0.04849	0.03738	0.02889	0.02237
30	0.09938	0.07537	0.05731	0.04368	0.03338	0.02557	0.01963
31	0.09202	0.06915	0.05210	0.03935	0.02980	0.02262	0.01722
32	0.08520	0.06344	0.04736	0.03545	0.02661	0.02002	0.01510
33	0.07889	0.05820	0.04306	0.03194	0.02376	0.01772	0.01325
34	0.07305	0.05339	0.03914	0.02878	0.02121	0.01568	0.01162
35	0.06763	0.04899	0.03558	0.02592	0.01894	0.01388	0.01019
40	0.04603	0.03184	0.02209	0.01538	0.01075	0.00753	0.00529
45	0.03133	0.02069	0.01372	0.00913	0.00610	0.00409	0.00275
50	0.02132	0.01345	0.00852	0.00542	0.00346	0.00222	0.00143

Present Value of Ordinary Annuity of \$1 per Period $= \dfrac{1 - \dfrac{1}{(1+i)^n}}{i}$

Periods	4.0%	4.5%	5%	5.5%	6%	6.5%	7%
1	0.96154	0.95694	0.95238	0.94787	0.94340	0.93897	0.93458
2	1.88609	1.87267	1.85941	1.84632	1.83339	1.82063	1.80802
3	2.77509	2.74896	2.72325	2.69793	2.67301	2.64848	2.62432
4	3.62990	3.58753	3.54595	3.50515	3.46511	3.42580	3.38721
5	4.45182	4.38998	4.32948	4.27028	4.21236	4.15568	4.10020
6	5.24214	5.15787	5.07569	4.99553	4.91732	4.84101	4.76654
7	6.00205	5.89270	5.78637	5.68297	5.58238	5.48452	5.38929
8	6.73274	6.59589	6.46321	6.33457	6.20979	6.08875	5.97130
9	7.43533	7.26879	7.10782	6.95220	6.80169	6.65610	6.51523
10	8.11090	7.91272	7.72173	7.53763	7.36009	7.18883	7.02358
11	8.76048	8.52892	8.30641	8.09254	7.88687	7.68904	7.49867
12	9.38507	9.11858	8.86325	8.61852	8.38384	8.15873	7.94269
13	9.98565	9.68285	9.39357	9.11708	8.85268	8.59974	8.35765
14	10.56312	10.22283	9.89864	9.58965	9.29498	9.01384	8.74547
15	11.11839	10.73955	10.37966	10.03758	9.71225	9.40267	9.10791
16	11.65230	11.23402	10.83777	10.46216	10.10590	9.76776	9.44665
17	12.16567	11.70719	11.27407	10.86461	10.47726	10.11058	9.76322
18	12.65930	12.15999	11.68959	11.24607	10.82760	10.43247	10.05909
19	13.13394	12.59329	12.08532	11.60765	11.15812	10.73471	10.33560
20	13.59033	13.00794	12.46221	11.95038	11.46992	11.01851	10.59401
21	14.02916	13.40472	12.82115	12.27524	11.76408	11.28498	10.83553
22	14.45112	13.78442	13.16300	12.58317	12.04158	11.53520	11.06124
23	14.85684	14.14777	13.48857	12.87504	12.30338	11.77014	11.27219
24	15.24696	14.49548	13.79864	13.15170	12.55036	11.99074	11.46933
25	15.62208	14.82821	14.09394	13.41393	12.78336	12.19788	11.65358
26	15.98277	15.14661	14.37519	13.66250	13.00317	12.39237	11.82578
27	16.32959	15.45130	14.64303	13.89810	13.21053	12.57500	11.98671
28	16.66306	15.74287	14.89813	14.12142	13.40616	12.74648	12.13711
29	16.98371	16.02189	15.14107	14.33310	13.59072	12.90749	12.27767
30	17.29203	16.28889	15.37245	14.53375	13.76483	13.05868	12.40904
31	17.58849	16.54439	15.59281	14.72393	13.92909	13.20063	12.53181
32	17.87355	16.78889	15.80268	14.90420	14.08404	13.33393	12.64656
33	18.14765	17.02286	16.00255	15.07507	14.23023	13.45909	12.75379
34	18.41120	17.24676	16.19290	15.23703	14.36814	13.57661	12.85401
35	18.66461	17.46101	16.37419	15.39055	14.49825	13.68696	12.94767
40	19.79277	18.40158	17.15909	16.04612	15.04630	14.14553	13.33171
45	20.72004	19.15635	17.77407	16.54773	15.45583	14.48023	13.60552
50	21.48218	19.76201	18.25593	16.93152	15.76186	14.72452	13.80075

Present Value of Ordinary Annuity of $1 per Period $= \dfrac{1 - \dfrac{1}{(1+i)^n}}{i}$

Periods	8%	9%	10%	11%	12%	13%	14%
1	0.92593	0.91743	0.90909	0.90090	0.89286	0.88496	0.87719
2	1.78326	1.75911	1.73554	1.71252	1.69005	1.66810	1.64666
3	2.57710	2.53129	2.48685	2.44371	2.40183	2.36115	2.32163
4	3.31213	3.23972	3.16987	3.10245	3.03735	2.97447	2.91371
5	3.99271	3.88965	3.79079	3.69590	3.60478	3.51723	3.43308
6	4.62288	4.48592	4.35526	4.23054	4.11141	3.99755	3.88867
7	5.20637	5.03295	4.86842	4.71220	4.56376	4.42261	4.28830
8	5.74664	5.53482	5.33493	5.14612	4.96764	4.79677	4.63886
9	6.24689	5.99525	5.75902	5.53705	5.32825	5.13166	4.94637
10	6.71008	6.41766	6.14457	5.88923	5.65022	5.42624	5.21612
11	7.13896	6.80519	6.49506	6.20652	5.93770	5.68694	5.45273
12	7.53608	7.16073	6.81369	6.49236	6.19437	5.91765	5.66029
13	7.90378	7.48690	7.10336	6.74987	6.42355	6.12181	5.84236
14	8.22424	7.78615	7.36669	6.96187	6.62817	6.30249	6.00207
15	8.55948	8.06069	7.60608	7.19087	6.81086	6.46238	6.14217
16	8.85137	8.31256	7.82371	7.37916	6.97399	6.60388	6.26506
17	9.12164	8.54363	8.02155	7.54879	7.11963	6.72909	6.37286
18	9.37189	8.75563	8.20141	7.70162	7.24967	6.83991	6.46742
19	9.60360	8.95011	8.36492	7.83929	7.36578	6.93797	6.55037
20	9.81815	9.12855	8.51356	7.96333	7.46944	7.02475	6.62313
21	10.01680	9.29224	8.64869	8.07507	7.56200	7.10155	6.68696
22	10.20074	9.44243	8.77154	8.17574	7.64465	7.16951	6.74294
23	10.37106	9.58021	8.88322	8.26643	7.71843	7.22966	6.79206
24	10.52876	9.70661	8.98474	8.34814	7.78432	7.28288	6.83514
25	10.67478	9.82258	9.07704	8.42174	7.84314	7.32998	6.87293
26	10.80998	9.92897	9.16095	8.48806	7.89566	7.37167	6.90608
27	10.93516	10.02658	9.23722	8.54780	7.94255	7.40856	6.93515
28	11.05108	10.11613	9.30657	8.60162	7.98442	7.44120	6.96066
29	11.15841	10.19828	9.36961	8.65011	8.02181	7.47009	6.98304
30	11.25778	10.27365	9.42691	8.69379	8.05518	7.49565	7.00266
31	11.34980	10.34280	9.47901	8.73315	8.08499	7.51828	7.01988
32	11.43500	10.40624	9.52638	8.76860	8.11159	7.53830	7.03498
33	11.51389	10.46444	9.56943	8.80054	8.13535	7.55602	7.04823
34	11.58693	10.51784	9.60857	8.82932	8.15656	7.57170	7.05985
35	11.65457	10.56682	9.64416	8.85524	8.17550	7.58557	7.07005
40	11.92461	10.75736	9.77905	8.95105	8.24378	7.63438	7.10504
45	12.10840	10.88120	9.86281	9.00791	8.28252	7.66086	7.12322
50	12.23348	10.96168	9.91481	9.04165	8.30450	7.67524	7.13266

Appendix B

Revenue Recognition

Companies recognize revenue when services have been performed or products have been delivered to customers. For example, when **McDonald's (MCD)** sells a hamburger, the revenue is earned when the hamburger is delivered to the customer. In this example, revenue recognition is simple because the hamburger is delivered and cash is received at a single point in time.

Revenue recognition is more complex, however, when a transaction includes several items that are sold together, items that are delivered over time, or items whose prices depend upon future events. To address these more complex transactions, the Financial Accounting Standards Board (FASB) issued a new accounting standard in May 2014.[1] The new Standard uses a five-step method for determining when revenue should be recognized. The five steps are as follows:

- Step 1. *Identify the contract with the customer.* The new Standard treats every revenue transaction as a contract. A contract is an agreement by the seller to provide a good or service in exchange for payment from the buyer. A contract may be verbal and implicit, such as the purchase of a **McDonald's** hamburger, or written and explicit, such as a cell phone contract.
- Step 2. *Identify the separate performance obligations in the contract.* Every contract requires the seller and buyer to perform. For example, when you purchase a **McDonald's** hamburger, you (the buyer) perform by paying and McDonald's (the seller) performs by delivering a hamburger. When you purchase a cell phone from **Verizon (VZ)**, the transaction is more complex. You perform by paying cash or charging your credit card and signing a written contract. Verizon performs by delivering you the phone and promising to provide you cellular service in the future. In this case, Verizon has two performance obligations: (1) to provide the phone and (2) to provide cellular service in the future.
- Step 3. *Determine the transaction price.* The transaction price is the amount the seller is entitled to receive in exchange for the goods and services they have provided. In the case of the **McDonald's** hamburger, the transaction price is the amount paid for the hamburger. In the case of **Verizon**, the transaction price is the total price to be paid for the phone (the first performance obligation) and cellular service (the second performance obligation).
- Step 4. *Allocate the transaction price to the separate performance obligations.* Since the sale of a **McDonald's** hamburger involves the sale of a single item that is immediately delivered, the entire transaction price is allocated to the hamburger. In more complex transactions, such as a **Verizon** cellular service contract, the revenue received from the customer must be allocated among the performance obligations. This allocation is based on the stand-alone (separate) price of each good or service. For example, Verizon should allocate the revenue from the customer between the phone (first performance obligation) and the commitment to provide cellular service (second performance obligation).
- Step 5. *Recognize revenue when each separate performance obligation is satisfied.* The seller should recognize (record) revenue as each performance obligation is satisfied. The performance obligation could be satisfied either at a point in time or over time. In the case of **McDonald's**, the performance obligation is satisfied when the clerk delivers the hamburger to the customer. At this point, the control of the hamburger has passed to the customer. In the case of **Verizon**, it satisfies its first performance obligation when it delivers you the phone. Verizon satisfies its second performance obligation over time by providing you cellular service. Thus, Verizon should record a portion of the total revenue at the time you sign the contract and receive your phone and the remaining revenue over the period cellular service is provided.

---

[1] Accounting Standards Update, *Revenue from Contracts with Customers (Topic 606),* Financial Accounting Standards Board, May 2014, Norwalk, CT.

To illustrate, assume that on March 1, Chandler Evans upgrades (replaces) his cell phone with Star Cellular at no cost by signing a two-year agreement. The new agreement cannot be cancelled and requires a payment of $90 per month. The cell phone selected by Evans cost Star Cellular $250.

The five-step method for recognizing revenue from this transaction would be applied as follows:

- Step 1. *Identify the contract with the customer.* The contract with Chandler Evans is the two-year cellular service agreement that includes delivery of a new cell phone.
- Step 2. *Identify the separate performance obligations in the contract.* Star Cellular has two separate performance obligations under this contract. First, Star Cellular must deliver a new cell phone at the time that Evans signs the service agreement. Second, Star Cellular must provide Evans with cell service for two years.
- Step 3. *Determine the transaction price.* The transaction price is the total amount Star Cellular will receive over the contract period. In this case, Star Cellular will receive $2,160 ($90 × 24 months) over the contract period.[2]
- Step 4. *Allocate the transaction price to the separate performance obligations.* If Star Cellular sold the cell phone and cell service separately, the individual prices would be as follows:

Cell phone (sold separately)	$ 600
Cell service for two years	3,000
Total price if sold separately	$3,600

The transaction price is allocated to each performance obligation based upon what each obligation would sell for separately as a stand-alone product. To illustrate, the cell phone is allocated $360 of the transaction price of $2,160, computed as follows:

$$\text{Cell Phone} = \text{Transaction Price} \times \frac{\text{Price of Cell Phone Sold Separately}}{\text{Total Price of Cell Phone and Cell Service Sold Separately}}$$

$$= \$2,160 \times \frac{\$600}{\$3,600} = \$360$$

The cell service is allocated $1,800 of the transaction price of $2,160, computed as follows:

$$\text{Cell Service} = \text{Transaction Price} \times \frac{\text{Price of Cell Service Sold Separately}}{\text{Total Price of Cell Phone and Cell Service Sold Separately}}$$

$$= \$2,160 \times \frac{\$3,000}{\$3,600} = \$1,800$$

- Step 5. *Recognize revenue when each separate performance obligation is satisfied.* The $360 of revenue assigned to the cell phone is recognized when the customer signs the service agreement and receives the phone. At this point, the first performance obligation has been satisfied by Star Cellular and the control of the phone has passed to the customer. The journal entry to record revenue on March 1 is as follows:

Mar. 1	Accounts Receivable—Chandler Evans	360	
	Sales		360
1	Cost of Goods Sold	250	
	Inventory		250

[2] An interest component may need to be considered in long-term contracts. To simplify, we ignore interest.

The $1,800 of cell service revenue is recognized as the performance obligation is satisfied over the two-year term of the contract. For example, $75 ($1,800 ÷ 24 months) of service revenue would be recorded each month. The journal entry to record the service revenue for March is as follows:

Mar. 31	Cash	90	
	Accounts Receivable ($360 ÷ 24 months)		15
	Cell Service Revenue ($1,800 ÷ 24 months)		75

The preceding journal entries illustrate how over the life of the two-year contract the total revenue from the contract of $2,160 is divided between the sale of the cell phone ($360 of revenue) and providing of cell service ($1,800 of revenue). In addition, the journal entries illustrate when revenue from the phone and service is recorded.

Exhibit 1 summarizes the division of revenue and its recording over the two-year contract.

Exhibit 1 Recording Revenue over Two-Year Contract

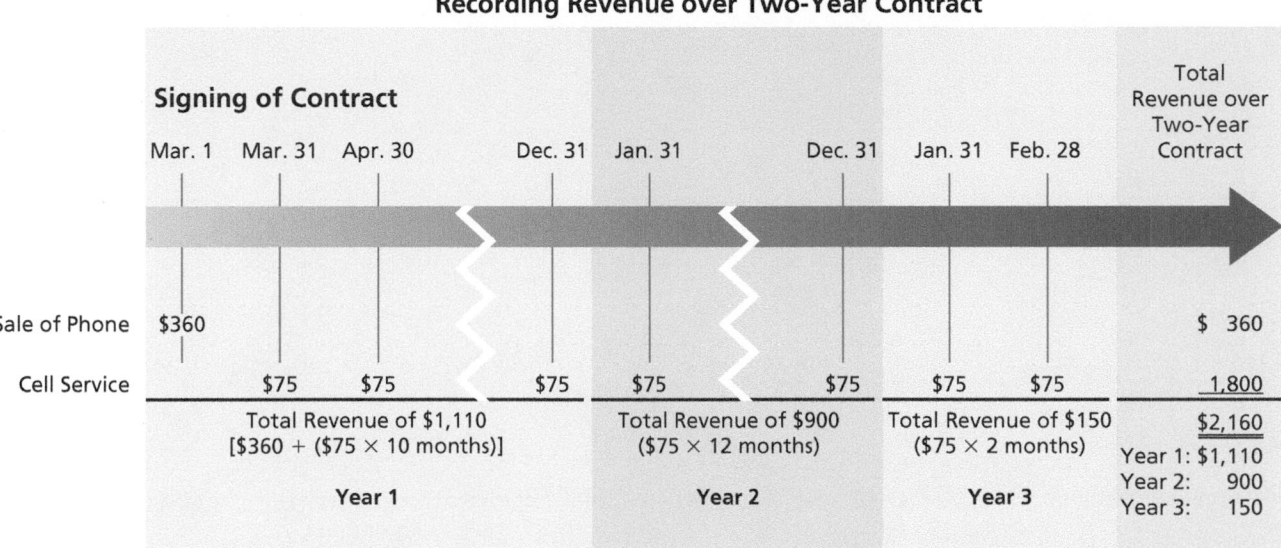

Recording Revenue over Two-Year Contract

Appendix C

International Financial Reporting Standards (IFRS)

IFRS

The Need for Global Accounting Standards

As discussed in Chapter 1, the Financial Accounting Standards Board (FASB) establishes generally accepted accounting principles (GAAP) for public companies in the United States. Of course, there is a world beyond the borders of the United States. In recent years, the removal of trade barriers and the growth in cross-border equity and debt issuances have led to a dramatic increase in international commerce. As a result, often companies are reporting financial results to users outside of the United States.

Historically, accounting standards have varied considerably across countries. These variances have been driven by cultural, legal, and political differences and resulted in financial statements that were not easily comparable and difficult to interpret. A common set of International Financial Reporting Standards (IFRS) has begun to emerge to reduce cross-country differences in accounting standards. While much of the world has migrated to IFRS, the United States has not. Because of the size of the United States and its significant role in world commerce, U.S. GAAP still has a global impact. As a result, there are currently two major accounting standard-setting efforts in the world, U.S. GAAP and IFRS. These two sets of accounting standards add cost and complexity for companies operating internationally.

Overview of IFRS

International Financial Reporting Standards are designed to meet the financial reporting needs of an increasingly global business environment.

What Is IFRS? International Financial Reporting Standards are a set of global accounting standards developed by an international standard-setting body called the International Accounting Standards Board (IASB). Like the Financial Accounting Standards Board, the IASB is an independent entity that establishes accounting rules. Unlike the FASB, the IASB does not establish accounting rules for any specific country. Rather, it develops accounting rules that can be used by a variety of countries, with the goal of developing a single set of global accounting standards.

Who Uses IFRS? IFRS applies to companies that issue publicly traded debt or equity securities, called **public companies**, in countries that have adopted IFRS as their accounting standards. For example, public companies in the European Union (EU) are required to prepare financial statements using IFRS. Exhibit 1 shows the approximately 140 countries and jurisdictions that have adopted or permit the use of IFRS for financial reporting.

Exhibit 1 IFRS Adopters

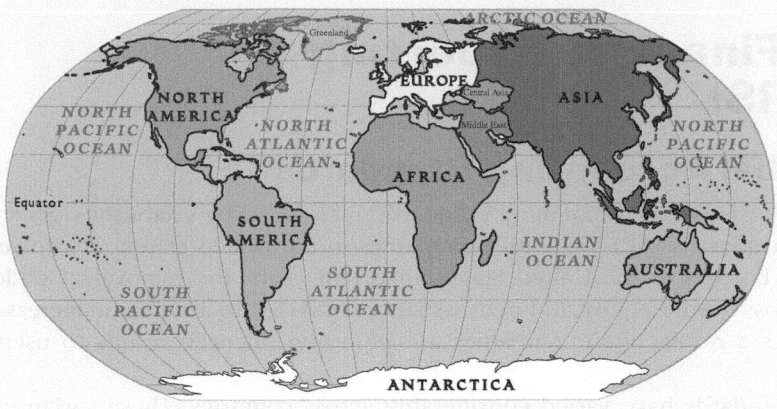

Afghanistan	Bulgaria	Ghana	Liechtenstein	Palestine	Sweden
Albania	Cambodia	Greece	Lithuania	Panama	Switzerland
Angola	Canada	Grenada	Luxembourg	Paraguay	Syria
Anguilla	Cayman Islands	Guatemala	Macao	Peru	Taiwan
Antigua and Barbuda	Chile	Guinea-Bissau	Macedonia	Philippines	Tanzania
Argentina	China	Guyana	Madagascar	Poland	Thailand
Armenia	Colombia	Honduras	Malaysia	Portugal	Trinidad and Tobago
Australia	Costa Rica	Hong Kong	Maldives	Romania	Turkey
Austria	Croatia	Hungary	Malta	Russia	Uganda
Azerbaijan	Cyprus	Iceland	Mauritius	Rwanda	Ukraine
Bahamas	Czech Republic	India	Mexico	Saint Lucia	United Arab Emirates
Bahrain	Denmark	Indonesia	Moldova	Saudi Arabia	United Kingdom
Bangladesh	Dominica	Iraq	Mongolia	Serbia	United States
Barbados	Dominican Republic	Ireland	Montserrat	Sierra Leone	Uruguay
Belarus	Ecuador	Israel	Myanmar	Singapore	Uzbekistan
Belgium	Egypt	Italy	Nepal	Slovakia	Venezuela
Belize	El Salvador	Jamaica	Netherlands	Slovenia	Vietnam
Bermuda	Estonia	Japan	New Zealand	South Africa	Yemen
Bhutan	European Union	Jordan	Nicaragua	Spain	Zambia
Bolivia	Fiji	Kenya	Niger	Sri Lanka	Zimbabwe
Bosnia and Herzegovina	Finland	Korea (South)	Nigeria	St Kitts and Nevis	
Botswana	France	Kosovo	Norway	St Vincent and the Grenadines	
Brazil	Georgia	Latvia	Oman	Suriname	
Brunei	Germany	Lesotho	Pakistan	Swaziland	

Source: *Financial Reporting Standards for the World Economy*, IFRS, June 2015.

U.S. GAAP and IFRS: The Road Forward

The United States has not formally adopted IFRS for U.S. companies. The wide acceptance being gained by IFRS around the world, however, has placed considerable pressure on the United States to align U.S. GAAP with IFRS. There are two possible paths that the United States could take to achieve this: (1) adoption of IFRS by the U.S. Securities and Exchange Commission or (2) convergence of U.S. GAAP and IFRS. These two options are briefly discussed in this section.

Adoption of IFRS by the SEC The U.S. Securities and Exchange Commission (SEC) is the U.S. governmental agency that has authority over the accounting and financial disclosures for U.S. public companies. Only the SEC has the authority to adopt IFRS for U.S. public companies. After considerable deliberation over a period of nearly five years, the SEC published a Final

Report on the issues surrounding IFRS adoption.[1] Notably, this report did not include a final policy decision or recommendation in favor of U.S. public companies adopting IFRS. Indeed, since this report, the SEC has distanced itself from the adoption position, and it is now acknowledged as unsupported.

Convergence of U.S. GAAP and IFRS Convergence involves aligning IFRS and U.S. GAAP one topic at a time, by slowly merging IFRS and U.S. GAAP into two broadly uniform sets of accounting standards. To this end, the FASB and IASB have agreed to work together on a select number of difficult and high-profile accounting issues. These issues frame a large portion of the disagreement between the two sets of standards and, if accomplished, will significantly reduce the differences between U.S. GAAP and IFRS. The projects selected for the convergence effort represent some of the more technical topics in accounting and are covered in intermediate and advanced accounting courses.

One of the major limitations of convergence is that both the FASB and IASB continue to operate as the accounting standard-setting bodies for their respective jurisdictions. As such, convergence would not result in a single set of global accounting standards. Only those standards that go through the joint FASB–IASB standard-setting process would be released as uniform. Standards that do not go through a joint standard-setting process may create inconsistencies between U.S. GAAP and IFRS.

Differences Between U.S. GAAP and IFRS

U.S. GAAP and IFRS differ both in their approach to standard setting, as well as their financial statement presentation and recording of transactions.

Rules-Based Versus Principles Approach to Standard Setting U.S. GAAP is considered to be a "rules-based" approach to accounting standard setting. The accounting standards provide detailed and specific rules on the accounting for business transactions. There are few exceptions or varying interpretations of the accounting for a business event. This structure is consistent with the U.S. legal and regulatory system, reflecting the social and economic values of the United States.

In contrast, IFRS is designed to meet the needs of many countries. Differences in legal, political, and economic systems create different needs for and uses of financial information in different countries. For example, Germany needs a financial reporting system that reflects the central role of banks in its financial system, while the Netherlands needs a financial reporting system that reflects the significant role of outside equity in its financial system.

To accommodate economic, legal, and social diversity, IFRS must be broad enough to capture these differences while still presenting comparable financial statements. Under IFRS, there is greater opportunity for different interpretations of the accounting treatment of a business event across different business entities. To support this, IFRS often has more extensive disclosures that support alternative assumptions. Thus, IFRS provides more latitude for professional judgment than typically found in comparable U.S. GAAP. Many countries find this feature attractive in reducing regulatory costs associated with using and auditing financial reports. This "principles-based" approach presents one of the most significant challenges to adopting IFRS in the United States.

Technical Differences Between IFRS and U.S. GAAP Although U.S. GAAP is similar to IFRS, differences arise in the presentation format, balance sheet valuations, and technical accounting procedures. A comprehensive summary of the key differences between U.S. GAAP and IFRS that are relevant to an introductory accounting course is provided in Exhibit 2.

---

[1] Work Plan for the Consideration of Incorporating International Financial Accounting Standards into the Financial Reporting System for U.S. Issuers: Final Staff Report, U.S. Securities Exchange Commission, July 13, 2012.

Exhibit 2   Comparison of Accounting for Selected Items Under U.S. GAAP and IFRS

	U.S. GAAP	IFRS	Text Reference
General:			
Financial statement titles	Balance Sheet Statement of Stockholders' Equity Statement of Cash Flows	Statement of Financial Position Statement of Changes in Equity Statement of Cash Flows	General
Financial periods presented	Public companies must present two years of comparative information for income statement, statement of stockholders' equity, and statement of cash flows	One year of comparative information must be presented	General
Conceptual basis for standard setting	"Rules-based" approach	"Principles-based" approach	General
Internal control requirements	Sarbanes-Oxley Act (SOX) Section 404		Ch 7
Balance Sheet:	**Balance Sheet**	***Statement of Financial Position***	
Terminology differences	"Payable" "Stockholders' Equity" "Net Income (Loss)"	"Provision" "Capital and Reserves" "Profit or (Loss)"	Ch 10 Ch 12 General
Inventory—LIFO	LIFO allowed	LIFO prohibited	Ch 6
Inventory—valuation	Reversal of lower-of-cost-or-market write-downs not allowed	Reversal of lower-of-cost-or-market write-downs allowed	Ch 6
Long-lived assets	May NOT be revalued to fair value	May be revalued to fair value on a regular basis	Ch 9

(Continued)

Exhibit 2 Comparison of Accounting for Selected Items Under U.S. GAAP and IFRS (*Concluded*)

	U.S. GAAP	IFRS	Text Reference
Land held for investment	Treated as held for use or sale, and recorded at historical cost	May be accounted for on a historical cost basis or on a fair value basis with changes in fair value recognized through profit and loss	Ch 9
Property, plant, and equipment—valuation	Historical cost	May select between historical cost or revalued amount (a form of fair value)	Ch 9
	If impaired, impairment loss may NOT be reversed in future periods	If impaired, impairment loss may be reversed in future periods	Ch 9
Cost of major overhaul (Capital and revenue expenditures)	Different treatment for ordinary repairs and maintenance, asset improvement, extraordinary repairs	Typically included as part of the cost of the asset or asset component if future economic benefit is probable and can be reliably measured	Ch 9
Intangible assets—valuation	Acquisition cost, unless impaired	Fair value permitted if the intangible asset trades in an active market	Ch 9
Intangible assets—impairment loss reversal	Prohibited	Prohibited for goodwill but allowed for other intangible assets	Ch 9
Income Statement:	*Income Statement*	*Statement of Comprehensive Income*	
Classification of expenses on income statement	Public companies must present expenses on the income statement by function (e.g., cost of goods sold, selling, administrative)	Expenses may be presented based either by function (e.g., cost of goods sold, selling) or by the nature of expense (e.g., wages expense, interest expense)	Chs 3, 4, 5
Statement of Cash Flows:	*Statement of Cash Flows*	*Statement of Cash Flows*	
Classification of interest paid or received	Treated as an operating activity	Interest paid may be treated as either an operating or a financing activity; interest received may be treated as an operating or investing activity	Ch 13
Classification of dividend paid or received	Dividend paid treated as a financing activity, dividend received treated as an operating activity	Dividend paid may be treated as either an operating or a financing activity; dividend received may be treated as an operating or investing activity	Ch 13

Discussion Questions

1. Briefly discuss why global accounting standards are needed in today's business environment.

2. What are International Financial Reporting Standards? Who uses these accounting standards?

3. What body is responsible for setting International Financial Reporting Standards?

4. Briefly discuss the differences between (a) adoption of IFRS by the U.S. Securities and Exchange Commission and (b) convergence of U.S. GAAP with IFRS.

5. Briefly discuss the difference between (a) a "rules-based" approach to accounting standard setting and (b) a "principles-based" approach to accounting standard setting.

6. How is property, plant, and equipment measured on the balance sheet under IFRS? How does this differ from the way property, plant, and equipment is measured on the balance sheet under U.S. GAAP?

7. What inventory costing methods are allowed under IFRS? How does this differ from the treatment under U.S. GAAP?

Appendix D

Investments

Most companies generate cash from their operations. This cash can be used for the following purposes:

- Investing in current operations
- Investing in temporary investments to earn additional revenue
- Investing in long-term investments in stock of other companies for strategic reasons

Cash is often used to support the current operating activities of a company. For example, cash may be used to replace worn-out equipment or to purchase new, more efficient, and productive equipment. In addition, cash may be reinvested in the company to expand its current operations. For example, a retailer based in the northwest United States might decide to expand by opening stores in the Midwest.

A company may temporarily have excess cash that is not needed for use in its current operations. This is often the case when a company has a seasonal operating cycle. For example, a significant portion of the annual merchandise sales of a retailer occurs during the fall holiday season. As a result, retailers often experience a large increase in cash during this period, which is not needed until the spring buying season.

Instead of letting excess cash remain idle in a checking account, most companies invest their excess cash in temporary investments. In doing so, companies invest in securities such as:

- **Debt securities**, which are notes and bonds that pay interest and have a fixed maturity date.
- **Equity securities**, which are preferred and common stocks that represent ownership in a company and do not have a fixed maturity date.

Investments in debt and equity securities, termed **investments** or *temporary investments*, are reported in the "Current assets" section of the balance sheet.

The primary objective of investing in temporary investments is to:

- earn interest revenue.
- receive dividends.
- realize gains from increases in the market price of the securities.

A company may invest cash in the debt or equity of another company as a long-term investment. Long-term investments may be held for the same investment objectives as temporary investments. However, long-term investments often involve the purchase of a significant portion of the stock of another company. Such investments usually have a strategic purpose, such as reduction of costs or expansion into new markets.

Equity Investments[1]

A company may invest in the preferred or common stock of another company. The company investing in another company's stock is the **investor**. The company whose stock is purchased is the **investee**.

The percent of the investee's outstanding stock purchased by the investor determines the degree of control that the investor has over the investee. This, in turn, determines the accounting method used for the stock investment, as shown in Exhibit 1.

---

[1]The discussion in this Appendix is consistent with *Financial Instruments, Subtopic 825-10, FASB Accounting Standards Update,* Financial Accounting Standards Board, Norwalk, CT, January 2016.

Exhibit 1 Stock Investments	**Percent of Outstanding Stock Owned by Investor**	**Degree of Control of Investor over Investee**	**Accounting Method**
	Less than 20%	No control	Fair value method
	Between 20% and 50%	Significant influence	Equity method
	Greater than 50%	Control	Consolidation

Fair Value Method: Less Than 20% Ownership

If the investor purchases less than 20% of the outstanding stock of the investee, the investor is considered to have no control over the investee. In this case, it is assumed that the investor purchased the stock primarily to earn dividends or to realize gains on price increases of the stock.

All equity investments of less than 20% of the investee's outstanding stock are accounted for using the **fair value method.** Under the fair value method, entries are recorded for the following:

- Purchase of stock
- Receipt of dividends
- Sale of stock
- Change in fair value

Purchase of Stock The purchase of stock is recorded at its cost. To illustrate, assume that on May 1, Tindell Company purchases 2,000 shares of Lisa Company common stock at $49.90 per share plus a broker fee of $200. The entry to record the purchase of the stock is as follows:

May 1	Investments—Lisa Company Stock		100,000	
	Cash			100,000
	Purchased 2,000 shares of Lisa Company common stock [($49.90 × 2,000 shares) + $200].			

Receipt of Dividends On July 31, Tindell Company receives a dividend of $0.40 per share from Lisa Company. The entry to record the receipt of the dividend is as follows:

July 31	Cash		800	
	Dividend Revenue			800
	Received dividend on Lisa Company common stock (2,000 shares × $0.40).			

Dividend Revenue is reported as part of "Other revenue" on Tindell Company's income statement.

Sale of Stock The sale of a stock investment normally results in a gain or loss. A gain is recorded if the proceeds from the sale exceed the balance of the investment account. A loss is recorded if the proceeds from the sale are less than the balance of the investment account.

To illustrate, on September 1, Tindell Company sells 1,500 shares of Lisa Company stock for $54.50 per share, less a $160 commission. The sale results in a gain of $6,590, computed as follows:

Proceeds from sale	$ 81,590*
Book value (cost) of the stock	(75,000)**
Gain on sale	$ 6,590

*($54.50 × 1,500 shares) – $160
**($100,000 ÷ 2,000 shares) × 1,500 shares

The entry to record the sale is as follows:

Sept. 1	Cash	81,590	
	Gain on Sale of Investments		6,590
	Investments—Lisa Company Stock		75,000
	Sold 1,500 shares of Lisa Company common stock.		

The gain on the sale of investments is reported as part of "Other revenue" on Tindell Company's income statement.

Change in Fair Value At the end of the accounting period, an adjusting entry is made to record the increase in the fair value of the investment. **Fair value** is the market price that the company would receive for a security if it were sold. A change in fair value of an equity investment is recognized in net income as an **unrealized gain or loss** for the period.[2]

To illustrate, on December 31, the remaining 500 shares of Lisa Company stock have a fair value of $55 per share. The increase in fair value results in an unrealized gain of $2,500, computed as follows:

Fair value of investment	$ 27,500*
Balance in the investment account	(25,000)**
	$ 2,500

*500 shares × $55
**$100,000 − $75,000

In order to maintain a record of the original cost of the securities, a valuation account, called Valuation Allowance for Trading Investments, is debited for $2,500, and Unrealized Gain on Trading Investments is credited for $2,500.[3] The adjusting entry to record the increase in fair value of the equity investment is as follows:

Dec. 31	Valuation Allowance for Trading Investments	2,500	
	Unrealized Gain on Trading Investments		2,500

Equity Method: Between 20%–50% Ownership

If a company (investor) purchases between 20% and 50% of the outstanding stock of another company (investee), the investor is considered to have a *significant influence* over the investee. Investments of between 20% and 50% of the investee's outstanding stock are accounted for using the **equity method**.

Under the equity method, a stock investment is recorded at its initial cost. However, the investor's share of the investee's operating results and dividends are also recorded in the investment account as follows:

- *Net Income:* The investor records its share of the net income of the investee as an increase (debit) in the investment account. Its share of any net loss is recorded as a decrease (credit) in the investment account.
- *Dividends:* The investor's share of cash dividends received from the investee are recorded as decreases (credits) to the investment account.

[2] Under *Financial Instruments, Subtopic 825-10, FASB Accounting Standards Update*, all equity securities for which an investor has purchased less than 20% of the outstanding stock are reported as trading securities. The financial statement reporting of trading securities are discussed in a later section of this Appendix.
[3] We assume that the valuation allowance account has a beginning balance of zero to simplify our illustrations.

Purchase of Stock To illustrate, assume that Simpson Inc. purchased its 40% interest in Flanders Corporation's common stock on January 2, 20Y7, for $350,000. The entry to record the purchase is as follows:

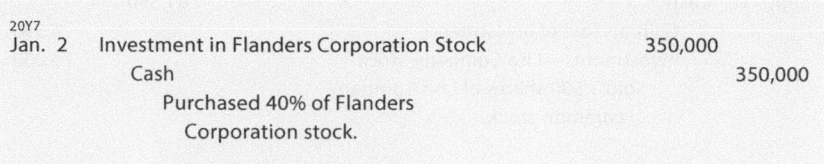

20Y7			
Jan. 2	Investment in Flanders Corporation Stock	350,000	
	Cash		350,000
	Purchased 40% of Flanders		
	Corporation stock.		

Recording Investee Net Income For the year ended December 31, 20Y7, Flanders Corporation reported net income of $105,000. Under the equity method, Simpson Inc. (the investor) records its share of Flanders net income, as follows:

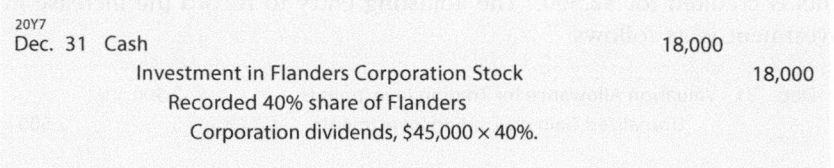

20Y7			
Dec. 31	Investment in Flanders Corporation Stock	42,000	
	Income of Flanders Corporation		42,000
	Recorded 40% share of Flanders		
	Corporation net income, $105,000 × 40%.		

Income of Flanders Corporation is reported on Simpson Inc.'s income statement separately or as part of "Other revenue." If Flanders had a loss during the period, the loss would be recorded as a debit to Loss of Flanders Corporation and a credit to the investment account.

Recording Investee Dividends During the year, Flanders Corporation declared and paid cash dividends of $45,000. Under the equity method, Simpson Inc. (the investor) records its share of Flanders dividends as follows:

20Y7			
Dec. 31	Cash	18,000	
	Investment in Flanders Corporation Stock		18,000
	Recorded 40% share of Flanders		
	Corporation dividends, $45,000 × 40%.		

The effect of recording 40% of Flanders Corporation's net income and dividends is to increase the investment account by $24,000 ($42,000 − $18,000). Thus, Investment in Flanders Corporation Stock increases from $350,000 to $374,000, as shown in Exhibit 2.

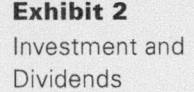

Exhibit 2

Investment and Dividends

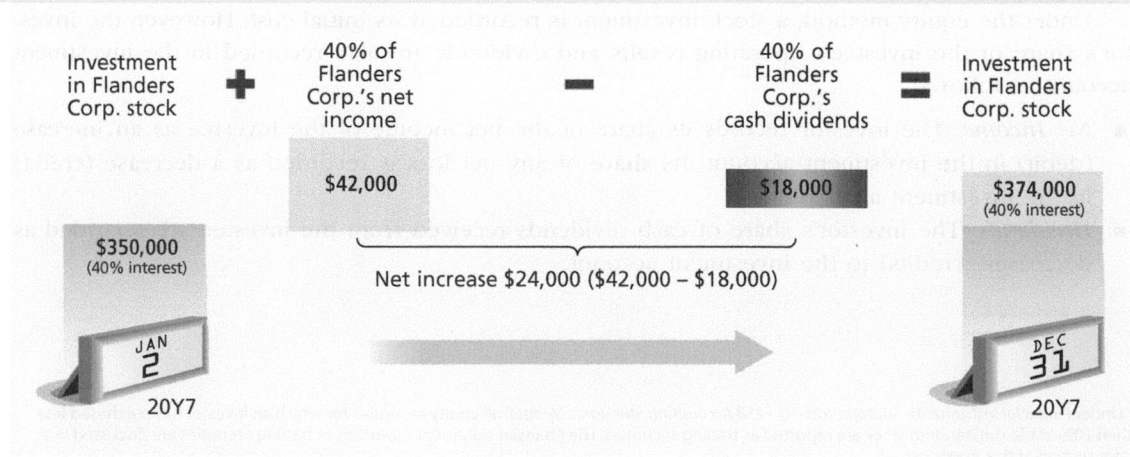

Investments accounted for under the equity method are classified on the balance sheet as noncurrent assets.

Sale of Stock Under the equity method, a gain or loss is normally recorded from the sale of an investment. A gain is recorded if the proceeds exceed the balance of the investment account. A loss is recorded if the proceeds are less than the balance of the investment account.

To illustrate, if Simpson Inc. sold Flanders Corporation's stock on January 1, 20Y8, for $400,000, a gain of $26,000 would be reported, computed as follows:

Proceeds from sale	$ 400,000
Book value of stock investment	(374,000)
Gain on sale	$ 26,000

The entry to record the sale is as follows:

20Y8			
Jan. 1	Cash	400,000	
	Investment in Flanders Corporation Stock		374,000
	Gain on Sale of Flanders Corporation Stock		26,000
	Sold Flanders Corporation stock.		

Consolidation: More Than 50% Ownership

If the investor purchases more than 50% of the outstanding stock of the investee, the investor is considered to have *control* over the investee. The purchase of more than 50% ownership of the investee's stock is termed a **business combination**. The corporation owning all or a majority of the voting stock of another corporation is called a **parent company**. The corporation that is controlled is called the **subsidiary company**.

Parent and subsidiary corporations normally continue to maintain separate accounting records and prepare their own financial statements. In such cases, at the end of the year, the financial statements of the parent and subsidiary are combined and reported as a single company. These combined financial statements are called **consolidated financial statements**. Such statements are normally identified by adding *and Subsidiary(ies)* to the name of the parent corporation or by adding *Consolidated* to the statement title.

Consolidated financial statements are more meaningful than separate statements for each corporation. This is because the parent company, in substance, controls the subsidiaries. The accounting for business combinations, including preparing consolidated financial statements, is described and illustrated in advanced accounting courses and textbooks.

Debt Investments

Debt securities include notes and bonds issued by corporations and governmental organizations. Most companies invest excess cash in bonds as investments to earn interest revenue.

Cost Method

Many debt investments[4] are reported at cost.[5] Typical transactions for debt investments include the following:

- Purchase of debt
- Interest revenue
- Sale of bonds

Purchase of Bonds The purchase of bonds is recorded by debiting an investments account for the cost of acquiring the bonds. This cost includes any fees charged by a broker in acquiring the bonds. If bonds are purchased between interest dates, the buyer must also pay the seller any accrued interest

---

[4] Debt investments may also include installment notes and short-term notes. The accounting for these debt investments is covered in intermediate and advanced accounting courses.

[5] When debt investments are reported at cost, they are called held-to-maturity investments. The reporting of held-to-maturity investments is covered in a later section of this appendix.

since the last interest payment date. Any accrued interest is debited to an interest receivable account rather than to the investment account.

To illustrate, assume that Homer Company purchases $18,000 of bonds at their face amount on March 17, 20Y3, plus accrued interest. The bonds have an interest rate of 6%, payable on July 31 and January 31.

The entry to record the purchase of the bonds is as follows:

20Y3			
Mar. 17	Investments—Bonds	18,000	
	Interest Receivable	135	
	Cash		18,135
	Purchased $18,000, 6% U.S. Treasury bonds.		

Because Homer Company purchased the bonds on March 17, it is also purchasing the accrued interest for 45 days (January 31 to March 17), as shown in Exhibit 3. The accrued interest of $135 is computed as follows:[6]

$$\text{Accrued Interest} = \$18,000 \times 6\% \times (45 \div 360) = \$135$$

The accrued interest is recorded by debiting Interest Receivable for $135. Investments is debited for the purchase price of the bonds of $18,000.

Interest Revenue On July 31, Homer Company receives a semiannual interest payment of $540 ($18,000 × 6% × ½). The $540 interest includes the $135 accrued interest that Homer purchased with the bonds on March 17. Thus, Homer has earned $405 ($540 − $135) of interest revenue since the purchase date, as shown in Exhibit 3.

Exhibit 3

Interest Timeline

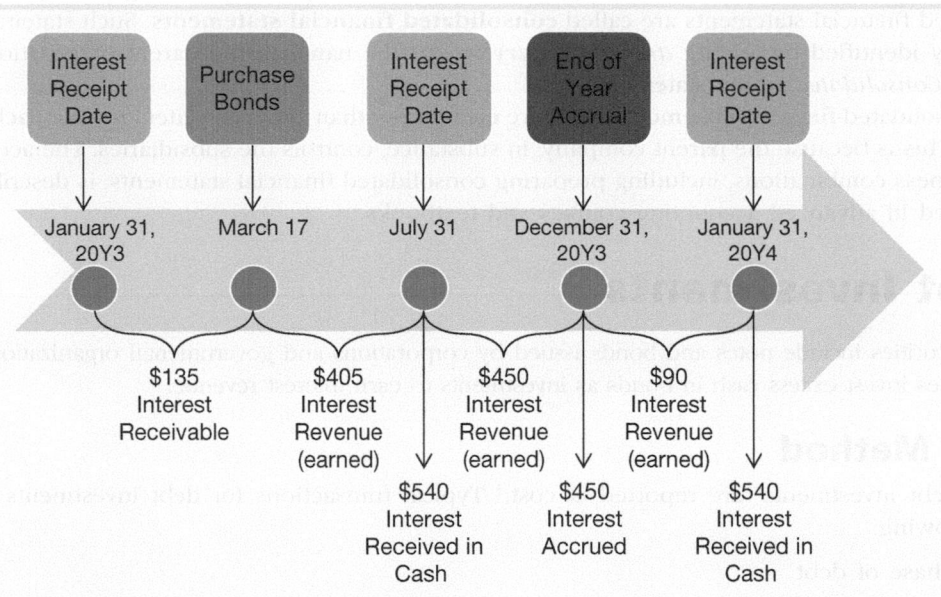

The receipt of the interest on July 31 is recorded as follows:

20Y3			
July 31	Cash	540	
	Interest Receivable		135
	Interest Revenue		405
	Received semiannual interest.		

---

[6] To simplify, a 360-day year is used to compute interest.

Homer Company's accounting period ends on December 31. Thus, an adjusting entry must be made to accrue interest for five months (August 1 to December 31) of $450 [$18,000 × 6% × (5 ÷ 12)], as shown in Exhibit 3. The adjusting entry to record the accrued interest is as follows:

20Y3			
Dec. 31	Interest Receivable	450	
	Interest Revenue		450
	Accrued 5 months of interest.		

For the year ended December 31, 20Y3, Homer Company would report Interest Revenue of $855 ($405 + $450) as part of "Other revenue" on its income statement.

The receipt of the semiannual interest of $540 on January 31, 20Y4, is recorded as follows:

20Y4			
Jan. 31	Cash	540	
	Interest Revenue		90
	Interest Receivable		450
	Received semiannual interest.		

Sale of Bonds The sale of bond investments normally results in a gain or loss. If the proceeds from the sale exceed the balance of the investment account, then a gain is recorded. If the proceeds are less than the balance of the investment account, a loss is recorded.

To illustrate, on January 31, 20Y4, Homer Company sells the bonds at 98, which is a price equal to 98% of their face amount. The sale results in a loss of $360, computed as follows:

Proceeds from sale	$ 17,640*
Book value (cost) of the bonds	(18,000)
Loss on sale of bonds	$ (360)
*$18,000 × 98%	

The entry to record the sale is as follows:

20Y4			
Jan. 31	Cash	17,640	
	Loss on Sale of Investment	360	
	Investments—Bonds		18,000
	Sold bond investment.		

There is no accrued interest upon the date of the sale because the interest payment date is also January 31. If the sale were between interest dates, interest accrued since the last interest payment date would be added to the sale proceeds and credited to Interest Revenue. The loss on the sale of bond investments is reported as part of "Other revenue (loss)" on Homer Company's income statement.

Fair Value Method Debt investments may also be reported at fair value.[7] Under the fair value method, the purchase of debt and the receipt of interest is recorded in a similar manner to the cost method. At the end of the year, an adjusting entry is made to record the change in fair value of the debt investment. This entry is similar to the adjusting entry required for equity investments. We illustrate this entry later in the appendix.

[7] When debt investments are reported at fair value, they are called either trading securities or available-for-sale securities. The reporting of these securities is covered in a later section of this appendix.

Reporting Investments

Generally accepted accounting principles (GAAP) classify equity and debt securities as:

- Trading securities
- Held-to-maturity securities
- Available-for-sale securities

Trading Securities

Trading securities are equity and debt securities that are purchased to earn profits from changes in their market prices. Trading securities are reported as a current asset on the balance sheet if management expects to sell the securities within a year. Otherwise, the securities are reported as a noncurrent asset. Trading securities are valued as a portfolio (group) of securities using the securities' fair values (the fair value method).

To illustrate, assume Maggie Company purchased a portfolio of trading securities during 20Y1. On December 31, 20Y1, the cost and fair values of the securities were as follows:

Name	Number of Shares	Total Cost	Total Fair Value
Armour Company	400	$ 5,000	$ 7,200
Maven, Inc.	500	11,000	7,500
Polaris Co.	200	8,000	10,600
Total		$24,000	$25,300

The portfolio of trading securities is reported on the balance sheet as a current asset with a fair value of $25,300. As illustrated earlier, an adjusting entry is necessary to record the increase in the fair value of $1,300 ($25,300 − $24,000). The adjusting entry on December 31, 20Y1, to record the fair value of the portfolio of trading securities is as follows:

20Y1			
Dec. 31	Valuation Allowance for Trading Investments	1,300	
	Unrealized Gain on Trading Investments		1,300
	To record increase in fair value of trading securities.		

Unrealized Gain on Trading Investments is reported on the income statement. Depending on its significance, it may be reported separately or as "Other revenue" on the income statement. The valuation allowance is reported on the December 31, 20Y1, balance sheet as follows:

Maggie Company
Balance Sheet (selected items)
December 31, 20Y1

Current assets:		
Cash...		$120,000
Trading investments (at cost).............................	$24,000	
Valuation allowance for trading investments	1,300	
Trading investments (at fair value)		25,300

If the fair value of the portfolio of trading securities was less than the cost, then the adjustment would debit Unrealized Loss on Trading Investments and credit Valuation Allowance for Trading Investments for the difference. Unrealized Loss on Trading Investments would be reported on the income statement as Other expenses. Valuation Allowance for Trading Investments would be shown on the balance sheet as a *deduction* from Trading Investments (at cost).

Over time, the valuation allowance account is adjusted to reflect the difference between the cost and the fair value of the portfolio. Thus, increases in the valuation allowance account from the beginning of the period will result in an adjustment to record an unrealized gain, similar to the preceding journal entry. Likewise, decreases in the valuation allowance account from the beginning of the period will result in an adjustment to record an unrealized loss.

Held-to-Maturity Securities

Held-to-maturity securities are debt investments, such as notes or bonds, that a company intends to hold until their maturity date. Only securities with maturity dates, such as corporate notes and bonds, are classified as held-to-maturity. Held-to-maturity securities are primarily purchased to earn interest revenue.

If a held-to-maturity security will mature within a year, it is reported as a current asset on the balance sheet. Held-to-maturity securities maturing beyond a year are reported as noncurrent assets.

Held-to-maturity debt investments are recorded using the cost method, as illustrated earlier in this appendix. If the interest rate on the bonds differs from the market rate of interest, the bonds may be purchased at a premium or discount. In such cases, the premium or discount is amortized over the life of the bonds as an increase (discount) or decrease (premium) to the investment account.

Held-to-maturity bond investments are reported on the balance sheet at their amortized cost. The accounting for held-to-maturity investments, including premium and discount amortization, is described in advanced accounting texts.

Available-for-Sale Securities

Available-for-sale securities are debt securities that a company intends to sell in the future, but not in the near term. Thus, the investment cannot be classified as trading securities or held-to-maturity securities. Available-for-sale securities are recorded at fair value using the fair value method discussed earlier in this appendix. However, changes in the fair values are not reported on the income statement but are reported directly in stockholders' equity.

To illustrate, assume that Campbell Company purchased three debt securities during 20Y1 as available-for-sale securities. On December 31, 20Y1, the cost and fair values of the securities were as follows:

Name	Total Cost	Total Fair Value
Armour Company	$30,000	$32,200
Maven, Inc.	10,000	6,500
Polaris Co.	50,000	52,600
Total	$90,000	$91,300

The portfolio of available-for-sale securities is reported at its fair value of $91,300. An adjusting entry is necessary to record the increase in fair value of $1,300 ($91,300 − $90,000). In order to maintain a record of the original cost of the securities, a valuation account, called *Valuation Allowance for Available-for-Sale Investments*, is debited for $1,300. This account is similar to the valuation account used for trading securities.

Unlike trading securities, the December 31, 20Y1, adjusting entry credits a stockholders' equity account instead of an income statement account. The $1,300 increase in fair value is credited to Unrealized Gain (Loss) on Available-for-Sale Investments.

The adjusting entry on December 31, 20Y1, to record the fair value of the available-for-sale securities is as follows:

20Y1			
Dec. 31	Valuation Allowance for Available-for-Sale Investments	1,300	
	Unrealized Gain (Loss) on Available-for-Sale Investments		1,300
	To record increase in fair value of available-for-sale investments.		

A credit balance in Unrealized Gain (Loss) on Available-for-Sale Investments is added to stockholders' equity, while a debit balance is subtracted from stockholders' equity.[8]

The valuation allowance and the unrealized gain are reported on the December 31, 20Y1, balance sheet as follows:

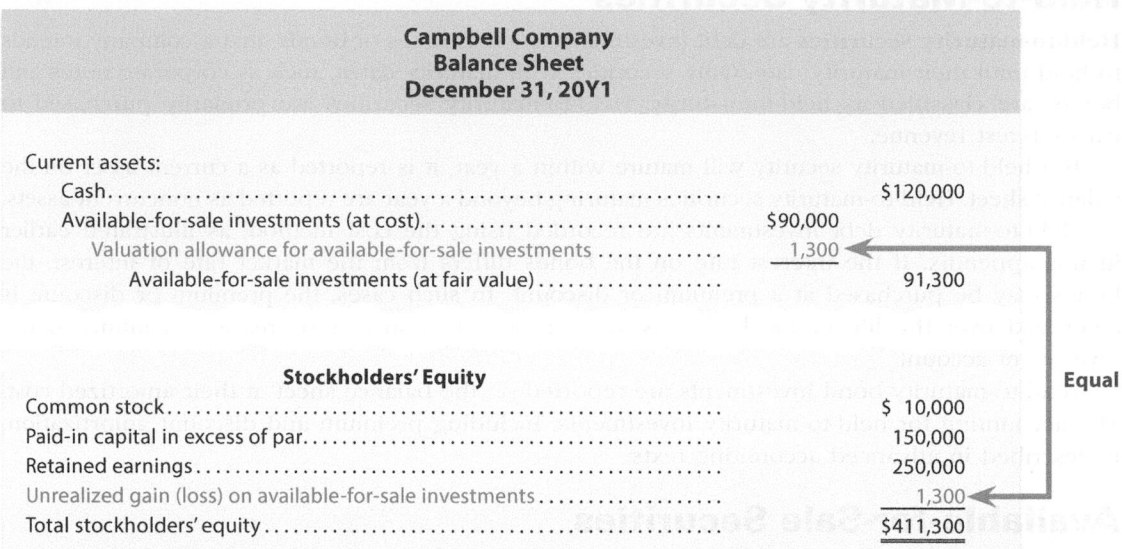

Campbell Company Balance Sheet December 31, 20Y1		
Current assets:		
Cash..		$120,000
Available-for-sale investments (at cost)................	$90,000	
Valuation allowance for available-for-sale investments	1,300	
Available-for-sale investments (at fair value).............		91,300
Stockholders' Equity		
Common stock..		$ 10,000
Paid-in capital in excess of par........................		150,000
Retained earnings.....................................		250,000
Unrealized gain (loss) on available-for-sale investments..........		1,300
Total stockholders' equity.............................		$411,300

As shown, Unrealized Gain (Loss) on Available-for-Sale Investments is reported as an addition to stockholders' equity. In future years, the cumulative effects of unrealized gains and losses are reported in this account.

If the fair value was less than the cost, then the adjustment would debit Unrealized Gain (Loss) on Available-for-Sale Investments and credit Valuation Allowance for Available-for-Sale Investments for the difference. Unrealized Gain (Loss) on Available-for-Sale Investments would be reported in the "Stockholders' Equity" section as a negative item. Valuation Allowance for Available-for-Sale Investments would be shown on the balance sheet as a deduction from available-for-sale investments (at cost).

Over time, the valuation allowance account is adjusted to reflect the difference between the cost and the fair value of the portfolio. Thus, increases in the valuation allowance from the beginning of the period will result in an adjustment to record an increase in the valuation and unrealized gain (loss) accounts, similar to the journal entry illustrated earlier. Likewise, decreases in the valuation allowance from the beginning of the period will result in an adjustment to record decreases in the valuation and unrealized gain (loss) accounts.

Summary

Exhibit 4 summarizes the valuation and balance sheet reporting of trading, available-for-sale, and held-to-maturity securities.

Exhibit 4 Summary of Valuing and Reporting of Investments		**Trading Securities**	**Available-for-Sale Securities**	**Held-to-Maturity Securities**
	Valued at:	Fair value	Fair value	Amortized cost
	Changes in valuation are reported as:	Unrealized gain or loss on the income statement as Other revenue (loss).	Accumulated unrealized gain or loss in stockholders' equity on the balance sheet.	Not applicable. Reported at cost.
	Reported on the balance sheet as:	Fair value: Cost of investments plus or minus valuation allowance.	Fair value: Cost of investments plus or minus valuation allowance.	Amortized cost of investment.
	Classified on balance sheet as:	Either a current asset or noncurrent asset, depending on management's intent.	Either a current or noncurrent asset, depending on manage- ment's intent.	Either a current or noncur- rent asset, depending on remaining term to maturity.

[8] The balance in the Unrealized Gain (Loss) on Available-for-Sale Investments account is reported on the balance sheet as an element of other comprehensive income. See Chapter 14, Appendix 2 for further discussion.

Exercises

SHOW ME HOW

EX D-1   Stock investment transactions

On September 12, 4,000 shares of Aspen Company were acquired at a price of $50 per share plus a $400 brokerage commission. On October 15, a $0.60-per-share dividend was received on the Aspen stock. On November 10, 3,000 shares of the Aspen stock were sold for $40 per share less a $200 brokerage commission. Journalize the entries to record the original purchase, the dividend, and the sale under the fair value method.

SHOW ME HOW

EX D-2   Entries for stock investments, dividends, and sale of stock

Seamus Industries Inc. buys and sells investments as part of its ongoing cash management. The following investment transactions were completed during the year:

Feb. 24.   Acquired 2,000 shares of Tett Co. stock for $80 per share plus a $200 brokerage commission.

May 16.   Acquired 2,000 shares of Issacson Co. stock for $40 per share plus a $100 commission.

July 14.   Sold 500 shares of Tett Co. stock for $100 per share less a $50 brokerage commission.

Aug. 12.   Sold 1,000 shares of Issacson Co. stock for $34 per share less an $80 brokerage commission.

Oct. 31.   Received dividends of $0.30 per share on Tett Co. stock.

Journalize the entries for these transactions under the fair value method.

SHOW ME HOW

EX D-3   Bond investment transactions

Starks Products uses the cost method to account for investments in bonds. Journalize the entries to record the following selected bond investment transactions for Starks Products:

a.   Purchased for cash $150,000 of Iceline, Inc., 6% bonds at 100 plus accrued interest of $1,500.

b.   Received first semiannual interest payment.

c.   Sold $90,000 of the bonds at 102 plus accrued interest of $900.

SHOW ME HOW

EX D-4   Entries for investment in bonds, interest, and sale of bonds

Parilo Company acquired $200,000 of Makofske Co., 5% bonds on May 1, 20Y5, at their face amount. Interest is paid semiannually on May 1 and November 1. On November 1, 20Y5, Parilo sold $80,000 of the bonds for 98.

Journalize the entries to record the following under the cost method:

a.   The initial acquisition of the bonds on May 1.

b.   The semiannual interest received on November 1.

c.   The sale of the bonds on November 1.

d.   The accrual of $1,000 interest on December 31, 20Y5.

SHOW ME HOW

EX D-5   Entries for investments in bonds, interest, and sale of bonds

Kalyagin Investments acquired $150,000 of Jerris Corp., 8% bonds at their face amount on October 1, 20Y2. The bonds pay interest on October 1 and April 1. On April 1, 20Y3, Kalyagin sold $50,000 of Jerris bonds at 102.

Journalize the entries to record the following under the cost method:

a.   The initial acquisition of the Jerris Corp. bonds on October 1, 20Y2.

b.   The adjusting entry for three months of accrued interest earned on the Jerris Corp. bonds on December 31, 20Y2.

c.   The receipt of semiannual interest on April 1, 20Y3.

d.   The sale of $50,000 of Jerris Corp. bonds on April 1, 20Y3, at 102.

SHOW ME HOW

EX D-6 Equity method

On January 2, Yorkshire Company acquired 40% of the outstanding stock of Fain Company for $800,000. For the year ended December 31, Fain earned income of $180,000 and paid dividends of $60,000. Journalize the entries for Yorkshire Company for the purchase of the stock, the share of Fain income, and the dividends received from Fain Company.

✔ **b. $5,040,000**

SHOW ME HOW   EXCEL TEMPLATE

EX D-7   Equity method for stock investment

On January 4, 20Y6, Spandella Company purchased 160,000 shares of Filington Company directly from one of the founders for a price of $30 per share. Filington has 400,000 shares outstanding, including the Spandella shares. On July 2, 20Y6, Filington paid $600,000 in total dividends to its shareholders. On December 31, 20Y6, Filington reported a net income of $1,200,000 for the year. Spandella uses the equity method in accounting for its investment in Filington.

a. Journalize the Spandella Inc. entries for the transactions involving its investment in Filington Company during 20Y6.

b. Determine the December 31, 20Y6, balance of the investment in Filington Company stock account.

SHOW ME HOW

EX D-8   Valuing trading securities at fair value

On January 1, 20Y9, Valuation Allowance for Trading Investments had a zero balance. On December 31, 20Y9, the cost of the trading securities portfolio was $42,500 and the fair value was $48,400. Journalize the December 31, 20Y9, adjusting journal entry to record the unrealized gain or loss on trading investments.

SHOW ME HOW

EX D-9   Fair value journal entries, trading investments

The investments of Charger Inc. include a single investment: 18,500 shares of Raiders Inc. common stock purchased on February 24, 20Y1, for $46 per share including brokerage commission. These shares were classified as trading securities. As of the December 31, 20Y1, balance sheet date, the share price had increased to $52 per share.

a. Journalize the entries to acquire the investment on February 24, and record the adjustment to fair value on December 31, 20Y1.

b. How is the unrealized gain or loss for trading investments reported on the financial statements?

SHOW ME HOW

EX D-10   Fair value journal entries, trading investments

Jets Bancorp Inc. purchased a portfolio of trading securities during 20Y3. The cost and fair value of this portfolio on December 31, 20Y3, was as follows:

Name	Number of Shares	Total Cost	Total Fair Value
Dolphins Inc.	1,600	$28,800	$32,000
Marino Company	1,400	35,000	30,800
Namath Company	600	21,000	19,800
Total		$84,800	$82,600

Journalize the entry to record the adjustment of the trading security portfolio to fair value on December 31, 20Y3.

EXCEL TEMPLATE

EX D-11   Fair value journal entries, trading investments

Storm, Inc. purchased the following trading securities during 20Y9, its first year of operations:

Name	Number of Shares	Cost
Dust Devil, Inc.	1,900	$ 81,700
Gale Co.	850	68,000
Whirlwind Co.	2,850	114,000
Total		$263,700

The market price per share for the trading security portfolio on December 31, 20Y9, was as follows:

	Market Price per Share, Dec. 31, 20Y9
Dust Devil, Inc.	$40
Gale Co.	75
Whirlwind Co.	42

a. Journalize the entry to adjust the trading security portfolio to fair value on December 31, 20Y9.

b. ➤ Describe the income statement impact from the December 31, 20Y9, journal entry.

EX D-12 Balance sheet presentation of trading investments

During 20Y8, its first year of operations, Galileo Company purchased two trading investments as follows:

Security	Shares Purchased	Cost
Hawking Inc.	900	$44,000
Pavlov Co.	1,780	38,000

Assume that as of December 31, 20Y8, the Hawking Inc. stock had a market value of $50 per share, and the Pavlov Co. stock had a market value of $24 per share. Galileo Company had net income of $300,000 and paid no dividends for the year ended December 31, 20Y8. All of the trading investments are classified as current assets.

a. Prepare the "Current assets" section of the balance sheet presentation for the trading investments.

b. What impact would the change in fair value have on the "Stockholders' Equity" section of the balance sheet?

EX D-13 Valuing available-for-sale securities at fair value

On January 1, 20Y5, Valuation Allowance for Available-for-Sale Investments had a zero balance. On December 31, 20Y5, the cost of the available-for-sale securities was $22,280 and the fair value was $25,450. Journalize the adjusting entry to record the unrealized gain or loss on available-for-sale investments on December 31, 20Y5.

EX D-14 Fair value journal entries, available-for-sale investments

The investments of Steelers Inc. include a single investment: $400,000 of Bengals Inc. 5% bonds purchased at 100 on January 1, 20Y7. These bonds were classified as available-for-sale securities. As of the December 31, 20Y7, balance sheet date, the fair value of the bonds declined to $392,800.

a. Journalize the entries to acquire the investment on January 1, 20Y7, and record the adjustment to fair value on December 31, 20Y7.

b. How is the unrealized gain or loss for available-for-sale investments disclosed on the financial statements?

Nike Inc., Form 10-K for the Fiscal Year Ended May 31, 2017 Selected Excerpts*

NIKE, Inc .

(Exact name of Registrant as specified in its charter)

Management's Annual Report on Internal Control Over Financial Reporting

Management is responsible for establishing and maintaining adequate internal control over financial reporting, as such term is defined in Rule 13(a)—15(f) and Rule 15(d)—15(f) of the Securities Exchange Act of 1934, as amended. Internal control over financial reporting is a process designed to provide reasonable assurance regarding the reliability of financial reporting and the preparation of the financial statements for external purposes in accordance with generally accepted accounting principles in the United States of America. Internal control over financial reporting includes those policies and procedures that: (i) pertain to the maintenance of records that, in reasonable detail, accurately and fairly reflect the transactions and dispositions of assets of the Company; (ii) provide reasonable assurance that transactions are recorded as necessary to permit preparation of financial statements in accordance with generally accepted accounting principles, and that receipts and expenditures of the Company are being made only in accordance with authorizations of our management and directors; and (iii) provide reasonable assurance regarding prevention or timely detection of unauthorized acquisition, use or disposition of assets of the Company that could have a material effect on the financial statements.

While "reasonable assurance" is a high level of assurance, it does not mean absolute assurance. Because of its inherent limitations, internal control over financial reporting may not prevent or detect every misstatement and instance of fraud. Controls are susceptible to manipulation, especially in instances of fraud caused by the collusion of two or more people, including our senior management. Also, projections of any evaluation of effectiveness to future periods are subject to the risk that controls may become inadequate because of changes in conditions, or that the degree of compliance with the policies or procedures may deteriorate.

Under the supervision and with the participation of our Chief Executive Officer and Chief Financial Officer, our management conducted an evaluation of the effectiveness of our internal control over financial reporting based upon the framework in *Internal Control — Integrated Framework (2013)* issued by the Committee of Sponsoring Organizations of the Treadway Commission (COSO). Based on the results of our evaluation, our management concluded that our internal control over financial reporting was effective as of May 31, 2017.

PricewaterhouseCoopers LLP, an independent registered public accounting firm, has audited (1) the Consolidated Financial Statements and (2) the effectiveness of our internal control over financial reporting as of May 31, 2017, as stated in their report herein.

Mark G. Parker

Chairman, President and Chief Executive Officer

Andrew Campion

Chief Financial Officer

* The entire Nike Inc., Form 10-K is available on the companion website at cengage.com.

Report of Independent Registered Public Accounting Firm

To the Board of Directors and Shareholders of NIKE, Inc.:

In our opinion, the consolidated financial statements listed in the index appearing under Item 15(a)(1) present fairly, in all material respects, the financial position of NIKE, Inc. and its subsidiaries as of May 31, 2017 and 2016, and the results of their operations and their cash flows for each of the three years in the period ended May 31, 2017 in conformity with accounting principles generally accepted in the United States of America. In addition, in our opinion, the financial statement schedule listed in the index appearing under Item 15(a)(2) presents fairly, in all material respects, the information set forth therein when read in conjunction with the related consolidated financial statements. Also in our opinion, the Company maintained, in all material respects, effective internal control over financial reporting as of May 31, 2017, based on criteria established in *Internal Control — Integrated Framework (2013)* issued by the Committee of Sponsoring Organizations of the Treadway Commission (COSO). The Company's management is responsible for these financial statements and financial statement schedule, for maintaining effective internal control over financial reporting and for its assessment of the effectiveness of internal control over financial reporting, included in Management's Annual Report on Internal Control over Financial Reporting appearing under Item 8. Our responsibility is to express opinions on these financial statements, on the financial statement schedule and on the Company's internal control over financial reporting based on our integrated audits. We conducted our audits in accordance with the standards of the Public Company Accounting Oversight Board (United States). Those standards require that we plan and perform the audits to obtain reasonable assurance about whether the financial statements are free of material misstatement and whether effective internal control over financial reporting was maintained in all material respects. Our audits of the financial statements included examining, on a test basis, evidence supporting the amounts and disclosures in the financial statements, assessing the accounting principles used and significant estimates made by management and evaluating the overall financial statement presentation. Our audit of internal control over

financial reporting included obtaining an understanding of internal control over financial reporting, assessing the risk that a material weakness exists and testing and evaluating the design and operating effectiveness of internal control based on the assessed risk. Our audits also included performing such other procedures as we considered necessary in the circumstances. We believe that our audits provide a reasonable basis for our opinions.

A company's internal control over financial reporting is a process designed to provide reasonable assurance regarding the reliability of financial reporting and the preparation of financial statements for external purposes in accordance with generally accepted accounting principles. A company's internal control over financial reporting includes those policies and procedures that (i) pertain to the maintenance of records that, in reasonable detail, accurately and fairly reflect the transactions and dispositions of the assets of the company; (ii) provide reasonable assurance that transactions are recorded as necessary to permit preparation of financial statements in accordance with generally accepted accounting principles, and that receipts and expenditures of the company are being made only in accordance with authorizations of management and directors of the company; and (iii) provide reasonable assurance regarding prevention or timely detection of unauthorized acquisition, use, or disposition of the company's assets that could have a material effect on the financial statements.

Because of its inherent limitations, internal control over financial reporting may not prevent or detect misstatements. Also, projections of any evaluation of effectiveness to future periods are subject to the risk that controls may become inadequate because of changes in conditions, or that the degree of compliance with the policies or procedures may deteriorate.

/S/ PRICEWATERHOUSECOOPERS LLP

Portland, Oregon

July 20, 2017

NIKE, Inc. Consolidated Statements of Income

(In millions, except per share data)		Year Ended May 31,				
		2017		2016		2015
Revenues	$	34,350	$	32,376	$	30,601
Cost of sales		19,038		17,405		16,534
Gross profit		15,312		14,971		14,067
Demand creation expense		3,341		3,278		3,213
Operating overhead expense		7,222		7,191		6,679
Total selling and administrative expense		10,563		10,469		9,892
Interest expense (income), net		59		19		28
Other (income) expense, net		(196)		(140)		(58)
Income before income taxes		4,886		4,623		4,205
Income tax expense		646		863		932
NET INCOME	$	**4,240**	$	**3,760**	$	**3,273**
Earnings per common share:						
Basic	$	2.56	$	2.21	$	1.90
Diluted	$	2.51	$	2.16	$	1.85
Dividends declared per common share	$	0.70	$	0.62	$	0.54

The accompanying Notes to the Consolidated Financial Statements are an integral part of this statement.

NIKE, Inc. Consolidated Statements of Comprehensive Income

(In millions)	Year Ended May 31,		
	2017	2016	2015
Net income	$ 4,240	$ 3,760	$ 3,273
Other comprehensive income (loss), net of tax:			
Change in net foreign currency translation adjustment	16	(176)	(20)
Change in net gains (losses) on cash flow hedges	(515)	(757)	1,188
Change in net gains (losses) on other	(32)	5	(7)
Total other comprehensive income (loss), net of tax	(531)	(928)	1,161
TOTAL COMPREHENSIVE INCOME	$ 3,709	$ 2,832	$ 4,434

The accompanying Notes to the Consolidated Financial Statements are an integral part of this statement.

NIKE, Inc. Consolidated Balance Sheets

(In millions)	May 31,	
	2017	2016
ASSETS		
Current assets:		
Cash and equivalents	$ 3,808	$ 3,138
Short-term investments	2,371	2,319
Accounts receivable, net	3,677	3,241
Inventories	5,055	4,838
Prepaid expenses and other current assets	1,150	1,489
Total current assets	16,061	15,025
Property, plant and equipment, net	3,989	3,520
Identifiable intangible assets, net	283	281
Goodwill	139	131
Deferred income taxes and other assets	2,787	2,422
TOTAL ASSETS	$ 23,259	$ 21,379
LIABILITIES AND SHAREHOLDERS' EQUITY		
Current liabilities:		
Current portion oflong-term debt	$ 6	$ 44
Notes payable	325	1
Accounts payable	2,048	2,191
Accrued liabilities	3,011	3,037
Income taxes payable	84	85
Total current liabilities	5,474	5,358
Long-term debt	3,471	1,993
Deferred income taxes and other liabilities	1,907	1,770
Commitments and contingencies		
Redeemable preferred stock	—	—
Shareholders' equity:		
Common stock at stated value:		
Class A convertible — 329 and 353 shares outstanding	—	—
Class B — 1,314 and 1,329 shares outstanding	3	3
Capital in excess of stated value	8,638	7,786
Accumulated other comprehensive (loss) income	(213)	318
Retained earnings	3,979	4,151
Total shareholders' equity	12,407	12,258
TOTAL LIABILITIES AND SHAREHOLDERS' EQUITY	$ 23,259	$ 21,379

The accompanying Notes to the Consolidated Financial Statements are an integral part of this statement.

NIKE, Inc. Consolidated Statements of Cash Flows

(In millions)	Year Ended May 31,		
	2017	2016	2015
Cash provided by operations:			
Net income	$ 4,240	$ 3,760	$ 3,273
Income charges (credits) not affecting cash:			
Depreciation	706	649	606
Deferred income taxes	(273)	(80)	(113)
Stock-based compensation	215	236	191
Amortization and other	10	13	43
Net foreign currency adjustments	(117)	98	424
Changes in certain working capital components and other assets and liabilities:			
(Increase) decrease in accounts receivable	(426)	60	(216)
(Increase) in inventories	(231)	(590)	(621)
(Increase) in prepaid expenses and other current assets	(120)	(161)	(144)
(Decrease) increase in accounts payable, accrued liabilities and income taxes payable	(364)	(889)	1,237
Cash provided by operations	3,640	3,096	4,680
Cash used by investing activities:			
Purchases of short-term investments	(5,928)	(5,367)	(4,936)
Maturities of short-term investments	3,623	2,924	3,655
Sales of short-term investments	2,423	2,386	2,216
Investments in reverse repurchase agreements	—	150	(150)
Additions to property, plant and equipment	(1,105)	(1,143)	(963)
Disposals of property, plant and equipment	13	10	3
Other investing activities	(34)	6	—
Cash used by investing activities	(1,008)	(1,034)	(175)
Cash used by financing activities:			
Net proceeds from long-term debt issuance	1,482	981	—
Long-term debt payments, including current portion	(44)	(106)	(7)
Increase (decrease) in notes payable	327	(67)	(63)
Payments on capital lease and other financing obligations	(17)	(7)	(19)
Proceeds from exercise of stock options and other stock issuances	489	507	514
Excess tax benefits from share-based payment arrangements	177	281	218
Repurchase of common stock	(3,223)	(3,238)	(2,534)
Dividends — common and preferred	(1,133)	(1,022)	(899)
Cash used by financing activities	(1,942)	(2,671)	(2,790)
Effect of exchange rate changes on cash and equivalents	(20)	(105)	(83)
Net increase (decrease) in cash and equivalents	670	(714)	1,632
Cash and equivalents, beginning of year	3,138	3,852	2,220
CASH AND EQUIVALENTS, END OF YEAR	$ 3,808	$ 3,138	$ 3,852
Supplemental disclosure of cash flow information:			
Cash paid during the year for:			
Interest, net of capitalized interest	$ 98	$ 70	$ 53
Income taxes	703	748	1,262
Non-cash additions to property, plant and equipment	266	252	206
Dividends declared and not paid	300	271	240

The accompanying Notes to the Consolidated Financial Statements are an integral part of this statement.

NIKE, Inc. Consolidated Statements of Shareholders' Equity

| | Common Stock | | | | Capital in Excess of Stated Value | Accumulated Other Comprehensive Income | Retained Earnings | Total |
| | Class A | | Class B | | | | | |
(In millions, except per share data)	Shares	Amount	Shares	Amount				
Balance at May 31, 2014	355	$ —	1,385	$ 3	$ 5,865	$ 85	$ 4,871	$ 10,824
Stock options exercised			27		639			639
Repurchase of Class B Common Stock			(58)		(9)		(2,525)	(2,534)
Dividends on common stock ($0.54 per share) and preferred stock ($0.10 per share)							(931)	(931)
Issuance of shares to employees, net of shares withheld for employee taxes			3		87		(3)	84
Stock-based compensation					191			191
Net income							3,273	3,273
Other comprehensive income (loss)						1,161		1,161
Balance at May 31, 2015	355	$ —	1,357	$ 3	$ 6,773	$ 1,246	$ 4,685	$ 12,707
Stock options exercised			22		680			680
Conversion to Class B Common Stock	(2)	—	2	—				—
Repurchase of Class B Common Stock			(55)		(8)		(3,230)	(3,238)
Dividends on common stock ($0.62 per share) and preferred stock ($0.10 per share)							(1,053)	(1,053)
Issuance of shares to employees, net of shares withheld for employee taxes			3		105		(11)	94
Stock-based compensation					236			236
Net income							3,760	3,760
Other comprehensive income (loss)						(928)		(928)
Balance at May 31, 2016	353	$ —	1,329	$ 3	$ 7,786	$ 318	$ 4,151	$ 12,258
Stock options exercised			17		525			525
Conversion to Class B Common Stock	(24)	—	24	—				—
Repurchase of Class B Common Stock			(60)		(9)		(3,240)	(3,249)
Dividends on common stock ($0.70 per share) and preferred stock ($0.10 per share)							(1,159)	(1,159)
Issuance of shares to employees, net of shares withheld for employee taxes			4		121		(13)	108
Stock-based compensation					215			215
Net income							4,240	4,240
Other comprehensive income (loss)						(531)		(531)
Balance at May 31, 2017	329	$ —	1,314	$ 3	$ 8,638	$ (213)	$ 3,979	$ 12,407

The accompanying Notes to the Consolidated Financial Statements are an integral part of this statement.

NOTE 1 — Summary of Significant Accounting Policies

Description of Business

NIKE, Inc. is a worldwide leader in the design, development and worldwide marketing and selling of athletic footwear, apparel, equipment, accessories and services. NIKE, Inc. portfolio brands include the NIKE Brand, Jordan Brand, Hurley and Converse. The NIKE Brand is focused on performance athletic footwear, apparel, equipment, accessories and services across a wide range of sport categories, amplified with sport-inspired sportswear products carrying the Swoosh trademark as well as other NIKE Brand trademarks. The Jordan Brand is focused on athletic and casual footwear, apparel and accessories using the Jumpman trademark. Sales and operating results of Jordan Brand products are reported within the respective NIKE Brand geographic operating segments. The Hurley brand is focused on surf and action sports and youth lifestyle footwear, apparel and accessories, using the Hurley trademark. Sales and operating results of Hurley brand products are reported within the NIKE Brand's North America geographic operating segment. Converse designs, distributes, markets and sells casual sneakers, apparel and accessories under the Converse, Chuck Taylor, All Star, One Star, Star Chevron and Jack Purcell trademarks. In some markets outside the U.S., these trademarks are licensed to third parties who design, distribute, market and sell similar products. Operating results of the Converse brand are reported on a stand-alone basis.

Basis of Consolidation

The Consolidated Financial Statements include the accounts of NIKE, Inc. and its subsidiaries (the "Company"). All significant intercompany transactions and balances have been eliminated.

On November 19, 2015, the Company announced a two-for-one split of both NIKE Class A and Class B Common Stock. The stock split was in the form of a 100 percent stock dividend payable on December 23, 2015 to shareholders of record at the close of business on December 9, 2015. Common stock began trading at the split-adjusted price on December 24, 2015. All share and per share amounts presented reflect the stock split.

Reclassifications

Certain prior year amounts have been reclassified to conform to fiscal 2017 presentation.

Revenue Recognition

Wholesale revenues are recognized when title and the risks and rewards of ownership have passed to the customer, based on the terms of sale. This occurs upon shipment or upon receipt by the customer depending on the country of the sale and the agreement with the customer. Retail store revenues are recorded at the time of sale and online store revenues are recorded upon delivery to the customer. Provisions for post-invoice sales discounts, returns and miscellaneous claims from customers are estimated and recorded as a reduction to revenue at the time of sale. Post-invoice sales discounts consist of contractual programs with certain customers or discretionary discounts that are expected to be granted to certain customers at a later date. Estimates of discretionary discounts, returns and claims are based on (1) historical rates, (2) specific identification of outstanding claims and outstanding returns not yet received from customers and (3) estimated discounts, returns and claims expected, but not yet finalized with customers. As of May 31, 2017 and 2016, the Company's reserve balances for post-invoice sales discounts, returns and miscellaneous claims were $643 million and $789 million, respectively.

Cost of Sales

Cost of sales consists primarily of inventory costs, as well as warehousing costs (including the cost of warehouse labor), third-party royalties, certain foreign currency hedge gains and losses and research, design and development costs. Outbound shipping and handling costs are expensed as incurred and included in *Cost of sales*.

Demand Creation Expense

Demand creation expense consists of advertising and promotion costs, including costs of endorsement contracts, television, digital and print advertising, brand events and retail brand presentation. Advertising production costs are expensed the first time an advertisement is run. Advertising communication costs are expensed when the advertisement appears. Costs related to brand events are expensed when the event occurs. Costs related to retail brand presentation are expensed when the presentation is completed and delivered.

A significant amount of the Company's promotional expenses result from payments under endorsement contracts. Accounting for endorsement payments is based upon specific contract provisions. Generally, endorsement payments are expensed on a straight-line basis over the term of the contract after giving recognition to periodic performance compliance provisions of the contracts. Prepayments made under contracts are included in *Prepaid expenses and other current assets* or *Deferred income taxes and other assets* depending on the period to which the prepayment applies.

Certain contracts provide for contingent payments to endorsers based upon specific achievements in their sports (e.g., winning a championship). The Company records demand creation expense for these amounts when the endorser achieves the specific goal.

Certain contracts provide for variable payments based upon endorsers maintaining a level of performance in their sport over an extended period of time (e.g., maintaining a specified ranking in a sport for a year). When the Company determines payments are probable, the amounts are reported in *Demand creation expense* ratably over the contract period based on the Company's best estimate of the endorser's performance. In these instances, to the extent that actual payments to the endorser differ from the Company's estimate due to changes in the endorser's performance, increased or decreased demand creation expense may be recorded in a future period.

Certain contracts provide for royalty payments to endorsers based upon a predetermined percent of sales of particular products. The Company expenses these payments in *Cost of sales* as the related sales occur. In certain contracts, the Company offers minimum guaranteed royalty payments. For contracts for which the Company estimates it will not meet the minimum guaranteed amount of royalty fees through sales of product, the Company records the amount of the guaranteed payment in excess of that earned through sales of product in *Demand creation expense* uniformly over the contract period.

Through cooperative advertising programs, the Company reimburses customers for certain costs of advertising the Company's products. The Company records these costs in *Demand creation expense* at the point in time when it is obligated to its customers for the costs. This obligation may arise prior to the related advertisement being run.

Total advertising and promotion expenses were $3,341 million, $3,278 million and $3,213 million for the years ended May 31, 2017, 2016 and 2015, respectively. Prepaid advertising and promotion expenses totaled $558 million and $540 million at May 31, 2017 and 2016, respectively, of which $311 million and $272 million, respectively, was recorded in *Prepaid expenses and other current assets*, and $247 million and $268 million, respectively, was recorded in *Deferred income taxes and other assets*, depending on the period to which the prepayment applies.

Operating Overhead Expense

Operating overhead expense consists primarily of wage and benefit-related expenses as well as other administrative costs, such as rent, depreciation and amortization, professional services and meetings and travel.

Cash and Equivalents

Cash and equivalents represent cash and short-term, highly liquid investments, that are both readily convertible to known amounts of cash, and so near their maturity that they present insignificant risk of changes in value because of changes in interest rates, including commercial paper, U.S. Treasury, U.S. Agency, money market funds, time deposits and corporate debt securities with maturities of 90 days or less at the date of purchase.

Short-Term Investments

Short-term investments consist of highly liquid investments, including commercial paper, U.S. Treasury, U.S. Agency, time deposits and corporate debt securities, with maturities over 90 days at the date of purchase. Debt securities that the Company has the ability and positive intent to hold to maturity are carried at amortized cost. At May 31, 2017 and 2016, the Company did not hold any short-term investments that were classified as trading or held-to-maturity.

At May 31, 2017 and 2016, *Short-term investments* consisted of available-for-sale securities. Available-for-sale securities are recorded at fair value with unrealized gains and losses reported, net of tax, in *Accumulated other comprehensive income*, unless unrealized losses are determined to be other than temporary. Realized gains and losses on the sale of securities are determined by specific identification. The Company considers all available-for-sale securities, including those with maturity dates beyond 12 months, as available to support current operational liquidity needs and therefore classifies all securities with maturity dates beyond 90 days at the date of purchase as current assets within *Short-term investments* on the Consolidated Balance Sheets.

Refer to Note 6 — Fair Value Measurements for more information on the Company's short-term investments.

Allowance for Uncollectible Accounts Receivable

Accounts receivable, net consist primarily of amounts receivable from customers. The Company makes ongoing estimates relating to the collectability of its accounts receivable and maintains an allowance for estimated losses resulting from the inability of its customers to make required payments. In determining the amount of the allowance, the Company considers historical levels of credit losses and makes judgments about the creditworthiness of significant customers based on ongoing credit evaluations. Accounts receivable with anticipated collection dates greater than 12 months from the balance sheet date and related allowances are considered non-current and recorded in *Deferred income taxes and other assets*. The allowance for uncollectible accounts receivable was $19 million and $43 million at May 31, 2017 and 2016, respectively.

Inventory Valuation

Inventories are stated at lower of cost or market and valued on either an average or specific identification cost basis. For inventories in transit that represent direct shipments to customers, the related inventory and cost of sales are recognized on a specific identification basis. Inventory costs primarily consist of product cost from the Company's suppliers, as well as inbound freight, import duties, taxes, insurance and logistics and other handling fees.

Property, Plant and Equipment and Depreciation

Property, plant and equipment are recorded at cost. Depreciation is determined on a straight-line basis for land improvements, buildings and leasehold improvements over 2 to 40 years and for machinery and equipment over 2 to 15 years.

Depreciation and amortization of assets used in manufacturing, warehousing and product distribution are recorded in *Cost of sales*. Depreciation and amortization of all other assets are recorded in *Operating overhead expense*.

Software Development Costs

Internal Use Software: Expenditures for major software purchases and software developed for internal use are capitalized and amortized over a 2 to 12 year period on a straight-line basis. The Company's policy provides for the capitalization of external direct costs of materials and services associated with developing or obtaining internal use computer software. In addition, the Company also capitalizes certain payroll and payroll-related costs for employees who are directly associated with internal use computer software projects. The amount of capitalizable payroll costs with respect to these employees is limited to the time directly spent on such projects. Costs associated with preliminary project stage activities, training, maintenance and all other post-implementation stage activities are expensed as incurred.

Computer Software to be Sold, Leased or Otherwise Marketed: Development costs of computer software to be sold, leased or otherwise marketed as an integral part of a product are subject to capitalization beginning when a product's technological feasibility has been established and ending when a product is available for general release to customers. In most instances, the Company's products are released soon after technological feasibility has been established. Therefore, software development costs incurred subsequent to achievement of technological feasibility are usually not significant, and generally most software development costs have been expensed as incurred.

Impairment of Long-Lived Assets

The Company reviews the carrying value of long-lived assets or asset groups to be used in operations whenever events or changes in circumstances indicate that the carrying amount of the assets might not be recoverable. Factors that would necessitate an impairment assessment include a significant adverse change in the extent or manner in which an asset is used, a significant adverse change in legal factors or the business climate that could affect the value of the asset or a significant decline in the observable market value of an asset, among others. If such facts indicate a potential impairment, the Company would assess the recoverability of an asset group by determining if the carrying value of the asset group exceeds the sum of the projected undiscounted cash flows expected to result from the use and eventual disposition of the assets over the remaining economic life of the primary asset in the asset group. If the recoverability test indicates that the carrying value of the asset group is not recoverable, the Company will estimate the fair value of the asset group using appropriate valuation methodologies, which would typically include an estimate of discounted cash flows. Any impairment would be measured as the difference between the asset group's carrying amount and its estimated fair value.

Goodwill and Indefinite-Lived Intangible Assets

The Company performs annual impairment tests on goodwill and intangible assets with indefinite lives in the fourth quarter of each fiscal year or when events occur or circumstances change that would, more likely than not, reduce the fair value of a reporting unit or an intangible asset with an indefinite life below its carrying value. Events or changes in circumstances that may trigger interim impairment reviews include significant changes in business climate, operating results, planned investments in the reporting unit, planned divestitures or an expectation that the carrying amount may not be recoverable, among other factors. The Company may first assess qualitative factors to determine whether it is more likely than not that the fair value of a reporting unit is less than its carrying amount. If, after assessing the totality of events and circumstances, the Company determines that it is more likely than not that the fair value of the reporting unit is greater than its carrying amount, the two-step impairment test is unnecessary. The two-step impairment test first requires the Company to estimate the fair value of its reporting units. If the carrying value of a reporting unit exceeds its fair value, the goodwill of that reporting unit is potentially impaired and the Company proceeds to step two of the impairment analysis. In step two of the analysis, the Company measures and records an impairment loss equal to the excess of the carrying value of the reporting unit's goodwill over its implied fair value, if any.

Indefinite-lived intangible assets primarily consist of acquired trade names and trademarks. The Company may first perform a qualitative assessment to determine whether it is more likely than not that an indefinite-lived intangible asset is impaired. If, after assessing the totality of events and circumstances, the Company determines that it is more likely than not that the indefinite-lived intangible asset is not impaired, no quantitative fair value measurement is necessary. If a quantitative fair value measurement calculation is required for these intangible assets, the Company utilizes the relief-from-royalty method. This method assumes that trade names and trademarks have value to the extent that their owner is relieved of the obligation to pay royalties for the benefits received from them. This method requires the Company to estimate the future revenue for the related brands, the appropriate royalty rate and the weighted average cost of capital.

Operating Leases

The Company leases retail store space, certain distribution and warehouse facilities, office space and other non-real estate assets under operating leases. Operating lease agreements may contain rent escalation clauses, renewal options, rent holidays or certain landlord incentives, including tenant improvement allowances. Rent expense for non-cancelable operating leases with scheduled rent increases or landlord incentives are recognized on a straight-line basis over the lease term, beginning with the effective lease commencement date, which is generally the date in which the Company takes possession of or controls the physical use of the property. Certain leases also provide for contingent rent, which is generally determined as a percent of sales in excess of specified levels. A contingent rent liability is recognized together with the corresponding rent expense when specified levels have been achieved or when the Company determines that achieving the specified levels during the period is probable.

Fair Value Measurements

The Company measures certain financial assets and liabilities at fair value on a recurring basis, including derivatives and available-for-sale securities. Fair value is the price the Company would receive to sell an asset or pay to transfer a liability in an orderly transaction with a market participant at the measurement date. The Company uses a three-level hierarchy established by the Financial Accounting Standards Board (FASB) that prioritizes fair value measurements based on the types of inputs used for the various valuation techniques (market approach, income approach and cost approach).

The levels of the fair value hierarchy are described below:

- Level 1: Quoted prices in active markets for identical assets or liabilities.

- Level 2: Inputs other than quoted prices that are observable for the asset or liability, either directly or indirectly; these include quoted prices for similar assets or liabilities in active markets and quoted prices for identical or similar assets or liabilities in markets that are not active.

- Level 3: Unobservable inputs for which there is little or no market data available, which require the reporting entity to develop its own assumptions.

The Company's assessment of the significance of a particular input to the fair value measurement in its entirety requires judgment and considers factors specific to the asset or liability. Financial assets and liabilities are classified in their entirety based on the most conservative level of input that is significant to the fair value measurement.

Pricing vendors are utilized for a majority of Level 1 and Level 2 investments. These vendors either provide a quoted market price in an active market or use observable inputs without applying significant adjustments in their pricing. Observable inputs include broker quotes, interest rates and yield curves observable at commonly quoted intervals, volatilities and credit risks. The fair value of derivative contracts is determined using observable market inputs such as the daily market foreign currency rates, forward pricing curves, currency volatilities, currency correlations and interest rates and considers nonperformance risk of the Company and that of its counterparties.

Level 1 investments include U.S. Treasury securities. Assets and liabilities included within Level 2 include commercial paper, U.S. Agency securities, money market funds, time deposits, corporate debt securities and derivative contracts. Level 3 investments are valued using internally developed models with unobservable inputs and are an immaterial portion of our portfolio.

The Company's fair value measurement process includes comparing fair values to another independent pricing vendor to ensure appropriate fair values are recorded.

Refer to Note 6 — Fair Value Measurements for additional information.

Foreign Currency Translation and Foreign Currency Transactions

Adjustments resulting from translating foreign functional currency financial statements into U.S. Dollars are included in the foreign currency translation adjustment, a component of *Accumulated other comprehensive income* in *Total shareholders' equity*.

The Company's global subsidiaries have various assets and liabilities, primarily receivables and payables, which are denominated in currencies other than their functional currency. These balance sheet items are subject to re-measurement, the impact of which is recorded in *Other (income) expense, net*, within the Consolidated Statements of Income.

Accounting for Derivatives and Hedging Activities

The Company uses derivative financial instruments to reduce its exposure to changes in foreign currency exchange rates and interest rates. All derivatives are recorded at fair value on the Consolidated Balance Sheets and changes in the fair value of derivative financial instruments are either recognized in *Accumulated other comprehensive income* (a component of *Total shareholders' equity*), *Long-term debt* or *Net income* depending on the nature of the underlying exposure, whether the derivative is formally designated as a hedge and, if designated, the extent to which the hedge is effective. The Company classifies the cash flows at settlement from derivatives in the same category as the cash flows from the related hedged items. For undesignated hedges and designated cash flow hedges, this is primarily within the *Cash provided by operations* component of the Consolidated Statements of Cash Flows. For designated net investment hedges, this is within the *Cash used by investing activities* component of the Consolidated Statements of Cash Flows. For the Company's fair value hedges, which are interest rate swaps used to mitigate the change in fair value of its fixed-rate debt attributable to changes in interest rates, the related cash flows from periodic interest payments are reflected within the *Cash provided by operations* component of the Consolidated Statements of Cash Flows. Refer to Note 16 — Risk Management and Derivatives for more information on the Company's risk management program and derivatives.

Stock-Based Compensation

The Company estimates the fair value of options and stock appreciation rights granted under the NIKE, Inc. Stock Incentive Plan and employees' purchase rights under the Employee Stock Purchase Plans (ESPPs) using the Black-Scholes option pricing model. The Company recognizes this fair value, net of estimated forfeitures, as *Operating overhead expense* in the Consolidated Statements of Income over the vesting period using the straight-line method.

Refer to Note 11 — Common Stock and Stock-Based Compensation for more information on the Company's stock-based compensation programs.

Income Taxes

The Company accounts for income taxes using the asset and liability method. This approach requires the recognition of deferred tax assets and liabilities for the expected future tax consequences of temporary differences between the carrying amounts and the tax basis of assets and liabilities. The Company records a valuation allowance to reduce deferred tax assets to the amount management believes is more likely than not to be realized. United States income taxes are provided currently on financial statement earnings of non-U.S. subsidiaries that are expected to be repatriated. The Company determines annually the amount of undistributed non-U.S. earnings to invest indefinitely in its non-U.S. operations.

The Company recognizes a tax benefit from uncertain tax positions in the financial statements only when it is more likely than not that the position will be sustained upon examination by relevant tax authorities. The Company recognizes interest and penalties related to income tax matters in *Income tax expense*.

Refer to Note 9 — Income Taxes for further discussion.

Earnings Per Share

Basic earnings per common share is calculated by dividing *Net income* by the weighted average number of common shares outstanding during the year. Diluted earnings per common share is calculated by adjusting weighted average outstanding shares, assuming conversion of all potentially dilutive stock options and awards.

Refer to Note 12 — Earnings Per Share for further discussion.

Management Estimates

The preparation of financial statements in conformity with generally accepted accounting principles requires management to make estimates, including estimates relating to assumptions that affect the reported amounts of assets and liabilities and disclosure of contingent assets and liabilities at the date of financial statements and the reported amounts of revenues and expenses during the reporting period. Actual results could differ from these estimates.

Recently Adopted Accounting Standards

In April 2015, the FASB issued Accounting Standards Update (ASU) No. 2015-03, *Interest — Imputation of Interest (Subtopic 835-30): Simplifying the Presentation of Debt Issuance Costs*. The updated guidance requires debt issuance costs to be presented as a direct deduction from the carrying amount of the corresponding debt liability on the balance sheet. The Company adopted the standard on a retrospective basis in the first quarter of fiscal 2017. The adoption of this standard reduced both *Deferred income taxes and other assets* and *Long-term debt* by $17 million on the Consolidated Balance Sheet as of May 31, 2016.

Recently Issued Accounting Standards

In October 2016, the FASB issued ASU No. 2016-16, *Income Taxes (Topic 740): Intra-Entity Transfers of Assets Other Than Inventory*. The updated guidance requires companies to recognize the income tax consequences of an intra-entity transfer of an asset other than inventory when the transfer occurs. Income tax effects ofintra-entity transfers ofinventory will continue to

be deferred until the inventory has been sold to a third party. The ASU is effective for the Company beginning June 1, 2018, using a modified retrospective approach, with the cumulative effect recognized through retained earnings at the date of adoption. Early adoption is permitted as of the beginning of an annual reporting period for which interim or annual financial statements have not been issued. The Company is evaluating the impact this update will have on its existing accounting policies and the Consolidated Financial Statements. The Company anticipates the updated guidance could have a material impact on the Consolidated Financial Statements at adoption through the recognition of a cumulative-effect adjustment to retained earnings of previously deferred charges.

In March 2016, the FASB issued ASU No. 2016-09, *Compensation — Stock Compensation (Topic 718): Improvements to Employee Share-Based Payment Accounting*, which changes how companies account for certain aspects of share-based payment awards to employees. The updated guidance requires excess tax benefits and deficiencies from share-based payment awards to be recorded in income tax expense in the income statement. Currently, excess tax benefits and deficiencies are recognized in shareholders' equity on the balance sheet. This change is required to be applied prospectively. In addition, the updated guidance also changes the accounting for statutory tax withholding requirements, classification in the statement of cash flows and provides an option to continue to estimate forfeitures or account for forfeitures as they occur. The Company will adopt the standard on June 1, 2017 and will elect to continue to estimate forfeitures. The ASU is expected to result in increased volatility to the Company's income tax expense in future periods dependent upon, among other variables, the price ofits common stock and the timing and volume of share-based payment award activity, such as employee exercises of stock options and vesting of restricted stock awards.

In February 2016, the FASB issued ASU No. 2016-02, *Leases (Topic 842)*, that replaces existing lease accounting guidance. The new standard is intended to provide enhanced transparency and comparability by requiring lessees to record right-of-use assets and corresponding lease liabilities on the balance sheet. The new guidance will require the Company to continue to classify leases as either operating or financing, with classification affecting the pattern of expense recognition in the income statement. The Company will adopt the standard on June 1, 2019. The ASU is required to be applied using a modified retrospective approach at the beginning of the earliest period presented, with optional practical expedients. The Company is in the process of evaluating the effect the guidance will have on its existing accounting policies and the Consolidated Financial Statements, but expects there will be an increase in assets and liabilities on the Consolidated Balance Sheets at adoption due to the recording of right-of-use assets and corresponding lease liabilities, which may be material. Refer to Note 15 — Commitments and Contingencies for information about the Company's lease obligations.

In January 2016, the FASB issued ASU No. 2016-01, *Financial Instruments — Overall (Subtopic 825-10): Recognition and Measurement of Financial Assets and Financial Liabilities*. The updated guidance enhances the reporting model for financial instruments, which includes amendments to address aspects of recognition, measurement, presentation and disclosure. The update to the standard is effective for the Company beginning June 1, 2018. The Company does not expect the adoption to have a material impact on the Consolidated Financial Statements.

In May 2014, the FASB issued ASU No. 2014-09, *Revenue from Contracts with Customers (Topic 606)*, that replaces existing revenue recognition guidance. The updated guidance requires companies to recognize revenue in a way that depicts the transfer of promised goods or services to customers in an amount that reflects the consideration to which the entity expects to be entitled in exchange for those goods or services. In addition, the new standard requires that reporting companies disclose the nature, amount, timing and uncertainty of revenue and cash flows arising from contracts with customers. The Company will adopt the standard on June 1, 2018 using a modified retrospective approach with the cumulative effective ofinitially applying the new standard recognized in retained earnings at the date ofinitial application. The Company is in the process of evaluating the new standard against its existing accounting policies, including the timing of revenue recognition, and its contracts with customers, to determine the effect the guidance will have on the Consolidated Financial Statements.

Notes 2-17 are available on the companion website at cengage.com

Glossary

A

accelerated depreciation method A depreciation method that provides for a higher depreciation amount in the first year of the asset's use, followed by a gradually declining amount of depreciation. (Ch. 9)

account An accounting form used to record the increases and decreases in each financial statement item. (Ch. 2)

account payable The liability created by a purchase on account. (Ch. 1)

accounting An information system that provides reports to stakeholders about the economic activities and condition of a business. (Ch. 1)

accounting assumptions Assumptions that provide the framework upon which accounting standards are constructed. (Ch. 1)

accounting cycle The accounting process that begins with analyzing and journalizing transactions and ends with the post-closing trial balance. (Ch. 4)

accounting equation Assets = Liabilities + Owner's Equity. (Ch. 1)

accounting principles Principles that provide the framework upon which accounting standards are constructed. (Ch. 1)

accounting standards The rules that determine the accounting for individual business transactions. (Ch. 1)

Accounting Standards Codification An electronic database maintained by the Financial Accounting Standards Board (FASB) that contains all of the accounting standards that make up the generally accepted accounting principles (GAAP). (Ch. 1)

Accounting Standards Updates Published changes to accounting standards that are the source of updates to the Accounting Standards Codification. (Ch. 1)

accounts payable subsidiary ledger The subsidiary ledger containing the individual accounts with suppliers (creditors). (Ch. 5)

accounts receivable An asset, which is a claim against the customer created by selling merchandise or services on credit. (Chs. 1, 2, 8)

accounts receivable analysis The evaluation of a company's ability to collect its accounts receivable. (Ch. 14)

accounts receivable subsidiary ledger The subsidiary ledger containing the individual accounts with customers. (Ch. 5)

accounts receivable turnover A measure of how frequently during the year the accounts receivable are being converted to cash, computed as sales divided by average accounts receivable. (Chs. 8, 14)

accrual A revenue that has been earned or an expense that has been incurrd but has not been recorded. (Ch. 3)

accrual basis of accounting A basis of accounting under which revenues and expenses are reported on the income statement in the period in which they are earned or incurred. (Ch. 3)

Accumulated Depreciation The contra asset account credited when recording the depreciation of a fixed asset. (Ch. 3)

accumulated other comprehensive income The cumulative effect of other comprehensive income items, which is reported separately in the "Stockholders' Equity" section of the balance sheet. (Ch. 14)

adjusted trial balance The trial balance prepared after all the adjusting entries have been posted. (Ch. 3)

adjusting entries The journal entries that bring the accounts up to date at the end of the accounting period. (Ch. 3)

adjusting process An analysis and updating of the accounts when financial statements are prepared. (Ch. 3)

administrative expenses (general expenses) Expenses incurred in the administration or general operations of the business. (Ch. 5)

aging the receivables The process of analyzing the accounts receivable and classifying them according to various age groupings, with the due date being the base point for determining age. (Ch. 8)

allowance for doubtful accounts A contra asset account for accounts receivable in which is recorded the estimate for uncollectible accounts when using the allowance method. (Ch. 8)

allowance method The method of accounting for uncollectible receivables that recognizes an expense by estimating future uncollectible accounts at the end of the accounting period. (Ch. 8)

amortization The periodic transfer of the cost of an intangible asset to expense or of a bond discount to interest expense. (Chs. 9, 11)

analytical methods Techniques that involve the examination of changes in the amount and percentage of financial statement items within and across periods. (Ch. 14)

annuity A series of equal cash receipts spaced equally in time. (Ch. 11)

arm's-length transactions Transactions between two independent parties. (Ch. 1)

asset turnover A profitability ratio that measures how effectively a business is using its assets to generate sales, computed as sales divided by average total assets (excluding long-term investments). (Ch. 14)

asset turnover ratio A profitability ratio that measures how effectively a business is using its assets to generate sales, computed as sales divided by average total assets. (Ch. 5)

assets The resources owned by a business. (Chs. 1, 2)

B

bad debt expense The operating expense incurred because of the failure to collect receivables. (Ch. 8)

balance of the account The amount of the difference between the debits and the credits that have been entered into an acccount. (Ch. 2)

balance sheet A list of the assets, liabilities, and stockholders' equity as of a specific date, usually at the close of the last day of a month or a year. (Ch. 1)

bank reconciliation The analysis that details the items responsible for the difference between the cash balance reported on the bank statement and the balance of the cash account in the ledger. (Ch. 7)

bank statement A summary of all checking account transactions mailed to the depositor or made available online by the bank each month. (Ch. 7)

bond A form of interest-bearing note used by corporations to borrow on a long-term basis. (Ch. 11)

bond indenture The underlying contract between the company issuing bonds and the bondholders. (Ch. 11)

book value (of the asset) The difference between the cost of a fixed asset and its accumulated depreciation. (Chs. 3, 9)

boot The remaining amount a buyer owes after the trade-in allowance when a fixed asset is traded in for a similar asset. (Ch. 9)

business An organization in which basic resources (inputs), such as materials and labor, are assembled and processed to provide goods or services (outputs) to customers. (Ch. 1)

business entity assumption A concept of accounting that limits the economic data in the accounting system to data related directly to the activities of the business. (Ch. 1)

business transaction An economic event or condition that directly changes an entity's financial condition or directly affects its results of operations. (Ch. 1)

C

capital expenditures The costs of acquiring fixed assets, adding to a fixed asset, improving a fixed asset, or extending a fixed asset's useful life. (Ch. 9)

carrying amount The balance of the bonds payable account (face amount of the bonds) less any unamortized discount or plus any unamortized premium. (Ch. 11)

cash Coins, currency (paper money), checks, money orders, and money on deposit that is available for unrestricted withdrawal from banks and other financial institutions. (Ch. 7)

cash basis of accounting A basis of accounting under which revenues and expenses are reported on the income statement in the period in which cash is received or paid. (Ch. 3)

cash dividend A cash distribution of earnings by a corporation to its shareholders. (Ch. 12)

cash equivalents Highly liquid investments that are usually reported with cash on the balance sheet. (Ch. 7)

cash flow per share The cash flow from operations divided by the number of common shares outstanding. (Ch. 13)

cash flows from financing activities The cash flows from transactions that affect the debt and equity of the company. (Ch. 13)

cash flows from investing activities The cash flows from transactions that affect the investments in the noncurrent assets of the company. (Ch. 13)

cash flows from operating activities The cash flows from transactions that affect the net income of the company. (Ch. 13)

cash refund An amount paid by the seller to the buyer for merchandise that is defective, is damaged during shipment, or does not meet the buyer's expectations. (Ch. 5)

cash short and over account An account in which are recorded errors in cash sales or errors in making change causing the amount of actual cash on hand to differ from the beginning amount of cash plus the cash sales for the day. (Ch. 7)

Certified Public Accountants (CPAs) Public accountants who have met a state's education, experience, and examination requirements. (Ch. 1)

chart of accounts A list of the accounts in the ledger. (Ch. 2)

closing entries The journal entries that transfer the balances of temporary accounts to permanent accounts at the end of the accounting period. (Ch. 4)

closing process The process of transferring the balances of temporary accounts to permanent accounts at the end of the accounting period. (Ch. 4)

closing the books The process of transferring the balances of temporary accounts to permanent accounts at the end of the accounting period. (Ch. 4)

common-sized statement A financial statement in which all items are expressed as percentages with no dollar amounts shown. (Ch. 14)

common stock Certificates issued by a corporation to investors as proof of their ownership rights; an account representing the ownership rights of investors in a corporation; a class of stock issued by a corporation that bears no preference rights. (Chs. 1, 2, 12)

compensating balance A minimum cash balance required by some banks to be maintained in a bank account. (Ch. 7)

comprehensive income All changes in stockholders' equity during a period, except those resulting from dividends and stockholders' investments. (Ch. 14)

consigned inventory Merchandise that is shipped by manufacturers to retailers who act as the manufacturer's selling agent. (Ch. 6)

consignee The retailer in a consigned inventory arrangement. (Ch. 6)

consignor The manufacturer in a consigned inventory arrangement. (Ch. 6)

contingent liabilities Liabilities that may arise from past transactions if certain events occur in the future. (Ch. 10)

contra accounts An account offset against another account. (Ch. 3)

contra asset accounts An account offset against another account. (Ch. 3)

contract rate The interest rate to be paid on the face amount of a bond as specified in the bond indenture. (Ch. 11)

control environment The overall attitude of management and employees about the importance of controls. (Ch. 7)

controlling account The account in the general ledger that summarizes the balances of the accounts in a subsidiary ledger. (Ch. 5)

copyright The exclusive right to publish and sell a literary, artistic, or musical composition. (Ch. 9)

corporation A business organized under state or federal statutes as a separate legal entity. (Ch. 1)

correcting journal entry An entry that is prepared to correct an error to an entry that has already been journalized and posted. (Ch. 2)

cost of goods sold The cost of merchandise sold recognized as an expense. (Ch. 5)

credit Amount entered on the right side of an account. (Ch. 2)

credit memorandum (credit memo) A form used by a seller to inform the buyer of the amount the seller proposes to credit to the account receivable due from the buyer. (Ch. 5)

credit period The amount of time the buyer is allowed in which to pay the seller. (Ch. 5)

credit terms Terms for payment on account by the buyer to the seller. (Ch. 5)

cumulative preferred stock Stock that has a right to receive regular dividends that were not declared (paid) in prior years. (Ch. 12)

current assets Cash and other assets that are expected to be converted to cash or sold or used up, usually within one year or less, through the normal operations of the business. (Ch. 4)

current liabilities Liabilities that will be due within a short time (usually one year or less) and that are to be paid out of current assets. (Ch. 4)

current position analysis The evaluation of a company's ability to pay its current liabilities. (Ch. 14)

current ratio A financial ratio that expresses the relationship between current assets and current liabilities, computed by dividing current assets by current liabilities. (Chs. 4, 14)

customer allowance A reduction from the initial selling price due to merchandise that is defective, is damaged during shipment, or does not meet the buyer's expectations, which reduces the amount owed by customer. (Ch. 5)

customer discounts A variety of discounts offered by the seller as incentives for the customer to act in a way benefitting the seller. (Ch. 5)

Customer Refunds Payable A liability account for estimated refunds and allowances that will be paid or granted to customers in the future. (Ch. 5)

D

days' cash on hand A measure of how long a company could survive if its sources of revenue were to decline significantly, computed as cash and short-term investments divided by daily cash operating expenses. (Ch. 7)

debit Amount entered on the left side of an account. (Ch. 2)

debit memorandum (debit memo) A form used by a buyer to inform the seller of the amount the buyer proposes to debit to the account payable due the seller. (Ch. 5)

deferral A future revenue or expense initially recorded as a liability or asset. (Ch. 3)

defined benefit plan A pension plan that promises employees a fixed annual pension benefit at retirement, based on years of service and compensation levels. (Ch. 10)

defined contribution plan A pension plan in which the contributions into the plan are defined but the employee's pension may vary depending on investment performance. (Ch. 10)

depletion expense The process of transferring the cost of natural resources to an expense account. (Ch. 9)

depreciable cost The amount of an asset's cost that will be allocated to depreciation expense over its useful life, determined by the difference between the asset's initial cost and its residual value. (Ch. 9)

depreciate To lose value or usefulness over time. (Ch. 3)

depreciation The systematic periodic transfer of the cost of a fixed asset to an expense account during its expected useful life. (Chs. 3, 9)

depreciation expense The portion of the cost of a fixed asset that is recorded as an expense each year of its useful life. (Ch. 3)

direct method A method of reporting the cash flows from operating activities as the difference between the operating cash receipts and the operating cash payments. (Ch. 13)

direct write-off method The method of accounting for uncollectible receivables that recognizes an expense only when an account is determined to be worthless. (Ch. 8)

discount The excess of the face amount of bonds over their issue price or the excess of the par value of stock over its issue price. (Chs. 11, 12)

dishonored note receivable A note that the maker fails to pay on the due date. (Ch. 8)

dividend yield A profitability ratio that measures the rate of return to common stockholders from cash dividends, computed by dividing the dividends per share of common stock by the market price per share of common stock. (Ch. 14)

dividends Distributions of earnings to stockholders; an account representing the distribution of a corporation's earnings to stockholders. (Chs. 1, 2)

dividends per share A profitability ratio that measures the extent to which earnings are being distributed to common shareholders, computed as dividends on common stock divided by shares of common stock outstanding. (Ch. 14)

double-declining-balance method A method of depreciation that provides for a declining periodic depreciation expense over the expected useful life of an asset. (Ch. 9)

double-entry accounting system A system of accounting for recording transactions, based on recording increases and decreases in accounts so that debits equal credits. (Ch. 2)

E

earnings The amount by which revenues exceed expenses. (Ch. 1)

earnings per common share (EPS) Net income per share of common stock outstanding during a period, computed as net income less preferred dividends divided by the average number of common shares outstanding. (Ch. 12)

earnings per share (EPS) on common stock The profitability ratio that measures the share of profits that are earned by a share of common stock, computed as net income less preferred dividends divided by the shares of common stock outstanding. (Ch. 14)

effective interest rate method (of amortization) A method of amortizing a bond discount or premium that provides for a constant rate of interest over the life of the bonds. (Ch. 11)

effective rate of interest The market rate of interest at the time bonds are issued. (Ch. 11)

electronic funds transfer (EFT) A system in which computers rather than paper (money, checks, etc.) are used to effect cash transactions. (Ch. 7)

elements of internal control The elements that together sustain internal control and include the control environment, risk assessment, control activities, information and communication, and monitoring. (Ch. 7)

employee fraud The intentional act of deceiving an employer for personal gain. (Ch. 7)

equity The rights of the owners of a business (Ch. 1)

Estimated Returns Inventory A current asset account for the estimated amount of merchandise that will be returned by customers. (Ch. 5)

ethics Moral principles that guide the conduct of individuals. (Ch. 1)

expected useful life The estimated length of time an asset will be used in normal business operations. (Ch. 9)

expense recognition principle A principle, sometimes called the matching principle, that requires expenses to be recorded in the same period as the related revenue; a concept of accounting in which expenses are matched with the revenue generated during a period by those expenses. (Chs. 1, 3)

expenses Amounts used to generate revenue; assets used up or services consumed in the process of generating revenues. (Chs. 1, 2)

F

face amount The amount specified on the face of a bond and the amount for which it will sell if the market rate of interest equals the contract rate. (Ch. 11)

fair value The price that would be received for an asset if it were sold today. (Ch. 14)

faithful representation A characteristic of financial reports that pertains to information accurately reflecting an entity's economic activity or condition. (Ch. 1)

fees earned Revenue from providing services. (Ch. 1)

FICA tax Federal Insurance Contributions Act tax used to finance federal programs for old-age and disability benefits (social security) and health insurance for the aged (Medicare). (Ch. 10)

financial accounting The branch of accounting that is concerned with recording transactions using generally accepted accounting principles (GAAP) for a business or other economic unit and with a periodic preparation of various statements from such records. (Ch. 1)

Financial Accounting Standards Board (FASB) The authoritative body that has the primary responsibility for developing accounting principles. (Ch. 1)

financial statements Financial reports that summarize the effects of events on a business. (Ch. 1)

first-in, first-out (FIFO) inventory cost flow method The method of inventory costing based on the assumption that the first units purchased are the first units sold. (Ch. 6)

fiscal year The annual accounting period adopted by a business. (Ch. 1)

fixed asset turnover ratio The number of sales dollars earned per dollar of fixed assets, computed by dividing sales by the average book value of fixed assets. (Ch. 9)

fixed assets Physical resources that are owned and used by a business and are permanent or have a long life; long-term or relatively permanent tangible assets such as equipment, machinery, buildings and land that are used in normal business operations. (Chs. 3, 4, 9)

FOB (free on board) destination Freight terms in which the seller pays the transportation costs from the shipping point to the final destination. (Ch. 5)

FOB (free on board) shipping point Freight terms in which the buyer pays the transportation costs from the shipping point to the final destination. (Ch. 5)

free cash flow The amount of operating cash flow available to a company after it purchases the property, plant, and equipment necessary to maintain its current operations, computed as cash flows from operating activities less cash used to purchase property, plant, and equipment. (Ch. 13)

fringe benefits Benefits provided to employees in addition to wages and salaries. (Ch. 10)

future value The value of an asset or cash at a specified date in the future that is equivalent in value to a specified sum today. (Ch. 11)

G

general expenses Expenses incurred in the administration or general operations of the business. (Ch. 5)

general ledger The primary ledger, when used in conjunction with subsidiary ledgers, that contains all of the balance sheet and income statement accounts. (Ch. 5)

general-purpose financial statements A type of financial accounting report that is distributed to external users. The term "general purpose" refers to the wide range of decision-making needs that the reports are designed to serve. (Ch. 1)

generally accepted accounting principles (GAAP) Generally accepted guidelines for the preparation of financial statements. (Ch. 1)

going concern assumption An assumption that requires that financial reports be prepared assuming that the entity will continue operating in the future. (Ch. 1)

goodwill An intangible asset that is created from such favorable factors as location, product quality, reputation, and managerial skill. (Ch. 9)

gross method (of recording sales discounts) A method of recording a sales invoice at the gross amount rather than the amount net of any discounts offered for early payment. (Ch. 5)

gross pay The total earnings of an employee for a payroll period. (Ch. 10)

gross profit Sales minus the cost of goods sold. (Ch. 5)

gross profit method A method of estimating inventory cost that is based on the relationship of gross profit to sales. (Ch. 6)

H

historical cost principle, or cost principle A concept of accounting that states that an asset should be recorded and maintained in the accounting records at its initial transaction price. (Ch. 1)

horizontal analysis Financial analysis that compares an item in a current statement with the same item in prior statements in terms of the amount and percentage of change. (Chs. 2, 14)

I

in arrears In a state of being behind; cumulative preferred stock dividends that have not been paid in prior years are said to be in arrears. (Ch. 12)

income from operations (operating income) The difference between gross profit and operating expenses. (Ch. 5)

income statement A summary of the revenue and expenses for a specific period of time, such as a month or a year. (Ch. 1)

indirect method A method of reporting the cash flows from operating activities that begins with net income and adjusts for revenues and expenses that do not involve the receipt or payment of cash. (Ch. 13)

initial cost The purchase price of an asset plus all costs to obtain and ready it for use. (Ch. 9)

installment note A debt that requires the borrower to make equal periodic payments to the lender for the term of the note. (Ch. 10)

intangible assets Long-term assets that are used in the operations of a business, are not held for sale, and are without physical qualities. (Ch. 9)

interest revenue Earnings received for interest. (Ch. 1)

internal control The policies and procedures used to safeguard assets, ensure accurate business information, and ensure compliance with laws and regulations. (Ch. 7)

International Accounting Standards Board (IASB) An organization that issues International Financial Reporting Standards for many countries outside the United States. (Ch. 1)

inventory Merchandise on hand (not sold) at the end of an accounting period. (Ch. 5)

inventory analysis The evaluation of a company's ability to manage its inventory effectively. (Ch. 14)

inventory shrinkage (inventory shortage) The amount by which the merchandise for sale, as indicated by the balance of the inventory account, is larger than the total amount of merchandise counted during the physical inventory. (Ch. 5)

inventory subsidiary ledger A supporting ledger to the inventory account, containing an individual account for each inventory item. (Ch. 5)

inventory turnover A measure of the number of times inventory is turned into goods sold during the year, computed by dividing the cost of goods sold by the average inventory. (Chs. 6, 14)

invoice The bill that the seller sends to the buyer. (Ch. 5)

J

journal The initial record in which the effects of a transaction are recorded. (Ch. 2)

journal entry The record of a transaction entered in a journal, made up of at least one debit and one credit. (Ch. 2)

journalizing The process of recording a transaction in a journal. (Ch. 2)

L

last-in, first-out (LIFO) inventory cost flow method A method of inventory costing based on the assumption that the last units purchased are assumed to be sold and the ending inventory is made up of the first purchases. (Ch. 6)

ledger A group of accounts for a business. (Ch. 2)

leverage The use of debt to increase the return on an investment. (Ch. 14)

liabilities The rights of creditors that represent debts of the business. (Chs. 1, 2)

limited liability company (LLC) A business form consisting of one or more persons or entities filing an operating agreement with a state to conduct business with limited liability to the owners, yet treated as a partnership for tax purposes. (Ch. 1)

liquidity A company's ability to convert assets into cash. (Chs. 4, 14)

long-term liabilities Liabilities that will not be due for a long time (usually more than one year). (Ch. 4)

lower-of-cost-or-market (LCM) method A method of valuing inventory that reports the inventory at the lower of its cost or current market value (net realizable value). (Ch. 6)

M

management accounting, or managerial accounting The branch of accounting that uses both historical and estimated data in providing internal users (management) with information relevant to decision making. (Ch. 1)

Management's Discussion and Analysis (MD&A) An annual report disclosure that provides management's analysis of the results of current operations and financial condition, as well as plans for the future. (Ch. 14)

manufacturing businesses A type of business that changes basic inputs into products that are sold to individual customers. (Ch. 1)

market rate of interest The rate determined from sales and purchases of similar bonds. (Ch. 11)

matching principle A concept of accounting in which expenses are matched with the revenue generated during a period by those expenses. (Ch. 3)

maturity value The amount that is due at the maturity or due date of a note, which is the sum of the face amount and any interest. (Ch. 8)

measurement principle A principle that requires that amounts be objective and verifiable. (Ch. 1)

monetary unit assumption An accounting assumption that requires that financial reports be expressed in a single monetary unit, or currency. (Ch. 1)

multiple-step income statement A form of income statement that contains several sections, subsections, and subtotals. (Ch. 5)

N

natural business year A fiscal year that ends when business activities have reached the lowest point in an annual operating cycle. (Ch. 1)

net book value The difference between the cost of a fixed asset and its accumulated depreciation. (Ch. 3)

net income, or net profit The amount by which revenues exceed expenses. (Ch. 1)

net loss The amount by which expenses exceed revenues. (Ch. 1)

net method (of recording sales discounts) A method of recording a sales invoice at the amount net of any discounts for early payment. (Ch. 5)

net pay The amount paid the employee, calculated as gross pay less payroll deductions. (Ch. 10)

net realizable value The estimated selling price of an item of inventory less any direct costs of disposal, such as sales commissions; the value of the receivables reduced to the amount that is expected to be collected or realized, computed as accounts receivable less allowance for doubtful accounts. (Chs. 6, 8)

normal balance of an account The side of an account (debit or credit) in which the balance normally appears based on the type of account and whether it is increased by debits or credits. (Ch. 2)

notes receivable A customer's written promise to pay an amount and possibly interest at an agreed-upon rate; amounts that customers owe for which a formal, written instrument of credit has been issued. (Chs. 4, 8)

number of days' sales in inventory The measure of the length of time it takes to acquire, sell, and replace inventory, computed by dividing the average inventory by the average daily cost of goods sold. (Chs. 6, 14)

number of days' sales in receivables An estimate of the length of time the accounts receivable have been outstanding, computed as average accounts receivable divided by average daily sales. (Chs. 8, 14)

O

operating cycle The process by which a company spends cash, generates revenues, and receives cash from customers. (Ch. 5)

operating income The difference between gross profit and operating expenses. (Ch. 5)

other comprehensive income Specified items that are reported separately from net income, including foreign currency items, pension liability adjustments, and unrealized gains and losses on investments. (Ch. 14)

other expense Expenses that cannot be traced directly to operations. (Ch. 5)

other revenue Revenue from sources other than the primary operating activity of a business. (Ch. 5)

outstanding stock Issued stock that has not been reacquired but remains in the hands of stockholders. (Ch. 12)

owner's equity The equity for a proprietorship, partnership, or a limited liability company. (Ch. 1)

P

par value A dollar amount assigned to each share of stock. (Ch. 12)

partnership An unincorporated business form consisting of two or more persons conducting business as co-owners for profit. (Ch. 1)

patents Exclusive rights to produce and sell goods with one or more unique features. (Ch. 9)

payroll The total amount paid to employees for services they provided during a certain period. (Ch. 10)

pension A cash payment to retired employees. (Ch. 10)

periodic inventory system An inventory system in which the inventory records are updated only after a physical count has been taken at periodic intervals, usually at the end of an accounting period. (Ch. 5)

permanent accounts or real accounts Term for balance sheet accounts because they are relatively permanent with balances that carry forward from year to year. (Ch. 4)

perpetual inventory system The inventory system in which each purchase and sale of merchandise is recorded in the inventory account and related subsidiary ledger; therefore, the inventory records are updated continuously. (Ch. 5)

petty cash fund A special cash fund to pay relatively small amounts. (Ch. 7)

physical inventory A detailed listing of merchandise on hand. (Chs. 5, 6)

plant assets Physical resources that are owned and used by a business and are permanent or have a long life; long-term or relatively permanent tangible assets such as equipment, machinery, and buildings that are used in normal business operations. (Chs. 3, 4)

posting The process of transferring the debits and credits from the journal entries to the accounts. (Ch. 2)

preferred stock A class of stock issued by a corporation that bears preference rights, such as a preference to dividends before common stockholders. (Ch. 12)

premium The excess of the issue price of bonds over their face amount; the excess of the issue price of stock over its par value. (Chs. 11, 12)

prepaid expense(s) Assets created by making advanced payments for expense items, such as insurance premiums or supplies, that will be used in the business in the future. (Chs. 1, 2, 3)

present value The value of an asset or cash at present that is equivalent in value to a specified sum in the future. (Ch. 11)

present value of an annuity The sum of the present values of a series of equal cash receipts spaced equally in time. (Ch. 11)

price-earnings (P/E) ratio A profitability ratio that measures a company's future earnings prospects, computed as the market price per share of common stock divided by earnings per shar on common stock. (Ch. 14)

prior period adjustment Corrections of material errors related to a prior period or periods, excluded from the determination of net income. (Ch. 12)

private accounting The field of accounting whereby accountants are employed by a business firm or a not-for-profit organization. (Ch. 1)

profit The difference between the amounts received from customers for goods or services provided and the amounts paid for the inputs used to provide the goods or services. (Ch. 1)

profitability The ability of a firm to earn income. (Ch. 14)

property, plant, and equipment Long-term or relatively permanent tangible assets such as equipment, machinery, and buildings that are used in normal business operations. (Ch. 4)

proprietorship A business owned by one individual. (Ch. 1)

public accounting The field of accounting where accountants and their staff provide services on a fee basis. (Ch. 1)

Public Company Accounting Oversight Board (PCAOB) A new oversight body for the accounting profession that was established by the Sarbanes-Oxley Act. (Ch. 1)

purchase order The document authorizing the purchase of the inventory from an approved vendor. (Ch. 6)

purchases discounts Discounts taken by the buyer for early payment of an invoice. (Ch. 5)

purchases returns and allowances From the buyer's perspective, returned merchandise or an adjustment for defective merchandise. (Ch. 5)

Q

quick assets Cash and other current assets that can be easily converted to cash, such as temporary investments and accounts receivable. (Chs. 10, 14)

quick ratio A financial ratio that measures a company's "instant" debt-paying ability, computed as quick assets divided by current liabilities. (Chs. 10, 14)

R

ratio The expression of a financial statement item or set of items as a percentage of another financial statement item in order to measure an important economic relationship as a single number. (Ch. 14)

ratio of fixed assets to long-term liabilities A solvency ratio that provides a measure of how much fixed assets a company has to support its long-term debt, calculated as net fixed assets divided by long-term liabilities. (Ch. 14)

ratio of liabilities to stockholders' equity A comprehensive leverage ratio that measures the relationship of the claims of creditors to stockholders' equity; a solvency ratio that measures how much of the company is financed by debt and equity, computed as total liabilities divided by total stockholders' equity. (Chs. 1, 14)

receivables All money claims against other entities, including people, business firms, and other organizations. (Ch. 8)

receiving report The document used by the receiving personnel to indicate that materials have been received and inspected. (Ch. 6)

relevant A characteristic of financial reports that pertains to information having the potential to impact decision making. (Ch. 1)

rent revenue Earnings from property that is leased to others for use. (Ch. 1)

report form (of balance sheet) A form of balance sheet with the "Liabilities" and "Stockholders' Equity" sections presented below the "Assets" section. (Ch. 1)

residual value The estimated value of a fixed asset at the end of its useful life. (Ch. 9)

restrictions Amounts of retained earnings that have been limited for use as dividends. (Ch. 12)

retail businesses A type of business that purchases products from other businesses and sells them to customers. (Ch. 1)

retail inventory method A method of estimating inventory cost that is based on the relationship of cost to retail price. (Ch. 6)

retained earnings The stockholders' equity created from business operations through revenue and expense transactions; an account representing the net income retained in a corporation. (Chs. 1, 2)

retained earnings statement A summary of the changes in the retained earnings in a corporation that have occurred during a specific period of time, such as a month or a year. (Chs. 1, 12)

return on common stockholders' equity A profitability ratio that measures the rate of profits earned on the amount invested by common stockholders, computed as net income less preferred dividends divided by average common stockholders' equity. (Ch. 14)

return on stockholders' equity A profitability ratio that measures the rate of income earned on the amount invested by the stockholders, computed as net income divided by average total stockholders' equity. (Ch. 14)

return on total assets A profitability ratio that measures the profitability of total assets without considering how the assets are financed, computed as income plus interest expense divided by average total assets. (Ch. 14)

revenue(s) Increases in owner's equity as a result of providing services or selling goods to customers. (Chs. 1, 2)

revenue expenditures Costs that benefit only the current period or costs incurred for normal maintenance and repairs of fixed assets. (Ch. 9)

revenue recognition principle A concept of accounting that states that revenues are recorded when earned, which is when the services have been performed or products have been delivered to customers. (Chs. 1, 3)

reversing entries Journal entries that are recorded on the first day of the next period that are the exact opposite of the related adjusting entry from the last day of the prior period. (Ch. 4)

rules of debit and credit In the double-entry accounting system, specific rules for recording debits and credits based on the type of account. (Ch. 2)

S

sales How revenue from the sale of merchandise is recorded; the total amount charged customers for merchandise sold, including cash sales and sales on account. (Chs. 1, 5)

sales discount From the seller's perspective, a discount that a seller may offer the buyer for early payment. (Ch. 5)

Sarbanes-Oxley Act (SOX) An act passed by Congress to restore public confidence and trust in the financial statements of companies. (Chs. 1, 7)

Securities and Exchange Commission (SEC) An agency of the U.S. government that has authority over the accounting and financial disclosures for companies whose shares of ownership (stock) are traded and sold to the public. (Ch. 1)

selling expenses Expenses that are incurred directly in the selling of merchandise. (Ch. 5)

service businesses A business providing services rather than products to customers. (Ch. 1)

single-step income statement A form of income statement in which the total of all expenses is deducted from the total of all revenues. (Ch. 5)

slide An error in which the entire number is moved one or more spaces to the right or the left, such as writing $542.00 as $54.20 or $5,420.00. (Ch. 2)

solvency The ability of a firm to pay its debts as they come due. (Chs. 4, 14)

special journals Journals designed to be used for recording a single type of transaction. (Ch. 5)

special-purpose funds Cash funds used for a special business need. (Ch. 7)

specific identification inventory cost flow method The method of inventory costing in which a unit sold is identified with a specific purchase. (Ch. 6)

standard four-column account A form of account that has Debit and Credit columns for recording transactions as well as Balance (Debit and Credit) columns for indicating the account balance after each transaction. (Ch. 2)

statement of cash flows A summary of the cash receipts and cash payments for a specific period of time, such as a month or a year. (Chs. 1, 13)

statement of stockholders' equity A summary of the changes in the stockholders' equity in a corporation that have occurred during a specific period of time, such as a month or a year. (Chs. 1, 12)

stock Shares of ownership of a corporation. (Ch. 12)

stock dividend A distribution of additional shares of stock by a corporation to its stockholders. (Ch. 12)

stock split A process by which a corporation reduces the par or stated value of its common stock by issuing a proportionate number of additional shares. (Ch. 12)

stockholders The owners of a corporation. (Ch. 12)

stockholders' equity The ownership rights of stockholders in a corporation; the stockholders' rights to the assets in a corporation. (Chs. 1, 2)

straight-line method A method of depreciation that provides for equal periodic depreciation expense over the estimated life of a fixed asset. (Ch. 9)

straight-line method (of amortization) A method of amortizing a bond discount or premium that provides for equal amounts of discount (or premium) to be written off to interest expense each period. (Ch. 11)

subsidiary inventory ledger The subsidiary ledger containing individual accounts for items of inventory. (Ch. 6)

subsidiary ledger Individual accounts with a common characteristic grouped together in a separate or secondary ledger, which is used to support a controlling account in the general ledger. (Ch. 5)

T

T account The simplest form of an account, which consists of an account title, a debit side, and a credit side. (Ch. 2)

temporary accounts or nominal accounts Term for income statement accounts because their balances relate to only one period and are not carried forward to the next period. (Ch. 4)

time period assumption An accounting assumption that allows a company to report its economic activities on a regular basis for a specific period of time. (Ch. 1)

times interest earned A ratio that assesses the risk that bondholders will not receive their interest payments or that interest payments will not be made if earnings decrease. The ratio is computed as income before income tax expense plus interest expense divided by interest expense. (Chs. 11, 14)

trade discounts Discounts from the list prices in published catalogs or special discounts offered to certain classes of buyers. (Ch. 5)

trade-in allowance The amount a seller allows a buyer for a fixed asset that is traded in for a similar asset. (Ch. 9)

trademark A name, term, or symbol used to identify a business and its products. (Ch. 9)

transposition An error in which the order of the digits is changed, such as writing $542 as $452 or $524. (Ch. 2)

treasury stock Stock that a corporation has issued and then reacquired. (Ch. 12)

trial balance A summary listing of the titles and balances of accounts in the ledger, which is used to verify that debits equal credits. (Ch. 2)

two-column journal A form of journal in which there are only two amount columns, one for debits and one for credits. (Ch. 2)

U

unadjusted trial balance A trial balance prepared at the end of an accounting period before adjusting entries are made. (Ch. 2)

unearned revenue The liability created by receiving revenue in advance. (Chs. 2, 3)

units-of-activity method A method of depreciation that provides the same amount of depreciation expense for each unit of an asset's activity, which may be expressed in hours, miles driven, or quantity produced. (Ch. 9)

unrealized gain An increase in the fair value of equity or debt securities for a period. (Ch. 14)

V

vertical analysis An analysis that compares each item in a current statement with a total or key amount within the same statement. (Chs. 3, 14)

voucher Any document that serves as proof of authority to pay cash or issue an electronic funds transfer, but for many businesses, is a special form used to record data about a liability and the details of its payment. (Ch. 7)

voucher system A set of procedures that uses vouchers for authorizing and recording liabilities and cash payments. (Ch. 7)

W

weighted average inventory cost flow method A method of inventory costing in which the cost of the units sold and in ending inventory is a weighted average of the purchase costs. (Ch. 6)

working capital The excess of the current assets of a business over its current liabilities. (Chs. 4, 14)

Index

The Basics

Accounting Equation:

Assets = Liabilities + Stockholders' Equity

T Account:

Account Title	
Left side	Right side
debit	credit

Rules of Debit and Credit, Normal Balances:

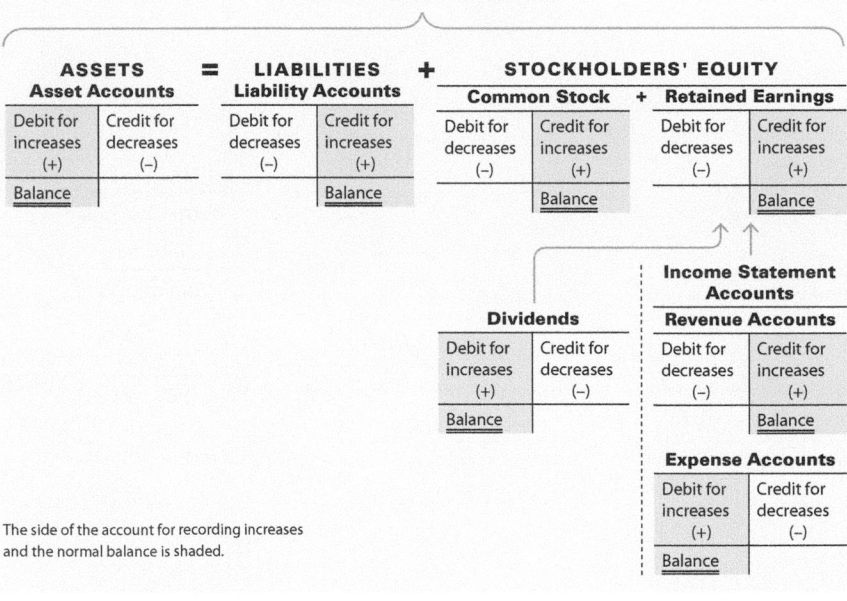

The side of the account for recording increases and the normal balance is shaded.

Analyzing and Journalizing Transactions

1. Carefully read the description of the transaction to determine whether an asset, liability, common stock, retained earnings, revenue, expense, or dividends account is affected.
2. For each account affected by the transaction, determine whether the account increases or decreases.
3. Determine whether each increase or decrease should be recorded as a debit or a credit, following the rules of debit and credit.
4. Record the transaction using a journal entry.
5. Periodically post journal entries to the accounts in the ledger.
6. Prepare an unadjusted trial balance at the end of the period.

Financial Statements:

- **Income statement:** A summary of the revenue and expenses for a specific period of time, such as a month or a year.
- **Statement of stockholders' equity:** A summary of the changes in stockholders' equity that have occurred during a specific period of time, such as a month or a year.

- **Balance sheet:** A list of the assets, liabilities, and stockholders' equity as of a specific date, usually at the close of the last day of a month or a year.
- **Statement of cash flows:** A summary of the cash receipts and cash payments for a specific period of time, such as a month or a year.

Accounting Cycle:

1. Transactions are analyzed and recorded in the journal.
2. Transactions are posted to the ledger.
3. An unadjusted trial balance is prepared.
4. Adjustment data are assembled and analyzed.
5. An optional end-of-period spreadsheet is prepared.
6. Adjusting entries are journalized and posted to the ledger.
7. An adjusted trial balance is prepared.
8. Financial statements are prepared.
9. Closing entries are journalized and posted to the ledger.
10. A post-closing trial balance is prepared.

Types of Adjusting Entries:

- Accrued revenue (accrued asset)
- Accrued expense (accrued liability)
- Unearned revenue (deferred revenue)
- Prepaid expense (deferred expense)
- Depreciation expense

Each entry will always affect both a balance sheet account and an income statement account.

Closing Entries:

1. Revenue and expense account balances are transferred to the retained earnings account.
2. The balance of the dividends account is transferred to the retained earnings account.

Shipping Terms:

	FOB Shipping Point	FOB Destination
Ownership (title) passes to buyer when merchandise is...............	delivered to freight carrier	delivered to buyer
Freight costs are paid by..........................	buyer	seller

Format for Bank Reconciliation:

Cash balance according to bank statement	$ XXX
Add: Deposits in transit	XXX
Deduct: Outstanding checks not paid by bank	(XXX)
Adjusted balance	$ XXX

Cash balance according to company's records	$ XXX
Add: Credit memos that have not been recorded (notes collected by bank)	XXX
Deduct: Debit memos that have not been recorded (NSF checks, service charges)	(XXX)
Adjusted balance	$ XXX

Inventory Costing Methods:

- First-in, First-out (FIFO)
- Last-in, First-out (LIFO)
- Average Cost

Interest Computations:

$$\text{Interest} = \text{Face Amount (or Principal)} \times \text{Rate} \times \text{Time}$$

Methods of Determining Depreciation:

Straight-Line: $\dfrac{\text{Cost} - \text{Estimated Residual Value}}{\text{Estimated Life}}$

Units-of-Activity: $\dfrac{\text{Cost} - \text{Estimated Residual Value}}{\text{Total Estimated Units of Activity}} \times \text{Units of Activity}$

Double-Declining-Balance: Rate* × Book Value at Beginning of Period

*Rate is commonly twice the straight-line rate   (1 ÷ Estimated Life).

Adjustments to Net Income (Loss) Using the Indirect Method:

Net income (loss)	$ XXX
Adjustments to reconcile net income to net cash flow from operating activities:	
Depreciation of fixed assets	XXX
Amortization of intangible assets	XXX
Losses on disposal of assets	XXX
Gains on disposal of assets	(XXX)
Changes in current operating assets and liabilities:	
Increases in noncash current operating assets	(XXX)
Decreases in noncash current operating assets....	XXX
Increases in current operating liabilities	XXX
Decreases in current operating liabilities	(XXX)
Net cash flow from operating activities	$XXX

Subtract	**Add**
Increases in accounts receivable	Decreases in accounts receivable
Increases in inventory	Decreases in inventory
Increases in prepaid expenses	Decreases in prepaid expenses
Decreases in accounts payable	Increases in accounts payable
Decreases in accrued expenses payable	Increases in accrued expenses payable
Decreases in income taxes payable	Increases in income taxes payable

Summary of Analytical Measures

Liquidity Measures

Working Capital $=$ Current Assets − Current Liabilities

Current Ratio $= \dfrac{\text{Current Assets}}{\text{Current Liabilities}}$

Quick Ratio $= \dfrac{\text{Quick Assets}}{\text{Current Liabilities}}$

Accounts Receivable Turnover $= \dfrac{\text{Sales}}{\text{Average Accounts Receivable}}$

Numbers of Days' Sales in Receivables $= \dfrac{\text{Average Accounts Receivable}}{\text{Average Daily Sales}}$

Inventory Turnover $= \dfrac{\text{Cost of Goods Sold}}{\text{Average Inventory}}$

Number of Days' Sales in Inventory $= \dfrac{\text{Average Inventory}}{\text{Average Daily Cost of Goods Sold}}$

Solvency Measures

Ratio of Fixed Assets to Long-Term Liabilities $= \dfrac{\text{Fixed Assets (net)}}{\text{Long-Term Liabilities}}$

Ratio of Liabilities to Stockholders' Equity $= \dfrac{\text{Total Liabilities}}{\text{Total Stockholders' Equity}}$

Times Interest Earned $= \dfrac{\text{Income Before Income Tax} + \text{Interest Expense}}{\text{Interest Expense}}$

Profitability Measures

Asset Turnover $= \dfrac{\text{Sales}}{\text{Average Total Assets (excluding long-term investments)}}$

Return on Total Assets $= \dfrac{\text{Net Income} + \text{Interest Expense}}{\text{Average Total Assets}}$

Return on Stockholders' Equity $= \dfrac{\text{Net Income}}{\text{Average Total Stockholders' Equity}}$

Return on Common Stockholders' Equity $= \dfrac{\text{Net Income} - \text{Preferred Dividends}}{\text{Average Common Stockholders' Equity}}$

Earnings per Share (EPS) $= \dfrac{\text{Net Income} - \text{Preferred Dividends}}{\text{Shares of Common Stock Outstanding}}$

Price-Earnings (P/E) Ratio $= \dfrac{\text{Market Price per Share of Common Stock}}{\text{Earnings per Share on Common Stock}}$

Dividends per Share $= \dfrac{\text{Dividends on Common Stock}}{\text{Shares of Common Stock Outstanding}}$

Dividend Yield $= \dfrac{\text{Dividends per Share of Common Stock}}{\text{Market Price per Share of Common Stock}}$

Abbreviations and Acronyms Commonly Used in Business and Accounting

AAA	American Accounting Association
AICPA	American Institute of Certified Public Accountants
B2B	Business-to-business
B2C	Business-to-consumer
CFO	Chief Financial Officer
CMA	Certified Management Accountant
COGM	Cost of goods manufactured
COGS	Cost of goods sold
CPA	Certified Public Accountant
Cr.	Credit
Dr.	Debit
EFT	Electronic funds transfer
EPS	Earnings per share
FASB	Financial Accounting Standards Board
FICA tax	Federal Insurance Contributions Act tax
FIFO	First-in, first-out
FOB	Free on board
FUTA	Federal unemployment compensation tax
GAAP	Generally accepted accounting principles
IASB	International Accounting Standards Board
IFRS	International Financial Reporting Standards
IMA	Institute of Management Accountants
IRC	Internal Revenue Code
IRR	Internal rate of return
IRS	Internal Revenue Service
LIFO	Last-in, first-out
LCM	Lower of cost or market
MACRS	Modified Accelerated Cost Recovery System
MD&A	Management's Discussion and Analysis
n/30	Net 30
n/eom	Net, end-of-month
NSF	Not sufficient funds
P/E Ratio	Price-earnings ratio
POS	Point of sale
R&D	Research and development
SEC	Securities and Exchange Commission
SOX	Sarbanes-Oxley Act
W-4	Employee's Withholding Allowance Certificate

Classification of Accounts

Account Title	Account Classification	Normal Balance	Financial Statement
Accounts Payable	Current liability	Credit	Balance sheet
Accounts Receivable	Current asset	Debit	Balance sheet
Accumulated Depletion	Contra fixed asset	Credit	Balance sheet
Accumulated Depreciation	Contra fixed asset	Credit	Balance sheet
Advertising Expense	Operating expense	Debit	Income statement
Allowance for Doubtful Accounts	Contra current asset	Credit	Balance sheet
Amortization Expense	Operating expense	Debit	Income statement
Bad debt expense	Operating expense	Debit	Income statement
Bonds Payable	Long-term liability	Credit	Balance sheet
Building	Fixed asset	Debit	Balance sheet
Cash	Current asset	Debit	Balance sheet
Cash Dividends	Stockholders' equity	Debit	Statement of stockholders' equity
Cash Dividends Payable	Current liability	Credit	Balance sheet
Common Stock	Stockholders' equity	Credit	Balance sheet
Cost of Goods Sold	Cost of goods sold	Debit	Income statement
Customer Refunds Payable	Current liability	Credit	Balance sheet
Delivery Expense	Operating expense	Debit	Income statement
Depletion Expense	Operating expense	Debit	Income statement
Discount on Bonds Payable	Long-term liability	Debit	Balance sheet
Dividend Revenue	Other income	Credit	Income statement
Dividends	Stockholders' equity	Debit	Statement of stockholders' equity
Employees Federal Income Tax Payable	Current liability	Credit	Balance sheet
Equipment	Fixed asset	Debit	Balance sheet
Estimated Returns Inventory	Current asset	Debit	Balance sheet
Federal Income Tax Payable	Current liability	Credit	Balance sheet
Federal Unemployment Tax Payable	Current liability	Credit	Balance sheet
Fees Earned	Revenue	Credit	Income statement
Finished Goods	Current asset	Debit	Balance sheet
Freight In	Cost of goods sold	Debit	Income statement
Freight Out	Operating expense	Debit	Income statement
Gain on Disposal of Fixed Assets	Other income	Credit	Income statement
Gain on Redemption of Bonds	Other income	Credit	Income statement
Gain on Sale of Investments	Other income	Credit	Income statement
Goodwill	Intangible asset	Debit	Balance sheet
Income Tax Expense	Income tax	Debit	Income statement
Income Tax Payable	Current liability	Credit	Balance sheet
Insurance Expense	Operating expense	Debit	Income statement
Interest Expense	Other expense	Debit	Income statement
Interest Receivable	Current asset	Debit	Balance sheet
Interest Revenue	Other income	Credit	Income statement
Inventory	Current asset/Cost of goods sold	Debit	Balance sheet/Income statement
Investment in Bonds	Investment	Debit	Balance sheet
Investment in Stocks	Investment	Debit	Balance sheet
Investment in Subsidiary	Investment	Debit	Balance sheet
Land	Fixed asset	Debit	Balance sheet
Loss on Disposal of Fixed Assets	Other expense	Debit	Income statement
Loss on Redemption of Bonds	Other expense	Debit	Income statement

Account Title	Account Classification	Normal Balance	Financial Statement
Loss on Sale of Investments	Other expense	Debit	Income statement
Marketable Securities	Current asset	Debit	Balance sheet
Medicare Tax Payable	Current liability	Credit	Balance sheet
Notes Payable	Current liability/Long-term liability	Credit	Balance sheet
Notes Receivable	Current asset/Investment	Debit	Balance sheet
Patents	Intangible asset	Debit	Balance sheet
Paid-In Capital from Sale of Treasury Stock	Stockholders' equity	Credit	Balance sheet
Paid-In Capital in Excess of Par (Stated Value)	Stockholders' equity	Credit	Balance sheet
Payroll Tax Expense	Operating expense	Debit	Income statement
Pension Expense	Operating expense	Debit	Income statement
Petty Cash	Current asset	Debit	Balance sheet
Preferred Stock	Stockholders' equity	Credit	Balance sheet
Premium on Bonds Payable	Long-term liability	Credit	Balance sheet
Prepaid Insurance	Current asset	Debit	Balance sheet
Prepaid Rent	Current asset	Debit	Balance sheet
Purchases	Cost of goods sold	Debit	Income statement
Purchases Discounts	Cost of goods sold	Credit	Income statement
Purchases Returns and Allowances	Cost of goods sold	Credit	Income statement
Rent Expense	Operating expense	Debit	Income statement
Rent Revenue	Other income	Credit	Income statement
Retained Earnings	Stockholders' equity	Credit	Balance sheet/Statement of stockholders' equity
Salaries Expense	Operating expense	Debit	Income statement
Salaries Payable	Current liability	Credit	Balance sheet
Sales	Revenue	Credit	Income statement
Sales Tax Payable	Current liability	Credit	Balance sheet
Social Security Tax Payable	Current liability	Credit	Balance sheet
State Unemployment Tax Payable	Current liability	Credit	Balance sheet
Stock Dividends	Stockholders' equity	Debit	Statement of stockholders' equity
Stock Dividends Distributable	Stockholders' equity	Credit	Balance sheet
Supplies	Current asset	Debit	Balance sheet
Supplies Expense	Operating expense	Debit	Income statement
Treasury Stock	Stockholders' equity	Debit	Balance sheet
Unearned Rent	Current liability	Credit	Balance sheet
Utilities Expense	Operating expense	Debit	Income statement
Vacation Pay Expense	Operating expense	Debit	Income statement
Vacation Pay Payable	Current liability/Long-term liability	Credit	Balance sheet
Work in Process	Current asset	Debit	Balance sheet